THE ROUGH GUIDE TO
CANADA

This tenth edition updated by
**Stephen Keeling, Rachel Mills, AnneLise Sorensen
and Christian Williams**

**ROUGH
GUIDES**

Contents

Introduction to

Canada

The home of ice hockey, the Niagara Falls, Mounties and maple syrup – not to mention Ryan Gosling, Céline Dion, Drake and of course, Justin Bieber – almost everyone on the planet knows something about Canada. Yet first-time visitors should expect some surprises, beginning with the immense size of the country, hard to appreciate until you get here. Canada's cities – enchanting Québec, trendy Vancouver, cosmopolitan Toronto and stylish Montréal among them – are rich with historical and cultural treasures, but above all Canada is a land of stunningly beautiful landscapes, from the spectacular fjord-slashed coastlines of Newfoundland and the Maritimes, to the Rockies' glittering lakes and majestic peaks, and the rippling prairie expanse with all the sky for a ceiling in between.

The second largest country in the world (after Russia), Canada covers an area the United Kingdom could fit into 41 times over. Much of this expanse is sparsely inhabited and the majority of the 36 million Canadians live in its southern half, relatively close to the US border. Like its neighbour to the south, Canada is a spectrum of cultures, a hotchpotch of immigrant groups who supplanted the continent's many Aboriginal peoples.

For the visitor, the mix that results from this mostly exemplary tolerance is an exhilarating experience, offering such widely differing cultural, artistic and culinary experiences as Vancouver's huge Chinatown, the Inuit heartlands of the far north, the austere religious enclaves of Manitoba or the Celtic-tinged warmth of the Maritimes.

Yet – in stark contrast to their southern neighbours – some Canadians are often troubled by the lack of a clear self-image, tending to emphasize the ways in which their country is different from the US as a means of self-description. The question "What is a Canadian?" continues to linger, with the on-again, off-again and always acrimonious debate over Québec's secession, but ultimately there can be no simple characterization

BELLWOODS BREWERY, TORONTO

of a people whose country is not so much a single nation as it is a committee on a continental scale. Pierre Berton, one of Canada's finest writers, wisely ducked the issue: "A Canadian", he quipped, is "someone who knows how to make love in a canoe."

Despite this balancing act, one thing is clear: Canadians have an overwhelming sense of pride in their history, their culture and the mesmerizing beauty of their land. Indeed, Canada embraces all this – as well as its own clichés – with an energy that's irresistible.

Where to go

Ontario contains not only the country's manufacturing heart and its largest city, **Toronto**, but also **Niagara Falls**, the premier tourist sight. North of Toronto there's **Georgian Bay**, a beautiful waterscape of pine-studded islets set against crystal-blue waters. The bay is also accessible from the Canadian capital, **Ottawa** – not as dynamic as Toronto, but still well worth a stay for its galleries, museums and handful of superb restaurants.

Québec, set apart by the depth of its French culture, is anchored by its biggest city, **Montréal**, which is for many people the most vibrant place in the country, a fascinating mix of old-world style and commercial dynamism. The pace of life is more relaxed in the historic provincial capital **Québec City**, and more easygoing

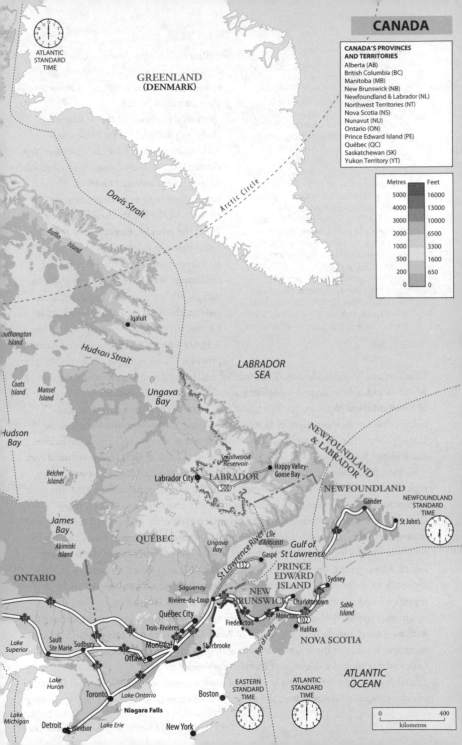

CANADA

ATLANTIC
STANDARD
TIME

GREENLAND
(DENMARK)

Davis Strait

Arctic Circle

**CANADA'S PROVINCES
AND TERRITORIES**
Alberta (AB)
British Columbia (BC)
Manitoba (MB)
New Brunswick (NB)
Newfoundland & Labrador (NL)
Northwest Territories (NT)
Nova Scotia (NS)
Nunavut (NU)
Ontario (ON)
Prince Edward Island (PE)
Québec (QC)
Saskatchewan (SK)
Yukon Territory (YT)

Metres	Feet
5000	16000
4000	13000
3000	10000
2000	6500
1000	3300
500	1600
200	650
0	0

Baffin Island

Iqaluit

Southampton
Island

Hudson Strait

LABRADOR
SEA

Coats
Island

Mansel
Island

Ungava
Bay

Hudson
Bay

NEWFOUNDLAND
& LABRADOR

Belcher
Islands

Smallwood
Reservoir

Happy Valley-
Goose Bay

Labrador City   LABRADOR

500

NEWFOUNDLAND

Gander

NEWFOUNDLAND
STANDARD
TIME

St John's

James
Bay

Akimiski
Island

QUÉBEC

Ungava
Bay

L'Île
d'Anticosti

Gulf of
St Lawrence

Gaspé

132

PRINCE
EDWARD
ISLAND

Sydney

ONTARIO

Saguenay

Rivière-du-Loup

NEW
BRUNSWICK

Charlottetown

Sable
Island

Québec City

Fredericton

Moncton   102

Trois-Rivières

105

Lake
Superior

Sault
Ste Marie

Sudbury

Montréal

Sherbrooke

Halifax

NOVA SCOTIA

Ottawa

Bay of Fundy

Lake
Huron

Toronto   Lake Ontario

Boston

EASTERN
STANDARD
TIME

ATLANTIC
STANDARD
TIME

ATLANTIC
OCEAN

Lake
Michigan

Niagara Falls

Detroit   Windsor   Lake Erie

New York

0   400

kilometres

FACT FILE

- Canada has the 10th largest economy in the world; the country's richest person is David Thomson (chairman of Thomson Reuters), worth around $25 billion.
- It's true: the Canadian province of Québec is by far the largest producer of maple syrup in the world (accounting for three-quarters of global output).
- Established in 1964, Tim Hortons is a Canadian icon, with over 4000 doughnut and "double-double" (coffee with two sugars and two creams) stores nationwide.
- Unbeknown to most Americans, Hollywood is crammed with Canadians: Michael Cera, Ryan Gosling, Evangeline Lily, Rachel McAdams, Mike Myers, Ellen Page, Keanu Reeves, Ryan Reynolds, Seth Rogen, Kiefer Sutherland and William Shatner (Captain Kirk!) among them.
- Since 1952, Saturday nights have been home to *Hockey Night in Canada* on CBC, when thousands are glued to the TV to pay homage to the national winter sport.

still in the villages dotted along the St Lawrence lowlands, where glittering spires attest to the enduring influence of the Catholic Church.

Across the mouth of the St Lawrence River, the pastoral **Gaspé Peninsula** – the easternmost part of Québec – borders **New Brunswick**, a densely forested introduction to the three **Maritime Provinces**, whose people have long been dependent on timber and the sea for their livelihood. Here, the tapering **Bay of Fundy** boasts mind-blowing tides – rising and falling by 9m or more – and superb maritime landscapes, while the region's tiny fishing villages are at their most beguiling near **Halifax**, the busy capital of **Nova Scotia**. Connected to New Brunswick by bridge is **Prince Edward Island**, Canada's smallest province – a picturesque place of rolling farmland and Victorian homes. Even prettier are the land and seascapes of **Cape Breton Island**, whose rugged topography anticipates that of the Atlantic province of **Newfoundland** to the north. The island's isolation has spawned a distinctive culture that's at its most lively in **St John's**, where the local folk music scene among Canada's best. The island also boasts some of the Atlantic seaboard's finest landscapes, particularly the flat-topped peaks and glacier-gouged lakes of **Gros Morne National Park**.

Back on the mainland, the prairie provinces of **Manitoba** and **Saskatchewan** have a reputation for dullness that's unfair: even in the flat southern parts there's the diversion of **Winnipeg**, whose traces of its early days make it a good place to break a trans-Canadian journey. Numerous lakes and gigantic forests offer magnificent canoeing and hiking, and in the far north, beside Hudson Bay, **Churchill** – remote, but accessible by train – is famous for its polar bears, beluga whales and easy viewing of the **Northern Lights**. Moving west, the wheatfields of **Alberta** ripple into ranching country on the approach to the province's two main cities, **Edmonton** and **Calgary**, grown fat on the region's oil and gas fields. Calgary is especially known for its cowboys, rodeos and sumptuous steaks. Both cities provide useful springboards for trips into the **Canadian Rockies** – most popularly to the resorts of **Banff**, **Lake Louise** and **Jasper** – and the most incredible scenery in the country, from mighty glaciers to the serene beauty of Moraine Lake and the rugged wilderness of Icefields Parkway.

Further west, **British Columbia** is a land of snow-capped summits, rivers and forests, pioneer villages, gold-rush ghost towns, and some of the greatest hiking, skiing, fishing

SUNSET SURFERS AT SOUTH CHESTERMAN BEACH, BRITISH COLUMBIA

ABORIGINAL PEOPLES

The British and French were latecomers to Canada, a country that for thousands of years was home to a vast **Aboriginal population** (or "First Nations"). Today, almost a million Canadians claim descent from these first peoples, from the so-called "Indians" of the central and western heartlands, to the Inuit, inhabitants of the great sweep of Canada's north. A third group, the Métis – descendants of mixed unions of white and Aboriginal people – also have a distinct identity, part of a rich cultural, social and artistic mosaic that provides a beguiling complement to the mainstream. You'll find evidence of Canada's former Aboriginal life in many museums and galleries, and plenty of areas nurturing living Aboriginal cultures, though there's no escaping the fact that many Aboriginal people are among the most marginalized of Canadians.

and canoeing in the world. Its urban focus, **Vancouver**, is the country's third largest city, known for its spectacular natural setting, fabulous food and a laidback West Coast hedonism. Off the coast lies **Vancouver Island**, a microcosm of the province's immense natural riches and home to **Victoria**, a devotedly anglophile little provincial capital. It's also well worth journeying over to the island's west coast to take in the rugged beauty of Pacific Rim National Park's **Long Beach**, **Clayoquot Sound** and surf town of **Tofino**.

North of British Columbia, wedged alongside Alaska, is the **Yukon Territory**, half grandiose mountains, half subarctic tundra, and full of evocative echoes of the Klondike gold rush. **Whitehorse**, its capital, and **Dawson City**, a gold-rush relic, are the major towns here, each accessed by dramatic frontier highways. The **Northwest Territories** and **Nunavut**, covering the Canadian Arctic, are an immensity of forest, lakes, tundra and ice, the realm of Dene and Inuit Aboriginal peoples. Roads are virtually nonexistent in the deep north, and only the frontier city of **Yellowknife**, plus a handful of ramshackle villages, offer the air links and resources necessary to explore this wilderness.

When to go

Canada's climate is hugely varied; areas near the coast generally have milder winters and cooler summers than the interior – although winter in the **Maritimes Provinces** is extremely cold. **July and August** are reliably warm throughout the country, even in the

HIKING THROUGH BRANDYWINE MEADOWS, WHISTLER

AVERAGE TEMPERATURES AND SNOWFALL

	Jan	Feb	Mar	Apr	May	Jun	Jul	Aug	Sep	Oct	Nov	Dec
CALGARY, AB												
Max/min (°C)	-3/-16	-1/-12	3/-8	11/-2	17/3	21/7	23/9	23/9	17/4	13/-1	3/-9	-2/-14
Max/min (°F)	26/4	31/10	38/17	51/28	62/37	69/45	74/49	73/48	63/39	55/30	37/16	28/6
Precipitation (mm)	13	10	15	25	53	76	71	48	48	15	13	13
HALIFAX, NS												
Max/min (°C)	-1/-9	-1/-9	3/-5	8/-1	13/4	18/9	22/13	22/13	18/10	13/5	8/1	2/-6
Max/min (°F)	31/16	30/15	37/23	46/31	55/39	65/48	71/55	71/56	65/50	55/41	46/33	36/21
Precipitation (mm)	130	107	112	109	104	104	99	102	91	122	140	150
MONTRÉAL/OTTAWA, ON												
Max/min (°C)	-7/-16	-5/-14	2/-7	11/1	18/7	23/12	26/15	24/14	19/9	13/3	4/-2	-4/-11
Max/min (°F)	20/4	23/6	35/19	51/33	65/45	74/54	79/59	76/57	67/49	55/38	40/28	25/12
Precipitation (mm)	51	51	56	66	76	84	86	89	84	74	81	74
TORONTO, ON												
Max/min (°C)	-3/-11	-2/-11	3/-6	11/1	18/6	23/11	27/14	25/13	21/9	14/3	7/-1	0/-8
Max/min (°F)	27/12	29/12	38/22	52/33	65/43	74/52	80/57	77/56	69/48	57/38	45/30	32/18
Precipitation (mm)	46	46	56	64	66	69	76	84	74	64	71	66
VANCOUVER, BC												
Max/min (°C)	6/0	8/1	9/2	12/4	16/8	19/11	22/12	22/13	18/10	13/6	9/3	6/1
Max/min (°F)	42/32	46/34	49/36	54/40	61/46	66/51	71/54	71/55	65/50	56/43	48/37	43/33
Precipitation (mm)	150	125	109	76	61	46	36	38	64	114	170	178

far north, making these the busiest months to visit, with **September** also warm (and busy) in the south (note also that the sun sets much later in the far north in summer). In Newfoundland, the Maritime Provinces and the **North**, much of the tourist infrastructure closes from October to May, although winter sports still draws some visitors. The long autumn can be the best time to visit **Ontario** and **Québec**, when there are equable temperatures and few crowds. **November to March** is an ordeal of subzero temperatures almost everywhere except on the West Coast, though winter days in many areas are clear and dry, and all large Canadian towns are geared to the challenge of cold conditions, with covered walkways and indoor malls protecting their inhabitants from the worst of the weather.

The southwestern parts of **British Columbia** enjoy some of Canada's best weather: the extremes are less marked and the overall temperatures generally milder than elsewhere. Much of the province, though, bears the brunt of Pacific depressions, so this is one of the country's damper regions: visiting between late spring and early autumn offers the best chance of missing the rain.

Author picks

Scaling the snow-tipped heights of its awe-inspiring national parks, enduring Atlantic storms and driving some of Canada's most challenging and isolated roads, our hard-travelling authors have visited every corner of this vast, magnificent country – from the outports of Newfoundland to the pristine wilderness of Yukon. Here are their personal favourites:

Live music In the land of Arcade Fire, Leonard Cohen and k.d. lang, see upcoming Canadian stars at the *Horseshoe Tavern* in Toronto (see page 93), *Club Soda* in Montréal (see page 227), and the *Commodore Ballroom* in Vancouver (see page 717).

Go wild Soak up Canada's pristine wilderness beachcombing Wonderstrand, Labrador (see page 457), driving the Dempster Highway to the Arctic Circle (see page 839) or hiking the Canol Heritage Trail in the North West Territories (see page 847).

Watching whales Enjoy hefty doses of minke, finback, grey and humpback from Westport in Nova Scotia (see page 351); St Lawrence River in Québec (see page 308); Bay Bulls in Newfoundland (see page 422); Battle Harbour in Labrador (see page 456); and Victoria in BC (see page 739).

Iceberg spotting In spring and early summer the chance is high you'll spy these blue-white giants at Twillingate (see page 441) and St Anthony (see page 450) in Newfoundland.

Aboriginal culture Visit the Metepenagiag Heritage Park in New Brunswick (see page 391) to learn about the local Mi'kmaq tribe, the Woodland Cultural Centre in Ontario (see page 117) and Haida Gwaii (see page 803), the island home of the Haida people.

Best microbreweries Fredericton's Picaroons is New Brunswick's high-quality microbrewery (see page 387), while Newfoundland's Quidi Vidi Brewery makes beer with real icebergs (see page 418) and À l'abri de la Tempête in Québec's Îles-de-la-Madeleine serves distinctive award-winning ales (see page 298). One of a very long list in BC is Vancouver's dependable Granville Island Brewing (see page 716).

> Our author recommendations don't end here. We've flagged up our favourite places – a perfectly sited hotel, an atmospheric café, a special restaurant – throughout the Guide, highlighted with the ★ symbol.

AN EMPTY DEMPSTER HIGHWAY, YUKON
ICEBERGS IN WOLF COVE, NEWFOUNDLAND AND LABRADOR

30

things not to miss

It's not possible to see everything that Canada has to offer in one trip – and we don't suggest you try. What follows, in no particular order, is a selective and subjective taste of the country's highlights: beautiful landscapes, alluring cities, outdoor adventures and spectacular events. All entries have a page reference to take you straight into the Guide, where you can find out more. Coloured numbers refer to chapters in the Guide.

1 VANCOUVER
See page 687
Canada's Pacific capital is one of the nation's most enticing cities, with a dazzling location, fine beaches and world-class cuisine.

2 DAWSON CITY
See page 833
Take a step back into history in this iconic frontier town, the centre of the great 1898 Klondike gold rush.

3 POLAR BEARS IN CHURCHILL
See page 492
Bleak and solitary, this northern town bills itself as the "polar bear capital of the world" – with justification.

4 WHALE-WATCHING
See pages 292, 308, 351, 358, 351, 423, 739, 769, 771 and 783
On both the East and West coasts, venturing out to view whales – from orcas to humpbacks and minke to belugas – at close quarters is an unforgettable experience.

5 JASPER
See page 590
Explore the Canadian Rockies' largest national park – by ice-climbing, hiking, biking or skiing.

6 NIAGARA FALLS
See page 105
Millions come to see the Falls – three great sheets of water thundering over a 50m precipice.

7 OTTAWA'S CANADIAN WAR MUSEUM
See page 168
This impressive homage to Canada's military history competes with the National Gallery as cultural centrepiece of the nation's agreeable capital.

8 SNOWBOARDING IN WHISTLER
See page 728
Hit the slopes where Olympians triumphed at North America's largest ski resort, with hundreds of acres of mind-blowing terrain.

9 LUNENBURG
See page 340
Of all the old fishing towns along the Nova Scotian coast, Lunenburg is the prettiest.

10 ART GALLERY OF ONTARIO
See page 71
With an outstanding collection of works by Canada's Group of Seven and an architectural revamp by Frank Gehry, Toronto's main art gallery is a must.

ART GALLERY OF ONTARIO MUSÉE DES BEAUX-ARTS DE L'ONTARIO

AGO

11 VIEUX-QUÉBEC
See page 249
With its clutch of fine old buildings, handsome location and great restaurant scene, Québec City's historic old town feels more European than Canadian.

12 WESTERN BROOK POND, GROS MORNE NATIONAL PARK
See page 446
Take a boat trip on Newfoundland's most jaw-dropping lake, hemmed in by 600m walls of rock.

13 MOUNT ROBSON
See page 600
The highest peak in the Canadian Rockies, set amid stunning scenery on the Alberta–BC border.

14 NEWFOUNDLAND FOLK MUSIC
See page 421
St John's is an enclave of live music excellence, especially noted for the quality of its folk artists, Celtic bands and fiddlers.

15 LOBSTER SUPPERS IN PEI
See page 400
End a day lounging on the reddish sands of PEI's National Park with one of the island's celebrated seafood feasts.

MOUNT
ROBSON
PARK

13

14

15

17

21 CALGARY STAMPEDE
See page 541
Let your inner cowboy (or -girl) loose at this annual bonanza of all things rodeo and Western.

22 GEORGIAN BAY ISLANDS
See page 143
Get a taster of the Great Lakes at Ontario's most scenic spot – easily explored by boat or kayak.

23 FOGO ISLAND, NEWFOUNDLAND
See page 438
Wild and unspoiled, this is Newfoundland at its most traditional, with gorgeous fishing villages clinging to the rocky shore.

24 CANOE IN ALGONQUIN PROVINCIAL PARK
See page 148
The wild tracts of this enormous park – the largest in Ontario – are best explored by canoe.

25 HIKING IN BANFF
See page 567
Countless trails make it easy to escape the crowds and explore the great outdoors around the Rockies' bustling summer capital.

26 BATTLE HARBOUR, LABRADOR
See page 456
Step back into the world of *Moby Dick* at this beautifully preserved nineteenth-century fishing port.

27 SEE A GLACIER UP CLOSE
See page 588
The largest collection of snow and ice in the Canadian Rockies is at the Columbia Icefield, home of the famed Athabasca Glacier.

28 MONTRÉAL'S JUST FOR LAUGHS
See page 197
Catching some of the thousands of acts at the world's largest comedy festival is just one of the ways to enjoy this city's many delights.

29 DRIVE THE ICEFIELDS PARKWAY
See page 585
Taking in the dramatic Rockies for over 200km, this is one of the world's most beautiful drives..

30 GRIZZLY BEAR SANCTUARY
See page 800
Take a boat trip from Prince Rupert to this remote, lush preserve, which is home to at least sixty grizzlies.

29

30

Itineraries

The following itineraries span the entire length of this vast and incredibly diverse country. You won't be able to cover everything, but even picking a few highlights will give you a deeper insight into Canada's natural and historic wonders...

CLASSIC CANADA

This three-week tour gives a taster of Canada's main highlights from coast to coast, travelling by train, bus and plane.

❶ Québec City Savour the baguettes, cobbled streets, café au lait and rich French heritage of Canada's oldest settlement. See page 244

❷ Montréal Head south to this hip and cosmopolitan city to enjoy the street artists, museums, smoked meats, bagels and North America's largest jazz festival. See page 193

❸ Ottawa The Canadian capital is worth a day or two for its outstanding museums and galleries, with a side trip to the distinctive geography of Gatineau Park. See page 161

❹ Toronto Canada's biggest city and commercial capital is best known for the cloud-scraping CN Tower, art from the Group of Seven and pulsing nightlife. See page 56

❺ Niagara Falls Canada's major show-stopper is just a short ride from Toronto. See page 105

❻ Take the train to Jasper Fly from Toronto to Edmonton and take the VIA Rail service to Jasper, home to gorgeous Maligne Lake and Canada's highest cable car. See page 591

❼ The Icefields Parkway Spend a few days immersed in the grandeur of the Rockies on the road to Banff, via the Columbia Icefield and Lake Louise. See page 585

❽ Banff The capital of the Canadian Rockies is surrounded by mesmerizing scenery, mountain trails and soothing hot springs. See page 563

❾ Vancouver After stops in Yoho and Revelstoke national parks, end your trip at the Pacific Ocean with a scenic stay at Canada's dynamic western capital. See page 687

BEST OF THE MARITIMES

Maritime Canada – called the Atlantic Provinces when you include Newfoundland and Labrador – is a land apart, with a distinct culture, stunning scenery and invariably empty roads. This two- to three-week tour is best experienced by car.

❶ Halifax The hip capital of Nova Scotia offers great museums, the notorious "donair" kebab, hundreds of pubs and the best live music in the east. See page 326

❷ Lunenburg and the south shore Take a day or two to see the best of Nova Scotia's rugged coastline south of Halifax, ending at the charming fishing port of Lunenburg. page 340

Create your own itinerary with Rough Guides. Whether you're after adventure or a family-friendly holiday, we have a trip for you, with all the activities you enjoy doing and the sights you want to see. All our trips are devised by local experts who get the most out of the destination. Visit **www.roughguides.com/trips** to chat with one of our travel agents.

❸ Bay of Fundy Drive to the New Brunswick side of the Bay of Fundy, where Hopewell's flowerpot rocks and the misty forests of the Fundy National Park await. See page 370

❹ Prince Edward Island Cross over the Confederation Bridge for the bucolic charms of *Anne of Green Gables* country. See page 392

❺ Cape Breton Back in Nova Scotia, drive north to Cape Breton Island, where the jaw-dropping Cabot Trail takes in the best scenery, and Acadian and Gaelic cultures. See page 358

❻ Gros Morne National Park Catch the ferry from Cape Breton to Newfoundland and drive up to this sensational national park. See page 445

❼ L'Anse aux Meadows Continue north to St Anthony and this remarkable historic site, home to Vikings some 500 years before Columbus. See page 451

❽ Fogo Island Cut across the vast wilderness of central Newfoundland to this untouched slice of traditional port life. See page 438

❾ St John's End up at Newfoundland's boisterous capital, where you can whale-watch, picnic at a lighthouse and get "screeched in". See page 412

THE GREAT NORTH

Only when you travel in Canada's immense northern wilderness will you begin to grasp just how big – and rich in wildlife – this nation is. Come in summer to enjoy the sunshine and take three to four weeks to complete this trip.

❶ Winnipeg Fly into the underrated capital of Manitoba and gateway to the prairies, home to the world's largest Inuit art collection. See page 471

❷ Churchill Take the train to this Hudson Bay outpost to see hordes of beluga whales and – while you still can – polar bears up close. See page 490

❸ Alaska Highway Fly or drive to Edmonton and then Dawson Creek before following the epic stretch of Alaska Highway up to the lively capital of the Yukon, Whitehorse. See page 813

❹ Klondike Highway Continue north from Whitehorse through the wilderness on the Klondike Highway, enjoying the toasty pools at Takhini Hot Springs. See page 830

❺ Dawson City Take a break from the road at this iconic northern frontier town, centre of the Klondike gold rush. See page 833

❻ Prince Rupert This port town is the stepping-off point for the Grizzly Bear Sanctuary and whale-watching tours. See page 799

❼ Haida Gwaii Take the ferry across to this magical island archipelago in the Pacific, rich in Aboriginal culture, flora and fauna. See page 803

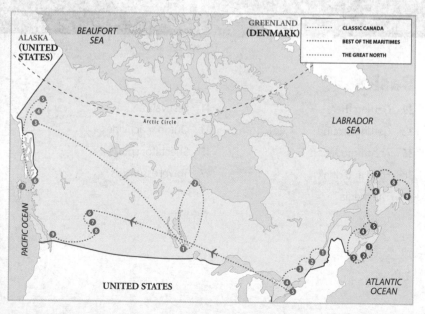

MONTREAL BAGELS

Basics

Getting there

Most US travellers visit Canada by car, but there are plenty of flights, buses, ferries and trains that cross the border. Other travellers, including those from the UK, Australia, New Zealand and South Africa, have little choice but to fly.

Airfares from the UK, Australia and New Zealand to Canada tend to be highest around mid-June to early September, the peak tourist season. You'll get the best prices during the low season, mid-November to April (excluding Christmas and New Year, when seats are at a premium).

Flights from the UK and Ireland

Most nonstop scheduled flights **from Britain** to Canada depart from London Heathrow or London Gatwick with a handful of departures from airports around Britain supplemented by holiday charter flights. The main gateways are Montréal, Toronto and Vancouver, but there are also nonstop scheduled flights to Calgary, Edmonton, Ottawa, Halifax and St John's (Newfoundland) in summer. Connecting flights from these airports delve into every corner of the country.

A standard return from London to Toronto with Air Canada (Ⓦ aircanada.com) can cost anywhere between £450 and £800 (low/high season), and £800 and £1100 to Vancouver (US carriers offer cheaper rates to the latter, usually with a change in Chicago). The cheapest nonstop rates – as low as £330 to Toronto – are offered by Air Transat (Ⓦ airtransat.co.uk). Most airlines also offer good-value **open-jaw** deals that enable you to fly into one Canadian city and back from another – useful if you want to make your own way across the country.

From Ireland, the only daily nonstop flights are in the summer (mid-April to mid-Oct) with Air Canada and Aer Lingus from Dublin to Toronto and on Air Transat to Toronto and Montréal; on all other flights you will have to change planes, usually either in the UK or US. Cheapest **return fares** on direct Dublin–

Toronto flights (7hr) are around €500 on Air Transat, and €1000 with connections to Vancouver.

Flights from the US

From the US to Canada there are plenty of nonstop **flights** on Air Canada and most US airlines, though prices, especially on east-coast routes, are relatively expensive. WestJet (Ⓦ westjet.com) offers flights primarily from the American West, and with the exception of Las Vegas routes, most of these are seasonal. Porter Airlines (Ⓦ flyporter.com) connects Toronto with New York, Boston, Chicago, Pittsburgh and DC, and is generally the cheapest carrier. Fares change drastically depending on season and when you purchase: in summer, expect to pay at least US$250 for New York to Toronto; US$450 for New York to Halifax; at least US$500 from Chicago to most of the big cities; US$450 for LA to Calgary; and US$400 for LA to Vancouver. WestJet flights between Las Vegas and Toronto can be as low as US$175 one way, even in summer.

Because **domestic flights** wholly within the US or Canada can cost less than flights between the two countries, you could save money by crossing the border before or after your flight. This is especially true of long-haul flights: a transcontinental flight from New York to Vancouver can be considerably more expensive than a similar flight to Seattle (which lies only 160km south of Vancouver).

Flying north/south is reasonably quick: New York to Montréal takes around 1hr 15min; New York to Toronto 1hr 30min; New York to Halifax 1hr 50min; LA to Vancouver 2hr 45min; and LA to Calgary 3hr. Flying east/west between countries usually involves a stopover or onward connection, so New York–Vancouver can take 7–8hr.

Flights from Australia, New Zealand and South Africa

The Air Canada service from Sydney to Vancouver is the only nonstop connection between Canada and Australia – high-season rates are around Aus$2100–3000 return (depending on how far ahead you buy).

A BETTER KIND OF TRAVEL

At Rough Guides we are passionately committed to travel. We believe it helps us understand the world we live in and the people we share it with – and of course tourism is vital to many developing economies. But the scale of modern tourism has also damaged some places irreparably, and climate change is accelerated by most forms of transport, especially flying. We encourage our authors to consider the carbon footprint of the journeys they make in the course of researching our guides.

For other parts of Canada, airlines tend to quote you fares via LA or Vancouver to your chosen destination; Air Canada flies through Vancouver, charging around Aus$2100 return from Sydney to Toronto, even in summer. Qantas flies through LA, with the onward portion to Toronto via codeshare with WestJet. Flights from other cities in **Australia route through** Sydney.

Air New Zealand (W airnewzealand.com) runs nonstop flights **from Auckland, New Zealand** to Vancouver just three times a week, and most other flights usually end up routing through LA: you can get flights from Auckland to Vancouver from NZ$2100 return via Air New Zealand. Flights to Toronto pass through Vancouver – expect to pay around NZ$3000 in peak season.

South Africa has no nonstop flights to Canada, and your cheapest options are usually to fly on KLM (W klm. com) via Amsterdam or via Frankfurt on Lufthansa (W lufthansa.com) to Toronto (up to R20,000) in high season, or via London (BA) and Frankfurt (Lufthansa) to Vancouver (up to R25,000).

By car

The **US highway** system leads into Canada at thirteen points along the border. The busiest corridors are from Blaine, WA, to White Rock, BC; from Detroit, MI, to Windsor, ON; from Buffalo, NY, to Fort Erie, ON; and at Niagara Falls. You may encounter traffic jams at the border, particularly at weekends, in the summer and on US or Canadian holidays, but given that most border posts are open 24hr, you can usually beat the lines by starting early. From New York to Montréal (380 miles/612km) or Toronto (490 miles/790km) reckon on eight to nine hours' driving; from San Francisco to Vancouver (955 miles/1536km), around nineteen hours. Mapmaker Rand McNally's website (W randm-cnally.com) has a good road-trip tool, with routes and mileage charts.

Vehicle insurance is compulsory and it's also advisable to obtain a yellow Non-Resident Inter-Province Motor Vehicle Liability Card from your insurance company before you go. Make sure you have documents establishing proof of insurance and proof of vehicle ownership with you at all times.

By bus

The Greyhound bus network extends into Canada from several points on the US East Coast and one from the West; prices below are for cheap **fourteen-day advance tickets**.

Travelling overland from San Diego to Montréal, say, is an epic, three-day journey (with at least three bus changes), but if you're on a tight budget, the US$192 fare is a bargain – though be sure to factor in three days' worth of food and drink. Greyhound and Trailways buses compete on the busy runs **from New York** to Montréal and Toronto, offering half a dozen trips per day. Fares for the eight-hour journey to Montréal are around US$80 one way; the twelve- to thirteen-hour marathon to Toronto can be as low as US$50 for advance tickets (US$75 regular). Trips **from Boston** to Montréal start at US$55 one way and the journey takes around seven hours.

Other cross-border connections include **from Burlington**, VT, to Montréal (4 daily; 2hr 30min–3hr; from US$21); and **from Seattle** to Vancouver (4 daily; 4hr 10min; US$18–25).

For real bargains, check out Mega Bus, which runs between New York and Toronto in eleven to twelve hours (fares can be as low as US$29 one way if you book two months ahead).

By train

For specific journeys, the **train** is usually more expensive than the bus (and often the plane), though special deals, especially in off-peak periods, can bring the round-trip cost down considerably.

Two routes on **Amtrak** from the northeastern US have direct connections with **VIA Rail**, Canada's national rail company: the "Maple Leaf" from New York to Toronto via Buffalo and Niagara Falls (1 daily; 12hr 30min; from US$131 one way); and the "Adirondack" from New York to Montréal via Albany and Plattsburgh (1 daily; 11hr; from US$70 one way). In the Northwest, the "Amtrak Cascades" runs from Seattle to Vancouver (2 daily; 4hr; US$40–77 one way). All these fares are for travel in economy class, where pillows are provided for overnight journeys.

Reserve as far as possible in advance, as it is compulsory to have a seat and some of the eastern-seaboard trains in particular get completely booked. Some rail passes for the US network are also valid as far as a Canadian gateway like Vancouver or Montréal.

By ferry

Several US–Canada ferry routes serve the West Coast, while two operate on the East Coast. Apart from the enjoyment of the ride, the boats can save you hours of driving. Always **book ahead where possible**.

On the **East Coast**, tiny car ferries link Deer Island, New Brunswick, to Eastport in Maine (late June to mid-Sept hourly 9am–6pm; 20min; car and driver $20, foot passenger $4; no reservations). From 2019 the Yarmouth (Nova Scotia) to Maine (US) car ferry is likely to switch ports to Bar Harbor from Portland, with "The Cat" services operated by Bay Ferries (☎ 877 762 7245, ⓦ ferries.ca). One-way high season rates start at around US$107 per adult, plus US$199 for a standard car. Ferries sail daily from early June to early October; rates are cheapest Monday to Wednesday and through June, September and October.

On the **West Coast**, the *Victoria Clipper* catamaran for foot passengers runs between Seattle and Victoria on Vancouver Island, three times daily from late June to August, twice daily in May, June and September and once daily for the rest of the year (2hr 45min; from US$99–119 one way). The most useful West Coast ferry is the Washington State Ferries service from Anacortes to Sidney, on Vancouver Island. The ferry travels twice daily in summer, and once daily in winter via the San Juan archipelago (average-sized vehicle with driver $57.05 each way, extra adult passengers $20.25 each; bicycles $6; 3hr). Further north, Alaska Marine Hwy ferries link several Alaskan towns with Prince Rupert, British Columbia.

AGENTS AND OPERATORS

Backroads US ☎ 510 527 1555, ☎ 800 462 2848, ⓦ backroads. com. Cycling, hiking and multisport tours in the Rockies, Québec and Nova Scotia.

Cosmos US ☎ 800 276 1241, ⓦ cosmos.com. Planned vacation packages with an independent focus.

ebookers UK ☎ 0871 223 5000, Republic of Ireland ☎ 01 431 1311; ⓦ ebookers.com. Low fares on an extensive selection of scheduled flights and package deals.

Ecosummer Expeditions Canada & US ☎ 800 465 8884, International ☎ 250 674 0102; ⓦ ecosummer.com. Wilderness expeditions and ecotourism focusing on BC, especially the Gulf and Haida Gwaii.

Exodus UK ☎ 0845 863 9600, ⓦ exodus.co.uk. Adventure and action-oriented vacation packages focused on low-impact tourism, mostly in western Canada.

Frontier Ski UK ☎ 020 8776 8709, ⓦ frontier-ski.co.uk. Leading Canadian ski holiday specialist, with trips to the Rockies and Québec.

G Adventures US ☎ 1 888 800 4100, UK ☎ 0344 272 2060, Australia ☎ 1300 853 325, New Zealand ☎ 0800 333 415; ⓦ gadventures.com. Adventure travel company taking small groups on specialist programmes that include walking, biking, overlanding, adventure and cultural trips. Québec, the Rockies and BC focused.

Go Fishing Worldwide UK ☎ 020 8742 1566, ⓦ gofishingworldwide.co.uk. Fishing trips to Labrador, New Brunswick, Québec, the Yukon, Alberta, BC, Ontario and NWT.

Great Rail Journeys UK ☎ 01904 521 936, ⓦ greatrail.com. Canada coast-to-coast by train.

Kuoni Travel UK ☎ 01306 747 002, ⓦ kuoni.co.uk. Major tour operator running long-haul package holidays. Especially good deals for families.

Moose Travel Network Canada ☎ 888 244 6673 or ☎ 855 741 7318 ⓦ moosenetwork.com. Outfit that runs backpacker mini-coach tours in BC, Alberta, New Brunswick, Nova Scotia, Ontario and Québec. See also page 34.

North America Travel Service UK ☎ 020 7569 6710, ⓦ northamericatravelservice.co.uk. Various itineraries cater to city breaks, cruises, spa vacations, guided tours and more.

North South Travel UK ☎ 01245 608 291, ⓦ northsouthtravel. co.uk. Friendly, competitive travel agency, offering discounted fares worldwide. Profits are used to support projects in the developing world, especially the promotion of sustainable tourism.

Rod and Reel Adventures US ☎ 800 356 6982, ⓦ rodandreeladventures.com. Fishing holidays.

Ski Independence UK ☎ 0845 310 3030, ⓦ ski-i.com. Wide range of ski packages, mostly to the Rockies.

Ski Safari UK ☎ 01273 224 060, ⓦ skisafari.com. Tailor-made ski and snowboarding holidays to the Rockies and Québec.

STA Travel US ☎ 800 781 4040, UK ☎ 0871 230 0040, Australia ☎ 134 782, New Zealand ☎ 0800 474 400, SA ☎ 0861 781 781; ⓦ statravel.com. Worldwide specialists in independent travel; also student IDs, travel insurance, car rental, rail passes and more. Good discounts for students and under-26s.

Trailfinders UK ☎ 0845 058 5858, Republic of Ireland ☎ 01 677 7888; ⓦ trailfinders.com. One of the best-informed and most efficient agents for independent travellers.

Travel Cuts Canada ☎ 800 667 2887, ⓦ travelcuts.com. Popular, long-established student-travel organization.

Travelplan Ski Australia ☎ 1300 130 754, ⓦ travelplan.com.au. Holidays in the snow worldwide, plus extreme heli-skiing trips.

Travelsphere UK ☎ 0800 567 7372, ⓦ travelsphere.co.uk. Wide range of options includes cruises, activity-based vacations and short trips.

TrekAmerica UK ☎ 0845 313 2614, ⓦ trekamerica.co.uk. Offers small-group adventure vacations.

Wildlife Worldwide UK ☎ 0845 130 6982, Ireland ☎ 01 440 7477; ⓦ wildlifeworldwide.com. Trips for wildlife and wilderness enthusiasts, including whale- and polar bear-watching packages.

RAIL CONTACTS

Amtrak US ☎ 800 872 7245, ⓦ amtrak.com.
VIA Rail Canada ☎ 888 842 7245, ⓦ viarail.ca.

BUS CONTACTS (US)

Greyhound US ☎ 800 231 2222, ⓦ greyhound.com.
Mega Bus US and Canada ☎ 877 462 6342, ⓦ megabus.com.
Trailways US ☎ 800 776 7548, ⓦ trailwaysny.com.

BUS CONTACTS (CANADA)

Coach Canada ☎ 800 461 7661, ⓦ coachcanada.com. Assorted services in Ontario and Québec.
DRL Coachlines ☎ 709 263 2171, ☎ 888 263 1854; ⓦ drl-lr.com. Newfoundland's only long-distance bus company.
Greyhound Canada ☎ 800 661 8747, ⓦ greyhound.ca. Long-distance buses in Québec, Ontario, central and western Canada.

Maritime Bus ☎ 800 575 1807, ⓦ maritimebus.com. Services throughout the Maritimes.
Ontario Northland ☎ 800 461 8558, ⓦ ontarionorthland.ca. Long-distance bus (and train) services in Ontario.
Orléans Express ☎ 888 999 3977, ⓦ orleansexpress.com. Long-distance bus services in Québec.
Red Arrow ☎ 800 232 1958, ⓦ redarrow.ca. Services to and from Calgary, Edmonton, Banff and Lake Louise.

FERRY CONTACTS

Alaska Marine Hwy US ☎ 800 382 9229, International ☎ 907 235 7099; ⓦ akferry.org.
Bay Ferries Canada ☎ 877 762 7245, ⓦ ferries.ca.
Black Ball Ferries Canada ☎ 360 457 4491, ⓦ cohoferry.com.
East Coast Ferries Canada ☎ 506 747 2159, ⓦ eastcoastferriesltd. com.
Victoria Clipper US ☎ 800 888 2535, ⓦ clippervacations.com/clipper-experience.
Washington State Ferries US ☎ 206 464 6400, ☎ 888 808 7977; ⓦ wsdot.wa.gov/ferries.

Getting around

Beyond the cities, getting around Canada by public transport can be tough: train services are limited to a light scattering of routes, and although buses are much more plentiful and cheap, bus stations and stops can be miles from the nearest hotel or campsite. Flying is far more expensive, and the vast bulk of visitors rent cars and drive.

By plane

Canada has a comprehensive network of **domestic flights** that covers every corner of the country. The big carriers are **WestJet** (☎ 888 937 8538, ⓦ westjet.com) and **Air Canada** (☎ 888 247 2262, ⓦ aircanada.com) and its subsidiary airlines, although there are a number of smaller airlines operating regionally. Throughout the Guide, we have given details of the most useful services.

Prices remain generally high, though new budget airlines are gradually changing things. A one-way fare from Toronto to Winnipeg (2hr 30min) with Air Canada can cost $300 (high season), and a little less on WestJet, though flights with Swoop (ⓦ flyswoop.com) and Flair Air (ⓦ flairair.ca) can be as low as $100 one-way. Standard fares to the more remote settlements in the north are still prohibitively expensive for non-business travellers: one-way flights from Toronto to Goose Bay are at least $350 in the summer, and $1600 for Montréal to Iqaluit. One way

around this particular cost is the **Yukon Advantage Air Pass** (☎ 800 661 0407, ⓦ flyairnorth.com) from Yukon-based Air North, which allows you to fly ten one-way flight segments, valid on any Air North route, starting from $3150. For a way to cut costs outside of the north, consider an **Air Canada Flight Pass** (you must be a member of Air Canada's Aeroplan mileage programme, which you can join online). There are endless permutations, but the principle is that you buy a fixed or unlimited number of flight credits, each of which is valid for an internal flight; the larger the area covered by the pass, the more expensive it is. For example, a Western Canada Pass offers ten flight coupons starting at $4068 for western Canada.

By car

Travelling by **car** is the best way to see Canada. Any US, UK, Australian or New Zealand national over 21 with a full driving licence is allowed to drive in Canada, though rental companies may refuse to rent to a driver who has held a full licence for less than one year, and under-25s almost invariably get lumbered with a higher insurance premium. Car-rental companies will expect you to have a credit card; if you don't, they may refuse to rent to you.

Petrol (gas)

Most of Canada's vehicles – and almost every rental car – run on **unleaded fuel**, which is sold by the litre. Petrol stations thin out markedly in the more remote regions, where you should fill up where you can. Petrol is heavily taxed in Canada and is usually twenty percent more expensive than the US (though still cheaper than the UK). Prices can vary widely throughout the country: Ontario petrol is often 20–30¢ cheaper (per litre) than Newfoundland and the northern territories.

Roads and hazards

Canada has a superb road network and although **multilane highways** radiate from every city, the bulk of the system is comprised of (lightly used) **two-lane highways**. Exits on multilane highways are numbered by the kilometre distance from the beginning of the highway, not sequentially – thus exit 55 is 10km beyond exit 45. In the north and off the beaten track, highways may be entirely composed of **gravel**. After rain, gravel and dirt roads are especially treacherous; if you're planning a lot of dirt-road driving, you'd be well advised to rent a four-wheel-drive.

Rural road hazards include moose and other large animals trundling into the road – particularly in the summer at dawn and dusk, when the beasts crash through the undergrowth onto the highway to escape the flies, and in winter, when they want to lick the road salt. Warning signs are posted in the more hazardous areas. Headlights can dazzle wild animals and render them temporarily immobile.

Parking

In cities, parking meters are commonplace, charging 25¢–$1.50 or more per hour. Car parks charge up to $35 a day. If you park in the wrong place (such as within 5m of a fire hydrant) your car may be towed away – if this happens, the police will tell you where your car is impounded and then charge you upwards of $350 to hand it back. When parking, ensure you park in the same direction as the traffic flow.

Rules of the road

Traffic drives on the **right-hand side** of the road. In most urban areas, streets are arranged on a grid system, with traffic lights at most intersections; at **junctions without traffic lights** there will be either yellow triangular "Yield" signs or red octagonal "Stop" signs ("Arrêt" in Québec) at all four corners. In the latter case, priority is given to the first car to arrive, and to the car on the right if two or more cars arrive at the same time. Except in Québec, you can **turn right on a red light** if there is no traffic approaching from the left. Traffic in **both directions** must stop if a **yellow school bus** is stationary with its flashing lights on, as this means children are getting on or off.

Driving laws are made at provincial level, with the maximum speed limit ranging 100–110kmph on major highways, 80kmph on rural highways and 50kmph or less in built-up areas. On-the-spot fines are standard for speeding violations, for failing to carry your licence with you and for having a passenger not wearing a seat belt.

Canadian law requires that any **alcohol** be carried unopened in the boot of the car. There are also limits on how much alcohol can be carried across provincial borders; amounts vary, so check in order to avoid it being confiscated .On the road, **spot checks** are frequently carried out, particularly at the entrances and exits to towns, and the police do not need an excuse to stop you.

Renting a car or RV

The least expensive way to **rent a car** is usually to take a fly-drive package or book in advance with a major rental company (see page 33). Competition is fierce and special deals are more commonplace in the shoulder and low seasons.

In Canada itself, expect to pay from around $300 a week for a two-door economy saloon in low season

---

TOP 5 SCENIC DRIVES

Alaska Highway See page 813
Cabot Trail See page 358
Dempster Highway See page 839
Gaspé Peninsula See page 285
Icefields Parkway See page 585

---

to $500 in high season, though throughout the year special promotions are offered by the major companies, which can get rates down to as low as $200 per week. Provincial **taxes** and GST or HST (see page 48) are not included in the rates, but the biggest hidden surcharge is often the **drop-off charge**, levied when you intend to leave your car in a different place from where you picked it up. Check if **unlimited mileage** is offered – an important consideration in a country where towns are so widely dispersed. The usual free quota, if you don't get unlimited mileage, is 150–200km per day, woefully inadequate if you're contemplating some serious touring – after which an extra charge of around 13–20¢/km is standard. You should also check your **insurance policy** for the excess applied to claims and ensure that, in general terms, it provides adequate levels of financial cover. Additionally, the **Loss Damage Waiver (LDW)**, a form of insurance that isn't included in the initial rental charge, is well worth the expense. At around $25 per day, it can add substantially to the total cost, but without it you're liable for every scratch to the car – even if it wasn't your fault.

A **recreational vehicle (RV)** can be rented through most travel agents specializing in Canadian holidays. It's best to arrange rental before getting to Canada, as RV-rental outlets are not too common. You can rent a huge variety of RVs right up to giant mobile homes with two bedrooms, showers and fully fitted kitchens. A price of around $1400 in low season, $2500 in high season, for a five-berth van for one week is fairly typical. On top of that you have to take into account the **cost of fuel** (some RVs do less than 25km to the litre), extra kilometre charges, drop-off charges, and the cost of spending the night at designated RV parks. Canada also has strict regulations on the size of vehicle allowed; in British Columbia and Ontario the maximum length for a trailer is 12.5m/41ft (in Ontario it's 23m or 75.5ft for trailer plus car, but just 20m or 65.6ft in BC) – if you are coming from the US check that your RV isn't over the limit.

CAR RENTAL AGENCIES

Alamo Ⓦ alamo.com.
Avis Ⓦ avis.com.
Budget Ⓦ budget.com.

MOOSE TRAVEL

Aimed at backpackers, the **Moose Travel Network** (eastern office ☎416 546 7344, ☎855 741 7318, western office ☎604 297 0255, ☎888 244 6673, ⓦmoosenetwork.com) provides a completely different experience from regular tour buses. Its mini-coaches (seating 15–21 passengers) hit the major destinations on the travellers' circuit in both western and eastern Canada (but not the centre) between May and mid-October; there are some additional winter packages, and also links with VIA Rail.

Moose's tours range from day-trips to twenty-day excursions; you don't need to book your own accommodation, since Moose ensures that a hostel dorm bed is available for every passenger at all major stopovers. There's no age limit, although most travellers tend to be in the 19–34 age bracket; to match this, there's an array of adventure activities offered as add-ons. Moose has a range of **tours** with its ten-day Big West tour (May–Sept only) costing around $959 and its nine-day Big East tour $1229 (May–Oct only).

Dollar ⓦ dollar.com.
Hertz ⓦ hertz.com.
Holiday Autos ⓦ holidayautos.co.uk.
National ⓦ nationalcar.com.
Thrifty ⓦ thrifty.com.

Driveaways

A variation on car rental is a **driveaway**, where you deliver a car from one place to another on behalf of the owner. The same rules apply as for renting – but look the car over beforehand as you'll be lumbered with any repair costs and a large fuel bill if it's a gas guzzler. Most driveaway companies (such as ⓦcanadadriveaway.com) will want a Canadian, US or international driving licence and personal reference as well as a deposit of up to $500. The most common routes are Toronto or Montréal to Vancouver, or to Florida and Arizona/New Mexico in the autumn and winter. Not a lot of leeway is given – around eight days is the time allowed for driving from Toronto to Vancouver.

By bus

Greyhound Canada runs most of the long-distance **buses** west of Toronto, including a service along the Trans-Canada Highway from Toronto to Vancouver, and is well represented in the east of the country, though here a network of smaller companies rules the roost. Long-distance buses run on a fairly full timetable (at least during the day), stopping only for meal breaks and driver changeovers.

Fares are pretty standard for all **Canadian bus companies** (see page 31): for example, Montréal to Toronto, an eight-and-a-half-hour (540km) ride, costs $47–60 one way.

DRIVING DISTANCES IN KILOMETRES

The figures shown on this chart represent the total distances **in kilometres** between selected rather than straight lines drawn on a map. For conversion, the figure **in miles** is roughly two-thirds

	Calgary	Chicago	Edmonton	Halifax	Montréal	New York	Ottawa	Regina
Calgary	–	2760	299	4973	3743	4294	3553	764
Chicago	2760	–	2750	2603	1362	1280	1220	2000
Edmonton	299	2750	–	5013	3764	4315	3574	785
Halifax	4973	2603	5013	–	1249	1270	1439	4225
Montréal	3743	1362	3764	1249	–	610	190	2979
New York	4294	1280	4315	1270	610	–	772	3534
Ottawa	3553	1220	3574	1439	190	772	–	2789
Regina	764	2000	785	4225	2979	3534	2789	–
St John's	6334	3950	6767	1503	2602	2619	2792	5581
Seattle	1204	3200	1352	5828	4585	4478	4334	1963
Toronto	3434	825	3455	1788	539	880	399	2670
Vancouver	977	3808	1164	5970	4921	5382	4531	1742
Whitehorse	2385	4854	2086	7099	5850	6427	5660	2871
Winnipeg	1336	1432	1357	3456	2408	2966	2218	571
Yellowknife	1828	4240	1524	6537	5268	5800	5098	2309

By train

Canadian **passenger trains** are now few and far between, though at least the national carrier, **VIA Rail** (📞888 842 7245, 🌐viarail.ca), runs speedy and efficient services between Montréal and Toronto. VIA also runs several prestige routes through some of Canada's finest scenery, the long, thrice-weekly (four-day) haul between Toronto and Vancouver and the two-day journey from Jasper to Prince Rupert being the prime examples.

There's always a choice of **ticket** on these flagship routes. The most basic entitles passengers to a reclining seat and access to a public lounge and dome car, but not much else. Top-of-the-range tickets include meals in the restaurant car, access to comfortable lounges, hot showers and accommodation in either a bunk-bedded sleeper, a "roomette" for one, or a bedroom for two. For more information, check with VIA or consult 🌐seat61.com. To give an idea of peak-season **fares**, Toronto-to-Vancouver tickets cost anywhere between $480 (economy) and $3250 for a single cabin; expect to pay about 25 percent less for off-peak travel.

VIA sells a number of **rail passes**, which can reduce costs considerably. Perhaps the most tempting is the **Canrailpass**, which allows seven (from $329), ten (from $439) or unlimited (from $769) one-way trips between Québec and Ontario for 21 consecutive days ("Corridor pass") or unlimited trips across Canada for sixty consecutive days ("System pass") for $1429.

Other, smaller companies offer **scenic rail trips**: **Rocky Mountaineer** trains (📞604 606 7245, 📞877 460 3200, 🌐rockymountaineer.com) run from Vancouver to several western destinations, including Jasper, Kamloops, Banff and Calgary; Ontario Northland's **Polar Bear Express** (📞800 461 8558, 🌐ontarionorthland.ca) goes from Cochrane to Moosonee (near James Bay); **Algoma Central Railway** (📞705 946 7300, 📞800 242 9287, 🌐agawatrain.com) has excursions through the Agawa Canyon (see page 178); the **White Pass & Yukon Railroad** trains (📞907 983 2217, 📞800 343 7373, 🌐wpyr.com) run from Fraser to Skagway (see page 821); and the epic **Tshiuetin Rail** (🌐tshiuetin.net) travels between Sept-Îles in Québec and Emeril Junction in Labrador (see page 452).

By ferry

You'll likely make the most use of Canadian ferries in BC, travelling between Vancouver, Vancouver Island, the Gulf Islands and north up the Inside Passage as far as Prince Rupert. BC Ferries (📞250 386 3431, 🌐bcferries.com) runs all these services and fares are reasonable. To go from Vancouver to Victoria, for example, costs $17.20 per passenger, plus another $57.50 with car ($2 for bicycles).

On the East Coast, you might take a ferry (see page 396) between Caribou, Nova Scotia, and Prince Edward Island (📞877 635 7245, 🌐ferries.ca), which costs $20, plus another $78 with car. Yet the more useful route would be from Sydney, Nova Scotia (see page 364), to points in Newfoundland (📞800 341 7981, 🌐marine-atlantic.ca). A trip to Channel-Port aux Basques, Newfoundland, from Sydney costs $35.65, plus another $119.24 with car.

cities in the Canada and the US. They are calculated on the shortest available route by road, of that given in kilometres: 8km equals five miles.

St John's	Seattle	Toronto	Vancouver	Whitehorse	Winnipeg	Yellowknife
6334	1204	3434	977	2385	1336	1828
3950	3200	825	3808	4854	1432	4240
6767	1352	3455	1164	2086	1357	1524
1503	5828	1788	5970	7099	3456	6537
2602	4585	539	4921	5850	2408	5268
2619	4478	880	5382	6427	2966	5800
2792	4334	399	4531	5660	2218	5098
5581	1963	2670	1742	2871	571	2309
–	7200	3141	7323	8452	5010	7891
7200	–	4050	230	2796	2548	2500
3141	4050	–	4412	5528	2099	4979
7323	230	4412	–	2697	2152	2620
8452	2796	5528	2697	–	3524	1927
5010	2548	2099	2152	3524	–	2681
7891	2500	4979	2620	1927	2681	–

TOP 5 CYCLING TRAILS

P'tit Train du Nord Québec. See page 231
Traversée de Charlevoix Québec. See page 301
Confederation Trail PEI. See page 394
Sundance Canyon Trail Banff. See page 568
Stanley Park Seawall Vancouver. See page 694

By bike

City cyclists are reasonably well catered for in Canada: most cities have cycling lanes and produce special maps, and long-distance buses, ferries and trains will allow you to transport your bike either free or at a minimal charge. An interesting ongoing project is the development of a **coast-to-coast recreational path**, the 23,000km Trans Canada Trail, aka "The Great Trail" (W thegreattrail.ca), which now crosses the nation from Newfoundland to the Yukon. Cycling Canada (T 613 248 1353, W cyclingcanada.ca) has lots of information on cycling. Standard bike-rental costs start at around $15–35 per day, plus a sizeable cash sum or a credit card as deposit; outlets are listed throughout the Guide.

Accommodation

Given the vast size of the country, it's no surprise that the price of accommodation in Canada varies widely. The least expensive options are camping and dormitory beds in hostels, where prices start at around $25. Prices for hotels and motels are less predictable, though you'll be lucky to get a double room for less than $100 in high season wherever you are.

If you're heading into remote parts of the country, check the availability of accommodation before setting off. Places that look large on the map often have few facilities at all, and US visitors will find chain motels far scarcer than in similar regions back home.

It's best to try to **book a room** before you arrive, particularly in summer. Also look out for local events and festivals such as the Calgary Stampede, when accommodation is always at a premium. Most places have a 24-hour-notice cancellation policy, but in places like Banff it can be as much as three days. **Room taxes** (see page 48) are around two to three percent. This is in addition to regular sales tax, which is always in addition to the quoted price. The highest rates tend to be in the Maritime Provinces (thirteen to fifteen percent), the lowest in Alberta (nine percent).

Local **tourist information offices** will invariably help out with accommodation if you get stuck: most offer free advice and will book a place free of charge, but few are willing to commit themselves to specific recommendations.

Hotels

Canadian **hotels** tend to fall into one of three categories: high-class establishments, plain downtown places and roadside motels. In the cities, the emphasis is often on the business traveller rather than the tourist. **Top-notch** hotels charge anywhere between $150 and $600, though $250 would get you a fairly luxurious double in most places.

Mid-price hotels are often part of a chain, such as *Holiday Inn* or *Best Western*, and usually offer a touch more comfort than middling motels. You should be able to find a high-season double in such places from around $120; more if you're in a well-known resort or the downtown area of a major city.

Bottom-bracket hotels – those costing anything from $65–90 – are mostly hangovers from the days when liquor laws made it difficult to run a bar without an adjoining restaurant or hotel. Found in most medium- and small-sized towns, they usually have the advantage of being extremely central but the disadvantage is that the rooms are mostly an afterthought.

Motels

Although variously called inns, lodges, resorts or motor hotels, **motels** all amount to much the same thing: driver-friendly, reasonably priced and reliable places on the main highways almost always on the edge of town. The simplest rooms start at around $85, with the **average price** nearer $100 – though in resorts and more remote areas it's not unusual to find well over this being charged for what are fairly basic rooms. Prices usually drop in the larger centres the further you move from downtown. Many offer **off-season rates**, usually between October and April, some have triple- or quadruple-bedded rooms, and

---

TOP 5 GRAND OLD RAILWAY HOTELS

Fairmont Château Laurier Ottawa. See page 173
Le Château Frontenac Québec City. See page 253
Prince of Wales Hotel Waterton Lakes National Park. See page 630
Banff Springs Hotel See page 565
The Empress Victoria. See page 743

ACCOMMODATION PRICES

Throughout this guide, **accommodation prices** quoted are (unless stated otherwise) for the cheapest double room in high season. However, there's rarely such a thing as a set rate for a room. A basic motel in a seaside or mountain resort may double its prices according to the season, while a big-city hotel in Québec or Vancouver that charges $200 per room during the week will often slash its tariff at the weekend when all the business visitors have gone home. For camping, prices are given for "sites", and in hostels, dormitory bed prices are indicated as well as private rooms.

most are fairly relaxed about introducing an extra bed into "doubles" for a nominal charge. Many also offer a **family plan**, whereby youngsters sharing their parents' room stay free. You may also be able to negotiate cheaper deals if you're staying more than one night, and especially if you're staying a week – many places advertise weekly rates.

Bed and breakfasts (B&Bs)

Recent years have witnessed a dramatic increase in the number of **B&Bs** – or **Gîtes du Passant** – both in the big cities and in the towns and villages of the more popular resort areas. **Standards** are generally very high, and prices are around $85 and upwards per couple including breakfast. There are no real savings over cheaper hotels and motels – B&Bs in Canada are more like their posh American counterparts than the budget European version – but you'll often end up with a wonderful room in a heritage building in a great location, with the chance to meet Canadians on closer terms.

Hostels, Ys and student accommodation

Canada has around sixty **Hostelling International (HI)** hostels and around 140 non-affiliated hostels, with almost all of the latter members of the Backpackers Hostels Canada network – these can range from small, typical dormitory-type hostels to summer student accommodation and budget guesthouses with private rooms. Many unaffiliated hostels still give discounts for HI members or students. Quality varies considerably, but most of the hostels listed on the websites below should be of a reasonably high standard, and we've described the best ones in this guide. For HI members dorm beds usually cost $25–30, with basic private rooms starting at $40 (nonmembers will usually pay $5–15 more).

Both the **YMCA** and **YWCA** also offer hotel accommodation in many Canadian cities. Some of them, such as the *YWCA Hotel* in Vancouver, are part of the Backpackers Hostels network, while others – like the *Hôtel Y Montréal* – are more like smart, private hotels. Most Ys in Canada are focused on providing community activities and affordable housing for locals – tourist accommodation, where offered, is usually a related but separate business.

In Canada's university cities it's usually possible to stay in **student accommodation** during the summer vacation. The accommodation is adequate and functional, if soulless, and you'll have access to the campus's sports facilities; on the downside, most places are a good distance from city centres. Prices for single and double rooms start at around $50. It's a good idea to call well ahead to be sure of a room – many places are part of the Backpackers Hostels network (see website below).

YOUTH HOSTEL AND Y ASSOCIATIONS

Backpackers Hostels Canada ☎ 888 920 0044, ⓦ backpackers.ca.
Hostelling International Canada ☎ 800 663 5777, ⓦ hihostels.ca.
YMCA Canada ☎ 416 967 9622, ⓦ ymca.ca.
YWCA Canada ☎ 416 962 8881, ⓦ ywcacanada.ca.

Farm vacations

Farm vacations, where you spend time as a paying guest on a working farm, give you the chance to eat well, sleep cheaply – and even work (if you want) – as well as mingle with your hosts. Ontario has a range of farm-based B&Bs with reasonably priced accommodation. In western Canada, it's possible to stay on a ranch and work as a ranch-hand. Due to the isolation of these places prices are usually for full board and include riding (from $140/day). For further details, consult tourist offices and provincial accommodation guides. See also the **Cowboy Trail Tourism Association** (ⓦ thecowboytrail.com/travel-category/farm-and-ranch-vacations) and **BC Guest Ranchers' Association** (ⓦ bcguestranches.com).

Camping

Few countries offer as much scope for **camping** as Canada. Many urban areas have a campground (in Canada the convention is to term the whole site a "campground" and individual pitches as "campsites");

all national parks and the majority of provincial parks have government-run sites, and in most wilderness areas and in the vast domain of Canada's federally owned Crown Lands you can camp rough more or less where you please. If you're travelling with a **tent**, check a campground's small print for the number of **unserviced** (tent) campsites, as many places cater chiefly to **RVs**, providing them with full or partial hook-ups for water and electricity.

During July and August campgrounds can become as busy as all other types of accommodation in cities, and particularly near mountain, lake or river resorts. Either aim to arrive early in the morning or book ahead. Generally reservations can only be made with ease at **private campgrounds**, not – crucially – at national park or provincial park campgrounds, where access is often, but certainly not always, on a first-come, first-served basis (you can make reservations at some national parks; check ⓦreservation.pc.gc.ca for more details). Finally, check that your chosen site is open: many only open seasonally, usually from May to October.

Types of campground

At the bottom of the camping pile are **municipal campgrounds**, usually basic affairs with few facilities, which are either free or cost only a few dollars – typically $7–10 per tent, $20 per RV. **Private campgrounds** run the gamut: some are as basic as their municipal cousins, others are like huge outdoor pleasure complexes with shops, restaurants, laundries, swimming pools and tennis courts. Private campgrounds have several ways of **charging** – some do so by the vehicle, others per couple and comparatively few on a tent or per-person basis. Two people sharing a tent might pay anything between $5 and $25 each, though an average price would be nearer $20.

Campgrounds **in national and provincial parks** are run respectively by Parks Canada and by individual provincial governments. All are immaculately turned out and most, in theory, are open only between May and September. In practice, most are available year-round, though key facilities are offered and fees

collected only in the advertised period: off season you may be expected to leave fees in an **honesty box**. You'll usually find at least one site serviced for **winter camping** in the bigger national parks, particularly in the Rockies. **Prices** vary from about $20–45 per pitch for full amenities (electricity, sewage, water and showers), depending on location and the time of year, and $16–25 for basic pitches (wood, water and pit toilets). Most parks also have basic **backcountry sites** usually providing only fire pits and firewood (see below). If you want to use an official backcountry campground or just camp rough in parks, you must obtain an overnight permit from the park centre ($9.80).

Primitive camping

Though commonplace in all the larger national and provincial parks, **primitive camping** (or backcountry/wilderness camping as it's known in Canada) has certain rules that must be followed. In particular, check that fires are permitted: in large parts of Canada they aren't allowed in summer because of the risk of forest fire. If they are permitted, use a fire pit (if provided), or a stove in preference to local materials. In wilderness areas, try to camp on previously used sites. Be especially aware of the precautions needed when in **bear** country (see page 576). Where there are no toilets, bury human waste at least 10cm into the ground and 30m from the nearest water supply and campsite. Canadian parks ask for all rubbish to be carried away; elsewhere burn rubbish, and what you can't burn, carry away. **Never drink** from rivers and streams, however clear and inviting they may look. If you have to drink **water** that isn't from taps, you should boil it for at least ten minutes, or cleanse it with an iodine-based purifier or a Giardia-rated filter, available from camping or sports shops.

oTENTik tents

In recent years Parks Canada has started offering more comfortable accommodation at national park campgrounds. Dubbed **oTENTik tents**, these are a cross between a tent and cabin (canvas roof and walls on a wood frame, and hardwood floors, bedframes and basic furniture), with room for three beds and up to six people. Bathrooms are still shared, however, and no food or cooking is permitted inside the tent. Rates range $100–200 per night depending on the park and the season.

Food and drink

The sheer number of restaurants, bars, cafés and fast-food joints in Canada is

---

TOP 5 CAMPING DESTINATIONS

staggering, though at first sight there's little to distinguish mainstream Canadian urban cuisine from that of any American metropolis: the shopping malls, main streets and highways are lined with pan-American food chains, trying to outdo each other with their bargains and special offers.

However, it's easy to leave the chain restaurants behind for more interesting options, as the standard of **Canadian cuisine** has improved dramatically in the last few years. In the big cities there's a plethora of international and speciality restaurants; on either seaboard the availability of fresh fish and shellfish enlivens many menus, and even out in the country there's a liberal supply of first-rate, family-run cafés and restaurants, especially in the more touristy areas. **Smoking** in restaurants (and all indoor public places) is banned throughout Canada.

Breakfast

All over Canada **breakfast** is taken very seriously, and with prices averaging between $8 and $15 it's often the best-value and most filling meal of the day. Whether you go to a café, coffee shop or hotel snack bar, the breakfast menu, on offer until around 11am (although some places offer an all-day breakfast), is a fairly standard fry-up: eggs in various guises, ham or bacon. Whatever you order, you nearly always receive a dollop of fried potatoes, called **hash browns** or, sometimes, home fries. Other favourite breakfast options include English muffins or, in posher places, bran muffins, a glutinous fruitcake made with bran and sugar, and waffles or pancakes, swamped in butter with lashings of maple syrup. Also, because the breakfast/lunch division is never hard and fast, mountainous meaty sandwiches are common too.

Ubiquitous coffee and doughnut chain *Tim Hortons* (ⓦ timhortons.com) is a staple all over Canada, but in the big cities, look out also for specialist **coffee shops**, where the range of offerings verges on the bewildering. As a matter of course, coffee comes with cream or half-and-half (half-cream, half-milk) unless you specifically ask for skimmed milk. **Tea**, with either lemon or milk, is also drunk at breakfast, especially in the Maritimes.

Lunch

Between about 11.30am and 2.30pm, many big-city restaurants offer special **set menus** that are generally excellent value. In Chinese and Vietnamese establishments, for example, you'll frequently find rice and noodles, or buffets for $10–15, and many Japanese

restaurants serve sushi very reasonably for under $20. Pizza is also widely available, from larger chains to family-owned restaurants and pavement stalls. Favourites with white-collar workers are café-restaurants featuring wholefoods and vegetarian meals, though few are nutritionally dogmatic, serving traditional meat dishes and sandwiches too; most have an excellent selection of daily lunch specials for around $10–12.

Dinner

If you're in a large city or town, choosing where to eat **dinner** is really just a matter of whatever takes your fancy – and is within your budget. Outside these areas, you're more likely to end up at smaller, family-owned restaurants, cafés or bistros, where prices might be cheaper but the quality of the food is often no less impressive than what you'd find in a big city. Pubs and bars aren't a bad place to grab a meal either, and if what they offer is not overly inventive (chicken wings, variations of burger, fish and chips) you can bet it will be filling.

You can find pretty much any type of cuisine in Canada's larger cities, with Montréal, Toronto and Vancouver especially standing out for their choice of **international** restaurants. Most run a dinner service starting at 5 to 7pm and ending at around 10 to 11pm. Expect to pay anywhere from $15–45 for a main dish at most places, and considerably more at fancier establishments. The average cost of a dinner for two, with wine, would be roughly $80–100.

Regional dishes

Largely swamped by the more fashionable regional European and international cuisines, **traditional Canadian cooking** relies mainly on local game and fish, with less emphasis on vegetables and salads. In terms of price, decent meals for two without wine average between $40 and $50.

Newfoundland and Labrador

Newfoundland's staple food has traditionally been cod fish, usually in the form of fish and chips, though with supplies dwindling, this has become more of a luxury. More common are salmon, haddock, halibut and hake, supplemented by more bizarre dishes like "cod tongues" (actually the meat in the cheek), "jiggs dinner" (salted beef and vegetables), fish and brewis (salt cod with hard bread, softened by pork fat and molasses) and seal flipper pie. The island's restaurants rarely serve seal or moose (hunters can only sell cooked moose meat to restaurants, thereby making it almost impossible for them to serve it fresh), but many islanders join in the annual licensed shoot and, if you befriend a hunter, you may end up across the table from a hunk of either animal. Caribou meat from **Labrador** is far more common, often turning up in burgers, and local bakeapples (cloudberries) and partridgeberries (loganberries) are used in jams, desserts and sauces.

The Maritimes

In the Maritimes, lobster is excellent everywhere, as are mussels, oysters, clams, scallops and herring, either on their own or in a fish stew or clam chowder; best value are the lobster suppers, especially on Prince Edward Island, where you'll get mountains of seafood for around $35. **Nova Scotia** is famous for its blueberries, Annapolis Valley apple pie, "fat archies" (a Cape Breton molasses cookie) and rappie pie (an Acadian dish of meat or fish and potatoes). **New Brunswick** is known for its fiddleheads (fern shoots) and dulse (edible seaweed).

Québec

Québec is renowned for its outstanding French-style cuisine, and **pork** forms a major part of the local diet, both as a spicy pâté known as *creton*, and in *tourtière*, a minced pork pie. There are also splendid thick pea and cabbage soups, beef pies (*cipâte*), and all sorts of ways to soak up maple syrup – *trempette* is bread drenched with it and topped with fresh cream. Quicker **snacks** include smoked meat sandwiches (the best of which can be had in Montréal), chewy Montréal-style bagels and *poutine*, fries covered in melted mozzarella cheese or cheese curds and gravy.

> ## TOP 5 REGIONAL DISHES
> **Poutine** Montréal. See page 220
> **Digby scallops** Nova Scotia. See page 350
> **Lobster suppers** PEI. See page 394
> **Fish and chips** St John's. See page 420
> **Steaks** Calgary. See page 548

Ontario

Fish is Ontario's most distinctive offering, though the pollution of the Great Lakes has badly affected the freshwater catch. Try the whitefish, lake trout, pike and smelt, but bear in mind that these are easier to come by in the north of the province than in the south.

The west and far north

Northern Saskatchewan and **Manitoba** are the places to try fish like the goldeye, pickerel and Arctic char, as well as pemmican (a mixture of dried meat, berries and fat) and fruit pies containing the Saskatoon berry. The **Arctic** regions feature caribou steak, and **Alberta** is also noted for its beef. **BC** features Pacific fish and shellfish of many different types, from cod, haddock and salmon to king crab, oysters and shrimp. Here and there, there's also the odd **Aboriginal peoples**' restaurant, most conspicuously at the Wanuskewin Heritage Park in Saskatoon, Saskatchewan, where the restaurant serves venison, buffalo and -black-husked wild rice. **Vancouver** is also one of the best places in North America for Chinese and Japanese food; other international cuisines are also well represented.

Drinking

Canadian **bars** are mostly long and dimly lit counters with a few customers perched on stools or the surrounding tables and booths. Yet, despite the similarity of layout, bars vary enormously, from the male-dominated, rough-edged drinking holes concentrated in the blue-collar parts of the cities and the mining and oil towns of the North, to more fashionable city establishments that provide food, live entertainment and an inspiring range of cocktails.

The **legal drinking age** is 18 in Alberta, Manitoba and Québec, and 19 in the rest of the country, though it's rare for anyone to have to show ID, except at the government-run liquor stores (closed Sun), which exercise a virtual monopoly on the sale of alcoholic beverages of all kinds direct to the public; the main exception is Québec, where beer and wine (not spirits) are sold at retail grocery stores.

Beer and wine

By and large, the major Canadian **beers** are unremarkable, designed to quench your thirst rather than satisfy your palate. Everywhere they're served ice-cold, and light, fizzy concoctions rule the roost. The three largest Canadian brewers, **Molson** (now Molson Coors), Japanese-owned **Sleeman** and Anheuser-Busch owned **Labatts**, market a remarkably similar brew under all sorts of names. In the 1990s these companies pioneered the gimmicky **ice beer** concept: by lowering the temperature of beer to just below the freezing point of water and skimming the resulting layer of ice off the top, they created a brew with a higher alcohol content.

The slightly tastier beers of still independent **Great Western Brewing**, one of the country's largest regional brewers, are produced in Saskatoon, Saskatchewan, while the heavily marketed **Moosehead** beer is produced in Saint John, New Brunswick. A welcome trend is the proliferation of independent **micro-breweries**, whose products are sold either in a pub on the brewery premises or are available in local restaurants, bars and pubs – these remain pretty much confined to the bigger cities.

Canadian wines are fast developing an excellent reputation, particularly those from Ontario's Niagara-on-the-Lake region and BC's Okanagan Valley. Imported wines from a wide range of countries are also readily available and not too pricey.

The media

Despite the all-pervasive influence of the US media, Canada's vibrant free press, local radio and – to a lesser extent – national TV stations demonstrate a high degree of independence from their southern neighbour, retaining an often subtle but distinctive voice.

Newspapers and magazines

Canada's only national daily **newspapers** are the *National Post* and the outstanding *Globe and Mail*, whose coverage of domestic politics and contemporary issues is superb. Every major city has at least one daily newspaper and standards are generally high – the *Toronto Star* and *Calgary Herald* being two cases in point. In Québec, the tabloid *Journal de Montréal* is the bestselling French-language paper in North America, competing with the more highbrow *La Presse* (now published electronically only) and the intellectual (and separatist) *Le Devoir*.

Most of Canada's major cities also have **free weekly listings papers**, often with news and features with an alternative slant. The small-c conservative *Maclean's* and French-language *L'actualité* are the most popular weekly news magazines, while *The Walrus* – a highbrow, Canadian equivalent of *The New Yorker* – is also a good read.

> **TOP 5 NEWSPAPERS**
> (by circulation)
> **Globe and Mail** (Toronto)
> **Toronto Star**
> **Le Journal de Montréal**
> **National Post** (Toronto)
> **Le Journal de Québec**

TV and radio

The **Canadian Broadcasting Corporation** (CBC) is the primary national and regional **TV** provider. The main commercial network is CTV Television (**CTV**), a mix of Canadian, American and regional output. Most US stations can also be picked up in every part of Canada thanks to cable and satellite.

The majority of Canadian **radio stations** stick to a bland commercial format. Most display little -originality – though they can be good sources of local nightlife and entertainment news, and road and weather reports. On the other hand, the state-subsidized CBC channels provide diverse, listenable and well-informed programmes. Driving through rural areas can be frustrating, as for hundreds of kilometres you might only be able to receive one or two very dull stations, if anything at all.

Festivals

Every province chips in with its share of festivals, from pageants and parades celebrating local events, through to more prestigious theatrical seasons and film festivals. For further details of the festivals listed below, including more precise dates, see the relevant account in the Guide. Provincial tourist offices (see page 52) can provide free festival and events calendars for each region.

JANUARY

Polar Bear Swim Vancouver, BC (Ⓦ vancouver.ca). A New Year's Day swim in the freezing waters of English Bay Beach – said to bring good luck for the year (if you survive).

Banff/Lake Louise Ice Magic Festival Banff and Lake Louise, AB (Ⓦ banfflakelouise.com/ice-magic-festival). Ski races, skating parties and the incredible International Ice Sculpture Competition on the shores of Lake Louise.

FEBRUARY

Winterlude Ottawa, ON (Ⓦ ottawatourism.ca). Winter-warming activities such as ice sculpting, snowshoe races, ice boating and skating for all on the canal.

Winter Carnival Québec City, QC ($\mathbb{W}$ carnaval.qc.ca). Two-week festival of winter-sports competitions, ice-sculpture contests and parades. Includes the Canadian ski marathon when skiers race between Lachute and Gatineau.

Montréal En Lumière Montréal, QC ($\mathbb{W}$ montrealenlumiere.com). Festival that, like Québec City's, tries to make the most of winter with a multitude of shows and food events.

APRIL

Shaw Festival Niagara-on-the-Lake, ON ($\mathbb{W}$ shawfest.com). Highly regarded theatre festival featuring the work of George Bernard Shaw and his contemporaries. Performances from April to late Oct.

MAY

Apple Blossom Festival Annapolis Valley, NS ($\mathbb{W}$ appleblossom. com). Community-oriented festival held in the small towns and villages of this apple-producing valley in Nova Scotia.

Stratford Festival Stratford, ON ($\mathbb{W}$ stratfordfestival.ca). A first-class Shakespeare Festival. Runs from May to early Nov.

Canadian Tulip Festival Ottawa, ON ($\mathbb{W}$ tulipfestival.ca). Three million tulips in a riot of colour all over the city.

JUNE

Banff Summer Arts Festival Banff, AB ($\mathbb{W}$ banffcentre.ca). Young-artist showcase: music, opera, dance, drama, comedy and visual arts, from June to Aug.

Edmonton International Jazz Festival Edmonton, AB ($\mathbb{W}$ edmontonjazz.com). Ten days of jazz concerts, free outdoor events and workshops.

Pride Week Toronto, ON ($\mathbb{W}$ pridetoronto.com). Gigantic celebration of LGBTQ culture, with huge parades and street parties that attract a million spectators.

Festival International de Jazz de Montréal Montréal, QC ($\mathbb{W}$ montrealjazzfest.com). The world's largest jazz festival (ten days) features over five hundred shows, including the world's top names; most outdoor performances are free; more than two million people attend.

JULY

Canada Day Ottawa, ON, and nationwide. Fireworks, parades and a day off for patriotic shenanigans every July 1.

Pow Wows Nationwide ($\mathbb{W}$ powwows.com). Traditional Aboriginal Canadian celebrations taking place on reserves across the country in July and Aug.

Calgary Stampede Calgary, AB ($\mathbb{W}$ calgarystampede.com). One of the biggest rodeos in the world: all the usual cowboy trappings, plus chuck-wagon rides, craft exhibitions, Aboriginal dancing and much more.

K-Days Edmonton, AB ($\mathbb{W}$ k-days.com). Family-targeted festival featuring theme park and fairground games, a food festival, parades, live music shows and the replica Chilkoot Gold Mine.

Antigonish Highland Games Antigonish, NS ($\mathbb{W}$ antigonishhighlandgames.ca). All sorts of traditional Scottish sports and activities recall the settlement of the area by Highlanders.

Halifax Jazz Festival Halifax, NS ($\mathbb{W}$ halifaxjazzfestival.ca). First-class jazz festival pulling in big names from round the world.

Toronto Caribbean Carnival (Caribana) Toronto, ON ($\mathbb{W}$ caribanatoronto.com) Large-scale three-week West Indian festival culminating in a carnival weekend with music, dance and a flamboyant parade.

Festival d'Été Québec City, QC ($\mathbb{W}$ infofestival.com). Arts performances, live bands and other shows on and off the streets and parks of Québec City.

Glengarry Highland Games Maxville, ON ($\mathbb{W}$ glengarryhighlandgames.com). Tucked away in the corner of Eastern Ontario are the North American Pipe Band Championships, Highland dancing, Gaelic sport competitions and an overall rollicking good time. Usually the last weekend in July or early August.

Just for Laughs Montréal, QC and Toronto, ON ($\mathbb{W}$ hahaha.com). Internationally acclaimed comic get-together with comedians from around the world performing in theatres and on outdoor stages.

AUGUST

Fringe Theatre Festival Edmonton, AB ($\mathbb{W}$ fringetheatre.ca). One of North America's most prestigious alternative-theatre festivals.

Montréal Pride Montréal, QC ($\mathbb{W}$ fiertemontrealpride.com). Québec's turn to celebrate LGBTQ pride, with another huge parade and street parties.

Squamish Days Loggers Sports Festival Squamish, BC ($\mathbb{W}$ squamishdays.ca). The continent's biggest lumberjacks' convention with impressive logging competitions.

Festival Acadian Caraquet, NB ($\mathbb{W}$ festivalacadien.ca). Celebration of Acadian culture in the northeast of New Brunswick.

Miramichi Folk Song Festival Newcastle, NB ($\mathbb{W}$ miramichifolksongfestival.com). New Brunswick's folk festival, featuring many of the finest fiddlers in the Maritimes.

SEPTEMBER

Toronto International Film Festival Toronto, ON ($\mathbb{W}$ tiff. net). Internationally acclaimed film festival spread over ten days, inundated with Hollywood stars.

OCTOBER

Vancouver International Film Festival Vancouver, BC ($\mathbb{W}$ viff. org). Another of Canada's highly rated film fests.

Okanagan Fall Wine Festival Okanagan, BC ($\mathbb{W}$ thewinefestivals. com). One of the many wine events in this vine-growing region.

Oktoberfest Kitchener-Waterloo, ON ($\mathbb{W}$ oktoberfest.ca). Alcohol and cultural events in honour of the twin towns' roots.

Black and Blue Montréal, QC ($\mathbb{W}$ bbcm.org). Major gay arts festival in Montréal.

NOVEMBER

Canadian Finals Rodeo Red Deer, AB ($\mathbb{W}$ cfrreddeer.ca). Pure Canuck rodeo. Late October into early November.

DECEMBER

Carol Ships Parade of Lights Vancouver, BC. When carol singers sail around Vancouver harbour in sparkly boats.

New Year's Eve Nationwide, but celebrated in style in St John's, Newfoundland, where everyone heads from the pub to the waterfront for a raucous midnight party.

Outdoor activities

Canada's mountains, lakes, rivers and forests offer the opportunity to indulge in a vast range of outdoor pursuits. We've concentrated on fishing, hiking, skiing and canoeing – four of Canada's most popular activities – and on the national parks, which have been established to preserve and make accessible the best of the Canadian landscape.

Other popular activities such as whale-watching, riding and rafting are covered in some detail in the main text. Once in Canada you can rely on finding outfitters, equipment rental, charters, tours and guides to help you in most areas; tourist offices invariably carry full details or contact numbers.

The national parks

Canada's 39 **national parks** and eight **national park reserves** are administered by Parks Canada (🌐 pc.gc.ca), and local staff based at **park information centres**. Visit these to pick up special **permits** if you intend to fish or camp in the backcountry, and for information and -audiovisual displays on flora, fauna and outdoor activities. Many offer talks and nature walks presented by park naturalists, as well as reports on snow, weather and recent bear sightings. The national parks system also administers 171 **National Historic Sites** – important historical sites dotted around the country.

Supplementing the national parks is a network of **provincial parks** in every province in the country. Entry to these parks is sometimes free, though often you'll have to pay a small fee of around $5 (often per car). You'll also have to pay for fishing and hunting permits as well as campgrounds on top of this; specifics vary from province to province.

National park permits

All those entering Canada's national sites and parks require a **park permit**, regardless of their mode of transport, though permits are usually sold to cover all those entering in a particular vehicle from a roadside booth on the park boundary. This costs around $7.80 to $9.80 per person per day, per adult; as of 2018,

THE BEST PARKS TO ...

Canoe It's pure paddling pleasure in Ontario, with Point Pelee National Park's winding freshwater marshes and Algonquin Provincial Park's network of lakes. See pages 126 and 148

Island hop The islets of Québec's Mingan Archipelago or BC's lush Southern Gulf Islands are both national park reserves. See pages 317 and 750

Drive Jasper's Icefields Parkway is a superlative mountain drive, but the Cabot Trail in Nova Scotia's Cape Breton Highlands is a fine maritime alternative. See pages 585 and 358

Hike Banff's credentials can't be denied, but to escape the crowds, head to Gros Morne National Park, Newfoundland. See pages 561 and 445

Soak in Radium or Banff Upper Hot Springs in the Rockies: both offer steaming waters to soothe the tired traveller. See pages 611 and 566

Raft Nahanni National Park in the Northwest Territories just edges Jasper for wild whitewater thrills. See pages 850 and 610

admission for youth 17 and under is free. If you intend to visit a number of national parks and sites, it might be worth investing in an annual Discovery Pass, which provides one adult unlimited admission to all parks and national historic sites for $67.70 (seniors $57.90); family or group passes, covering a whole car-load of people, cost around double.

Additional permits are also required to fish (see page 45) and backcountry camp in national parks: both are generally available from park information centres.

Hiking

Canada boasts some of North America's finest **hiking**, and whatever your ability or ambition you'll find a walk to suit almost anywhere in the country. All of the national and many provincial parks have well-marked and well-maintained trails, and a visit to any park centre or local tourist office will furnish you with adequate **maps** of the usually very easily followed local paths. If you're venturing into the backcountry try to obtain the appropriate 1:50,000 sheet from the Canadian Topographical Series. For key hiking areas we've given a brief summary of the best trails in the appropriate parts of the Guide, though with over 1500km of paths in Banff National Park alone, these recommendations only scratch the surface. Park staff can advise on other good walks, and detailed trail guides are widely available for most popular regions.

Before setting off on anything more than a short stroll be properly informed of local conditions and be **properly equipped**. Hiking at lower elevations should present few problems, though swarms of **blackflies** in the spring and **mosquitoes** near water can drive you crazy; anything containing DEET should be a fairly reliable repellent. For more on specific health problems, see page 49.

Main hiking areas

The most extensive and rewarding hiking-trail networks are in the **Rockies national parks** of Alberta and BC. Thousands of kilometres of well-kept and well-tramped paths crisscross the four main parks – Banff, Jasper, Yoho and Kootenay – as well as the smaller enclaves of Glacier, -Revelstoke and Waterton Lakes. Scope for hiking of all descriptions is almost limitless. More modest areas dotted all over **BC** boast walking possibilities out of all proportion to their size: we pay less attention to these, but by most relative standards hiking here is still among the best in North America.

In **Manitoba**, the Riding Mountain National Park offers about thirty hiking trails, but though there's plenty of upland walking to be had in the prairie provinces, you have to move east to **Québec**'s Mauricie, Forillon and Gatineau parks for a taste of mountains comparable to the western provinces. In **Ontario**, Lake Superior Provincial Park and Algonquin Park are the most challenging terrains. **New Brunswick**'s Fundy National Park offers coastal walks, while **Newfoundland**'s hiking centres on its two national parks: Terra Nova on the East Coast, and the high plateau and fjords of the West Coast's Gros Morne. For the truly bold, however, nothing can match the **Arctic** extremes of Baffin Island, whose principal trail lies over an icecap that never melts.

Long-distance trails

In areas with highly developed trail networks, seasoned backpackers can blaze their own **long-distance walking routes** by stringing together several longer trails. Recognized long-haul paths are relatively rare, though more are being designated yearly. One of the best is the **Chilkoot Trail** from Dyea in Alaska to Bennett in BC, a 53km hike that closely follows the path of prospectors en route to the Yukon during the 1898 gold rush (see page 822). The most popular is probably Vancouver Island's demanding **West Coast Trail**, which runs for 75km along the edge of the Pacific Rim National Park (see page 767).

More far-reaching walks include the **Rideau Trail**, which follows paths and minor roads for 387km from Kingston to Ottawa (🌐 rideautrail.org); the 895km **Bruce Trail** from Niagara to Tobermory on the Bruce Peninsula, (🌐 brucetrail.org); and the **Voyageur Trail** along the north shores of lakes Superior and Huron, which is the longest and most rugged route in the province (🌐 voyageurtrail.ca). In the Maritimes, the **Confederation Trail** (see page 394) cuts a bucolic path across PEI, while the **Fundy Trail** (see page 370) in New Brunswick and, in particular, the **East Coast Trail** (see page 422) in Newfoundland offer a more rugged experience.

Skiing

Wherever there's good hiking in Canada, there's also usually **skiing**. The increasingly popular resorts of the Rockies and BC are the main areas and the country's leading resorts are at Whistler, Banff and Lake Louise. But there's also great skiing in Québec, and a few good runs at the minor day-resorts that dot the other provinces. Most cities are also close to excellent cross-country trail networks.

Canadian ski packages are available from travel agents worldwide, but it's perfectly feasible to organize your own trips, as long as you book well ahead if you're

---

BEARS, COUGARS AND SNAKES

Realistically, your biggest irritations while hiking are likely to be mosquitoes, flies and blackflies and hiking in the Canadian wilderness is far safer than wandering around most cities – but make no mistake, **bears** (see page 576) are potentially very dangerous, and most people blow a whistle while walking in bear country to warn them off. If confronted don't run, make loud noises or sudden movements, all of which are likely to provoke an attack.

Cougars pose a somewhat lesser threat, with most attacks occurring in BC – unlike bears, the best strategy with cougars is to try and fight them off (they usually avoid groups altogether).

Snake bites are more common in some parts of Canada (there are rattlesnakes in Georgian Bay Islands National Park for example), but even then only a handful are reported each year and fatalities are rare – wear proper boots and if you do disturb a snake back away so that it has room to move freely. Even the most venomous bites can be treated successfully if you receive immediate medical attention (call ☎911 or notify park staff).

hoping to stay in some of the better-known resorts. **Costs** for food, accommodation and ski passes are still fairly modest by US and European standards: expect to pay $65–80 per day (depending on the quality and popularity of the resort) for lift passes, plus another $30 or more per day to rent equipment.

TOP 5 SKI RESORTS

Mont-Tremblant See page 232
Banff (Norquay, Sunshine and Lake Louise). See pages 566, 576 and 579
Kicking Horse See page 608
Big White See page 664
Whistler See page 726

Fishing

Canada is **fishing** nirvana. While each region has its specialities, from the Arctic char of the Northwest Territories to the Pacific salmon of BC, excellent fishing can be found in most of the country's abundant lakes, rivers and coastal waters. Many towns have a fishing shop for equipment, and any spot with fishing possibilities is likely to have companies running boats and charters. Most provinces publish detailed booklets on everything that swims within the area of their jurisdiction.

Fishing is governed by a range of **regulations** that vary between provinces and are usually baffling at first glance, but usually boil down to the need for a nonresident permit for freshwater fishing, and another for saltwater fishing. These are increasingly available online (search the provincial government websites) or from most local fishing or sports shops for $60 and up, and are valid for a year. Short-term (one- or six-day) licences are also available in some provinces ($15–30).

For non-Canadians, fishing in Ontario requires an Outdoors Card for $11.94, plus a fishing licence: one year is $87.22, while one day is $25.83 (for one-day you don't need the Outdoors Card; see Ⓦontario.ca/page/get-outdoors-card). Alberta fishing licences (for foreign non-residents) are $85 (one year) and $26.63 (one day; Ⓦmywildalberta.ca/buy-licences/fishing-licenses-fees/default.aspx); Northwest Territories charges $40 per season and $30 for three days (Ⓦenr.gov.nt.ca/en/services/apply-fishing-licence); while BC charges $80 annually ($20 for one day; Ⓦfishing.gov.bc.ca). Newfoundland licences are required for salmon ($80 per season for non-residents) and trout ($12 per season), with seasons strictly regulated (Ⓦnfl.dfo-mpo.gc.ca/NL/AG/LicenseFees). Additional permits are required to fish in national parks (where fishing is allowed); available from park administration centres, these cost around $34.30 annually or $9.80 daily. There may well be quotas on the types and numbers of fish you can catch, which you can find out when you buy a permit.

Canoeing

Opportunities for **canoeing** are limited only by problems of access and expertise: some of the rapids and portages on the country's more challenging routes are for real pros only. The most straightforward regions to canoe are in **Ontario**, with its estimated 250,000 lakes and 35,000km of waterways, some 25,000km of which have been documented as practical canoe routes. The key areas are the Algonquin, Killarney and Quetico provincial parks, though the single most popular run is the 190km Rideau Canal, a tame stretch from Kingston to Ottawa.

The rivers of **BC** offer generally more demanding whitewater routes, though the lake canoeing – in Wells Gray Provincial Park, for example – is among the country's most beautiful. One of the province's other recognized classics is the 120km trip near Barkerville on the Cariboo River and the lakes of the Bowron Lakes Provincial Park. More challenging still are the immense backcountry lakes and rivers of the Mackenzie River system and the Barrenlands of the **Northwest Territories**, where you can find one of the continent's ultimate river challenges – the 300km stretch of the South Nahanni River near Fort Simpson. Growing in popularity, partly because of improved road access, are trips on and around the **Yukon** River system, particularly the South Macmillan River east of Pelly Crossing. Other areas that will test the resources of any canoeist are to be found in **Manitoba** and **Labrador** – all detailed in this guide.

Once you've decided on an area, provincial tourist offices (see page 52) can provide full lists of **outfitters**. These will rent out equipment, organize boat and plane drop-offs, and arrange provisions for longer trips. **Costs** range from $150 to $250 for weekly canoe rental.

Spectator sports

Most Canadians are sports mad – so much so that they have two national sports: ice hockey in winter and lacrosse in summer. But it's the former that's the real national obsession; in 2004, CBC's "Greatest Canadian" top ten included two retired hockey players: Don Cherry (best known for his irascible sports-commentary) and Wayne Gretzky (aka "The Great One"),

regarded as the best player of all time and afforded god-like status in Canada. Dropping in on a hockey game can give visitors an unforgettable insight into a city and its people.

back in 1993 (though the Vancouver Canucks were runners-up in 2011). Regardless of who makes it to the final, don't expect to get much done the night of a Stanley Cup match – most of Canada shuts down to watch the games.

Ice hockey

With players hurtling around and the puck clocking speeds of over 160kph, ice hockey would be a high-adrenaline sport even without its relaxed attitude to combat on the rink (as an old Canadian adage has it: "I went to see a fight and an ice-hockey game broke out"). The **National Hockey League** (Ⓦnhl.com), founded in Montréal in 1917, currently consists of 31 teams (likely to be 32 by 2020), seven of which are from Canada and the remainder from the US (though Canadians usually make up over half the players in the league). Each team plays over eighty games a season, which lasts from October to May. **Tickets** start at around $50 for ordinary games, rise to well over $200 for play-offs and nearly always need to be bought in advance. The **Montréal Canadiens** are the most successful team in the league, with 24 Stanley Cup championships, and were the last Canadian winners,

Canadian football

Professional **Canadian football** (similar to the American variety) – played under the aegis of the **Canadian Football League** (Ⓦcfl.ca) – is largely overshadowed by the National Football League in the US, chiefly because the best home-grown talent moves south in search of better money while NFL castoffs move north to fill the ranks. The two countries' games vary slightly – Canada's uses a longer, wider field, has fewer "downs" and uses bigger balls – but the Canadian version is faster-paced, higher-scoring and more exciting. The season lasts from June to November, each team (there are nine) playing a match a week. The play-offs at the end of the season culminate with the hotly contested Grey Cup – Edmonton Eskimos have won the most titles (eleven). **Tickets** are fairly easy to buy online and start at around $45.

CANADA'S MAJOR-LEAGUE PROFESSIONAL SPORTS TEAMS

Specific details for the most important teams in all the sports are given in the various city accounts. They can also be found through the major-league websites.

ICE HOCKEY – NHL
Calgary Flames Ⓦnhl.com/flames.
Edmonton Oilers Ⓦnhl.com/oilers.
Montréal Canadiens Ⓦnhl.com/fr/canadiens.
Ottawa Senators Ⓦnhl.com/senators.
Toronto Maple Leafs Ⓦnhl.com/mapleleafs.
Vancouver Canucks Ⓦnhl.com/canucks.
Winnipeg Jets Ⓦnhl.com/jets.

CANADIAN FOOTBALL – CFL
BC Lions (Vancouver) Ⓦbclions.com.
Calgary Stampeders Ⓦstampeders.com.
Edmonton Eskimos Ⓦesks.com.
Hamilton Tiger Cats Ⓦticats.ca.
Montréal Alouettes Ⓦmontrealalouettes.
com.
Ottawa Redblacks Ⓦottawaredblacks.com
Saskatchewan Roughriders (Regina)
Ⓦriderville.com.
Toronto Argonauts Ⓦargonauts.ca.
Winnipeg Blue Bombers Ⓦbluebombers.
com.

BASEBALL – MLB
Toronto Blue Jays Ⓦmlb.com/bluejays.

BASKETBALL – NBA
Toronto Raptors Ⓦnba.com/raptors.

LACROSSE – NLL
Calgary Roughnecks Ⓦcalgaryroughnecks.
com.
Saskatchewan Rush Ⓦsaskrush.com.
Toronto Rock Ⓦtorontorock.com.
Vancouver Warriors Ⓦvancouverwarriors.
com.

SOCCER – MLS
Montréal Impact Ⓦimpactmontreal.com
Toronto FC Ⓦtorontofc.ca.
Vancouver Whitecaps FC Ⓦwhitecapsfc.
com.

**CANADIAN WOMEN'S HOCKEY LEAGUE
– CHWL**
Calgary Inferno Ⓦcalgary.thecwhl.com.
Canadiennes de Montréal Ⓦmontreal.
thecwhl.com.
Markham Thunder Ⓦmarkham.thecwhl.
com.
Toronto Furies Ⓦtoronto.thecwhl.com.

Baseball

The **Toronto Blue Jays** (World Series champions in 1992 and 1993) are the only Canadian team in North America's **Major League Baseball** (Ⓦmlb. com). Even if you don't understand the rules, visiting a game can be a pleasant day out, drinking beer and eating burgers and popcorn in the sun, among a friendly, family-oriented crowd. There are over eighty home games each season, played from April to late September, with play-offs continuing through October. Blue Jays tickets can be hard to come by (starting at $50), so buy them in advance via the website.

Basketball

Basketball was invented in Springfield, Massachusetts by Canadian sports coach Dr James A. Naismith in 1891, but since then Canadian interest has been fairly low with teams coming and going and national leagues foundering. Canada does have one team – the **Toronto Raptors** – in the US **National Basketball Association** (Ⓦnba.com). Despite making the play-offs every year from 2014 to 2018, the team has yet to win a major championship. The season lasts from November to April and **tickets** cost from $10–15 (standing room only) to well over $1000 for VIP areas.

Lacrosse

Canada has four teams in the **National Lacrosse League**, or NLL (Ⓦnll.com) – the Toronto Rock (who won in 2011), the Calgary Roughnecks (winners 2009), the Saskatchewan Rush (in Saskatoon; winners 2016 and 2018) and Vancouver Warriors. This is the indoor version of the game and (perhaps because its level of speed and activity matches that of ice hockey) all four draw good crowds. **Tickets** aren't hard to get in any of the four cities, with the cheapest ranging from $22–30.

Soccer (football)

Canada has three teams in the **Major Soccer League**, or MLS (Ⓦmlssoccer.com) – Toronto FC, Montréal Impact and Vancouver Whitecaps FC. The season runs March to October and the sport is gaining in popularity in Canada, with especially lively crowds in Vancouver and a roster of mainly US and (older) foreign players (Spain's David Villa, England's Ashley Cole and Wayne Rooney and Sweden's Zlatan Ibrahimović were all playing in 2019). **Tickets** aren't hard to get in any of the four cities, with the cheapest ranging $20–30.

Women's professional sports

Women's professional sports in Canada have so far lagged behind the US, with one predictable exception – ice hockey. The **Canadian Women's Hockey League** (CHWL; Ⓦcwhl.ca) is currently a six-team league, including Calgary Inferno, Canadiennes de Montréal, Markham Thunder and Toronto Furies (the Worcester Blades, USA, and the Shenzhen KRS Vanke Rays in China, are the other two). League attendance is usually low, but the play-offs and finals can attract decent crowds. Though Canada's national soccer team is pretty good, there are as yet no Canadian sides in the **National Women's Soccer League** (there are several Canadian teams in the lower level W-League and Women's Premier Soccer League).

Rodeo

Professional **Canadian rodeo tournaments** are as big as their US counterparts, and just as much fun. If you're looking for an alternative to big-league -professional sports, this is a good option – and something you're not likely to see matched if coming from Europe. Rodeos generally take place in the western provinces (Alberta, BC and Saskatchewan), and are organized by the Canadian Professional Rodeo Association (☎403 250 7440, Ⓦrodeocanada.com). The season starts in March and ends in November. Prices can be as low as $10 in some venues, rising to well over $100 for the finals.

Travel essentials

Costs

The commodity-fuelled Canadian economy is one of the world's richest, and though most things in Canada are **reasonably priced** by western European standards, food and drink, even basic items and snacks, can be relatively expensive. In remote areas such as Labrador and the far north, everything starts to get significantly more expensive – travel here is much harder on a budget. Accommodation, almost certainly your major outlay, can be very pricey in any of the country's cities and towns – especially if you're after a degree of comfort – but there are plenty of bargains to be had, not least in the burgeoning hostel and B&B market.

On **average**, if you're prepared to buy your own picnic lunch, stay in hostels and stick to the least expensive bars and restaurants, you could get by on around £38/US$50/C$66 a day. Staying in a good B&B,

CANNABIS IN CANADA

Despite making cannabis (marijuana) legal in 2018, Canada maintains strict rules regulating the use of the drug. Under 19s are prohibited from using it (with the exception of Alberta and Québec, where you must be 18 and over), and there are provincial regulations determining where adults can buy it (authorized retailers only), where adults can use it and how much adults can possess (usually a maximum of 30 grams). Any breach of these rules could lead to arrest and up to fourteen years in jail – needless to say, attempting to take any cannabis out of the country (especially across the US border) is illegal and a very bad idea, even if you purchased the drug legally in Canada.

eating out in medium-range restaurants most nights and drinking regularly in bars, you'll get through at least £98/US$125/C$166 a day, with the main variable being the cost of your room. On £152/US$195/C$260 a day, you'll be limited only by your energy reserves – though if you're planning to stay in the best hotels and make every night a big night out, this still won't be enough.

Taxes

Virtually all prices in Canada for everything from bubble gum to hotel rooms are quoted **without tax**, which means the price you see quoted is not the price you'll end up paying. With the exception of Alberta, the Yukon, Nunavut and NWT, each province levies a **Provincial Sales Tax (PST)** of between six (Saskatchewan) and ten (the Maritimes) percent on most goods and services, including hotel and restaurant bills; this is supplemented by the **Goods and Services Tax (GST)**, a five percent Federal levy applied nationwide. In New Brunswick, Nova Scotia, Ontario, PEI and Newfoundland and Labrador, the two taxes are amalgamated into the so-called **Harmonized Sales Tax (HST)** at a rate of thirteen to fifteen percent.

All of this means Alberta (and the territories) have the lowest total sales tax of just five percent (though hotels are slapped with an additional four percent in Alberta), while the Maritime provinces have the highest, at fifteen percent.

Crime and personal safety

Canada is one of the safest countries in the world and although there are a few crime hot-spots, these are confined to the peripheries of the country's three big cities – Toronto, Montréal and Vancouver. Few Canadian citizens carry **arms**, muggings are uncommon, and even in the cities, street crime is infrequent. Since 2018, cannabis has been legal throughout Canada, but stiff penalties are imposed for all other drugs and the rules surrounding the use of cannabis are strictly enforced (see page 48). Police are also diligent in enforcing **traffic laws**.

Electricity

In Canada **electricity** is supplied at an alternating current of 110 volts and at a frequency of 60Hz, the same as in the US. Appliances such as shavers and hairdryers from most other countries need transformers – most phones, laptops and tablets can usually handle both 220/240 and 110 volt currents. For all appliances, you'll need a plug converter for Canada's two-pin sockets.

Entry requirements

Canada requires all visa-exempt foreign nationals who fly to Canada to get **Electronic Travel Authorization** (eTA) in advance. This applies to citizens of the EU, Norway, Iceland and most Commonwealth countries, including the UK, Australia and New Zealand – passport holders from South Africa must still apply for formal visas in advance. You must apply for eTA online and pay a $7 fee – most are approved within minutes and are valid for five years (multiple entry). You'll need a valid passport, an email address and a credit card (not debit card) to complete the online form. Visit **Ⓦ** cic.gc.ca for the latest requirements and forms. **US citizens** only need a passport or approved alternative to enter Canada (and can stay for up to six months without a visa). Note that eTA is also not required for anyone visiting Canada by land and sea from the US – border formalities at these entry points remain unchanged.

At the border itself the **immigration officer** decides the **length of stay permitted** – usually not more than six months. The officers rarely refuse entry, but they may delve deep, asking you for details of your schedule and enquiring as to how much money you have and what job you do; they may also ask to see a return or onward ticket.

For visits of more than six months, study trips and stints of (temporary) employment, contact the nearest Canadian embassy, consulate or high commission for authorization prior to departure. Once inside Canada, if you need an extension of your stay or want to change the basis on which you were admitted, you must apply to the nearest Canada Immigration Centre at least thirty days before the expiry of the authorized visit. Most visitors to Canada cannot work or study in the country without a special permit.

For **duty-free**, the standard allowance is 1.5 litres of wine or 1.14 litres of liquor or 24 355ml bottles/cans of beer, plus two hundred cigarettes, fifty cigars or cigarillos, and 200g of tobacco.

Health

Canada has an excellent **health service**, but nonresidents are not entitled to **free** health care, and medical costs can be astronomical – get insurance before you go (see page 50). If you have an accident, medical services will get to you quickly and charge you later. If you are carrying medicine prescribed by your doctor, also bring a copy of the prescription – first, to avoid problems at customs and immigration and, second, for renewing -medication with Canadian doctors, if needed. Most larger towns and cities should have a 24-hour or late-opening pharmacy. For general information on public health, and a list of **travel clinics** across Canada, the Public Health Agency of Canada is a good resource (W phac-aspc.gc.ca).

You are unlikely to face any special health issues in Canada, though there are certain dangers in the **backcountry**. Tap water is generally safe to drink, but at campgrounds water is sometimes good for washing only. You should **always boil backcountry water** for at least ten minutes to protect against the

EMERGENCIES

In a medical **emergency**, call ☎911.

Giardia parasite, which thrives in warm water, so be equally careful about swimming in hot springs – if possible, keep nose, eyes and mouth above water. Symptoms are intestinal cramps, flatulence, fatigue, weight loss and vomiting, all of which can appear up to a week after infection. If left untreated, more unpleasant complications can arise.

Blackflies and **mosquitoes** are notorious for the problems they cause walkers and campers, and are especially bad in areas near standing water and throughout most of northern Canada. Late April to June is the blackfly season, and the mosquito season is from June until about October. If you're planning an expedition into the wilderness, take three times the recommended daily dosage of vitamin B complex for two weeks before you go, and to take the recommended dosage while you're in Canada; this cuts down bites by up to 75 percent.

Once you're there, **repellent creams and sprays** may help: the best are those containing DEET. Don't go anywhere near an area marked as a blackfly mating ground – although it's very rare, people have died from bites sustained when the creatures are in heat. Also dangerous is **West Nile virus** (mid-April to Oct), a mosquito-borne affliction with life-threatening properties; the virus has infected people as far west as BC and has killed over forty since 2002, so pay attention to local advice.

CANADIAN HIGH COMMISSIONS, EMBASSIES AND CONSULATES ABROAD

Australia Commonwealth Ave, Canberra ☎02 6270 4000, Wcanadainternational.gc.ca/australia-australie. Consulates in Melbourne, Perth and Sydney.
Germany Leipziger Platz 17, 10117 Berlin ☎030 203120, Wcanadainternational.gc.ca/germany-allemagne. Consulates in Düsseldorf, Munich and Stuttgart.
Ireland 7–8 Wilton Terrace, Dublin 2 ☎01 234 4000, Winternational.gc.ca/world-monde/ireland-irlande/splash.aspx.
New Zealand Level 11, 125 The Terrace, Wellington ☎04 473 9577, Wcanadainternational.gc.ca/new_zealand-nouvelle_zelande. Consulate in Auckland.
South Africa 1103 Arcadia St, Hatfield, Pretoria ☎012 422 3000, Wcanadainternational.gc.ca/southafrica-afriquedusud. Consulate in Durban.
UK Macdonald House, 1 Grosvenor Square ☎020 7258 6600, Wcanadainternational.gc.ca/united_kingdom-royaume_uni. Honorary consulates in Belfast, Cardiff and Edinburgh.
USA 501 Pennsylvania Ave NW, Washington, DC 20001 ☎202 682 1740, Wcanadainternational.gc.ca/world-monde/country-pays/united_states-etats_unis. Consulate Generals in Atlanta, Boston, Buffalo, Chicago, Dallas, Denver, Detroit, Los Angeles, Miami, Minneapolis, New York, San Francisco and Seattle; consulates in Anchorage, Houston, Raleigh, Philadelphia, Phoenix and San Diego.

If you develop a large rash and flu-like symptoms, you may have been bitten by a tick carrying Lyme borreliosis, or **Lyme disease**. This is easily curable, but if left untreated can lead to nasty complications. It's spreading in Canada, especially in the more southerly and wooded parts of the country, so you should check on its prevalence with the local tourist authority. It also may be advisable to buy a strong tick repellent and to wear long socks, trousers and sleeved shirts when walking.

In backcountry areas, look out for **poison ivy**, which grows in most places, but particularly in a belt across southern Ontario and Québec. If you're likely to be walking in affected areas, ask at tourist offices for tips on where it is and how to recognize it. The ivy causes itchy open blisters and lumpy sores up to ten days after contact. If you do come into contact with it, wash your body and clothes as soon as possible, smother yourself in calamine lotion and try not to scratch. In serious cases, hospital emergency rooms can give antihistamine or adrenaline jabs.

Insurance

Prior to travelling, you should take out an **insurance policy** to cover against theft, loss and illness or injury. You'll probably want to contact a **specialist travel insurance company**, or consider the travel insurance deal we offer (see box above). Most policies exclude so-called **dangerous sports** unless an extra premium is paid: in Canada this can mean whitewater rafting, mountain climbing and so on. If you need to make a claim, keep **receipts** for medicines and medical treatment. In the event you have anything stolen, you must obtain a **crime report** statement or number from the police.

Internet

Internet access is commonplace at Canadian hotels, hostels and B&Bs, and there are also plenty of cafés with free wi-fi in cities and towns. Free internet access is also available at all major libraries.

Mail

Every Canadian city, town and village of any significant size has its own **post office**, operated by **Canada Post** (ⓦ canadapost.ca). Opening hours are usually Monday to Friday 8.30am to 5.30pm, though a few places open on Saturday from 9am to noon. Much more numerous are Canada Post **service counters** inside larger stores, especially pharmacies, and here opening hours vary considerably, though core hours are the same as those of the post offices. To check for the nearest postal outlet, call ☏ 800 267 1177, or consult the website. Apart from Canada Post outlets, **stamps** can be purchased from automatic vending machines, the lobbies of larger hotels, airports, train stations, bus terminals and many retail outlets and newsstands. Current **postal charges** are 85¢ for letters and postcards up to 30g within Canada, $1.20 for the same weight to the US and $2.50 for international mail (also up to 30g).

Maps

In addition to the maps in this guide, the **free maps** issued by each provincial tourist office (see page 52) are excellent for general driving and route planning, especially as they provide the broad details of ferry connections. The best of the **commercially produced maps** are those published by Rand McNally (ⓦ randmcnally.com), though Google Maps are also fairly accurate for most areas of Canada.

Measurements

Canada uses the **metric system**, though many people still use the imperial system. Distances are in kilometres, temperatures in degrees Celsius, and foodstuffs, petrol and drink are sold in grams, kilograms or litres.

Money

Canadian currency is the **Canadian dollar** ($), made up of 100 cents (¢). Coins come as 5¢ (nickel), 10¢ (dime), 25¢ (quarter), $1 and $2. The 1¢ (penny) is no longer in circulation – so if you are paying in cash the price is rounded up or down to the nearest 5¢. If you pay by credit or debit card, you pay the exact amount. The $1 coin is known as a "loonie", after the loon bird on one face; the $2 coin is known as a "toonie". There are notes of $5, $10, $20, $50 and $100. **US dollars** are widely accepted near the border, but generally – banks, etc apart – on a one-for-one basis, which can be a very bad deal for US dollar holders. For up-to-date **exchange rates**, check ⓦ xe.com; at the time of writing, one Canadian dollar was worth 0.58 British pounds (£), 0.67 euros (€), 0.75 US dollars (US$), 1.04 Australian dollars (Aus$), 1.11 New Zealand dollars (NZ$) and 10.5 South African Rand (R).

Banking hours are a minimum of Monday to Friday 10am to 3pm, but many have late opening – till 6pm – on one night a week; others are open on Saturday mornings.

ATMs are commonplace. Most accept a host of **debit cards**, including all those carrying the Cirrus coding. All major credit and charge cards are widely accepted.

Phones

When **dialling** any Canadian number, either local or long-distance, you must include the area code. Long-distance calls – to numbers beyond the area code of the telephone from which you are making the call – must be prefixed with "1".

Since 2018 all **mobile** providers in Canada (including the big three; Bell Mobility, Rogers Wireless and Telus Mobility) use GSM, HSPA or LTE,

which means that mobiles bought in the **UK** and **Europe** can also be used in Canada (assuming you have a roaming option and your phone is tri-band) – in this case you'll definitely be charged international rates for incoming calls that originate from home. UK providers that have roaming agreements with Rogers include Orange, T-Mobile, Vodafone and 3. If you have an iPhone these should work in Canada, but you'll need to be extra careful about roaming charges, especially for data, which can be extortionate; even checking voicemail can result in hefty charges. Many travellers turn off voicemail and data roaming before they travel. Most phone companies will provide cheaper options for customers travelling to Canada, so check in advance. If you have a GSM phone and intend to use it a lot, it can be much cheaper to **buy a Canadian SIM card** ($10 or less) to use during your stay (you can also buy a micro-SIM for iPhone 4, 4S, or any compatible smartphone, or a nano-SIM for iPhone 5 and above). In Canada, **mobile networks** cover every city and town, but in rural areas you'll struggle to get a signal.

Public telephones are becoming harder to find due to the popularity of mobile phones. The cost of a local call is usually 50¢ for three or four minutes, depending on the carrier (each phone company runs their own booths). Long-distance calls are much pricier, and you're better off using a prepaid calling card ($5, $10 or $20), which you can buy at most grocery stores and newsstands.

USEFUL PHONE NUMBERS

Police, fire, ambulance ☎ 911.
Operator ☎ 0.
Information Within North America ☎ 411; international, call the operator ☎ 0.

METRIC CONVERSIONS

All figures are approximate:

1 centimetre = 0.39 inches	1 inch = 2.5cm	1 foot = 30cm
1 metre (100cm) = 1.1 yards or 39 inches	1 yard = 0.9m	
1 kilometre (1000m) = 0.6 miles	1 mile = 1.6km	8km = 5 miles
1 hectare (10,000sq m) = 2.5 acres	1 acre = 0.4ha	
1 litre = 2.1 US pints	1 US pint = 0.5 litres	1 US quart = 0.9 litres
1 litre = 0.3 US gallons	1 US gallon = 3.8 litres	
1 litre = 1.8 UK pints	1 UK pint = 0.6 litres	
1 litre = 0.2 UK gallons	1 UK gallon = 4.5 litres	
1 kilogramme or kilo (1000g) = 2.2lb	1lb = 45g/0.45kg	1oz = 28g

TEMPERATURES

°C	-10	-5	0	5	10	15	20	25	30	35
°F	14	23	32	41	50	59	68	77	86	95

Time zones

Canada has six **time zones**, but only four-and-a-half hours separate the eastern extremities of the country from the western.

Newfoundland is on **Newfoundland time** (3hr 30min behind the UK and 1hr 30min ahead of the eastern US).

The Maritimes and Labrador are on **Atlantic** (4hr behind the UK and 1hr ahead of the eastern US), though southeastern Labrador follows -Newfoundland time.

Québec and most of Ontario are on **Eastern** (5hr behind the UK) – the same zone as New York and the eastern US.

Manitoba, the northwest corner of Ontario, and Saskatchewan are on **Central** (6hr behind the UK; same as US Central).

Alberta, the Northwest Territories and a slice of northeast BC are on **Mountain** (7hr behind the UK – same as US Mountain).

In the west, the Yukon and the remainder of BC are on **Pacific** (8hr behind the UK and 1hr ahead of Alaska – same as US Pacific).

Nunavut spans a number of time zones, from Mountain to Atlantic.

For **daylight savings** (used in all regions except Saskatchewan, parts of Québec and northeast BC), clocks go forward one hour on the first Sunday of April, and back one hour on the last Sunday in October.

Tourist information

All of Canada's provinces have their own tourist **website** and these, along with those run by **Parks Canada**, covering the country's national parks and historic sites, and **Travel Canada**'s generic website (Ⓦtravelcanada.ca), are the most useful source of information before you set out. Each province and territory operates a **toll-free visitor information line** for use within mainland North America. In Canada itself, there are **provincial and territorial tourist -information centres** along the main highways, especially at provincial boundaries and along the US border; -**information centres** at every national and many provincial parks, selling fishing and backcountry permits and giving help on the specifics of hiking, canoeing, wildlife-watching and so forth; and **tourist offices** in every city and town.

PROVINCIAL TOLL-FREE INFORMATION NUMBERS AND WEBSITES

Alberta Ⓣ 800 252 3782, Ⓦ travelalberta.com.
British Columbia Ⓣ 800 435 5622, Ⓦ hellobc.com.
Manitoba Ⓣ 800 665 0040, Ⓦ travelmanitoba.com.
New Brunswick Ⓣ 800 561 0123, Ⓦ tourismnewbrunswick.ca.
Newfoundland and Labrador Ⓣ 800 563 6353, Ⓦ newfoundlandlabrador.com.
Northwest Territories Ⓣ 800 661 0788, Ⓦ spectacularnwt.com.
Nova Scotia Ⓣ 800 565 0000, Ⓦ novascotia.com.
Nunatsiavut Ⓣ 709 922 2942, Ⓦ tourismnnunatsiavut.com
Nunavut Ⓣ 866 686 2888, Ⓦ nunavuttourism.com.
Ontario Ⓣ 800 668 2746, Ⓦ ontariotravel.net.
Prince Edward Island Ⓣ 800 463 4734, Ⓦ tourismpei.com.
Québec Ⓣ 877 266 5687, Ⓦ quebecoriginal.com.
Saskatchewan Ⓣ 877 237 2273, Ⓦ tourismsaskatchewan.com.
Yukon Ⓣ 800 661 0494, Ⓦ travelyukon.com.

GOVERNMENT WEBSITES

Australian Department of Foreign Affairs Ⓦ dfat.gov.au.
British Foreign & Commonwealth Office Ⓦ gov.uk.
Canadian Department of Foreign Affairs Ⓦ international. gc.ca.
Irish Department of Foreign Affairs Ⓦ dfa.ie.
New Zealand Ministry of Foreign Affairs Ⓦ mfat.govt.nz.
South African Department of International Relations Ⓦ dirco.gov.za.
US State Department Ⓦ travel.state.gov.

OTHER USEFUL WEBSITES

Assembly of First Nations Ⓦ afn.ca. Lobbying organization of Canada's Aboriginal peoples, with plenty to get you briefed on the latest situation.
Canadian Ice Hockey Ⓦ hockeycanada.ca. The official site of the amateur governing body for the national obsession.
The Globe and Mail Ⓦ theglobeandmail.com. Canada's premier newspaper online.
National Atlas of Canada Online Ⓦ atlas.nrcan.gc.ca. Maps, stats and plenty of details on Canada's geographic features.
National Library of Canada Ⓦ collectionscanada.gc.ca. Information on all things Canadian, ordered by subject. Includes Canadian arts, literature and history.

CALLING HOME FROM ABROAD

Note that the initial zero is omitted from the area code when dialling the UK, Ireland, Australia and New Zealand from abroad.

Australia international access code + 61
New Zealand international access code + 64
UK international access code + 44
US and Canada international access code + 1
Ireland international access code + 353
South Africa international access code + 27

PUBLIC HOLIDAYS

NATIONAL HOLIDAYS

New Year's Day Jan 1
Good Friday Varies; March/April
Easter Sunday Varies; March/April
Easter Monday Varies; March/April (widely observed, but not an official public holiday)
Victoria Day Third Mon in May
Canada Day July 1
Labour Day First Mon in Sept
Thanksgiving Second Mon in Oct
Remembrance Day Nov 11 (only a partial holiday; government offices and banks are closed, but most businesses are open)
Christmas Day Dec 25
Boxing Day Dec 26

PROVINCIAL HOLIDAYS

Alberta Third Mon in Feb (Alberta Family Day); first Mon in Aug (Heritage Day)
British Columbia First Mon in Aug (British Columbia Day)
Manitoba First Mon in Aug (Civic Holiday)
New Brunswick First Mon in Aug (New Brunswick Day)
Newfoundland and Labrador March 17 (St Patrick's Day); third Mon in April (St George's Day); third Mon in June (Discovery Day); first Mon in July (Memorial Day); third Mon in July (Orangeman's Day)
Northwest Territories First Mon in Aug (Civic Holiday)
Nova Scotia First Mon in Aug (Civic Holiday)
Nunavut April 1 (Nunavut Day)
Ontario First Mon in Aug (Civic Holiday)
Québec Jan 6 (Epiphany); Ash Wednesday; Ascension (forty days after Easter); June 24 (Saint-Jean-Baptiste Day); Nov 1 (All Saints' Day); Dec 8 (Immaculate Conception)
Saskatchewan First Mon in Aug (Civic Holiday)
Yukon Third Mon in Aug (Discovery Day)

Parks Canada ⓦ pc.gc.ca. Excellent website with detailed information on all of Canada's national parks and national historic sites. Reserve space at some national parks at ⓦ pccamping.ca.
Weather – Environment Canada ⓦ weather.gc.ca. Get the most accurate weather forecasts at this government site.

Travellers with disabilities

At least in its cities and towns, Canada is one of the best places in the world to travel if you have limited mobility or other **physical disabilities**. All public buildings are required to be wheelchair-accessible and provide suitable toilet facilities, almost all street corners have dropped kerbs and public phones are specially equipped for hearing-aid users. Wheelchair users may encounter problems when travelling on urban public transport, but this is changing rapidly.

Out in the wilds, things are inevitably more problematic, but almost all the national parks have accessible visitor and information centres and many have specially designed, accessible trails. In addition, VIA Rail offers a good range of services for travellers with disabilities – and the larger **car-rental companies** (see page 33) can provide vehicles with hand controls at no extra charge, though these are usually only available on their most expensive models; book one as far in advance as you can. Provincial tourist offices (see page 52) are the prime source of information on accessible hotels, motels and sights. To obtain a parking privilege permit, drivers with disabilities must apply to a provincial authority, though the permit itself, once issued, is valid across Canada. Useful websites include ⓦ otc-cta.gc.ca/eng/take-charge.

Toronto

TORONTO FROM LAKE ONTARIO

1 Toronto

Toronto sprawls along the northern shore of Lake Ontario, its pulsating centre encased by a jangle of satellite townships and industrial zones which cover – as the Greater Toronto Area (GTA) – no less than one hundred square kilometres. In recent decades, successive city administrations and a raft of wealthy benefactors have lavished millions of dollars on glitzy architecture, slick museums, an excellent public transport system and the reclamation and development of the lakefront. As a result, few would argue that the GTA has become the cultural and economic focus of English-speaking Canada, and its six million inhabitants share what must surely be one of North America's most likeable, liveable cities.

The city has its share of attention-grabbing sights and the majority are conveniently clustered in the centre – either Downtown or Uptown. The most celebrated of them is the **CN Tower** (until 2010 the world's tallest freestanding structure) which stands next to the modern hump of the **SkyDome** stadium, now the Rogers Centre. The **Art Gallery of Ontario**, which possesses a first-rate selection of Canadian painting, and the **Royal Ontario Museum**, where pride of place goes to the Chinese and First Peoples collections, lead the city's other prestige attractions. Yet it's the pick of Toronto's smaller galleries that really add to the city's charm. There are a superb collection of ceramics at the **Gardiner Museum**, a fascinating range of footwear at the **Bata Shoe Museum** and the small but eclectic **Gallery of Inuit Art**. You'll find absorbing period homes too, most memorably the mock-Gothic extravagances of **Casa Loma** and the Victorian gentility of **Spadina House**, as well as the replica colonial fortress of **Fort York**, where Toronto began. Spare some time also for the good-looking buildings of the lively **St Lawrence** neighbourhood with its sprawling, colourful St Lawrence Market, and the **Distillery District**, the city's brightest arts complex, sited in a capacious former distillery. Indeed, there is an outstanding programme of **performing arts**, from dance to theatre and beyond, as well as exciting festivals, a vibrant club scene and literally hundreds of cafés and restaurants.

Toronto's sights illustrate different facets of the city, but in no way do they crystallize its **identity**. The city remains opaque, too big and diverse to allow for a defining personality, and this adds an enticing air of excitement and unpredictability to the place. Neither is its layout predictable: Toronto may have evolved from a lakeside settlement, but its growth has been sporadic and mostly unplanned, resulting in a cityscape that can seem a particularly random mix of the old and the new. This apparent disarray, when combined with the city's muggy summers, means most visitors spend their time hopping from sight to sight on the transit lines rather than walking. Yet, if you've the time and determination to get under the skin of the city, take to your feet and Toronto will slowly reveal itself.

Brief history

Situated on the slab of land separating Lake Ontario and Georgian Bay, **Toronto** was on one of the early portage routes into the interior, its name taken from the Huron for "place of meeting". The first European to visit the district was the French explorer Étienne Brûlé in 1615, but it wasn't until the middle of the eighteenth century that the French made a serious effort to control Lake Ontario with the development of a simple settlement and stockade, **Fort Rouillé**. The British pushed the French from the northern shore of Lake Ontario in 1759, but then chose to ignore the site for almost

CAFÉS IN THE DISTILLERY DISTRICT

Highlights

❶ Queen Street West Groove away in the liveliest part of the city, awash with boho cafés, restaurants and idiosyncratic shops. See page 61

❷ Distillery District In a sprawling, one-time Victorian distillery, this enjoyable arts and entertainment complex comes complete with a raft of cafés, bars, art galleries, theatres and shops. See page 68

❸ St Lawrence Market Sample your way across Toronto's most popular food market, which unfolds with fragrant stalls selling everything from heirloom tomatoes to pungent cheeses. See page 68

❹ Art Gallery of Ontario A superb collection of Canadian art with the Group of Seven very much to the fore. See page 71

❺ Royal Ontario Museum The ROM has a magnificent hoard of applied and fine art drawn from every corner of the globe – but the Native Canadian galleries takes top honours. See page 75

❻ Casa Loma The grand stone "House on the Hill" doesn't fail to disappoint, its eight dozen rooms kitted out in the height of early twentieth-century style. See page 80

❼ Toronto International Film Festival (TIFF) North America's biggest (by number of flicks) and most important film festival is a star-studded ten-day affair held in September. See page 92

HIGHLIGHTS ARE MARKED ON THE MAP ON PAGE 58

1

forty years until the arrival of hundreds of **United Empire Loyalists** (see page 329) in the aftermath of the American Revolution.

In 1791 the British divided their remaining American territories into two, Upper and Lower Canada. The first capital of Upper Canada was Niagara-on-the-Lake (see page 112), but this was too near the American border for comfort and the province's new lieutenant-governor, **John Graves Simcoe**, moved his administration to the relative safety of Toronto in 1793, calling the new settlement **York**. Simcoe had grand classical visions of colonial settlement, but was exasperated by the conditions of frontier life, noting "the city's site was better calculated for a frog pond … than for the residence of human beings". Nicknamed "Muddy York", the capital was little more than a village when, in 1812, the Americans attacked and burnt its main buildings.

The Family Compact – and William Lyon Mackenzie

In the early nineteenth century, effective economic and political power lay in the hands of an anglophile oligarchy christened the **Family Compact** by the radical polemicists of the day. The Compact's most vociferous opponent was a radical Scot, **William Lyon Mackenzie**, who promulgated his views both in his newspaper, the *Colonial*

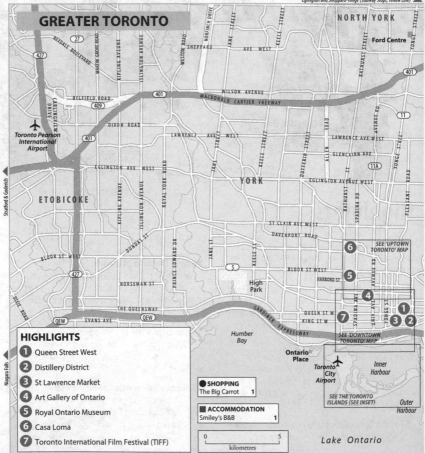

GREATER TORONTO

Eglington and Sheppard-Yonge (Subway Stops, Yellow Line)

NORTH YORK

Ford Centre

Toronto Pearson International Airport

ETOBICOKE

YORK

SEE 'UPTOWN TORONTO' MAP

High Park

Humber Bay

SEE 'DOWNTOWN TORONTO' MAP

Ontario Place

Toronto City Airport

Inner Harbour

SEE THE TORONTO ISLANDS (SEE INSET)

Outer Harbour

Lake Ontario

HIGHLIGHTS

1. Queen Street West
2. Distillery District
3. St Lawrence Market
4. Art Gallery of Ontario
5. Royal Ontario Museum
6. Casa Loma
7. Toronto International Film Festival (TIFF)

● **SHOPPING**
The Big Carrot 1

■ **ACCOMMODATION**
Smiley's B&B 1

0   5
kilometres

1

Advocate, and as a member of the legislative assembly. Mackenzie became the first mayor of Toronto, as the town was renamed in 1834, but the radicals were defeated in the elections two years later and a frustrated Mackenzie drifted towards the idea of armed revolt. In 1837, he staged a poorly organized **insurrection**, during which a few hundred farmers marched down the main drag, Yonge Street, fought a couple of half-hearted skirmishes and then melted away. Mackenzie fled across the border and two of the other ringleaders were executed, but the British parliament, mindful of similar events that led to the American Revolution, moved to liberalize Upper Canada's administration instead of taking reprisals. In 1841, they granted Canada **responsible government**, reuniting the two provinces in a loose confederation, prefiguring the final union of 1867 when Upper Canada was redesignated as **Ontario**.

Toronto the Good

By the end of the nineteenth century, Toronto had become a major **manufacturing centre** dominated by a conservative mercantile elite, which was exceedingly loyal to the British interest and maintained a strong Protestant tradition. This elite was sustained by the working-class **Orange Lodges**, whose reactionary influence was a key feature of municipal

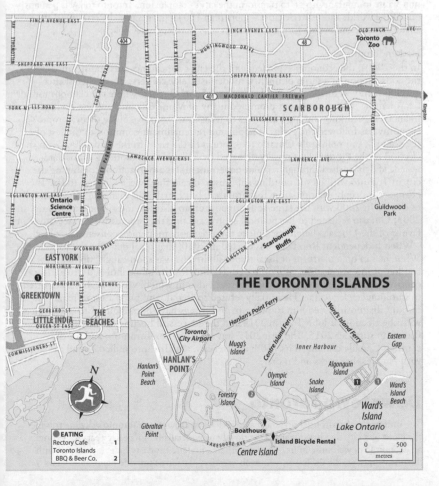

THE TORONTO ISLANDS

N

● EATING
Rectory Cafe 1
Toronto Islands BBQ & Beer Co. 2

0   500
metres

1

ORIENTATION AND STREET NUMBERS

Yonge Street is Toronto's principal north–south artery. Main drags perpendicular to Yonge use this intersection to change from west to east – Queen Street West, for example, becomes Queen Street East when it crosses Yonge. Therefore, 1000 Queen Street West is a long way from 1000 Queen Street East.

politics, prompting a visiting Charles Dickens to complain about the city's "rabid Toryism". Other commentators were equally critical, referring to Toronto at one time or another as "Hogtown" and – with more than a slice of irony – "Toronto the Good". Nevertheless, these same Protestants were enthusiastic about public education, just like the Methodist-leaning middle classes, who spearheaded social reform movements, principally suffrage and temperance. The trappings, however, remained far from alluring – well into the twentieth century Sunday was preserved as a "day of rest" and Eaton's department store drew its curtains to prevent Sabbath window-shopping. Indeed, for all its capital status, the city was strikingly provincial by comparison with Montréal until well into the 1950s, when the opening of the **St Lawrence Seaway** gave the place something of a jolt and the first wave of non-white immigrants began to transform the city's complexion. Toronto today is perhaps one of the world's most diverse cities – more than 130 languages and dialects crowd the airstream here, and half of Toronto's residents were born outside Canada.

Modern Toronto

In the 1960s, the economy exploded, and the city's appearance was transformed by the construction of a series of mighty, modernistic **skyscrapers**. This helter-skelter development was further boosted by the troubles in Québec, where the clamour for fair treatment by the francophones prompted many of Montréal's anglophone-dominated financial institutions and big businesses to transfer to Toronto. Since then, Toronto's economy has followed the cycles of boom and retrenchment common to the rest of the country, but politically Ontario took a turn to the right in the mid-1990s with the election of the **Progressive Conservatives** led by Mike Harris. Nothing if not hard-nosed, Harris pushed through a major **governmental reorganization**, combining the city of Toronto with its surrounding suburbs to create the "Mega City" of today. The change was deeply unpopular in Toronto itself, but Harris still managed to get himself re-elected in 2000 with the large-scale support of small-town and suburban Ontario. In 2003, Ontario returned to the political centre, ejecting the Progressive Conservatives in favour of the Liberals, heralding a move towards more moderate, consensual politics.

When Independent Rob Ford was elected in 2010, that ideal flew out the window. While he ran on a platform of fiscal responsibility, he was soon caught up in a conflict of interest scandal, and others concerning his use of alcohol and drugs. The controversies reached a climax in an internet video in which, visibly high, he admitted to smoking crack cocaine. He initially refused to step down, but a stint in rehab and a tumour diagnosis forced him to pull out, and things have been a bit more stable since, with the election of John Tory in 2014 and the successful hosting of the Pan American Games in summer 2015. The year 2017 was a big one for Toronto – and for the country. Canada celebrated its 150th anniversary, and Toronto pulled out all the stops, with parades, fireworks and more.

Downtown Toronto

The uniformly glass-fronted skyscrapers etched across **Downtown Toronto**'s skyline trumpet the clout of a city that has discarded the dowdy provincialism of its early years to become an economic powerhouse in its own right. There's no false modesty here, kicking off with Toronto's mascot, the **CN Tower**, whose observation platforms provide panoramic views over the city and its immediate surroundings. From here, it's a brief stroll to the handsome symmetries of **Union Station**, which stands on the edge of the **Banking District**, where striking high-rises march north up Yonge Street as far as Queen Street with one of their number, the Toronto Dominion Centre, holding the delightful **Toronto Dominion Gallery of Inuit Art**. Beyond Queen Street lies the main shopping area, revolving around the enormous **Eaton Centre** – one of the busiest malls in North America – which is itself a stone's throw from the neo-Romanesque intricacies of the **Old City Hall** and the modernism of **Nathan Phillips Square**. From the square, it's another short haul to the **Art Gallery of Ontario**, holding the city's finest collection of paintings, and another, slightly longer trek west to **Fort York**, an accurate and intriguing reconstruction of the British outpost established here in 1793.

TORONTO'S NEIGHBOURHOODS

One of Toronto's most striking features is its division into distinct **neighbourhoods**, many of them based on the residents' ethnic origin. The following rundown will help you get the most from the city's demographic mosaic, whether you want to shop, eat or just take in the atmosphere.

The Beaches South of Queen Street East between Woodbine and Victoria Park Ave. A prosperous and particularly appealing district with chic boutiques, leafy streets and a sandy beach trimmed by a popular boardwalk.

Cabbagetown East of Jarvis and roughly bounded by Gerrard Street East on its south side, Wellesley to the north and the Don River to the east, it's noted for its trim Victorian housing. Its name comes from the district's nineteenth-century immigrants, whose tiny front gardens were filled with cabbages.

Chinatown Spreads west along Dundas Street West from Beverley and then north up Spadina to College. This section is crowded with busy restaurants and stores selling anything from porcelain and jade to herbs and pickled seaweed.

The Danforth (Greektown) Eat your way through buzzing Greektown, which is filled with superb Greek and Mediterranean restaurants, as well as world cuisine including Thai, Japanese and Brazilian. The Greek legacy goes back over one hundred years – in 1907 this neighbourhood emerged as a small Greek community, and is now one of the largest in North America. The best time to visit? The annual Taste of the Danworth in mid-August, a celebration of food, art, entertainment and more.

The Gay Village The Village's plethora of bars, restaurants and bookshops radiate out from the intersection of Church and Wellesley streets. Jammed to the gunnels during Toronto Pride held in the last week of June.

Kensington Market Just north of Dundas between Spadina and Augusta. Likely the most ethnically diverse part of town, combining Portuguese, West Indian and Jewish Canadians, who pack the streets with a ramble of small shops, cafés and open-air stalls.

Leslieville In the east end, lively Leslieville is dotted with cafés, bistros, restaurants, bars and antique shops. The vibrant Gerrard India Bazaar, known as Little India, is in the neighbourhood's northeast wedge – browse the area for South Asian cuisine, spices and more. Strolling around is a joy – Leslieville's tree-lined charm has made it a favourite backdrop for TV and film productions.

Little Italy The so-called Corso Italia, which runs along College between Bathurst and Ossington, is one of Toronto's liveliest neighbourhoods, with a gaggle of good restaurants and bars.

Little Portugal A crowded, vital area packed with shops and home-grown food joints, focused on Dundas Street West from Ossington to Lansdowne Ave.

Queen West Queen Street West, between University and Spadina, was once the grooviest part of town, but rising rents have long since pushed its crew of uber-cool Torontonians further west to what is often called "**West Queen West**", running west from Strachan Street to Dufferin. West Queen West is the city's star turn, with great bars, restaurants and shops.

Yorkville Just above Bloor between Bay Street and Avenue Road, Yorkville was "alternative" in the 1960s, with regular appearances by the leading lights of the counterculture like Gordon Lightfoot and Joni Mitchell. Today, the alternative jive is long gone, and the district holds some of Toronto's most showy clothing shops and art galleries.

1

CN Tower

301 Front St West • Daily 8:30am–11pm, sometimes later • Look Out Level deck & glass floor $38, Sky Pod $15 extra; discount with Toronto CityPass and combination ticket • ☎ 416 868 6937, Ⓦ cntower.ca • Subway: Union Station

The **CN Tower** has emerged as the city's symbol – it's touted on the city's promotional literature, features on thousands of postcards and holiday snaps and has become the obligatory start to most tourist itineraries. From almost anywhere in the city, it's

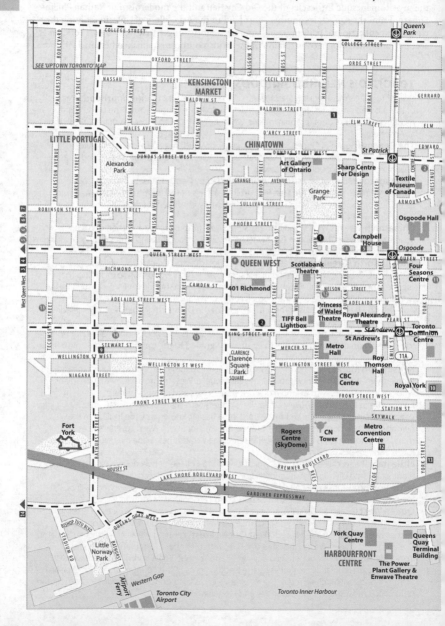

impossible to miss its slender form poking high above the skyline, reminding some of French novelist Guy de Maupassant's quip about another famous tower: "I like to lunch at the Eiffel Tower because that's the only place in Paris I can't see it."

Unlikely as it may seem, the celebrity status of the CN Tower was entirely unforeseen, its origins plain and utilitarian. In the 1960s, the Canadian Broadcasting Corporation (CBC) teamed up with the railway conglomerate Canadian National (CN) to propose

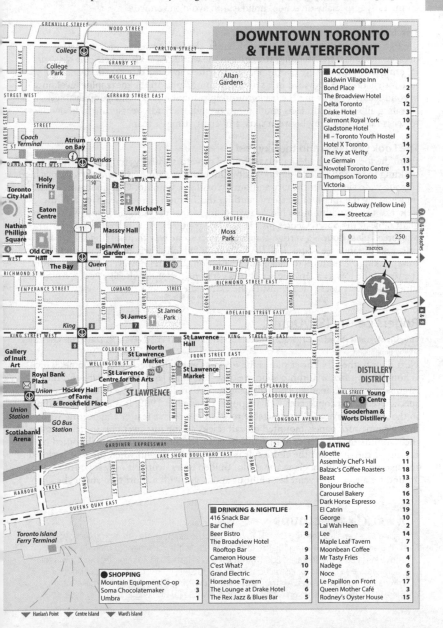

DOWNTOWN TORONTO & THE WATERFRONT

■ ACCOMMODATION	
Baldwin Village Inn	1
Bond Place	2
The Broadview Hotel	6
Delta Toronto	12
Drake Hotel	3
Fairmont Royal York	10
Gladstone Hotel	4
HI – Toronto Youth Hostel	5
Hotel X Toronto	14
The Ivy at Verity	7
Le Germain	13
Novotel Toronto Centre	11
Thompson Toronto	9
Victoria	8

— Subway (Yellow Line)
- - - Streetcar

0 ——— 250
metres

N

● EATING	
Aloette	9
Assembly Chef's Hall	11
Balzac's Coffee Roasters	18
Beast	13
Bonjour Brioche	8
Carousel Bakery	16
Dark Horse Espresso	12
El Catrin	19
George	10
Lai Wah Heen	2
Lee	14
Maple Leaf Tavern	7
Moonbean Coffee	1
Mr Tasty Fries	4
Nadège	6
Noce	5
Le Papillon on Front	17
Queen Mother Café	3
Rodney's Oyster House	15

■ DRINKING & NIGHTLIFE	
416 Snack Bar	1
Bar Chef	2
Beer Bistro	8
The Broadview Hotel Rooftop Bar	9
Cameron House	3
C'est What?	10
Grand Electric	7
Horseshoe Tavern	4
The Lounge at Drake Hotel	6
The Rex Jazz & Blues Bar	5

● SHOPPING	
Mountain Equipment Co-op	2
Soma Chocolatemaker	3
Umbra	1

Hanlan's Point   Centre Island   Ward's Island

1

the construction of a bigger and better transmission antenna. The CBC eventually withdrew from the project, but CN forged ahead. To the company's surprise, they found the undertaking stirred intense public interest – so much so that long before the tower was completed, in 1975, it was clear its potential as a tourist sight would be huge. Today, broadcasting only accounts for about twenty percent of the tower's income, with the rest provided by the two million tourists who throng here annually. Come early (especially on school holidays) to avoid the crowds.

The tower

Though now eclipsed by Dubai's Burj Khalifa, the CN Tower was for several decades the **tallest freestanding structure in the world**, its sleek and elegant structure tapering like a minaret to a point 553m (1815ft) above the city centre. Details of its construction are provided in a series of photographs on the **mezzanine level**, just beyond security check-in. The background information is extremely interesting, revealing all sorts of odd facts and figures, though it's hardly reassuring to know the tower is hit by lightning between sixty and eighty times a year.

The Look Out Level and the Sky Pod

From the foot of the building, **glass-fronted elevators** whisk you up the outside of the building to the indoor and outdoor **Look Out Level** at 346m. The circular galleries here provide wide views over the city and out across Lake Ontario. Certain features stand out, notably the splash of greenery banding the Toronto Islands (see page 83), the welter of new condominium blocks marauding across the lakeshore, and Will Alsop's giant table at the Sharp Centre for Design (see page 73). At this level also is the reinforced **glass floor** – a vertigo shock that goes some way to justifying the column's pricey admittance fee – and *360 The Restaurant*, which slowly revolves around the tower, taking 72 minutes to make one revolution. You are, however, still 100m from the top of the tower: a separate set of lifts carry visitors up to the **Sky Pod**, a confined little gallery that doesn't really justify the extra expense.

Rogers Centre (SkyDome)

1 Blue Jays Way • Call or visit website for schedule of guided tours • $17, game tickets from $17 • ☎ 416 341 2770, ⓦ rogerscentre.com • Subway: Union Station

Next door to the CN Tower stands the **Rogers Centre**, formerly the **SkyDome**, which is home to two major Toronto sports teams – the Blue Jays baseball team and the Argonauts of the Canadian Football League. The stadium seats 53,000 and is used for special events and concerts as well as sports. Opened in 1989, it was the first stadium in the world to have a fully retractable roof, an impressive feat of engineering with four gigantic roof panels mounted on rail tracks taking just twenty minutes to cover the stadium's three hectares of turf and terrace. The SkyDome was much touted by the city at the time, but the end result is rather unsightly and when the roof is closed the stadium looks like a giant armadillo. **Guided tours**, worth it only if you're sticking around for a sporting event, last an hour and begin with a short film about the

---

A WALK IN THE CLOUDS

Calling all adrenaline seekers: The CN Tower offers the ultimate rush: In high season, you can walk along the rim of the restaurant's roof, 356m above the pavement (tethered to a track above for safety). The so-called Edgewalk itself ($225) lasts 20 to 30 minutes, but allow a total of one-and-a-half hours for instructions and prep; further, there are a number of physical criteria that you must meet. And yes, sometimes low-lying wispy clouds will make the trip a more atmospheric one. Refer to ⓦ edgewalkcntower.ca for booking and further details.

stadium's construction; pick up tour tickets at the Jays Shop Stadium Edition store, which is packed with unique Jays merchandise from caps to autographed memorabilia.

Union Station

The city's transport hub, **Union Station**, at Front Street West and Bay Street, is a distinguished Beaux Arts structure designed in 1907 and completed in 1927. The station's exterior is imposing, with its long row of Neoclassical columns, but the interior is the real highlight, the vast **main hall** boasting a coffered and tiled ceiling of graceful design. Like other North American railway stations of the period, Union Station has the flavour of a medieval cathedral, with muffled sounds echoing through its stone cloisters and daylight filtering through its high-arched windows. The station's grandiose quality was quite deliberate; in the days when the steam train was the most popular form of transport, architects were keen to glorify the train station, and, in this case, to conjure up images of Canada's vastness – a frieze bearing the names of all the Canadian cities reachable by rail at the time of construction runs around the hall.

The Banking District

Opposite the east end of Union Station, the **Banking District**, which extends north as far as Queen Street, kicks off with the **Royal Bank Plaza**, at 200 Bay St, where the two massive towers were designed by local architect Boris Zerafa. Each tower is coated with a thin layer of gold, and despite Zerafa's assertion that the gold simply added texture to his creation, it's hard not to believe the Royal Bank just wanted to show off.

To the left of the Royal Bank – and to the right of the *Royal York* hotel (see page 88) – a gated **stone stairway** climbs up from Front Street West to a tiny plaza overseen by a phalanx of skyscrapers. It's a delightful spot, in a heart-of-the-city sort of way, and **Catherine Widgery**'s *City People*, a folksy set of life-size aluminium figures attached to the stairway's walls, adds a touch of decorative élan. The walkway continues down to Wellington Street West, just a few metres from the southern tower of the **Toronto Dominion Centre**, whose four reflective black blocks straddle Wellington Street between Bay and York streets. Arguably the most appealing of the city's modern skyscrapers, the four towers are without decoration, but as an ensemble they achieve an austere beauty that can't help but impress. The south tower holds the Gallery of Inuit Art (see below) and the other three, on the north side of Wellington Street, rise high above a small lawn on which have been placed seven extraordinarily realistic bronze cows, the work of Saskatchewan's **Joe Fafard**.

Toronto Dominion Gallery of Inuit Art

South Tower of the Toronto Dominion Centre • 79 Wellington St West • Mon–Fri 8am–6pm, Sat & Sun 10am–4pm • Free • ☏ 416 982 8473, ⓦ art.td.com • Subway: King

The **Toronto Dominion Gallery of Inuit Art** boasts an outstanding collection of over a hundred pieces of Inuit sculpture. Spread over two levels – and beginning in the foyer – the collection is owned by the Toronto Dominion (TD) Bank, who commissioned a panel of experts to celebrate Canada's Centennial in 1965 by collecting the best of postwar Inuit art. All the favourite themes of Inuit sculpture are here, primarily animal and human studies, supplemented by a smattering of metamorphic figures, in which an Inuk adopts the form of an animal, either in full or in part. Other sculptures depict deities, particularly **Sedna** (or Nuliayuk), the sea goddess. Inuit religious belief was short on theology, but its encyclopedic animism populated the Arctic with spirits and gods, the subject of all manner of Inuit folk tales. Most of the pieces are in soapstone, but there are also bone, ivory and caribou-antler pieces, as well as vibrant prints and drawings. A free introductory booklet, available from the rack at the entrance of the gallery, provides some background information.

1

St Andrew's Presbyterian Church

73 Simcoe St, at King • Sun 10.30am–1pm, Mon–Fri 9am–5pm • Free • ☎ 416 593 5600, ⓦ standrewstoronto.org • Subway: St Andrew

Marooned among the city's skyscrapers, **St Andrew's Presbyterian Church** is a handsome sandstone structure, whose Romanesque Revival towers and gables have a distinctly Norman appearance. Built in 1876 for a predominantly Scottish congregation – and now an isolated reminder of an older Toronto – the church has a delightful interior, its cherrywood pews and balcony sloping down towards the chancel with dappled light streaming in through the stained glass windows. St Andrew's has an admirable history of social action and since the earliest days of the city's settlement it has played a leading role in the fight against poverty and homelessness.

Roy Thomson Hall

60 Simcoe St • ☎ 416 872 4255, ⓦ roythomson.com • Subway: St Andrew

Across the street from St Andrew's Presbyterian Church is **Roy Thomson Hall**, the home of the Toronto Symphony Orchestra (see page 94). The Hall also hosts a wide range of celebrity lectures, benefit concerts and unique shows – check website for schedule. Completed in 1982 to a design by Arthur Erickson (1924–2009), the hall looks like an upturned soup bowl by day, but at night its appearance is transformed, its glass-panelled walls radiating a skein of filtered light high into the sky. A native of British Columbia, Erickson was one of the leading architects of his generation, a modernist who designed, among much else, Toronto's Eglington West Subway station and King's Landing, a luxury condominium block down on the waterfront at 470 Queen's Quay West.

CBC Centre

250 Front St West, at John • Hours may vary; daily 9am–5pm• Free • ☎ 416 205 5574, ☎ 866 306 4636, ⓦ cbc.ca • Subway: St Andrew

The **CBC Centre** occupies a ten-storey high-rise with painted gridiron beams. A highlight of the Centre is the soaring Barbara Frum Atrium, named for a legendary Canadian journalist, which is topped with a spectacular skylight. Since its foundation in 1936, the **CBC** – the Canadian Broadcasting Corporation – has built up an international reputation for the impartiality of its radio and television news and, although it carries commercials unlike the UK's BBC, it remains in public ownership. Guided tours of the Centre are occasionally available – check the website for information.

Fort York

250 Fort York blvd • Mid-May to Aug daily 10am–5pm; Sept to mid-May Mon–Fri 10am–4pm, Sat & Sun 10am–5pm • $14 • ☎ 416 392 6907, ⓦ fortyork.ca • Harbourfront streetcar (#509) from Union Station to Fleet St, then a 10min walk via Fort York blvd

Modern-day Toronto traces its origins to **Fort York**, a colonial stockade built in 1793 on the shores of Lake Ontario to bolster British control of the Great Lakes. Since then, landfill has pushed the lakeshore southwards and marooned the fort, which was

---

STRANGE TALES FROM THE NORTH – SEDNA, THE SEA GODDESS

Half-woman, half-seal, **Sedna**, the goddess of the sea and sometimes of life itself, is one of the key figures of Inuit mythology. Her story is a sad one. She was deceived by a young man, who posed as a hunter, but was in fact a powerful shaman. Sedna married him and he promptly spirited her away from her family. Sedna's father gave chase and rescued his daughter, but on the return journey they were assailed by a violent storm conjured by the shaman. Terrified, the father threw his daughter overboard, and when she repeatedly attempted to get back into the boat, he chopped off her fingers and then her hands. These bits and pieces became whales, seals, walruses and fish, but Sedna herself sank to the depths of the ocean, where she remains.

reconstructed in the 1930s, under the shadow of the (elevated) Gardiner Expressway just to the west of Bathurst Street. Fort York was initially a half-hearted, poorly fortified affair, too remote to command much attention – never mind that the township of York was the capital of Upper Canada. In 1811, deterioration in Anglo-American relations put it on full alert, but the British realized it was rather too weak to rebuff the American army that marched on York in 1813 and they decided to withdraw. In a desperate hurry, the British blew up the gunpowder magazine to stop its contents falling into enemy hands, but underestimated the force of the explosion, killing or wounding ten of their own men in addition to 260 of the advancing enemy.

After the war, the fort was rebuilt and its garrison made a considerable contribution to the development of Toronto, as York was renamed in 1834. The British army moved out in 1870 and their Canadian replacements stayed for another sixty years; the fort was opened as a **museum** in 1934. Throughout the year, costumed guides give the low-down on colonial life and free plans of the fort are issued at reception.

The fort

The **fort**'s carefully restored, thick, earth-and-stone **ramparts** are low-lying and constructed in a zigzag pattern, both to mitigate against enemy artillery and to provide complementary lines of fire. They enclose a haphazard sequence of log, stone and brick buildings, most notably a couple of well-preserved **blockhouses**, complete with heavy timbers and snipers' loopholes. There are also reconstructions of the stone and brick powder **magazine**, which has 2m-thick walls and spark-proof copper and brass fixtures; the **Blue Barracks**, the former junior officers' quarters; and the old **officers' quarters and mess**, which hold two original money vaults, hidden away in the cellar. Of the several buildings featuring exhibitions on the fort and its history, the most diverting is the archeological display exhibiting various bits and pieces unearthed at the fort, including buckles, brooches, plates, clay pipes and tunic buttons, and a substantial collection of colonial armaments. The latter includes a rare, cumbersome Gatling gun like the one used against the Métis (see page 505) and a furnace for heating up cannon balls – hence the term "hot shot".

Hockey Hall of Fame

Brookfield Place, 30 Yonge St at Front St West; enter through lower concourse of Brookfield Place • July & Aug Mon–Sat 9.30am–6pm & Sun 10am–6pm; rest of year Mon–Fri 10am–5pm, Sat 9.30am–6pm & Sun 10.30am–5pm • $20, ages 4–13 $14, over-65s $16 • ☎ 416 360 7765, Ⓦ hhof.com • Subway: Union Station

The **Hockey Hall of Fame** is a large and adulatory tribute to Canada's national obsession – ice hockey. The game arouses deep passions across the country and parts of the Hall of Fame have the tenor of a shrine, nowhere more so than the **Trophy Room**, where the very first Stanley Cup, donated by Lord Stanley, the Governor General of Canada in 1893, is displayed: the Stanley Cup is the award given to a season's championship team.

The main body of the museum, housed in the lower concourse of Brookfield Place, a glass-roofed retail centre, holds a string of exhibition areas, including one featuring a replica of the Montréal Canadiens' locker room, and another on Hometown Hockey, celebrating local teams across Canada and the US, with photos, jerseys, artefacts and more. A couple of mini-theatres show film of key hockey games and interviews with hockey stars, and there are a pair of miniature ice rinks where youngsters can practise either shooting or goal-minding.

St Lawrence District

The **St Lawrence District**, lying just to the east of Yonge Street, between The Esplanade, Adelaide Street East and Frederick Street, is one of the city's oldest neighbourhoods, enjoying its first period of rapid growth after the War of 1812. In Victorian times, St Lawrence became one of the most fashionable parts of the city, and although it hit the skids thereafter, it was revamped and partly gentrified in the late 1990s.

1

St Lawrence Market

92 Front St East, at Market • Tues–Thurs 8am–6pm, Fri 8am–7pm & Sat 5am–5pm • ☎ 416 392 7219, ⓦ stlawrencemarket.com • Subway: Union Station

The St Lawrence District is home to **St Lawrence Market**, easily the city's best food and drink market, housed in a capacious red-brick building dating to 1844. Spread out across the main and lower levels are stalls selling everything from fish and freshly baked bread to international foodstuffs, all sorts of organic edibles and Ontario specialities, including cheese, jellies, jams and fern fiddleheads. The market is at its busiest on Saturday, when you can also drop by the **North St Lawrence Market**, an authentic farmers' market (Sat 5am–3pm) – a tradition that, impressively, dates back to 1803. The St Lawrence Market also regularly offers cooking classes at the Market Kitchen ($60 per person), which include everything from making salsa and sauces with local vegetables to pie-baking.

St Lawrence Hall

157 King St East, at Jarvis • ☎ 416 392 7809 • Subway: Union Station

St Lawrence Hall is one of Toronto's most attractive Victorian buildings, a palatial edifice whose columns, pilasters and pediments are surmounted by a dinky little cupola. Dating from 1850, the hall was built with oodles of space for balls, public lectures and concerts; it also became the city's main meeting place for big events like the anti-slavery rallies of the 1850s. The bad taste award goes to the American showman and circus proprietor **P.T. Barnum**, one-time mayor of his home town of Bridgeport, Connecticut. It was here in St Lawrence Hall (among other spots) where Barnum saw the potential of the diminutive (60cm) Charles Sherwood Stratton, aka **Tom Thumb**, exhibiting him as a curiosity to stump up a few dollars.

St James Anglican Cathedral

65 Church St, at King • Mon–Fri 7.30am–5.30pm, Sat 9am–5pm & Sun 8am–5.30pm • Free • ☎ 416 364 7865, ⓦ stjamescathedral.on.ca • Subway: Union Station

The graceful bulk of **St James Anglican Cathedral** rises high above its immediate surroundings, its yellowish stone fetchingly offset by copper-green roofs and a slender spire. An excellent example of the neo-Gothic style once popular in every corner of the British Empire, the cathedral boasts scores of pointed-arch windows and an abundance of sturdy buttressing. Inside, the **nave** is supported by elegant high-arched pillars and flanked by an ambitious set of **stained glass windows** that attempts to trace the path by which Christianity reached Canada from Palestine via England. It's all a little confusing, but broadly speaking, the less inventive windows depict Biblical scenes, whereas those which focus on English history are the more ingenious. The nave's stained glass windows were inserted at the end of the nineteenth century, but those of **St George's Chapel**, in the southeast corner of the church, were added in 1935 to celebrate the Silver Jubilee of George V. They exhibit an enthusiastic loyalty to the British Empire that is echoed in many of the cathedral's funerary plaques: take, for example, that of a certain **Captain John Henry Gamble**, who was born in Toronto in 1844 but died on active service in the Khyber Pass in 1879; his stone is in the west transept. Spare a thought also for poor old **William Butcher**, a native of Suffolk, England, who fell to his death when he was working on the cathedral spire in 1839, aged just 27; his stone is in the main entranceway.

Distillery District

55 Mill St, near the foot of Parliament St • Most of the galleries and shops here open daily at 9am or 10am and close at 6pm, though the cafés and bars stay open later • ☎ 416 364 1177, ⓦ thedistillerydistrict.com • King streetcar (#504) east to Parliament St, then a 5min walk

The **Distillery District** is home to Toronto's most original and diverse arts centre, sited in the former **Gooderham and Worts Distillery**, an appealing industrial "village" on Mill Street. This rambling network of over forty brick buildings once constituted the largest distillery in the British Empire. In operation until 1990 the distillery was founded in

1832, when ships could sail into its own jetty, though landfill subsequently marooned it in the lee of the railway lines and the tail end of the Gardiner Expressway.

Since its demise, the distillery has been sympathetically redeveloped by a small group of entrepreneurs, who chose to integrate many of the original features into the revamp – including its quirky walkways and bottle runways – and, with refreshing integrity, to exclude all multinational chains. One of the architectural highlights is the **Pure Spirits** building, which features French doors and a fancy wrought-iron balcony. Among much else, the complex holds art galleries and artists' studios, hand-made-jewellery stores, designers, a chocolatier, bakeries, shops, a microbrewery, restaurants (serving an array of global cuisine, from French to Italian) and a couple of performance venues.

Nathan Phillips Square

One of the city's most important gathering points, **Nathan Phillips Square**, just west of Yonge Street, on Queen Street West, is also a distinctive landmark, the whole caboodle designed in the 1960s by a Finnish architect, the determined functionalist **Viljo Revell**. The square is framed by an elevated walkway and focuses on a reflecting pool, which becomes a skating rink in winter, and to the rear is Toronto's modernist **City Hall** with its curved glass-and-concrete towers. Revell won all sorts of awards for this project, which was then considered the last word in urban design, though today its rain-stained blocks look a tad dejected. Had his grand scheme been fully implemented, the city would have bulldozed the **Old City Hall**, a flamboyant pseudo-Romanesque building on the east side of the square. Completed in 1899, it was designed by **Edward J. Lennox**, who developed a fractious relationship with his city council paymasters. They had a point: the original cost of the building had been estimated at $1.77m, but Lennox spent an extra $750,000 and took eight years to finish it. Lennox had the last laugh however, carving gargoyle-like representations of the city fathers on the arches at the top of the front steps and placing his name on each side of the building – something the city council had expressly forbidden him to do.

Eaton Centre

220 Yonge St • Mon–Fri 10am–9.30pm, Sat 9.30am–9.30pm & Sun 10am–7pm • ☎ 416 598 8560, ⓦ cfshops.com • Subway: Queen Street or Dundas

Beginning on the north side of Queen Street West at Yonge, the **Eaton Centre**, owned and operated by Cadillac Fairview, is a three-storey assortment of shops and restaurants spreading out underneath a glass-and-steel arched roof. By shopping-mall standards, the design is appealing and the flock of fibreglass Canada geese suspended from the ceiling adds a touch of decorative flair; the general rule is the closer to the flock, the more expensive the shop. The centre takes its name from **Timothy Eaton**, an Ulster, Ireland immigrant who opened his first store here in 1869. Eaton kept a grip on the pioneer settlements in the West through his mail-order catalogue, known as the "homesteader's bible" – or the "wish book" among native peoples – while Eaton department stores sprang up in all of Canada's big cities. The Eaton's chain struggled to maintain its profitability in the later years of the twentieth century, and in 1999 dissolved into bankruptcy; the store was taken over by Sears, but they've since vacated as well, and a three-floor Nordstrom has now taken its place.

Elgin and Winter Garden Theatre

189 Yonge St, just north of Queen • Guided tours only: Thurs at 5pm & Sat at 11am • $12 (cash only) • 1hr 30min • ☎ 416 314 2871, ⓦ heritagetrust.on.ca • Subway: Queen Street

The **Elgin and Winter Garden Theatre** is one of the city's most unusual attractions. The first part of the guided tour covers the **Elgin**, an old vaudeville theatre whose ornate

1

furnishings and fittings have been restored after years of neglect. The Elgin was turned into a cinema in the 1930s and, remarkably enough, the top-floor **Winter Garden**, also a vaudeville theatre, was sealed off. When it was rediscovered, its original decor was intact, the ceiling still hung with thousands of preserved and painted beech leaves illuminated by coloured lanterns. Some items had to be replaced, but the restoration work was painstakingly thorough and the end result is delightful. The theatre hosts a variety of events throughout the year, including opera, theatre and the annual Toronto International Film Festival in mid-September.

Campbell House and around

160 Queen St West, at University • Tues–Fri 9.30am–4.30pm, Sat noon–4.30pm; plus June to Sept Sun noon–4.30pm • $10 • ☎ 416 597 0227, ⓦ campbellhousemuseum.ca • Subway: Osgoode

---

GLENN GOULD

In the 1970s, anyone passing the Eaton's department store around 9pm on any day of the year might have seen the door unlocked for a distracted-looking figure swaddled in overcoat, scarves, gloves and hat. This character, making his way to a recording studio set up for his exclusive use inside the store, was perhaps the most famous citizen of Toronto and certainly the most charismatic pianist in the world – **Glenn Gould**.

Not the least remarkable thing about Gould was that very few people outside the CBS recording crew would ever hear him play live. In 1964, aged just 32, he retired from the concert platform, partly out of a distaste for the accidental qualities of any live performance, partly out of hatred for the cult of the virtuoso. Yet no pianist ever provided more material for the mythologizers. He possessed a memory so prodigious that none of his acquaintances was ever able to find a piece of music he could not instantly play perfectly, but he loathed much of the standard piano repertoire, dismissing Romantic composers such as Chopin, Liszt and Rachmaninoff as little more than showmen. Dauntingly cerebral in his tastes and playing style, he lived at night and kept in touch by phoning his friends in the small hours of the morning, running up a monthly bill of thousands of dollars. He detested all blood sports, a category in which he also included concert performance. He travelled everywhere with bags full of medicines and would never allow anyone to shake his hand, yet soaked his arms in almost scalding water before playing in order to get his circulation going. At the keyboard, he sang loudly to himself, swaying back and forth on a creaky little chair. And even in a heatwave he was always dressed as if a blizzard were imminent. To many of his colleagues, Gould's eccentricities were maddening, but what mattered was that nobody could play like Glenn Gould. As one exasperated conductor put it, "The nut's a genius."

Gould's **first recording**, Bach's *Goldberg Variations*, was released in 1956, and became the bestselling classical record of that year. Soon after, he became the first Western musician to play in the Soviet Union, where his reputation spread so quickly that for his final recital more than a thousand people were allowed to stand in the aisles of the Leningrad hall. The technique always dazzled, but Gould's fiercely wayward intelligence made his interpretations controversial, as can be gauged from an announcement by **Leonard Bernstein**, who, when he was conducting Gould on one occasion, informed the audience that what they were about to hear was the pianist's responsibility, not his. Most notoriously of all, he had a very low opinion of Mozart's abilities – and went so far as to record the **Mozart** sonatas in order to demonstrate the legendary composer died too late rather than too soon. Gould himself **died** suddenly in 1982 at the age of 50 – the age at which he had previously stated he would give up playing the piano entirely.

Gould's **legacy of recordings** is not confined to music. He made a trilogy of radio documentaries on the theme of solitude: *The Quiet in the Land*, about Canada's Mennonites; *The Latecomers*, about the inhabitants of Newfoundland; and *The Idea of North*, for which he taped interviews with people who spent much of their time amid Canada's harshest landscapes. But Gould's **eighty-odd piano recordings** are the basis of his enduring popularity. One of the most poignant is his second version of the *Goldberg Variations*, the last record issued before his death.

Just outside the Osgoode station stands the handsome Georgian **Campbell House.**
Originally built on Adelaide Street for Sir William Campbell, Chief Justice and Speaker
of the Legislative Assembly, the building dates to 1822, and is the oldest standing
structure from the original town of York; it was transported to this corner in 1972.
There are regular guided tours of the period interior and these provide a well-researched
overview of early nineteenth-century Toronto.

East across University Avenue, the glassy and glossy **Four Seasons Centre for the
Performing Arts** is home to both the Canadian Opera Company (see page 94) and
the National Ballet of Canada (see page 94). **Osgoode Hall**, an attractive Neoclassical
pile built for the Law Society of Upper Canada early in the nineteenth century, owns
the block across Queen Street West. Looking like a cross between a Greek temple and an
English country house, it's protected by a wrought-iron **fence** that was originally erected
to keep cows and horses off its immaculate lawn. To check out the beautiful library,
rotunda or the late 1800s courtrooms, contact the Law Society at Ⓦlsuc.on.ca/visit.

Art Gallery of Ontario

317 Dundas St West, at Beverley • Tues & Thurs 10.30am–5pm, Wed & Fri 10:30am–9pm, Sat & Sun 10.30am–5.30pm • $19.50, but free
Wed 6–9pm & extra for temporary exhibitions • ☎ 416 979 6648, Ⓦ ago.net • Subway: St Patrick

The **Art Gallery of Ontario**, or **AGO**, is celebrated both for its extensive collection of
Canadian art and its excellent temporary exhibitions. In 2008 it was feted after a
thorough revamp in which the architect Frank Gehry (perhaps most famous for Bilbao's
Guggenheim Museum) transformed its appearance with a startling glass-and-wood
north facade on Dundas Street, and a four-storey titanium-and-glass wing overlooking
Grange Park to the south. The end result can be a little confusing, however, and it takes
a little time to get oriented. There are **six floors**: the Concourse Level holds a theatre and
learning centre. Level 1 is largely devoted to European art; Level 2 holds a wonderful
collection of Canadian paintings as well as a battery of Henry Moore sculptures; Level 3
offers the Galleria Italia, a soaring, airy, gallery-linking wood-and-glass hall which hosts
sculpture exhibits (and an espresso bar, too); Level 4 has a regularly rotated selection
of contemporary art, as does Level 5. There is a café, a restaurant, a large gift- and
bookshop, and a first-rate programme of guided tours free with admission.

Level 1: the European collection

The AGO possesses an eclectic sample of **European fine and applied art**, including ivory
and alabaster pieces, illuminated manuscripts, exquisite cameos and fine porcelain,
much of it the gift of the newspaper tycoon Kenneth Thomson, aka Lord Thomson of
Fleet (1923–2006). Early **paintings** include some rather pedestrian Italian altarpieces,
Pieter Brueghel the Younger's fine *Moses Breaking Pharaoh's Crown*, and a strong showing
for Dutch painters of the Golden Age, including Rembrandt, Van Dyck, Frans Hals and
Jan Van Goyen. Look out also for **Rubens**' exquisite *Massacre of the Innocents*, a typically
stirring canvas from the middle of his career, populated with writhing, muscular figures.

Level 2: Canadian eighteenth- and nineteenth-century painting

Distributed among forty numbered galleries on Level 2, the AGO has the finest
collection of **Canadian paintings** in the world. From the **eighteenth century**, one
particular highlight is a curiously unflattering *Portrait of Joseph Brant* by William
Berczy. A Mohawk chief, Brant (see page 117) is shown in a mix of European and
native gear, an apt reflection of his twin loyalties. From the **early to mid-nineteenth
century** comes the cheery *Passenger Pigeon Hunt* by Antoine Plamondon and the bright
and breezy *The Ocean Bride leaving Halifax Harbour* by John O'Brien, who specialized
in maritime scenes. Equally enjoyable is the work of the prolific Cornelius Krieghoff
(see page 73). The AGO owns a large sample of Krieghoff's paintings, including
characteristic winter scenes like his *The Portage Aux Titres*. Look out also for the

1

canvases of one of the era's most fascinating figures, Paul Kane, notably his *Landscape in the Foothills with Buffalo Resting* and *At Buffalo Pound*, where bison are pictured in what looks more like a placid German valley than a North American prairie.

Folksy and/or romanticized country scenes and landscapes ruled the Canadian artistic roost from the **1850s to the early twentieth century**. By and large this was pretty routine stuff, but Homer Watson's glossy Ontario landscapes, with their vigorous paintwork and dynamic compositions, made him a popular and much acclaimed artist – Queen Victoria even purchased one of his paintings, and Oscar Wilde dubbed him "the Canadian Constable". The AGO possesses several Watson paintings, including the handsome and well-composed canvas *The Old Mill*, but his *Death of Elaine* – inspired by a Tennyson poem – is a bizarrely unsuccessful venture into ancient legend, the eponymous maiden looking something like a stick insect.

Level 2: Canada's Group of Seven

A seminal work, the AGO's *West Wind* by **Tom Thomson** is an iconic rendering of the northern wilderness that is perhaps the most famous of all Canadian paintings. Thomson was the first to approach the wilderness with the determination of an explorer and a sense that it could encapsulate a specifically Canadian identity. A substantial sample of his less familiar (but no less powerful) works are also part of the AGO collection, including the moody *A Northern Lake, Maple Saplings, October* and the Cubist-influenced *Autumn Foliage 1915*. There is also a whole battery of preparatory sketches of lakes and canyons, waterfalls and forests, each small panel displaying the vibrant blotches of colour that characterize Thomson's work.

One of the most distinctive artists of the **Group of Seven** (see page 74) was **Lawren Harris**, whose 1924 *Above Lake Superior* is a pivotal canvas, its clarity of conception, with bare birch stumps framing a dark mountain beneath Art Deco clouds, quite exceptional. Equally stirring is his surreal *Lake Superior*, one of an army of paintings inspired by the wild, cold landscapes of the lake's north shore. Harris was also partial to urban street scenes and the AGO has several – including two of Toronto – each painted in a careful pointillist style very different from his wilderness works.

A contemporary of the Group – but not a member – the gifted **Emily Carr** focused on the Canadian west coast in general, and its dense forests and native villages in particular, as in her dark and haunting *Thunderbird* and the deep green foliage of both *In a Circle* and *Yellow Moss*.

Level 2: the Henry Moore Sculpture Centre

The AGO owns the world's largest collection of sculptures by **Henry Moore** (1898–1986), with the emphasis firmly on his plaster casts, alongside a few of his bronzes. Given a whole gallery, the sheer size and volume of Moore's output is impressive, but it was something of an accident his work ended up here at all. In the 1960s, Moore thought London's Tate Gallery was going to build a special wing for his work. When the Tate declined, Moore negotiated with the AGO instead, after being persuaded to do so by the gallery's British representative, Anthony Blunt – the art expert who was famously uncovered as a Soviet spy in 1979.

Levels 4 and 5: contemporary art

Spread over two levels, the AGO's collection of **contemporary art** showcases work by European, British and American artists from 1960 onwards. Around two hundred pieces are exhibited and they cover a wide range of media, from painting, sculpture and photography through to film and installation. These displays are changed fairly regularly. Recent temporary exhibitions include works by Japanese artist and sculptor Yayoi Kusama and an overview on painter Georgia O'Keeffe.

THE ARTIST DEFEATED: CORNELIUS KRIEGHOFF

Born in Amsterdam in 1815, **Cornelius Krieghoff** trained as an artist in Düsseldorf before emigrating to New York, where, at just 21, he joined the US Army, serving in the Second Seminole War in Florida. Discharged in 1840, Krieghoff immediately re-enlisted, claimed three months' advance pay and deserted, hot-footing it to Montréal with the French-Canadian woman he had met and married in New York. There, he picked up his brushes again, but without commercial success – quite simply no one wanted to buy his paintings. That might have been the end of the matter, but Krieghoff moved to **Québec City** in 1852 and found a ready market for his paintings among the well-heeled officers of the British garrison, who liked his folksy renditions of Québec rural life. This was the start of Krieghoff's most productive period and over the next eight years he churned out dozens of souvenir pictures – finely detailed, anecdotal scenes, many of the same tableau, that are his best work. In the early 1860s, however – and for reasons that remain obscure – he temporarily packed in painting, returning to Europe for five years before another stint in Québec City. However, this time, with the officer corps gone, he failed to sell his work. In 1871, he went to live with his daughter in **Chicago** and died there the following year, a defeated man.

Grange Park

In a wonderful display of teamwork – between the Art Gallery of Ontario, the City of Toronto and the local community – Grange Park received a makeover in 2017, solidifying its place as one of the city's most popular small urban parks. The five-acre park, just south of the museum, was originally part of the 1820 Grange estate, owned by the Boulton family. In 1910, the family bestowed The Grange house and estate to the newly opened *Art Gallery of Toronto*. The revitalized park, which reopened in 2017, was planted with more than 80 new trees, while paving stones inscribed with quotes by local authors and musicians were added to park paths. The highlight of the park is the museum's Henry Moore sculpture, *Large Two Forms*, which was relocated to the park from its former location at McCaul and Dundas streets.

Sharp Centre for Design

100 McCaul St, near Dundas St West · Ⓦ ocadu.ca · Subway: St Patrick

The **Ontario College of Art & Design** once occupied a plain brick building immediately to the south of the AGO along McCaul Street – but all that changed when the English architect **Will Alsop** got the go-ahead to transform the place in 2004. This was Alsop's first building in North America and he was not inclined to compromise, adding the extraordinary **Sharp Centre for Design**, which comprises a giant rectangular black-and-white-checkered "table-top", perched high up at roof level and supported by mammoth, multicoloured steel legs; it holds art studios, theatres and so forth, and has variously been described as "adventurous" and "ludicrous".

Chinatown

The AGO is fringed by **Chinatown**, a bustling neighbourhood cluttered with shops, restaurants and street stalls. The boundaries of Chinatown are somewhat undefined, but its focus is on Dundas Street west of Beverley and north along Spadina Avenue. The first Chinese to migrate to Canada arrived in the mid-nineteenth century to work in BC's goldfields. Subsequently, a portion of this population migrated east, and a sizeable Chinese community sprang up in Toronto in the early 1900s. Several more waves of migration – the last influx following the British handover of Hong Kong to mainland China in 1997 – have greatly increased the number of Toronto's Chinese, bringing the population to approximately 300,000.

1

THE GROUP OF SEVEN

In the autumn of 1912, a commercial artist by the name of **Tom Thomson** returned from an extended trip to the Mississauga country, north of Georgian Bay (see page 143), with a bag full of sketches that were to add new momentum to Canadian art. His friends, many of whom were fellow employees of the art firm of Grip Ltd in Toronto, saw Thomson's naturalistic approach to indigenous subject matter as a pointer away from the influence of Europe, declaring the "northland" as the true Canadian "painter's country". World War I and the death of Thomson – who drowned in 1917 – delayed these artists' ambitions, but in 1920 they formed the **Group of Seven**. Initially, the group comprised Franklin H. Carmichael, Lawren Harris, A.Y. Jackson, Arthur Lismer, J.E.H. MacDonald, F.H. Varley and Frank Johnston; later, they were joined by A.J. Casson, LeMoine Fitzgerald and Edwin Holgate. Working under the unofficial leadership of **Harris**, they explored the wilds of Algoma in northern Ontario, travelling around in a converted freight car, and later foraged even further afield, from Newfoundland and Baffin Island to British Columbia.

They were immediately successful, staging forty shows in eleven years, a triumph due in large part to Harris's many influential contacts. Yet there was also a genuine popular response to the intrepid frontiersman element of their aesthetic. Art was a matter of "taking to the road" and "risking all for the glory of a great adventure", as they wrote in 1922, while "nature was the measure of a man's stature", according to Lismer. Symbolic of struggle against the elements, the Group's favourite symbol was the lone pine set against the sky, an image whose authenticity was confirmed by reference to the "manly" poetry of Walt Whitman.

The **legacy** of the Group of Seven was – and perhaps still is – double-edged. On the one hand, they established the autonomy of Canadian art, but on the other, well into the 1950s it was difficult for Canadian painters to establish an identity that didn't conform to the Group's precepts. Despite the Group's unpopularity among many later painters, Ontario artist Graham Coughtry (1931–99) was, for one, generous: "They are the closest we've ever come to having some kind of romantic heroes in Canadian painting."

Kensington Market

Adjacent to Chinatown, just north of Dundas Street West, between Spadina and Augusta avenues, lies one of Toronto's most ethnically diverse neighbourhoods, the pocket-sized **Kensington Market**. It was here, at the beginning of the twentieth century, that Jewish Eastern European immigrants squeezed into a patchwork of modest little brick-and-timber houses that survive to this day. On Kensington Avenue they established a lively **open-air street market**, and though the market proper is no longer here, successive waves of immigrants from the Middle East, the Caribbean and from Asia have contributed to a lively hotchpotch of storefronts and shops. Purveyors of secondhand clothes can be found in the lower section of the neighbourhood, just off Dundas Street, while the upper part has an abundance of cafés and fresh-food stalls of every ethnic stripe.

Uptown Toronto

Spreading north from Gerrard Street, **Uptown Toronto** is something of an architectural hotchpotch, with perhaps the handiest starting point being **University Avenue**, whose bristling, monochromatic office blocks stomp up towards the imposing Victorian stonework of the **Ontario Legislative Assembly building**. The Assembly Building marks the start of a small but impressive **museum district**, made up of the delightful **Gardiner Museum of Ceramic Art**, the large but somewhat rambling **Royal Ontario Museum**, which possesses one of the country's most extensive collections of cultural artefacts, and the fanciful **Bata Shoe Museum**. The Assembly Building, flanked by the northern and southern sections of the green Queen's Park, is also close to the prettiest part of the sprawling **University of Toronto** campus, on and around King's College Circle, and is but a short subway ride away from the city's two finest historic homes: the neo-baronial **Casa Loma** and the debonair **Spadina House** next door.

Ontario Legislative Assembly

Queen's Park • Frequent 30min guided tours of building: Jan to mid-May & Sept–Dec Mon–Fri 9am–5pm; mid-May to June Mon–Fri 9am–5pm, Sat & Sun 9am–4.30pm; July to Aug Mon–Fri 9am–5.30pm, Sat & Sun 9am–4.30pm; visitors' gallery open when provincial legislature is in session late Sept to late June, when main chamber is not included in tours (call for details and times) • Free • ☎ 416 325 0061, Ⓦ ontla.on.ca • Subway: Queen's Park

Peering down University Avenue, the pink sandstone mass of the **Ontario Legislative Assembly** dates to the 1890s. Elegant it certainly isn't, but although the building is heavy and solid, its ponderous symmetries do have a certain appeal, with block upon block of roughly dressed stone assembled in the full flourish of the Romanesque Revival style. Seen from close up, the design is even more engaging, its intricacies a pleasant surprise: above the chunky columns of the main entrance is a sinuous filigree of carved stone, adorned by mythological creatures and gargoyle-like faces. The main facade also sports a Neoclassical frieze in which the Great Seal of Ontario is flanked by allegorical figures representing Art, Music and Agriculture. Inside, the foyer leads to the **Grand Staircase**, whose massive timbers are supported by gilded iron pillars. Beyond, among the long corridors and arcaded galleries, is the **Legislative Chamber**, where the formality of the mahogany and sycamore panels is offset by a series of whimsical little **carvings**: look for the owl overlooking the doings of the government and the hawk overseeing the opposition benches.

University of Toronto

Opened in 1843, and long the province's most prestigious academic institution, the assorted buildings of the **University of Toronto** are concentrated between Bloor Street West and College Street to the west of Queen's Park. The university's older buildings, with their quadrangles, ivy-covered walls and Gothic interiors, deliberately evoke Oxford and Cambridge with **Hart House**, at the west end of Wellesley Street on **Hart House Circle**, being a prime example. Hart House is attached to the **Soldiers' Tower**, a neo-Gothic memorial erected in 1924 to honour those members of the university community who had served Canadian forces in World War I. It adjoins an arcaded **gallery**, which is inscribed with a list of those university students, staff and alumni killed in World War I along with Canadian **John McCrae**'s *In Flanders Fields*, the war's most famous poem. Optimistically, the builders of the memorial didn't leave any space to commemorate the dead of any subsequent war: so the names of locally significant World War II casualties had to be inscribed on the walls at the foot of the tower.

Royal Ontario Museum

100 Queen's Park (enter on Bloor St West) • Daily 10am–5.30pm; summer Fridays (July–Sept) 10am–8.30pm • $20, but $12 after 5.30pm on summer Fridays; temporary exhibitions extra • ☎ 416 586 8000, Ⓦ rom.on.ca • Subway: Museum

A must-see, the **Royal Ontario Museum**, or **ROM**, is Canada's largest and most diverse museum, holding a vast hoard of fine and applied art, natural world exhibits, and cultural artefacts drawn from every corner of the globe. What's more, the permanent collection is supplemented by an ambitious programme of temporary exhibitions which

---

ART – AND COMMUNITY – FLOURISH AT 401 RICHMOND

Explore Toronto's vibrant contemporary art scene – all under one roof. A former tin lithography factory just south of Chinatown, 401 Richmond (Spadina Ave and Richmond St W; Mon–Fri 9am–7pm, Sat 9am–6pm, ☎ 416 595 5900, Ⓦ 401richmond.com) has become the model of an urban art space, with thriving art galleries and affordable studios for working artists, filmmakers, architects, fashion designers, milliners and more. The art hub is crowned by a relaxing leafy rooftop garden. Pick up a gallery guide upon arrival and browse the art and photography, including at the Abbozzo Gallery, which showcases more than 25 local and international artists. Refuel at the Roastery Coffee House, which serves soup, salad and potent espresso.

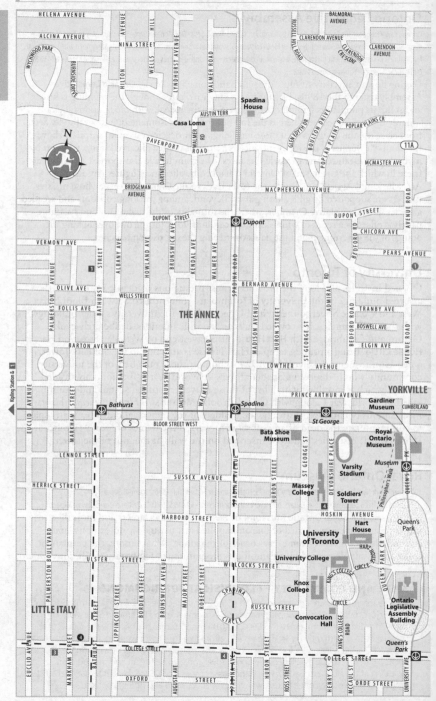

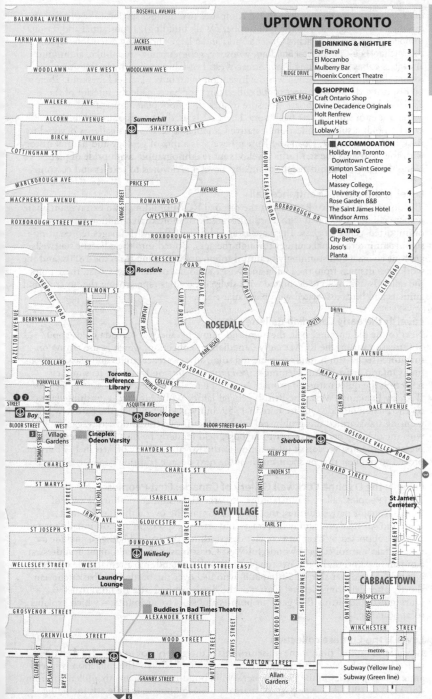

UPTOWN TORONTO

■ **DRINKING & NIGHTLIFE**
Bar Raval	3
El Mocambo	4
Mulberry Bar	1
Phoenix Concert Theatre	2

● **SHOPPING**
Craft Ontario Shop	2
Divine Decadence Originals	1
Holt Renfrew	3
Lilliput Hats	4
Loblaw's	5

■ **ACCOMMODATION**
Holiday Inn Toronto Downtown Centre	5
Kimpton Saint George Hotel	2
Massey College, University of Toronto	4
Rose Garden B&B	1
The Saint James Hotel	6
Windsor Arms	3

● **EATING**
City Betty	3
Joso's	1
Planta	2

1

often generate rave reviews. The ROM comprises two distinct sections: the original building (now referred to as the Philosopher's Walk building), a substantial and serious-minded stone structure facing Queen's Park; and a large and flashy extension, known as the **Michael Lee-Chin Crystal Building**, whose six geometrically crystal-like, aluminium-and-glass cubes march along Bloor Street West. Lee-Chin, a wealthy businessman, footed the bill, and the design was the invention of architect Daniel Libeskind. There's no disputing the visual impact of the cubes, but they have made the interior of the ROM rather hard to negotiate – be sure to pick up a **floor plan** at reception.

The museum spreads over **five floors**: Level B2 is used for temporary exhibitions; Level 1 holds a superb collection of native Canadian artefacts plus galleries devoted to Asia, including China, Japan and Korea; Level 2 is a mix of geology and natural history with the dinosaurs the star turn; Level 3 is more ethnographic, with pride of place being the ancient Egyptian collection; and Level 4 is devoted to textiles and costume.

Level 1: the old ROM entrance hall

The domed and vaulted **Rotunda** of the original ROM building is an extravagant affair, whose ceiling is decorated with a brilliant mosaic of more than a million tiny pieces of imported Venetian glass. These are arranged in 16 fields, with images representing significant international cultures through the ages. Bolted into the adjacent stairwells are four colossal and stunningly beautiful **totem poles**. Dating from the 1880s, and the work of craftsmen from the Haida and Nisga'a peoples of the West Coast, these poles – the tallest is 24.5m – are decorated with stylized carvings representing the supernatural animals and birds associated with particular clans.

Level 1: the early Canadian galleries

Next to the old entrance hall, the Sigmund Samuel Gallery of Canada holds about 560 treasures from the ROM's **early Canadian** art collection, which is also strong on furniture (see Karim Rashid's notable red sofa), silverware, ceramics and glass. You can find Ontario artist Arthur Heming's *The Hunter's Camp* on this level, its simplicity reflecting the quiet nature of primal Canada. Here also is the iconic *Death of General Wolfe* by Benjamin West. The British general James Wolfe inflicted a crushing defeat on the French outside Québec City in 1759, but was killed during the battle. West's painting transformed this grubby colonial conflict into a romantic extravagance, with the dying general in a Christ-like pose, held tenderly by his subordinates. West presented the first version of his painting to the Royal Academy of Arts in 1771 and it proved so popular that he spent much of the next decade painting copies.

Level 1: the Daphne Cockwell Gallery of Canada: First Peoples

The **First Peoples** gallery is outstanding, its large glass cabinets examining each of Canada's major native cultures; the exhibits, containing over a thousand artefacts related to spiritual and family life, travel and artistic expression are continually rotated, and are supported by clear and concise descriptions. Particular highlights include a rare buffalo war robe; some wonderful West Coast masks and ceremonial headdresses; a bunch of paintings by the artist-explorer Paul Kane; and, most remarkable of all, the war bonnet and war shirt of **Sitting Bull**, who fled over the border into Saskatchewan shortly after defeating General Custer at the Battle of the Little Bighorn in 1876. During his exile Sitting Bull gave his bonnet and shirt to a Mountie – which explains its appearance here.

Level 1: the Chinese collection

If you have limited time at the museum, this is the gallery not to miss. It's the largest collection of Chinese architectural artefacts outside of China. The collection is spread among four galleries in the Philosopher's Walk building, and spans six millennia, from 4500 BC to 1900 AD. Key parts of it are devoted to **Chinese temple art**, including three large and extraordinarily beautiful Yuan Dynasty wall paintings dating from 1300 AD. Other key exhibits in this section include a stunning collection of luxury objects (furniture, silk garments, porcelain). The most popular component of the Chinese collection is the **Ming tomb**. The aristocracy of the Ming Dynasty (1368–1644) evolved an elaborate style of monumental funerary sculpture, and the ROM holds the only example outside of China, though it is actually a composite tomb drawn from several sources rather than an intact, original whole.

Level 2: the Dinosaurs
Among the assorted natural history galleries on Level 2, the highlight, in the Lee-Chin Crystal building, is the **Dinosaurs** section, which holds the ROM's splendid collection of fossil skeletons, the pick being those retrieved from the Alberta Badlands near Calgary in western Canada. The Badlands are the richest source of dinosaur fossils in the world, having yielded over three hundred complete skeletons and 35 dinosaur species – ten percent of all those known today. Among the accumulated beasties, look out for the pig-sized, super-armoured armadillo, the T-Rex, and its smaller relative Albertosaurus, a Jurassic-period carnivore of large-proportioned head and ferocious appearance with ridiculously tiny hands. Also spare a moment for the Parasaurolophus (with a cranial crest reminiscent of a certain movie alien), and "Gordo", the museum's impressive Barosaurus, a wondrous 27m long and one of only three complete skeletons of the species in the world.

Level 3: the Egyptian collection
The ROM is solid when it comes to **ancient Egypt**, owning several finely preserved mummies, including the richly decorated sarcophagus of Djed-maat-es-ankh, a court musician who died from a dental infection around 850 BC. Even more unusual is the assortment of mummified animals, including a crocodile, a hawk and (sometimes) an odd-looking cat. There is also the intriguing Punt Wall, a 1905 plaster cast of the original in Queen Hatshepsut's temple in Deir el-Bahri, Egypt. The events depicted on the wall occurred in the year 1482 BC, and represent a military expedition to Punt, which lay south of Egypt near present-day Somalia.

Gardiner Museum
111 Queen's Park • Mon–Thurs 10am–6pm, Fri 10am–9pm, Sat & Sun 10am–5pm; free guided tours Mon–Thurs & Sat 2pm, Fri 2pm & 7pm, Sun 2pm & 3pm • $15, half-price Fri after 4pm • ☎ 416 586 8080, ⓦ gardinermuseum.com • Subway: Museum

The **Gardiner Museum**, just across the street from the Royal Ontario Museum, holds a superb collection of **ceramics**, beautifully presented and displayed over three intimate floors. On the main floor, the **pre-Columbian** section, composed of over three hundred pieces from Mexico and Central America through to Peru, is one of the most comprehensive collections of its kind in North America, providing an intriguing insight into the lifestyles and beliefs of the Maya, Inca and Aztec peoples. Also on this floor is an exquisite sample of fifteenth- and sixteenth-century tin-glazed **Italian majolica**, mostly dishes, plates and jars depicting classical and Biblical themes designed by Renaissance artists.

The second floor features a superb collection of Japanese and Chinese porcelain. In addition, the stunning European gallery on this level, reformatted in 2015 – the first such reformation in three decades allowed over 400 new pieces from the collection to be displayed – brings the history of porcelain to life with examples and stories of how it figured in the lives of the rich and powerful. At the heart of the space is a sumptuous re-creation of a late eighteenth-century dessert table, complete with a sugar temple, sculptures crafted by what was then the royal factory in Sèvres, France, and a model dessert presented on botanical-themed Derby plates. (The gallery ends with a presentation about maker's marks, determining provenance, and how professionals can detect a forgery.) The third floor holds a reliable selection of visiting and temporary special exhibitions. Refuel

1

at the top-notch restaurant *Clay*, which opened in 2018, and serves hearty food like lamb burgers, steak frites and a fudge brownie topped with coffee ice cream and sesame brittle.

Bata Shoe Museum

327 Bloor St West, at St George • Mon–Sat 10am–5pm, Thurs until 8pm, Sun noon–5pm • $14, pay what you wish (suggested $5) on Thurs evening • ☎ 416 979 7799, ⓦ batashoemuseum.ca • Subway: St George

The **Bata Shoe Museum** was built at the behest of the late Sonja Bata, of the Bata shoe manufacturing family, to display the extraordinary assortment of footwear she has spent a lifetime collecting. The museum begins on **Level B1** with an introductory section entitled, appropriately enough, "All About Shoes", which presents an overview on the evolution of footwear. Among the more notable exhibits in this section are pointed shoes from medieval Europe, where different social classes were allowed different lengths of toe, and tiny Chinese silk shoes used by women whose feet had been bound. A small adjoining section is devoted to **specialist footwear**, most memorably French chestnut-crushing clogs from the nineteenth century and a pair of 1940s Dutch smugglers' clogs with the heel and sole reversed to leave a footprint intended to hoodwink any following customs officials.

Level G features a large glass cabinet showcasing all sorts of **celebrity footwear**. The exhibits are rotated regularly, but look out for Buddy Holly's loafers, Marilyn Monroe's stilettos, Robert Redford's cowboy boots, Nureyev's ballet shoes and Elton John's shocking platforms. Level 2 and Level 3 are used for temporary exhibitions which draw extensively on the museum's permanent collection – there isn't enough room to show everything at once.

Casa Loma

1 Austin Terrace • **House** Daily 9.30am–5pm, last admission 4pm • **Gardens** Daily 9.30am 4pm May–Oct • $30; parking $10/vehicle • ☎ 416 923 1171, ⓦ casaloma.org • Subway: Dupont, then 5min walk north up the slope of Spadina Ave to Davenport Rd and up a flight of steps

A folly to outdo almost any other, **Casa Loma** is undoubtedly Toronto's most bizarre attraction, an enormous towered and turreted mansion built for **Sir Henry Pellatt** between 1911 and 1914. Every inch the self-made man, Pellatt made a fortune by pioneering the use of hydroelectricity, harnessing the power of Niagara Falls to light Ontario's expanding cities. Determined to construct a house no one could ignore, Pellatt gathered furnishings from all over the world and even imported Scottish stonemasons to build the wall around his 2.5-hectare property. He spent more than $3m fulfilling his dream, but business misfortunes – and the $100,000 spent on upkeep every year – forced him to move out in 1923, earning him the nickname "Pellatt the Plunger". His legacy is a strange mixture of medieval fantasy and early twentieth-century technology: secret passageways, an elevator, and claustrophobic wood-panelled rooms baffled by gargantuan pipes and plumbing.

The ground floor

A clearly numbered, self-guiding route goes up one side of the house and down the other. It begins on the ground floor in the **great hall**, a pseudo-Gothic extravaganza with an 18m-high cross-beamed ceiling, a Wurlitzer organ and enough floor space to accommodate several hundred guests. Hung with flags, heavy-duty chandeliers and a suit of armour, it's a remarkably cheerless place, but in a touch worthy of an Errol Flynn movie, the hall is overlooked by a balcony at the end of Pellatt's second-floor bedroom: presumably he could, like some medieval baron, welcome his guests from on high.

Next is the **library**, followed by the walnut-panelled **dining room**, which leads to the **conservatory**, an elegant and spacious room with a marble floor and side-panels set beneath a handsome Tiffany domed-glass ceiling. This is perhaps the mansion's most

1

appealing room, its flowerbeds kept warm even in winter by the original network of steam pipes. The nearby **study** was Pellatt's favourite room, a serious affair engulfed by mahogany panelling and equipped with two secret passageways, one leading to the wine cellar, the other to his wife's rooms – a quintessential choice for any self-made man.

The second and third floors

On the second floor, **Sir Henry's suite** has oodles of walnut and mahogany panelling, which stands in odd contrast to the 1910s white-and-blue marble, high-tech bathroom, featuring both a tub and an elaborate shower with water streaming from overhead and a vertical multi-nozzle unit, from which his servant could direct streams of water along his body all at once. **Lady Pellatt's suite** wasn't left behind in the ablutions department either – her bathroom had a bidet, a real novelty in George V's Canada – though she had a lighter decorative touch, eschewing wood panelling for walls painted in her favourite colour, Wedgwood Blue.

The third floor holds a mildly diverting display on Pellatt's one-time regiment, the **Queen's Own Rifles**, tracing their involvement in various campaigns from the 1885 suppression of the Métis rebellion in western Canada (see page 505) through to World War I and beyond. From the third floor, wooden staircases clamber up to two of the house's **towers**, from where there are pleasing views over the house and gardens.

The lower level and the gardens

On the ground floor, stairs lead down to the **lower level**, which was where Pellatt's money ran out and his plans ground to a halt. Work never started on the bowling alleys and shooting range he'd designed, and the swimming pool only got as far as the rough concrete basin that survives today. Pellatt did manage to complete the 250m-long **tunnel** running from the house and pool to the **carriage room** and **stables**, where his thoroughbred horses were allegedly better treated than his servants, chomping away at their oats and hay in splendid iron-and-mahogany stalls, each with the appropriate equine nameplate. The stables are a dead end, so you'll have to double back along the tunnel to reach the house and the exit.

Before you leave, spare time for the **terraced gardens**, which tumble down the ridge at the back of the house. They are parcelled up into several different sections and easily explored along a network of footpaths, beginning on the terrace behind the great hall. From June to October, the fragrant rose gardens are in brilliant bloom.

Spadina House

285 Spadina Ave • Guided tours: Jan–March Sat & Sun noon–5pm; April–Aug Tues–Sun noon–5pm; Sept–Dec Tues–Fri noon–4pm, Sat & Sun noon–5pm • $10 • ☎ 416 392 6910, ⓦ toronto.ca • Subway: Dupont, then 5min walk north up the slope of Spadina Ave to Davenport Rd and up a flight of steps

Quite what the occupants of **Spadina House** must have thought when Casa Loma went up next door can only be imagined, but there must have been an awful lot of curtain-twitching. The two houses are a study in contrasts: Casa Loma a grandiose pile, Spadina an elegant Victorian property of genteel appearance dating from 1866. Spadina was built by James Austin, a wealthy banker of Irish extraction whose descendants lived here until 1983, when the house was bequeathed to the city. The Austins' long and uninterrupted occupation means the house's furnishings are nearly all genuine family artefacts, and they provide an intriguing insight into their changing tastes and interests.

Particular highlights of the **guided tour** include the conservatory trap-door that allowed the gardeners to come and go unseen by their employers, an assortment of period chairs designed to accommodate the largest of bustles, the original gas chandeliers and a couple of canvases by Cornelius Krieghoff (see page 73). Pride of place, however, goes to the **Billiard Room**, which comes complete with an inventive Art Nouveau decorative frieze.

The waterfront and the Toronto Islands

There is much to enjoy on the north shore of **Lake Ontario**, despite the platoon of condominium tower blocks and the concrete brow of the Gardiner Expressway. Footpaths and cycling trails now nudge along a fair slice of the **waterfront** and the **Harbourfront Centre** offers a year-round schedule of activities. Even better are the **Toronto Islands**, whose breezy tranquillity attracts droves of city-dwellers during the city's humid summers. It only takes fifteen minutes to reach them by municipal ferry, but the contrast between the city and the islands could hardly be more marked, not least because the islands are almost entirely **vehicle-free**. You'll find a couple of food venues with casual fare (see page 91).

Harbourfront Centre

Harbourfront (#509) or Spadina (#510) streetcar from Union Station to York St (the second stop)

Toronto's grimy docks once disfigured the shoreline nearest the city centre, a swath of warehouses and factories that was unattractive and smelly in equal measure. Today it's another story: the port and its facilities have been concentrated further east, beyond the foot of Parliament Street, while the **waterfront** west of Yonge Street has been redeveloped in grand style, sprouting luxury condominium blocks, jogging and cycling trails, offices, shops and marinas. The focus of all this activity is the **Harbourfront Centre**, stretching west from the foot of York Street, whose various facilities include an open-air performance area and the **Power Plant Contemporary Art Gallery** (231 Queens Quay West; Tues–Sun 10am–5pm, Thurs until 8pm; free; ☎416 973 4949, ⓦthepowerplant. org). Every year, the gallery presents about a dozen exhibitions of contemporary art, often featuring emerging Canadian artists, as well as lectures and symposiums The art is mostly cutting-edge stuff: indecipherable to some, thrilling to others.

Toronto Islands

Originally a sandbar peninsula, the **Toronto Islands**, which arch around the city's harbour, were cut adrift from the mainland by a violent storm in 1858. First used as a summer retreat by the Mississauga Nation, the islands went through various incarnations during the twentieth century: they once hosted a baseball stadium, where slugger Babe Ruth hit his first professional home run, saw funfairs featuring horses diving from the pier, and even served as a training base for the Norwegian Air Force during World War II. Today, this archipelago, roughly 6km long and totalling around 3.2 square kilometres, seems worlds away from the bustle of downtown, a perfect spot to relax and unwind – and a place where visitors' cars are **banned**; many locals use wheelbarrows or golf buggies to move their tackle, while others walk or cycle.

The city side of the archipelago is broken into a dozen tiny **islets** dotted with cottages, leisure facilities, verdant gardens and clumps of wild woodland. By comparison, the other side is a tad wilder and more windswept, consisting of one long sliver of land, which is somewhat arbitrarily divided into three "islands". From the east these are: **Ward's Island**, a quiet residential area with parkland and wilderness; **Centre Island**, the busiest and most developed of the three; and **Hanlan's Point**, which leads round to Toronto City Centre Airport, known as Billy Bishop. Hanlan's Point also holds the city's best **sandy beach** – though, as Lake Ontario is generally regarded as being too polluted for swimming, most visitors stick to sunbathing.

ARRIVAL AND DEPARTURE	TORONTO ISLANDS

BY FERRY

Passenger ferries bound for the Toronto Islands depart from the mainland ferry terminal, located behind the conspicuous *Westin Harbour Castle* hotel, between the foot of Yonge and Bay streets. To get to the ferry terminal from Union Station, take the #509 or #510 streetcar and get off at the first stop, Queen's Quay. The Toronto Islands have three ferry docks – one each on Ward's Island, Centre Island and Hanlan's Point. The ferries to Ward's Island run year-round, whereas there's a limited winter service to Hanlan's Point and nothing at all in winter to Centre Island. During peak season (May to early Sept), ferries to all three islands depart at regular intervals, generally every 45min; at other times of the year, it's usually hourly. Ferries begin running between 8am and 9am and finish between 9pm and 11.30pm, depending on the service and the season; adult return fare $7.87. For schedule details, call ☎ 416 392 8193 or check ⓦ toronto.ca/parks/island/ferry-schedule.htm.

GETTING AROUND

Several hours are needed to explore the islands by bike, a full day if you are on foot or you can overnight at an island B&B (see page 89).

By bike Cyclists are allowed to take their bikes on the ferry, unless it is jam-packed. On Centre Island, a 5–10min walk from the ferry dock at the foot of the pier, is Toronto Island Bicycle Rental (May to mid-June & Sept daily 11am–5pm; mid-June to Aug daily 10.30am–6pm; ☎ 416 203 0009, ⓦ torontoislandbicyclerental.com). It stocks ordinary bicycles, tandems and even quadracycles, but doesn't take reservations except for groups of thirty or more. It sometimes closes if the weather is bad – call ahead to double-check opening times.

By boat Canoe, kayak and stand-up paddleboat rental is available from the Harbourfront Canoe & Kayak Centre (☎ 416 203 2277, ⓦ paddletoronto.com) at 283 Queens Quay West, on the lakefront. Renting a canoe or kayak allows you to paddle round the islands' network of mini-lagoons and reach a couple of tiny wooded islets that are otherwise inaccessible.

By tram A free and fairly frequent tram runs from Centre Island to Hanlan's Point and back throughout the summer; you can board the train at any point along its circuitous route.

The suburbs

The satellite **suburbs** and industrial areas that make up most of the **GTA** (the Greater Toronto Area) are of little general appeal, a string of formless settlements sprawling over a largely flat and dreary landscape, which extends from Oshawa in the east to Mississauga and Burlington in the west and north towards Barrie. Nevertheless, the suburbs are home to several prestige attractions, most notably the **Ontario Science Centre**, which showcases dozens of interactive science displays, and the **Toronto Zoo**.

Ontario Science Centre

770 Don Mills Rd • Mon–Fri 10am–4pm, Sat 10am–7pm, Sun 10am–5pm • $22, seniors & ages 13–17 $16, ages 4–12 $13; OMNIMAX $9 extra • ☎ 416 696 1000, ⓦ ontariosciencecentre.ca • From downtown Toronto, take the Don Valley Parkway and follow signs from the Don Mills Rd North exit; by public transport, take the Yonge Street subway line north to Eglington station, then transfer to the Eglington East bus (#34) to Don Mills Rd

Featuring more than eight hundred exhibits on science and technology, the **Ontario Science Centre** draws over a million visitors per year. One of the most popular exhibits is **The Human Edge**, where visitors can discern the inner workings of human biology through life-sized three-dimensional displays and various quizzes and games. There's also easily understood information on complex medical advances, including bioengineering, how bias can affect scientific research, DNA fingerprinting and immunology. Two other big pulls are the **OMNIMAX Theatre**, which boasts a 24m-high wraparound screen with digital sound, and the only public planetarium in the city.

Toronto Zoo

2000 Meadowvale Rd • Daily: May–Aug 9.30am–6pm; Sept–April 9.30am–4.30pm • $29, kids 3–12 $19, seniors $24; parking $12; in winter (Oct–May) $23, ages 3–12 $14, seniors $18• ☎ 416 392 5932, ⓦ torontozoo.com • By car, take Hwy-401 to Scarborough (exit 389) and drive north on Meadowvale Rd, following the signs for the zoo; by public transport (about 50min from downtown), take the Sheppard East #85B bus from Sheppard-Yonge subway station

Set on the hilly edge of the Rouge Valley, **Toronto Zoo** encompasses a sprawling site of 287 hectares (and six miles of walking trails) that does its best to place animals in their own environments. Representing different geographic regions, **seven pavilions** are filled with indigenous plants and more than five thousand animals. Hardy species live outside in large paddocks, and an open train, the **Zoomobile**, zips around between the pavilions. Get the adrenaline pumping on the Wild Rouge Zipline and Canopy Tour (Thurs–Sun; $29.95) at the Indo-Malayan Pavilion, where you can zip through the air and take a canopy walk amid the trees. The zoo also has an extensive breeding, recovery and reintroduction programme.

ARRIVAL AND DEPARTURE   TORONTO

Some 25km northwest of the city centre, **Toronto Pearson International Airport** has flights to a wide variety of international destinations as well as every major Canadian town and city. The vast majority of visitors to Toronto arrive by plane. Toronto's bus and train stations are conveniently located downtown and link Toronto to a wide range of Canadian and American cities. Those arriving by car will find the city encircled by motorways, a straightforward drive except during rush hour when traffic congestion can be a real pain.

BY PLANE

TORONTO PEARSON INTERNATIONAL
Arriving by plane, you'll almost certainly land at the city's main airport, Toronto Pearson International (ⓦ toronto pearson.com). There are two passenger terminals (Terminals 1 and 3), both with the usual full range of facilities, including currency exchange offices and ATMs; the two terminals are connected by the free, 24hr LINK Train.

Getting into town A taxi from the airport to the city centre is about $60, a few dollars less if you take the airport limo service (a shared taxi system). Unlike taxis, the price of a limo is fixed, an important consideration if you arrive (or leave) during rush hour; the disadvantage is that they usually only leave when they're full. The least expensive way into town is to catch the Airport Rocket bus (#192; daily every 10–30min: Mon–Sat 5.30am–1.30am, Sun 9am–1.30am; $3.25 one way), which takes about 25min to reach Kipling subway station, at the west end of the subway network; from there, it takes another 30min by subway to get downtown. The TTC (Toronto Transit Commission) operates the Rocket, which stops outside both terminals. Perhaps the easiest, most comfortable way into town is by Union Pearson Express train (UP Express), departing from Terminal 1 ($12.35 one way, reduced price using the PRESTO card; ⓣ 416 869 3300, ⓣ 844 438 6687, ⓦ upexpress.com). Trains take only about 15min to hit the Bloor stop, and 25min to reach Union Station (see below), with a smooth connection onto the subway.

BILLY BISHOP TORONTO CITY AIRPORT
The much smaller Toronto City Airport (ⓦ torontoport.com/ airport.aspx) is close to downtown on Hanlan's Point, one of the Toronto Islands (see page 83). There are flights to the airport from a number of Canadian and US cities with the main carrier being Porter Airlines (ⓣ 416 619 8622, ⓣ 888 619 8622, ⓦ flyporter.com).

Getting into town A passenger ferry to and from the

airport leaves from the foot of Bathurst St, departing every 15min; the journey – all of 121m – only takes a couple of minutes. There's also a pedestrian tunnel, and a free minibus to and from the airport from the *Fairmont Royal York* hotel, on the corner of Front St West and York St.

BY TRAIN
All incoming and outgoing trains use **Union Station**, at the corner of Bay St and Front St West. The Union Station complex is also the hub of the city's public transportation system, incorporating both a subway station and the main GO Transit train terminal: GO trains connect Union Station with the city's suburbs and are geared up for the city's commuters.
VIA Rail ⓣ 888 842 7245, ⓦ viarail.ca.
Destinations Brockville (3–8 daily; 3hr); Kingston (5–10 daily; 2hr 30min); London (7 daily; 2hr); Montréal (3–7 daily; 4hr 40min); Niagara Falls (1 daily; 2hr); Ottawa (3–7 daily; 4hr 15min); Stratford (2 daily; 2hr 15min); Sudbury Junction (3 weekly; 7hr 15min); Windsor (4 daily; 4hr 15min); Winnipeg (3 weekly; 35hr).

BY BUS
Well connected to most of the major towns of eastern and central Canada, Toronto's **coach terminal** is conveniently located downtown at 610 Bay St, metres from Dundas St West – and a 5min walk from the subway station at the corner of Yonge and Dundas. The three main carriers are Greyhound, Coach Canada and the bus company Ontario Northland. If you're arriving late at night, note that the bus station's immediate environs are unsavoury. It only takes a couple of minutes to reach more reassuring parts of downtown, but if you're travelling alone it's probably sound advice to take a taxi. In addition, GO Transit operates buses from a number of commuter towns, including Hamilton, to the GO bus station at Front and Bay streets.
Coach Canada ⓣ 800 461 7661, ⓦ coachcanada.com.
Destinations Niagara Falls (every 1hr to 2hr; 1hr 30min–2hr 30min).
GO Transit ⓣ 416 869 3200, ⓣ 888 438 6646, ⓦ gotransit.com.
Destinations Hamilton (1–2 hourly; 1hr 20min).
Greyhound ⓣ 800 661 8747, ⓦ greyhound.ca.
Destinations Hamilton (3 daily; 1hr); Kitchener (every 1hr; 1hr 45min); London (8–10 daily; 2hr 10min–3hr 50min); Niagara Falls (4 daily; 1hr 30min–2hr); Ottawa (12 daily; 5–6hr); Owen Sound (1 daily; 4hr); Sault Ste Marie (2 daily; 11hr); Thunder Bay (2 daily; 21hr); Wawa (2 daily; 14hr 15min); Windsor (3–5 daily; 4–5hr).

1

Ontario Northland ☎ 800 461 8558, ⓦ ontarionorthland.ca. Destinations Bracebridge (4 daily; 3hr); Gravenhurst (4 daily; 2hr 45min); Huntsville (4 daily; 3hr 45min); North Bay (4–5 daily; 5hr 20min); Orillia (4 daily; 2hr 10min); Parry Sound (3 daily; 3hr 25min); Port Severn (2 daily; 2hr 10min); Sudbury (3 daily; 5hr 45min).

BY CAR

On all routes you can expect delays during rush hours (roughly 7.30–9.30am and 4.30–6.30pm).

From the west Driving into Toronto from Niagara Falls and points west along Lake Ontario, most traffic arrives via the Queen Elizabeth Way (QEW), which funnels into the Gardiner Expressway, an elevated motorway (notorious for delays) that cuts across the southern side of downtown, just south of Front St.

From the east Most drivers coming from this direction opt for the busy Hwy-401, which sweeps along Lake Ontario before veering off to slice through the city's suburbs north of downtown.

From the north Driving in from the north, take Hwy-400, which intersects with Hwy-401 northwest of the centre, or Hwy-404, which meets Hwy-401 northeast of the centre.

Hwy-407 ETR (ⓦ 407etr.com) This toll road has been built further north on the city's outskirts to relieve congestion on Hwy-401. This was North America's first all-electronic toll highway with each vehicle identified by a transponder fixed to the interior – the invoice is posted later. Toll charges are fixed but vary by section of road and time of day – at peak times vehicles are charged 29–35¢/km – and there's also a supplementary charge per trip for any vehicle without a transponder; these vehicles are identified by licence plate photos. Rental companies add an extra administration charge if you take their vehicles on this road.

GETTING AROUND

The **Toronto Transit Commission**, or **TTC** (☎ 416 393 4636 helpline, ⓦ ttc.ca), operates the city's public transportation, which is fast, frequent and efficient, with an integrated network of subways, buses and streetcars serving virtually every corner of the city. With the exception of downtown, where all the major sights are within easy walking distance of each other, your best option is to use public transport to hop between attractions – especially in the cold of winter or the sultry summer. The TTC has gone to great lengths to assure the safety of its passengers: all subway stations have **designated waiting areas (DWAs)**, which are well lit, have an intercom connection with TTC staff and are monitored by closed-circuit TV. TTC buses also operate a **Request Stop Program**, which allows women travelling alone late at night (9pm–5am) to get off buses wherever they want, and not just at regular TTC stops. A similarly positive approach has been adopted for passengers with **disabilities**, who can use a dedicated service, **Wheel-Trans** (☎ 416 393 4222, ⓦ mywheel-trans.ttc.ca). In addition to taxis, which fan out across the city, Uber and other ride services also operate in Toronto.

ESSENTIALS

Fares Throughout the TTC system a single journey costs $3.25. This can be paid in cash at every subway station and to bus and streetcar drivers, but the drivers do not give change – exact fare only.

Tokens and tickets Adults (non-concessionary passengers) can purchase metallic tokens at reduced rates at subway stations: three tokens minimum at $9. Seniors and students can opt to receive tickets in multiples of 5 for $10.25. Each ticket or token entitles passengers to one complete journey of any length on the TTC system. If this involves more than one type of transport, it is necessary to get a paper transfer at your point of entry. Streetcar and bus drivers issue transfers, as do the automatic machines located at every subway station.

Day-passes and family tickets A day-pass costs $12.50 and provides one adult with unlimited TTC travel on any day of the week. At weekends, the same pass can also be used as a family ticket, covering up to six people with a maximum of two adults. Day-passes can be purchased at any subway station.

BY SUBWAY

Toronto's subway, the core of the city's public transportation network, is basically a simple, two-line system: one line cuts east to west along Bloor St and Danforth Ave, while the other forms a loop with Union Station at its base; north of Union, one part of this subway line runs along University Ave, the other along Yonge St. Transferring between the two subway lines is possible at three stations only: Spadina, St George and Bloor-Yonge.

Opening times The subway operates Mon–Sat 6am–1am & Sun 9am–1am.

BY BUS AND STREETCAR

The bus and streetcar network couldn't be simpler, as bus and/or streetcar stops or stations adjoin every major subway station. Hours of operation vary with the route, but are comparable with subway times; there is also a limited network of night buses running along key routes roughly hourly between 1am and 6am.

BY COMMUTER TRAIN AND BUS

GO Transit (☎ 416 869 3200, ⓦ gotransit.com) operates trains and buses into the city centre from various suburbs and satellite towns, including Hamilton (see page 103). Trains arrive and depart from Union Station, buses from close by at Bay and Front streets. There are no free transfers from the TTC system to GO train lines.

BY TAXI

Taxis cruise the city in numbers. Fares are reasonable and are based on a fixed tariff of $1.75/km plus an initial charge of $4.25 (which covers the first 143m). As an example, a ride from Union Station to the corner of Bloor and Yonge streets should cost around $15. Taxis can also be reserved in advance. **Companies** There are a multitude of firms to choose from, but two of the more dependable are Co-op Cabs (☎416 504 2667, ⓦco-opcabs.com) and Diamond Taxicab (☎416 366 6868, ⓦdiamondtaxi.ca). Toronto taxi drivers anticipate a tip of ten to fifteen percent.

BY BIKE

Toronto has its own municipal bike rental scheme (ⓦbikesharetoronto.com) with docking stations dotted around the city centre – and there's a spiderweb-like network of bicycle lanes to match. Register online. Costs are reasonable and passes begin at $7 per 24hr; each 30min or less trip is free, but longer ones incur usage fees beginning at $1.50 for first extra 30min period. A three-day pass is $15, which is ideal for short visits.

INFORMATION

Ontario Tourism The Ontario Tourism travel information centre (Mon–Sat 10am–6pm & Sun noon–5pm; ☎800 ONTARIO, or within Toronto ☎416 314 5899, ⓦontariotravel.net) is located inside Union Station. It stocks a comprehensive range of information on all the major attractions in Toronto and throughout Ontario. Among much else, it issues free city maps, the *Ride Guide* to Toronto's transport system, and the official and very detailed *Toronto Visitor Guide*. It also supplies entertainment details in the monthly magazine *Where* (ⓦwhere.ca) and will book hotel accommodation on your behalf both in Toronto and most of Ontario. Its website is particularly strong on practical information.

Tourism Toronto The city's official visitor and convention bureau does not have an information office per se, but does run a telephone information line (Mon–Fri 8:30am–5pm; ☎800 499 2514, ☎416 203 2500, ⓦseetorontonow.com), whose operators can handle most city queries and will make hotel reservations on your behalf. You can also scour bags of information and book accommodation on its website.

ACTIVITIES AND TOURS

Toronto and its suburbs are great if you are a biking enthusiast and there's a city-wide rental scheme (see above); cycle maps can be found at ⓦbikingtoronto.com. Those more inclined towards watersports should visit the Toronto Islands (see page 83) or one of several YMCAs in the city. Walkers and hikers will find paths In Queen's Park in the centre of town (see page 74) and trails that crisscross the vast High Park (with a small, free zoo) on the city's southwestern fringe (ⓦhighparktoronto.com; subway: High Park then 2min walk).

Beer Lover's Tours ☎416 662 6312, ⓦbeerloverstour. com. In business for almost 20 years, the company's all-day Saturday beer tours ($149) are a Toronto staple, and include a charcuterie lunch; for an additional $50, you can add on a four-course "beer dinner".

Gone Sailing Adventures ☎416 529 4361, ⓦgone sailingadventures.com. Cruise Toronto Harbour and Lake Ontario on one of Gone Sailing's smooth three-hour tours ($150, mid-May to Sept daily 10am, 2pm, 6pm); other options include a jaunt with wine and cheese (July–Aug), a sailing during the full moon, or the Summer Sailstice (all $195). Charters available as well.

Heritage Toronto ☎416 338 1338, ⓦheritagetoronto. org. This division of the city government offers tours (some sponsored & free, some suggested $10 donation) on a variety of topics throughout the year that can range from local musical history to architecture to the social development of city neighbourhoods.

Tasty Tours ⓦtastytourstoronto.com. Very sweet hosts guide guests on a multicultural dessert-themed stroll in the Kensington Market district ($59) or on visits to chocolate-related purveyors on Queens West and Dundas West around Trinity Bellwood Park ($49).

Toronto Architecture Tours ⓦtorontosocietyof architects.ca. A variety of distinct tours are on the Toronto Society of Architects' schedule from May to early October (Sat or Sun, $10 each) – tours focus on museums and cultural centres, the University of Toronto St George campus and the towers that compose the Toronto skyline.

Urban Expeditions ☎416 427 7227, ⓦurbanexpeditions. com. The company (which also sponsors a sort of get-to-know-the-city scavenger hunt) puts on regular walking and bike tours of Toronto, with sights grouped on common themes (Green Toronto, Cultural Toronto, etc).

ACCOMMODATION

Toronto is filled with a wide variety of lodging, from contemporary hotels in skyscrapers to **boutique properties to lakefront resorts**. Availability can be a challenge, especially during the city's big festivals, but booking in advance is recommended at any time of the year. Prices fluctuate wildly, but in general double rooms in the city centre start at about $150–180. Most hotels now offer free wi-fi. **Bed and breakfast** accommodation tends to be less expensive and although most of these places are not as central as the city's hotels, they often take you out

1

into Toronto's quainter/quieter neighbourhoods. Budget-conscious travellers might want to consider a **hostel** or opt instead for a **student room** in one of the university's halls of residence, available – with some variation – from the second week in May to late August. The Ontario Tourism travel information centre (see page 87) will help in **finding a hotel room**, as will Tourism Toronto (see page 87).

DOWNTOWN

HOTELS

Bond Place 65 Dundas St East ☎ 416 362 6061, ☎ 800 268 9390, ⓦbondplace.ca; Subway: Dundas; map p.62. This straightforward, tower-block hotel is handily located, just a couple of minutes' walk from the Eaton Centre and Queen Street. It has simple doubles done up in light wood and shades of cream, and there are often weekend reductions. $215

★ **The Broadview Hotel** 106 Broadview Ave ☎ 416 362 8439, ⓦthebroadviewhotel.ca; Queen streetcar (#301); map p.62. Old is new again at this impeccably restored boutique hotel in a landmark 1891 building with a salacious past (infamous strip club Jilly's used to be on the ground floor). The Romanesque Revival-style architecture displays beautiful details inside and out, from terracotta carvings to vaulted ceilings to a dazzling glass-box rooftop. The elegant rooms have wooden floors, colourful artwork and vinyl record players. The hotel's food and drink options are equally alluring: dine on seasonal Ontario cuisine at The Civic and toast the Toronto night on the roof bar (see page 92), which offers 360-degree views of the skyline. $330

Delta Toronto 75 Lower Simcoe St at Front ☎ 416 849 1200, ☎ 888 890 3222, ⓦdeltatoronto.com; Subway: Union; map p.62. This sleek hotel lives in a striking 46-storey tower. Near the CN Tower and Rogers Centre, the hotel's 567 rooms have blond wood, clean lines and vertigo-inducing glass-wall bathrooms with city or harbour views. On-site is the SOCO restaurant (open 'til late), a clubby lobby whisky bar (Char No. 5), all with a fun cosmopolitan atmosphere. $350

Drake Hotel 1150 Queen St West at Beaconsfield ☎ 416 531 5042, ☎ 866 372 5386, ⓦthedrakehotel. ca; Queen streetcar (#501); map p.62. Part of a Drake microcommunity that's also by turns nightclub, restaurant, bar and arts venue, this hotel in an 1890s building is one of the most fashionable spots in town. The nineteen rooms are a mixture of ultra luxurious and kitsch/bizarre, from the handcrafted furniture and big beds through to the peculiar dolls left on the pillows. Free fitness passes. $229

Fairmont Royal York 100 Front St West ☎ 416 368 2511, ☎ 800 257 7544, ⓦfairmont.com; Subway: Union Station; map p.62. When it was completed in 1927, the Royal York was the largest hotel in the British Empire and it still retains much of its original grandeur, especially in the sprawling lobby, which is decked out with mosaic floors, coffered ceilings and massive chandeliers. The good-sized rooms aren't as pricey (or as stylish) as you might expect, and there are substantial off-season and weekend discounts. $269

★ **Gladstone Hotel** 1214 Queen St West at Gladstone ☎ 416 531 4635, ⓦgladstonehotel.com; Queen streetcar (#501); map p.62. Befitting its West Queen West digs, this handsome, red-brick building dating from the 1880s hides something hipster-cool. In this beehive of activity, all 37 rooms have been designed by different local artists, right down to the wallpaper, communal areas serve as art galleries, and the splendid cage elevator has survived intact and in full working order. This is in the most fashionable part of town, and the hotel bar heaves – so forget it if you're after a quiet night: people come here to razzle it up. $220

The Ivy at Verity 111D Queen St East ☎ 416 368 6006 x300, ⓦtheivyatverity.ca; Subway: Queen Street; map p.62. Toronto's classiest hotel is also one of the most distinctive: it's part of an old brick-walled chocolate factory and comes complete with an excellent restaurant – George (see p.88). There are only four guest rooms, but each is decorated immaculately, in a canny mix of the creative and the stylish. Each of the guest rooms has its own sit-out balcony and continental breakfast is served to the rooms on a tray. Unbeatable – and family owned. $369

★ **Le Germain** 30 Mercer St ☎ 416 345 9500, ☎ 866 345 9501, ⓦgermaintoronto.com; Subway: St Andrew; map p.62. Immaculate, swanky boutique hotel kitted out in the full flourish of modern style, from the handsome foyer, with its soaring ceiling, open fire and masses of glass, through to the stylish, well-appointed reasonably spacious guest rooms with Frette linens, and Moulton Brown shower products. After a long day, head to the leafy rooftop bar for a cocktail amid the city lights. Enjoy "deluxe" continental breakfast. $325

Novotel Toronto Centre 45 The Esplanade ☎ 416 367 8900, ⓦaccorhotels.com; Subway: Union Station; map p.62. In a splendidly converted old building, with an elegant arcaded facade and other Art Deco flourishes, this chain hotel offers excellent service at moderate prices. Its relative affordability may be linked to its noisy location – it abuts the railway – but the location is excellent, close to the downtown core and the St Lawrence Market. $160

Thompson Toronto 550 Wellington St ☎ 416 640 7778, ⓦthompsonhotels.com; Subway: St Andrew; map p.62. Chic from top to bottom, with airy rooms decked out in dark wood with pops of bright orange, a trendy rooftop pool and lounge with stunning views. The Thompson Diner serves comfort food with a twist. $280

Victoria 56 Yonge St ☎ 416 363 1666, ☎ 800 363 8228, ⓦhotelvictoria-toronto.com; Subway: King; map p.62. This long-established, welcoming hotel occupies a historic high-rise in the heart of downtown. The fifty-odd rooms are decorated in crisp modern style and the foyer is an idiosyncratic attempt at vintage. $230

1

B&B

Baldwin Village Inn 9 Baldwin St ☎416 591 5359, ⓦbaldwininn.com; Subway: St Patrick; map p.62. Well-established B&B in a handy location a brief walk from Chinatown and the AGO. Has six a/c guest rooms with shared facilities, a lounge with satellite TV, and a dining room. The house is a pleasant two-storey affair, painted yellow, with a small courtyard. $115

HOSTEL

HI – Toronto Youth Hostel 76 Church St, at King ☎416 971 4440, ☎877 848 8737, ⓦhostellingtoronto.com; Subway: King; map p.62. The surrounding neighbourhood may have resisted gentrification, but the hostel is clean, well-run and a 5min walk from the subway. Four- to ten-person dorms and family rooms are available, along with quads and private rooms, plus free internet access, coin-operated laundry, an on-site café and shared kitchen and TV lounge. Rates include bedding and towels. Dorms from $36, private doubles $173

UPTOWN

HOTELS

Holiday Inn Toronto Downtown Centre 30 Carlton St ☎416 977 6655, ☎877 410 6777, ⓦholidayinn.com/ toronto; Subway: College; map p.76. Superbly located, this chain hotel is better-than-average value with good service, restaurant, and nicely proportioned rooms. $155

Hotel X Toronto 111 Princes' Blvd, ☎647 943 9300, ⓦhotelxtoronto.com; Exhibition GO Transit station and Exhibition Loop Streetcar #509; map p.62. One of Toronto's splashiest openings in 2018, this resort-style complex rises over the grounds of Exhibition Place. The handsome rooms offer sweeping views of the Toronto skyline, and a wealth of upscale amenities including indoor tennis and squash courts, an activity centre for kids and a three-level rooftop bar. Plus, the Lake Ontario waterfront is within easy walking distance. $363

★ **Kimpton Saint George Hotel** 280 Bloor St West ☎416 968 0010, ⓦkimptonsaintgeorge.com; Subway: St George; map p.76. Kimpton hotels are known for their whimsy and charm – and this is vibrantly evident in their first Toronto branch. The impeccable, inviting hotel features elegant rooms and a host of great amenities, like a hosted evening "wine hour" and free use of bicycles. $314

The Saint James Hotel 26 Gerrard St East ☎416 645 2200, ⓦthesaintjameshotel.com; Subway: College; map p.76. Simple and central, with sizeable rooms, this welcoming hotel is a comfortable, affordable base for exploring Toronto. Yonge Street is a short walk away, as are a multitude of lively restaurants and bars. $229

Windsor Arms 18 St Thomas St ☎416 971 9666, ☎877 999 2767, ⓦwindsorarmshotel.com; Subway: Bay Street; map p.76. One of the city's more striking hotels, the *Windsor* occupies a striking brick-and-stone-trimmed neo-Gothic building. Open fires, columns, stained glass windows and Georgian-style furniture characterize the interior, as do the creams and browns of the extremely comfortable guest suites. There's a no-expense-spared spa here too, as well as a pretty tea room. $379

B&B

Rose Garden B&B 1030 Bathurst St ☎416 992 0746, ⓦrosegardenbandb.ca; Subway: Dupont; map p.76. Relax at this cosy B&B, which has well-maintained, spotless rooms. Greet the morning over the tasty breakfast with strong coffee. $150

STUDENT ROOMS

Massey College, University of Toronto 4 Devonshire place ☎416 978 2895, ⓦmasseycollege.ca/summer-rentals; Subway: Museum; map p.76. The one-time stomping ground of author Robertson Davies, this old and distinguished college reportedly also boasts the presence of at least one ghost. Simple singles and doubles are available, with breakfast included, from May to late August. Book online. Singles $70; doubles $90

TORONTO ISLANDS

B&B

Smiley's B&B 4 Dacotah Ave, Algonquin Island, Toronto Islands ☎416 203 8599, ⓦerelda.ca; map p.58. Semirural bliss on Algonquin Island, a short ferry ride (see page 83) from the city centre. *Smiley's* offers the self-contained Studio Suite, with its own entrance, sitting area, bathroom and kitchen (June–Sept only), as well as Eric's Room, a simple double room with shared bathroom. Cash deposit required upon reservation. No cards. Studio Suite $308; Eric's Room $125

EATING

Toronto's dazzling cultural diversity translates into rich and varied food scene, with cuisine from around the globe. The entire city – especially the areas around King St West, Queen St West and West Queen West – simply heaves with cafés and restaurants, from upscale, chandelier-filled dining rooms to casual neighbourhood joints. Many restaurants incorporate local ingredients, including fresh vegetables, fish and wild game. Toronto is also a city of colourful food markets – top among them is Kensington Market and St Lawrence Market– where you can sample the best of the season.

Prices range from upwards of $80 for a meal at fancier restaurants, to bargain-basement cafés where a decent-sized snack or sandwich works out at just a few dollars. The majority of places fall somewhere in between – a $40 bill per person for a two-course meal, excluding drinks.

1

DOWNTOWN

CAFÉS

Balzac's Coffee Roasters 60, 55 Mill St ☎416 207 1709, ⓦbalzacscoffee.com; King streetcar (#504); map p.62. The popular *Balzac's* has a relaxed, arty feel and occupies the old pump room of the Gooderham & Worts Distillery, in the heart of the Distillery District (see page 68). It churns out nicely presented espresso-type coffees, plus matching cakes and light bites. Balzac's also has other cafes around the city – check the website for locations. Daily 8am–7pm.

Bonjour Brioche 812 Queen St East, at DeGrassi ☎416 406 1250, ⓦbonjourbrioche.com; Queen streetcar (#501); map p.62. This patisserie-café draws hordes from all over the city on account of its fruit tarts, buttery croissants, puffy brioche and delectable *pissaladière*. The sit-down menu is a blackboard full of soups, sandwiches, tarts, omelettes and quiche. There's always a queue for Sunday brunch, and almost everything's gone by 2pm, so come early. No reservations, no cards. Tues–Sun 8am–4pm.

Carousel Bakery 93 Front St East ☎416 363 4247; Subway: Union Station; map p.62. St Lawrence Market has a bunch of choice vendors, but *Carousel* is especially noted as the top place to snag Toronto's famed peameal bacon sandwich and a butter tart.

Dark Horse Espresso 125 John St at Nelson ☎416 748 7700, ⓦdarkhorseespresso.com; Queen streetcar (#501); map p.62. This local chainlet, with locations around the city, supplies knowledgeable caffeine addicts with quality, top-strength coffee and espresso drinks, as well as homemade baked goods and paninis. Mon–Fri 7am–7pm, Sat & Sun 10am–5pm.

Moonbean Coffee 30 St Andrew's St ☎416 595 0327, ⓦmoonbeancoffee.com; Spadina streetcar (#510); map p.62. One of a dwindling band of cafés that still roast their own beans, this is a Kensington Market institution, a laidback, slightly dishevelled sort of place whose patio is a perfect spot to watch the world go by while sampling the tasty soups and sandwiches – plus, of course, the outstanding coffee. Daily 7am–9pm.

Mr Tasty Fries Outside City Hall on Queen St ☎416 803 1955 Subway: Queen Street; map p.62. As his blue van proudly announces, *Mr Tasty Fries* has been feeding office workers for thirty years – feeding them with outstanding (and very large) German sausages, first-rate *poutines*, and chunky chips. Something of an institution; come early to avoid the queues. Mon–Fri 11.30am/noon to around 3/3.30pm.

Nadège 780 Queen St West ☎416 368 2009, ⓦnadege-patisserie.com; Queen streetcar (#501); map p.62. Croissants, cakes and tarts are taken to a high art at this smart little café that really get the taste buds going; pricey perhaps, but simply superb. Eat in or take away. Mon–Fri 9am–6pm, Sat 9am–4pm.

RESTAURANTS

★ **Aloette** 163 Spadina Ave ☎416 260 3444, ⓦaloetterestaurant.com; Subway: Osgoode; map p.62. Toronto's celebrated *haute cuisine* French restaurant Alo (tasting menu from $135; ⓦalorestaurant.com) now has a casual sibling, which is the perfect way to experience chef Patrick Kriss's masterful culinary vision at gentler prices. The menu – and ambiance – is, in their apt words, "the neighbourhood bistro reimagined". Try roast squid with pork belly and Granny Smith apples, beef carpaccio with truffles and one of the finest burgers in town, crowned with Beaufort cheese. The cocktails and wine list are equally inventive. Sip the Aloette Punch (for two) – aromatized wine, plum, champagne syrup and jasmine tea. Stop by for Aloette Hour (weekdays 3–4.30pm) when cocktails and wines by the glass are $10. Mains $18–26. Daily 11.30am–10.30pm.

Assembly Chef's Hall 111 Richmond St W ☎647 557 5993, ⓦassemblychefshall.com; Subway: Osgoode; map p.62. Sample cuisine from Toronto's top chefs at this lively food hall, from Mediterranean mezze platters and juicy barbecued meat to hand-tossed aubergine pizzas and lobster rolls. Top it off with desserts like caramel apple crumble and *alfajores* (dulce de leche sandwich cookies). Main dishes $14–25. Mon–Fri 7am–10pm, Sat 10am–10pm.

★ **Beast** 96 Tecumseth St, off King St ☎647 340 8224, ⓦthebeastrestaurant.com; King streetcar (#504); map p.62. What many outsiders have heard about the Toronto food scene consists of five letters: *Beast*. Chef Scott Vivian's meat-heavy operation is renowned for its whole animal dinners (advance notice required) in which six courses are spun from every corner of the creature. You can also find fish and, to a lesser extent, vegetables, variously boldly flavoured or finessed as necessary. Wed–Fri 5–10pm, Sat 10am–3pm & 5–10pm, Sun 10am–3pm.

El Catrin 18 Tank House Lane ☎416 203 2121, ⓦdelcatrin. ca; King streetcar (#504); map p.62. Not only coolly curated with a stunning mural, punched metal lights on the patio and a wall of multicoloured Day of the Dead skulls, this eatery in the Distillery District has won awards for its mix of traditional and contemporary Mexican cuisine, including huevos and ceviches. Mon–Thurs 11.30am–11pm, Fri & Sat 11.30am–1am, Sun 10.30am–11pm.

★ **George** 111 Queen St East ☎647 496 8275, ⓦgeorgeonqueen.com; Subway: Queen Street; map p.62. This excellent restaurant has a bijou interior and a charming outside terrace. The inventive menu is international by disposition, with prominence given to Asian and Italian dishes – try for example the salmon with wasabi cream and veal with bell peppers and apricots. Mains average $25, $20 at lunch, and advance reservations in the evening are recommended. Mon noon–2.30pm, Tues–Fri noon–2.30pm & 5.30–10.30pm, Sat 5.30–10.30pm.

Lai Wah Heen Metropolitan Hotel, 108 Chestnut St ☎416 977 9899, ⓦlaiwahheen.com; Subway: St

Patrick; map p.62. The name means "elegant meeting place", which this Chinese restaurant most certainly is. The high-end dining room atmosphere is matched by the complex menu, best described as Hong Kong modern, with, for example, the daily catch served steamed with soy sauce, ginger and scallions. The restaurant is also noted for its dim sum (lunch only). Main courses begin at $19. Daily 11.30am–3pm (Sat & Sun 'til 4pm) & 6–10.30pm.

Lee 603 King St West, at Portland ☎ 416 504 7867, ⓦ susur.com/lee; King streetcar (#504); map p.62. The brain child of super-chef Susur Lee, this high-octane restaurant-cum-bar, with its dappled lighting and lots of space, is gastronomically ambitious: the menu is Asian fusion with bells on – try the superb caramelized black cod and diver scallops in a jasmine crust, served with plantain, bacon hash and pickled aubergine. Pick-and-mixing several dishes together is the way to go. Mains $25–32. Reservations advised. Mon–Wed 5.30–10.30pm, Thurs–Sat 5.30–11.30pm.

Maple Leaf Tavern 955 Gerrard St East ☎ 416 465 0955, ⓦ mapleleaftavern.ca; College/Carlton streetcar (#506); map p.62. An ancient Leslieville dive bar now has a new lease on life, courtesy of a stylish makeover that's rivalled by the imaginative bistro menu and cocktails. Settle in amid the gleaming dark wood, and dig into pork belly with birch syrup, a wedge of lasagne made with veal and bone marrow; and a velvety chocolate and peanut butter mousse. Classic cocktails with a twist include coconut Sazerac. Mains $20–30. Tues–Wed 5–10pm, Thurs 3–10pm, Fri 3–11pm, Sat 11am–11pm, Sun 11am–10pm.

Noce 875 Queen St West, at Walnut Ave ☎ 416 504 3463, ⓦ nocerestaurant.com; Queen streetcar (#501); map p.62. First-rate Italian restaurant, where the pasta is rolled by hand, the beef *carpaccio* melts on the tongue and the meat tumbles right off the bone. Mains average $25. Reservations advised. Daily 6–11pm.

Le Papillon on Front 69 Front St East ☎ 647 977 6302, ⓦ papillononfront.com; Subway: Union Station; map p.62. Attractive, French-cum-Québécois restaurant where the house speciality is crêpes (sweet or savoury), though the bistro-style menu covers all the French classics with gusto. Mains average $25, less at lunch, crepes from $16. Tues–Wed 11.30am–10pm, Fri–Sat 11.30am–11pm, Sun 11am–10pm.

Queen Mother Café 208 Queen St West, at Nelson ☎ 416 748 7700, ⓦ queenmothercafe.ca; Queen streetcar (#501); map p.62. Queen West mainstay serving a mix of Asian-influenced (*pad Thai*, *khao soy gai*) and classic (burgers, calamari, spinach cannelloni) comfort food (mains $15–26) and amazing desserts. Great brunch on Sundays too. Mon–Sat 11.30am–1am, Sun 11.30am–11pm.

Rodney's Oyster House 469 King St West, at Spadina ☎ 416 363 8105, ⓦ rodneysoysterhouse.com; King streetcar (#504); map p.62. Toronto's favourite oyster

bar, ensconced in a handsomely modernized old basement, serves up tonnes of the slippery delicacies, plus scallops, mussels, crab and shrimp. There's a good range of fresh fish too, always including salmon and trout. Main courses average around $25. Mon–Tues 11.30am–10pm, Wed–Thurs 11.30am–11pm, Fri–Sat 11.30am–midnight.

UPTOWN

RESTAURANTS

City Betty 1352 Danforth ☎ 647 271 3949, ⓦ citybetty. com; Subway: Greenwood; map p.76. The dining room may look simple, but the farm-to-fork cuisine is anything but. Local seasonal vegetables are taken to a high art, with dishes such as colourful salads sprinkled with Middle Eastern spices; corn fritters topped with guacamole, and tangy shrimp ceviche tossed with quinoa. Wed 5–9pm, Thurs–Fri 5–10pm, Sat 10am–3pm & 5–10pm, Sun 10am–3pm.

Joso's 202 Davenport Rd ☎ 416 925 1903, ⓦ josos.com; 15min walk north from Bay Subway; map p.76. This celebrated restaurant, described at length by Margaret Atwood in her novel *The Robber Bride*, is famous for two things: its squid-ink risotto and the plethora of breasts and buttocks in owner Joso Spralja's paintings and statues. Reservations are essential and mains cost around $28. It's a 15min walk north of Bloor St West along Avenue Rd, so you may prefer to take a taxi. Mon–Fri 11.30am–2pm & 5.30–11pm, Sat 5.30–11pm.

Planta 1221 Bay St ☎ 647 348 7000 ⓦ plantarestaurants. com; Subway: Bay; map p.76. The name says it all: The menu is entirely plant-based. Robust, richly flavoured vegan dishes include stuffed mushrooms with artichoke hearts, spinach and tree nut butter; Singapore fried noodles, and avocado lime cheesecake with a cashew date crust. Main dishes $19–$22. Mon–Sat 11.30am–3pm & 5–10pm, Sun 10.30am–3pm & 5–10pm.

TORONTO ISLANDS

CAFÉ

Rectory Café Ward's Island ☎ 416 203 2152, ⓦ therectory cafe.com; map p.58. For eating and drinking on the islands, it's mostly all fast-food except for this cosy little café, where they serve tasty snacks and light meals ($14–20) such as soups, salads and sandwiches. Sun–Thurs 11am–9pm, Fri & Sat 11am–10pm, but may close during bad weather or for private functions.

RESTAURANT

Toronto Island BBQ & Beer Co. Centre Island ☎ 416 203 0405; map p.58. The huge outdoor patio with a panoramic city view is the perfect setting for some barbecued food washed down with a cold brew. June–Aug Mon–Fri 11.30am–8pm. Sat–Sun 11.30am–9pm

1

TORONTO'S LEADING FESTIVALS

The city is always putting something on, from beer festivals to a Caribbean carnival to a celebration of ice and winter; visit ⓦ seetorontonow.com for a full list. The **Toronto International Film Festival** or **TIFF** (ⓦ tiff.net) is one of the most respected film festivals in the world, established in 1976. Over a week and a half in September, the celebration usually features close to 400 films, and queues to get into them can be fearsome. Single, same-day **tickets** are available from the TIFF box offices (or as **rush tickets** immediately before screenings), but regular TIFF attendees mostly buy **books of tickets in advance** or opt for one of several **passes**, which can be purchased from the website. In all cases, book well ahead. In June, there's the outstanding **Toronto Jazz Festival** (ⓦ tojazz.com), which usually overlaps with the week-long LGBTQ **Pride** (ⓦ pridetoronto.com) that culminates in a whopping Pride Day Parade with one million spectators. Also in mid-June is North by Northeast, a splashy music and arts festival that's modelled on the wildly popular South by Southwest in Austin, Texas. The Fringe Festival (ⓦ fringetoronto.com) in early July is also great fun; more than 150 inexpensive productions (encompassing plays, dance, alternative musicals and busking) take place all over the city, inside and out.

DRINKING AND NIGHTLIFE

As befits the largest city in Canada, Toronto lights up with thriving nightlife as the sun sets, from dusty dive bars to cocktail lounges and craft beer halls. And then there's the music: The city that gave us The Weeknd, Rush and, of course, Drake, continues to exhibit a flourishing **live music scene** both for big-name and up-and-coming bands and artists, and **jazz** is well represented too. The **club scene** is vibrant, if not exactly earth-shattering, but there's more than enough to keep anyone going for days (and nights) on end. For **listings**, consult NOW (ⓦ nowtoronto.com), a free weekly magazine widely available.

BARS

416 Snack Bar 181 Bathurst St, at Queen St West ☏ 416 364 9320, ⓦ 416snackbar.wordpress.com; Queen streetcar (#501) map p.62. Cosy and ultra-fashionable gastropub, where both the decor and the menu give multiple nods to all things Torontonian – from the TTC memorabilia to the steamed pork buns (Chinatown) and the salads (Greektown). Microbrews on tap and great cocktails too. Mon–Sat 5pm–2am.

Bar Chef 472 Queen St West, at Augusta ☏ 416 868 4800, ⓦ barcheftoronto.com; Queen streetcar (#501); map p.62. Cool, candlelit bar where the big deal is the cocktails – served and prepared every which way and costing $16 and up. Particularly impressive is the variety of European absinthe. Dress up – it's the place to see and be seen. Sun–Wed 6pm–midnight, Thurs–Sat 6pm–2am.

Bar Raval 505 College St, at Palmerston ⓦ thisisbarraval. com; College streetcar (#506); map p.76. This intimate Spanish bar furnished with an abundance of sexy curved wood has a full drinks menu (plus sherries and vermouths), but a big selling point is their tapas (squash tortilla, anchovies, ham croquetas, and deserts like crema catalana). Expect to stand, as they do in Barcelona. Mon–Fri 11am–2am, Sat–Sun 10am–2am.

Beer Bistro 18 King St East, at Yonge ☏ 416 861 9872, ⓦ beerbistro.com; Subway: King; map p.62. In a large and attractive older building, this bar-restaurant specializes in beer – both imported and domestic, bottled and on tap. Among the rotating local beer is the delightfully named Life in the Clouds by Collective Arts in Hamilton, Ontario. The food goes far beyond bar bites, and includes truffled potato perogies, mussels and, on Saturdays, applewood-smoked suckling pig. Mon–Wed 11.30am–1am, Thurs–Fri 11:30am–2am, Sat 11am–2am, Su 11am–midnight.

The Broadview Hotel Rooftop Bar 106 Broadview Ave ☏ 416 362 8439, ⓦ thebroadviewhotel.ca; Subway: Queen streetcar (#301); map p.62. A night here is defined by the spectacular 360-degree views of Toronto's twinkling skyline. Crowning The Broadview Hotel (see page 88), this buzzy rooftop terrace offers colourful cocktails and elevated bar snacks, like beet salad with candied pecans and beef tartare with egg and pickled chilies. Mon–Fri 4pm–1am, Sat–Sun noon–1am.

C'est What? 67 Front St East, at Church ☏ 416 867 9499, ⓦ cestwhat.ca; Subway: Union Station; map p.62. In a dark, low-ceilinged basement in the St Lawrence District, C'est What? has over forty microbrews on tap plus an impressive selection of single malt Scotch and hearty pub food. The performance space here has seen the likes of Barenaked Ladies and Jeff Buckley. Sun–Mon 11.30am–1am, Tues–Sat 11.30am–2am.

★ **Grand Electric** 1330 Queen St West, at Brock Ave ☏ 416 627 3459, ⓦ grandelectrictoronto.com; Queen streetcar (#501); map p.62. Uber-cool bar attracting a hipster crew, drawn here by the cocktails and the bourbons (one of the widest selections in the city) plus the tacos – the best thing on the menu. Go early to avoid the crowds. Mon–Wed noon–midnight, Thurs & Fri noon–1am, Sat 11am–1am, Sun 11am–midnight.

The Lounge at the Drake Hotel 1150 Queen St West, at Beaconsfield ☏ 416 531 5042, ☏ 866 372 5386,

Ⓦthedrake.ca; Queen streetcar (#501); map p.62. This booming lounge-bar serves up delicious cocktails like the Ginger Rogers (whisky, rhubarb, strawberry, ginger) to a crowd that sprawls on sofas and loungers. The basement performance space, Drake Underground, features hopping live music. Mon–Fri 11am–2am, Sat & Sun 10am–2am.

Mulberry Bar 828 Bloor St West Ⓔmulberryto@gmail. com, Ⓦmulberry.bar; Subway: Ossington; map p.76. Parisian flair abounds at this charming bar. Greenery sprouts from all corners – a perfect backdrop for the tart and frothy cocktails, like the Palm Court (tequila, *crème de banane*, cava, lemon, saffron and mint) and the Que Syrah Syrah (syrah, blackberry liqueur, cracked pepper). The owners also run the nearby *Northwood* bar and café. Sun–Mon 5pm–midnight, Tues–Thurs 5pm–2am, Fri–Sat 4pm–2am.

LIVE MUSIC VENUES

Cameron House 408 Queen St West, at Cameron ☎416 703 0811, Ⓦthecameron.com; Queen streetcar (#501); map p.62. This legendary place, located just west of Spadina Ave, is unmissable – you can't fail to notice the colourful murals on the outside. The interior is a clash of Beaux Arts boudoir and honky-tonk bar, and the stage at the back of the room has long provided a showcase for emerging talent of every genre. Opening times vary with performances – check the website, but in general daily 4pm–2am.

El Mocambo 464 Spadina Ave, at Oxford ☎647 748 5959, Ⓦelmocambo.ca; College streetcar (#506); map p.76. Toronto's iconic rock-and-roll bar – which has hosted the biggest names in music, including The Rolling Stones, Jimi Hendrix, BB King and Blondie – shuttered in

2014, to the great sadness of music fans across the city. But, hope is here: Investors came in to resurrect this hallowed music hall, with a projected opening date of late 2019. Check the website for details. Opening hours vary with performances.

Horseshoe Tavern 370 Queen St West, at Spadina ☎416 598 4226, Ⓦhorseshoetavern.com; Queen streetcar (#501); map p.62. Many Toronto bands got their start here, and it's still a favourite for the newly famous to play a set or one-off concert. The interior of the *Horseshoe Tavern* (on the scene since 1947) is relentlessly unglamorous, but the low cover charge is a major compensation. Daily from 8.30pm.

Phoenix Concert Theatre 410 Sherbourne St, just north of Carlton ☎416 323 1251, Ⓦphoenixconcerttheatre. com; Carlton streetcar (#506); map p.76. This flashy, five-bar, three-venue concert emporium specializes in booking big-name acts longing for intimate gigs. Everyone from Sharon van Etten to Richard Thompson, Cesaria Evora and Green Day has performed here. Opening times vary with performances, but sets usually start at 6.30pm Mon–Thurs, 5pm Fri, noon Sat & Sun.

★ **The Rex Jazz & Blues Bar** 194 Queen St West, at St Patrick ☎416 598 2475, Ⓦtherex.ca; Subway: Osgoode; map p.62. In arguments about which is the best jazz club in town, this one (with an attached restaurant and hotel as well) is consistently near the top of the list. A well-primped crowd lounges in the spiffed-up interior, but any reservations about pretensions evaporate once the (always top-notch) music begins. Usually two shows a night, at 6.30pm and 9.30pm – see website.

PERFORMING ARTS AND FILM

Toronto sustains a wide-ranging programme of theatre, opera, ballet and classical music. Its particular strength is the **theatre scene**, the third-largest in the English-speaking world after London and New York. For movies, Toronto's mainstream **cinemas** show Hollywood releases before they reach Europe and the city has an excellent art-house cinema – as befits a city that hosts what is often regarded as the world's best film fest, the renowned **Toronto International Film Festival** (see page 92).

THEATRE

Buddies in Bad Times Theatre 12 Alexander St, off Yonge ☎416 975 8555, Ⓦbuddiesinbadtimes.com; Subway: St Andrew. The longest-established queer theatre company on the planet, the organization continues to generate critical and popular acclaim. This is the place for searing gay and alternative theatre in the city. Saturday nights, it opens its doors for bar party After Hours, and all proceeds are channelled back into the theatre.

Princess of Wales Theatre 300 King St West, at John ☎416 872 1212, Ⓦmirvish.com; Subway: St Andrew. Built

in the 1990s to accommodate the helicopter in *Miss Saigon*, this addition to Toronto's more traditional playhouses manages to have a surprisingly intimate feel, despite its 2000 seats.

Royal Alexandra Theatre 260 King St West at Simcoe ☎416 872 1212, Ⓦmirvish.com; Subway: St Andrew. The "Royal Alex" is a charming Edwardian theatre from 1906 that has been fully restored to its original, gilt-edged glory. It puts on everything from classical theatre to exuberant musicals to dramatic plays

St Lawrence Centre for the Arts 27 Front St East, at Scott ☎416 366 7723, Ⓦstlc.com; Subway: Union Station. Home to the Canadian Stage Company (Ⓦcanadianstage.com), the centre contains two stages: the Bluma Appel Theatre, the facility's main stage, where primarily new works by contemporary artists are shown, and the upstairs, studio-sized Jane Mallett Theatre, which presents experimental and workshop productions.

Young Centre for the Performing Arts 50 Tank House Lane, enter at 55 Mill St, Distillery District ☎416 866 8666, Ⓦyoungcentre.ca; King streetcar (#504). A lively and adventurous programme of performing arts that concentrates

1

on Toronto artists. Its main company is Soulpepper Theatre (☏416 203 6264, ⓦsoulpepper.ca), a youthful troupe that performs the classics from Miller to Molière.

CLASSICAL MUSIC

Glenn Gould Studio 250 Front St West, at John ☏416 205 5000, ⓦcbc.ca/glenngould; Subway: Union Station or King streetcar (#504). Named after the great pianist himself (see page 70), this small, boxy hall, which is located downtown in the CBC Centre (see page 66), is so sprung for sound that enthusiastic performances leave audiences literally vibrating. The programming is first-rate, generally showcasing Canadian talent.

Massey Hall 178 Victoria St, at Yonge ☏416 872 4255, ⓦmasseyhall.com; Subway: Queen. Built in the late 1800s, this recital hall boasts great acoustics and has hosted a wide variety of performers – everyone from Maria Callas to Jarvis Cocker.

Roy Thomson Hall 60 Simcoe St ☏416 872 4255, ⓦroythomson.com; Subway: St Andrew. Home to the Toronto Symphony Orchestra (☏416 598 3375, ⓦtso.ca), this modern hall has a circular auditorium with excellent sightlines and its acoustics have been tweaked to rave reviews.

OPERA AND BALLET

Canadian Opera Company Four Seasons Centre for the Performing Arts, 145 Queen St West ☏416 363 8231, ⓦcoc.ca; Subway: Osgoode. Canada's national opera has impressed international audiences for years with its ambitious productions and devotion to young talent. Seats are often scarce, particularly for the eagerly anticipated season premieres, so reserve as far in advance as possible; ticket prices range from $22–80 for ring 5 to $55–233 for orchestra level.

National Ballet of Canada Four Seasons Centre for the Performing Arts, 145 Queen St West ☏416 345 9595, ⓦnational.ballet.ca; Subway: Osgoode. The NBC's prima ballerinas are much admired, as is the company itself, performing classical ballet and contemporary dance with equal artistry; tickets $37–265.

CINEMAS

Cineplex Odeon Varsity 55 Bloor St West, at Balmuto ☏416 961 6304, ⓦcineplex.com; Subway: Bloor-Yonge. Multi-screen behemoth with good sight-lines, great sound and sink-in-able seats.

Scotiabank Theatre 259 Richmond St West, at John ☏416 368 5600, ⓦcineplex.com; Queen streetcar (#501). Never mind the film, half the spectacle is in the theatre experience itself, with a mammoth, outdoor pixel-board cube showing film clips, an almost vertical ride up the escalator to the cinemas and a sound system for its fourteen screens that will blast you out of your seat.

TIFF Cinémathèque Bell Lightbox, 350 King St West, at John ☏416 968 3456, ⓦtiff.net/cinematheque; King streetcar (#504). Cinémathèque is a year-round extension of the Toronto International Film Festival (see page 92) with an imaginative and far-reaching programme of international and, more especially, Canadian films.

SHOPPING

Canada's most popular leisure-time pursuit would seem to be **shopping** – and Toronto bristles with shops and stores. The largest city-centre shopping mall is the Eaton Centre (see page 69), but this is largely the preserve of the big chains and there are lots of more individual offerings – we give a sample below. Furthermore, more than four dozen buildings, providing access to 1200 shops and services (and sites like CN Tower and Roy Thomson Hall), are connected via 30km of **underground walkways** (referred to as PATH) – superb for milling about and shopping when cold Canadian winds are blowing outside.

The Big Carrot 348 Danforth Ave, at Jackman Ave ☏416 466 2129, ⓦthebigcarrot.ca; Subway: Chester; map p.58. A long-established collective, this wholefood supermarket offers one-stop shopping for organic food and earth-friendly household items. It has a popular vegetarian deli-counter/café, and a top-notch wellness section, with a body care department, holistic dispensary and herbalist shop. Mon–Fri 9am–9pm, Sat 9am–8pm & Sun 10am–6pm.

Craft Ontario Shop 1106 Queen Street W, ☏416 921 1721, ⓦcraftontario.com; Subway: Queen streetcar (#501); map p.76. The retail location of the Ontario Crafts Council showcases the work of Canadian artisans. They mix newcomers with collectible veterans and carry glass, ceramics, textiles, jewellery and wood. The store is also Toronto's oldest Inuit and First Nations art dealer. Mon

---

SPECTATOR SPORTS IN TORONTO

Baseball The Blue Jays (ⓦbluejays.com) play at the Rogers Centre (see page 64).
Basketball The Toronto Raptors (ⓦtorontoraptors.com) of the (American) NBA dribble down the court at the Scotiabank Arena, behind Union Station.
Canadian football The Argonauts (ⓦargonauts.ca) also play at the Rogers Centre.
Ice hockey The Maple Leafs (ⓦmapleleafs.nhl.com) skate at home in the Scotiabank Arena.

11am–6pm, Tues–Wed 10am–6pm, Thurs–Sat 10am–7pm, Sun 11am–5pm.

Divine Decadence Originals Upper Level, 128 Cumberland St, at Bellair ☎416 324 9759, ⓦdivinedecadenceoriginals.com; Subway: Bay; map p.76. An unmatched collection of vintage *haute couture*, including Chanel from the 1930s, Dior from the 1950s, Pucci from the 1960s, and museum-quality accessories, jewellery, beaded bags, fragile cocktail-hats plus vintage bridal. Essential browsing for connoisseurs. Mon–Sat 11am–7pm.

Holt Renfrew 50 Bloor St ☎416 922 2333, ⓦholtrenfrew; Subway: Bloor-Yonge and Bay; map p.76. Canada's iconic luxury department store has all the usual high-end brands, but it's also one of the best places to find luxe fashion by Canadian designers, including Line the Label (worn by Meghan Markle for her engagement announcement to Prince Harry), Pink Tartan and Greta Constantine. Mon–Wed & Sat 10am–8pm, Thurs–Fri 10am–9pm, Sun 11am–7pm.

Lilliput Hats 462 College St at Bathurst ☎416 536 5933, ⓦlilliputhats.ca; College/Carlton streetcar (#506); map p.76. Millinery is almost a lost art, so Toronto is particularly blessed to have Karen Gingras and her Lilliput Hats in its midst. In addition to the breathtaking variety of finished headwear, the open studio is in the shop, steaming, stitching and forming fabrics into each unique creation. Special orders are welcome. Mon–Fri 10am–6pm, Sat 11am–6pm.

Loblaw's 60 Carlton St ☎416 593 6154, ⓦloblaws.ca; Subway: College; map p.76. Think of this as a normal supermarket with the volume pumped up to 1000. In addition to a massive grocery and produce section, you can get all manner of prepared foods – sushi to order, pizzas, grilled meats and veggies, salads, dozens of varieties of tea, cheese galore, pastries and cakes in every colour – in a truly tremendous 8000 sq m box that formerly held Maple Leaf Gardens, where hockey contests were held. You can eat your bounty in a few installed stadium seats, and rumour has it there's a red spot in the spice aisle marking centre ice, where the puck was dropped. Daily 7am–11pm.

Mountain Equipment Co-op 400 King St West, at Peter St ☎416 340 2667, ⓦmec.ca; King streetcar (#504); map p.62. If you're planning to dog-sled in the Arctic, bike across China, climb mountains or go deep-sea diving, you can buy everything you need here at better-than-average prices. Mountain Equipment Co-op also does daily rentals of bicycles, cross-country skis, canoes and kayaks. The building itself is of interest too: it's made from recycled materials and has a wildflower garden on the roof. Mon–Fri 10am–9pm, Sat 9am–9pm, Sun 10am–6pm.

Soma Chocolatemaker 32 Tank House Lane, Mill St, Distillery District ☎416 815 7662, ⓦsomachocolate. com; King streetcar (#504); map p.62. A serious business, this chocolate-making – and nobody in Toronto does it better than Soma. Prize products, with truffles and pralines to tickle your fancy. Mon–Sat 10am–8pm, Fri–Sun 11am–6pm.

Umbra 165 John St, at Renfrew Pl ☎416 599 0088, ⓦumbra.com; Subway: Osgoode; map p.62. Umbra, a Toronto-born global design company, trades in intelligent, creative, colourful homeware products with a bit of whimsy to them; this is its flagship and its only physical store. You might find here copper butterflies wall art, their award-winning soap dispensers reminiscent of penguins or chairs that can be folded and hung in the closet when not in use. Items often are multi-purpose; designers are sometimes credited on the object; and even the packaging can be inventive. Mon–Fri 11am–7pm, Sat 10am–7pm, Sun 11am–6pm.

DIRECTORY

Car rental As you might expect, Toronto has scores of car hire companies. Three downtown locations are: Discount, 134 Jarvis St (☎416 864 0632); National, 200 Wellington St West (☎877 222 9058); Enterprise, Simcoe Place, 200 Front St West (☎416 751 1342).

Consulates Australia, Suite 1100 South Tower, 175 Bloor St East ☎416 323 1155; UK, 777 Bay St ☎416 593 1290; USA, 360 University Ave, entrance at 225 Simcoe St ☎416 595 1700.

Internet Almost all city hotels provide internet access for their guests either free or at minimal charge. The Toronto Reference Library (see below) also provides free internet access.

Laundry The Laundry Lounge, 527 Yonge St at Maitland, just south of Wellesley (daily 8am–10pm; ☎416 975 4747).

Left luggage Union Station, Front St at Bay, has lockers for passengers, as does the Toronto Coach Terminal, 610 Bay St at Dundas.

Library The main library is the Toronto Reference Library, 789 Yonge St, one block north of Bloor (Mon–Fri 9am–8.30pm, Sat 9am–5pm, Sun 1.30–5pm; ☎416 395 5577, ⓦtorontopubliclibrary.ca).

Pharmacies Shopper's Drug Mart, multiple locations including 66 Wellington St West (☎416 365 0927) and 10 Dundas St (☎416 591 1733). For a holistic pharmacy, including herbal and traditional treatments, try the Big Carrot Wholistic Dispensary, 348 Danforth Ave (☎416 466 8432, ⓦthebigcarrot.ca).

Post offices Canada Post (ⓦcanadapost.ca) operates branches in scores of locations, with many inside pharmacies. One handy location is downtown inside the Royal Bank Plaza, 200 Bay St at Front.

Ontario

CANADIAN HORSESHOE FALLS AT NIAGARA FALLS

Ontario

Ontario may not have the tourist profile of the Rockies out west, but the province still boasts many of Canada's top attractions: Niagara Falls is the country's most visited sight; Ottawa makes an engaging capital, while Toronto (see page 56) is one of the most visited cities in North America; and Algonquin Provincial Park is an especially fine tract of pristine wilderness. It's also very, very big – a giant slab of land, Canada's second-largest province, stretching all the way from the St Lawrence River and the Great Lakes to the frozen shores of Hudson Bay. The thousands of lakes that dot the landscape gave rise to the province's name – "Ontario" is based on a word meaning "glittering waters" in the language of the Iroquois, its earliest inhabitants.

Spreading along the northern shore of **Lake Ontario** to either side of Toronto is a chain of towns that are often lumped together as the **Golden Horseshoe**, a misleadingly evocative name that refers simply to the area's geographic shape and economic success. This is Ontario's manufacturing heartland, a built-up strip whose most notable attraction is the **Royal Botanical Gardens**, close to steel-town **Hamilton**. Further round the lake are the famous **Niagara Falls**, easily Ontario's most popular attraction, and **Niagara-on-the-Lake**, one of the province's quaintest towns. West of the Golden Horseshoe, much of Southwest Ontario is profoundly rural, an expanse of farmland sandwiched between lakes Huron and Erie. High points here include **Goderich** and **Bayfield**, two charming little towns tucked tight against Lake Huron; **Stratford**, with its much-vaunted theatre festival; and **Georgian Bay**, whose **Severn Sound** is the location of the astoundingly beautiful **Georgian Bay Islands National Park**, an elegiac land- and waterscape of rocky, pine-dotted islets and crystal-blue lake. The national park – and its campsites – are best approached by boat from tiny **Honey Harbour**, but you can sample the scenery on a variety of island cruises from Penetanguishene, Midland and the dinky little port of **Parry Sound**. Also here on Severn Sound are a pair of top-notch historical reconstructions, the one-time British naval base at **Discovery Harbour** and the former Jesuit mission at **Sainte-Marie among the Hurons**.

Central Ontario, inland from the coastal strip bordering Georgian Bay, is largely defined by the **Canadian Shield**, whose endless forests, myriad lakes and thin soils dip down from the north in a giant wedge. This hostile terrain has kept settlement down to a minimum, though latterly the very wildness of the land has attracted Canadian holiday-makers, who come here to hunker down in their lakeside cottages – hence the moniker "cottage country". The centre of this is the **Muskoka Lakes**, a skein of narrow lakes and rivers, and their main supply towns, **Gravenhurst** and **Bracebridge**. The Muskoka Lakes may be relatively domesticated, but neighbouring **Algonquin Provincial Park** is certainly not, comprising a wilderness tract with abundant wildlife and a mind-bogglingly large network of canoe routes.

The implacability of the Shield breaks up as it approaches the **St Lawrence River** at the east end of Lake Ontario, and it's here you'll find a string of historic towns and villages. The pick is **Kingston**, renowned for its fine limestone buildings and a pleasant stepping stone on the road east to either Montréal (see page 188) or **Ottawa**, Canada's appealing capital city, which boasts some of the country's finest museums and a first-rate restaurant and bar scene.

Stretching north from the shores of Lake Huron and Lake Superior, **northern Ontario** is almost entirely flat, give or take the odd ridge and chasm, an endless expanse of forest and lake pouring over the mineral-rich rocks of the Canadian Shield. It was the north which once produced the furs that launched Canada's economy, but the

THE TOWN OF NIAGARA-ON-THE-LAKE

Highlights

❶ Niagara Falls One of the most celebrated tourist attractions in North America, this thunder of foaming water is spread over two falls – one American, one Canadian. See page 105

❷ Niagara-on-the-Lake With its antique clapboard houses immaculate gardens, this is one of Ontario's prettiest towns. See page 112

❸ Bayfield All leafy streets and elegant homes, the lakeside hamlet of Bayfield is a perfect place to unwind. See page 129

❹ Diving at Fathom Five National Marine Park Clear waters and some surprisingly well-

preserved shipwrecks make for outstanding diving. See page 135

❺ Georgian Bay Islands Ontario at its most beautiful – crystal waters studded with pine-dusted islands. See page 143

❻ Ottawa Amiable capital city, with a lively restaurant and café scene, plus a clutch of outstanding museums, galleries and theatres. See page 161

❼ Riding the Algoma Central Railway Arguably the best of Ontario's train rides, from Sault Ste Marie deep into the northern wilderness. See page 178

HIGHLIGHTS ARE MARKED ON THE MAP ON PAGE 100

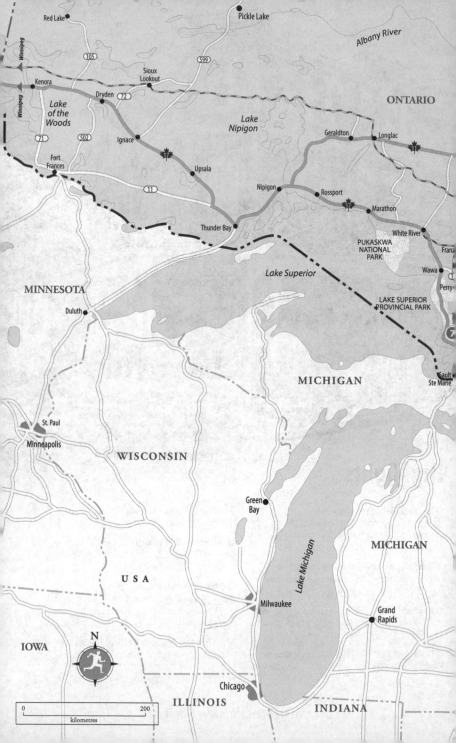

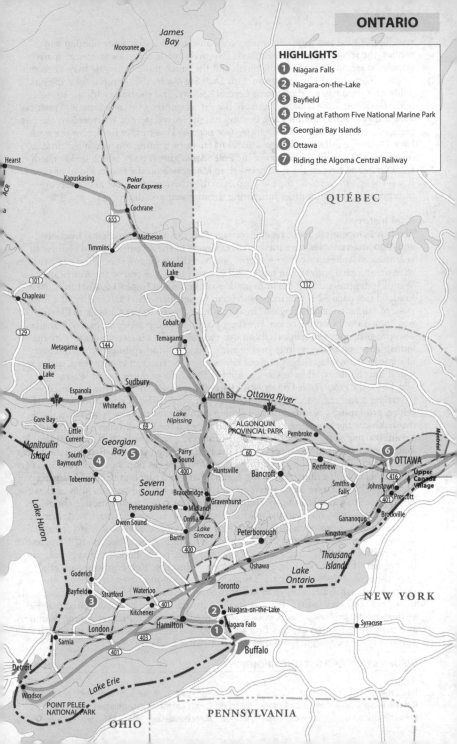

ONTARIO

James Bay

Moosonee

QUÉBEC

Hearst

Kapuskasing

Polar Bear Express

Cochrane

ACR a

655

Matheson

Timmins

101

Kirkland Lake

Chapleau

117

129

Cobalt

Temagami

Metagama

144

11

Elliot Lake

Sudbury

Espanola

North Bay

Ottawa River

Whitefish

69

Lake Nipissing

ALGONQUIN PROVINCIAL PARK

Pembroke

Montreal

Gore Bay

Little Current

Georgian Bay

5

Parry Sound

60

OTTAWA

6

Manitoulin Island

South Baymouth

4

400

Huntsville

Bancroft

Renfrew

416

Upper Canada Village

Tobermory

Severn Sound

Bracebridge

Gravenhurst

Smiths Falls

Johnstown

401

Prescott

6

Penetanguishene

Midland

7

Gananoque

Brockville

Lake Huron

Owen Sound

Orillia

Lake Simcoe

Peterborough

Kingston

Thousand Islands

Goderich

Barrie

400

NEW YORK

Bayfield

3

Stratford

Waterloo

Oshawa

Lake Ontario

London

401

Kitchener

Hamilton

Toronto

2

Niagara-on-the-Lake

Syracuse

Sarnia

403

1

Niagara Falls

Detroit

401

Buffalo

Windsor

Lake Erie

POINT PELEE NATIONAL PARK

OHIO

PENNSYLVANIA

2

travelling is hard and time-consuming and, unless you're after some **hunting and fishing**, the region's charms are limited. Two main roads cross this immense, sparsely populated region, Hwy-11 in the north and the much more enjoyable **Hwy-17** to the south. Highlights of Hwy-17 begin with **Sault Ste Marie**, the terminus for a splendid wilderness train trip on the **Algoma Central Railway**, and continue with the string of parks bordering **Lake Superior**, notably the extravagantly wild **Lake Superior Provincial Park** and **Pukaskwa National Park**. Beyond lies the inland port of **Thunder Bay**, the last place of much appeal before Winnipeg (see page 471), a further 680km to the west. **Hwy-11**, on the other hand, links a series of far-flung mining towns and has little to offer with the possible exception of the **Polar Bear Express train**, which strikes north from **Cochrane** beyond the road network to **Moosonee** on the frozen shores of James Bay – though to be frank, the rail journey across these northern wastes can seem interminable, the mosquitoes infuriating the moment you disembark.

Brief history

The first **Europeans** to make regular contact with the region's Aboriginal **Iroquois and Algonquin peoples** were the French explorers of the seventeenth and eighteenth centuries, most famously Étienne Brûlé and Samuel de Champlain. These early visitors were preoccupied with the **fur trade**, and it wasn't until the end of the American War of Independence and the immigration of the **United Empire Loyalists** from New England (see page 329) that mass settlement began. Between 1820 and 1850 a further wave of migrants, mostly English, Irish and Scots, made **Upper Canada**, as Ontario was known until Confederation, the most populous and prosperous part of Canada. This pre-eminence was reinforced towards the end of the nineteenth century by the **industrialization** of the region's larger towns, a process underpinned by the discovery of some of the world's richest mineral deposits: in the space of twenty years, nickel was found near Sudbury, silver at Cobalt, gold in Red Lake and iron ore at Wawa.

In 1943, the **Progressive Conservative Party (PCs)** took control of the provincial government and remained in power for over forty years. The PCs followed a right-of-centre, pro-business agenda and their skill in handling the popular vote earned them the nickname the "Big Blue Machine". Nevertheless, the PCs did move with the times, passing a string of **progressive acts** such as, for example, Canada's first Fair Employment Practices Act against discrimination and the Female Employees Fair Remuneration Act, both in 1951. In 1985, the PCs finally lost a provincial election, but returned to power ten years later with a flinty right-wing agenda that owed much to Britain's Margaret Thatcher. The PCs were much taken up with privatization and tax cuts (plus endless carping about welfare scroungers), but this did not play well with a sizeable chunk of the population and, much to the relief of the Left, the Liberals have defeated them in the last four elections, with 2014 seeing Kathleen Wynne elected as the first female leader of the majority winner. In the June 2018 Ontario general election, the Progressive Conservative Party of Ontario won the majority vote, led by populist Doug Ford, who is the brother of the infamous late former mayor of Toronto, Rob Ford (see page 60).

On the economic front, Ontario's timber and mining industries, massive hydroelectric schemes and myriad factories continue to keep the province at or near the top of the economic ladder. The province's industrial success has also created massive **environmental problems**, most noticeable in the wounded landscapes around Sudbury and the polluted waters of lakes Erie and Ontario – problems which the provincial government has begun to focus on albeit somewhat tardily.

INFORMATION AND GETTING AROUND   ONTARIO

INFORMATION
Ontario Travel A string of excellent information centres at key locations across the province (visitor helpline: Mon–Fri

8am–8pm, Sat & Sun 9am–6pm; ☎ 800 668 2746 within Canada and the US, ⊕ ontariotravel.net).
Accommodation Many B&Bs are members of the

Federation of Ontario Bed and Breakfast Accommodation (ⓦfobba.com). Almost all Ontario's one hundred provincial parks have campsites; for details, and an online reservation service, see ⓦontarioparks.com or call ☎800 668 2746.

PUBLIC TRANSPORT
There are fast and fairly frequent buses and trains between Toronto and Niagara Falls, and a similarly efficient service between the region's other major settlements, like Ottawa, Windsor, London and Kitchener. Transport, once patchy in the smaller towns and villages, has been evolving, with new transit options like the Linx Transit Service (ⓦsimcoe. ca), which launched in 2018 in Penetanguishene and Midland.Towns and villages can sprawl over several kilometres. So if you're heading for a particular park, hotel, motel or campsite, you can still be dropped miles from your destination – check before you set out.

Long-distance buses There are two principal long-distance bus companies: Greyhound (☎800 661 8747, ⓦgreyhound.ca) and Ontario Northland (☎800 461 8558, ⓦontarionorthland.ca).

Trains The main train company is VIA Rail (☎888 842 7245, ⓦviarail.ca). Ontario Northland operates the Polar Bear Express (☎800 265 2356; see page 152) from Cochrane to Moosonee on James Bay.

2

Hamilton

With a population of around 500,000, **HAMILTON** lies at the extreme western end of Lake Ontario, about 70km from Toronto. The city takes its name from George Hamilton, a storekeeper-turned-landowner who surveyed the area after he moved here following the destruction of his homestead during the War of 1812. By the early 1900s, Hamilton had become a major **steel producer** and today its mills churn out about half the country's output, though the city's industrial heyday has faded and in the last couple of decades it has struggled to keep itself afloat. Industrial cities are rarely high on tourist itineraries and Hamilton is no exception, but it does have a couple of quality attractions, including the sprawling **Royal Botanical Gardens** and the family-friendly **Dundurn Castle.** Other than the gardens, all the city's key attractions are in – or within comfortable walking distance of – a surprisingly compact **downtown core**. This runs east to west parallel to the lakeshore along King Street West and Main Street West, between Bay Street North and James Street North. Beyond here, Hamilton becomes a large and sprawling city.

Whitehern
41 Jackson St West, one block south of Main Street West • Tues–Sun noon–4pm • $7 • ☎905 546 2018, ⓦhamilton.ca/attractions/culture

The long-time home of the McQuesten family, who established Hamilton's first foundry, **Whitehern** is an excellent example of Victorian architecture, its good-looking, columned portico set against the precise symmetries of the house's windows and imposing stonework. The interior holds an eccentric mix of styles, ranging from a splendid mid-nineteenth century circular stairway to a dingy wood-panelled 1930s basement – all the garbled legacy of the McQuestens, who lived here until the 1960s. Seasonal events are held throughout the year, including the McQuesten Family Christmas, when the house is decked out in festive finery.

Art Gallery of Hamilton
123 King St West • Wed & Fri 11am–6pm, Thurs 11am–8pm, Sat & Sun noon–5pm • $10, free on first Fri of month after 4pm• ☎905 527 6610, ⓦartgalleryofhamilton.com

The **Art Gallery of Hamilton,** founded in 1914, is one of the oldest museums in Southern Ontario. Exhibits feature an excellent representative sample of Canadian painting drawn from its permanent collection, including a good selection of works by Emily Carr as well as the Group of Seven (see page 74). It also offers a first-rate programme of temporary exhibitions with Canadian artists to the fore.

Dundurn Castle

610 York blvd • Tues–Sun noon–4pm • $11.50 • ☏ 905 546 2872, ⓦ hamilton.ca/attractions/culture

In its own grounds on the western edge of the city centre, **Dundurn Castle** is an impressive villa with an interior in which it's easy to imagine the lives of the upstairs and downstairs residents, the former living among fine contemporaneous furnishings, and the dozens of servants who once worked here scurrying below within a warren of poorly ventilated rooms. The house was built in the 1830s for Sir Allan Napier MacNab, a soldier, lawyer and land speculator, who became one of the leading

SOUTHWEST ONTARIO

conservative politicians of the day. He was knighted for his loyalty to the Crown during the Upper Canada Rebellion of 1837, when he employed bands of armed men to round up supposed rebels and loot their property. The castle also hosts a wide array of workshops and events, including the perennially popular Historic Cooking Workshops, where you'll cook using traditional methods and recipes.

The Royal Botanical Gardens (RBG)

680 Plains Rd West, Burlington • Daily 10am–dusk • $18 • **Visitor Centre** Daily: May–Sept 10am–8pm; Oct–April 10am–5pm • ☎ 905 527 1158, ⓦ rbg.ca • Most Hamilton–Burlington buses stop outside the Visitor Centre from where there's a seasonal shuttle bus to all the other sections – check website for details

The delightful **Royal Botanical Gardens** cover some twelve square kilometres just across Burlington Bay from downtown Hamilton, its several sections spread over 15km of wooded shoreline. The flower displays here are simply gorgeous with highlights including **Hendrie Park's Rose Gardens** (best June–Oct) and nearby **Laking Garden** with its irises and peonies (May & June). Hendrie Park adjoins the main **RBG Visitor Centre**, where there's a shop, café and several inside areas featuring forced bulbs, orchids and cacti. Wilder parts of the RBG are round to the west with the 800-hectare **Cootes Paradise Sanctuary** latticed with hiking trails.

ARRIVAL AND INFORMATION   HAMILTON

By bus Hamilton's GO Transit Centre, a couple of blocks south of Main St at 36 Hunter St East and James, serves as the town's combined bus and train station; note that VIA Rail does not currently have trains to or from Hamilton. Destinations (GO Transit) Toronto (every 30min; 1hr–1hr

40min).
Tourist office On the ground floor of the Lister Block, downtown at 28 James St North (Mon–Fri 9am–4pm, Sat & Sun 11am–3pm; ☎ 905 546 2424, ☎ 800 263 8590, ⓦ tourismhamilton.com).

ACCOMMODATION AND EATING

Brux House 137 Locke St ☎ 905 527 2789, ⓦ bruxhouse. com. Home to craft beers and ciders, along with a modest menu of mains ($19–29) like duck confit, mussels and fries, and pork schnitzel. Tues–Thurs 11am–11.30pn, Fri–Sat 11.30am–midnight, Sun 11.30am–9pm.
The Burnt Tongue 10 Cannon St East ☎ 905 536 1146, ⓦ theburnttongue.com. The burger/salad/sandwich menu is hearty, but what people come for (and rave about) are the soups: a daily choice of several classics and more exotic ones, some vegan or dairy-free, all stupendously flavourful. Mon–Sat 11.30am–8pm.

Sheraton Hamilton 116 King St West ☎ 905 529 5515, ⓦ marriott.com. This large modern affair slap-bang in the centre has large, well-appointed rooms. $149
La Spaghett 970 Upper James St ☎ 905 318 8211, ⓦ laspaghett.com. Hamilton has a large Italian community, and *La Spaghett* stands out among the city's dozens of Italian restaurants for its superb range of home-made pastas (mains around $18). It's a couple of kilometres south of the centre. Mon–Fri 11.30am–2pm & daily 4.30–10pm.

Niagara Falls and the Niagara River

In 1860, thousands watched as **Charles Blondin** walked a tightrope across **Niagara Falls** for the third time. Midway, he paused to cook an omelette on a portable grill, and then had a marksman shoot a hole through his hat from the *Maid of the Mist* boat, fifty metres below. As attested by Blondin – and the innumerable lunatics and publicity seekers who have gone over the Falls in every craft imaginable – the Falls simply can't be beat as a theatrical setting. Yet, in truth, the stupendous first impression doesn't last long and to prevent the thirteen million visitors who arrive each year from getting bored by the sight of a load of water crashing over a 52m cliff, the Niagarans have ensured that the Falls can be seen from every angle imaginable – from boats, viewing towers, helicopters, cable cars, tunnels in the rock face behind the cascade – and even azipline. The tunnels and boats are the most exciting, with the entrance to the former

2

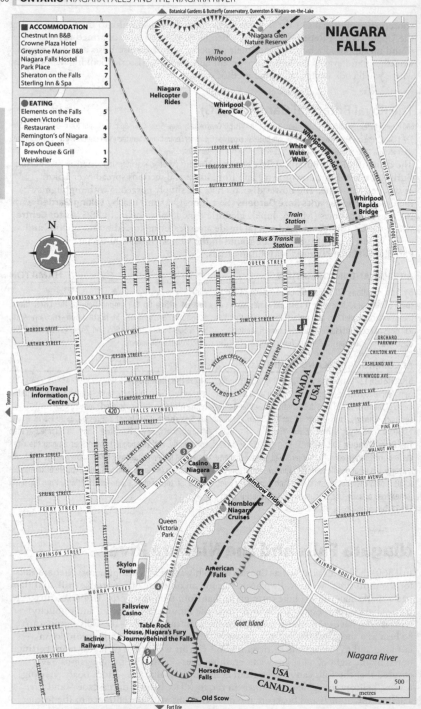

Botanical Gardens & Butterfly Conservatory, Queenston & Niagara-on-the-Lake

NIAGARA FALLS

■ ACCOMMODATION

Chestnut Inn B&B	4
Crowne Plaza Hotel	5
Greystone Manor B&B	3
Niagara Falls Hostel	1
Park Place	2
Sheraton on the Falls	7
Sterling Inn & Spa	6

● EATING

Elements on the Falls	5
Queen Victoria Place Restaurant	4
Remington's of Niagara	3
Taps on Queen Brewhouse & Grill	1
Weinkeller	2

Niagara Glen Nature Reserve

The Whirlpool

Niagara Helicopter Rides

Whirlpool Aero Car

White Water Walk

Whirlpool Rapids

NIAGARA PARKWAY

LEADER LANE
FERGUSON STREET
BUTTREY STREET

Whirlpool Rapids Bridge

VICTORIA AVENUE

WHIRLPOOL STREET

LEWISTON DRIVE

Train Station

Bus & Transit Station

BRIDGE STREET

Queen Street

ZIMMERMAN AVE
ERIE AVE
ONTARIO AVE
CATARACT

MORRISON STREET

SIXTH AVE
FIFTH AVE
FOURTH AVE
THIRD AVE
SECOND AVE
FIRST AVE
BUCKLEY STREET
ST LAURENCE AVE

SIMCOE STREET
ARMOURY ST

8TH ST

MORDEN DRIVE
ARTHUR STREET

VALLEY WAY

JEPSON STREET

RYERSON CRESCENT

EASTWOOD CRESCENT

ORCHARD PARKWAY
CHILTON AVE
ASHLAND AVE
ELMWOOD AVE
SPRUCE AVE
CEDAR AVE

STANLEY AVENUE

MCRAE STREET

STAMFORD STREET

Ontario Travel Information Centre

VICTORIA AVENUE

RIVER ROAD NIAGARA PARKWAY

ONTARIO AVENUE

PINE AVE

CANADA
USA

420 (FALLS AVENUE)

KITCHENER STREET

WALNUT AVE

NORTH STREET

BUCHANAN AVENUE

DIXSON AVENUE

MCGRAIL AVENUE

LEWIS AVENUE

MAGDALEN STREET

ELLEN AVENUE

VICTORIA AVENUE

CLIFTON HILL

FALLS AVENUE

Casino Niagara

Rainbow Bridge

FERRY AVENUE

SPRING STREET

FERRY STREET

Hornblower Niagara Cruises

MAIN STREET

NIAGARA STREET

1ST STREET

RAINBOW BOULEVARD

ROBINSON STREET

FALLSVIEW BOULEVARD

Queen Victoria Park

Skylon Tower

American Falls

MURRAY STREET

Fallsview Casino

DIXON STREET

Table Rock House, Niagara's Fury & JourneyBehind the Falls

Goat Island

Niagara River

Incline Railway

DUNN STREET

ALLANThALE AVE

PORTAGE ROAD

FALLS VIEW BOULEVARD

Horseshoe Falls

USA
CANADA

0   500
metres

Old Scow

Toronto

N

Fort Erie

right next to the Falls at Table Rock House and the latter leaving from the foot of the cliff at the end of Clifton Hill, 1100m downriver. Both give a real sense of the extraordinary force of the waterfall, a perpetual white-crested thundering pile-up that supposedly had Austrian composer Gustav Mahler shouting "At last, fortissimo" over the din. After the Falls themselves, be sure to allow enough time to explore the Niagara River along either the Niagara Parkway road or the Niagara River Recreation Trail (see page 108), an easy-to-follow jogging and cycle path. Both road and trail stretch the length of the Niagara River from Fort Erie, 32km upstream from the Falls, to Niagara-on-the-Lake.

A day is more than enough time to see the Falls and its immediate surroundings, but if you do decide to spend the night hereabouts, quaint **Niagara-on-the-Lake** (see page 112), 26km downstream beside Lake Ontario, is a much better option than the crassly commercialized town of Niagara Falls itself. That said, Niagara-on-the-Lake gets very crowded in high season, so try to book at least a couple of days in advance.

The Falls

Even if you've seen all the postcards and watched all the films, nothing quite prepares you for your first glimpse of the **Falls**, a fearsome white arc shrouded in clouds of dense spray with the river boats struggling down below, mere specks against the surging cauldron. There are actually two cataracts, as tiny **Goat Island** divides the accelerating water into two channels: on the far side, across the frontier, the river slips over the precipice of the **American Falls**, 320m wide but still only half the width of the **Horseshoe Falls** on the Canadian side. The spectacle is even more extraordinary in winter, when snow-covered trees edge a jagged armoury of freezing mist and heaped ice blocks. Even after the sun goes down, the Falls are a splendid sight, thanks to the Falls Illumination, a multi-coloured light and water show. In 2016, existing lights were replaced with blazing LED technology, which has vastly improved the experience. The Falls Illumination has seasonal hours (generally from 7 or 8pm until midnight to 2am) – check ⓦ niagaraparks.com.

All this may look like a scene of untrammelled nature, but it isn't. Since the early twentieth century, hydroelectric schemes have greatly reduced the water flow, and all sorts of tinkering has spread what's left of the river more evenly over the crest line. As a result, the process of erosion, which has moved the Falls some 11km upstream in 12,000 years, has slowed down from one metre per year to just 30cm. This obviously has advantages for the tourist industry, but the environmental consequences of harnessing the river in such a way are still unclear. More positively, the cardsharps and charlatans who overran the riverside in Blondin's day are long gone with the **Niagara Parks Commission** (ⓦ niagaraparks.com), which controls the area along the Canadian side of the river and beside the Falls, ensuring the immaculately tended tree-lined gardens and parkland remain precisely so.

Table Rock Welcome Centre

Niagara Parkway • **Journey Behind the Falls** Daily 9am to dusk, sometimes later • $19.95, children 6–12 $13 • **Niagara's Fury** Daily 9am–dusk, sometimes later • $15, ages 6–12 $9.75 • Both on Adventure Pass (see page 108) • ⓦ niagaraparks.com

At **Table Rock House**, you can get disarmingly close to the crest line of the Horseshoe Falls at a free **observation platform** and from here you can also spy the rusting remains of the **Old Scow**, stuck against the rocks in the middle of the river just upstream. In 1918, this flat-bottomed barge was being towed across the Niagara River when the lines snapped and the boat – along with the two-man crew – hurtled towards the falls. There must have been an awful lot of praying going on, because – just 750m from the precipice – the barge caught against the rocks, and it's stayed there ever since.

Inside Table Rock House, lifts travel to the base of the cliff, where the tunnels of the **Journey Behind the Falls** lead to platforms directly beside the cascade. It's a magnificent

2

ADVENTURE PASS AND NIAGARA HERITAGE TRAIL PASS

Niagara Parks offers the **Adventure Pass** ($65 children 6–12 $43; ⓦniagaraparks.com), which saves you money on a combination of four different activities. There are several varieties to choose from, but the most popular Classic formulation encompasses the Journey Behind the Falls, Hornblower Niagara Cruise, White Water Walk and Niagara's Fury, as well as coupons that can be used at local restaurants and shops, and two-day WEGO bus access. There is also a Nature Pass (covers Hornblower Niagara Cruise, Whirlpool Aero Car, Floral Showhouse, Butterfly Conservatory and two-day WEGO access; same price), and Plus Pass ($99, children 6–12 $65), which covers seven sites and includes a two-day pass for the often-convenient Incline Railway. The pass can be purchased at any of the associated attractions. Niagara Parks also has the Niagara Heritage Trail Pass ($20.95), which covers four historic sites, including Laura Secord Homestead and Old Fort Erie.

---

sight, which is more than can be said for Table Rock's other attraction, **Niagara's Fury**, a self-billed "4-D experience" that aims to re-create the formation of the Falls.

Hornblower Niagara Cruises

Clifton Hill • Daily: April to late June 9.45am–5.45pm; late June to early Sept 9am–7pm; early Sept to late Oct 9.45am–4.45pm • Boats leave every 15min in high season, otherwise every 30min • $25.95, ages 6–12 $15.95, including waterproofs • Covered on Adventure Pass (see page 108) • ☎ 905 358 5781, ⓦ niagaracruises.com

From Table Rock House, a wide path leads north along the edge of the river gorge, with the manicured lawns of **Queen Victoria Park** to the left and views over towards the American Falls to the right. At the end of the park is Clifton Hill, the main drag linking the riverside with the town of Niagara Falls. From the jetty below Clifton Hill, the former *Maid of the Mist* boats, now run by **Hornblower Niagara** (*Maid of the Mist* now solely refers to those departing from the American side), edge out into the river and push up towards the Falls, an exhilarating trip no one should miss.

WildPlay Mistrider Zipline

5920 Niagara Parkway, Grandview Marketplace, near the Hornblower tower • Hours vary throughout the year; generally daily 10am–4pm • $59 • ☎ 800 263 7073, ⓦ niagarafalls.wildplay.com.

Get the adrenaline pumping on this popular zipline, where you'll dangle from 67 metres in the air. Soar through the Niagara gorge and take in the vast views of the thundering falls.

Clifton Hill and around

For better or worse – probably the latter – **Clifton Hill** is the centre of the tourist action in Niagara Falls, comprising a short, steep slope flanked by a tawdry collection of fast-food joints and bizarre attractions, from the innocuous Dinosaur Adventure Golf (yes, that's right) to the eminently missable Ripley's Believe It or Not! Or, climb aboard the Niagara Skywheel, where you can twirl 53 metres above the falls in climate-controlled gondolas. Close by, near the Rainbow Bridge off Victoria Avenue, is one of the town's two 24hr **casinos**, Casino Niagara, a bristlingly modern structure where kids can watch their parents fritter away their inheritance; the other is Fallsview Casino Resort on Fallsview Boulevard. If you're keen to avoid all this commercialization, then stick to the well-kept **riverside** area, where a string of much more agreeable attractions begins downstream with the White Water Walk, 3km from Clifton Hill.

Downstream from the Falls

The **Niagara River Recreation Trail** is a combined bicycle and walking track that travels the entire length of the Niagara River from Lake Erie to Lake Ontario; for most of its 58km it runs parallel to the main road, the scenic **Niagara Parkway**. Downstream from the Falls, trail and parkway cut across the foot of Clifton Hill before continuing north to a series of viewpoints and attractions that culminate in Niagara-on-the-Lake.

White Water Walk

Daily: April to late June 10am–5pm; late June to early Sept 9am–8pm; early Sept to Oct 10am–5pm • $13 • Covered on Adventure Pass (see page 108) • ⓦ niagaraparks.com

Three kilometres on from Clifton Hill, **White Water Walk** comprises an elevator and then a tunnel, which leads to a boardwalk overlooking the Whirlpool Rapids, where the river seethes and fizzes as it makes an abrupt turn to the east.

Whirlpool Aero Car

Daily: early March to late June 10am–5pm; late June to early Sept 9am–8pm; early Sept to early Nov 10am–5pm • $15, ages 6–12 $9.75 • ⓦ niagaraparks.com

From the White Water Walk, it's 1km further along the parkway to the brightly painted **Whirlpool Aero Car**, a cable-car ride across the gorge that's as near as you'll come to emulating Blondin's tightrope antics.

Niagara Helicopters

3731 Victoria Ave • Daily 9am–sunset • $145, ages 3–12 $89 • ☎ 905 357 5672, ⓦ niagarahelicopters.com.

Take to the skies for the ultimate view of the Falls. Niagara Helicopters offer breathtaking twelve-minute excursions that follow the Niagara River, over Whirlpool Rapids and the Rainbow Bridge.

Niagara Glen Nature Reserve

Daily dawn to dusk, weather permitting • Free • ⓦ niagaraparks.com

Pushing on from the Niagara Helicopter landing strip, it's a short 2.5km hop to the **Niagara Glen Nature Reserve**, where paths lead down from the clifftop to the bottom of the gorge. It's a hot and sticky trek in the height of the summer, and strenuous at any time of the year, but rewarding for all that – here at least (and at last) you get a sense of what the region was like before the tourist hullabaloo.

Niagara Parks Botanical Gardens and the Butterfly Conservatory

Niagara Parks Botanical Gardens Daily dawn to dusk • Free • **Butterfly Conservatory** Daily: Jan to late June 10am–5pm; late June to early Sept 10am–7pm; early Sept to Oct 10am–5pm; Nov & Dec 10am–4pm • $15, children $9.75 • ⓦ niagaraparks.com

From Niagara Glen, it's about 800m downstream along the parkway to the Niagara Parks Commission's pride and joy, the immensely popular **Niagara Parks Botanical Gardens**, whose various themed gardens – including rose, bog and parterre – flank the huge, climate-controlled **Butterfly Conservatory**, which houses over two thousand exotic butterflies in a tropical rainforest setting.

Queenston Heights Park

From the Botanical Gardens, it's about 3km to **Queenston Heights Park**, which marks the original location of the Falls, before the force of the water – as it adjusts to the hundred-metre differential between lakes Erie and Ontario – eroded the river bed to its present point, 12km upstream. A pleasant expanse of greenery, the park's cardinal feature is a grandiloquent monument to **Sir Isaac Brock**, the Guernsey-born general who was killed here in the War of 1812, leading a head-on charge against the invading Americans.

Queenston

From beside Queenston Heights Park, the Niagara Parkway begins a curving descent down to the little village of **Queenston**, whose importance as a transit centre disappeared in 1829 when the Falls were bypassed by the Welland Canal, which runs a few kilometres to the west between lakes Erie and Ontario. Perhaps surprisingly,

Queenston has managed to avoid the tourist excesses nearby, its scattering of old timber houses trailing back from the river amid a dense canopy of mature trees.

Laura Secord Homestead

29 Queenston St at Partition • Guided tours: early May to early Sept daily 10am–5pm; early Sept to mid-Oct Wed–Sun 11am–5pm • $9.70 • ☎ 905 262 5841, ⓦ niagaraparks.com

In the centre of Queenston, the **Laura Secord Homestead** is a reconstruction of the substantial timber-frame house once owned by Massachusetts-born **Laura Ingersoll Secord**. It was from here, during the War of 1812, that Secord proved her dedication to the imperial interest by walking 30km through the woods to warn a British platoon of a surprise attack planned by the Americans. As a result, the British and their Aboriginal allies laid an ambush and captured over five hundred Americans at the Battle of Beaver Dams. Secord had good reason to loathe the Americans – during the war they looted her house, and her husband was badly wounded at the battle of Queenston Heights – but in the years following her dramatic escapade she kept a low profile, possibly fearing reprisals in what was then a wild frontier area. The tour provides an intriguing introduction to Secord's life and times, and the house itself is of elegant proportions with a full crop of period furnishings and fittings.

Upstream from Niagara Falls to Fort Erie

Old Fort Erie 350 Lakeshore Rd • Early May to Oct daily 10am–5pm • $12.50 • ☎ 905 871 0540, ⓦ niagaraparks.com

Heading upstream from Niagara Falls past the **Old Scow** (see page 107), both the **Niagara Parkway** and the **Niagara River Recreation Trail** stay close to the river, giving pleasant views over to the US. Nonetheless, this portion of the river is much less appealing than the stretch to the north of the Falls – especially so beyond humdrum **CHIPPAWA**, which is where America's Grand Island divides the river into two drowsy channels. Further upriver, just 26km from the falls, the Niagara Parkway peters out at **FORT ERIE**, a small industrial town that also marks the end of the Queen Elizabeth Way linking Toronto with the American city of Buffalo. The one noteworthy site here is **Old Fort Erie**, which overlooks Lake Erie from the mouth of the Niagara River just 2km south of town. The Americans razed the original fort in 1814, but it was painstakingly rebuilt in the 1930s as a Depression make-work scheme. The layout is similar to that of Fort George (see page 113) with a dry ditch, earth-and-stone ramparts and protruding bastions encircling a central compound, though here the outer gate is much more imposing, comprising a pair of huge double doors strengthened by iron studs. The central compound holds the usual spread of army buildings, including officers' quarters, barracks and a powder magazine, plus a modest museum that explores the fort's history.

ARRIVAL AND DEPARTURE

NIAGARA FALLS AND THE NIAGARA RIVER

Trains and buses **from Toronto** and many of southern Ontario's larger towns serve the town of Niagara Falls, 3km to the north of the watery action. From Toronto, both take a couple of hours and although the train is more scenic, delays on the return leg – on which the evening train originates in New York – can be a real pain.

By train The station (☎ 888 842 7245, ⓦ viarail.ca) is on Bridge St at Erie Ave, 3km north of the Falls.

Destinations Buffalo (2 daily; 40min); Toronto (2 daily; 2hr).

By bus Niagara Falls bus station is across the street from the train station (see above). The main carrier is Coach Canada

(☎ 800 461 7661, ⓦ coachcanada.com), with buses to Toronto (every 1–2hr; 1hr 40min–2hr 40min).

By car Parking anywhere near the Falls can be a major hassle in the summer. Try to arrive before 9.30am when there's usually space in the car park beside Table Rock House, metres from the waterfall; any later and you can expect a long queue. Another hassle can be crossing the international border over to the US; it only takes a few minutes to walk or drive across Rainbow Bridge from Canada into the US, but the return journey can take literally hours, depending on the officials at border control – be sure to bring your passport.

INFORMATION

Niagara Parks Welcome Centre Steer clear of the gaggle of privately run tourist centres that spring up here and there across Niagara Falls and head instead for the main Niagara Parks Welcome Centre (daily 9am–5pm; ⓦ niagaraparks.com), at the Table Rock complex right beside the Falls. Discount coupon books for the city's multitude of attractions can be found here and elsewhere.

Ontario Travel information centre 5355 Stanley Ave, at the intersection of Hwy-420, the main road to the Falls from the QEW Hwy (daily: 8.30am–5pm; June–Aug 8am–8pm; ☎ 905 358 3221, ⓦ ontariotravel.net); with a wide range of free literature on Ontario in general and Niagara Falls in particular.

GETTING AROUND

Incline Railway This handy Niagara Parks service transports visitors from the rear of Table Rock House up the bluff to Portage Rd for access to Fallsview blvd (daily every 15min; $2.50, all-day ticket $7). Check schedule for hours, but generally: mid-May to early Oct 9am–9:30pm; early Oct to mid-May Mon–Fri 9am–8:30pm, Sat & Sun 9amam–10:30pm.

Niagara Transit A limited range of town and suburban services is operated by Niagara Transit (☎ 905 356 1179, ⓦ niagarafalls.ca) from the main bus station, just opposite the train station on Bridge St at Erie Ave, 3km north of the Falls. Runs mid-May to early Oct, daily 9am–10pm, every 30min–1hr; $3, or all-day ticket $7.

WEGO Niagara Parks'WEGO service is a four-line shuttle bus system; the most convenient Green line (daily: early April to early May & Sept to mid-Oct 10am–6pm; early May to late June 9am–5pm; late June to Aug 9am–10pm; adult one-day pass $8, children 6–12 $5; adult two-day pass $12.50, children 6–12 $9) travels 30km along the Niagara Parkway between Queenston Heights Park, downriver (north) from the Falls – and a little more than halfway to Niagara-on-the-Lake – and the Rapids' View car park just to the south, pausing at all the major attractions in between. There is no public transport upriver beyond the Rapids' View car park. The Orange line connects (with a transfer) the end of the Green line with Fort George (25min) in Niagara-on-the-Lake (you must transfer in Queenston Heights.)

ACCOMMODATION

Niagara Falls is billed as the "Honeymoon Capital of the World", which means many of its **motels and hotels** have an odd mix of cheap, basic rooms and gaudy suites with heart-shaped bathtubs, waterbeds and the like. In summer, hotel and motel rooms fill up fast, so book ahead, but out of season it's a buyer's market so haggle away. The least expensive choices are mostly out along **Lundy's Lane**, a dispiriting motel strip that extends west of the Falls for several kilometres, but you're much better off spending a little more to stay on leafy **River Road**, where there are several good **B&Bs**. If you want a room with a decent **view of the Falls**, you'll be paying premium rates. The premier hotels on **Falls Avenue**, beside Clifton Hill, and **Fallsview Boulevard**, on top of the ridge directly above the Falls, offer the best views but you should always check the room first: descriptions can be fairly elastic and some rooms claiming to be in sight of the Falls require minor gymnastics for a glimpse.

HOTELS

Crowne Plaza Hotel 5685 Falls Ave ☎ 905 374 4447, ☎ 800 263 7135, ⓦ niagarafallscrowneplazahotel.com; map p.106. Just metres from the foot of Clifton Hill, this is one of Niagara's older and most attractive hotels, a tidy tower block with Art Deco flourishes whose upper storeys (and more expensive rooms) have splendid views over the American Falls. Marilyn Monroe stayed here in Room #801 while filming *Niagara* – and you can stay there too for no extra charge. **$110**

★ **Sheraton on the Falls** 5875 Falls Ave ☎ 905 374 4445, ☎ 888 229 9961, ⓦ sheratononthefalls.com; map p.106. Walloping skyrise, whose upper floors have wondrous views of the American Falls. Large and well-appointed rooms with supremely comfortable beds. **$159**

B&BS

Chestnut Inn B&B 4983 River Rd ☎ 905 374 7623, ⓦ chestnutinnbb.com; map p.106. Tastefully updated nineteenth-century house, surrounded by 100-year-old chestnut trees (hence the name), located a short drive from Clifton Hill along the river. Holds four ornately decorated, period-style en-suite rooms with fireplaces. Continental breakfast included. **$130**

Greystone Manor B&B 4939 River Rd ☎ 905 357 7373, ⓦ greystone-manor.ca; map p.106. There are four bright and cheerful guest rooms at this well-maintained B&B, which occupies a pleasant older house.Smashing, hot home-cooked breakfasts too, including everything from quiches to frittatas. **$110**

Park Place 4851 River Rd ☎ 905 358 0279, ⓦ park placeniagara.ca; map p.106. This elegant B&B occupies a handsome house in Niagara, an elaborate, nineteenth-century edifice of yellow-white brickwork with a fancy turret-tower and a gorgeous curving veranda. Has two superbly appointed suites kitted out in a modern version of period style, as well as a cosy carriage house. Full breakfast. Minimum two-night stay. **$205**

2

★ **Sterling Inn & Spa** 5195 Magdalen St ☎ 289 292 0000, ⊛ sterlingniagara.com; map p.106. This charming boutique hotel is a refreshing departure from the chain hotels that fill the area. Sterling Inn doesn't have the spot-on views of the Falls like the biggies, but it makes up for it with spacious rooms decked out with elegant dark wood and cosy fireplaces. The soothing spa offers a wide range of treatments, from honey-and-wine body wraps to facials. **$144**

HOSTEL

Niagara Falls Hostel 4549 Cataract Ave ☎ 905 357 0770, ⊛ hihostels.ca; map p.106. In a brightly painted building up near the train and bus station, this HI hostel has self-catering facilities, a laundry, free wi-fi, lounge, free breakfast, and even a backyard with fire pit. April–Dec. Dorms **$31**, non-members **$36**; doubles **$78** (same price for members and non-members)

EATING

The restaurant scene in Niagara Falls is hardly pulsating, with cheap chains and fast-food joints ruling the local roost, though there are a few breaks in the gastronomic gloom.

Elements on the Falls 6650 Niagara Parkway ☎ 905 354 3631, ⊛ niagaraparks.com; map p.106. This room, with a fantastic vantage point across from Horseshoe Falls, is one of five dining venues operated by Niagara Parks. It focuses on local produce and purveyors. Lunch (average $22) can amount to a sandwich, salad or veggie stir-fry; at night, try veal tenderloin, lamb mixed grill or rainbow trout. (about $39). Great selection of cool cocktails and Niagara-sourced wines. Generally open year-round, but check website for hours. Daily 11.30am–dusk.

Queen Victoria Place Restaurant 6345 Niagara Parkway ☎ 905 356 2217, ⊛ niagaraparks.com; map p.106. This inviting restaurant offers elevated comfort food, including maple-brined pork burgers, sandwiches and soups. Mains ($28–30). The terrace is a great option for testing out the craft beer and wine tasting flights. Check the website, as the opening hours are variable. May to mid-Oct daily 11.30am–dusk.

Remington's of Niagara 5657 Victoria Ave ☎ 905 356

4410, ⊛ remingtonsofniagara.com; map p.106. Big and brassy – with wood panelling and Wild West statuettes – there's nothing subtle about this restaurant, where the waiters chip in with a bit of impromptu karaoke, but there's no gainsaying the quality of the steaks, which start at $25. Near the top of Clifton Hill. Daily 4–10pm.

Taps on Queen Brewhouse & Grill 4680 Queen St ☎ 289 477 1010, ⊛ tapsbeer.ca; map p.106. Among the assorted cafés and restaurants on Queen St near the train station, this is one of the most distinctive, selling an excellent range of locally manufactured brews, as well as hearty bar food, like pulled pork and cheddar chili Live music Tues and Sat. Daily noon–1am.

Weinkeller 5633 Victoria Ave ☎ 289 296 8000, ⊛ weinkeller.ca; map p.106. This warmly inviting, brick-walled restaurant offers a trio of pleasures – craft wines, local cuisine and excellent service. Start off with the charcuterie board, and tuck into generous main dishes like grilled pork loin with maple mustard or chicken with woodland mushrooms. Prix-fixe menu, from $55 for three courses. Sun–Thurs 5pm–midnight, Fri–Sat 5pm–1am.

Niagara-on-the-Lake

Boasting elegant clapboard houses and verdant, mature gardens, all spread along tree-lined streets, **NIAGARA-ON-THE-LAKE**, 26km downstream from the Falls, is one of Ontario's most charming little towns, much of it dating from the early nineteenth century. The town was originally known as Newark and became the first capital of Upper Canada in 1792, but four years later it lost this distinction to York (Toronto) because it was deemed too close to the American frontier, and therefore vulnerable to attack. The US army did, in fact, cross the river in 1813, destroying the town, but it was quickly rebuilt and renamed. Since then, it has managed to avoid all but the most sympathetic of modifications, maintaining an impressive level of historic appeal.

Niagara-on-the-Lake attracts too many day-trippers for its own good, but the crowds stick religiously to the souvenir and knick-knack shops that line the main street, and they mostly melt away by 5 or 6pm. The town is also popular as the location of one of Canada's most acclaimed theatre festivals, the **Shaw Festival**, which celebrates the works of George Bernard Shaw with performances from April to late October, and it is also surrounded by **wineries**, many of which welcome visitors (see page 116).

Queen Street and around

It's the general flavour of Niagara-on-the-Lake that appeals, rather than any specific sight, but **Queen Street**, the main drag, does hold a pretty **clock tower** and the **Niagara**

Apothecary Museum (mid-May–June noon–6pm, July–Aug daily 11am–6pm; Sept to mid-Oct Sat & Sun noon–6pm; free; ☎905 468 3845, ⓦocp.info), which is worth a peep for its beautifully carved walnut and butternut cabinets, crystal gasoliers and porcelain jars. Nearby, the town's finest building is the church of **St Andrews**, at Simcoe and Gage streets, a splendid illustration of the Greek Revival style dating to the 1830s. The church has a well-proportioned portico and the interior retains the original high pulpit and box pews. Also of interest is the fenced **burial plot** behind **Simcoe Park**, on Byron Street midway between King and Wellington streets, which holds the earthly remains of 25 Polish soldiers who died here during the great influenza epidemic of 1918–19.

Niagara Historical Museum

43 Castlereagh St, at Davy • Daily: May–Oct 10am–5pm; Nov–April 1–5pm • $5 • ☎ 905 468 3912, ⓦ niagarahistorical.museum

The lovingly maintained **Niagara Historical Museum** holds an enjoyable potpourri of military artefacts as well as an entertaining selection of old photographs, faded sepias featuring local bigwigs and early settlers at work and play. One of the photos is of a very grumpy looking Prince of Wales – the future George V – taken outside a local hotel with his retinue in 1901: a gas leak inside the hotel forced the royals to sit outside on the veranda till 3am the night before; hence the bad mood. The museum also offers a lively programme of temporary exhibitions on all things local.

Fort George

51 Queen's Parade, 700m southeast of the centre • May–Oct daily 10am–5pm; April & Nov Sat & Sun 10am–5pm • $11.70 • ☎ 905 468 6621, ⓦ pc.gc.ca

The British built **Fort George** as one of a line of stockades that they slung across the Great Lakes to protect Canada from the US. For the redcoats, it was a popular posting – but only because the US was so near: indeed so many of the fort's early soldiers hightailed it off to the States (where soldiers were better paid) that the British were

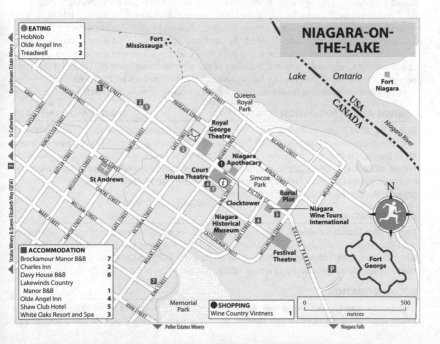

2

THE STRANGE TALE OF THE POLES IN NIAGARA-ON-THE-LAKE

In the later stages of World War I, over twenty thousand **Polish soldiers** mustered in the US to form a Polish brigade. It was a delicate situation, as the Allies needed the soldiers but the Poles were committed to the creation of an independent Poland at a time when their country was ruled by Russia, an ally of the US. In any event, policy differences with the US government prompted the Poles to move over the border to Niagara-on-the-Lake, where they established a base camp. Paid and equipped by France, the Poles were trained by Canadian officers and then shipped off in batches to fight on the Western front, thereby deferring their attempts to create an independent Poland. At the end of the war, with the Tsar gone and the Bolsheviks in control of Russia, the Polish brigade – or "Blue Army" as it was called, from the colour of their uniform – crossed Germany to return to their homeland, where they played a key role in the foundation of an independent Poland. The graves of the 25 Polish soldiers in Niagara-on-the-Lake (see page 112) recall these historical complexities, and a small shrine has been erected in their honour.

obliged to outfit it with a troop of married men approaching retirement, who were unlikely to forfeit their pensions by deserting. If they did try and were caught, they were branded on the chest with the letter "D" (for "Deserter"), and were either lashed, transported to a penal colony, or shot. The original Fort George was destroyed during the War of 1812, but the site was thoroughly excavated and the fort reconstructed in splendid style in the 1930s. There are ninety-minute, lantern-light **ghost tours** of the fort – good fun with or without an apparition (May, June & Sept Sun 8.30pm; July & Aug Tues, Thurs & Sun 8.30pm, Sept Sun 7:30pm; $20; ☎905 468 6621, ⏹niagaraghosts. com). Tours begin at the car park in front of the fort; tickets can be purchased either in advance at the fort's gift shop, or from the guide thirty minutes before the start.

The fort

Today's palisaded **compound**, complete with its protective bastions, holds about a dozen buildings, among them the officers' quarters and two log **blockhouses**, which doubled as soldiers' barracks. The difference between the quarters and the barracks is striking. The former are comparatively spacious and were once furnished with fancy knick-knacks, while the latter housed the men and some of their wives in the meanest of conditions. A tunnel links the main part of the fort with one of the exterior bastions, called **ravelins**. The only original building is the **powder magazine** of 1796, its interior equipped with wood and copper fittings to reduce the chances of an accidental explosion; as an added precaution, the soldiers working here went barefoot.

ARRIVAL AND INFORMATION
NIAGARA-ON-THE-LAKE

By bus The WEGO Niagara-on-the-Lake Shuttle ($6 one way) connects with the Green line to Niagara Falls (see page 111) at Queenston Heights.

Tourist office Niagara-on-the-Lake tourist office is in the basement of the Court House Theatre, 26 Queen Street (daily: mid-May to mid-Oct 10am–7.30pm; mid-Oct to mid-May 10am–5pm; ☎905 468 1950, ⏹niagaraonthelake. com). They issue free town maps and operate a free room reservation service, which can be a great help in the summer when the town's hotels and B&Bs – of which there are dozens – get very busy.

GETTING AROUND

Niagara Wine Tours International 92 Picton St ☎905 468 1300, ☎800 680 7006, ⏹niagaraworldwinetours. com. It only takes a few minutes to stroll from one end of Niagara-on-the-Lake to the other, but to venture further afield – especially to the Falls – you might consider renting a bicycle here. They have several types to choose from, starting at $30/day, $20/half-day.

ACCOMMODATION

Niagara-on-the-Lake has over one hundred **B&Bs** and **hotels**, with a few dotted round the leafy streets of the centre and the majority on the outskirts of town. The most distinctive occupy lovely old villas dating from the early nineteenth century, but these tend to be expensive – reckon on $150–$175 per double room per night. Reservations are essential throughout the summer, when the tourist office's free room reservation service is most valuable.

Brockamour Manor B&B 433 King St, at Mary ☎ 905 468 5527, ⓦ brockamour.com; map p.113. This appealing B&B has six en-suite guest rooms ranging from the commodious Sir Brock's Bedchamber to the two smaller rooms in the old servants' quarters. With its high gables and wide porch, the house itself is a splendid affair dating from 1812 and it's surrounded by an attractive wooded garden. **$189**

★ **Charles Inn** 209 Queen St ☎ 905 468 4588, ☎ 866 556 8883, ⓦ niagarasfinest.com/properties/charleshotel; map p.113. This charming old inn, dating from the 1830s, has all sorts of idiosyncratic features, from lovely verandas to old cast-iron fireplaces. There are twelve guest rooms, each decorated in a fetching version of period style, and the beds are super-comfortable. Unlike many of its rivals, the inn has not been overly spruced up, which gives it real character – but at a price. **$245**

Davy House B&B 230 Davy St ☎ 905 468 5307, ☎ 888 314 9046, ⓦ davyhouse.com; map p.113. Cosy two-storey clapboard house with a particularly pleasant veranda. Each of the bedrooms is decorated in a plush, country-house version of retro style, which works very well indeed. Within easy strolling distance of the town centre. **$185**

Lakewinds Country Manor B&B 328 Queen St, at Dorchester ☎ 905 468 1888, ☎ 866 338 1888, ⓦ lakewinds. ca; map p.113. Expansive and lavishly modernized 1880s Victorian mansion with six a/c guest rooms and suites, each of which is decorated in a particular style – Florentine or Singaporean, for example. The house is surrounded by a well-kept garden with an outdoor heated pool. **$195**

Olde Angel Inn 224 Regent St, off Queen ☎ 905 468 3411, ⓦ angel-inn.com; map p.113. Dating from the 1820s, this is the oldest inn in town, an infinitely cosy little place with a handful of equally cosy guest rooms and suites, one of which is equipped with an "Irish fertility bed" – you have been warned. Substantial discounts in winter (Nov–April). **$145**

Shaw Club Hotel 92 Picton St ☎ 905 468 5711, ☎ 800 511 7070, ⓦ niagarasfinest.com; map p.113. This hotel, with a luxe spa attached, may be owned by the same people who run the *Charles Inn* (see opposite) but the two are chalk and cheese. The *Shaw* is a sharply decorated, ultramodern place, from the chic entrance to the minimally designed guest rooms – with plasma-screen TVs and feather-top beds – and beyond; the nicest rooms have balconies. **$250**

White Oaks Resort and Spa 253 Taylor Rd, Niagara-on-the-Lake ☎ 800 263 5766, ⓦ whiteoaksresort. com; map p.113. Relax at this stylish resort, which has amenity-rich rooms and a blissful spa, featuring a range of pampering services from facials to body wraps. **$169**

EATING

By sheer weight of numbers, the day-trippers set the gastronomic tone in Niagara-on-the-Lake, but nonetheless one or two **cafés** and **restaurants** have survived the flood to offer tasty meals and snacks.

HobNob 209 Queen St ☎ 905 468 4588, ☎ 866 556 8883, ⓦ niagarasfinest.com/properties/hobnob; map p.113. This smart and mildly formal restaurant, in one of the ground-floor rooms of the *Charles Inn* (see above), has a carefully crafted menu: try the pork belly and scallop, the Ontario rack of lamb or the vegetarian beet and mushroom chili. Mains average $32. Reservations recommended. Daily noon–10pm.

★ **Olde Angel Inn** 224 Regent St ☎ 905 468 3411, ⓦ angel-inn.com; map p.113. With its low-beamed

ceilings and flagstone floors, this is the town's most atmospheric pub, serving a first-rate range of draught imported and domestic beers, and playing live music Wed–Sat. Also offers filling and very affordable bar food – Guinness steak-and-kidney pies are $17 – and has an à la carte restaurant at the back (mains $17–30). Daily 11am–1am.

Treadwell 114 Queen St ☎ 905 934 9797, ⓦ treadwell cuisine.com; map p.113. Feast on farm-to-fork cuisine, from roasted red pepper soup with lime yogurt sorbet to pork belly with smoked apple to halibut with smoked Ontario heirloom risotto. The local wines are equally excellent. Mon–Sat 11am–2.15pm & 5pm– 11pm, Sun 11.30am–2.15pm & 5pm– 11pm.

THE SHAW FESTIVAL

Showcasing the work of one of Canada's largest repertory theatre companies, the **Shaw Festival** is the only one of its kind devoted to the works of **George Bernard Shaw** and his contemporaries – and a rich repertoire it is too. The festival runs from April to late October and performances are held in three Niagara-on-the-Lake theatres. The largest is the **Festival Theatre**, a modern structure seating 850, at 10 Queen's Parade; the other two, both holding around 300, are the **Court House**, a nineteenth-century stone building at 26 Queen St, and the **Royal George**, with its fancy Edwardian interior, at 85 Queen St. **Ticket prices** for the best seats at prime weekend performances hit $125, but most seats go for $40–75. The box office for all three theatres is: ☎ 800 511 7429, ⓦ shawfest.com.

2

ONTARIO WINES

Until the 1980s, **Canadian wine** was something of a joke. The industry's most popular product was a sticky, fizzy concoction called "Baby Duck", and other varieties were commonly called "block-and-tackle" wines, after a widely reported witticism of a member of the Ontario legislature: "If you drink a bottle and walk a block, you can tackle anyone." This sorry state of affairs was transformed by the **Vintners Quality Alliance** (VQA; ⓦ vqaontario.ca), who have, since 1989, come to exercise tight control over wine production in Ontario, which produces around eighty percent of Canadian wine. The VQA's appellation system distinguishes between – and supervises the quality control of – two broad types of wine: those carrying the **Provincial Designation** on their labels must be made from one hundred percent Ontario-grown grapes from an approved list of European grape varieties and selected hybrids; those bearing the **Geographic Designation** (eg Niagara Peninsula, Pelee Island) can only use *Vitis vinifera*, the classic European grape varieties, such as Riesling, Chardonnay and Cabernet Sauvignon. As you might expect from a developing wine area, the results are rather inconsistent, but the **Rieslings** have a refreshingly crisp, almost tart flavour with a mellow, warming aftertaste – and are perhaps the best of the present range, white or red.

More than twenty **wineries** are clustered in the vicinity of **Niagara-on-the-Lake**. Most of them have showrooms, others offer guided tours and just about all of them have tastings. The town's tourist office carries a full list with opening times and prices. Here are a few options.

VINEYARDS AND SHOPS

Konzelmann Estate Winery 1096 Lakeshore Rd ⓣ 905 935 2866, ⓦ konzelmann.ca. This lush lakefront winery, whose origins are in the German town of Uhlbach, produces top-notch wines – including superb ice wines – and offers an array of informative tours ($10) and tastings ($15). May–Oct daily 10am–6pm, Nov–April Mon–Fri 11am–5pm, Sat–Sun 10am–6pm.

Peller Estates Winery 290 John St East, 2.5km from Queen St ⓣ 905 468 4678, ⓣ 888 673 5537, ⓦ peller. com. With a vineyard and a large modern showroom on the edge of town, Peller has produced a clutch of much-praised vintages. They also do a good line in one of Canada's specialities, ice wine, a sweet dessert wine made from grapes that are left on the vine until winter, then hand-picked at night while frozen. The picking and

the crushing of the frozen grapes is a time-consuming business and this is reflected in the price – from about $50 per 375ml bottle. Tour and samples $15. June–Aug Mon–Thurs 10am–9pm, Fri–Sun 10am–10pm, Oct–May Sun–Thurs 10am–7pm, Fri–Sat 10am–9pm.

Stratus Winery 2059 Niagara Stone Rd, just southwest of town ⓣ 905 468 1806, ⓦ stratuswines. com. Handily located not far from the centre of Niagara-on-the-Lake, Stratus has pioneered a more environmentally friendly approach to wine production. Tours and guided tasting $25. Daily 11am–5pm.

Wine Country Vintners 27 Queen St ⓣ 905 468 1881, ⓦ waynegretzkyestates.com; map p.113. The best wine shop in town, it carries a variety of Peller-associated wines and offers shuttles to the Peller winery as well. Mon–Sat 10am–8pm, Sun 11am–6pm.

Brantford

BRANTFORD, a quick 40km west of Hamilton on Hwy-403, takes its name from **Joseph Brant**, an Iroquois chieftain who was one of the most intriguing figures of colonial Canada (see page 117). Brant helped the British during the American War of Independence and, after their defeat, he and his followers were obliged to make a hasty exit from New York State before the Americans could take their revenge. The British stayed loyal to their ally (just about) and in 1784 Brant was ceded a large tract of land beside the Grand River on the site of what is today Brantford. European settlers reached the area in numbers in the 1850s, and after that Brantford developed as a manufacturing centre churning out agricultural equipment by the wagonload. By the 1980s, however, the town was in decline as many of its factories and foundries went bust or relocated. Brantford still bears the scars of this deindustrialization, but a concerted effort has been made to breathe new life into the centre, and for the most part this has been a success, with a batch of leisure facilities and shopping malls. For Canadians, Brantford is most famous as the home town of **Wayne Gretzky**, probably the greatest ice-hockey player of all time; for everyone else, the town is best known as being the one-time home of the inventor of the telephone, **Alexander Graham Bell**.

Harmony Square

Nicely refreshed, Brantford's **town centre** is at its most attractive on and around **Harmony Square**, an airy plaza with flower beds and fountains adjoining one of the main drags, Colborne Street. The square is also just a few metres from several splendid Victorian buildings, with the grand Neoclassical **Post Office** at 58 Dalhousie St leading the municipal charge.

Woodland Cultural Centre

184 Mohawk St, 2km south of the centre • Mon–Fri 9am–4pm, Sat & Sun 10am–5pm (late Dec to late May closed Sun) • $7, no cards • ☎ 519 759 2650, ⓦ woodland-centre.on.ca

Acting as a sort of historical primer, the **Woodland Cultural Centre** is one of the most comprehensive First Nations' museums in Ontario. A series of displays concentrates on the Six Nations of the Grand River, **Mohawks** who started out in New York State as members of the Iroquois League before retreating north at the end of the American War of Independence. The collection is displayed chronologically, beginning with an assortment of trade goods, plus several wampum belts recording treaties between the British and the Mohawks. There's also a portrait of Joseph Brant (see box below) in Aboriginal gear and an incisive section on racist representations of Native Americans in popular culture from the nineteenth century onwards. The centre also offers a programme of temporary exhibitions with a focus on contemporary Mohawk artists.

TROUBLE IN THE COLONIES – THE LIFE AND TIMES OF JOSEPH BRANT

Born in modern-day Ohio as Thayendanega, **Joseph Brant** (1742–1807) was a **Mohawk** leader whose stepfather had close ties with the British. This connection was reinforced when Joseph's sister, **Molly**, married the British Superintendent for Indian Affairs, William Johnson, who subsequently sponsored Brant's college education. Brant learnt to read and write English, took to wearing European clothes and even became an Anglican and Freemason, but he had another life too, odd-jobbing as a member of Mohawk war parties. By the mid-1760s, Brant had established himself as a farmer in New York State and was so well regarded by the British that, in 1776, they took him to London, where he was presented to King George III and became something of a celebrity, the subject of a string of official portraits. In each of them, Brant is shown in a mix of European and Aboriginal gear – typically, he carries a tomahawk and has a Mohawk hairdo, but wears a dress coat with a sash – an apt reflection of his twin loyalties. Duly impressed by the power and wealth of the imperial capital, Brant remained loyal to the British during the **American War of Independence**, his repeated, large-scale raids – and alleged savagery – earning him the soubriquet "**Monster Brant**" among the colonials.

After the war, when neither the British nor the Americans felt militarily secure, both sides tried to woo Brant, who became adept at playing them off against each other; despite his blood-curdling reputation, he was even invited to Philadelphia to meet President Washington in 1792. From the British, Brant secured a sizeable chunk of land beside the **Grand River** in modern-day Brantford, where his followers moved in 1784, but back in the US he was unable to protect his Aboriginal allies from further American encroachment. Sensing failure, Brant withdrew to Burlington, near Hamilton, to live the life of a gentleman farmer (complete with servants and slaves) and it was here he died. In 1850, Mohawks carried Brant's **coffin** the 55km from Burlington to Brantford's Royal Chapel of the Mohawks (see page 118).

2

Her Majesty's Royal Chapel of the Mohawks

301 Mohawk St • Mid-May to mid-Oct Tues–Sun 10am–3pm; other times by appointment • $7, guided tours $10 • ☎ 519 756 0240,
Ⓦ mohawkchapel.ca

From the Woodland Centre, it's a further 700m along Mohawk Street to **Her Majesty's Royal Chapel of the Mohawks**, a spindly clapboard structure in a lovely, lightly wooded location with the Grand River snaking along behind. Dating back to 1785, the church was built both to celebrate the Mohawk–British alliance and to replace the original chapel in New York, which the Mohawks were forced to abandon when they moved north. They did, however, retrieve the inscribed **plaques** that now stand behind the altar, religious inscriptions of the Lord's Prayer and the Creed written in a phonetic (and technically inaccurate) version of Iroquois. The stained glass **windows** depicting events in the history of the Six Nations were added in the 1950s. Beside the church is the large tomb-table of Joseph Brant, though his coffin was only moved here (from Burlington) in 1850.

The Bell Homestead

94 Tutela Heights Rd, N3T 1A1 • Tues–Sun 9.30am–4.30pm • $7 • ☎ 519 756 6220, Ⓦ bellhomestead.ca • The Bell Homestead is hard to find: take Colborne St West from the town centre; this leads into Mount Pleasant St and then Mount Pleasant Rd, where you should watch for the sign; no public transport

Brantford's most popular attraction, the **Bell Homestead National Historic Site** is located about 4km south of the centre, among the low wooded hills overlooking the Grand River. Soon after his arrival from Edinburgh in 1870, **Alexander Graham Bell** took a job as a teacher of the deaf, motivated by his mother's loss of hearing and, in his efforts to discover a way to reproduce sounds visibly, he stumbled across the potential of transmitting sound along an electrified wire. The consequence was the first long-distance call, made in 1876 from Brantford to the neighbouring village of Paris. The Bell Homestead consists of two simple, clapboard buildings. The first, moved to this site from downtown in 1969, housed Canada's original Bell company office

---

THE MENNONITES OF KITCHENER–WATERLOO AND ST JACOBS

The twin industrial cities of **Kitchener** and **Waterloo** hog a slab of flatland to the west of the Grand River. They have a distinctive pedigree, as the first white settlers to arrive in the area in numbers were the **Mennonites**, a tightly knit Protestant sect who migrated here in the 1790s from the US, where their pacifist beliefs had incurred the wrath of their neighbours during the American Revolution. Over the years, the Mennonites gradually drifted out of the twin cities and now own much of the farmland immediately to the north. They are unmistakeable, with the men wearing traditional black suits and broad-brimmed hats, or deep-blue shirts and braces, the women ankle-length dresses and matching bonnets; many navigate the roads in black, horse-drawn buggies. Despite appearances, however, the Ontario Mennonites are far from a homogeneous sect – over twenty different groups are affiliated to the **Mennonite Central Committee (MCC)**. For more information, check the website: Ⓦ mcccanada.ca. They all share certain religious beliefs reflecting their Anabaptist origins – the sole validity of adult baptism being crucial – but precise practices and dress codes vary from group to group; for instance, members of the traditional wing of the Mennonite movement, sometimes called **Amish**, own property communally and shun all modern machinery. To explain their history and faith, the MCC runs a small but intriguing interpretation centre, **The Mennonite Story**, at 1406 King St North (Jan–March Sat 11am–4.30pm & Sun 2–4.30pm; April–Dec Mon–Sat 11am–5pm & Sun 1.30–5pm; donation expected of $5; ☎ 519 664 3518, Ⓦ stjacobs.com) in the village of **St Jacobs**, just north of Waterloo via Hwy-85. Also in St Jacobs, along the short main street, are several **Mennonite stores** selling home-made farm produce – the maple syrup is simply magnificent. Mennonite traders are also prominent at the much-lauded **Farmers' Market**, back in the centre of Kitchener on King Street East (Sat 7am–2pm; ☎ 519 741 2287, Ⓦ kitchenermarket.ca). The upper level features vendors selling international cuisine (Tues–Fri 8am–3pm, Sat 7am–2pm).

2

KITCHENER'S OKTOBERFEST

In the early nineteenth century, German farmers followed the trail blazed by the Mennonites, settling here in Kitchener by the hundreds. The Mennonites had called their settlement **Sand Hills**, but the new arrivals renamed the place **Berlin** in 1826, changing it yet again during World War I to "Kitchener" (after the British field marshal) at a time when it was prudent to prove their patriotism. Today around sixty percent of Kitchener's inhabitants are descendants of German immigrants, a heritage celebrated every year during **Oktoberfest** (ⓦoktoberfest. ca; admission to Oktoberfest Haus $8), nine days of alcoholic stupefaction when even the most reticent of men can be seen wandering the streets in Lederhosen.

and features a series of modest displays on the history of the telephone. The second, the cosy family home, fronts a second small exhibition area devoted to Bell's life and research.

ARRIVAL AND INFORMATION   BRANTFORD

There are **buses** and **trains** to Brantford from several neighbouring cities, but to see the town's key sights you'll need a car. The town centre fans out from Dalhousie and Colborne streets, which run parallel to each other (east/west) for about 1.5km.

By train The VIA train station is a 10min walk north of Dalhousie – on Wadsworth St, just off Market St.

Destinations London (5 daily; 1hr); Toronto (5 daily; 1hr 10min); Windsor (3–4 daily; 3hr).

By bus Buses to Brantford pull in on the west side of the centre, one block north of Dalhousie at Darling and Market streets.

Destinations London (3 daily; 1hr 40min); Niagara Falls (3 daily; average 6hr with one change); Toronto (5 daily; 1hr 50min).

Brantford Visitor Centre On Wayne Gretzky Parkway, to the north of the centre – just off (and signposted from) Hwy-403 (mid-May to Sept Mon–Fri 9am–6pm, Sat 10am–6pm, Sun 10am–5pm; Oct to mid-May Mon–Fri 9am–5pm, Sat 10am–4pm; ☎519 751 9900, ☎800 265 6299, ⓦdiscoverbrantford.com). Among much else, they supply free city maps, which are extremely useful, as Brantford can be difficult to negotiate.

ACCOMMODATION AND EATING

Al Dente 250 King George Rd ☎519 753 4303, ⓦaldentebrantford.ca. Good, long-established Italian dining spot with a few more French-skewing starter options on the menu, along with steak and burgers. Pasta mains – try the shrimp with creamy garlic tossed in linguini – and medium pizzas $17–19. They also offer local brewery and winery tours combined with a dinner back at the restaurant. Daily 4–10pm, plus Thurs & Fri 11.30am–2.30pm.

Best Western Brant Park Inn 19 Holiday Drive ☎519 753 8651, ⓦbestwesternbrantford.com. The pick of Brantford's handful of chain hotels is this large, modern affair to the north of the centre just off Wayne Gretzky Parkway, with a good range of facilities, including an indoor pool, sauna and fitness centre. <u>$145</u>

★ **Café Troy** 2190 Highway 5 W ☎519 647 2117, ⓦdonnzver.com. Feast on homemade local cuisine at this delightful restaurant that adjoins the well-known Donn Zver Pottery Studio. A dinner for two ($60) includes fresh bread, soup or salad and main dishes like chicken cacciatore or prime rib. Tues–Thurs & Sun 11.30–3pm, Fri–Sat 11.30–3pm & 5–8pm.

Coffee Culture 75 Dalhousie St, on Harmony Square ☎519 304 5772, ⓦcoffeeculturecafe.com. Spick-and-span café with tasty panini, wraps, salads and pastries. One of a large Ontario-centric chain. Mon–Sun 7am–10pm.

ENTERTAINMENT

Sanderson Centre for the Performing Arts 88 Dalhousie St ☎519 752 9910, ☎800 265 0710, ⓦsandersoncentre.ca. This is Brantford's leading performance arts venue and it occupies a creatively recycled vaudeville and silent-movie house that dates back to 1919. Offers a varied programme of entertainment: theatre performances, comedy nights and concerts by Canadian heroes or the Brantford Symphony Orchestra.

Stratford

STRATFORD, some 150km west of Toronto, is a likeable country town of thirty thousand people, which rises head and shoulders above its neighbours as the host of the

2

THE STRATFORD FESTIVAL

Each year, North America's largest classical repertory company puts on the **Stratford Festival** (☎519 273 1600, ☎800 567 1600, ⓦstratfordfestival.ca), featuring two of Shakespeare's tragedies and one of his comedies; this programme is augmented by other classical staples – Molière, Chekhov, Jonson and so forth – as well as by the best of modern and musical theatre. The festival also hosts a lecture series, various tours (of backstage and a costume warehouse, for example), music concerts, an author reading series and meet-and-greet sessions with the actors. The festival runs from mid-April to late October and there are performances in four downtown theatres – the Festival, the Tom Patterson, the Avon and the Studio. Regular **tickets** cost between $50 and $90 depending on the performance and seat category, though there are all sorts of discount deals for students, seniors, same-day performances and previews; many plays are sold out months in advance. Call or check the website to book.

Stratford Festival (see box), originating in 1953 and now one of the most prestigious theatrical occasions in North America, attracting no fewer than half a million visitors every year. It only takes an hour or so to work out what is where in Stratford, beginning with the town's **downtown** core, on and around the junction of Ontario and Downie streets. Here a handsome set of nineteenth-century brick facades reaches an idiosyncratic hiatus in the grandiose **city hall**, a brown-brick fiesta of cupolas, towers and limestone trimmings. The town is also bisected by the meandering **Avon River**, whose leafy banks are lined with immaculately maintained footpaths and overlooked by the largest of the town's four theatres, the **Festival Theatre**.

ARRIVAL AND INFORMATION   STRATFORD

By train From Stratford's station, on Shakespeare Street, it's a dull 15min stroll north via Downie St to the town's main crossroads, where Downie, Ontario and Erie streets meet. Alternatively take a taxi from outside the station building.
Destinations (VIA Rail) Kitchener (2–3 daily; 35min); London (2 daily; 1hr 10min); Toronto (2 daily; 2hr 10min).

Information Stratford has a seasonal visitor information centre beside the River Avon, on York St, metres from the main town crossroads (June–Sept daily 10am–6pm; ☎519 271 5140, ☎800 561 7926, ⓦvisitstratford.ca). There's also an all-year visitor information centre downtown at 47 Downie St (Mon–Fri 9am–5pm, Sat 10am–5pm; June–Dec also Sun 10am–4pm). Both offices issue free town maps and a comprehensive visitors' guide.

ACCOMMODATION

Stratford has a small army of **B&Bs** plus around a dozen **hotels** and **motels**, but vacant rooms can still be hard to find during the festival's busiest weekends, when the tourist office's **accommodation booking service** is particularly useful.
Acrylic Dreams B&B 66 Bay St ☎519 271 7874, ⓦacrylicdreams.com. Handily located a 10min walk from the main crossroads, this cottage-style timber house, which dates from the 1870s, has four intimate guest rooms decorated in pastel browns and creams. The owners serve up home-made breakfasts with the vegetarian in mind and also offer chair massages and reflexology sessions. $155
Blue Spruce B&B 297 Erie St ☎519 271 0068, ⓦthe-blue-spruce.com. Welcoming B&B in a handsome old house south of the main crossroads. Each of the three guest

rooms has been carefully decorated in an attractive vintage style and the beds are super-comfortable. $185
The Bruce Hotel 89 Parkview Dr ☎519 508 7100, ⓦthebruce.ca. Welcoming and well-maintained, this elegant hotel sits in the centre of town near the Festival Theatre. The hotel hosts an array of fun events, including wine tastings, afternoon tea and dinners like "Coast to Coast", which features cuisine from across Canada. $210
Stone Maiden Inn 123 Church St ☎519 271 7129, ⓦstonemaideninn.com. Immaculately maintained 1873 Victorian house with a variety of guest rooms of varying size and luxury, though all have period trimmings. Complimentary coffee and tea. Good location too, a short walk south of the main crossroads. $159

EATING AND DRINKING

Stratford's festival-goers support a hatful of excellent **cafés** and **restaurants** and several of the best are just a stone's

throw from the town's main crossroads, at the junction of Downie, Ontario and Erie streets.

Balzac's Coffee Roastery 149 Ontario St ☎ 519 273 7909, ⓦ balzacscoffee.com. This branch, the original of a small Ontario chain, sells a first-rate range of fair-trade coffees plus pastries and cakes. Prides itself on the quality of its coffee beans. Mon–Fri 6.30am–8pm, Sat–Sun 7am–8pm.

Fellini's 107 Ontario St ☎ 519 271 3333, ⓦ fellinis stratford.com. This large Italian/Mediterranean restaurant with a kitsch decor offers a competent range of pizzas and pasta dishes with main courses averaging $18–22. Tues–Fri 11.30am–3pm & 4.30–8pm, Sat 11.30–8pm,

Sun 11.30am–7pm.

Sirkel Foods 40 Wellington St ☎ 519 273 7084, ⓦ sirklefoodstratford.com. Kick off the morning at this bustling café-restaurant across from City Hall, which serves the heartiest breakfasts in town. Try the Eggs Florentine or the lentil pancakes with salmon and sour cream. The sandwiches and salads are equally tasty, including the chicken pesto sandwich and the spinach salad with poached pears and blue cheese. Breakfast $6–9, sandwiches and salads $7–13. Daily 8am–3pm.

London

The citizens of **LONDON**, 60km southwest of Stratford, are proud of their clean streets, efficient transport system and neat suburbs, but to the outsider the main attractions of this university town are the leafiness of the centre and its location – slap bang in the heart of rural, agricultural Ontario. The town owes its existence to a one-time governor of Upper Canada, **John Graves Simcoe**, who arrived in 1792 determined to develop the wilderness far to the west of Lake Ontario. Because of its river connections, he chose the

ACCOMMODATION

Idlewyld Inn	3
Hotel Metro	2
Woodfield Bed & Breakfast	1

EATING

Budapest	4
The Church Key	2
David's Bistro	3
Garlic's of London	1
Idlewyld Inn	4

2

site of London as his new colonial capital and promptly renamed its river the Thames. Simcoe's headlong approach to his new job irritated his superior, Governor Dorchester, who vetoed his choice with the wry comment "I presume the approach to be by hot-air balloon." When York (present-day Toronto) was selected as the capital instead, Simcoe's chosen site lay empty until 1826, yet by the 1880s London was firmly established as the economic and administrative centre of a prosperous farming area. With a population of some 350,000, it remains so today – despite the lightning: London has more lightning strikes than anywhere else in Canada, running at thirty to forty per year.

Museum London

421 Ridout St North • Tues–Sun 11am–5pm, Thurs till 9pm; Sept–May Tues–Sun noon–5pm, Thurs till 9pm • Free tours Sun at 2pm • Donation expected • ☎ 519 661 0333, ⓦ museumlondon.ca

At the west end of Dundas Street, close to the river, **Museum London** occupies a chunkily modernist structure that looks a bit like a giant bicycle shed. The building was designed by famed Canadian architect Raymond Moriyama, whose work is often characterized by a preference for contorted curves and circles rather than straight lines – the museum is not perhaps his finest achievement. The gallery's permanent collection features a somewhat indeterminate mix of lesser eighteenth- and nineteenth-century Canadian painters, but there's an interesting section devoted to contemporary photography and the temporary modern art exhibitions – some of which come here straight from Toronto – are usually excellent.

Eldon House

481 Ridout St North • Jan–April Thurs–Sun noon–5pm; May & Oct–Dec Wed–Sun noon–5pm; June–Sept Tues–Sun noon–5pm • Donation expected • ☎ 519 661 5169, ⓦ eldonhouse.ca

London's oldest residence, the **Eldon House** is a graceful clapboard dwelling built in the 1830s for John Harris, a retired Royal Navy captain. The house remained the property of the Harris family until the 1960s, when it was bequeathed to the city, and its interior has now been returned to its nineteenth-century appearance, from the mounted animal horns in the front hall to the four-poster beds up above.

Two churches – St Paul's and St Peter's

The British influence is easy to pick out among the handsome Victorian homes that dot the centre of London and more especially in **St Paul's Anglican Cathedral**, a simple red-brick structure on Richmond Street that was built in the English Gothic Revival style in 1846. The church is in marked contrast to the nearby and rival **St Peter's Catholic Cathedral**, a flamboyant, high-towered, pink-stone edifice typical of the French Gothic style popular among Ontario's Catholics in the same period.

ARRIVAL AND INFORMATION   LONDON

By train London's train station is centrally situated at York and Richmond streets.

Destinations (VIA Rail) Kitchener (2 daily; 1hr 45min); Stratford (2 daily; 1hr 10min); Toronto (7–10 daily; 2hr 10min–3hr 20min); Windsor (4 daily; 2hr).

By bus The bus station is near the train station at York and Talbot streets, served by Greyhound.

Destinations Toronto (12–15 daily; 2hr–4hr 30min); Windsor (5 daily; 2hr 30min).

Tourist office There are two nearby: 267 Dundas St and Wellington (Mon–Fri 8.30am–4.30pm) and 969 Wellington Rd South (Mon–Fri 8.30am–4.30pm, Sat & Sun 10am–5pm), both ☎ 519 661 5000, ⓦ londontourism.ca.

ACCOMMODATION

Idlewyld Inn 36 Grand Ave ☎ 519 432 5554, ⓦ idlewyld inn.com; map p.121. The most appealing hotel in town, the *Idlewyld* occupies a rambling blonde-brick Victorian mansion whose public rooms retain many of their original fittings. Each of the twenty-or-so en-suite guest rooms is pleasantly furnished in a modern rendition of period style and all are quite comfortable. A 20min walk south of the centre. First-rate restaurant too. $155

Hotel Metro 32 Covent Market Pl ☎ 519 518 9000, ⓦ hotelmetro.ca; map p.121. This inviting boutique hotel offers loft-style accommodation with exposed-brick walls and wooden floors. The Gnosh Dining & Cocktails

serves a fresh, seasonal menu, including seared salmon and filo-wrapped brie. $144

Woodfield Bed & Breakfast 499 Dufferin Ave ☎ 519 675 9632, ⓦ woodfieldbb.com; map p.121. A grand-looking home from 1873 in the heritage district, nestled under the leafy shade of a large tree, this three-room B&B (two with fireplaces) is very central, and its hosts are most gracious. $100

2

EATING

Budapest 348 Dundas St at Waterloo ☎ 519 439 3431, ⓦ oo5.com/bpr; map p.121. Long-established family-run restaurant offering Hungarian food in convivial surroundings since 1965 – though there are mixed opinions on the early-evening live music. This is the place to come when you're hungry – enjoy generous servings of chicken paprikash, wiener schnitzel and goulash. Mains $19–23. Mon–Sat 11am–10pm & Sun 4–9pm.

The Church Key 476 Richmond St ☎ 519 936 0960, ⓦ thechurchkey.ca; map p.121. Smart and modern bistro-cum-pub with an inventive menu – anything from island chicken to lamb curry to "Game of the Week". Has a pleasant mini-terrace and stocks a good range of beers. Kitchen till 10pm. Mon & Tues 11am–10pm, Wed & Thurs 11am–11pm, Fri & Sat 11.30am–2am, Sun 11am–10pm.

David's Bistro 432 Richmond St ☎ 519 667 0535, ⓦ davidsbistro.ca; map p.121. This amiable bistro with checkered tablecloths serves an eclectic, seasonal menu, including ricotta gnocchi with lobster and peas, and duck

confit draped in lingonberry sauce. Wed–Fri 11.30am–2.30pm & 5–10pm, Sat–Tues 5–10pm.

Garlic's of London 481 Richmond St ☎ 519 432 4092, ⓦ garlicsoflondon.com; map p.121. One of London's most tempting restaurants, this smart and modern Italian place offers all the classics and more – all prepared from scratch – and a good wine-cellar too. Try the Ontario trout with potato salad, or the duck confit with fettuccine in a cream sauce. Pizza, pasta and dinner main courses range from $17 to $35. Sun–Fri 11.30am–10pm, Fri 11am–11pm.

Idlewyld Inn 36 Grand Ave ☎ 519 432 5554, ⓦ idlewyldinn.com; map p.121. This hotel (see page 122) restaurant can lack a little atmosphere, but there's no denying the quality of the food with nicely presented dishes like almond-crusted Ontario lamb with garbanzo bean purée. hitting all the right gastronomic buttons. Mains £24–44. Mon–Sat 7–10am, 11am–3pm & 5–9pm, Sun 11am–3pm.

St Thomas and Port Stanley

Heading south from London towards the **Lake Erie shoreline**, it's about 30km to **ST THOMAS**, a sprawling town that was once a major railway junction – which was mighty bad luck for **Jumbo the Elephant**. A widely-travelled animal, Jumbo was born in what is now Mali before being transferred to a Paris zoo and then London zoo, where he became a much-loved fixture, famous for giving rides to children. In 1881, the London zoo sold him to P.T. Barnum's travelling circus – despite more than 100,000 children writing to Queen Victoria to object – and it was in St Thomas that Jumbo met his maker after being hit by a train in a marshalling yard.

From St Thomas, it's a further 15km or so south to **PORT STANLEY**, whose tiny centre straddles a slow-moving creek as it nears the lake. The main pull here is the port's long

---

A COUNTRY DETOUR – LONDON TO WINDSOR ON HWY-3

The 190km-long romp along **Hwy-401** from London to Windsor is fast but really rather dreary, whereas the much prettier **Hwy-3** cuts a parallel if slightly slower route through the rural heart of the region. The most enjoyable part of Hwy-3 is the section between London and **Leamington** (where you can turn south for Point Pelee National Park). It's here that the highway slips through a string of one-horse villages, passing pioneer graveyards, overgrown wooded dells, antique timber farmhouses and wheat fields that stretch as far as the eye can see. It's a handsome, relaxing drive, but you won't see much of **Lake Erie**, which is, for the most part, hidden from view by a long, rolling bluff.

2

and sandy **beach** just to the west of town, thronged with sunbathers whenever the weather permits.

Kettle Creek Inn 216 Joseph St ☎ 519 782 3388, ☎ 866 414 0417, ⓦ kettlecreekinn.com. In the centre of Port Stanley, close to the harbour, this charming inn consists of a huddle of well-maintained timber chalet-cottages. Also has an excellent restaurant featuring such delights as chicken pot pie ($15), pan-seared perch fillets with grilled citrus ($30) or rich poutine with crispy pork ($10). Daily 11.20am–8pm. $145

Windsor and around

"I'm going to Detroit, Michigan, to work the Cadillac line" growls an old blues number, but if the singer had crossed the river from Detroit he'd have been equally at home among the car plants of **WINDSOR**, 190km southwest of London. The factories were established as subsidiaries of the American auto industry and for many years the forceful Canadian Automobile Workers Union made sure there were thousands of well-paid jobs. Some years back, the trials of Detroit-based American auto companies cast a long shadow over the city, but Windsor is focusing on diversifying to boost the local economy – and morale.

For the casual visitor, Windsor has a certain appeal as a border town with both an attractive riverside setting, asurprisingly compact downtown core focused on Ouellette Avenue between the river and Wyandotte Street and an interesting art museum It also has a clutch of good restaurants, a lively edges bar scene, and, as a bonus, it's within easy driving distance of **Point Pelee National Park**, about 60km away to the southeast.

The waterfront

Windsor's most appealing feature is its elongated **waterfront**: from here, there are striking views of Detroit and its platoon of skyscrapers and it's here you'll also find the manicured lawns and borders of **Dieppe Gardens**, stretching along the waterfront from the foot of Ouellette Avenue – and named in honour of the many Canadians who died in an amphibious attack on Dieppe, when that French port was occupied by the Germans in World War II. The gardens are part of a longer riverside park, which extends west for 3.5km as far as the Ambassador Bridge, incorporating the whimsical modern statues of the open-air, open-access **Windsor Sculpture Park**.

Art Gallery of Windsor

401 Riverside Drive West • Wed–Sun 11am–5pm, first Thurs of month open until 9pm • Free • ☎ 519 977 0013, ⓦ agw.ca

Housed in a flashy modern structure, the **Art Gallery of Windsor** has a well-deserved reputation for the excellence of its temporary exhibitions, most of which focus on things Canadian. The permanent collection is substantial too – and is noted for its late nineteenth- and early twentieth-century Canadian paintings, especially the Group of Seven (see page 74).

By bus Windsor bus station is on Church St at Pitt, a couple of minutes' walk from the main downtown drag, Ouellette Ave. Also at the bus station is Transit Windsor (☎ 519 944 4111, ⓦ citywindsor.ca), which operates a shuttle bus service (2 hourly, about 30min; $5) over to downtown Detroit. Remember to bring passport or proof of citizenship, which you'll need to show when crossing the border.

Destinations (Greyhound) London (4 daily; 2hr); Toronto (4–5 daily; 5hr).

By train Windsor's shed-like train station is 3km east of the city centre along the riverfront at 298 Walker Rd at Riverside Drive East; to get into the centre, take a taxi ($12–14). Destinations (VIA Rail) London (4 daily; 2hr); Toronto (4 daily; 4hr).

Ontario Travel This provincial information centre is beside the Detroit tunnel at 110 Park St East, at Goyeau (daily 8.30am–5pm; June to Aug 8am–8pm; ☎ 519 973 1338). **The Windsor Convention and Visitors' Bureau** The local information bureau is across the street from the bus station at 333 Riverside Drive West (Mon–Fri 8.30am–4.30pm; ☎ 519 255 6530, ☎ 800 265 3633, ⓦ visitwindsoressex.com).

ACCOMMODATION

Best Western Plus Waterfront Hotel 277 Riverside Drive West ☎ 877 973 7829, ⓦ windsor-hotel.ca; map p.125. Tower-block chain hotel distinguished by its location – the views of the audacious Detroit skyline across the river are simply wonderful from the upper floors. The rooms themselves are fairly routine, but they're large and the beds comfortable. **$135**

EATING AND DRINKING

★ **The Blind Owl** 430 Ouellete Ave, no phone, ⓦ facebook.com/blindowlbar; map p.125. This charming cocktail lounge is a breath of fresh air in the Windsor after-dark scene. Styled after a speakeasy, with no sign out front, the craft cocktails rival the best in the business, made with fresh juice, unique herbs and spices and top-shelf alcohol. Tues–Thurs 4pm–midnight, Fri 4pm–2am, Sat 6pm–2am.

★ **F&B Walkerville** 2090 Wyandotte St E ☎ 519 915 8147, ⓦ fandbwalkerville.com; map p.125. This stylish restaurant and bar serves delectable small plates, including elk tartare with black garlic and smoked duck with dry-roasted edamame. The cocktails are equally inventive. Small plates $8–20. Sun & Tues–Thurs 5pm–midnight, Fri–Sat 5pm–1am.

Phog Lounge 157 University Ave West ☎ 519 253 1605, ⓦ phoglounge.com; map p.125. Downtown Windsor has a hatful of rough-and-ready bars and this is perhaps the pick, a dark and cramped bar-cum-club with a varied programme of live music – some good, some bad and some outstanding. Popular with university students. Daily from 5pm.

Spago 690 Erie St East ☎ 519 252 2233, ⓦ spagos. ca; map p.125. In the heart of Little Italy, about 1.5km

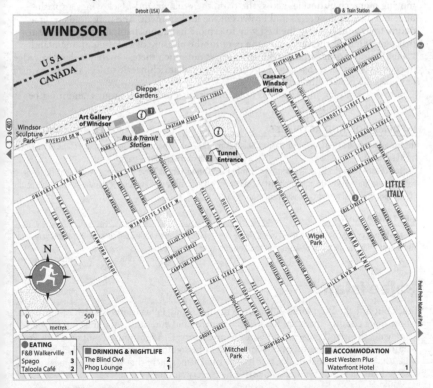

2

southeast of the city centre, this large and very popular, ground-floor restaurant covers all the Italian classics with meat and seafood mains averaging $21, pizzas $14. Electric-fast service too. The trattoria on the first floor is a little more formal. Mon–Thurs 11.30am–10pm, Fri–Sat 11.30am–11.30pm, Sun 1–9pm.

★ **Taloola Café** 396 Devonshire Rd ☎ 519 254 6652, ⓦ taloolacafe.com; map p.125. Lovely boho café –

something of a surprise in Windsor – with modern art on the walls and vintage furnishings squeezed into an old red-brick row house. Does a great line in sandwiches and light meals – both eat-in and take-out – as well as salads and stews, all with local, organic products wherever possible. Live music of various types Friday and Saturday evenings. Near the Hiram Walker distillery, about 2km east of downtown. Tues–Fri 8am–10pm, Sat 9am–10pm, Sun 10am–4pm.

Point Pelee National Park

Daily: April to early Oct 6am–10pm; early Oct to March 7am–7pm • $7.80

Heading southeast from Windsor on Hwy-3, it's about 50km to **Leamington**, a workaday agricultural town that bills itself as the "Tomato Capital of Canada" – with a massive Heinz factory to prove the point. From the town, it's just 8km or so to **Point Pelee National Park**, which occupies the southernmost tip of Canada's mainland, filling out half of a 20km-long sand spit at the same latitude as Rome and Barcelona. The park boasts a variety of habitats rarely matched in Canada, including marshlands and open fields, but most remarkably it is one of the few places where the ancient **deciduous forest** of eastern North America has survived. One-third of the park is covered by this jungle-like forest, packed with a staggering variety of trees, from hackberry, red cedar, black walnut and blue ash to vine-covered sassafras. The park's mild climate and its mix of vegetation attract thousands of **birds** on their spring and autumn migrations. In September, the sand spit also funnels thousands of southward-moving **monarch butterflies** across the park, their orange-and-black wings a splash of colour against the greens and browns of the undergrowth. The park holds several **nature trails** and these are the best way to explore its various habitats; but most visitors make a beeline for the very tip of the park for the pleasure of standing on mainland Canada's southernmost point, though there is not much there – merely a slender wedge of coarse brown sand that can't help but seem a tad anticlimactic unless, that is, a storm has piled the beach with driftwood.

Note that camping in the park is only for not-for-profit adult groups, and must be arranged beforehand.

INFORMATION AND ACTIVITIES   POINT PELEE NATIONAL PARK

Information kiosk At the entrance to the park about 8km from Leamington.

Visitor centre From the kiosk, it's a further 7km to the visitor centre (mid-March to mid-April Sat & Sun only 10am–5pm; mid-April to mid-Oct daily 10am–5pm; ☎ 519

322 2365, ⓦ pc.gc.ca), at the beginning of the Tilden Woods and Woodland nature trails.

Canoe rental There is a canoe rental spot (June–Sept) 3km from the park entrance at the Marsh Boardwalk nature trail.

GETTING AROUND

By shuttle Propane-powered shuttle "trains" leave the visitor centre for the 2km trip down to the southern tip

of the park from early April to early Oct; times vary – call ahead for schedule.

Pelee Island

Stuck out in Lake Erie, some 20km from the mainland, **Pelee Island** is a slab of farmland, whose quiet country roads are flanked by orchards and vineyards. About 15km long and 6km wide, the island possesses a pair of nature reserves – Lighthouse Point and Fish Point – at its northern and southern extremities and one significant settlement, **PELEE ISLAND VILLAGE**, where the boat docks, but it's the rural atmosphere that is of most appeal to the assorted ramblers and cyclists who arrive here every summer.

ARRIVAL AND INFORMATION

PELEE ISLAND

By ferry Ontario Ferries (☎ 800 661 2220, ⓦ ontarioferries. com) operates car ferries to Pelee Island from Kingsville, on the mainland 10km to the west of Leamington. There are sailings between April and mid-Dec (1–3 daily; 1hr 30min; $7.50/person one way; bicycles $3.75; cars $16.50). Ferry schedules usually make it easy to visit the island on a day-trip.

Information For maps and information, check out ⓦ pelee.org.

GETTING AROUND

By bike Given the flatness of the terrain, the best way to explore the island is by bike; these can be rented from Comfortech, metres from the dock ($10 an hour or $25 per day; ☎ 519 724 2828, ⓦ peleebikerental.com); advance booking is required. Explore Pelee (☎ 519 325 8687, ⓦ explorepelee.com) offers guided bike (from $40, not including bike rental) and motor tours ($30).

ACCOMMODATION

The Wandering Dog Inn 1060 East West Rd ☎ 519 724 2270, ⓦ thewanderingdoginn.com. In a pretty, two-storey house in the southeast corner of the island, this appealing inn has twelve well-appointed rooms, most en suite, each decorated in a bright and breezy manner. The inn is also a brief walk from the beach and there's an outdoor Jacuzzi. Open May–November. **$125**

Hwy-21: Dresden to Petrolia

The large chunk of farmland rolling 100km west from **London** (see page 121) to the inconsequential border town of **Sarnia** is one of the less absorbing parts of the province. It was also one of the last parts of southern Ontario to be cleared and settled, its heavy clay soil difficult to plough and almost impassable in rain. The district is bisected by **Hwy-21**, which serves as a handy short-cut between both Windsor (see page 124) and Point Pelee National Park (see page 126) and the good-looking towns of Lake Huron's shoreline, primarily Bayfield and Goderich (see page 129). Fortunately, Hwy-21 also passes by the area's three points of interest. These are – from south to north – **Uncle Tom's Cabin Historic Site**, where a group of escaped US slaves found refuge in the 1830s; the **Oil Museum of Canada**, recalling the local oil boom of the middle of the nineteenth century; and small-town **Petrolia**, also a result of the oil rush. You'll need a car, as **no buses** run along Hwy-21.

Uncle Tom's Cabin Historic Site

29251 Uncle Tom's Rd, Dresden • Mid-May to June & Sept to late Oct Tues–Sat 10am–4pm, Sun noon–4pm; July & Aug Mon–Sat 10am–4pm, Sun noon–4pm • $7 • ☎ 519 683 2978, ⓦ heritagetrust.on.ca

Hwy-21 begins its appealing, albeit convoluted, journey across this part of Ontario at its junction with Hwy-401, about 110km east of Windsor and 80km west of London. From this intersection, it's around 30km northwest to **DRESDEN**, a small agricultural community in a gentle loop of the Sydenham River. Here, on the edge of Dresden in a rural setting, is **Uncle Tom's Cabin Historic Site**, comprising a small visitor centre with a handful of old wooden buildings, including a lovely little church and the clapboard house that was once the home of the **Reverend Josiah Henson** (1789–1883). A slave who fled from Maryland to Canada in 1830 by means of the Underground Railroad (see page 128), Henson and a group of abolitionist sympathizers bought 200 acres of farmland here in Dresden and founded a vocational school for runaway slaves known as the British American Institute. Unable to write, Henson dictated his life experiences, and in 1849 these narrations were published as *The Life of Josiah Henson – Formerly a Slave*. It's a powerful tract, unassuming and almost matter of fact in the way it describes the routine savagery of slavery, and it was immediately popular. One of its readers was **Harriet Beecher Stowe**, who met Henson and went on to write the most influential

THE UNDERGROUND RAILROAD

The **Underground Railroad** started in the 1820s as a loose and secretive association of abolitionists dedicated to smuggling slaves from the southern states of the US to Canada. By the 1840s, it had become a well-organized network of routes and safe houses, but its real importance lay not so much in the number of slaves rescued – the total was comparatively small – but rather in the psychological effect it had on those involved in the smuggling operation. The movement of a runaway slave usually involved very few people, but many more, particularly neighbours and friends, knew what was happening and therefore were complicit in breaking the law. To the extent that white Americans could be persuaded to accept even the most minor role in the Underground Railroad, the inclination to compromise with institutional slavery was undermined, though the psychology of racism remained intact: like Beecher Stowe's Uncle Tom, the freed negroes were supposed to be humble and grateful, simulating childlike responses to please their white parent-protectors.

abolitionist text of the day, *Uncle Tom's Cabin* (1852), basing her main character on Henson's accounts. Most of the Dresden refugees returned to the US after the Civil War, but Henson stayed on, accumulating imperial honours that must have surprised him greatly. He was even presented to Queen Victoria and, in commemoration of this royal connection, a crown surmounts his **tombstone**, which stands just outside the complex. Henson's book is hard to find, but copies are sold here at the visitor centre, where there's also a small **interpretation centre** on slavery in the US, plus an intriguing film giving more details on Henson's life and times.

Oil Museum of Canada

2423 Kelly Rd, just off Hwy-21, 1km south of Oil Springs • May–Oct daily 10am–5pm; Nov–April Mon–Fri 10am–5pm • $5 • ☎ 519 834 2840, ⓦ lambtonmuseums.ca/oil

Some 25km north of Dresden, **Hwy-21** scuttles past the intriguing **Oil Museum of Canada** just before it reaches the hamlet of **OIL SPRINGS**. The museum tells the tale of the local oilfields, beginning in the modern visitor centre, which is jam-packed with artefacts, from distinctive old oil cans and fascinating sepia photos taken during the initial boom, through to a receipt singed brown by an explosion and all sorts of elaborate tools designed to keep the oil flowing. There are also potted biographies of the leading oil men of the day and details of who drilled where, why and when. Outside, a scattering of sights includes a mock-up of James Williams' original well on the site where he first hit oil, a replica of Shaw's "gusher" (though this was actually elsewhere), and a small patch of crusty gum-bed. Oil is still produced in the fields around the museum, drawn to the surface and pushed on into an underground system of pipes by some five hundred pumpjacks. You can get a glimpse of all this activity by following the side-road driving route recommended by the museum – they supply a free map and it only takes about fifteen minutes.

Petrolia

The grand stone-and-brick buildings of tiny **PETROLIA**, just off Hwy-21 about 10km north of Oil Springs, speak volumes about the sudden rush of wealth that followed the discovery of the region's oil. This was Canada's first oil town and as the proceeds rolled in, the Victorian mansions and expansive public buildings popped up all over. Several have survived along and around the main drag, **Petrolia Line**. Three prime examples are the former **railway station**, now a library, whose extravagant, pagoda-like roof is on the corner of Station Street; the **Municipal Offices**, just opposite at the intersection with Greenfield Street; and **St Andrew's Presbyterian church**, where Petrolia Line and Queen Street cross, awash with neo-Gothic gables and towers. To emphasize the town's origins, its streetlamps are cast in the shape of oil derricks, but once you've admired the architecture there's no reason to hang around.

From Petrolia, it's about 12km north along Hwy-21 to **Hwy-402**, the motorway linking London to the east and **Sarnia** away to the west, and a further 80km to Lake Huron's Bayfield (see below).

The Lake Huron shoreline

A popular holiday spot, the southern section of the **Lake Huron shoreline** is Ontario at its most alluring, with long sandy beaches and a steep bluff trailing along the lakeshore – all interrupted by the occasional river valley and a string of pretty country towns. The water is much less polluted than Lake Ontario, the sunsets are fabulously beautiful, and in **The Pinery** the region possesses one of the most beautiful provincial parks. Of the towns, **Bayfield** and **Goderich** stand head and shoulders above the rest, charming little places with great hotels and B&Bs. The only fly in the ointment is the almost total lack of public transport.

Pinery Provincial Park

9526 Lakeshore Rd • Day-entry $11.25 • ☎ 519 243 8574, ⊚ pinerypark.on.ca

Anchoring the Lake Huron shoreline at the point where it turns west, **Pinery Provincial Park** occupies a slab of coastline with a magnificent, dune-backed sandy **beach**. Behind the beach is a mixed area of forest, savanna and wetland, which extends either side of a long and slender waterway – the Old Ausable Channel. The park holds a handful of short hiking trails that explore this varied habitat as well as a gentle 14km-long bike trail.

ARRIVAL AND INFORMATION   PINERY PROVINCIAL PARK

By car Hwy-21 trims the southern edge of The Pinery, which is about 50km from Petrolia (see page 128) and 40km from Bayfield (see below).

Visitor centre In the middle of The Pinery and can only be reached along the circuitous one-way road that travels the park's length (Mon–Fri 1–4pm, Sat & Sun 10am–5pm; ☎ 519 243 8574). It sells park maps, has lots of information on hiking and canoeing and rents canoes and bikes (both from 1hr; from $10/hr).

ACCOMMODATION

Campsites ☎ 888 668 7275, ⊚ ontarioparks.com. The Pinery has three campsites; reservations can be made, though generally for a minimum of three nights. Of the three, the *Riverside Campground*, located along the Old Ausable Channel, is open all year; the other two – the *Dunes* and the *Burley* – are open from May to Sept. Sites **$36**

Bayfield

Sloping along the edge of Lake Huron, beguiling **BAYFIELD**, about 90km north of London, is a charming village whose handsome timber villas nestle among well-tended gardens beneath a canopy of ancient trees. The local citizenry have kept modern development at arm's length – there's barely a neon sign in sight, never mind a concrete apartment block – and almost every old house has been beautifully maintained: look out for the scrolled woodwork, the fanlights and the graceful verandas. Historical plaques give the low-down on the older buildings that line Bayfield's short **Main Street**, which started out in the 1830s as a supply centre for local farmers with a blacksmith's, a tannery, a saw mill or two, a brickyard and a distillery. Short Hill Road, off the west end of Main Street, leads to pint-sized **Pioneer Park**, which perches on the bluff overlooking the lake and is a fine spot to take in the sunset. From the park, a flight of wooden steps leads down to the pebbly **beach**, from where it is a short stroll to the harbour and the marina. If you have the time, ramble up from the harbour along the banks of the Bayfield River where, in season, you can pick wild mushrooms and fiddlehead ferns.

ARRIVAL AND INFORMATION BAYFIELD

By car From London take Ontario 4 north before turning off on County Rd 3 for the last 28km.
Tourist office In a kiosk beside Hwy-21 on the south side of town (May–Sept daily 10am–5pm; ☎ 519 565 2499, ☎ 866 565 2499, ⓦ villageofbayfield.com).

ACCOMMODATION

Bayfield Boutique Bed and Breakfast 12 The Square ☎ 519 955 2121, ⓦ secretgardenbandb.com. Bayfield possesses several charming B&Bs, but this is the pick with three immaculate, vintage-style guest rooms in a meticulously maintained old house beside the attractive Clan Gregor Square. Great breakfasts, too. **$224**
★ **Little Inn of Bayfield** 26 Main St North ☎ 519 565 2611, ☎ 800 565 1832, ⓦ littleinn.com. Offering some of Ontario's finest lodgings, this superb, medium-sized hotel occupies an early nineteenth-century timber-and-brick building with a handsome second-floor veranda. Wherever possible, the original fittings have been left intact, which gives the place a homey, intimate feel, but there are discreet additions too – for example most of the guest rooms have baths. A modern, two-storey timber guest cottage across the street serves as an annexe. Good restaurant, too (see below). **$235**; cottage rooms **$279**

EATING

★ **Little Inn of Bayfield** 26 Main St North ☎ 519 565 2611, ☎ 800 565 1832, ⓦ littleinn.com. Smart and chic restaurant, the best for miles around, with an inventive menu that makes good use of local, seasonal ingredients. They also serve a superb Sunday brunch ($25/person). Mains range from $28 to $42. Part of an excellent hotel (see above). Daily 7:30am–10pm.

Goderich

GODERICH, at the mouth of the Maitland River 20km north of Bayfield, is a delightful country town, whose pleasant centre perches on a bluff behind and above its working harbour. It began life in 1825, when the British-owned Canada Company bought two and a half million acres of southern Ontario – the **Huron Tract** – from the government at the ridiculously low rate of twelve cents an acre, amid rumours of bribery and corruption. Eager to profit on their investment, the company pushed the **Huron Road** through from Stratford (see page 119) in the east to Goderich in the west, an extraordinary effort chronicled by a certain Mr Moffat – "The trees were so tall, the forest was eternally dark and with the constant rains it was endlessly damp... Since each man was responsible for cooking his own food after a hard day's work, the men sometimes ate the fattest pork practically raw... To make up for such fare, a barrel of whisky with a cup attached always stood at the roadside." Completed in 1828, the road attracted the settlers the company needed. Indeed, within thirty years the Huron Tract had two flourishing towns, Stratford (see page 119) and Goderich, and was producing large surpluses of grain for export, as it continues to do today. Perfect for an overnight stay, Goderich has several good B&Bs, two intriguing museums and several well-attended festivals throughout the year.

Courthouse Square

The centre of Goderich is very different from almost any other town in Ontario, its wide, tree-lined avenues radiating out with geometrical precision from **Courthouse Square**, a grand, octagonal central circle dominated by the town's white-stone Courthouse. From the square, the four main streets follow the cardinal points, though the general aspect of the centre was severely disrupted in August 2011 when a waterspout tornado came ashore from Lake Huron and ripped through the town, killing one person and damaging many buildings.

Huron County Museum & Historic Gaol

Museum 110 North St • Jan–April & Nov–Dec Tues–Fri 1 0am–4.30pm (until 8pm on Thurs), Sat 1–4.30pm; May–Oct Mon–Sat 10am–4.30pm (until 8pm on Thurs), Sun 1–4.30pm • **Gaol** 181 Victoria St North; take North St from Courthouse Square, turn right at the end • May–Aug Mon–Fri 10am–4.30pm, Sat 1–4.30pm, Sept–Oct Sun–Fri 1–4pm, Sat 10am–4.30pm • Museum $6, $10 with Gaol • ☎ 519 524 2686, ⓦ huroncountymuseum.ca

One of the best museums of its sort in the province, the large and comprehensive **Huron County Museum** has over thirty galleries covering every aspect of the county's history, from the terrifying equipment of an early dentist's surgery to a log cabin, a massive 1913 steam locomotive, an old dress shop and displays on both world wars. There are also a number of period rooms and a feature on the worst storm on record to hit the Great Lakes region – the 1913 "Great Storm" that sunk twelve ships and killed 250 people.

The **Huron Historic Gaol** is among Ontario's most intriguing attractions, With its thick and strong stone walls, the Gaol was constructed as a combined courthouse and jail between 1839 and 1842. Visits begin on the **third floor** of the main block, whose claustrophobic courtroom was originally situated next to a couple of holding cells. There were two problems: the design was most unpopular with local judges, who felt threatened by the proximity of those they were sentencing; the other was the odour emanating from the privies in the exercise yard below. In 1856, the administration finally gave way and built a new courthouse in the town centre, separating the jail and the judiciary once and for all. The jail's **first and second floors** hold the original jailer's apartment and a string of well-preserved prison cells, reflecting various changes in design between 1841 and 1972, when the prison was finally closed. The worst is the leg-iron cell for "troublesome" prisoners, where unfortunates were chained to the wall with neither bed nor blanket. End your tour at the **Governor's House**, with its attractively restored, late Victorian interior. In the summer (Tues–Thurs eves), the museum hosts Behind the Bars interactive tours ($10, $5 children), where you can meet the faces of the Gaol.

West Street and the harbour

From Courthouse Square, **West Street** leads the 1km through a cutting in the bluffs to the Lake Huron shoreline at the south end of the **harbour**, which is flanked by disused grain elevators and home to the industrial tackle of Goderich **salt mine**, whose subterranean workings extend 7km out under the lake. At the moment, you can't walk north round the harbour to the Tiger Dunlop Heritage Trail (see below), but you can stroll south along some 1.5km of tidied-up shoreline to a picnic area and a sandy if notably scrawny **beach**, where the sunsets can be spectacular.

Tiger Dunlop Heritage Trail

CPR Station at Goderich Harbour

Reached along North Harbour Road, which runs west from Hwy-21 on the north side of the town centre, the **Tiger Dunlop Heritage Trail** is a 3.2km-long hiking and cycling trail that loops round the north bank of the Maitland River before intersecting with Hwy-21. Near the start, the trail crosses the river by means of the old CPR railway bridge, the **Menesetung Bridge**, a splendid structure offering lovely views.

ARRIVAL AND INFORMATION

GODERICH

By car Currently Goderich is not connected to any cities by bus; it's best to come by car.

Tourist office Beside Hwy-21 at the intersection of Nelson and Hamilton, a couple of minutes' walk from Courthouse Square (mid-May to Sept daily 9am–6pm; Oct to mid-May Mon–Fri 9am–4.30pm; ☎ 519 524 6600, ☎ 800 280 7637, ⓦ goderich.ca).

ACCOMMODATION

Colborne B&B 72 Colborne St ☎ 519524 7400, ☎ 800 390 4612, ⓦ colbornebandb.com. One of the most appealing B&Bs in town, the *Colborne* occupies a large, red-brick house and former manse near Courthouse Square. It has four guest rooms – all en suite – and each is decorated in a pleasant modern version of period style. $105

Point Farms Provincial Park 82491 Bluewater Hwy, off Hwy-21 ☎519 524 7124, camping reservations ☎888 668 7275, ⓦontarioparks.com. Backing onto the bluff that overlooks Lake Huron just 7km north of Goderich, this park has a sandy beach, walking trails and two medium-sized, seasonal campgrounds (mid-May to Oct). Pitches with hook-up, vehicle and two adults from $55

EATING

Thyme on 21 80 Hamilton St ☎519 524 4171, ⓦthymeon21.com. In a Victorian house opposite the tourist office, this smart little place features such delights as pecan-crusted chicken breast ($26) and pork wrapped in bacon with maple mustard ($27), helping make it Goderich's best restaurant. There's a nice wine list, too. Wed–Thurs 11.30am–1.30pm & 5–7.30pm, Fri 11.30am–1.30pm & 5–8pm, Sat 5–8pm, Sun

Owen Sound

OWEN SOUND occupies the ravine around the mouth of the Sydenham River, at the foot of the Bruce Peninsula. In its heyday, Owen Sound was a rough and violent port packed with brothels and bars, prompting the Americans to establish a consulate whose main function was to bail out drunk and disorderly sailors. For the majority it was an unpleasant place to live, and the violence spawned an especially active branch of the Women's Christian Temperance Organization, whose success was such that an alcohol ban was imposed in 1906 and only lifted in 1972. The town was in decline long before the return of the bars, its port facilities undercut by the railways from the 1920s, but it's managed to reinvent itself and is now an amiable sort of place well worth at least a pit stop. Getting around town can be confusing; however, it helps to know that avenues run north–south and streets east–west, while the river, which bisects the town centre, separates avenues and streets East from those marked West.

Tom Thomson Art Gallery

840 1st Ave West • Wed–Sat 11am–4pm • Free, but donation suggested • ☎519 376 1932, ⓦtomthomson.org

Owen Sound's prime attraction is the **Tom Thomson Art Gallery**, whose permanent collection includes a strong sample of the artist's work with his wilderness landscapes to the fore. Arguably Canada's greatest painter, and certainly the inspiration for the Group of Seven (see page 74), Thomson (1877–1917) was born just outside Owen Sound in Leith. The gallery also offers a lively programme of temporary exhibitions, most of which feature Canadian artists.

Billy Bishop Museum

948 3rd Ave West • Jan–March & Sept–Dec Tues–Fri noon–4pm; April–May Tues–Sun noon–4pm; June–Aug Mon–Sat 10am–5pm, Sun noon–5pm • $5 suggested donation • ☎519 371 0031, ⓦbillybishop.org

---

BLUE MOUNTAIN SKI RESORT

The small-time port of **Collingwood**, 65km east of Owen Sound on Nottawasaga Bay, is the gateway to the **Blue Mountain**, a segment of the Niagara Escarpment whose steepish slopes are now a major wintersports area, mainly for **alpine skiing**, though several cross-country trails have also been developed. To get there from Collingwood, take the Blue Mountain Road (Hwy-19) which reaches – after about 10km – the *Blue Mountain Resort* (☎705 445 0231, ☎877 445 0231, ⓦbluemountain.ca), a large and modern sprawl comprising hotels, shops, restaurants and cafés. In total, the Blue Mountain ski area has 36 downhill ski slopes of varying difficulty with a maximum vertical drop of 219m. The prime season is from mid-December to mid-March.

Born in Owen Sound, the son of a lawyer, **Billy Bishop** (1894–1956) was one of the finest fighter pilots of World War I, thought to have disposed of 72 enemy aircraft and awarded the VC for a particular piece of derring-do. It seems that Bishop had amazingly good eyesight and he was definitely a crack-shot, but perhaps most important of all he appears to have been absolutely without fear. The **Billy Bishop Museum** occupies Bishop's boyhood home and a series of exhibits track through his aerial exploits.

ARRIVAL AND INFORMATION

OWEN SOUND

By bus The bus station, served by Greyhound, is a brief walk east of the Sydenham River at 1020 3rd Ave East and 10th St East. From here, it's a 10min walk to the tourist office. There are 2 buses daily to Toronto (4hr).

Tourist office On the west side of the river just north of 10th St East at 1155 1st Ave West (Mon–Thurs 9am–5pm, Fri 9am–6pm, Sat 10am–5pm, Sun 10am–4pm; ☏ 519 371 9833, ☏ 888 675 5555, ⓦ owensoundtourism.com).

ACCOMMODATION AND EATING

Highland Manor 867 4th Ave West ☏ 519 372 2699, ⓦ highlandmanor.ca. This enticing inn occupies a grand Victorian mansion with high ceilings and a handsome garden veranda, and each of the four large and comfortable guest rooms comes complete with original features. Advance booking is strongly recommended at the height of the season (mid-July to mid-Aug). **$190**

Jazzmyns Tapas & Taps 261 9th St East ☏ 519 371 7736, ⓦ jazzmyns.com. Coolest place in town with live music, riveting decor and a wide-ranging, inexpensive menu – anything from tapas and coconut shrimp to *pad Thai* noodles and pulled pork sandwiches. Mains for as little as $9. Mon–Sat noon to 1am; kitchen till 9 or 10pm.

The Bruce Peninsula

Separating the main body of Lake Huron from Georgian Bay, the **Bruce Peninsula** holds two of Ontario's national parks. The more distinctive is the **Fathom Five National Marine Park**, at the northern tip of the peninsula, which provides wonderful sport for divers. The second is the **Bruce Peninsula National Park**, comprising two slabs of forested wilderness on either side of Hwy-6, its northern portion offering magnificent coastal hiking on a small section of the Bruce Trail (see below). There's camping at both parks and a reasonable choice of hotel and motel accommodation at lively **Tobermory**, from where you catch the car ferry over to Manitoulin Island (see page 134).

The Bruce Peninsula National Park

Heading northwest from Owen Sound, **Hwy-6** scoots up the middle of the Bruce Peninsula to reach – after about 100km – the turning for the **Bruce Peninsula National Park** at **Cyprus Lake**. The park is a mixture of limestone cliff, rocky beach, wetland and forest that's best visited in June when the wildflowers are in bloom and it's not too crowded. Four **hiking trails** start at the northern edge of Cyprus Lake and three of them connect with one of the most dramatic portions of the **Bruce Trail**, a long-distance footpath which follows the route of the Niagara Escarpment as it weaves its way across Ontario from Queenston (see page 109) to Tobermory (see below). Canoes can be rented at Cyprus Lake too, and you are just 15km from Tobermory.

Tobermory

Just 11km or so beyond the Cyprus Lake turning, Hwy-6 slips into **TOBERMORY**, a quaint fishing village and holiday resort at the northern tip of the peninsula. There are no sights as such, but it's an attractive spot with a tiny centre focused on a slender inlet, **Little Tub harbour**, where **car ferries** (see below) leave for South Baymouth on Manitoulin Island and **passenger boats** shuttle out to Flowerpot Island within Fathom Five National Marine Park.

2

Fathom Five National Marine Park

Fathom Five National Marine Park comprises a scattering of twenty uninhabited islands and the waters that surround them at the end of the Bruce Peninsula, offshore from Tobermory. To protect the natural habitat, only **Flowerpot Island**, 4km from the mainland, has any amenities, with limited space for **camping** – six sites only – and a couple of short hiking trails that explore its eastern reaches. A delightful spot, Flowerpot takes its name from two pink-and-grey rock pillars that have been eroded away from its eastern shore; these are readily seen on the islet's hiking trails.

ARRIVAL AND INFORMATION

THE BRUCE PENINSULA

By bus There are no scheduled buses up along the Bruce Peninsula – the nearest you'll get is Owen Sound (see page 132).

By boat to Flowerpot Island From May to mid-October, Flowerpot Island is easily reached by boat from Tobermory. Several operators run regular services, either dropping passengers off and then collecting them later or pausing at Flowerpot as part of a longer excursion – just stroll along Little Tub harbour until you find the service that suits. One reliable company is Blue Heron (☎ 519 596 2999, ⬤ blueheronco.com). The return fare is $30–45, depending on whether you're getting off at the island. Campers need to make reservations at and get permits from the park office in Tobermory. Both hikers and campers need to pack their own food and drink.

National Park office The office, covering both Fathom Five and the Bruce Peninsula national parks, is on the southeast edge of Tobermory on Chi sin tib dek Rd (late June to Aug daily 8am–8pm; Sept to early Oct Thurs–Mon 9am–5pm; ☎ 519 596 2233, ⬤ pc.gc.ca). It has park maps, will advise on hiking and canoeing, and sells backcountry camping permits (from $15 per person per night), which are compulsory if you're heading off to a backcountry campsite.

Tobermory Visitor Information Centre The village tourist office is down by the harbour (May, June & Sept to mid-Oct daily 9am–5pm; July & Aug daily 9am–9pm; ☎ 519 596 2452, ⬤ tobermory.com).

ACCOMMODATION AND EATING

There are a dozen or so **hotels** and **motels** in and around Tobermory, mostly brisk, modern affairs that are comfortable without being especially distinctive. Advance reservations are essential in the season. Most visitors eat where they sleep.

BRUCE PENINSULA NATIONAL PARK

Cyprus Lake off Hwy-6 ☎ 519 596 2263, ⬤ pccamping. ca/parkscanada. There are three campsites in the environs of Cyprus Lake with a total of 240 pitches. Reservations can be made online or via the visitor centre (see above). Camping is permitted all year. Charges vary with the season and with the facilities offered, but there are no hook-ups. Two adults, a tent and a car. $35

TOBERMORY

★ **Ancient Cedars Café** 7178 Hwy-6 ☎ 519 596

8626. Cute café serving delicious burgers, sandwiches and pasta dishes with local ingredients – there are several excellent vegan options, too. It's attached to a golf course, but well worth a stop even if going out on the greens is not in your plans. Mon & Sun 11am–4pm, Tues–Sat 11am–7pm.

Blue Bay Motel 32 Bay St ☎ 519 596 2392, ⬤ bluebay-motel.com. Family owned and operated, this well-kept two-storey, balconied motel with a variety of comfortable guest rooms on the east side of the harbour. $125

Grandview Motel 11 Earl St ☎ 519 596 2220, ⬤ grandview-tobermory.com. The *Grandview* has around twenty bright and airy rooms and suites, each of which is decorated in a cheerful modern style. The motel is on the east side of the harbour. $105

Manitoulin Island

The **Ojibwa** believed that when Gitchi Manitou (the Great Spirit) created the world he reserved the best bits for himself and created **Manitoulin** (God's Island) as his home. Divine intervention or not, Manitoulin is strikingly different from the harsh grey rocks of the Canadian Shield that surrounds it, its white cliffs, wide lakes, gentle woodland and stretches of open, prairie-like farmland presenting an altogether more welcoming aspect. This rural idyll has long attracted hundreds of summer **sailors**, who ply the lakes that punctuate the island, and has also proved increasingly popular with motorized city folk, who arrive here in numbers on the car ferry from Tobermory (see page 133).

DIVING IN FATHOM FIVE NATIONAL MARINE PARK

Fathom Five is known across Canada for its excellent **diving** – the waters are clear, there are extraordinary rock formations and you can see several well-preserved shipwrecks. Prospective divers must register in person at the National Park office (see page 134). Divers Den (3 Bay St, ☎ 519 596 2363, ⓦ diversden.ca), near the Tobermory harbour, offers a wide range of diving services, including four-hour dives with equipment (from $150), Padi courses (from $185), snorkel tours (from $80) and more.

2

These visitors fan out across the island, exploring its sleepy nooks and crannies, but Manitoulin is at its most diverting along **Hwy-6**, which drifts across the eastern edge of the island for 70km from the South Baymouth ferry dock to Little Current via **Manitowaning** and **Sheguiandah**.

Brief history

Manitoulin is the world's largest freshwater island (at over 2700 square kilometres) and about a quarter of its twelve thousand inhabitants are Aboriginals, descendants of groups believed to have arrived here over ten thousand years ago. Archeologists have uncovered evidence of these Paleoamericans at **Sheguiandah**, on the east coast, and the small display of artefacts at the museum here contains some of the oldest human traces found in Ontario. Much later, in 1836, the island's Aboriginal peoples – primarily Ojibwa and Odawa – reluctantly signed a **treaty** that turned Manitoulin into a refuge for several Georgian Bay bands, who had been dispossessed by white settlers. Few of them came, which was just as well because the whites soon revised their position and wanted the island all for themselves. In 1862, this pressure culminated in a second treaty that gave most of the island to the newcomers. It was all particularly shabby and, to their credit, the Ojibwa band living on the eastern tip of the island at **Wikwemikong** refused to sign. Their descendants still live on this so-called "unceded reserve" and, during the third weekend in August, hold the largest **pow wow** in the country (ⓦ wikwemikong.ca).

Manitowaning and Wikwemikong

Assiginack Museum Bay Rd · June & Sept Mon–Fri 10am–5pm, July & Aug daily 10am–5pm · $4 · ☎ 705 859 3905, ⓦ manitoulin-island.com/museums

The hamlet of **MANITOWANING**, on Hwy-6 about 30km north of the South Baymouth ferry dock, lies on the lakeshore, its tidy streets home to the **Assiginack Museum**, whose pioneer bygones, such as glassware are pottery, are mostly housed within the sturdy limestone building that once served as the local jail. The museum also owns the SS *Norisle*, a 1940s Canadian ferry that has ended up moored here.

From Manitowaning, a side road runs the 14km east to the village of **WIKWEMIKONG**, on Smith Bay and the focus of the eponymous First Nations Reserve. Canada's foremost Aboriginal theatre group, **De-Ba-Jeh-Mu-Jig** (meaning "story teller") is based here and holds regular bilingual (English & Ojibwa) performances of native legends and contemporary plays by Aboriginal playwrights during the summer (call for dates, venues and reservations; ☎ 705 859 2317, ⓦ debaj.ca).

Sheguiandah

Centennial Museum May & Sept to early Oct Tues–Sat 9am–4.30pm; June–Aug daily 9am–4.30pm, Thurs till 8pm · $4 · ☎ 705 368 2367, ⓦ manitoulin-island.com/museums

Hwy-6 pushes on north from Manitowaning, cutting across rolling farmland en route to pint-sized **SHEGUIANDAH**, where the **Centennial Museum** is mainly concerned with the pioneer families who first farmed and traded here. Named photographs tell you who was who – and who was related to whom – in what was once an extremely

2

isolated and tightly knit community, where the inhabitants were called "Haweaters" by outsiders after their liking for the scarlet fruit of the hawthorn tree. It was in this wooded bayshore setting that archeologists found the remains of a Paleoamerican settlement around 10,000 years old. It was a remarkable find but most of the artefacts were carted off to big museums elsewhere, leaving this museum with a modest display of crudely fashioned quartzite tools. The museum also hosts a variety of events, including a Historic Sheguiandah Walking Tour in the summer as well as Pioneer Evenings, which includes a guided tour, pioneer crafts and a butter-making demonstrations (check website for dates; donations encouraged for both).

Little Current

At the northeast tip of Manitoulin, the gridiron streets of **LITTLE CURRENT** nudge up against the bridges and causeways that span the scattering of islands lying between Manitoulin and the mainland. Founded in the middle of the nineteenth century, Little Current once made a healthy living supplying wood for the boilers of the lake steamers as they paused here on their long journeys east and west, but no-one could quite decide what to call the place – Waebijewung and Shaftsbury were both tried before the locals settled on "Little Current".

Hikes on Manitoulin

Heading west from Little Current, Hwy-540 ducks and weaves its way right along the northern edge of Manitoulin, giving long, lingering views over the North Channel. The road also accesses several popular **hiking trails**, notably the 12km-long **Cup and Saucer Lookout Trail**, which starts near – and is signposted from – the junction of Hwy-540 and Bidwell Rd, about 20km from **Little Current**. The trail reaches the highest point of the island (460m) and involves climbing rough wooden ladders and squeezing through natural rock chimneys.

ARRIVAL AND INFORMATION
MANITOULIN ISLAND

By ferry (from the south) Car ferries from Tobermory (see page 133) dock at South Baymouth, on the island's south coast (May to mid-Oct 2–4 daily; $16.50 one way, cars $36.95; 2hr; ☎ 800 265 3163, ⓦ ontarioferries.com).

By road (from the north) From the north, the island is accessible by road (and bridge) from Hwy-17 to the west of Sudbury (see page 176). There are no bus or train services to or around the island.

Tourist office The island's main tourist office is by the bridge, on Hwy-6, in Little Current (early May to June & Sept to early Oct daily 10am–4pm; July & Aug daily 8am–8pm; early Oct to early May Wed–Sat 10am–4pm; ☎ 705 368 3021, ⓦ manitoulintourism.com).

ACCOMMODATION AND EATING

GORE BAY
Queen's Inn B&B 19 Water St ☎ 705 282 0665, ⓦ thequeensinn.ca. Immaculately maintained Victorian mansion with a large communal veranda offering stunning views over the bay. Has eight well-appointed, en-suite guest rooms decorated in an elegant version of period style with lots of antique furnishings. Gore Bay is about 60km west of Little Current on Hwy-540. Note that it only operates May–Dec. **$165**

LITTLE CURRENT
Loco Beanz 7 Water St ☎ 705 368 2261. The best café in town, selling a good range of coffees, and wraps (from $7) and snacks as well as bagels and freshly baked cookies. Mon–Fri 7am–5pm, Sat 7am–4pm, Sun 8am–3pm.

SOUTH BAYMOUTH
Southbay Gallery & Guesthouse B&B 15 Given Rd ☎ 705 859 2363, ☎ 877 656 8324, ⓦ southbay guesthouse.com. A long stone's throw from the ferry dock, this well-kept B&B has four warm and welcoming guest rooms, either en suite or with shared facilities; there's also a tidy cottage that sleeps four. The home-cooked breakfasts are delicious and the attached gallery specializes in locally made jewellery, pottery and so forth. Open May to

September. Shared bathroom $119; en suite $179; cottage $169

TEHKUMMAH
Garden's Gate Hwy-542 ☎ 705 859 2088, ⓦ garden sgate.ca. Distinctive cosy little place that features home-cooking – from the salad dressings to the bread – and regional ingredients. The menu is full of hearty dishes such as the signature chicken in tangy blueberry sauce ($23) and there is a good cellar of Ontario wines. Tehkummah is just west of Hwy-6, 13km north of the ferry dock. To get to the restaurant, follow the signs along Hwy-542 as it branches off from Hwy-6. May–June & Sept–Oct Tues–Sun 5–10pm; July & Aug daily 5–10pm.

Severn Sound

Severn Sound, the southeastern inlet of Georgian Bay, is one of the most beautiful parts of Ontario. The bay's sheltered southern shore is lined by tiny ports and studding its deep-blue waters are the skeletal outcrops of the **Georgian Bay Islands National Park**, whose glacier-smoothed rocks and wispy pines were much celebrated by the Group of Seven painters. There are **cruises** to and around the waters of the national park from all the larger ports bordering Severn Sound, but a hike on the park's **Beausoleil Island** is the best way to enjoy its stunning scenery – and there are boats to the island from the delightfully named hamlet of **Honey Harbour**.

Severn Sound also possesses two of the province's finest historical reconstructions – **Discovery Harbour**, a British naval base on the edge of **Penetanguishene**, and **Sainte-Marie among the Hurons**, a Jesuit mission located near **Midland**. There's more lovely Canadian Shield scenery on the road north to **Parry Sound** (see page 144), an agreeable little port that also serves as a convenient stepping point on the long road north to Sudbury and Northern Ontario. Public transport hereabouts is sketchy with the exception of Parry Sound, which can be reached by both bus and train.

Penetanguishene

The most westerly town on Severn Sound, **PENETANGUISHENE** – "place of the rolling white sands" in Ojibwa – was the site of one of Ontario's first European settlements, a Jesuit mission founded in 1639, then abandoned in 1649 following the burning of Sainte-Marie (see page 141). Europeans returned some 150 years later to establish a trading station, where local Ojibwa exchanged pelts for food and metal tools, but the settlement remained insignificant until just after the War of 1812, when the British built a naval base that attracted a bevy of French and British shopkeepers and suppliers – and is now re-created as **Discovery Harbour**. Penetanguishene itself is an agreeable sort of place, one of the few towns in southern Ontario that maintains a bilingual (French–English) tradition, and one where a string of vintage red-brick facades trail along the town's **Main Street** as it slopes up from Severn Sound.

Centennial Museum
13 Burke St, at Beck blvd, 3min walk east of Main St along the waterfront • July–Aug daily 9am–4.30pm; Sept–June Tues–Fri 9am–4.30pm, Sat 9am–12.30pm & 1–4.30pm. • Free, but donation appreciated • ☎ 705 549 2150, ⓦ pencenmuseum.com
Penetanguishene's interesting **Centennial Museum** occupies the old general store and offices of the Beck lumber company, whose yards once stretched right along the town's waterfront. The company was founded in 1865 by Charles Beck, a German immigrant who made himself immensely unpopular by paying his men half their wages in tokens that were only redeemable at his stores. The museum has several displays on the Beck lumber company, including examples of these "Beck dollars", and there's also a fascinating selection of old photographs featuring locals at work and play in the town and its forested surroundings.

Discovery Harbour
Jury Drive, a signed 5km drive north of Penetanguishene • Mid-May to Aug daily 10am–5pm • $7 • ☎ 705 549 8064, ⓦ discoveryharbour.on.ca

Discovery Harbour, Penetanguishene's prime attraction, is an ambitious reconstruction of the important British naval base established here in 1817. The principal purpose of the base was to keep an eye on American movements on the Great Lakes following the War of 1812, and between 1820 and 1834 up to twenty Royal Navy vessels were stationed here. Ships from the base also supplied the British outposts further to the west and, to make navigation safer, the Admiralty decided to chart the Great Lakes. This monumental task

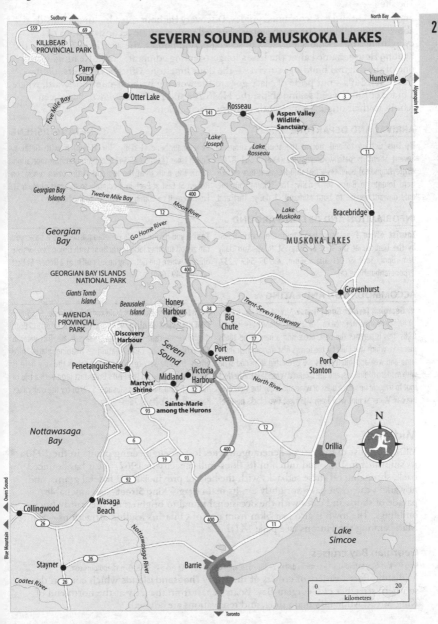

fell to **Lieutenant Henry Bayfield**, who informed his superiors of his determination "to render this work so correct that it shall not be easy to render it more so". He lived up to his word, and his charts remained in use for decades. The naval station was more short-lived. By 1834, relations with the US were sufficiently cordial for the Navy to withdraw, and the base was turned over to the Army, who maintained a small garrison here until 1856.

The site

Staffed by enthusiastic costumed guides, **Discovery Harbour** spreads along a hillside above a tranquil inlet, its green slopes scattered with accurate reconstructions of everything from a sailors' barracks to several period houses, the prettiest of which is the **Keating House**, named after the base's longest-serving adjutant, Frank Keating. Only one of the original buildings survives – the dour limestone **Officers' Quarters**, dating from the 1840s – but pride of place goes to the working harbour-cum-dockyard, where a brace of fully rigged **sailing ships**, the HMS *Bee* and HMS *Tecumseth*, have been rebuilt to their original nineteenth-century specifications.

ARRIVAL AND DEPARTURE
PENETANGUISHENE

By bus Getting to and around the southern shore of Severn Sound is patchy. Greyhound (☎ 800 661 8747, ⓦgreyhound.ca) operates a fast and frequent bus service from Toronto to Barrie (4–7 daily; 1hr 30min), but the only onward service to both Midland (1 daily; 1hr) and Penetanguishene (1 daily; 1hr 15min) is with Getaway Coach Lines (☎ 705 645 5431, ⓦhammondtransportation. com). This pulls in at the top end of the town centre, on Robert St East at Peel, immediately to the east of Main St. From here, it's a 10min stroll down to the harbour.

INFORMATION AND GETTING AROUND

Tourist office Penetanguishene tourist office is down by the harbour at the foot of Main St (May–Aug daily 9am–6pm; Sept & Oct 10am–6pm; ☎705 549 2232, ⓦpenetanguishene.ca).

Taxi If you decide to use Penetanguishene as a base, you can zip off to other local attractions with Union Taxi, whose office is where the Getaway buses pull in at 2 Robert St East (☎705 549 7666).

ACCOMMODATION AND EATING

★ **Georgian Terrace Guest House** 14 Water St ☎705 549 2440, ⓦgeorgianterrace.ca. Of Penetanguishene's several B&Bs, this is perhaps the best, occupying a handsome 1860s mansion, which was built for the town's first mayor. Their three large and well-appointed suites are decorated in period style with modern trimmings, and the splendid veranda is the perfect spot to snuggle up with a glass of wine and enjoy the view over the bay. Water St runs west from Main just two blocks north of the main town crossroads at Main and Robert streets. $155

Phil's Casual Dining 48 Main St ☎705 549 7858, ⓦphilsrestaurant.ca. The name says it all: This veteran diner is all about casual eating – heaping plates, nice prices, friendly service. The best meal of the day here is breakfast – fill up on the Phil's Breakfast (egg with a trio of meats - bacon, ham, and sausage; $12) or try the crab cakes Benedict ($15). Daily 7am–9pm.

Midland

MIDLAND, just to the east of Penetanguishene, lost its engineering plants in the 1930s, its shipyards in 1957 and much of its flour-mill capacity in 1967. Yet it has bounced back, shrugging off these setbacks with the help of provincial and federal grants, and nowadays the town has a sprightly air, its main drag – **King Street** – an amenable parade of shops and cafés with the occasional mural to brighten up the sturdy brick buildings. The town is also just 5km from one of Ontario's leading attractions – Sainte-Marie among the Hurons (see page 141).

Georgian Bay cruises

King St • Mid-May to mid-Oct 1–3 cruises daily • 2–3hr • $36, with dinner $55 • ☎ 705 549 3388, ⓦmidlandtours.com

Midland offers a variety of cruises of the **Thirty Thousand Islands** which confetti the southern stretches of Georgian Bay. Boats depart from the jetty at the north end of King Street, Midland's main drag, and reservations are advised.

Huronia Museum & Huron–Ouendat Village

549 Little Lake Park Rd, off King St, a 20min walk south of the harbour • Mid-May to mid-Oct daily 9am–5pm; mid-Oct to mid-May Mon–Fri 9am–5pm • $12 • ☎ 705 526 2844, ⓦ huroniamuseum.com

First stop for visitors to the **Huronia Museum & Huron–Ouendat Village** is the museum, which holds a number of Huron artefacts and also displays a series of photos tracing the pioneer settlement of Midland. Rather more interesting is the adjacent **village**, a replica of a sixteenth-century Huron settlement, its high palisade encircling storage pits, drying racks, a sweat bath, a medicine man's lodge and two long houses. These longhouses are characteristic Huron constructions, their bark-covered walls of cedar poles bent to form a protective arch. They hold tiers of rough wooden bunks, draped with furs, while up above herbs, fish, skins and tobacco hang from the roof to dry. It all feels surprisingly authentic, though it still lags behind the comparable section of the nearby Sainte-Marie among the Hurons (see below).

ARRIVAL AND INFORMATION

MIDLAND

By bus From Barrie and Penetanguishene (see page 138), the once-daily Getaway bus (1hr from Barrie; ☎ 705 645 5431, ⓦ hammondtransportation.com) to Midland pulls in down by the harbour near the foot of King Street.

Southern Georgian Bay Chamber of Commerce Midland's tourist office is down by the harbour at 208 King St (Mon–Fri 9am–5pm; ☎ 705 526 7884, ⓦ southerngeorgianbay.on.ca).

METTING AROUND

Taxi To visit the attractions surrounding Midland you'll need a taxi – call or drop by Central Taxi, metres from the tourist office at 207 King St, at Bay (☎ 705 526 2626, ⓦ centraltaximidland.ca).

ACCOMMODATION

Victorian Inn B&B 670 Hugel Ave, at 5th St ☎ 705 526 4441, ☎ 877 450 7660, ⓦ victorianinn.ca. In a good-looking Victorian house with a large veranda, this well-established B&B has three en-suite guest rooms decorated in an appealing modern version of period style. Fairly central location, a few blocks to the west of King St. **$129**

EATING

Ciboulette et Cie 248 King St ☎ 705 245 0410, ⓦ cibouletteetcie.ca. On the main street, in a handsomely modernized old general store, this large café does a good line in sandwiches and snacks – both eat-in and take-out. Mon 8am–4pm, Tues–Sat 8am–9pm, Sun 11am–4pm.

The Explorers Café 345 King St ☎ 705 527 9199, ⓦ theexplorerscafe.com. This idiosyncratic little place – in a timber shack tucked away down an alley off the main drag, King St – is part restaurant, part bar. The menu is ambitious, dipping into several types of cuisine (Italian and Indian, for example), and mains average $25–30. Try the salmon with a chipotle maple glaze. Tues–Sat noon–10pm.

Sainte-Marie among the Hurons

Hwy-12, 5km south of Midland • Early April to mid-May & mid- to late Oct Mon–Fri 10am–5pm; mid-May to mid-Oct daily 10am–5pm • $12 • ☎ 705 526 7838, ⓦ saintemarieamongthehurons.on.ca • No buses; a taxi from Midland costs $20 or so

Without a shadow of a doubt, **Sainte-Marie among the Hurons** is one of the province's most arresting historical attractions, comprising the carefully researched and immaculately restored site of a seventeenth-century Jesuit mission to the Huron (also known as Wendat). The mission site is also just across the highway from the **Martyrs' Shrine**, built in the 1920s to commemorate those Jesuits from the mission who came to a very sticky end at the hands of the Iroquois.

Brief history

In 1608, the French explorer and trader **Samuel de Champlain** returned to Canada believing that the only way to make the fur trade profitable was by developing alliances with Aboriginal hunters. The **Huron** (or **Wendat**) were the obvious choice, as they already acted as go-betweens in the exchange of corn, tobacco and hemp from the Aboriginal groups to the south and west of their territory, for the pelts collected to the north. In 1611, having participated in Huron attacks on the Iroquois, Champlain cemented the alliance by a formal exchange of presents. Yet his decision to champion one tribe against another – and particularly his gifts of **firearms** to his allies – disrupted the balance of power among the Aboriginal societies of the St Lawrence and Great Lakes, setting the stage for the destruction of Sainte-Marie almost forty years later.

Meanwhile, the **Jesuits**, who established their centre of operations at Sainte-Marie in 1639, had converted a substantial minority of the Huron community to Christianity, thereby undermining traditional social patterns and obligations. The Hurons had also been enfeebled by the arrival of three European sicknesses – measles, smallpox and influenza. Then, in 1648, the Dutch on the Hudson River began to sell firearms to the **Iroquois**, who launched a full-scale invasion of Huronia in March 1649, slaughtering their enemies as they moved in on Sainte-Marie. Fearing for their lives, the Jesuits of Sainte-Marie burnt their settlement and fled. Eight thousand Hurons went with them; most starved to death on Christian Island, in Georgian Bay, but a few made it to Québec. During the campaign two Jesuit priests, fathers **Brébeuf and Lalemant**, were captured at the outpost of Saint-Louis, near present-day Victoria Harbour, where they were bound to the stake and tortured, as per standard Iroquois practice. The image of Catholic bravery and Indian cruelty lingered in the minds of French-Canadians long after the sufferings of the Hurons had been forgotten.

The mission site

A visit to Sainte-Marie begins in the **visitor centre** with a video that provides some background information before the screen lifts dramatically to reveal the handsomely restored **mission site**. There are 31 wooden buildings here, divided into two main sections: the Jesuit area with its watchtowers, chapel, forge, living quarters, well-stocked garden and farm buildings full of pigs, cows and hens; and the Aboriginal area, including a hospital and a pair of bark-covered long houses – one for Christian converts, the other for "heathens". Costumed guides act out the parts of Hurons and Europeans with great gusto, answering questions and demonstrating crafts and skills, though they show a certain reluctance to eat what was once the staple food of the region, **sagamite**, a porridge of cornmeal seasoned with rotten fish. The grave in the simple wooden **church of St Joseph** between the Christian and Aboriginal areas is the place where the (remaining) flesh of Brébeuf and Lalemant was interred after the Jesuits had removed many of the bones for future use as reliquaries.

The museum

A path leads from the mission site back to the visitor centre, where the excellent **museum** traces the story of the early exploration of Canada with maps and displays on such subjects as fishing and the fur trade, seen in the context of contemporary European history. This leads into a section on the history of the missionaries in New France, with particular reference to Sainte-Marie. Information on the archeology of the site follows: the mission's whereabouts were always known even though Victorian settlers helped themselves to every chunk of stone – from what was known locally as "the old Catholic fort" – because the Jesuits had deposited the necessary documentation in Rome. Excavations began on the site in the 1940s and work is still in progress.

The Martyrs' Shrine

Hwy-12, overlooking Sainte-Marie • Early May to late Oct daily 8am–9pm • $5 • ☎ 705 526 3788, ⓦ martyrs-shrine.com

The eight Jesuits who were killed in Huronia between 1642 and 1649 are commemorated by the **Martyrs' Shrine**, a twin-spired, 1920s church that overlooks Sainte-Marie from the other side of Hwy-12. Blessed by Pope John Paul II in 1984 – when he bafflingly remarked that it was "a symbol of unity of faith in a diversity of cultures" – the church, along with the assorted shrines and altars in its grounds, is massively popular with pilgrims. Inside, the transepts hold a number of saintly reliquaries, most notably the skull of Brébeuf, and a stack of crutches discarded by healed pilgrims.

Port Severn and around

Sitting on the northeastern shore of Severn Sound at the mouth of the Severn River, **PORT SEVERN** is a sprawl of a village that serves as the gateway to the **Trent–Severn Waterway**, a 400km canalized route connecting Georgian Bay with Lake Ontario. With a maximum depth of only 2m, it's of little commercial importance today, but until the late nineteenth century this was one of the region's principal cargo routes. You can view one set of its many **locks** at Port Severn and sign up for a short taster cruise at the *Inn at Christie's Mill* (see below), but otherwise you'll need your own boat to navigate the system. The other watery sight hereabouts is the **Big Chute Marine Railway**, where boats are lifted over the 18m drop between the upper and lower levels of the Severn River. The Big Chute is something of a yawn, but it certainly attracts its share of visitors, most of whom drive here – just follow the signs off Hwy-400 (Exit 162) north of Port Severn.

ARRIVAL AND GETTING AROUND

By bus Port Severn spreads east from Hwy-400. The Ontario Northland bus service from Toronto to Parry Sound and Sudbury (3–4 daily) pulls off the highway to drop passengers at the H&S Gas Bar, on Lone Pine Rd, on the edge of Port Severn, but this leaves you pretty much in the middle of nowhere; neither are there any buses onto Honey Harbour for the Georgian Bay Islands National Park (see

below), 13km to the northwest along Route 5.
By boat You will need your own boat to navigate the Waterway, which is open from the middle of May to the middle of October and takes about a week to travel from one end to the other. For information on fees, lock times and other nautical-related regulations, check with Parks Canada (☎ 888 773 8888, ⓦ pc.gc.ca).

ACCOMMODATION AND EATING

Inn at Christie's Mill 263 Port Severn Rd North ☎ 705 538 2354, ☎ 800 465 9966, ⓦ christiesmill.com. A smart and briskly modern hotel that makes a sound choice, with large, well-appointed rooms which are for the most part decorated in a surprisingly pleasant vintage style. The inn also has the district's best restaurant, with views out across the river. The menu has a seasonal and local bent with mains averaging around $25. Reservations are advised – and the restaurant operates restricted hours out of season. Located just east off Hwy-400. Breakfast not included. **$184**

★ **Severn Lodge** 116 Gloucester Trail ☎ 705 756 2722, ☎ 800 461 5817, ⓦ severnlodge.on.ca. This luxurious lodge has a wonderful solitary location amid a dense forest overlooking a wide and quiet section of the Trent–Severn Waterway. The main lodge and chalets have all the facilities of a mini-resort, including canoe and motorboat rental, an artificial beach, a restaurant and an outdoor swimming pool. To get there, leave Hwy-400 at Exit 162, also the turning for the Big Chute Marine Railway (see above); the lodge is 7km along Route 34. Minimum two-night stay in the summer; price includes meals. **$360**

Georgian Bay Islands National Park

The **Georgian Bay Islands National Park** consists of a scattering of about sixty islands spread out between Honey Harbour and Twelve Mile Bay, about 50km to the north. The park's two distinct landscapes – the glacier-scraped rock of the Canadian Shield and the hardwood forests and thicker soils of the south – meet at the northern end of the largest and most scenic island, **Beausoleil**. Cruises of the waters surrounding the park's islands depart from Penetanguishene (see page 138), Midland (see page 140) and Parry Sound (see page 144), but the only way of making landfall is from **Honey Harbour**, little more than a couple of shops, a liquor store and a few backcountry houses just 13km northwest of Port Severn (see above) across the mouth of the river and along Route 5. Several of the park's islands can be reached by boat from Honey Harbour, but Beausoleil is the obvious objective.

2

Hiking in the park

Beausoleil Island has twelve short **hiking trails**, including two that start at the **Cedar Spring landing stage**, on the southeastern shore. These include the Treasure Trail (3.8km), which heads north behind the marshes along the edge of the island, and the Christian Trail (1.5km), which cuts through beech and maple stands to the balsam and hemlock groves overlooking the rocky beaches of the western shoreline. At the northern end of Beausoleil, within comfortable walking distance of several other **jetties**, are the Cambrian (2km) and Fairy (2.5km) trails, two delightful routes through the harsher scenery of the Canadian Shield. Nearby, just to the west, is the Dossyonshing Trail (2.5km), which tracks through a mixed area of wetland, forest and bare granite in the transitional zone between the two main landscapes.

ARRIVAL AND INFORMATION   GEORGIAN BAY ISLANDS NATIONAL PARK

There are no buses to Honey Harbour – the nearest you will get is Port Severn (see page 143).

By boat Organized by Parks Canada, the DayTripper boat leaves for Beausoleil from the jetty in front of the Honey Harbour visitor kiosk (mid-May to mid-June & early Sept to mid-Oct Mon, Tues & Fri–Sun; mid-June to early Sept daily; 3 daily in each direction; $15.70 including return and park admission; ☎ 705 526 8907). The trip takes 15min and you are left with a maximum of 4hr 30min on the island. Reservations are strongly recommended.

By water taxi Several Honey Harbour operators run a water taxi service over to several of the park's other islands – for example Centennial Island ($60–75) and Island 95

($60–75). The Honey Harbour visitor kiosk can supply operator details. Water taxi prices are negotiable as are drop-off and pick-up times.

Cedar Spring Visitor Centre kiosk There's a small visitor centre near the Cedar Spring dock on Beausoleil (mid-May to mid-June & early Sept to mid-Oct Mon, Tues & Sun 9.30am–5pm, Fri 9am–7pm, Sat 9am–6pm; mid-June to early Sept Mon–Thurs & Sun 9.30am–5pm, Fri 9am–7pm, Sat 9am–6pm; ☎ 705 527 7200, ⓦ pc.gc.ca).

Honey Harbour visitor kiosk There's also a visitor kiosk down by the main jetty in Honey Harbour (mid-May to mid-Oct daily 9am–5pm; ☎ 705 527 7200, ⓦ pc.gc.ca), operated by Parks Canada.

ACCOMMODATION

Camping on Beausoleil ☎ 705 526 9804. There are nine campsites on Beausoleil Island and all except one operate on a self-registration, first-come, first-served basis. The exception is *Cedar Spring* ($25.50), where the visitor centre takes reservations on half the sites for a small additional fee for bookings between May and September. You can also reserve on the official Parks Canada site – pc.gc.ca. For everywhere else, ask about current availability at the Honey

Harbour visitor kiosk or call ahead. Don't forget the insect repellent. $15.70

Rustic cabins on Beausoleil ☎ 705 526 9804. The Cedar Spring landing stage has a handful of rustic cabins, comfortable, if rudimentary, affairs that sleep between two and five visitors. Minimum stay is two nights. Smallest cabins $175

Parry Sound and around

A chirpy little place, **PARRY SOUND** sits beside an inlet of Georgian Bay some 70km north of Port Severn – and well on the way to Sudbury (see page 176). Parry Sound takes its name from the Arctic explorer Sir William Edward Parry, but it earned the nickname "Parry Hoot" on account of the swarms of water-bound log-drivers, who once chose this as the place to get drunk in. The logs and the loggers are long gone and Parry Sound is short on sights, but its slender harbour is overshadowed by a splendid Edwardian railway **trestle bridge** and the few blocks that make up the commercial centre – along and around **James Street** – are dotted with good-looking, old brick and stone buildings. Nowadays, the town is mainly popular for the **boat cruises** that leave the harbour bound for the **Thirty Thousand Islands** out in the bay and for its proximity to one of the region's most impressive parks, **Killbear**.

Georgian Bay cruises

Government Wharf, Bay St • **Afternoon cruise** June to mid-Oct 1 daily • $40 • **Morning cruise** July & Aug 1 daily • $34 • ☎ 705 746 2311, ☎ 800 506 2628, ⓦ islandqueencruise.com

Parry Sound is the home port of the **Island Queen**, which squeezes through the **Thirty Thousand Islands** of Georgian Bay in a spectacular cruise of either two or three hours' duration. The two-hour morning cruise heads north to weave its way through the inner islands, which are dotted with summer cottages, while the three-hour afternoon cruise sails south to a remoter batch of islands, thereby providing a better chance of spotting wildlife. Both cruises pass through the **Hole in the Wall**, a narrow channel with hardly any space to spare. In 2018, Island Queen launched Islander Adventure Tours, cruising to Huckleberry Island, where a naturalist guides you across the island to a quiet beach for a dip in the water.

Killbear Provincial Park

Visitor Centre Mid-May to late June daily 10am–3pm; late June to early Sept daily 10am–5pm; early Sept to mid-Oct daily 10am–3pm • Day-entry with car $11.25 • ☎ 705 342 5492, ⓦ ontarioparks.com • From Parry Sound, head north on Hwy-69 for about 18km until Route 559, the 20km side road that leads to the park entrance

The wild and glacier-scoured Georgian Bay shoreline is seen to fine advantage at **Killbear Provincial Park**, which fills out a tapering, 10km-long peninsula, its spindly cedars and black spruce clinging precariously to a shoreline of pink-granite outcrops, the classic Canadian Shield scenery so beloved by Tom Thomson (see page 150). The best of the park's three short **hiking trails** is the easy 3.5km loop of the **Lookout Point Trail**, which slips through the maple, beech and yellow birch forest of the park's rugged interior to reach a lookout across Parry Sound; allow a couple of hours. The park also has a long stretch of sandy **beach**, a perfect spot for some sunbathing.

ARRIVAL AND INFORMATION

By bus Parry Sound is on the Ontario Northland (☎ 800 461 8558, ⓦ ontarionorthland.ca) bus route from Toronto to Sudbury. Buses pull into *Richard's Coffee House*, 119 Bowes St, 1km or so to the east of the town centre. To get downtown from here, call Parry Sound Taxi (☎ 705 746 1221). There is no public transport to Killbear Provincial Park.
Destinations Port Severn (2–3 daily; 1hr); Sudbury (3 daily; 2hr); Toronto (3 daily; 3hr 30min).
By train VIA Rail's (☎ 888 842 7245, ⓦ viarail.ca) infrequent Toronto–Winnipeg train stops at Parry Sound:

PARRY SOUND AND AROUND

eastbound trains stop at the old CN station on Station St, about 800km from the town centre: walk to the foot of Station St, turn right along Church St and then turn left at McMurray. Westbound trains pull into the old CP station on Avenue Rd, just to the west of the town centre.
Destinations Toronto (3–4 weekly; 4hr 40min); Winnipeg (3 weekly; 30hr).
Tourist office Seasonal office down by the harbour, 70 Church St, next to the *Island Queen* cruise boat jetty (June–Sept daily 9am–8pm; ☎ 705 746 1287, ⓦ gbcountry.com).

ACTIVITIES

White Squall 19 James St ☎ 705 746 4936, ⓦ white squall.com. Highly regarded outdoor pursuits company with an office in the centre of Parry Sound. Specializes in kayaking the waters of Georgian Bay and offers both day-

long and overnight wilderness excursions. A full day of kayaking costs $165, and multi-day trips include 4-day Northeast Coast Ecology, where you'll explore the flora and fauna of this coast.

ACCOMMODATION

★ **Bayside Inn** 10 Gibson St ☎ 705 746 7720, ☎ 866 833 8864, ⓦ psbaysideinn.com. This excellently run, enticing hotel occupies an attractively modernized nineteenth-century house just above the harbour. The rooms are decorated in soothing shades of grey, cream and ruddy brown and the bespoke furniture is contemporary Mennonite handiwork of the finest order. Rooms have air-con and LCD televisions. Off- and shoulder-season discounts. **$113**

Killbear Provincial Park Killbear ☎ 888 668 7275, ⓦ ontarioparks.com. A shortish drive north of Parry Sound, this provincial park (see above) has no fewer than seven campgrounds open from mid-May to early Oct. There are both regular pitches and ones with hook-ups – and reservations are recommended. Most of the campgrounds are on or close to the water. Pitches **$44**; with hook-up **$51**

EATING

Bay St Café 22 Bay St ☎ 705 746 2882. Informal café-restaurant down by the harbour with a pleasant, laidback

feel and cosy decor. Simple dishes include clam chowder, juicy burgers and pasta dishes. July–Aug daily 11am–

11pm, Sept–June daily 11am–9pm, but restricted hours in winter.

★ **Bistro by the Bay** 2 James St ☎ 705 746 3712, ⊚ bistrobythebay.com. A dinner at Parry Sound's most attractive restaurant is one of the area's real treats; choose from well-executed dishes such as a rack of lamb with sweet potato gratin ($39) and blackened salmon ($32); there are also more low-key options such as *poutine* ($9). Don't skip the appetizers, which are meals unto themselves – try the braised pork belly and grilled octopus ($19). Wed–Sun 4–9pm.

★ **Gilly's** Snug Harbour Rd, Snug Harbour ☎ 705 342 5552, ⊚ gillyssnugharbour.com. In a timber shack beside a narrow cove, *Gilly's* serves the best and freshest seafood for miles around – all served with the minimum of fuss. The place heaves at the weekend, when you should expect to wait. To get there from Parry Sound, take Hwy-69 north for about 18km to Route 559 – the Killbear Provincial Park turning; follow Route 559 and watch for the sign to Snug Harbour – a 5km-long detour west. May to mid-June Thurs–Sun noon–9pm; mid-June to Aug Tues–Sun noon–9pm.

The Muskoka Lakes

Hwy-11, the main route from Toronto and Barrie to Algonquin Provincial Park (see page 148), zips past **Orillia**, the one-time home of Stephen Leacock (see page 147), before slicing through the **Muskoka Lakes**, a region of more than 1500 lakes and hundreds of cottage retreats – for this is **cottage country**. The Muskoka Lakes were named after an Ojibwa chief, Mesqua-Ukee, who settled here with his people after aiding the British during the War of 1812. Thereafter, the area was opened to tourism in 1860, when two hikers made the two-day trek from Toronto to a small Ojibwa settlement at what is now the town of Gravenhurst. By the 1890s, the lakes had become the haunt of wealthy families from southern Ontario and although things are more democratic today, this is still primarily the preserve of the well heeled. The main access towns to the Muskoka Lakes – **Gravenhurst**, **Bracebridge** and Huntsville – are strung out along Hwy-11. None has much to offer the passing visitor, with the notable exception of the **Aspen Valley Wildlife Sanctuary** near Huntsville, and you're much better off either heading for one of the area's deluxe hotel resorts or befriending a cottage-owning Canadian, who can show you the local ropes.

Gravenhurst

Sandwiched between two lakes, the gridiron streets of downtown **GRAVENHURST**, some 170km north of Toronto, are surprisingly leafy, but the busiest part of town is down by the harbour, where cottagers whizz in and out to collect supplies. In its early days, the town prospered from logging and for a while it was even called "Sawdust City", until the local council had second thoughts.

Bethune Memorial House National Historic Site

235 John St North, one block west of main drag, Muskoka Rd • June & late Oct Wed–Sun 10am–4pm; July to mid-Oct daily 10am–4pm • $3.90 • ☎ 705 687 4261, ⊚ pc.gc.ca

Gravenhurst's prime historical attraction is the recently upgraded **Bethune Memorial House National Historic Site**, the birthplace of the remarkable Norman Bethune (1890– 1939), a doctor who introduced Western medicine to the Chinese in the 1930s and invented mobile blood-transfusion units. The house has been restored to its appearance in 1890 and has displays on Bethune's considerable accomplishments – he was even praised by Chairman Mao – all detailed in English, French and Chinese.

ARRIVAL AND DEPARTURE   **GRAVENHURST**

By bus Ontario Northland (☎ 800 461 8558, ⊚ ontario northland.ca) operates a regular bus service (5–6 daily) from Toronto through the Muskoka Lakes, calling at Barrie, Orillia, Gravenhurst, Bracebridge, Huntsville and ultimately North Bay (see page 151). In Gravenhurst, it pulls into the station on the south side of the centre at 150 2nd St South. Destinations Bracebridge (4 daily; 15–30min); North Bay (4 daily; 2hr 35min); Toronto (4 daily; 3hr).

ORILLIA: THE HOME OF STEPHEN LEACOCK

Small-town **Orillia**, beside Hwy-11 on the road north to Algonquin Provincial Park (see page 148), is far from riveting, but it is home to the intriguing **Stephen Leacock Museum and National Historic Site**, 50 Museum Drive (mid-May to mid-Sept daily 10am–4pm, late Sept to early Dec 10am–4pm; $5; ⓦ leacockmuseum.com), which stands on the lakeshore about 3km southeast of the town centre – just follow the signs. Built in 1928 in the colonial style, this was the summer home of the humourist and academic **Stephen Leacock** (1869–1944), whose most famous book, *Sunshine Sketches of a Little Town*, gently mocks the hypocrisies and vanities of the people of Mariposa, an imaginary town so clearly based on Orillia that it caused great local offence. The museum itself contains furnishings and fittings familiar to Leacock, while other exhibits shed light on his career, interests and attitudes – and there's a striking contrast here: his books are engagingly whimsical, but you can't help but wonder about a man who had concealed spyholes in his library so that he could watch his guests and, perhaps worse, carefully positioned his favourite living-room chair so that he could keep an eye on his servants in the pantry via the dining-room mirror.

2

EATING

Blue Willow Tea Shop 900 Bay St ☎ 705 687 2597, ⓦ bluewillowteashop.ca. Much of Gravenhurst's old harbour has been redeveloped and rebranded as Muskoka Wharf and it's here you'll find this pleasant café in an old timber building. They sell wraps, sandwiches, soups, quiches and other light meals – standouts include a sizeable ploughman's lunch ($16.25) and shrimp and scallop salad ($15.50). Variable hours, but normally Wed–Sat 11am–3pm.

Bracebridge and around

Straddling the Muskoka River, **BRACEBRIDGE**, a quick 20km north of Gravenhurst, boasts of its location on the 45th Parallel, halfway between the North Pole and the equator – perhaps not much to get excited about, but it does for starters. The town's most distinctive feature is the **waterfall** at the foot of the main street, and it was this ready source of energy that attracted the town's first settlers in the 1860s. Otherwise, the prettiest part of Bracebridge is the short main drag, **Manitoba Street**, which is flanked by a pleasant ensemble of Victorian red-bricks. Bracebridge is also within comfortable striking distance of both Algonquin Provincial Park (see page 148), about 100km away, and the **Aspen Valley Wildlife Sanctuary**.

Aspen Valley Wildlife Sanctuary

1116 Crawford St, Rosseau • Four open houses annually May–Sept (no reservation needed; check website for dates) • Free, but donation expected • Private tours by appointment only from $30 for 2 people • ☎ 705 732 6368, ⓦ aspenvalley.ca • From Bracebridge, take Hwy-11 north to Exit 219; turn west along the Aspdin Rd (County Road #3); continue west until you reach the signed turning, about 2km short of Rosseau; total journey about 65km

The fascinating **Aspen Valley Wildlife Sanctuary** gives you a chance to see many of Canada's wild species in a natural habitat. Audrey Tournay founded the sanctuary over forty years ago and it's now the largest **black bear rehabilitation centre** in the world. Spread over a thousand acres, the sanctuary houses orphaned bear cubs – often rescued in the hunting season – nursing them until they're strong enough to be released back into the wild. You won't get up close and personal with the cubs, as they need to be kept shy of humans, but the permanent residents (animals unfit ever to be released) more than compensate. Look out for the Arctic wolves, raccoons, white-tailed deer, birds of prey, beavers and otters.

ARRIVAL AND DEPARTURE   BRACEBRIDGE AND AROUND

By bus Ontario Northland's Toronto-to-North Bay bus pulls in on the south side of the Muskoka River at 300 Ecclestone Drive, about 1km southwest of the main street.

Destinations Gravenhurst (4–5 daily; 15–30min); North Bay (5 daily; 2hr 15min); Toronto (5 daily; 3hr 15min).

2

ACCOMMODATION AND EATING

Inn at the Falls 1 Dominion St ☎705 645 2245, ⓦinnatthefalls.ca. This unusual hotel is Bracebridge's star turn, comprising a substantial Victorian mansion, complete with a battery of original furnishings and fittings, and six old houses nearby – altogether a bit like an open-air museum. The updating has been done sympathetically, though guest rooms vary considerably in terms of size and facilities (which is reflected in the pricing). The on-site restaurant (daily for lunch and dinner) is a cosy spot for filling cuisine – pork tenderloin, Milford Bay trout – and offers excellent views of the Muskoka River. Mains $18–26. **$109**
Sherwood Inn 1090 Sherwood Rd, Port Carling ☎705

765 3131, ☎ 1 866 844 2228, ⓦsherwoodinn.ca. A handsome complex of deluxe chalet-villas set deep in the Muskoka woods beside Lake Joseph. The decor is traditional – plush country house is the best description – and each of the guest rooms is comfortable and suitably lush. The food is first-rate too – try the rosemary-scented rack of lamb. Mains $25–35 To get there, take Hwy-118 west from Bracebridge and after 25km you reach Port Carling; stay on Hwy-118 and keep going till you hit Hwy-169, where you turn right – and shortly afterwards you'll see the sign. Full- and half-board deals are available. Rooms only **$235**

Algonquin Provincial Park

Created in 1893 at the behest of logging companies keen to keep farmers out, **Algonquin Provincial Park** is Ontario's oldest and largest provincial park and for many it comprises the quintessential Canadian landscape. Located on the southern edge of the Canadian Shield, the park straddles a **transitional zone**, with the hilly two-thirds to the west covered in a hardwood forest of sugar maple, beech and yellow birch, while in the drier eastern part jack pine, white pine and red pine predominate. Throughout the park, the lakes and rocky rounded hills are interspersed with black spruce bogs, a type of vegetation typical of areas far further north. **Canoeing** is very popular here and with an astounding 1600km of routes there's a good chance of avoiding all contact for days on end. **Wildlife** is as varied as the flora – any trip to Algonquin is characterized by the echo of birdsong, from the loons' ghostly call to the screech of ravens. Beavers, moose, black bears and raccoons are all resident, as are white-tailed deer, whose population thrives on the young shoots that replace the trees felled by the park's loggers. Public "howling parties" – which can attract up to two thousand people – set off into the wilderness during August in search of **timber wolves**, or rather their howls: many of the rangers are so good at howling that they can get the animals to reply.

Whether you're after the full wilderness experience or just a quick dabble, access to Algonquin's backcountry is via the 56km **Parkway Corridor** – also known as the Frank McDougall Parkway (Hwy-60) – the park's only significant road linking the West Gate, 45km east of Hwy-11, and the East Gate, on the long road to and from Ottawa.

The Parkway Corridor

Entering Algonquin Park from the west along the **Parkway Corridor**, the location of trailheads and campsites is indicated by distances from the **West Gate**. Fifteen **day-hikes** begin beside the road; the 2km **Beaver Pond Trail** (Km45) is a rugged but easy trail that takes you past huge beaver dams, while the equally short but somewhat steeper **Lookout Trail** (Km39) offers fine views. For a longer trail with greater chances of spotting wildlife, the 11km **Mizzy Lake Trail**(Km15) is recommended, and it also skirts nine ponds. Spare time also for both the **Algonquin Art Centre** (Km20; late June to mid-Oct daily 10am–5pm; donation; ⓦalgonquinartcentre.com), which has regularly rotated exhibitions on the park's flora and fauna, as well as events like art classes and lectures, and the **Algonquin Logging Museum** (late May to mid-Oct daily 9am–5pm; free with park day-pass; ⓦalgonquinpark.on.ca), near the East Gate at Km54.5. Here, the namesake 1.3km gentle loop trail threads past some fascinating old logging leftovers, including a tugboat, a locomotive, a saw-log camp and sleighs.

ARRIVAL AND DEPARTURE

By public transport Ontario Northland (☎ 800 461 8558, ⓦ ontarionorthland.ca) operates a regular bus service (4 daily) from Toronto to Bracebridge (see page 147) and Huntsville (3–4 daily; 3hr 30min), from where there is a limited bus service on into the park (July & Aug 3 weekly; $40 each way) with Hammond Transportation (☎ 705 645 5431, ⓦ hammondtransportation.com).

ALGONQUIN PROVINCIAL PARK

By car Access to the park is via either the West Gate, 45km from Huntsville along Hwy-60, or – if you're arriving from Ottawa and points east – the East Gate. The two gates are linked by the 56km-long Parkway Corridor – also known as the Frank McDougall Parkway – the park's only road. Away from the corridor, walking and canoeing are the only means of transport.

INFORMATION

Algonquin Visitor Centre The main visitor centre is 43km inside the park from the West Gate and 11km from the East Gate (late April to mid-May & mid to late Oct daily 10am–5pm; late May to June & Sept to mid-Oct daily 10am–6pm; July & Aug daily 9am–8pm; Nov to late April Sat & Sun 10am–4pm; ☎ 705 633 5572, ⓦ ontarioparks.com). It holds a series of dioramas explaining the park's general and natural history. It also stocks a comprehensive range of literature describing every aspect of the park, from maps and detailed hiking trail and canoeing route guides through to booklets on Aboriginal folklore.

West & East Gates There are park offices at both gates (same hours as the visitor centre). They have trail descriptions and park information, but there's not so wide a range as at the main visitor centre; individual trail guides are also available at most trailheads.

Entry A day-pass costs $17 per vehicle including occupants.

Permits and food If you're heading for the backcountry, pick up food and water before you get here as outlets in the park are few and far between. Backcountry camping requires a permit, available at both gates and at the visitor centre (from $12 per person per night).

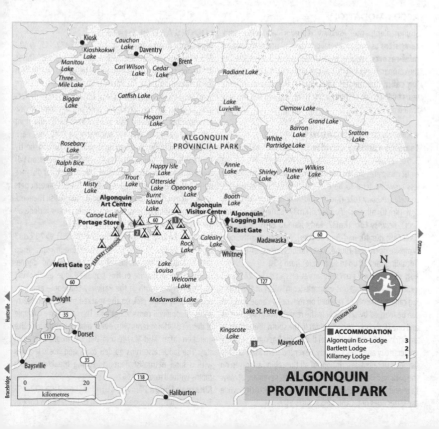

2

THE MYSTERY OF TOM THOMSON

Arguably Canada's greatest painter, **Tom Thomson** drowned in Canoe Lake in Algonquin Park in 1917. He was last seen setting out across the lake on a fishing trip, but a few hours later his empty canoe was spotted bobbing around on the water and his body was finally discovered one week later. No one knows what happened to Thomson – and his death may well have been an accident – but he was an expert canoeist and an experienced backwoodsman, skills that would seem to make his accidental death unlikely. The result has been all sorts of theories to explain his early demise – from the conceivable (suicide) to the bizarre (shot by a World War I deserter hiding in the woods). Whatever the truth, there's a cairn **monument** to Thomson overlooking Canoe Lake a forty-minute paddle from the Portage Store.

TOURS AND ACTIVITIES

Call of the Wild For all-in adventure tours of Algonquin throughout the year, the outstanding operator is Call of the Wild, 23 Edward St, in Markham, a suburb of Toronto (☎ 905 471 9453, ☎ 800 776 9453, ⓦ call-wild.com). Among a varied programme, they run personalized and relaxed canoe trips in the park (3/4/5 days: $480/630/775) with experienced guides. Prices include all meals, permits and equipment. dvance reservations are essential.

Canoe rental The park interior is best explored by canoe,

and there are several outfitters dotted along the Parkway Corridor. One of the best is the Portage Store at Canoe Lake (Km14; summer ☎ 705 633 5622, winter ☎ 705 789 3645, ⓦ portagestore.com). Rates vary enormously depending on the sort of canoe you rent, but the simplest models cost about $30 per day (or $25 per day for five days and over). The Portage Store also rents tents, life vests and all the associated canoeist's tackle, and organizes guided canoe trips; in all cases, reservations are essential.

ACCOMMODATION

Strung along the Parkway Corridor are nine park **campsites** as well as several privately owned **lodges and mini-resorts**, ranging from the simple and unaffected to the comparatively lavish. You can also stay in a backcountry **log cabin**: the rangers who roamed the park in its early years built dozens of them; some have survived and are now rented out.

CAMPSITES AND CABINS

Camping Parkway Corridor Reservations ☎ 519 826 5290, ☎ 888 668 7275, ⓦ ontarioparks.com. Of the eight campsites dotted out along the Parkway Corridor, the less crowded tend to be those that prohibit motorboats, namely *Canisbay Lake* (Km23; mid-May to early Oct); *Mew Lake* (Km30; all year); *Pog Lake* (Km37; early June to early Sept); *Kearney Lake* (Km37; early June to early Sept); and *Coon Lake* (Km40; mid-June to Aug). *Mew Lake* is the only campsite open year-round. Reservations are essential. Sites (including car and up to six people) from **$30**

Log cabins and yurts Reservations ☎ 519 826 5290, ☎ 888 668 7275, ⓦ ontarioparks.com. Most of the park's log cabins can only be reached on foot or by canoe, but five can be reached by car – four in the remote north of the park and one (*Rain Lake Ranger Cabin*) in the south (but not from the Parkway Corridor). None of the cabins has running water or electricity and they can only be rented from May to early October. Detailed descriptions of all the cabins are given on the park website. Of the park's eight yurts, seven are at Mew Lake and one is at Achray; the former have electricity, while the latter does not. Cabins **$62**; yurts **$97**

LODGES AND RESORTS

Algonquin Eco-Lodge Maynooth ☎ 905 471 945, ☎ 800 776 9453, ⓦ algonquinecolodge.com; map p.149. This is the remotest lodge in the Algonquin, located far away from the (relative) bustle of the Parkway Corridor at the southern tip of the park. Built to high ecological standards, it's a perfect base for canoeing and hiking, and is very comfortable. Access is convoluted: leave the park via the East Gate, turn right onto Hwy-127 after Whitney and carry on until you reach Maynooth. At Maynooth, turn right onto Hwy-62 and shortly afterwards turn right again onto County Rd 10 (Peterson Rd) and watch for the lodge sign after 18km. The total distance from the East Gate to the lodge is about 70km. Domestic pets are not allowed – as the wolves would soon polish them off. Two-night minimum stay in the summer. Prices include all meals. **$140**; two-night stay in summer **$320**

Bartlett Lodge Parkway Corridor (Km23) ☎ 705 633 5543, ☎ 866 614 5355, ⓦ bartlettlodge.com; map p.149. Modern log cabins of varying size and degree of luxury are a feature of this popular lodge overlooking Cache Lake just south of the Parkway Corridor – and only accessible by boat: pick up the marked phone at the jetty and someone will come to get you. They also have a couple of deluxe platform tents with every mod con – it's a bit like going on safari. Mid-May to mid-Oct. Two-night minimum stay. The lodge also runs guided tours and hosts lectures with a local naturalist. Tents, including breakfast **$165**; cabins with all meals **$295**

Killarney Lodge Parkway Corridor (Km32) ☎ 877 767 5935, ⓦ killarneylodge.com; map p.149. Dating back to the 1930s, the comfortable log cabins of this lovely resort dot a spindly promontory that hooks out into the Lake of Two Rivers. Has a splendid wilderness setting. Early May to mid-Oct. Full board only. $\overline{\$339}$

North Bay

Once an important halting point on the canoe route running from Montréal to the west, **NORTH BAY**, about 160km from Bracebridge and 100km from Sudbury (see page 176), is a relative giant hereabouts with a population of about 64,000. Settlement got under way in the 1880s and the town flourished on the back of its lumber and mining industries, but more recently it's moved into health and education.

Cruising Lake Nipissing

200 Memorial Drive, Kings Landing · Cruises: Mid-May to mid-June Sat & Sun only, 1 daily; mid-June to early Sept 1 daily; early Sept to early Oct Sat only, 1 daily · 90min · $29 · ☎ 705 494 8167, ⊕ georgianbaycruise.com

North Bay is glued to the shores of Lake Nipissing and the town's star turn is a modern passenger vessel that makes scheduled **cruises** around the Manitou Islands in the middle of the lake. There are other types of cruise, such as dinner and sunset, but the Manitou cruise does very nicely.

ARRIVAL AND INFORMATION NORTH BAY

By bus Both Ontario Northland and Greyhound buses stop at the Intermodal station at 100 Station Rd, to the east of – and a local cab ride from – the downtown core, which zeroes in on Main St, one block from the lakeshore.

Destinations (Greyhound) Ottawa (3 daily; 5hr); Sudbury (3 daily; 2hr).

THE BEAVER

The **beaver** is Canada's national animal: it appeared on the first postage stamp issued by the colony in 1851, and now features on the back of the 5¢ piece. There was nothing sentimental about this choice – beaver pelts kick-started the colonial economy – and only recently has the beaver been treated with some restraint and protected from being indiscriminately polished off.

Beavers are aquatic rodents, growing to around 75cm in length and weighing about 35kg. Aboriginal peoples hunted the beaver for its thick, soft **pelt**, composed of long guard hairs and a dense undercoat, to use for clothing. In the seventeenth century, European fur traders realized the value of beaver pelts, particularly in the manufacture of the all-weather, all-purpose **hat** worn by every man of any substance. To keep up with demand the beaver was extensively trapped, and the French *voyageurs* pushed further and further west along the lake and river systems in pursuit of the animal, thereby opening up much of the interior. The beaver was hunted to the point of extinction in much of eastern Canada, but had a reprieve when the beaver hat went out of fashion in the late nineteenth century; today beavers are comparatively commonplace.

Beavers start to build their **dams**, which can be up to 700m wide, by strategically felling one tree across a stream. This catches silt and driftwood and the beaver then reinforces the barrier with sticks and stones plus grass and mud, which is laboriously smoothed-in as a binding element. The **lodge** is constructed simultaneously; sometimes it forms part of the dam and sometimes it is fixed to the shore or an island in the pond. It is about 2m in diameter and has two entrances – one accessible from land and one from underwater – both for its own convenience and to be able to escape predators in any emergency, along with a lot of tail slapping to give the alarm. Lodges are topped with grass thatch and a good layer of mud, which freezes in winter, making them virtually impenetrable. During the autumn, the beaver stocks its **pond** with the soft-bark trees and saplings that make up its diet. It drags them below the water line and anchors them to the mud at the bottom before retiring to the lodge for the winter, only emerging to get food from the pond or repair the dam.

2

Destinations (Ontario Northland) Bracebridge (4 daily; 2hr); Cochrane (2–3 daily; 6hr 15min); Gravenhurst (4 daily; 2hr 30min); Orillia (4 daily; 3hr 15min); Toronto (4 daily; 6hr).
Tourist office Beside Hwy-11 on the south side of town at 1375 Seymour St (July & Aug daily 9am–7pm; Sept–June Mon–Fri 9am–5pm, Sat & Sun 10am–4pm; ☎705 472 8480, ⊛cityofnorthbay.ca).

ACCOMMODATION

Most of North Bay's **accommodation** is concentrated on **Lakeshore Drive**, a crowded strip of motels and fast-food joints strung along the sandy shore of Lake Nipissing.

Best Western North Bay Hotel 700 Lakeshore Drive ☎705 474 5800, ⊛book.bestwestern.com. Not far from the lake, this substantial hotel has no-nonsense modern rooms at competitive prices. There's also a fitness centre and hot-tub. **$116**

Lakeshore (North Bay) Travelodge 718 Lakeshore Drive ☎705 472 7171, ⊛travelodge.com. No surprises here at this modern chain hotel, whose general layout is reminiscent of a motel. It has a good location, metres from Lake Nipissing, and the guest rooms are kept in good order. **$75**

Sunset Inn 641 Lakeshore Drive ☎705 472 8370, ⊛sunsetinn.ca. Just south along the lakeshore from North Bay, this inn occupies a prime location. It's made up of a substantial two-storey modern lodge, decorated in bright and cheerful colours, and a scattering of smaller chalets surrounding it (two bedrooms; $239). Dine at the top-notch on-site restaurant, *White Owl Bistro* (see below). **$120**

EATING

Urban Café 101b Worthington St East ☎705 472 0032, ⊛urbancafenorthbay.com. The town's best café, a lively downtown joint with a varied menu – everything from salads and wraps to burgers and teriyaki. The salads average about $11–14. Mon–Fri 10am–3.30pm & Sat 11am–3pm.

The White Owl Bistro 639 Lakeshore Dr ☎705 472 2662, ☎thewhiteowlbistro.ca. This welcoming, lakeshore restaurant serves seasonal dishes made with fresh ingredients from local farms, including watermelon and cucumber salad with chunks of feta, and rainbow trout with pineapple-lime salsa. Mains $23–35. Mon–Sat 11am–9pm, Sun 10am–3pm & 5–9pm.

Kingston

Birthplace of the rock singer Bryan Adams but prouder of its handsome limestone buildings, the city of **KINGSTON**, a fast 260km east of Toronto along Hwy-401, is the largest and most enticing of the communities along the northern shore of Lake Ontario. The town occupies an attractive and strategically important position where the lake narrows into the St Lawrence River, its potential first recognized by the French who built a fortified fur-trading post, **Fort Frontenac**, here in 1673. It was not a success, but struggled on until 1758 when it fell to a combined force of British, Americans and Iroquois, a victory soon followed by an influx of United Empire Loyalists (see page 329), who promptly developed Kingston – as they renamed it – into a major shipbuilding centre and naval base. The money rolled in and the future looked rosy when the completion of the Rideau Canal (see page 166), linking Kingston with Ottawa in 1832, opened up its hinterland. Kingston became Canada's **capital** in 1841 and although it lost this distinction just three years later it remained the region's most important town until the end of the nineteenth century. Over the last decade, Kingston – and its 160,000 inhabitants – has had as many economic downs as ups, but it does benefit from the presence of **Queen's University**, one of Canada's most prestigious academic institutions, and of the **Royal Military College**, the country's answer to Sandhurst and West Point.

Central Kingston's medley of old houses and offices displays every architectural foible admired by the Victorians, from neo-Gothic mansions with high gables to elegant Italianate villas, but the cream of the architectural crop is the city's Neoclassical limestone buildings, especially **City Hall** and the **Cathedral of St George**. Kingston also holds the first-rate **Agnes Etherington Art Centre** gallery and **Bellevue House**, once the home of prime minister Sir John A. Macdonald. Add to this several superb B&Bs, a cluster of good restaurants and bars and scenic **boat trips** round the **Thousand Islands** just offshore, and you have a city that is well worth a couple of days.

Kingston's elongated centre slopes up from Lake Ontario. Most of the key sights and the pick of the city's bars and restaurants nudge together along the first few blocks of the main commercial drag, **Princess Street**.

City Hall and around

Ontario St · Mid-May to Aug 30–45min guided tours Mon–Sat 10am–4pm; Sept to mid-Oct Mon–Thurs 10am–4pm; self-guided tours of first two floors year-round Mon–Fri 8.30am–4.30pm groups Mon–Fri year-round by appointment · Free · ☎ 613 546 4291, Ⓦ cityofkingston.ca

The obvious place to start a visit to Kingston is **City Hall**, a copper-domed, stone extravagance which, with its imposing Neoclassical columns and portico, dominates the waterfront as was intended – a suitably grand structure for what was scheduled to be the Canadian Parliament. By the time the building was completed in 1844, however, Kingston had lost its capital status and – faced with colossal bills – the city council had to make some quick adjustments, filling the empty corridors with shops and stalls and even a saloon. Things are more sedate today, with municipal offices occupying most of the space, but the tour does provide a fascinating insight into the development of the city and includes a trip up the **clock tower** via a magnificent circular stairway.

At the back of City Hall is the **Market Square**, which is home to an excellent open-air **market** (April–Nov Tues, Thurs & Sat 8am–6pm) and on summer Sundays the square is given over to craft and antiques stalls. In front of City Hall is the site of the original French outpost and this is now marked by the pocket-sized **Confederation Park**, whose manicured lawns run behind the harbour with its marina and squat, nineteenth-century Martello tower.

Anglican Cathedral of St George

270 King St East · Tues–Fri 9am–4.30pm · Free · ☎ 613 548 4617, Ⓦ stgeorgescathedral.ca

It's a five-minute walk from City Hall to Kingston's finest limestone building, the **Anglican Cathedral of St George**, hogging the skyline at King and Johnson streets. Dating from the 1820s, the stirring lines of the cathedral, with its Neoclassical portico and dainty domes, are deceptively uniform, for the church was remodelled on several occasions, notably after severe fire damage in 1899. The capacious interior holds some delightful Tiffany stained glass windows and, attached to the wall of the nave, a plain **memorial** to Molly Brant (1736–97), a Mohawk leader and sister of Joseph Brant (see page 117).

EXPLORE KINGSTON WITH A K-PASS

Discover Kingston with a K-Pass (kpass.ca), which covers a wide variety of sights, tours and cruises, including Fort Henry (see page 156), a Kingston 1000 Islands Cruise (see page 155), Kingston Trolley Tours and more. A 24-hour pass is $89, 48 hours is $109 and 72 hours is $129. You can buy your pass online, and then pick it up at 248 Ontario Street when you arrive in town.

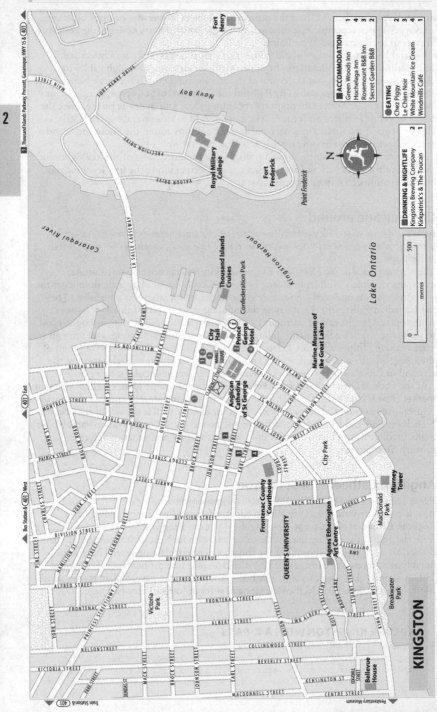

2

◀ 1 Thousand Islands Parkway, Prescott, Gananoque, HWY 15 & 401

Fort Henry

FORT HENRY DRIVE

Navy Bay

PRECISION DRIVE

Royal Military College

VALOUR DRIVE

Fort Frederick

Point Frederick

MAIN STREET

LA SALLE CAUSEWAY

Cataraqui River

Thousand Islands Cruises

Confederation Park

Kingston Harbour

Lake Ontario

PLACE D'ARMES
BARRACK STREET
WELLINGTON ST
City Hall
Prince George Hotel
MARKET SQUARE
Anglican Cathedral of St George
CLARENCE STREET
RIDEAU STREET

N

0   500
     metres

ACCOMMODATION
Green Woods Inn   1
Hochelaga Inn   4
Rosemount B&B Inn   3
Secret Garden B&B   2

EATING
Chez Piggy   2
Le Chien Noir   3
White Mountain Ice Cream 4
Windmills Café   1

DRINKING & NIGHTLIFE
Kingston Brewing Company 2
Kirkpatrick's & The Toucan 1

◀ 401 East

MONTREAL STREET

BAY STREET
ORDNANCE STREET
SYDENHAM STREET
QUEEN STREET
PRINCESS STREET
BROCK STREET
WILLIAM STREET
JOHNSON STREET
EARL STREET

ONTARIO STREET
KING STREET EAST
GORE STREET
WELLINGTON ST
KING STREET
LOWER UNION STREET
WEST STREET

Marine Museum of the Great Lakes

City Park

Murney Tower

MacDonald Park

RAGLAN ROAD
JOHN STREET
PATRICK STREET

CHARLES STREET
YORK STREET
COLBORNE STREET
DIVISION STREET

BARRIE STREET
COURT STREET
ARCH STREET
GEORGE ST

Frontenac County Courthouse

UNIVERSITY AVENUE

◀ Bus Station & 401 West

PINE STREET
HAMILTON ST
ELM STREET

ALFRED STREET

FRONTENAC STREET

DIVISION STREET

QUEEN'S UNIVERSITY

Agnes Etherington Art Centre

UNIVERSITY AVE

STUART STREET
BARRIE LANE
QUEEN'S CRESCENT
KING STREET WEST

Breakwater Park

Victoria Park

ALFRED STREET
FRONTENAC STREET
ALBERT STREET
COLLINGWOOD STREET
BEVERLEY STREET
KENSINGTON ST
MACDONNELL STREET
CENTRE STREET

PRINCESS STREET (HWY 2)
NELSON STREET

VICTORIA STREET
DUNDAS ST
MACK STREET
BROCK STREET
JOHNSON STREET
EARL STREET
COLLINGWOOD STREET

Bellevue House

COLLINGWOOD STREET
LWR ALBERT STREET

KINGSTON

◀ 401 East

▲ Train Station & 401   Penitentiary Museum ▶

GUIDED TOURS IN KINGSTON BY LAND AND RIVER

Kingston offers a full complement of **guided tours**. Top of the list are **cruises** out among the **Thousand Islands** (see page 160) from the dock at the foot of Brock Street. The islands, which speckle the St Lawrence River as it leaves Lake Ontario, range from tiny hunks of rock to much larger islets with thick forest and lavish second homes. It's a pretty cruise at any time of the year, but especially so in autumn when the leaves turn.

Kingston 1000 Islands Cruises ☎ 613 549 5544, ⓦ 1000islandscruises.ca. Several local companies offer cruises, but the benchmark is set by Kingston 1000 Islands Cruises, whose three-hour sightseeing excursions are as good as any (late June–Oct 1–3 daily; $45). They leave from the dock at the foot of Brock St,

near City Hall.

Haunted Walk of Kingston ☎ 613 549 6366, ⓦ hauntedwalk.com. An enjoyable 90min narrated stroll through the older parts of town beginning at the Haunted Walk Ticket Office at 200 Ontario St (Feb–Nov 1–2 daily; $23.75).

Marine Museum of the Great Lakes

53 Yonge St, Portsmouth Olympic Harbour • Daily Mon–Fri 10am–4pm • Free • ☎ 613 542 2261, ⓦ marmuseum.ca

The **Marine Museum of the Great Lakes** tracks through the region's maritime history with ship models and a huge miscellany of nautical artefacts, from navigational instruments and rigging gear to boat-building tools and steam engines.

Murney Tower

MacDonald Park • Mid-May to early Sept daily 10am–5pm • $5 • ☎ 613 507 5181, ⓦ kingstonmuseums.ca

Murney Tower is by the lake at the foot of Barrie Street. The most impressive of four such towers built to defend the Kingston dockyards against an anticipated US attack during the Oregon Crisis of 1846–47, this one is packed with military memorabilia including old weapons, uniforms and re-created nineteenth-century living quarters. The design of the tower, built as a combined barracks, battery and storehouse, was copied from a Corsican tower (at Martello Point) that had proved particularly troublesome to the British navy. A self-contained, semi-self-sufficient defensive structure with thick walls and a protected entrance, the Martello design proved so successful that towers like this were built throughout the empire, only becoming obsolete in the 1870s with advances in artillery technology. Incidentally, on Christmas Day 1885, members of the Royal Canadian Rifles regiment set out to skid around the frozen lake equipped with their **hockey sticks** and a **lacrosse ball**, thereby inventing (or at least so Kingstonians assert) the sport that has become a national passion – ice hockey.

Queen's University: the Agnes Etherington Art Centre

University Ave • Tues–Fri 10am–4.30pm (Thurs till 9pm), Sat & Sun 1–5pm • Free; donations welcome • ☎ 613 533 2190, ⓦ agnes.queensu.ca

The campus of **Queen's University** spreads west from Barrie Street between Earl and Stuart streets. There's a clutch of handsome limestone buildings here too, but the place to aim for is the first-rate **Agnes Etherington Art Centre**, on the corner of University Avenue and Bader Lane. The gallery has an excellent reputation for its temporary exhibitions, so the paintings are regularly rotated, but the first two rooms usually kick off in dramatic style with a vivid selection of Canadian Abstract paintings. Beyond, a healthy slice of gallery space is mostly devoted to the **Group of Seven**, with two highlights being a striking *Evening Solitude* by **Lawren Harris** and the carpet-like, rolling fields of **Arthur Lismer's** *Québec Village*, while **Tom Thomson** chips in with his studied *Autumn, Algonquin Park*. Other exhibits to look out for are the **Inuit** prints of Kenojuak and Pitseolak – two of the best-known Inuit artists of modern times;

a satisfying collection of Dutch seventeenth-century paintings; heritage **quilts** from eastern Ontario; and the work of **Jack Bush** (1909–77), who began painting in the style of the Group of Seven, but graduated to forceful, strongly coloured abstracts.

Bellevue House

35 Centre St, 2km west of the city centre along King St West · Late May to end June & early Sept to early Oct Thurs–Mon 10am–5pm; July to early Sept daily 10am–5pm · $3.90 · ☎ 613 545 8666, ⓦ pc.gc.ca

Born in Glasgow, **Sir John Alexander Macdonald** (1815–91) emigrated to Canada in his youth, settling in Kingston, where he became a successful corporate lawyer, an MP – representing the town for nearly forty years – and ultimately prime minister (1867–73 and 1887–91). A shrewd and forceful man, Macdonald played a leading role in Canada's Confederation, with a little arm-twisting here and a little charming there to ensure the grand plan went through. In the 1840s, Macdonald rented **Bellevue House**, a bizarrely asymmetrical, pagoda-shaped building that had been built for a local grocer. The idea was that the country air would improve the health of Macdonald's wife, Isabella, whose tuberculosis was made worse by the treatment – laudanum. Isabella never returned to good health and died after years as an invalid, leaving Macdonald alone (with the bottle). Both the house and gardens have been restored to the period of the late 1840s, when the Macdonalds lived here.

The Penitentiary Museum

555 King St West, 1km west of Bellevue House · May–Oct Mon 9am–4pm, Tues–Sun 10am–7pm; last admission one hour before closing · Donation · ☎ 613 530 3122, ⓦ penitentiarymuseum.ca

Across the street from Kingston penitentiary, one of Canada's most important prisons, the intriguing **Penitentiary Museum** occupies the old prison warden's house, a trim limestone structure dating from the 1870s. The house was built by the prisoners and seven of its rooms now hold a fascinating assortment of exhibits, from examples of inmate arts and crafts to contraband the prisoners smuggled. Escape devices by which means they intended to get out are also displayed – and no wonder the "Punishment and Restraint" section has examples of the sort of fate awaiting them, from the simple wooden easel to which prisoners were tied for a good old flogging through to the large and cumbersome contraption for a touch of water-boarding.

East of the centre: Fort Frederick and Old Fort Henry

Royal Military College Museum Fort Frederick · Late June to early Sept daily 10am–5pm · Donation · ☎ 613 541 6000, ⓦ rmcc-cmrc. ca · Fort Henry Fort Henry Drive · Mid-May to early Sept daily 9.30am–5pm; early Sept to mid-May daily 10am–4pm · $20 · ☎ 613 542 7388, ⓦ forthenry.com

The twin headlands on the far side of **La Salle Causeway** to the east of downtown Kingston have long been used by the military. The first is home to the **Royal Military College**, the training academy for officers of all three services, and the **Royal Military College Museum**, housed in the old Martello tower at **Fort Frederick** and stuffed with military bric-a-brac. The second headland holds **Fort Henry**, a large and imposing fortress built to keep the Americans at bay after the War of 1812. The fort's thick stone-and-earth ramparts are flush with the lie of the land to protect against artillery bombardment, but as it turned out it was all a waste of time and money. Anglo-American relations improved and the fort never saw a shot fired in anger, so when the last garrison departed at the end of the nineteenth century, the fortress fell into disrepair. Restored in 1938, the fort's focus is the large **parade ground**, where volunteers periodically dress up in military gear and fill the fort with the smoke of musket and cannon and the racket of bugles, drums and fifes. These enactments are firmly aimed at families, and there's lots for kids to do, from joining in on drill parades and helping with the gun salute to participating in lessons in a Victorian schoolroom. You can also explore the ramparts, with views over the St Lawrence River; examine the fort's magazines, kitchens and officers' quarters; and visit the Discovery Centre, whose interactive exhibits put more flesh on the historical bone.

ARRIVAL AND INFORMATION
KINGSTON

By train VIA trains pull into the station just off John Counter St (and near Hwy-2), an inconvenient 7km northwest of the city centre. You can get a taxi from the station to downtown for about $20 or catch Kingston Transit bus #18, whose schedule is designed to meet train arrivals (☎613 546 0000, ⓦkingstontransit.ca).

Destinations Brockville (5–6 daily; 1hr); Montréal (5–8 daily; 2hr 45min); Ottawa (5–8 daily; 2hr); Toronto (11–15 daily; 2hr 20min).

By bus The long-distance bus station for both Greyhound (☎800 661 8747, ⓦgreyhound.ca) and Coach Canada (☎800 461 7661, ⓦcoachcanada.com) is on John Counter St, just west of Division St, about 5km to the north of the city centre. Taxis to the centre cost around $17; alternatively, catch Kingston Transit bus #18 (there should be a transit bus waiting).

Destinations (Greyhound) Montréal (1–4 daily; 5hr 20min); Ottawa (1–4 daily; 2hr 45min).

Destinations (Coach Canada) Montréal (10–14 daily; 3hr 20min); Toronto (10–14 daily; 3hr).

Tourist office On the harbourfront at 209 Ontario St (Jan–April daily 10am–4pm; early May to mid-May Mon–Wed & Sun 10am–4pm, Thurs–Sat 9.30am–5pm; mid-May to June Mon–Wed & Sun 9.30am–6pm, Thurs–Sat 9.30am–7pm; July to early Sept Mon–Wed & Sun 9.30am–8pm, Thurs–Sat 9.30am–9pm; early Sept to mid-Oct Sun–Wed 9.30am–5pm, Thurs–Sat 9.30am–6pm; mid-Oct to Dec Sun–Thurs 10am–4pm, Fri & Sat 10am–5pm; ☎613 548 4415, ☎888 855 4555, ⓦkingstoncanada.com).

ACCOMMODATION

Green Woods Inn 1368 Highway 15 ☎613 544 1922, ⓦgreenwoods-inn.ca; map p.154. Just east of Kingston, this beautifully restored country home offers charming rooms, well-appointed bathrooms and an included full gourmet breakfast. **$189**

Hochelaga Inn 24 Sydenham St South ☎613 549 5534, ☎877 933 9433, ⓦhochelagainn.com; map p.154. This sprawling inn, located in a residential area within easy walking distance of the centre, occupies a good-looking

Victorian mansion with a playful central tower, bay windows and wraparound veranda. There are 21 comfortable guest rooms, all en suite. **$160**

★ **Rosemount B&B Inn** 46 Sydenham St South ☎613 531 8844, ☎888 871 8844, ⓦrosemountinn.com; map p.154. An eminently appealing B&B, which occupies a strikingly handsome, distinctively Italianate old limestone villa – one of Kingston's finest buildings. The *Rosemount* has eleven en-suite guest rooms, including two in the adjacent

A WATERY DETOUR: THE RIDEAU CANAL

If you're travelling **from Kingston to Ottawa**, the obvious route is east along Hwy-401 and then north up Hwy-416, a journey of 175km. With more time, however, it's worth considering a slower route along two country roads – **Hwy-15** and then **Hwy-7**. En route, you'll pass a battery of signs to the 24 lock stations of the 202km-long **Rideau Canal** (☎613 283 5170, ⓦpc.gc.ca), which cuts through the slab of coniferous and deciduous forest, bogs, limestone plains and granite ridges that separate Ottawa and Kingston. Completed in 1832 after a mere six years' work, the canal was built to provide safe inland transport at a time of poor Anglo-American relations, but after the political situation improved it developed as an important route for regional commerce. The canal's construction led to the development of **Bytown**, renamed **Ottawa** in 1855, but in the second half of the nineteenth century the railways made the canal obsolete and today it's plied by holiday boats. For the motorist, one of the more impressive **lock stations** is **Kingston Mills** (Locks 46–49), 12km inland from Kingston on Hwy-15, where a steep flight of locks negotiates a wooded ravine overlooked by a blockhouse and lock offices. It's a lovely spot and there's more of the same, albeit in a wilder setting, at **Jones Falls** (Locks 39–42), 3km off Hwy-15 and about 40km from Kingston. Here, a huddle of old timber buildings is a prelude to a rickety footbridge that leads over a lake to a steep flight of locks guarded by several old stone buildings. By boat it takes five days to get from Kingston to Ottawa on the Rideau Canal with **Ontario Waterways** (☎705 327 5767, ☎800 561 5767, ⓦontariowaterwaycruises.com); there are between three and six cruises monthly from mid-May to mid-September, the cost is around $2000, and reservations are essential.

2

coach house, and each is decorated in attractive period style. The breakfasts are delicious and there's an on-site "vinotherapy" spa (which uses wine-based products). **$185**

Secret Garden B&B 73 Sydenham St South ☎ 613 531 9884, ☎ 877 723 1888, ⊛ thesecretgardeninn.com; map p.154. One of Kingston's most enjoyable B&Bs, with

seven extremely comfortable rooms, all en suite and each decorated in charming antique style. The house is a fetching Victorian building of timber and brick with verandas, porches and a splendid bay-windowed tower. The excellent included breakfast features fresh lemon ricotta pancakes, quiches and more. **$149**

EATING

Kingston has a good supply of quality **restaurants** and a wide range of inexpensive **cafés**, many of which prosper from its large student population.

Chez Piggy 68R Princess St ☎ 613 549 7673, ⊛ chezpiggy.com; map p.154. Something of a Kingston institution, where locals bring their kith and kin to celebrate high days and holidays, this large, split-level restaurant is housed in restored stables dating from 1810. The patio is packed in summer and the attractive interior has kept its rough stone walls. The wide-ranging menu features all manner of main courses served in bountiful helpings, from Thai and Korean through to South American and standard North American dishes – try the lamb prepared three ways (ribs, confit and sausage). Mains average around $30. Mon–Sat 11.30am–10pm, Sun 10am–9.30pm.

Le Chien Noir 69 Brock St ☎ 613 549 5635, ⊛ lechien noir.com; map p.154. Spirited bar-cum-bistro with smart, modern decor and a first-rate menu featuring local, seasonal ingredients in creative combinations; try the free-

range chicken with cheddar grits and asparagus. Mains average around $28, less at lunchtime. Mon–Wed & Sun 11.30am–9.30pm, Thurs–Fri 11.30am–10pm, Sat 11am–10pm.

White Mountain Ice Cream 176 Ontario St ☎ 613 545 3474; map p.154. Seriously rich home-made ice cream and waffle cones – try the White Mountain special: vanilla dotted with chocolate, pecan and maple brittle ($7). Daily 10am–11pm.

★ **Windmills Café** 184 Princess St ☎ 613 544 3948, ⊛ windmills-cafe.com; map p.154. The best café-restaurant in town, with attractive modern decor – the paintings on the wall are a delight – and a tasty, lively menu: the burgers, for example, are made with local beef and topped with dressings such as roasted red pepper mayo and ancho chile mayo ($14). Also tasty is the braised Québec duck with red wine-braised cabbage. Great desserts too. Mon & Tues 7.30am–10pm, Wed 7.30am–10.30pm, Thurs & Fri 7.30am–11pm, Sat 8am–11pm, Sun 8am–10pm.

DRINKING AND NIGHTLIFE

Kingston has several lively **pubs** and a modest live music scene: for **listings**, see the twice-monthly freebie *Key to Kingston*, available from major hotels, B&Bs, restaurants and the tourist office.

★ **Kingston Brewing Company** 34 Clarence St ☎ 613 542 4978, ⊛ kingstonbrewing.ca; map p.154. The best pub in town, serving ales and lagers brewed on the premises, as well as filling bar food. The patio is a great

place to park yourself and enjoy a brew in summer. Mon–Sat 11.30am–2am, Sun 11am–2am.

Kirkpatrick's & The Toucan 76 Princess St ☎ 613 544 1966, ⊛ thetoucan.ca; map p.154. Two ersatz Irish bars in one building, offering a wide range of domestic and imported beers, plus live gigs and DJ nights. The bar snacks and small plates are a cut above, including sweet potato fries with curried ketchup and vegetable dumplings. Daily 11am–2am.

The upper St Lawrence River

East of Kingston, Hwy-401 and the calmer, prettier Hwy-2 follow the northern shore of the **St Lawrence River**, whose island-studded waters were tricky going until the 1950s when the US and Canadian governments created the **St Lawrence Seaway**. An extraordinarily ambitious project, the Seaway extends 3790km inland from the Atlantic by means of lakes, rivers and locks to the west end of Lake Superior. Fifteen locks were installed on the St Lawrence River alone, each big enough to handle massive ocean-going freighters, while a string of dams harnessed the river's hydroelectric potential. But it all came at a price: the Seaway necessitated the relocation of many riverside towns and there were long-term **environmental** costs, too, with the ships transporting species previously unknown here on their hulls and in their bilge. What's more, the Seaway has been something of a flop, its decline directly related to the move towards road and air.

Leaving Kingston, **Hwy-2** begins by cutting across rolling farmland and offering fleeting views of the region's scenic highlight, the **Thousand Islands**, a confetti of lightly forested granite islands poking out of the river for the 80km between Kingston and Brockville. The islands are best seen on a **cruise**, available at most riverside towns, including Kingston (see page 152), though those from **Gananoque** are generally rated the best. Among the towns dotting the river, **Brockville** and tiny **Prescott** are the most enjoyable, but still most people pass on by with Ottawa (see page 161), just 175km from Kingston, the most obvious target. The most scenic part of the drive is along the **Thousand Islands Parkway**, a 40km stretch of Hwy-2 beginning just to the east of Gananoque, where the road is shadowed by a combined cycle- and footpath.

2

Gananoque and the Thousand Islands Parkway

From Kingston it's 30km east to **GANANOQUE** (pronounced Gan-an-owkee), a steady little hamlet that gets overrun by tourists in the summer on account of its boat trips out into the Thousand Islands (see box opposite). Just beyond Gananoque, the 40km-long **Thousand Islands Parkway** loops off Hwy-2 to slip along the north bank of the river, threading its way over narrow creeks and passing the greenest of riverine meadows. The Parkway ends at the delightfully named **Butternut Bay**, a few kilometres short of Brockville.

Brockville

Named after the Canadian general Isaac Brock, who was killed near Niagara Falls during the War of 1812, **BROCKVILLE** is a substantial little town, whose good-looking centre strings up the slope from the river. The town boasts a platoon of handsome Victorian buildings, self-confident neo-Gothic structures at their proudest on and around **Court House Avenue**, the site of an especially ambitious war memorial.

ARRIVAL AND DEPARTURE
BROCKVILLE

By train Brockville train station is on Perth St, about 1km northwest of the town centre.
Destinations Kingston (5–7 daily; 40min); Montréal (3–5 daily; 3hr); Ottawa (4–5 daily; 1hr 20min); Toronto (5–8 daily; 3hr 20min).

ACCOMMODATION AND EATING

Buell Street Bistro 27 Buell St, just west of Court House Ave along George ☎ 613 345 2623, ☜ buellstreetbistro. com. Intimate bistro with a lovely patio and a wide-ranging menu including Canadian, Italian and French dishes, from Ontario pork with mashed potatoes to seafood fettuccini. Occasional jazz gigs too. Main courses around $24. Mon–Fri 11.30am–10pm, Sat–Sun 5–10pm

Sir Isaac Brock B&B 89 Church St ☎ 613 865 8924, ☜ sirisaacbrockbb.com.
Relax at this handsome B&B set in a beautifully restored historic Georgian house. The two comfortable suites have high ceilings, wooden floors and wingback chairs. **$149**

Prescott

Fort Wellington, 370 Vankoughnet St • Late May to early July & early Sept to early Oct Thurs–Mon 10am–5pm; early July to early Sept daily 10am–5pm • $3.90 • ☎ 613 925 2896, ☜ pc.gc.ca

Stringing along the river, pocket-sized **PRESCOTT**, 20km east of Brockville, was rendered almost obsolete by the St Lawrence Seaway, but previously it had been important as a deep-water port and trans-shipment centre. Beside Hwy-2 on the east side of town, the crumbling, partly submerged dark-black **timbers** of the old town jetty recall busier days, as do the grassy ramparts of **Fort Wellington**. Work started on the fort in 1812 during the Anglo-American war, but by the time it was finished the war was over. The military moved out in 1869 and, after years of neglect, the fort has been returned to its 1830s appearance, complete with a two-storey blockhouse-cum-barracks, an officers' quarters, powder magazine and a cookhouse.

2

THE THOUSAND ISLANDS

Geologically, the **Thousand Islands** form part of the Frontenac axis, a ridge of million-year-old rock that stretches down into New York State. Aboriginal peoples called the islands *Manitouana* – the "Garden of the Great Spirit" – in the belief they were created when petals of heavenly flowers were scattered on the river; more prosaically, the islands later gave their name to a salad dressing. The **Thousand Islands** first hit the national headlines in the late 1830s, when they were the haunt of an irascible Canadian pirate, William Johnston, whose irritation with the British prompted him and his gang to spend several years harrying British shipping and Canadian farmers until he retired (with his booty) to New York State. Thereafter, the islands became a popular retreat for the rich and famous – including Irving Berlin and Jack Dempsey – but it was **George Boldt**, the owner of New York's *Waldorf Astoria*, who outdid them all. In 1899, he bought one of the islands and reshaped it into a heart as a tribute to his wife; hence the name **Heart Island**. He then plonked a whopping – and whoppingly expensive – ersatz medieval castle on top of the island, but promptly abandoned **Boldt Castle** (daily: early May to late June & late Aug to late Sept 10am–6.30pm; late June to late Aug 10am–7.30pm; late Sept to early Oct 10am–5.30pm; early to mid-Oct 11am–5pm; US$10; ☎ 315 482 9724, 🌐 boldtcastle.com) when his wife died, taking his new salad-dressing recipe with him back to New York.

For **cruises** out into the Thousand Islands, you're spoiled for choice, but one obvious place to aim for is **Gananoque**, 30km east of Kingston, where the main **cruise boat** operator is the **Gananoque Boat Line** (1hr trips: mid-May to late Sept 4–6 daily; early May to mid-May & late Sept to early Nov by appointment; from $24.95; 2hr 30min trips: early May to mid-Oct 2–5 daily; $37.60; ☎ 613 382 2144, ☎ 888 717 4837, 🌐 ganboatline.com). Highlights of the longer cruise include a good look at **Just Room Enough Island**, with its single tiny home, and, at the other extreme, Millionaire's Row on much larger **Wellesley Island**. The same company also does five-hour cruises (mid-May to late June Sat & Sun only, 2 daily; late June to early Sept 2 daily; early Sept to late Sept Mon–Fri 1 daily and Sat & Sun 2 daily; late Sept to early Oct 1 daily; mid-Oct Mon, Sat & Sun 1 daily; $48.80, but castle extra), which include a two-hour stop at Boldt Castle; the castle is in US waters, so bring your **passport**.

The Battle of the Windmill

The Americans never attacked Fort Wellington, but it did serve as the muster station for the militia in the lead-up to the **Battle of the Windmill** in 1838. In the aftermath of the shambolic Rebellion of 1837, hundreds of refugee rebels took off into the Ontario bush or fled to the US. One of the larger groups hunkered down in the Thousand Islands and, together with their American sympathizers, planned an attack on Canada, hoping this would stir a general rebellion. Two hundred of them landed beside a stone **windmill** 2km east of Prescott, but there was no widespread uprising and the invaders ended up occupying the windmill instead. The militia surrounded them and, after a dogged fight, they were forced to surrender: eleven were executed and most of the rest were transported to Australia. The windmill – which subsequently saw service as a lighthouse – has survived and a peep at it makes for a pleasant excursion: follow the signs from Hwy-2.

ARRIVAL AND DEPARTURE — PRESCOTT

By bus Greyhound buses pause down near the river at Mr   Destinations Ottawa (2–3 weekly; 1hr 15min).
Gas, on Prescott's main drag at 152 King St East.

Johnstown and the Upper Canada Village

Upper Canada Village • 13740 Hwy-2 • Early May to early Sept daily 9.30am–5pm; early Sept to late Sept Wed–Sun 9.30am–5pm; in spring and fall, visit is via guided tour only – check website for times • $20 • ☎ 613 543 4328, 🌐 uppercanadavillage.com

East of Prescott, it's just 5km to **JOHNSTOWN**, where there's a **choice of routes** with Hwy-416 cutting north to Ottawa and Hwy-401 continuing along the St Lawrence River bound for Montréal. About 35km east of Johnstown, Hwy-401 passes **Upper Canada Village**, one of the region's most popular attractions, only ninety minutes' drive from Ottawa. In the 1950s, the construction of the St Lawrence Seaway raised the river level, threatening many of the old buildings along the river bank. The best were painstakingly relocated to this purpose-built, sixty-acre complex, which re-creates 1860s rural Ontario life with a wide range of buildings, from farmhouses and farm outhouses to a bakery, a parsonage, a church, a wool factory, a saw mill and a blacksmith's. It is all very well done and the staff dress up in period gear to demonstrate traditional skills, producing cheeses, quilts, brooms, bread and cloth in exactly the same way as their pioneer ancestors. They also have the Play Dress Up offer, where you can dress up in period clothing and have your picture taken ($23.99) and/or tour the village in full costume ($35). In the adjacent riverside park is the **Battlefield Monument**, which – along with a visitor centre – commemorates the Battle of Crysler Farm in 1813, when a small force of British and Canadian soldiers drove off American invaders; Crysler Farm was itself submerged by the Seaway.

Ottawa

Proud of its capital status, **OTTAWA** is a lively cosmopolitan city of around one million inhabitants, whose attractions include a clutch of outstanding **national museums**, a pleasant riverside setting and superb cultural facilities like the National Arts Centre. Throw in acres of parks and gardens, miles of bicycle and jogging paths – many of them along the **Ottawa River** – lots of good hotels and B&Bs and a busy café-bar and restaurant scene and you have enough to keep the most diligent sightseer going for a day or three, maybe more. It's also here that Canada's bilingual laws really make sense: French-speaking **Gatineau**, just across the river in Québec, is commonly lumped together with Ontario's Ottawa as the "Capital Region", and on the streets of Ottawa you'll hear as much French as English.

Almost all of Ottawa's major sights are clustered on or near the south bank of the Ottawa River to either side of the Rideau Canal. It's here you'll find the monumental Victorian architecture of **Parliament Hill**, the outstanding art collection of the **National Gallery**, and the **Byward Market**, the hub of the restaurant and bar scene. Many visitors only cover these, but there are a clutch of other attractions, most memorably the fascinating **Canadian War Museum**, housed in a striking building a couple of kilometres to the west of the centre, and **Laurier House**, packed with the possessions of the former prime minister William Lyon Mackenzie King and located 1.5km southeast of downtown. There are also some minor attractions to the east of the centre, on the far side of the Rideau River, principally the governor-general's mansion, **Rideau Hall**, and the **Canada Aviation Museum**.

Brief history

The one-time hunting ground of the Algonquian, Ottawa received its first recorded European visitor in 1613 in the shape of Samuel de Champlain. The French explorer pitched up, paused to watch his Aboriginal guides make offerings of tobacco to the misty falls (which now lie submerged beneath the river), and then took off in search of more appealing pastures. Later, the **Ottawa River** became a major transportation route, but the Ottawa area remained no more than a camping spot until 1800, when **Philemon Wright** snowshoed up here along the frozen Ottawa River from Massachusetts. Wright founded a small settlement, which he called Wrightstown and subsequently **Hull** (now **Gatineau**) after his parents' birthplace in England. Hull flourished but nothing much happened on the other (Ottawa) side of the river until 1826, when the completion of the **Rideau Canal** (see page 157) linked the site of present-day Ottawa to Kingston and the St Lawrence River. The canal builders were under the command of **Lieutenant-Colonel John By** and it was he who gave his name to the new settlement, **Bytown**, which soon became a hard-edged lumber town characterized by drunken brawls and broken bones.

In 1855 Bytown re-christened itself **Ottawa** in a bid to become the capital of the Province of Canada, hoping a change of name would relieve the town of its tawdry reputation. As part of their pitch, the community stressed the town's location on the border of Upper and Lower Canada and its industrial prosperity. **Queen Victoria**

2

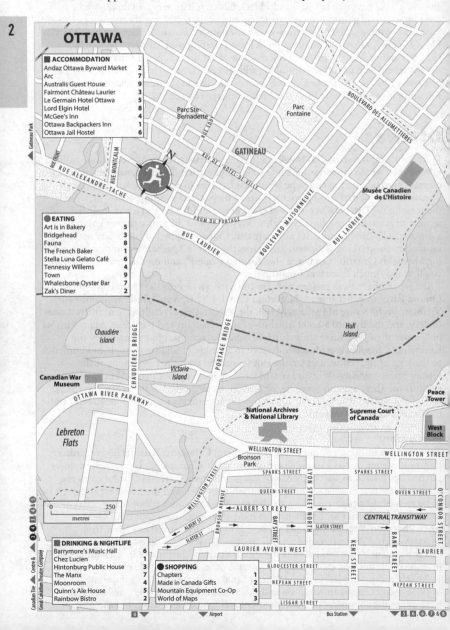

OTTAWA

■ ACCOMMODATION
Andaz Ottawa Byward Market	2
Arc	7
Australis Guest House	9
Fairmont Château Laurier	3
Le Germain Hotel Ottawa	5
Lord Elgin Hotel	8
McGee's Inn	4
Ottawa Backpackers Inn	1
Ottawa Jail Hostel	6

● EATING
Art is in Bakery	5
Bridgehead	3
Fauna	8
The French Baker	1
Stella Luna Gelato Café	6
Tennessy Willems	4
Town	9
Whalesbone Oyster Bar	7
Zak's Diner	2

■ DRINKING & NIGHTLIFE
Barrymore's Music Hall	6
Chez Lucien	1
Hintonburg Public House	3
The Manx	7
Moonroom	4
Quinn's Ale House	5
Rainbow Bistro	2

● SHOPPING
Chapters	1
Made in Canada Gifts	2
Mountain Equipment Co-Op	4
World of Maps	3

granted their request in 1857, though this had little to do with their efforts and much more to do with her artistic tastes: the Queen had been looking at some romantic landscape paintings of the Ottawa area and decided this was the perfect spot for a new capital. Few approved: Montréal and Toronto smarted at their rebuff and Canada's politicians fumed at the inconvenience – former prime minister Sir Wilfred Laurier found it "hard to say anything good" about the place.

2

OTTAWA'S FESTIVALS

Federal funding ensures national holidays – especially Canada Day on July 1 (Ⓦcanadascapital. gc.ca) – are celebrated in style, while seasonal **festivals** are as lavish as any in the country. The tourist office (see page 172) has the full calendar of events, and you can check out Ⓦottawafestivals.ca. The selection below is arranged chronologically.

Winterlude Jan and Feb Ⓦcanadascapital.gc.ca. A snow-and-ice extravaganza spread over three weekends from late January to mid-February. Concentrated around the frozen Rideau Canal, it includes ice sculptures at Confederation Park – renamed the Crystal Garden for the duration – and snow sculptures around Dows Lake. Other events include speed-skating, bed- and dog-sled races.

Canadian Tulip Festival Eleven days beginning in early May Ⓦtulipfestival.ca. This is the oldest of Ottawa's festivals. It began in 1945 when the Dutch sent 100,000 tulip bulbs to the city both to honour Canadian soldiers who had liberated the Netherlands and as a thank-you for sheltering Queen Juliana, who had taken refuge in Ottawa during the war. The bulbs are planted around Parliament, along the canal and around Dows Lake, a gigantic splash of colour accompanied by concerts, parades, fireworks and a huge craft show.

Ottawa Chamberfest Two weeks in late July/early Aug Ⓦchamberfest.com. The largest chamber festival in the world, which celebrated its 25th anniversary in 2018, fills the city with classical tunes, at historic churches, theatres and concert venues.

Ottawa Jazz Festival Two weeks in late June/early July Ⓦottawajazzfestival.com. One of Ottawa's most popular festivals, showcasing more than four hundred musicians. The main stage is in Confederation Park with concerts several times daily. In addition, local bands play around Byward Market and at city clubs.

Bluesfest Twelve days in July Ⓦottawabluesfest.ca. This is Canada's largest festival of blues and gospel with concerts held in various venues, and free shows in Confederation Park.

Give or take some federal buildings – including the splendid trio of neo-Gothic buildings that make up today's Parliament – Ottawa remained a workaday town until the late 1940s, when the Paris city planner **Jacques Greber** was commissioned to beautify the city with a profusion of parks, wide avenues and tree-lined pathways. The scheme transformed the city, defining much of its current appearance, and today Greber's green and open spaces confine a city centre that is, at least for the most part, a fetching mix of Victorian architecture and modern concrete-and-glass office blocks.

Parliament Hill

Perched high above the Ottawa River, on the limestone bluff that is **Parliament Hill**, Canada's postcard-pretty **Parliament Buildings** have a distinctly ecclesiastical air, their spires, pointed windows and soaring clock tower amounting to "a stupendous splodge of Victoriana" as travel writer Jan Morris expressed it. Begun in 1859 and seventy years in the making, the complex comprises a trio of sturdy neo-Gothic structures, whose architectural certainties were both a statement of intent for the emergent country and a demonstration of the long reach of the British Empire. The Parliament Buildings were designed to be both imperial and imperious, but they certainly didn't overawe the original workmen, who urinated on the copper roof to speed up its oxidization.

Two popular events are staged on Parliament Hill: the **Changing of the Guard**, when the Governor General's Foot Guards march onto the Hill dressed in full ceremonial uniform of bright-red tunics and bearskin helmets (late June to late Aug daily 10–10.30am); and a free summer-evening **sound and light show** (early July to mid-Sept), illustrating Canada's history with alternate French and English performances nightly.

Centre Block

Guided tours Times and duration (20min to 1hr) vary, but guideline times when parliament is in session are: Mon–Tues & Thurs 9.20am–12.50pm & 3.20pm, Wed 12.30–3.20pm, Fri 9–9.50am & 12.50–3.20pm; when parliament is not in session, Mon–Fri 9.20am–7.20pm, Sat–Sun 9am–4.20pm; early July–early Sept daily 9am–4.30pm • Tickets (first-come, first-served) from the main entrance at the foot of the Peace Tower or, in summer, from the Info-Tent outside • Free • **Peace Tower** Same times; self-guided visits • Free • ☎ 613 992 4793, ⓦ parl.gc.ca/visitors

Dominating architectural proceedings on Parliament Hill is **Centre Block**, home of the Senate and the House of Commons and in fact a replacement for the original building, which was destroyed by fire in 1916. This second structure was supposed to be the same as its predecessor, but it ended up about twice the size. The **Peace Tower**, rising from the middle of the facade, was added in 1927 as a tribute to Canadians who served in World War I. The tower, which offers fine views over the Ottawa River, holds some superb fan vaulting and a Memorial Chamber complete with a Book of Remembrance. The tower is not part of the **guided tour**, whose (changeable) itinerary includes a quick gambol round the **House of Commons**, where the Speaker's chair is partly made of English oak from Nelson's flagship *Victory*, and the red-carpeted **Senate**, which, with its murals of scenes from World War I, is surmounted by a beautiful gilded ceiling. Time your visit to the Peace Tower for the playing of the carillon, one of the best-known in Canada. The carillon is rung July to August (Mon–Fri 11am–noon) and September to June (Mon–Fri noon–12.15pm). At the back of the Centre Block is the **Library**, the only part of the building to have survived the fire of 1916; the circular design and the intricately carved wooden galleries make it parliament's most charming space.

The **debates** in both the House of Commons and the Senate are open to the public, who can observe proceedings from the public galleries. Most of the gallery seats are pre-booked, but a small number are allocated on the day, on a first-come, first-served basis: ask for further information on arrival. To check what is being debated and when, consult the website. Parliament's liveliest debates are usually during **Question Period**, when the Opposition interrogates the prime minister.

West Block and East Block

East Block guided tours early July to early Sept daily 9.45am–4.45pm; around 20min • Free

Flanking Centre Block are West Block and East Block. **West Block** is used as parliamentary offices and there's no public access, but **East Block** contains four Confederation-era rooms, most memorably the original governor-general's office and the Privy Council Chamber. Costumed guides give the low-down.

The grounds

The manicured lawns surrounding the Parliament Buildings are dotted with **statues** and two of the more interesting occupy a tiny hillock just to the west of Centre Block. Here, **Queen Victoria** has been stuck on a plinth guarded by a lion and offered laurels from below, while **Lester Pearson** (prime minister 1963–68) lounges in an armchair, the epitome of the self-confident statesman. Round the back of Centre Block there are pleasant views across the Ottawa River to Gatineau (see page 171) with the low green hills of Québec rolling away into the distance.

Confederation Square

Triangular **Confederation Square**, a brief stroll from Parliament Hill, is a breezy open space dominated by the magnificent **National War Memorial**, in which a soaring stone arch is surmounted by representations of Liberty and Peace. Down below, a swirling, finely executed bronze depicts returning service men and women passing through the arch – from war to peace – and manages to convey both their exultation and sorrow. To the square's west, across Elgin Street, is **Sparks Street**, a pedestrianized strip of shops and restaurants, but probably most notable as the site of Canada's most famous **political assassination**: a suspected Fenian sympathizer shot Thomas D'Arcy McGee, a father of Confederation, here in 1868; a pub on the corner of Sparks and Elgin streets now bears McGee's name. On the southeast side of the square is the complex of low concrete buildings that houses the **National Arts Centre** (see page 175), which clunks down to the Rideau Canal. Opposite, across the canal, rise the stirring lines of Ottawa's former **railway station**, now – rather sadly – a conference centre.

The Rideau Canal in Ottawa

Bytown Museum, Rideau Canal locks • Jan by appointment only; mid-May to early Oct daily 10am–5pm (until 8pm Thurs); end June to early Sept daily 10am–7pm (until 8pm Thurs); early Oct to early May Thurs–Mon 11am–4pm • $8, free on Thurs after 5pm • ☎ 613 234 4570, ⓦ bytownmuseum.com

A narrow sliver of water that becomes the **world's longest skating rink** in winter, the **Rideau Canal** runs past the National Arts Centre (see page 175) before it slides down into the Ottawa River via a pretty flight of **locks**, with Parliament Hill rising on one side, the *Fairmont Château Laurier* hotel on the other. Beside the foot of the locks is the **Bytown Museum**, Ottawa's oldest building, where military supplies were stored during the construction of the canal. Here, a short film explores the history of the waterway and the difficulties involved in its construction; afterwards you can take a peek at a scattering of bygones from the city's earliest days. From mid-May to early October, **canal boat trips** leave from the top of the locks, **river trips** from the bottom. The main operator is Paul's Boat Lines (4–6 of each trip daily; canal trips 1hr, $20; river trips $25; reservations recommended; ☎613 225 6781, ⓦpaulsboatcruises.com).

Major's Hill Park and Nepean Point

On the east side of the Rideau Canal, just to the west of Sussex Drive, is **Major's Hill Park**, whose assorted greenery rolls across a small hill above the Ottawa River. This was where Colonel By decided to build his house and the extant foundations bear a plaque attesting to its history. Major's Hill Park slopes down towards **Nepean Point**, a pint-sized headland that nudges out into the river bisected by the main road – and bridge – to Gatineau (see page 171). On the far side of the road a path climbs up the headland to an outside theatre and, at the tip, a statue of Champlain, from where there are wide river views. The statue is actually a cock-up dating back to 1915: Champlain is shown holding his astrolabe – his navigational aid – aloft, but it is in fact upside down.

National Gallery of Canada

380 Sussex Drive • Oct–April Tues–Sun 10am–5pm (Thurs until 8pm); May–Sept daily 10am–6pm (Thurs until 8pm) • $15, free Thurs after 5pm • ☎ 613 990 1985, ⓦ gallery.ca

The **National Gallery of Canada** occupies a cleverly conceived building whose acres of glass reflect the turrets and pinnacles of Parliament Hill. The collection was founded in 1880 by the then-governor general, the Marquis of Lorne, who persuaded each member of the Royal Canadian Academy to donate a painting or two. Over the next century artworks were gathered from all over the world, resulting in a permanent collection now numbering more than 25,000 pieces. There's not enough space for all the paintings to be exhibited at any one time, so although the general layout of the museum stays pretty constant, the individual works mentioned below may not be on display; the gallery also holds world-class **temporary exhibitions**. The collection spreads over two main levels and free plans are issued at the reception desk; the gallery shop sells guides to both the permanent collection and the exhibitions.

The Canadian galleries: 1750 to 1880

The **Canadian galleries**, laid out in roughly chronological order on **Level 1**, are the finest in the building, following the history of Canadian painting from the mid-eighteenth century to modern times. After an initial room of early Aboriginal art, the collection focuses on religious art from Québec, including a flashy gilded high altar of basswood and butternut by **Paul Jourdain**. A further section is devoted to the emergence of secular art in early nineteenth-century Québec, with paintings by immigrant artists trained in Europe. The most notable of these was **Joseph Légaré**, a painter, politician and nationalist; his *Cholera Plague, Québec* is a typical example of his fastidiously romantic work. For popularity, though, none could match **Cornelius Krieghoff** (see page 73), who could turn his hand to anything requested by his middle-class patrons – as illustrated by his *Winter Landscape* and *White Horse Inn by Moonlight*. Close by is one of the gallery's more unusual exhibits, the **Rideau Street Convent Chapel**, rebuilt piece by piece after it was threatened with demolition in 1972. Designed in the 1880s by the architect and priest Canon Georges Bouillon for a local convent school, it has slender cast-iron columns supporting a fan-vaulted ceiling – one of the few extant examples of its kind in North America.

Further on, a small collection of early nineteenth-century paintings from the Maritimes and Ontario occupies Room A104. The highlight here is the unique **Croscup Room** from Nova Scotia. Once the living room of a shipping family, it's altogether a peculiar affair, its bright and cheerful murals juxtaposing an apparently haphazard mix of images from mid-nineteenth century North America and Europe – portraits of Micmac Indians, bagpipe-playing Scots and so forth. Here also, look out for the evocative frontier scenes of **Paul Kane**, Canada's first artist-explorer.

The Canadian galleries: 1880s to 1920s

In the second half of the nineteenth century Canadians were still in thrall to European masters and it was to be the **Group of Seven** (see page 74) who developed a Canadian aesthetic in a style that aimed to capture the spirit and vastness of the northern landscape, rather than rendering it into a tamer European version and vision. The three rooms devoted to the Group's canvases feature the seminal paintings of **Tom Thomson**, whose startling *Jack Pine* was in effect the Group's clarion call – trees, often windswept or dead, are a constant symbol in the Group's landscape paintings. Using rapid, brash and often brutal brushstrokes, the Group's works are faithful less to the landscape itself than to the emotions it evoked – **Lawren Harris**'s phallic *North Shore, Lake Superior*, A.Y. Jackson's *Red Maple* and J.E.H. MacDonald's *The Solemn Land* are all memorable examples.

The Canadian galleries: 1930s to 1960s

After MacDonald's death in 1932, the Group of Seven formed the **Canadian Group of Painters**, embracing all Canadian artists of the time whatever their style. Landscape remained the dominant genre in this period, but the effects of the Depression forced politics to the fore; *Ontario Farm House* by **Carl Schaefer**, which turns a landscape into a social statement, is a first-rate example.

Room 111 marks a change of artistic direction, displaying a selection of **abstract paintings** produced in Montréal from the 1940s to the 1970s. In Canada, it was the **Montréal Automatistes** who first explored abstraction, though the **Platiciens**, who hit the artistic big-time in the 1950s, rejected their emphasis on the expressive qualities of colour, choosing geometrical and analytical forms instead. Elsewhere in Canada, other painters chose a very different route, most strikingly **Alex Colville**, whose magic realism is seen to good advantage in his *To Prince Edward Island*, an acrylic emulsion on masonite from 1965.

Contemporary art

Beginning with the 1960s, the gallery's collection of **contemporary art** is spread over Levels 1 and 2. The highlights here are almost exclusively the work of American artists, most notably **Andy Warhol**'s *Brillo Soap Pads Boxes*, his serigraphs of Chairman Mao, and George Segal's life-size assemblage *The Gas Station*. Canadians pop up here and there, but they almost always seem to take the lead from foreigners – witness the shadow of New York's Abstract Expressionists falling over Charles Gagnon's *Cassation/Open/Ouvert*.

2

The European galleries

On Level 2, the **European galleries** begin with a medley of medieval Gothic and Renaissance paintings and panel-paintings from Northern Europe, though it's the collection of **seventeenth-century** works that is most impressive. There's Bernini's sculpture of his patron Pope Urban VIII, Claude Lorrain's *Landscape with a Temple of Bacchus*, an *Entombment* by Rubens, Rembrandt's sumptuous *Heroine from the Old Testament* and Van Dyck's *Suffer the Little Children to Come Unto Me*.

From Britain in the **eighteenth century** there are portraits by Reynolds and Gainsborough plus the iconic *Death of General Wolfe* by **Benjamin West**, an American who became George III's official painter. West depicts Wolfe in a Christ-like pose, lying wounded and surrounded by his adjutants – and the painting made Wolfe an imperial hero.

The final European galleries feature **twentieth-century** works, showcasing a range of paintings and sculpture, including works by Klimt, Matisse, Picasso and Dalí.

American Abstract Expressionists

One room on Level 2 is devoted to **American Abstract Expressionists**. This is where you'll usually find **Barnett Newman**'s *Voice of Fire*, the very mention of which causes some Canadians to froth at the mouth – not because of its artistic significance but because it cost a cool $1.76m. The artist intended the 5.5m-high piece to give the viewer a "feeling of his own totality, of his own separateness, of his own individuality, and at the same time of his connection to others, who are also separate". Such blandishments did not satisfy everyone; one Tory MP ranted that it took "… two cans of paint and two rollers and about ten minutes" – and indeed it really is just three parallel lines, two blue and one red in the middle. The same room also contains lesser works by Jackson Pollock and Mark Rothko.

The Inuit collection

The gallery's small but eclectic collection of **Inuit art and sculpture** is displayed in the basement. The kernel of the Inuit material is its soapstone sculptures, but there are whale bone and ivory pieces, as well as brightly coloured drawings. Two particular sculptors to look out for are **Charlie Inukpuk**, who carved the elemental *Woman who Killed a Bear with a Mitten*, and **Jackoposie Oopakak**, whose superb *Nunali* is a representation of the whole Arctic world delicately carved onto a set of caribou antlers.

Notre Dame Basilica

385 Sussex Drive • May–Oct Mon 11.30am–6pm, Tues–Sat 9am–6pm, Sun 8am–8.30pm; Nov–April Mon 11.30am–6pm, Tues–Sat 9am–6pm, Sat 2–6pm, Sun 8am–8.30pm • Free • **Guided tours** Mid-May to mid-Oct Mon–Fri by appointment; 30–40min • Call for fee • ☎ 613 241 7496, ⓦ notredameottawa.com

The twin silver spires of the capital's Catholic cathedral, the **Notre Dame Basilica**, poke high into the sky across the street from the National Gallery. Completed in 1890, the neo-Gothic cathedral has a nave that reaches a sort of ecclesiastical crescendo in a massive high-altar piece, flanked by a herd of pious wooden sculptures, many of which were carved by the carpenters and masons who worked on the Parliament Buildings.

The Canadian War Museum

1 Vimy Place • Mon–Wed & Fri–Sun 9.30am–5pm, Thurs 9.30am–8pm • $17, free Thurs after 4pm • ☎ 819 776 7000, ⓦ warmuseum.ca • OC Transpo bus #8 from Albert St

The exemplary **Canadian War Museum** is housed in a striking modern building on Lebreton Flats, a somewhat desolate parcel of land beside the Ottawa River about 2km west of Confederation Square. The museum is divided into four main display areas, which work their way through Canada's military history with accompanying text and

2

quotations. The first gallery, the "Battleground: Wars on Our Soil, earliest times to 1885", features a good selection of Native Canadian weaponry – tomahawks, muskets and so forth – plus a particularly well-researched section on the War of 1812. However, the museum really gets into its stride when it reaches **World War I** in the second gallery. There are lots of fascinating photographs, but it's the incidental detail that impresses most: Canada was keen for its soldiers to use a Canadian rifle, but the end product – the Ross Rifle – often jammed, while the rum ration came in barrels labelled "SRD" (Service Regimental Depot), which the troops rebranded as "Seldom Reaches Destination". The section on World War II is similarly intriguing and there's good stuff on the Cold War too – including details of the strange case of the Russian defector **Igor Gouzenko**, who was so scared of retribution that he was often interviewed with a bag over his head. Finally, the **Lebreton Gallery** is a large hangar packed with all sorts of military hardware, such as tanks, armoured cars and artillery pieces.

Laurier House

335 Laurier Ave East • Early May to June Thurs–Mon 10am–5pm; July to early Sept daily 10am–5pm • $3.90 • ☎ 613 992 8142, ⊚ pc.gc.ca

A national historic site, the **Laurier House**, 1km east of the Laurier Bridge, is the former home of prime ministers Sir Wilfred Laurier and William Lyon Mackenzie King. **Laurier**, Canada's first French-speaking prime minister, served from 1896 to 1911, while **Mackenzie King**, his self-proclaimed "spiritual son", was Canada's longest serving – from 1921 to 1930 and 1935 to 1948. Notoriously pragmatic, King enveloped his listeners in a fog of words through which his political intentions were barely discernible. The perfect illustration – and his most famous line – was "not necessarily conscription, but conscription if necessary", supposedly a clarification of his plans at the onset of World War II. Even more famous than his obfuscating rhetoric was his personal eccentricity. His fear that future generations would view him simply as the heir of his grandfather William Lyon Mackenzie – who led the Upper Canada rebellions of the 1830s (see page 58) – eventually led him into spiritualism. He held regular séances to tap the advice of great dead Canadians, including Laurier, who allegedly communicated to him through his pet dog.

King's possessions dominate the **house**; look for his crystal ball and a portrait of his obsessively adored mother, in front of which he placed a red rose every day. The house also contains a reconstruction of a study belonging to prime minister **Lester B. Pearson**, who was awarded the Nobel Peace Prize for his role in resolving the Suez Crisis. Pearson also had a stab at devising a new flag for his country and, although it was rejected, the mock-up he commissioned, with blue stripes at either end to symbolize the oceans, is on display here.

Rideau Falls and Rideau Hall

Take **Sussex Drive** north out of the city centre and you soon reach **Rideau Falls**, at the mouth of the Rideau River, where the twin cataracts are separated by Green Island. It's a pleasant spot and you can stroll out into the **Rideau Falls Park** or press on, following the **Rockcliffe Parkway**, which sticks close to the river bank on its way to the Aviation Museum (see below). En route, you'll pass the riverside **Prime Minister's Residence**, a stately stone mansion barely visible through the trees at 24 Sussex Drive, and then the Neoclassical **Rideau Hall** (free guided tours; 45min; reservations sometimes required; ☎613 991 4422, ☎866 842 4422, ⊚gg.ca), home of Canada's governors general since Confederation. The hall's **gardens** of maples and fountains are usually open from 8am to one hour before sunset; call ahead to be certain.

Canada Aviation and Space Museum

11 Aviation Parkway • Early May to early Sept daily 9am–5pm; early Sept to April Mon & Wed–Sun 10am–5pm • $15 • ☎ 613 991 3044, ⊚ ingeniumcanada.org.

Along the Rockcliffe Parkway, 5km from downtown, is the huge hangar of the **Canada Aviation and Space Museum**. Highlights include a replica of the *Silver Dart*, which made the first powered flight in Canada in 1909; it flew for a full nine minutes, a major achievement for a contraption that seems to be made out of spare parts and old sheets. There are also bombers and fighters from both world wars and later, including a Harrier jet.

Gatineau

Though firmly incorporated within the Capital Region, **GATINEAU** (formerly **Hull**), lying just across the river from Ottawa in the province of Québec, remains quite distinct and predominantly francophone. For years it served mainly as Ottawa's nightspot as its bars were open two hours longer than those in the capital, but with this alcoholic advantage now gone – and its paper mills relegated to minor importance – Gatineau struggles to compete with its neighbour. It does, however, have one major museum, the **Musée Canadien de L'Histoire**, and it also edges the handsome scenery of **Gatineau Park**, whose assorted lakes and forested hills cover no fewer than 360 square kilometres; the park is a prime spot for hiking, mountain biking and cross-country skiing.

Musée Canadien de L'Histoire (Canadian Museum of History)

100 Laurier St • Late June to early Sept daily 9.30am–6pm (Thurs till 8pm); early Sept to March daily 9.30am–5pm (Thurs till 8pm) • $20, free Thurs after 5pm • ☏ 819 776 7000, ⦿ historymuseum.ca • OC Transpo bus #8 from Albert St or 10min walk from the National Gallery

Standing on the far side of the Alexandra Bridge from the National Gallery is Gatineau's pride and joy, the whopping **Musée Canadien de L'Histoire** whose distinctive, curvy limestone contours are supposed to represent the rocky sweep of the Canadian Shield; the best view is from the Ottawa side of the river. In 2013, Canada's largest museum changed its name from the Musée Canadien des Civilisations to the Musée Canadien de L'Histoire – and to coincide with Canada's 150th birthday celebrations in 2017, the museum changed its angle too, focusing on Canada's history, with the splashy opening of the Canadian History Hall. On Level 3, it's divided into three galleries, each covering a different era in Canadian history – Early Canada, Colonial Canada and Modern Canada.

The museum spreads over four floors and the entrance, where you can pick up a free plan, is on Level 2. The museum website also has an excellent map of the museum. On Level 2, you'll find a mixed bag of attractions, including a Children's Museum and an IMAX screen showing nature and adventure films (for a supplementary fee). Level 4 holds temporary exhibitions and then it's down to Level 1 for the **Grand Hall**, easily the largest room in the museum and perfectly designed to display a magnificent collection of around twenty Pacific Coast **totem poles**. The main line of poles stands outside six Aboriginal "houses" which explore Pacific Coast Aboriginal culture, including displays on trade, religious beliefs, tribal gatherings and art.

Gatineau Park

Visitor centre Southern entrance near Gatineau • May to early Nov & late Dec to early Jan daily 9am–5pm; early Nov to late Dec & early Jan to April Mon–Fri 10am–4pm, Sat & Sun 9am–5pm • ☏ 819 827 2020, ⦿ canadascapital.gc.ca • Plans and hiking leaflets available here and at Ottawa tourist office (see page 172)

Long popular with the capital's hikers and cyclists, the forested hills and lakes of **Gatineau Park** begin just 3km to the west of the Musée Canadien de L'Histoire – follow the signs. The park was founded in 1938 when the government snapped up the land to stop its deforestation for firewood during the hard years of the Depression. Nowadays, it's latticed with **hiking trails**, many of which are readily reached along the park's most scenic road, the **Champlain Parkway**, which is a turning off the park's main road, the **Gatineau Parkway**. The Champlain Parkway meanders its way across the southern reaches of the park before reaching its conclusion at the **Champlain Lookout**, 24km from the park's southern entrance. There's a grand view of a distinctive landscape from here, with the granite outcroppings of the Canadian Shield transitioning down to the rich green fields of the St Lawrence lowlands.

ARRIVAL AND INFORMATION

By plane Ottawa International Airport (☎613 248 2125, ⓦottawa-airport.ca) is located about 15km south of the city centre. From the airport, OC Transpo (☎613 741 4390, ⓦoctranspo.com) operates bus #97 (daily 6am–1am, every 20–30min) to several downtown stops including the Albert St Transitway (see below); en route, there are no easy-to-recognize landmarks, so it's a good idea to ask the driver to drop you off at the right stop. A taxi from the airport to downtown costs about $45.

By train Ottawa's train station (☎888 842 7245, ⓦviarail.ca) is on the southeastern outskirts of the city, about 4km from the centre, off the Queensway (Hwy-417) at 200 Tremblay Rd. OC Transpo buses #94 and #95 go downtown from the station; the same journey by taxi costs about $15.
Destinations Brockville (4–6 daily; 1hr 20min); Kingston (5–8 daily; 2hr); Montréal (4–6 daily; 2hr); Toronto (5–8 daily; 4hr 20min).

By bus Long-distance buses, including Greyhound (☎800 661 8747, ⓦgreyhound.ca), use the bus station, 1.5km south of the city centre at 265 Catherine St at Kent. Take OC Transpo bus #4 to get downtown.
Destinations Kingston (1–4 daily; 2hr 45min); Montréal (14–23 daily; 2hr 30min); North Bay (2–4 daily; 5hr); Sudbury (1–3 daily; 7hr 30min); Toronto (6–13 daily; 5–6hr).

Capital Information Kiosk This staffed kiosk (daily 9am–6pm; ☎844 878 8333, ⓦcanadascapital.gc.ca) is at 90 Wellington Street. It has free leaflets, including a useful *Visitor Guide*, and issues free public transport maps. It also sells the Capital Museums Passport.

Capital Museums Passport Valid for three days from the first museum visit, and covers admission into your choice of three museums from Ottawa's and Gatineau's seven leading museums. The cost is $35, and it is sold at participating museums and at Capital Information Kiosk.

GETTING AROUND

Most of Ottawa's key attractions – as well as many of its better restaurants, bars and hotels – are clustered in the downtown area within comfortable walking distance of Confederation Square.

By bus OC Transpo (☎613 741 4390, ⓦoctranspo.com) provides a comprehensive network of bus services across Ottawa and its suburbs. The hub of the OC Transpo system is the Transitway, which runs one-way west along Albert St and one-way east on Slater St – in both cases between Bay and Elgin streets. Key bus services operate daily from 5am or 6am to around midnight. Gatineau and its immediate surroundings, on the north side of the river, are covered by STO buses (☎819 770 3242, ⓦsto.ca).

Tickets A standard single bus fare within the city limits costs $3.50 – pay the driver (exact fare only) or use a ticket machine (there's one at most bus stops). Express buses cost a shade more. A DayPass, which allows unlimited travel on the OC Transpo system, costs $10.50; these are available from bus drivers (exact fare only), who also issue free transfers, which are essential if you're travelling on an ordinary ticket and need to change buses to complete your journey.

By O-Train The O-Train is an 8km-long commuter line linking Greenboro station to the south of the centre with the Bayview Transitway station just to the west.

By bike Rentabike, Plaza Bridge, East Arch, 2 Rideau St at Colonel By Drive (☎613 241 4140, ⓦrentabike.ca), rents bicycles of various specifications and sells cycling maps.

By car Rental companies include: Discount, 1749 Bank St (☎613 667 9393, ⓦdiscountcar.com); Hertz, 30 York St, Byward Market (☎613 241 7681 and airport ☎613 521 3332); National, at the airport (☎613 737 7023).

Taxis Blue Line ☎613 238 1111; Capital Taxi ☎613 744 3333.

ACTIVITIES AND SPORTS

Ice hockey From September to April, the Ottawa Senators (☎613 599 0250, ⓦsenators.nhl.com) play NHL home games at the Canadian Tire Centre (see page 175).

Whitewater rafting Owl Rafting (☎800 461 7238, ⓦowl-mkc.ca) offers an excellent programme of whitewater rafting on the Ottawa River, near Pembroke, about 170km northwest of Ottawa. From May to September, a one-day excursion costs $115–155 with rental of all the necessary tackle and a buffet lunch included.

ACCOMMODATION

Ottawa hosts dozens of business conferences and conventions and although there are hundreds of **rooms** in the city, things can still get tight – with prices rising accordingly. The best bet for a reasonably priced room is often in an **inn** or **B&B**, the pick of which offer prime lodgings close to the centre; the cheapest beds in town are at the two downtown **hostels**. Staff at the main visitor centre (see above) will supply a list of local accommodation and you can make a booking at the Capital Information Kiosk's free computers.

HOTELS

★ **Andaz Ottawa Byward Market** 325 Dalhousie St ☎613 321 1234, ⓦhyatt.com; map p.162. This sleek hotel covers most items on a top hotel checklist: great location, style and amenities. The hotel is in the heart of it all, at Byward Market, a short stroll to the Parliament and National Gallery of Canada. The rooms are elegant, with Canadian touches, natural colours and views of the skyline thorough floor-to-glass windows. And, the rooftop lounge,

Copper Spirits and Sights, is the highest bar in town, with stunning vistas that rival the expert cocktail menu. $205

★ **Arc** 140 Slater St ☎ 613 238 2888, ☎ 800 699 2516, ⓦ arcthehotel.com; map p.162. Designer hotel in a handy downtown location, with minimalist decor. The guest rooms are kitted out in style, all wood and leather with Egyptian cotton sheets, though they can be a little on the small side (for Canada). The *Arc Lounge & Bar* features locally sourced cuisine, from frittatas with goat cheese and kale in the morning to scallops and pork belly with spiced grapes for dinner. $169

★ **Fairmont Château Laurier** 1 Rideau St ☎ 613 241 1414, ☎ 800 257 7544, ⓦ fairmont.com; map p.162. Keen to impress, the Grand Trunk Pacific Railway built this prestige hotel in the 1910s and it remains Ottawa's finest, comprising a wonderful example of the French Renaissance – or château – style: the exterior is a forest of copper-clad turrets, spires and towers, and inside the public areas boast marble floors, high ceilings, chandeliers and soaring columns, plus extravagantly embossed lifts. The guest rooms are thoroughly comfortable, done up in a muted palette of creams and browns, and the best offer delightful views towards the Ottawa River. The fitness centre is top-notch, and has a pool. Discounts are legion. $299

Le Germain Hotel Ottawa 30 Daly Ave ☎ 613 691 3230, ⓦ legermainhotels.com; map p.162. *Le Germain* lives up to its chic reputation at this stylish hotel that opened in 2018. Airy rooms are filled with natural light and done up in earthy tones. Wake up to a complimentary hearty breakfast – and then work it off at the sleek fitness center. $299

Lord Elgin Hotel 100 Elgin St ☎ 613 235 3333, ☎ 800 267 4298, ⓦ lordelginhotel.ca; map p.162. This long-established hotel occupies a handsome château-meets-Art-Deco-style 1940s high-rise near Confederation Square. The 300 guest rooms are large and well appointed and decorated in a traditional version of country-house style.

Often has discounts at weekends. $139

INNS AND B&BS

Australis Guest House 89 Goulburn Ave ☎ 613 235 8461, ⓦ bbcanada.com/1463.html; map p.162. Self-billed as "A touch of Australia", this cosy B&B is in a pleasant, three-storey house a couple of kilometres east of the Rideau Canal, just off (and to the south of) Laurier Ave East. It has just two guest rooms (one en suite), both decorated in a folksy style. $129

★ **McGee's Inn** 185 Daly Ave ☎ 613 237 6089, ☎ 800 262 4337, ⓦ mcgeesinn.com; map p.162. On a leafy side-street a short walk from downtown, *McGee's* occupies a grand old Victorian redbrick The interior is decorated in attractive period style and the guest rooms are charming, a nice mix of the old and the new. The two best rooms have their own balcony. Breakfasts are first rate – and home cooked. $119

HOSTELS

Ottawa Backpackers Inn 203 York St ☎ 613 241 3402, ☎ 888 394 0334, ⓦ ottawahostel.com; map p.162. Spartan, informal, medium-sized hostel in a chalet-like building on a side street close to Byward Market. Self-catering facilities, internet access and linen supplied (free); dorms are for eight to ten people. Dorms $28; doubles $80

Ottawa Jail Hostel 75 Nicholas St, at Daly ☎ 613 235 2595, ☎ 866 299 1478, ⓦ hihostels.ca; map p.162. Ottawa's old prison has been converted into a HI hostel with guests sleeping in former cells, complete with bars on the windows, in six- or eight-bed dorms, twin cells and double rooms. The old admissions area is now a kitchen, the former chapel a TV and games lounge, and there's also a laundry, self-catering facilities, free bedding, and free wi-fi. The hostel is handily located downtown, just south of Rideau Street's Rideau Shopping Centre. Reservations recommended. Dorms $38; twins $101; doubles $106

EATING

Ottawa has an excellent range of **restaurants**, some geared firmly to the expense account, but the majority reasonably priced. The city also has a small army of **bars**, some dog-eared and dog-tough, others selling an excellent range of local ales in eminently inviting surroundings. There's a high concentration of restaurants in **Byward Market** (see page 174), the main tourist zone, but there are other enclaves too. Most notable are **Hintonburg**, a downbeat, low-rise neighbourhood to the southwest of the city centre, and the southern reaches of **Bank Street**.

BAKERIES, CAFÉS AND DINERS

Art is in Bakery 250 City Center Ave ☎ 613-695-1226, ⓦ artisinbakery.com; map p.162. Follow your nose to this perennially popular industrial-chic bakery, breakfast and lunch joint. Try the decadent croissants and the sandwiches served on the superb bread, like chicken

Caesar on cheddar, jalapeño and chive bread. Breakfast and sandwiches $9–16. Mon–Fri 7am–3pm & 5–9.45pm, Sat 8am–3pm, Sun 8am–2pm.

Bridgehead 96 Sparks St at Metcalfe ☎ 613 232 4936, ⓦ bridgehead.ca; map p.162. Competing with the multinationals may be difficult, but this coffee house, one of a smallish local chain, does the business supremely well – supplying tasty coffee with good beans as well as cold-press juices, kombucha, croissants, granola – including banana peanut butter overnight oats – and excellent bread like a cherry-lemon loaf. Mon–Fri 6am–6pm, Sat & Sun 8am–6pm.

The French Baker 119 Murray St ☎ 613 789 7941, ⓦ frenchbaker.ca; map p.162. Much-lauded bakery, with a handful of seats for in-house eating, that does a great line in French bread and sells what many local thinks are the best croissants in town. Mon–Fri 7am–6.30pm, Sat & Sun 7am–5.30pm.

2

BYWARD MARKET

Since the 1840s, **Byward Market** (known simply as "The Market" to locals), just east of Sussex Drive and north of Rideau Street, has been a centre for the sale of farm produce, but it's now also Ottawa's busiest district, buzzing until the early hours. At its heart, the 1920s **Byward Market building** (Mon–Wed, Fri & Sat 9.30am–6pm, Thurs 9.30am–8pm, Sun 9.30am–5pm; ⓦ byward-market.com) is home to cafés and delis, specialist food and fresh fruit and vegetable stalls and these merge with the street stalls and kiosks outside. These stalls and kiosks are something of an Ottawa institution, mainly on account of their *poutine* (fries covered in gravy and cheese curds), but **Beavertails**, at the junction of George and William streets, weighs in with its eponymous offering, a flat, deep-fried dough sprinkled with all sorts of sweet toppings. Look for the Savour Ottawa (ⓦ savourottawa.ca) logo as you're shopping – this indicates food that comes that's grown or raised in and around Ottawa.

Stella Luna Gelato Café 1103 Bank St at Sunnyside ☎613 523 1116, ⓦ slgelato.com; map p.162. In airy premises – the place used to be a general store – this neighbourhood café does a great line in Italian snacks and light meals. Also offers a wide range of home-made ice creams and sorbets in alarming colours. Bus #1 or #7 from downtown. Mon–Sat 8am–10pm & Sun 9am–10pm.

Zak's Diner 14 Byward Market Square ☎613 241 2401, ⓦ zaksdiner.com; map p.162. A 1950s-style time warp with chrome decor, rock 'n' roll blaring from the jukebox and all-American food – stick to the shakes. Open 24hr, seven days a week.

RESTAURANTS

★ **Fauna** 425 Bank St ☎613 563 2862, ⓦ faunaottawa. ca; map p.162. *Fauna* is all about creative new Canadian cuisine, serving innovative dishes inspired by the country's natural bounty, from red deer tartare with green strawberry chutney and quail yolk to duck breast with scallion pancakes. Don't miss the dark chocolate tart with black pepper ganache and cherries. Mains $18–30. Mon–Thurs 11.30am–2pm & 5.30pm–10pm, Fri 11.30am–2pm & 5.30pm–11pm, Sat 5.30pm–11pm, Sun 5.30pm–10pm. Bar open late.

Tennessy Willems 1082 Wellington St West at Melrose

☎613 722 0000, ⓦ twpizza.com; map p.162. Pizzas are the big deal here – arguably the best in the city – large and cooked in a wood-fired oven. Wash it down with a craft beer. Pizzas average $16. In Hintonburg – bus #2 from Rideau St. Mon–Wed 11.30am–10pm, Thurs–Sat 11.30am–10.30pm, Sun 4–10pm.

★ **Town** 296 Elgin St ☎613 695 8696, ⓦ townlovesyou. ca; map p.162. Feast on creative, artisanal Italian cuisine with a Canadian twist at this spirited restaurant that lives up to its website name. Start off with small bites like lavender almonds and fried Brussels sprouts with vegan cashew crema and then launch into main dishes, like ricotta-stuffed meatballs and pork cheek ragu. Nearby, Town has a new sibling in Citizen (207 Gilmour St), a lively wine bar. Mains $17–30. Sun–Thurs 5–10pm, Fri–Sat 5–11pm.

Whalesbone Oyster Bar 430 Bank St at Gladstone ☎613 231 8569, ⓦ thewhalesbone.com; map p.162. The best seafood joint in town, offering the freshest of fish in its antique, highly varnished premises. Famous for its oysters – but the other seafood dishes also impress, including the excellent shellfish risotto. Bus #1 or #7 from downtown. Most mains around $30. Mon–Wed 11.30am–2pm & 5–10pm, Thurs & Fri 11.30am–2pm & 5–11pm, Sat 5–11pm, Sun 5–10pm.

DRINKING AND NIGHTLIFE

Byward Market has a number of inviting **bars** and **clubs**, making it an obvious first choice for a night out; in the warmer months it heaves with people strolling from one stop to the next. Ottawa has also become a major port of call for big-name **rock** and **pop** acts, most of whom appear at Scotiabank Place.

BARS AND PUBS

Chez Lucien 137 Murray St, at Dalhousie ☎613 241 3533; map p.162. Smashing, Québec-style joint with a well-chosen selection of craft beers plus great burgers, *escargot* and a (free) jukebox. Daily 11am–2am.

Hintonburg Public House 1020 Wellington St West, at

Fairmont ☎613 421 5087, ⓦ hintonburgpublichouse.ca; map p.162. Cameronbeers and ales ring the alcoholic bells here at this modern pub, but it's the bar food which pulls in many of the punters – try the fish and chips and the juicy burger. Mains $16–23. In Hintonburg – bus #2 from Rideau St. Mon–Fri 11.30am–2am, Sat & Sun 11am–2am.

The Manx 370 Elgin St, at Frank ☎613 231 2070, ⓦ manxpub.com; map p.162. This basement pub packs the locals in tight with a boisterous crew having an energetic bash at all the twenty-odd beers on draught. Bus #14 from Rideau St. Mon–Wed 11.30am–1am, Thurs & Fri 11.30am–2am, Sat 10am–2am, Sun 10am–1am.

Moonroom 442 Preston St ☎613 231 2525, no website;

map p.162. Creative cocktails, tasty tapas – bacon-wrapped olives, parmesan popcorn – and a casually stylish vibe make this a prime spot to kick off the evening (or end it). Daily 5pm–2am.

Quinn's Ale House 1170 Bank St ☎613 523 2200; map p.162. Not much from the outside perhaps, but this small, cosy bar is an amenable sort of place that serves local and international draught beers. Bus #1 or #7 from downtown. Mon–Thurs 4pm–2am, Fri 3pm–2am, Sat & Sun 11am–2am.

CLUBS

Barrymore's Music Hall 323 Bank St, at Gilmour ☎613 695 8488, ⓦbarrymores.tunestub.ca; map p.162. Big and brassy club in what was once a theatre, *Barrymore's* features everything from live acts to DJ specials as well as themed retro nights. Check website for what's on, when. Bus #1 or #7 from downtown. Mon–Thurs 11am–midnight, Fri–Sun 11am–2.30am.

Rainbow Bistro 76 Murray St ☎613 241 5123, ⓦtherainbow.ca; map p.162. Atmospheric blues and jazz club with regular jam sessions and good sidelines in reggae, funk, rock and ska. Daily 8pm–2am.

ENTERTAINMENT

Ottawa has a good programme of **performing arts**, with several venues regularly holding a wide variety of events.

CINEMAS

Bytowne Cinema 325 Rideau St, at Nelson ☎613 789 3456, ⓦbytowne.ca. The capital's most popular art house cinema, which shows a mix of international and independent releases.

Canadian Film Institute 2 Daly Ave, at Nicholas ☎613 232 6727, ⓦcfi-icf.ca. Shows art-house and independent films from every corner of the globe. Specializes in themed nights and events.

THEATRES AND VENUES

Canadian Tire Centre 1000 Palladium Drive ☎613 599 3267, ⓦcanadiantirecentre.com. Located about 15km west of downtown at Kanata, this is Ottawa's big-deal concert arena attracting big-name rock and pop acts from Barbra Streisand to Madonna. Also home to the Ottawa Senators ice-hockey team (see page 172).

Great Canadian Theatre Company 1233 Wellington St West, at Holland ☎613 236 5196, ⓦgctc.ca. Quality, not-for-profit theatre company offering a lively and adventurous programme with modern Canadian playwrights to the fore. In Hintonburg – bus #2 from downtown.

National Arts Centre 53 Elgin St ☎613 947 7000, ⓦnac-cna.ca. This is Ottawa's cultural focus, presenting plays by its resident theatre company as well as touring groups, concerts by its resident orchestra, and opera and dance from (among others) the National Ballet of Canada and the Royal Winnipeg Ballet; the acoustics are outstanding.

Ottawa Little Theatre 400 King Edward Ave, at Rideau ☎613 233 8948, ⓦottawalittletheatre.com. Top-of-the-range community theatre showcasing a varied programme of modern classics (and not-so-classics) from Agatha Christie to Noël Coward and Arthur Miller. Downtown location.

SHOPPING

Chapters 47 Rideau St, at Sussex Drive ☎613 241 0073, ⓦchapters.indigo.ca; map p.162. Large, downtown bookshop spread over two floors. Has a comprehensive selection of Canadian titles and authors – both fiction and nonfiction. Mon–Sat 9.30am–10pm, Sun 10am–9pm.

Made in Canada Gifts 50 Rideau St ☎613 729 6378, ⓦmadeincanadagifts.ca; map p.162. This is one-stop-shopping for unique Canadian gifts and souvenirs, from Canadian pottery and art to the maple leaf in multiple forms, including printed on colourful socks. Mon–Sat 9.30am–9pm, Sun 11am–6pm.

Mountain Equipment Co-Op 366 Richmond Rd, at Churchill Ave North ☎613 729 2700, ⓦmec.ca; map p.162. Outdoor specialist with a huge selection of all sorts of activity gear both for sale and rental. Occupies an old movie theatre to the west of the centre. Mon–Wed 10am–7pm, Thurs & Fri 10am–9pm, Sat 9am–6pm, Sun 11am–5pm; special hours late May to early Sept.

World of Maps 1191 Wellington St West, at Parkdale ☎613 724 6776, ⓦworldofmaps.com; map p.162. Map and travel guide specialist, whose stock includes detailed maps of Ontario and its larger settlements. Also maps of the province's parks, canoe routes, hiking trails and cycling routes. In Hintonburg – bus #2 from Rideau St. Mon–Fri 9am–6pm, Sat 10am–5pm, Sun 11am–4pm.

DIRECTORY

Embassies Australia, 50 O'Connor St (☎613 236 0841); Ireland, 130 Albert St (☎613 233 6281); New Zealand, 99 Bank St (☎613 238 6097); UK, 80 Elgin St (☎613 237 1530); US, 490 Sussex Drive (☎613 238 5335).

Laundry Rideau Coinwash, 436 Rideau St, at Chapel (☎613 789 4400).

Sudbury

An economic centre in its own right, sprawling **SUDBURY**, some 165km north of Parry Sound (see page 144) and 130km northeast of Little Current on Manitoulin Island (see page 134), is parked on the edge of the **Sudbury Basin**, a pit created either by a volcano or, the preferred theory, by a giant **meteor**. Whatever did the damage, the effect was to throw one of the world's richest deposits of **nickel and copper** towards the surface. It was the nickel – used to temper steel – that made Sudbury's fortune, but its by-products caused acute environmental degradation. Most of the damage was done by a smelting method known as **heap roasting**, used until the 1920s, which spread clouds of sulphurous fumes over forests already ravaged by lumber firms and mineral prospectors, who often started fires to reveal the traces of metal in the bare rocks below. Likened to Hell and Hiroshima, the bleak landscape had only one advantage: in 1968 it enabled Buzz Aldrin and Neil Armstrong to practise their great leap for mankind in a ready-made lunar environment. Having continued to produce sulphur-laden smoke from the stacks of their nickel smelters, the mining companies were finally forced to take action when a whole community of workers from **Happy Valley**, just northeast of Sudbury (and now ringed off by a large steel fence), were evacuated in the 1970s because of the number of sulphur-induced illnesses. Since then, pollutants have been greatly reduced and the city has implemented an ambitious re-greening programme, which has been widely acclaimed by environmentalists.

Sudbury's key attractions are located to the south and west of the **downtown core**, which is focused on Elm Street between Notre Dame Avenue and Durham Street.

Science North

100 Ramsey Lake Rd • Daily: April–June & Sept–Dec 10am–4pm; July & Aug 9am–6pm • $22 • ☎ 705 522 3701 or ☎ 800 461 4898, ⓦ sciencenorth.ca

Making the most of the city's unusual geology, **Science North**, a huge snowflake-shaped structure south of the centre on Ramsey Lake Road, is installed in a cavern blasted into the rock of the Canadian Shield. The hands-on displays enable you to simulate a miniature hurricane, gauge your fitness, lie on a bed of nails, learn to lip-read, call up amateur radio hams worldwide and tune in to weather-tracking stations, all under the guidance of students from the city's university. The museum also has a collection of insects and animals, some of which can be handled, an IMAX Theatre, various virtual-reality rides and a planetarium.

Dynamic Earth

122 Big Nickel Rd • Daily: April–June & Sept–Dec 10am–4pm; July & Aug 9am–6pm • $22 • ☎ 705 522 3701 or ☎ 800 461 4898, ⓦ sciencenorth.ca

The town's symbol, a nine-metre-high steel replica of a five-cent piece, known as the **Big Nickel**, stands near the Trans-Canada Highway on the western approach to town. The nickel marks the entrance to **Dynamic Earth**, where an imaginative range of attractions has been located in an old nickel mine, from multimedia features on the world's cultures through to an exploration of old mine shafts and stories exploring Sudbury's history.

ARRIVAL AND INFORMATION

SUDBURY

By train Served by VIA Rail, Sudbury's principal train station – Sudbury Junction – is about 10km northeast of the town centre on Lasalle Boulevard. There are no buses into town – you have to take a taxi from the rank outside the terminal.

Destinations Toronto (3–4 weekly; 7hr); Winnipeg (3 weekly; 27hr).

By bus The Greyhound bus depot is at 854 Notre Dame, about 3km north of the centre. The Ontario Northland bus depot is northeast of the centre at 1663 The Kingsway at 2nd Ave North. Greater Sudbury Transit (☎ 705 675 3333)

operates an extensive network of bus routes throughout the area ($3; exact fare required).

Destinations (Greyhound) North Bay (3 daily; 2hr); Ottawa (3–4 daily; 7hr 30min); Sault Ste Marie (3 daily; 4hr 30min); Thunder Bay (2 daily; 15hr).

Destinations (Ontario Northland) Cochrane (1 daily; 6hr 45min); Hearst (1 daily; 9hr); Parry Sound (3 daily; 2hr); Port Severn (3 daily; 3hr 15min); Toronto (3 daily; 6hr).

Tourist office Downtown on Market Square at 200 Brady St (June–Aug daily 8.30am–6.30pm; Sept–May Mon–Fri 8.30am–4.30pm; ☎ 877 304 8222, ⊛ sudburytourism.ca).

ACCOMMODATION

SUDBURY

Best Western Downtown Sudbury 151 Larch St ☎ 705 673 7801, ⊛ bestwestern.com. Modern chain hotel in the heart of town with spacious, well-appointed rooms and fitness facilities. **$130**

SURROUNDING REGION

The Lodge at Pine Cove 1013 Hwy-528A Noëlville

☎ 705 898 2500, ⊛ frenchriver.com. Heading north from Parry Sound to Sudbury, it's a longish but manageable detour east to this chalet-cottage complex, deep in the forest, about 80km south of Sudbury via the Trans-Canada Hwy (Hwy-69). Set in an exquisite riverside location, there's hiking here but the main deal is kayaking and canoeing – and good-quality food. Early May to end Oct. **$337**

EATING

Laughing Buddha 194 Elgin St ☎ 705 673 2112, ⊛ laughingbuddhasudbury.com. The folksy interior of this lively little place makes it a welcoming pit stop, with a mix of vegetarian and meat-friendly fare, from the loaded chicken sandwich, smeared with balsamic-pesto mayonnaise and topped with a chicken breast and double-cream brie to a sesame quinoa salad with seaweed, cashew crumble and grilled tofu. Mains $12–15. Liver-bashing range of beers too. Sun–Wed 11am–midnight, Thurs 11am–1am, Fri–Sat 11am–2am.

Respect Is Burning 82 Durham St ☎ 705 675 5777, ⊛ ribsupperclub.com. A large and stylish warehouse-style downtown lounge serving mainly Italian food, with mains from around $18; try the fettuccine with shrimp and scallops. Tues–Thurs 5–10pm, Fri–Sat 5pm–1am.

Teklenburg's 1893 Lasalle Boulevard ☎ 705 560 2662. Well-established seafood restaurant, which does a good line in lake trout and pickerel. Is also popular for its "surf and turf" dishes from $25. Mains from $20–30. Mon–Sat 11am–9pm, Sun 3–9pm.

Sault Ste Marie

Strategically situated beside St Mary's River, the tortuous link between lakes Superior and Huron, industrial **SAULT STE MARIE** – more popularly **The Soo** – sits opposite the Michigan town of the same name and sees constant two-way traffic, with two sets of tourists keen to see how the other lot lives. The Soo, 300km from Sudbury, is northern Ontario's oldest community, originally settled by Ojibwa fishing parties. The French called these Ojibwa *Saulteux* ("people of the falls") and the Jesuit missionaries who followed added the Christian sobriquet to give the town its present name. Initially, The Soo flourished as a gateway to the fur-rich regions inland, but it was the construction of a **lock** and **canal** in the nineteenth century that launched its career as a Great Lakes port and industrial centre, churning out pulp, paper and steel.

Some 2km long and three blocks wide, The Soo's downtown core runs parallel to the waterfront to either side of the main drag, **Queen Street East**. All the principal sights and most visitor facilities are located here, the pick of which stretch along the **waterfront**, but its real appeal is as the starting point for a splendid wilderness train ride on the **Algoma Central Railway**.

2

THE ALGOMA CENTRAL RAILWAY

The 476km-long **Algoma Central Railway** (**ACR**) was constructed in 1901 to link The Soo's timber plants with the forests of the interior. The first recreational users were members of the Group of Seven (see page 74), who shunted up and down the track in a converted boxcar, stopping to paint whenever the mood took them. The ACR's timber days are long gone, but today the railway offers one of Ontario's finest excursions, with the train snaking through a wonderful wilderness of deep ravines, secluded lakes and plunging gorges. To see it all, sit on the left-hand side – otherwise you'll end up looking at an awful lot of rock. There are **several tours** to choose from, though only two stand out, and all depart from the Algoma Central Railway Terminal, in downtown Soo at 129 Bay St, at Dennis (☎ 705 946 7300, ☎ 800 242 9287, ⓦ agawacanyontourtrain.com).

The **Agawa Canyon Tour Train** takes a day to cover the first 200km of track and back (late June to mid-Oct departs daily at 8am, returns 6pm; $100; $121 in autumn). **Reservations** are strongly advised and essential in autumn, when the leaves turn. A two-hour stop within the canyon's 180m-high walls allows for a **lunch break** and a wander around the well-marked nature trails, which include a lookout post from where the rail line appears as a thin silver thread far below. Unless you are properly equipped, don't miss the train back – the canyon gets very cold at night, even during the summer, and the blackflies are merciless.

The waterfront

The spruced-up section of The Soo's elongated **waterfront** extends west for a couple of kilometres from the Art Gallery of Algoma, at the foot of East Street. En route, it incorporates a series of modest attractions – nothing too riveting perhaps, but enough for a pleasant stroll until you reach the **Station Mall**, a sprawling shopping centre that has sucked the commercial heart out of downtown; on the other side of the mall, away from the lake, is the Algoma Central Railway station (see box above).

Art Gallery of Algoma

10 East St • Tues–Sat 9am–5pm • $7 • ☎ 705 949 9067, ⓦ artgalleryofalgoma.com

Housed in a neat and trim modern building, the **Art Gallery of Algoma** has a strong permanent collection with modern Canadian painters to the fore, including a number of works by the Group of Seven (see page 74), Emily Carr, and the strikingly original Norval Morrisseau (1932–2007), aka Copper Thunderbird, an Ojibwa from Thunder Bay. The gallery also offers an inventive programme of temporary exhibitions, usually featuring local artists.

Sault Ste Marie Canal National Historic Site

Open access • Free

A good twenty-minute walk west of Station Mall, Canal Drive crosses one of the river's narrow channels to reach St Mary's Island, home to the **Sault Ste Marie Canal National Historic Site**. Here, you can stroll along the lock and investigate the old stone buildings that surround it with the help of a series of explanatory plaques.

ARRIVAL AND INFORMATION   SAULT STE MARIE

By bus The Greyhound bus station is at 73 Brock St – in the centre between Queen St East and the waterfront.
Destinations Kenora (2 daily; 16hr); Thunder Bay (2 daily; 9–10hr); Toronto (3–4 daily; 10hr 30min); Wawa (2 daily; 3hr); White River (1 daily; 4hr 15min); Winnipeg (2 daily; 20hr).

Tourism Sault Ste Marie Centre This first-rate information centre (daily: mid-May to June 8am–6pm; July to early Sept 8am–8pm; early Sept to mid-May 8.30am–5pm; ☎ 705 759 5442, ☎ 800 461 6020, ⓦ saulttourism.com) is located near the waterfront at 99 Foster Drive.

ACCOMMODATION AND EATING

Aurora's Westside 300 2nd Line W ☎ 705 949 3000, ⓦ aurorarestaurant.com. At this lively family-run

restaurant, sink your teeth into tasty pizza and other Italian favourites, including heaping platters of lasagne and baked tortellini. Mon–Thurs 11am–11pm, Fri–Sat 11am–midnight, Sun 4–10pm.

Comfort Inn 333 Great Northern Rd ☎705 759 8000, ⓦchoicehotels.com. One of the more appealing hotels in this giant chain, this particular *Comfort Inn* occupies a modern, two-storey building just to the north of the city centre. Perks include a fitness centre, an indoor heated pool and complimentary hot breakfast. $140

Delta Sault Ste Marie Waterfront Hotel 208 Saint Mary's Drive ☎705 949 0611, ⓦmarriott.com. Large, modern waterfront property with a restaurant and lounge, spacious rooms, a pool and a fitness centre. As it's a popular spot for conferences, advance reservations are recommended. $131

Lake Superior's north shore

More like an inland sea than a lake, the steely waters of **Lake Superior** comprise the largest freshwater lake in the world – and one of the wildest. Its northern shore between Sault Ste Marie and **Thunder Bay** is a windswept, rugged region formed by volcanoes, earthquakes and glaciers, its steep, forested valleys often overhung by a canopy of grey sky. In 1872 Reverend George Grant wrote of Superior: "It breeds storms and rain and fog. It is cold… wild, masterful and dreaded." The indigenous Ojibwa lived in fear of the storms that would suddenly break on the lake they knew as Gitche Gumee, the Big-Sea-Water, and white sailors were inordinately suspicious of a lake whose icy waters caused its victims to sink like stones: Lake Superior never gives up its dead. For the most part, **Hwy-17** sticks close to the north shore of Lake Superior between Sault Ste Marie and Thunder Bay, but a screen of trees almost always keeps the lake out of view. This stretch of road is 690km long, so unless you're up for a gruelling thrash, it's much better to dawdle and dally. Along the way are two magnificent parks, **Lake Superior Provincial Park** and **Pukaskwa National Park**, where there's camping and hiking – though the insects can be unbearable from May to August, sometimes longer. The small towns dotted along the highway mostly fail to inspire, but low-key **Wawa**, about a third of the way along, has several good places to stay, while diminutive **Rossport**, a further 300km west, is easily the prettiest settlement hereabouts.

Greyhound **buses** regularly travel Hwy-17 between Toronto and Thunder Bay en route to Winnipeg, but don't expect them to drop you exactly where you want: if you are aiming for a specific motel or campsite, check how far you'll have to walk.

Lake Superior Provincial Park

Hwy-17 cuts through the park for around 100km, giving access to all key facilities; no park services Nov–April, when service roads (but not Hwy-17) are barred and gated • Mid-May to late Oct $14.50 day-entry • ☎705 882 2026, ⓦlakesuperiorpark.ca

Heading north from Sault Ste Marie on Hwy-17, it's about 130km to the southern perimeter of **Lake Superior Provincial Park**, which offers ready access to Lake Superior's granite shoreline and its immediate hinterland. Autumn is the best time to visit, when the blackflies have abated and the forests of sugar maples and yellow birch flash with colour, but the scenery and wildlife are enthralling year-round. Moose, chipmunk and beaver are the most common, sharing their habitat with the more elusive white-tailed deer, woodland caribou, coyote, timber wolf and black bear, as well as myriad migratory and resident birds.

The Coastal Trail

The finest of the park's many trails, the **Coastal Trail** begins some 140km from Sault Ste Marie at **Sinclair Cove** and runs north to **Chalfant Cove**. It comprises a challenging 48km-long route of high cliffs, sand and cobbled beaches, sheltered coves and exposed granite ledges. There are numerous designated backcountry campsites on the trail and the burnt-out fires on the beaches indicate where most people choose to pitch. The entire trek takes about five to seven days but access points enable you to do shorter sections; the southern part of the trail is not as demanding, with fewer climbs and easier going on sand rather than cobbled beach. Maps and trail guides are available at the park office and the visitor centre (see below).

INFORMATION   LAKE SUPERIOR PROVINCIAL PARK

Both the visitor centre and the park office sell park maps as well as hiking and canoe route maps and backcountry camping permits ($10 per person per night), which are compulsory if you're heading off into the wilderness. The rangers will warn you if weather conditions look perilous, but always expect the worst – the park receives more rain and snow than any other in Ontario.

Lake Superior Provincial Park Visitor Centre Just off Hwy-17 about 15km from the southern edge of the park in the same location as the *Agawa Bay* campground (daily: May, June & Sept to early Oct 9am–5pm; July & Aug 9am–8pm; ☎705 882 2026).

Lake Superior Provincial Park Office Also off Hwy-17, about 60km to the north of the park's visitor centre (daily May–Oct 8am–4.30pm; ☎705 856 2284).

ACCOMMODATION

Lake Superior Provincial Park has two major **campsites**. Reservations can be made online (🌐lakesuperiorpark.ca) or via either the park office or the visitor centre.

Agawa Bay Just off Hwy-17, about 15km from the park's southern entrance. Midsize campsite with 146 pitches, some of which are right beside the lake ($5 extra), 38 hook-ups, showers and laundry facilities. Mid-May to early Oct. Vehicle and site $41

Rabbit Blanket Lake Near the park office (see above). Ideal for forays into the interior, there are sixty pitches here with twenty hook-ups, showers and laundry. Mid-May to late Oct. Vehicle and site $41

Wawa

The unassuming, former iron-mining town of **WAWA**, 14km north of Lake Superior Provincial Park, was named after the Ojibwa word for **wild goose** – and to hammer home the point there's a great big steel model of the bird at the entrance to town. The model has helped to make Wawa a busy stopping point on the Trans-Canada Highway (Hwy-17), which was just the idea. In the 1960s, much to the chagrin of local businessfolk, the highway was routed a couple of kilometres to the west of town – hence the goose to attract passing motorists.

ACCOMMODATION AND EATING   WAWA

Kinniwabi Pines Restaurant 136 Hwy-17 South ☎705 856 7226. According to many a local, a stay here in Wawa isn't complete without eating at the *Kinniwabi*. The place is famous hereabouts for its Caribbean dishes, a speciality of the Trinidadian chef. Mains, such as jerk chicken and *rotis*, from $20. May–Oct daily 8am–10pm.

★ **Rock Island Lodge** RR #1, Lake Superior ☎705 856 7168, ☎800 203 9092, 🌐rockislandlodge.ca. This appealing wooden lodge sits beside a sandy beach, its patio literally hanging over Lake Superior. The four modern and straightforward guest rooms have no phones and no TV, but they are popular all the same and reservations are advised. The lodge also offers kayaking trips and teepee-camping. The lodge is located 10km from Wawa: take the Trans-Canada Hwy south from town and turn right (west) after 5km along Michipicoten River Village Road. $128

Wawa Motor Inn 118 Mission Rd ☎705 856 2278, ☎800 5612278, 🌐wawamotorinn.com. On the main drag, this large and modern motel has a variety of options, from standard rooms with double beds to log chalets with a fireplace and a full kitchen. Doubles $106; chalets $248

White River

Beyond Wawa, it's 90km of forest until you reach the next settlement of any interest, **WHITE RIVER**. There's nothing much to the place, but it does have two claims to fame. First, in 1935 the temperature here dropped to a mind-boggling -57°C (-72°F), the lowest ever recorded in the whole of mainland Canada – hence the whopping thermometer hanging by Hwy-17. Second, this was the home of a small bear cub named Winnipeg who was exported to London Zoo in 1914 and became the inspiration for **Winnie-the-Pooh**. To emphasize the connection, you'll spot a fibreglass Winnie up a tree beside the highway.

Pukaskwa National Park

Open year-round, but limited services in winter • $5.80 per vehicle and passengers • ☎ 807 229 0801, ⓦ pc.gc.ca

Beyond White River, Hwy-17 turns west, heading back towards the Lake Superior shoreline. After about 85km, just short of the little lakeshore town of **Marathon**, Hwy-17 clips past **Hwy-627**, the 15km-long side road that provides the only access to **Pukaskwa National Park**, a large chunk of hilly boreal forest interspersed by muskeg and loch that fills out an enormous headland with a stunningly wild and remote coastline. Apart from a scattering of facilities beside the road at **Hattie Cove**, the park is untrammelled wilderness, attracting a mixed bag of canoeists and backcountry campers.

2

The trails

At Hattie Cove, most visitors embark on the **Coastal Hiking Trail**, which travels 60km south through the boreal forest and over the ridges and cliffs of the Canadian Shield. It is not an easy hike, but it is magnificent and there are regular backcountry campsites on the way. In the summer, McCuaig Marine Services (☎ 807 229 0193) offers a **water taxi** service to Swallow River, so you can just hike one-way back to Hattie Cove. Far less arduous are the short trails departing from or near the visitor centre. Of these, the rocky **Southern Headland Trail** (2.2km) offers superb views over Lake Superior before hitting Horseshoe Beach, where you can continue on the **Beach Trail** (1.5km) leading you back to the campsite.

INFORMATION	**PUKASKWA NATIONAL PARK**
Hattie Cove Visitor Centre Pukaskwa National Park's visitor centre (late May to early Oct daily 8.30am–4.30pm; ☎ 807 229 0801, ⓦ pc.gc.ca) is on the northern edge of	the park reached along Hwy-627. They sell trail guides and backcountry camping permits (from $9.80 per night).

ACCOMMODATION	
Hattie Cove campsite ☎ 807 229 0801, ⓦ pc.gc.ca. This is the national park's only campsite with both unserviced and serviced sites with electrical hook-ups ($5 extra).	Reservations can be made online or at the Hattie Cove Visitor Centre. **$25.50**

Rossport

Some 130km beyond the Pukaskwa turning, Hwy-17 passes close to **ROSSPORT**, a pretty little village draped around a tiny, sheltered bay. Originally a Hudson's Bay Company trading post, the settlement prospered as a fishing port until the 1960s, when a combination of overfishing and a sea-lamprey attack on the lake trout led to the industry's decline. Today Rossport is the quietest of villages and one that makes for a useful pit stop on the long trek north.

A CANADIAN HERO: TERRY FOX

West of Nipigon, highways 17 and 11 combine as the **Terry Fox Courage Highway**, named after **Terrance Stanley Fox** (1958–81), one of modern Canada's most remarkable figures. At the age of 18, Fox developed cancer and had to have his right leg amputated. Determined to advance the search for a cure, he planned a money-raising run from coast to coast and on April 12, 1980, he set out from St John's, Newfoundland. For 143 days he ran 26 painful miles a day, covering five provinces by June and raising $34m. In September, at mile 3339, just outside Thunder Bay, lung cancer forced Terry to abandon his run; he returned home to Port Coqitlam, BC, where he died the following summer. Several hundred million dollars have now been raised for cancer research in his name and, in his honour, the **Terry Fox Monument**, a finely crafted bronze statue, has been placed on top of a ridge in a little park above the highway just to the east of Thunder Bay.

Serendipity Café 222 Main St ☎807 824 2890, ⓦserendipitygardens.ca. The best place to eat in Rossport, a cosy and surprisingly sophisticated spot where you can sample locally caught lake trout, among other tasty dishes (mains from $14). You can also stay here, in one of four stylish studios, which occupy an unusual high-gabled modern building with views of the lake. Daily 11am–9pm. **$125**

Ouimet Canyon Provincial Park

Daylight hours only; no camping · $10 daily vehicle permit · ☎807 977 2526, ⓦ ontarioparks.com

From Rossport, it's 80km west to **NIPIGON**, where Hwy-11 finishes its mammoth trek across northern Ontario to merge with Hwy-17. After a further 35km or so, Hwy-11/17 reaches the 11km-long turning that leads north away from the lake to one of the region's more spectacular sights in **Ouimet Canyon Provincial Park**. The canyon was formed during the last ice age, when a sheet of ice 2km thick crept southward, bulldozing a fissure 3km long, 150m wide and 150m deep. Nearly always deserted, the canyon has two interconnected lookout points that hang over the terrifyingly sheer sides with the permanently dark base lurking below – an anomalous frozen habitat whose perpetual snow supports some very rare arctic plants.

Thunder Bay

The Lake Superior port of **THUNDER BAY**, some 110km from Nipigon, is much closer to Winnipeg than to any other city in Ontario, and consequently its 120,000 inhabitants are prone to see themselves as Westerners. Economics as well as geography define this self-image, for this was once a booming grain-handling port – for grain harvested in the Prairies. Some grain still arrives here by rail to be stored in the town's gigantic grain elevators on its way to the Atlantic, but since the 1990s the economics of the trade have favoured Canada's Pacific ports and many of the elevators that dominate the harbourfront are now literally rotting away.

Thunder Bay makes a pleasant stopover on the long journey to or from Winnipeg and points west. The most agreeable part of town is the few blocks stretching inland from behind the marina in **Thunder Bay North**, north of Central Avenue, where you'll also find several good cafés and restaurants. **Thunder Bay South** is much less appealing, but on its outskirts is the city's star turn, the replica fur-trading post of **Fort William Historical Park**.

Brief history

Thunder Bay was created in 1970 when the two existing towns of Fort William and Port Arthur were brought together under one municipal roof. **Fort William** was the older of the two, established in 1789 as a fur-trading post and then becoming the upcountry headquarters of the North West Company. It lost its pre-eminent position when the North West and Hudson's Bay companies merged, but it remained a fur-trading post until the end of the nineteenth century. In the middle of the nineteenth century, rumours of a huge **silver** lode brought prospectors to the Lake Superior shoreline just north of Fort William, where **Port Arthur** was established. The silver didn't last and the Port Arthur, Duluth & Western Railway (PD&W), which had laid the lines to the mines, was soon nicknamed "the Poverty, Distress & Welfare". The Canadian Northern Railway, which took over the abandoned PD&W lines, did much to rescue the local economy, but did not bring Fort William and Port Arthur closer together. Rudyard Kipling noted that, "The twin cities hate each other with the pure, passionate, poisonous hatred that makes cities grow. If Providence wiped out one of them, the other would pine away and die." Fortunately, the 1970 amalgamation bypassed Kipling's prediction and nowadays these parochial rivalries have all but vanished.

The waterfront

Thunder Bay's 5km-long **waterfront** is home to a string of **grain elevators**, whose striking architecture – all modernist lines and pure functionalism – can't fail to impress. In the middle of the industrial jangle is the **marina** and behind it the former CN **railway station**, whose distinctive high-pitched gables, turrets and dormer windows were built to resemble a French château. The station was erected in 1906 and three years later CN dipped into their pockets again to create the **Pagoda**, a fanciful bandstand just across the street, that now houses a tourist office (see page 184).

Little Suomi

Thunder Bay North's most appealing enclave is the Finnish district of **Little Suomi**, focused on the Bay and Algoma streets intersection, about ten minutes' walk southwest from the Pagoda. There are over forty ethnic groups in Thunder Bay and several of them maintain their own institutions, but none more so than the Finnish. Arriving in the 1870s, the first Finns to get here were left-wing refugees escaping the Tsar, whereas those who arrived after 1917 were right-wing opponents of the Bolsheviks (plus the odd anarchist), leading to a political divide within the community that still echoes today. Little Suomi's architecture is resolutely suburban, but the town's most atmospheric restaurants are here (see page 184). Head west along Bay Street from Algoma Street and you'll soon reach **Hillcrest Park**, perched on a low ridge, offering great views out across the lake.

Fort William Historical Park

1350 King Rd • Daily mid May to early Oct 10am–5pm • Mid-May to mid-June & mid-Aug to early Oct $12, mid-June to mid-Oct $14 • ☎ 807 473 2347, ⓦ fwhp.ca

Thunder Bay's tour de force is the reconstructed fur-trading post of **Fort William Historical Park**, in a loop of the Kaministiquia River about 15km southwest of the town centre – and 13km upriver from its original site. At the entrance is a **visitor centre**, where a first-rate film traces the history of the fort and explains its workings. From here, it's a quick stroll or bus ride to the fort, a large palisaded compound which has been restored to its appearance in 1815, when it was the inland headquarters of the North West Company and their major trans-shipment base. Impeccably researched and staffed by students dressed in period gear, the forty-odd buildings that fill out the compound illuminate the fort's original purpose with everything from simple storehouses to the capacious Great Hall. Look out for the **fur warehouse**, festooned

---

SEEING STARS IN ONTARIO

Gaze up at the skies through one of the largest telescopes in Central Canada. The **David Thompson Astronomical Observatory** (hours vary; check website for schedule; $10; ☎ 807 473 2344, ⓦ fwhp.ca), in the Fort William Historical Park. The well-equipped observatory offers a wide range of astronomical activities, including the Star Walk Experience, which includes a tour of the centre and star-gazing workshops. Make a weekend of it, and stay at the observatory campground (May–Nov; from $45), near the Kaministiquia River, and visit the observatory at night, when they offer a "journey through the cosmos". To book the campground, call the observatory or email reservations@fwhp.ca.

2

with the pelts of beaver, lynx and arctic fox, and the **canoe workshop**, where birch-bark canoes are made to traditional designs for museums all over Canada. There are demonstrations of contemporary trades and crafts, a working kitchen, a kitchen garden and a farm complete with sheep, pigs and cows.

ARRIVAL AND DEPARTURE

THUNDER BAY

By plane Thunder Bay Airport (�🌐 tbairport.on.ca) is on the southwest edge of the city, about 13km from Thunder Bay North, which is where you want to be. To get from one to the other by public transport, take local bus #3 Airport (every 40min; 30min; $2.75) to the City Hall transit terminal, on Brodie St in Thunder Bay South, and then either change or stay on the bus (depending on the service) for onward transportation to Thunder Bay North, where buses pull into the Water St terminal behind the marina.

By bus The long-distance Greyhound bus station (☎ 800 661 8747, 🌐 greyhound.ca) is located about 3km south of Thunder Bay North at 815 Fort William Rd; there are no trains.

Destinations Kenora (2 daily; 6hr 30min); Sault Ste Marie (2 daily; 9–10hr); Sudbury (2–3 daily; 15hr); Toronto (2 daily; 21hr); Winnipeg (2 daily; 9hr).

INFORMATION AND GETTING AROUND

Downtown tourist office In the landmark Pagoda building on Water St at the foot of Red River Rd (mid-June to early Sept Tues–Sat 10am–6pm; ☎ 807 684 3670, 🌐 thunderbay.ca), this tourist office is well stocked with a full range of brochures and area maps.

Terry Fox Centre The Terry Fox Centre tourist office (daily: mid-June to early Sept 8.30am–7.30pm; Sept to mid-June 9am–5pm; ☎ 807 983-2041), by the Terry Fox Monument on Hwy-17 just north of town, can be a useful stop as you head out of town.

Buses Thunder Bay Transit (☎ 807 684 3744, 🌐 thunderbay.ca) operates all city buses with a flat fare of $2.75 (exact fare); ask the driver for a transfer if you need more than one bus to complete your journey.

ACCOMMODATION

Lakehead University 955 Oliver Rd ☎ 807 343 8485, 🌐 conferenceservices.lakeheadu.ca. With its manicured lawns and miniature lake – students call it Lake Inferior – the campus is a pleasant spot. Rooms, town houses or apartments are available May–Aug. Access to the university's extensive sports facilities is a few dollars extra. The campus is located about 4km southwest of the Pagoda; the #2 Crosstown bus from the Water St terminal by the marina goes right past it. Singles $50; doubles $65; basic apartments $150; fully equipped apartments $210

Prince Arthur Waterfront Hotel & Suites 17 Cumberland St North ☎ 807 345 5411, ☎ 800 267 2675, 🌐 princearthurwaterfront.com. Built by the CNR in 1908, this imposing stone-and-brick block is bang in the centre of town. Inside, there are flashes of its original Edwardian elegance, but most of the furnishings are modern and the rooms are similar, as well as being large and comfortable. $135

TownePlace Suites 550 Harbour Expressway ☎ 807 346 9000, 🌐 marriott.com. Large Marriott property with clean rooms and a wide range of amenities, including full kitchens, a fitness room and large LCD TVs. Breakfast is included. $145

EATING

Hoito Restaurant 314 Bay St ☎ 807 345 6323. Established in 1918, Thunder Bay's best-known Finnish café-cum-canteen is always full and the specials on the board should not be missed. The salt fish, potatoes

---

WEST FROM THUNDER BAY TO WINNIPEG

Heading west from Thunder Bay, it's almost 700km to **Winnipeg** in Manitoba. The logical place to break your journey is **Kenora**, almost 500km away along Hwy-17, through the interminable pine forests of the Canadian Shield. Remember to put your watch back one hour when you cross into the **Central time zone**, about 60km west of Thunder Bay.

ACCOMMODATION IN KENORA

Clarion Lakeside Inn & Conference Centre 470 1st Ave South ☎ 807 465 1120, 🌐 choicehotels. ca. The eleven-storey Lakeside Inn has comfortable rooms, and panoramic views over the town and its surroundings. $160

and *viili* (buttermilk) are delicious, as is the open-faced pickled herring sandwich and the creamy rice pudding. Breakfasts start around $7, dinners at $18. Daily 8am–8pm.

Lot 66 66 South Court St ☎807 683 7708, ⓦlot66.ca. Dark and intimate restaurant with an ambitious, wide-ranging menu, featuring everything from fried chicken ($12) and pizza to herb-crusted rack of lamb. Mains $26–38. Excellent wine cellar too. When the eating is finished

(about 10pm), the place morphs into a bar. Tues & Wed 5–11pm, Thurs 5pm–midnight, Fri & Sat 5pm–1am.

Prospector Steak House 27 South Cumberland St ☎807 345 5833, ⓦprospectorsteakhouse.com. A local favourite, the *Prospector* has pictures of old-time Thunder Bay on the walls and serves chowder from brass prospectors' vats, along with such dishes as prime rib, steak and locally caught fish, all from $24. Mon–Thurs & Sun 4–9pm, Fri & Sat 4–10pm.

Moosonee and Moose Factory Island

The Crees have been hunting and fishing James Bay, a southerly extension of Hudson Bay, for several thousand years and they make up the majority of the population of **MOOSONEE**, which occupies an incredibly remote and solitary bayside location well to the north of the road network. A French fur-trading company, Révillon Frères, founded Moosonee in 1903 and the **Révillon Frères Museum** (late June to early Sept daily 10am–6pm; free; ☎705 336 1209), in one of the original company buildings, traces the history of the settlement and its largely unsuccessful attempt to challenge the local monopoly of the **Hudson's Bay Company**. The latter had established the trading post of **Moose Factory Island**, just offshore, in 1673, which makes it the oldest English-speaking community in Ontario. **Water taxis** ($10 one way) zip travellers from the jetty at Moosonee to the island, where the **Moose Factory Centennial Museum Park** (late June to early Sept daily 9am–5pm; free; ☎705 658 2733) holds the original blacksmith's shop, graveyard, powder magazine (the island's only stone building) and a teepee where the locals sell bannock (freshly baked bread). South of here, **St Thomas Anglican Church**, built in 1860, has an altar cloth of beaded moose hide, prayer books written in Cree and removable floor plugs to prevent the church floating away in floods.

ARRIVAL AND DEPARTURE

MOOSONEE AND COCHRANE

Whichever way you cut it, Moosonee is expensive to get to: most visitors fly in, but the determined can get here with Ontario Northland, a long-winded, two-leg journey by bus from North Bay (see page 151) to Cochrane and then the Polar Bear Express Train.

By plane AirCreebec (☎819 825 8375, ⓦaircreebec.ca) flies to Moosonee from Fort Albany (2 daily except Sat; 25min) and Timmins (2 daily except Sat; 50min), a large resource town in northern Ontario. There are flights to Timmins from most of Ontario's bigger cities.

By train Ontario Northland's Polar Bear Express Train (☎800 461 8558, ⓦontarionorthland.ca) cuts across 300km of desolate backwoods on its

way from Cochrane to Moosonee (Mon–Fri 1 daily; 4hr 50min). This is as far north as anyone can easily (or reasonably) go in Ontario – but, despite the name, you won't see any polar bears. The train departs Cochrane at 9am and arrives in Moosonee at 1.50pm, departing Moosonee 5pm and arriving back in Cochrane at 9.45pm. The return fare is $118 and reservations are compulsory.

By bus Ontario Northland (☎800 461 8558, ⓦontario northland.ca) runs a twice-daily bus service from North Bay to Cochrane (6hr 15min), but note that it does not connect with the Polar Bear Express Train – you have to overnight in Cochrane. A return bus ticket is $175.

ACCOMMODATION

MOOSE FACTORY ISLAND

Cree Village Ecolodge ☎705 658 6400, ⓦcreevillage. com. This ecolodge in an attractive wood-and-glass structure has light and spacious rooms with fabulous views. The restaurant offers a mix of contemporary and Aboriginal cuisine, including baked trout and caribou. **$185**

COCHRANE

Station Inn 200 Railway St ☎705 272 3500, ☎800 265 2356, ⓦontarionorthland.ca. In the same complex as Cochrane's train and bus station, you could not get anywhere more convenient if you are heading on to Moosonee. The rooms are short on frills, but perfectly adequate, with comfortable beds and plump duvets. **$98**

Montréal and Southwest Québec

MONTREAL CITY

Montréal and Southwest Québec

One of the first signs (literally) that you've arrived in proudly French-speaking Québec is the octagonal red traffic warnings displaying "ARRÊT" rather than "STOP". Québec is the only French-speaking society in North America, and from the language to the cuisine, it's distinct from the rest of the continent – so distinct, in fact, that its political elite have long been focused on secession, though voter views have shifted considerably of late. The province was ceded to the British after the conquest of the French in 1759 and yet more than two hundred years later the legacy of "New France" is as tangible as ever. After the colony was transferred to British rule, the Québécois were allowed to maintain their language and Catholic religion, which ensured large families and a prevalence of French-speakers – a political move termed the *revanche du berceau* ("revenge of the cradle"). Centuries later, the result is a unique blend of North American and European influence and a province with an interesting dual personality. Nowhere is this more evident than in Montréal and Southwest Québec. Within striking distance of Ottawa, and nudging up against the US border, this corner of the province has led both the economic and political resurgence of French-speaking Canada throughout the last century.

Home to over a third of all Québécois, the island metropolis of **Montréal** celebrates both its European heritage and its reputation as a truly international city. There can be few places in the world where people on the street flit so easily between two or more languages – sometimes within the same sentence – or whose cafés and bars ooze such a cosmopolitan feel.

From downtown Montréal, the mirrored skyscrapers that vie for space with colony-era cathedrals are privy to views of the St Lawrence River and the wilderness beyond that was once the source of the city's wealth and power. These days, though, the vast wilds of **Southwest Québec** are admired for their natural beauty rather than their promise of furs and minerals, and there are several carefully groomed rural getaways just an hour's drive out of the city. To the north, the hilly and forested **Laurentians** offer outdoor activities year-round, including cycling, hiking and horseriding trails in the summer and downhill ski centres and more than 2000km of cross-country ski trails in the winter. To the south and east of Montréal, the **Eastern Townships (Cantons-de-l'Est)**, which spread across the foothills of the Appalachian mountains, lure city dwellers into the country with a more opulent approach to the outdoors.

Train services within the region run from Montréal to Ontario, New Brunswick and into the US as well as connecting Québec City and the north of Québec. For most destinations, buses are your best bet for getting around, with the major places connected by regular services, supplemented by a network of smaller local lines.

QUÉBEC INFORMATION

The superb, province-wide website of **Tourisme Québec** (☎ 877 266 5687, ⍵ bonjourquebec.com) has up-to-date information on everything from current events and festivals to outdoor activities.

OLD MONTREAL

Highlights

❶ Vieux-Montréal Wander around cobblestone streets lined with lively bars and centuries-old buildings and monuments. See page 195

❷ Quartier des Spectacles Montréal's entertainment hub hosts the city's most exciting events, including the world's largest comedy and jazz festivals. . See page 209

❸ Plateau Mont-Royal Montréal's cultural melting pot has innovative restaurants, wild nightlife and relaxed cafés. See page 211

❹ Musée des Beaux-Arts Explore Canada's oldest museum, which showcases the country's most impressive collection of Canadian art. See page 208

❺ Poutine and Québécois cuisine Sample the province's beloved comfort food of *poutine*, as well as innovative Québécois cuisine, at the city's extraordinary variety of restaurants. See page 220

❻ Mont-Tremblant Eastern Canada's premier ski resort is a great spot year-round for outdoor pursuits. See page 232

❼ La Route des Vins Sip your way across the Eastern Townships on this wine route that connects the region's lush vineyards. See page 237

HIGHLIGHTS ARE MARKED ON THE MAP ON PAGE 190

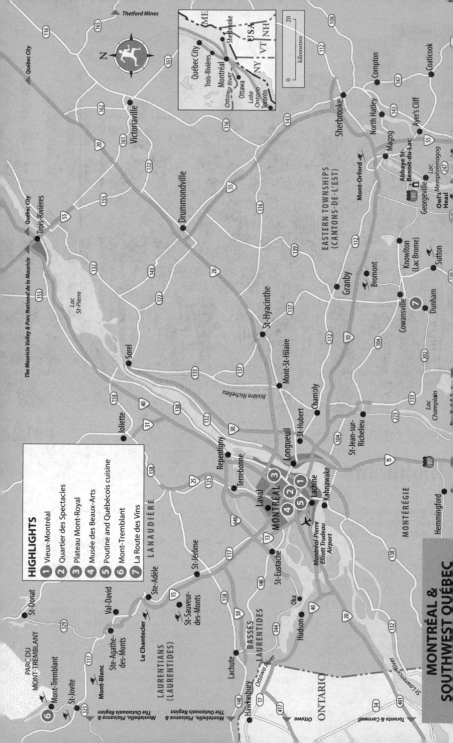

MONTRÉAL & SOUTHWEST QUÉBEC

HIGHLIGHTS

1. Vieux-Montréal
2. Quartier des Spectacles
3. Plateau Mont-Royal
4. Musée des Beaux-Arts
5. Poutine and Québécois cuisine
6. Mont-Tremblant
7. La Route des Vins

ONTARIO

Toronto & Cornwall

Ottawa

Thetford Mines

Québec City

Trois-Rivières

Victoriaville

Drummondville

St-Hyacinthe

Mont-St-Hilaire

Chambly

Longueuil

St-Hubert

St-Jean-sur-Richelieu

Sorel

Joliette

Repentigny

Terrebonne

Laval

MONTRÉAL

Lachine

Kahnawake

Montréal-Pierre Elliott Trudeau Airport

St-Eustache

Oka

Hudson

Lachute

Hawkesbury

Ste-Adèle

St-Jérôme

St-Sauveur-des-Monts

Le Chantecler

Ste-Agathe-des-Monts

Val-David

Mont-Blanc

St-Jovite

Mont-Tremblant

St-Donat

PARC DU MONT-TREMBLANT

Sherbrooke

EASTERN TOWNSHIPS (CANTONS-DE-L'EST)

Compton

North Hatley

Coaticook

Ayer's Cliff

Magog

Mont-Orford

Abbaye St-Benoît-du-Lac

Georgeville

Owl's Head

Knowlton (Lac Brome)

Sutton

Dunham

Cowansville

Bromont

Granby

Hemmingford

MONTÉRÉGIE

Rivière Richelieu

Lac St-Pierre

The Maurice Valley & Parc National de la Mauricie

LAURENTIANS (LAURENTIDES)

BASSES LAURENTIDES

LANAUDIÈRE

Montebello, Plaisance & The Outaouais Region

Ottawa River

St Lawrence River

Lac Champlain

Lac Memphrémagog

N

Québec City

Trois-Rivières

Montréal

Ottawa

Ottawa River

Lake Ontario

Toronto

Sherbrooke

ME

QC

VT

NH

NY

USA

0   20
kilometres

Brief history

Although various **First Nations** have lived in pockets of the province for millennia and there was sporadic European contact to the east, Québec's history really begins with Jacques Cartier's 1535 voyage. He sailed up the St Lawrence stopping at Stadacona and Hochelaga – present-day Québec City and Montréal, respectively. The early days of the colony revolved around the fur trade and attempts to convert the Aboriginal peoples to **Christianity**. The priests' tasks were made more difficult by the fact that the French had aligned with the Algonquin and Huron nations to gain access to their **fur-trading networks**, while those groups' traditional enemies, the Iroquois Confederacy, had formed alliances with the Dutch and then the British. Louis XIV made **New France** a royal province in 1663, dispatching troops and, subsequently, unmarried Frenchwomen, the so-called **filles du roi**. Periodic skirmishes between the French and British and their Aboriginal allies continued to be a destabilizing factor, stunting the growth of the colony. Matters were resolved somewhat when twelve hundred colonists met with an even greater number of Aboriginal peoples from across eastern North America at Pointe-à-Callière in Montréal to sign **La Grande Paix**, the Great Peace treaty of 1701.

The Seven Years' War and its aftermath

It wasn't until mid-century that further serious conflict broke out, with the British and French again at odds in the **Seven Years' War** (also known as the French and Indian War). The turning point took place in 1759 with the Battle of the Plains of Abraham (see page 259). The British consolidated their hold with the 1774 Québec Act (see page 874), a pre-emptive move that helped resist American attempts to take over the colony. After the Americans won independence from Britain, a flood of **United Empire Loyalists** fled across the Canadian border, settling primarily in the Eastern Townships and present-day Ontario.

The creation of Lower and Upper Canada in 1791 emphasized the inequalities between anglophones and francophones, and later led to rebellion. Investigating its causes, Lord Durham concluded that English and French relations were akin to "two nations warring within the bosom of a single state". His prescription for peace was immersing French-Canadians in the English culture of North America; the subsequent 1840 Act of Union joining Lower and Upper Canada can be seen as a deliberate attempt to marginalize francophone opinion within an English-speaking state.

Industrialization and urbanization

French-Canadians remained insulated from the economic mainstream until nineteenth-century **industrialization**, financed and run by the better-educated anglophones, led to a mass francophone migration to the cities. By the mid-twentieth century, a French-speaking middle class had begun to articulate the grievances of the workforce and to criticize the suffocating effect the Church was having on francophone opportunity. The shake-up of Québec society finally came about with the so-called **Quiet Revolution** in the 1960s, spurred by the provincial government under the leadership of Jean Lesage and his Liberal Party of Québec. The provincial government took control of welfare, health and education from the Church and, under the slogan *Maîtres chez-nous* ("Masters of our own house"), established state-owned industries that reversed anglophone financial domination.

The rise against federalism

In order to implement these fiscal policies, Québec needed to administer its own taxes, and the provincial Liberals, despite being staunchly federalist, were constantly at loggerheads with Ottawa. Encouraged and influenced by other nationalist struggles, Québécois' desire for recognition and power reached a violent peak in 1970, when the terrorist **Front de Libération du Québec (FLQ)** kidnapped a provincial government

INDIGENOUS PEOPLES IN QUÉBEC

Francophone–anglophone relations may be the principal concern of most Québécois – eighty percent of them have French as their mother tongue – but the province's population also includes eleven nations of **Indigenous peoples**, the majority of whom live on reservations. Aboriginal grievances are particularly acute in Québec as most of the province's tribes are English-oriented – the **Mohawks** near Montréal even fought on the side of the British during the conquest. Still, relations are even bad between the authorities and French-speaking groups. The **Hurons** (see page 141) near Québec City battled in courts for eight years to retain their hunting rights; while around James Bay the **Cree** fought and won the right to block the expansion of Québec's hydroelectric network which, had it been completed as planned, would have covered an area the size of Germany. Begun in 1971, the project nonetheless resulted in the displacement of Cree and **Inuit**.

Indigenous peoples have categorically voted against separation and have used mostly peaceful methods to register their land claims, which amount to 85 percent of the province's area. There was violence at the Mohawk uprising at Oka near Montréal in 1990, which, though condemned by most, drew attention to the concerns of Indigenous Canadians.

3

minister and a British diplomat in Montréal (see page 881). Six years later, a massive reaction against the ruling provincial Liberals brought the separatist **Parti Québécois (PQ)** to power. Led by René Lévesque, the PQ accelerated the process of social change, particularly with unilingual language law **Bill 101** and held a referendum on sovereignty that 6.5 million people voted 60:40 against (see page 881).

In 1993, Québec's displeasure with federalism was evident in the election of the Bloc Québécois – a federal party committed to shattering federalism – to the ironic status of Her Majesty's Loyal Opposition in Ottawa. The separatist cause received added support in 1994 when the PQ was returned to provincial power after vowing to hold another **referendum** on separation from Canada. The 1995 vote was so close – Québec opted to remain within Canada by a margin of less than one percent – that calls immediately arose for a third referendum (prompting pundits to refer to the process as the "neverendum").

In 2003, the PQ lost to the Liberals, which at the time left little hope of achieving the dream of independence. Yet the "National Question" rumbled on, as evidenced by the PQ's return to power in 2012, helmed by Pauline Marois, the province's first female Premier. But the victory was short-lived: in the 2014 general elections, the PQ lost heavily to the Liberal Party, led by Philippe Couillard. The PQ's focus on secession was partly blamed for its failure by an electorate seemingly less interested in independence. In May 2015, the controversial Pierre Karl Péladeau was elected head of the PQ, proclaiming "Independence is more alive than ever!" as he accepted the leadership. But, public enthusiasm for an outright split had been on the decline. Indeed, Canada's prime minister, Justin Trudeau, whose 2015 campaign headquarters were in Montréal and who is a champion of the province, had long spoken out against secession, though he does believe that Québec needs to be more involved in the governance of Canada to keep the country culturally and politically relevant. In May 2016, Péladeau resigned as leader of PQ, and Jean-François Lisée took the reins until 2018.

The 2018 Québec general election was a historic one. In a defining sign of the changing times, separatism was not on the ballot for the first time in decades. And, nearly fifty years of two-party rule by PQ and Liberal was brought to a crushing end with the stunning victory of the right-leaning Coalition Avenir Québec, helmed by François Legault, who was sworn in as the Premier of Québec on October 18, 2018. The PQ, longtime advocates of an independent Québec, didn't just lose the election – they also didn't win enough votes to maintain official party status. Secession, for now, has been sidelined – but there is good news at the root of it: The Québec economy is booming, and unemployment is among the lowest in Canada.

Montréal

It's a travel-writing cliché to describe a destination as a "juxtaposition of old and new", but in **MONTRÉAL** this is spectacularly evident. Canada's second-largest city is geographically as close to the European coast as to Vancouver, and in look, taste and feel it combines some of the finest aspects of the two continents. Its North American skyline of glass and concrete rises above churches and monuments in a melange of European styles as varied as Montréal's social mix. This is also the world's second-largest French-speaking city after Paris, but only two-thirds of the citizens are of French extraction, the other third being a cosmopolitan mishmash of *les autres* ("the others"), including British, Eastern Europeans, Chinese, Italians, Greeks, Jews, Latin Americans and Caribbeans. The memorable result is a truly multidimensional city, with a global variety of restaurants, bars and clubs, matched by a calendar of festivals that makes this one of the most vibrant places in Canada. In 2017, Montréal celebrated its 375th anniversary with much fanfare, including special exhibits, events, concerts, parades and more.

It is also here that the two main linguistic groups c anglophones and francophones – come into greatest contact with one another. In the wake of the "francization" of Québec, English-Canadians hit Hwy-401 in droves, tipping the nation's economic supremacy from Montréal to Toronto. Though written off by Canada's English-speaking majority, the city did not sink into oblivion. Instead, it has undergone an extraordinary resurgence, becoming one of the driving forces behind the high-tech industries helping transform Canada's economy.

Everywhere are signs of civic pride and prosperity, from the historic quarter of **Vieux-Montréal** to the once-disused **Vieux-Port**, which has been turned into a summer playground with landscaped parklands and urban beaches facing onto the St Lawrence.

To the northwest unfolds the **downtown** area, where the modern glass frontages of the office blocks reflect Victorian terraces and the spires of numerous churches. Here, the boulevards and leafy squares buzz from the morning rush hour right through to the wee hours, when clubbers return from the establishments of **rue Ste-Catherine** and the diverse bars and lounges of the **Plateau** and **Quartier Latin** districts. The dazzling **Quartier des Spectacles** serves as the city's cultural hub, booming with performing arts venues, lively restaurants and outdoor public spaces and walkways.

Rising above downtown, the city's landmark, **Mont Royal** – known by residents as "The Mountain" – is best accessed from the easterly Plateau Mont-Royal. The cafés, restaurants and bars of **The Main** and rue St-Denis throng with people day and night. Further out to the east, the enormous **Stade Olympique** complex and the vast green space of the **Jardin Botanique** – second in international status only to London's Kew Gardens – are the main pull. The islands facing the Vieux-Port that make up Parc Jean-Drapeau and the westerly Lachine Canal offer all manner of activities, many of them family-friendly.

Brief history

The island of Montréal was first occupied by the St Lawrence **Iroquois**, whose small village of Hochelaga ("Place of the Beaver") was situated at the base of Mont-Royal.

CITY ORIENTATION

Montréal island may be sizeable (measuring 51km by 16km), but the heart of the city itself is very manageable. It's divided into **Vieux-Montréal** along the St Lawrence River, a **downtown** business core on the south side of **Mont Royal** and the lively **Plateau** and **Quartier Latin** neighbourhoods to the east. The main east–west arteries are rue Sherbrooke, boulevard de Maisonneuve, rue Ste-Catherine and boulevard René-Lévesque, all divided into east (*est*) and west (*ouest*) sections by the north–south **boulevard St-Laurent**, known locally as "The Main". North–south street numbers increase as you progress north from the St Lawrence River.

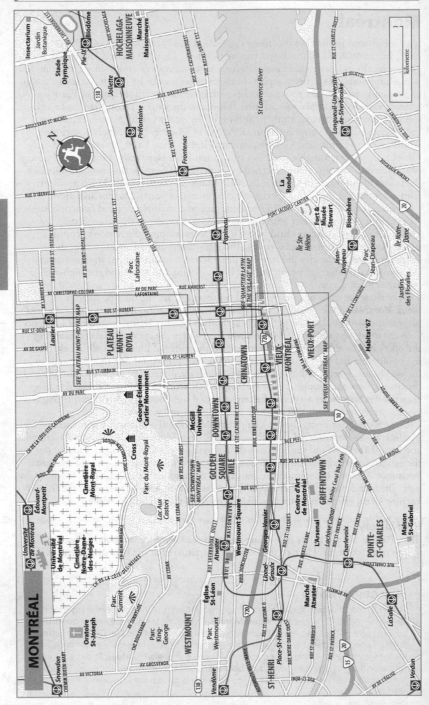

The first European contact occurred in 1535 when Jacques Cartier was led here while searching for a northwest route to Asia. A permanent European presence was not established until 1611; the French settlement was little more than a small garrison, and it wasn't until 1642 that the colony of Ville-Marie was founded. Bloody conflict with the Iroquois, fanned by the European fur-trade alliances with the Algonquins and Hurons, was constant until the **Great Peace treaty** of 1701 prompted the growth of Montréal into the main embarkation point for the fur and lumber trades. When Québec City fell to the British in 1759, Montréal briefly served as the capital of New France. The ensuing **British occupation** saw a flood of Irish and Scottish immigrants who soon made Montréal North America's second-largest city.

Rising fortunes

With the creation of the **Dominion of Canada** in 1867, Montréal emerged as the nation's premier port, railroad nexus, banking centre and industrial producer. Its population reached half a million in 1911 and doubled in the next two decades with an influx of émigrés from Europe. It was also during this period that Montréal acquired its reputation as Canada's "sin city". During Prohibition in the US, Québec became the main alcohol supplier to the entire continent: the Molsons and their ilk made their fortunes here, while prostitution and gambling thrived under the protection of the authorities. Only in the wake of World War II and the subsequent economic boom did a major anti-corruption operation begin, tied in with rapid architectural growth. The most glamorous episode in the city's face-lift came with **Expo '67**, the World's Fair that attracted fifty million visitors to Montréal. Yet it was the city's anglophones who were benefiting from the prosperity, and beneath the smooth surface, francophone frustrations were reaching dangerous levels. These reached an apex with the 1970 FLQ crisis, the reverberations of which shook the nation (see page 881).

Francophone upsurge

The combination of the PQ's election in 1976, the consequent Bill 101 language laws they introduced and the threat of sovereignty prompted an anglophone exodus in the tens of thousands from the city, chiefly to Toronto.

A Canada-wide economic recession in the mid-1990s saw Québec lag behind the rest of the country in economic growth. After the 1995 referendum a tacit truce was made on the issue of separation and the boarded-up shops lining rue Ste-Catherine gradually reopened, while the derelict pockets on the edges of downtown and Vieux-Montréal were renovated. But perhaps the most enduring change is that the gaps left by departing anglophones have been filled by young **bilingual** francophones, who feel in charge of their own culture and economy. At the same time, many anglophones who stayed have also become bilingual, and these days it's perfectly normal to hear the two languages intermingling wherever you may be.

Vieux-Montréal

Severed from downtown by the Autoroute Ville-Marie, the gracious district of **Vieux-Montréal** was left to decay until the early 1960s, when developers started to step in with generally tasteful renovations that brought colour and vitality back to the area. North America's greatest concentration of seventeenth-, eighteenth- and nineteenth-century buildings has its fair share of tourists, but it's popular with Montréalers, too – formerly as a symbolic place to air francophone grievances; more recently as a spot to check out the buskers on place Jacques-Cartier, take in the historic monuments and roam the port's waterfront. Place-d'Armes is the most central Métro station, although Square-Victoria or Champ-de-Mars are handier for the western and eastern ends of the district.

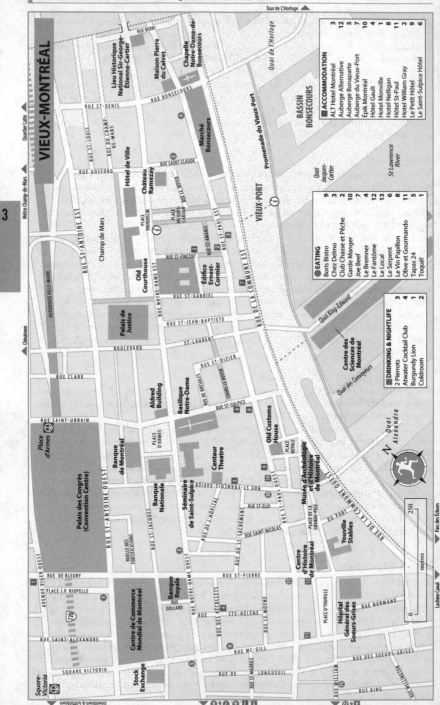

VIEUX-MONTRÉAL

ACCOMMODATION
ALT Hotel Montréal	3
Auberge Alternative	12
Auberge Bonaparte	5
Auberge du Vieux-Port	7
Épik Montréal	10
Hôtel Gault	4
Hotel Monville	1
Hotel Nelligan	8
Hôtel St-Paul	11
Hotel William Gray	2
Le Petit Hôtel	9
Le Saint-Sulpice Hôtel	6

EATING
Boris Bistro	9
Chez Delmo	3
Club Chasse et Pêche	2
Garde Manger	10
Joe Beef	7
Le Bremner	4
Le Fantôme	12
Le Local	13
Le Serpent	6
Le Vin Papillon	8
Olive et Gourmando	11
Tapas 24	5
Toqué!	1

DRINKING & NIGHTLIFE
2 Pierrots	3
Atwater Cocktail Club	4
Burgundy Lion	1
Coldroom	2

Place d'Armes

The focal point of Vieux-Montréal is **place d'Armes**, its centre occupied by a century-old statue of Maisonneuve, whose missionary zeal raised the wrath of the displaced Iroquois. The mutt that you see represents the animal who warned the French of an impending attack in 1644; legend says the ensuing battle ended when the supposedly unarmed Maisonneuve killed the Iroquois chief on this very spot.

Basilique Notre-Dame

110 rue Notre-Dame ouest • Mon–Fri 8am–4.30pm, Sat 8am–4pm, Sun 12.30–4pm • $6, includes 20min guided tour that departs half-hourly during open hours; special Aura music and light show $26.50, generally 6pm daily, with additional times in summer and on weekends; check website ⓦ aurabasiliquemontreal.com for schedule • ☎ 514 842 2925, ⓦ basiliquenddm.org • Métro: Place-d'Armes

The twin-towered, neo-Gothic **Basilique Notre-Dame**, the cathedral of the Catholic faithful since 1829, looms over place d'Armes. Its architect, the Protestant Irish-American James O'Donnell, was so inspired by his creation that he converted to Catholicism in order to be buried under the church. The western tower, named Temperance, holds the ten-tonne Jean-Baptiste bell, whose booming could once be heard 25km away. The breathtaking gilt and sky-blue interior, flooded with light from three rose windows unusually set in the ceiling, and flickering with multicoloured votive candles, was designed by Montréal architect Victor Bourgeau. Most notable of the detailed furnishings are Louis-Philippe Hébert's fine wooden carvings of the

3

GET FESTIVE

In many cities, festivals are special occasions; in Montréal, they're a way of life. In the summer, especially, the city explodes with festivals, many taking place in the gleaming entertainment quarter, **Quartier des Spectacles** (see page 209). For festival news and updates, consult the excellent ⓦ tourism-montreal.org. You can buy festival tickets via a variety of sources, including the festival websites (worth checking frequently for special deals); at the the Quartier des Spectacles' central info and ticket centre (see page 209); and **Admission**, a division of TicketMaster (☎ 514 790 1245, ☎ 800 361 4595, ⓦ admission.com). The world-renowned **Cirque du Soleil** (ⓦ cirquedusoleil.com), based in Montréal, regularly puts on shows. Here's a selective list of the best events:

Fête des Neiges de Montréal Late Jan ⓦ fetedesneiges.com. Île Ste-Hélène hosts ice-sculpting and general seasonal carousing.

Vues d'Afrique Late April ⓦ vuesdafrique.org. Brings a rich variety of African and Caribbean films to Montréal.

International Fireworks Competition Throughout June and July ⓦ internationaldesfeuxloto-quebec.com. The most visually spectacular of the city's shindigs, featuring breathtaking, music-coordinated pyrotechnics from countries around the globe at the La Ronde amusement park on Île Sainte-Hélène.

Francofolies Mid-June ⓦ francofolies.com. Dance to international tunes at this festival, which brings French musicians from around the world to various downtown stages.

Festival International de Jazz de Montréal Late June and early July ⓦ montrealjazzfest. com. North America's largest jazz event, with more than four hundred shows, most of them free at huge open-air stages in the Quartier des Spectacles.

Montréal First Peoples' Festival Generally in July ⓦ nativelynx.qc.ca. A lively event celebrating Aboriginal peoples' history and featuring traditional activities, from throat-singing to stonecutting.

Juste pour Rire ("Just For Laughs") Mid-July ⓦ hahaha.com. The world's largest comedy festival, with past headliners including Tim Allen, Louis CK, Jerry Seinfeld, Rowan Atkinson, Jim Carrey, John Candy, Lily Tomlin and Whoopi Goldberg.

Festival International Nuits d'Afrique July ⓦ festivalnuitsdafrique.com. The sounds of African beats fill the city to full effect.

Montreal International Reggae Festival Mid-Aug ⓦ montrealinternationalreggaefestival. com. Lively reggae festival drawing fans from around the globe.

MUSEUM PASSES AND THE PASSEPORT MTL

Montréal offers three types of **Carte Musées Montréal** (Montréal Museums Pass; wmuseesmontreal.org), which grant free admission to 39 museums in the city: a three-day pass without public transport ($75); a three-day pass with unlimited public transport, including bus, subway and airport shuttle ($80); and a one-year pass with transport ($225). The passes also offer various other discounts, including on walking tours.

There's also the **Passeport MTL** card (Ⓦ passeportmtl.com). Available in 48hr ($85) or 72hr ($10) versions, this allows access to 28 of the city's attractions – including the Musée d'art Contemporain de Montréal, Musée des Beaux-Arts, the Bateau-Mouche at the Montréal port and the Biosphère – and unlimited use of the public transport system. You can skip the queue at most attractions, but reservations are recommended for cruises and other major exhibitions.

You can buy Carte Musées Montréal and the Passeport MTL online, from tourist offices, participating museums, La Vitrine at the Quartier des Spectacles (see page 209), various hotels and other points of purchase around the city.

---

prophets on the pulpit and the awe-inspiring main altar by French sculptor Bouriché. Imported from Limoges in France, the stained glass windows depict the founding of Ville-Marie. Behind the main altar is the **Chapelle Sacré-Coeur**, destroyed by a serious fire in 1978 but rebuilt with an impressive modern bronze reredos by Charles Daudelin. The Aura sound and light show offers the chance to see the architectural details artfully lit up, though it's not really worth the high price tag.

Séminaire de St-Sulpice

110 rue Notre-Dame ouest • Not open to public • ☎ 514 849 6561, Ⓦ sulpc.org • Métro: Place-d'Armes

The mock-medieval **Séminaire de St-Sulpice** sits behind fieldstone walls and wrought-iron gates to the west of Notre-Dame. The low-lying seminary features a portal that's topped by North America's oldest public timepiece, which began chiming in 1701. Generally considered Montréal's oldest building, it was founded in 1685 by the Paris-based Sulpicians, who instigated the establishment of Montréal by Maisonneuve as a religious mission. They liked the place so much they bought the whole island, and until 1859 were in charge of religious and other affairs as the *seigneurs* of the colony. The seminary is still the Canadian headquarters of the Sulpicians (and thus not open to the public), but their duties are now limited to maintaining the basilica.

Rue St-Jacques

British names once controlled the finances of the continent from the stately limestone institutions along **rue St-Jacques**, once the Wall Street of Canada, but French businesses now dominate. The red-sandstone building on the northeast corner of place d'Armes and rue St-Jacques was built for the New York Life Insurance Co in 1888 and, at eight storeys high, was the city's first skyscraper. Looming over place d'Armes, the **Aldred Building** is among the city's finest examples of the Art Deco style. Both are dwarfed today by the black monolith on the west side of the square that houses the **Banque Nationale**, built in 1967 as a symbol of new-found francophone business strength.

Rue Notre-Dame

The city's first street, **rue Notre-Dame**, was laid out in 1672 and runs east to west. Head east along Notre-Dame from the top of rue St-Sulpice, past the black glass behemoth of the **Palais de Justice** on the corner of boulevard St-Laurent. It overshadows its forerunner, the imposing **Old Courthouse**, erected by the British to impress upon the French population the importance of abiding by their laws; today it serves as municipal offices. Criminal trials took place across the street, at 100 rue Notre-Dame est, in the **Édifice Ernest Cormier**, built in 1925, and now used as an appellate court.

Place Vauquelin

Centred on a pretty fountain and statue of the naval commander Jean Vauquelin, the 1858 place Vauquelin gives views of the **Champ de Mars** to the north. Digging to build a car park here hit rock, which turned out to be the original city walls; they were excavated, restored, and the area made into a pleasant grassy space instead.

Hôtel de Ville

275 rue Notre-Dame est, east of place Vauquelin • Mon–Fri 8am–5pm; 45min guided tours depart hourly in summer Mon–Fri 11am–4pm; Sept–July Fri 1pm (in French) and 2pm (in English) • Free • ☎ 514 872 0311, ⓦ ville.montreal.qc.ca • Métro: Champ-de-Mars

The ornate **Hôtel de Ville** (City Hall) was built in the 1870s and is a typical example of the area's civic buildings of the time when French-speaking architects looked to the mother country for inspiration. On a visit to Expo '67, General de Gaulle chose its second-floor balcony to make his "Vive le Québec libre!" speech, which left the city's anglophones reeling at the thought that Québec was on its way to independent status and infused francophones with a political fervour (see page 881). The areas open to visitors include the Council Chamber, with its striking stained glass windows, and the Hall of Honour, featuring changing history and art exhibits.

Place Jacques-Cartier

A popular gathering spot for locals and tourists, the lively, cobbled **place Jacques-Cartier**, originally built as a market in 1804, slopes down towards the river, giving views of the Vieux-Port. The square is filled with outdoor restaurants and cafés, along with buskers, street artists and caricaturists. The city-run **tourist office** (see page 217) occupies a stone building at the northwest corner. Your best bet for souvenirs here is the small courtyard market tucked away from the street, where jewellery stalls offer some decent artisan-crafted pieces, while the narrow **rue St-Amable** to the west is often dotted with artists selling watercolours and tinted photos of Montréal scenery. A few buildings on the square – Maison Vandelac, Maison del Vecchio and Maison Cartier – show the features typical of Montréal architecture in the 1800s, with pitched roofs designed to shed heavy snowfall and small dormer windows to defend against the cold.

At the top of the square itself looms the controversial **Nelson Monument**. The city's oldest monument – the column is a third the height of its more famous London counterpart, but predates it by a few years – was funded by anglophone Montréalers delighted with Nelson's 1805 defeat of the French at Trafalgar. Québec separatists adopted it as a rallying point in the 1970s. Ironically, the anglophones never liked the monument much anyway, because it faced away from the water.

Musée Château Ramezay

280 rue Notre-Dame est, east of place Jacques-Cartier • June–Nov daily 9.30am–6pm; Dec–May Tues–Sun 10am–4.30pm; guided tours July–Sept daily noon–3pm, Oct–June Sat–Sun noon–3pm • $11, including a fifty-percent discount on entry to the Musée Stewart, within ten days of visit • ☎ 514 861 3708, ⓦ chateauramezay.qc.ca • Métro: Champ-de-Mars

The long and low fieldstone manor of the **Musée Château Ramezay**, set in stately gardens, looks much as it did in 1705 when it was built for Montréal's eleventh governor, Claude de Ramezay. It later served as the North American headquarters for the Compagnie des Indes, before passing into the hands of the British in 1760. During the fleeting American invasion fifteen years later, Benjamin Franklin stayed here in an attempt to persuade Montréalers to join the United States, but he lost public and church support by not promising the supremacy of the French language in what would have been the fourteenth state. Its collection of oil paintings, domestic artefacts, tools, costumes and furniture from the eighteenth and nineteenth centuries is thorough and informative. The most impressive room is a reconstruction of the Salle des Nantes, complete with eighteenth-century mahogany walls and woodwork imported from the Compagnie des Indes headquarters in France. Another highlight is the immaculately landscaped gardens, including the formal French garden, inspired by the manicured greenery of Versailles. The leafy grounds include a kitchen garden, with cabbage, squash and Jerusalem artichokes, and a fragrant orchard, with pear and apple trees. The museum also hosts lectures and summer craft workshops.

Lieu historique national de Sir-George-Étienne-Cartier

458 rue Notre-Dame est • June–Aug Wed–Sun 10am–5pm; Sept–Dec & May Fri–Sun 10am–5pm • $3.90 • ☎ 514 283 2822, ⓦ pc.gc.ca/cartier • Métro: Champ-de-Mars

The **Lieu historique national de Sir-George-Étienne-Cartier** comprises two adjoining houses inhabited by the Cartier family from 1848 to 1871. The cocky Sir George-Étienne Cartier was one of the fathers of Confederation, persuading the French-Canadians to join the Dominion of Canada by declaring: "We are of different races, not for strife but to work together for the common welfare." Today, leaders of French-Canadian nationalism decry Cartier as a collaborator, and the displays in the east house diplomatically skirt over the issue of whether he was right or wrong and emphasize instead his role in the construction of Canada's railways. The quirky exhibits – many of which have an educational angle, catering to school kids – include white-painted papier-mâché models of Cartier sitting at a round table, and stuffily decorated rooms filled with more than a thousand original artefacts and furnishings to evoke the period when Cartier lived here.

Rue St-Paul

Rue St-Paul, one of Montréal's most attractive thoroughfares, is lined with nineteenth-century commercial buildings and Victorian lampposts, the buildings little changed from when Charles Dickens stayed here, although they now house restaurants, art galleries and specialist shops selling everything from Inuit crafts to Québécois arts.

Chapelle Notre-Dame-de-Bonsecours

400 rue St-Paul est • March–April & early Oct to early Jan Tues–Sun 11am–4pm; May to early Oct Tues–Sun 10am–6pm • Chapel free; museum $12 • ☎ 514 282 8670, ⓦ marguerite-bourgeoys.com • Métro: Champ-de-Mars

Mark Twain noted that, in Montréal, "you couldn't throw a brick without hitting a church", and near rue St-Paul's eastern end is Montréal's favourite: the delicate and profusely steepled **Chapelle Notre-Dame-de-Bonsecours**, or the Sailors' Church. The outstretched arms of the Virgin on the tower became a landmark for ships on the St Lawrence and, once safely landed, the mariners would endow the chapel with wooden votive lamps in the shape of ships, many of which are still here. The chapel dates back to the earliest days of the colony, when Maisonneuve helped cut the wood for what was Ville-Marie's first church, under the instigation of Marguerite Bourgeoys, who had been summoned to Ville-Marie to teach the settlement's children. The devout Bourgeoys also founded the nation's first religious order and was in charge of the *filles du Roi* – orphaned French girls sent to marry bachelor settlers and multiply the colony's population. She was canonized in 1982, becoming Canada's first saint. Today's chapel contains a small museum devoted to her life, as well as temporary exhibits on early explorers, missionaries and traders. The entry price lets you climb the narrow stairs leading to the summit of the tower above the apse, where the "aerial chapel" gives sweeping views.

Marché Bonsecours

350 rue St-Paul est • Jan to early May & early Nov to Dec daily 10am–6pm; early May to late June Mon–Thurs & Sun 10am–6pm, Fri & Sat 10am–9pm; late June to early Sept daily 10am–9pm; early Sept to early Nov Mon–Wed & Sun 10am–6pm, Thurs & Fri 10am–9pm, Sat 10am–7pm • ☎ 514 872 7730, ⓦ marchebonsecours.qc.ca • Métro: Champ-de-Mars

The striking, silver-domed **Marché Bonsecours**, built in the mid-nineteenth century, sparkles over Vieux-Montréal. For years this elegant building was used for municipal offices, but for the city's 350th birthday in 1992 it was restored and transformed to house restaurants, boutiques, and a number of shops specializing in Québécois crafts, leatherwork, jewellery, antiques and artwork. You can also pick up local delicacies, including a huge variety of maple products (syrup, candles, tea), ice cider and more. The Marché also hosts festivals and events throughout the year.

Vieux-Port

Extends along the waterfront, from rue McGill to rue Berri • Vieux-Port Jacques-Cartier information booth at Centre des Sciences ticket booth (see page 202): early May to mid-June daily 10am–8pm; mid-June to early Sept daily 10am–10pm; early Sept to mid-Sept daily 10am–7pm; mid-Sept to early Oct Sat & Sun 10am–7pm • ☎ 514 496 7678, ⓦ oldportofmontreal.com • Métro: Champ-de-Mars, Place-d'Armes, Square-Victoria

The **Vieux-Port de Montréal** was once the principal import and export conduit of the continent. When the main shipyards shifted east in the 1970s they left a lot of vacant space, which in 1992 was fully renovated for public use, with parks, a breezy promenade, biking and jogging paths, exhibitions in the quayside hangars and outdoor restaurants and cafés. The Vieux-Port comes into its own in the summer, with a variety of festivals and activities, including an outdoor film festival, obstacle courses and circus and trapeze acts. It is also the launch area (see box) for a range of boat trips.

La Grande Roue de Montréal

Vieux Port (enter Vieux Port via Quai de l'Horloge) • Daily 10am–11pm • $25 • ☎ 514 325 7888, ⓦ lagranderouedemontreal.com

Want to rise above it all? Climb aboard La Grande Roue de Montréal, the tallest observation wheel in Canada, which opened in 2017 as part of Montréal's 375th anniversary festivities. Take in sweeping views, from the waterfront to the skyline. The observation wheel runs year-round – the gondolas are air-conditioned in summer, and heated in winter.

Tour de l'Horloge

Quai de l'Horloge, at the Vieux-Port's easternmost point • **Tour de l'Horloge** End May to mid-Sept daily 11am–7pm • Free • **Plage de l'Horloge** Hours can vary, but generally end May to mid-June Fri–Sun 11am–9pm; mid-June to early Sept Mon & Tues 11am–5pm, Wed–Sun 11am–9pm; $2; fireworks night and other special events $5 • ⓦ oldportofmontreal.com • Métro: Champ-de-Mars, Place-d'Armes, Square-Victoria

Rising 51m above sea level, the **Tour de l'Horloge** (Clock Tower) was built in 1922 to commemorate the men of the Merchant Fleet who died in World War I; ships were recorded as having entered the harbour as soon as they had passed it. The 192 steps

---

FIVE TERRIFIC WATER TOURS

When you're in the urban centre of Montréal, it can be easy to forget that it is, in fact, an island. One of the best ways to remind yourself is by taking to the waters. The Vieux-Port is the major departure point for various **boat trips**.

Amphi-bus Corner of rue de la Commune and blvd St-Laurent ☎ 514 849 5181, ⓦ montreal-amphibus-tour.com; four to ten departures daily May–Oct; 1hr–1hr 30min; $35. A bus that trundles through the city and then morphs into a boat on entering the river.

Bateau-Mouche Quai Jacques-Quartier ☎ 514 849 9952, ☎ 800 361 9952, ⓦ bateau-mouche.ca; up to five daily departures mid-May to mid-Oct; 1hr–1hr 30min; $25–130. Meandering river cruises in glass-topped vessels, with sunrise breakfast cruises and gourmet dinner cruises also available.

Croisières AML Quai King-Edward ☎ 855 284 7842, ⓦ croisieresaml.com; daily departures mid-May to mid-Oct; brunch cruise 1hr 30min, $59; sunset dinner cruise, $73; and a lively three-course dinner and circus cruise, with artistic circus performances, $99. This family-run company offers a variety of comfortable and informative river cruises.

Le Petit Navire Quai Jacques-Cartier ☎ 514 602 1000, ⓦ lepetitnavire.ca; daily departures mid-May to mid-Oct; 45min; $20. Ecofriendly, electric-powered boats for short tours around the Vieux-Port, with special trips during the annual International Fireworks Competition (1hr 30min; $42).

Saute-Moutons Quai de l'Horloge ☎ 514 284 9607, ⓦ jetboatingmontreal.com; daily departures May–Sept; 1hr; from $50. Get wet in the Lachine Rapids on these exciting jet-boat trips.

leading up to the observatory will reward you with excellent views of the harbour, the St Lawrence Seaway, Vieux-Montréal, the islands and Mont Royal. In the summer, a sandy beach, **Plage de l'Horloge**, opens at the foot of the clock tower, with an outdoor bar.

Centre des Sciences de Montréal

Quai King-Edward • Mon–Fri 9am–4pm, Sat–Sun 9am–5pm • Exhibit $20; film $12; combo tickets (exhibit and film) $30 • ☎ 514 496 4629, ⓦ montrealsciencecentre.com • Métro: Place-d'Armes and Champ-de-Mars

The kid-friendly **Centre des Sciences de Montréal**, an interactive science and entertainment complex, features a variety of exhibition halls that cover everything from the earth and environment to technology, with plenty of hands-on exhibits, including the Fabrik – Creativity Factory, where visitors are invited to develop and build creative tools The centre also houses an IMAX theatre (English screening times vary).

Musée d'Archéologie et d'Histoire de Montréal

350 place Royale • Tues–Fri 10am–5pm, Sat & Sun 11am–5pm • Free guided tours generally offered three times daily– check the website for current times • $22 • ☎ 514 872 9150, ⓦ pacmuseum.qc.ca • Métro: Square-Victoria

Once the site of duels, whippings and public hangings amid the peddlers and hawkers who sold wares from the incoming ships, **place Royale** is dominated by the neat classical facade of the **Old Customs House** and **Musée d'Archéologie et d'Histoire de Montréal**, on the site of the original colony, Pointe-à-Callière. The sleek, superbly curated museum, which spreads underground below place Royale as far as the Old Customs House, focuses on the development of Montréal as a meeting and trading place, as told through the archeological remains excavated here at the oldest part of the city, as well as high-tech audiovisual presentations. Early remnants include the city's first Catholic cemetery, eighteenth-century water conduits and sewage systems, and walls dating from different centuries. Be sure to leave time for the often superb temporary shows, which cover everything from local gastronomy to the history of the telephone in Québec. The gift shop has a decent stock of distinctive souvenirs.

Centre d'Histoire de Montréal

335 place d'Youville • Wed–Sun 10am–5pm • $7.50 • ☎ 514 872 3207, ⓦ ville.montreal.qc.ca/chm • Métro: Square-Victoria

Explore multimedia exhibits of the city's history at the engaging **Centre d'Histoire de Montréal** in place d'Youville, within a converted century-old red-brick fire station. Daily life in the early days of Montréal are evoked via films, period furnishings and crafts. Temporary exhibitions are generally stimulating, and might feature photographic

---

GRIFFINTOWN: FROM FACTORIES TO FASHION

This gritty wedge in the southwest of Montréal was once the domain of Irish labourers – now, it's one of Montréal's hippest residential neighbourhoods. An ever-growing array of design shops and fashion retailers, as well as restaurants and bars, have sproutedto cater to the neighbourhood's new demographic.

At ther heart of Griffintown's artistic renaissance is the Centre d'Art de Montréal (Montréal Art Centre; 1844 rue William, ☎ 514 667 2270, ⓦ montrealartcenter.com; Mon–Sat 11am–5pm, Sun 11am–3pm). This community arts centre features a variety of exhibits by local artists, and also runs the popular Griffintown Art School, with workshops and classes in all forms of art, from sculpture to ceramics to painting. **L'Arsenal** (2020 rue William; ☎ 514 931 9978, ⓦ arsenalmontreal.com; Wed–Fri 10am–6pm, Sat 10am–5pm; $10), housed in a former shipyard, also occasionally hosts exhibits; check website for details.

Griffintown, which rubs up against another evolving neighbourhood, **Little Burgundy**, lies a little over 1km west of Vieux-Montréal; one of the most enjoyable ways to reach it is by walking or biking along the Lachine Canal from the Vieux-Port. Explore by sauntering the streets, including **rue Notre-Dame**, dubbed the **Quartier des Antiquaires**, for all its antiques and vintage shops.

essays on the city's neighbourhoods, nightlife and cuisine, and diverse ethnic and cultural communities. The museum is outgrowing its home: By the end of 2019, it will close, to prepare for a big move (and name change). In 2121, the museum will reopen as MEM (Mémoire des Montréalais), with a focus on the evolution of Montréal, in the Quartier des Spectacles.

Place d'Youville features the Founders' Obelisk, a monument to the city founders. The eastern portion of the square was renamed **place de la Grande-Paix** in 2001, to mark the tercentennial of the Great Peace of Montréal, a treaty signed here in 1701 to end the conflict between the First Nations and French settlers. Additionally, the square was once a marketplace, which also served as the Parliament of United Canada from 1844 until it was torched by Tory rioters in 1849.

Square Victoria

This urban square is marked by an **Art Nouveau grille** adorning the Métro station entranceway – which once graced a station on the Paris Métro – donated to the city for Expo '67. Also look for the 1872 statue of Queen Victoria created by English sculptor Marshall Wood. The imposing skyscraper bracketing the west side of the square used to be the digs of the **Montréal Stock Exchange**, but futures are traded there now instead of shares.

Centre de Commerce Mondial de Montréal

747 rue Square Victoria • Generally open daily; hours vary for restaurants and stores • Free • ☎ 514 982 9888, Ⓦ centredecommercemondial.com • Métro: Square-Victoria

Inaugurated in 1991 to revive a former business district – an area dubbed "Quartier International" – the massive **Centre de Commerce Mondial de Montréal** is an architectural tour de force, incorporating facades of centuries-old buildings. Inside, the **ruelle des Fortifications**, so named because the former alley marked the location of the city's stone walls, has been transformed into a lofty interior arcade adorned with boutiques, restaurants, occasional noonday live classical music, a soothing fountain and a statue of Amphitrite, Poseidon's wife. At its easternmost end is a chunk of the Berlin Wall. Nearby on place Jean-Paul-Riopelle, and also forming part of the Quartier International, is the **Palais des Congrès** (Convention Centre). It's hard to miss: look for the multicoloured glass panel-walls by Montréal architect Mario Saia.

Downtown Montréal

Montréal's **downtown** lies roughly between rue Sherbrooke and rue St-Antoine to the north and south, towards rue St-Denis in the east and overlapping with an area known as the Golden Square Mile (see page 207) as it stretches west beyond rue Guy. Of the main streets, **rue Ste-Catherine** offers the most in the way of **shopping**, dining and entertainment, while **boulevard de Maisonneuve** is more business-oriented. The **Quartier des Spectacles** (see page 209) functions as Montréal's entertainment hub. A number of Métro stations provide easy access to downtown's attractions – most are linked to the so-called Underground City (see page 207). The area is also dotted with old churches, museums and public squares filled with activity from buskers, artists and market vendors.

Square Dorchester

Formerly a Catholic cemetery, leafy **Square Dorchester** is right in the centre of downtown and a good spot to get your bearings – the Art Deco-inspired Dominion Square Building on the north side of the square is the site of the Infotouriste office (see page 217) and the starting point for various guided tours; there are also occasional lunchtime concerts here in summer. The southern half of the square is partitioned off as **place du Canada**, which commemorates the 1967 centennial.

3

St George's Anglican Church

1101 rue Stanley, west side of Square Dorchester • Tues–Fri 9am–4pm, Sat & Sun 9am–3pm • Free • ☎ 514 866 7113, ⓦ st-georges.org
• Métro: Bonaventure

The area's oldest building is the Victorian **St George's Anglican Church**. Its solid neo-Gothic exterior gives way to a lofty interior, where trusses that rise in a series of arches support the gabled roof. Also worth a look are the striking stained glass windows.

Centre Bell

1909 av des Canadiens-de-Montréal • **Centre Bell** Daily noon–6pm (open later for hockey games, concerts etc) • ☎ 514 932 2582,
ⓦ centrebell.ca • One-hour guided tours of Centre Bell, generally 11.30am–3.30pm •$20 (not available on concerts and game days) •
☎ 514 925 7777, ⓦ hall.canadiens.com • Métro: Lucien-L'Allier

The city's legendary ice-hockey team, the **Montréal Canadiens** (ⓦ canadiens.nhl.com), known as "the Habs", short for "Habitants", can claim plenty of superlatives: founded in 1909, it is the longest continually operating ice hockey team in the world; it's the only existing National Hockey League (NHL) team that predates the league's foundation; and it has won the coveted Stanley Cup more times than any other. The team plays at the 21,000-plus-seat **Centre Bell**, and if you can catch a game jump at the chance: chanting for The Habs until your throat is raw, alongside thousands of giddy home-town fans, as the Montréal winter swirls outside, is an experience to remember. Additionally, the centre is a venue for rock concerts, classical music performances and family entertainment. For those who want a full overview of Centre Bell, it's best to

▲ Oratoire St-Joseph

DOWNTOWN MONTRÉAL

● EATING
Bouillon Bilk	3
Café Myriade	2
Maison Boulud	1
Reuben's Deli	5
Ruby Rouge	7
Taverne F	4
Tiradito	6

■ ACCOMMODATION
Auberge les Bons Matins	8
Auberge de Jeunesse Internationale de Montréal	7
Hotel 10	1
Hôtel Bonaventure Montréal	10
Hotel Le Crystal	6
Hôtel Le Germain	3
Le Dauphin Centre Ville	9
Le Mount Stephen	5
Le St-Martin Hôtel Particulier Centre-Ville	4
McGill University Residences (Bishop Mountain Hall)	2

take a guided tour, which includes all main areas, including the arena, the Canadiens' dressing room, the luxury suites and more.

Basilique-Cathédrale Marie-Reine-du-Monde

1085 rue de la Cathédrale • Mon–Fri 7am–7pm, Sat & Sun 7.30am–7pm • Free • ☎ 514 866 1661, ⓦ diocesemontreal.org • Métro: Bonaventure

Dwarfed by its high-rise neighbours, the **Basilique-Cathédrale Marie-Reine-du-Monde** was commissioned by Bishop Ignace Bourget in 1875 as a reminder that Catholicism still dominated the largest city in the new Dominion of Canada. Impressed by St Peter's while visiting Rome, Bourget created a scaled-down replica of the famous church. While the statues crowning St Peter's facade are of the Apostles, the thirteen statues atop its smaller cousin represent the patron saints of the parishes that donated them. The inside is not as opulent as you might expect, though the high altar of marble, onyx and ivory is surmounted by a gilded copper reproduction of Bernini's baldachin over the altar in St Peter's. To your left on entering, the Chapelle des Souvenirs contains various relics, including the wax-encased remains of St Zoticus, a patron saint of the poor.

Centre Canadien d'Architecture

1920 rue Baile, west of Centre Bell • Wed & Fri Sun 11am–6pm, Thurs 11am–9pm • $10; free Thurs after 5.30pm & first Sun of the month • ☎ 514 939 7026, ⓦ cca.qc.ca • Métro: Guy-Concordia

3

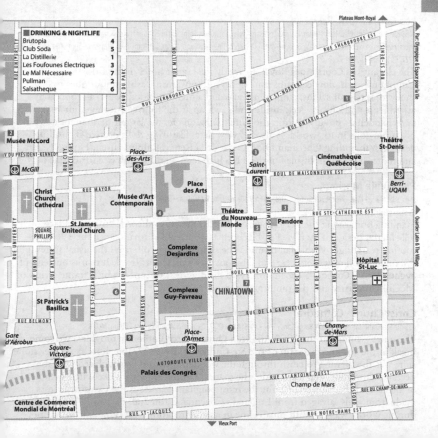

The **Centre Canadien d'Architecture (CCA)** inhabits a wonderfully sleek building with a curiously windowless facade and vast glass doors. The design incorporates the beautifully restored Shaughnessy House (the former residence of a president of the Canadian Pacific Railway) and its Art Nouveau conservatory, while the light-filled galleries display the museum's vast collection of prints, drawings and books in exhibitions ranging from individual masters to whole movements from all cultures and periods. In the early 1970s, when other buildings in the area were being demolished, Montréal-based photographer Brian Merrett documented the house in a series of beautiful photos that saved it from the wrecking ball; those photos are on display today. Behind the museum on the south side of boulevard René-Lévesque are the whimsical **CCA Sculpture Gardens**, designed by prominent Montréal artist and architect Melvin Charney.

Rue Ste-Catherine and around

The city's main commercial thoroughfare since the early 1900s, **rue Ste-Catherine** stretches for 12km across the island, with the part east of rue Guy serving as the main shopping artery. For all its consumerist gloss the road still has its seedy bits, with the occasional strip club enlivening the streetscape, though most have been phased out. Further along, the street passes through the Quartier Latin, forms the heart of the gay village, and then cuts through the Quartier des Spectacles (see page 209), the splashy entertainment district.

Les Cours Mont-Royal

1455 rue Peel • Mon–Wed 10am–6pm, Thurs & Fri 10am–9pm, Sat 10am–5pm, Sun noon–5pm (occasionally stores have extended hours; confirm on website) • Barbie Expo: Mon–Wed 9am–8pm, Thurs–Fri 9am–10pm, Sat 9am–6pm, Sun 9am–5pm • free • ☎ 514 842 7777, ⓦ lcmr.ca • Métro: Peel

The elegant **Les Cours Mont-Royal**, formerly the largest hotel in the British Commonwealth, now contains four floors of shops, from fashion boutiques to shoe stores to hair salons, along with spas and a high-end food court, all topped by apartments and offices. Peek inside and gawk up at the fourteen-storey-high atria and chandeliers preserved from the hotel. *Barbie Expo*, the largest permanent exhibit of Barbie dolls in the world, is also on view here, featuring dolls dressed by leading designers, including Christian Dior, Oscar de la Renta, Ralph Lauren, Donna Karan and more. It's a lavish display of the 11.5-inch icon – and a must-see for Barbie fans.

Place Ville Marie

Place Ville Marie • Mon–Wed 9.30am–6pm, Thurs & Fri 9.30am–9pm, Sat 9.30am–5pm, Sun noon–5pm • ☎ 514 861 9393, ⓦ placevillemarie.com • Métro: McGill

Standing out among the skyscrapers and malls, the cross-shaped, 46-storey **Place Ville Marie**, designed by I.M. Pei, has been a Montréal landmark since the 1960s, its rooftop searchlight visible far around. The shopping mall offers all the usual stores, plus restaurants and other services, and fabulous views of Mont Royal. It marks one end of **avenue McGill College**, a broad boulevard lined with skyscrapers which frame a view of McGill University and the mountain beyond.

Christ Church Cathedral

635 rue Ste-Catherine ouest • Daily 8am–6pm • Free • ☎ 514 843 6577, ⓦ montrealcathedral.ca • Métro: McGill

The quiet grounds of the 1859 Anglican **Christ Church Cathedral** provide a welcome break in the commercial strip of rue Ste-Catherine. By 1927, the church's slender stone spire was threatening to crash through the wooden roof and was replaced with the peculiar aluminium replica. Inside, the soaring Gothic arches are decorated with heads of angels and the Evangelists, but the most poignant feature is the Coventry Cross, made from nails salvaged from England's Coventry Cathedral, destroyed by bombing during World War II. With the decline in its congregation, the cathedral authorities'

THE UNDERGROUND CITY

Place Ville Marie marks the beginning of Montréal's famous **Underground City** (officially called RÉSO – a homophone of *réseau*, the French word for "network" – or La Ville Souterraine, in French), planned as a refuge from the weather – outrageously cold in the winter and humid in the summer. The underground network began with the construction of Place Ville-Marie in the 1960s. Montréalers flooded into the first climate-controlled shopping arcade, and the Underground City duly spread. Today its 33km of passages provide access to the Métro, major hotels, shopping malls, transport termini, thousands of offices, apartments and restaurants and a good smattering of cinemas and theatres. Everything underground is signposted, but you're still likely to get lost on your first visit – pick up a map of the ever-expanding system from the tourist office. While the pamphlets make the Underground City sound somewhat exotic, it's a pretty banal place – most Montréalers just use it to get from place to place, or drop in on a number of fairly standard shopping malls. If you're on a budget, check out the inexpensive food courts on the lowest floor of any of the malls (also handy for public toilets).

3

desperation for money led them to lease all the land around and beneath the church. For nearly a year, Christ Church was known as "the floating church" – it was supported on concrete struts while the developers tunnelled out the glitzy Promenades de la Cathédrale, a boutique-lined part of the Underground City. To fully experience the church, stop by on Sundays at 10am for the Choral Eucharist or at 4pm for Choral Evensong. The church also features concerts throughout the year, including the L'Oasis Musicale on Saturdays at 4:30pm, which features local emerging musicians ($10 suggested donation).

Musée d'Art Contemporain de Montréal (MAC)

18 rue Ste-Catherine ouest • Tues 11am–6pm, Wed–Fri 11am–9pm, Sat & Sun 10am–6pm • $19; $7 Wed 5–9pm • ☎ 514 847 6226, Ⓦ macm.org • Métro: Place-des-Arts

Occupying the west side of the place des Arts, the **Musée d'Art Contemporain de Montréal** is Canada's first museum devoted entirely to contemporary art. It showcases Québécois artists, such as Paul-Émile Borduas, Jean-Paul Riopelle, Fernand Leduc, Guido Molinari and Claude Tousignant, and also works by other Canadian and international artists. The daring temporary exhibits are consistently excellent, and have covered everything from digital installations to Canadian Abstract Expressionist art. The sculpture garden holds a Henry Moore amid the greenery. Throughout the year, generally on the first Friday night of the month, the museum features "Nocturnes" (5pm–2am), with live music, cocktails, tours and gallery talks (regular admission). Refuel at the *Restaurant du MAC*, which serves a fresh, organic menu, including salmon tartare and chicken tacos.

Rue Sherbrooke and around

Rue Sherbrooke crosses half of the island of Montréal but, other than the Stade Olympique far out east, its most interesting part is the few blocks from McGill University to rue Guy, an elite stretch of private galleries, exclusive hotels and **boutiques**, including Yves Saint-Laurent, Ralph Lauren and Giorgio Armani.

The Ritz-Carlton

1228 rue Sherbrooke ouest, near rue Drummond • ☎ 514 842 4212, Ⓦ ritzcarlton.com • Métro: Peel

Montréal's most ornate hotel is the **Ritz-Carlton** – Elizabeth Taylor married Richard Burton here – and it remains a symbol of what was once known as the **Golden Square Mile**; although downtown has encroached upon its southern precincts, the area between rue Sherbrooke, chemin de la Côte-des-Neiges, the mountain and McGill University retains many of the sumptuous mansions (though many now do duty as commercial or university buildings). From the late nineteenth century to World War II, about seventy percent of Canada's wealth was owned by a few hundred people who lived here. Known as the Caesars of the Wilderness, the majority were Scottish immigrants who made their fortunes in brewing, fur trading and banking, and who financed the railways and steamships that contributed to Montréal's industrial growth. After a lavish renovation of its rooms and public spaces, the *Ritz-Carlton* hotel reopened in 2012 for its hundredth anniversary, reintroducing its popular afternoon tea (daily, at 12.30pm and 3.30pm), and boasting the superb *Maison Boulud* (see page 222) and the Dom Pérignon Bar (1pm–11pm)

Musée des Beaux-Arts

1380 rue Sherbrooke ouest • Daily 10am–5pm, main exhibits Wed till 9pm • $15 for permanent collection, $23 for major temporary exhibits (includes free admission the following day to the permanent collection), $11.50 Wed after 5pm • ☏ 514 285 1600, ⓦ mmfa.qc.ca • Métro: Guy-Concordia

The superb **Musée des Beaux-Arts** is Canada's oldest museum – and Montréal's largest – and features the country's most impressive Canadian art collection. It covers the full spectrum, from the devotional works of New France, through paintings of the local landscape by, among others, James Wilson Morrice, Maurice Cullen and Clarence Gagnon, to the more radical canvases by the Automatistes – Paul-Émile Borduas and Jean-Paul Riopelle – who transformed Montréal's art scene in the 1940s. The museum also has a breathtaking collection of European art and sculpture, with works by such masters as El Greco, Rembrandt, Rodin, Picasso, Monet and Cézanne. The Pavilion of Québec and Canadian Art – with over six hundred pieces – also houses the 450-seat Bourgie Concert Hall. The dazzling marble-and-glass pavilion, built as an extension of the restored Erskine and American Church, is as impressive as the art within, designed by a local architectural firm. The pavilion also displays the church's eighteen Tiffany stained glass windows, the largest collection of Tiffany's work outside the US. In 2016, the museum unveiled the stunning new Hornstein Pavilion for Peace, which showcases over 750 international works, including 100 Old Master paintings, donated by Michal and Renata Hornstein. Two floors of the pavilion are devoted to education and art therapy. The museum's temporary exhibits are consistently superb, and have included everything from Cuban art and history to the music and dance in Andy Warhol's work. The gorgeous sculpture garden features one of the largest collections of public art in Montréal, including works by Jim Dine, Jaume Plensa, Dale Chihuly and Dominique Blain.

McGill University

845 rue Sherbrooke ouest • Free • ☏ 514 398 4455, ⓦ mcgill.ca • Métro: McGill

The city's most prestigious seat of learning, **McGill University**, is entered through a Neoclassical stone gate at the top of avenue McGill College, a principal boulevard with wide pavements adorned with sculptures, most notably Raymond Mason's *The Illuminated Crowd*, portraying a mass of larger-than-life people – generally faced by an equally large crowd of tourists. The university was founded in 1813 from the bequest of James McGill, a Glaswegian immigrant fur trader, and the university is now world-famous for its medical and engineering schools. The ornate limestone buildings and their modern extensions are perfect for relaxing or for a walk above the street level of downtown. A boulder on the campus near Sherbrooke marks the spot where the original Iroquois village of Hochelaga stood before European penetration.

Musée Redpath

859 rue Sherbrooke ouest, on the McGill campus • Mon–Fri 9am–5pm, Sat–Sun 11am–5pm (in July & June–Aug 1–5pm) • Free • ☏ 514 398 4086, ⓦ mcgill.ca/redpath • Métro: McGill

The **Musée Redpath**, one of the first custom-built Canadian museums, features an eclectic anthropological collection of Egyptian mummies and coffins, dinosaur bones and marine vertebrates, and ancient musical instruments and ceremonial items from

QUARTIER DES SPECTACLES

Montréal's astoundingly varied theatre, music, dance and art – and its formidable festival season – centres on the **Quartier des Spectacles (ⓦ**quartierdesspectacles.com), a square kilometre spreading out from the central intersection of Ste-Catherine and St-Laurent. Initially proposed in the early 2000s, construction on the Quartier began in earnest in 2008, and has continued since: in 2019, the National Film Board of Canada is due to move in, in a new building next to the main square. Overall, the Quartier's approach has been two-pronged: to revitalize and renovate already existing venues; and to add new ones, from art galleries to theatres to, most impressively, numerous public spaces, squares, gardens and walkways. Dubbed the "Broadway of Montréal", it has over eighty cultural venues and hosts more than forty festivals, including the renowned Jazz Festival, Just for Laughs and Francofolie, and is served by three Métro stations: St-Laurent, Place-des-Arts and Place-d'Armes. Its signature symbol is a playful red dot, which you'll see throughout – and on the website – a reference to the neighbourhood's former red-light district. The Quartier's many highlights include:

2-22 & La Vitrine Culturelle 2 rue Ste-Catherine est ☎514 285 4545, Ⓦlavitrine.com. Unveiled in 2012, the dashing 2-22 building – designed by the esteemed Montréal company Moment Factory – houses nine different cultural and community venues, including the glass-walled studios of CIBL, Montréal's French-language radio. Also here is La Vitrine Culturelle (the Cultural Window; Sun–Mon 11am–6pm, Tues–Sat 11am–8pm), a superb, tech-savvy information and ticket centre with the city's most extensive information on arts and entertainment offerings.

La Place des Arts 175 rue Ste-Catherine ☎514 285 4200, Ⓦlaplacedesarts.com. Montréal's longtime leading performing-arts centre forms the core of the Quartier, and features everything from opera to ballet to films.

Place des Festivals Opened in 2009 as one of the first major hubs of the Quartier, this hosts most of the bigger festivals, and features the largest animated fountains in Canada, with 235 water jets and four massive lighting towers.

Promenade des Artistes A prime example of the Quartier's well-designed public spaces, this paved promenade is created out of old traffic lanes and lined with planters and "event vitrines", room-sized glass boxes that feature different art installations throughout the year. Lying between Ave du Président-Kennedy and blvd de Maisonneuve, the Promenade also hosts different outdoor exhibits including the annual, popular *21 Balançoires* (21 Swings), a set of 21 musical swings.

3

around the world. The Geological Garden displays minerals and fossils from across Canada. There's also a superb array of events, including the lively Freaky Fridays lecture series, where "scientists bust myths and clarify science", plus weekend family workshops and activities

Musée McCord d'Histoire Canadienne

690 rue Sherbrooke ouest, facing McGill campus • Tues, Thurs & Fri 10am–6pm, Wed 10am–9pm, Sat & Sun 10am–5pm; late June to early Sept, also open Mon 10am–6pm • $19; free Wed 5–9pm • ☎514 398 7100, ⓦmccord-museum.qc.ca • Métro: McGill

The **Musée McCord d'Histoire Canadienne**, in a handsome, early twentieth-century McGill Union building, offers an extensive and fascinating overview of Canadian history. The main part of the collection was amassed by the Scots-Irish McCord family over an eighty-year period from the mid-nineteenth century and represents a highly personal vision of the development of Canada, which they saw as a fusion of colonial and declining Aboriginal elements. The museum is particularly strong on Aboriginal artefacts; highlights include First Nations items such as furs, ivory carvings and superb beadwork. In other rooms, jewellery and other memorabilia from elite Montréal families contrast with the gritty floor-to-ceiling black-and-white pictures of the city taken by famed photographer William Notman in the mid-1800s. The museum currently only has the space to show a fraction of its collection, and it has long been exploring a move to a new, larger location; though nothing has been officially announced. Check the website before visiting to confirm.

MONTRÉAL: PLATEAU MONT-ROYAL

DRINKING & NIGHTLIFE

Barfly	9
Bar Henrietta	1
Bily Kun	7
Blizzarts	10
Casa del Popolo	2
Club Balattou	8
Datcha	4
Isle de Garde	6
Muzique	11
Notre-Dame des Quilles	5
Whisky Café	3

EATING

Au Pied de Cochon	16	Le Jardin de Panos	15	Patati Patata	13		
Beautys	8	Leméac	1	Schwartz's	19		
Café Santropol	17	Maestro SVP	20	Soy	3		
Fairmount Bagel Bakery	5	Maison Publique	12	St-Viateur Bagel & Café	11		
La Banquise	14	Milos	2	Vin Mon Lapin	6		
La Binerie Mont-Royal	9	Moishes	18	Wilensky's Light Lunch	4		
Le Filet	10	Montréal Plaza	7				

ACCOMMODATION

A la Carte B&B	1
Anne ma Soeur Anne	2
Château de l'Argoat	3
Gîte Plateau Mont-Royal	4

Plateau Mont-Royal

Boulevard St-Laurent – The Main – leads all the way up from Vieux-Montréal to the northern extremities of the city. North of rue Sherbrooke is the absorbing **Plateau Mont-Royal** district, where Montréal's cosmopolitan diversity is evident in distinct enclaves of immigrant neighbourhoods. At the southern end of boulevard St-Laurent, which runs parallel to **rue St-Denis**, the Plateau's other main artery, is the heart of the upbeat studenty **Quartier Latin**.

The lively, historical, culturally rich neighbourhood of Plateau Mont-Royal is an absorbing jumble of sights, sounds and smells, filled with delis, bars, nightclubs, cafés and bookshops, and an ever-growing number of trendy boutiques. Traditionally, **boulevard St-Laurent** divided the English in the west from the French in the east of the city. Montréal's immigrants, first Russian Jews, then Greeks, Portuguese, Italians, East Europeans and, more recently, Latin Americans, settled in the middle and, though many prospered enough to move on, the area around The Main is still a cultural mix where neither of the two official languages dominates.

Wandering north from rue Sherbrooke on The Main, you'll pass through the strip's flashiest block, filled with see-and-be-seen restaurants and clubs, before arriving at one of Montréal's few pedestrianized streets, **rue Prince-Arthur**, thronged with buskers and caricaturists in the summer. Its eastern end leads to the beautiful fountained and statued **Square St-Louis**, the city's finest public square. Designed in 1876, the square was originally the domain of bourgeois Montréalers, and the magnificent houses were subsequently occupied by artists, poets and writers. The east side of the square divides the lower and upper areas of **rue St-Denis**.

St Denis and Quartier Latin

The busy rue St-Denis, a major north–south artery, is the traditional francophone strip of Montréal, lined with bars, clubs, cafés, restaurants and eclectic shops. The **Quartier Latin**, which covers the part of rue St-Denis that leads south from rue Sherbrooke to rue Ste-Catherine, is the traditional student quarter, colonized by terrace cafés and bars crammed with students from the nearby Université du Québec à Montréal (UQAM) well into the early hours. By contrast, the Plateau stretch of rue St-Denis north of Square St-Louis is the stomping ground of the stylish set, all boutiques and restaurants.

Parc du Mont-Royal

Little more than a hill to most tourists but a mountain to Montréalers, **Mont Royal** reaches just 233m but its two square kilometres of greenery are visible from almost anywhere in the city. Mont Royal holds a special place in the history of the city – it was here that the Iroquois established their settlement and that Maisonneuve declared the island to be

---

WALKS UP MONT ROYAL

There are various access points for a walk up the mountain but the most popular starting point is at the **George-Étienne Cartier monument** along avenue du Parc, most easily accessed by following rue Rachel westward from boulevard St-Laurent. You can also take the Métro to Mont-Royal station, walk west along avenue du Mont-Royal and turn left on avenue du Parc; or, get off the Métro at Place-des-Arts and take bus #80, disembarking halfway along the park. However you get there, the angel-topped monument is hard to miss on summer Sundays, when buskers and locals congregate until the sun goes down. From here, several paths lead towards the summit and the illuminated cross, Croix sur la Montagne, that commemorates Maisonneuve placing a wooden cross here in 1642. The gentlest slope is along chemin Olmsted, a carriage trail that winds lazily up from the monument, past the top of rue Peel (the easiest access from downtown), and along the summit to a lookout point offering fine views of downtown and the St Lawrence beyond. Guided hikes and walks are offered throughout the year; check the website for details.

French – but for centuries the mountain was privately owned. Then, during an especially bitter winter, one of the inhabitants cut down his trees for extra firewood. Montréalers were outraged at the desecration, and in 1875 the city bought the land for the impressive sum of $1 million. Frederick Law Olmsted, designer of New York's Central Park and San Francisco's Golden Gate Park, was hired to landscape the hill, which now provides 56km of jogging paths and 20km of skiing trails to keep city inhabitants happy year-round.

The city has steadfastly refused any commercial developments on this lucrative site, the only construction being **Lac aux Castors**, built in the 1930s as a work-creation scheme for the unemployed; it now serves as a skating rink in the winter and pedal-boat playground in the summer. In the 1950s, protection of the mountain reached a puritanical extreme when a local journalist revealed young couples were using the area for amatory pursuits and, even worse, that people were openly drinking alcohol. Consequently all of the underbrush was uprooted, which only succeeded in killing off much of the ash, birch, maple, oak and pine trees. Within five years Mont Royal was dubbed "Bald Mountain" and a replanting campaign had to be instigated. The park is now very well-maintained thanks to a community of enthusiastic volunteers, and is especially popular on the weekends, when Montréalers take to the walking paths (see page 211) to escape the bustle of the city.

Maison Smith

1260 chemin Remembrance • Daily: mid-June to early Sept 9am–6pm; early Sept to mid-June 9am–5pm • Free • ☎ 514 843 8240, Ⓦ lemontroyal.com • Métro: Mont-Royal

Maison Smith houses an information centre with trail maps, brochures, books, info on the local flora and fauna and an exhibit on the park's history and conservation efforts. There's a café, too, and from mid-May to mid-October you can sit on the outdoor terrace, which makes a pleasant vantage point.

Oratoire St-Joseph

3800 chemin Queen-Mary, on northwest side of mountain • **Basilica** Hours generally daily 7am–9pm • **Museum** Daily 10am–4.30pm (July & Aug, also open Sat & Sun until 5.30pm) • Basilica free; museum $4; for both: suggested donation for parking $5 • ☎ 514 733 8211, Ⓦ saint-joseph.org • Métro: Côtes-des-Neiges • Buses #51 or #165 also stop nearby

TRACE HISTORY AT CANADA'S LARGEST CEMETERY

"Much more than a cemetery" is the apt tagline at the vast, leafy Cimitière Notre-Dame-Des-Nieges (4601 Côte-des-Neiges Rd, ☎514 735 1361, ⓦcimetierenotredamedesneiges.ca, daily 8am–5pm), which sprawls near the Oratoire St-Joseph. Founded in 1854, this is the largest cemetery in Canada (and third largest in North America). Over a million people are buried here – including 20 Montréal mayors, as well as local artists, painters and poets – offering a fascinating overview of the history and evolution of Montreal. But most of all, the cemetery is a place for reflecting amid lush nature. It's hard to believe that you're in the middle of a city as you wander the cemetery, where French Baroque architecture, romantic statuary and elegant mausoleums blend with flourishing nature, including Norway maples, oaks, ash trees, elms, cedars and, of course, weeping willows. Check the website for a map, or pick one up upon arrival at the cemetery.

The formidable **Oratoire St-Joseph** rises from its green surroundings near Montréal's highest point. In 1904, Brother André – canonized as Québéc's **first saint** in early 2010 – built a small chapel here to honour St Joseph, Canada's patron saint. Before long, Brother André's ability to heal people had earned him the sobriquet "The Miracle Man of Montréal", and huge numbers of patients took to climbing the outside stairs on their knees to receive his grace. Satisfied clients donated so much money that in 1924 he could afford to begin work on this immense granite edifice, which was completed in 1967, thirty years after his death. It is topped by a dome second in size only to St Peter's in Rome.

The splendid Italianate exterior gives way to a chapel in the apse, which is richly decorated with green marble columns and a gold-leaf ceiling. In the adjoining anteroom, thousands of votive candles burn along the walls, and proof of Brother André's curative powers hang everywhere: crutches, canes and braces are crammed into every available space. The roof terrace, above the portico, has excellent views of the city and provides access to the gardens. A small upstairs museum displays items relating to Brother André's life, including the room where he died, shifted here from a local hospice. Brother André's heart is enclosed in a glass case; the devout believe it quivers occasionally. Throughout the year, Oratoire St-Joseph hosts Sunday concerts (generally at 3:30pm), celebrating famous composers such as Bach or local organists.

Outside, the **Way of the Cross** has some particularly beautiful sculptures in smooth, white Carrara marble and Indiana buff stone by Montréal artist Louis Parent – a tranquil site used as a setting for the Denys Arcand film *Jésus de Montréal*. You can also visit the small building a few metres away from the Oratory containing the original chapel and Brother André's tiny room.

Parc Olympique and Espace pour la vie

The Parc Olympique lies east of the city, an easy hop on the Métro to either Pie-IX (pronounced "pee-nuhf") or Viau, or a twenty-minute drive on rue Sherbrooke. The Parc encompasses several main sights, including the striking **Stade Olympique** and the sprawling **Espace pour la vie (Space for Life)** complex, which includes the lush **Jardin Botanique**, the environmental centre **Biodôme** and the **Planétarium Rio Tinto**.

Stade Olympique

4141 av Pierre-de-Coubertin • **Tower** Mon 1pm–6pm (until 7pm end June to early Sept), Tues–Sun 9am–7pm; winter: Tues–Sun 9am–5pm; closed early Jan to early March• $23.25 • **Stade** Guided tours depart regularly early March to mid-April Tues–Sun 10.30am–4pm; early May to mid-Oct Mon 1pm–4pm, Tues– Sun 10.30am–4pm • $14.50 • **Centre sportif** Pools usually open July & Aug Mon–Fri 6.30am–8.55pm, Sat & Sun 9am–4.25pm; Sept–June hours vary (note that mornings are usually adults-only) • $7 • ☎514 252 4141, ⓦ parcolympique.qc.ca • Métro: Pie-IX

The Parc Olympique's main attraction, the **Stade Olympique**, is known by Montréalers as the "Big O" for several reasons: its name, its circular shape and the fact that it took the city thirty years to pay for it. The main facilities for the 1976 Summer

3

> ### PACKAGE TICKETS
>
> If you plan on spending a full day in the Parc Olympique and Espace pour la vie (a good bet if you're visiting with kids), it's worth buying a **package ticket** from any of the participating venues. You can buy these in various combinations, with prices starting at $40, and they are generally valid for sixty consecutive days.

Olympics were designed by Roger Taillibert, who was told money was no object. The complex ended up costing $1.4 billion (over $2 billion with subsequent interest and maintenance) – and it was not even completed in time for the games. After the Olympics, it was used sporadically, and in a continuing attempt to pay off debts, the schedule featured everything from football to trade shows. But the area around the stadium has evolved into an urban park and user-friendly public space, with a surprisingly varied series of events, particularly in the summer. The highest inclined tower in the world, the stadium's 175m **tower** was erected to hold a retractable 65-tonne roof, but the retraction process never really worked properly. The main attraction here is the **funicular** that takes you up the tower to an observation deck with 60km views and an exhibition of historic photos of Montréal. Also here is the *Since 1976* exhibition (included with admission), an overview on Parc Olympic, from construction to today. Looking to do a quick workout? The **Centre sportif** (Sports Centre), with a slew of pools, from a water-polo pool to a diving pool, offers well-priced day rates (from $7). For guidance in exploring the Parc Olympique, check the helpful self-circuits section of the website, which covers routes you can follow.

Rio Tinto Alcan Planetarium

4801 av Pierre-de-Coubertin • End June to early Sept Mon–Wed & Sun 9am–6pm, Thurs–Sat 9am–9.30pm; early Sept to end June Mon–Wed & Sun 9am–5.30pm, Thurs–Sat 9am–8.30pm • $20.50; ticket combos available (see above) • ☎ 514 863 3000, ⓦ espacepourlavie. ca • Métro: Viau

In 2013, the **Rio Tinto Alcan Planetarium** celebrated its splashy opening, unveiling not one but two state-of-the-art circular theatres. The permanent exhibit, *EXO, Our Search for Life in the Universe*, is filled with kid-friendly interactive displays on everything from space exploration to mighty meteorites.

Biodôme de Montréal

4777 av Pierre-de-Coubertin • End June to early Sept daily 9am–6pm; early Sept to mid-Feb Tues–Sun 9am–5pm; mid-Feb to end June daily 9am–5pm • $20.50; ticket combos available (see above) • ☎ 514 868 3000, ⓦ biodome.qc.ca • Métro: Viau

The **Biodôme de Montréal**, housed in a building shaped like a bicycle helmet, started life as the Olympic velodrome. Now it is an environmental masterpiece – one of Montréal's most popular musueums – comprising a variety of ecosystems: tropical, Laurentian forest, St Lawrence maritime, Labrador coast and polar. You can wander freely through the different zones, which are planted with appropriate flourishing vegetation and inhabited by the relevant birds, animals and marine life. It's both entertaining and educational, for kids and adults alike. Closed for renovations at the time of writing but due to reopen end of 2019.

Jardin Botanique

4101 rue Sherbrooke est, just north of Stadium • May–Aug daily 9am–6pm; Sept & Oct Mon–Thurs & Sun 9am–9pm, Fri–Sat 9am–10pm; Nov–April Tues–Sun 9am–5pm • $20.50; ticket combos available (see above) • ☎ 514 872 1400, ⓦ ville.montreal.qc.ca/jardin • Métro: Pie-IX

The grounds and greenhouses of the **Jardin Botanique** contain some thirty types of garden, from medicinal herbs to orchids. Highlights include a Japanese garden, its ponds of water lilies bordered by greenish sculptured stone and crossed by delicate bridges, while the nearby Chinese garden is especially resplendent during the autumn lantern festival. Also popular are the well-curated temporary exhibits. The bug-shaped

Insectarium forms part of the same complex and features insects of every shape and size, from brightly coloured butterflies to ink-black, fuzzy spiders.

Parc Jean-Drapeau

The former Parc des Îles, renamed **Parc Jean-Drapeau** following the death in 1999 of the longtime mayor, comprises **Île Ste-Hélène** and the artificial **Île Notre-Dame**, constructed from fill dredged from the river and from the construction of the Métro (whose yellow line includes the Jean-Drapeau stop, located on Île Ste-Hélène). The islands, east of downtown Montréal in the St Lawrence River, feature beaches, canals, gardens and more. The site of the Expo '67 World's Fair, they have since hosted multiple sporting and musical events, including the annual summertime Canadian Grand Prix on Île Notre-Dame, where cars tear their way along the Circuit Gilles-Villeneuve that rings the island. The park also features a wonderful array of public art, many from the Expo '67, including *Iris*, a flowering aluminium sculpture by Montréal artist Raoul Hunter.

Tour de Lévis

Pavilion du Canada, Île Ste-Hélène • mid-May to June Sat–Sun 10am–4.45pm, July–Aug Sat–Sun 10am–8.45pm, Sept Sat–Sun 10am–7.30pm, Oct 10am–5.45pm • free • ☎ 514 872 9013, ⓦ parcjeandreapeau.com • Métro: Jean-Drapeau

Take in 360-degree views, from the river to the downtown Montreal skyline, at the Tour de Lévis, a historical landmark built in the 1930s to house a water tower. Climb the indoor 157-step staircase to the observation deck.

Biosphère

160 chemin Tour-de-l'Isle, Île Ste-Hélène • June–Oct daily 10am–5pm; Nov–May Wed–Sun 10am–5pm • $15 • ☎ 514 283 5000, ⓦ biosphere.ec.gc.ca • Métro: Jean-Drapeau

The **Biosphère** looms as a giant sphere of interlocking aluminium triangles designed by Buckminster Fuller for Expo '67. Today, it's an interactive museum focusing on the environment, with exhibits on climate change, sustainable development and transport, and more. Kids especially will delight in the interactive touch-screens, skill-testing games and movies and multimedia displays. On the fourth floor, a stupendous lookout point takes in the St Lawrence River and the city, foregrounded by the giant Alexander Calder stabile, *Man* – one of many pieces of public art dotted about the island.

Musée Stewart

Vieux-Fort, 20 chemin du Tour-de-l'Isle, Île Ste-Hélène • End June to early Sept Tues–Sun 10am–5pm; early Sept to end June Wed–Sun 10am–5pm • $15 • ☎ 514 861 6701, ⓦ stewart-museum.org • Métro: Jean-Drapeau

Montréal's only **fort**, a U-shaped building situated close to the river's edge, was built by the British between 1820 and 1824 as a defence against the threat of American invasion – which never came. Over the decades, this fortified arsenal commissioned by the Duke of Wellington played a number of roles, including as a World War II prison camp, before opening as the **Musée Stewart** in 1955. The museum focuses on the history of Île Ste-Hélène. Its well-curated permanent collection showcases military and cultural artefacts as related to Canada's history, including weaponry; maps, globes and navigational instruments; and household items from the sixteenth to nineteenth centuries. The fort isthe summer venue for the re-enactment of seventeenth- to eighteenth-century military manoeuvres by actors dressed as the Fraser Highlanders and Compagnie Franche de la Marine. The museum also features creative temporary themed exhibits.

ARRIVAL AND DEPARTURE

MONTRÉAL

BY PLANE

Aéroport International Pierre-Elliott-Trudeau de Montréal Montréal's main international airport (code YUL; ☎ 514 394 7377, ☎ 800 465 1213, ⓦ admtl.com), occasionally referred to by its old name of Dorval, or Montréal-Trudeau for short, is 22km southwest of the city.

3

BIXI: PEDAL YOUR WAY ACROSS MONTRÉAL

Montréal's public bike system – the first launched in North America – features over 5000 self-service bikes available 24hr across the city at 450-plus stations, from April to November. Montréal researched similar bike programmes in other cities, including Paris and Barcelona, to emerge with the well-oiled, wonderfully accessible **Bixi** (ⓦ bixi.com; the name comes from "bike" plus "taxi"). Renting a bike is simple: at a Bixi stand (which are liberally scattered across the city), swipe your credit card and ride off. A ride of 30 minutes or less is $2.95; 24hr access pass is $5; during that period, you can borrow bikes as often as you like, and the first 30min is free. Beyond that, you pay additional charges. Also on offer are thirty-day ($34) and one-year ($94) subscriptions.

The cheapest ride between the airport and Montréal's city centre is the Express Bus 747 (24hr, departures every 30min, during rush hour every 7min; travel time 45min–1hr; $10 one way, which is valid for 24hr of travel on all STM bus and Métro lines; ☎ 514 288 6287, ⓦ stm.info). The bus makes eleven stops in town, including a first stop at the Lionel-Groulx Métro, and then throughout downtown along René-Lévesque, including rue Peel, Jeanne-Mance and St-Laurent, with a final stop at the main bus station, the Gare d'Autocars de Montréal, on the eastern edge of the Quartier Latin. You can buy the 747 tickets in the airport, at all Métro stations and at Stationnement de Montréal pay stations (look for the blue P$ sign), which are dotted along the bus route on René-Lévesque. Note that if you buy a ticket at a Stationnement, it is only valid for the one-way ride to the airport, and you must board the bus on René-Lévesque. You can also buy the ticket on the bus, but note that you'll need exact change – no notes are accepted, only coins. A taxi from the airport to downtown is around $35–47.

Destinations Baie-Comeau (3–4 daily; 1hr 30min); Calgary (3–5 daily; 4hr 30min); Chicoutimi (5 daily; 1hr 5min); Gaspé (2–3 daily; 2hr 40min); Halifax (10–12 daily; 1hr 25min); Îles-de-la-Madeleine (1–3 daily; 3hr 50min); Moncton (3–4 daily; 1hr 20min); Mont Joli (3–4 daily; 1hr 25min); Ottawa (9–10 daily; 40min); Québec City (13–20 daily; 50min); Saint John, NB (3–5 daily; 1hr 35min); Sept-Îles (3–6 daily; 2hr 45min); Toronto (19–40 daily; 1hr 15min); Vancouver (4–6 daily; 5hr 20min); Wabush (2–3 daily; 4hr 5min); Winnipeg (2–4 daily; 2hr 55min).

BY TRAIN

Montréal's main train station, Gare Centrale, is centrally located downtown at 895 rue de la Gauchetière ouest (☎ 514 989 2626). The station is the major terminus for Canada's VIA Rail trains (☎ 514 989 2626, ☎ 888 842 7245,

ⓦ viarail.ca) from Halifax, Toronto, Ottawa, Québec and the Gaspé, as well as US Amtrak trains from Washington and New York. It's linked to the Métro system at Bonaventure Métro station.

Destinations Bonaventure (3 weekly; 13hr 10min); Carleton (3 weekly; 12hr); Cornwall (4–5 daily; 1hr 5min); Gaspé (3–4 weekly; 17hr 30min); Jonquière (3 weekly; 8hr 55min); Kingston (4–5 daily; 2hr 30min); Matapédia (6 weekly; 10hr 10min); New York (1 daily; 11hr 30min); Ottawa (4–6 daily; 2hr 10min); Percé (3 weekly; 16hr 5min); Québec City (4–5 daily; 3hr); Rimouski (5–6 weekly; 7hr 40min); Rivière-du-Loup (5–6 weekly; 5hr 55min); Toronto (4–5 daily; 4hr–5hr 30min); Washington, DC (1 daily; 16hr 10min).

BY BUS

Long-distance buses use the Gare d'Autocars de Montréal (1717 rue Berri; ☎ 514 842 2281 for info on all bus lines). The Berri-UQAM Métro station is beneath it. A number of bus lines – including Orléans Express (☎ 888 999 3977, ⓦ orleansexpress.com), one of Québec's main coach companies – serve various destinations.

Destinations Bromont (2 daily; 2hr); Chicoutimi (4 weekly; 4hr 55min); Granby (4–7 daily; 1hr 30min); Jonquière (4 weekly; 5hr 25min); Kingston (7 daily; 3hr); Magog (7–10 daily; 1hr 30min); Mont-Tremblant (3 daily; 2hr 40min); Montebello (6 daily; 1hr 30 min); New York (6 daily; 8hr 30min); North Bay (2 daily; 7hr 40min); Orford (3 daily; 3hr); Ottawa (hourly; 2hr 20min); Québec City (hourly; 3hr); Rimouski (3 daily; 7hr); Rivière-du-Loup (4 daily; 5hr 30min); Ste-Adèle (6 daily; 1hr 25min); Ste-Agathe (5 daily; 1hr 45min); St-Jovite (5 daily; 2hr 15min); St-Sauveur (6 daily; 1hr); Sherbrooke (7–10 daily; 2hr 5min); Tadoussac (2 daily; 7hr 30min); Toronto (8 daily; 6hr 45min); Trois-Rivières (6–8 daily; 2hr); Val-David (5–6 daily; 1hr 30min).

GETTING AROUND

BY MÉTRO

Montréal's Métro system is efficient, speedy and clean. Run by the STM (Société de Transport de Montréal; ☎ 514 288 6287, ⓦ stm.info), it operates Mon–Thurs & Sun (6.30am–12.30am) & Fri–Sat (6am–1.30am). Some of the Métro's major interconnecting stations are Berri-UQAM, Lionel-Groulx, and Snowdon and Jean-Talon. A one-way fare on either Métro or bus is $3.25 (exact change needed on the bus); you can also get two trips for $6 or ten trips for $28. Tickets can also be used to transfer from Métro to bus; tickets are good for 2hr from first use. A good bet for visitors is the one-day pass for $10, the weekend pass for $13.75 or three consecutive days for $19. Locals often use OPUS cards, with a reloadable smart chip; these cost a one-time fee of $6, and you can then recharge your card at all Métro stations from fare vending machines or fare collectors.

BY BUS
Montréal has an efficient fleet of buses that covers the entire city, though most visitors will find the Métro sufficient for exploring. Fares are the same as the Métro ($3.25); buses also have a similar schedule to the Métro, though some run all night.

BY TAXI
Taxis are plentiful and you can hail them on the street or call. Taxi Diamond (☎514 273 6331, ⊛taxidiamond.com) is a reliable service.

CAR RENTAL
Avis, 1225 rue Metcalfe (☎514 866 7906, ⊛avis.com); Budget, 895 rue de la Gauchetière (☎514 938 1000, ⊛budget.com); Hertz, 1073 rue Drummond (☎514 938 1717, ⊛hertz.com); and Thrifty, 845 rue Ste-Catherine est (☎514 845 5954, ⊛thrifty.com).

INFORMATION AND TOURS

Infotouriste Montréal's main information centre, Infotouriste, is at 1255 rue Peel (early May to early Oct daily 9am–6pm; early Oct to early May daily 9am–5pm; ☎514 873 2015, ☎877 266 5687, ⊛bonjourmontreal.com; Métro: Peel). It has heaps of useful information and offers an accommodation service.

Tourist Information Centre of Vieux-Montréal On the northwest corner of place Jacques-Cartier at 174 rue Notre-Dame est (daily: May & Oct 10am–6pm; June–Sept 9am–7pm; ⊛ntl.org; Métro: Champ-de-Mars); information on the city only.

Walking tours Montréal boasts numerous top-notch walking tours, including Local Montréal Food Tours ⊛localfoodtours.com; $60), where you can sample your way across Montréal's neighbourhoods, including Plateau and The Main. and Free Old Montréal Walking Tour (5369 blvd St-Laurent; ☎514 613 1940, ⊛freemontrealtours.com; 1 daily Mon–Thurs year-round; 1hr 45min; free).

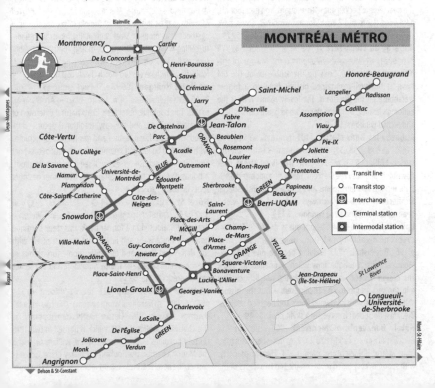

ACCOMMODATION

Montréal has a wide range of **accommodation**, from five-star palaces to moderately priced B&Bs to stylish hotels to rock-bottom hostels and university residences. **Vieux-Montréal** is easily one of the most popular neighbourhoods for bedding down, in large part because of the ever-growing number of boutique hotels, many housed in charming historical buildings, and offering the inviting combination of ancient facades and stone walls plus high-thread-count sheets, and rooftop bars **Downtown** is very central, with easy access to most parts of the city, and features an extensive variety of accommodation, from big-name chain hotels to smaller but no less elegant properties. For cosy B&Bs, head to the Plateau neighbourhood, while the student-thronged **Quartier Latin** has a number of simple and cheap residences and hostels.

HOTELS AND B&BS

VIEUX-MONTRÉAL

Auberge Bonaparte 447 rue St-François-Xavier ☎ 514 844 1448, ⓦ bonaparte.com; Métro: place-d'Armes; map p.196. Sleep amid history at this handsome inn, steps from the Basilique Notre-Dame, which was built in 1886 and is shaded by smart burgundy awnings. Inside, the quarters are decked out with wrought-iron headboards, hardwood floors and French dormer windows; some have views of the Basilique's gardens. Breakfast included. **$279**

Auberge du Vieux-Port 97 rue de la Commune ☎ 514 876 0081, ⓦ aubergeduvieuxport.com; Métro: place-d'Armes; map p.196. Soak up the ambience of the old town at this well-maintained historic hotel in a former warehouse on the riverfront. The lovely rooms reflect the building's history, with pine floors, wood beams, brass beds and arched windows. **$270**

Auberge les Bons Matins 1401 av Argyle ☎ 514 931 9167, ☎ 800 588 5280, ⓦ bonsmatins.com; Métro: Lucien-L'Allier; map p.204. On a tree-lined street near downtown and busy rue Crescent, this well-appointed B&B-style inn has spacious rooms and suites, each with special architectural features (archways, exposed brick, wood beams, fireplace) and large windows. **$133**

Épik Montréal 171 rue St-Paul ouest ☎ 514 842 2634, ⓦ epikmontreal.com; Métro: place-d'Armes; map p.196. This historic 1723 building became one of Vieux-Montréal's first boutique inns when it opened in 1989. The design is sleek – and amenities top-notch, including rain showers and in-room coffeemakers – but the history shines through, with hardwood floors and beamed ceilings. Breakfast (included) is served in a skylit nook. **$249**

Hôtel Bonaventure Montréal 900 rue de la Gauchatière ouest ☎ 514 878 2332, ⓦ hotelbonaventure. com; Métro: Bonaventure; map p.204. Elegant property, with spacious, cool-toned rooms on the top two floors of the Place Bonaventure, a retail and office complex adjacent to the main train station. There's a pool and fitness centre too. **$219**

Hôtel Gault 449 rue Ste-Hélène ☎ 514 904 1616, ☎ 866 904 1616, ⓦ hotelgault.com; Métro: Square-Victoria; map p.196. This is the very definition of a boutique hotel – the individually designed loft-style rooms in an 1871 warehouse are a design-junkie's dream, with Arne Jacobsen fixtures and white-oak panelling, while the bathrooms have sleek freestanding tubs and heated floors. **$279**

Hotel Le Crystal 1100 rue de la Montagne ☎ 514 861 5550, ⓦ hotellecrystal.com; Métro: Lucien-L'Allier; map p.204. The sparkling chandelier and soaring windows in the lobby set the tone for this chic hotel, with spacious, sophisticated rooms and suites and an indoor saltwater pool and outdoor hot tub on the twelfth floor. **$279**

★ **Hôtel Le Germain** 2050 rue Mansfield ☎ 514 849 2050, ⓦ germainmontreal.com; Métro: McGill or Peel; map p.204. Long one of downtown's finest boutique hotels, *Le Germain* is awash in distinctive details, from local artwork to bamboo-and-cotton towels in the stylish bathrooms to goose-down duvets on the comfortable beds. The excellent complimentary breakfast is served at the on-site restaurant *Le Bisco*. Pet-friendly, too. **$240**

Hotel Monville 1041 rue De Bleury ☎ 514 379 2000, ⓦ hotelmonville.com; Métro: map p.196. *Hotel Monville* may be in the heart of the old town, but its entire aesthetic is all modern: sleek, minimalist rooms with floor-to-ceiling windows; online check-in and -out; and a robot (yes, really) for room service. Kick off your night in the stylish lobby bar, which serves top-notch classic cocktails. **$180**

★ **Hotel Nelligan** 106 rue St-Paul ouest ☎ 514 788 2040, ⓦ hotelnelligan.com; Métro: place-d'Armes; map p.196. This boutique hotel feels like a natural extension of its neighbourhood, and the cosy, traditional decor – dark wood, chocolate-hued leather and gas fireplaces – chimes with the 1850 building. It's named after the Québécois poet Emile Nelligan, whose verses you'll see printed throughout. A bonus: *Nelligan*'s bar and restaurants rival other designer spots in town. **$265**

Hôtel St-Paul 355 rue McGill ☎ 514 380 2222, ☎ 866 380 2202, ⓦ hotelstpaul.com; Métro: Square-Victoria; map p.196. Housed in a former bank, this sleek boutique hotel has white walls and linens that contrast nicely with the dark-wood floors and elegantly simple furnishings of the rooms and suites. The trendy *Hambar* restaurant serves market-fresh cuisine. **$239**

★ **Hotel William Gray** 421 rue St-Vincent ☎ 514 656 5600, ⓦ hotelwilliamgray.com; Métro: place-d'Armes; map p.196. Classic meets contemporary at this charming boutique hotel, which is housed in two 18th century buildings – the Maison Edward-William Gray and the Maison Cherrier. Overlooking the buzzy place Jacques-Cartier, the hotel features elegant rooms, as well as two roof terraces with old town views, a lovely spa, the *Maggie Oaks* brasserie and the lively *Living Room*, which invites lounging while sipping hand-crafted cocktails. $260

Le Dauphin Centre Ville 1025 rue De Bleury ☎ 514 788 3888, ⓦ hotelsdauphin.ca; Métro: place-d'Armes; map p.204. As central as it gets: one block from the Palais des Congrès, and within walking distance of the Quartier des Spectacles, Chinatown and Vieux-Montréal. The rooms are straightforward but well maintained and each is equipped with an iMac computer. $175

Le Mount Stephen 1440 Drummond St ☎ 514 313 1000, ⓦ lemountstephen.com; Métro: Peel; map p.204. *Le Mount Stephen* has an impressive pedigree. The 1880 George Stephen House – which housed the upscale Mount Stephen Club for nearly a century – is now this new neoclassical mansion hotel. After a detailed renovation, the luxury hotel opened in 2017, and features luxurious rooms with heated floors and rainforest showers. The hotel's grand Bar George restaurant serves UK cuisine with a Québécois twist. $289

Le Petit Hôtel 168 rue St-Paul ouest ☎ 514 940 0360, ⓦ petithotelmontreal.com; Métro: place-d'Armes; map p.196. Bright orange accents play against old stone at this whimsical Vieux-Montréal hotel, housed in an elegant nineteenth-century building. Stylish rooms come in clothing sizes – S, M, L, XL; the lobby café serves up ink-black espressos and robust red wines; and the glass front doors swing open onto the cobblestone streets of the old town. Bicycles available for guests' use. $190

★ **Le Saint-Sulpice Hôtel** 414 rue St-Sulpice ☎ 514 288 1000, ☎ 877 785 7423, ⓦ lesaintsulpice.com; Métro: place-d'Armes; map p.196. It would be hard to find a better-placed hotel in Vieux-Montréal, in the shadow of the Basilique Notre-Dame. The hotel is all suites, each with a fireplace and kitchenette, and some with an ample terrace. The *Sinclair* serves contemporary French cuisine, in a leafy courtyard overlooking the neighbouring Sulpician seminary gardens. $260

Le St-Martin Hôtel Particulier Centre-Ville 980 blvd de Maisonneuve ouest ☎ 514 843 3000, ⓦ lestmartin montreal.com; Métro: Peel; map p.204. Some downtown hotels can be stuffy and antiseptic; not this one. Blending elegance with a homely, service-oriented atmosphere, its spacious rooms boast top-notch amenities, such as Keurig coffee machines, ample work desks with ergonomic chairs and thick robes. There's also a fitness centre and heated outdoor pool (open year-round). $229

PLATEAU MONT-ROYAL

Anne ma Soeur Anne 4119 rue St-Denis ☎ 514 281 3187, ⓦ annemasoeuranne.com; Métro: Mont-Royal; map p.210. On a prime stretch of rue St-Denis, this comfy hotel features well-tended studio-style rooms with kitchenettes and large bathrooms; some have private terraces and balconies overlooking the sun-dappled

backyard. Staff can also arrange longer stays at apartments around the city; rates vary. $126

Château de l'Argoat 524 rue Sherbrooke est ☎ 514 842 2046, ⓦ hotel-chateau-argoat.com; Métro: Sherbrooke; map p.210. The attractive rooms at this fanciful, cream-coloured fortress have high ceilings and quaint chandeliers. There's local artwork throughout, much of it for sale. Parking is included, as is breakfast – enjoy Fairmount bagels and fresh croissants. $125

Hotel 10 10 Sherbrooke ouest ☎ 514 843 6000, ☎ 855 390 6787, ⓦ hotel10montreal.com; Métro: St-Laurent; map p.204. Stylish hotel in an artfully modernized 1914 building, handy for nightlife – within strolling distance of the Plateau and club-crammed blvd St-Laurent. The hotel has its own lively after-dark offerings, including the *Blvd44* club and *Bar20* wine bistro. $169

EAST OF THE CITY

★ **A la Carte B&B** 5477 av 10, Rosemont, near the Jardin Botanique ☎ 514 593 4005, ⓦ alacartebnb.com; Métro: Ste-Michelle and Joliette; map p.210. It's not just the rooms that are warm and inviting – so are owners Daniel, Petra and miniature poodle Monsieur Petit. This delightful B&B offers two colourful, wooden-floored rooms, a second-floor apartment that can sleep six, and a hearty Québécois breakfast. It's a bit out of the centre of town, but there's plenty of public transport. Rooms $130; apartment $185

GRIFFINTOWN

ALT Hotel Montréal 120 rue Peel ☎ 844 823 8120, ⓦ althotels.com; Métro: Bonaventure; map p.196. This hip hotel reflects its equally hip neighbourhood, with chic furnishings, colourful art, recycled brick from the district's old buildings and polished rooms with plump beds and cotton sheets. $175

HOSTELS

Auberge Alternative 358 rue St-Pierre ☎ 514 282 8069, ⓦ auberge-alternative.qc.ca; Métro: Square-Victoria; map p.196. This comfortable, arty hostel is in a refurbished 1875 Vieux-Montréal warehouse and has a range of dorms, and private rooms. The hostel celebrates the local art community, with a small gallery showcasing emerging artists. They also offer bike and camping equipment rental. Dorms $17; private rooms that fit three 108

Auberge de Jeunesse Internationale de Montréal 1030 rue Mackay ☎ 514 843 3317, ☎ 866 843 3317, ⓦ hostellingmontreal.com; Métro: Lucien-L'Allier; map p.204. This large, well-located hostel has simple but clean dorms and private rooms. Staff are friendly and helpful, and offer fun activities including pub crawls, games nights and a bike and beer tour. Dorms from $20; non-members $25

3

Gîte Plateau Mont-Royal 185 rue Sherbrooke est ☎ 514 284 1276, ☎ 877 350 4483, ⊛ hostelmontreal. com; Métro: Sherbrooke; map p.210. Bright dorms and private rooms (with shared bath), a chilled-out common room and great Plateau location make this a popular backpacker spot. Continental breakfast included. They also offer long-term stays and in summer it operates the *Gîte du Parc Lafontaine*, near leafy Parc Lafontaine in Plateau Mont-Royal, with similar prices and accommodation. Dorms $\underline{\$24}$; doubles $\underline{\$80}$; month-long stays in private room from $\underline{\$810}$

STUDENT ROOMS

Les Résidences Universitaires UQAM East Lodge: 303 blvd René-Lévesque est ☎ 514 987 6669; Métro: Berri-UQAM; West Lodge: 100 rue St-Urbain ☎ 514 987 7747; Métro: St-Laurent; ⊛ residences-uqam.qc.ca; map p.212. Clean and basic rooms and studios, some with kitchenette, as well as apartments, in these two Quartier Latin student residences. Access to fitness centre. Mid-May to mid-Aug. $\underline{\$70}$

McGill University Residences (Bishop Mountain Hall) 3935 rue University ☎ 514 398 5200, ⊛ mcgill.ca/students/housing/summer; Métro: McGill; map p.204. The university runs four popular residences in the summer that range from simple student-style rooms, each with a small refrigerator, to suites and apartments. Residences include Bishop Mountain Hall on the slopes of Mont Royal; New Residence Hall in downtown; La Citadelle and Royal Victoria College near the campus; and Solin Hall, off-campus near the Atwater Market. The website has an overview on each residence hall and also offers up-to-date information on closures, rates and more. Enquire about weekly rates, which are often a good deal. Mid-May to mid-Aug. $\underline{\$110}$

EATING

A culinary destination that rivals the gourmet capitals of the world, Montréal is said to have the highest number of restaurants per capita in North America after New York City. It was *Toqué!* (see page 222) – helmed by master chef Normand Laprise – that catapulted the city to the top culinary ranks, and since then numerous home-grown chefs have captured the world's attention, from Martin Picard of *Au Pied de Cochon* (see page 222) to Derek Damann of *Maison Publique* (see page 224).

Montréal's ethnic diversity is amply displayed by the variety of **cuisines** available. The city has its own **Chinatown** just north of Vieux-Montréal, a **Little Italy** around Jean-Talon Métro (near the excellent **Jean-Talon market**; ⊛ marchespublics-mtl.com) and a **Greek** community whose cheaper restaurants are concentrated along Prince Arthur; for more traditional Greek cuisine, head further north along avenue du Parc.

Most prominent of the international restaurants are the **Eastern European** establishments dotted around the city. Opened by Jewish immigrants, their speciality is **smoked meat**, served between huge chunks of rye bread with pickles on the side. Another Montréal speciality is **poutine**, fries smothered in gravy and cheese curds, generally served in diners and snack joints (see page 225). Montréal comes a close second to New York as the **bagel** capital of the world; they're sold everywhere. Montréal's coffee scene has always been robust, but a new wave of **coffee shops** is bringing even more innovative variety to the caffeinated city. The city has also long embraced the concept of *apportez votre vin* ("bring your own wine"), with a wide variety of lively "BYOW" restaurants.

CAFÉS, BAKERIES, DELIS AND DINERS

Beautys 93 av du Mont-Royal ouest ☎ 514 849 8883, ⊛ beautys.ca; Métro: Mont-Royal; map p.210. A beloved diner with wonderful 1950s decor – and delicious breakfasts, including the dizzyingly rich Mish-Mashan omelette studded with salami and hot dog; and the Beautys Bonjoura bagel heaped with egg, bacon and Cheddar cheese. Get up early at the weekend to avoid the queue. Mains $7–$15. Mon–Fri 7am–3pm, Sat & Sun 8am–4pm.

★ **Café Myriade** 1432 rue Mackay, ☎ 514 939 1717, ⊛ cafemyriade.com; Métro: Guy-Concordia; map p.204. Helmed by top baristas, this is a place for seriously good coffee, including ink black espressos and single-origin filtered coffees ($3–7), along with croissants, tarts and other freshly baked goods ($4–9) from Québécois purveyors. Two other locations, in Mile End and Vieux-Montréal. Mon–Fri 7.30am–7pm, Sat & Sun 9am–7pm.

Café Santropol 3990 rue St-Urbain ☎ 514 842 3110, ⊛ santropol.com; Métro: Sherbrooke or Mont-Royal; map p.210. Feast on big sandwiches – including such tasty vegetarian concoctions as the CBLT (coconut bacon, tomatoes, lettuce) – salads, and home-made vegetarian chilli, as well as various herbal teas and excellent organic coffees. In the summer its blooming back terrace is a welcome oasis from the busy streets, while the atrium is cosy in winter. Mains $10–18. Daily 11am–10pm.

Fairmount Bagel Bakery 74 av Fairmount ouest ☎ 514 272 0667, ⊛ fairmountbagel.com; Métro: Laurier; map p.210. Possibly the best bagel outlet in Montréal, with over twenty varieties. There is nowhere to sit, but grab a bag of bagels, a pot of cream cheese and some smoked salmon and perch on the nearest kerb. Bagels $3–9. Open 24hr.

La Binerie Mont-Royal 367 av du Mont-Royal est ☎ 514 285 9078, ⊛ labineriemontroyal.com; Métro: Mont-Royal; map p.210. This Montréal institution first opened in 1938, and with just a few tables and a chrome counter, not much has changed – including the menu. Feast on beans, beans and more beans with ketchup, vinegar and maple syrup. Also served is *tourtière* (a minced pork pie) and *pouding chômeur* ("unemployed pudding"), a variation on bread pudding. Mains $8–15. Tues–Wed 6am–2pm, Thurs–Fri 6am–2pm & 5pm–8pm, Sat 7.30–3pm & 5–8pm, Sun 7.30am–3pm.

Olive et Gourmando 351 rue St-Paul ☎ 514 350 1083, ⊕ oliveetgourmando.com; Métro: Square-Victoria; map p.196. The smell of fresh baguettes greets you at this delightful café-bakery. Cosy up at a wooden table and enjoy homemade ricotta with honey and orange zest, and sandwiches like the Cajun chicken, with mango and homemade guacamole. Mains $10–15. Mon–Fri 8am–5pm, Sat–Sun 8am–6pm.

Reuben's Deli 1116 rue Ste-Catherine ouest ☎ 514 866 1029; Métro: McGill or Peel; map p.204. Dine on smoked meats, tasty fries and barbecue short rib poutine at this casual deli that gets packed at lunch. Mains $10–18. Sun–Thurs 8am–midnight, Fri–Sat 8am–1.30am.

Schwartz's 3895 blvd St-Laurent ☎ 514 842 4813, ⊕ schwartzsdeli.com; Métro: Sherbrooke; map p.210. A Montréal institution: a small, narrow deli serving up colossal smoked-meat sandwiches, with sometimes surly service thrown in as part of the package. All sorts of stars have dined here, from Céline Dion to the Rolling Stones. Sandwiches and mains $7–17. Line up out the door at weekends. Mon & Thurs–Sun 8am–12.30am, Fri 8am–1.30am, Sat 8am–2.30am.

St-Viateur Bagel & Café 1127 av Mont-Royal est ☎ 514 276 8044, ⊕ stviateurbagel.com; Métro: Mont-Royal; map p.210. If a bagel war broke out, it would come down to *Fairmount* (see page 220) versus *St-Viateur*, which is also known to have the choicest bagels in town. The original bakery is in Mile End, but this is where you can sit and enjoy the hand-rolled, baked wonders. Bagels and mains $4–12. Daily 6am–11pm.

Wilensky's Light Lunch 34 av Fairmount ouest ☎ 514 271 0247, ⊕ wilenskys.com; Métro: Laurier; map p.210. Used for countless film sets because the decor hasn't changed since 1932 – and that includes the till, grill and drinks machine. The Wilensky Special, which the *Montréal Gazette* declared a local icon, includes bologna and three types of salami and costs around $4. Plus, sink your teeth into hot dogs with Swiss cheese or a chopped-egg sandwich and top off the meal with an egg-cream soda. Mains $4–10. Mon–Fri 9am–4pm, Sat 10am–4pm.

RESTAURANTS

VIEUX-MONTRÉAL

Boris Bistro 495 rue McGill ☎ 514 848 9575, ⊕ borisbistro.com; Métro: Square-Victoria; map p.196. Locals flock to this large, bustling outdoor terrace – one of the most inviting in the downtown area. The menu ranges from steak tartare to grilled trout with caramelized walnuts, plus don't miss the signature duck-fat fries, along with

a fine list of wines. Mains $20–24. Summer Mon–Fri 11.30am–11pm, Sat & Sun noon–11pm; winter Mon–Fri 11.30am–2pm, Tues–Fri 5–11pm, Sat 6–11pm.

Chez Delmo 275 rue Notre-Dame ouest ☎ 514 288 4288, ⊕ chezdelmo.com; Métro: place-d'Armes; map p.196. Montréalers of a certain age used to go on date nights at *Chez Delmo*. Now a new generation is flirting over the grilled scallops. The seafood palace, which first opened in 1932, reopened in 2011 after a glamorous renovation – and the addition of an eye-catching mural splashed on the back wall that was inspired by the restaurant's original frieze. Try the famous tomato soup and Atlantic salmon, and then order a cocktail at the bar, where you can sit on the original bar stools, each printed with the name of a longtime regular. Mains $19–35. Mon–Fri 11.45am–3pm & 5.30–10pm, Sat 5.30pm–midnight.

★ **Club Chasse et Pêche** 423 rue St-Claude ☎ 514 861 11122, ⊕ leclubchasseetpeche.com; Métro: Champ-de-Mars; map p.196. The name – "Hunting and Fishing Club" – is quaintly rural; the food is anything but. One of Canada's top restaurants, with a seasonally changing menu that may include venison with polenta and aged Cheddar and rabbit ravioli. The setting is handsome and clubby, with leather chairs, dark wood and animal-inspired lighting. Tues–Sat 6–10.30pm

Garde Manger 408 rue St-Francois-Xavier ☎ 514 678 5044, ⊕ crownsalts.com/gardemanger; Métro: Square-Victoria; map p.196. A festive, familial atmosphere fills this popular restaurant helmed by celebrity chef Chuck Hughes. Seafood is the speciality – try the lobster *poutine* – but equal care is given to the braised short ribs. Lively tunes, a bustling bar and a cocktail-fuelled crowd make for one of the more vibrant, if crowded, dining spots in Vieux-Montréal. Mains $25–40. Tues–Sun 5.30–11.30pm.

Le Bremner 361 Saint-Paul E ☎ 514 544 0446, ⊕ crownsalts.com; Métro: Champ-de-Mars; map p.196. Chef Chuck Hughes (a popular TV personality, and owner of Garde Manger – see above) injects Vieux Montréal with his edgy comfort food at this brick-walled French-Canadian bistro. Mains $18–35. Mon–Sat 5.30–11pm.

Le Local 740 rue William ☎ 514 397 7737, ⊕ resto-lelocal.com; Métro: Square-Victoria; map p.196. The hipness quotient is high at this lively restaurant with a rustic-industrial interior. Sit amid artfully angled glass and steel and enjoy locally sourced dishes like duck breast with carrots and figs to halibut with blood orange. Mains $29–33. Mon–Fri & Sun 11.30am–10pm, Sat–Sun 5.30pm–11pm; hours may vary; call ahead.

Le Serpent 257 rue Prince ☎ 514 316 4666, ⊕ leserpent. ca; Métro: Square-Victoria; map p.196. The soaring setting with massive windows and striking monochrome decor rivals the grandly presented Italian-inspired dishes, which include rabbit tart with porcini foam and smoked gouda; oysters and maple mignonette; and lobster risotto

3

3

with yellow beets and mascarpone. Mains $17–32. Mon & Wed–Sat 6–11pm, Tues 11.30am–2pm.

★ **Tapas 24** 420 rue Notre-Dame ouest ☎ 514 849 4424, ⓦ tapas24.ca; Métro: Square-Victoria; map p.196. Light-filled, rollicking tapas joint. The Catalan chef produces superbly authentic dishes ($6–22) with a Québécois twist: try fried eggplant with maple syrup; clams, artichokes, and Iberian ham; or suckling pig with seasonal mushrooms. The wine list shows off the best of Spain. Mon–Wed 5pm–11pm, Thurs–Fri 11.30am–2.30pm & 5–11pm, Sat 5–11pm.

Toqué! 900 place Jean-Paul-Riopelle ☎ 514 499 2084, ⓦ restaurant-toque.com; Métro: Square-Victoria; map p.196. Renowned chef Normand Laprise holds court here and the dining experience is ultra chic and unforgettable – if you can get a seat. Call far ahead to book – it's worth it; this is the restaurant that pushed Montréal to the top of the culinary ranks. Innovative dishes include a starter of a venison carpaccio with goats cheese followed by a main dish of suckling pig with squash gnocchi. Mains $48–58. Tues–Fri 11.30am–1.45pm & 5.30–10pm, Sat 5.30–10.30pm.

DOWNTOWN

★ **Bouillon Bilk** 1595 blvd St-Laurent ☎ 514 845 1595, ⓦ bouillonbilk.com; Métro: St-Laurent; map p.204. "Dish after dish is a knockout," gushed the *Montréal Gazette* about *Bouillon Bilk*, where the eclectic French-inspired cuisine includes guinea fowl with pistachios and duck with celery root and hazelnuts. The minimalist setting is a quiet contrast to the creativity bursting from the plates. Mains $28–36. Mon–Fri 11.30am–2.30pm & 5.30–11pm, Sat & Sun 5.30–11pm.

Maison Boulud 1228 rue Sherbrooke ouest ☎ 514 842 4224, ⓦ maisonboulud.com; Métro: Peel; map p.204. Chef Daniel Boulud may have made his name in New York City, but his cuisine – and star power – translates beautifully to Montréal, especially amid the regal home of the renovated *Ritz-Carlton* (see page 207). The cuisine – French, with a Québécois style and New York twist – includes dishes such as veal with asparagus and lemon saffron clams with linguine. Mains $39–$42. Mon–Fri 7–10.30am, noon–2pm & 6–10.30pm, Sat & Sun 7–10.30am, noon–2.30pm & 6–10.30pm.

Ruby Rouge 1008 rue Clark ☎ 514 390 8828, ⓦ restaurantrubyrouge.com; Métro: place-d'Armes; map p.204. A temple to dim sum, right in the heart of Chinatown. Try everything from shrimp and cashews to stir-fried snow peas. Mains $8–17. Daily 8.30am–11pm.

Taverne F 1485 rue Jeanne-Mance ☎ 514 289 4558, ⓦ tavernef.ca; Métro: place-des-Arts; map p.204. Well-known Portuguese chef Carlos Ferreira, who runs the longtime and popular restaurant *Ferreira Café* on rue

Peel, has opened this bustling trattoria in the Quartier des Spectacles. In the summer, join the crowds outside and dig into dishes like grilled shrimp with garlic and brandy; sardines with *fleur de sel*; and a dessert of chocolate and orange ganache. Mains $27–29. Mon–Wed 11.30am–2.30pm & 5–10pm, Thurs–Sat 11.30am–2.30pm & 5–10.30pm.

Tiradito 1076 rue de Bleury ☎ 514 866 6776, ⓦ tiraditomtl.com; Métro: place-d'Armes; map p.204. This smashing restaurant is bringing heat, flavor and culinary sass to downtown Montréal. The exciting small-plates menu is rooted in Nikkei – Japanese-Peruvuian fare – and includes octopus anticucho with panka peppers, Peruvian ramen and the excellent Butifarra Sandwich, with duck breast and salsa criolla. The setting and ambiance is equally unique: Seats encircle a large kitchen in the centre of the high-ceilinged dining room, which gives it both a communal and intimate feel. Note: For now, the restaurant is not open to minors due to the fact that it is legally only a bar. Dishes $8–$18. Wed–Fri 11.30am–2pm & 5–11pm, Sat–Tues 5–11pm.

PLATEAU MONT-ROYAL

Au Pied de Cochon 536 av Duluth est ☎ 514 281 1114, ⓦ aupieddecochon.ca; Métro: Mont-Royal or Sherbrooke; map p.210. What happens when you tamper with a national dish? If you're chef Martin Picard, it makes you into a household name – and inspires dozens of copycats. Picard, whose approach to Québécois cuisine is as playful as his hair, famously added foie gras to *poutine* – *quelle scandale!* – at his breakout restaurant. Since then, he has continued to challenge the norm, with a robustly meat-centric menu, which includes juicy pork chops, ribs, duck and *foie gras* served a dozen different waysand, of course, stuffed pig's feet (*pieds de cochon*). Mains $17–33. Experience Picard's cuisine in the woods at this sugar shack (see page 230). Wed–Sun 5pm–midnight.

★ **La Banquise** 994 rue Rachel Est, Plateau Mont-Royal ⓦ labanquise.com; Métro: Mont-Royal; map p.210. This shrine to *poutine* – Québec's earthy, folksy culinary symbol – was opened by local fireman Pierre Barsalou in 1968 as an ice-cream shop, and soon became a 24hr snack bar serving hot dogs and "legendary fries". *Poutine* first graced the menu in the early 1980s and there are now thirty different varieties ($7–17) – from classic *poutine* to La Hot-Dog to La Reggae (with ground beef, guacamole, diced tomatoes and hot peppers) – with the place now run by Barsalou's youngest daughter, Annie. Daily 24hr.

Le Filet 219 av du Mont-Royal ouest ☎ 514 360 6060, ⓦ lefilet.ca; Métro: Mont-Royal; map p.210. The chefs at this sleek seafood restaurant wisely let the fresh fish and shellfish shine on their own merits, with minimal but

3

well-selected garnishes: try the octopus with pepper and chorizo, cold corn soup with oysters and local lamb with tomato jam. Enjoy views of the nearby Parc Jeanne-Mance, with Mont Royal looming beyond. Mains $18–30. Tues–Fri 5.45–10.30pm, Sat 5.30–10.30pm.

Le Jardin de Panos 521 av Duluth est ☎514 521 4206; Métro: Sherbrooke or Mont-Royal; map p.210. Beats out the numerous cheap Greek *brochetteries* on rue Prince Arthur in taste and has a garden to boot. An average meal will cost $20–35. Bring your own wine. Sun–Thurs 11.30am–10.30pm, Fri–Sat 11.30am–11pm

Maestro SVP 3615 blvd St-Laurent ☎514 842 6447, ⓦmaestrosvp.com; Métro: Sherbrooke; map p.210. This is the place for oysters, with over sixty varieties served in myriad ways. Try them fresh, baked or in a shooter with vodka and horseradish sauce for a quick kick. Oysters are $12 for a pair, or go for magnificent seafood platters (from $65), heaped with snow crab, black tiger shrimp, calamari and, of course, oysters. Mon–Wed & Sun 4–10pm, Thurs–Sat 4–11pm.

Maison Publique 4720 rue Marquette ☎514 507 0555, ⓦmaisonpublique.com; Métro: Laurier; map p.210. The best of several worlds meet in this wildly popular restaurant helmed by local chef Derek Dammann (and backed by Jamie Oliver). The food is British gastropub – Welsh rarebit, baked oysters, roasted root vegetables – the wine list is Canadian, the microbrews are Québécois and the atmosphere is fully Montréal – warm, casual, quirky. Brunch fans: this is the place, with comfort food like pancakes and bacon or a full English breakfast (blood pudding, sausages, baked beans). Mains $15-30. Wed–Fri 6–10.30pm, Sat–Sun 10.30am–2pm & 6–10.30pm.

Milos 5357 av du Parc ☎514 272 3522, ⓦmilos.ca; Métro: Laurier; map p.210. Feast on halibut with olive oil and juicy lamb chops with roasted potatoes at this warm, fine-dining Greek restaurant. Mains $27–46. For a great deal, come by for the late-night prix-fixe menus (Thurs–Sat; around $25) served after 10pm. Mon–Fri noon–3pm & 5.30pm–midnight, Sat 5.30pm–midnight, Sun 5.30–11pm.

Moishes 3961 blvd St-Laurent ☎514 845 3509, ⓦmoishes.ca; Métro: Sherbrooke; map p.210. Since 1938, this favourite haunt of Montréal's business community has been slinging excellent (and huge) steaks, upwards of $30. Stop by for its After 9 + Wine menu (Wed–Sun, 9pm–midnight), which offers a starter, main dish and coffee/tea for $29. The wine list features robust, top-notch wines. Mon–Tues 5.30–10pm, Wed–Fri 5.30pm–midnight, Sat 5pm–midnight, Sun 5–10pm.

Patati Patata 4177 blvd St-Laurent ☎514 844 0216; Métro: Mont-Royal; map p.210. With only enough room for a dozen people, this tiny spot serves excellent and cheap home-made food. The *poutine* – among the best in Montréal – is well worth a try. Mon–Fri 9am–11pm, Sat & Sun 11am–11pm.

Soy 5258 blvd St-Laurent ☎514 499 9399, ⓦrestaurant soy.com; Métro: St-Laurent; map p.210. Sample your way through a tasty Chinese menu, from pan-fried BBQ duck dumplings to crispy tofu with a ginger-teriyaki sauce to juicy Szechwan duck. Main dishes at lunch are $11–14, and at dinner $22–25. Mon–Fri 11.30am–11pm, Sat 5–11pm, Sun 5–10pm.

★**Vin Mon Lapin** 150 rue Saint-Zoutique E (no phone), ⓦvinmonlapin.com; map p.210. The *Joe Beef* (see page 225) magic now extends to Little Italy: In 2018, this vivacious wine bar opened, unveiling innovative small plates that live up to the famous Joe Beef culinary creativity. The ever-changing seasonal menu might include fried oysters, snails with salami and, of course, *lapin* (rabbit). Dishes $7–25. Tues–Sat 5pm–midnight.

QUARTIER LATIN AND THE VILLAGE

O'Thym 1112 blvd de Maisonneuve est ☎512 525 3443, ⓦothym.com; map p.212. It's BYOB at this spirited restaurant serving classic-with-an-edge French cuisine, from lobster mushroom rolls with crunchy homemade pickles to duck in a sea buckthorn sauce. Try the crème brûlée with maple liquor for dessert. Mon–Fri 5.30pm–11pm, Sat–Sun 10am–2pm & 5.30–11pm.

Le Resto du Village 1310 rue Wolfe, just off rue Ste-Catherine ☎514 524 5404; Métro: Beaudry; map p.212. This small diner serves filling comfort food that's perfect after a night at the bars, like fat burgers, spaghetti with meat sauce and *poutine* for under $20. Popular with the LGBTQ crowd. Open 24hr.

MILE END AND OUTREMONT

Leméac 1045 av Laurier ouest ☎514 270 0999, ⓦrestaurantlemeac.com; Métro: Laurier; map p.210. Of Montréal's plentiful top-notch French restaurants, *Leméac* is one of the finest – as much for the classic food as for the classic ambience. Try the duck confit with fingerling potatoes, and Icelandic cod with fennel. The desserts are deservedly popular, including a chocolate tart with ginger ice cream and *pain perdu* (French for "lost bread," because it was once a method to make old bread palatable), which is a sumptuously thick slice of French bread drizzled in maple caramel. A particularly good deal is the late-night menu (daily after 10pm), which includes a starter and main dish for $28. Mains $22–39; desserts $8–14. Mon–Fri noon–midnight, Sat & Sun 10am–midnight.

Montréal Plaza 6230 St-Hubert ☎514 903 6230, ⓦmontrealplaza.com; Métro: Beaubien; map p.210. "Innovative" is putting it mildly at this lively restaurant in Plaza St-Hubert, with a bold, whimsical menu by Charles-Antoine Crête and partner Sheryl Johnson (both formerly of the esteemed *Toqué*). The locavore bistro cuisine includes delights like whelk *gratinée* with miso butter, *cavatelli* with silky foie gras, venison hearts and fried Brussels sprouts. Splurge on the tasting menu (from $80), which is the perfect way to sample the kitchen's culinary riches. Daily 5pm–11pm.

RESTAURANT PICKS

TOP 5 LOCAL AND QUÉBÉCOIS CUISINE
Au Pied de Cochon See page 222
Vin Mon Lapin See page 224
La Banquise (for the poutine) See page 222
Schwartz's See page 221
Leméac See page 224

TOP 5 FOR CARNIVORES
Le Fantôme See below
Au Pied de Cochon See page 222

Moishes See page 224
Joe Beef See below
Reuben's Deli See page 221

TOP 5 FOR SEAFOOD
Chez Delmo See page 221
Le Filet page 222
Maestro SVP See page 224
Riverain at Ripplecove Lakefront Hotel See page 238
Tiradito See page 222

GRIFFINTOWN

Joe Beef 2491 rue Notre-Dame ouest ☎514 931 3999, ⓦjoebeef.ca; Métro: Lionel-Groulx; map p.196. The daily changing specials are scrawled on a blackboard at this popular Griffintown bistro named after Charles "Joe-Beef" McKiernan, a nineteenth-century innkeeper and a Montréal "working class hero". The chefs take advantage of the nearby Atwater Market to compose their simple but inspired dishes, from Prince Edward Island oysters to juicy steak with bone marrow. Mains $23–45. Tues–Sat 5.30–10.30pm.

★ **Le Fantôme** 1832 rue William ☎514 846 1832, ⓦrestofantome.ca; Métro: Lucien l'Allier; map p.196. Some restaurants are showered with accolades right out of the gate, which was the case with this delightful Griffintown restaurant. Amid flickering candles, dine on a menu that is equal parts playful and masterful, like the signature peanut butter, jelly and foie gras toasted sandwich. The ever-changing tasting menu (from $65) features seasonal greatest hits, and might include beef tartare with pink garlic, and tender duck breast. Tues–Sun 6–8pm.

Le Vin Papillon 2519 rue Notre-Dame oust; no phone, ⓦvinpapillon.com; Métro: Lionel-Groulx; map p.196. The *Joe Beef* team has triumphed again with the charming *Le Vin Papillon*, which was born as a wine bar and has since expanded into a full restaurant. The innovative menu celebrates vegetable-focused small plates, like tender roast cauliflower, delicately fried courgette flowers and ricotta cheese and anchovies. The wine list spans the globe, from France to Croatia and beyond. Small plates $8–19. Tues–Sat 3pm–midnight.

DRINKING AND NIGHTLIFE

Montréal has elevated *joie de vivre* to a high art – and nowhere more so than at the bars and clubs. The city's **nightlife** keeps going strong into the small hours of the morning – **bars** are generally open until 3am. One of the liveliest after-dark areas is the bar-packed **Plateau**. Cutting a wide swath through the Plateau – and into the adjacent neighbourhood of Mile-End – is **blvd St-Laurent**, lined on both sides with an eclectic array of nightspots, from sleek lounges to dive bars. **Downtown**, the action centres on rue Crescent, while **Vieux-Montréal** is increasingly buzzing with new hotel lounges, restaurant-bars and breezy terraces. Also popular are the student-packed **Quartier Latin** bars and the nearby **Village**, heart of the gay scene (see page 226). **Griffintown** (see page 202) is also establishing itself as an after-dark hangout, with an array of hip bars. For up-to-date listings, check out the English-language daily *Montréal Gazette* (ⓦmontrealgazette.com).

BARS

★ **Atwater Cocktail Club** 512 av Atwater ☎438 387 4252, ⓦatwatercocktailclub.com; Métro: Lionel-Groulx; map p.196. Scoot up to the elegant marble bar and indulge in inventive cocktails at this low-lit place in St-Henri. The changing drinks list incorporates seasonal flavours; try Patagonia Secret, made with ginger beer, Luxardo Fernet, lime and maté. Daily 5pm–3am.

Barfly 4062 blvd St-Laurent ☎514 284 6665; Métro: St-Laurent; map p.210. The epitome of a dive bar, which is precisely why everyone loves it. Local bands – from punk to blues to rockabilly – nearly every night of the week. Daily 4pm–3am.

Bar Henrietta 115 av Laurier oust ☎514 276 4282, ⓦbarhenrietta.com; Métro: Laurier; map p.210. Kick off the night at this spirited, low-lit Portuguese tavern, filled with lots of dark and amber woods, a top-notch menu of Mediterranean wine and cava and colourful cocktails. The bonus is a tasty array of small plates, which are perfect for soaking up the alcohol. A highlight is the Manchego popcorn, tuna and swordfish ceviche, chorizo in a romesco sauce and Portugal's famous dessert, a delectable pasteis de nata. Daily 4.30pm–midnight.

Bily Kun 354 av du Mont-Royal est ☎514 845 5392, ⓦbilykun.com; Métro: Mont-Royal; map p.210. Youthful, packed brasserie-pub, with stuffed ostrich heads overlooking tables and booths. A great world beer selection,

3

LGBTQ MONTRÉAL

Montréal has an excellent **LGBTQ** scene, with the action concentrated in the area known as **The Village** – roughly located on rue Ste-Catherine est between rue Amherst and the Papineau Métro station. *Fugues* (ⓦ fugues.com) is one of the city's main monthly French gay and lesbian magazines and websites. In early August, **Divers Cité** (ⓦ diverscite.org), the gay and lesbian pride parade, is the event of the year, while in October the massive **Black & Blue** circuit party (ⓦ bbcm.org) is one of the city's – if not Canada's – biggest and wildest gay parties.

Most of the **restaurants** and hangouts in The Village cater to an LGBTQ crowd in the evening, but are more mixed during the day.

BARS, CLUBS AND DISCOS

Cabaret Mado 1115 rue Ste-Catherine est ☎ 514 525 7566, ⓦ mado.qc.ca; Métro: Beaudry; map p.212. Local drag celebrity Mado and her cohorts camp it up for a mixed, fun-loving clientele, who inevitably end up partying the night away on the huge dancefloor. Entry starts around $5–10. Shows generally nightly starting around 10pm.

Complexe Sky 1474 rue Ste-Catherine est ☎ 514 529 6969, ⓦ complexesky.com; Métro: Beaudry; map p.212. The choice is yours at this glamorous after-dark complex: drink cocktails under the stars on the roof terrace, hit the unfailingly pounding dancefloor or sing along to drag cabaret. Nightly from 4pm until

close (between 1am–3am); most shows from 11pm onwards.

Notre-Dame des Quilles 32 rue Beaubien ☎ 514 507 1313; Métro: Rosemont; map p.210. Friendly little joint that draws a mixed crowd with its jaunty tunes, miniature bowling, Mac and cheese, karaoke nights. Mon–Wed & Sun 3pm–1am, Thurs–Sat 3pm–3am.

Unity 1171 rue Ste-Catherine est ☎ 514 523 2777, ⓦ clubunitymontreal.com; Métro: Beaudry; map p.212. A young, mixed and outgoing crowd fills the large dancefloor – and when it gets too hot, head to the rooftop terrace to cool off and take in an unforgettable view of the city. Generally open Fri & Sat 10pm–3am, but sometimes open other nights for special events.

plus DJs and occasional live bands, from jazz to funk to classical quartets. Daily 3pm–3am.

Blizzarts 3956A blvd St-Laurent ☎ 514 843 4860, ⓦ blizzarts.ca; Métro: Mont-Royal; map p.210. Funked-out lounge-bar with retro furnishings, colourful lighting and a tiny dancefloor. Potent, creative cocktails include such fun inventions as rye and rootbeer and bison grass vodka with a splash of apple flavour. Daily 9.30pm–3am; hours may vary.

Brutopia 1219 rue Crescent ☎ 514 393 9277, ⓦ brutopia.net; Métro: Lucien-L'Allier; map p.204. This welcoming pub is spread over three floors, with a terrace and balcony. Exotic beers – from chocolate stout to honey wheat – are brewed on-site in the copper drums behind the bar. Live bands most nights as well as lively open-mic nights and happy hour tiriva. Mon–Thurs, Sat & Sun 5pm–3am, Fri noon–3am.

Burgundy Lion 2496 rue Notre-Dame ouest ☎ 514 934 0888, ⓦ burgundylion.com; Métro: Lionel-Groulx; map p.196. It may call itself a pub – but it's funkier than that. The casual icon of the emerging Little Burgundy neighbourhood has a British sensibility – as interpreted by hipster Montréalers. Yes, there are darts, dark beer and sports on the telly, but also resident DJs, banquettes and even high tea, served on Sundays with a reservation. Also has one of the largest whisky collections in Québec, with four hundred varieties. Mon–Fri 11.30am–3am, Sat & Sun 9am–3am.

Coldroom 155 Saint-Paul E ☎ 514 294 6911, ⓦ the coldroommtl.com; Métro: Champ-de-Mars; map p.196. This smooth cocktail bar lives inside a former industrial coldroom from 1877. Cozy up on the leather sofas, surrounded by brick walls and gilded mirrors, and sample your way through the inventive cocktails, such as Duck, made with dark rum, amaretto, angostura bitters and duck fat. A tiny new addition opened in 2018: the adorable, Cuban-themed *El Pequeño* bar, which seats just nine, and is accessible via a door in the *Coldroom*. Daily 5pm–3pm.

Isle de Garde 1039 rue Beaubien est ☎ 514 831 0181; Métro: Jean-Talon; map p.210. This cosy bar pours a wonderful array of suds, from Berliner Melon Weisse (from Dunham, Québec) to dry, tart ciders to the house-made Isle de Garde Brown Porter Ale. Mon–Wed 3.30pm–1.30am, Thurs & Fri 11.30am–3am, Sat 1pm–3am, Sun 1–11.30pm.

La Distillerie 300 rue Ontario est ☎ 514 288 7915, ⓦ pubdistillerie.com; Métro: Berri-UQAM; map p.204. Drink innovative cocktails – many made with seasonal ingredients – from mason jars at this trendy but welcoming bar. Get here early – or be prepared to wait in line. There's *Distillerie 2* in the Plateau, and *Distillerie 3* in Rosemont. Daily 4pm–3am.

Le Mal Nécessaire 1106B blvd St-Laurent ☎ 514 439 91991, ⓦ lemalnecessaire; Métro: Champ-de-Mars; map p.204. A subterranean tiki bar incongruously located in Chinatown (look for the glowing green pineapple), this laidback hipster joint channels old-school Hawaii, serving fruity drinks to a funky hip-hop and house soundtrack. Tues & Sun 6pm–2am, Wed 4.30pm–2am, Thurs & Fri 4.30pm–3am, Sat 6pm–3am.

Pandore 1300 rue Ste-Dominique ☎514 439 4451, ⓦpandore.ca; Métro: St-Laurent; map p.212. This lively nightspot in the Quartier des Spectacles' sleek 2-22 building (see page 209) offers multiple experiences: from a low-lit cocktail lounge to a breezy terrasse to various stages showcasing everything from burlesque to jazz. Thurs 5pm–3am, Fri 6pm–3am, Sat 7pm–3am.

★**Pullman** 3424 av du Parc ☎514 288 7779, ⓦpullman-mtl.com; Métro: place-des-Arts; map p.204. Much like the premium wine it pours, this bar hits all the right notes: warm, elegant, casual. The innovative interior matches the superb international wine selection, with a wine-glass chandelier, rich woods and industrial-chic exposed concrete walls. Among the vast wine repertoire, you'll find some Québécois vintages; it can be challenging to find local wines at the bars, so this is a good place to sample them. Sun–Tues 4.30pm–midnight, Wed–Sat 4.30pm–midnight.

Whisky Café 5800 blvd St-Laurent ☎514 278 2646, ⓦwhiskycafe.ca; Métro: Outremont; map p.210. Sleek lounge where the top-shelf liquor includes over 150 Scotch whiskies. The next-door cigar lounge is one of the few spots where you can light up. Mon–Wed 5pm–1am, Thurs & Fri 5pm–3am, Sat 6pm–3am, Sun 7pm–1am.

CLUBS AND MUSIC VENUES

2 Pierrots 104 rue St-Paul est ☎514 861 1270, ⓦ2spierrots.com; Métro: Champ-de-Mars; map p.196. Québécois folk singers are the mainstay of this club (especially on Fri & Sat) and everyone sings along. Other fun nights include karaoke with a live band. The atmosphere is fun and friendly,, and the pitchers of beer flow freely. Outside terrace in the summer. Daily 8.30pm–3am.

Bistro à Jojo 1627 rue St-Denis ☎514 843 5015, ⓦbistroajojo.com; Métro: Berri-UQAM; map p.212. This longtime joint calls itself the "Blues Temple of Montréal" – and it's an apt title. Since 1975, this low-lit, unpretentious spot has been serving up nightly blues shows. Daily 1pm–3am.

Casa del Popolo 4873 blvd St-Laurent ☎514 284 3804, ⓦcasadelpopolo.com; Métro: Laurier; map p.210. "The House of the People" is a sofa-strewn, low-key Plateau spot with high-calibre spoken-word evenings, folk, rock and other concerts and events. It also has lively DJ nights and by day serves vegetarian soups and salads – try the goats cheese and red peppers with nachos – making it a mingle-worthy spot any time. Hours vary, but generally daily noon–3am.

Club Balattou 4372 blvd St-Laurent ☎514 845 5447, ⓦbalattou.com; Métro: St-Laurent; map p.210. This popular club heats up with live world music, from Africa to the Caribbean, most nights of the week. Tues–Sun 9pm–3am.

Club Soda 1225 blvd St-Laurent ☎ 514 286 1010, ⓦclubsoda.ca; Métro: St-Laurent; map p.204. Large live-music venue that attracts all the best acts and has reached almost legendary status in Montréal. The club also hosts Jazz Festival and Just for Laughs shows and events. Tickets from $15–20. Open nightly for shows, generally from 8pm until closing, though times vary.

Datcha 98 av Laurier oust ☎514 279 3555, ⓦbardatcha. com; Métro: Laurier; map p.210. This slender, sexily lit Russian-themed bar and club heats up with Euro techno and other dance tunes.Thurs–Sat 11pm–3am.

Les Foufounes Électriques 87 rue Ste-Catherine est ☎514 844 5539, ⓦfoufounes.qc.ca; Métro: St-Laurent; map p.204. A bizarre name ("The Electric Buttocks") for a wonderfully bizarre bar-club venue. Known as *Foufs*, it's the best place in Québec for alternative bands, attracting a crowd from ravers to punks. Huge outside terrace perfect for summer evenings, and pitchers of beer are cheap. Daily 3pm–3am.

Muzique 3781 blvd St-Laurent ☎514 282 2224, ⓦmuziquemontreal.com; Métro: St-Laurent; map p.210. The cool kids flock to this dance club which throbs with DJ-spun hip-hop, house and pop. Fri–Sun 10pm–3am.

Salsatheque 1220 rue Peel ☎514 875 0016, ⓦsalsatheque.com; Métro: Peel; map p.204. Leave your inhibitions at the door: *Salsatheque* sizzles with spirited revellers who come to dance, dance, dance to *"muy caliente"* Latino tunes. Wed–Sat 8/9pm–3am.

SPECTATOR SPORTS IN MONTRÉAL

Canadian football The Montréal Alouettes (ⓦmontrealalouettes.com) represent the city in the Canadian Football League (CFL). Home games are at McGill University's Percival Molson Stadium, 475 av des Pins ouest. On game days, a free shuttle operates to the stadium from the Square-Victoria and McGill Métro stations. Tickets start at $25.

Ice hockey The Montréal Canadiens (see page 46) play at the Centre Bell, 1250 rue de la Gauchetière ouest (Métro: Bonaventure). Tickets start at $25.

Soccer Montréal Impact (☎514 328 3669, ⓦmontrealimpact.com), the city's professional soccer team, play at the Saputo Stadium, 4750 Sherbrooke est (Métro: Viau). Tickets start at $10–15.

3

ENTERTAINMENT

Montréal's gleaming entertainment quarter, the **Quartier des Spectacles** (see page 209), is the hub of the city's performing arts scene. The world-famous **Cirque du Soleil** (ⓦ cirquedusoleil.com) is headquartered in Montréal, and though it doesn't feature a permanent show, the circus generally performs in late spring and early summer in the Vieux-Port, where it erects its famous blue-and-yellow tents. Montréal also has numerous excellent **dance** troupes, from **Les Grands Ballets Canadiens** (ⓦ grandsballets.qc.ca) and **Les Ballets Jazz de Montréal** (ⓦ bjmdanse.ca) to the avant-garde **La La La Human Steps** (ⓦ lalalahumansteps.com). For cinema check in the *Montréal Gazette* for show times; English films are indicated by **v.o.** (*version originale*), not v.f. (*version français*), which means it's dubbed.

Segal Centre for Performing Arts 5170 chemin de la Côte-Ste-Catherine ☎ 514 739 7944, ⓦ segalcentre. org; Métro: Côte-Ste-Catherine. This esteemed theatre features English (and Yiddish) music, dance, film and theatre.

Théâtre Rialto 5723 av du Parc ☎ 514 770 7773, ⓦ theatrerialto.ca; Métro: Laurier. This grand old theatre with a glorious Beaux Arts facade dates back to 1923–24, and is designated a National Historic Site of Canada. Revitalized in 2010, it now hosts varied programming throughout the year, from theatre to opera to concerts.

Théâtre St-Denis 1594 rue St-Denis ⓦ 514 849 4211, ⓦ theatrestdenis.com; Métro: Berri-UQAM. This eclectic venue presents everything from blockbuster musicals to big-name concerts to comedy shows.

THEATRE

Centaur Theatre 453 rue St-François-Xavier ☎ 514 288 3161, ⓦ centaurtheatre.com; Métro: place d'Armes. Montréal's main English-language theatre showcases a wide range of theatre, from the classics to contemporary.

Place des Arts Quartier des Spectacles. A massive complex with a comprehensive year-round programme of dance, music and theatre. The Orchestre Symphonique de Montréal (ⓦ osm.ca), Orchestre Métropolitain (ⓦ orchestremetropolitain.com) and L'Opéra de Montréal (ⓦ operademontreal.com) stage regular concerts here.

CINEMAS

Cinéma Parallèle 3536 blvd St-Laurent ⓦ cinema parallele.ca. Features a wide range of indie flicks.

Cinémathèque Québécoise 335 blvd de Maisonneuve est ⓦ cinematheque.qc.ca. Has excellent screening and exhibition programmes.

CineRobotheque 1564 rue St-Denis ⓦ nfb.ca. The main repertory cinema in English, run by the NFB (National Film Board).

DIRECTORY

Consulates UK, 1000 rue de la Gauchetière ouest (☎ 514 866 5863); US, 1155 rue St-Alexandre (☎ 514 398 9695); Germany, 1250 blvd René-Lévesque ouest, Suite 4315 (☎ 514 931 2277); for Australia, Ireland, New Zealand and South Africa, contact the embassy in Ottawa (see p.173).

Hospitals Central hospitals include the Montréal General Hospital, 1650 av Cedar, on the mountain's slope northwest of downtown (☎ 514 934 1934), and Royal Victoria Hospital, 687 av des Pins ouest, up the hill from McGill University (☎ 514 934 1934).

Weather and road conditions Environment Canada (☎ 514 283 3010, ⓦ weatheroffice.gc.ca) for weather and winter road conditions; Transports Québec (☎ 514 284 2363, ⓦ mtq.gouv.qc.ca) for roadworks.

Montebello and around

The small town of **MONTEBELLO**, 135km west of Montréal on the scenic Hwy-148, in the lush Outaouais region, has a distinctive claim to fame: the world's largest log building – the **Fairmont Le Château Montebello** (see page 229). The town was named after the grand estate of seigneur, politician and Rebellion leader Louis-Joseph Papineau, which abuts the Château. Montebello also draws plenty of holiday-makers, thanks to a resort-friendly atmosphere that includes horseriding and boating. The largely wilderness stretch of the Outaouais region begins around 130km west of Montréal and extends along the north side of the Rivière Outaouais (Ottawa River). Once the domain of Algonquin tribes, the region was not developed until the 1800s, when it became an important centre for the lumber industry. The bulk of the activities here are of an outdoorsy nature – hiking, snowmobiling, cycling and cross-country skiing.

THE BATTLE OF ST-EUSTACHE

In the early 1800s, British immigrants to Lower Canada were offered townships (cantons), while francophones were not allowed to expand their holdings, exacerbating the resentment caused by the favouritism extended to English-speaking businesses in Montréal. The situation was worsened by high taxes on British imports and a savage economic depression in 1837. Wearing Canadian-made garments of *étoffe du pays* as a protest against British imports, the leaders of Lower Canada reform – known as the **Patriotes** – rallied francophones to rebel in Montréal. As Louis-Joseph Papineau, the Outaouais region seigneur whose speeches in the Assembly had encouraged the rebellions, fled the city, fearful that his presence would incite more rioting, the government sent military detachments to the countryside, the hotbed of the Patriotes. Two hundred Patriotes took refuge in the church of **St-Eustache**, a town that lies about 35km west of Montréal. Eighty of them were killed by British troops, who went on to raze much of the town. The bloody rebellion became known as the **Battle of St-Eustache**, and the town's riverside historic centre, Vieux St-Eustache, still holds the scars of this tragic past. The church, **Église St-Eustache** (123 rue St-Louis; ☎ 450 974 5170), restored in 1841 after the battle, offers free guided tours (mid-June to mid-Aug: hours vary, but generally Tues–Fri 9.30am–4.30pm, Sun noon–4.30pm). St-Eustache can be reached by driving through the suburbs northwest of Montréal by Hwy-13 or 15, then southwest on Hwy-640.

Manoir Papineau National Historic Site

In the grounds of the *Fairmont Le Château Montebello* • **Estate** Mid-May to mid-June & early Sept to mid-Oct Fri–Sun 10am–5pm; mid-June to early Sept daily 10am–5pm • $7.80 • **Chapel** July & Aug Wed–Sun 10am–noon & 1–5pm • Free • ☎ 819 423 6965, Ⓦ pc.gc.ca/manoirpapineau

Papineau's tranquil estate, the **Manoir Papineau National Historic Site**, encompasses his manor house, chapel and granary over a sizeable tract of land. Exhibits explore Papineau's life and times, including displays of old photographs. Papineau and other family members are buried in the quiet chapel, which sits amid pine trees on the estate's forest. The Manoir also hosts a wide variety of events, including summer garden parties and culinary-themed walks.

INFORMATION   MONTEBELLO

Tourist office 502 rue Notre-Dame (late June to early Sept daily 9am–6pm; early Sept to late June Tues–Sat 9am–4pm; ☎ 819 423 5602, Ⓦ tourismeoutaouais.com).

ACCOMMODATION AND EATING

Fairmont Le Château Montebello 392 rue Notre-Dame ☎ 819 423 6341, ☎ 800 441 1414, Ⓦ fairmont.com/montebello. *The* place to spend a night in Montebello, it was built by the Seigneury Club in 1930 in just ninety days, and the original three buildings are made up of a whopping ten thousand red-cedar logs. Plenty of famous folks have stayed, from Canadian prime ministers to Harry S. Truman, Bing Crosby and Bette Davis. The hotel exudes a rustic-chic vibe, with handsome rooms and a large indoor pool. Even if you don't stay, it's worth coming by to check out the six-hearthed fireplace in the massive hexagonal lobby. The hotel offers several options for riverside meals, including locally sourced dishes at the stylish *Aux Chatignoles* restaurant (mains $20–30) or a cocktail at *Le Riverain Lounge*. **$343**

The Laurentians (Les Laurentides)

Looming mightily on the north side of the St Lawrence from the Ottawa River to the Saguenay River, the **Laurentians** are one of the world's oldest ranges. Five hundred million years of erosion have moulded a rippling landscape of undulating hills and valleys, and a vast sweep of coniferous forest dotted with hundreds of tranquil lakes and rivers. The most accessible stretch lies north of Montréal, even though settlement in the upper Laurentians did not begin until the 1830s, when the construction of the **P'tit Train du Nord** railway tracks let in the mining and lumber industries. When the

3

THE ULTIMATE SUGAR SHACK

The only thing better than dining on Martin Picard's celebrated food at Au Pied de Cochon in Montréal? Doing so amid the rustic wilderness. At the Cabane à Sucre Au Pied de Cochon (ⓦaupiedducochon.com), in St-Benoît de Mirabel (58km west of Montréal), Picard and his team dish out lavish feasts (from $65/person), built around maple syrup. The menu – which is influenced by Picard's travels – changes every season, and might include squid stuffed with pork, salmon mousse kefta and foie gras – all with lashings of maple syrup, of course. The Cabane à Sucre is open during sugar season (mid-Feb to early May) and the harvest (mid-Aug to end-Oct), Thursday to Friday for dinner, and Saturday to Sunday for lunch and dinner. Reservations are essential. Check the website for the date and time that reservations open – and pounce. Most are snapped up right away. In 2018, Picard introduced a romantic sibling to Cabane à Sucre, with the opening of La Cabane d'à Côté ($56/person; Wed–Sun 5pm–close, generally open year-round, except for a few months in winter), which sits next door ("à côté"), amid an apple and pear orchard. The menu is countrified Quebéçois with a twist – the requisite pea soup, for example, has chunks of bacon and foie gras.

---

decline in both industries left the area in a depression, salvation came in the form of the recreational demands of the growing populace of Montréal. The region is now one of North America's largest ski areas, helmed by the esteemed, stylish Mont-Tremblant, and the train tracks have been replaced by a terrific cycling trail. Even with the ski crowds, much of the land has remained relatively untouched – like the **Parc National du Mont-Tremblant** – and the area is a must-see when autumn colours arrive. Other than Tremblant – which is pricey – rates for **ski passes** are around $50 a day in the decent areas, a few dollars more at weekends.

ARRIVAL AND INFORMATION
THE LAURENTIANS

By bus Galland buses (ⓣ514 333 9555, ⓦautobusgalland. com) offers regular bus service from the Gare d'Autocars de Montréal to most of the main towns in the Laurentians, including Saint-Saveur (1hr) and Mont-Tremblant (3hr).

Tourist offices Exit 52, off Hwy-15 (daily 8.30am–5pm; in summer, sometimes open until 7 or 8pm; ⓣ450 224 7007, ⓣ800 561 6673, ⓦlaurentians.com). This regional office, Tourisme Laurentides, has information on everything from accommodation to ski conditions.

Saint-Sauveur-des-Monts

There's a good reason for the Laurentians' appeal to the Montréal vacationing crowds: the ski resorts start at just 60km from the city, an easy day- or weekend trip. The first of these is **SAINT-SAUVEUR-DES-MONTS**, with over 35 pistes in its immediate vicinity. The main drag, rue Principale, reflects the influx of visitors with restaurants of all stripes, as well as shops and boutiques.

INFORMATION
SAINT-SAUVEUR-DES-MONTS

Tourist office 30 Fillon St (daily 9am–5pm; ⓣ450 2272564, ⓣ877 528 2553, ⓦvalleesaintsauveur.com).

TOURISM INFORMATION FOR SOUTHWEST QUÉBEC

Eastern Townships ⓣ819 820 2020, ⓣ800 355 5755, ⓦeasterntownships.org.

Laurentides ⓣ450 436 8532, ⓣ800 561 6673, ⓦlaurentides.com.

Mauricie ⓣ819 536 3334, ⓣ800 567 7603, ⓦtourismemauricie.com.

Outaouais ⓣ819 778 2222, ⓣ800 265 7822, ⓦoutaouais-tourism.ca.

Association de l'Agrotourisme et du Tourisme Gourmand ⓦterroiretsaveurs.com. Québec's top-notch association of agritourism and food tourism features recommended accommodation, farm tours and more.

ACCOMMODATION AND EATING

Bistro St Sauveur 146 rue Principal ☏ 7450 227 1144, ⓦ bistrostsauveur.com. Simple French food, such as salmon poached in white wine, snails with garlic and duck confit., at this central, buzzy BYOW restaurant. Hours vary but generally daily 5–11pm.

Le Relais St-Denis 61 rue St-Denis ☏ 450 227 4766, ☏ 888 997 4766, ⓦ relaisstdenis.com. This friendly hotel, within strolling distance of the centre of town, has traditionally cosy rooms, an outdoor pool that is heated year-round and an inviting French restaurant. **$169**

Val-David

About 80km north of Montréal **VAL-DAVID** is the vaguely bohemian resort (its motto: "A world apart") of the Laurentians, favoured by artists and craftspeople. The main street, rue de l'Église, has galleries and shops, many run by the artisans themselves, and the village thrums with energy during the popular midsummer festival 1001 Pots (ⓦ 1001pots.com), which features ceramic workshops, creative classes for kids and plenty of crafts shopping. The **Centre d'exposition de Val-David** (2495 rue de l'Église; ☏ 819 322 7474, ⓦ culture. val-david.qc.ca; hours depend on temporary exhibits; free) features temporary exhibits, from painting to photography to sculpture, throughout the year. The town abounds with activities year-round, from skiing and snowboarding – check out the family-friendly Centre de Ski Vallée-Bleue (ⓦ vallee-bleue.com) – to hiking, rock climbing and pedalling along the justly popular P'tit Train du Nord bicycle path (see box).

ARRIVAL AND INFORMATION VAL-DAVID

By bus Galland buses (☏ 514 333 9555, ⓦ autobusgalland. com) offers regular bus service from the Gare d'Autocars de Montréal (1–2hr).

Tourist office 2525 rue de l'Église (daily 9am–5pm; ☏ 819 324 5678, ☏ 888 322 7030, ⓦ valdavid.com).

ACCOMMODATION

Le Chalet Beaumont 1451 rue Beaumont ☏ 819 322 1972, ⓦ chaletbeaumont.com. This massive chalet serves as Val-David's hostel, with both dorm and private rooms. Curl up by the fire in the winter and enjoy great outdoor views. They can also arrange for outdoor activities. Dorms **$26**; doubles from **$70**

La Maison de Bavière 1470 chemin de la Rivière ☏ 819 322 3528, ⓦ maisondebaviere.com. You can watch the river rapids from the fireplace-warmed sitting room in the winter or sit outside on the terrace and sip away on a glass of wine in the summer at this pleasant, small, Bavarian-themed B&B. It also has two studio apartments, with kitchen, for those interested in longer stays (from $160 per night). **$159**

EATING

Au Petit Poucet 1030 Hwy-117, just south of the village ☏ 819 322 2246, ⓦ aupetitpoucet.com. Fill up on home-made Québécois cuisine at this longtime favourite, from smoked ham to *tourtière* (a minced pork pie) to baked beans. Mains $15–30. Daily 6.30am–4pm.

THE P'TIT TRAIN DU NORD BICYCLE TRAIL

Québec is prime cycling territory, as wonderfully exemplified by the **Le P'tit Train du Nord** trail. This disused railway line, which once ferried Montréalers to the Laurentians' resorts, is now a major bicycle trail, running up to 230km, north from St-Jérôme to Mont-Laurier, with sweeping mountain vistas along the way. The route forms part of the superb **Route Verte** (Green Route; ⓦ routeverte.com), a nearly 2500km bike network that snakes its way across the province. Le P'tit Train du Nord's former rail stations have been renovated and now often house information centres, some with facilities such as showers and snack bars. In winter, the route is used by cross-country skiers who can explore numerous side-trails branching off into the hills between St-Jérôme and Val-David, and to snowmobilers. For more information, maps and a list of services (including cycle repair, baggage transport and accommodation), check out ⓦ laurentians.com/parclineaire, or visit the regional tourist office (see page 230).

Mont-Tremblant

MONT-TREMBLANT (ⓦtremblant.ca), some 130km north of Montréal, is the Laurentians' oldest and most renowned ski area. The impressive range is crowned by its highest peak, **Mont-Tremblant** (960m), so called because the indigenous population believed it was the home of spirits that could move the mountain. In the 1990s, the company that developed British Columbia's ski resort of Whistler (see page 726) pumped large amounts of money into Tremblant, and the resulting European-style ski village has made it a premier ski destination. The ski runs cater to all levels, with a maximum vertical drop of more than 650m and the longest ski run in Québec. One-day **ski passes** cost $82.

Mont-Tremblant comprises the ski resort itself plus the merged town of **St-Jovite**, the area's commercial centre (referred to as Centre-Ville Mont-Tremblant) and the pedestrian-only **Mont-Tremblant Village**, 10km north, which has the feel of a Québécois "toy village" and is dotted with ritzy boutiques, cute little walkways and après-ski bars. Around 5km northwest of the resort is an area that was once the town centre, which is often called the old village of Mont-Tremblant. The resort also hosts the excellent Mont Tremblant Snow School and a glitzy **Casino de Mont-Tremblant** (Mon–Wed & Sun 11am–1am, Thurs–Sat 11am–3am; ⓦcasinosduquebec.com/mont-tremblant), which you can reach by an aerial gondola or daily shuttle.

Parc National du Mont-Tremblant

North of Mont-Tremblant Village • Open year-round • $8.60; campgrounds from $30; must be reserved in advance • ☎ 819 688 2281, ☎ 800 665 6527, ⓦ sepaq.com

The **Parc National du Mont-Tremblant**, a large wilderness area that spreads northwards from the villages, is a favourite with the Québécois. Skiing, snowmobiling, snowshoeing and sledding are favoured winter sports; in summer the park attracts campers, canoeists, hunters and hikers – in remote areas you may see bear, deer and moose.

ARRIVAL AND INFORMATION
MONT-TREMBLANT

By bus Galland buses (☎ 514 333 9555, ⓦ autobusgalland. com) offers regular bus service from the Gare d'Autocars de Montréal (1hr).

Tourist office 48 chemin de Brébeuf, just off Hwy-117 as you enter St-Jovite (Centre-Ville Mont-Tremblant; daily 9am–5pm; ☎ 819 425 3300, ☎ 800 322 2932, ⓦ tourismemonttremblant.com). A second tourist office is further north at 5080 Montée Ryan (daily 9am–5pm; ☎ 819 425 2434, ⓦ tremblant.ca).

ACCOMMODATION

Auberge de Jeunesse International du Mont-Tremblant 2213 chemin du Village, old village of Mont-Tremblant ☎ 819 425 6008, ☎ 866 425 6008, ⓦ hostellingtremblant.com. An excellently kitted out hostel, with a café and bar, swimming in the lake behind the hostel, free canoe rental and organized treks and ski packages. Dorms $25, non-members $29; doubles $75, non-members $85

Ermitage du Lac 150 chemin du Cure-Deslauriers, Mont-Tremblant resort ☎ 819 681 2222, ☎ 800 461 8711, ⓦ tremblant.ca. One of the many options available in the resort itself, this pleasant hotel has spacious rooms and suites, each equipped with a kitchenette; some rooms also have a fireplace and balcony. There is an outdoor pool, and breakfast is included. $190

Fairmont Tremblant 3045 chemin de la Chapelle, Mont-Tremblant resort ☎ 819 681 7000, ☎ 800 441 1414, ⓦ fairmont.com/tremblant. One of the more glamorous choices in the area, by Lac Tremblant and facing the base of the mountain. Elegant, sunny rooms feature memorable views, and you can relax variously at the soothing spa, heated indoor and outdoor pool and whirlpools and outdoor terraces with lovely views Additionally, it has a fitness centre, ski rental, an excellent restaurant and a ski-in, ski-out lounge. $249

Quintessence Tremblant Sur le Lac 3004 chemin de la Chapelle ☎ 819 425 3400, ⓦ hotelquintessence. com. Nature and nurture come together splendidly in this all-suite boutique hotel: nature with the views of the glistening Lac Tremblant; nurture from the concierge who can arrange for ski lessons or personally deliver wood for your in-room fireplace, and from the heated marble floors in the bathroom. Indulge in further pampering at the Spa Sans Sabots or at the inviting wine bar. $295

EATING, DRINKING AND NIGHTLIFE

Antipasto 855 rue de Saint-Jovite, Centre-Ville Mont-Tremblant ☎819 425 7580, ⓦrestaurantantipasto.com. Feast on hearty servings of Italian pastas, veal cutlet, sausage with spicy tomato sauce and pizzas made in a wood-burning oven at this welcoming restaurant set in the former St-Jovite train station. Mains $15–27. Daily 11am–10pm.

Le P'tit Caribou 125 chemin Kandahar ☎819 681 4500, ⓦptitcaribou.com. At the height of the ski season, Mont-Tremblant buzzes with a lively après-ski scene, especially at popular *Le P'tit Caribou*, which is consistently voted one of Canada's best ski bars. Join the cocktail-fuelled crowd until the wee hours. There's also a wide range of live music throughout the year. Daily 2pm–3am.

La Savoie 117 chemin Kandahar ☎819 681 4573, ⓦrestaurantlasavoie.com.
There's nothing like fondue when you're in the mountains. This inviting Swiss chalet restaurant serves rich cheese fondue (from $40 per person) and raclette (from $47 per person), as well as a robust wine list. Daily 5–10pm.

Microbrasserie La Diable 117 chemin Kandahar, at the base of the slopes ☎819 681 4546, ⓦmicroladiable.com. After a long day of skiing (or hiking), kick back at this comfortable brewpub, where you can guzzle everything from black stout to Belgian wheat beer. It also serves hearty grub, like burgers, chunky chili, barbecue ribs and hot soups. Dinner menu under $30. Daily 11.30am–2am.

The Eastern Townships (Cantons-de-l'Est)

The Eastern Townships were once Québec's quietest corner, with swaying fields and farmland punctuated by time-capsule villages. But these settlements – many spruced up with luxury inns, art galleries and antique shops – have since become a readily accessible country getaway for Montréalers: the **Cantons-de-l'Est** begin 80km east of Montréal – a leisurely drive – and extend to the US border. A continually growing ski industry – concentrated around Mont Sutton, just north of the Vermont border – is making its mark on the land. Yet the region's agricultural roots are still evident, especially in spring, when the maple trees are tapped for syrup. At this time of year, remote *cabanes à sucre* offer sleigh rides and traditional Québécois treats such as maple taffy – strips of maple syrup frozen in the snow. You can also sample Québécois wines on La Route des Vins, which snakes through the region's lush vineyards, and eat at superb restaurants: look for the designation of Créateurs de Saveurs Cantons-de-l'Est (Eastern Townships Creators of Flavour; ⓦcreateursdesaveurs.com), a network of local, home-grown restaurants and cafés.

The land of the Eastern Townships, once the domain of scattered groups of Aboriginal peoples, was settled by United Empire Loyalists hounded out of the US after the American Revolution. Their loyalty to the Crown resulted in freehold land grants from the British, and townships with very English names like **Sherbrooke** and **Granby** were founded. In the mid-nineteenth century the

---

PEDALLING THE CANTONS DE L'EST

Rolling hills punctuated by parish churches; quiet rivers winding through the countryside; snow-capped mountains rising beyond: the Cantons de l'Est are ideal for exploring on two wheels. And now it's much easier to do so: the region, in partnership with Vélo Québec, has designed a new *Véloroute des Cantons* cycling map (ⓦeasterntownships.org), with six routes that show off the best of Cantons de l'Est, from panoramic views to gourmet spots where you can refuel to bike shops. Top routes include the 79km Memphrémagog to Massawippi trail; the 96km Sutton Mountain Tour; and the 55km Lake Mégantic loop. The Véloroute des Cantons, which unfolds for a total of 225km, from Farnham to Danville, is linked to the Route Verte (Green Route; ⓦrouteverte.com) that crosses Québec. This, in turn, connects to the Trans Canada Trail. The region is dotted with bike clubs and rental shops, including the Centre National de Cyclisme de Bromont (400 rue Shefford; ☎450 534 3333, ⓦcentrenationalbromont.com; hours vary, but generally open April–Sept daily 9am–5pm), which has a velodrome for everything from mountain to BMX biking.

townships opened up to industry, which attracted an influx of French-Canadians seeking work: today, nearly 95 percent are francophone. For the most part, relations between the linguistic groups have been amicable, though pockets like the towns and villages around **Knowlton** and **North Hatley** remain staunchly tied to their anglophone heritage.

ARRIVAL AND INFORMATION
THE EASTERN TOWNSHIPS

By car Cantons-de-l'Est is an easy drive from Montréal: head east on Autoroute 10, which is a straight shot towards Sherbrooke and into Cantons-de-l'Est.

By bus Transdev Limocar (☎ 514 842 2281, ☎ 866 700 8899, ⓦ transdev.ca) links Montréal with Magog (1hr 30min), Sherbrooke (2hr), Granby (1hr 15min) and Bromont (1hr).

Tourist information For in-depth information on the region, from local events to top restaurants to organized outdoor tours, check the excellent ⓦ easterntownships.org. Most towns have a local tourist office, for information on the town and around.

Zoo de Granby

1050 blvd David-Bouchard, Granby • Daily: late May to mid-June & mid-Aug to early Nov 10am–5pm; mid-June to late July 10am–7pm; mid-July to mid-Aug 10am–9pm; note that hours may vary, so check website first • Noctamble: Generally Fri–Sun 7–10pm • $36.95, sometimes lower rates in the fall season; Noctamble: $14.99, or $5.99 addition to regular daytime ticket • ☎ 450 372 9113, ☎ 877 472 6299, ⓦ zoodegranby.com

The **Zoo de Granby**, Québec's foremost attraction of its kind, is the main redeeming feature of the somewhat unexceptional town of **Granby**, on the Montréal side of the Cantons-de-l'Est. The zoo caters to kids and has a rich array of exhibits and activities, from a gorilla park to tigers to underwater creatures. Also on-site, an aquatic park features a popular wave pool and water slides. The zoo also features the fun Noctamble, an evening walk through the zoo, where you can observe the creatures' nocturnal habits.

Bromont

Just south of Granby, **BROMONT** is focused on the 405m ski and snowboarding hill at its centre, **Ski Bromont** (☎ 450 534 2200, ☎ 866 276 6668, ⓦ skibromont. com). In summer, the hill metamorphoses into a hiking and mountain-biking centre and watery playground at the slides and pools of the **Bromont Water Park** (same phone and email as Ski Bromont; daily: early to late June & mid- to late Aug 10am–5pm; late June to early July 10am–6pm; early July to mid-Aug 10am–6.30pm; from $24). Less energetic options include the tiny **Musée du Chocolat**, 679 rue Shefford (Mon–Fri 8am–5pm, Sat & Sun 8am–5.30pm; ☎ 450 534 3893, ⓦ lemuseeduchocolatdelaconfiseriebromont.com; free), where you can learn about chocolate-making while nibbling on some fine specimens.

ACCOMMODATION AND EATING
BROMONT

Auberge Nuits St-Georges 792 Shefford St ☎ 450 534 0705, ⓦ auberge-georges.com. Relax in rustic comfort in the heart of the village at this inviting auberge. The airy rooms have hardwood floors, stone walls and comfortable beds made with crisp linens. **$160**

Le Cellier du Roi par Jérôme Ferrer Le Royal Bromont, 400 chemin Compton ☎ 450 534 4653, ⓦ royalbromont. com. Chef Jérôme Ferrer brings his creative, Québec-inspired cuisine to the Eastern Townships at this eponymous

restaurant. The menu is deeply rooted in the surrounding region, highlighting everything from local cheeses to home-grown garden vegetables. The prix fixe dinner menu ($64.50) includes dishes like foie gras with smoked bison and sea bream with carrots and gingerbread. The setting matches the cuisine: the elegant restaurant sits amid the landscaped grounds of Le Royal Bromont, a public golf course just north of Bromont that's ranked among the best in Canada. Wed–Fri 11.30am–9pm, Sat 5–9pm.

Knowlton

The serene, leafy township of Lac Brome, named after the lake in its centre, encompasses several hamlets, the most inviting of which is the petite Knowlton, known for its Loyalist history. Knowlton's main draw is the chance to spend a peaceful weekend just milling about, sipping coffee and perusing antique shops and art galleries, which you'll find on the two main thoroughfares, chemins Lakeside and Knowlton and other smaller streets. Knowlton also buzzes with performing arts thanks to **Theatre Lac Brome** (9 chemin Mont-Écho; ☎450 242 2270, ⓦtheatrelacbrome.ca), which showcases English-language plays, often comedies, in July and August, as well as an excellent line-up of live music, from folk to classical, throughout the year. Among the various lively festivals throughout the year is the late-September Lac Brome Duck Festival (ⓦcanardenfete.ca), with culinary demonstrations, a fragrant produce market and plenty of local libations.

Société Historique du Comté du Brome

130 chemin Lakeside • Mid-May to Oct daily 10am–5pm, Sun 11am–4.30pm • $8 • ☎450 243 6782, ⓦbromemuseum.com

This county museum, the oldest historical society in the Eastern Townships, features several floors crammed with regional cultural artefacts, many of which reveal the province's Loyalist history. It also holds a number of military pieces, as well as the star of the museum, a Fokker DVII airplane. The historical society also runs a children's museum in the Marion Phelps building on the grounds, which invites the younger set to step back into the past, with an array of interactive exhibits and more.

ACCOMMODATION   KNOWLTON

Le Pleasant 1 Pleasant Rd, Sutton, about 25km south of Knowlton ☎450 538 6188, ⓦlepleasant.com. Kick back at this relaxing spot near Sutton, a sleek departure from what can sometimes feel like the oppressively quaint B&B. Dark-wood ceilings are offset by snow-white sofas and the occasional pop of colour. The café is an inviting spot for cocktails and small plates, including pungent cheese with local honey. *Le Pleasant* capitalizes on its proximity to Mont Sutton with excellent ski deals. __$120__

Manoir Maplewood 26 rue Clark, Waterloo, 14km north of Knowlton ☎450 920 1500, ⓦmanoirmaplewood.com. This lovely inn was once the 1864 mansion of Senator Asa Belknap Forster, who was one of Canada's railroad tycoons. The beautifully restored inn features ten elegant rooms with cream-coloured linens and hardwood floors, a restaurant that celebrates the local bounty, , and a wine cellar that hosts tastings. The inn is in the quiet town of Waterloo, which was founded by Loyalists in the 1790s. __$199__

Magog and around

The summer resort town of **MAGOG**, about 40km east of Bromont, gets its name from a corruption of an Aboriginal word meaning "great expanse of water" – now known as **Lac Memphrémagog**, one of the township's largest lakes, on which it borders. A strange beast known as Memphré supposedly lurks in its waters (the subject of various fishy tales since 1798).

Magog itself is a lively spot with plenty of bars and restaurants along its main street, rue Principale. Various boat cruises ply the river in the summer, like Escapades Memphrémagog (☎819 843 7000, ☎888 422 8328, ⓦescapadesmemphremagog.com), which offers a variety of trips, including a brunch cruise (Sun 10am–1pm; $51) and the "Offshore 4 to 6" ($42), when you can enjoy an evening sail with complimentary cocktail You can also go fishing on the lake with Lomechuse (☎819 209 5633, ⓦlomechuse.com), which offers a full day of trout fishing from $300.

Abbaye Saint-Benoît-du-Lac

1 rue Principale, Saint-Benoît-du-Lac, 25km southwest of Magog via Hwy-245 • **Abbey** Hours vary, generally daily 5am–9pm; Gregorian chant daily 11am & 5pm (Thurs at 7pm); schedule can differ in summer • **Shop** Mon–Sat 9–10.45am & 11.45am–6pm, Sun 12.15–6pm; winter closed Sun • ☎819 843 4080, ⓦst-benoit-du-lac.com

As you explore the shores of Lac Memphrémagog, it's hard to miss this elegant abbey, which is marked by white-granite turrets that loom over the quiet waters. The abbey is home to sixty Benedictine monks, renowned for their Gregorian chants and for producing Québec's famous L'Ermite *fromage* as well as apple cider and fruit jams.

ARRIVAL AND INFORMATION   MAGOG

By bus Transdev Limocar (☎514 842 2281, ☎866 700 8899, ⓦtransdev.ca) travels regularly between Magog and other main towns in the Eastern Townships.

Tourist office 55 rue Cabana (daily: June to mid-Oct 8.30am–7pm; mid-Oct to May 9am–5pm; ☎800 267 2744, ⓦtourisme-memphremagog.com).

ACCOMMODATION AND EATING

Abbaye Saint-Benoît-du-Lac 1 rue Principale, Saint-Benoît-du-Lac, 25km southwest of Magog ☎819 843 4080, ⓦst-benoit-du-lac.com. The abbey has two budget hostels (one for men and one for women; reservation by phone only). These are less about a cheap bed, and more about silence, spirituality and exploring monastic life. Room and board **$60**

Microbrasserie La Memphré 12 rue Merry Sud ☎819 843 3405, ⓦmicrobrasserielamemphre.com. Kick back at this pleasant bar with views of the lake from the veranda.

Enjoy tasty local beer and quality pub food, including juicy burgers, *poutine* and onion soup with red ale beer and melted cheese (mains $12–15). Mon–Wed 11.30–midnight, Thurs–Sun 11.30am–3am.

Ô Bois Dormant 205 rue Abbot ☎819 843 0450, ⓦoboisdormant.qc.ca. Inviting, cosy B&B in a lovely 1889 Queen Anne house, with a breezy veranda. A hearty breakfast is included. They also run the nearby 1927 cottage, with a suite and adjoining room (from $155) that's perfect for families or groups. **$120**

Parc National du Mont-Orford

10km north of Magog via Hwy-141 • ☎819 843 9855, ☎800 655 6527, ⓦsepaq.com

A mature sugar-maple forest blankets three-quarters of the small **Parc National du Mont-Orford**. Ski on Mont Orford (859m) in winter or hike in the summer: the chair-lift operates year-round. You can also **camp** at one of the park's sites or off in the woods.

ACCOMMODATION   PARC NATIONAL DU MONT-ORFORD

Auberge du Centre d'Arts Orford 3165 chemin du Parc, off exit 118 from Autoroute 10 ☎819 843 3981, ☎800 567 6155, ⓦorford.mu. A renowned music academy set on verdant grounds, which hosts summer concerts, and has a well-run inn with comfortable rooms. **$70**

Parc National du Mont-Orford ☎819 843 9855, ☎800 655 6527, ⓦsepaq.com. Well-maintained campgrounds are dotted around the park. Sites from **$30**

LA ROUTE DES VINS (THE WINE ROUTE)

Sip your way through the Eastern Townships on the 120km **La Route des Vins** Brome-Missiquoi (ⓦlaroutedesvins.ca), connecting the region's lush vineyards, many of which are notable for their ice wines. The route website has an easy-to-follow map. The wine route snakes across the southwest wedge of the townships, and along the way you can indulge in Québécois wines at over a dozen vineyards. The **Wines of Québec** group (ⓦwinesofquebec.com) also features several wine routes throughout the region, including in Cantons de l'Est.

Domaine Les Brome ☎450 242 2665, ⓦleoncourville.com. West of Lac Brome, in Ville de Lac-Brome, this features a superb array of wines – and a gorgeous view of vineyards with the lake shimmering in the distance. Explore on a guided tour (45min, $10). Sat & Sun 10am–5pm.

Union Libre Cidre & Vin ☎450 295 2223, ⓦunionlibre.com. Near Vignoble L'Orpailleur in Dunham, this lively spot produces sparkling cider, ice cider and,

uniquely, fire cider, made from heated fermented apples. Half-hour guided visits daily 11am–2pm & 3.30pm (from $5, includes tasting for three ciders).

Vignoble L'Orpailleur ☎450 295 2763, ⓦorpailleur.ca. Southwest of Knowlton near the village of Dunham, this friendly vineyard is well primed for visitors, with a small museum and sunny restaurant. Guided tours June to Oct three or four times daily (from $10).

North Hatley and Lake Massawippi

It's here that the unique flavour of the Magog region – anglophone pride and gorgeous lakes – really come together. **Lake Massawippi**, which extends for 19km, offers some of the region's most idyllic waterfront spots, with a couple of splendid lakeside inns. The tiny town of **NORTH HATLEY**, which sits at the northern tip of the lake, a thirty-minute drive east from Magog along Hwy-108, charmingly reveals its anglophone roots, with boutiques selling teas and tweeds. The village is also home to the lively theatre company **The Piggery**, 215 chemin Simard (☎819 842 2431, ⟁piggery.com), which puts on an eclectic array of shows, from musicals to bluegrass, throughout the summer. Several art galleries and antique shops cluster along the waterfront. The family-friendly **Parc du Mont Hatley** (☎819 842 2447, ⟁monthatley.com), north of North Hatley, offers outdoor activities, including snow tubing and snowshoeing, as well as hiking and mountain biking.

ACCOMMODATION   NORTH HATLEY AND LAKE MASSAWIPPI

★ **Manoir Hovey** 575 chemin Hovey, North Hatley ☎819 842 2421, ☎800 661 2421, ⟁manoirhovey. com. This classy nineteenth-century colonnaded inn, modelled after George Washington's Mount Vernon, sits in sloping grounds on the banks of Lake Massawippi and offers a variety of outdoor activities, from kayaking and windsurfing to snowshoeing and ice-skating. Or go for pamper treatments, from deep-tissue massages to facials. Plush alpine rooms feature four-poster beds, woollen blankets piled on wicker chairs and burnished wood floors. You can dine on market-fresh Québécois and French cuisine at *Le Hatley* restaurant, and then ease into the evening over a chess game and mulled wine in the oak-panelled library,

surrounded by well-thumbed books, tasselled curtains and mallard decoys. <u>$200</u>

★ **Ripplecove Lakefront Hotel** 700 Ripplecove, Ayer's Cliff ☎819 838 4296, ☎800 668 4296, ⟁ripplecove. com. This beautiful, family-run inn on the southern shores of Lake Massawippi celebrated its seventieth year in 2015. The inviting rooms and chalets have thick carpets, historic furnishings and plump beds, and activities on offer include kayaking and lake cruises to skating and sleigh rides, as well as indulgent spa treatments The *Le Riverain* restaurant celebrates local seafood and produce, with dishes like scallops and blood sausage with watercress sauce. Mains $37–41. <u>$230</u>

EATING

Café Massawippi 3050 chemin Capelton ☎819 842 4528, ⟁cafemassawippi.com. *Foie gras*, Lac Brome duck and other local dishes are specialities at this esteemed restaurant, whose humble exterior – a wooden porch, specials scrawled on a blackboard, gauzy white curtains –

belies the daring country cuisine prepared within. Dishes include foie gras banana split (foie gras with friend banana panko), braised rabbit with sundried tomatoes. Mains $27–32. Daily 6–10pm; in summer sometimes also Thurs–Sun 11.30–3pm.

Compton

One of the great appeals of the Eastern Townships is its agricultural bounty: look in one direction, and you'll see verdant vineyards; in another direction, fragrant orchards and fields dotted with placid cows. The small farming town of **COMPTON**, about 16km northeast of Hatley, is particularly well-placed to experience the fertile outdoors, as it's surrounded by farmland, from apple orchards to cheese factories – and, it's an easy day-trip from any of the other main cities, including Magog, Sherbrooke and Hatley. Compton also has a place in Canada's political history: former prime minister Louis S. St-Laurent was born here, and you can visit his childhood home. In town, you'll also find a number of inviting spots to sample the local goods.

Louis S. St-Laurent National Historic Site

6335 route Louis S. St-Laurent • End June to Aug daily, Sept Sat–Sun 10am–5pm • $3.90 • ☎819 835 5448, ⟁pc.gc.ca

Tour the childhood home of Louis S. St-Laurent, the twelfth Prime Minister of Canada from 1948 to 1957. The draw here is as much about St-Laurent himself (a lively short film chronicles his life and career) as it is about an authentic glimpse into life in small-town Québec at the turn of the century. The house has been lovingly restored, as has the general store that belonged to Louis S. St-Laurent's father, Jean-Baptiste-Moïse, with such period items as an iron stove, whalebone corsets and chamber pots.

Fromagerie la Station

440 chemin de Hatley (Route 208), southwest of Compton • Mid-June to mid-Oct daily 10am–6pm; mid-Oct to mid-June Thurs & Fri 10am–5pm • Guided tour $5; guide nature walks free • ☎ 819 835 5301, ⓦ fromagerielastation.com

If you've ever doubted if organic tastes better, one bite of the cheese here will clear that up. The fromagerie's signature Alfred Le Fermier, a hefty round of pale orange, washed-rind cheese, comes from a single herd of Holsteins, which you see roaming in the surrounding fields. This is organic cheese at its finest, as its many awards will attest, and history has a lot to do with it: four generations of the Bolduc family have worked the farm, which includes pastureland, stables, a ripening room and a store. The farm offers guided tours through all the stages of production, topped off by a sampling. Or, embark on the free nature walks, guided by the owners, where you'll roam the fields, taste herbs and more.

Le Gros Pierre

6335 route Louis S. St-Laurent, north of Compton • End June to end July & Nov to mid-Dec Thurs–Sat 10am–6pm, end July to early Nov daily 9am–6pm; three or four guided tours daily • ☎ 819 835 5549, ⓦ grospierre.com

Sink your teeth into juicy apples at this fragrant, kid-friendly orchard with more than eight thousand dwarf apple trees – and over fifteen varieties of apple. Tours may include apple-picking, tractor rides, touring the factory and, of course, tasting apple products, from jams to juice.

EATING   COMPTON

Le Cinquième Element 6815 route Louis S. St-Laurent ☎ 819 835 0052, ⓦ lecinquiemeelement.ca. Enjoy crêpes laiden with fresh cheese, grilled trout with maple spices and cheese risotto and orange-scented crème brûlée. at this charming restaurant. Mains start at $12; table d'hôte from $35. Wed–Sun 11am–3pm and 5–10pm; closing times are flexible, depending on when last diners leave.

Sherbrooke

The university town of **SHERBROOKE**, 147km east of Montréal, has a youthful energy and is evolving from a gritty commercial hub to a lively city with some worthwhile sights and innovative restaurants. Most of the city's attractions are clustered in Vieux-Sherbrooke, around the 1.5km gorge carved by the Rivière Magog.

Musée des Beaux Arts de Sherbrooke

241 rue Dufferin • Tues–Sun noon–5pm• $10 • ☎ 819 821 2115, ⓦ mbas.qc.ca

This absorbing museum, housed in a handsome nineteenth-century building that used to be the Eastern Townships Bank, displays a range of works by Québécois artists, from the nineteenth century to today, including Frederick Simpson Coburn, Charles Daudelin and Michel Goulet. The museum also features interesting temporary exhibits, often with a focus on local art and sculpture.

Centre d'interprétation de l'histoire de Sherbrooke

275 rue Dufferin • Tues–Fri 9am–noon & 1–5pm, Sat & Sun 1–5pm • $7 • ☎ 819 821 5406, ⓦ histoiresherbrooke.org

This well-run museum delves into Sherbrooke's history, from permanent exhibits on the evolution of Sherbrooke's urban sprawl to temporary shows that delve into topics like the town's musical history. The museum also offers walking tours of historic Sherbrooke.

By bus Transdev Limocar (☎514 842 2281, ☎866 700 8899, ⓦtransdev.ca) travels regularly between Sherbrooke and other main towns, including Trois-Rivières (2hr 10min) and Québec City (3hr).

Tourist office 785 rue King ouest (mid-June to mid-Aug daily 9am–7pm; mid-Aug to mid-June Mon–Sat 9am–

5pm, Sun 9am–3pm; ☎819 821 1919, ☎800 561 8331, ⓦdestinationsherbrooke.com).

Tours With the wonderful Sherbrooke Greeters programme (☎819 821 1919, ⓦsherbrookegreeters.com), local volunteers take visitors around their city for free, sharing personal knowledge and insights.

ACCOMMODATION AND EATING

★ **Auguste** 82 rue Wellington Nord ☎819 565 9559, ⓦauguste-restaurant.com. Innovative, farm-to-fork Québécois cuisine, including sweet potato ravioli, black sausage served with red cabbage, and other superb grilled meats and fish. Mains $25–36. Tues & Wed 11.30–2.30 & 5–10pm, Thurs & Fri 11.30am–2.30pm & 5pm–11pm, Sat 10.30am–2.30pm & 5–11pm, Sun 10.30am–2.30pm & 5–10pm.

La Table du Chef 11 rue Victoria ☎819 562 2258, ⓦlatableduchef.ca. Helmed by renowned chef Alain Labrie, this elegant restaurant excels at French-accented

regional cuisine, including grilled bison with creamy polenta and elk tartare with chipotle peppers. Mains $26–35. Tues–Fri 11.30am–2pm & 5.30–9pm, Sat 5.30–9pm.

Marquis de Montcalm 797 rue du Général-De Montcalm ☎819 823 7773, ⓦmarquisdemontcalm. com. This lovely B&B near the gorge features comfortable rooms, hardwood floors and goose-down comforters. A robust breakfast – from fresh fruits to vegetable quiche to scrambled eggs with sundried tomatoes – is included. **$119**

Trois-Rivières

Midway between Montréal and Québec City, **TROIS-RIVIÈRES** is the lively hub of the Mauricie region. The town sits at the point where the Rivière St-Maurice splits into three channels – hence the name "Three Rivers" – before meeting the St Lawrence. The European settlement dates from 1634, when it established itself as an embarkation point for the French explorers of the continent and as an iron-ore centre. Lumber followed, and today Trois-Rivières is one of the world's largest producers of paper, the delta chock-full of logs to be pulped. It's often dismissed as an industrial city and little else, but its shady streets of historic buildings – neither as twee as Québec City, nor as monumental as Vieux-Montréal – are worth a wander, and the town is a good starting point for exploring the Mauricie Valley.

Cathédrale de l'Assomption

363 rue Bonaventure • Mon–Fri 9–11.30am & 1.30–5.30pm, Sat 9–11am & 1.30–5.15pm, Sun 9.30–noon & 2–6pm • Free • ☎819 374 2409

Trois-Rivières' compact downtown core branches off from the small square of Parc du Champlain and extends south down to the waterfront. Facing the park to the east looms the stately **Cathédrale de l'Assomption**, which is notable for its stained glass windows by Guido Nincheri, and massive Gothic Revival style reminiscent of London's Westminster Abbey.

Musée Québécois de Culture Populaire

200 rue Laviolette • **Museum** Late June to early Sept daily 10am–6pm; early Sept to late June Tues–Sun 10am–5pm; **Prison** Late June to early Sept daily 10am–6pm; early Sept to mid-Oct & mid-April to end June Tues–Sun 10am–5pm; mid-Oct to mid-April Thurs–Sun 10am–5pm • $13 prison or museum, combined ticket $21 • ☎819 372 0406, ⓦenprison.com

The **Musée Québécois de Culture Populaire** features folk and pop culture exhibitions, including everything from local crafts to an overview of sports stars of the province. The museum's real highlight is the **Vielle Prison of Trois-Rivières**; dating from 1822, it housed up to eighty inmates at a time until 1980, and while the decades of graffiti tell a story, it's nothing compared to the tales of the guides – many of them once served time here.

ARRIVAL AND INFORMATION

By bus The Orléans Express (☎ 514 395 4000, ☎ 888 999 3977, ⓦ orleansexpress.com) travels regularly between Montréal and Québec City, and services many cities in the area, including Trois-Rivières.

Tourist office 1457 rue Notre-Dame (mid-June to late Aug daily 9am–7pm; late Aug to mid-Oct & mid-May to mid-June Mon–Fri 9am–5pm, Sat & Sun 10am–4pm; mid-Oct to mid-May Mon–Fri 9am–5pm; ☎ 819 375 1122, ☎ 800 313 1123, ⓦ tourismetroisrivieres.com).

ACCOMMODATION

Manoir De Blois 197 rue Bonaventure ☎ 819 373 1090, ☎ 800 397 5184, ⓦ manoirdeblois.com. Relax in the elegant rooms of this 1828 stone house with original wood floors and an antique-strewn salon. The family-run inn also serves a filling breakfast. <u>$109</u>

3

Québec City and Northern Québec

RUE DU PETIT-CHAMPLAIN, QUEBEC CITY

Québec City and Northern Québec

Forming the greater part of Canada's largest province, Northern Québec stretches from the temperate farmland in the south to the Arctic tundra in the north, covering over one million square kilometres. Nature rules supreme in this area and the influence of the Arctic is strong – winters are long and among the coldest in eastern Canada, and the blazing summers are clipped short by northern frosts. Moose, caribou, wolverine and bears fill the forests and in many places humans have barely made inroads. Towns and villages are largely concentrated on the shores of the St Lawrence River, around the main coastal highways radiating eastward from historic Québec City.

The regal provincial capital is the undisputed highlight of the region, perched commandingly above and alongside the narrowing of the St Lawrence River like a symbolic gateway to the north (the city's name actually derives from the Algonquin word *kebek*, meaning "where the river narrows"). It is also the most easterly point that connects the north and south shores of the river. Beyond the city, the waterway broadens dramatically and the only connection between shores is by ferry.

The southern shore of the St Lawrence is less remote than its counterpart, with the agricultural **Bas-Saint-Laurent** (Lower St Lawrence) the gateway to the rugged and lightly populated **Gaspé Peninsula**. East of here, stuck out in the middle of the Gulf of St Lawrence, are the majestic, treeless landscapes of the **Îles-de-la-Madeleine**, most easily reached by air or a ferry from Prince Edward Island. The islands' fine shores and strikingly eroded sandstone cliffs will appeal particularly to cyclists, walkers and solitude-seeking beach-goers.

From the north shore of the St Lawrence trim farmland gives way to a vast forest bordering a barren seashore. Immediately northeast of Québec City is the beautiful **Charlevoix** region and its idyllic villages and towns that bear the marks of Québec's rural beginnings. The beguiling hills and valleys lead to dramatic ravaged rock just beyond the Charlevoix borders, where the **Saguenay River** crashes into the immense fjord that opens into the St Lawrence at **Tadoussac**, a popular resort for whale-watching and hiking. Inland, **Lac Saint-Jean** – source of the Saguenay River – is an oasis of fertile land in a predominantly rocky region, and its peripheral villages offer glimpses of First Nations as well as Québécois life. Adventurous types following the St Lawrence can head beyond Tadoussac along the **Côte-Nord** through a sparsely populated region of spectacular empty beaches and dramatic rockscapes. In the far northeast the supply ship *M/V Bella Desgagnés* serves the **Île d'Anticosti** and the roadless lower north shore as far as the Labrador border. The remoteness of the Île d'Anticosti and the sculptured terrain of **l'Archipel-de-Mingan** – a national park well served by boats from **Havre-Saint-Pierre** – is matched by the isolation of the fishing communities along the **Basse Côte-Nord**, where no roads penetrate and visits are possible only by supply ship, plane or snowmobile.

Québec City

Spread over the promontory Cap Diamant and the banks of the St Lawrence River, **QUÉBEC CITY** (sometimes referred to just as "Québec") is one of Canada's most beautifully located cities, and certainly its most historic one. Vieux-Québec, surrounded by solid fortifications, is the only walled city in North America, and a UNESCO World Heritage Site. Throughout the old city winding cobbled streets

CAP-AUX-MEULES, THE MAGDALEN ISLANDS

Highlights

❶ Festival d'Été Québec City is awash in a celebratory reverie during its acclaimed summer music festival. See page 247

❷ Vieux-Québec The only walled city in North America is full of romantic nooks and crannies. See page 249

❸ Mont-Sainte-Anne A boggling number of ski runs in the winter as well as world-class mountain biking and hiking during the summer just north of Québec City. See page 279

❹ Parc National Forillon At the very tip of the Gaspé Peninsula, this exquisite national park has t all: spectacular setting, iconic wildlife and a restored fishing village. See page 288

❺ Îles-de-la-Madeleine Explore the distinctive red dunes and sample the fresh seafood of these secluded islands in the Gulf of St Lawrence. See page 295

❻ Tadoussac Base yourself at this lively village and explore the Saguenay Fjord and join a whale-watching trip. See page 305

❼ Cycling the Véloroute des Bleuets Take in some of Québec's most scenic countryside while cycling this thoroughly enjoyable circuit of Lac Saint-Jean. See page 311

❽ Kayaking the Mingan Archipelago Kayak around the eerie "flowerpot" islands dotted by immense wind-sculpted rock formations and teeming with wildlife. See page 317

HIGHLIGHTS ARE MARKED ON THE MAP ON PAGE 246

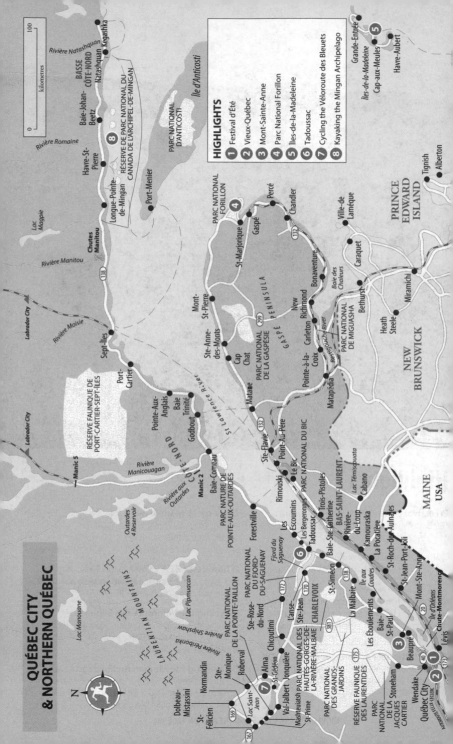

QUÉBEC CITY & NORTHERN QUÉBEC

HIGHLIGHTS

1. Festival d'Été
2. Vieux-Québec
3. Mont-Sainte-Anne
4. Parc National Forillon
5. Îles-de-la-Madeleine
6. Tadoussac
7. Cycling the Véloroute des Bleuets
8. Kayaking the Mingan Archipelago

100

0 kilometres

QUÉBEC CITY FESTIVALS

Québec City is renowned for its excellent annual **festivals**, the best of which are listed below.

Carnaval de Québec Feb ☎418 626 3716, ⓦcarnaval.qc.ca. Held in the depths of winter, when large quantities of the warming Caribou – a lethal mix of red wine, spirits and spices – are consumed amid parades and ice-sculpture competitions.

St-Jean Baptiste Day June 24. The provincial holiday sees an outpouring of Québécois pride spilling onto the streets in a massive celebration, with thousands of fleur-de-lis flags adorning the entire city.

★ **Festival d'Été** Eleven days in July ☎418 529 5200, ☎888 992 5200, ⓦinfofestival.com. The largest festival of francophone culture in North America and the biggest outdoor music festival in Canada features several major international acts. Everyone is roped in to the celebration, with restaurants offering discounts and Québec's major performers leading the party from open-air stages all over town.

Fêtes de la Nouvelle-France Aug ☎418 694 3311, ☎866 391 3383, ⓦnouvellefrance. qc.ca. Great fun, as Basse-Ville returns to the seventeenth and eighteenth centuries: thousands of Québécois from around the province dress up in period costume, often ones they've sewn themselves.

---

are flanked by seventeenth- and eighteenth-century stone houses and churches, graceful parks and squares, and countless monuments. Although some districts have been painstakingly restored to give tourists as seductive an introduction to Québec as possible, this is nevertheless an authentically and profoundly French-Canadian city. Over ninety percent of its 800,000 population are francophone, and it is often difficult to remember which continent you are in as you tuck in to a croissant and a steaming bowl of *café au lait* in a Parisian-style café. Moreover, despite the fact that the city's symbol is a hotel, the **Château Frontenac**, the government remains the main employer.

None of Québec City's highlights are far from the St Lawrence River, with the main attractions being evenly distributed between the upper and lower portions of what is known as **Vieux-Québec** (Old Québec). Within the quarter's walls reminders of the days when the city was the bastion of the Catholic Church in Canada are discernible at almost every corner. The Church can claim much of the credit for the creation and preservation of its finest buildings, from the quaint **Église Notre-Dame-des-Victoires** to the **Basilique-Cathédrale Notre-Dame de Québec** and the vast **Séminaire**.

On the Cap Diamant, **Haute-Ville** (Upper Town) continues along the river from the old city walls and from here you should wander at least to the **Musée National des Beaux-Arts du Québec**, home to the finest art collection in the province. The museum is set in the expansive battlefield of the **Plaines d'Abraham**, a national historic park that unfurls west of the massive and magnificent **Citadelle**, an austere defensive structure that reveals the military pedigree of a city dubbed by Churchill the "Gibraltar of North America". At the foot of the *Château Frontenac*, **Terrasse Dufferin** is also worth a stroll to watch street entertainers and for the arresting views over the river, but it gets crowded in the evening. It also overlooks the second part of Vieux-Québec, **Basse-Ville** (Lower Town), connected to Haute-Ville by funicular and several winding streets and stairs.

Brief history

For centuries the clifftop site of what is now Québec City was occupied by the **Iroquois** village of Stadacona, and although **Jacques Cartier** visited in the sixteenth century, permanent **European settlement** did not begin until 1608, when **Samuel de Champlain** established a fur-trading post here. To protect what was rapidly developing into a major inland trade gateway, the settlement shifted to the clifftop in 1620 when Fort St-Louis was built on the present-day site of the *Château Frontenac*.

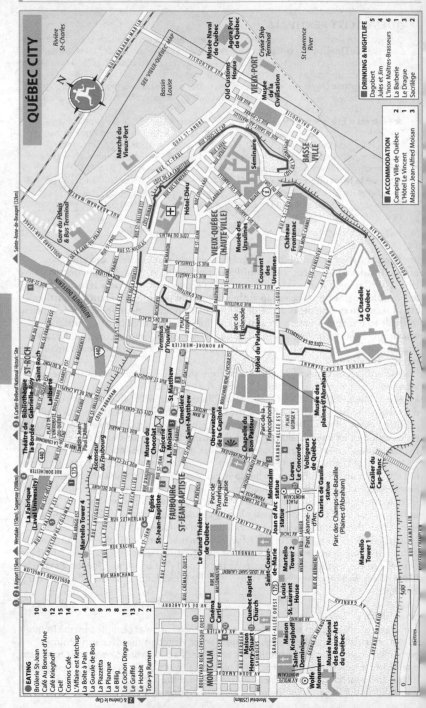

QUÉBEC CITY

DRINKING & NIGHTLIFE

Dagobert	5
Jules et Jim	4
L'Inox Maîtres-Brasseurs	6
La Barberie	1
Le Drague	3
Sacrilège	2

ACCOMMODATION

Camping Ville de Québec	2
L'Hôtel Le Vincent	1
Maison Jean-Alfred Moisan	3

EATING

Brûlerie St-Jean	10
Café Au Bonnet d'Âne	6
Café Krieghoff	12
Ciel!	15
Cosmos Café	14
L'Affaire est Ketchup	1
La Boîte à Pain	4
La Gueule de Bois	5
La Piazzetta	9
La Planque	3
Le Billig	8
Le Cochon Dingue	11
Le Graffiti	13
Le Hobbit	7
Tora-ya Ramen	2

Catholicism and commercial might

Missionaries began arriving in 1615, and by the time **Bishop Laval** arrived in 1659 Québec City and the surrounding province were in the grip of the **Catholic Church**. Yet in the city's earliest days the merchants of the fur trade wielded the most power and frequently came into conflict with the priests, who wanted a share in the profits in order to spread their message among the Indigenous peoples. **Louis XIV** resolved the wrangles, after being advised to take more interest in his kingdom's mercantile projects. In 1663 the entire French colony, which officially stretched from Newfoundland to the Gulf of Mexico and was known as New France, became a royal province, administered by a council appointed directly by the Crown and answerable to the king's council in France. Before the century ended, the long-brewing European struggles between Britain and France spilled over into the colony. It was at this time that the **Comte de Frontenac**, known as the "fighting governor", replaced Champlain's Fort St-Louis with the sturdier Château St-Louis, and began work on the now-famous fortifications that ring Vieux-Québec. In 1690, Admiral Phipps' Anglo-American invasion force laid siege to the city, but gave up when winter set in.

British takeover

In 1759, during the **Seven Years' War** (also known as the French and Indian War), the most significant battle in Canada's history took place here, between the British under General **James Wolfe** and the French commander general Louis Joseph, **Marquis de Montcalm**. The city had already been under siege from the opposite shore for three months when Wolfe and his four thousand troops scaled the cliff of Cap Diamant and engaged the hastily organized and ill-prepared French. The twenty-minute battle on the **Plaines d'Abraham** left both leaders mortally wounded and the city of Québec in the hands of the British, a state of affairs ultimately confirmed by the Treaty of Paris in 1763.

In 1775 – the year after the **Québec Act**, which allowed French-Canadians to retain their Catholic religion, language and culture – the town was attacked again, this time by the Americans, who had already captured Montréal. The British won the **Battle of Quebec**, and for the next century the city quietly earned its livelihood as the centre of a **timber-trade and shipbuilding** industry, in addition to being made capital of Lower Canada by the Constitutional Act of 1791. Yet by the 1840s the accessible supplies of timber had run out. The final blow came with the appearance of steamships that could travel as far as Montréal (earlier sailing ships had found it difficult to proceed beyond Québec City). Ceasing to be a busy seaport, the city declined into a centre of small industry and local government, its way of life still largely determined by the Catholic Church. The **Québec Conference on Canadian Confederation** was held in the city in 1864, and three years later Québec City became the capital of the newly created province of Québec.

The rise of Québécois nationalism

With the **Quiet Revolution** in the 1960s under premier **Jean Lesage** and the rise of Québec **nationalism**, Québec City became a symbol of the glory of the French heritage: the motto *Je me souviens* ("I remember"), for instance, placed above the doors of its parliament buildings, was transferred to the licence plates of Québec cars, to carry the message across Canada. Though the city played little active part in the changes, it has grown with the upsurge in the francophone economy, developing a suburbia of shopping malls and convention centres as slick as any in the country – the old centre is largely given over to **tourism** these days (the city is a major cruise ship destination), with most commercial activity focussed on **Saint-Roch** (especially for IT), and along Boulevard Laurier in **Sainte-Foy**.

Basse-Ville

The birthplace of Québec City, Vieux-Québec's **Basse-Ville** is an exceedingly charming area, a warren of cobbled streets lined with historic houses whose appearances have changed little since the city was founded on the banks of the St Lawrence.

Funiculaire de Québec

16 rue du Petit-Champlain • Daily: Jan–March & Dec 7.30am–10.30pm; April to late June & Sept–Oct 7.30am–11pm; late June to Aug 7.30am–11.30pm; Nov Mon–Fri 7.30am–9pm, Sat & Sun 10am–7pm • $3.50 • ☎ 418 692 1132, ⓦ funiculaire.ca

Basse-Ville can be reached from Terrasse Dufferin either by the steep **L'Escalier Casse-Cou** (Breakneck Stairs) or by the short (64m) **Funiculaire de Québec** alongside. First established in 1879, the (now modernized) funicular shoots up the 60m high cliff in a couple of minutes. The Basse-Ville station of the funicular is the 1683 **Maison Louis-Jolliet**, built for the retired discoverer of the Mississippi, Louis Jolliet; it now houses a souvenir shop.

Quartier du Petit-Champlain

Shopping hours Mon–Wed 9.30am–5.30pm, Thurs & Fri 9.30am–9pm, Sat & Sun 9.30am–5pm • ⓦ quartierpetitchamplain.com

Dating back to 1685, the narrow, cobbled **rue du Petit-Champlain** is the city's oldest street, and the surrounding area – known as **Quartier du Petit-Champlain** – is the oldest shopping area in North America. The quaint seventeenth- and eighteenth-century houses now hold restaurants, boutiques and galleries selling arts and crafts.

Place Royale

Champlain built New France's first permanent settlement in 1608 in **Place Royale** (ⓦ placeroyale.ca) in order to begin trading fur with the First Nations peoples. Known as place du Marché until the **bust of Louis XIV** was erected here in 1686, the square remained the focal point of Canadian commerce until 1759, and after the fall of Québec the British continued using the area as a lumber market. After 1860 place Royale was left to fall into disrepair, but in the 1970s it was renovated. Its pristine stone houses, most of which date from around 1685, are undeniably photogenic, with their steep metal roofs, numerous chimneys and pastel-coloured shutters, but it's a Legoland townscape, devoid of the scars of history. Happily, the atmosphere is enlivened in summer by entertainment from classical orchestras to juggling clowns, and by the **Fêtes de la Nouvelle-France** (see page 247), when everyone dresses in period costume and it once again becomes a chaotic marketplace. Just to the north along Rue Notre Dame, check out the building–sized **La Fresque des Québécois** (Québéc city mural), a dramatic *trompe-l'oeil* work unveiled in 1999 telling the story of the city.

Église Notre-Dame-des-Victoires

32 rue Sous-le-Fort (Place Royale) • Mid-May to late June daily 9.30am–5pm; late June to Aug daily 9.30am–6.30pm; Sept–Oct Wed–Sat noon–4pm, Sun 9.30am–4.30pm • Free • ☎ 418 692 6464, ⓦ notre-dame-de-quebec.org

The **Église Notre-Dame-des-Victoires**, on the west side of place Royale, nearly always has a wedding in progress during the summer. Established by Laval in 1688, it has been completely restored twice – after destruction by shellfire in 1759 and a fire in 1969. Inside, the fortress-shaped altar alludes to the two French victories over the British navy (in 1690 and 1711) that gave the church its name. Paintings depicting these events hang above the altar, while the aisles are lined with copies of religious paintings by Van Dyck, Van Loo and Rubens, gifts from early settlers to give thanks for a safe passage. The large model ship suspended in the nave has a similar origin.

Place de Paris

From Place Royale, cobbled Rue du Marché Finlay runs east down onto **Place de Paris**, where a white cubic sculpture called *Dialogue with History* marks the disembarkation place of the first settlers from France. To the south (and also accessible from the end of rue St-Pierre), the crenellated **Batterie Royal** rampart was used to defend the city during the siege of 1759.

Musée de la Civilisation

85 rue Dalhousie • Late June to early Sept daily 10am–5pm; early Sept to late June Tues–Sun 10am–5pm • $17; Nov–May free on Tues • ☎ 418 643 2158, ⓦ mcq.org

One of Québec City's most impressive museums, the **Musée de la Civilisation** was designed by prominent Israeli-Canadian architect Moshe Safdie and opened in 1988. The structure gives a nod to the steep-pitched roofs of the early settlers by incorporating a rooftop terrace with great views and three historic buildings – don't miss the vaulted cellars in the 1751 **Maison Estèbe**, which survived the British bombardment to eventually become the **museum's gift shop** (the rest of the house is off-limits).

Concentrating primarily on Canadian subjects but also diversifying into a worldwide perspective, the museum presents engaging temporary exhibitions that have ranged from whimsical pop-culture interests to serious looks at earlier historical periods. The two **permanent exhibitions** offer very different perspectives of Québec history. **People of Québec…Then and Now** (ground floor) is a fascinating chronological account of life in Québec from the Neolithic era to the present (including the 2012 "Maple Spring" protests), enhanced with rare artefacts (such as stone tools from the La Martre archeological site dating from 10,000 years ago) and video booths. It does an especially good job of showing how the painstakingly gradual process of uniting disparate colonies into one Canada in the nineteenth century came about.

On the upper floor, the beautifully presented **This Is Our Story** was created in consultation with all eleven of the First Nations of Québec. The exhibition uses a variety of themes and over 450 objects (from artwork to traditional dress and musical instruments) to portray contemporary First Nations life, their very different version of Québec history, beginning some 12,500 years ago, and their experience of colonization from the seventeenth century.

4

Vieux-Port

Near the confluence of the St Charles and the St Lawrence rivers north of Basse-Ville lies the **Vieux-Port de Québec**, the busiest port in the province until its gradual eclipse by Montréal at the end of the nineteenth century. Much of the old dockland has been renovated as a recreational area, with theatres, apartments, sheltered walkways, restaurants and a marina packed with pleasure boats and yachts. The views across the Bassin Louise are still marred by industrial development, mitigated somewhat at night when the Bunge grain silos are illuminated with the colours of the northern lights.

Musée naval de Québec

170 rue Dalhousie • Daily 9am–4pm • Free • T 418 694 5387, W museenavaldequebec.com

The tiny one-room **Musée naval de Québec** is a poignant homage to some of the province's naval heroes, particularly those that served on Atlantic convoys in World War II. The Frédérick Rolette sword is also displayed, awarded to the eponymous lieutenant for bravery during the War of 1812. Nearby lies the **Agora** amphitheatre (venue for summer shows) and the grand Neoclassical **New Québec Custom House**, designed by prominent Toronto architect William Thomas in the 1860s.

Marché du Vieux-Port

160 Quai St-André • Mon–Fri 9am–6pm, Sat & Sun 9am–5pm • W mvpq.ca

A block east from the train station, the **Marché du Vieux-Port** is a throwback to how the port used to be – its busy market stalls selling fresh produce, cheeses and seafood from the local area. It's not terribly big, but in the summer it can have a good variety of stands, and the prices are usually surprisingly cheap.

L'îlot des Palais

8 rue Vallière • Late June to Aug daily 10am–5pm, Sept Tues–Sun 10am–5pm, Oct to late June Thurs 1–4.30pm, Fri 10am–4.30pm, Sat & Sun 10am–5pm • $8 • T 418 692 1441, W ilotdespalais.ca

Once a quiet cove on the northern side of the city, **L'îlot des Palais** (literally "Islet" or "lot" of the palaces) was the site of three mansions built in succession to lodge the

4

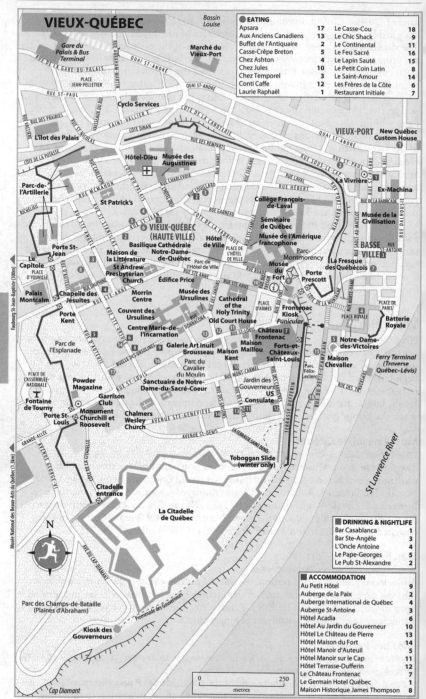

VIEUX-QUÉBEC

Bassin
Louise

EATING

Apsara	17	Le Casse-Cou	18
Aux Anciens Canadiens	13	Le Chic Shack	9
Buffet de l'Antiquaire	2	Le Continental	11
Casse-Crêpe Breton	5	Le Feu Sacré	16
Chez Ashton	4	Le Lapin Sauté	15
Chez Jules	10	Le Petit Coin Latin	8
Chez Temporel	3	Le Saint-Amour	14
Conti Caffe	12	Les Frères de la Côte	6
Laurie Raphaël	1	Restaurant Initiale	7

DRINKING & NIGHTLIFE

Bar Casablanca	1
Bar Ste-Angèle	3
L'Oncle Antoine	4
Le Pape-Georges	5
Le Pub St-Alexandre	2

ACCOMMODATION

Au Petit Hôtel	9
Auberge de la Paix	2
Auberge International de Québec	4
Auberge St-Antoine	3
Hôtel Acadia	6
Hôtel Au Jardin du Gouverneur	10
Hôtel Le Château de Pierre	13
Hôtel Maison du Fort	14
Hôtel Manoir d'Auteuil	5
Hôtel Manoir sur le Cap	11
Hôtel Terrasse-Dufferin	12
Le Château Frontenac	7
Le Germain Hotel Québec	1
Maison Historique James Thompson	8

Intendants of New France between 1675 and 1760 (the *intendant* was head of the colony's civil administration). Little remains of those structures today – the current red-brick warehouse on the site was built in the 1880s as a brewery, though the stone foundations and vaulted cellars inside are original to the 1720s second palace. The brewery closed in 1968, and the building now contains some enlightening exhibits on life in early Québec, as well as the varied history of the building, enhanced by multimedia displays and artefacts found in situ (including the bones of poor "Samy", a small eighteenth-century poodle that somehow ended up in the latrines).

Haute-Ville

The ten square kilometres of Vieux-Québec's **Haute-Ville**, encircled by the city walls, form the Québec City of the tourist brochures. Dominated by the **Château Frontenac**, it holds a glut of historic architecture and several compelling museums. The whole area is undeniably enchanting, and simply strolling along its maze of streets is one of the city's great pleasures.

Place d'Armes

Haute-Ville's centre of gravity is the main square, the **Place d'Armes**, with benches around the central fountain serving in the summer as a resting place for throngs of weary sightseers. Champlain established his first fort here in 1620, on the site now occupied by the gigantic **Château Frontenac**, probably Canada's most photographed building. On the west side of the square is the former **Palais de Justice**, a Renaissance-style courthouse completed in 1887 to a design by Eugène-Étienne Taché, architect of the province's Parliament buildings (it's now a Ministry of Finance building).

Musée du Fort

10 rue Ste-Anne (Place d'Armes) • May–Oct daily 10am–5pm (shows alternate in English and French every 30min), Nov–April daily 11am–4pm • $8.50 • ☎ 418 692 2175, ⓦ museedufort.com

On the north-east corner of Place d'Armes lies the **Musée du Fort**, whose sole exhibit is a 37-square-metre model of Québec City circa 1750 (replete with tiny ships and soldiers). You can only see it as part of the quaint but illuminating thirty-minute **sound and light show**, when the city's six major battles, beginning with the English siege of 1690 and including the battle of the Plaines d'Abraham and the American invasion of 1775, are re-enacted. Hard to believe today, but the opening of the museum in 1965 jump-started the city's tourist industry.

Rue du Trésor and the artisans' stalls

Parallel to rue du Fort is the narrow alley of **rue du Trésor** where French settlers once paid their taxes to the Royal Treasury; nowadays it is a touristy artists' market. You will probably fare better at the row of **stalls** manned by local artisans in the churchyard running alongside the portraitists on the pedestrianized stretch of rue Ste-Anne.

Château Frontenac

1 rue des Carrières (Place d'Armes) • Guided tours $20 ($15 for guests) • ☎ 418 977 8977, ⓦ fairmont.com/frontenac-quebec

New York architect Bruce Price drew upon the French-Canadian style of the surroundings to produce the **Château Frontenac**, a pseudo-medieval pile crowned with a copper roof. Although the hotel was inaugurated by the Canadian Pacific Railway in 1893, its distinctive main tower was only added in the early 1920s, resulting in an over-the-top design that makes the most of the stupendous location atop Cap Diamant. Numerous notables, including Queen Elizabeth II, have stayed here, and suites have been named after Churchill and Roosevelt who were holed up in the hotel during the **First and Second Quebec Conferences** of World War II. A small exhibit charts the history of the hotel in the ornate **lobby**, but you can also take a **guided** tour (daily; visit ⓦcicerone.ca/en/guided-tours for the latest schedule), or connect to the hotel wi-fi (free to the public) and download the **virtual tour app**. You can also sample the hotel's gourmet **afternoon tea** (Sat 2–3.30pm; $41.95/person; reservations advised) at *Place Dufferin* restaurant, or try its three other restaurants and bars, open to the public.

Terrasse Dufferin

Up the slope at the east side of Place d'Armes lies the clifftop boardwalk of the **Terrasse Dufferin** that runs in front of the Château Frontenac, a spectacular vantage point over Basse-Ville and the St Lawrence. It begins at the **Frontenac Kiosk** (where you buy tickets for the Forts-et-Châteaux-Saint-Louis and the city fortifications guided tours). Here also is a romantic statue of **Champlain** and, beside it, a modern sculpture symbolizing Québec City's status as a UNESCO World Heritage Site. Behind here the **funicular** descends to Vieux-Québec's Basse-Ville (see page 249). You can also take the stairs down to the **Porte Prescott**, one of the city's four rebuilt gates.

Lieu historique national des Forts-et-Châteaux-Saint-Louis

Terrasse Dufferin (Frontenac Kiosk) • Mid-May to early Oct daily 9am–6pm (usually also open to early Nov 9am–5pm) • $3.90 • ⓣ418 648 7016, ⓦpc.gc.ca/fr/lhn-nhs/qc/saintlouisforts

Underneath part of the Terrasse Dufferin boardwalk are the foundations of Frontenac's **Château St-Louis**, which served as the governor's residence for two centuries until a fire destroyed it in 1834. Today, little remains at the well-presented **Lieu historique national des Forts-et-Châteaux-Saint-Louis** (St Louis Forts and Châteaux National Historic Site), but the foundations (excavated 2005–2007), weathered stone walls and 120 artefacts found on site (including pipes dating back to Champlain's time) are enigmatic enough, enhanced with audio and plenty of information. Features such as a 1771 icehouse and 1760s brick oven are clearly visible. Buy tickets at the **Frontenac Kiosk**.

Promenade des Gouverneurs

At the southern end of the Terrace Dufferin, a long flight of 310 steps leads up to the 655-metre long **Promenade des Gouverneurs**, a narrow boardwalk perched precariously on the cliff face below the Citadelle. Built in 1958, the incredibly scenic route ends at the **Kiosk des Gouverneurs**, a short walk from the Musée des Plaines d'Abraham (see page 259). From the kiosk you can just spy the **Québec Bridge** to the south, still the longest cantilever bridge span (549m) in the world, despite being completed in 1919.

THE FORTIFICATIONS OF QUÉBEC

The **Fortifications of Québec National Historic Site** (ⓣ418 648 7016, ⓦpc.gc.ca/en/lhn-nhs/qc/fortifications) brings together several sections of the 4.6km city walls and associated buildings. The main wall sections can be viewed on a 1hr 30min **guided tour**, while the Parc de l'Artillerie (see page 257), can be visited independently. Though parts of the wall may be under renovation, it's also possible to walk large sections independently (free).

Tours usually start at the **Frontenac Kiosk** (late May to early Nov 9am–5.30pm; $4.90; daily 10.30am, 1.30pm & 3.30pm; early Oct to early Nov 10.30am & 3.30pm) and proceed clockwise around the walls, making special stops at the Jardin des Gouverneurs, a soldier's casemate in the Citadelle and a nearby powder magazine (otherwise closed to visitors),ending at Porte St-Louis – one of the four city gates. You can also take 45-minute guided tours (late June to early Sept only; $3.90) of the ramparts between Porte St-Louis (departing 1.30pm) and Parc de l'Artillerie (departing 10.30am & 3pm). In August, special "Lantern Tours" ($18) run at 7.30pm nightly from Frontenac Kiosk, enlivened by costumed actors. Special discounts are usually offered for combinations of various tours.

Cathedral of the Holy Trinity

31 rue des Jardins • Daily late May to Oct 10am–5pm (tours Mon–Sat 11am & hourly 1pm–4pm, Sun 1pm, 3pm & 4pm) • Free; guided tours (25min) $6 • ☎ 418 692 2193, ⓦ cathedral.ca

By the corner of rue Ste-Anne and rue des Jardins stands the first Anglican cathedral built outside the British Isles, the **Cathedral of the Holy Trinity**. Constructed between 1800 and 1804 on orders from George III, it followed the lines of London's church of St Martin-in-the-Fields. The simple interior houses the 1845 bishops' throne, reputedly made from the wood of the elm tree under whose branches Samuel de Champlain conferred with the Iroquois. Many of the church's features came from London, including lavish silverware from George III (displayed in the special "**King's Gift**" exhibit along with rare Bibles; $2 donation requested) and Victorian stained glass, shipped in vats of molasses for protection. The brass bars on the balcony denote the seats for the exclusive use of British sovereigns (or their representatives); humbler parishioners had wooden doors on the box pews to keep the winter cold out. In the courtyard (summer only) are Les Artisans de la Cathédrale, Québec-based artisans whose small crafts and clothes stalls avoid tourist tat.

Place de l'Hôtel de Ville and around

Haute-Ville's civic heart remains the **Place de l'Hôtel de Ville**, dominated by the **Monument Cardinal-Taschereau** in the centre and scene of numerous live summer shows. Facing each other on opposite sides of the square lie the edifices of the colony's once-powerful Church and the home of democratic power in the city today – the **Hôtel de Ville** (City Hall) of 1883. To the north, the shops on **Côte de la Fabrique** extend down the hill to the lively restaurants and bars of rue St-Jean. The **Atelier Les Trois Corbeaux** (Three Crow Glass Studio) at no. 41 (daily 10am–6pm; ⓦ troiscorbeaux. com) is best known for its demonstrations of traditional **glass-blowing**. To the south, the square is overlooked by the impressive Art Deco buildings of the **Hôtel Clarendon** and the 82-metre high **Édifice Price** (the city's first skyscraper in 1931, and an official residence for the Premier of Quebec,), on rue Ste-Anne.

Basilique-Cathédrale Notre-Dame de Québec

20 rue De Buade (Place de l'Hôtel de Ville) • Mon–Fri 7am–4pm, Sat 7am–6pm, Sun 8am–5pm • Guided tours daily every 30min 8.30am–3.30pm; reservations required • Free; guided tours $2 • ☎ 418 692 2533, ⓦ notre-dame-de-quebec.org

The impressive bulk of the **Basilique-Cathédrale Notre-Dame de Québec** constitutes the oldest parish north of Mexico; the church burnt to the ground in 1922 – one of many fires it has suffered – and was rebuilt to the original plans of its seventeenth-century forebear. Absolute silence within the cathedral heightens the impressiveness of the Rococo-inspired interior, culminating in a ceiling of blue sky and billowy clouds. The altar, a gilded replica of St Peter's, is surmounted by an elaborate baldachin uncharacteristically supported by angelic caryatids rather than columns due to the narrow space, and is topped by a statue of Jesus standing on a gilded sphere. In the **crypt** more than nine hundred bodies, including three governors and most of Québec's bishops, are interred. Champlain is also rumoured to be buried here, though archeologists are still trying to work out which body is his (you can visit on **guided tours** only). On the right side of the basilica lies the focus of much local veneration, the **tomb of Saint François de Laval** (see page 256), one of Québec's founding fathers. Visit the **Centre d'Animation François-de-Laval** (daily 9am–5pm; free; ⓦ francoisdelaval.com) in the chapel beyond the tomb to learn more about Laval, through a short video and displays of period artefacts.

Musée de l'Amérique francophone

2 Côte de la Fabrique • Late June–Aug daily 10am–5pm, Sept to late June Sat & Sun 10am–5pm • $10 • ☎ 418 643 2158, ⓦ mcq.org/en/informations/maf

The core of the **Musée de l'Amérique francophone** is the gorgeous **chapel** that once served the Petit Séminaire and Université Laval, consecrated in 1900 in Second Empire

4

MONSEIGNEUR LAVAL

François-Xavier de Montmorency-Laval – aka **Saint François de Laval** – was born into a wealthy aristocratic family in northeast France in 1623. Educated by Jesuits, he briefly studied in Paris before giving up his hefty patrimony to join the Church, and was ordained a priest in 1647 at the age of 24. When ten years later the Pope needed someone to oversee the spiritual development of New France, the Jesuits proposed Laval, who before long was made a bishop and sent to Québec. During his incumbency, from 1659 to 1688, Laval founded the Séminaire de Québec (1663) to increase the supply of priests. He also secured more power than the governor and intendant put together – any officer dispatched from France found himself on the next boat home if Laval did not care for him. Ill health, brought about by his religious fervour denying him blankets and proper food, caused his early retirement. But, unhappy with his successor, Bishop de St-Valier, he continued to exert a stubborn influence on the running of the colony well into his dotage. Death finally came in 1708 after complications arising from a frozen foot. Laval was beatified by Pope John Paul II in 1980, and was finally **canonized in 2014** by **Pope Francis**. His tomb lies in the Notre-Dame de Québec (see page 255).

style to replace one that burnt down (Laval was originally buried here before being moved to the Basilique-Cathédrale in 1993 – a memorial side-chapel commemorates the connection). Inside, the **Rediscovered Colony** exhibit traces the history of the first France in America (1541–1543) through artefacts found at the Cartier-Roberval archeological site. The museum occupies part of the giant **Séminaire de Québec**, founded by Laval in 1663 – much of the site today serves as the **Université Laval**.

Musée du Monastère des Augustines

77 rue des Remparts • Tues–Sun 10am–5pm • $10 (guided tours $15, check the website for times) • ☎ 418 694 8565, ⓦ monastere.ca/en/pages/museum

Seemingly tagged on to the mammoth Hôtel-Dieu de Québec (hospital), looming behind it, Québec's old Augustinian convent has been tastefully converted into a boutique hotel and the intriguing **Musée du Monastère des Augustines**. Though offering a similar experience to the Ursulines convent (see below), this site blends old stone, wooden floors and timber ceilings with stylish contemporary design, parts of the old structure completely enveloped by the new. The museum tells the story of the Augustinian Sisters, who came to Québec in 1639 primarily to nurse the sick – they went on to establish twelve hospitals in the province (some eight nuns still live on the premises). Objects displayed include an original mortar and pestle brought from France in 1639, letters patent signed by Louis XIII, and scary looking surgical instruments from the eighteenth century. Le Monastère's **restaurant** and boutique **store** are also worth checking out.

Couvent des Ursulines

12 rue Donnacona

South along of the Hôtel de Ville within narrow rue Donnacona, a sculptured hand holding a quill – a monument to the women who have dedicated their lives to teaching young Québécois – rests on a pedestal. It seems to point the way to the **Couvent des Ursulines**, built by a tiny group of Ursuline nuns in 1642 calling themselves "the Amazons of God in Canada". Their task was to bring religion to the First Nations peoples and later to the daughters of the settlers, a mission carried out in the classrooms of North America's **first girls' school** – the buildings still house a private school.

Musée des Ursulines

Tues–Sun: May–Sept 10am–5pm; Oct–April 1–5pm • $10 • ☎ 418 694 0694, ⓦ museedesursulines.com

A likeness of the Ursulines' first mother superior, **Marie l'Incarnation**, can be seen in a posthumous portrait attributed to Pommier in the interesting little **Musée des**

Ursulines, housed on the site of the home of one of the first nuns, just outside the convent (the current building dates from 1836). The ground floor examines the heritage of the site, while the second and third floors take an unusually in-depth look at life inside the convent and the school – novice nuns and boarders endured a similarly rigorous routine. However, exhibits suggest that the education provided was relatively progressive, even by the nineteenth-century. Other paintings, documents and household items testify to the harshness of life in the early days of the colony, but lacework and embroidery are the highlights, particularly the splendid liturgical ornaments and vestments produced by the early Ursulines and shot through with gold and silver thread.

Chapelle des Ursulines

10 rue Donnacona • May–Oct Tues–Sat 10–11.30am & 1.30–4.30pm, Sun 1.30–4.30pm • Free

Marie de l'Incarnation's remains are entombed in the oratory adjoining the **Chapelle des Ursulines** next to the museum, rebuilt in 1902 but retaining sumptuous altar and sculptures, created between 1726 and 1736 by wood carver Noël Levasseur, and seventeenth- and eighteenth-century paintings acquired from post-Revolution France in the 1820s. A plaque indicates **General Montcalm**'s former resting place below the chapel (only his skull was found there during renovations, and this has subsequently been reinterred in a suburban military cemetery). The rest of the church (the "Sister's Choir") is off-limits, through visible through a grill in the oratory. For more on the life of Marie de l'Incarnation (who, like Laval, was **declared a saint** by Pope Francis in 2014), visit the **Centre Marie-de-l'Incarnation** (May–Nov Tues–Sat 10.30am–noon & 12.30–4.30pm, Sun 1.30–4.30pm; free), just down the street at 6 rue du Parloir.

Parc de l'Artillerie (Artillery Park)

2 Rue d'Auteuil • Mid-May to early Oct daily 10am–5pm • $3.90 • ☎ 418 648 7016, ⓦ pc.gc.ca/en/lhn-nhs/qc/fortifications

The northwest corner of the old town contains the various defensive structures of **Parc de l'Artillerie** (Artillery Park), parts of which were substantially renovated between 2017 and 2019. Though officially part of the Fortifications of Québec National Historic Site, access to the park is managed separately to the city wall tours offered at the Frontenac Kiosk (see page 254), with most of its buildings open for self-guided visits.

Just north of Porte St-Jean is the **Arsenal Foundry**, completed in 1903, and now housing an interpretation centre, with displays on the military pedigree of the city, including a vivid **model of Québec City** completed in 1808. You can also sign up for **fortifications tours** (see page 254) here that lead south along the walls to Porte-Ste-Louis. The adjacent **Gun Carriage Warehouse** dates from 1815.

The northern section of the park, across Rue McMahon, contains the **Officers' Quarters**, furnished as it was in 1830, and the massive **Dauphine Redoubt**, which was completed by the French in 1748. The latter typifies the changes of fortune here: used by the French as the barracks for their garrison, it became the officers' mess under the British and then the residence of the superintendent of the Arsenal. The **Celtic Cross** at the northeastern corner of the park was a gift from the people of Ireland to the people of Québec in 1997, part-recognition of the large scale Irish emigration that took place here during the Great Famine of the 1840s.

New Barracks (Nouvelles-Casernes)

The huge edifice at the northern end of the park is the **New Barracks** (*Nouvelles-Casernes*), built by the French between 1749 and 1752 and later serving as a barracks for the Royal Artillery Regiment until 1871. In 1879 it became a munitions factory, supplying the Canadian army in both world wars and only closing in 1964 – **the massive renovation** of this section is unlikely to be complete until 2021.

Chalmers-Wesley United Church

78 rue Ste-Ursule • Late June to late Oct Wed–Sat 10.30am–4.30pm, Sun 12.30–4.30pm • Free • ☏ 418 692 2640,
Ⓦ chalmerswesleyunited.ca

Completed in 1853, **Chalmers-Wesley United Church** is one of the most beautiful in the city. Its slender, Gothic Revivalist spires are a conspicuous element of the skyline and, inside, the stained glass windows are worth a look (there's also a small historical exhibition on the balcony upstairs). Originally a Presbyterian church, the English-speaking congregation united with the local Wesleyan church in 1931 (Congregationalist, Methodist and Presbyterian churches had merged in 1925 to form the **United Church of Canada**).

Citadelle de Québec

1 Côte de la Citadelle • Guided tours (hourly; late June–Aug every 30min) daily: May–Oct 9am–5pm; Nov–April 10am–4pm • $16 •
☏ 418 694 2815, Ⓦ lacitadelle.qc.ca

Dominating the southern section of Vieux-Québec, the massive star-shaped **Citadelle de Québec** can only be visited on one of the worthwhile **guided tours**. The *tour de force* of Québec City's fortifications, the Citadelle occupies the highest point of Cap Diamant, 100m above the St Lawrence. This strategic site was first built on by the French, but the British constructed most of the buildings from the 1820s under orders from the Duke of Wellington, who was anxious about American attack after the War of 1812. The complex of 25 buildings is the largest North American fort still occupied by troops – being home to the **Royal 22nd Regiment**, Canada's only French-speaking regiment, since 1920. You can visit the extensive museum dedicated to the celebrated "Van-Doos" *(vingt-deux)* – the **Musée Royal 22e Régiment** – independently before or after the tours, to learn about its formation in 1914 and campaigns during the two World Wars, Korean War and various UN missions, most notably Afghanistan 2004 to 2011 (where it lost 15 men).

The tour

The enthusiastic **tours** (1hr) take in various buildings and monuments around the **central parade ground**, including a claustrophobic **powder magazine** under the Prince of Wales Bastion and plaques to the **Quebec Conferences of 1943 and 1944**. You'll see the **noon-day gun** (fired daily), and from the outside only, the old hospital (now regiment headquarters) and the observatory (with a time-ball tower). Tours also stop at the cannon-heavy **King's Bastion** which offers spectacular views of the old town and St Lawrence, before passing the base Chapel, remembrance hall (which can be visited on a VIP tour; $25) and Vimy Ridge Memorial. The French-built Cap Diamant Redoubt (1693), the East Casemate (1831), and the military prison (1842) may also feature – routes sometimes vary.

You'll also pass the **second residence of Canada's governor general** (who normally resides in Ottawa); to see the immaculate state rooms inside, you'll need to reserve a **separate tour** (mid-May to mid-June daily 10am–4pm, mid-June to Aug daily 11am–4pm, Sept to mid-Oct Sat & Sun 10am–4pm; 1hr; free; ☏ 418 648 4322, ✉ citadelle@gg.ca).

In addition to the guided tours, the admission price includes the colourful **Changing of the Guard** (late June to first Mon in Sept daily 10am), which you can catch at the end of a 9am tour (otherwise arrive by 9.45am), and the **Beating of the Retreat** (30min; July & Aug Wed 4pm).

Beyond Vieux-Québec

With so much to take in within Vieux-Québec it's easy to feel compelled to remain there for the duration of your stay. But venture outside the walls and you'll find a cosmopolitan city gradually shedding its provincial reputation as well as offering plenty worth exploring. Paramount of the sights is the excellent **Musée National des Beaux-Arts du Québec**, showcasing Québécois and Inuit art. This lies at the western fringes of the expansive **Parc des Champs-de-Bataille**, site of a decisive battle in the city's history and a pleasant place for a picnic. A few blocks north of the park is stately **Grande-Allée** – many of the city's best restaurants and bars can be found on or just off it. To the east, **Faubourg Saint-Jean-Baptiste** is a lively and progressive neighbourhood with a number of stylish shops and restaurants, and is a great spot for a stroll.

Parc des Champs-de-Bataille

Ⓦ ccbn-nbc.gc.ca/en

West of the Citadelle are the rolling grasslands of the **Parc des Champs-de-Bataille (Battlefields Park)**, a sizeable chunk of land stretching along the cliffs above the St Lawrence River. The park encompasses the historic **Plaines d'Abraham**, named after Abraham Martin, the first pilot of the St Lawrence River in 1620, and is the site of a **battle** that rewrote Canada's history (see box).

The park is littered with monuments and statues – the dead of 1759 are commemorated, rather provocatively, by a beloved statue of **Joan of Arc** (the French saint burned at the stake by the English in 1431), anonymously donated to the city in the 1930s and placed in a beautifully maintained sunken **garden** just off Wilfrid-Laurier avenue at place Montcalm.

Musée des Plaines d'Abraham

835 Wilfrid-Laurier ave • Daily 9am–5.30pm • $13.50 (July & Aug $17; includes Martello Tower 1 and "Abraham's Bus" tour of the park) • ☏ 418 649 6157, Ⓦ theplainsofabraham.ca

The park's **Musée des Plaines d'Abraham** is the best place to gain an understanding of the events of 1759–1760 – the **Battle of the Plains of Abraham** was the most consequential, leading to the deaths of French commander **Marquis de Montcalm**, and British commander **General James Wolfe**, but was not the only engagement of the Québec campaign (see box). Unfolding over two floors, the slickly presented "**Battles 1759-1760**" exhibition features a 30min video, interactive displays and plenty of artefacts found on the site, from animal bones to clay pipes. In July and August, the **Abraham's Bus tour** departs the museum for a guided 40–45min ride around the park.

> ## THE BATTLE OF THE PLAINS OF ABRAHAM
>
> In June of 1759 a large British force led by **General Wolfe** sailed up the St Lawrence to besiege **General Montcalm** in Québec City. After their initial assault was pushed back at the **Battle of Montmorency** at the end of July, the British forces shuttled up and down the south side of the river, raking the city with cannon fire until early September. Montcalm and the governor, Vaudreuil, became convinced Wolfe was planning a direct assault on the citadel from Anse de Foulon (Wolf's Cove), the only handy break in the cliff face; this was confirmed when lookouts observed a British detachment surveying Cap Diamant from across the river in Lévis. Montcalm thus strengthened the defences above Anse de Foulon, but made the mistake of withdrawing the regiment stationed on the Plains themselves. The following night the British performed the extraordinary feat, which even Wolfe had considered "a desperate plan", of scaling the cliff below the Plains via Anse de Foulon, and on the morning of September 16 Montcalm awoke to find the British drawn up a couple of kilometres from the city's gate. The hastily assembled French battalions, flanked by native (mostly Odawa) warriors, were badly organized and rushed headlong at the British, whose volleys of gunfire mortally wounded Montcalm. On his deathbed Montcalm wrote a chivalrous note of congratulations to Wolfe, not knowing he was dead. Québec City surrendered four days later. The following April, the French under the **Chevalier de Lévis** defeated the British at the **Battle of Sainte-Foy**, but were unable to retake the city after British reinforcements arrived up the river – Lévis retreated to Montréal, where the whole of Québec was finally surrendered in September 1760.

Martello Tower 1

South of av Wilfrid-Laurier • July to early Sept daily 9am–5.30pm • $17 (includes Musée des Plaines d'Abraham & Abraham's Bus)

Standing out amid the wooded park, scenic drives, jogging paths and landscaped gardens, are two Martello towers, built between 1808 and 1812 for protection against the potential American attack. **Martello Tower 2**, on the corner of Wilfrid-Laurier and Taché, hosts period dinner events and Halloween festivities (☎418 649 6157 for information and tickets), while **Martello Tower 1**, further south in the park, has superb views of the river from its rooftop lookout and an interactive exhibition on the history of the towers. Martello Tower 3 was demolished in 1905, while Martello Tower 4 still stands on Rue Lavigueur, further north.

Grande-Allée

Sweeping out from Porte St-Louis and flanked by grand Victorian mansions, the tree-lined boulevard of **Grande-Allée** features bustling restaurants, hotels and bars. Adjacent to the hulking *Loews Le Concorde* hotel, Place Montcalm has a monument to **Montcalm** and a more recent statue of **Charles de Gaulle**, the French president who declared from Montréal "Vive le Québec libre" in the 1960s, much to the separatists' delight. On the other side of the street, the neo-Byzantine tower and ornamentation of **Saint-Coeur-de-Marie**, completed in 1920, seems somewhat out of place, though it's no longer a church – at the time of writing it harboured a hip flea market, though its new owner was controversially attempting to build condos on the site.

Musée National des Beaux-Arts du Québec

179 Grande Allée Ouest • June to early Sept daily 10am–6pm; early Sept to May Tues–Sun 10am–5pm, Wed until 9pm year-round • $20 ($10 Wed 5–9pm) • ☎ 418 643 2150, ⬤ mnba.qc.ca • Bus #11

Canadian art had its quiet beginnings in Québec City and the full panoply of this output can be found in the **Musée National des Beaux-Arts du Québec**. The Pavillon Central connects the museum's three main buildings (its original 1933 home, the Pavillon Gérard-Morisset; a renovated Victorian prison renamed the Pavillon Charles-Baillairgé; and the glass-covered Pavillon Pierre Lassonde, on Grande Allée itself, completed to a design by Rem Koolhaas' OMA cpmpany in 2016). The museum's permanent holdings are best seen over the course of a couple of days, and there are compelling temporary exhibitions throughout the year. You can enter via the Pavillon Pierre Lassonde or the Pavillon Central.

Pavillon Pierre Lassonde

Dedicated to **contemporary art** in all mediums, the stylish **Pavillon Pierre Lassonde** displays the best of the museum's post-1960 collections. The first floor features an excellent café, shop and temporary exhibitions, while the permanent Contemporary Art gallery lies on the second floor. The sixty or so works displayed sometimes rotate, but multimedia work from the likes of BGL (Québec City's lauded art collective), Pierre Dorion, Claudie Gagnon, Nadia Myre and sculptor Valérie Blass should all be represented. The third floor features a selection of more than 100 works from the remarkable **Brousseau Inuit Art collection**, tracing the development of Inuit art from the naive works of the mid-twentieth century to highly narrative and intricately carved stone and whalebone sculptures by contemporary artists. The few ancient items include simple whalebone and antler works from the nomadic Dorset and Thulé cultures. Also up here is the absorbing **Decorative Arts and Design in Québec** gallery, featuring Patrick Messier's futuristic, *Mamma Rocking Chair*, the wacky *Vase chinois bachelier avec bananes* by Richard Milette and the bizarre, lobster-like Clipper computer workstation by Douglas Ball.

From the lower level you can stroll to the other buildings via the underground **Passage Riopelle**, decorated with **Jean-Paul Riopelle**'s *L'Hommage à Rosa Luxembourg*, a 40m-long triptych in thirty segments, with ghostly spray-painted outlines of birds and man-made objects.

Pavillon Gérard-Morisset

In 2018 the **Pavillon Gérard-Morisset** reopened after an ambitious renovation to provide an enlightening survey of Québécois "ancient and modern" art. The core *350 ans de pratiques artistiques au Québec* ("350 Years of Artistic Practices in Québec") exhibit features 650 works (paintings, sculptures, the work of silversmiths and goldsmiths, furnishings, the graphic arts and photography) from New France to the counterculture of the 1960s. As Québec churches were the primary art commissioners at the time, most of the earliest works are **religious** in nature, including the output of **Frère Luc**, represented here by *The Guardian Angel*. The most notable contributions to the collection are by two dynasties: the works of brothers **Pierre-Noël and François-Noël Levasseur** from the mid-1700s and the three generations of **Baillairgés** who succeeded them, their copious output including the architecture of churches as well as their interior decoration. Under the British, the subject matter broadened to include portraiture, seen here in **Antoine Plamondon**'s poised *Madame Tourangeau*, and Canadian landscapes by Québec-born **Joseph Légaré** and, more famously, Amsterdam-born **Cornelius Krieghoff** (see page 73), noted for his romanticized landscapes of landmarks in the region. Of the more modern works, urban life is admirably recorded by **Adrien Hébert**'s *Rue St-Denis*, which wonderfully captures the spirit of Montréal in the 1920s.

Pavillon Charles-Baillairgé

Armand Vaillancourt's *Tree on rue Durocher* sweeps up into the atrium of the former jail, a red-brick edifice completed in 1867 (the prison closed in 1970), now dedicated to **Modern Art**. Exhibits begin on the second floor where a few of the exceedingly cramped, bare **prison cells** have been opened up, enlivened by audio recordings of ex-inmates. The rest of the building is primarily dedicated to four of Québec's greatest artists, beginning on this floor with abstract expressionist **Fernand Leduc** (1916–2014) and **Jean-Paul Riopelle** (1923–2002). Leduc's boldly coloured, geometric abstracts begin simply enough (with plenty of stereotypical "modern" monochromatic canvases), but his more complex compositions, such as *The Path and its Obstacles* and *Napoleon's Last Campaign* are well worth viewing. Riopelle's work often resembles that of Jackson Pollock, with giant abstract canvases such as *Sunspray* and *Chicago II,* and especially his *Spain* a mass of paint splats – yet his *Guy-Bleue Viau* is more like an Australian Aboriginal vision of Dreamtime.

The fourth floor continues with **Jean-Paul Lemieux** (1904–1990) and **Alfred Pellan** (1906–1988). The Lemieux gallery begins with his famous *Self-portrait* of 1974 (made into a Canadian stamp), then displays his wildly varying style, from landscapes inspired by the Group of Seven, such as the Charlevoix-set *Afternoon Sun*, through a phase of folk-art-style painting (including *La Fête-Dieu à Québec*, a fun look at the Corpus Christi parade winding down côte de la Montagne), and ending with a series of uncluttered Expressionist portraits. The impact of Pellan, who returned from Paris in 1940 to teach at Montréal's École des Beaux-Arts, plays out in the development of postwar **figurative** and **abstract art**. His comparative radicalism, evident in his Cubist-influenced still life, *Flowers and Dominoes*, was the catalyst for a generation of Québécois artists to pick up on the avant-garde movements of the time. His *Jardin bleu* and *Jardin vert* are especially striking.

Finally, accessed via the fifth floor and a small spiral staircase to the prison tower, Montréal sculptor **David Moore** has created a unique two-storey sculpture of bodies scaling walls – just what you might expect in an old prison.

Hôtel du Parlement

Late June to first Mon of Sept Mon–Fri 8.30am–4.30pm; Sat & Sun 9.30am–4.30pm; first Mon of Sept to late June Mon–Fri 8am–5pm • Free guided tours (English) every 45min 9.15am–3.45pm • ☎ 418 643 7239, ☎ 866 337 8837, ⓦ assnat.qc.ca

Upon Parliament Hill, at the eastern end of Grande-Allée, stand the stately buildings of the **Hôtel du Parlement**, designed by Eugène-Étienne Taché and completed in 1886, using the Louvre for inspiration. The ornate facade includes niches for twelve bronze statues by Québécois sculptor Louis-Philippe Hébert, of Canada's and Québec's major statesmen, while finely chiselled and gilded walnut panels in the entrance hall depict important moments in Québec's history, coats of arms and other heraldic features. From here the corridor of the Presidents' Gallery, lined with portraits of all the Legislative Assembly's speakers and presidents, leads to the Chamber of the National Assembly, where the 125 provincial representatives meet for debate. You can't see much unless you take one of the absorbing **guided tours** (you must pick up passes for these in person, on a first come, first served basis; photo ID required).

Observatoire de la Capitole

1037 rue de la Chevrotière • Feb–June & Sept daily 10am–5pm; July & Aug daily 10am–6pm; Oct–Jan Tues–Sun 10am–5pm • $14.75 • ☎ 418 644 9841, ⓦ observatoire-capitale.com

Among the government buildings clustered to the west of the Hôtel du Parlement, the brutalist **Édifice Marie-Guyart** (at 132m) is the tallest structure in the city, completed in 1972. On its 31st floor, the **Observatoire de la Capitole** offers a 360-degree panoramic view over Vieux-Québec, the Citadelle, the Laurentians, Québec Bridge and beyond (at 221m above sea level), with artsy "Horizon" panels designed by celebrated local designer Olivier Dufour and touch-screens usefully providing background info on what you can see.

Faubourg Saint-Jean-Baptiste

West of Porte St-Jean and across place d'Youville, rue St-Jean passes through the former *faubourg* – the name given to the settlements that once stood undefended outside the city walls – of **Saint-Jean-Baptiste**. The quarter's studenty atmosphere is more relaxed than the rest of Québec, with cheaper restaurants and great nightlife spots. A five-minute walk brings you to the **Cimetière Saint-Matthew** (755 Rue Saint-Jean; May to mid-Nov daily 7am–8pm), Québec City's first Protestant cemetery and now the oldest one remaining in the province. Many historical figures were buried here between 1772 and 1860, including Lt Col James Turnbull, Queen Victoria's presumed half-brother. The neo-Gothic **church of St Matthew** (this incarnation dates from 1848) has long since lost its parishioners – it was converted into a library, now the Bibliothèque Claire-Martin (Fri–Tues 10am–5pm, Wed & Thurs 1–8pm) in 1980.

Further along at no. 695, **Maison Jean-Alfred Moisan** has been in the grocery trade since 1871, making it the oldest grocery store in North America. The tin ceilings and wooden furnishings provide a backdrop for fine foods and baked goods, while on the top floors it runs a quaint B&B (see page 265) – grab a coffee in its on-site café.

On the other side of the street at no.634, **Érico**, one of the city's popular chocolate shops, has established the **Le Musée du Chocolat** (Mon–Wed & Sat 10.30am–6pm, Thurs & Fri 10.30am–9pm, Sun 11am–6pm; free; ☎418 524 2122, ⓦericochocolatier.com), with displays on the history of chocolate and the chance to see sweet treats being made. The district's namesake, the **Église Saint-Jean-Baptiste** (late June to mid-Sept Mon–Fri & Sun 11am–4pm, Sat 9am–4pm), at 410 rue St-Jean, dominates the *faubourg*, its spire rising to 73m. Completed in 1882 in grand Second Empire style, the church's elegant facade is a close reproduction of the Église de la Trinité in Paris.

Saint-Roch

To find out where most Québécois work today, head down to the city's distinctly non-touristy business district in **Saint-Roch**, just northwest of Saint-Jean-Baptiste. Until relatively recently, this was one of the most deprived neighbourhoods in the city, but its regeneration has been startling. Take the stairs at the end of Rue Sainte-Claire or the **Ascenseur du Faubourg** (Mon–Wed 7am–7pm, 7am–10pm Thurs & Fri, 10am–10pm Sat, 10am–7pm Sun), an elevator that whisks up and down the cliff-face for free. Pretty **Jardin Jean-Paul L'Allier** leads on to the main drag, Boulevard Charest, but one block further lies the far more appealing **Rue Saint-Joseph**, lined with hip cafés and boutiques. Dominating its central section, the **Église Saint-Roch** is a twin-towered Gothic Revival behemoth completed in 1923 – it's the city's largest church, with 2000 seats. Inside, try to spot the tiny fossils that appear in the Saskatchewan marble fixtures, and a rare work by seventeenth-century painter **Jacques Blanchard**, *La vision de Saint Roch*.

Cartier-Brébeuf National Historic Site

175 rue de l'Espinay • Late June to early Sept daily 1–5pm • Free • ☎ 418 648 4038, ⊛ pc.gc.ca/en/lhn-nhs/qc/cartierbrebeuf • Buses #3, #4 and #801

Some 3km north-west of Vieux-Québec, on the banks of the Saint-Charles River, the **Cartier-Brébeuf National Historic Site** has a double claim to fame. It marks the spot where Jacques Cartier spent the winter of 1535–36 in friendly contact with the people of the surrounding Iroquoian villages – a relationship Cartier later soured by taking a local chief and nine of his men hostage. It is also where **Jean de Brébeuf** (best known for his martyrdom near today's Midland in Ontario; see page 140), with his Jesuit friends, built his first Canadian residence in 1625. The **interpretation centre** features an excellent account of Cartier's voyages and of the hardship he and his crew endured during the winter, and background information on the Jesuits' role in New France.

ARRIVAL AND DEPARTURE QUÉBEC CITY

BY PLANE

Québec City's Aéroport Jean-Lesage (☎ 877 769 2700, ⊛ aeroportdequebec.com), 20km west of the city, caters almost exclusively for domestic flights; most international flights arrive at Montréal. The 20min trip to Vieux-Québec by taxi is fixed at $35.10; other than Uber, there's no alternative transport.

Destinations Baie-Comeau (1–3 daily; 1hr 35min); Gaspé (2 daily; 2hr 10min); Îles-de-la-Madeleine (2–3 daily; 3hr 20min); Montréal (14–15 daily; 50min); Ottawa (1–2 daily; 1hr 10min); Sept-Îles (3–4 daily; 1hr 30min); Toronto (9–10 daily; 1hr 30min); Wabush (1–2 daily; 2hr 50min).

BY TRAIN

VIA Rail trains from Montréal arrive at the central Gare du Palais in Basse-Ville, while services from the Atlantic provinces stop and depart at Sainte-Foy Station, 11km southwest of the Gare du Palais; a taxi shuttle is available between the two stations but reservations must be made in advance.

Destinations Montréal (5 daily Mon–Fri; 3 daily Sat & Sun; 3hr 10min–3hr 34min); Ottawa (4 daily; 5hr 50min–6hr).

BY BUS

The long-distance bus terminal (☎ 418 525 3000) is at 320 rue Abraham-Martin, adjoining the Gare du Palais. Intercar (☎ 418 525 3030, ☎ 800 363 7279, ⊛ intercar.qc.ca) operates out of here and serves points throughout Northern

and Eastern Québec. Orléans Express (⊛ orleansexpress. com) serves the south bank of the St Lawrence, the Gaspé, Montréal, Trois-Rivières and the Maritimes through Rivière-du-Loup via Maritime Bus (⊛ maritimebus.com). La Québécoise (⊛ autobus.qc.ca) serves Sherbrooke.

Destinations Alma (2 daily; 2hr 45min); Baie-Comeau (2 daily; 6hr 5min–7hr); Forestville (2 daily; 5hr–5hr 45min); Fredericton (2 daily; 8hr 30min); Gaspé (2 daily, via Rimouski; 11hr); La Malbaie (3 daily; 2hr 20min); Les Escoumins (2 daily; 4hr 10min–4hr 50min); Montréal (9–10 daily; 3hr 45min); Rimouski (4 daily; 4hr 20min); Rivière-du-Loup (4 daily; 2hr 35min); St-Siméon (2 daily; 2hr 45min–3hr 20min); Saguenay (Chicoutimi; 4 daily; 2hr 20min); Sherbrooke (2 daily; 3hr 40min); Tadoussac (2 daily; 3hr 35min–4hr 15min); Trois-Rivières (6 daily; 1hr 50min); Val-Jalbert (1–2 daily; 3hr 45min).

BY CAR

Parking in Vieux-Québec can be a pain: it's best to leave your vehicle outside the walls, near the tourist office off Grande-Allée or in the Vieux-Port area.

BY FERRY

The ferry to Lévis (2–3 hourly 6.20am–2.20am; 10min; ☎ 877 787 7483, ⊛ traversiers.com; $3.60 one way; $8.50 with a car) leaves from the waterfront just to the southeast of the Place de Paris.

GETTING AROUND

Québec City's sights and hotels are packed into a small area, so **walking** is the best way to get around. Motorcycles are banned in Vieux-Québec.

By bus For sights further out, like the Musée National des

Beaux-Arts du Québec, RTC local buses (☎ 418 627 2511, ⊛ rtcquebec.ca) run from around 6am–1am (certain routes until 3am Fri & Sat). Fares are a standard $3.05 per journey by prepaid ticket, available at newsstands, grocery stores and

4

supermarkets across town, as are one-day passes ($8.60); the cash fare per journey is $3.50, exact fare only. If you need more than one bus to complete your journey, pick up a transfer (une correspondance) from the driver, which enables you to take the second bus for no extra charge. The main bus terminal in Vieux-Québec is on its west side at place d'Youville, near Porte St-Jean. The main transfer points for RTC buses are here and at place Jacques-Cartier; many buses stop at both locations.

By taxi It's best to call in advance for a taxi, as it's not always easy to find one available when strolling around town. Try Taxi Coop ☎418 525 5191.

Bike rental Cyclo Services, 289 Rue Saint-Paul (☎418 692 4052, ☎877 692 4050, ⓦcycloservices.net; $10–20/hr, $25–50/day).

INFORMATION

Centre Infotouriste 12 rue Ste-Anne, on the other side of place d'Armes from the *Château Frontenac* (daily: late June to Aug 9am–6pm; Sept to late June 9am–5pm; ☎877 266 5687, ⓦquebecoriginal.com). Province-wide information.

ACCOMMODATION

Vieux-Québec still has some reasonably priced **accommodation** options, though prices continue to rise. The only downside to staying there is the difficulty in finding cheap parking – expect to pay at least $25 a day for a spot in a garage. Basing yourself outside the city walls is worth considering, too – the rates are usually better, parking is cheaper and there are some good choices within easy walking distance of the old city. As Québec City is one of Canada's prime tourist destinations, try to reserve in advance, particularly during the summer months and the Carnaval in February.

BASSE-VILLE

★ **Auberge St-Antoine** 8 rue St-Antoine ☎418 692 2211, ☎888 692 2211, ⓦsaint-antoine.com; map p.252. Contemporary hotel divided into two buildings next to the Musée de la Civilisation. All rooms are exceedingly spacious, tastefully decorated (some with a historic theme) and several have views of the river. Massage therapy, a private cinema, gym, babysitters and indoor valet parking ($30/day) are among the top-notch services. **$370**

Le Germain Hotel Québec 126 rue St-Pierre ☎418 692 2224, ☎888 833 5253, ⓦlegermainhotels.com; map p.252. Fabulous boutique hotel with all the touches – feather pillows and duvets, subdued lighting, stylish modern decor and cool frosted-glass sinks lit from below. Some rooms have river views. Amenities include terrace bar service and a fitness centre. **$225**

HAUTE-VILLE (WITHIN THE WALLS)

Au Petit Hôtel 3 ruelle des Ursulines ☎418 694 0965, ⓦaupetithotel.com; map p.252. Situated in a peaceful cul-de-sac just off rue Ste-Ursule, the beds and rooms are a bit small but all are en suite. **$115**

Auberge de la Paix 31 rue Couillard ☎418 694 0735, ⓦaubergedelapaix.com; map p.252. Situated just off rue St-Jean this is by far the better of the city's two hostels, with three floors of cheery dorm rooms that sleep up to eight and five private rooms. There's a large courtyard to hang out in, and shared kitchen. The rate includes breakfast. Nearby parking $17.50/day. **$30**; private rooms **$85**

Auberge International de Québec 19 rue Ste-Ursule ☎418 694 0755, ⓦaubergeinternationaledequebec. com; map p.252. The 300-bed HI hostel, in a former hospice run by nuns, is often full and can be impersonal, though it offers laundry facilities, luggage lockers, kitchens and a bar. Dorms **$31.50**, non-members **$35**; private rooms **$73.80**, non-members **$82**

Hôtel Acadia 43 rue Ste-Ursule ☎418 694 0280, ☎800 463 0280, ⓦhotelacadia.com; map p.252. Over forty attractive rooms with bare-brick walls, original fireplaces, period furniture and the odd stained glass window. A few have shared bathrooms. A buffet breakfast is included in the rate for online bookings. **$135**

Hôtel Au Jardin du Gouverneur 16 rue Mont-Carmel ☎418 692 1704, ☎877 692 1704, ⓦleshotelsduparc. com; map p.252. On the corner of the Jardin des Gouverneurs, the seventeen decent-sized rooms here come with modern furnishings and adjoining bathrooms. **$210**

Hôtel Le Château de Pierre 17 av Ste-Geneviève ☎418 694 0429, ☎888 694 0429, ⓦchateaudepierre. com; map p.252. An 1853 mansion with fifteen plush rooms; all are en suite and those without a/c have balconies. **$169**

★ **Hôtel Manoir d'Auteuil** 49 rue d'Auteuil ☎418 694 1173, ☎866 662 6647, ⓦmanoirdauteuil.com; map p.252. Lavish 1835 town house by the city walls, with stylish Art Deco rooms, free breakfast and a cheery owner. **$170**

★ **Hôtel Maison du Fort** 21 av Ste-Geneviève ☎418 692 4375, ☎888 203 4375, ⓦhotelmaisondufort.com; map p.252. Charming hotel with eleven impeccably designed, spacious rooms, some with exposed brick walls and wooden floors; all rooms have cable TV. There's also a two-room apartment with kitchenette. Doubles **$150**; apartment **$287**

TOP 5 PLACES TO STAY

Auberge St-Antoine See above
Le Château Frontenac See page 265
Hotel Maison du Fort See opposite
Hôtel Manoir d'Auteuil See opposite
L'Hôtel Le Vincent See page 265

Hôtel Manoir sur le Cap 9 av Ste-Geneviève ☎418 694 1987, ☎866 694 1987, ⓦmanoir-sur-le-cap.com; map p.252. Nineteenth-century townhouse (once the home of painter Théophile Hamel), with fourteen bright rooms of varying size, all with a private bath and TV, with exposed beams or stone walls; a few have kitchenettes. **$139**

Hôtel Terrasse-Dufferin 6 place Terrasse-Dufferin ☎418 694 9472, ⓦterrassedufferin.net; map p.252. The better rooms in this 1830 private mansion have some of the finest views in town, overlooking the St Lawrence, which makes up for the slightly plain decor; book months ahead. **$89**; river view **$160**

Le Château Frontenac 1 rue des Carrières ☎418 692 3861, ⓦfairmont.com/frontenac-quebec; map p.252. This opulent Victorian "castle" opened in 1893 (see page 253) and is the symbol of the city. Thanks to its location and history it's the most expensive place in town, with splendid rooms and views, antique furnishings, first-class service and the several stately restaurants and bars. Parking is $36/day extra. **$519**

Maison Historique James Thompson 47 rue Ste-Ursule ☎418 694 9042, ⓦbedandbreakfastquebec.com; map p.252. A B&B in a historic 1793 house with sleigh beds, antiques throughout, a lovely sitting room and filling breakfasts. **$135**

HAUTE-VILLE (OUTSIDE THE WALLS)

★ **Camping Ville de Québec** 2050 rte de l'Aéroport ☎418 871 1574, ☎800 294 1574, ⓦcampingquebec enville.com; map p.248. Although not in the most scenic of settings, this is well run and the closest camping option to the city. The decent range of services includes wi-fi. Take exit 305 nord off Hwy-440 onto rte de l'Aéroport – the campsite is around 5km north of the airport itself. **$35**

★ **L'Hôtel Le Vincent** 295 rue St-Vallier est ☎418 523 5000, ⓦaubergelevincent.com; map p.248. Upscale boutique hotel in Saint-Roch boasting ten exquisitely designed and spacious rooms, each with exposed brick walls, tall windows and cable TV. A full breakfast is included. **$199**

Maison Jean-Alfred Moisan 699 rue St-Jean ☎418 529 9764, ⓦjamoisan.com; map p.248. Occupying a historic residence dating from 1846 and above a long-running general store (see page 262), this friendly B&B has four cosy rooms and elegant public areas with period furniture. **$160**

EATING

It is when you start **eating** in Québec City that the French ancestry of the Québécois hits all the senses. The city's restaurants present an array of culinary delights adopted from the mother country, from humble baguettes to sumptuously presented gourmet dishes. The lively **cafés** are ideal starting points for immersing yourself in the city, as you wash down bowls of soup and *croûtons* (toasted baguettes dripping with cheese) with plenty of coffee.

Vieux-Québec (upper and lower) is home to most of the gourmet **restaurants** and cafés; in Haute-Ville you'll generally find better value along rue St-Jean than rue St-Louis. Other areas have their fair share of eating spots as well – notably Faubourg Saint-Jean-Baptiste and Saint-Roch (both eclectic and cheaper) and, just outside the walls, Grande-Allée (generally touristy and expensive). Although prices in the city tend to be rather high, even the poshest restaurants have cheaper lunchtime and table d'hôte menus.

CAFÉS

Brûlerie St-Jean 881 rue St-Jean ☎418 704 4420, ⓦlesbruleries.com; map p.248. On the eastern edge of Saint-Jean-Baptiste, this local mini-chain has a strong selection of fair-trade roasts as well as soups, sandwiches and free wi-fi. Mon–Thurs & Sun 6.30am–10pm, Fri & Sat 6.30am–11pm.

★ **Café Au Bonnet d'Âne** 298 rue St-Jean ☎418 647 3031, ⓦnew.aubonnetdane.com; map p.248. While away a few hours at this hip café-bar, where you can enjoy omelettes (from $10.95), burgers (from $15.25) and enormous salads (from $16.50) at the quieter end of rue St-Jean. April–Oct daily 8am–11pm; Nov–March Mon–Wed & Sun 8am–10pm, Thurs–Sat 8am–11pm.

Café Krieghoff 1089 av Cartier ☎418 522 3711, ⓦcafekrieghoff.qc.ca; map p.248. This inviting bistro serves up some of the city's best coffee and iconic French fare, including the "quiche du chef" ($13.95) and croque-madame ($14.95). Good spot to sit and read or write in the day, especially on the terrace. Mon–Thurs 7am–9pm, Fri 7am–11pm, Sat 8am–11pm, Sun 8am–9pm.

Casse-Crêpe Breton 1136 rue St-Jean ☎418 692 0438, ⓦcassecrepebreton.com; map p.252. Diner-style restaurant where filling crêpes are prepared in front of you. Choose from stalwarts like turkey, mushrooms, egg and mozzarella ($9.45) or build your own (from $6.95 for two ingredients). There's often a queue, but it moves quickly. Daily 7am–11pm.

★ **Chez Temporel** 25 rue Couillard ☎418 694 1813; map p.252. This cosy café, near the *Auberge de la Paix* hostel, offers bowls of steaming café au lait, croissants and *chocolatines*, but is also a perfect place for soups and sandwiches (from $10–12, desserts from $5). Daily 11am–8.30pm (closed Jan).

★ **La Boîte à Pain** 289 rue St-Joseph est ☎418 647 3666, ⓦboiteapain.com; map p.248. Small locals' haven in Saint-Roch serving buttery croissants stuffed with a variety of fillings, such as a vegetable pâté, or ham and cheese ($7.95), and smoked salmon with capers and red onions ($8.50). The assorted breads and pastries

4

TOP 5 PLACES TO EAT

L'Affaire est Ketchup See page 267
Café Au Bonnet d'Âne See page 265
Chez Jules See opposite
Le Lapin Sauté See below
Restaurant Initiale See below

are all baked daily and justifiably revered; expect a wait at breakfast and lunch. Mon–Sat 6.30am–8pm, Sun 6.30am–5.30pm.

Le Casse-Cou 90 rue du Petit-Champlain ☎418 694 1121; map p.252. Cute little spot at the end of pedestrianized rue du Petit-Champlain, with basic options such as $10 poutine and fish and chips for around $17. Mon–Wed 9.30am–5.30pm, Thurs & Fri 9.30am–10pm, Sat & Sun 9.30am–5pm.

RESTAURANTS

BASSE-VILLE AND VIEUX-PORT

★ **Buffet de l'Antiquaire** 95 rue St-Paul ☎418 692 2661, ⓦlebuffetdelantiquaire.com; map p.252. An old-school diner with cosy tables and bar stools, popular with locals for breakfast (huge plates $12–15) plus home-cooked comfort food like *poutine* (from $7) and *l'assiette Québécoise* (meat pie with beans, $18.70). Daily 6am–10pm.

Laurie Raphaël 117 rue Dalhousie ☎418 692 4555, ⓦlaurieraphael.com; map p.252. Warm but formal atmosphere in a restaurant focusing on *cuisine du marché*. Specialities include fish, sweetbreads, Québec venison and lobster from the Îles-de-la-Madeleine. The three-course chef menu starts at $110 for dinner; it's $155 for five courses. Tues–Sat 5.30–10pm.

★ **Le Lapin Sauté** 52 rue du Petit-Champlain ☎418 692 5325, ⓦlapinsaute.com; map p.252. Very popular, reasonably priced informal bistro specializing in rabbit – even on the breakfast menu ($12–20). Dinner mains include a rabbit *poutine* ($17) and an excellent cassoulet with rabbit confit and duck sausage ($28). Mon–Thurs 11am–10pm, Fri 11am–10.30pm, Sat 9am–10.30pm, Sun 9am–10pm.

★ **Restaurant Initiale** 54 rue St-Pierre ☎418 694 1818, ⓦrestaurantinitiale.com; map p.252. One of Québec City's best restaurants (and priced accordingly – $115–165 for tasting menus), this chic place does a local take on fine French classics, from roasted scallops with sea urchin cream, to roast duckling with rutabaga purée. Tues–Sat 5.30–9pm.

HAUTE-VILLE (WITHIN THE WALLS)

Apsara 71 rue d'Auteuil ☎418 694 0232, ⓦrestaurant apsara.com; map p.252. Cambodian, Vietnamese and Thai dishes such as lobster tail with sautéed broccoli and a rich *pad Thai* in a muted dining room across from the Parc de l'Esplanade. Three-course lunch is around $30, most dinner mains from $17–21. Mon–Fri 11am–2pm & 5.30–10pm; Sat & Sun 5.30–10pm (closed Mon Nov–April).

Aux Anciens Canadiens 34 rue St-Louis ☎418 692 1627, ⓦauxancienscanadiens.qc.ca; map p.252. This overly expensive and touristy restaurant (table d'hôte from $49.95) is nevertheless in Maison Jacquet, one of the oldest and most atmospheric homes in Québec City. It serves refined Québécois specialities like *tourtière* (meat pie) and *pattes de cochon* (pigs' trotters) and house inventions such as duck glazed with maple syrup and caribou in blueberry-wine sauce. Daily noon–9pm.

Chez Ashton 54 Côte du Palais ☎418 692 3055; map p.252. If you're looking to sample some of the best *poutine* in the city, consider this late-night location of the chain *Chez Ashton* an essential stop. Served in a veritable tub, the several *poutine* varieties (from around $5 to $10) are all surefire artery cloggers but worth it just the same. Mon–Thurs & Sun 11am–10pm, Fri & Sat 11am–4am.

★ **Chez Jules** 24 rue Ste-Anne ☎418 694 7000, ⓦchez jules.ca; map p.252. You're spoiled for choice across the board at this lively French brasserie. The superb menu includes exquisitely prepared items such as sole fillet with rice ($22), a sumptuous croque-madame ($18) and duck foie gras ($19). Not a place to skip dessert, particularly the heavenly crème brulee ($7). Monday is all-you-can-eat frog legs for $25 (seriously). Mon–Fri 7.30am–10pm, 11.30am–1.30pm & 5.30–10pm; Sat & Sun 7.30am–10pm & 5.30–10pm.

Conti Caffe 32 rue St-Louis ☎418 692 4191, ⓦconti caffe.com; map p.252. Sharing the kitchen of *Le Continental* next door, this casual and hip Italian restaurant is the best choice on a street swamped with mediocre, touristy restaurants. Veal is a speciality – the medallions in porcini mushroom sauce are rich and succulent. Most mains from $15–17. Daily 11.30am–11pm.

Le Chic Shack 15 rue du Fort ☎418 692 1485; map p.252. On the corner of Place d'Armes, this laidback spot is one of the better cheaper options – and guilty pleasures – within the city walls. Bulging burgers ($12–14) and heaping *poutines* ($7–11) fill the menu (and fresh salads, too), including Le P'tit Dej', a brioche bun stuffed with Canadian bacon, Cheddar, fried egg, pickled onions and Tabasco hollandaise. Local ingredients are used and the quality is blessedly equal to the quantity served. Daily 11am–9pm.

Le Continental 26 rue St-Louis ☎418 694 9995, ⓦrestaurantlecontinental.com; map p.252. Old-school French restaurant – excellent seafood, veal and table-side flambéed dishes are among the options on the table d'hôte (four courses from $65). Mon–Wed 11.30am–10.30pm, Thurs & Fri 11.30am–11pm, Sat 5–11pm, Sun 5–10.30pm.

Le Feu Sacré 68½ rue St-Louis ☎418 694 9022, ⓦfeusacre.com; map p.252. Handsome restaurant with stone walls and leather seating that specializes in divine steak and seafood dishes such as a decent 250g skirt steak ($28) and monkfish with ham, onions saffron cake, basil cream ($25). Daily: May to mid-Oct 7am–midnight; late Oct to April 11.30am–midnight.

Les Frères de la Côte 1129 rue St-Jean ☎418 692 5445, ⓦrestaurantlesfreresdelacote.com; map p.252. A friendly and crowded bistro that draws locals as well as tourists for steaks, pizzas, smoked salmon and fresh shellfish. Mains are priced between $19 and $29 and the eight-course table d'hôte is a bargain at $32. Tues–Fri 11.30am–10pm, Sat–Mon 4–10pm.

★ Le Petit Coin Latin 8½ rue Ste-Ursule ☎418 692 0700, ⓦlepetitcoinlatin.ca; map p.252. Cosy café-bistro with a secluded courtyard. *Raclette* (heated cheese slivers with dried meats; $23–29) is a speciality, but they also serve steaks and a caribou *tourtière* (meat pie; $17) for heartier appetites. Breakfast (7.30–11.30am, until 4pm weekends) ranges from straightforward fry-ups to eggs Benedict. Daily 7.30am–11pm.

Le Saint-Amour 48 rue Ste-Ursule ☎418 694 0667, ⓦsaint-amour.com; map p.252. Romantic French restaurant from celebrity chef Jean-Luc Boulay, with a glass-roofed winter garden and a top-notch wine list. Excellent and inventive cuisine at around $120 for two; the house speciality is a seared foie gras ($35). Mon–Fri 11.30am–1.30pm & 5.30–10pm, Sat & Sun 5.30–10pm.

HAUTE-VILLE (OUTSIDE THE WALLS)

★ Ciel! 1225 cours du Général-De Montcalm ☎418 640 5802, ⓦcielbistrobar.com; map p.248. This rotating bistro on the top floor of the *Hôtel Loews Le Concorde*, overlooking Grande-Allée, offers unbeatable views across the city. For dinner choose from hearty mains such as smoked beef cannelloni with mushrooms and spinach or foie gras (mains $22–32), while the excellent lunch menu is a lot cheaper. Mon–Wed 11.30am–10pm, Thurs & Fri 11.30am–11pm, Sat 9am–11pm, Sun 9am–10pm.

Cosmos Café 575 Grande-Allée est ☎418 640 0606, ⓦlecosmos.com; map p.248. By far the best spot on the Grande-Allée – cool decor, great breakfasts (such as omelette with prosciutto, asparagus, pesto and Parmesan cheese; $14) and menu of tasty poutines ($7.50 to $19.95 for one with foie gras), sandwiches ($16.75–18.75) and burgers ($14.75–18.95), though it definitely feels more like a bar than a restaurant. Crowded and lively for the *cinq à sept* cocktail hour. Mon & Tues 7am–10pm, Wed & Thurs 7am–11pm, Fri 7am–midnight, Sat 8am–midnight, Sun 8am–10pm.

Le Cochon Dingue 46 blvd René-Lévesque ouest ☎418 523 2013, ⓦcochondingue.com; map p.248. Near av Cartier, this branch draws locals, not tourists, as in Basse-Ville. Home-style French cooking, such as a seafood pot pie ($27.50) and a half-rack of maple-smoked ribs ($24.95). Mon–Thurs 7am–10pm, Fri 7am–11pm, Sat & Sun 8am–10pm.

Le Graffiti 1191 av Cartier ☎418 529 4949; map p.248. Chic French–Italian restaurant with decent lunch specials that also does a good Sunday brunch. The dinner menu includes mains ($21–42) such as a succulent bison medallion with sausages in a red wine sauce and a salmon risotto; there's an impressive wine list as well. Mon–Fri 11.30am–2.30pm & 5–11pm, Sat 5–11pm, Sun 11am–2.30pm & 5–11pm.

SAINT-JEAN-BAPTISTE

La Piazzetta 707 rue St-Jean ☎418 521 4393, ⓦlapiazzetta.ca; map p.248. Trendy pizzeria with funky furnishings – the numerous pizza options come close to perfection and are reasonably priced (pizzas range $11–19). Mon–Thurs 11am–10.30pm, Fri 11am–11pm, Sat 11.30am–11pm, Sun 11.30am–10.30pm.

★ Le Billig 481 rue St-Jean ☎418 524 8341; map p.248. Friendly and folksy restaurant that serves enormous mouthwatering buckwheat crêpes (from $9.50). Among the dozen or so house specialities is the decadent Béarn – duck confit, spinach, Swiss and goat cheeses with an onion marmalade ($16). Mon–Fri 11am–10pm, Sat & Sun 10am–10pm.

Le Hobbit 700 rue St-Jean ☎418 647 2677, ⓦhobbit bistro.com; map p.248. A popular local spot where a mixed studenty crowd comes for the great vegetarian options, bistro dishes, burgers and pasta like bison ravioli with mushrooms, diced bacon and a creamy port sauce (mains $19.75–25). Mon–Fri 8am–10pm, Sat & Sun 9am–10pm.

SAINT-ROCH AND BEYOND

★ L'Affaire est Ketchup 46 rue St-Joseph est, Saint-Roch ☎418 529 9020, ⓦen-gb.facebook.com/laffaireest.ketchup; map p.248. What this place pulls off on a nightly basis would seem insane were it not for the good times the small staff – and rapturous diners – are clearly having. With just two domestic-sized ovens and a food prep area not much larger than a cutting board, *L'Affaire est Ketchup* creates exquisite, revelatory Québécois dishes such as seared scallops, sweetbreads and duck (most mains $24–32). The menu rotates nightly; reservations are essential. Open Tues–Sun for dinner seating at 6pm & 8.30pm.

La Gueule de Bois 207 rue St-Vallier est, Saint-Roch ☎418 353 0505, ⓦlagueuledebois.ca; map p.248. Surprisingly affordable French bistro with an understated elegance and a dinner menu full of inventive dishes, none of which make for light eating. Choose from meals such as duck breast with shallots and elk steak (mains $23–32). Reservations recommended. Tues–Thurs 5–10pm, Fri & Sat 5–10.30pm.

4

★ **La Planque** 1027 3e Av ☎ 418 914 8780, ⓦ laplanque restaurant.com; map p.248. The effort it takes to get here is a small price to pay for some of the finest and most inspired French-Canadian meals in the city. Supremely satisfying mains, such as Cap St-Ignace guinea fowl with butternut squash ($27) and Turlo pork with Basque blood pudding and beets puree ($25), are backed by an extensive wine list. The urban-rustic decor wouldn't feel out of place in Montréal, nor would the nightly buzz. Reservations recommended (check the website for lunch hours). Tues–Sat 5.30–10pm.

Tora-ya Ramen 75 rue St-Joseph est, Saint-Roch ☎ 418 780 1903, ⓦ torayaramen.com; map p.248. The ramen noodle has been elevated beyond all recognition at this Saint-Roch institution. Choose from substantial and surprisingly flavourful ramen bowls like miso ($12.25) and *kimchi* ($14.25) as well as bite-size *tsumami* snacks ($4–13.25). Tues–Fri 11.30am–3pm & 5–10pm, Sat 5–10pm.

DRINKING AND NIGHTLIFE

Québec City has far more relaxed **nightlife** than Montréal: an evening spent in an intimate bar or a jazz or blues soiree is more popular than a big gig or disco. Outside of the Festival d'Été in July (see page 247), few major bands tour here, though there are plenty of spots to catch Québécois bands. Québec City's main bar and nightclub strips are around rue St-Jean in Saint-Jean-Baptiste and rue St-Joseph in Saint-Roch; both have lively bars and gay nightspots oozing atmosphere. Places on Grande-Allée tend to cater to tourists, though with the closure of long-time club Maurice in 2017, even this strip is more bar-restaurant focused these days.

BARS AND MUSIC VENUES

Bar Ste-Angèle 26 rue Ste-Angèle ☎ 418 692 2171; map p.252. A dark and smoky neighbourhood bar with a beamed ceiling and cosy nook that hasn't noticed it's in the middle of Tourist Central. Daily 8pm–3am.

Jules et Jim 1060 av Cartier ☎ 418 524 9570; map p.248. A long-time local hangout, this small, quiet place amid all the restaurants on av Cartier serves beers from the province and has patio seating. Mon & Sun 1pm–1am, Tues–Sat 1pm–3am.

★ **La Barberie** 310 rue St-Roch ☎ 418 522 4373, ⓦ labarberie.com; map p.248. Inviting microbrewery in Saint-Roch with a small selection of standout ales. With a large terrace, it's a great spot to relax with a few pints or, better still, the carousel – an assortment of glasses or flutes that has helped make this brewery revered across the province. Daily noon–1am.

★ **Le Drague** 815 rue St-Augustin ☎ 418 649 7212, ⓦ ledrague.com; map p.248. Popular gay bar, café, cabaret and club with cheap imported beers and a full calendar of events and DJ sets most nights. Sunday-night drag shows are great fun. Daily 10am–3pm.

★ **L'Inox Maîtres-Brasseurs** 655 Grande-Allée est ☎ 418 692 2877, ⓦ brasserieinox.com; map p.248. The city's original brewpub serves artisanal cheeses and European sausages; a nice match with the fine ales and ample terrace seating. Daily 11am–3am.

★ **L'Oncle Antoine** 29 rue St-Pierre ☎ 418 694 9176, ⓦ facebook.com/oncleantoine; map p.252. Dark and claustrophopia-inducing stone brewpub tucked inside a historic residence that somehow rarely feels overrun; the sidewalk seating is a great spot for people-watching. There's an excellent choice of Québécois ales on tap and a stellar Scotch selection, too. Daily 11am–1am.

Le Pape-Georges 8 rue Cul-de-Sac ☎ 418 692 1320; map p.252. Tiny cellar of a bar near Place Royale with acoustic acts and pavement terrace serving wines by the glass, cheeses and smoked meats. Popular with the locals. Daily 11am–3am.

Le Pub St-Alexandre 1087 rue St-Jean ☎ 418 694 0015, ⓦ pubstalexandre.com; map p.252. Over two hundred reasonably priced beers and forty single malts in this boisterous English-style pub with frequent jazz and folk nights. There's plenty of choice on the food menu as well; the juicy smoked meat sandwich ($19.95) is hard to pass up. Daily 11am–3am.

Sacrilège 447 rue St-Jean ☎ 418 649 1985, ⓦ lesacrilege. com; map p.248. Friendly and cheap watering hole in the Saint-Jean-Baptiste with a popular terrace in back. Daily noon–3am.

CLUBS

Bar Casablanca 1169 rue St-Jean ☎ 418 692 4301; map p.252. Weekend dance club playing reggae, African and Arabic beats hidden away down a passageway off rue St-Jean (it's part of the *Maison Marocaine* restaurant). No cover. Sat 11pm–3am only.

Dagobert 600 Grande-Allée est ☎ 418 522 0393, ⓦ dagobert.ca; map p.248. This sprawling old house has been one of the city's most raucous nightspots for decades. Young dressed-up clubbers head upstairs for the large Eighties-ish dancefloor. Downstairs a slightly older crowd sits at tiered tables to catch cover bands from 10.30pm. There's rarely a cover charge. Thurs–Sun 10.30pm–3am.

ENTERTAINMENT

For **information** on the city's goings-on, check out the listings section in the French daily newspapers *Le Soleil* (ⓦ lesoleil.com) and *Journal de Québec* (ⓦ journaldequebec. com) and the free weekly newspaper *Voir* (ⓦ voir.ca). The

quarterly bilingual magazine for tourists *Voilà Québec* (ⓦvoilaquebec.com) also carries information, as does the English *Québec Chronicle-Telegraph* (ⓦqctonline.com), published every Wednesday.

running theatre for well-attended small-scale plays. **Théâtre Le Capitole** 972 rue St-Jean ☎418 694 4444, ⓦlecapitole.com. Just outside the city walls, Le Capitole hosts dinner theatre, cabaret and flashy musicals.

THEATRE
Grand Théâtre de Québec 269 blvd René-Lévesque est ☎418 643 8131, ⓦgrandtheatre.qc.ca. The city's main theatre for the performing arts is the Grand Théâtre de Québec, which has a programme of drama, opera, dance shows and classical music.
Théâtre de la Bordée 315 rue St-Joseph est, Saint-Roch ☎418 694 9721, ⓦbordee.qc.ca. Head to this long-

CINEMAS
Cinéma Cartier 1019 av Cartier ⓦcinemacartier.com. Large multiplex showing the latest blockbusters and independent French-language films.
Cinéma le Clap 2360 chemin Ste-Foy ⓦclap.qc.ca; bus #7. The city's repertory cinema, Cinéma le Clap is in Sainte-Foy, and has the odd English film – pick up its monthly programme at cafés and bookstores.

DIRECTORY
Consulate US, 2 place Terrasse-Dufferin (Mon–Fri 9am–4pm; ☎418 692 2095).
Emergencies 24hr medical advice and referral service ☎418 648 2626. Hôtel-Dieu Hospital, 11 côte du Palais (☎418 691 5042), is in Vieux-Québec; Jeffrey Hale Hospital, 1250 chemin Ste-Foy (☎418 683 4471, ⓦjhsb.ca/en), is better for English-speakers.
LGBTQ Gai Écoute and Gay Line (☎888 505 1010; ⓦcaeoquebec.org/gay-line in English 7–11pm only).

Laundry Lavoir Ste-Ursule, 17b av Ste-Ursule (daily 8am–8pm; $4, drying $1/12min).
Post office, 5 rue du Fort (Mon–Fri 8am–7.30pm; Sat 9.30am–5pm) and 698 rue St-Jean (Mon–Fri 9am–7pm, Sat noon–5pm).
Weather and road conditions Environment Canada (☎418 648 7766, ⓦweather.gc.ca) for recorded weather forecast; Transports Québec (☎888 355 0511, ⓦtransports.gouv.qc.ca) for road construction and winter road conditions.

Around Québec City

Options for day-trips on the fringes of the city include **Wendake**, to see Canada's only surviving Huron community, and **Lévis**, on the opposite shore of the St Lawrence River, less inundated by visitors than Québec City and with great views of its more illustrious neighbour. Also in easy striking distance of the city is tranquil, charming **Île d'Orléans** where the agricultural landscape is dotted with *gîtes* and *auberges*. The island is just offshore of the bucolic **Côte-de-Beaupré** further to the northeast, which, though something of a city annexe, boasts the spectacular waterfalls of **Chute-Montmorency** and the **Canyon Sainte-Anne**, as well as the gigantic **Basilique de Sainte-Anne-de-Beaupré**, which attracts millions of pilgrims annually and is one of the most impressive sights in Québec. For those in search of a longer jaunt into the great outdoors, the **Réserve Faunique des Laurentides** is within easy reach and there are a number of **ski hills** in the area.

Wendake

Just northwest of Québec City lies **WENDAKE**, the only **Huron reservation** in Canada (officially the *Nation Huronne-Wendat*). Its name derives from the Hurons' own name for their people – *Wendat*, meaning "people of the island". In 1650, French Jesuit missionaries led three hundred Huron-Wendat from Ontario's Georgian Bay to the shores of the St Lawrence around today's Vieux-Québec, thereby saving the smallpox-weakened population from extermination at the hands of the Iroquois. As more French settlers arrived, the Hurons were successively relocated, ending up here beside the Saint-Charles River in 1697. Today, the central village core of the reserve retains typical Québécois wooden houses with sloping and gabled roofs.

WINTER SPORTS AROUND QUÉBEC CITY

You'll find good opportunities for everything from **cross-country skiing** to **ice-climbing** around Québec City in the winter, but most popular are the **skiing** and **snowboarding** at three resorts – Stoneham, Mont-Sainte-Anne and Le Massif. Some experts in search of big bowls and deep powder might find the terrain limited, but for most, the fine mogul fields, tricky glades, well-thought-out terrain parks and extensive night-skiing more than compensate.

THE SKI RESORTS

Only 6km beyond the city limits off Rte-73 is **Stoneham** (Dec to mid-March Mon–Fri 9am–9.30pm, Sat & Sun 8.30am–9.30pm; late March to mid-April Mon–Wed 9am–4pm, Thurs & Fri 9am–7pm, Sat 8.30am–7pm & Sun 8.30am–4pm; day-pass $69; ☎418 848 2415, ☎800 463 6888, ⓦski-stoneham.com), which has limited expert terrain, but is set in a wind-protected horseshoe valley. Despite a minimal vertical drop of 421m and a modest 322 acres of terrain, it has been sculpted into an impressive ski area, thanks partly to its night-skiing operation, which keeps around two-thirds of the resort open after dark; the après-ski can get wild.

The largest of Québec City's ski areas is **Mont-Sainte-Anne** (Dec to mid-April Mon–Fri 9am–4pm, Sat & Sun 8.30am–4pm (late Dec to mid-March Wed–Sat till 9pm); day-pass $83; ☎888 827 4579, ⓦmont-sainte-anne.com), 40km away via Rte-440, which becomes Hwy-138, northeast of town. It offers a well-balanced mix of terrain and comprehensive facilities. Centred on a single peak and covering 428 acres, it's easily navigable yet still provides a remarkably varied high-density trail system. The presence of novice runs extending from summit to base on both sides of the mountain is handy, while first-timers benefit from free access to bunny slopes adjoining the base area. The resort's greatest strength is its wealth of intermediate-level runs that make up almost half the ski zone. Most start from the resort's rapid gondola and follow a smooth and steep grade back to the minimal lift queues. Those hunting for steeper slopes, moguls, trees and high-speed carving should make for a cluster of black diamonds on the south side.

The third main mountain in the area is **Le Massif** (early Dec to early April opening hours vary throughout the season but are at least 9am–3pm, longer at weekends; day-pass $85; ☎418 632 5876, ☎877 536 2774, ⓦlemassif.com), 75km along Hwy-138 from Québec City. It has some of the most spectacular views of any resort in the world, and despite the presence of a couple of narrow, tricky and busy beginner runs, it's best at providing wonderful intermediate-level carving slopes. The mountain's grooming regime puts several black diamond runs within the capacity of intermediates – but watch out for the terrifying triple-diamond La Charlevoix.

OTHER WINTER SPORTS

Tubing, ice-skating and an indoor climbing wall are available at Stoneham, while Mont-Sainte-Anne offers ice-skating, snowshoeing, dog-sledding, paragliding, sleigh-riding and snowmobiling. The **Mont-Sainte-Anne Cross-Country Ski Center** (mid-Dec to mid-April Mon–Fri 9am–4pm, Sat & Sun 8.30am–4pm), 7km east of the main ski area, is a splendid local resource and the largest of its kind in Canada, boasting over 220km of cross-country trails. Day-tickets cost $31, rentals another $22/day. For more of a wilderness experience cross-country skiers should also explore the rolling hills around Camp Mercier (see page 280). On the fringes of Québec City at Montmorency Falls (see page 273) is the world's largest **ice-climbing** school, L'Ascensation École d'escalade (reservations necessary; from $99 a day; ☎418 647 4422, ☎800 762 4967, ⓦrocgyms.com).

PRACTICALITIES

Mont-Sainte-Anne and Stoneham have on-site **accommodation**, but more convenient are Québec City's hotels (see page 264), linked to Mont-Sainte-Anne and Le Massif via a **ski shuttle** operated by Tours du Vieux-Québec (round-trips $28–32.15; ☎418 664 0460, ⓦtoursvieuxquebec.com). Services run from Place d'Armes (8am, return 4–4.30pm) – at the time of research the only way to reach Stoneham was by car or taxi. All three resorts **rent** equipment (skis or snowboards around $32/day, full gear $47–50). There's a better selection of higher-end gear and lower prices in the stores along the highway in Beaupré.

4

Musée Huron-Wendat and around

15 Place de la Rencontre • Late May to late Oct daily 9.30am–noon & 1–5pm; late Oct to late May Wed–Sun 10am–noon & 1–4pm; $14.50; ⓦ tourismewendake.ca

Part of a striking complex that includes a boutique hotel, the **Musée Huron-Wendat** opened in 2008, it's design inspired by traditional longhouses and including a cylindrical structure that looks like a giant tipi. Permanent and temporary interactive exhibits shed light on Huron-Wendat culture, some of which include ceremonial attire beaded with pearls and porcupine quills, drums of moose hide and feathered headdresses used for festive occasions. A colourful **audio-guide** (included) adds context. On the museum's grounds (and included in the audio tour) is the **National Longhouse Ekionkiestha**, a replica of a traditional Huron dwelling that could hold up to eighty clan members, surrounded by a solid timber stockade and enhanced with flickering camp fires.

The village

From the museum it's a short stroll to the 1730 church of **Notre Dame-de-Lorette** on boulevard Bastien in the centre of the village. This is Canada's only Huron church, and you'll find snowshoes on the altar and a small sanctuary dedicated to **Saint Kateri Tekakwitha**, the first Native American to become a saint, canonized by Pope Benedict in 2012 (ask about entry to the church at the museum). Nearby, the Saint-Charles River shoots through a tiny gorge and down a small but powerfull waterfall dubbed **Kabir Kouba** (see ⓦ chutekabirkouba.com for tours and activities in the summer). Trails provide viewpoints and information boards on the ruins of the mills that once stood here.

Onhoüa Chetek8e

575 rue Stanislas-Koska • Mid-May to mid-Oct daily 9am–5pm (last tour 4pm); mid-Oct to mid-May 10am–4pm (last tour 3pm) • $14.50 • ☎ 418 842 4308, ⓦ huron-wendat.qc.ca

In the northern half of Wendake is one of its main highlights, the **Onhoüa Chetek8e**. This replica of a seventeenth-century Huron village consists of wooden longhouses, smokehouses and sweat lodges with Hurons in traditional garb providing talks on making traditional canoes and snowshoes. You're greeted by a traditional welcome dance; participatory activities such as shooting arrows ($6.50) and working on animal skins ($7.50) cost extra.

ARRIVAL AND DEPARTURE   WENDAKE

By bus The STCUQ #801 bus runs from Place d'Youville to its terminus at Charlesbourg, from where the #72 goes to Wendake (stopping at the bridge over the Saint-Charles River); get a transfer (*une correspondance*) and the 45min or so journey will set you back $3.50.

By shuttle From late May to early Oct a direct shuttle runs between the tourist information centre at 12 rue Ste-Anne (page 264) and the museum (9am, 11am, 1pm & 4pm; return 10am, noon, 2pm & 5pm; $10 one-way, ☎ 418 847 2222; reservations required; get tickets at the tourist centre).

By bike In good weather, the most enjoyable way to get here is by bike – a 25km round-trip along the bike path (La Route Verte 6) from the Vieux-Port; all the climbing is on the way.

EATING

Nek8arre (Onhoüa Chetek8e) 575 rue Stanislas-Koska ☎ 418 842 4308, ⓦ huron-wendat.qc.ca/restaurant. Choose from delicious indigenous foods such as bison sausages ($21), rainbow trout ($22.25) and sunflower seed soup ($6.50) at this relaxed restaurant in a wood cabin. Daily May–Oct 9am–5pm; Nov–April 10am–4pm.

Lévis

Although an attractive Victorian town in its own right, the key appeal of **LÉVIS** is the view across the river of Québec. Most tourists promptly get on the next ferry back to the city, but those willing to scale the staircase (5min walk, to the right as you exit the ferry terminal) to the **Terrasse de Lévis** (a landscaped park created in the 1930s) on the heights of Lévis are rewarded with an even greater panorama. The Terrasse lies at the southwestern end of the old quarter, **Vieux-Lévis**, whose sleepy main drag, **avenue Bégin**, has a small-town feel with low-rise mostly modernized buildings. Towering above the town to the north, the huge **Église Notre-Dame-de-la-Victoire** (18 Rue Notre Dame; usually open Sat & Sun only) was built in 1850 to a solid Neoclassical design by renowned architect Thomas Baillairgé.

Maison Alphonse-Desjardins

6 rue du Mont-Marie • Tues–Fri 10am–noon & 1–4.30pm, Sat & Sun noon–5pm (late June to Aug daily 10am–5pm) • Free • ☎ 418 835 2090, ⓦ desjardins.com/maisonalphonsedesjardins

Around the corner from Église Notre-Dame, **Maison Alphonse-Desjardins** is a particular delight with its cake-frosting-like facade looking onto a leafy park whose centrepiece is a statue of Father Joseph David Déziel, founder of Lévis. Inside, a permanent exhibition explains the evolution of the *caisse populaire* (cooperative credit union) in Québec, and the early twentieth-century interior furnishings convey the lifestyle of the period. **Alphonse Desjardins** was born in Lévis in 1854, going on to co-found the Caisses Populaires Desjardins (today Desjardins Group) with his wife **Dorimène Roy Desjardins** in this house in 1900. From here you can walk east a couple of blocks to rue St-Jean, where a second staircase leads back to the ferry terminal.

ARRIVAL AND INFORMATION

LÉVIS

By ferry The regular ferry leaves day and night (6.20am–2.20am) from near Québec City's place Royale, and costs $3.50 (☎ 418 643 8420, ⓦ traversiers.com) for the 10min crossing – double that if you go back (you must disembark and re-enter the terminal to return).

Tourist office There's a seasonal tourist office outside the ferry terminal (mid-May to mid-June Sat & Sun 10am–4pm; late June to mid-Oct daily 9am–7pm; ☎ 418 838 6026, ⓦ levis.chaudiereappalaches.com).

EATING AND DRINKING

Aux P'tits Oignons 45 av Bégin ☎ 418 835 1816, ⓦ auxptitsoignons.ca. For freshly baked breads and pastries, sandwiches (most $9–12) and salads, stop at this popular café and fine-foods grocery. Mon–Wed 9am–6pm, Thurs & Fri 9am–9pm, Sat & Sun 9am–5pm.

★ **Corsaire Pub** 5955 Rue Saint-Laurent ☎ 418 380 2505, ⓦ corsairemicro.com. Lévis has its very own microbrew pub, conveniently located opposite the ferry terminal. Pair your fish and chips or sticky toffee pudding with a pint of Levisienne (a British-style IPA), "Tanaka",

wheat beer (with ginger) or the Anne Bonny pilsner. Daily 11.30am–3am.

★ **Les Chocolats Favoris** 32 av Bégin ☎ 418 833 2287, ⓦ chocolatsfavoris.com. Sure, the views of Québec City are worth the ferry crossing alone, but chocolate-lovers will find the decadent offerings at *Les Chocolats Favoris* just as enticing. It's understandable then that the queues for a bewildering variety of home-made chocolates and ice cream are often out the door. Mon–Thurs & Sun 11am–9.30pm, Fri & Sat 11am–10pm.

Parc de la Chute-Montmorency

5300 Sainte-Anne Blvd (main entrance), 12km northeast of Québec City • Site open year-round, parking & facilities open Feb to mid-April Thurs–Sun 10am–4pm; mid-April to late May Mon–Fri 9am–5pm, Sat & Sun 9am–6pm; late May to mid-June daily 9am–6pm; mid-June to mid-Aug daily 8.30am–6.45pm; mid-Aug to Oct daily 8.30am–5.15pm; closed Jan, Nov & Dec • Free; parking $10.65/car (Nov–April $7.18); cable car $14.35 return ($12.18 Nov to late April) • ☎ 418 663 3330, ⓦ sepaq.com/destinations/parc-chute-montmorency

The waters of the Montmorency River cascade 83m down from the Laurentians into the St Lawrence River, making the spectacular falls at **Parc de la Chute-Montmorency** one and a half times the height of Niagara (though the volume of water is considerably less). The falls, named by Champlain in honour of the governor of New France, were the site of Wolfe's first attempted attack on the colony, but Montcalm's superior forces repelled the British at the **Battle of Montmorency** in 1759 (Wolfe's redoubt is visible off the main trail above the falls). In those days – before a hydroelectric dam cut off much of the flow – the falls were far more impressive, but the cascade remains a mesmerizing spectacle, especially in winter, when the water and spray create a gigantic cone of ice at the base, known locally as the "sugar loaf".

From the main car park a **cable car** runs to the **interpretation centre** in the **Manoir Montmorency**, which also contains the *Pub Kent House* (daily mid-June to mid-Sept) and a restaurant with a terrace (daily mid-May to mid-Oct), famed for its Sunday brunch (April–Dec 10am–5pm) The elegant mansion was rebuilt after a fire in 1993 to replicate the 1780 original built by British governor Frederick Haldimand as a country retreat. The interpretation centre chronicles the history of the site, which includes a period of residence by Queen Victoria's father in the 1790s. Hard to believe today, but a giant cotton mill operated at the foot of the falls until 1985. From the centre, a cliffside walkway leads to the suspension bridge over the falls (wooded trails follow the river upstream) and onto the zigzag staircase down the other side, offerings sensational (and often saturated) views of the cascade. Along the way a 300-metre **zipline** ($26) and **via ferrata** ($32.50–48.50) are offered in the summer.

ARRIVAL AND DEPARTURE   PARC DE LA CHUTE-MONTMORENCY

By bus Local STCUQ bus #800 terminates just before the top of the falls; you can catch the bus at the Place d'Youville station in Québec; it takes around 40min, costing $3.50. Other buses run here, but you'll have to change in order to get to Québec City centre.

By train The tourist-oriented Train de Charlevoix (ⓦ traindecharlevoix.com) runs from the park's Chute-Montmorency station north to La Malbaie via Baie-Saint Paul (2–3 daily mid-June to mid-Oct; from $98 one-way). Shuttle buses ($5 one-way or $10 return) depart Gare du Palais and Place d'Youville in Québec City to connect with the trains – check the website for the latest schedule.

By bike It's a 25km round-trip from the Vieux-Port and the Corridor du Littoral bike path passes the Domaine Maizerets park, good for a pleasant break.

Île d'Orléans

From just northeast of Québec City to a short distance beyond Sainte-Anne-de-Beaupré, the St Lawrence River is bottlenecked by the **ÎLE D'ORLÉANS**, a fertile islet whose bucolic atmosphere and handy location make it a popular spot for holiday-making Québécois. More than most places on the mainland, the island, with its old stone churches, little cottages and seigneurial manors, has kept a flavour of eighteenth-century French Canada; it was only joined to the mainland in 1935, when a suspension bridge was constructed from Hwy-440, opposite the Montmorency falls, connecting it to the west end of the island. Tourism and agriculture are mainstays: **roadside stalls** heave under the weight of **fresh fruit** (especially raspberries and apples), vegetables, jams, dairy products, home-made bread and maple syrup, and the island's restaurants and B&Bs are some of the best in the province.

Encircling the island, Hwy-368 – called the chemin Royal for most of its length – dips and climbs over gentle slopes and terraces past acres of neat farmland and orchards, passing through the six villages with their churches evenly spaced around the island's periphery. A counterclockwise tour of the island (turn right on chemin Royal from the highway) and its principal villages is described below.

Sainte-Pétronille

The island's oldest and most beautifully situated settlement, riverside **SAINTE-PÉTRONILLE** is characterized by the grand white clapboard homes of the merchants who made their fortunes trading farm produce with Québec City. At the heart of the village lies the mouth-watering treats of the **Chocolaterie de l'Ile d'Orleans** (ⓦ chocolaterieorleans.com), while some of the best views of Québec City and the Montmorency falls can be had from nearby rue Horatio-Walker, which runs along the riverside promenade. Known unofficially as the grand seigneur of Sainte-Pétronille, artist **Horatio Walker** lived here from 1904 until his death in 1938. His subject matter was almost entirely based on the Île d'Orléans and many of his paintings now grace Canada's larger galleries.

Saint-Laurent

Until the 1950s the south shore of the island was the domain of sailors and navigators, with the village of **SAINT-LAURENT** being the island's supplier of *chaloupes*, the long rowing boats that were the islanders' only means of getting to the mainland before the bridge was built. At the **Parc maritime de Saint-Laurent** (120 chemin de la Chalouperie; mid-June to mid-Oct daily 10am–5pm; $5; ☎418 828 9672, ⓦparcmaritime.ca) you can take a guided tour of the island's shipbuilding history and the interpretation centre provides details of attractions like **La Forge à Pique-Assaut** (2200 chemin Royale; June to mid-Oct daily 9am–5pm; rest of year Mon–Fri 9am–noon & 1.30–5pm; free; ☎418 828 9300, ⓦforge-pique-assaut.com), which features a blacksmith's shop and an eighteenth-century bellows, and sells forged metal crafts. Today Saint-Laurent is more notable for its **art galleries**, a couple of tiny roadside chapels (the "**Chapelle de procession**" common on the island, often used here as art galleries) and the 1860s **Église de Saint-Laurent** (open daily mid-May to Sept), picturesquely situated right on the river with a handsome interior created by the architect Charles Baillargé.

Saint-Jean

The nautical roots of the island's prettiest village, **SAINT-JEAN**, are plain to see; the cemetery of the red-roofed **Eglise de Saint-Jean-de-l'île-d'Orléans** contains gravestones of numerous mariners. Dating back to the 1730s, the interior of the church was worked on by **Jean Baillairgé**, patriarch of the famous family of architects. Don't miss **Confiturerie Tigidou** (5508 chemin Royal) at the southern end of the village, which sells high-quality homemade berry jams throughout the summer (free jam-tasting, or $2 with a scone).

Manoir Mauvide-Genest

1451 chemin Royal • mid-May to mid-June & mid-Sept to mid-Oct Sat & Sun 11am–5pm; late June to early Sept daily 11am–5pm • $9 • ☎418 829 2630, ⓦmanoirmauvidegenest.com

Saint-Jean's museum of antique furniture and domestic objects is housed in the stately **Manoir Mauvide-Genest**, a huge mansion built between 1734 and 1752 for ship's surgeon and later "seigneur de l'île d'Orléans" Jean Mauvide. The metre-thick walls withstood the impact from Wolfe's bombardment in 1759 – you can still see dents in the wall.

Saint-François

The northernmost village of **SAINT-FRANÇOIS** is best known for its wooden observation tower (**Tour d'observation St-François**), providing clear views (via 98 steps) of the smaller river islands to the north, and **La Seigneurie** (mid-May to early Oct; $7–20; ⓦseigneurieiledorleans.com) a fragrant lavender farm and varied gardens where you can do guided tours (lavender best in July; tours from $38).

Sainte-Famille

Among the French wood and stone buildings in **SAINTE-FAMILLE** (which straggles along the hilltop rather than the river), two particularly fine examples are open to the public. Make a stop also at **Les Fromages de l'isle d'Orléans** (daily: late June to early Sept 10am–6pm, early Sept to mid-Oct 11am–5pm; ☎418-829-0177, ⓦfromagesdeliledorleans.com) at 2950 chemin Royal, **where you can see** traditional **cheesemaking** and sample artisanal cheeses. Look out for **viewpoints** of the river along the road here – the Basilique de Sainte-Anne-de-Beaupré (see page 277) should be clearly visible on the far bank.

Maison de nos Aïeux

2485 chemin Royal • Mid-Feb to early June Mon–Fri 10am–4pm; early June to Aug daily 10am–6pm; Sept to early Oct daily 10am–4pm; early Oct to Nov Sun–Fri 10am–4pm • $5 • ☎418 829 0330, ⓦfondationfrancoislamy.org

Next to the ornate eighteenth-century **Église Sainte-Famile-de-l'île-d'Orléans**, the 1896 rectory is now the **Maison de nos Aïeux**. Displays inside offer a fine introduction to the island's history and traditions, with exhibits on the early colonists, the role of the Catholic Church and local cuisine.

Maison Drouin

4700 chemin Royal • Mid-June to Aug daily 10am–6pm; Sept to early Oct Sat & Sun noon–4pm • $6 • ☎ 418 829 0330, ⓦ fondationfrancoislamy.org

The handsome **Maison Drouin** was built by the Canac dit Marquis family around 1730 (the Drouin family acquired the house in 1872). Today it contains exhibits on the architecture of the island's early houses.

Saint-Pierre

The largest village on the island, **SAINT-PIERRE** also runs along the hilltops for several kilometres, notable for its stone **Église de Saint-Pierre** (1445 chemin Royal; June to early Oct 10am–4pm), the oldest church in rural Québec. Constructed in 1718, it has pews with special hot-brick holders for keeping bottoms warm on seats, while Thomas Baillairgé worked on the interior in the nineteenth century. A modern church was built next door in 1955, and services are no longer held here.

Before you leave the island make a stop at **Isle de Bacchus** (1335 chemin Royal; daily 10am–6pm; ☎ 418 828 9562, ⓦ isledebacchus.com), one of several island vineyards that produces an excellent series of ice wines, and **Cidrerie Bilodeau** (1868 chemin Royal, ☎ 418 828 9316, ⓦ en.cidreriebilodeau.com) a family-run apple orchard and cider mill (which also sells apple butter and sugar pie).

Espace Félix-Leclerc

1214 chemin Royal • Mid-May to early Oct daily 9.30am–5.30pm; early Oct to last weekend in Oct Sat & Sun 9.30am–5.30pm • $8 • ☎ 418 828 1682, ⓦ felixleclerc.com

Saint-Pierre is also known as the long-time home and final resting place of **Félix Leclerc**, the poet and singer-songwriter who penned *P'tit Bonheur* and the first musician to bring Québécois music international acclaim. The **Espace Félix-Leclerc** covers a site that pays homage to Leclerc's life and work, and has several hiking trails and picnic tables.

ARRIVAL AND INFORMATION ÎLE D'ORLÉANS

By car Hwy-368, 2.5km to the east of the Chute-Montmorency, bridges the St Lawrence (no toll) and arrives at the southern end of Sainte- Pierre.

By bus PLUMobile buses depart from av d'Estimauville and blvd Monseigneur Gauthier (near Terminus Beauport) in Québec City and stop at multiple points on the island (Mon–Fri 8.05am, 2.10pm & 5.20pm; $5 one-way to/from Québec; $4 for rides within Île d'Orléans).

Visitor centre 490 côte du Pont, on the right at the top of the hill after the bridge from the mainland (Jan–March, Nov & Dec Mon–Fri 8.30am–4.30pm; April & mid-Oct to end Oct Mon–Fri Mon–Fri 8.30am–4.30pm, Sat & Sun 11am–3pm; May to mid-June & Sept to mid-Oct Mon–Fri Mon–Fri 8.30am–4.30pm, Sat & Sun 9am–5pm; mid-June to Aug daily 8.30am–6pm; ☎ 418 828 2335, ⓦ tourisme. iledorleans.com); provides comprehensive details on the island's B&Bs and has details on self-guided driving tours (English available).

ACCOMMODATION

Auberge L'Île Flottante 7127 chemin Royal, Saint-Laurent ☎ 418 828 9476, ⓦ ileflottante.com. Pretty and cheerful B&B occupying an ancestral dwelling with five comfortable rooms and friendly and helpful owners Annie and Michel. Local ingredients are used to prepare the filling breakfasts that are served in a handsome dining room furnished with antiques. $93

Camping Orléans 357 chemin Royal, Saint-François near the village jetty ☎ 418 829 2953, ⓦ camping orleans.com. Scenic campsite set on the river with a good range of services, including a small on-site pool and free wi-fi. Showers $1 (8min). Mid-May to early Oct. Two-night minimum. Unserviced $37; hook-up $43

Le Vieux Presbytère 1247 av Monseigneur D'esgly, Saint-Pierre ☎ 418 828 9723, ⓦ presbytere.com. A charming inn with low ceilings, beams and antiques in an old presbytery just behind the village church. It has terrific river views, rents bicycles and has a good restaurant serving game dishes. Breakfast is included. $95

4

EATING AND DRINKING

★ **La Boulange** 4624 chemin Royal, Saint-Jean ☎418 829 3162, ⓦ laboulange.ca. One of the island's best *boulangeries* and justifiably popular, with irresistible bread, pastries and pizzas. Stock up for a picnic or savour the baked goods on the terrace with views of the river. April & early Oct to Dec Fri & Sat 7.30am–5.30pm; May to late June Thurs–Sat 7.30am–5.30pm; late June to Aug Mon–Sat 7.30am–5.30pm; Sept to early Oct Wed–Sat 7.30am–5.30pm; year-round Sun 7.30am–5pm.

La Goéliche 22 rue du Quai, Sainte-Pétronille ☎418 828 2248, ⓦ goeliche.ca. This historic inn right on the water serves dishes such as pork fillet with a strawberry and honey sauce and salmon steak marinated in *crème de cassis* (mains $24–29). Mon, Wed & Thurs 8.30am–7.30pm, Tues 8.30am–2.30pm, Fri & Sat 8.30am–8.30pm; (hours change seasonally).

Les Ancêtres 1101 chemin Royal, Saint-Pierre ☎418 828 2718, ⓦ lesancestres.ca. Excellent restaurant with stone walls and superb vistas over the St Lawrence serving creative takes on traditional French-Canadian cuisine, such as veal medallions with mushrooms and hazelnuts (mains $21–40). Tues–Sun from 5pm.

Pub Le Mitan 2471 chemin Royal, Sainte-Famille ☎418 829 0408, ⓦ microorleans.com. An inviting microbrewery and just about an essential stop in summer, *Pub Le Mitan* has a terrace overlooking the river from which you can enjoy a fine selection of home-brewed ales. May & Oct–Nov Fri 4.30–11pm, Sat 11.30am–11pm, Sun 11.30am–6pm; June–Sept daily 4–11pm.

Un des 2 (Canard Huppé) 7326 chemin Royal, Saint-Laurent ☎418 828 2292, ⓦ undes2.com. A gourmand's treat, the deli and cafe attached to the Canard Huppé inn serves freshly-ground coffee, ready-to-eat meals and all sorts of artisanal food products from the island. Mon–Wed & Sat–Sun 8am–5pm, Thurs & Fri 8am–7pm.

Côte-de-Beaupré

The **Côte-de-Beaupré** stretches along the St Lawrence River past the **Basilique de Sainte-Anne-de-Beaupré**, 40km northeast of Québec City, as far as the migratory bird sanctuary on **Cap Tourmente**, where you can see the greater snow goose in spring and autumn. There are two roads along the coast: the speedy autoroute Dufferin-Montmorency (Hwy-440, then Hwy-138) and the slower avenue Royale (Hwy-360), which local buses serve. The latter road gives a far better introduction to the province's rural life, passing through little villages with ancient farmhouses and churches lining the way. Beyond Sainte-Anne-de-Beaupré, Hwy-360 leads to one of the best ski resorts in the province – **Mont-Sainte-Anne** (see page 279), which has everything from golf to world-championship mountain biking in summer.

Au Trois Couvents

7976 Ave Royale, Château-Richer • Daily 10am–5pm • $6 • ☎418 826 3677, ⓦ auxtroiscouvents.org

Acting as a modest gateway to the region, **Au Trois Couvents** ("the three convents") lies in the sleepy village of **CHÂTEAU-RICHER**, just off the highway to Sainte-Anne-de-Beaupré (25km northeast of central Québec City). The grand three-storey building served as the third convent in the village – this Second Empire-style version dates from 1907 but was rebuilt twice. Inside bilingual exhibits chronicle the history of the Côte-de-Beaupré, region, from the arrival of the first French families in the 1630s.

Basilique de Sainte-Anne-de-Beaupré and around

10018 Ave Royale, Sainte-Anne-de-Beaupré • Basilica Daily: May–Aug 7am–9.30pm, Sept 8am–5.30pm; Oct–April 8.30am–5pm • **Information centre** Daily: May–Sept 8am–5.30pm, Oct 8.30–5.30pm, Nov–April 8.30am–4.30pm • ☎418 827 3781, ⓦ sanctuairesainteanne.org

Pretty much the only reason to stop in **SAINTE-ANNE-DE-BEAUPRÉ** is to see Québec's equivalent of Lourdes – the **Basilique de Sainte-Anne-de-Beaupré**. It dominates the immediate area, its twin spires soaring above the St Lawrence shore. The church began in 1658 as a small wooden chapel devoted to **St Anne** (traditionally the Virgin Mary's mother). The current Romanesque Revival confection with lofty symmetrical spires is the fifth church to stand here (consecrated only in 1976), fires and floods having destroyed the first four. The statue of St Anne between the steeples miraculously survived the 1922 destruction of the fourth church, even though the roof and both steeples fell in the blaze. The basilica seats 1500, though on **St Anne's feast day (July 26)** up to five thousand crowd in. Most of its mesmerizing decoration – countless stained glass windows and massive murals – depict the miraculous powers of St Anne, while the wooden pews bear delightful animal carvings. Behind the ornate golden statue of St Anne itself, depicted holding her daughter Mary, is a chapel said to contain a portion of Anne's forearm, donated by the pope in 1960. Those who have been cured by her intervention have left a vast collection of crutches and wooden limbs hanging on the basilica's pillars near the entrance. Be sure to visit the basement **Chapelle de l'Immaculée Conception**, a far more intimate space dedicated to the Virgin Mary, adorned with paintings of the saints. Of to the side down here is the small but beautifully decorated

Chapelle du Très-Saint-Sacrement, as well as a faithful replica of Michelangelo's statue **La Pietà**.

The outer shrines

Chapelle Commémorative & Scala Santa May to mid-Oct daily 8am–5pm

Several little chapels lie outside in the basilica's shadow. The simple **Chapelle Commémorative**, across the street behind the basilica, contains some of the stones from the second chapel and was built in the nineteenth century on the foundations of the transept of the third church (1676–1877), hence its north–south orientation. Nearby, the small white chapel of the **Scala Santa** contains stairs that supposedly replicate those climbed by Christ on his meeting with Pontius Pilate. Glass boxes, embedded in each stair, contain lumps of earth from various holy places, and the devout accomplish the ascent on their knees. Another obligatory part of the penitential route is the nearby **Way of the Cross** (Chemin de Croix), which curves steeply up the hillside. There are two daytime processions, and on some summer evenings torchlit processions wend their way through each station. The **Musée de Sainte-Anne**, on the other side of the basilica, closed in 2017, and at the time of writing seemed unlikely to reopen.

ARRIVAL AND DEPARTURE   SAINTE-ANNE-DE-BEAUPRÉ

By bus The journey 39km northeast from Québec City takes 25–35min by Intercar bus from central Gare du Palais (3 daily; $8.65 one-way) or 35min on the local PLUMobile bus from Gare du Palais and Place d'Youville (Mon–Fri 3 daily; $5 one-way).

By train The tourist-oriented Train de Charlevoix (ⓦ traindecharlevoix.com) runs from Chute-Montmorency station to Sainte-Anne (2–3 daily mid-June to mid-Oct; from $29 one-way).

THE MIRACLE OF ST ANNE

According to Christian tradition, **St Anne** was the mother of Mary and the grandmother of Jesus (though she's not mentioned in the Gospels). Despite having no physical connection with Canada, the reason her shrine is so revered today (and the reason she's a patron saint of the nation) is thanks to the Catholic belief in **miracles** – specifically the belief that St Anne grants miracles to the faithful through her intercession. During the construction of the first chapel on the site of the **Basilique de Sainte-Anne-de-Beaupré**, a crippled peasant – one Louis Guimond – was allegedly cured of rheumatism; but the legend of St Anne's intercession didn't really get going until some Breton sailors were caught in a storm on the St Lawrence River in 1661 and vowed to build a chapel to St Anne if she saved them. The ship capsized at nearby Cap Tourmente, but the sailors survived. Word of this miracle spread, and from then on everyone caught in the river's frequent storms prayed to St Anne. In 1876, the same year St Anne was declared **patron saint of Québec**, the church was distinguished as a basilica, to which the devout came on their knees from the beach or walked shoeless from Québec City; today, one and a half million pilgrims flock to the site every year in comfortable coaches.

ACCOMMODATION AND EATING

Auberge Baker 8790 av Royale, Château-Richer ☎ 418 824 4478, ⓦ aubergebaker.com. A wonderfully atmospheric B&B occupying a 150-year-old farmhouse set well back from the busy Hwy-138 (about half-way between central Château-Richer and Sainte-Anne). Rooms have rough-hewn beams and gloriously mismatched antique furnishings; guests have use of a communal kitchen. $99
La Camarine 10947 blvd Ste-Anne, Beaupré ☎ 418 827 5703, ⓦ camarine.com. The restaurant of this rambling inn (3km from the basilica in Beaupré) is the best in the area, serving an eclectic variety of French, Italian and Asian dishes, often fused and off a frequently changing menu. The

food is of the highest standard – mains run $16.95–45.95 (most $20–30). Mon–Thurs & Sun 7am–2pm & 4–9pm, Fri & Sat 7am–2pm & 4–10pm.

★ **Microbrasserie Des Beaux Prés** 9430 blvd Ste-Anne (Rte-138) ☎ 418 702 1128, ⓦ mdbp.ca. By far the most enticing option in Saint-Anne itself, this brewpub lies just under 2km from the basilica (20min walk). Try the beef chilli ($12) or smoked meat Panini ($12), washed down with "Bonne Sainte-Anne" blonde ale or "Route 138" double IPA. Tues 3–10pm, Wed noon–11pm, Thurs & Sat noon–midnight, Fri noon–1am, Sun noon–10pm.

Mont-Sainte-Anne

Just up the highway from Sainte-Anne-de-Beaupré is the town of Beaupré, which provides access to **MONT-SAINTE-ANNE** (see page 278; ⓦ mont-sainte-anne.com). The ski resort has successfully marketed itself as an off-season destination and is now the longest-standing venue on the **mountain bike** world-cup circuit. **In summer** you can explore the extensive cross-country mountain-bike trails ($19), either staying around the base area to test your trials skills on the North Shore-style wooden obstacles, or using the gondola ($21.74 round-trip) to explore one of the hardest downhill mountain-bike courses in the world (there are easier routes down the mountain). Bikes can be rented at the base area with front-suspension models going for $40 for four hours, full-suspension for $75.

Hikers wanting to enjoy the remarkable views over the St Lawrence River and Québec City, as well as try out the several marked trails, can also take the gondola up the mountain. Yet one of the best hiking trails leaves out of the car park at the base area – head down the hill and over the bridge along the main road – to the **Chutes Jean-Larouse**, a twenty-minute walk. The trail leads to a series of dramatic waterfalls, though the latticework stairway that's been constructed alongside is just as dizzying and almost more impressive.

ACCOMMODATION   MONT-SAINTE-ANNE

Camping Mont-Sainte-Anne 300 Rang Saint-Julien, Saint-Ferréol-les-Neiges ☎ 418 827 5281, ☎ 800 463 1568, ⓦ mont-sainte-anne.com/en/summer/campground.

Seven kilometres east of the resort is its pleasantly wooded campsite which has a nice range of services and free wi-fi. To reach it, take a left off av Royale. $37

Canyon Sainte-Anne

On Hwy-138 6km east from the Mont-Sainte-Anne base area • Mid-May to late June & early Sept to mid-Oct daily 9am–5pm; late June to early Sept daily 9am–6pm • $14 • ☎ 418 827 4057, ⓦ canyonsa.qc.ca

For an especially grand waterfall head to **Canyon Sainte-Anne** about a 30min drive from Québec City. Here, the Saint-Anne River has carved a gorge where the water tumbles 74m, flanked by a chasm fringed with woodlands and short nature trails. A bridge crosses just before the precipice, giving views down the canyon, while in front of the falls a suspension bridge allows for splendid – and terrifying – views. Project Vertical (☎ 418 647 4422, ⓦ projetvertical.com) leads a variety of adrenaline-fuelled activities in the canyon, including a thrilling 60m zip-line over the gorge and a challenging *via ferrata* climb ($50–77), also open in the winter.

Réserve Faunique des Laurentides

Park entry $8.60 • ☎ 418 848 2422, ☎ 800 665 6527, ⓦ sepaq.com/rf/lau

The zone of the Laurentians 40km to the north of Québec City – via Hwy-73 and Hwy-175 – is considerably wilder than the mountains near Montréal, thanks to the creation of the **Réserve Faunique des Laurentides**. The vast wooded terrain, with summits of more than 1000m towards the east, was once a hunting ground of the Montagnais, until the Hurons, armed by the French, drove the small population further north. The wildlife reserve became a protected area in 1895 to conserve the caribou herds, an intervention that was not a great success – very few exist today. Although it allows controlled moose-hunting, the reserve's main function is still to preserve native animals such as the beaver, moose, lynx, black bear and deer, all of which you may see in remote areas.

The heavy snowfall makes the park an excellent place for **cross-country skiing** on a 120km network (day pass $15.44; equipment rental $28.50/day). Hwy-175 traverses the reserve; halfway through is **L'Étape**, the only spot to fill your tank (or yourself) until just before Chicoutimi or Alma.

Parc national de la Jacques-Cartier

Park entry $8.60 · **Discovery and Visitors Centre** April to mid-May Sun–Fri 9am–4pm; Sat 9am–5pm; mid-May to mid-June & late Aug to early Oct Mon–Thurs 9am–7pm, Fri 9am–10pm, Sat 8am–8pm, Sun 8am–7pm; mid-June to late Aug daily 7.30am–10pm; early Oct to mid-Dec daily 9am–4pm; mid-Dec to March Mon–Fri 9am–4.30pm, Sat & Sun 9am–5pm

The southernmost sector of the reserve is set off as the **Parc national de la Jacques-Cartier**. The **Discovery and Visitors Centre**, 10km west of Hwy-175, serves as the gateway to the Jacques-Cartier River valley, enclosed by 550m-high forested slopes. The park is ideal for canoeing, although the river runs beside a road for part of the way, detracting from the wilderness experience. You can rent canoes, kayaks, inflatable rafts and bicycles at the visitors centre, where you can also reserve a space at the **campsite**.

ARRIVAL AND INFORMATION

By bus Intercar (see page 263) runs a bus service through the reserve from Québec City's main terminal to Alma (2 daily; 2hr 45min) and Saguenay (Chicoutimi; 4 daily; 2hr 30min).

Registration centre The reserve's main entry point is at its southern end, along Hwy-175. At Km94, 9km north of the entrance, the Camp Mercier registration centre (hours vary though at minimum daily 8.30am–4pm; ☏ 418 848 2422, ☏ 800 665 6527, ⓦ sepaq.com) gives out information, including trail maps.

RÉSERVE FAUNIQUE DES LAURENTIDES

ACCOMMODATION

Parc national de la Jacques-Cartier campsites The national park has two serviced campgrounds near the visitor centre, four primitive campgrounds further into the park and two campsites reachable only by canoe. Primitive sites $24; sites with electricity $31

Réserve Faunique des Laurentides campsites ☏ 800 665 6527. It's possible to pitch a tent beside Lac Jacques-Cartier at the rustic *Camping La Loutre* and 4km from the northern boundary at *Camping Belle-Rivière*. Cabins are available at each. Late May to early Sept. Primitive sites $30; sites with electricity $42; cabins $115

TOURIST INFORMATION IN NORTHERN QUÉBEC

The areas to the north of Québec City and the offshore islands are divided into the following regional tourist associations, each providing an excellent free guide (including basic maps) of the region. All the main offices in each region will usually have guides for other regions. For general information contact Tourisme Québec (☏ 514 873 2015, ☏ 877 266 5687, ⓦ quebecoriginal.com).

Bas-Saint-Laurent ☏ 418 867 1272, ☏ 800 563 5268, ⓦ bassaintlaurent.ca.

Charlevoix ☏ 418 665 4454, ☏ 800 667 2276, ⓦ tourisme-charlevoix.com.

Côte-Nord ☏ 418 962 0808, ☏ 888 463 0808, ⓦ tourismecote-nord.com.

Gaspésie ☏ 418 775 2223, ☏ 800 463 0323, ⓦ tourisme-gaspesie.com.

Îles-de-la-Madeleine ☏ 418 986 2245, ☏ 877 624 4437, ⓦ tourismeilesdelamadeleine.com.

Saguenay–Lac-Saint-Jean ☏ 418 543 9778, ☏ 877 253 8387, ⓦ saguenaylacsaintjean.ca.

Bas-Saint-Laurent

Heading east from Québec City along the southern shore of the St Lawrence, the most scenic route is Hwy-132, which sticks close to the shoreline showcasing the highlights of **Bas-Saint-Laurent (Lower St Lawrence)**, a region of fertile lands with farming and forestry covering gently rolling hills. The landscape is agricultural and dominated by long, narrow fields that are remnants of the old seigneurial system. The stops worth making on the trip to the Gaspé Peninsula are the woodcarving centre of **Saint-Jean-Port-Joli**, the seigneurial **Saint-Roch-des-Aulnaies**, the architecturally quaint **Kamouraska**, the regional centre of **Rivière-Du-Loup** and the stunning coastal landscapes of **Parc national du Bic**.

Saint-Jean-Port-Joli

Some 80km east of Lévis on Hwy-132 is **SAINT-JEAN-PORT-JOLI**, where the long main street accommodates the galleries of the region's most popular **woodcarvers**. The traditional Québécois folk art of woodcarving flourished in the eighteenth and nineteenth centuries, but had almost expired by the 1930s, when the three Bourgault brothers (Médard, Jean-Julien and André) established their workshop here. Initially, religious statuary was their main source of income, but their folksy style and francophile themes were adopted and popularized by the nationalists in the 1960s.

Musée des Anciens Canadiens

332 av de Gaspé ouest, on Hwy-132 • Daily: mid-May to mid-July 9am–5.30pm; mid-July to Aug 8.30am–7pm; Sept to mid-Oct 9am–5pm • $8 • ☎ 418 598 3392, ⓦ museedesancienscanadiens.com

The **Musée des Anciens Canadiens** has an interesting collection of woodcarvings cut in white pine and walnut, many of which are the work of the Bourgaults. Aside from odes to pop culture – including The Beatles onstage and Harry Potter with his owl Hedwig – the most eye-catching piece is the giant *Les Patriotes*, a tribute to the Québécois rebels of 1837 who, under the leadership of Louis-Joseph Papineau, tried to drive out the British.

4

ACCOMMODATION AND EATING   **SAINT-JEAN-PORT-JOLI**

Camping de La Demi-Lieue 589 Hwy-132 est ☎ 418 598 6108, ☎ 800 463 9558, ⓦ campingunion.com/fr/saint-jean-port-joli-demi. Choose from several cosy cottages on the grounds of a former seigneury, any one of which is a great alternative to the numerous, mostly bland motels that line Hwy-132 hereabouts. Located alongside the river, *de La Demi-Lieue* is a friendly and well-run site with a variety of campsites; cyclists camping pay a reduced rate, too. Mid-May to Sept. Sites $33; sites for cyclists $25; cottages $175

La Boustifaille 547 av de Gaspé ouest ☎ 418 598 3061, ⓦ rocheaveillon.com. For gigantic portions of Québécois

food (*planches à partager* to share, $22–24; menu de jour from $16.75), head to this cheerful restaurant that shares a building with La Roche à Veillon theatre on the east side of town. Mid-May to early Oct daily 8am–9pm (closed Mon–Wed in May).

★ **La Maison de L'Ermitage** 56 rue de l'Ermitage ☎ 418 598 7553, ⓦ maisonermitage.com. Friendly B&B with a lot of character and a few alpaca, too. The house has five charming rooms, including one inside a red-and-white turret. Three of the bedrooms share a bathroom; the other two are en suite. $90; en suite $95

La Seigneurie des Aulnaies

525 Hwy-132 ouest, Saint-Roch-des-Aulnaies, 14km east of Saint-Jean-Port-Joli • Late May to early Oct daily 9.30am–6pm; early Oct to mid-Nov Sat & Sun 9.30am–6pm • $14 (grounds only $6) • ☎ 418 354 2800, ⓦ laseigneuriedesaulnaies.qc.ca

At the village of **SAINT-ROCH-DES-AULNAIES**, a gorgeous water mill and manor house have survived on an eighteenth-century seigneurial estate, **La Seigneurie des Aulnaies**, formerly the home of a rich merchant. Named after the alder trees that grow along the banks of the Ferrée River, it offers a fascinating glimpse into that era. The river still powers Québec's largest bucket wheel in the estate's three-storey communal grist mill, the Moulin Banal. Now refurbished and fully operational, the mill has frequent flour-grinding displays and mouthwatering muffins and pancakes in the café. Just upstream, the veranda-wrapped Victorian manor house has period rooms, guides in costume and diverting interactive displays on the seigneurial system.

Kamouraska

Some 40km east of Saint-Roch-des-Aulnaies along Hwy-132, **KAMOURASKA** is a pleasant village where well-heeled citizens of Québec City once congregated to take the air. While they no longer visit to the same degree, it's not for lack of good air, which still has its way with the town's current residents, many of whom live to over 100. The village boasts many examples of the Bas-Saint-Laurent region's most distinctive architectural feature, the **Kamouraska roof**. Extended to keep the rainwater off the walls, the arched and rounded eaves project from the houses in a design borrowed from the shipyards. One of the best examples is the **Villa Saint-Louis**, at 125 av Morel, a private residence once home to Adolphe Basile-Routhier, the man who penned the words to Canada's national anthem.

TOURS   KAMOURASKA

Boat trips From the pier, Kamouraska Zodiac Aventure (☎ 418 863 3132, ⓦ zodiacaventure.com) leads ten-passenger Zodiacs out on the St Lawrence for a 90min trip ($40) to the Îles de Kamouraska to spot local bird and marine life.

ACCOMMODATION AND EATING

★ **Café du Clocher** 90 av Morel ☎ 418 492 7365. Head to this bistro (set in a nineteenth-century stable) to try the excellent coffee or local delicacy, smoked eel, on a bagel with cream cheese and capers ($8.75) as well as a range of vegetarian dishes under $20. June–Oct 8am–10pm.

La Grand Voile 168 av Morel ☎ 418 492 2539, ⓦ lagrandvoile.ca. One of the village's best B&Bs, this regal choice has cheerful rooms with an abundance of natural light; all have balconies with views of the river and private bathrooms. The on-site spa offers a full range of services. **$174**

Motel Cap Blanc 300 av Morel ☎ 418 492 2919, ⓦ motelcapblanc.com. A simple motel with river views, *Cap Blanc* capitalizes on its location with tall windows in the eleven rooms, all of which have a private terrace and a kitchenette. May–Nov. **$90**

Rivière-du-Loup

A prosperous-looking place, whose hilly centre is complete with broad streets and handsome Victorian villas, **RIVIÈRE-DU-LOUP** owes its development to the timber industry and the coming of the railway in 1859. This established Rivière-du-Loup as a crossroads for traffic between the Maritimes, the Gaspé Peninsula and the rest of Québec. Its significance as an administrative and commercial centre has grown accordingly and today it is easily the most thriving town in the region.

ARRIVAL AND INFORMATION   RIVIÈRE-DU-LOUP

By bus Orléans Express (☎ 418 862 4884, ☎ 888 999 3777, ⓦ orleansexpress.com) buses leave from 317 blvd de l'Hôtel de Ville ouest (Petro-Canada on Hwy-132) to points throughout Bas-Saint-Laurent, the Gaspé Peninsula (via Rimouski) and back to Québec City and Montréal. This is also the western terminus for Maritime Bus (ⓦ maritimebus.com) with onward services to points in New Brunswick and Nova Scotia.
Destinations Fredericton, NB (1–2 daily; 4hr 15min); Gaspé (1–2 daily via Rimouski; 8hr 30min–9hr 15min); Montréal (4 daily; 4hr 50min–5hr 50min); Québec City (4 daily; 2–2hr 45min); Rimouski (4 daily; 1hr 30min–2hr 5min).

By train The train station (☎ 888 842 7245) is on rue Lafontaine and rue Fraserville and only open when VIA Rail trains arrive here (Halifax to Montréal only; the Montreal–Gaspé service was suspended in 2013).
Destinations Halifax, NS (1 daily; 15hr 38min); Montréal (1 daily; 6hr 10min); Québec City (Sainte-Foy only; 1 daily 3hr 17min).

By ferry A car ferry (☎ 418 862 5094, ⓦ traverserdl.com; 1–4 daily; 1hr 5min; $19.50/person, cars an additional $46.30) provides a service to and from the marina to Saint-Siméon on the north shore of the St Lawrence.

Tourist office 189 blvd de l'Hôtel-de-Ville (mid-June to Aug daily 8.30am–7pm, Sept Mon–Fri 8.30am–4.30pm, Sat & Sun 11am–4pm; Oct to mid-June Mon–Fri 8.30am–4.30pm ☎ 418 862 1981, ⓦ tourismerivieredeloup.ca).

TOURS AND ACTIVITIES

Boat trips Rivière-du-Loup is one of the better spots on the St Lawrence River to take a boat trip, with several options to choose from. Beginning at around $70/person, these excursions are not cheap, but are well organized; you may see beluga, minke and finback whales throughout the summer. All the companies are located by the marina at 200 rue Hayward. Croisières AML (mid-June to mid-Oct; ☎ 418 867 3361, ☎ 800 563 4643, ⓦ croisieresaml.com) specializes in whale-watching trips (3hr 30min) on large boats. La Société Duvetnor (June–Sept; ☎ 418 867 1660, ⓦ duvetnor.com) has daily cruises to various midstream sea-bird and mammal sanctuaries, with overnight stops offered (from $25; reservations required).

Cycling The longest cycling trail of its kind in Québec, the Petit Témis (ⓦ en.petit-temis.ca) begins in Rivière-du-Loup and ends 134km later in Cabano in the Gaspé Peninsula. The route follows a flat disused railroad bed, which makes for a gentle ride through bucolic countryside. The trailhead is on rue Fraserville, adjacent to Hwy-85 and the Petro-Canada petrol station.

Hiking The area has a few good opportunities for shoreline hiking, including the Québec segment of the Trans Canada Trail (ⓦ tctrail.ca), which picks up on the south shore of the Saint Lawrence at Rivière-du-Loup, before continuing southeast toward Cabano and eventually New Brunswick.

ACCOMMODATION

Auberge de la Pointe 10 blvd Cartier ☎ 418 862 3514, ⓦ aubergedelapointe.com. Sprawling resort with over a hundred comfortable and well-appointed rooms spread across several buildings. Also on-site are a restaurant, café, health spa and indoor pool. Mid-April to early Oct. **$97**

Auberge Internationale de Rivière-du-Loup 46 rue de l'Hôtel-de-Ville ☎ 418 862 7566, ⓦ aubergerdl.ca. This pretty HI hostel in an attractive wooden building has pleasant dorms and a few rooms and offers cycling and hiking packages, including treks on the nearby Trans Canada Trail. Breakfast is included and the kitchen is available for use. Dorms **$28.67** (HI members **$24.33**); private rooms **$60.88** (HI members **$54.36**).

Camping municipal de la Pointe de Rivière-du-Loup 2 Côte-des-Bains ☎ 418 862 4281, ⓦ campingmunicipaldelapointe.ca. Quiet campsite with a nice range of services, free wi-fi throughout and spacious pitches. Most sites lack a river view, but a beach is just a few minutes' walk away. Mid-May to late Sept. **$26**; sites with electricity **$37.95**

EATING AND DRINKING

Café du Clocher 419 rue Lafontaine ☎ 418 862 1616, ⓦ cafeduclocherrdl.com. A great spot for coffee (from local roasters Brûlerie de l'Est), croissants and bagel sandwiches with mixed fruit ($5.95) and home-made baked goods. Mon–Fri 7am–9pm, Sat 8am–9pm, Sun 8am–8pm (reduced hours Sept–April).

L'Estaminet 299 rue Lafontaine ☎ 418 867 4517, ⓦ restopubestaminet.com. A bustling bar near the centre, with 150 types of beer and fine pub food, including *moules frites* (most mains around $20). Mon–Wed 7am–11pm, Thurs 7am–midnight, Fri 7am–1am, Sat 8am–1am, Sun 8am–11pm.

Le Saint-Patrice 169 rue Fraser ☎ 418 862 9895, ⓦ restaurantlestpatrice.ca. Stylish restaurant devoted to serving expertly prepared and arranged regional dishes, such as smoked fish, lamb and shellfish (most mains $24–32). It's also earned a reputation for its thin-crust pizza, with options such as smoked salmon ($17–22). Mon–Fri 11.30am–2pm & 5–9pm, Sat 5–9.30pm, Sun 5–8pm.

Trois-Pistoles

Heading 46km northeast from Rivière-du-Loup along Hwy-132, with the far bank of the St Lawrence clearly visible, the coastal highway passes through a succession of farming and fishing villages on its way to **TROIS-PISTOLES**, said to be named after a silver goblet worth three *pistoles* (gold coins) that a French sailor dropped into the river while trying to fill it with water in 1621.

Notre-Dame-des-Neiges-de-Trois-Pistoles

30 Notre-Dame est • Daily 9am–5pm • ☎ 418 851 1391, ⓦ eglisetrois-pistoles.com

The enormous church of **Notre-Dame-des-Neiges-de-Trois-Pistoles**, built between 1882 and 1887, dominates Trois-Pistoles itself. From a distance the church looks like something out of Disneyland, with a silver roof surmounted by four pinnacles. Inside, the vaulted ceiling is supported by massive marble columns, while the walls are dotted with nineteenth-century devotional paintings.

ARRIVAL, INFORMATION AND ACTIVITIES

By car A car ferry crosses to Les Escoumins (1–3 daily mid-May to mid-Oct; 90min; ☎418 851 4676, ☎877 851 4677, ⓦ traversiercnb.ca; $21.75 one way; $48.50 additional for a car; $36 for a bike round-trip, including passenger fare) on the Côte-Nord (see page 313).
Information centre The information centre is on Hwy-132, on the southern edge of town, with a miniature

windmill and lighthouse outside (late June to early Sept daily 9am–7pm, early Sept to early Oct Fri–Sun 9am–4pm; ☎418 851 3698, ⓦtourismelesbasques.com).
Sea-kayaking Kayak de Mer des Îles, 60 av du Parc, offer guided trips from 3hr to two days (July & Aug; 3hr trips from $60; ☎418 851 4637, ☎877 851 4637, ⓦkayaksdesiles.com).

ACCOMMODATION AND EATING

Camping Municipal de Trois-Pistoles 100 rue du Chanoine Côté ☎418 851 4515, ⓦcampingtrois-pistoles.com. The town's campsite spreads out along the river, a couple of blocks from Hwy-132. The sites vary a good bit in size and attractiveness; most have a nice amount of shade and open views of the St Lawrence. Late May to late Sept. $\overline{33}$
★ **La Belle Excuse** 138 rue Notre-Dame ouest ☎418 857 3000. Cosy restaurant in a pretty red house serving

exceptional regional cuisine such as smoked fish. Mains are from $23–27, the Sunday brunch (mains $14–$17) is a steal and there's terrace seating. June–Sept Wed–Sat 5–9pm, Sun 10am–9pm.
La Fromagerie des Basques 69 Hwy-132 ouest ☎418 851 2189, ⓦfromageriedesbasques.ca. For a picnic lunch or hefty snack stop by this gourmet deli for exceptional artisanal cheeses, bread, pastries and traditional beer, all made on-site. Open daily 24hr.

Parc national du Bic

3382 Hwy-132 Ouest • Year-round • Park entry $8.60, levied year-round • ☎418 736 5035, ⓦsepaq.com/pq/bic

Heading 40km northeast from Trois-Pistoles, Hwy-132 crosses fertile agricultural landscape until it reaches the rocky wooded hummocks of the shoreline's **Parc national du Bic**. At this naturalists' paradise, whose headlands push up tight against the river, it's possible to see herds of grey and harbour seals, particularly during August and September in the park's main sector, Rivière-du-Sud-Ouest. Shuttle buses (late June to late Aug daily every 30min 12.30–2.30pm; $5.50 one way, $9.25 return) leave from the Pic Champlain parking area up to **Pic Champlain**, a 346m lookout in the park's western sector.

INFORMATION AND ACTIVITIES

Visitor centre At the entrance to the Rivière-du-Sud-Ouest sector, the Visitors Centre (hours vary throughout the year; ☎418 736 5035) provides maps of the park, sells supplies and can book campsites; the Discovery and Visitors Centre at Rioux Farm in the centre of the park also offers information, convenience store and shop.
Hiking The park has a dozen hiking trails of varying length; almost all are fairly flat. The Chemin-du-Nord (4km round-trip; 1hr 20min) is a gentle stroll along the estuary's shoreline and provides a great introduction to the park.

Cycling Three cycle paths depart from the Discovery and Visitors Centre; if you're pressed for time choose La Coulée Blanchette (10km round-trip; 1hr 30min), which provides great views of Pic Champlain and Baie des Ha! Ha!; rental is $14.25/hr or $41/day.
Sea-kayaking Guided sea-kayak tours explore the park's shoreline and nearby islands with Aventures Archipel (☎418 736 5232, ⓦaventuresarchipel.com; late May to early Oct; from $60.84 for half-day outings).

ACCOMMODATION

Rivière-du-Sud-Ouest Campground ☎418 736 5035, ⓦsepaq.com. The park's serviced campsite abuts the visitor centre and spreads west along the eponymous river. It's unfortunately adjacent to Hwy-132 and therefore road

noise can be a problem. Still, it's scenic, very well run and close to all the main spots in the park, as well as Le Bic. Early June to early Sept. $\overline{30}$; serviced $\overline{31}$

Le Bic

Just 4km northeast of the Parc national du Bic along Hwy-132, the elongated village of **LE BIC**, perched on a low ridge above its snout-shaped harbour, is a handsome medley of old and modern architecture. It's a good spot to stop for a bite to eat or to use as a base for longer visits to the park. Classical music lovers will also want to check out the town in early August for the **Concerts aux Îles du Bic** (Ⓦbicmusique.com), a four-day outdoor chamber music festival that features performances, mostly here and in Rimouski, by leading national and regional musicians.

ACCOMMODATION AND EATING   LE BIC

Auberge du Mange Grenouille 148 rue Ste-Cécile Ⓣ418 736 5656, Ⓦaubergedumangegrenouille.qc.ca. Graceful inn with a superb restaurant (reservations advised) with a decidedly upscale and expensive table d'hôte ($44–49; tasting menu $65) and attractively furnished double rooms. May to mid-Oct. **$99**

★ **Folles Farines** 113 rue St-Jean Baptiste Ⓣ418 736 8180, Ⓦfollesfarines.com. Be wary of entering this long-running bakery on an empty stomach – a wicked selection of tasty breads, croissants and thin-crust pizzas (from $13) awaits. Late June to Aug Mon–Sat 8am–6pm, Sun 8am–5pm; Sept to mid-Oct & May to late June Wed–Sat 8am–6pm, Sun 8am–5pm; mid-Oct to April Fri & Sat 8am–6pm, Sun 8am–5pm.

Gîte de la Baie Hâtée 2271 Hwy-132 Ⓣ418 736 5668, Ⓦgitedelabaiehatee.wordpress.com. Stately B&B with period furnishings, views of the river, a restaurant and massage services. **$95**

The Gaspé Peninsula

Bounded by the Gulf of St Lawrence to the north and west, and by the Baie des Chaleurs to the south and east, the **Gaspé Peninsula** is roughly 550km long, with a chain of mountains and rolling highlands dominating the interior and the northern shore. It has always been sparsely inhabited with limited economic opportunities, its remote communities eking out an existence from the turbulent seas and the rocky soil. But the landscape provides some truly spectacular scenery, especially in the the peninsula's two outstanding parks: the extravagantly mountainous **Parc national de la Gaspésie**, inland from **Sainte-Anne-des-Monts**, and the **Parc national Forillon**, at the tip of the peninsula, with its mountain and coastal hikes and wonderfully rich wildlife. Just to the south of the latter, the village of **Percé** is famous for the offshore **Rocher Percé**, an extraordinary limestone monolith that has been a magnet for travellers for more than a hundred years.

   As a major summer holiday spot, the Gaspé gets especially busy during the last two weeks of July for Québec's **construction holiday**; if you travel during this period, book your accommodation and activities well in advance.

Rimouski

Running parallel to Hwy-132, the Trans-Canada Highway (Hwy-20) is a much faster route to the university town of **RIMOUSKI**, effectively the start of the Gaspé Peninsula. Some 20km northeast of Le Bic, "Riki" appears quite unattractive from the highway, thanks to a major fire that destroyed one-third of the buildings from the river to midtown in 1950, forcing the city to rebuild in 1960s strip-mall style. Forge past the highway and into the town, the administrative capital of Eastern Québec, and you'll find a youthful city (thanks to the number of educational institutions), but not much in terms of sights, bar the interesting **Musée régional de Rimouski** (35 rue St-Germain ouest; mid-June to early Sept daily 10am–5.30pm, Thurs until 8pm; early Sept to mid-June Wed–Sun noon–5pm, Thurs until 8pm; $6; Ⓣ418 724 2272, Ⓦmuseerimouski.qc.ca). It's housed in the oldest church in Eastern Québec with an intact exterior; the three floors inside have been renovated and now focus on rotating exhibits on local history and contemporary art.

ARRIVAL AND INFORMATION   RIMOUSKI

By bus The Orléans Express bus station (Ⓣ418 723 4923) is at 90 av Léonidas.

Destinations Carleton (1 daily; 3hr 30min); Gaspé via Carleton (1 daily; 8hr 15min); Gaspé via Matane (1 daily;

6hr 35min); Matane (1 daily; 1hr 30min); New Richmond (1 daily; 5hr); Rivière-du-Loup (4 daily; 1hr 30min); Percé (1 daily; 7hr 25min); Québec City (3–4 daily; 4hr 5min–4hr 40min); Ste-Anne-des-Monts (1 daily; 2hr 30min).

By train The train station is at 57 de l'Évêché est (☎418 722 4737, ☎800 361 5390).

Destinations Halifax (1 daily; 13hr 50min); Moncton (1 daily; 9hr 22min); Montréal (1 daily; 8hr 2min); Rivière-du-Loup (1 daily; 1hr 37min).

By ferry There's a car ferry to Forestville (1hr) on the Côte-Nord (late May to late Sept 2–4 trips daily; ☎418 725 2725, ☎800 973 2725, ☜traversier.com; 1hr; $25 one-way, cars

$49), which only holds thirty vehicles so reservations are essential. The *M/V Bella Desgagnés* (see page 320) departs Rimouski every Mon at 10pm (mid-Oct to April usually 9.15pm) to: Blanc-Sablon (1 weekly; 78hr 30min); Sept-Îles (downstream only; 1 weekly; 11hr 30min).

Tourist office In the centre of town at 50 rue St-Germain ouest, on the waterfront (early May to mid-June Mon–Fri 9am–4.30pm; mid-June to early Sept daily 8.30am–7.30pm; early Sept to early Oct Mon–Fri 8.30am–5.30pm, Sat & Sun 11am–4pm; early Oct to early May Mon–Fri 9am–noon & 1–4.30pm; ☎418 723 2322, ☜tourismerimouski.com); has accommodation listings.

ACCOMMODATION

Camping de l'Île Saint-Barnabé ☎418 723 2280, ☜ilestbarnabe.com/camping. If you're considering camping, take the crossing to l'Île Saint-Barnabé, a tranquil island and popular bird migration site 3km offshore, where there are twelve sites. The ferry departs from the marina on Hwy-132 (daily every 30min 9am–2.30pm mid-June to early Sept; $19). <u>$25</u>

Hotel Rimouski 225 blvd René-Lepage est ☎418 725 5000, ☎800 463 0755, ☜hotelrimouski.com. A peach-coloured behemoth catering mostly to convention centre visitors, the *Rimouski* has comfortable rooms and suites; health centre, pool and bikes available for guest use. The location is central and the sunset views from the rooms are not to be missed. <u>$139</u>

EATING AND DRINKING

Central Café 31 rue de l'Évêché ouest ☎418 722 4011, ☜centralcaferimouski.com. Somehow, despite a bewildering number of birdcages and avian wall art at this inviting bistro, it's possible to concentrate on the food, which thankfully isn't quite as kooky. Choose from tasty salads (from $7.50) and pizzas (from $11), with a few beers on tap. Mon–Sat 11am–10pm, Sun 4–10pm.

La Brûlerie d'Ici 91 rue St-Germain ouest ☎418 723 3424, ☜bruleriedici.com. A local favourite, this warm, relaxed café serves heady coffee made with roasts from around the world. The lip-smacking food, like croissant sandwiches (from $7.50) and salads for lunch, is reasonably priced. Mon–Wed 7am–10pm, Thurs & Fri 7am–11pm, Sat 8am–11pm, Sun 8am–10pm.

★ **La Réserve Bistro** 150 av de la Cathédrale ☎418 730 6525, ☜bistrolareserve.com. Down the block from the city's cathedral, *La Réserve* is one of the area's unmistakeable and unmissable culinary treats. The menu features inventive and beautifully arranged meals, such as beef shoulder braised in an oatmeal stout ($28) and salmon tartare ($24). Desserts such as crème brûlée ($8) and chocolate tart ($8) are well worth any guilty pangs that may follow. Tues–Fri 11am–10pm, Sat 5–10pm.

Le Bien, le Malt 141 av Belzile, just off Hwy-132 ☎418 723 1339, ☜lebienlemalt.com. This hip brewpub with outdoor seating has an impressive selection of house-brewed ales made with local ingredients and frequent live music. Mon–Wed & Sun 3–11pm, Thurs–Sat 3pm–2am.

Site historique maritime de la Pointe-au-Père

1000 rue du Phare, Pointe-au-Père • Museum: early June to late Oct daily 9am–6pm; late Oct to late Nov Wed–Sun 10am–5pm • $10 • Onondaga: June to early Oct daily 9am–6pm • $16, or $22 with museum • ☎418 724 6214, ☜shmp.qc.ca

A few kilometres east from Rimouski along Hwy-132, the small town of **POINTE-AU-PÈRE** contains the absorbing **Site historique maritime de la Pointe-au-Père**, featuring a museum, submarine and lighthouse. **The Empress of Ireland Museum,** housed in a modern building resembling a tilting ship, tells the story of the *Empress of Ireland*, a luxury liner that sank offshore here in 1914 – with more than a thousand lives lost, it was a disaster second only to the *Titanic*. In summer you can also visit the 90-metre **HMCS Onondaga submarine,** beached on the nearby pier. The sub patrolled the North Atlantic for the Canadian navy between 1967 and 2000, its claustrophic interior open for self-guided tours.

Lieu historique national du Phare-de-Pointe-au-Père

1034 rue du Phare • Early June to early Oct daily 9am–6pm • $4 ($19 with submarine; $13 with museum; $25 for all three) • ☜pc.gc.ca/fr/lhn-nhs/qc/pointeaupere

---

THE LAST FERRIES ACROSS THE ST LAWRENCE

The only reason to come to industrial Matane, 96km northeast of Rimouski, is to catch one of the **car ferries** (☏418 562 2500, ☏877 562 6560, ⊛traversiers.com) to **the Côte-Nord** (see page 313) – this is the last chance to cross the St Lawrence as you head north. Two destinations are served: **Godbout** (late Oct to April 1 daily except Thurs & Sun; April to early June 1 daily; early June to late Oct 1–2 daily; 2hr 10min; $20, cars $48.80); and **Baie-Comeau** (late Oct to April 1 daily except Tues & Sat; April to early June 1 daily; early June to late Oct 1–2 daily; 2hr 20min; same fares).

The **Lieu historique national du Phare-de-Pointe-au-Père** offers fantastic views from the top of its 1909 **lighthouse**, the second tallest in the country (at 33m). The adjacent keeper's house contains an exhibit on the lighthouses of the St Lawrence, while the Fog Alarm Shed has a display on sound signals.

Sainte-Anne-des-Monts

Unenticing **SAINTE-ANNE-DES-MONTS**, 180km northeast from Rimouski, sprawls along the coastline, its untidy appearance only offset by its relaxed atmosphere and its convenience – it's an easy place to break your journey before heading on to the cape, or inland to the Parc national de la Gaspésie.

Exploramer

1 rue du Quai • Early June to mid-Oct daily 9am–5pm • $18; Zodiac excursions $58 • ☏ 418 763 2500, ⊛ exploramer.qc.ca

Sainte-Anne-des-Monts' lone attraction is the **Exploramer** marine and birdlife discovery centre. Head to the aquarium downstairs, where you can handle sea stars, sea cucumbers and scallops. The centre also offers ninety-minute covered **Zodiac excursions** on the St Lawrence River to observe marine life.

ACCOMMODATION	SAINTE-ANNE-DES-MONTS

★ Auberge Festive Sea Shack 292 blvd Perron est ☏418 763 7844, ⊛aubergefestive.com. The best budget choice in the region – and certainly the liveliest – this cheerful hostel, with views over the river, has several tidy cabins, cavernous yurts and beach campsites. It frequently hosts events and offers kayak rental and a shuttle to Parc national de la Gaspésie. HI members get a $5 discount. March–Oct only. Site $25; dorms $40; cabins $96; yurts (for eight) $320

Motel Beaurivage 245 1ère av ouest ☏418 763 2291, ⊛motelbeaurivage.com. A good-value motel right on the beach with clean, spacious rooms, cabins with kitchens and a filling breakfast served in the dining room. May to mid-Oct. $99; cabins $130

Parc national de la Gaspésie

Year-round • Park entrance fee $8.60

As you travel south from Sainte-Anne-des-Monts on Hwy-299, the snowcapped **Chic-Choc Mountains** – which make up most of the **Parc national de la Gaspésie** – can be spotted in the distance, a stark and forbidding backdrop to the coastal plain. The Chic-Chocs are the most northerly protrusions of the Appalachian Ridge, which extends deep into the US, and the serpentine road reveals the full splendour of their alpine interior. The sequence of valleys framed by thickly wooded slopes culminates in the staggering ravine that lies at the foot of the towering **Mont Albert**.

If you are intending to **hike**, you should come equipped with warm clothes, food and water, and log your intended route at the centre. The trails ascend to the summits of the area's highest mountains – including Mont Jacques-Cartier (1270m), Mont Richardson (1180m) and Mont Albert (1088m) – and remarkably climb through three distinctive habitats: herds of Virginia deer thrive in the rich vegetation of the lowest zone, while moose live in the boreal forest, and caribou in the tundra near the peaks. This is the only place in Québec where the three species exist in close proximity.

ARRIVAL AND INFORMATION	PARC NATIONAL DE LA GASPÉSIE

By shuttle bus A shuttle bus (late June to early Sept daily; early Sept to end Sept Sat & Sun only; 8am, return 5pm; $7.50 round-trip) links the park to Sainte-Anne-des-Monts; buses travel between the town's tourist office and the Discovery and Visitors Centre. Shuttles also link the Visitors Centre with the Mont-Jacques-Cartier trailhead (late June to early Sept daily; early Sept to end Sept Sat & Sun only; 9am; 1hr; return 4pm; $18 round-trip).

Discovery and Visitors Centre The park's extremely helpful visitors centre (late June to early Sept daily 8am–8pm; check website for seasonal opening times; ☏ 418 763 5435, ⊚ sepaq.com/pq/gas) is in a ravine about 40km from Sainte-Anne-des-Monts. It rents hiking equipment, kayaks and canoes and has details and maps of half a dozen well-signposted hiking trails; most are about a day's duration, though a couple around the centre are shorter.

ACCOMMODATION

Camping Mont Albert ☏ 418 763 1333. Conveniently near the interpretation centre, this beautifully located campsite offers a number of serene pitches, all of which have plenty of shade. Primitive sites $24; with services $32

★ **Gîte du Mont-Albert** ☏ 418 763 2288, ☏ 866 727 2427, ⊚ sepaq.com. The exquisite *Gîte du Mont-Albert* offers the only fixed lodgings in the park, with 60 rooms and

18 cabins boasting a much more contemporary aesthetic and furnishings to match. Room prices rocket during the summer and skiing seasons, but the location is very handy. It also has an excellent (if pricey) restaurant specializing in regional produce such as pan-seared rabbit, caribou medallions and home-smoked salmon. Early June to early Oct (cabins year-round). Rooms $115; cabins $154

Mont-Saint-Pierre

Heading east from Sainte-Anne-des-Monts towards the tip of the Gaspé Peninsula, the road often squeezes between the ocean and the sheer rock faces of the mountains, its twists and turns passing tumbling scree and picturesque coves. The view as you approach **MONT-SAINT-PIERRE** is particularly majestic, the curving seashore and the swelling mountains together framing this little community set at the mouth of a wide river valley. It's an unassuming resort dedicated to bathing and fishing, except during the colourful four-day **Fête du Vol libre** (☏ 418 797 2222, ⊚ tourisme-mont-saint-pierre. com) at the end of July, when hang-gliders and paragliders fill the skies.

ACTIVITIES	MONT-SAINT-PIERRE

Carrefour Aventure 106 rue Prudent-Cloutier ☏ 418 797 5033, ⊚ facebook.com/carrefouraventure. This friendly outfit runs 4WD tours to the top of the village's

eponymous mountain (from $25) and rents sea-kayaks and mountain bikes. Mid-June to Aug.

ACCOMMODATION AND EATING

Camping municipal 103 rue Pierre-Godfroie-Coulombe ☏ 418 797 2250, ⊚ mont-saint-pierre.ca. Set south of Hwy-132 along a river, this secluded campsite has large pitches spaced well apart and a pool. Mid-June to early Sept. $25

Le Délice 100 rue Prudent-Cloutier ☏ 888 797 2955, ⊚ audelice.com. The best motel around, this friendly place has comfortable rooms and offers a nice range of amenities and guided trips up the mountain. Its restaurant dishes up typical Gaspésien classics (mains $15–25). Daily 6–10pm. $106

Parc National Forillon

June to early Oct • $7.80 (late June to early Sept); $5.65 (June 1 to late June & early Sept to early Oct)

At the very tip of the peninsula, the federally run **PARC NATIONAL FORILLON** is the scenic culmination of the Gaspé, encompassing thick forest and mountains, crossed by hiking trails and fringed by stark cliffs along a deeply indented coastline. The splendour of the landscape is complemented by the **wildlife**: black bear, moose, beaver, porcupine and red fox are all common to the area. More than two hundred species of bird have also been seen, ranging from sea birds like gannet, cormorant and guillemot, to songbirds such as the skylark and chaffinch. From the coastal paths around Cap Gaspé itself, **whales**, such as humpback, fin and minke, and **harbour porpoise** can also be spotted (May–Oct).

Roughly triangular in shape, the park is sandwiched between the Gulf of St Lawrence and the Baie de Gaspé and encircled by highways 197 and 132: the former crossing the interior to delineate the park's western limits, the latter mostly keeping to the seashore and threading through L'Anse-au-Griffon and **Cap-des-Rosiers** – tiny coastal villages with views onto the river and Forillon's wooded parkland. Make the time to take this route, as the views are spectacular, and the much-photographed **lighthouse** at Cap-des-Rosiers is the tallest in Canada.

Les Graves trail

Dolbel-Roberts house Late June to early Sept daily 1-5pm • **Hyman & Son's General Store and Warehouse** Daily: June & Sept to early Oct 10am–4pm; July & Aug 10am–5pm • **L'Anse-Blanchette** Mid-July to early Sept daily 10am–5pm • All free with park entry

The park has nine hiking trails, the best of which, Les Graves, takes you to the tip of **Cap Gaspé**, otherwise known as "Land's End" (4hr 30min; 15km round-trip). The trail extends from the end of the paved road beyond **Grande-Grave**, a restored fishing village originally founded by immigrants from Jersey and Guernsey; in 1798, the Jersey-based company Janvrin set up for business here and encouraged fishermen to settle there permanently. Inside the **Dolbel-Roberts house** the "Gaspesians from Land's End" exhibit sheds light on their history, including how their property was controversially expropriated to form the park 1970. Also in Grande-Grave, **Hyman & Son's General Store and Warehouse** occupies the ground floor of the original home built by William Hyman in 1864. A little further along the trail, **L'Anse-Blanchette**, a fisherman's house, fish shed and various structures used by the Blanchette family to dry cod, has also been painstakingly restored; the on-site barn screens "We Always Looked to the Sea" telling the story of the family. The path rises and falls until it reaches the **Cape Gaspé lighthouse** (fully-automated), which is set on a 95m cliff with the sea on three sides; from here you can descend down a steep path to the ocean around Land's End itself.

INFORMATION AND TOURS   PARC NATIONAL FORILLON

Visitor Centres There are two visitors' centres off Hwy-132: one at Anse-au-Griffon (daily: late June to early Sept 9am–5pm; ☎418 368 5505, ⓦpc.gc.ca/en/pn-np/qc/forillon); the other on the south coast at Penouille (daily: late June to early Oct 9am–5pm; ☎418 892 5661).

Whale-watching Excursions depart from Grande-Grave (June to early Oct 1–4 daily; $80; ☎418 892 5500, ☎888 617 5500, ⓦbaleines-forillon.com).

ACCOMMODATION AND EATING

Café de L'Anse 557 blvd Griffon, in L'Anse-au-Griffon's cultural centre ☎418 892 0115, ⓦcafedelanse.com. A nice spot to eat, offering mostly seafood dishes (mains $18–26), including a traditional *brandade de morue* (codfish brandade); it also has internet access. Daily 8am–9pm.

Camping Parc National Forillon ☎418 368 6050, ⓦreservation.pc.gc.ca. The park's half-dozen campsites are pleasantly situated and well maintained; *Cap-Bon-Ami* (late June to early Sept) has a particularly delightful setting just south of the lighthouse, while the *Petit-Gaspé* (late June to early Oct) campsite in the Secteur Sud has shaded sites, modern facilities and serves as the start of a few hikes. $25.50; serviced $29.40

L'Auberge Internationale Forillon 2095 blvd Grande-Grève, Cap-aux-Os ☎418 892 5153, ⓦauberge internationaleforillon.com. Just outside the national park's southern sector, this well-run hostel has a café, campsites, laundry facilities, mountain-bike rental; it also can book sea-kayaking and whale-watching tours. Camping $20; Dorms $30; private rooms $70

Motel le Noroît 589 blvd Griffon, L'Anse-au-Griffon ☎418 892 5531, ⓦmotellenoroit.com. Located steps from the beach and one of the best options within a short drive to Parc national Forillon, *Le Noroît* has ten simple, clean rooms with fridge and microwave. $75

Gaspé

The town of **GASPÉ** – its name derived from *Gespeg*, "the end of the land" in the Mi'kmaq language – straddles the hilly estuary of the York River and is a disappointment after the scenic drama of the national park. It's a humdrum settlement

---

JACQUES CARTIER IN GASPÉ

Gaspé is thought to be the spot where the French navigator and explorer **Jacques Cartier** landed in July 1534, on the first of his three trips up the St Lawrence River. He stayed here for just eleven days, time enough to erect a wooden cross engraved with the escutcheon of Francis I, staking out the king's – and Christianity's – claim to this new territory. Cartier's first aim was to find a sea route to the Orient, but he also had more extensive ambitions – to acquire land for himself and his men, exploit the Indigenous peoples as fur gatherers and discover precious metals to rival the loot the Spaniards had taken from the Aztecs. Naturally, Cartier had to disguise his real intentions on the first trip and his initial contacts with the Iroquois were cordial. Then, in the spring of 1536, he betrayed their trust by taking two of the local chief's sons back with him to Francis I. They were never returned, and when Cartier made his third trip in 1541 the Iroquois were so suspicious that he was unable to establish the colony he had been instructed to found. Desperate to salvage his reputation, Cartier sailed back to France with what he thought was a cargo of gold and diamonds; it turned out to be iron pyrite and quartz crystals.

---

of about seventeen thousand people, whose hard-pressed economy is reliant on its deep-water port.

Jacques Cartier Monument National Historic Site and Musée de la Gaspésie

Musée de la Gaspésie 80 blvd Gaspé · June–Oct daily 9am–5pm; Nov–May Wed–Fri 10am–5pm, Sat & Sun 12.30–5pm · $11.25 · ☎ 418 368 1534, ⊛ museedelagaspesie.ca

Just to the east of the town centre, the **Jacques Cartier Monument National Historic Site** looks out over the bay from the grounds of the town museum. It consists of six striking bronze dolmens carved in relief that record Cartier's visit (see above) and treatment of the indigenous peoples in ambivalent terms, along with anodyne homilies on the nature and unity of humankind. The adjacent **Musée de la Gaspésie** illuminates the social issues that have confronted the inhabitants of the peninsula: isolation from the centres of power, depopulation and, more recently, unemployment.

Cathédrale du Christ-Roi

20 rue de la Cathédrale

Near the top of rue Jacques-Cartier stands the **Cathédrale du Christ-Roi**, built in 1969. It's the only wooden cathedral in North America and, after recent renovations have given it new life, its angular exterior now looks strikingly modern. Inside the nave – all straight lines and symmetrical simplicity – is bathed in warm, softly coloured light that pours in through an enormous stained glass window.

Birthplace of Canada ("Berceau du Canada")

179, montée de Wakeham · Late June to mid-Sept daily 10.30am–6pm · Leboutillier House $5, other buildings by donation · ☎ 418 368 9423, ⊛ pointeoharagaspe.ca/en

Down on the York River waterfront the **Birthplace of Canada** ("Berceau du Canada") is Gaspé's newest attraction. A living museum, it comprises one original building (the 1850s **Leboutillier House**) and six reconstructed structures (Davis Warehouse, Baker Tavern, old photo shop, Collas & Slous Store, Jacques de Lesseps Seaplane Base and navy base), designed to replicate the village as it was in 1900. Historic artifacts, interpretive panels and costumed characters bring the plca to life in the summer. The site also contains **Jacques Cartier's Cross Monument** (aka the **Cross of Gaspé**), a granite monolith raised in 1934 to commemorate Cartier's arrival around here in 1534.

Sanctuaire Notre-Dame-de-Pointe-Navarre

765 blvd Pointe-Navarre · Late May to mid-Oct daily 9am–5pm; mid-Oct to late May by appointment only · Free · ☎ 418 368 2133

Just outside town, the white **Sanctuaire Notre-Dame-de-Pointe-Navarre** has been a popular pilgrimage site since 1940 due to its alleged healing powers, supported by the collection of crutches, braces and canes found in the **Chapelle du Souvenir** entombing **Father Watier** (1897–1968), the sanctuary's founder. Up a slight incline behind the church, the replica of the Lourdes Grotto (replete with outdoor altar) and the Garden of Mary's Sorrows are both attractive, with remarkable religious sculptures.

ARRIVAL AND INFORMATION

GASPÉ

By bus Buses stop on rue Jacques-Cartier, at the *Motel Adams*.

Destinations Carleton (1 daily; 4hr 10min); Matane (1 daily; 5hr 20min); Montréal (1 daily; 14hr 5mon); Percé (1 daily; 55min); Rimouski (2 daily; 6hr 40min–8hr 35min); Rivière-

du-Loup (1–2 daily; 9hr 5min–11hr).

Tourist office 8 rue de la Marina, on the far side of the river from the town centre along Hwy-198 (daily 8.30am–6pm; ☎ 418 368 6335, ⊚ gogaspeforillon.com).

ACCOMMODATION AND EATING

Brise-Bise 135 rue de la Reine ☎ 418 368 1456, ⊚ brisebise.ca. A great bistro and a swinging bar at night with terraces on each of its two floors and serving a variety of dishes (mains $18–34, pizzas from $16). Daily 11am–midnight.

Café des Artistes 101 rue de la Reine Gaspé ☎ 418 368 2255, ⊚ cafedesartistes.co/index.php. A great spot for a morning bagel ($3) and coffee as well as a variety of sandwiches (from $10.95) and pasta (from $9.50). Mon–Fri 7am-10.30pm Sat & Sun 8am–10.30pm.

Hôtel Plante 137 rue Jacques-Cartier ☎ 418 368 2254, ⊚ hotelplante.com. One of the better-value motels in town, this modern place has sweeping bay views and basic

doubles or two-storey suites with a kitchen. Doubles $95; suites $125

★ **La Maison William Wakeham** 186 rue de la Reine ☎ 418 368 5537, ⊚ maisonwakeham.ca. Set in a historic stone house overlooking the bay, this good-looking inn has plenty of charm and exceedingly helpful owners. The rooms vary in size and furnishings, but all have a/c and queen or king beds; the more expensive choices have fantastic views. Breakfast is included, and the elegant dining room is easily the best spot around to sample regional cuisine, made with local ingredients (mains $18–34; open Mon–Fri 11.30am–2pm & 5.30-10pm, Sat 5.30–10pm, Sun 9am–2pm). $99

Percé

Once a humble fishing community, **PERCÉ** is a prime holiday spot, bisected by Hwy-132, thanks to the tourist potential of the gargantuan limestone rock that rears up from the sea here facing the reddish cliffs of the shore. One of Canada's most celebrated natural phenomena, the **Rocher Percé** – so named for the hole at the western end – is nearly 500m long and 90m high, and is a surreal sight at dawn, when it appears bathed in an eerie golden iridescence. The town is now replete with tacky gift shops and mediocre restaurants and bars; off-season, when much of the resort closes down, Percé maintains a delightfully relaxed and sleepy feel.

Musée le Chafaud

142 Hwy-132 • Late June to late Sept daily 10am–8pm • $5 • ☎ 418 782-5100, ⊚ musee-chafaud.com

Facing the shore near the main wharf (and housing the Discovery & Visitors Center for Rocher Percé) the **Musée le Chafaud** occupies the old Charles Robin Company building formerly used for processing and storing cod. The museum displays traditional and contemporary art and occasionally gets high-calibre travelling exhibitions.

Parc national de l'Île-Bonaventure-et-du-Rocher-Percé

Discovery & Visitors Center 4 Rue du Quai • Late May to early Oct daily 10am–5pm (July & Aug 8am-5pm) • $8.60 (ferries $25 return) • ☎ 418 782 2240, ⊚ sepaq.com/pq/bon/index.dot

Four trails (for a total of 15km) criss-cross the wild headlands of the **Parc national de l'Île-Bonaventure-et-du-Rocher-Percé**, taking in the island's main sights, from its famous colony of **Northern Gannets** (over 110,000 of them) to the now abandoned homes of its former inhabitants (incuding Le Boutillier, a restored nineteenth-century fisherman's home). **Ferries** depart from the wharf next to the Discovery & Visitors Center (in Le Chafaud) on the mainland, where you can also take boat trips or kayak around the island (see page 292).

Hiking trails

One of the most spectacular longer-range views of Rocher Percé is from the top of **Mont-Sainte-Anne**, which rises directly behind Percé Town; the path is signposted from behind the church on rue de l'Église. The steep 3km walk takes about an hour each way. A separate trail leads from the path to **La Grotte**, a lovely spot with waterfalls and statues of the Virgin Mary nestled into the mountain's crevasses.

ARRIVAL AND INFORMATION   PERCÉ

By bus Arriving from Carleton or Gaspé, Orléans Express buses drop passengers in the centre of Percé in front of the tourist office.
Destinations Carleton (1 daily; 3hr 5min); Gaspé (1 daily; 55min).

Tourist office For Rocher Percé ferry timetables, stop by the tourist office (late May to late Oct daily 9am–7pm; ☎418 782 5448, ☎855 782 5448, ⓦperce.info) on the main drag (142 Hwy-132).

TOURS

Boat trips From the wharf, ferry operators to Rocher Percé also run boat trips around the island and the nearby Île-Bonaventure bird reserve (daily: mid-May to early Oct 8.15am–4pm; 3–5 times daily), whose precipitous cliffs are favoured by gannets, kittiwakes, razorbills, guillemots, cormorants and puffins. Les Bateaux de Croisières Julien Cloutier (1hr 30min–3hr; $38; ☎418 782 2161, ⓦcroisieres-julien-cloutier.com) and Les Bateliers de Percé (1hr 30min–3hr; $35; ☎418 782 2974; ⓦlesbateliersdeperce.com) offer similar rates and schedules.

Sea-kayaking From the nearby Parc national Forillon to Rocher Percé, there are some tremendous possibilities for sea-

kayaking off the coast of Percé, where you stand a reasonable chance of spotting seals and several species of sea bird. Avolo (☎418 782 5403, ⓦavolo.qc.ca) offers guided trips (from 2hr 30min; $60) as well as lessons (full-day lesson $125).

Whale-watching The wharf is also the departure point for whale-watching excursions (June–Oct); blue and humpback whales are often in the area, and you may also see porpoises, seals and the rarer white-sided dolphins. Zodiacs speed out with Les Bateliers de Percé (3hr; $85), which also offer excursions in larger boats ($80). Les Croisières Julien Cloutier also offers 2hr 30min whale-watching trips ($80), or 2hr trips by zodiac ($85).

ACCOMMODATION

Most of Percé's **accommodation** is open during the summer months only, when you should book in advance; in the off-season, you'll likely have to stay in Gaspé. There are numerous charming motels along Hwy-132.

Hôtel La Normandie 221 Hwy-132 ouest ☎418 782 2112, ☎800 463 0820, ⓦnormandieperce.com. There's been a hotel on this site since 1937 – no wonder, given its cliff-top location offering superb views of the bay and that rock. Thirty-seven of the 45 bright and modern rooms have balconies. The on-site restaurant (early June to early Oct 7.30–10.30am & 6–8.30pm) offers table d'hôte for $24–58. **$129**

La Maison Rouge 125 Hwy-132 ☎418 782 2227, ⓦlamaisonrouge.ca. A dynamic hostel that rents kayaks

and runs excursions to l'Île-Bonaventure. Dorm beds are in a renovated barn, while private rooms are in the main building. Dorms **$30**; private rooms **$105**

Le Mirage 288 Hwy-132 ☎418 782 5151, ☎800 463 9011, ⓦhotellemirageperce.com. One of the larger hotels in town, this rather pretty establishment has seventy rooms (some suites), all of which have great views of the Rocher Percé. There's also an on-site restaurant. **$106**

Tête d'Indien 1669 Hwy-132 est ☎418 645 2333, ⓦteteindien.com. Though this campsite is about 30km west of town toward Gaspé, it's a popular choice thanks to the friendly vibe, scenic location and services offered, which include kayak tours and lessons. Minimum 2–3 nights. **$26**

EATING AND DRINKING

Boulangerie Le Fournand 194 Hwy-132 ☎418 782 2211, ⓦboulangerielefournand.com. Very much a quintessential French bakery and an essential morning stop, cheery and bustling *Le Fournand* tempts with a wide assortment of brownies, loafs, cakes, croissants and tarts. It also serves tasty soups, sandwiches and quiches ($6–14). May–Oct Mon–Sat 7am–2pm.

La Maison du Pêcheur 157 Hwy-132 ☎418 782 5331. Top-notch seafood restaurant with pleasant decor and locally-sourced produce, with most mains, such as boiled

lobster, filet mignon, seafood chowder and seared scallops, costing $19–47. Reservations recommended. Late May to late Oct daily noon–10pm.

Pub Pit Caribou 182 Hwy-132 ☎418 782 1444, ⓦpitcaribou.com. After a day out on the water, this popular microbrewery is the perfect place to recap the day's activities. Set inside a historic white-tiled building, the pub oozes a relaxed charm and serves its five beers on tap, of which the blonde and IPA are standouts (pints $6). Daily noon–midnight.

New Carlisle

The south shore of the peninsula runs along the **Baie des Chaleurs**, a long wedge of sheltered ocean with relatively warm waters that separates the Gaspé from New Brunswick. Some 116km southwest of Percé on Hwy-132, the small bilingual settlement of **NEW CARLISLE** is best known as the childhood home of **René Lévesque** (1922–1987), ex-premier of Québec, founder of the Parti Québécois in 1968 and all-round local hero. Established by former British soldiers in 1784, today the town remains 62 percent English-speaking, like many of the settlements on this side of the Gaspé.

Espace René-Lévesque

120 boul. Gérard-D-Lévesque • June–Sept daily 9am–6pm • $12 • ☎ 581 357 3355, ⓦ espacerenelevesque.com

The spanking new **Espace René-Lévesque** is a stylish tribute to the Québécois political giant, with displays (mostly in the gardens outside, aided with audioguide) and a fifteen-minute video shedding light on his momentous career as Liberal Party then pro-independence leader.

Kempffer Cultural and Interpretation Center

125 boul. Gérard-D-Lévesque • Late June–Aug daily 9am–5pm • $10 • ☎ 418 752 1334

The history of New Carlisle is chronicled by small but enlightening displays at the **Kempffer Cultural and Interpretation Center**, housed in a grand Victorian pile built in 1868 by local businessman Robert Kempffer. The centre organizes cultural events throughout the summer and runs an on-site tea room on Wednesdays.

Bonaventure

A further 15km along Hwy-132 from New Carlisle, you'll reach **BONAVENTURE**, founded by Acadian refugees near the mouth of the Bonaventure River in 1760. Today, Bonaventure is still known for being a stronghold of **Acadian** culture (see page 354).

Musée Acadien du Québec

95 av Port-Royal • Late June to early Oct daily 9am–5pm; early Oct to mid-Nov Mon–Fri 9am–noon & 1–4pm, Sun 1–4.30pm; mid-Nov to end Nov Mon–Fri 9am–noon & 1–4pm; Dec Mon–Wed & Sat 9am–5pm, Thurs & Fri 9am–5.30pm, Sun noon–5pm; Jan to early May Tues–Fri 9am–noon & 1–4pm, Sun 1–4.30pm; early May to late June Mon–Fri 9am–noon & 1–4.30pm, Sat & Sun 1–4.30pm • $12 • ☎ 418 534 4000, ⓦ museeacadien.com

Acadian traditions and heritage are celebrated at the **Musée Acadien du Québec**, set in an imposing blue-and-white wooden building in the town centre. Highlights of the collection include some delightful handmade furniture dating from the eighteenth century and a range of intriguing photographs that encapsulate something of the hardships of Acadian rural life.

Le Bioparc de la Gaspésie

123 rue des Vieux-Ponts • Daily: June to mid-Oct 9am–5pm; mid-July to mid-Aug until 6pm • $24 • ☎ 866 534 1997, ⓦ bioparc.ca

The wildlife observation centre **Le Bioparc de la Gaspésie** showcases the region's animals – caribou, lynx, otter and mountain lion – in their respective ecosystems. It's possible to tour the park in a couple of hours on a visit and it's a great opportunity to learn more about many of the animals endemic to the peninsula and the efforts being made to protect them. For $99 you can stay "**Overnight with the Wolves**", sleeping in tents inside the park.

INFORMATION AND TOURS   **BONAVENTURE**

Tourist office 93 av Port-Royal, behind Musée Acadien (mid-June to Oct daily 9am–6pm; ☎ 418 534 4014, ⓦ tourismebonaventure.com). Free wi-fi.

Lobster and crab harvesting For a unique experience, join a local fishing crew as they gather their lobster and crab traps with Excursions l'Omirlou on rue Beaubassin (☎ 418 534 2955, ☎ 581 886 0472, ⓦ lomirlou.com). Passengers can assist (to a moderate degree) and learn about the livelihood of area fishermen (May–Sept 2hr–6hr; $50–70).

ACCOMMODATION AND EATING

Café Acadien 168 rue de Beaubassin ☎418 534 4276, ⓦ cafeacadien.com. This cute café (June–Sept daily 7am–11pm) right on the water serves imaginative French-Canadian food and also offers five comfy B&B rooms. $90

★ **Cime Aventure** 200 chemin Arsenault ☎418 534 2333, ☎800 790 2463, ⓦ cimeaventures.com. Excellent ecolodge (linen is $8/night per bed) that also has campsites and tipis alongside the Bonaventure River and comfortable cottages nestled in the woods. It rents kayaks and canoes, and runs guided trips, including snorkelling, on the river (3hr–6 days). June–Sept. Sites $32; tipis $80; lodges $160; cottages $240

Le Bioparc de la Gaspésie 123 rue des Vieux-Ponts ☎418 534 1997, ⓦ bioparc.ca. The reserve has nine immaculate and sunny chalets with high ceilings and a striking design located between the sea and the Bonaventure River estuary. During summer (mid-June to Aug) they're generally available by the week only, but can be reserved at the last minute if not already booked (two-night minimum). $195; weekly rental $1249

Carleton

Around 37km northwest of Bonaventure, Hwy-299 runs north along the banks of the Cascapédia towards the Parc national de la Gaspésie (see page 287), while the coastal Hwy-132 continues for another 24km to the popular bayside resort of **CARLETON**, where the mountains of the interior return to dominate the landscape. Founded in 1756 by Acadian refugees, Carleton is an unassuming little place that stands back from the sea behind a broad lagoon, linked to the narrow coastal strip by a couple of long causeways. The town has a bird sanctuary – a favourite haunt of wading species like the sandpiper and plover – and several accessible bathing **beaches** where you can rent kayaks.

Oratoire Notre-Dame-du-Mont-Saint-Joseph

837 rue de la Montagne • Daily: mid-June to late Aug 8am–6pm; late Aug to mid-Oct 9am–5pm • $8.50 • ☎418 364 2256, ⓦ montsaintjoseph.com

What makes Carleton special is the contrast between the coastal flatlands and the backdrop of wooded hills that rise up behind the town. At 582m, Mont Saint-Joseph is the highest of these and is presided over by the **Oratoire Notre-Dame-du-Mont-Saint-Joseph**, a church that incorporates the walls of a stone chapel built on the site in 1935. A 3km maze of steep footpaths slip past streams and waterfalls before they reach the summit (worth it for the view rather than the building). You can also take the less adventurous option and drive up to see the splendid panoramic views over the bay and across to New Brunswick. To access the mountain (including the chapel) and bike trails you must purchase a "Fidèle au Mont-Saint-Joseph" pass for $8.50, at the Pavillon Desjardins on the summit.

Parc national de Miguasha

231 Route Miguasha Ouest • Park entrance fee $8.60 • Exhibition Halls May & early Oct to late Oct Mon–Fri 8.30am–noon & 1–4.30pm; June to early Oct daily 9am–5pm • $10.65 • ⓦ sepaq.com/pq/mig/index.dot

The hilly **Miguasha Peninsula**, some 20km to the west of Carleton off Hwy-132, makes a pleasant excursion. Famous for its fossils, this tiny peninsula is home to the **Parc national de Miguasha**, where some of the area's better findings are displayed at the "From Water to Land" and "Elpistostege: the origins of a quest" **Exhibition Halls**. Frequent and free guided tours take in the exhibitions, the research area and a walk along the beach and cliffs.

ARRIVAL AND DEPARTURE

CARLETON

By bus Orléans Express buses stop in the centre of Carleton at *Restaurant Le Héron*, 561 blvd Perron (☎418 364 3881).

ACCOMMODATION AND EATING

Auberge du Château Bahia 152 blvd Perron, Pointe-à-la-Garde ☎418 788 2048, ⓦ chateaubahia.com. Located 36km west of town and signposted off Hwy-132 is this eccentric Renaissance-style wooden castle (built by the owner in the 1980s). Rates include breakfast and banquet-style dinners of hearty Québécois fare are served ($21) – all is delicious. May to early Oct. Dorms $̄31; private room $̄35; camping $̄20

La Mie Véritable 578 blvd Perron ☎ 418 364 6662. An excellent bakery that uses organic ingredients and serves coffee at its café upstairs, *La Mie d'en Haut*. Mon–Sat 7am–5.30pm, Sun 8am–2pm.

Le Pub St-Joseph 482 blvd Perron ☎ 418 364 3355, ⓦ pubstjoseph.com. Lively brewpub in the *Hotel Baie Bleue* that is a popular spot to watch sports on one of the four large-screen TVs. The beer on tap is from a local

brewery and heaped portions of agreeable pub fare are moderately priced (most dishes $14–25). Mon–Fri 7am–2pm & 4–10pm, Sat & Sun 7am–11pm.

Manoir Belle Plage 474 blvd Perron ☎ 418 364 3388, ☎ 800 463 0780, ⓦ manoirbelleplage.com. A large, pretty, yellow inn with a touch of class, a wide range of amenities and a range of supremely comfortable rooms. *Le Courlieu*, the inn's maritime-themed restaurant, serves grilled seafood dishes ($17–35). Restaurant May–Sept Mon–Fri 7–10am, 11.30am–2pm & 5–8.30pm; Sat & Sun 7–10am & 5–8.30pm (open for breakfast year-round). $̄99

Îles-de-la-Madeleine

The archipelago of the **Îles-de-la-Madeleine** (Magdalen Islands), in the middle of the Gulf of St Lawrence some 200km southeast (and one hour ahead) of the Gaspé Peninsula and 100km northeast of Prince Edward Island (see page 392), consists of twelve main islands, seven of which are inhabited. Six of these are connected by narrow sand spits and crossed by paved and gravel roads, while the last is only accessible by boat. Together these dozen islands form a crescent-shaped series of dunes, lagoons and low rocky outcrops that measures about 80km from end to end, with the main village and ferry port roughly in the middle at **Cap-aux-Meules**. The islands lie in the Gulf Stream, which makes the winters warmer than those of mainland Québec, but they are subject to almost constant winds, which have eroded the red-sandstone cliffs along parts of the shoreline into an extraordinary array of arches, caves and tunnels. These rock formations, the archipelago's most distinctive attraction, are at their best on the central **Île du Cap-aux-Meules** and the adjacent **Île du Havre-aux-Maisons**.

The islands' 15,000 inhabitants (most descended from Acadian settlers) are largely dependent on **fishing**, the lobster catch in particular. Despite international pressure, the annual seal hunt in late winter also still supports many islanders (seals can be easily spotted on the ice floes in March). Other sectors of the fishery are now suffering because of fish-stock depletion, and the islands' future livelihood revolves around **tourism**. Still, many residents worry about preserving their way of life and the fragile ecology of their beautiful islands.

Visitors are drawn to the archipelago for its wide-open **landscapes** and sense of **isolation** – it's easy to find a dune-laden **beach** where you can be alone with the sea. The islands' big attraction for many adventure travellers is the strong winds that blow here: between late August and late October conditions for **windsurfing** and **kitesurfing** are exemplary and the Canadian Professional and Amateur Windsurf Championship heads here every year. Throughout the islands, **powerful currents** and changeable weather conditions can make swimming dangerous, and the waters are occasionally home to stinging jellyfish.

Île du Cap-aux-Meules

The ferry from Souris, Prince Edward Island (see page 392), docks in the middle of the archipelago, at **Île du Cap-aux-Meules**, which boasts the islands' largest community – **CAP-AUX-MEULES**, on the eastern shore. A useful base for exploring the neighbouring islands, the town is the islands' administrative and business centre and their least attractive enclave. Yet just a couple of kilometres west of the village, there are fine views of the entire island chain from the **Butte du Vent**, the area's highest hill. Further west, on the other end of the island near the fishing port of **L'ÉTANG-DU-NORD**, you'll find

4

OUTDOOR ACTIVITIES IN ÎLES-DE-LA-MADELEINE

Unsurprisingly, the opportunities to get on, and in, the water around the islands – from wreck diving to horseriding on a beach – are plentiful and every bit worth setting aside time for, if not making them the focus of your trip.

ÎLE DU CAP-AUX-MEULES

Boat and fishing trips Outings depart from near the ferry terminal in Étang-du-Nord during summer. Excursions en mer (☎418 986 4745, ⓦ excursionsenmer.com) and Excursions Le Pluvier (☎418 986 5681, ⓦ telebecinternet.com/lepluvier) offer similar services, which include marine wildlife-watching trips and explorations of coves and uninhabited islands (from $35).

Windsurfing, kitesurfing and kayaking The island boasts Canada's first kitesurfing school, Aerosport Carrefour d'Aventures (late June to early Sept; ☎418 986 6677, ⓦ aerosport.ca), at 1390 chemin de La Vernière in Étang-du-Nord. If you're looking to windsurf or kitesurf, stop here first; it's an indispensable source of advice and rentals (kitesurfing lessons from $250 for 2–3hr). It also offers excellent guided kayak tours to some of the islands' geographical highlights, including the red sandstone caves of Gros-Cap (3hr; $44).

Horseriding In Cap-aux-Meules, La Crinière au Vent (Mon–Sat 9am–5pm; ☎418 986 6777, ⓦ lacriniereauvent.sitew.com), 115 chemin John-Aucoin, leads scenic horseback rides along the beach (3hr 30min; $162). It also offers pony rides and day-camps.

ÎLE DU HAVRE-AUBERT

Kayaking and windsurfing The Centre nautique de l'Istorlet (☎418 937 5266, ⓦ istorlet.com), at 100 chemin de l'Istorlet, offers sea-kayak outings (June–Sept; 3hr; $55), windsurfing lessons (2hr; $95) and kayak rentals (from $20/hr).

some extravagant coastal rock formations and a port where kayaking tours take off. In the opposite direction, the main road skirts the southern tip of the islands' longest lagoon before heading on across the Île du Havre-aux-Maisons.

Île du Havre-aux-Maisons

The **Île du Havre-aux-Maisons**' smooth green landscapes contrast with the red cliffs of its southern shore. Crisscrossed by narrow country roads and littered with tiny, straggling villages, this island is best known for a unique oral tradition. The Acadians that settled here post-deportation were so irate with their treatment they decided never to utter the word "king" (*roi* in French) again, and eventually wound up dropping the letter "r" from their language altogether.

The striking arches and shapes of the coastal rocks around **Dune-du-Sud** are an understandably popular draw, as is the **Fumoir d'Antan** (guided tours mid-June to Aug daily 9am–5pm; $5; April to mid-June & Sept self-guided tours 9am–5pm $4.50; ☎418 969 4907, ⓦ fumoirdantan.com), at 27 chemin du Quai, the last remaining traditional herring smokehouse on the islands. Deserted twin beaches edge the hamlet islet of **Pointe-aux-Loups** north of here, across the sand spit and along Hwy-199.

Grosse-Île and Île de la Grande-Entrée

At the far northern end of the archipelago, the twin islets of anglophone **Grosse-Île** and francophone **Île de la Grande-Entrée**, the last island to be inhabited, border the wildlife reserve of the **Pointe-de-l'Est**, whose entrance is beside the main road. On its south side, the reserve is edged by the enormous sandy expanse of **La Grande Échouerie beach**, whose southern end is framed by yet more splendid rock formations at Old Harry's Point. This is where Europeans first came to the islands in order to slaughter walruses, depleting the stock by 1800. Today, the 10km walk down the beach offers a good chance to spot seals, and there have been some – albeit very rare – walrus sightings. A kilometre past the rustic wharf at **Old Harry**, the pretty white church of **St. Peter's-by-the-Sea** with beautifully sculptured doors uses the islands as backdrop for biblical tales – it's the oldest Anglican church on the islands.

Council for Anglophone Magdalen Islanders (CAMI)

787 chemin Principal • July & Aug daily 8am–4pm; Sept–June Mon–Fri 9am–4.30pm • $5 (includes both museums) • ☎418 985 2116,
Ⓦmicami.org

The **Council for Anglophone Magdalen Islanders (CAMI)** operates a couple of worthwhile
museums in Old Harry, beginning with the **Little Red School House**, a one-room school
built in 1922. The museum's collection of old photographs and historic artifacts tells
the history of the local anglophone population, most of whom are of Scottish descent.
The adjacent **Veterans' Museum** houses a collection of uniforms, medals, swords and
equipment used by former soldiers from the Magdalen Islands, including the diary of
local William Welsh, kept just before he died in a prisoner of war camp in Hong Kong.

Île du Havre-Aubert

To the south of Île du Cap-aux-Meules, **Île du Havre-Aubert** has one significant
community, **HAVRE-AUBERT**, edged by round, sloping hills. It's the most attractive
and scenically sited of the islands' communities, and attracts a lot of visitors. It
is situated around **La Grave**, a pebbly beach flanked by a boardwalk and wooden
buildings once used by sailors and fishermen and now transformed into bars, cafés,
restaurants, souvenir shops and art galleries; the best spot to buy souvenirs is **Atelier
Cotier** (Mon–Fri 10am–5pm; ☎418 937 2917, Ⓦateliercotier.com), at 907 chemin
de la Grave, which has an impressive collection of decorative sandstone housewares
crafted by local artists.

Île d'Entrée

The tiny anglophone **Île d'Entrée** is the only inhabited island not linked by land to the
rest of the archipelago. Home to fewer than 150 people, this grassy hillock is encircled
by footpaths and makes a pleasant day out, providing the sea is calm on the hour-long
ferry trip from Cap-aux-Meules (Mon–Sat 7.30am & 3pm, return 9am & 4.30pm;
$16.95 one-way; ☎418 986 3278, Ⓦtraversierctma.ca). Horses and cows roam freely
on the slopes of the Îles-de-la-Madeleine's highest point, **Big Hill** (174m), accessible
from the port by taking chemin Main and then chemin Post Office, and following
the path across the fields to the top for a view of the whole archipelago. On your way
towards the path, the tiny **Musée de l'Île d'Entrée** (June–Sept hours vary; free; ☎418
986 6622, Ⓦmicami.org) displays island artefacts and historical household items.

ARRIVAL AND DEPARTURE

ÎLES-DE-LA-MADELEINE

By ferry Every month a CTMA ferry sails to Cap-aux-
Meules from Souris on Prince Edward Island (☎418 986
3278, ☎888 986 3278, Ⓦtraversierctma.ca) – the number
of weekly departures varies from three to eleven depending
on the season (a one-way ticket is $53.25 mid-June to mid-
Sept, otherwise $34.40; plus $99.25 for a car mid-June to
mid-Sept, otherwise $69.80; $15.30 for a bicycle year-
round; 5hr). Reservations are mandatory in July and Aug
and need to be made several months in advance.
By plane The Îles-de-la-Madeleine Airport is at the north
end of Île du Havre-aux-Maisons, some 20km from Cap-aux-
Meules. Some flights have connecting buses to Cap-aux-
Meules, but otherwise you'll have to take a taxi (about $28),

or rent a car from Hertz (☎418 969 4229) at the airport;
book in advance in the summer.
Destinations Daily scheduled flights on Air Canada Express-
Jazz leave Gaspé (2–3 daily; 55min), Québec City (2–3 daily;
2hr 50min, via Gaspé) and Montréal (1 daily; 2hr 30min; or
via Gaspé and/or Québec City). The other option is Pascan
Aviation (☎450 443 0500, ☎888 313 8777, Ⓦpascan.
com), which flies from Bonaventure (2 daily; 1hr), Mont-
Joli (1 daily; 1hr 20min) and Québec City (2hr 20min, via
Bonaventure). Air Saint-Pierre operates a useful connection
to Saint-Pierre and Miquelon (page 354) in July and August
(Mon & Fri; 1hr 10min).

GETTING AROUND AND INFORMATION

By bike and moped The best way to tour the principal
islands is by bike; you can rent these at Le Pédalier (from

$24/day, $85/week; ☎418 986 2965, Ⓦlepedalier.com),
at 545 chemin Principal in Cap-aux-Meules. It and the

tourist office have an excellent map of the island's many well-marked routes. Mopeds can be rented from Agence de Location des Îles, 357 rue Principal, in Cap-aux-Meules (☎ 418 986 6565).

By bus RÉGÎM (☎ 877 521 0841, ⊚ regim.info) runs a limited bus service throughout the main islands; just wave them down. Flat fares are $4, with tickets sold in books of ten (at just $30). Several routes run Mon–Fri from Cap-aux-

Meules, but infrequently (often once a day in each direction).

Information The ferry terminal at Cap-aux-Meules is near the tourist office, at 128 chemin Principal (daily: late June to late Aug 7am–9pm; late Aug to late Sept 9am–8pm; Oct–May Mon–Fri 9am–noon & 1–5pm; first three weeks of June 9am–8pm; ☎ 418 986 2245, ☎ 877 624 4437, ⊚ tourismeilesdelamadeleine.com), which operates a free room-reservation service with an emphasis on B&Bs.

ACCOMMODATION

With few inns, motels and hotels on the islands, it's advisable to book a bed before you arrive. The tourist office also has details of cottage and apartment rentals, starting at roughly $250 per week (⊚ airbnb.com also covers the island). The cheapest way to stay is either at the hostel on Île du Cap-aux-Meules (where you can also camp) or one of the other half-dozen commercial campsites on the islands.

ÎLE DU CAP-AUX-MEULES

Château Madelinot 323 Hwy-199, Fatima ☎ 418 986 3695, ☎ 855 986 2211, ⊚ hotelsaccents.com/chateau. Large, immaculate hotel with fine sea views, great food, comfortable rooms and an indoor pool. $144; suites $174

Hostel and Camping Gros Cap 74 chemin du Camping ☎ 418 986 4505, ☎ 800 986 4505, ⊚ parcdegroscap.ca. The dramatically sited and wind-swept hostel in L'Étang-du-Nord has private rooms, dorm rooms, five cottages and several campsites overlooking the water. It also offers expertly guided kayak tours from $54, kayak rentals (a double for 3hr is $45). June to mid-Sept. Dorms (including breakfast) $34; sites $26 (serviced $32); private rooms $72; cottages $95

ÎLE DU HAVRE-AUX-MAISONS

Auberge la Petite Baie 187 Hwy-199 ☎ 418 937 8901, ⊚ www3.telebecinternet.com/auberge.petitebaie. A former customs station, this inn is the best bet on the island, with lovely rooms of varying size and sea vistas. Breakfast is included. Late June to late Sept. $112

Au Vieux Couvent 292 Hwy-199 ☎ 418 969 2233, ⊚ domaineduvieuxcouvent.com. A restored convent and one of the more elegant accommodation options on the islands, with ten airy rooms facing the sea, luxurious

furnishings and a stellar seafood restaurant (see page 300). $225

Camping Des Sillons 436 chemin Dune-du-Sud ☎ 418 969 2134, ⊚ chaletscampingdessillons.com. You can camp by the beach on the east side of the island at Camping Des Sillons, which also has several dated, but tidy chalets. June to Sept. Sites $26; chalets $120

ÎLE DE LA GRANDE-ENTRÉE

La Salicorne 377 Hwy-199 ☎ 418 985 2833, ⊚ salicorne. ca. Friendly inn with comfortable rooms furnished with pieces made by local artists. There's camping space on the grounds as well as a great restaurant, Madelinot. The food is expensive but you can save money by opting to pay for full board (from $145 per person); it's also open to non-guests. The inn offers hikes and cave trips ($59), as well as a shuttle service to and from the airport on Île du Havre-aux-Maisons ($28). Sites $24; doubles $148

ÎLE DU HAVRE-AUBERT

Auberge Chez Denis à François 404 chemin d'en Haut ☎ 418 937 2371, ⊚ aubergechezdenis.com. Located at the end of La Grave, Chez Denis à François offers fine views of the strip and has fourteen sunny rooms (breakfast included). $145

ÎLE D'ENTRÉE

Chambres Josey 289 chemin Main ☎ 418 986 5629, ⊚ goo.gl/rtYi51. There are three basic rooms with antique furnishings on the upper floor of this quaint inn, one of a couple of the island's official lodging choices and on the trail to the Big Hill. $89

EATING AND DRINKING

ÎLE DU CAP-AUX-MEULES

★ **À l'abri de la Tempête** 286 chemin Coulombe ☎ 418 986 5005, ⊚ alabridelatempete.com. Housed in an old fish factory just short of the Dune de l'Ouest and well worth a detour, this fantastic microbrewery serves several award-winning beers made from ingredients grown on the islands. May to June & Sept daily 4–10pm; July & Aug daily noon–midnight; Oct–May Tues & Fri 4–10pm.

Café la Côte 499 chemin Boisville ouest, L'Étang-du-Nord ☎ 418 986 6412, ⊚ lecafelacote.com. One of the island's more creative restaurants, with filling mains such as lobster poutine and smoked mackerel pizza (from $12). There's a nice selection of wines and the views of the water can't be beat. Mid-May to Sept Mon–Sat 11am–9pm, Sun 9am–9pm.

La Table des Roy 1188 chemin de La Verniére in La

Vernière just west of Cap-aux-Meules ☎ 418 986 3004, ⓦ restaurantlatabledesroy.com. An outstanding, if pricey, option for seafood dishes (mains from $32), such as a scallop stew with lobster and sweetbread. June to late Sept Mon–Sat 6–10pm.

ÎLE DU HAVRE-AUX-MAISONS

La Moulière (Au Vieux Couvent) 292 Hwy-199 (see page 298). The island's prime place to splurge on seafood, with creative mains like a scallop salad with a balsamic vinaigrette and honey dressing ($28). It also has an energetic basement bar with regular live music – even without, the place gets packed nightly. April–May & late Nov to Dec Thurs–Sun 5–9pm; June to late Oct daily 5–9pm (closed late Oct to late Nov).

ÎLE DU HAVRE-AUBERT

Auberge Chez Denis à François 404 chemin d'en Haut ☎ 418 937 2371, ⓦ aubergechezdenis.com. The expertly prepared seafood dishes served in the cosy dining room of this inn are well worth sampling even if you're not staying here, with mains from around $22. May–Oct daily 5–9pm.

★ **Café de la Grave** 969 Hwy-199 ☎ 418 937 5765. For chunky sandwiches, clam chowder served in a bread bowl ($15.50), local beers and free wi-fi, head for this convivial café in the old general store. Mon–Fri 11am–11pm, Sat 9am–11pm (June–Oct Sun 9am–11pm).

Charlevoix

Stretching along the **north shore** of the St Lawrence River east of Québec City, from the Beaupré coast to the Fjord du Saguenay, the region of **Charlevoix**, named after the Jesuit historian François Xavier de Charlevoix, is a UNESCO World Biosphere Reserve. Species like the **arctic caribou** and **arctic wolf**, not usually associated with such southerly latitudes, can be seen in the more remote areas, and because the Ice Age that shaped the rest of eastern Canada missed this breathtaking portion of the Canadian Shield, numerous pre-glacial plants still thrive here. It consists of gently sloping hills, sheer cliffs and vast valleys veined with rivers, brooks and waterfalls, a landscape that Québec's better-known artists – Clarence Gagnon, Marc-Aurèle Fortin and Jean-Paul Lemieux – chose for inspiration. Though Charlevoix has been a tourist destination for years and especially popular with people from Québec City on weekend breaks, the land has been carefully preserved, and quaint villages and tin-roofed churches still nestle in an unspoiled countryside.

Highway 138, the main route through Charlevoix, travels 225km from Québec City to Baie-Sainte-Catherine on the Saguenay. The main towns along this highway are served by Intercar **buses** from Québec City, but many of the quintessential Charlevoix villages – in particular those along the coastal Hwy-362 which starts from Baie-Saint-Paul – are not served by public transport. Be prepared to rent a car or bike; the expense is worth it.

Baie-Saint-Paul

One of Charlevoix's earliest settlements and longtime gathering place for Québec's landscape painters, the picture-perfect **BAIE-SAINT-PAUL** is tucked into the Gouffré Valley at the foot of the highest range of the Laurentian mountains. Dominated by the twin spires of the **Église de Baie-Saint-Paul** (the fifth church to stand here, inaugurated in 1964), winding streets radiate out from the Rivière Gouffré, flanked by houses that are more than two hundred years old. From beside the church, the main road **rue St-Jean-Baptiste** slips through the commercial heart of the town edged by numerous quaint cottages characteristic of Québec's earliest houses, with curving roofs and wide verandas, many converted into commercial galleries. The collective effect is reason enough to make wandering around Baie-Saint-Paul the main attraction.

Maison de René-Richard

58 rue St-Jean-Baptiste (entrance on Rue Clarence Gagnon) • Daily 11am–6pm • Free • ☎ 418 435 5571

The **Maison de René-Richard** offers an insight into the works of René Richard, an associate of the Group of Seven. The 1852 house has been left exactly the same since

---

TRAVERSÉE DE CHARLEVOIX

Attracting hikers, mountain-bikers and cross-country skiers, the long-distance **Traversée de Charlevoix** (☎418 639 2284, ⓦtraverseedecharlevoix.qc.ca) begins near the Parc des Grands-Jardins on Hwy-381, crossing 105km of mountainous terrain including the Parc national des Hautes-Gorges-de-la-Rivière-Malbaie (see page 304) before ending at Mont Grand-Fonds near La Malbaie. Accommodation starts at $35 per day for cabins or $37 per day for cottages for the six nights needed to complete the hike.

Richard died in 1982; though it's more of a gallery than museum (all the art on display is for sale), you can usually wander around his studio and living quarters, a rare glimpse at the Charlevoix of the 1940s when some of Québec's finest painters hung out here.

Musée d'art contemporain de Baie-Saint-Paul

23 rue Ambroise-Fafard • Late June to early Sept daily 10am–5pm; early Sept to late June Tues–Sun 11–5pm • $10 • ☎418 435 3681, ⓦmacbsp.com

For an overview of the works of art produced in Charlevoix, visit the plush **Musée d'art contemporain de Baie-Saint-Paul**, which has an international reputation for the excellence of its temporary exhibitions of Québécois and international paintings, scultptures and photography in particular. Throughout the year it showcases works created by local artists at symposiums in town.

Parc national des Grands-Jardins

Hours vary at Mont-du-Lac-des-Cygnes Visitors Centre but are generally daily: June–Aug 8.30am–8pm; Sept, Oct & March–May 9am–4pm (Nov–Feb Sat & Sun only) • $8.60 • ☎418 439 1227, ⓦsepaq.com/pq/grj

Baie-Saint-Paul makes a good base to explore the **Parc national des Grands-Jardins**, 42km away on Hwy-381 but with no public transport. Within the forests and lakes of the park, the 900m Mont-du-Lac-des-Cygnes gives the best of all Charlevoix panoramas. It's a 4hr (8km) climb from the **Mont-du-Lac-des-Cygnes Visitors Centre** on Hwy-381 (21km) to the top and back along a clear but rocky path; you will need proper footgear. You can rent canoes ($46.50/day) at Mont-du-Lac-des-Cygnes or at **Arthabaska Discovery and Visitors Centre** (open late May to mid-Oct only, daily 9am–8pm) and accommodation is available (see page 302).

ARRIVAL AND INFORMATION   BAIE-SAINT-PAUL

By bus The Intercar bus stops at the petrol station at 909 boul Mgr de Laval (☎418 435 0101) on the edge of town. Destinations Baie-Comeau (2 daily; 4hr 55min–5hr 45min); La Malbaie (3 daily; 1hr); Québec City (3 daily; 1hr 20min); Sainte-Anne-de-Beaupré (3 daily; 45min); Tadoussac (2 daily; 2hr 25min–3hr).
By train The tourist-oriented Train de Charlevoix (ⓦtraindecharlevoix.com) runs from Chute-Montmorency station to Baie-Saint Paul (2–3 daily mid-June to mid-Oct; from $59 one-way), and on to La Malbaie (from $39 one-way).

Tourist offices The main Charlevoix Tourist Information Office is at 444 boul Mgr-De Laval (daily: mid-May to late June 9am–5pm, late June to early Sept 8.30am–7pm, early Sept to early Oct 8.30am–5pm, early Oct to mid-May 9am–4pm; ☎418 665 2276, ⓦtourisme-charlevoix.com) off Hwy-138 before you descend into town from the west. The Baie-Saint-Paul Tourist Information Office lies in the heart of town at 6 rue St-Jean-Baptiste (daily: mid-May to late June & early Sept to early Oct 9am–5pm, late June to early Sept 9am–6pm, early Oct to mid-May 9am–4pm; ☎418 665 4454, ⓦbaiesaintpaul.com).

ACCOMMODATION

Auberge La Muse 39 rue St-Jean-Baptiste ☎418 435 6839, ⓦlamuse.com. Right in the centre of town, this beautiful Victorian-era inn has twelve large, prettily decorated rooms – including an "energizing suite". Facilities include a restaurant, health centre and gift shop selling food made on-site. **$149**

L'estampilles 24 chemin du Cap-aux-Corbeaux-Nord ☎418 435 2533, ⓦlestampilles.com. A few minutes out of town off Hwy-362, this graceful inn has eleven nicely appointed rooms; the rooms on the upper floor have a/c. There's a sauna, outdoor spa, bar and on-site restaurant; the latter serves a scrumptious table d'hôte nightly at around

---

OUTDOOR ACTIVITIES AROUND BAIE-SAINT-PAUL

Some of the province's most dramatic **skiing** is at **Le Massif** (see page 271) perched over the St Lawrence River 20km to the west of town.

Hiking Randonnées Nature-Charlevoix (☎418 435 6275, ⓦrandonneesnature.com) runs excellent hiking tours in the Parc national des Grands-Jardins (see page 301) and tours around the **Charlevoix Crater** – to the east of town and one of the planet's largest – by bus (year-round; reservations required; 2hr 30min; $195)

Helicopter tours To really get a sense of the crater's immense scale and beauty see it from above on a helicopter tour from Héli Charlevoix (May–Oct daily 9.30–5.30pm; Nov–April by Mon–Sat 9.30am–4pm; two-person minimum; from $129; ☎418 435 4071,

ⓦheli-charlevoix.com), which has an office just outside town at 735 boul Mgr de Laval (Hwy-138).

Kayaking At the marina, Katabatik, at 210 rue Ste-Anne (☎418 435 2066, ⓦkatabatik.ca), is one of the top outfitters in the region, capable of guiding or providing equipment for just about any outdoor activity you might have in mind. Rent bicycles, kayaks, canoes and paragliders or choose courses in kayaking and paragliding; it also runs guided **kayak trips** along the coast and toward Cap-à-l'Aigle (from $64/half-day).

$49.95. **$165**

Maison Otis 23 rue St-Jean-Baptiste ☎418 435 2255, ⓦmaisonotis.com. One of the best hotels in town, with a pleasant, country-house feel (the property dates back to 1836). The twenty rooms and five suites (some with exposed beams) were completely renovated in 2018; some have baths and fireplaces. There's also an on-site restaurant

and bar. Doubles **$160**

Parc national des Grands-Jardins ☎418 439 1227, ☎800 665 6527, ⓦsepaq.com. A range of accommodation is available within the park but must be reserved in advance. Cabins (two people; late May to mid-Sept) **$115**; huts (per adult; late May to mid-Sept) **$28.95**; rustic camping (late May to mid-Sept) **$23.80**

EATING AND DRINKING

Belle-Plage 192 rue Ste-Anne ☎418 435 3321, ⓦbelleplage.ca. The restaurant of the *Domaine Belle-Plage* serves traditional Québécois cuisine, with a buffet for around $22. Open nightly for dinner.

Joe Smoked Meat 54 rue St-Jean-Baptiste ☎418 240 4949, ⓦjoesmokedmeat.com. A menu stocked with hearty dishes aimed squarely at carnivores packs in people at this lively chain restaurant. The signature sandwich, a sub ("sous-marins") stuffed with smoked meat, steak slices, cheese and peppers ($15.40), is a veritable gut buster. Daily 11am–9pm.

Le Café des Artistes 25 rue St-Jean-Baptiste ☎418 435

5585, ⓦlecafedesartistes.com. Popular bistro that serves desserts, coffees and thin-crust pizzas, and frequently hosts art openings. Its adjoining club is the place to go to catch live local and regional acts. Mon–Thurs 10.30am–10pm, Fri 10.30am–11pm, Sat 10am–11pm, Sun 10am–10pm.

Le Saint-Pub 2 rue Racine, corner of St-Jean-Baptiste ☎418 240 2332, ⓦsaint-pub.com. A terrific brewpub with a few ales on tap, such as the Dominus Vobiscum, that are wildly popular throughout Québec as well as a selection of ales that are brewed seasonally or for shorter runs. Mon–Thurs 11.30am–10pm, Fri & Sat 11.30am–11pm, Sun 11.30am–9.30pm.

L'Isle aux Coudres

The 16km-long island of **l'Isle aux Coudres**, where Jacques Cartier celebrated Canada's first Mass in 1535, is named after its numerous hazelnut trees. Missionaries were the first permanent settlers, arriving in 1748, and the growing population came to depend on shipbuilding and beluga-whale hunting for their livelihoods. Ship- and canoe-building still takes place here, but the main industry of its 1600 inhabitants is harvesting peat moss from the bogs in the centre of the island.

The island's stone manors and cottages attract huge numbers of visitors, who drive and **cycle** around the 24km peripheral road that connects – in a clockwise direction – the three villages of **SAINT-BERNARD**, **LA BALEINE** and **SAINT-LOUIS**. The only real diversions along the way are the restored and working windmill and adjacent water mill, **Les Moulins de l'Isle-aux-Coudres** (mid-May to early Oct daily 10am–5pm; $8.70; ☎418 760 1065, ⓦlesmoulinsdelisleauxcoudres.com) in the southwest corner of the island, both dating from the early nineteenth century.

ARRIVAL, GETTING AROUND AND INFORMATION — L'ISLE AUX COUDRES

By ferry The island is reached year-round via a free, 20min car ferry ride (number of daily trips vary 6am–11.30pm, but at least 1 per hour; ⓣ 877 787 7483 option 5, ⓦ traversiers.com) at 750 chemin du Quai in Saint-Joseph-de-la-Rive (20km from Baie-Saint-Paul).

By bike and moped Bikes can be rented (from $12/hr and $40/day) from Vélo-Coudres (May–Oct; ⓣ 418 438 2118, ⓦ velocoudres.com), 2926 chemin des Coudriers, which has a wide selection (including quadricycles) and rents mopeds ($110/day), too, but is 5km from the dock at the eastern tip of the island (most visitors drive and leave their car here).

Tourist Welcome Center at 1024 chemin des Coudriers, near the ferry dock in Saint-Bernard, with maps of the island (mid-May to late June & early Sept to early Oct Sat 9am–5pm & Sun 9am–2.30pm, late June to early Sept daily 9am–5pm; ⓣ 418 665 4454, ⓦ tourismeisleauxcoudres.com).

ACCOMMODATION AND EATING

Boulangerie Bouchard 1648 chemin des Coudriers ⓣ 418 438 2454, ⓦ boulangeriebouchard.com. Before heading off the island pay a visit to this historic bakery, which has all manner of freshly baked breads and pies. Mid-June to mid-Oct daily 8am–6pm; mid-Oct to mid-June Mon, Tues & Thurs–Sat 9am–5pm, Wed & Sun 10am–4pm.

Camping Leclerc 333 chemin de la Baleine ⓣ 418 438 2217, ⓦ famille-leclerc.charlevoix.net. A variety of sites can be booked at this pleasant campsite in La Baleine, most with views of the river. There are also basic motel rooms and the 1750s ancestral House Leclerc on the grounds (only viewable from the outside). Mid-May to mid-Oct. Sites **$35**; rooms **$88**

Hôtel Cap-aux-Pierres 444 chemin de la Baleine ⓣ 418 438 2711, ⓦ hotelcapauxpierres.com. This posh spot with immaculate landscaped grounds provides half-board accommodation; offers hotel and motel rooms; and has indoor and outdoor pools, a tennis court and a good restaurant. **$154**

La Malbaie

4

Highways 362 and 138 converge about 50km from Baie-Saint-Paul at **LA MALBAIE** ("Bad Bay"), so called because Champlain ran aground here in 1608. Situated at the mouth of the Rivière Malbaie, the town – an amalgamation of five villages – sprawls along the riverfront with little to detain you, though it's a good base for a day-trip to the **Hautes-Gorges** (see page 304); and the ritzy resort area **POINTE-AU-PIC** – back along Hwy-362 – is worth a look for its grand **Le Manoir Richelieu** (see page 303), once a regular haunt of early twentieth-century high society. This French château-style incarnation of the hotel was completed in 1929 and makes for a delightful overnight stay – and you can wager the rest of your travel budget at the immense Casino de Charlevoix next door.

ARRIVAL AND INFORMATION — LA MALBAIE

By bus Buses (ⓣ 418 665 2264) stop and pick up at the Familiprix (west side) and Depanneur Julien Lavoie, 170 Blvd Malcolm Fraser (east side of town)

Destinations Baie-Comeau (2 daily; 3hr 40min–4hr); Baie-Saint-Paul (3 daily; 1hr); Québec City (3 daily; 2hr 10min–2hr 20min); Tadoussac (2 daily; 1hr 15min).

By train The tourist-oriented Train de Charlevoix (ⓦ traindecharlevoix.com) runs from Chute-Montmorency station to La Malbaie (2–3 daily; mid-June to mid-Oct; from $98 one-way).

By ferry The nearest car ferry across the St Lawrence leaves from the hillside village of Saint-Siméon 25km northeast on Hwy-138, towards Rivière-du-Loup (see page 282).

Tourist office Along the St Lawrence River at 495 blvd de Comporté (daily: early Jan to mid-May & mid-Oct to mid-May 9am–4pm; mid-May to mid-June & early Sept to mid-Oct 9am–5pm; mid-June to early Sept 8.30am–7pm; ⓣ 418 665 4454); has a full range of info on Charlevoix.

ACCOMMODATION

Auberge des 3 Canards 115 côte Bellevue ⓣ 418 665 3761, ⓦ auberge3canards.com. Graceful inn with 48 comfortable rooms – most have their own private balcony overlooking the river – and one of the area's finest restaurants. **$145**

Camping Chutes Fraser 500 chemin de la Vallée ⓣ 418 665 2151, ⓦ campingchutesfraser.com. If you have transport, head for Charlevoix's oldest and most beautifully situated campsite by the falls of the same name about 3km north of La Malbaie. Sites (camping mid-May to late Oct) **$32**; chalets (year-round) **$130**

Le Manoir Richelieu 181 rue Richelieu ⓣ 418 665 3703, ⓦ fairmont.com/richelieu-charlevoix. A luxurious and historic château replete with a golf course, spa with indoor and outdoor pools, a handful of restaurants and bars, and a full range of high-end amenities. The 405 rooms and suites are exceedingly comfortable and spacious, and many have spectacular views over the St Lawrence. **$209**

EATING AND DRINKING

Auberge des 3 Canards 115 côte Bellevue ☎418 665 3761, ☎800 461 3761, ⓦauberge3canards.com. The inn's restaurant is known for its exquisite table d'hôte ($60), but its breakfasts are a great bet, too. Choose from plates such as maple butter crêpes and poached eggs à la Florentine with smoked salmon served on a potato pancake; all options include a cold buffet ($19). Daily 7–10.30am & 5.30–9pm.

Maison du Bootlegger 110 Rang du Ruisseau des Frênes, just off Hwy-138 (14km north of Malbaie) ☎418 439 3711, ⓦmaisondubootlegger.com. For pub food head to this fun steakhouse and hopping bar with frequent

live music. The table d'hôte ($47–57) includes a quirky tour (nightly in summer) of some of the house's rooms, connected by a warren of passageways added when alcohol was forbidden by the Church (guided tours otherwise $10). July–Sept daily 10am–11.30pm, June & Sept Sat & Sun 10am–11.30pm.

Restaurant l'Orchidée 439 rue St-Étienne ☎418 665 1070, ⓦrestolorchidee.com. Authentic Charlevoix mainstays fill the menu of this appealing restaurant that uses local ingredients. Choose from a few tables d'hôte ($32–48) and dishes like venison osso bucco ($31). Daily 5.30–10pm.

Parc national des Hautes-Gorges-de-la-Rivière-Malbaie

Park entry $8.60

One sight not to be missed in the Charlevoix region is the **Parc national des Hautes-Gorges-de-la-Rivière-Malbaie**, a network of valleys slicing through a maze of lofty peaks 45km west of La Malbaie. As you enter the park, cliff faces on all sides rise up to more than 700m, making it Canada's deepest canyon east of the Rockies. Its uniqueness lies not just in this astounding geology but also in the fact that all of Québec's forest species grow in this one comparatively small area. The best way to take in a sampling of the park's natural bounty is hiking the **L'Acropole-des-Draveurs** trail, a tiring but rewarding 11.2km (round-trip) trek from Pin-Blanc campground to the canyon's highest point. It passes through a Laurentian maple grove on the way to the arctic–alpine tundra of the 800m **Montagne des Érables** ("Maple Mountain") summit and affords stunningly expansive views of the gorge (reckon 5–6hr round-trip). Shorter trails from the **Le Draveur Visitors Centre** offer less strenuous alternatives, as well as boat tours and kayaking.

ARRIVAL AND INFORMATION   HAUTES-GORGES-DE-LA-RIVIÈRE-MALBAIE

By car To get there take Hwy-138 to Saint-Aimé-des-Lacs, a small town 13km northwest of La Malbaie from where the way to the park is well marked.

Félix-Antoine-Savard Discovery and Visitors Centre The park's excellent visitor centre (late May to Nov; ☎418 439 1227, ⓦsepaq.com/pq/hgo), is located beside the Rivière Malbaie, just off rue Principale. You must leave your car here and rent a bike (late May to mid-Oct; $17.75/hr, $51/day) or take the frequent, free shuttle bus (every 7–30min; late May to mid-Oct) into the park as far as the Le

Draveur Visitors Centre.

Le Draveur Visitors Centre In the centre of the park, near several of the park's trailheads (open Dec to mid-Oct; Sat & Sun only Dec–April). A good source of information and offers several rentals (see below).

Cruises and kayaking From Le Draveur Visitors Centre you can take a leisurely 90min river cruise ($36; late May to early Oct) or rent canoes ($17.25/hr, $49.50/day) or kayaks ($17.50/hr, $50.50/day) for the 8km paddle along the calm "Eaux Mortes" of the river.

ACCOMMODATION

National park camping ☎418 439 1227, ⓦsepaq. com. At the Félix-Antoine-Savard Centre you can reserve

sites at the park's three campsites, and get permits for wild camping. Late June to mid-Oct. Sites <u>$30.45</u>; cabins <u>$155</u>

The Saguenay and Lac Saint-Jean

The **Saguenay** is Québec's most diverse region, encompassing some of the province's most spectacular scenery, tremendous marine life and also the dreariest of industrial towns. Fortunately, the two extremes are kept nicely separate along the Saguenay River, so that you can explore the rich landscapes along its fjord and source – **Lac Saint-Jean** – in peace.

The main tourist centre of the region, **Tadoussac**, is best known as a **whale-watching** centre but also makes a great base to explore a number of other outdoor attractions in the vicinity. Many of these are centred on the national parks along the **Fjord du Saguenay**, another prime whale-watching spot, where both the land and sea are protected as a provincial park.

If you have time, continue west to the Upper Saguenay past the industrial centres of Chicoutimi and Jonquière and make a circuit of the flat farming country of Lac Saint-Jean. It's an ideal location to cycle, and the excellent **Véloroute des Bleuets** allows you to travel the 256km around the lake without trucks forcing you off the road.

Tadoussac

One of Canada's oldest villages, **TADOUSSAC** is beautifully situated at the neck of the Fjord du Saguenay and its confluence with the St Lawrence River, beneath rounded hills that gave the place its name; the Algonquian word *tatoushak* means "breasts". Basque whalers were the first Europeans to live here and by the time Samuel de Champlain arrived in 1603 it was a thriving seasonal trading post. The mid-nineteenth century saw Tadoussac evolve into a popular summer resort for the anglophone bourgeoisie, but today it's the best place in Québec, along with Les Bergeronnes and Les Escoumins just north along the coast, for **whale-watching** (see page 308). Mid- to late June is a good time to be here, when traditional Québécois folk singers, jazz pianists and rock guitarists all play a part in the popular **Festival de la Chanson de Tadoussac** (⟨w⟩chansontadoussac.com).

The waterfront

The waterfront rue du Bord-de-l'Eau is dominated by the red roof and green lawns of the *Hôtel Tadoussac*, a landmark since 1864 and the focus of the historic quarter. Across the road is the oldest wooden church in Canada, the tiny **Chapelle de Tadoussac** (mid-June to early Oct daily generally 10am–6pm; donation accepted; ☎418 235 1415, ⟨w⟩chapelledetadoussac.com), built in 1747 and now containing a multimedia exhibit on the lives of New France missionaries.

Centre d'Interprétation des Mammifères Marins

108 rue de la Cale-Sèche • Daily: mid-May to mid-June & early Oct to early Nov noon–5pm; mid-June to late Sept 9am–8pm; late Sept to early Oct 11am–6pm • $12 • ☎418 235 4701, ⟨w⟩gremm.org

Following the waterfront towards the harbour brings you to the modern **Centre d'Interprétation des Mammifères Marins**, run by the nonprofit Group for Research and Education on Marine Mammals (GREMM). This is highly recommended if you intend to go whale-watching; its excellent documentary films and displays explain the life cycles of the whales and the efforts being made to save their ever-diminishing numbers.

The Tadoussac dunes

Considered the best place in Québec to observe migrating hawks (Sept & Oct), the **Tadoussac dunes** sector of the Parc national du Fjord-du-Saguenay (known locally as *le desert*) fold majestically into Baie-du-Moulin-à-Baude, 4.5km northeast from Tadoussac village. Near the Chapelle there is a 2hr walk to the dunes along the beach; check tide times, as you'll have to clamber over rocks at high tide. To reach the 112m-high dunes, you can also drive along chemin du Moulin-Baude to the **Sentier du Belvédère**, an ideal spot for a picnic with its expansive views of the river below and the dunes to the north.

ARRIVAL AND DEPARTURE   **TADOUSSAC**

By bus Tadoussac's bus station (☎418 235 4733) is at 414 rue du Bâteau-Passeur on Hwy-138 at Motel Chantmartin.

Destinations Baie-Comeau (2 daily; 2hr 30min–2hr 45min); Baie-Saint-Paul (2 daily; 3hr); Les Escoumins (2 daily; 35min), La Malbaie (2 daily; 1hr 15min); Québec City (2 daily; 4hr 25min); Saguenay (Chicoutimi; 4 weekly; 1hr 40min); Rivière Sainte-Marguerite (4 weekly; 30min).

By ferry Traffic crosses the neck of the fjord by a free car ferry from Baie-Sainte-Catherine to Tadoussac (10min; year-round 24hr), but you may have to wait as long as an hour or two to board in midsummer. The nearest ferries across the St Lawrence River depart and arrive from Les Escoumins in the

north (see page 307) and Saint-Siméon in the south (see page 309). From July to early Sept, Navettes maritimes du Fjord (☎418 543 7630, ⍟navettesdufjord.com) operates a boat shuttle service to a handful of villages along the Fjord du Saguenay (from $72 round-trip).

Destinations Baie-Sainte-Catherine (1–3 hourly; 10min); L'Anse-Saint-Jean (1–3 hourly; 1hr 30min).

INFORMATION

Information centre The information centre for the Côte-Nord is in a red-brick manor at 197 rue des Pionniers (daily: late June to early Sept 8am–9pm; early Sept to late June

9am–noon & 1–5pm; ☎418 235 4744, ☎866 235 4744, ⍟tadoussac.com) and provides an accommodation service.

ACCOMMODATION

★**Auberge la Sainte Paix** 102 rue du Saguenay ☎418 235 4803, ⍟aubergelasaintepaix.com. The best of the town's many inns (breakfast is $9 extra), this attractive house is set on a hill overlooking the bay and has six comfortable rooms, a loft and a sunny lounge area. The exceedingly helpful owners can reserve whale-watching cruises with all of the town's operators. **$100**

Camping Tadoussac 428 rue du Bâteau-Passeur ☎418 233 2266, ☎855 708 4501, ⍟vacancesessipit.com. About 2km from the ferry terminal on Hwy-138, this is the best spot in the area for family-style camping– just make sure you arrive early during summer to get a spot. It also features five charming cottages and several larger, fully equipped houses ("Condo-Hotels" with 1 or 2 bedrooms). Sites **$30**; cottages **$145**; houses **$192**

Hôtel Tadoussac 165 rue du Bord-de-l'Eau ☎418 235 4421, ⍟hoteltadoussac.com. This rambling red-roofed hotel, established back in 1864, is the pick of the town's accommodation options, with surcharged river-view rooms, refined restaurants, swimming pool, miniature golf and tennis courts. **$179**

Le Roupillon 141 rue du Parc ☎418 235 4353,

⍟leroupillon.ca. A friendly, bilingual B&B with five themed rooms (including "Safari" and "Astral"), antique furnishings throughout and a relaxing lounge area with wood-burning stove; bathrooms are shared. The included breakfast is delicious and makes for a great start to the day. The owners can help arrange whale-watching tours. **$93**

Maison Hovington 285 rue des Pionniers ☎418 235 4466, ⍟maisonhovington.com. A century-old B&B with five beautifully decorated rooms. The bilingual owners will pick you up from the bus station. May–Oct. **$145**

Maison Majorique 158 rue du Bâteau-Passeur ☎418 235 4372, ⍟ajtadou.com. This hostel is one of the oldest and cheapest in Québec and – thanks to its own bar – determinedly lively, though it's definitely getting worn around the edges and English is rarely spoken. Canoes, cross-country skis, snowmobiles and snowshoes are all available for rent; various activities – guided hikes, snowshoe excursions and dogsled trips – are organized in their relative seasons. All-you-can-eat breakfasts ($8.50) are optional. Private and family rooms also available – call for prices. Dorms **$26.50**

EATING AND DRINKING

★**Café Bohéme** 239 rue des Pionniers ☎418 235 1180, ⍟lecafeboheme.com. Charming café and bistro that serves breakfast items, fresh salads and inventive dinners using local ingredients (dinner mains $22–29); it also has free wi-fi. Daily: May–June & Sept–Oct 8am–10pm; July & Aug 7am–11pm.

Café du Fjord 152 rue du Bâteau-Passeur, near the hostel ☎418 235 4626. A popular hangout with regular live music and DJs, this spot also serves food, including a $22 dinner buffet. Daily noon–11pm.

★**Chez Mathilde** 227 rue des Pionniers ☎418 235 4443, ⍟chezmathildebistro.com. There always seems to be a buzz about this hip restaurant which specializes in fresh local seafood. Though the choices are few, the dishes, such as snow crab and filet mignon, are uniformly divine.

The prices (most mains around $30) are more than in most places in town, but a meal here is well worth it. June–Oct daily noon–3pm & 6–11pm.

Le Coverdale 165 rue du Bord-de-l'Eau ☎418 235 4421, ☎800 561 0718, ⍟hoteltadoussac.com. Inside the *Hôtel Tadoussac*, *Le Coverdale* is one of the property's two restaurants (there's also a café) and features a breakfast buffet ($25) and a deluxe meat, seafood and pasta dinner buffet ($47).

★**Microbrasserie Tadoussac** 115 rue Coupe-de-L'Islet ☎418 235 1170, ⍟microtadoussac.com. Tadoussac's very own brewpub knocks out some excellent craft beers, from the tasty IPA de la Traverse to the refreshing Ponton 5 pilsner, paired with a simple menu of pizzas, sandwiches, cheese and charcuterie. Daily noon–11pm.

North of Tadoussac

The landscape **north of Tadoussac** takes in lakes surrounded by granite outcroppings and boreal forest, interspersed with stretches of sandy beach and salt marsh. The craggy terrain is the chief attraction here with lookout points and short trails in many of the villages, as well as interpretation centres for just about everything. The area is particularly known for cheaper and more convenient **whale-watching**, spectacular **diving** and first-rate **birdwatching**, particularly during the migratory seasons.

Les Bergeronnes

When accommodation fills up in Tadoussac in high season, you may wind up having to stay in **LES BERGERONNES**, 22km along Hwy-138. Otherwise if you're here it's generally for the whales – either the cheaper whale-watching tours or the good vantage point by a popular feeding ground beside the Cap-de-Bon-Désir lighthouse. The lighthouse now serves as the **Centre d'Interprétation et d'Observation de Cap-de-Bon-Désir** (13 chemin du Cap-Bon-Désir; $7.80; mid-June to early Sept daily 9am–6pm; ⓦpc.gc.ca/en/amnc-nmca/qc/saguenay/Cap-de-Bon-Desir), which has informative displays on whales.

ACCOMMODATION   LES BERGERONNES

Camping Bon Désir 198 Hwy-138 ☎418 232 6297, ☎877 632 6297, ⓦcampingbondesir.com. Overlooking the St Lawrence, this large campsite has a number of scenic pitches (and charges more for those with a view) and chalets, too. Bikes are available for rent and a cycling path leads to Les Escoumins. June–Sept. Sites __$28__; chalets __$140__

Le Bergeronnette 65 rue Principale ☎418 232 6642, ☎877 232 6605, ⓦbergeronnette.com. Welcoming B&B occupying a historic house that has simple rooms and apartments that accommodate from four to eight. May–Oct. Doubles __$85__; apartments __$130__

Les Escoumins

Though **whale-watching** is also popular at **LES ESCOUMINS**, another 16km north on Hwy-138 from Bergeronnes, the big deal here is the **diving**, especially at night when bioluminescence produced by offshore microorganisms creates an eerie underwater landscape. Marine-related exhibits, videos and activities are on offer at the **Centre de découverte du milieu marin** (mid-June to early Sept daily 9am–6pm; early Sept to early Oct Fri–Sun 9am–5pm; $7.80; ⓦparcmarin.qc.ca), at 41 rue des Pilotes, which highlights the fauna and flora of the Parc marin du Saguenay–Saint-Laurent. If you intend to dive (diving card required), head to the dive shop downstairs, **Base de plongée** (same hours; ☎418 233 4025, ⓦbaseplongeefqas.com), which rents out a complete set of gear for $90 per day. The other reason to visit is for the excellent **birdwatching**; the Promenade du Moulin brings you to a rugged shoreline with hundreds of birds.

ARRIVAL AND DEPARTURE   LES ESCOUMINS

By ferry Compagnie de Navigation des Basques (CNB) ferries depart from Les Escoumins to Trois-Pistoles (mid-May to mid-Oct 1 daily; 1hr 30min; $20.25 one way; $48.50 additional for a car; $36 round-trip for a bike, including passenger fare; ☎418 851 4676, ☎877 851 4677, ⓦtraversiercnb.ca) from the wharf; turn right at rue de la

Réserve. To catch the ferry to Rimouski (see page 285), drive 58km north to Forestville.
By bus Intercar runs south to and from Tadoussac (2 daily; 30min) and Québec City (2 daily; 4hr 40min–4hr 55min); and north to Baie-Comeau (2 daily; 1hr 55min–2hr 10min).

ACCOMMODATION AND EATING

Auberge Manoir Bellevue 27 rue de l'Église ☎418 233 3325, ⓦmanoirbellevue.com. A block off Hwy-138, this pleasant B&B serves filling breakfasts and has comfortable rooms, some more dated than others. __$99__

★ **Poissonnerie Escoumins** 152 rue Marcellin est

☎418 233 3122, ⓦfruitsdemeretpoissons.com. An essential stop for fish and seafood lovers, this cavernous cafeteria-style restaurant prepares dishes that couldn't be fresher; the tasty clam chowder and seafood pie are easily worth a stop alone. There's not much in the way of

WHALE-WATCHING FROM THE TADOUSSAC AREA

Whale-watching trips from Tadoussac and the surrounding communities are best done from mid-May to mid-October. Generally, prices for 2–3hr trips from Tadoussac are around $70–75 in a large, sturdy and comfortable boat and $75–80 in a Zodiac, which provides a more exciting ride. The price drops the more northerly the starting-point: similar excursions from **Les Bergeronnes** and **Les Escoumins** cost around $55–58 in a Zodiac. You'll spend less time on the water from points of departure north of Tadoussac, but they are closer to where the whales are most likely to be, so you get about the same amount of contact time for less money. If you're worried about missing a reservation in **Tadoussac** because of the ferry queue, ask to board at the quay in **Baie-Sainte-Catherine** instead – many of the companies fill up their boats on both shores of the mouth of the Saguenay before heading off to see the whales.

Alternatively, take the short **hike** around the Pointe de l'Islet from the marina in Tadoussac, which has lookout points for beluga-spotting. Improve your chances for a sighting by heading to even better lookout points along the shore: **Baie-Sainte-Marguerite** (see page 310), west of Tadoussac, and **Cap-de-Bon-Désir** (see page 307), just past Les Bergeronnes, are the best.

FROM TADOUSSAC AND BAIE-SAINTE-CATHERINE

Croisières AML ☎ 866 856 6668, ⌨ croisieresaml. com. Offers the largest selection of boats and packages, including large boat or Zodiac tours that last 2–3hr.
Otis Excursions 77, rue des Pionniers, Tadoussac ☎ 418 235 4197, ⌨ otisexcursions.com. For trips in large catamarans and 12- and 36-person Zodiacs.

FROM BERGERONNES AND LES ESCOUMINS

Les Croisière Essipit ☎ 418 233 2266, ⌨ vacance sessipit.com. Uses the quay in Les Bergeronnes and runs 2hr trips aboard twelve-person Zodiacs (early June to early Oct).
Croisières Neptune 507 rue du Boisé, Les Bergeronnes ☎ 418 232 6716, ☎ 877 763 7886, ⌨ croisieresneptune. ddns.net. Trips in small and large Zodiacs. There's also a location in Les Escoumins at 50 Hwy-138 (☎ 418 233 4343).
Les Écumeurs 31 rue des Pilotes, Les Escoumins ☎ 418 233 2141, ⌨ lesecumeurs.com. The least expensive of the options north of Tadoussac ($50–55); launches its Zodiacs from Les Escoumins, just south of the marine park (see page 307).

atmosphere, but the prices are very reasonable (most mains around $14) and there's terrace seating and free wi-fi, too. Be sure to stock up in the adjoining *poissonnerie* (fish shop) before moving on. Mon–Thurs & Sun 8am–8pm, Fri 11am–9pm, Sat 8am–9pm (shop Mon–Wed 9am–6pm, Thurs & Fri 9am–8pm, Sat & Sun 8am–6pm).

Fjord du Saguenay

The **Fjord du Saguenay** is one of the world's longest fjords, cutting through the Canadian Shield before merging with the **St Lawrence River**. A stupendous expanse of rocky outcrops, sheer cliffs and thick vegetation, the land flanking the fjord on both sides is protected as the **Parc national du Fjord-du-Saguenay** (⌨ sepaq.com) and **Parc marin du Saguenay–Saint-Laurent** (☎ 418 235 4703, ☎ 888 773 8888, ⌨ parcmarin. qc.ca), whose main entry is at Baie-Éternité. The marine park contains six different ecosystems and supports hundreds of marine species, but has had its work cut out. Since the park's creation, government initiatives have eliminated ninety percent of the pollutants from industrial plants in the immediate vicinity. Still, pollutants remain in the sediment and the number of St Lawrence River **beluga whales** is currently at one thousand, down from five thousand a century ago, placing them on Canada's list of endangered species. The area continues to attract whales because the mingling of the cold Labrador Sea waters with the highly oxygenated freshwater of the Saguenay River produces a uniquely rich crop of krill and plankton. The white St Lawrence River beluga lives in the area year-round, and from May to October it is joined by six species of migratory whale, including the **minke**, **finback** and **blue**.

The walls of the fjord itself extend to a depth of 270m in places, almost as much as the height of the cliffs above the waterline. Wedged between the two halves of the Parc du Saguenay are some of the most attractive parts of the Parc marin du Saguenay–Saint-Laurent. But since no bridges cross the Saguenay for the 126km between Tadoussac and Chicoutimi, you may need to backtrack to explore both shores.

The southern shore

Coming from Charlevoix, the best approach to the Parc national du Fjord-du-Saguenay is to drive along the wriggling Hwy-170 from **Saint-Siméon**, a road that strikes the **southern shore** of the Fjord du Saguenay after about 50km, close to L'Anse-Saint-Jean. Both this town and Rivière-Éternité, 33km further west, are easy entry points to the park and arguably the most attractive places on the fjord to take a boat trip.

L'Anse-Saint-Jean

L'ANSE-SAINT-JEAN is famous for its **Pont du Faubourg**, a covered bridge. The village has a terrific view of the Fjord du Saguenay and surrounding hills from the marina, and makes a good base to explore the park. L'Anse-Saint-Jean also boasts a particularly fine view of the Saguenay from the **L'Anse-de-Tabatière lookout**; the 500m trail begins at the lookout's car park.

ARRIVAL AND DEPARTURE   L'ANSE-SAINT-JEAN

By ferry During summer the Croisières du Fjord shuttle stops at the marina.

Destinations La Baie (daily; 2.5hr); Tadoussac (daily; 1.5hr).

TOURS AND ACTIVITIES

Cruises and kayak trips From the quay in L'Anse-Saint-Jean you can take cruises of the fjord with Croisières du Fjord: from 1hr 30min; June to early Oct; from $75; or join Fjord en kayak (late May to mid-Oct; ☎ 418 272 3024, ⓦ fjordenkayak.ca), 359 rue St-Jean-Baptiste, for 3hr trips ($62) or one- to five-day excursions (from $139).

Horseriding You can ride along the fjord on horseback: the Centre équestre des Plateaux (☎ 418 272 3231, ⓦ cedp.ca), 34 chemin des Plateaux, offers 3hr rides ($85) and 6hr rides ($160).

Skiing Inland at 67 rue Dallaire, you can ski at Mont-Édouard (☎ 418 272 2927, ⓦ montedouard.com; $49 for full-day pass), with a 450m vertical and 31 trails.

ACCOMMODATION AND EATING

★ **Bistro L'Anse** 319 rue St-Jean-Baptiste ☎ 418 272 4222, ⓦ bistrodelanse.com. At this excellent cultural and culinary repository you can grab a seat on a terrace overlooking the fjord and munch on dishes such as *poutine*, fish and chips, and shrimp risotto ($14.50–20.50), as well as salads and burgers, and wash it all down with one of the regional beers on tap. Works by local artists are displayed, and the bistro hosts frequent live acts. Mid-May to mid-Oct generally 11am–2pm & 5–9pm.

Camping de l'Anse 325 rue St-Jean-Baptiste ☎ 418 272 2554, ⓦ campingdelanse.ca. Serene campsite in a good position close to the fjord with excellent facilities including a pool. **$30.05**

Chez Montagner 354 rue St-Jean-Baptiste ☎ 418 608 8870. Opened by Québec City restauranteur Frédérick Montagner in 2018, this creative spot with fine views of the fjord offers locally-sourced seasonal dishes (think duck confit or salmon with three varieties of carrot), superb cocktails and an excellent Sunday brunch menu for $15.95. Tues 5–9pm, Wed 8am–9pm, Thurs 8am–10pm, Fri 8am–11pm, Sat 8.30am–11pm, Sun 8.30am–9pm.

Les Gîtes du Fjord 354 rue St-Jean-Baptiste ☎ 418 272 3430, ⓦ chalets-sur-le-fjord.com. The wood clifftop cottages and condos share a heated pool and an on-site bistro with outdoor seating. Significant discounts for longer stays. Studios **$150**; cottages **$243**

Parc national du Fjord-du-Saguenay: southern shore

Park entry $8.60

Scrappy **Rivière-Éternité**, 83km from Saint-Siméon on Hwy-138 and 61km east of Chicoutimi, is the main gateway to the **Parc national du Fjord-du-Saguenay** and its Baie-Éternité sector. From the main information centre (see page 310), a couple of short **hikes** and a long one branch out through this sector of the park. The best short hike is the **Sentier de la Statue**, a fairly easy 4hr (7km) round-trip up the massive bluff of Cap Trinité, which flanks the deep-blue water of the Baie-Éternité. The summit is topped by a huge statue known as *Our Lady of the Saguenay*, erected in 1881 by Charles-Napoléon Robitaille after he was saved from drowning in the river.

The long-distance **Les Caps trail** (25km) follows the bay of the Éternité River back to L'Anse-Saint-Jean via massive plateaus, ravines, waterfalls and stunning views. It is an intermediate walk along clear paths and the full hike takes about three days. There are wilderness campsites and a couple of refuges along the way; registration with the information centre is required. A number of companies offer water-taxi services for backpackers (enquire at the information centre), enabling you to hike as far as Tadoussac (one week) – you can even have your vehicle sent on to your destination by boat.

INFORMATION PARC NATIONAL DU FJORD-DU-SAGUENAY: SOUTHERN SHORE

Discovery and Visitors Centre 91 rue Notre-Dame, 8km northeast from Rivière-Éternité and Hwy-170 (late May to Oct; ☎ 418 272 1556, ⓦ sepaq.com) on the fjord itself; has trail maps and kayak routes and expert naturalists on hand.

The smaller Baie-Éternité Information Kiosk (late May–Oct) lies just 1.5km from Rivière-Éternité on the same road, on the park's border.

ACCOMMODATION

Baie-Éternité camping ☎ 418 272 1556, ⓦ sepaq. com. The sector's main campsite is located right on the bay; reservations can be made at the information centre. Blackflies love this area, though the worst is over by late

July; dress appropriately and bring repellent. Several rustic campsites set along the shore can be reached by kayak; the information centre has details and a kayaking map. $23.80

The northern shore

Running parallel to the Fjord du Saguenay, Hwy-172 is a dramatic route along the less-frequented **northern shore** of the Saguenay that gives occasional panoramas over the water and provides access to a couple of pretty towns en route, where cruises are available or kayaks can be rented. The Intercar **bus** from Tadoussac follows the highway, terminating at Saguenay (Chicoutimi).

Parc national du Fjord-du-Saguenay: northern shore

Park entry $8.60 • Discovery and Visitors Centre late May to early Oct 8am–6pm • ☎ 418 272 1556, ⓦ sepaq.com

A 42km hiking trail from Tadoussac (follow the signs for "Sentier Le Fjord") ends at **Baie-Sainte-Marguerite**, where the **Le Béluga Discovery and Visitors Centre** covering the northern part of the Parc national du Fjord-du-Saguenay is located. By car, you need to travel 3km down a dusty gravel road that exits the highway just after tiny **RIVIÈRE-SAINTE-MARGUERITE**, itself worth a quick stop for its covered bridge, **Pont Louis-Gravel**. The main draw here is **belugas**, and the visitors centre has displays on them as well as the fjord in general; ask at the desk for an English-language guidebook. An easy 3km walk through the woods along the long-distance Sentier le Fjord leads to an observation platform, from where the belugas can frequently be spotted.

ACCOMMODATION BAIE-SAINTE-MARGUERITE

Baie-Ste-Marguerite camping ☎ 418 272 1556, ☎ 800 665 6527, ⓦ sepaq.com. There is a serviced campsite near the information centre and a more primitive one about a 15min walk along the Sentier le Fjord. $23.80

Saguenay

The Fjord du Saguenay's source – the vast **Lac Saint-Jean** – sits 210km inland, linked to it by the Rivière Saguenay. Along this 65km stretch, a glut of aluminium and paper plants using the river as a power source has resulted in the growth of a sprawling industrial city, **SAGUENAY**, created in 2002 through the merging of the cities of Chicoutimi and Jonquière and the town of La Baie. If travelling on public transport you may have to pass through, but if you are driving you won't miss much by skipping it.

By bus Saguenay's main bus station is in Chicoutimi (☎ 418 543 1403), 55 rue Racine est. Buses from Montréal, Québec City, Lac Saint-Jean and Tadoussac all connect here. Destinations Alma (1–2 daily; 1hr 15min–1hr 30min); Dolbeau (1–2 daily; 3hr 45min); Montréal (4–5 daily; 6hr 10min–6hr 45min); Québec City (4–5 daily; 2hr 15min–2hr 30min); Riviere Sainte-Marguerite (4 times weekly; 1hr 10min); Saint-Félicien (1–2 daily; 3hr); Tadoussac (4 times weekly; 1hr 40min); Val-Jalbert (1–2 daily; 2hr 5min–2hr 15min).

Lac Saint-Jean

West of Saguenay, the huge, glacial **Lac Saint-Jean** is fed by most of the rivers of northeastern Québec and – unusually for an area of the rocky Canadian Shield – is bordered by sandy beaches and a lush, green terrain that has been farmed for over a century. It's a relatively untouched area with tranquil lakeshore villages linked by Hwy-169, the circular route that offers a unique zoo at **Saint-Félicien**, the strange sight of **Val-Jalbert**, Québec's most accessible ghost town, and the picturesque shorelines of **Parc national de la Pointe-Taillon**.

Better still, the **Véloroute des Bleuets** (bike trail; see pBOX) connects the lake's towns and is an increasingly popular option for cyclists. Many come as well for the **local cuisine**, especially the delicious coarse meat pie called a *tourtière* and the thick **blueberry pie**. The itinerary outlined below begins at Alma and heads west around the lake.

Alma

The dull aluminium-producing city of **ALMA**, 50km west of Saguenay, is useful for its **buses** – to Saguenay and Québec City and various points around Lac Saint-Jean – and is a practical starting point for the Véloroute des Bleuets. In a clockwise direction beyond Alma, the Véloroute des Bleuets follows a shoreline inaccessible by road, joining up with Hwy-170 beyond Saint-Gédéon, a popular beach town.

Val-Jalbert

95 rue St-Georges • Daily: late May to mid-June & late Aug to mid-Oct 10am–5pm; mid-June to late Aug 9am–6pm • $28 (includes cable) • ☎ 418 275 3132, ⓦ valjalbert.com

One of the main attractions of the region, the historical village of **VAL-JALBERT** is 52km beyond Alma along the cycle route and 92km west of Saguenay along highways 170 and 169. The 72m-high **Ouiatchouan Falls**, which dominate the town, led to the

---

THE VÉLOROUTE DES BLEUETS

Easily the best way to take in the lake is on the relatively flat **Véloroute des Bleuets** (ⓦ veloroutedesbleuets.com), a 256km **bike route** that encircles the whole lake. Much of it is in the form of a wide paved shoulder, but 60km of the route is completely car-free. The path passes close to most of the major attractions and through many of the villages around Lac Saint-Jean and there are beaches all along the lakeshore where you can cool off. A number of **B&Bs** and other services cater to two-wheeled visitors, and even the locals lay out a warm welcome – some set up garden chairs to rest on near the bike path. Enquire at the information centre in Alma for a list of shuttle services that can transport your luggage around a portion of the lake; the fee for three to four days is typically $45.

BIKE COMPANIES IN ALMA

Equinox 1385 chemin de la Marina ☎ 418 480 7226, ⓦ equinoxaventure.ca. Bike rental from $9.13/hr to $36.40/day.

Liberté à Vélo 75 blvd St Luc ☎ 418 668 8430, ⓦ liberteavelo.ca. Guided tours along the cycle route, including luggage transport (from one night/$185).

Also offers kayak tours of similar length and price around some of the lake's islands.

Vélo Jeunesse 1691 av du Pont Nord ☎ 418 662 9785, ⓦ velo-jeunesse.ca. Bike and tandem rental ($15/half day, $28/day; tandem $45/day).

establishment of a pulp mill here more than a century ago, and by 1926 the village had around 950 inhabitants. In the following year, the introduction of chemical-based pulping made the mill redundant, and the village was closed down. Val-Jalbert was left to rot until 1985, when the government decided to renovate it as a tourist attraction. From the site entrance a bus (with on-board French commentary) runs around the main sights of the village, ending at the mill at the base of the falls. You can then wander around whatever catches your eye along the way – the abandoned wooden houses, a former convent (now a museum) or the general store (now a souvenir shop). From the mill, itself converted into an excellent crafts market and cafeteria, a **cable car** leads to the top of the falls, from where there are stunning views of the village and Lac Saint-Jean beyond. Though the site is officially closed from late October through April, you can still enter it then for free – it is a beautifully tranquil place to wander about.

Musée du fromage cheddar

148 av Albert-Perron, Saint-Prime • Daily: early to late June & late Aug to late Sept 10am–5pm; late June to late Aug 9.30am–6pm • $16 • ☏ 418 251 4922, ⓦ museecheddar.org

Saint-Prime village has a surprising little museum, the **Musée du fromage cheddar**, where four generations of cheese-makers have worked since 1895. The one-hour guided tour covers the whole process of cheddar production (some of which is still exported to England). The unexpected part of the tour is upstairs, where the Perron family residence appears as it would have in 1922; a very convincing "Marie Perron" describes her life, how the best piece of furniture was reserved for the priest who visited once a year and why kitchen counters used to be so low – so children could make themselves useful. You also get to try a bit of the cheese produced by the modern cheese factory.

Parc national de la Pointe-Taillon

835 Rang 3 Ouest, Saint-Henri-de-Taillon • Late May to mid-Oct • $8.60 • ☏ 418 347 5371, ⓦ sepaq.com/pq/pta

Occupying a finger of land that juts into Lac Saint-Jean, **Parc national de la Pointe-Taillon** is bordered by long and often deserted beaches, and there are 45km of cycle trails, a portion of which coincides with the Véloroute des Bleuets. **Cycling** is, unsurprisingly, the best way to take in the park on land; the ride throughout is almost uniformly flat and along the way you stand a decent chance of spotting **moose**, which thrive in the park. Pointe-Taillon is also an ideal spot to **kayak**, with several kilometres of shoreline, scenic inlets and the Île-Bouliane to explore; the possibilities for waterborne adventures will increase when current plans to expand the park's area with thirty small islands on the eastern shore of the lake is formally approved. Rent and kayaks from the Discovery and Visitor Centre (see page 313).

ARRIVAL AND DEPARTURE

LAC SAINT-JEAN

From Lac Saint-Jean's southern shore it's about 5hr to Montréal on Hwy-155 (via Trois-Rivières); from the southeast, you can take the moose-infested Hwy-169 until it joins up with Hwy-175 on its way to Québec City.

PARC NATIONAL DE LA POINTE-TAILLON

The park can be reached via the Véloroute des Bleuets and from Hwy-169.

By ferry To the northwest of the park and across the eponymous river, the village of Péribonka operates a shuttle ferry to the Pointe-Chevrette and Île-Bouliane sectors for cyclists and pedestrians (10min; mid-June to early Sept daily 10am–5.30pm hourly; $8 one-way).

INFORMATION

ALMA

1682 av du Pont-Nord (mid-May to late June & early Sept to mid-Oct Mon–Fri 8am–noon & 1–4pm, Sat & Sun 9am– noon & 1–5pm; late June to early Sept daily 8am–8pm; mid-Oct to mid-May Mon–Fri 8am–noon & 1–4 pm; ☏ 418 668 3611, ⓦ tourismealma.com).

SAINT-FÉLICIEN

1209 blvd Sacré-Coeur (mid-June to early Sept Mon–Thurs 8am–7.30pm, Fri–Sun 8.30am–7.30pm; early Sept to mid-Oct Mon–Fri 8.30am–noon & 1.30–5.30pm, Sat & Sun 10am–5.30pm; mid-Oct to mid-June Mon–Fri 8.30am–noon & 1.30–4.30pm; ☎418 679 9888, ⓦville.stfelicien.qc.ca).

PARC NATIONAL DE LA POINTE-TAILLON

The park's Discovery and Visitor Centre is situated on the eastern edge of the park on the lake (late May to mid-June & early Sept to early Oct 9am–5pm; late June to mid-Aug 8am–9pm; late Aug to early Sept 8am–8pm).

ACCOMMODATION, EATING AND DRINKING

SAINT-GÉDÉON

Auberge des Îles 250 Rang des Îles ☎418 345 2589, ⓦaubergedesiles.com. For a treat, head for this lakefront inn just north of Saint-Gédéon with a four-course menu of game and local flavours for around $40. $168

Microbrasserie du Lac Saint-Jean 120 rue de la Plage ☎418 345 8758, ⓦmicrodulac.com. One of the better stops for refreshment on the Véloroute des Bleuets, this lively microbrewery has a terrace and a small selection of stellar ales, such as a Belgian amber, all crafted with regional ingredients. June to early Sept Mon–Wed & Sun 11.30am–midnight, Thurs–Sat 11.30am–2am; early Sept to May Thurs–Sat 11.30am–2am, Sun 11.30am–6pm.

VAL-JALBERT

General store and period houses rue St-Georges ☎418 275 3132, ☎888 675 3132, ⓦvaljalbert.com. You can stay in one of eight rooms in Val-Jalbert's renovated hotel above the general store and in apartments in the converted houses on rue St-Georges; both options include breakfast and a table d'hôte dinner served in the mill. Late May to early Oct. $290

SAINT-FÉLICIEN

Auberge des Berges 610 blvd Sacré-Coeur ☎418 679 3346, ⓦhoteldesberges.ca. The quaint *Auberge des Berges* has fifteen comfortable rooms and views of the river, and can arrange bike and canoe rentals. $105

PÉRIBONKA

Auberge l'Île du Repos de Péribonka ☎418 347 5649, ⓦiledurepos.com. This peaceful hostel and campsite is set on its own little island. Sites $25; dorms $35; cabins $155

PARC NATIONAL DE LA POINTE-TAILLON

National park camping ☎418 347 5371, ⓦsepaq.com. The park has five beachfront campgrounds: three on Lac Saint-Jean and two on the Rivière Péribonka. Two of the campsites have large "ready-to-camp" Huttopia tents. Bike–camping packages are offered that include a cargo trailer. Late May to mid-Oct. Sites $24; Huttopia tents $92; bike–camping packages $104

The Côte-Nord

The St Lawrence River was the lifeline of the wilderness beyond Tadoussac until the 1960s, when **Highway 138** was constructed along the **Côte-Nord** to **Havre-Saint-Pierre**, 625km away, and later **Kegashka**, another 202km distant; the extension of the highway to (to the existing segment from Vieux Fort to the Newfoundland and Labrador border) is tabled to begin in 2019. The road sweeps from high vistas down to the rugged shoreline through the vast regions of Manicouagan and Duplessis. Traditional sightseeing diversions are thin on the ground in the villages and towns en route, but there is plenty to reward a journey to this remote region, not least the strong Innu and Mi'kmaq heritage and the panorama of spruce-covered mountains, the vast sky and the mighty St Lawrence. It is the river that holds much of what is most alluring in the Côte-Nord, from the striking beauty of the **Mingan Archipelago** to gazing at the Northern Lights aboard the **M/V Bella Desgagnés**.

GETTING AROUND
THE CÔTE-NORD

By bus The Intercar bus from Québec City to Tadoussac serves the Côte-Nord as far as Baie-Comeau, from where another travels to Sept-Îles, where you have no choice but to spend the night before continuing on to Havre-Saint-Pierre. There is presently no public road transport to Natashquan or Kegashka.

By ship At Kegashka the highway gives out altogether and the only onward transport is by snowmobile, plane or the supply ship from Rimouski, which serves the wildlife haven of Île d'Anticosti and undertakes a breathtaking journey along the inlets of the windswept coastline of the Basse Côte-Nord (Lower North Shore).

Baie-Comeau

The road into western **BAIE-COMEAU** may be a fairly drab landscape of strip malls, but it's nothing compared to the city's east side, where a monstrous, belching newsprint mill plant sits. There's no reason to hang around Baie-Comeau, but while waiting for a northward bus or a ferry to Gaspé's Matane you might stroll through the quartier Sainte-Amélie in the eastern Marquette sector, where the streets are lined with grand houses dating from the 1930s. Here you'll find the **Église Sainte-Amélie** (36 av Marquette; daily: late June to early Sept 9am–6pm; free; 45min audio tour $5), worth a peek for its vibrant frescoes and stained glass windows, designed by the Italian artist Guido Nincheri.

ARRIVAL AND INFORMATION
BAIE-COMEAU

By bus Buses stop and drop-off on Hwy-138 at the Petro-Canada petrol station at 675 Lafleche Blvd in Baie-Comeau (Hauterive), and also at Baie-Comeau (Marquette), Galeries Baie-Comeau, 300 Lasalle Blvd.
Destinations Baie-Saint-Paul (2 daily; 5hr 30min); Godbout (1 daily; 1hr); Port-Cartier (1 daily; 2hr); Sept-Îles (1 daily; 2hr 45min).
By ferry The departure point for the car ferry to Matane (see page 287) is beyond the eastern end of blvd Lasalle on rue Cartier.

By air Air Canada Jazz and Pascan Aviation operate out of Baie-Comeau's regional airport, 9km southwest of town. Destinations Mont-Joli (2 daily; 45min); Montréal (daily; 1hr 40min).

Tourist offices Bureau d'information touristique de Baie-Comeau is open daily 8am–8pm at 20 avenue Cartier, Secteur-Est (Marquette; ☎418 296 8178, ⓦtourisme baiecomeau.com).

ACCOMMODATION AND EATING

Hotel Le Manoir 8 av Cabot ☎418 296 3391, ⓦmanoirbc.com. A historic former manor, this rambling stone hotel overlooks the St Lawrence River and offers a variety of handsome rooms, including a suite with a fireplace. All rooms come with cable TV. Bikes are avilable for rent and there's a fitness room and tennis court. The on-site restaurant *Bistro la Marée Haute* (Mon–Fri 6.30am–10pm, 11.30am–2pm & 3–10pm; Sat & Sun 7am–10pm & 3–10pm) serves excellent, but pricey, seafood dishes; the table d'hôte starts at $29. $145

Pizza Royale 2674 blvd Laflèche ☎418 589 5427. For straightforward and filling pizzas, particularly the Royale Plus (laden with bacon, chopped steak and sausage; $18.99 for 12-inch), head to this downtown joint on Hwy-138. Mon–Thurs & Sun 11am–midnight, Fri & Sat 11am–5am.

Godbout

The attractive village of **GODBOUT**, situated on a crescent-shaped bay 54km from Baie-Comeau, is not just the most pleasant place hereabouts and a prime spot for salmon fishing, it also has the excellent **Musée Amérindien et Inuit** (134 rue Pascal-Comeau; late June to Sept daily 9am–5pm; by donation; ☎418 568 7306). The museum was founded by Claude Grenier, who spent ten years in the north in the 1970s on a government scheme to boost the Inuit economy by promoting First Nations culture. Consequent commercialism has diluted the output since then, but the private collection of Grenier features nothing but genuine pieces.

ARRIVAL AND INFORMATION
GODBOUT

By ferry The village is linked to Matane on the south shore by car ferry (see page 287).
Tourist office 144 rue Pascal-Comeau (mid-June to early Sept generally Mon–Fri 8am–6pm, Sat & Sun 9am–6pm; ☎418 568 7581, ⓦmunicipalitegodbout.ca).

Sept-Îles

Named after the seven-island archipelago just offshore in the Gulf of St Lawrence, **SEPT-ÎLES** is now the largest ore-exporting port in eastern Canada, a major aluminum processing centre and, in recent years, an unlikely cruise ship destination. The town itself has as much character as a pile of iron ore, but it's pleasantly situated on the river's shore and you could spend an enjoyable day here thanks to two museums and historic sites that explore Innu and early fur trading culture. A trip to Île Grande-Basque is also a worthwhile, easy adventure.

The waterfront

The town is best appreciated along the waterfront. A 27km bike path leads from **Parc Rivière des Rapides**, with a 3km walking trail and ice-fishing in winter, to the beaches east of town; rent **bikes** from Rioux Vélo Plein Air, 555 blvd Laure (Mon–Wed 9am–5pm, Thurs & Fri 9am–9pm, Sat 9.30am–5pm, Sun noon–5pm; ☎418 968 8356, ⓦriouxvelopleinair.com). The road down to the third beach, **Plage Routhier**, offers the best view of the seven islands that gave Sept-Îles its name. Along the way, the path passes through the Jardins de l'Anse – a good spot for birdwatching – and along the riverfront promenade in the **Parc du Vieux-Quai**, where evening concerts of Québécois music are held under the yellow tent (late June to late Aug; free).

Musée Shaputuan

290 blvd des Montagnais • Late June to early Sept Mon–Fri 8am–4.30pm, Sat & Sun 1–4pm; early Sept to late June Mon–Fri 8am–4.30pm • $5.50 • ☎ 418 962 4000, ⓦ itum.qc.ca

The absorbing **Musée Shaputuan** presents the traditional life of the **Innu** people as it is shaped by the seasons. Unlike most descriptive museums, the exhibits speak to the viewer – often literally via audio and video recordings.

Musée Régional de la Côte-Nord

500 boulevard Laure • Late June to early Sept daily 9am–5pm; early Sept to late June Tues–Thurs 10am–noon & 1–5pm, Fri 10am–5pm, Sat & Sun 1–5pm • $7 • ☎ 418 968 2070, ⓦ museeregionalcotenord.ca

The history of the region is chronicled at the **Musée Régional de la Côte-Nord** with a variety of permanent and temporary exhibits, covering everything from prehistoric arrow heads and Innu and Mi'kmaq artifacts (including caribou skin clothing), to a cache of local art from the likes of René Richard and Lucien-Gabriel Jourdain, an Innu artist from Uashat.

Le Vieux-Poste

Rue Shimun (western end of blvd des Montagnais) • Late June to Aug Mon 10am–5pm, Tues–Sun 10am–6pm • $12 • ☎ 418 968 6237, ⓦ vieuxposte.com

In the summer, **Le Vieux-Poste** comes alive as a recreation of a fur trading post in the nineteenth century, with costumed interpreters, timber trading desk, an interactive exhibition explaining the history of the site and an Innu encampment. The buildings were reconstructed near the site of the original seventeenth-century Sept-Îles trading post, long abandoned and only excavated in the 1960s.

Île Grande-Basque

Just offshore, the largest island in the Sept-Îles archipelago, **Île Grande-Basque**, has 11km of easy walking trails and picnic spots; from early June to early Sept you can buy camping permits for $11.30 at the **Kiosque d'interprétation du Tourisme Sept-Îles** on the marina (Parc du Vieux-Quai). From mid-June to early September, the marina is the departure point for regular Les Croisières du Capitaine **passenger ferries** (4 daily; 10min; $25 return; ☎418 968 2173, ⓦlescroisieresducapitaine.com).

ARRIVAL AND INFORMATION

SEPT-ÎLES

By bus The bus station (☎ 418 962 9736) is at 27 rue Comeau. Destinations Baie-Comeau (1 daily; 3hr 15min); Havre-Saint-Pierre (1 daily; 2hr 30min).

By train The QNS&L (train station is on rue Retty at the east end of town, with departures Mon & Thurs at 7am.

Destinations Emeril Junction (2 weekly; 8hr 30min–10hr 30min); Schefferville (2 weekly; 11hr 15min).

By ferry The *M/V Bella Desgagnés* supply ship from Rimouski leaves Sept-Îles every Tues at 1.30pm (for details see page 319).

Destinations Havre-St-Pierre (1 weekly; 15hr 15min); Port-Menier (1 weekly; 7hr 45min).

By air The airport is 8km east of town at 1000 blvd Laure est (☎418 962 8211).

Destinations Montréal (5 daily; 2hr 15min); Québec (3 daily; 1hr 30min); Wabush (3 daily; 2hr).

Tourist office 1401 blvd Laure, on the outskirts of town (daily: late May to mid-Sept 7.30am–9.30pm; mid-Sept to late May 8.30am–5pm; ☎418 968 1238, ⦿ tourismeseptiles. ca). This well-stocked office has details on numerous outdoor activities and can help book accommodation.

BOAT TOURS

Cruises Les Croisières du Capitaine (☎418 968 2173, ⦿ lescroisieresducapitaine.com) run cruises from the quay June to Sept. Whales and a sea-bird sanctuary are the main attractions, but fishing trips are also available.

ACCOMMODATION

★ **Auberge Internationale Le Tangon** 555 av Cartier ☎418 962 8180, ⦿ aubergeletangon.com. Friendly hostel two blocks from the waterfront, set inside a 1930s clapboard schoolhouse (which makes it a historic building up here). Features three dorms and 13 private rooms with shared bathrooms, bright shared kitchen and lounge, plus a tranquil courtyard outside. Dorms $\overline{\$22}$; doubles $\overline{\$55}$

Camping Laurent-Val 1000 rue Fournier, 25km east of town in Moisie, off Hwy-138 ☎418 927 2899, ⦿ campinglaurentval.com. Pleasant campground with 65 sites – most of which do not offer a great deal of shade – and set along the salmon-filled Rivière Moisie; boat rentals are available. Open mid-May to early Sept. $\overline{\$25}$

★ **Château Arnaud** 403 av Arnaud ☎855 960 5511, ⦿ chateauarnaud.com. Plush, modern accommodation right on the marina, with spectacular views of the islands and stylish rooms, some with kitchenettes, gym and spa treatments available. $\overline{\$155}$

EATING AND DRINKING

★ **Casse-Croûte du Pêcheur** 4 rue Maltais ☎418 968 6411. Fabulous seafood restaurant right on the marina (with its own min-lighthouse/gift shop), with piles of fresh crab, lobster and an incredible "poutine de la mer" (fries smothered in a creamy seafood sauce crammed with shrimp). Mains $16–25. June to early Sept daily 11am–8pm.

Chez Sophie 495 av Brochu ☎418 968 1616. A good spot for tasty seafood, pizza ($18–28) and pasta ($18–29), as well as a solid selection of coffee, beers and wine. Tues–Sat 3–11pm.

Pub St-Marc 588 av Brochu ☎418 962 7770. A surprisingly stylish bar serving microbrews, with a more expensive restaurant upstairs where there's great pasta and a vast selection of salads, all under $20. Mon–Fri 11.30am–11pm, Sat & Sun 4pm–3am.

The Mingan coast

There is little of specific interest along the stretch of shore east of Sept-Îles, known as the **Mingan coast** – blackfly-ridden in May and much of June – until you reach **Longue-Pointe-de-Mingan**, but the scenery changes dramatically with sand dunes followed by granite outcroppings of the Canadian Shield, then eerie landscapes of rounded grey boulders surrounded by scrubby vegetation. Most visitors make the journey for the stunning islands of l'**Archipel-de-Mingan**, a unique environment of sculptured rock formations and profuse wildlife lying off the coast between Longue-Pointe-de-Mingan and **Havre-Saint-Pierre**, the region's largest town and a good base for visiting the archipelago. As the tourist season is short here, accommodation can be at a premium, so book ahead.

Longue-Pointe-de-Mingan

Although Havre-Saint-Pierre is the more popular departure point for cruises of the Mingan Archipelago, it's worth stopping in **LONGUE-POINTE-DE-MINGAN** for the **Centre de recherche et d'interprétation de la Minganie** (378 rue du Bord de la Mer; mid-June to early Sept daily 9am–5pm; $10), a joint venture between Parks Canada and the Mingan Island Cetacean Study. In addition to a film and displays on whales and other marine life, the centre provides information on excursions to the islands, issues camping permits and, for the more adventurous, offers week-long adventures with **whale researchers** (mid-June to mid-Sept; $2645/week; ☎418 949 2845, ⦿ rorqual.

com). The latter are not cruises (though lodging, meals and transportation are included) – you are with a marine biologist in a small boat from dawn until whenever their work is finished – but it is a unique experience. Less taxing cruises are offered by Excursions du Phare (May–Sept; 3hr; $65; ☎418 949 2302, ⓦminganie.info), 126 rue de la Mer, who lead trips to the westernmost islands – an important consideration if you want to see **puffins**, as most of the cruises from Havre-Saint-Pierre only visit the islands in the central sector.

ACCOMMODATION	LONGUE-POINTE-DE-MINGAN

Camping de la Minganie 109 rue de la Mer ☎418 949 2307, ⓦtourisme-loiselle.com. At the eastern edge of town, this has large sites and a nice setting on the St Lawrence. $19

Havre-Saint-Pierre

The community of **HAVRE-SAINT-PIERRE** would have remained a tiny fishing village founded in 1857 by fleeing Acadians but for the discovery in the 1940s of a huge deposit of **ilmenite**, the chief source of titanium. The quarries are 45km north of town, where fishing and tourism provide employment for the non-miners, the latter industry having received a major boost when the forty islands of l'**Archipel-de-Mingan** (see page 316) were made into a national park in 1983. Before setting off to the park, check out the **interpretation centre**, which shares a building with the **tourist office** on the wharf at 1010 Promenade des Anciens. The centre has temporary photographic displays and information on the flora, fauna and geology of the islands. You can book cruises to the archipelago here or at one of the smaller kiosks further along the wharf.

4

ARRIVAL AND DEPARTURE	HAVRE-SAINT-PIERRE

By bus The bus station is at 843 rue de l'Escale (☎418 538 2033).
Destinations Longue-Pointe-de-Mingan (1 daily Mon–Fri; 25min); Sept-Îles (1 daily Mon–Fri; 2hr 30min).
By ferry The *M/V Bella Desgagnés* stops at the wharf and continues on further into the Côte-Nord.

Destinations Blanc-Sablon (1 weekly; 43hr 45min); Harrington Harbour (1 weekly; 24hr 45min); Kegaska (1 weekly; 11hr 30min); La Romaine (1 weekly; 16hr); La Tabatière (1 weekly; 32hr 45min); Natashquan (1 weekly; 6hr 15min); St-Augustin (1 weekly; 37hr 15min); Tête-à-la-Baleine (1 weekly; 29hr 15min).

ACCOMMODATION AND EATING	

Auberge de la Minganie 3980 Hwy-138 ouest ☎418 538 1538. An old fishing camp converted into a hostel on a pretty bay by the Romaine river with minimum renovations and lots of bugs. It doesn't serve breakfast, though there are kitchen facilities and canoes for rent. It's 17km west of town, but the bus from the west will let you off nearby, leaving you to walk the remaining 700m. Open May–Sept. Sites $10; dorms $25

Chez Julie 1023 Dulcinée ☎418 538 3070. A good bet for heaped portions of a wide selection of fresh seafood and tasty smoked-salmon pizza (mains $22–35). Daily 4–10pm.

Gîte Chez Françoise 1122 rue Boréale ☎418 538 3778, ⓦgitechezfrancoise.com. This pleasant B&B has one room with private bath and kitchenette, as well as three other immaculate rooms that share a bathroom. $68; en suite $95

La Promenade 1197 Promenade des Anciens ☎418 538 1720. Friendly seaside restaurant serving hearty meals for lunch and dinner with a view of the Mingan Archipelago (mains from $21–40). Daily 11am–11pm.

Mingan Archipelago National Park Reserve (Réserve de parc national de l'Archipel-de-Mingan)

Park entry $5.80

Immediately offshore from Havre-Saint-Pierre, the **Mingan Archipelago National Park Reserve** offers some of the most beautiful landscapes in Québec. Standing on the islands' white-sand shorelines are innumerable 8m-high **rocks** that have the appearance of ancient totem poles, with bright orange lichen colouring their mottled surfaces and bonsai-sized trees clinging to their crevices. These formations originated as underwater sediment near the equator. The sediment was thrust above sea level more than 250 million years ago and then covered in an ice cap several kilometres thick. As the drifting ice melted, the islands emerged again, seven thousand years ago, at their present location. The sea and wind gave the final touch by chipping away at the soft limestone to create the majestic monoliths of today.

Bizarre geology isn't the archipelago's only remarkable feature. The **flora** constitutes a unique insular garden of 452 arctic and rare alpine species, which survive here at their southerly limit due to the limestone soil, long harsh winters and cold Gulf of Labrador current. Other than the gulf's whale populations, the permanent **wildlife** inhabitants of the park include puffins, who build nests in the scant soil of three of the islands from early May to late August, and 199 other species of bird.

INFORMATION

L'ARCHIPEL-DE-MINGAN

Visitor centres 625 rue du Centre in Longue-Pointe-de-Mingan (mid-June to early Sept daily 8am–5pm; ☎418 949 2126, ⓦpc.gc.ca/mingan) and 1010 Promenade des Anciens in Havre-St-Pierre (mid-June to early Sept daily 8am–5pm; ☎418 538 3285).

TOURS AND ACTIVITIES

BOAT TOURS

Tours around portions of the archipelago (June–Sept) are available from the wharf at Havre-St-Pierre, but they must be booked in advance. Cruises to see puffins in the park's west depart from Longue-Pointe-de-Mingan (see page 316).

Services Maritimes Boréale 1039 rue du Titane, Havre-Saint-Pierre ☎418 538 2865, ⓦsmboreale.com. Umbrella tour company that coordinates various boat trips from Portail Pélagie Cormier, 1010 Promenade des Anciens, with rates ranging $70–90 for 3–6hr. Also arranges scuba diving trips.

ACCOMMODATION

★ **Île aux Perroquets** ☎418 949 0005, ⓦileaux perroquets.ca. It's now possible to spend the night in relative luxury inside this converted solar-powered lightkeeper's house on tiny île aux Perroquets – a remarkable experience, with puffins and razorbills flying around in the mornings. The nine rooms are simply decked out in 1950s style and adorned with local handicrafts; breakfast is included, as is boat transport (30min) and a tour of the 1888 lighthouse (free wi-fi is available). Late June to Aug. Per person $300

Island camping ☎418 538 3285. Primitive camping (dry toilets, no showers) is allowed on Île Quarry (where six oTENTik tents are also available) and five other islands, but the only transport besides a sea-kayak is on a Havre-St-Pierre-based Services Maritimes Boréale sea-bus or seza-taxi (around $70–90 return, depending on destination). Obtain camping permits from the interpretation centre in Longue-Pointe or the wharfside kiosk in Havre-St-Pierre. Mid-June to early Sept. $15.70; oTENTik $120

Île d'Anticosti

In the Gulf of St Lawrence between the Jacques Cartier and Honguedo straits, the remote 220km-long **Île d'Anticosti** was once known as the "Graveyard of the Gulf", as more than four hundred ships have been **wrecked** on its shores. The island's vast expanse is made up of windswept sea cliffs and forests of twisted pine, crisscrossed by turbulent rivers and sheer ravines. Known as *Notiskuan* – "the land where we hunt bears" – by the Innu, and a walrus- and whale-fishing ground by the Basques, Île d'Anticosti became the private domain of Henri Menier, a French chocolate millionaire, in 1873. He imported white-tailed Virginia deer, red fox, silver fox, beaver and moose in order to gun them down at his leisure. Today, a less exclusive horde of **hunters** and **anglers** comes here to blast away at deer from the back of four-wheel-drives and to hoist the salmon from the rivers. For other travellers it presents an opportunity to explore an untamed area that's still practically deserted.

Port-Menier

Menier established the tiny village of Baie-Sainte-Claire on the western tip in 1895; less than five years later the settlers moved to **PORT-MENIER** on the south side of this tip, and Baie-Sainte-Claire's homes were left to the ravages of the salt air (you can see the remains today). The Québec government bought the island in 1974, and its population of around 250 is still concentrated in the blue-roofed houses of Port-Menier, where the *M/V Bella Desgagnés* arrives once a week from Havre-St-Pierre and from Sept-Îles (see page 320). Before you head into the park, stock up on supplies at the **CCIA Grocery Store**.

Écomusée d'Anticosti

10 chemin des Forestiers • June–Aug daily 9am–5pm • Free

The tiny **Bureau d'accueil touristique Info-Anticosti** (tourist information centre; ☎418 535 0250, ⓦile-anticosti.org) at 7 chemin des Forestiers provides maps an information on the island but also access to the adjacent **Écomusée d'Anticosti**, a small museum that chronicles Menier's heyday as well as the habits and customs of the islanders.

Parc national d'Anticosti

Park entry $8.60 • ☎ 418 535 0156, ⓦ sepaq.com/pq/pan

Port-Menier edges the westerly portion of the **Parc national d'Anticosti** whose protected landscapes spread further east in the reserve's four sectors. The twisting gravel road crossing the island – jokingly called the "Trans-Anticostian" – provides access to the central and eastern portions of the reserve. Driving is the only way to get there: a four-wheel-drive is necessary, and it's not uncommon to get a few dents or a flat tyre. A few kilometres beyond the **McDonald Visitors Centre** (daily late June to mid-Aug), the park's principal entry point, a rough track leads from the "main" road to Québec's largest cave. Discovered in 1982, the glacial **Grotte à la Patate**, 120km east of Port-Menier, has a modest opening leading into a cathedral-like chamber and a warren of 500m-long passages (park naturalists run 3hr tours of the cave for $25; enquire at the McDonald Visitor Centre). Some 10km further on you can glimpse the **Canyon de l'Observation**, whose bleak walls rise to over 50m. Continuing about 20km east, pull off at the signed parking area for another of the park's highlights, the **Chute-Vauréal**, a 76m waterfall best taken in from the banks of the pool it surges into.

ARRIVAL AND GETTING AROUND ÎLE D'ANTICOSTI

By ferry The *M/V Bella Desgagnés* from Havre-St-Pierre to Port-Menier (Sundays) costs $58.24 one-way, from Sept-Îles $75.86 (Tuesdays). The boat returns to Havre-St-Pierre Tuesday night, and to Sept-Îles Sunday afternoon.

By air Sépaq Anticosti (☎418 890 0863, ⓦsepaq.com/anticosti) flies to the island as part of a package from Montréal, Québec City and Mont-Joli, which includes pick-up from the airport, 7km inland from Port-Menier. Pascan

Aviation (ⓦpascan.com) offers charter flights from Sept-Îles and Havre-St-Pierre.

Car rental In Port-Menier at Location Georges Lelièvre, Anticosti (8 rue des Eudistes; ☎418 535 0204). There are gas stations at McDonald Visitors Centre (daily 8am–7pm), Chicotte-la-Mer Visitors Centre (daily 7–8am & 4–6pm) and in Port-Menier (daily 8am–5pm). Beyond Port-Menier, no roads are paved.

ACCOMMODATION AND EATING

Auberge de la Pointe-Ouest 20km west of Port-Menier at Pointe de l'Ouest ☎418 535 0311. Two former houses of lighthouse caretakers have been converted to this idyllically located hostel. Each house has a fully equipped kitchen and accommodates up to six. The owner is an excellent source of island information and can lead guided tours into the park. June–Sept. **$40**

National Park accommodation ☎418 535 0156, ⓦsepaq.com. From late June until mid-Aug you can

camp at one of the park's rustic campsites; the most scenic overlooks a bay in the Baie-de-la-Tour sector. Check at the McDonald Visitor Centre for the current rates; three-night packages, which include rental car and flight from Mont-Joli, start at $560 for tent camping (meals and gas not included), $670 for cabins and at $975 for the comfy Auberge McDonald, 105km from Port-Menier.

THE BELLA DESGAGNÉS

When the road ends at **Kegashka** (200km east of Havre-Saint-Pierre), access further up the Basse Côte-Nord is by snowmobile in winter, floatplane or boat. The **M/V Bella Desgagnés** (mid-April to mid-Jan; ☎418 723 8787, ⓦ relaisnordik.com) makes a weekly journey here on a trip that affords stunning views of a rocky, subarctic landscape so cold that icebergs occasionally float past the ship even in the height of summer. The boat is evenly split between its role as a freighter and passenger ship; the majority of its passengers are locals skipping between settlements or heading for a longer jaunt to Québec's bigger towns. Its voyage begins in **Rimouski** on Monday nights, stopping in **Sept-Îles** and **Port-Menier** on Île d'Anticosti on Tuesdays and **Havre-Saint-Pierre** and **Natashquan** on Wednesdays before calling in at the roadless communities along the Basse Côte-Nord, reaching **Blanc-Sablon** (see page 454), Québec's most easterly village on the Labrador border, on Fridays. The same route is then followed in reverse to arrive back in Rimouski on Monday morning.

THE JOURNEY

The journey up this stretch of the St Lawrence is far more impressive than the destinations. During the day, whales, dolphins, seals and a wealth of sea birds are a common sight; at night the **Northern Lights** often present an unforgettable display. At some stops the village inhabitants surround the boat, as its twice-weekly arrival is about all that happens hereabouts. With careful planning you can arrange to spend a couple of days in one community and catch the boat on the return voyage; each village receives at least one daytime visit, but either the upstream or downstream stop may be in the middle of the night. Most travellers just hop off at each port of call for the couple of hours needed to load and unload freight. A rented bicycle is particularly handy if you want to see much.

   The first stop after **Kegashka** is **La Romaine**, a scrappy Innu town. Beyond here the land becomes increasingly rocky and picturesque, the coastline cut with many intriguing inlets. **Harrington Harbour**, a pretty village settled in 1871 by fishermen from Newfoundland and easily one of the sightseeing highlights of the trip, is set on an island whose topography of large rounded rocks made it necessary to make the pavements out of wood. **Tête-à-la-Beleine**, where boatmen are usually on hand to transport tourists from the ship out to the incongruous Chapelle de l'Île Providence perched on a nearby hill, and **St Augustine** have similarly picturesque settings. The Coasters Association at Tête-à-la-Beleine is the local residents' group and their website (ⓦ coastersassociation.com) is a useful resource.

FARES

It's possible either to travel all-inclusive (with three surprisingly good daily meals and a cabin berth) or to bed down on the aircraft-style seats and picnic on the deck or in the cafeteria. You can start and finish your journey from any of the stops along the coast; the standard inclusive fare to travel the entire length of the route on a return trip to Rimouski is $1627 versus just $339.52 for a seat and no meals (one-way). The same round-trip with a spot in a select plus two-berth cabin (with a private sink, shower, toilet and TV) is $2229. Plan on booking your trip at least thirty days in advance; summer voyages should be booked several months in advance. Non-round-trippers can bring their car, although it's inaccessible during the voyage; fares are based on distance and the weight of the car. For bikes, add $25 to the fare.

Basse Côte-Nord

Highway 138 used to end at Havre-Saint-Pierre, leaving the dozen or so villages along the rugged **Basse Côte-Nord** (Lower North Shore) cut off from the rest of Québec, as they had been for centuries – so much so that many inhabitants only speak English. Since 2013 Hwy-138 has linked Havre-Saint-Pierre with Natashquan and **Kegashka** on the final 200km stretch. If you make the lonely journey by car – as yet there is no bus – you will receive a welcome unique to a people not long connected by road to the rest of Canada.

Baie-Johan-Beetz

Some 69km east of Havre-Saint-Pierre, the village of **BAIE-JOHAN-BEETZ** was named after the painter and sculptor whose extraordinary and enormous house built in 1897, **La Pourvoirie Baie-Johan-Beetz**, is open to the public as hotel and restaurant (see below).

Natashquan

Some 83km from Baie-Johan-Beetz, a small church, wooden houses and the old weather-worn huts of cod fishermen (*Les Galets*) are about all there is to see in **NATASHQUAN**, one-time home of revered Québécois poet **Gilles Vigneault**. **La Vieille École** (24 chemin d'en Haut; late June to early Sept daily 10.30am–noon & 1.30–4.30pm; $5; ☎418 726 3054), a schoolhouse built in the early twentieth century (and which Vigneault attended), proudly displays memorabilia from his life's works.

Kegashka

In 2013, a new bridge was built over the Great Natashquan River extending Highway 138 to the small fishing village of **KEGASHKA** (48km east of Natashquan). Located between two tranquil bays and on an island (where the *M/V Bella Desgagnés* docks), connected by bridge to the mainland, the village is best known for its white sand **beaches** and hiking trails covered with crushed shells. Most of the villagers make a living from crab, lobster and scallop fishing.

ACCOMMODATION AND EATING   **BASSE CÔTE-NORD**

4

BAIE-JOHAN-BEETZ

★ **La Pourvoirie Baie-Johan-Beetz** ☎418 365 5021, ⓦ baiejohanbeetz.com. You can sleep in one of the seven historic bedrooms in the *Johan-Beetz House*, which also offers meal-inclusive rates ($120), a variety of salmon- and trout-fishing packages and kayaking tours. **$65**

NATASHQUAN

Auberge la Cache 183 chemin d'en Haut ☎418 726 3347, ⓦ aubergelacache.com. The ten-room *Auberge la Cache* is pleasantly furnished and a nice enough play to stay, though it's a little pricey. Its restaurant – also pricey – is open June to early Sept. **$185**

Camping Municipal Chemin Faisant ☎418 726 3697, ⓦ campingquebec.com. You can camp along Hwy-138 at this site, on the east side of town with views of the sea and nearby dunes. Mid-June to mid-Sept. **$33**

Maison Chevarie 77 rue du Pré ☎418 726 3541. The five rooms at this unassuming inn have TVs; there is a surcharge for the three that have private bathrooms. **$65**

KEGASHKA

Auberge Brion 17 rue Portage ☎418 726 3738. Cozy B&B in the heart of the village, open year-round, with 13 rooms with kitchenettes, satellite TVs and fabulous home-cooked meals. Usually no mobile phone signal up here, but there is free wi-fi. **$140**

The Maritime Provinces

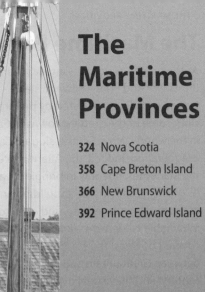

LUNENBURG, NOVA SCOTIA

5

The Maritime Provinces

As their name suggests, Canada's Maritime Provinces – Nova Scotia, New Brunswick and Prince Edward Island – are dominated by the sea, with a long, jagged coastline punctured by picturesque bays, sandy beaches, towering cliffs, some of the prettiest towns in Canada and the freshest, tastiest lobster in the world – Nova Scotia's slogan "Canada's ocean playground" is no exaggeration. Indeed, the Atlantic Ocean was crucial to the development of the Maritimes, not only in bringing waves of settlers but also accounting for its greatest industries: shipbuilding and fishing. Forestry became important in the nineteenth century, and even today, the bulk of the region remains intractable wilderness – 84 percent of New Brunswick, for example, is covered by trees. The Maritimes were also at the heart of the epic struggle between Great Britain and France for North America in the eighteenth century, and they boast a rich legacy of historic sights, many associated with the French-speaking Acadians, who were usually caught in the middle.

Most travellers focus on **Nova Scotia**, where the provincial capital of **Halifax** makes an appealing base from which to explore the picturesque coastline, then head north to **Cape Breton Island**. Driving from the US or the rest of Canada, you'll pass through the often overlooked province of **New Brunswick**, with plenty of world-class diversions of its own: the gritty, revitalized port of **Saint John** (never "St John", and not to be confused with St John's, Newfoundland), the **Acadian Coast** and the **Bay of Fundy**, whose taper creates tidal surges of up to 12m. **Prince Edward Island (PEI)** was linked to the mainland by the whopping Confederation Bridge in 1997 and possesses one of the region's most enticing culinary scenes. Leafy, laidback **Charlottetown** is well worth at least a couple of days, especially as it's just a short hop from the magnificent sandy beaches of the **Prince Edward Island National Park**.

Nova Scotia

Connected to the rest of Canada by the 24km-wide Isthmus of Chignecto, **Nova Scotia** juts into the North Atlantic like an upside-down anvil, its weathered coastline a whopping 7500km long and littered with gorgeous villages, beaches, rocky inlets and windblown headlands. Originally the home of the **Mi'kmaq** people, the French established the first permanent European settlement at Port Royal in 1605, laying the foundations for what would become French-speaking **Acadia**. The British established control over the region in the eighteenth century, and today the province displays mixed English, Scottish and French heritage, as well as Mi'kmaq.

Visits usually begin at the lively capital, **Halifax**, which sits beside a splendid harbour on the south coast. From here, the most beguiling parts of the province fall into three regions: the **South Shore**, with **Lunenburg** the most alluring target; the **Annapolis Valley**, stretching 110km northeast from Annapolis Royal to Wolfville, noted for whale-watching, fruit growing and winemaking; and rugged **Cape Breton Island**, best appreciated by driving the jaw-dropping **Cabot Trail**.

INFORMATION NOVA SCOTIA

Nova Scotia Department of Tourism Toll-free within 742 0511, ⓦ novascotia.com.
North America ☎ 1 800 565 0000; from elsewhere ☎ 902

ATLANTIC LOBSTER FOR DINNER

Highlights

❶ **Halifax** The largest city in the Maritimes, jam-packed with pubs, restaurants, museums and poignant memorials to the *Titanic*. See page 326

❷ **Lunenburg** This handsome fishing port is small-town Nova Scotia at its most romantic, its hilly streets dotted with charming Victorian mansions. See page 340

❸ **Acadian culture** Soak up one of Canada's most resilient cultures – distinct French heritage, tasty cuisine, vibrant music and tumultuous history – especially in New Brunswick. See page 354

❹ **Cabot Trail** Atlantic Canada's most scenic highway cuts across the searing coastal headlands and plunging forested valleys of

Cape Breton Island. See page 358

❺ **Fundy Coastal Drive** Explore this rugged and mesmerizing section of the Bay of Fundy coast, with swirling waters, fresh lobster and record-setting tides. See page 370

❻ **Prince Edward Island National Park** Explore the extensive legacy of *Anne of Green Gables* before lounging on splendid beaches of pristine, red-hued sand. See page 400

❼ **Lobster suppers** It's hard to resist the all-you-can-eat mussels, scallops, chowder and fresh lobster suppers served up in the Maritimes, but they're particularly good on Prince Edward Island. See page 402

HIGHLIGHTS ARE MARKED ON THE MAP ON PAGE 326

5

Halifax

Set beside one of the world's finest harbours, **HALIFAX** has become the financial, educational and transportation centre of the Maritimes, with its population of just under 400,000 making it almost four times the size of its nearest rival, New Brunswick's Saint John. This pre-eminence has been achieved since World War II, but long before then Halifax was a naval town par excellence. Founded by British settlers led by **Edward Cornwallis** in 1749, Halifax was primarily a fortified navy base well

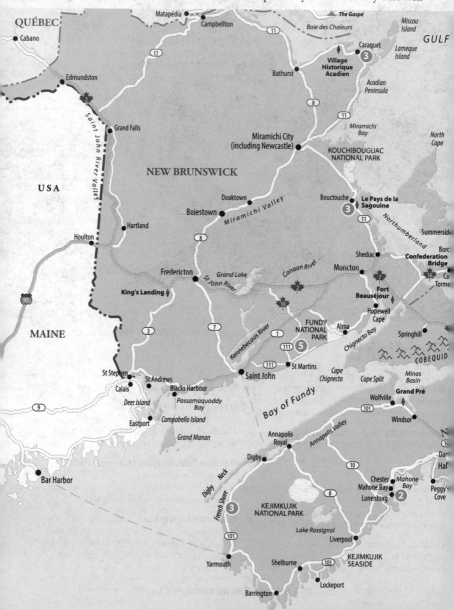

into the nineteenth century with most **Haligonians**, as the locals are known, at least partly employed in a service capacity. Today Halifax retains a compact, thriving centre, with artists, street performers and students from prestigious **Dalhousie University** adding a grungy, alternative balance to the bankers and fashionistas. Workaday office blocks reflect the city's new commercial success, tumbling down to the harbour from the **Citadel**, the old British fortress that remains the city's most significant sight. The city's other attractions – most notably the **Art Gallery**, the **Maritime Museum** and the

THE MARITIME PROVINCES

LAWRENCE

Îles-de-la-Madeleine
(Québec)

Newfoundland

Meat Cove

CAPE BRETON
HIGHLANDS
NATIONAL PARK

4

Cape North

INCE EDWARD ISLAND

endish

6 P.E.I. NATIONAL PARK

Souris

Chéticamp

Saint
Ann

Charlottetown

CABOT TRAIL

CABOT TRAIL

North
Sydney

Glace
Bay

Wood Islands

West Mabou

Baddeck

Sydney

rait

19

105

4

22

Caribou

Bras d'Or
Lake

Louisbourg

Pictou

Antigonish

**Cape Breton
Island**

NTAINS

104

Port
Hastings

104

New Glasgow

Isle Madame

Truro

*Chedabucto
Bay*

374

Sherbrooke

OTIA

Sheet Harbour

7

N

0 ————————————— 100
kilometres

ATLANTIC OCEAN

HIGHLIGHTS

1 Halifax

2 Lunenburg

3 Acadian culture

4 Cabot Trail

5 Fundy Coastal Drive

6 Prince Edward Island National Park

7 Lobster suppers

5

Georgian **Province House** – huddle together in the lower part of town beneath the fortress. The **waterfront**, once at the heart of Halifax commercial life, is now lined by a series of shops and tourist attractions linked by the traffic-free **Harbourwalk**.

The Citadel

5425 Sackville St • Daily: early May–June, Sept & Oct 9am–5pm; July & Aug 9am–6pm; free guided 45min tours early May–Oct from the information centre every hour or so • $11.70, $7.80 early May to June, Sept & Oct; parking $3.15 • Nov to early May grounds open 9am–5pm (free), but all exhibits closed • ☎ 902 426 5080

Crowning the hill overlooking downtown, the present fortifications of **Halifax Citadel National Historic Site** are Victorian, the fourth in a series dating from Edward Cornwallis's stockade of 1749. Although it never saw action, the fort was garrisoned by the British until 1906, and by Canadian forces during the two world wars. Today it's an

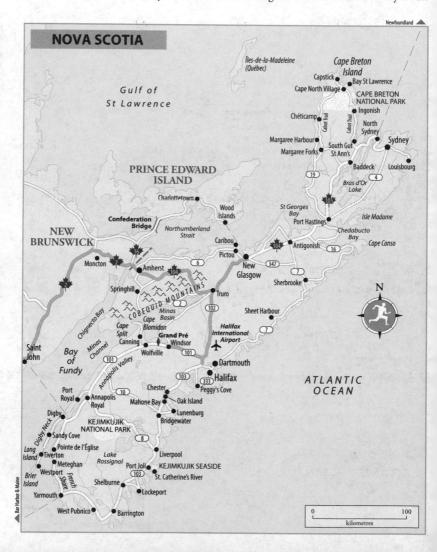

NOVA SCOTIA

THE LOYALISTS

The forty thousand **United Empire Loyalists** who streamed north from America to British Canada – primarily Nova Scotia and New Brunswick – in the aftermath of the American Revolutionary War (1775–83) accounted for a sizeable chunk of the New England population. Many had been subjected to reprisals by their revolutionary neighbours and most arrived virtually penniless in the 1780s. All but eight thousand settled in the Maritime Provinces, where they and their descendants formed the kernel of powerful commercial and political cliques. As a result, the Loyalists have frequently – and not altogether unfairly – been pilloried as arch-conservatives. In fact they were far from docile royalists: shortly after their arrival in Canada they were pressing the British for their own elective assemblies. Crucially, they were also to instil in their new country an abiding dislike for the American version of republican democracy – and this has remained a key sentiment threading through Canadian history.

Before their enforced exile, the Loyalists conducted a fierce debate with their more radical compatriots, but whereas almost everyone today knows the names of the American revolutionary leaders (aka "The Founding Fathers"), the Loyalists are forgotten. The Loyalist argument had several strands: loyalty to Britain, the "mother country"; fear of war and other European powers; the righteousness or otherwise of civil obedience and, rather more subliminally, the traditional English Tory belief that men live most freely in a hierarchical society where roles are clearly understood.

absorbing blend of museum, castle and historical re-enactment, with bagpipes blaring, marching "soldiers" of the Royal Artillery and 78th Highlanders in period kilts and uniform (c.1869), and an elaborate ceremony to **fire one of the old cannons every day at noon**, which makes a terrific bang. If all this militarism leaves you cold, the Citadel is still worth a visit for the grand view over the city and harbour, and the guided tours are entertaining. Just below the Citadel, the Palladian **Town Clock** of 1803 is a city landmark and obligatory photo op.

St Paul's Church

1749 Argyle St • Mon–Fri 9am–4.30pm • Free • ☎ 902 429 2240, ⊚ stpaulshalifax.org

The southern edge of Grand Parade – a tree-lined, elongated square – borders the handsome **St Paul's Church**, whose chunky cupola and timber frame date from 1750, making it both the oldest building in town and the first Protestant church in Canada. Look out for the debris embedded in the plaster above the inner entrance doors, a remnant of the 1917 Halifax Explosion (see page 331). At the other end of Grand Parade lies the stately **City Hall**, completed in 1888 in Second Empire style.

Province House

1726 Hollis St • July & Aug Mon–Fri 9am–5pm, Sat & Sun 10am–4pm; Sept–June Mon–Fri 9am–4pm • Free tours (photo ID required) • ☎ 902 424 5982, ⊚ nslegislature.ca

Charles Dickens, visiting in 1842, described the graceful sandstone **Province House**, a couple of minutes' walk from Grand Parade, as "a gem of Georgian architecture". Highlights of the free **guided tour** (self-guided in winter) include a peek into the old upper chamber, aka the **Red Chamber**, with its ornate plasterwork and assorted portraits, including a dandified King George III and Queen Charlotte. The Nova Scotian legislature has been meeting in the **Assembly Chamber** since the house opened in 1819, a cosy space that partly resembles a Georgian dining room rather than a provincial seat of government.

Art Gallery of Nova Scotia

1723 Hollis St • Mon–Wed & Fri –Sun 10am–5pm, Thurs 10am–9pm; free guided tours daily 2.30pm (Thurs also 7pm) • $12, free Thurs 5–9pm • ☎ 902 424 7542, ⊚ artgalleryofnovascotia.ca

Across the road from Province House, the **Art Gallery of Nova Scotia** occupies two adjacent buildings – one the stern Art Deco Provincial Building, the other an

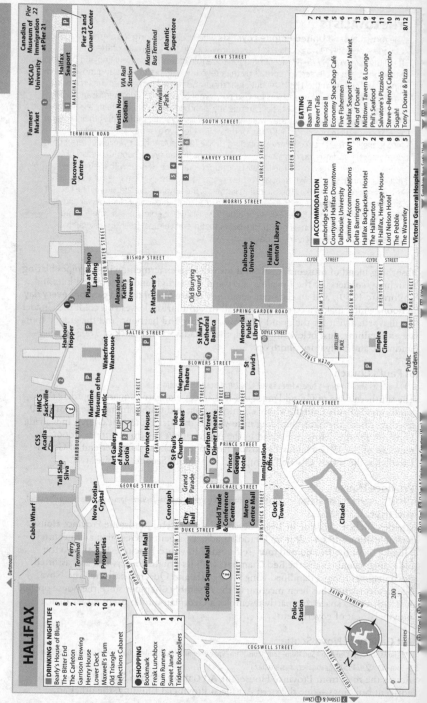

HALIFAX

● DRINKING & NIGHTLIFE

Bearty's House of Blues	5
The Bitter End	8
The Carleton	7
Garrison Brewing	1
Henry House	6
Lower Deck	2
Maxwell's Plum	10
Old Triangle	3
Reflections Cabaret	4

● SHOPPING

Bookmark	5
Freak Lunchbox	3
Rum Runners	1
Sweet Jane's	4
Trident Booksellers	2

■ ACCOMMODATION

Cambridge Suites Hotel	6
Courtyard Halifax Downtown	1
Dalhousie University	10/11
Summer Accommodations	10/11
Delta Barrington	3
Halifax Backpackers Hostel	7
The Halliburton	4
HI Halifax, Heritage House	11
Lord Nelson Hotel	8
The Pebble	9
The Waverley	5

● EATING

Baan Thai	7
BeaverTails	2
Bluenose II	4
Five Fishermen	6
Economy Shoe Shop Café	1
Halifax Seaport Farmers' Market	13
King of Donair	9
Midtown Tavern & Lounge	14
Phil's Seafood	11
Salvatore's Pizzaiolo	10
Steve-o-Reno's Cappuccino	3
Sugah!	8/12
Tony's Donair & Pizza	5

Victoria General Hospital

embellished Victorian edifice (the 1867 Dominion Building) that has previously served as a courthouse, police headquarters and post office. The gallery is attractively laid out and although there is some rotation of the exhibits most of the pieces described here should be on view. Pick up a free **gallery plan** at the entrance in the more southerly of the two buildings, Gallery South.

Floor 1 of **Gallery South** (Provincial Building) contains a delightful section devoted to the Nova Scotian artist **Maud Lewis** (1903–70), portrayed by British actress Sally Hawkins in the 2016 movie *Maudie*. Lewis overcame several disabilities, including rheumatoid arthritis, to become a painter of some renown, creating naive, brightly coloured works of local scenes. Lewis's tiny "Painted House" – awash with her bright paintwork – was removed from the outskirts of Digby (see page 349) for safe-keeping in 1984, and was finally placed here in 1997.

An underground passageway connects the Lower Floor of Gallery South with the Lower Floor of **Gallery North**. Here you'll find **Canadian historical paintings**, while room 4 holds several canvases by Cornelius Krieghoff (see page 73) and a small sample of the work of the **Group of Seven** (see page 74); here are Lawren Harris's haunting *Algoma* landscape and J.E.H. MacDonald's diminutive *Lake O'Hara*. Room 6 features an eclectic selection of modern Canadian paintings drawn from the permanent collection: *Island in the Ice* by the Nova Scotian artist Tom Forrestall is perhaps the most striking work here, its sharp, deep-hued colours and threatening ice- and seascape enhanced by a tight control of space. Look out also for the work of Forrestall's mentor, **Alex Colville**, whose disconcerting paintings demonstrate a sort of Magic Realism of passive, precisely juxtaposed figures caught, cinema-like, in mid-shot.

Maritime Museum of the Atlantic

1675 Lower Water St • May–Oct Mon & Wed–Sat 9.30am–5.30pm, Tues 9.30am–8pm (Sun 9.30am–5.30pm June–Oct only); Nov–April Tues 9.30am–8pm, Wed–Sat 9.30am–5pm, Sun 1–5pm • May–Oct $9.55, Nov–April $5.15 • ☎ 902 424 7490, ⓦ maritimemuseum. novascotia.ca

If the sun's out in Halifax make time to trawl along **Harbourwalk**, lined with ice cream shacks and boat-trip vendors and anchored by the absorbing **Maritime Museum of the Atlantic**. The ground floor holds a series of small displays, including one on the Allied convoys that used Halifax as a port during both world wars; a second on the cataclysmic **Halifax Explosion** of 1917, illustrated by a first-rate video; and a third on the perilously sited **Sable Island lighthouse**, stuck out in the Atlantic southeast of Nova Scotia. Upstairs, a collection of small boats and cutaway scale models details the changing technology of shipbuilding in the "Days of Sail", but it is the **Unsinkable Ship and Halifax** section that attracts most attention, a detailed display on the **Titanic**, which sank east of Halifax in 1912. Docked **outside** the museum are an early twentieth-century steamship, the **CSS Acadia** (part of the museum) and the World War II corvette, **HMCS Sackville** (see below).

HMCS Sackville

Sackville Jetty, Halifax Waterfront • Mid-June to late Oct daily 10am–5pm • $5 • ☎ 902 429 2132, ⓦ hmcssackville.ca

Canada's oldest fighting warship and the nation's official Naval Memorial, **HMCS Sackville** is the last of many convoy escort vessels built during World War II – Halifax was a key assembly point for convoys during the **Battle of the Atlantic**. Exploring the cramped decks and interior, restored to their 1944 configuration, brings home just how grim the war at sea must have been.

Discovery Centre

1215 Lower Water St • Daily 10am–5pm (Wed 10am–8pm) • $12, children 3 and above $10; free Wed 5–8pm • ☎ 902 492 4422, ⓦ thediscoverycentre.ca

From the Maritime Museum it's a fifteen-minute stroll along Harbourwalk to the Halifax Seaport development (ⓦ halifaxseaport.com) of shops, bars and condos at

5

the southern edge of downtown. First up is the **Discovery Centre**, a hands-on science museum targeted primarily at children. The immersive Dome Theatre ($2 extra) shows planetarium-style movies throughout the day.

Halifax Seaport Farmers' Market

1209 Marginal Rd, Pier 20 • July–Oct Mon–Fri 10am–5pm, Sat 7am–3pm, Sun 9am–3pm; Nov–June Tues–Fri 10am–5pm, Sat 7am–3pm, Sun 9am–3pm • ☎ 902 492 4043, ⓦ halifaxfarmersmarket.com

Just beyond the Discovery Centre lies **Halifax Seaport Farmers' Market**, a popular arts, crafts and artisan food market (see page 336). The market moved here from Alexander Keith's Brewery (see below) in 2010, but a more traditional version ("**Halifax Brewery Farmers' Market**") still takes place at the latter on Saturdays from 7am to 1pm (ⓦ halifaxbrewerymarket.com).

Canadian Museum of Immigration at Pier 21

1055 Marginal Rd • April Tues–Sun 10am–5pm; May–Oct daily 9.30am–5.30pm; Nov daily 9.30am–5pm; Dec–March Wed–Sun 10am–5pm • $14.50 • ☎ 902 425 7770, ⓦ pier21.ca

Just east along the wharf from the Farmers' Market is the Seaport's premier historic attraction, the **Canadian Museum of Immigration at Pier 21**. Around 1.5 million immigrants and Canadian military personnel passed through Pier 21 between 1928 and 1971, and the museum features recordings and video testimonies of many, enhanced with an assortment of interactive exhibits. Start with the thirty-minute multimedia presentation (shown frequently), which features compelling dramatizations of immigrant arrivals from the 1920s to the 1960s.

Alexander Keith's Brewery

1496 Lower Water St • **Tours** June–Oct Mon–Sat noon–7.30pm, Sun noon–5pm, every 30min; Nov–May Fri & Sat noon–7.30pm, Sun noon–5pm, hourly • $26.95 • ☎ 902 455 1474, ⓦ keiths.ca **Red Stag Tavern** Mon–Thurs & Sun 11.30–9pm, Fri & Sat 11.30am–10pm • ☎ 902 422 0275, ⓦ redstag.ca

Founded in 1820, **Alexander Keith's Brewery** is one of the oldest commercial beer-makers in North America (today it's owned by Labatt, a subsidiary of Anheuser-Busch InBev). Costumed actors, usually playing feisty bar wenches circa 1863 (singing, storytelling and joking in a highly convincing, bawdy manner), conduct pricey one-hour tours (two beers are included) of the historical premises, which can be rounded off by another beer or meal (burgers and pub grub $12–22) at the on-site **Red Stag Tavern**. Note that Nova Scotia's most popular beer, **Keith's Indian Pale Ale**, is more like a lager than the hoppy, British-style version.

Fairview Lawn Cemetery – The Titanic Graveyard

3720 Windsor St, at Connaught Ave • 24hr • Free

If you have a car, it's worth considering the short ride out to **Fairview Lawn Cemetery**, in the North End of Halifax. The cemetery is the largest resting place of **Titanic** victims (121), the plot marked with a simple white "Titanic" sign and small granite headstones, paid for by the White Star Line after the 1912 disaster. Most have their names engraved on the stones (some families have paid for larger memorials), but many occupants are still unidentified and wandering around the site can be a moving experience – you might see toys at the memorial to the Unknown Child. Fans of the movie *Titanic* came here in droves in 1997 to lay flowers at the headstone of one "J. Dawson", though director James Cameron later confirmed there was no connection with the film's main character.

Dartmouth

Founded in 1750, today **DARTMOUTH** is primarily a dormitory town for Halifax, just across the harbour. There's little to see, but the ferry ride over does provide the **best views** of the waterfront and downtown Halifax.

5

Quaker House

57 Ochterloney St • June–Aug Tues–Sun 10am–1pm & 2–5pm • $5 • ⓦ dartmouthheritagemuseum.ns.ca • Walk through the Alderney Gate mall at the ferry terminal, turn left at Alderney Drive and then take the first right

Little remains of historic Dartmouth, but a five-minute stroll from the ferry lies **Quaker House**, a small, grey-clapboard residence sitting three blocks up the hill. After the American War of Independence, 27 Quaker whaling families emigrated from Nantucket to Dartmouth to avoid paying British tariffs on whale oil – the home of William Ray, cooper, is the only one of their houses to survive. The interior has been painstakingly restored to its 1786 appearance, its spartan fittings reflecting Quaker values. Costumed guides explain the archaic bits and pieces on display – spinning wheels, kids' toys and the like – as well as the story behind 200-year-old shoes found in the wall during renovations in 1991, and the eye of a Sei whale, gruesomely preserved in formalin.

ARRIVAL AND DEPARTURE — HALIFAX

BY PLANE

Halifax Stanfield International Airport The airport (ⓦ halifaxstanfield.ca) is 35km northeast of the city centre and has free wi-fi and its own extremely efficient Nova Scotia Visitor Information Centre (June–Oct daily 10am–9pm, Nov–May Mon–Fri 9am–4.30pm; ☏ 902 873 1223). All the major car rental agencies have desks.

Getting into town Metro Transit operates the hourly MetroX service (bus #320; daily 4.30am–11.20pm; 1hr) between downtown at Duke/Albemarle St and the airport (every 30min 6–9am & 3–6pm, otherwise hourly); the fare is $3.50. Maritime Bus (☏ 902 429 2029, ⓦ maritimebus.com) run an express shuttle bus from the airport to the larger downtown hotels and Dartmouth (May–Oct only; 24hr; takes 40min–1hr depending on traffic; $22 one way, $40 return; reservations essential). From Nov–April there's a reduced schedule to the *Westin* in downtown Halifax. Taxis from the airport to the centre charge a flat fee of $63. Shuttle bus services run direct from the airport to numerous destinations, including Cape Breton, the Annapolis Valley and PEI (see airport website for details).

BY TRAIN

The train station is the East Coast terminus for VIA Rail, 1161 Hollis St at Cornwallis Park (☏ 888 842 7245, ⓦ viarail.ca), and handles just three trains to Montréal via Moncton a week. It's a 15min walk into the centre.
Destinations Moncton (Wed, Fri, Sun; 4hr 17min); Montréal (Wed, Fri, Sun; 22hr 18min); Truro (Wed, Fri, Sun; 1hr 26min).

BY BUS

Maritime Bus (☏ 902 429 2029, ⓦ maritimebus.com) runs long-distance services throughout the region from the VIA Rail Station at 1161 Hollis St.
Destinations Charlottetown (3 daily; 5hr 10min–5hr 30min); Fredericton (2 daily; 6hr 55min–7hr 15min); Moncton (3 daily; 4hr 15min); Montréal (1–2 daily; 17hr–18hr 5min); Québec City (1–2 daily; 14hr 30min–16hr 35min); Saint John (2 daily; 7hr 35min–7hr 10min); Sydney (1–2 daily; 6hr

30min–6hr 55min); Wolfville (2 daily; 1hr 40min).

BY SHUTTLE BUS

The Maritime Bus services are supplemented by shuttle buses that link Halifax with other areas of the province; note that these services normally require a minimum number of passengers to run. Kiwi Kaboodle (☏ 866 549 4522, ⓦ novascotiatoursandtravel.com) runs between Halifax Airport and Chester, Mahone Bay or Lunenburg for $140 plus tax (plus $9 curb fee), shared between all passengers (so if there are two of you it's $70). Kathleen's Shuttle (☏ 902 249 0086) runs between Halifax and Digby via the Annapolis Valley in just 2hr 30min ($75 one way), leaving Digby around 9am and departing Halifax around noon–2pm (mid-June to mid-Sept Sun–Fri; mid-Jan to mid-June & mid-Sept to mid-Dec Mon, Wed, Fri & Sun; mid-Dec to mid-Jan daily). Mariner Shuttle (☏ 855 586 6140, ⓦ marinershuttle.co) runs between Halifax and Yarmouth via the Annapolis Valley daily, departing the Yarmouth area 7am–7.30am, and heading back from Halifax and the airport 1–3pm (Halifax–Yarmouth $80; Halifax to *Digby Backpackers Inn* $65; cash only). Cloud Nine Shuttle (☏ 902 742 3992, ⓦ thecloudnineshuttle.com) also runs to Yarmouth (1 daily, 3pm; 4hr; $75; $80 from the airport) – note that trips can take up to seven hours if several stops are scheduled. Bay Luxury Shuttle (☏ 855 673 8083, ⓦ bayluxuryshuttle.com) runs between Glace Bay and Halifax ($70) via several locations in Cape Breton (including Baddeck and Sydney); pick-ups start at 6.30am from Glace Bay, with returns from Halifax starting at 1pm.

BY CAR

Most hotels have designated parking – otherwise aim for the convenient waterfront parking on Lower Water St ($3/hr or $16 daily 8am–6pm; $6 daily 6pm–8am) or the Park Lane Parkade at Dresden Row and Sackville St (Mon–Fri 6am–6pm; $2/30min or $20/day; Mon–Fri 6pm–6am, Sat & Sun 24hr; $1/hr, maximum $5). On-street metered parking is also available ($1.50/hr, $3/hr on the waterfront; free 6pm–8am and all day Sat & Sun).

5

GETTING AROUND

By bus The best way to see downtown Halifax is on foot, but for outlying attractions and accommodation buses operated by Metro Transit (☎902 490 4000, ⓦhalifax.ca/metrotransit) are reliable and efficient. The flat fare is $2.50 in the Halifax area (exact change only) or $20 for a book of ten tickets. If you need to change buses on the same journey, ask for a free transfer ticket at the outset. Free Metro Transit route maps and schedules are available from the tourist office.

By ferry The ferries that cross Halifax harbour to Dartmouth (Alderney Landing) depart the waterfront ferry terminal at 5077 George St; the journey takes about 10min (daily 6.45am–11.45pm every 15–30min; $2.50). Last departure from Dartmouth is 11.30pm.

Taxi Casino Taxi ☎902 429 6666; Yellow Cab ☎902 420 0000. Meters start at $3.20, and fares rarely top $10–15 for trips around downtown.

Bike rental I Heart Bikes, on the waterfront (officially 1507 Lower Water St; ☎902 406 7774, ⓦiheartbikeshfx.com), offers rentals ($12/hr, $17/2hr, $45/24hr) and guided tours for $44.

INFORMATION

Halifax Waterfront Visitor Information Centre Sackville Landing, 1655 Lower Water St (daily: June to Oct 9am–7pm; Nov–May 9am–4.30pm; ☎902 424 4248, ⓦdiscoverhalifaxns.com).

Guides and publications For entertainment listings and local news, grab a copy of free weekly *The Coast* (ⓦthecoast.ca), widely available around town, or Halifax's main daily newspaper, the *Chronicle-Herald* (ⓦthechronicleherald.ca); its Thursday listings are particularly good.

TOURS

Ambassatours Gray Line 6575 Bayne St ☎902 420 1015, ⓦambassatours.com. Choose from a wide range of boat trips on the waterfront, from the amphibious Harbour Hopper (May–Oct daily 10.15am–8pm every 1hr 15min; $36.75), to Tall Ship cruises (late June to Sept daily 2pm, 4.30pm & 6.30pm; 1hr 30min; $31.99).

Ghost Walks of Historic Halifax (Tattle Tours) ☎902 494 0525, ⓦtattletours.ca. Creepy tales, haunted buildings and even a cursed bridge on tours by local ghost guide Andy Smith. May–Oct Wed, Fri & Sun 7.30–9.30pm at the Old Town Clock ($15).

Local Tasting Tours ☎902 818 9055, ⓦlocaltastingtours.com. Bite-sized food tours (2hr; $50) of a range of lauded local shops and restaurants start at the Fish Shop at the Farmers' Market. May–Oct Mon & Sun 1.30pm.

ACCOMMODATION

DOWNTOWN

★ **Cambridge Suites Hotel** 1583 Brunswick St ☎902 420 0555, ⓦcambridgesuiteshalifax.com; map p.330. Large, luxurious hotel that offers spacious but affordable suites and studios, all decked out in swish, contemporary style; most rooms have superb views of the waterfront. Breakfast included. **$195**

Courtyard Halifax Downtown 5120 Salter St ☎902 428 1900, ⓦmarriott.com; map p.330. Family-friendly option with rooms and small balconies, next to Alexander Keith's near the waterfront. Gym and small pool; parking $25/day. **$258**

Dalhousie University Summer Accommodations ☎902 494 8840, ⓦstay.dal.ca; map p.330. Dalhousie University offers rooms to tourists from early May to mid-Aug in two principal locations: Howe Hall, 6230 Coburg Rd, and historic Shirreff Hall, 6385 South St, both on the main university campus, south of the centre along University Ave. Single and double rooms available (two single beds), usually with shared bathrooms – students and seniors receive substantial discounts. Note that rooms can get hot in the summer. Singles **$53**; doubles **$81**

Delta Barrington 1875 Barrington St ☎902 429 7410, ⓦmarriott.com; map p.330. Modern luxury, in the middle of downtown, with weekend discounts of up to thirty percent. Attached to one of the city's larger shopping malls. Parking $24/day. **$240**

The Halliburton 5184 Morris St ☎902 420 0658, ⓦthehalliburton.com; map p.330. Near the railway station off Barrington St, this long-established thirty-room inn occupies three adjacent buildings. The oldest, the original inn dating from 1809, has a Victorian period look to its public rooms, but the bedrooms beyond are firmly modern. The nicer – and larger – rooms, many of which have balconies, are in the other two buildings. Free breakfast but limited free parking. **$155**

HI Halifax, Heritage House 1253 Barrington St ☎902 422 3863, ⓦhihostels.ca; map p.330. Only 300m from the train station and more central than *Backpackers*, this clean and agreeable HI hostel with private rooms (which sleep up to three) and four- to six-bed male and female-only dorms has free phones, coin laundry, a kitchen, patio and parking. Dorms **$26**, non-members **$30**; private rooms **$62**, non-members **$68**

Lord Nelson Hotel 1515 South Park St ☎902 423 6331, ⊛lordnelsonhotel.ca; map p.330. With its high-coffered ceiling, the lobby of this popular brown-brick hotel is spacious and elegant, with Art Deco details dating from its 1920s construction. The two hundred-odd rooms do not quite live up to the lobby, but they are spacious, comfortable and furnished in a slick modern style. Parking $28/day. $230

The Waverley 1266 Barrington St ☎902 423 9346, ⊛waverleyinn.com; map p.330. Elegant Victorian mansion, with thirty en-suite a/c rooms, sympathetically refurbished with splendid period furnishings. Oscar Wilde stayed here on his 1882 North American lecture tour, apparently turning up in green velvet pantaloons. The inn is a 5min walk from the train station. Rates include breakfast and parking. $135

NORTH AND SOUTH ENDS

Halifax Backpackers Hostel 2193 Gottingen St, North End ☎902 431 3170, ⊛halifaxbackpackers.com; map p.330. These spacious six-bed dorms are the best deal in the city. *Alteregos Café* downstairs offers light meals, the shared kitchen is big and the owners invite all guests to a barbecue every Friday. Parking is $5/day. It's only a 10min walk to the Citadel, and there are plenty of student-friendly bars nearby. Dorms $26; doubles $55

★ **The Pebble** 1839 Armview Terrace, South End ☎902 423 6687, ⊛thepebble.ca; map p.330. Enjoy fine Irish hospitality in this quiet, leafy residential neighbourhood just south of the centre, with gorgeous views across the North West Arm and fabulous breakfasts (included). The two luxurious suites are beautifully furnished, and the free phone calls and glass of port in the evening are nice touches. $275

EATING

DOWNTOWN

Baan Thai 5234 Blowers St ☎902 446 4301, ⊛baanthai.ca; map p.330. There's often a queue here to sample the city's best Thai food at the weekends, but it's worth the wait. Good value, with mains (green curries, cashew chicken) around $13–19. Mon–Fri 11.30am–3pm & 3–10pm, Sat & Sun 3–10pm.

Bluenose II 1824 Hollis St, at Duke St ☎902 425 5092, ⊛bluenoseii.ca; map p.330. An institution since 1964, this diner serves filling and fairly tasty meals (breakfasts $12–19). Seafood, in various guises, is the real speciality ($13–21), along with Greek dishes (lamb chops, souvlaki $16–17), excellent burgers and the signature rice pudding ($3.50) – service can suffer at busy times. Free wi-fi. Mon–Fri 7am–9pm, Sat & Sun 8am–9pm.

★ **Economy Shoe Shop Café** 1663 Argyle St ☎902 423 7463, ⊛economyshoeshop.ca; map p.330. Everything here is imaginative – from the name and the offbeat decor through to the menu, offering tapas to Italian (mains $15–18), but best known for its addictive nachos ($18), topped with marble cheddar and banana pepper. Daily 11am–2am.

★ **Five Fishermen** 1740 Argyle St, at Carmichael St ☎902 422 4421, ⊛fivefishermen.com; map p.330. One of Halifax's best restaurants, where the house speciality is seafood (and Alberta Angus beef). It's expensive (mains $24–45), but the food is exceptional and the all-you-can-eat mussel bar is included in the price of any main dish. The restaurant is on the first floor of a gorgeous 1816 building and its cosy interior, with its booths and stained glass, is decked

---

HALIFAX: THE SWEET TREAT TOP 5

BeaverTails Harbourwalk, 1549 Lower Water St ☎902 789 0989, ⊛beavertails.com; map p.330. Deep-fried wholewheat dough, stretched to look like a beaver's tail, and smothered with sweet toppings; the original version is simply sprinkled with cinnamon and sugar, but the apple cinnamon, banana-chocolate and maple butter are totally addictive ($5–7). May–Oct daily 11am–8pm (July & Aug 10am–10pm).

Freak Lunchbox 1729 Barrington St ☎902 420 9151, ⊛freaklunchbox.com; map p.330. A hip candy store with a cult following, with a phenomenal range of sweets and chocs. June–Aug Mon–Thurs 9am–11pm, Fri & Sat 9am–midnight, Sun 10am–11pm; Sept–May Mon–Thurs 10am–11pm, Fri & Sat 10am–midnight, Sun 10am–11pm.

Rum Runners Bishop's Landing, 1479 Lower Water St ☎902 421 6079, ⊛theuncommongroup.com; map p.330. Free tasters of the classic, chocolate or whisky rum cake (whole cakes $22.95), made with spirits provided by Glenora Distillery on Cape Breton Island. May to mid-Nov daily 10am–6pm.

Sugah! Bishop's Landing, 1479 Lower Water St ☎902 421 6079; map p.330. Crammed with all sorts of sweet delights, chocolates and silky smooth hand-paddled ice cream – pick a topping for them to "paddle" into the creamy base (from $3). May–Oct daily 10am–6pm; Nov–April Fri & Sat 10am–6pm.

Sweet Jane's 1300 Queen St ☎902 425 0168, ⊛sweetjanes.com; map p.330. Old-fashioned sweet shop, stocking classic Canadian treats such as Acadian Maple Products' maple roasted peanuts ($5.99). Mon–Sat 9.30am–9pm, Sun 10am–6pm.

out in antique nautical style. Reservations required for the main restaurant, though not for bar, which offers a menu of fresh oysters and small plates. Restaurant daily 5–10pm; bar Mon–Fri 11.30am–10pm, Sat & Sun 4–10pm.

★ **Halifax Seaport Farmers' Market** Pier 20, 1209 Marginal Rd ☎ 902 429 6256, ⓦ halifaxfarmersmarket. com; map p.330. Choices, choices. *Stella's Antiguan Cuisine* is all about the jerk chicken ($13.50), while the *Cake Lady* will tempt you with her German-style desserts. Grab a coffee at *Java Blend* upstairs (Halifax roasters since 1938) or Lunenburg-based *Laughing Whale Coffee*. July–Oct Mon–Fri 10am–5pm, Sat 7am–3pm, Sun 9am–3pm; Nov–June Tues–Fri 10am–5pm, Sat 7am–3pm, Sun 9am–3pm.

Midtown Tavern & Lounge 1744 Grafton St ☎ 902 422 5213, ⓦ themidtown.ca; map p.330. This venerable diner and pub has been in business since 1949, but moved into smart new digs in 2009. Daily specials include roast beef dinner (Thurs; $14) and ribs (Sat; $14), and DJs add a party atmosphere Fri & Sat nights (mains average $11–18). Mon–Sat 11am–2am, Sun noon–2am.

Steve-o-Reno's Cappuccino 1536 Brunswick St, just off Spring Garden Rd ☎ 902 429 3034, ⓦ steveorenos. com; map p.330. New Age-ish café-bar with bohemian decor and laidback vibes. The breakfasts are tip-top, with a bewildering range of coffees from local roasters North

Mountain Fine Coffees. Mon–Fri 7am–5pm, Sat 7.30am–5pm, Sun 7.30am–4pm (seasonal hours).

NORTH END AND WEST END

★ **Phil's Seafood** 6285 Quinpool Rd ☎ 902 431 3474, ⓦ philsseafood.ca; map p.330. Fried-fish fans should make the modest pilgrimage out to this local diner, home to the best fresh, lightly breaded haddock and hand-cut chips ($7.95) in Halifax – it's a 20min walk from the Citadel, just beyond the Quinpool Centre. Try the gingerbread ($4.25) for dessert. Tues–Thurs & Sat 11.30am–8pm, Fri 11.30am–8.30pm, Sun 11.30am–7.30pm.

Salvatore's Pizzaiolo 5541 Young St, Hydrostone Market, North End ☎ 902 455 1133, ⓦ salvatorespizza. ca; map p.330. This homely place knocks out the best thin-crust pizzas in the province, and at reasonable prices considering the quality (large starts at $15.99); try the clam pie *marinato* ($13.98–21.98). Mon–Wed 11.30am–10pm, Thurs–Sat 11.30am–11pm.

DARTMOUTH

Two if By Sea Café 66 Ochterloney St ☎ 902 469 0721, ⓦ twoifbyseacafe.ca. Excellent, locally run café, the best place for breakfast or brunch; justly famed for its speciality coffee and huge, buttery croissants ($3.75). Mon–Fri 7am–6pm, Sat & Sun 8am–5pm.

DRINKING, NIGHTLIFE AND ENTERTAINMENT

Drinkers rejoice: Halifax has more **bars** per head than anywhere else in Canada except St John's, Newfoundland, and the listings below are merely a taster – you'll rarely be a few metres from a decent pub, especially on Argyle St. It also has a vibrant **live music scene** with around forty of its café-bars and pubs offering everything from blues and jazz through to indie and techno. Detailed **entertainment listings** are given in **The Coast** (see page 334). The main musical event is the five-day **Halifax Jazz Festival** (☎ 902 420 9943, ⓦ halifaxjazzfestival.ca), held in mid-July

and featuring many of the biggest international names.

BARS

The Bitter End 1572 Argyle St ☎ 902 425 3039, ⓦ bitterend.ca; map p.330. Well-known for its martinis, this polished cocktail bar provides a quietly cool beginning to – or end of – a night on the tiles. Daily 4pm–2am.

Garrison Brewing 1149 Marginal Rd ☎ 902 453 5343, ⓦ garrisonbrewing.com; map p.330. Award-winning microbrewery near Pier 21 and the Farmers' Market, with

---

THE HALIFAX "DONAIR"

What is the Halifax "donair", and why does it have (sort of) cult status? The donair is much like a typical doner kebab, but uses fresh, lean ground beef and a slightly sweet milk-based garlic sauce. Legend has it that it was created in a small tavern in Greece, and introduced to Canada in 1973. Today you can order donair pizza and donair subs in addition to the original – hard to believe, but Nova Scotian expats often experience severe homesickness for this eastern Mediterranean delight. See what the fuss is all about at these illustrious locations:

King of Donair 6420 Quinpool Rd ☎ 902 421 0000, ⓦ kingofdonair.ca; map p.330. The mini-chain that claims to have started the donair craze back in 1973 still knocks out some of the best ($6.99–12.99), as well as donair pizza (from $10.99). Mon–Wed & Sun 10am–1am, Thurs–Sat 10am–3am.

Tony's Donair & Pizza 2390 Robie St, North End (and 1735 Grafton St) ☎ 902 404 8669, ⓦ tonysdonair.ca; map p.330. Tony has provided friendly competition since 1976, with donairs $6.95–10.95. Sun–Tues 11am–2am, Wed & Thurs 11am–3am, Fri & Sat 11am–4am.

5

LGBTQ HALIFAX

Halifax has a small but vibrant **LGBTQ scene**, centred on places like **Menz & Mollyz Bar**, 2182 Gottingen St in the North End (daily 4pm–2.30am; W facebook.com/menznmollyz); check W gay.hfxns.org for the latest information. Halifax Pride Festival is every July (W halifaxpride.com).

tasty brews such as Imperial IPA, Jalapeño Ale and the raspberry wheat. Mon–Thurs & Sun 10am–8pm, Fri 10am–9pm, Sat 8am–9pm.

Henry House 1222 Barrington St, at South ☎902 423 5660, W henryhouse.ca; map p.330. British-style pub with a charmingly intimate bar occupying a handsome stone building dating from 1834 – it was once the home of Confederation "father" William A. Henry. Most of the ale is brewed on the premises – try the Peculiar, a fair approximation of the sultry grandeur of the legendary British ale. Daily 11.30am–12.45am.

Maxwell's Plum 1600 Grafton St, at Sackville ☎902 423 5090, W themaxwellsplum.com; map p.330. Beer drinkers' heaven, with an outstanding sixty ales on tap, and over 99 different types of beer on offer altogether. Traditional pitchers (from $21.95) and selected draughts (from $6.95). Daily 11am–2am.

Old Triangle 5136 Prince St, at Bedford St ☎902 492 4900, W oldtriangle.com; map p.330. An Irish-style pub with a whole network of cosy snugs and a warm and welcoming atmosphere. Live music every night, with Gaelic music at weekends. Mon, Tues & Sun 11am–midnight, Wed & Thurs 11am–12.30am, Fri & Sat 11am–2am.

LIVE MUSIC AND CLUBS

Bearly's House of Blues 1269 Barrington St ☎902 423 2526, W bearlys.ca; map p.330. Near the train station, this low-key bar has regular acts with the emphasis – you guessed it – on blues and bluegrass. Blues jam sessions on Sun nights, karaoke on Wed (10pm). Mon 4pm–midnight, Tues 11am–midnight, Wed, Fri & Sat 11am–2am, Thurs 11am–12.30am, Sun noon–1am.

The Carleton 1685 Argyle St ☎902 422 6335, W thecarleton.ca; map p.330. One of the best live venues (mostly urban folk) on the East Coast as well as a great bar

for wine, proper martinis and draught beer. Tues, Wed & Sun 4–11pm, Thurs 4pm–1am, Fri & Sat 4pm–2am.

Lower Deck 1887 Upper Water St (Historic Properties) ☎902 425 1501, W lowerdeck.ca; map p.330. Traditional Maritime folk music is the speciality here with daily live acts and pub food, while the Beer Market (on the upper floor) reverts to a conventional DJ club Thurs–Sun 5pm–2am. May–Sept daily 11.30am–12.30am; Oct–April Mon–Wed 5pm–midnight, Thurs & Sun 5pm–12.30am, Fri & Sat 11.30am–12.30am.

Reflections Cabaret 5187 Salter St ☎902 422 2957, W reflectionscabaret.com; map p.330. Halifax's biggest dance club with themed nights, both by music and disposition, though house tends to predominate. Mon 10pm–2.30am, Thurs–Sat 10pm–4am.

CLASSICAL MUSIC AND THEATRE

Grafton Street Dinner Theatre 1741 Grafton St ☎902 425 1961, W graftonstdinnertheatre.com. Music, comedy and interactive characters enhance a traditional Nova Scotian dinner – seafood chowder, salmon, haddock and steaks (3–6 shows Tues–Sun, depending on the season, from 6.30–10pm; $49).

Neptune Theatre 1593 Argyle St ☎902 429 7070, W neptunetheatre.com. The doyen of Halifax's live theatres since 1915, offering a wide range of mainstream dramatic productions; normally closes June–Aug. Tickets usually $32–75.

Symphony Nova Scotia Dalhousie Arts Centre Box Office, 6101 University Ave ☎902 494 3820, W symphony novascotia.ca. Professional orchestra that usually performs at the university's Rebecca Cohn Auditorium (University Ave and LeMarchant St). Concert season from Sept to May. Everything from Beethoven to Piaf, with tickets ranging $30–87. Box office Mon–Fri noon–6pm.

SHOPPING

Bookmark 5686 Spring Garden Rd ☎902 423 0419, W bookmarkreads.ca; map p.330. Great independent bookstore with a friendly vibe and lots of author events. Mon–Fri 9am–10pm, Sat 9am–6pm, Sun 11am–6pm.

Trident Booksellers 1256 Hollis St ☎902 423 7100; map p.330. Actress Ellen Paige's favourite café-cum-bookshop (she has a house nearby). Mon–Fri 8am–5pm, Sat 8.30am–5pm, Sun 10am–3pm.

DIRECTORY

Consulate US, Suite 904, Purdy's Wharf Tower II, 1969 Upper Water St ☎902 429 2480, W ca.usembassy.gov/embassy-consulates/halifax (Mon–Fri 8.30am–5pm).
Internet access Free internet access at the Halifax North

Memorial Public Library, 2285 Gottingen St (Tues–Thurs 9am–9pm, Fri & Sat 9am–5pm, Sat 10am–5pm; ☎902 490 5723).
Post office 1680 Bedford Row, at Prince St (Mon–Fri 7.30am–5.15pm; ☎866 607 6301).

5

Peggy's Cove

From Halifax, Rte-333 cuts south across dense forest before reaching the **South Shore**, a winding ribbon of Atlantic fishing villages, glacial boulders and indented rocky bays beginning with tiny **PEGGY'S COVE**, 45km from the capital. Founded in 1811, the hamlet, with a resident population of just 35 souls year-round, surrounds a rocky slit of a harbour, with the spiky Gothic Revival **St John's Anglican Church** of 1885, a smattering of clapboard houses and wooden jetties on stilts.

Drive to the end of the road where the solitary **Peggy's Point Lighthouse** stands against the sea-smoothed granite of the shore – built in 1914, its automated light still functions. Otherwise the main activity here is just wandering around the tiny harbour, soaking in the undeniable beauty of the place, despite the swarms of tourists in midsummer; try to visit early mornings or late afternoons.

DeGarthe Gallery

109 Peggy's Point Rd • May–Oct 9am–4pm • $1 • ☎ 902 823 2256

Finnish-born artist **William deGarthe** (1907–83) fell in love with Peggy's Cove in the 1930s, and moved here permanently in 1955. Today the **deGarthe Gallery**, built next to his former home, displays a collection of his work including the complex *Pax in Terra*, the *Tuna Trap*, *Doreyman*, and studies for the murals he painted inside St John's Anglican Church in 1963 (the church only opens for services on every third Sunday). His dramatic **Fishermen's Monument**, carved into the 30m granite rock-face in the garden outside, is an epic tribute to local fishermen, unfinished at the time of his death.

INFORMATION
PEGGY'S COVE

Nova Scotia Visitor Information Centre 96 Peggy's Point Rd (mid-May to late Oct daily 9am–5pm; July to late Sept closes 7pm; ☎ 902 823 2253, ⓦ peggyscoveregion. com); stocks local maps and heaps of information on the South Shore. Free wi-fi available.

ACCOMMODATION AND EATING

★ **DeeDee's Ice Cream** 110 Peggy's Point Rd ⓦ deedees. ca. This local ice-cream shack has garnered quite a reputation for its innovative flavours (cones $3.75–4.75), using organic fair-trade raw cane sugar, real fruit, nuts and European chocolate in its thick and creamy desserts. Try Mexican dark chocolate with a hint of cinnamon, nutmeg and cayenne, or the rhubarb ginger sorbet. May–Sept daily 10am–6pm.
Peggy's Cove B&B 17 Church Rd ☎ 902 823 2265, ⓦ peggyscovebb.com. Overlooking the harbour from the end of Church Rd, this B&B provides five simple but

adequate rooms, each with cable TV and its own sun deck; advance reservations are advised. Open mid-April to second week in Nov. $159
The Sou'wester 178 Peggy's Point Rd ☎ 902 823 2561, ⓦ peggys-cove.com. Behind the lighthouse, this basic canteen and touristy gift shop serves all the usual chowder, fish and chips, haddock and lobsters, home-made gingerbread and apple crisp. Hot cider in winter. Free wi-fi. Mains $13–36. Daily: June–Oct 8.30am–9pm; Nov–May 10am–6pm.

Chester

It's a 30min drive north from Peggy's Cove to Hwy-103 and a further 40km west to **CHESTER**, a handsome and prosperous-looking village tumbling over a chubby little peninsula. Officially founded in 1759 and initially settled by colonists from Massachusetts, the village, with its fine old trees and elegant frame houses, has long been the favoured resort of yachting enthusiasts, whose principal shindig is the **Chester Race Week** regatta held in mid-August (visit ⓦ tourismchester.ca for more information).

Big Tancook Island

Ferry Terminal at Water St • Mon–Fri 7am, 10.20am, 3.40pm, 5.30pm, Fri also 8.30pm & 11pm; Sat 1pm & 7pm, Sun 10am & 6pm; 50min • Last return Mon–Thurs 4.30pm, Fri 9.30pm, Sat 6pm, Sun 5pm • $7 return • Limited parking (free) near the pier

A **passenger ferry** sallies out from Chester bound for **Big Tancook Island** (as distinct from neighbouring Little Tancook Island, which most ferries also visit), whose quiet

OAK ISLAND: TRICK OR TREASURE?

In 1795, three boys discovered the top of an underground shaft on tiny **Oak Island**, a low-lying, offshore islet a few kilometres west of Chester, connected to the mainland by a causeway (it's signposted on Rte-3). The shaft, or "Money Pit", soon attracted the attentions of treasure-hunters, who were convinced this was where a vast horde of booty had been interred. At first the betting was on Drake, Kidd or Morgan, but present favourites include the Templars and even Elizabethan scientist Francis Bacon. No treasure has ever been found (only non-indigenous coconut fibres and a seventeenth-century Spanish coin), but the diggings became so dangerous (four men died here in 1965) the island's current owners (treasure-hunter Dan Blankenship and brothers Rick and Marty Lagina) have limited access to the public (though they restarted the search themselves in 2009 and run carefully guided tours). Several documentaries have featured the site, the most recent being *The Curse of Oak Island* on the History Channel – indeed, the TV series, which has been running continually since 2014, has become far more lucrative than any "treasure" so far found.

You can visit the *Oak Island Interpretation Centre*, just across the causeway itself (late May to late Oct 10am–5pm; free; ⓦoakislandtours.ca), which chronicles the story of the island and organizes **pre-booked weekend tours** (2hr; $30), the only way to visit the island. You must book tours on the website – reservations for the upcoming season open in February and often sell out in a few hours (partly because it's become a major venue for cruise ship tours).

country roads and rustic scenery are popular with walkers. In July and August, local "Tourism Ambassadors" welcome visitors on the wharf, while the **Tancook Tourism Center** (in the recreation centre, on the school road just a short walk from the wharf; open daily May–Sept) hands out island maps.

INFORMATION   CHESTER

Visitor centre The Chester Municipal Heritage Society (late May–Sept Wed–Sat 10am–5pm; rest of year Wed 1–3pm; ☎ 902 275 4616) in the old 1905 train station at 20 Smith Rd, just off Rte-3, acts as an information centre in the summer, also containing the Station 20 Handicraft Shoppe. The Chester Farmers' & Artisan Market opens outside the station every Friday 9am–1pm (June–Sept).

ACCOMMODATION AND EATING

Carolyn's Restaurant 656 Tancook Island Rd, Big Tancook Island (just opposite the jetty) ☎ 902 228 2749. Dine in or take out fresh seafood, burgers, sandwiches, salads, chowder, home-made fruit pies and ice cream. Late May to early Nov Mon–Fri 11am–7pm, Sat noon–8pm, Sun 11am–8pm.

Mecklenburgh Inn 78 Queen St ☎ 902 275 4638, ⓦ mecklenburghinn.ca. There's only a handful of B&Bs in town, including the affordable and rather modest *Mecklenburgh*, whose four guest rooms (all en suite, three with clawfoot tubs) are in a handsome 1902 clapboard house in the centre. **$139**

Rope Loft 36 Water St, Chester ☎ 902 275 3430, ⓦropeloft.com. Dockside restaurant and pub that serves up delicious seafood – fresh local lobsters, seafood chowder, Digby clams and haddock and chips – but also a decent burger. Lunch $12–17, dinner $13–35. May–Sept daily 11am–midnight.

ENTERTAINMENT

Chester Playhouse 22 Pleasant St ☎ 902 275 3933, ⓦ chesterplayhouse.ca. Chester is home to this first-rate theatre, which offers a lively programme of concerts and plays (mid-March to Dec; most tickets $30–40) and hosts the Summer Theatre Festival of contemporary music and Canadian-oriented drama (July & Aug).

Mahone Bay

Just 25km southwest of Chester, **MAHONE BAY** lines the Atlantic seashore, its elongated waterfront dominated by three adjacent **church towers**, which combine to create one of the region's most famous vistas: **Trinity United Church** (1861); **St John's Lutheran Church** (1903), with its ornate woodwork ceiling designed to resemble the inside of a ship's hull; and the Gothic Revival **St James Anglican Church** (1887).

5

Mahone Bay Museum

578 Main St • May to early Sept daily 10am–4pm (rest of year by appointment) • Free • ☏ 902 624 6263, ⓦ mahonebaymuseum.com

Founded in 1754 by "Foreign Protestants" (aka German and Swiss settlers from Lunenburg), there's not much to see in Mahone Bay today, though you might drop by the **Mahone Bay Museum** to examine its hotchpotch of period furniture, early nineteenth-century ceramics and displays on the early Protestant founders.

INFORMATION   MAHONE BAY

Mahone Bay Visitor Information Centre 165 Edgewater St, on the northern side of town on Rte-3, just off Hwy-103 exit 10 (daily: mid-May to June & Oct 10am–5pm; July & Aug 9.30am–7pm; Sept 10am–6pm; ☏ 902 624 6151, ⓦ mahonebay.com).

Parking You'll find plenty of free parking along the waterfront near the churches.

ACCOMMODATION

Heart's Desire B&B 686 Main St ☏ 902 624 8470, ⓦ heartsdesirebb.com. This well-tended B&B occupies an attractive 1922 "classic four-square" home with pleasant views out across the bay. $120

★ **Kip & Kaboodle Backpacker Hostel** Mader's Cove, 9466 Rte-3 ☏ 902 531 5494, ⓦ kiwikaboodle.com. This cosy hostel, 3.5km south of Mahone Bay, is an excellent budget option, charging just $30 for dorm beds (shared bath) with free breakfast, and shuttle into Lunenburg and Mahone Bay. Dorms $30; doubles $65

EATING AND DRINKING

★ **Biscuit Eater Café & Books** 16 Orchard St ☏ 902 624 2665, ⓦ thebiscuiteater.com. This friendly, alternative café in the oldest building in Mahone Bay (circa 1775) combines new and used books, free wi-fi, good coffee, light meals (from $12) and sublime oat cakes. Early May to early Nov Mon–Sat 9am–4pm, Sun 10am–3pm; early Nov to early May Wed–Sun 9.30am–4.30pm.

Jo-Ann's Deli, Market & Bakeshop 9 Edgewater St ☏ 902 624 6305, ⓦ joannsdelimarket.ca. Deli-cum-café *Jo-Ann's*, beside the main crossroads, sells a superb selection of fishcakes, lobster sandwiches, baguettes, muffins, cookies and sumptuous fruit pies. Early May to Oct daily 9am–7pm (July & Aug to 8pm Thurs–Sat).

Mug & Anchor 643 Main St ☏ 902 624 6378, ⓦ themugandanchorpubltd.com. For a beer or meal on the waterfront, aim for this congenial pub, with over 18 local and imported beers on tap and a menu of seafood, steaks and burgers (mains $12–24). Mon–Sat 11am–midnight, Sun noon–9pm.

Lunenburg

Comely **LUNENBURG**, 10km south of Mahone Bay, perches on a narrow, bumpy peninsula, its central gridiron of streets clambering up from the main harbourfront flanked by elegant churches and candy-coloured wooden houses. Dating from the late nineteenth century, the most flamboyant of these mansions display an arresting variety of architectural features from Gothic towers and classical pillars to elegant verandas and the so-called "**Lunenburg Bump**", where triple-bell cast roofs surmount overhanging window dormers, giving the town a vaguely European appearance – which is appropriate considering it was founded in 1753 by German and Swiss settlers, dubbed the "Foreign Protestants", on invitation of the British in Halifax. Starting out as farmers, they eventually created a prosperous community of fishermen with its own fleet of trawlers and scallop-draggers, though today the only fishing done here is for lobster; and since being declared a UNESCO World Heritage Site in 1995 the town earns far more from the tourist industry.

Fisheries Museum of the Atlantic

68 Bluenose Drive • Mid-May to June & Sept to mid-Oct daily 9.30am–5pm; July & Aug daily 9.30am–5.30pm • $12 (parking $4/hr or $20/day) • ☏ 902 643 4794, ⓦ fisheriesmuseum.novascotia.ca

Just about every visitor to Lunenburg eventually ends up at the pride and joy of the town, the **Fisheries Museum of the Atlantic**, housed in an old fish-processing plant by the quayside. The museum has an excellent aquarium, a room devoted to whales and whaling and displays on fishing and boat-building techniques. Another section explains the history of the locally built 1920s schooner **Bluenose** and its replica **Bluenose II** (see below), while the "August Gales" display has wondrous tales of mountainous seas and helmsmen tied to the mast to stop being swept overboard. Moored by the jetty, there's a trawler and a scalloper, but the real highlight is the **Theresa E. Connor**, a saltbank fishing **schooner** launched in 1938. Superbly restored, the schooner was one of the last boats of its type to be built, a two-masted vessel constructed to a design that had changed little since the early eighteenth century.

Bluenose II

68 Bluenose Drive • Cruises April–Sept 9.30–11.30am & 1.30–3.30pm (when in port) • $64 • ☎ 902 634 8483, ⓦ bluenose.novascotia.ca

Unless it's out for a tour, the schooner **Bluenose II** should be moored at the wharf adjacent to the Fisheries Museum. The original *Bluenose*, whose picture is on the 10¢ coin, was famed throughout Canada as the fastest vessel of its kind in the 1920s, although she ended her days ingloriously as a freighter, foundering off Haiti in 1946. The 1960s replica has spent years as a floating standard-bearer for Nova Scotia, based in Lunenburg, and embarks on a very popular cruise programme every summer.

Knaut-Rhuland House Museum

125 Pelham St • Early June to Aug Mon–Sat 11am–5pm, Sun noon–4pm; Sept daily noon–4pm • Free • ☎ 902 634 3498, ⓦ lunenburgheritagesociety.ca.

To take a peek inside an old Lunenburg home, visit the **Knaut-Rhuland House Museum**, a Georgian-style house built around 1793 for wealthy merchant Benjamin Knaut, and now staffed by guides dressed in period clothing. Free tours shed light on the bits and pieces on display (working spinning wheels, some rare old German Bibles and antique furnishings). Take time also to view the exhibition room upstairs, which chronicles the history of the house and the town (Conrad Rhuland became the second owner in 1813), including the notorious **Sack of Lunenburg** in 1782 by US privateers from Boston.

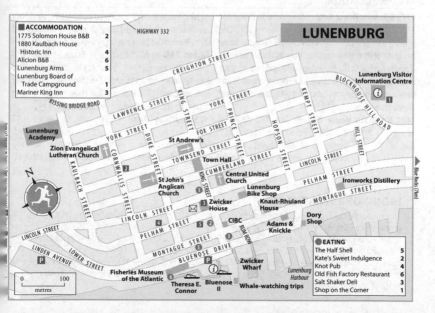

5

St John's Anglican Church

81 Cumberland St • May & early Sept to early Oct Sat & Sun noon–4pm; June to early Sept daily 10am–7pm • Donation $2 • ☎ 902 634 4994, ⓦ stjohnslunenburg.org

Lunenburg's most elegant building, **St John's Anglican Church**, whose original oak frame was imported from Boston in 1754, burnt down in 2001. It was faithfully rebuilt four years later – a superb illustration of decorative Gothic, its frilly wooden scrollwork punctuated by slender pinnacles that poke up from every one of its facades. The Anglicans seem to have stimulated the other religious communities in town, with all the major churches erected nearby: the **Zion Evangelical Lutheran Church** (65 Fox St; July & Aug Mon–Fri 10am–4pm; free; ☎ 902 634 4383) dates from 1891 and boasts a grand Victorian Gothic style, from its pointed windows to its soaring spire.

ARRIVAL AND DEPARTURE   LUNENBURG

By car Parking on the waterfront (next to the museum) costs $4 per hour; you can also find spaces (2hr free Mon–Fri 8am–6pm) on Linden Ave, just before the Fisheries Museum, and at the far end of Bluenose Drive. Most of the central street spaces in town are metered ($0.50/30min,

$1/1hr; 2–4hr maximum, Mon–Sat 10am–5pm).
By shuttle There is no public transport to Lunenburg, but Kiwi Kaboodle (☎ 866 549 4522, ⓦ novascotiatours andtravel.com) runs between Halifax and Chester, Mahone Bay and Lunenburg for $140.

INFORMATION AND ACTIVITIES

Visitor centre The Lunenburg Visitor Information Centre (daily: late May to Sept 9am–5pm; ☎ 902 634 8100, ⓦ lunenburgns.com) occupies an imitation blockhouse at 11 Blockhouse Hill Rd, a stiff 700m walk up from the harbourfront (driving you can follow the signs on Hwy-332 to avoid the town centre). It operates a free room-reservation service – especially useful in high season. There's a smaller, more convenient information kiosk on the waterfront (open similar hours).

Bike rental You can rent bikes from the Lunenburg Bike Shop (Tues–Sun 10am–5pm; $25/half-day, $40/full day; ☎ 902 521 6115, ⓦ lunenburgbikeshop.com) at 151 Montague St.
Whale-watching Two- to three-hour whale-watching cruises operate four times daily from May to October via Lunenburg Whale Watching Tours (☎ 902 527 7175, ⓦ novascotiawhalewatching.com; $58).

ACCOMMODATION

1775 Solomon House B&B 69 Townsend St ☎ 902 634 3477, ⓦ bbcanada.com/5511.html; map p.341. Clad in cedar shingles, this eighteenth-century Georgian house has many of its original features, from its double entrance stairway outside to the plank floors within. There are three guest rooms, bedecked with period furniture, antiques, and bathrooms with claw-foot tubs. The freshly baked scones at breakfasts are fabulous. **$135**
1880 Kaulbach House Historic Inn 75 Pelham St ☎ 902 634 8818, ⓦ kaulbachhouse.com; map p.341. One of the best preserved of Lunenburg's Victorian mansions, this comfortable inn, with its brightly painted

exterior, has seven well-appointed guest rooms, most with sea views and all decorated in an attractive version of period style. The creative European breakfasts are delicious. **$180**
Alicion B&B 66 McDonald St, at Green St ☎ 902 634 9358, ⓦ alicionbb.com; map p.341. Located a few minutes' drive from the central gridiron, this splendidly well-preserved 1911 mansion has three gorgeous guest rooms kitted out in a pleasing Edwardian style. **$149**
★ **Lunenburg Arms** 94 Pelham St ☎ 902 640 4040, ⓦ eden.travel; map p.341. Centrally located, boutique hotel with a maritime theme and 24 rooms (most overlooking the harbour) equipped with cable TV,

---

IRONWORKS DISTILLERY

To buy bottles of locally produced spirits (and the only rum made in Nova Scotia), visit **Ironworks Distillery**, thick with the aroma of distilled molasses. It also makes Annapolis apple vodka, and a rich apple brandy, aged in Hungarian oak barrels (local fruit supplies the liqueurs). Follow your nose to the 1893 Blacksmith's Shop, 2 Kempt St (Jan–March Thurs–Sat noon–5pm; April Thurs–Sun noon–5pm; May to mid-June & mid-Sept to Dec daily noon–5pm; mid-June to mid-Sept daily 10am–7pm; ☎ 902 640 2424, ⓦ ironworksdistillery.com). **Tours** ($15) of the distillery run daily at various times June–Dec.

hardwood floors and fluffy bathrobes. There's also a fancy spa on-site, Spa at Ninety4. **$154**

Lunenburg Board of Trade Campground 11 Blockhouse Hill Rd ☎ 902 634 8100, �🌐lunenburgns.com; map p.341. Plain campground with 55 pitches next door to the visitor centre on Blockhouse Hill. Water and free hot showers, plus free wi-fi. Great views – and big winds. Mid-May to early Oct. Unserviced **$36.80**; serviced **$52.90**

★ **Mariner King Inn** 15 King St ☎902 634 8509, ⓦmarinerking.com; map p.341. Built in 1830 bang in the centre of town, the luxurious *Mariner King* features oodles of stripped wood and crisply modern furnishings and fittings. Five pleasant guest rooms, all with wall-mounted TVs, fancy coffee-makers and claw-foot baths. The gourmet breakfast is included. **$155**

EATING

The Half Shell 108 Montague St ☎902 634 8503; map p.341. High-quality seafood served on an outdoor deck with fabulous views – everything from steamed mussels ($9) and fresh oysters ($3), to rich chowder ($12) and scallop carbonara ($18). Closes if it rains or is too cold! Late May to Sept daily noon–9pm (July & Aug noon–midnight).

★ **Kate's Sweet Indulgence** 242B Lincoln St ☎902 640 3399, ⓦsweetindulgence.ca; map p.341. *Kate's* knocks out the best salt cod fish cakes (from $10), as well as decent coffees and pastries (from $2.50). Free wi-fi. Mon–Fri 7.30am–6pm, Sat & Sun 8.30am–6pm (closes 5pm daily Oct–April).

Knot Pub 4 Dufferin St ☎ 902 634 3334, ⓦtheknotpub.ca; map p.341. Quirky wooden shack with cosy oak and brass interior serving delicious potato skins ($7), fish chowder ($9.50), seafood and salads (mains $6–17). Mon–Sat 10am–1am, Sun noon–1am.

★ **Old Fish Factory Restaurant** 68 Bluenose Drive ☎902 634 3333, ⓦoldfishfactory.com; map p.341.

This seafood place has long been considered the prime spot on the waterfront, but although it still serves a splendid range of fish and shellfish (and seafood chowder $9–12), it's a little canteen-like. Favourites include the Lunenburg fish fry ($26) and the local scallops ($25). Mid-May to mid-Oct daily 11am–9pm (July & Aug till 9.30pm).

Salt Shaker Deli 124 Montague St ☎902 640 3434, ⓦsaltshakerdeli.com; map p.341. A great standby in an 1863 clapboard with excellent views across the harbour, Propeller draught beers (brewed in Halifax), salads, Indian Point mussels, smoked seafood chowder and justly popular pizza ($12.50–17.50): try the seafood version or the Stinky Charlie's (garlic). Daily 11am–9pm.

Shop on the Corner 263 Lincoln St, at King ☎902 634 3434; map p.341. Easily the best place for a caffeine fix, this shop and coffee specialist sells Laughing Whale blends (roasted next door using only organically grown beans) and a tempting selection of snacks and pastries; try the oatcakes. Mon–Fri 8.30am–5pm, Sat 9am–5pm, Sun 10am–5pm.

Liverpool

Like its British namesake, **LIVERPOOL**, 70km from Lunenburg along Hwy-103, skirts the mouth of a Mersey River and has a strong seafaring tradition, but there the similarities end. Nova Scotia's Liverpool was founded in 1759 by New England emigrants enticed by free land, who later established a fearsome reputation for privateering during both the American Revolution and the War of 1812. The fine old houses grouped around the eastern end of **Main Street** are evidence of the prosperity this created, also commemorated by the gargantuan maritime-themed **murals** on Water Street. Those glory days are long gone, however; today the town has a population of under three thousand, with the closure of the **Bowater Paper Mill** in 2012 – once Liverpool's largest employer – an especially devastating blow.

Perkins House Museum

105 Main St • June to mid-Oct Mon–Sat 9.30am–5.30pm, Sun 1–5.30pm • $5 with Queens County Museum • ☎ 902 354 4058, ⓦ perkinshouse.novascotia.ca

Touring colonial homes can get a little monotonous in this part of Canada (having the term "sleep tight" explained for the tenth time, for example), but thanks to holographic "ghosts" **Perkins House Museum** offers a fresher approach. Note that the museum was closed for structural repairs and should reopen in 2019.

The pinewood house was completed in 1767 for **Simeon Perkins** (1735–1812), who moved here from Connecticut. Perkins became a shipowner, a merchant, a justice of the court and colonel in the militia; after initial sympathy for the American

5

MI'KMAQ ROOTS AT KEJIMKUJIK

Kejimkujik National Park has always been important to the local **Mi'kmaq** (also spelled Mi'kmaw here) community, with the "Connect with Mi'kmaw culture" programmes from the Acadia First Nation offering an illuminating glimpse into native traditions and myth. The one-hour "Mi'kmaw Encampment - Wejisqalia'ti'k" programme includes stories and songs and roasting *lu'sknikn* (a traditional bread) over an open campfire (July & Aug Mon, Tues & Fri 2pm, Sat 7pm; free with admission) at Merrymakedge. Mi'kmaq interpreters also offer guided tours (July to early Sept daily; free with admission; call ☎ 902 682 2772 for tour dates and times) of some of the park's 500-plus lakeside petroglyphs; carvings range from porpoise hunts and sail-rigged canoes to traditional clothing and adornments (humans have been living here for at least six thousand years). Birch Bark Canoe Building Workshops ($65) and Kejimkujik Lake Yoga ($22) are also offered. If you stay on a Saturday night be sure to participate in the various **Dark Sky Discovery** programmes, where interpreters connect legends and stories to a sensational view of the night sky.

Revolution, he became a dedicated Loyalist, leading the defence of the town against marauding New England privateers. He's best remembered today for his detailed and revealing **diary**. Copies of this four-volume work are on display inside, but it has also provided the basis for the "ghosts" of Perkins and his family (holographs of actors), enhancing the period rooms with their musings about life in the eighteenth century.

Queens County Museum

109 Main St • June to mid-Oct Mon–Sat 9am–5pm, Sun 1–5pm; mid-Oct to May Mon–Sat 9am–4.30pm • By donation • ☎ 902 354 4058, ⓦ queenscountymuseum.com

Just behind Perkins House lies the **Queens County Museum**, crammed with an eclectic ensemble of curios and artefacts which chronicle the history of the region from the Mi'kmaq to the world wars – old muskets, bank notes, cameras and minke whale bones included, as well as Simeon Perkins' original diaries (see page 343).

Fort Point Lighthouse

21 Fort Lane • June to early Oct Tues–Sun • Free • ☎ 902 354 3456

Built in 1855 overlooking Liverpool Harbour, **Fort Point Lighthouse** is a quirky wood and shingle structure 500m northeast of Perkins House. You can climb to the tiny tower and toot the foghorn, watch a short video narrated by the last lighthouse keeper's son, Bert McLeod, and grab a coffee and blueberry muffin at the on-site café. Tasty **Lighthouse Picnic Lunches** are also offered daily (11am–5pm; order at the lighthouse or Lane's Privateer Inn, see below).

INFORMATION   LIVERPOOL

Visitor centre On the waterfront at 32 Henry Hensey Drive (May–Oct daily 10am–6pm, open till 7pm July & Aug; ☎ 902 354 5421, ⓦ regionofqueens.com), where you can also park for free and use the wi-fi.

ACCOMMODATION AND EATING

Lane's Privateer Inn 27 Bristol Ave ☎ 902 354 3456, ⓦ lanesprivateerinn.wordpress.com. Just across the bridge from the centre of town, this inn occupies a spick-and-span, two-storey, motel-like structure built in the general style of an old timber house, with 27 guest rooms in the annexe. The inn is also the best place to eat, either in the restaurant (Mon–Fri 7am–10pm, Sat & Sun 8am–10pm), where well-prepared steak and seafood dishes cost $15–28, or in the adjoining bar, which serves good coffees, teas and gourmet treats, including handmade Belgian chocolates. **$120**

Kejimkujik National Park

50km south of Annapolis Royal • Park entrance mid-May to mid-Oct $5.80; mid-Oct to mid-May free

There's no better way to experience the solitude and scenery of Nova Scotia's hinterland than to head northwest 70km from Liverpool along Rte-8 to **Kejimkujik**

National Park. This magnificent tract of rolling wilderness, especially spectacular during the autumn foliage season, has a rich variety of forest habitat, interrupted by rivers and brooks linking about a dozen lakes; the main activities here are **kayaking**, **biking** and **canoeing**. In the spring and autumn the park is alive with wildflowers, whose brilliant colours provide cover for an abundance of porcupine, black bear, white-tailed deer and beaver, as well as three types of turtle. The best time to visit is in the early spring and autumn, when the insects aren't too troublesome: blackflies peak between mid-May and late June.

Exploring the park

Hiking trails crisscross Kejimkujik, but the easiest way to explore the park and its flat-water rivers and lakes is by **canoe**. A couple of clearly defined, day-long canoe trips begin at Jakes Landing, namely the delightful paddle among the islets of Kejimkujik Lake and an excursion up the Mersey River beneath a canopy of red maple.

INFORMATION AND ACTIVITIES   KEJIMKUJIK NATIONAL PARK

Visitor reception centre Near the park entrance (late June to Aug daily 8.30am–8pm; mid-May to late June & Sept–Oct Mon–Thurs 8.30am–4.30pm, Fri 8.30am–7pm, Sat & Sun 8.30am–6pm; ☎ 902 682 2772, ⊕ pc.gc.ca/en/pn-np/ns/kejimkujik); it has detailed maps and dispense trail advice.

Canoes, kayaks and bikes Canoes and kayaks can be rented from Keji Outfitters at Jakes Landing (mid-May to mid-Oct; $12–17/hr, $32–55/day; ☎ 902 682 2282, ⊕ whynotadventure.ca; reservations recommended), roughly 10km by road from the entrance to the park (there's a shuttle service throughout the park, with most trips $7–30). The same company also rents bikes for $40/day and 4-person tents ($17/night).

ACCOMMODATION

Jeremys Bay Campground ☎ 877 737 3783, ⊕ reservation.pc.gc.ca. The large park campground, some 10km from the main entrance, has clean washrooms, hot showers and internet (services May–Oct only). There are also fifty primitive campsites (reservations ☎ 902 682 2772) dotted along its canoe routes and hiking trails (get a free backcountry camping permit at the visitor centre), and posher

oTENTik cabins ($100). Unserviced $25.50; serviced $29.40

Whitman Inn 12389 Rte-8, Kempt ☎ 902 682 2226, ⊕ whitmaninn.com. If camping isn't your thing, the nearest beds are at the frayed but friendly *Whitman*, 2km south of the park entrance on Rte-8, with eight cosy rooms and even a small indoor pool. Add $8.50 for breakfast, $9 for packed lunch. $79

Kejimkujik's Seaside Adjunct

Southwest from Liverpool on Hwy-103, it's about 25km to tiny **Port Joli**, from where a bumpy, 6.5km-long gravel road leads to **St Catherine's River** and the more accessible, western side of **Kejimkujik National Park Seaside Adjunct** (information kiosk mid-June to mid-Oct 9.30am–5.30pm; free), a 22-square-kilometre parcel of pristine coastline that provides an ideal half-day or day's hike. The Adjunct straddles the end of a beautiful but inhospitable peninsula where the mixed forests and squelchy bogs of the interior back onto the tidal flats, lagoons, headlands and beaches of the coast. From the parking lot, the **Harbour Rocks Trail** follows the route of an old cart track straight down to the seashore, a fairly straightforward if sometimes wet and muddy 5.2km (return) hike. There are no facilities, so carry food and water.

Shelburne

Founded in 1783 by United Empire Loyalists (see page 329) – including two hundred freed black slaves – fleeing the American Revolution, historic **SHELBURNE** lies 70km southwest of Liverpool on Hwy-103. Once a major **shipbuilding** centre, the town's fine clapboard houses and shingle wharf buildings have been preserved in the pristine **Historic District** that strings down from **Water Street**, the main drag, to **Dock Street** and the waterfront. The biggest and most striking buildings on Dock Street are in fact the only fakes: the **Cox Building** (dating to the early twentieth century) was modified to look

5

BIRCHTOWN AND THE BOOK OF NEGROES

At the end of the American Revolutionary War in 1783, former black slaves who had fought for the British – on the condition they be freed – were shipped to New Brunswick and Nova Scotia, ostensibly to be settled as free men and women. The largest group (some 3000) came to Shelburne, where they were promptly shunted off to the rocky, worthless land at nearby **Birchtown**. Most were soon signed up as indentured servants to the Loyalists in Shelburne – essentially another form of slavery. Having suffered the largest race riot in Canadian history in 1784 and years of abuse, most of the ex-slaves sailed back to Africa in 1792, founding Freetown in Sierra Leone. Some were forced to stay, however, establishing a community that exists to this day. Learn about their story at the **Black Loyalist Heritage Centre** (the original was torched by arsonists in 2006) off Rte-3 in Birchtown (119 Old Birchtown Rd), 7km west of Shelburne; it's open June to mid-Oct daily 10am to 5pm, and mid-Oct to May Mon–Fri 9am–4pm (☎902 875 1293, ⓦblackloyalist.novascotia.ca and ⓦblackloyalist.com; $9.20). The shop sells copies of Lawrence Hill's excellent *Book of Negroes*, named after the register all those "freed" slaves had to sign in New York before travelling to Canada. You can also visit *St Paul's Church* and *Old School House* (which houses the Bunce Island exhibit and movie), and stroll the Heritage Trail to the *Pit House*.

---

like a church and the **Guild Hall** behind it was built from scratch to mimic a seventeenth-century market hall when the movie **Scarlet Letter** was filmed here in 1994.

Shelburne County Museum

20 Dock St • June to mid-Oct daily 9.30am–5.30pm; mid-Oct to May Wed–Sat 9am–1pm & 2–5pm • $4; joint ticket with Dory Shop Museum and Ross-Thomson House $10 • ☎902 875 3219, ⓦshelburnemuseums.com

The best place to start a tour of the town is **Shelburne County Museum**, which provides a broad overview of the region's history and its maritime heritage (pride of place goes to Canada's oldest fire pumper, made in London in 1740).

Ross-Thomson House

9 Charlotte Lane • June to mid-Oct daily 9.30am–5.30pm • $4; joint ticket with Dory Shop Museum and Shelburne County Museum $10 • ☎902 875 3219, ⓦshelburnemuseums.com

The clapboard **Ross-Thomson House** is a Loyalist merchant's store and home that originally opened in 1785, making it the oldest restored wooden shop in all North America (it finally closed in 1880). The creaky interior has been kitted out with sales goods and furniture circa 1820s.

Dory Shop Museum

11 Dock St • June to mid-Oct daily 9.30am–5.30pm • $4; joint ticket with Ross-Thomson House and Shelburne County Museum $10 • ☎902 875 3219, ⓦshelburnemuseums.com

Housed in an ageing waterfront boat factory, the **Dory Shop Museum** is a monument to Shelburne's most successful industry. The flat-bottomed **dory**, rarely more than 5m long and built to ride the heaviest of swells, was an integral part of the fishing fleet during the days of sail – production began in earnest here in the 1880s. Master dory builder Milford Buchanan still produces three a year, but only for private use – the few dories used today in the offshore fishery are steel-hulled.

INFORMATION   SHELBURNE

Visitor centre 43 Dock St (times vary, sometimes closing for lunch; May, June & Sept Mon–Fri 9am–5pm, Sat 10am–4pm, Sun noon–5pm; July & Aug daily 9am–7pm; ☎902 875 4547, ⓦshelburneandlockeport.com); operates a free room-reservation service and has free wi-fi.

ACCOMMODATION AND EATING

Beandock Coffee 10 John St/30 Dock St ☎902 875 1302. For coffee, cookies, Skor bar squares or tasty light lunches ($6.95–13.95) try *Beandock*, with tables inside and out. May–Sept Mon–Thurs 8.30am–8pm, Fri 8.30am–

5pm, Sat 10am–4pm, Sun 10am–2pm (reduced hours Oct–April).

★ **Charlotte Lane Café** 13 Charlotte Lane ☎ 902 875 3314, ⓦ charlottelane.ca. Just off Water St, this is one of the most enticing restaurants in the region, with pricey but exceptionally good pastas ($21.95), salads, seafood and Swiss-inspired specialities (dinner mains $20–42) from Chef Roland Glauser. Mid-May to late Dec Tues–Sat 11.30am–2.30pm & 5–8pm.

Cooper's Inn 36 Dock St ☎ 902 875 4656, ⓦ thecoopers inn.com. The most agreeable hotel in town occupies a lavishly refurbished old shingle house dating back to 1784, with cosy, period-style rooms and huge breakfasts. April–Oct. **$130**

Sea Dog Saloon 1 Dock St ☎ 902 875 2862, ⓦ thesea dog.com. The best place for a drink is the outdoor deck of this waterside pub, which also sells live lobsters, has free wi-fi and rents kayaks ($45/day). Mon–Sat 11am–8pm, open till 2am Fri & Sat.

Côtes acadiennes: West Pubnico

Just south of Hwy-103 and 60km west of Shelburne, **West Pubnico**, part of the **Côtes acadiennes** ("Acadian Shores"; see page 349), is home to an especially tenacious group of Acadians, most of whom eventually returned to their lands here in Nova Scotia after the deportations of the 1750s. The town was founded in 1653 by **Philippe Mius d'Entremont** (1609–99) – his surname is by far the most common around here today.

Musée des Acadiens des Pubnicos

898 Rte-335, West Pubnico • Mid-May to Aug Mon–Sat 9am–5pm; Sept & Oct Mon–Fri 12.30–4.30pm • $4 • ☎ 902 762 3380, ⓦ museeacadien.ca

Get a taster of a traditional Acadian homestead at the **Musée des Acadiens des Pubnicos**, where costumed guides explain the period bits and pieces on display: a French millstone (which may have belonged to d'Entremont), old toys, a Mi'kmaq feather fan made in 1850 and traditional Acadian kitchen tools and furniture. There's even a chunk of the original Pubnico *aboiteau* (wooden dyke), and the town's first printing press (1937). The red clapboard-and-shingle house dates from 1864.

Village Historique Acadien de la Nouvelle-Écosse

91 Old Church Rd (off Rte-335, Lower West Pubnico • June–Sept daily 9am–5pm • $8 • ☎ 902 762 2530, ⓦ levillage.novascotia.ca

A few kilometres south of the Musée des Acadiens (10.3km south of Hwy-103) is the more comprehensive **Village Historique Acadien de la Nouvelle-Écosse**, where a cluster of nineteenth-century Acadian homes from the region has been collected to act as a living museum re-creating the early 1900s. Each building is manned by costumed guide or artisan, happy to chat and provide background (in English): the girls in the Charles Duon House bake molasses cookies, while traditional crafts are on display in the blacksmith's, ship-making and net-making shacks. It's an evocative location, on a headland overlooking Pubnico harbour.

EATING WEST PUBNICO

Râpure d'Eon's 697 Rte-335, West Pubnico ☎ 902 762 2312, ⓦ deonsrappiepie.com. Get your fix of Rappie Pie (traditional Acadian meat pie made from grated potatoes or *patates râpées*) at this small takeaway (which has roots in 1927), with standard ready-cooked pies from $7.99 – ideally you'll need somewhere to heat these up later. Mon–Fri 6.30am–5pm.

Yarmouth

Founded in 1761 by settlers from Massachusetts, **YARMOUTH** boomed in the nineteenth century thanks to shipping, the cache of grand Victorian homes scattered around the town testimony to its once great wealth. Though it remains the largest settlement on the South Shore, these days the centre is an unassuming, workaday place, though gallant efforts have been made to freshen up the harbourfront.

5

THE MAINE FERRY

The troubled **Yarmouth-to-Maine (US) ferry** resumed after a five-year break in 2014, only to fold within two years due to lack of customers; in 2016 *Bay Ferries* (☎877 762 7245, ⓦ ferries.ca/thecat) started operating *The Cat,* a high-speed catamaran that speeds between Yarmouth and Portland in just 5hr 30min. One-way rates start at around US$80 per adult (June & mid-Sept–Oct), to $107 July to mid-Sept; discounts are available for returns. You'll pay another $149–199 for a standard car (one-way). Ferries only sail June to mid-October, departing daily from Yarmouth (58 Water St) in the morning and returning from Maine in the afternoon (check the website for the latest schedule). Note that from 2019, The Cat is likely to travel between *Yarmouth* and *Bar Harbor* (still in Maine, but 240km north of Portland, meaning a faster crossing).

Art Gallery of Nova Scotia, Western Branch

341 Main St • Thurs noon–8pm, Fri–Sun noon–5pm • $6 (free Thurs 5–8pm) • ☎ 902 749 2248, ⓦ artgalleryofnovascotia.ca

Efforts to brighten the appeal of Main Street are centred on the **Art Gallery of Nova Scotia, Western Branch**, which displays pieces from the main collection in Halifax (see page 329) over two floors of small but well-presented galleries. The gallery occupies the stately Royal Bank of Canada building, completed in 1913.

W. Laurence Sweeney Fisheries Museum

112 Water St • Mid-May to mid-Oct Mon–Sat 10am–5pm • $3 • ☎ 902 742 3457, ⓦ sweeneyfisheriesmuseum.ca

The **W. Laurence Sweeney Fisheries Museum** has preserved some of the actual wharf buildings and shacks that once dominated the Yarmouth waterfront, crammed with all sorts of fishing and sailing paraphernalia going back to the 1920s. Sweeney was once one of Yarmouth's biggest employers, but closed in 1994.

Cape Forchu Lightstation

1856 Cape Forchu (Rte-304) • Late May to Sept daily 9am–5pm (Fri to 7pm) • Free • ☎ 902 742 4522, ⓦ capeforchulight.com

A winding 11km around the harbour from Yarmouth stands windswept **Cape Forchu Lightstation** aka the Yarmouth Light, an iconic "applecore" shape lighthouse completed in 1962 at a height of 23m. The site includes a small museum, gift shop and *The Keeper's Kitchen* (Tues–Sun 11am–7pm), but even if these are closed you can wander the grounds, read the interpretive boards and soak up the views of fishing skiffs and rolling waves.

ARRIVAL AND INFORMATION   YARMOUTH

By shuttle bus Mariner Shuttle (☎855 586 6140, ⓦ marinershuttle.co) runs between Halifax and Yarmouth via the Annapolis Valley daily, departing the Yarmouth area 7am–7.30am, and heading back from Halifax and the airport 1–3pm ($80; cash only). Cloud Nine Shuttle (☎902 742 3992, ⓦ thecloudnineshuttle.com) also runs to Yarmouth (1 daily; 4hr; $75; $80 from the airport).

Visitor centre The regional Nova Scotia Visitor Information Centre (June to mid-Oct daily 9am–5pm, closes 7pm July & Aug; ☎902 742 5033) is at 228 Main St, just uphill from the ferry terminal, crammed with free leaflets and brochures.

ACCOMMODATION AND EATING

Comfort Inn 96 Starrs Rd ☎902 742 1119, ⓦ yarmouthcomfortinn.com This well-equipped chain, just off Rte-3 on the outskirts of town (3km from the centre), is the most popular option for drivers, with comfy rooms and free continental breakfast. **$180**

Lakelawn B&B & Motel 641 Main St ☎902 742 3588, ⓦ lakelawnmotel.com. This appealing B&B, a short drive from the ferry terminal, is a stately mansion built in 1864, with pleasant, antique-laden rooms in the main house (with cable TV; $139), and simpler efficiencies in the newer motel section. **$99**

Rudder's 96 Water St ☎902 742 7311, ⓦ ruddersbrewpub.com. The best place to eat and drink is *Rudder's* on the harbourfront, which has a patio, brews its own beer and serves decent lobster suppers. Daily 11am–midnight.

Côtes acadiennes: Baie Sainte-Marie

North from Yarmouth, Hwy-101 and the much slower Rte-1 slip across the flat coastline of the 50km **Baie Sainte-Marie** district, part of the **Côtes acadiennes** (Acadian Shores) whose straggling villages house the largest concentration of Acadians (see page 354) in the province, some eight to nine thousand. The best time to visit the region is late July or August, when the **Festival Acadien de Clare** (ⓦfestivalacadiendeclare.ca) features concerts, parades and special events celebrating Acadian culture.

Église Sainte-Marie

1713 Rte-1 • Mid-May to mid-Oct daily 9am–5pm • $2 donation • ☎ 902 769 2378, ⓦ museeeglisesaintemariemuseum.ca

At **POINTE-DE-L'ÉGLISE (Church Point)**, 65km from Yarmouth and right on the Bay of Fundy, is the massive **Église Sainte-Marie** whose soaring fairytale tower and steeple were finished in 1905 and reach a giddy 56m, making it the tallest wooden church in North America. The vast but simple interior is lined with vivid stained glass windows, while the **museum** section (to the right of the altar) holds a dusty collection of nineteenth-century vestments, religious artefacts, calvaries and statuary, all well labelled in English. Don't miss the box of medieval reliquaries beside the altar, among which are wooden shards purportedly from the Holy Cross and a lock of hair from St Bernadette.

Rendez-vous de la Baie

23 Lighthouse Rd, Université Sainte-Anne Campus (1695 Rte-1) • Mon–Fri 8am–6pm, Sat & Sun 9am–3pm (Oct–May Mon–Fri 8am–5pm) • Free • ☎ 902 769 2345, ⓦ rendezvousdelabaie.ca

Just across from the Église Sainte-Marie on the campus of the Université Sainte-Anne is the ultramodern **Rendez-vous de la Baie** cultural centre, containing the small Le Trécarré art gallery, gift shop, café, information centre and the excellent **Acadian Interpretive Centre & Museum**. Bilingual information boards and videos tell the history of the region beginning in the 1760s, when Acadians started to return after the deportations (see page 354). Special attention is paid to some of the more colourful characters (such as "Cy á Mateur", local drunk and womanizer thought to be in league with the devil), and there's an especially good section on contemporary Acadian culture.

EATING
POINTE-DE-L'ÉGLISE

Chez l'Ami 1730 Rte-1 ☎ 902 769 0001. You can eat cheaply at this food shack across the road from the church, selling gumbo, lobster *poutine*, old-fashioned ice cream, and even ice cream "pizza" (with brownie base). Most items $8–12. March–Dec daily 11am–10pm.

La Râpure Acadienne 1443 Rte-1 ☎ 902 769 2172. A local culinary gem just south of the village, where you can buy *râpure* to go ($9), a stodgy beef or chicken and potato concoction considered classic Acadian food, straight out of the oven. June–Sept daily 9am–5.30pm.

Digby

It's 42km from Pointe-de-l'Église to the fishing port of **DIGBY**, whose workaday centre spreads over a hilly headland that pokes out into the Annapolis Basin. The latter is connected to the Bay of Fundy by a narrow channel known as the **Digby Gut**, thereby subjecting Digby **harbour** to the swirling effects of the Fundy tides – and it's the pocket-sized harbour, with its rickety wooden piers, seafood restaurants and shops which is the most appealing part of town. Founded in 1783 by United Empire Loyalists led by Rear Admiral Sir Robert Digby, today the town is home to one of the world's largest **scallop** fleets.

Maud Lewis Memorial

If you've seen the "Painted House" of **Maud Lewis** at the Art Gallery of Nova Scotia in Halifax (see page 329), you might want to check out the poignant **Maud Lewis Memorial** on Hwy-101 in **Marshalltown**, just five minutes south of the Digby exit. The steel structure marks the spot where Maud lived and painted for 32 years; designed

5

by Brian MacKay-Lyons, it mimics the actual size of the house. It can be hard to spot: coming from Digby it's on the right side of the road at the sign for "Maud Lewis Lane" (it's a little tough to see coming in the other direction).

ARRIVAL AND INFORMATION   DIGBY

By car You can park along Water St (2hr; free), though spaces go fast in July and Aug.

By shuttle bus Kathleen's Shuttle, Mariner Shuttle and Cloud Nine Shuttle (see page 333) all run between Halifax and Digby via the Annapolis Valley in around 2hr 30min ($65–75 one way), leaving Digby around 9am and departing Halifax in the early afternoon. Local Kings Transit buses (Mon–Sat only; $3.50; ☎ 888 546 4442, ⊛ kbus.

ca) link Digby with Wolfville via Annapolis Royal, but this involves changing three times and takes around 4hr 20min.

By ferry Digby's ferry port is located 5km north of town; from here Bay Ferries (☎ 888 249 7245, ⊛ ferries.ca) runs regular car ferries (1–2 daily year-round; 3hr; adult passengers $38–48 one way, cars $111–116; bicycles $10) across the Bay of Fundy to Saint John, New Brunswick (see page 373), saving a long drive (around 6hr).

ACCOMMODATION

Bayside Inn 115 Montague Row ☎ 902 245 2247, ⊛ baysideinn.ca. This bargain inn occupies a nineteenth-century clapboard house on the bayfront, with ten cosy rooms (seven en suite), an airy patio, breakfast and gorgeous views. May to mid-Oct. Shared bath $105; private bath $120

★ **Harbourview Inn** 25 Harbourview Rd ☎ 902 245 5686, ⊛ theharbourviewinn.com. Just east of town on Hwy-1, this gorgeous B&B surrounded by gardens dates

back to 1899, rooms blending period decor with cable TV and a/c. May–Oct. $134

★ **Holdsworth House B&B** 36 Carleton St ☎ 866 643 1784, ⊛ holdsworthhousebandb.com. Canada's only "re-enactment" B&B is loads of fun, Tony, Margaret and the team setting up their B&B like a real eighteenth-century inn in the oldest house in Digby (built by Loyalist James Holdsworth c.1784); there are just three rooms (two en suite), with full breakfast included. $95

EATING

★ **Antonio's** 9066 Hwy-101, Brighton (Scotia Bay Motel) ☎ 902 245 5698. This no-frills diner just outside town has garnered a cult following in the province for its sumptuous haddock and chips ($13), scallops ($16) and clams ($14.50), as well as its pastas and pizzas. Mon–Fri 4–9pm, Sat & Sun noon–9pm.

The Fish Market 35 Birch St ☎ 902 245 6551. Digby is famed for two things: scallops and its smoked herring

or "Digby chicks", usually on sale at the north end of the harbour at this fish wholesaler, along with fresh haddock. Cash only. Mon–Fri 9am–5.30pm, Sat 9am–noon.

Fundy Restaurant 34 Water St ☎ 902 245 4950, ⊛ fundy restaurant.com. Digby's delicious scallops (seasonal prices, around $17) are the main event here, but fish and chips ($14), fried clams ($16) and a display of rare blue lobsters (live) are also a major plus. Daily 8.30am–8.30pm.

Digby Neck

Sheltering the Acadian Shore from the full effects of the ocean, the 70km-long **Digby Neck** is a narrow finger of land that gingerly nudges out into the Bay of Fundy south of Digby. The Neck's further reaches are broken into two little islands – **Long Island** and, at the tip, **Brier Island**, just 6.5km long and 2.5km wide – boasting tranquil hiking trails, two lighthouses and a seal colony, though most people only venture down here to join a **whale-watching trip** (see page 351). **Car ferries** shuttle across the narrow channels between the islands (5–10min), running every hour (seasonal and depends on traffic), 24hr a day and charging $7 each for the return trip (you only pay on the outward crossing). Ferry times are coordinated, so it takes about two hours to reach

---

GUY'S FRENCHYS

In 1972 the first **Guy's Frenchys** opened its doors in Digby (still at 343 Conway St, Hwy-303). Selling secondhand clothing was a relatively new concept in 1972, but the idea caught on and today Guy's is a local institution, with stores all over the Maritimes. Each store is open Mon–Fri 9am–9pm, Sat 9am–5pm, Sun noon–5pm; visit ⊛ guysfrenchys.com for the nearest branch.

DIGBY NECK WHALE-WATCHING

The nutrient-rich waters of the **Bay of Fundy** attract dozens of whales, and several local companies organize daily **whale-watching excursions** from **late May to mid-October**. Trips usually last between two and three hours, though those from Westport (Brier Island) tend to last longer – between three and five hours. No one can guarantee you'll spy a whale, but there's every chance, beginning with finback and minke in late spring, and humpback from mid- to late June. By the middle of July all three species are sighted and usually hang around the Bay of Fundy till late summer and autumn, which is when the rare North Atlantic right whale is seen.

Brier Island Whale & Seabird Cruises 223 Water St, Westport, Brier Island ☎ 902 839 2995, ⓦ brierislandwhalewatch.com. Variety of trips by boat ($50; 3–5hr) or Zodiac ($65; 2–3hr). **Mariner Cruises** 325 Water St, Westport, Brier Island ☎ 902 839 2346, ⓦ novascotiawhalewatching.ca.

Friendly competition is supplied by this local outfit, with trips at $49 (2hr 30min–4hr 30min). **Ocean Explorations Whale Cruises** Tiverton, Long Island ☎ 902 839 2417, ⓦ oceanexplorations.ca. On Long Island, this outfit only uses Zodiac boats, with tours from $85 (2hr 30min–3hr 30min) led by biologist Tom Goodwin.

Westport on Brier Island from Digby; ferry timetables are available at the Digby tourist office. The road along the Neck (Hwy-217) travels inland and is fairly monotonous, though make time for Long Island's premier attraction, **Balancing Rock**, some 4km from the ferry on Hwy-217; this soaring column of basalt lies at the end of a 1km trail that involves a scramble down 235 steps.

ACCOMMODATION AND EATING

DIGBY NECK

Brier Island Lodge 225 Water St, Westport, Brier Island ☎ 902 839 2273, ⓦ brierisland.com. Wonderfully located atop the cliffs, this friendly inn features en-suite rooms (some with hot-tubs ocean views and kitchenettes), on-site restaurant and TV lounge (no TVs in rooms). **$119**

Lighthouse Café 225 Water St, Westport, Brier Island ☎ 902 839 2273. Justly popular for its famous egg tarts, fish and chips ($12), scallops, shrimp and chowder. April–Oct daily 11am–8pm.

Annapolis Royal

With a population of just six hundred, **ANNAPOLIS ROYAL**, 40km northeast of Digby, spreads across a podgy promontory that lies tucked in between the Annapolis River and its tributary, the Allain River. The town maintains a relaxed and retiring air that's hard to resist, one that belies its turbulent past. Scots led by Sir William Alexander settled the district in 1629, but were forced to leave just three years later as part of an Anglo-French treaty. French forces occupied the town in 1636 (when it became the new Port Royal), and though subsequently it changed hands many times, this Acadian outpost prospered, even serving as the British capital of Nova Scotia after its capture in 1710 (Halifax assumed the role in 1749). The British – who had renamed the town again in honour of Queen Anne – finally expelled the Acadians in 1755, and the elegant wooden mansions you see today were built by Loyalist settlers in later years. Though its history may seem a little confusing, the current town is undeniably appealing, blessed with quality B&Bs, restaurants and antique shops.

Fort Anne National Historic Site

323 St George St • **Museum** late May to mid-June & mid-Sept to early Oct Tues–Sat 9am–5.30pm; mid-June to mid-Sept daily 9am–5.30pm • $3.90 • ⓦ pc.gc.ca • **Graveyard tours** June to mid-Oct daily 9.30pm • 1hr • $10 • ⓦ tourannapolisroyal.com

Edging St George Street just before it swings along the waterfront are the substantial remains of **Fort Anne National Historic Site** (open access), whose grass-covered ramparts date from 1702. A few military buildings remain inside, but the most significant survivor is the old **officers' quarters** in the centre. The British built these in 1797 and, surmounted by three outsized chimney stacks, they now house a small **museum**. Inside

5

there's a copy of the original charter by which James I incorporated "Nova Scotia" in 1621, and a cheerful community tapestry tracing the town's history. If you want more of the flavour of early Annapolis Royal, check-out the candlelight tours of the **old graveyard** next to the fort – they're good fun and a snip at the price.

Annapolis Royal Historic Gardens
441 St George St · Daily: May, June, Sept & Oct 9am–5pm; July & Aug 9am–8pm · $14.50 · ☎ 902 532 7018, ⓦ historicgardens.com

The **Annapolis Royal Historic Gardens** feature a string of enjoyable "theme gardens", from formal Victorian gardens to an extensive rose collection in which the different varieties are arranged broadly in chronological order. There's also **La Maison acadienne**, an authentic replica of an Acadian dwelling circa 1671. The whole site slopes gently down towards the Allain River, with a dyke-walk offering views of mudflats and salt marshes and also twisting through elephant grass, a reed imported by the Acadians to thatch their cottages.

ARRIVAL AND INFORMATION
ANNAPOLIS ROYAL

By shuttle bus Kathleen's Shuttle and Mariner Shuttle (see page 333) run between Halifax and Digby, and will stop at Annapolis Royal. Local Kings Transit buses (Mon–Sat only, every 2hr; $3.50) link Annapolis Royal with Digby and Wolfville.

Tidal Power Visitor Centre 236 Prince Albert Rd; on the other side of town, inside the tidal generating station on the Rte-1 bridge, about 1.4km north of the centre (daily: July & Aug 8am–8pm; mid-May to June & Sept to mid-Oct 10am–5pm; ☎ 902 532 5454).

ACCOMMODATION

Bread and Roses Inn 82 Victoria St ☎ 902 532 5727, ⓦ breadandroses.ns.ca. Well-tended inn, a late Victorian mansion completed in 1882 with canopy and antique beds in immaculate period rooms. May–Oct. **$139**

Dunromin Campground Granville Ferry ☎ 902 532 2808, ⓦ dunromincampground.ca. This well-equipped campsite, 1km beyond the tourist office on the far side of the Annapolis River, occupies a wooded, riverside location. Mid-May to mid-Oct. Tent sites (unserviced) **$30**; cabins **$70**

★ **Hillsdale House Inn** 519 St George St ☎ 902 532 2345, ⓦ hillsdalehouseinn.ca. The town's best accommodation options are its B&Bs, and this is one of the top choices, an elegant villa of 1859 with full breakfast and fifteen elegant rooms. **$142**

★ **Queen Anne Inn** 494 St George St ☎ 902 532 7850, ⓦ queenanneinn.ns.ca. This grand turreted and towered extravagance of the 1860s offers 12 fine rooms, en suite and kitted out in enchanting period style. May–Nov only. **$129**

EATING AND DRINKING

★ **Garrison Grill Restaurant** 350 St George St ☎ 902 532 5750, ⓦ garrisonhouse.ca. The best place for dinner, set in an old wooden house dating from 1854 and featuring local pan-fried haddock, Digby scallops with feta and

---

NOVA SCOTIAN WINE

The Annapolis Valley is Canada's up-and-coming wine destination – it's not the Rhône Valley of course, but these vineyards knock out some surprisingly decent vintages (tours May–Oct). See also ⓦ winesofnovascotia.ca.

Blomidon Estate Winery 10318 Hwy-221, Habitant ☎ 902 582 7565, ⓦ blomidonwine.ca. July–Oct Mon–Sat 10am–5pm, Sun 11am–5pm; tastings $8 (3 wines). Private tours from $300. Known for its very drinkable "Blow Me Down" blend of reds Leon Millot and Luci Kuhlmann.

Casa Nova Fine Beverages 2635 Clementsvale Rd, Bear River East ☎ 902 467 0363, ⓦ casanovafine beverages.com. Formerly Annapolis Highland Winery, Casa Nova Winery debuted in 2018, focusing on wines, craft ciders and cellos (fortified wines, made with local blueberries and strawberries), with complimentary vineyard and winery tours by pre-booking or by chance daily. June–Oct daily 10am–6pm.

Domaine de Grand Pré 11611 Rte-1 ☎ 902 542 7177, ⓦ grandprewines.ns.ca. See page 354.

Gaspereau Vineyards 2239 White Rock Rd, Gaspereau ☎ 902 542 1455, ⓦ gaspereauwine. ca. Offers tours (June–Sept; $8) and tastings ($7 for 3 wines). Daily: May & Oct 10am–5pm; June–Sept 10am–6pm; Nov–Dec Fri–Sun 10am–5pm.

5

WOLFVILLE FARMERS' MARKET

The orderly and well-heeled university town of **WOLFVILLE**, 110km northeast from Annapolis Royal, was originally called Mud Creek after the mudflats surrounding its tiny harbour. Today the town is best known for its **Farmers' Market** (ⓦ wolfvillefarmersmarket.ca), with more than 65 vendors (Wed 4–7pm; Sat 8.30am–1pm year-round at 24 Elm Ave).

lobster, as well as more standard but equally tasty meat dishes (mains $16–30). May–Nov daily 5.30–8.30pm.

Leo's Café 222 St George St ☎ 902 532 7424. There are several cafés along the town's waterfront, including this gem in a circa 1713 wood-framed house; it serves up first-rate snacks and lighter meals: try great sandwiches such as the curried chicken ($7.95) or Leo's "famous" veggie

sandwich ($7.50). June–Sept Mon–Sat 9am–8pm & Sun noon–5pm; Oct–May Mon–Sat 9am–4pm.

Ye Olde Towne Pub 9 Church St ☎ 902 532 2244. This olde-world pub – just down the street from *Leo's* and across from the boatyard – serves good draught beer but also great pub food, seafood chowders and Rappie Pie (the classic Acadian dish). Mon–Sat 11am–11pm, Sun noon–8pm.

Port-Royal National Historic Site

10.5km south of Rte-1, Granville Ferry • mid-June to mid-Sept daily 9am–5.30pm, mid-May to mid-June & mid-Sept to mid-Oct Tues–Sat 9am–5.30pm • $3.90 • ☎ 902 532 2898, ⓦ pc.gc.ca/en/lhn-nhs/ns/portroyal

In 1605, after their dreadful winter on the island of Saint-Croix in Passamaquoddy Bay, Samuel de Champlain and Pierre Sieur de Monts set up camp close to the current **Port-Royal National Historic Site**, on the north side of the Annapolis River – Nova Scotia's first European settlement. This was a commercial venture, not a colony or military installation; the hastily constructed **habitation**, designed by Champlain and similar to the fortified farms of France, was a square of rough-hewn, black-painted timber buildings where the French would trade with the Mi'kmaq for furs, particularly beaver pelts. Champlain left in 1607 (going on to found Québec), and the outpost was looted and destroyed by a party of desperate English colonists from Virginia in 1613.

The stronghold dominated the estuary from a low bluff, as does today's evocative **replica**, a painstaking reconstruction completed in 1940, relying solely on the building techniques of the early seventeenth century. Rooms inside have been furnished as they might have appeared at the time, with the Trading Room containing a selection of real beaver, timber wolf, bear, fox and raccoon hides.

Grand Pré National Historic Site

2241 Grand Pré Rd • Mid-May to mid-Oct daily 9am–5pm • $7.80 • ⓦ pc.gc.ca/en/lhn-nhs/ns/grandpre

The expulsion of the Acadians from Nova Scotia by the British in the 1750s is generally considered one of the darkest moments in Canadian history, which partly explains the reverence accorded the **Grand Pré National Historic Site**. Established in the 1680s, this Acadian village was totally destroyed in 1755; almost forgotten, the tragedy was dramatized by poet Henry Longfellow in 1847, when he chose Grand Pré as the setting for his epic poem **Evangeline – A Tale of Acadie**. The poem follows the star-crossed love of the fictional Evangeline for her Gabriel and, though horribly sentimental, it became extremely popular, turning the destruction of this particular community into a symbol of Acadian suffering and British callousness.

Displays in the visitor centre recount the history of the expulsions, but it's the multimedia presentation (every 30min) that really gets across just how devastating they were. Outside the site itself is a bit of an anticlimax – well-manicured gardens containing statues of Longfellow and Evangeline, and a memorial chapel built in 1922 displaying some vivid paintings of the expulsions. The most absorbing sights here are the ongoing archeological digs, which began in 2001; so far they have located the remains of a house next to the chapel, but as yet not the original church.

5

THE ACADIANS

Acadia – *Acadie* in French – has at different times included all or part of Maine, New Brunswick and Nova Scotia. The bulk of today's Acadians are the descendants of just forty French peasant families who arrived at Port Royal, Nova Scotia, in 1636; slowly spreading along the **Annapolis Valley**, they lived a semi-autonomous existence in which trading with their English-speaking neighbours was more important than grand notions of loyalty to the French Empire. Consequently, when the British secured control of Port Royal under the Treaty of Utrecht in 1713, the Acadians made no protest.

In **1755**, at the start of the Seven Years' War, British government officials attempted to make the Acadians swear an **oath of allegiance** to the Crown. They refused, so Governor Charles Lawrence decided – without consulting London – to **deport** them en masse to other colonies (the **"Grand Dérangement"** in French). The process of uprooting and removing a community of around thirteen thousand was achieved with remarkable ruthlessness.

By the end of the year over half the Acadians had arrived on the American East Coast, where they faced a cold reception – the Virginians even rerouted their allocation to England. Most of the rest spread out along the North Atlantic seaboard, establishing communities along New Brunswick's Miramichi Valley, on Prince Edward Island and in St-Pierre et Miquelon. Some went to Louisiana – these were the ancestors of the **Cajuns**, whose name is a corruption of "Acadian". Starting in 1763, Acadians were allowed to return to the Bay of Fundy region (provided they took the oath), but many farms had been given to British and New England colonists and they were forced to settle the less hospitable lands of the **Acadian Shore**, further west. Between 1860 and 1920, what's known as the **Acadian Renaissance** helped revive Acadian traditions and culture, encouraged, in part, by the global success of Longfellow's poem *Evangeline*.

Today, the Acadian communities of the Maritime Provinces have largely resisted the pressures of assimilation and have consolidated their cultural independence, most notably in New Brunswick, where the Université de Moncton has become their academic and cultural centre.

EATING AND DRINKING
GRAND PRÉ

Just Us! Café 11865 Hwy-1, Grand Pré ☎ 902 542 7474, ⓦ justuscoffee.com. There are good paninis, lip-smacking muffins and fair-trade coffee at this cool café; they also run a roastery for the national *Just Us!* chain, and coffee museum. Mon–Fri 7am–6pm, Sat 8am–6pm, Sun 9am–6pm.

Restaurant Le Caveau Domaine de Grand Pré winery, 11611 Hwy-1, Grand Pré ☎ 902 542 7177, ⓦ grandprewines.ns.ca. The best place to eat around here is at the Domaine de Grand Pré winery, where *Restaurant Le Caveau* utilizes seasonal produce and the on-site wines (mains $28–34). You can also take guided tours of the winery (May–Oct) daily at 11am & 4pm. May–Oct daily 11.30am–2pm & 5–9pm; Nov & Dec Thurs–Sat 5–9pm, Sun 11am–2pm.

Cape Blomidon and Cape Split

The rugged, hook-shaped peninsula stretching north of Grand Pré and its neighbouring town of Wolfville encompasses the dramatic scenery of **Cape Blomidon**, and of wilder and bleaker **Cape Split** beyond. To reach the peninsula from Wolfville, take Hwy-1 west for a couple of kilometres and then turn north along Rte-358.

Blomidon Provincial Park

3138 Pereaux Rd • Mid-May to early Oct 24hr • Free • ☎ 902 582 7319, ⓦ parks.novascotia.ca/content/blomidon

North of the small town of **Canning** there's a choice of routes: stay on Rte-358 for Cape Split, or take the signed 13km-long turning that leads down to **Blomidon Provincial Park**, a narrow slice of seashore where steep sea cliffs back onto a lush, coastal forest. It's an entrancing spot with around 14km of footpaths and a popular **campground** (see page 355).

Back on Rte-358 beyond the Blomidon turning, the road clambers 3km up to the peninsula's highest point, the **Look-off Provincial Park**, from where the views over the Annapolis Valley and the Minas Basin are spectacular.

Cape Split Provincial Park Reserve

999 Cape Split Rd, Scots Bay • Mid-May to mid-Oct 24hr • Free • ☎ 902 582 7319, ⓦ parks.novascotia.ca

From the Look-off, it's a further 10km to **SCOTS BAY**, a scattered farming village that straggles along the edge of a wide and muddy bay. The road ends abruptly just beyond the village at the start of one of the region's most popular and moderate hiking trails that leads the 8km (one way) to the tip of **Cape Split Provincial Park Reserve**. Reckon on two hours each way. The trail begins by threading up through thick forest beneath towering cliffs and passes heavily eroded rock formations before emerging onto a small open area, from where there are wondrous views across the Bay of Fundy.

ACCOMMODATION	CAPE BLOMIDON AND CAPE SPLIT
Blomidon Campground ☎ 902 582 7319, ⓦ parks. novascotia.ca. This seventy-site campground offers both woodland and open sites (unserviced), two picnic areas and access to the park beach and hiking trails. Mid-May to early Sept. Per person $27	**Look-off Campground** Rte-358, Canning ☎ 902 582 3022, ⓦ lookoffcamping.com. You can savour the gasp-inducing scenery at the Look-off at length if you bed down at the one of the best-sited campgrounds in the province. Mid-May to Sept. Sites (unserviced) $30; cabins $70

Pictou

Signs proclaim **PICTOU**, 170km from Halifax, as the "Birthplace of New Scotland". The title refers to the arrival in 1773 of the ship **Hector**, loaded with around two hundred Gaelic-speaking settlers from the Highlands, the advance guard of subsequent Scots migrations to the province which eventually topped five million. Though the area had actually been settled by colonists from Pennsylvania in 1767, Pictou's historic appeal today relates to this landmark Scottish event, and the town even has the **Hector Festival**, a five-day affair in August featuring Scottish traditional dancing and plenty of bagpipes.

Hector Heritage Quay

33 Caladh Ave • May–Aug daily 10am–4pm; Sept to mid-Oct Mon–Fri & Sun 10am–4pm • $8 • ☎ 902 485 5046, ⓦ shiphector.ca

Pictou's pride and glory is a replica of the **Hector**, an expensive ten-year project because the townsfolk insisted on using the original shipbuilding techniques. The boat was finally launched in 2000 and now either bobs around the harbour or can be viewed at the **Hector Heritage Quay** on the waterfront, which gives the lowdown on the original

---

RIDING THE TIDAL BORE RAPIDS

The Bay of Fundy is noted for its high tides, but while it can be intriguing to watch harbours around the bay fill up in a matter of minutes, don't confuse this with the hypnotic spectacle of the *Fundy tidal bore*. This only occurs higher up rivers towards the end of the bay: an advancing wave, ranging anything from 2m (very rare) to a few centimetres (the size depends on various factors, including the lunar cycle) powers upstream, smothering the river bank. One of the best places to see it is *Truro* in central Nova Scotia; aim for the new visitor information centre on the site of the former Palliser Motel (now demolished) on the edge of town (Tidal Bore Rd at Hwy-102, exit 14), which overlooks the Salmon River.

To get a closer look, you can take an exhilarating boat ride across the bore and crash through the 1–6m rapids temporarily formed as the tide rushes over rocks and boulders. Several operators run Zodiac boats on the Shubenacadie River, south of Truro, all offering a similar experience (May–Oct only; reservations are crucial; arrive 1hr in advance).

Shubenacadie River Adventure Tours 10061 Rte-215, South Maitland ☎ 888 878 8687, ⓦ shubie.com. Three-hour tours from $90, ending with all-you-can-eat hamburgers and hot dogs.

Tidal Bore Rafting Resort 12215 Rte-215, Urbania ☎ 902 758 8433, ⓦ raftingcanada.ca. Runs trips for $60–85 (2hr–4hr).

5

harrowing twelve-week voyage of those first Scottish settlers. Conditions on the boat must have been unbelievably grim – just take a look below deck. It's all excellently done and spruces up Pictou's unassuming centre, where the narrow streets slope up from the harbour dotted with stone buildings.

Northumberland Fisheries Museum

21 Caladh Ave • June–Sept Tues–Sat 10am–4pm • $8 • ☎ 902 485 8925, ⓦ northumberlandfisheriesmuseum.ca

The **Northumberland Fisheries Museum** lies just along the waterfront from the *Hector*, housing an eclectic mix of old photos, an authentic fisherman's bunkhouse and over a thousand artefacts from Pictou's heyday as a fishing port. Behind the main building on the wharf lies the Lighthouse Research & Interpretative Centre (a replica 1905 lighthouse stuffed with information about the province's lighthouses) while next door you can view cute (-ish) baby crustaceans at the Lobster Hatchery.

ARRIVAL
PICTOU

By car Plenty of free parking can be found along the waterfront (Caladh Ave), near the Hector Heritage Quay. Some 8km north of Pictou is Caribou, from where

Northumberland Ferries operates frequent car ferries over to Wood Islands on Prince Edward Island (see page 392).

ACCOMMODATION

Customs House Inn 38 Depot St ☎ 902 485 4546, ⓦ customshouseinn.ca. Eight spacious rooms with exposed brick walls and hardwood floors, in a stately 1870 red-brick and sandstone mansion on the waterfront, all with a/c and cable TV. April to late Nov. **$140**

Willow House Inn 11 Willow St ☎ 902 485 5740, ⓦ willowhouseinn.com. Another central choice, whose four well-priced rooms and two suites, in a pristine clapboard house built in 1840, are kitted out in a fetching version of late Victorian style. Open year-round. **$105**

EATING AND DRINKING

Alladin Syrian Canadian Restaurant 41 Water St ☎ 902 921 8615. This small shack run by a super-friendly Syrian family knocks out superb Middle Eastern staples from chicken shawarma ($12) and falafel ($8) to shish kebabs ($12). Daily 11am–5.30pm.

Mrs MacGregor's Shortbreads 59 Water St ☎ 902 382 1878, ⓦ mrsmacgregors.com. No longer a teashop, *MacGregor's* focuses on its renowned shortbread line, selling cakes and the delicious shortbreads themselves

(from classic Scottish and lavender and lemon to Canadian maple; $7.50). Wed–Sat noon–4pm (usually closed Jan–March).

Sharon's Place Family Restaurant 12 Front St ☎ 902 485 4669. The most popular diner in town and a real local hangout; cheap, home-cooked food featuring fresh fish (haddock) and delicious burgers for under $10. Great coffee and milkshakes also. Daily 6am–7pm.

ENTERTAINMENT

deCoste Centre 85 Water St ☎ 902 485 8848, ⓦ decostecentre.ca. Pictou's Scottish heritage is much in evidence at this waterfront arts centre, where much of

the summer season is taken up by ceilidhs, pipe bands and Highland dancing. Box office Mon–Fri 11.30am–5pm.

Sherbrooke

Established by Scottish settlers in the early 1800s, **SHERBROOKE** boomed when gold was found nearby in 1861, the start of a short-lived gold rush that fizzled out within twenty years. Sherbrooke returned to the lumber trade, but without much success: the decline of the industry gradually whittled the population down to the four hundred of today. In 1969 the old commercial heart of the settlement along Main Street was turned into **Sherbrooke Village Restoration area** to conserve the buildings that remained. Today the active part of the village lines Main Street only as far as Court Street – the rest is part of the museum.

5

Sherbrooke Village

42 Main St (off Rte-7) • Early June to late Sept daily 9.30am–5pm • $15.95 • ☎ 888 743 7845, ⓦ sherbrookevillage.novascotia.ca

The open-air museum of **Sherbrooke Village** offers an intriguing glimpse of rural life in Nova Scotia from 1860 to before World War I, its precious collection of nineteenth-century clapboard and shingle houses and shops enhanced by costumed guides and real artisans. The site is large, encompassing over eighty structures, though only around 25 are open to the public. Highlights include the surprisingly grand Neoclassical **Courthouse** of 1858, in use until 2000. Nearby is **Cumminger House**, the town's oldest cottage, dating from 1840, and the high-gabled **Greenwood Cottage** of 1871, the epitome of Victorian luxury and real contrast to the other homes on view. Elsewhere you'll see a blacksmith hammering away in his shop, weavers at the loom, newly shaved timbers in the wood turner's shop and plenty of (real) turkeys, cows and horses. Be sure to visit the creaky **old gaol**, used as a lock-up until 1968 – the ladies here are usually baking bread and cakes in the original stove. In the fields south of the main site a plaque marks the location of **Fort Sainte Marie**, a French trading post established here in 1655 and destroyed by the English in 1669. Note that at 5pm the gates are thrown open and you can wander the village for free (though the interiors are all locked up).

ARRIVAL AND DEPARTURE
SHERBROOKE

Sherbrooke is 243km northeast of Halifax via the relatively slow Rte-7, and 104km south of Pictou. There is no public transport.

ACCOMMODATION AND EATING

Daysago B&B 15 Cameron Rd ☎ 902 522 2811, ⓦ bbcanada.com/daysago. This congenial B&B is a 1920s house with views of the St Mary's River and four cosy rooms decorated with antique furnishings. __$100__

★ **St Mary's River Smokehouses** 8000 Hwy-7 ☎ 902 522 2005, ⓦ thebestsmokedsalmon.com. Not a restaurant but a store selling delectable Scottish-style smoked salmon to take away: cold-smoked slices, gravlax (with dill, salt and sugar) and smoked salmon pâtés. Mon–Fri 9am–5pm.

What Cheer Tea Room Sherbrooke Village ☎ 902 522 2254. Within Sherbrooke Village open-air museum (you can grab a bite here without paying the museum admission fee), this serves tasty fruit pies ($7) and soups and chowders ($7–11). June to late Sept Mon–Fri 9.30am–5pm.

Cape Breton Island

From the lakes, hills and valleys of the southwest to the ripe, forested mountains of the north, **CAPE BRETON ISLAND** offers the most exquisite of landscapes, reaching its melodramatic conclusion along the fretted, rocky coast of the **Cape Breton Highlands National Park**. Encircling the park and some of the adjacent shore is the **Cabot Trail**, reckoned to be one of the most awe-inspiring drives on the continent. The Trail begins at Hwy-105 (Exit 7) before weaving its way on a scenic loop of 298km around the northern tip of the island, passing through Cape Breton Highlands and ending in Baddeck, back on Hwy-105 (see ⓦ cabottrail.com). Allow time also for a **whale-watching cruise**: these are big business hereabouts and they are available at almost every significant settlement from May to October when fin, pilot, humpback and minke whales congregate off the island.

Cape Breton Island is also a major locus for **Scottish culture**; it attracted thousands of Scottish Highlanders at the end of the eighteenth century, and many of the region's settlements celebrate their Scots ancestry and Gaelic traditions in one way or another – museums, Highland Games and bagpipe-playing competitions.

Cape Breton's **weather** is notoriously unpredictable, even in summer. The Cabot Trail is pretty miserable in mist and rain, so if possible you should build a bit of flexibility into your itinerary.

ARRIVAL AND DEPARTURE

By car It's easy getting to Cape Breton, but without your own transport getting around the island once here is a struggle. To get onto the island, all traffic has to cross the 1.4km Strait of Canso causeway (free).

By plane Cape Breton's only airport is Sydney/J.A. Douglas McCurdy Airport (about 10km northeast of downtown Sydney), with regular flights to Halifax, Toronto and St-Pierre et Miquelon page 429).

By ferry Ferries to Newfoundland sail from Sydney (see page 364).

By bus Maritime Bus (☎ 902 429 2029, ⓦ maritimebus. com) runs long-distance bus services to Cape Breton (Sydney) from Halifax; you'll probably change at Truro for other locations in the Maritimes.

Destinations (from Sydney, Irving gas station at 565 George St); Charlottetown (1 daily; 9hr); Fredericton (1 daily; 11hr 15min); Halifax (1–2 daily; 7hr); Moncton (1 daily; 8hr 15min); Montréal (1 daily; 22hr); Saint John (1 daily; 11hr 10min); Wolfville (1–2 daily; 11hr 20min).

By shuttle bus The Maritime Bus services are supplemented by shuttle buses that link Halifax with Cape Breton. Bay Luxury Shuttle (☎ 855 673 8083, ⓦ bayluxuryshuttle.ca) runs between Glace Bay and Halifax ($70) via several locations in Cape Breton (including Baddeck and Sydney); pick-ups start at 6.30am from Glace Bay, with returns from Halifax starting at 1pm. A1 Shuttle Service (☎ 902 539 2700, ⓦ a1shuttleservice.com) also runs two daily minibuses to Halifax for similar rates ($75 for Halifax airport), leaving Sydney at 10.30am and 2.30pm, and departing Halifax 7.30am and 5.30pm; shuttles depart Halifax at 5.30pm.

INFORMATION

Port Hastings Visitor Information Centre 96 Hwy-104 ☎ 902 625 4201, ⓦ cbisland.com. Just up the hill

5

GAELIC MUSIC ON CAPE BRETON ISLAND

Cape Breton is not just about scenery and sights: the Scottish Highlanders who settled much of the island in the late eighteenth and early nineteenth centuries (many as a result of the Highland Clearances, where they were forcibly evicted by landowners) brought with them strong cultural traditions and today these are best recalled by the island's **musicians**, especially the fiddle players. Buddy MacMaster (1924–2014) was one of the greats, and current names to watch out for include his niece Natalie MacMaster, her cousin Ashley MacIsaac and the remaining members of the Rankin Family, not to mention Glenn Graham, Rodney MacDonald and Jackie Dunn MacIsaac – though it's impossible to pick out the "best" as each fiddler has their own particular style. Local tourist offices will gladly advise you on **gigs**, whether it be a ceilidh, concert or square dance, and listings are given in the weekly *Inverness Oran* (ⓦ invernessoran.ca), a local newspaper available at tourist offices and convenience stores. During the summer there's something happening almost every day – the Saturday-night **Family Square Dance** at West Mabou Hall is especially well regarded (9pm–midnight; $8). The largest festival is **Celtic Colours** (ⓣ 902 562 6700, ⓦ celtic-colours.com), with performances all across Cape Breton held over ten days in early to mid-October.

from the Canso causeway – a place to get your bearings and make advance room reservations on all of Cape Breton Island. Late May to late Oct daily 9am–5pm; closes 7pm mid-June to mid-Sept.

La Région Acadienne and Chéticamp

North from Hwy-105 and the Margaree Valley, the **Cabot Trail** offers captivating views of land and sea as it slices across the wide grassy littoral. The scattered dwellings hereabouts form **La Région Acadienne**, an Acadian enclave established in 1785 by French settlers deported from elsewhere in the Maritimes (see page 354). Despite being surrounded by English-speaking settlements, the region was connected to the rest of Nova Scotia by road only in 1947, partly explaining the survival of Acadian culture. After 30km or so, the road slips into the district's main village, **CHÉTICAMP**.

L'Église Saint-Pierre

15114 Main St (Cabot Trail) · Daily 8am–9pm

Dominating the heart of Chéticamp is the soaring silver steeple of l'**Église Saint-Pierre**, completed in 1893 with stones lugged across the ice from Chéticamp Island, just offshore. Inside, the lines of the cavernous nave are interrupted by two long galleries and oceans of elaborate plasterwork; the striking frescoes were added in 1957.

Les Trois Pignons

15584 Main St (Cabot Trail) · Daily: mid-May to June & Sept to mid-Oct 8.30am–5pm; July & Aug 8.30am–6.30pm · $5 · ⓣ 902 224 2642, ⓦ lestroispignons.com

There's a worthwhile exhibition of Acadian crafts at the north end of the village in **Les Trois Pignons**, a cultural centre and **Museum of the Hooked Rug & Home Life** that proudly displays Acadian artefacts (with detailed explanations) collected by local eccentric Marguerite Gallant, as well as the hooked mats of Elizabeth LeFort, an artist of some local renown. Hooked rugs are still made in the village today, and you'll usually be able to watch one of the amiable volunteers demonstrating the ancient technique.

INFORMATION CHÉTICAMP

Visitor centre Les Trois Pignons (see above) contains a visitor information centre with free wi-fi (mid-May to mid-Oct 9am–5pm; ⓣ 902 224 4207, ⓦ cheticampns.com).

ACCOMMODATION AND EATING

Chéticamp Outfitters Inn B&B 13938 Cabot Trail, Point Cross ⓣ 902 224 2776, ⓦ cheticampoutfitters.

com. This distinctive cedarwood B&B is perched on a hilltop just off the main road about 4km south of the village, with riveting views over the surrounding shoreline and six comfy rooms (three with shared bath; two with satellite TV). April–Nov. Shared bath $100; private bath $125

Le Gabriel 15424 Main St (Cabot Trail) ☎ 902 224 3685, ⓦ legabriel.com. Marked by a replica lighthouse, this Acadian restaurant is the best place in the region for seafood; sumptuous lobsters, crab legs, shrimp, scallops and a chowder thick with cream, bacon and shellfish. Also does fish cakes, meat pie and other Acadian favourites. Popular with tour groups, so best to avoid if buses are parked outside. Seafood mains average $19–20. Free wi-fi. Daily 11am–10pm.

Ocean View Motel & Chalets 15569 Main St (Cabot Trail) ☎ 902 224 2313, ⓦ oceanviewchalets.com. There are around twenty motels and B&Bs in and around Chéticamp with this being one of the best: well-maintained and spacious shingle-clad chalets right by the seashore, opposite Les Trois Pignons. May–Oct. $135

Cape Breton Highlands National Park

Park entry $7.80 • ⓦ pc.gc.ca/en/pn-np/ns/cbreton

The extensive **Cape Breton Highlands National Park**, beginning 9km north of Chéticamp, offers some of the most mesmerizing scenery anywhere in the Maritimes – a mix of deep wooded valleys, rocky coastal headlands, soft green hills and boggy upland. Although visitors get a taster of the park travelling by car – 120km of Cabot Trail trimming its northern edge – the essence of the place is only revealed on foot.

Hiking in the park

Though much of the park is actually off-limits to the public, land bordering the **Cabot Trail** can be explored by 25 **hiking trails** signposted from the road, some of them the easiest of woodland strolls, others offering steeper climbs to small lakes, waterfalls and rugged coastal viewpoints. One of the most popular is the 9.2km **Skyline Loop Trail** (2–3hr), which clambers up the coastal mountains north of Corney Brook, a few kilometres up the coast from Chéticamp. Another rewarding trail is the 7.4km **Franey Loop Trail** (3–4hr), a steep walk up through the mountains and lakes north of Ingonish Beach. Most of the wildlife inhabits the inner reaches of the park: garter snakes, red-backed salamanders, snowshoe hares and moose are common, while bald eagles, black bear and lynx are rarer. The only artificial sight is the **Lone Sheiling**, a somewhat battered 1930s replica of the stone shelters once built by Highlanders beside their mountain pastures. The hut is on the northern perimeter of the park in a valley that was settled by Scots in the early 1800s; it is accessible along a short and easy footpath from the road, providing a rare taster of the hardwood forests that make up the park's central (and strictly protected) zone.

INFORMATION **CAPE BRETON HIGHLANDS NATIONAL PARK**

Visitor centres The park has two visitor information centres (both daily: late June to late Aug 8.30am–7pm; mid-May to late June & late Aug to mid-Oct 9am–5pm) – Chéticamp Visitor Centre is the larger one, with exhibits on the park, at the west-coast entrance just beyond Chéticamp village (☎ 902 224 2306); the Ingonish Visitor Centre lies at the east-coast entrance near Ingonish Beach (same number).

Maps Both visitor centres sell 1:50,000 maps, have details of the park's hiking trails (which are in peak condition July–Sept), and issue backcountry camping permits ($9.80).

ACCOMMODATION

National Park campgrounds The park has six campgrounds ($17.60–38.20), all within easy reach of the road, and one backcountry campground – *Fishing Cove* – along one of the more arduous 8km trails. Chéticamp and Broad Cove also offer the posher oTENTik cabins for $100. Campground services vary and are only available from mid-May to mid-Oct, but you can camp in the park at any time of the year. Reservations (☎ 877 737 3783, ⓦ reservation. pc.gc.ca) are accepted at *Chéticamp* and *Broad Cove* campgrounds (the only two with serviced sites and hook-ups), but the others assign sites on first-come, first-served basis. $17.60

5

Cape North

Another 30km or so beyond the northern perimeter of the Cape Breton Highlands National Park is **Cape North**, a forested hunk of hill and valley that juts out into the sea where the Gulf of St Lawrence meets the Atlantic Ocean. The Cabot Trail threads its way across the base of the cape, passing through the tiny village of **CAPE NORTH**, no more than a few lonely buildings straggling along the road.

North Highlands Community Museum

29263 Cabot Trail • Mid-June to Aug daily 9am–5pm, Sept to late Oct Mon–Sat 10am–4pm • $5 • ☎ 902 383 2579, ⓦ northhighlandsmuseum.ca

In the centre of Cape North village, the **North Highlands Community Museum** is an enthusiastic attempt to document the history of the area, with displays on local industries, lighthouses, early settlers, and even a few bits and pieces recovered from the **Titanic**.

Meat Cove

To get off the beaten path, head up to **MEAT COVE** (Cape North itself is inaccessible), an incredibly picturesque spot at the end of a bumpy 8km-long gravel road from the hamlet of Capstick (22km north of the Cabot Trail). On the way, visit the windswept **Cabot Landing Provincial Park**, the spot where John Cabot may have "discovered" North America in 1497.

ACCOMMODATION

CAPE NORTH

MacDonald's Motel ☎ 902 383 2054, ⓦ macdonalds motel.ca. There are several places to stay in the area, beginning with this handy motel, offering ageing but cheap rooms at the Cape North village crossroads. Mid-May to mid-Oct. $75

The Markland 802 Dingwall Rd ☎ 902 383 2246, ⓦ themarkland.com. For a bit more comfort, follow the signs to Dingwall and the *Markland Coastal Beach Cottages*

(wi-fi in main building, but no TVs in rooms), which has its own private beach. $189

Meat Cove Campground 2479 Meat Cove Rd ☎ 902 383 2379, ⓦ meatcovecampground.ca. This idyllic campground is full of the roar of the ocean, has kayaks and even its own *Chowder Hut Restaurant* (June–Oct 8am–8pm). June–Oct. Sites $35; cabins $80

Ingonish

From Cape North village, heading east, the Cabot Trail skirts the edge of the national park for 30km, cutting across the interior before veering south along the coast to reach the pretty harbour at **INGONISH**. There's little in the village itself, though **Ingonish Beach**, around 10km further south (before the village of the same name), is one of the most enticing in the national park, a thin strip of silky sand facing South Bay. Nearby, the easy 3.8km hike along **Middle Head** (drive through the grounds of **Keltic Inn** to get there) offers sublime views across both South and North bays.

ACCOMMODATION

INGONISH

Glenghorm Beach Resort 36743 Cabot Trail ☎ 902 285 2049, ⓦ glenghorm.net. Among several places to stay in the area, this resort is on the main road halfway between Ingonish and the beach, its neat and trim motel rooms and more luxurious suites spreading out along a pleasant slice of seashore. Open May to late Oct. Rooms $140; suites $239

★ **Keltic Lodge Resort & Spa** 383 Keltic Inn Rd, Middle Head Peninsula, Ingonish Beach ☎ 902 285 2880, ⓦ kelticlodge.ca. The motels of Ingonish pale

in comparison with one of the province's finest hotel complexes, perched high above the cliffs amid immaculate gardens on Middle Head; features and facilities include beaches, restaurants, tennis courts and kayaks. You can stay in the main lodge, a handsome Edwardian mansion, or the modern inn, but the cottages are perhaps more enjoyable, the best of them prettily located among the woods that cover much of the promontory. Mid-May to mid-Oct. $246

The Gaelic Coast

On the east coast south of the Cape Breton Highlands National Park, the Cabot Trail threads its way down the 80km-long **Gaelic Coast** passing through **SOUTH GUT ST ANN'S**, the location of Gaelic College.

Great Hall of the Clans

51779 Cabot Trail Rd (Hwy-105), St Ann's • Late May to early Oct Mon–Fri 9am–5pm • $8 • ☎ 902 295 3411, ⊚ gaeliccollege.edu

The main focus of a visit to the Gaelic College (Colaisde na Gàidhlig) is the **Great Hall of the Clans**, which provides potted clan descriptions alongside wax models dressed in the appropriate tartan, exhibits tracing Scotland's military history, and pioneer artefacts from the nineteenth century. Also inside are eight interactive displays highlighting Gaelic language, dancing, piping, music, song, storytelling and textiles; you can even view *Faire Chaluim Mhic Leòid*, North America's first Gaelic-language short film.

Baddeck

The laidback resort and yachting village of **BADDECK**, some 90km north-east of the Canso causeway along Hwy-105, enjoys a tranquil lakeside setting on St Patrick's Channel, an inlet of the tentacular Bras d'Or Lake. The village was founded by Irish and Scottish settlers in 1839, and today has a year-round population of under a thousand.

Alexander Graham Bell National Historic Site

559 Chebucto St (Rte-205) • Late May to Oct daily 9am–5pm • $7.80 • ☎ 902 295 2069, ⊚ pc.gc.ca/en/lhn-nhs/ns/grahambell

Baddeck is home to the absorbing **Alexander Graham Bell National Historic Site**, which overlooks the water at the northern end of the village. The museum is a mine of biographical information about the Scottish-born Bell – who started spending his summers here in 1885 – and gives detailed explanations of all his inventions. Most famous for the **invention of the telephone** in 1876, Bell also made extraordinary advances in techniques for teaching hearing-impaired children, a lifelong interest inspired by the deafness of his mother. He also worked on aircraft and boats, culminating in the first Canadian air flight here in 1909 – a replica of the **Silver Dart** is displayed in a special exhibit area. Bell's exploits culminated in 1919 with the launch of the world's first hydrofoil, the **HD-4** (there's a full-scale replica as well as the original, in the same hall as *Silver Dart*), which reached a speed of 114kmph on the lake in front of town.

INFORMATION	BADDECK

Baddeck Visitor Information Centre 454 Chebucto St, at Shore Rd (daily: June & Sept to mid-Oct 10am–4pm; July & Aug 10am–6pm; ☎ 902 295 1911); has lots of useful local information and sits at the resort's main intersection.

ACCOMMODATION

Auberge Gisele's Inn 387 Shore Rd ☎ 902 295 2849, ⊚ giseles.com. Large, motel-like place overlooking the lake, with commodious bedrooms decked out in floral, modern style and an excellent dining room. The deluxe rooms have fireplaces. May to late Oct. **$145**

Baddeck Heritage House 121 Twining St ☎ 902 295 3219, ⊚ baddeckheritagehouse.ca. This justly popular B&B, built in the 1880s, offers four cosy rooms (three with four-posters), with flat-screen TV and delicious breakfasts including addictive fresh-baked scones. **$125**

Bras d'Or Lakes Campground Hwy-105 Km 80 ☎ 902 295 2329, ⊚ brasdorlakescampground.ca. The closest campground to Baddeck is around 6km west of the village on Hwy-105, a pleasant lakeside location with 93 RV and tent campsites, and a series of cabins. Mid-June to Sept. Sites **$40**; cabins **$67**

Inverary Resort 368 Shore Rd ☎ 902 295 3500, ⊚ invераryresort.com. This extensive and immaculately maintained complex is the most luxurious place in town. It dates back to 1850 and spreads down from Shore Rd to the bay. There are rooms in the main lodge, cheaper motel-like rooms and several different types of cottage. May–Nov. Doubles **$160**; cottages **$270**

Silver Dart Lodge 257 Shore Rd ☎ 902 295 2340, ⊚ maritimeinns.com. Popular hotel with spacious chalets spread over a hillside with decks and stunning views of the lake. Has a pool, hiking trails and free mountain bikes. Mid-May to mid-Oct. **$165**

5

FERRIES AND FLIGHTS FROM SYDNEY

Once the industrial dynamo of eastern Canada, **SYDNEY** sprawls along the east bank of the Sydney River, 80km north of Baddeck. Today it's the largest urban centre on Cape Breton Island, but there's not much to see in terms of sights. It is, however, a transport hub and the maritime gateway to Newfoundland. Buses connect the city with Halifax (see page 326).

By ferry Marine Atlantic (☎800 341 7981, ⓦmarine-atlantic.ca) operates two car-ferry routes to Newfoundland from North Sydney (149 Prince St), 21km northwest of Sydney proper. The first, to Channel-Port aux Basques (1–3 daily), takes 7hr (up to 8hr at night). One-way passenger tickets cost $45.57, with an additional $119.20 for cars (bikes are $18.70). A four-berth cabin (reserve in advance) costs an additional $53.50 for day-use, $126.50 at night. The second car ferry connects North Sydney to Argentia, Newfoundland, 130km southwest of

St John's (late June to late Sept, Wed, Fri & Sun 5.30pm; 16hr). One-way passenger tickets cost $121.26, plus $244.56 for cars. Vehicles must be booked in advance, as must four-berth cabins, which cost $176.75

By plane J.A. Douglas McCurdy Sydney Airport (ⓦsydneyairport.ca) lies 10km northeast of downtown Sydney, with regular flights to Halifax and Toronto with Air Canada and WestJet. The major car rental agencies have desks at the airport, and taxis (City Wide ☎902 564 5432) usually meet flights.

EATING AND DRINKING

Baddeck Lobster Suppers 17 Ross St, off Shore Rd ☎902 295 3307, ⓦbaddecklobstersuppers.ca. Located inside the old Armoury (1860), overlooking the lake, this place excels in "hot planked" smoked salmon ($29) as well as its signature fresh lobster suppers ($50; with unlimited chowder, fresh mussels, rolls, biscuits, salads and desserts). Early June to mid-Oct daily 4–9pm.

Bell Buoy Restaurant 536 Chebucto St ☎902 295 2581. Solid option for steaks and seafood, with fresh mussels

and lobster in season ($19.95 for lobster sandwiches, $9 for chowder, haddock and chips $17.50). Daily: late May to June 4–10pm; July–Oct 11.30am–10pm.

Highwheeler Café 470 Chebucto St ☎902 295 3006. The best café in town, serving up a tasty range of chowder, blueberry scones, pies, soups and grilled sandwiches (mains $8.95–12) – expect long lines for breakfast in July/Aug. May to mid-Oct Tues–Sun 7am–5pm.

Glace Bay

Coal mining in **GLACE BAY**, just 24km northeast of Sydney on Hwy-4, dates back to the 1860s, but the last mine closed in 1984 and today the only reminder of this mighty industrial past is the enlightening **Cape Breton Miners' Museum**.

Cape Breton Miners' Museum

17 Museum St (extension of Birkley St) just south of the town centre • Late May to mid-Oct daily 10am–6pm (rest of year by appointment) • $15; underground tour $16 (includes museum) • ☎902 849 4522, ⓦminersmuseum.com

The **Cape Breton Miners' Museum** features exhibits on the history of local coalfields, but the highlight is the underground tour (June to mid-Oct) of Ocean Deeps Colliery, led by retired but still energetic miners. It's also home to the local miners' choir, **The Men of the Deeps**, which performs at concerts here in the summer.

Marconi National Historic Site

15 Timmerman St, Table Head (north of the centre) • July & Aug daily 10am–6pm • Free • ☎902 295 2069, ⓦpc.gc.ca/en/lhn-nhs/ns/marconi/index

Glace Bay's other claim to fame apart from the mining museum is the **Marconi National Historic Site**, overlooking the cliffs at Table Head, which honours the first official wireless message sent from this site across the Atlantic to England in 1902 by Guglielmo Marconi. The station closed in 1946, and today there is a small exhibition at the visitor centre and a trail to the original transmitter site.

Louisbourg

Stringing along the seashore 34km southeast of Sydney, the modern village of **LOUISBOURG** comes alive in the summer months when tourism supplements modest incomes from lobster and crab fishing. The crowds come for the **Fortress of Louisbourg**, one of Canada's most enchanting historic monuments.

Fortress of Louisbourg National Historic Site

259 Park Service Rd · Late May to mid-Oct daily 9.30am–5pm; mid-Oct to late May Mon–Fri 9.30am–4pm (unstaffed) · Late May to mid-Oct $17.60; mid-Oct to late May $7.30 · ☎ 902 733 2280, ⓦ fortressoflouisbourg.ca

A visit to the remarkably restored **Fortress of Louisbourg National Historic Site** begins just 2km beyond the village of Louisbourg at the visitor centre, where there's a good account of the fort's history. The French began construction in 1719, a staggeringly ostentatious stronghold that covered a hundred acres, encircled by 10m-high stone walls, to guard the Atlantic approaches to New France. Louisbourg was only attacked twice, but it was captured on both occasions, the second time by the celebrated British commander, James Wolfe, on his way to Québec in 1758, and it was levelled in 1760. Rebuilt in the 1960s, today it offers an extraordinary window into eighteenth-century colonial life, its streets and buildings populated by a small army of costumed role-players – English visitors (those who admit their nationality), can expect some good-natured ribbing about being imprisoned for spying.

From the visitor centre, a free shuttle bus (June to early Sept only) runs to the fort and settlement, whose stone walls rise from the sea to enclose more than four dozen restored buildings as they were in the 1740s. There are powder magazines, forges, guardhouses, warehouses, barracks and the chilly abodes of the soldiers, with an effort to create a 'living history', including costumed actors – all enhanced by the dazzling coastal setting. Particular care has been taken with the **governor's apartments**, which have been splendidly furnished according to the inventory taken after the death of Governor Duquesnel here in 1744. Allow at least three hours to look round the fortress and sample the authentic refreshments available at the taverns and bakeries. The equally impressive story of Louisbourg's reconstruction is told in the small on-site museum.

INFORMATION

LOUISBOURG

Louisbourg Visitor Information Centre 7495 Main St (mid-June to mid-Oct daily 10am–6pm; ☎ 902 733 4636, ⓦ louisbourg.ca); well stocked with maps and leaflets from all over the province, and can help with accommodation.

ACCOMMODATION

★ **Cranberry Cove Inn** 12 Wolfe St ☎ 902 733 2171. Lavishly refurbished old house in fierce pink on the edge of the village (on the way to the fort), with seven gorgeous rooms, computer use and fine dining. Mid-May to Oct. **$130**

Louisbourg Harbour Inn 9 Lower Warren St ☎ 902 733 3222, ⓦ louisbourgharbourinn.com. Fabulous bed and breakfast in an old sea captain's house just off Main St, with eight bright and modern en-suite rooms (six with harbour views). **$130**

Point of View Suites 15 Commercial Ext ☎ 902 733 2080, ⓦ louisbourgpointofview.com. Most convenient option for the fortress, with large, well-equipped and modern suites, some overlooking the water, and all with cable TV and kitchen. **$130**

Stacey House B&B 7438 Main St ☎ 902 733 2317, ⓦ bbcanada.com/thestaceyhouse. An attractive, high-gabled Victorian home, with four well-priced guest rooms dressed with period furnishings, hardwood floors and drapes. Mid-June to mid-Oct. **$75**

EATING

Grubstake 7499 Main St ☎ 902 733 2308, ⓦ grubstake. ca. Lobster is usually served at the clapboard *Grubstake*, as well as decent fish platters (maple salmon, haddock) and home-baked pastries. Mid-June to mid-Oct daily noon–8pm.

Lobster is a real treat in Louisbourg; the season runs mid-May to mid-July and you can buy them cheap and fresh from H. Hopkins (Mon–Thurs 8am–noon; ☎ 902 733 2424) at 20 Marven St on the waterfront.

Lobster Kettle 41 Commercial St ☎ 902 733 2723, ⓦ lobsterkettle.com. Louisbourg's only waterfront restaurant is a solid bet for the local speciality (lobster dinners from $29), plus snow crab ($24) and signature seafood chowder (from $9). Mid-June to early Oct daily noon–8pm.

5

ENTERTAINMENT

Louisbourg Playhouse 11 Aberdeen St ☎ 902 733 2996, ⓦ louisbourgplayhouse.ca. This modern shingle theatre near the water hosts music, comedy, plays and dance. June to mid-Oct daily; shows at 8pm (box office from 2pm).

New Brunswick

The province of **NEW BRUNSWICK** attracts fewer tourists than its Maritime neighbours, despite sharing a border with the US and offering some spell-binding scenery. The only province in Canada that is constitutionally bilingual (English–French), around 33 percent of the population is francophone, a legacy of New Brunswick's turbulent history; settled by the French in the seventeenth century, the British occupied the region in the 1750s, its population swelled by English-speaking Loyalists fleeing the American Revolutionary War in 1783.

Today the booming city of **Moncton** – the effective capital of modern **Acadia** – acts as a gateway to the province from Nova Scotia (the border lies 54km to the southeast). Assuming you have a car, the best of New Brunswick can be experienced on three main routes from here. Travelling west along the coast to the **US state of Maine** you'll shadow the deeply indented **Bay of Fundy**, with a sparsely populated shoreline of forest, rock and swamp epitomized by the coastal **Fundy Trail Parkway** and **Fundy National Park**. The province's biggest city is **Saint John**, boasting a splendid sample of Victorian architecture, while easily the prettiest of the region's coastal towns is **St Andrews**, a Loyalist settlement turned seaside resort and equipped with a battery of tantalizing inns and B&Bs. The other main attraction is the **Fundy Islands** archipelago at the mouth of Passamaquoddy Bay, which includes **Campobello Island**, the site of Franklin Roosevelt's country retreat, and the far larger **Grand Manan Island**, a wild and remote spot noted for its imposing sea cliffs and rich birdlife.

Heading north to **Québec** from Moncton are two further routes: the first slices up the western edge of the province along the **St John River Valley** via **Fredericton**, the provincial capital, which offers the bonus of the Beaverbrook Art Gallery and a handsome historic district. The second route cuts north along the Gulf of St Lawrence to the cluster of small towns known collectively as **Miramichi City**. Near here are the untamed coastal marshes of the **Kouchibouguac National Park** and culture-rich attractions of the **Acadian Coast** and **Acadian Peninsula**, heartlands of the French-speaking Acadians today.

INFORMATION AND BORDER CROSSING

Tourism New Brunswick ☎ 800 561 0123, ⓦ tourism newbrunswick.ca.

CROSSING THE US–CANADA BORDER

New Brunswick is the Maritimes' gateway to the US, and crossing the land border to Maine is relatively stress-free (most crossings are open 24hr). Entering Canada by land, visitors (who don't need visas) do not need to apply for the Electronic Travel Authorization (eTA); just bring your passport. If you've entered the US on the visa waiver programme (EU, UK, Ireland etc), Canadian immigration officials may want proof of your onward ticket (the same applies heading back into the US); note that the 90 days granted by the US visa waiver includes time in Canada. If you've flown into Canada and then want to enter the US by land you'll need to fill in the I-94W visa waiver form at the border (US$6) – you do not require pre-approval through ESTA (same applies for ferries between New Brunswick and Maine). Visitors who require a visa to enter the US will need to obtain one in advance.

Border crossings From the US, I-95 is the fastest route into New Brunswick, crossing the border at Houlton, Maine. You'll pass a visitor information centre 2km into Canada (May–Sept only). There is nowhere to change money at the border; however, this crossing leads to the New Brunswick town of Woodstock, just across the Trans-Canada Highway, where there are banks for changing money. The Calais/St Stephen crossing, further south, is a more popular choice with tourists and can be busier in the summer: there are plenty of amenities and attractions on both sides (see page 380). The Lubec/Campobello Island crossing is also well-used, but to move on to the rest of Canada you need to take two ferries (see page 381). Houlton contains a few motels and petrol stations while Calais and Lubec (by far the nicest of the three border towns) offer the same. It's a 2hr drive from Houlton or Calais to Bangor, Maine – give at least 4–5hr for Boston (350 miles).

Time zones Maine is on Eastern Time, one hour behind New Brunswick's Atlantic Time.

Moncton

Founded in 1766 by Pennsylvania Dutch immigrants, **MONCTON** is a thriving commercial centre today – Greater Moncton (population 145,000) is bigger than Saint John. With outskirts of long strip malls and a centre of predominantly modern office

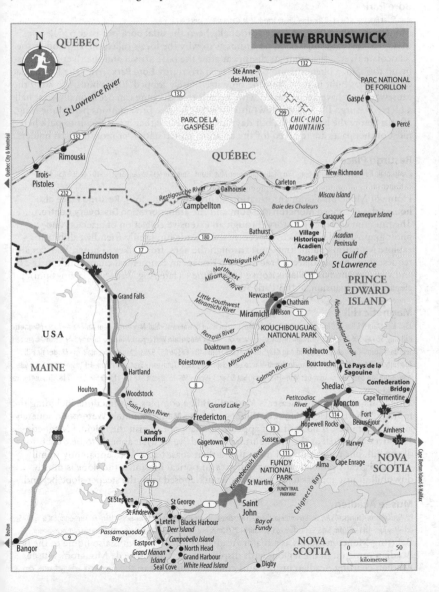

5

buildings (the iconic **Bell Aliant Tower**, at 127m, is the tallest radio tower in Atlantic Canada), the city might seem less appealing than the province's more rustic attractions, but it would be a mistake to skip Moncton. The Petitcodiac River provides the bizarre **tidal bore** that sweeps up twice a day from the Bay of Fundy, 35km downstream, and the **Musée Acadian** is one of the best museums in the region. Indeed Moncton's rejuvenation partly reflects the increasing confidence of local **Acadians**: the town hosts the province's only French-speaking university and is proud of becoming **Canada's first officially bilingual city** in 2002.

Bore Park

Main St, at Bendview Court • 24hr • Free • Bore schedule at ⓦ tourism.moncton.ca

Moncton's main attraction has traditionally been the **tidal bore** (see page 355), though at low tide you'll be in no doubt as to why the locals called the Petitcodiac the "chocolate river". The mudflats disappear after the bore arrives and the river level rises by up to 7.5m, a phenomenon best observed from tiny **Bore Park**. After the Petitcodiac causeway was built in the 1960s the bore itself rarely topped 20cm, but since 2010 the causeway gates have been opened with a result that the bore can occasionally crest half a metre. Resurgo Place (see below) interpreters give free presentations here (June–Aug, 30min before the bore arrives, but daytime only). Note that it is difficult to **park** here – most of the spaces are reserved for the adjacent police station or monthly pass holders.

Resurgo Place

20 Mountain Rd • Tues–Sat 10am–5pm, Sun noon–5pm (open Mon 10am–5pm late May to early Sept) • $10 • ☎ 506 856 4327, ⓦ resurgo.ca

Home of Moncton Visitor Information Centre (see page 369), **Resurgo Place** also houses the revamped **Moncton Museum** and the **Transportation Discovery Centre**. The museum charts city history through an extensive collection of artefacts and photographs, while the discovery centre uses hands-on, family-friendly exhibits to explore Moncton's public transport through the ages, from bikes to buses. You can also request tours of the adjacent **Free Meeting House**, an ecumenical chapel built in 1821, and visit the **Thomas Williams House** (early June to late Aug Wed–Sun 10am–6pm), an elegant 1883 mansion at 103 Park St.

Magnetic Hill

2875 Mountain Rd, Rte-126 (off Rte-2 Exit 450, about 9km northwest of downtown) • Mid-May to mid-Sept daily 8am–7pm • **Magnetic Hill** only, $6 • ☎ 506 389 5980, ⓦ magnetichillwharfvillage.ca • **Magic Mountain Waterpark** Mid-June to early July & mid-Aug to early Sept daily 10am–6pm; early July to mid-Aug daily 10am–7pm • From $48 • ☎ 506 857 9283, ⓦ magicmountain.ca • **Magnetic Hill Zoo** Early April to mid-May daily 10am–4pm; mid-May to early Sept daily 9am–7pm; early Sept to Oct Mon–Fri 10am–6pm, Sat & Sun 9am–6pm; Nov daily 10am–3pm; Dec Mon–Fri 5–9pm, Sat & Sun 3–9pm • $9–15, ages 4–12 $7–11 • ☎ 506 877 7718, ⓦ moncton.ca/magnetichillzoo

Moncton's major crowd-pleaser is **Magnetic Hill**, a complex of attractions including the touristy Wharf Village, **Magnetic Hill Zoo** and the **Magic Mountain Waterpark**, squarely aimed at families. If none of that appeals, you can opt to visit the original Magnetic Hill attraction itself at the main entrance; you drive to what appears to be the bottom of the hill, put your vehicle in neutral and then coast backwards, apparently uphill – which is really rather weird. In reality it's an optical illusion – the slope is mostly downhill, it just appears to be uphill when juxtaposed with the steeper slope beyond.

Musée Acadien

Pavillon Clément-Cormier, 405 Ave de l'Université (at the main entrance to Université de Moncton) • June–Sept Mon–Fri 9am–5pm, Sat & Sun 1–5pm; Oct–May Tues–Fri 1–4.30pm, Sat & Sun 1–4pm • $5, parking $1.25/30min; free Sat & Sun • ☎ 506 858 4088, ⓦ umoncton.ca/umcm-maum

Befitting Moncton's status as a major Acadian centre, the town is also home to the best Acadian museum in the region, with displays at the Université de Moncton's **Musée Acadien** charting Acadian history and culture from 1604 to the present. Artefacts on show include a cache of rare books, including a 1717 missionary Bible, and there's a special section on legendary heroine Evangeline (see page 353).

ARRIVAL AND DEPARTURE   MONCTON

By plane Greater Moncton International Airport (@cyqm. ca) is located 10km east of downtown near Dieppe, and hosts regular flights from Halifax, Montréal, Ottawa and Toronto (via Air Canada, Porter and WestJet). Avis, Budget, Hertz and National have car rental desks at the airport; the only other way to get into town is to take a taxi (Air Cab; around $20; ☎ 506 857 2000), or pre-arrange a pick-up with Maritime Bus (see below).

By bus Maritime Bus (☎ 506 854 2023, @maritimebus. com) runs long-distance bus services to and from Moncton

VIA Rail Station at 77 Canada St (and Moncton airport if arranged in advance).

Destinations Bathurst (1 daily; 3hr 15min); Charlottetown (3 daily; 3hr–3hr 20min); Fredericton (2–3 daily; 2hr 15min–3hr 30min); Halifax (3 daily; 3hr 45min–4hr 20min); Miramichi (1 daily; 2hr 5min); Montréal (1–2 daily; 11hr); Québec City (1–2 daily; 8hr 35min); Saint John (2–4 daily; 2hr 10min).

By train Moncton's VIA Rail train station is at 77 Canada St.

Destinations Halifax (1 daily except Tues; 4hr 25min); Montréal (1 daily except Tues; 15hr).

INFORMATION

Visitor centres The main Moncton Visitor Information Centre is inside Resurgo Place (daily: May–Sept Mon–Sat 10am–5pm, Sun noon–5pm; Sept–May Tues–Sat 10am–5pm, Sun noon–5pm; ☎ 800 363 4558, @tourism.

moncton.ca). There's a seasonal office in the historic Treitz Haus (the only surviving building from the Pennsylvania Dutch era), 10 Bendview Court, opposite Bore Park (mid-June to early Sept daily 9am–6pm).

ACCOMMODATION

Auberge C'mon Inn Hostel 47 Fleet St ☎ 506 854 8155, @monctonhostel.ca. Great budget option in a grand old house downtown, with dorm beds (mixed and female only) as well as simple doubles and singles (shared bathrooms). Laundry and shared kitchen; breakfast usually included. Dorms $32; private rooms $72

Delta Hotels by Marriott Beausejour 750 Main St ☎ 506 854 4344, @marriott.com. The most lavish hotel in town is this vast modern high-rise close to the centre, offering luxury rooms and all the extras. Parking $15/day, breakfast $16.95. $170

★ **Residence Inn** 600 Main St ☎ 506 854 7100, @marriott.com. One of the newer hotels in Moncton is also

one of the best, beating out the *Delta* in most departments, and the most centrally located, steps from Bore Park. Each spacious suite comes with sitting area, kitchen and flat-screen TV. Decent pool and gym; parking $15/day. $199

St. James Gate 14 Church St ☎ 506 388 4283, @st-jamesgate.ca. Boutique hotel with hardwood floors, flat-screen TVs, iPod docks, DVDs and full-length glass between bathroom (some with huge soaking -tubs) and bed, in the centre of town. It's definitely the coolest place to stay in Moncton, but there's no elevator and the bar below is very noisy at weekends (till 2am); the breakfast (included) is also rather basic. Parking $10/day. $179

EATING

★ **Jean's Restaurant** 1999 Mountain Rd ☎ 506 856 8988, @jeansrestaurants.com. No-frills diner located about 3km blocks from Magnetic Hill (west of downtown), worth the trip for its clams alone (it also does decent burgers and seafood plates from $13–20), not to mention its 1950s booths. Free parking on-site. Daily 5.45am–10pm.

★ **Little Louis'** 2/F, 245 Collishaw St (off Vaughan

Harvey) ☎ 506 855 2022, @littlelouis.ca. Something of a Moncton experience, this gourmet restaurant is tucked away on the second floor of a strip mall, but local chef Pierre A. Richard cooks up some real culinary delights; think pistachio-crusted rack of lamb, marinated salmon roe and squid-ink gnocchi, and a mouthwatering bouillabaisse (mains from $25). Daily 5–11pm.

DRINKING

Old Triangle Irish Alehouse 751 Main St ☎ 506 384 7474, @oldtriangle.com. Irish-themed pub food ($12–18) and plenty of live music (folk and Irish) accompany those fine pints of Guinness or local brews from Picaroons and Keith's in this sister pub of the Halifax stalwart. Happy hour Mon–Fri 4–7pm. Mon–Tues & Sun 11am–midnight, Wed–Sat 11am–2am.

★ **Pump House Brewery** 5 Orange Lane, just off Main

St ☎ 506 855 2337, @pumphousebrewery.ca. Popular brewpub that crafts some excellent seasonal beers; if the lauded blueberry cream ale is too fruity, try the hoppy IPA or Muddy River Stout. The pub food is pretty good too (beer bread for $6, beer-steamed mussels $13.95, and Moncton's only wood-fired pizza oven, pizzas from $10.25). Mon–Wed 11am–midnight, Thurs 11am–1am, Fri & Sat 11am–2am, Sun noon–midnight.

5

Fort Beauséjour

111 Fort Beauséjour Rd, Aulac • Late June to early Sept daily 9am–5pm • $3.90 • ☎ 506 364 5080, ⓦ pc.gc.ca/en/lhn-nhs/nb/beausejour

Providing panoramic views over the broad sweep of Chignecto Bay, **Fort Beauséjour** (officially the Fort Beauséjour-Fort Cumberland National Historic Site) is stuck on a grassy, treeless hill about 50km south of Moncton and just 2km from the junction of routes 2 and 16. The site's strategic value was first recognized by the French, who fortified the hill in 1751. Four years later, the British captured the fort (renaming it **Fort Cumberland**), and promptly deported the local Acadians, who they thought might rebel. The British garrison stayed on until 1835 as a defence against the Americans.

Flush with the brow of the hill, the **remains** of the star-shaped fort include much of the original earthwork, the concentric ditches and mounds typical of the period, as well as a sally port and a couple of deeply recessed casements, used for general storage. The site also has a **museum** with intriguing displays on the history of the fort and of the Acadian farmers who settled the region in the 1670s. Some of the most interesting exhibits, such as ancient clogs and farm tools, were recovered when the fort was repaired and restored in the 1960s. From Fort Beauséjour, it's just a few kilometres south to central Nova Scotia and about 50km east to the Confederation Bridge over to PEI (see page 392).

The Fundy coast

Some of the most alluring portions of New Brunswick's coastline can be found between Moncton and Saint John, a wild and mostly untouched region of rugged headlands, crumbling cliffs and dense, fog-bound forests trailing into the sea. The main sights are easily accessed via highways 114 and 111, collectively dubbed the **Fundy Coastal Drive**.

The Fundy coast is a popular holiday spot in the summer, so it's a good idea to book **accommodation** in advance – most things are closed between November and June. Be prepared for patches of pea-soup fog: the Bay of Fundy is notoriously prone to them. You'll need a car to make the most of the area, as there is **no public transport** to either St Martins or the Fundy National Park.

Hopewell Rocks

131 Discovery Rd, Hopewell Cape (Rte-114) • Daily: mid-May to late June & early Sept to mid-Oct 8am–5pm; late June to late Aug 8am–8pm; late Aug to early Sept 8am–7pm • $10 • ☎ 877 734 3429, ⓦ thehopewellrocks.ca

From Moncton, it's 50km south along the west bank of the Petitcodiac River on Rte-114 to the captivating shoreline of Hopewell Cape, contained within the privately managed **Hopewell Rocks park**. The interpretive centre at the park's upper section explains the cape's geology and the marine complexities of the Bay of Fundy, but you'll soon be wandering down the 828m footpath to the lower section – past several vantage points – to the gnarled red-sandstone pinnacles rising up to 15m above the beach known as the **Flowerpot Rocks** (golf carts shuttle back and forth for $2 one way). The rocks were pushed away from the cliff face by glacial pressure during the Ice Age, and the Bay of Fundy tides have defined their present, eccentric shape. At high tide they resemble stark little islands covered in fir trees, but at low tide they look like enormous termite hills. Steps lead down to the beach and you can safely walk round the rocks two to three hours either side of low tide, or paddle round them at high tide by taking a guided tour by **kayak** (June–Aug; 1–2hr tours from $69; ☎ 877 601 2660, ⓦ baymountadventures.com). Your ticket is valid for two days to ensure you see both tides. You can still wander around the site when the park is officially closed, but at your own risk.

Cape Enrage

650 Cape Enrage Rd, Waterside (off Rte-915) • Daily: mid-May to mid-June & early Sept to early Oct 9am–6pm; mid-June to early Sept 9am–8pm • $6; family $20 • ☎ 506 887 2273, ⓦ capeenrage.ca

Some 35km southwest of Hopewell Cape lies **Cape Enrage**, 6.5km down a side road off Rte-915, where the original 1848 lighthouse is glued to a great shank of rock soaring high above the sea. When the lighthouse was automated in 1988, the keepers moved away, and a Moncton schoolteacher initiated an ambitious plan to protect and develop the site with the enthusiastic help of his students. There's now a wooden walkway up to the foot of the lighthouse, a path down to the beach, and the old keeper's house has been converted into a pleasant café (try the fish chowder) and interpretive centre. Students staff the cape in the summer and help run a programme of **adventure sports**, principally rappelling ($95 for 2hr) and zip-lining (three runs; $50). In all cases, book ahead. Though the facilities are locked up from October to April, you can usually still wander around the site.

Alma

Just across the Salmon River from the east entrance to the Fundy National Park (see page 370) and some 14km from Cape Enrage, **ALMA** is a sleepy little village whose three hundred inhabitants make a tidy living from fishing, farming and tourism. The highlight here is food – the village contains three **lobster** pounds that sell the local Fundy Bay variety, prized for their firm, tasty meat, fresh from large saltwater tanks. Most shops also sell scallops, smoked salmon, oysters and fresh fish.

ACCOMMODATION   ALMA

★**Cleveland Place B&B** 8580 Main St (Hwy-114) ☎506 887 221, ⊛bbcanada.com/137.html. Beautiful clapboard B&B dating back to 1927 and hosted by gourmet chefs (dinner is also offered) – the warm hospitality and food are the highlights, but the airy, period rooms are very comfy and there's a bookstore at the back. $150

Falcon Ridge Inn 24 Falcon Ridge Drive ☎506 887 1110, ⊛falconridgeinn.nb.ca. This fine B&B is all about the mesmerizing views, perched high above the village and

the bay. The four rooms (satellite TV and DVD) are spacious and the breakfasts are divine. $115

Parkland Village Inn 8601 Main St (Hwy-114) ☎506 887 2313, ⊛parklandvillageinn.com. This is more of a standard two-storey, motel-like option on the main street, with breakfast included April–June & Sept–Oct. The ageing rooms are a little old-fashioned but come with cable TV – the deluxe rooms have ocean views. April–Nov only. $135

EATING

Alma Lobster Shop 36 Shore Lane, off Foster Rd ☎506 887 1987, ⊛thankfultoo.com. Overlooking the water, this shop sells live (by the pound, market price) and cooked lobsters (around $2–3 more); buy one to eat on the picnic tables outside (lobster rolls from $12, complete lobster dinners from $25). Daily 11am–9pm.

Fundy Take-Out Restaurant 21 Fundy View Rd ☎506 887 2261. Overlooking the Salmon River, this no-frills shack knocks out fried chicken ($9.50), fish and chips (medium $11.99), fried breaded clams ($10.95) and lobster rolls ($13.95) you can eat on picnic tables with *poutine*. May–Oct Mon–Thurs 11am–7pm, Fri & Sat 11am–10pm, Sun

11am–7.30pm.

Kelly's Bake Shop 8587 Main St (next to Alpine Motor Inn) ☎506 887 2460. For something sweet, visit this lauded bakery, best known for its enormous, delicious sticky buns and array of tempting cakes. Daily: May & June 10am–5pm, July & Aug 7am–6pm, Sept & Oct 8.30am–5pm.

Tides Restaurant 8601 Main St (Parkland Village Inn) ☎506 887 2313. The best place for a sit-down meal in Alma; the seafood chowder is a worthy house special and the views of the bay are fabulous. Mains $18–32. May–Oct daily 11am–7pm; Nov–April Thurs–Sun 11am–7pm.

Fundy National Park

Two entrances on Rte-114: one near Lake Wolfe, about 20km south of Rte-1; the other is about 20km to the east, on the coast next door to Alma • Open 24hr, but limited access in winter • Mid-May to Oct daily 8am–6pm $7.80, free at other times

Bisected by Rte-114, **Fundy National Park** encompasses a short stretch of the Bay of Fundy's pristine shoreline, all jagged cliffs and tidal mudflats, and the forested hills, lakes and river valleys of the central plateau behind. This varied scenery is crossed by more than 100km of **hiking trails**, mostly short and easy walks taking no more than three hours to complete – though the 45km Fundy Circuit links several of the interior trails and takes between three and five days. The pick of the hiking trails are along the Fundy shore,

5

where the shady **Point Wolfe Beach Trail** is a moderately steep, 600m hike down from the spruce woodlands above the bay to the grey-sand beach below (15min). Of equal appeal is the 4.4km loop of the **Coppermine Trail** (1hr 30min–2hr), which meanders through the forests with awe-inspiring views out along the seashore. Birdlife is more common in the park than larger **wildlife**, though you may see the odd moose, and several precocious raccoons in summer, which have become real pests – feeding them is illegal.

INFORMATION   FUNDY NATIONAL PARK

Visitor centre Rte-114 near the east entrance (late Jan to late May Tues & Wed 8.15am–noon & 12.45–4.15pm, Thurs–Mon 10am–6pm; late May to late June daily 8am–6.45pm; late June to early Sept daily 8am–9.45pm, early Sept to late Oct daily 8am–7.45pm; ☏ 506 887 6000, ⓦ pc.gc.ca/en/pn-np/nb/fundy); features displays on local flora and fauna, organizes guided walks (June–Aug), issues backcountry permits ($9.80) and sells hiking maps.
Trail map All the park's trails are described on a free map issued on arrival at either of the two Rte-114 entrance kiosks.

ACCOMMODATION

Fundy Highlands Inn & Chalets 8714 Rte-114 ☏ 506 887 2930, ⓦ fundyhighlands.com. If either camping or staying in Alma (see page 371) doesn't appeal, opt for one of these twenty comfortable, a/c motel studios and 24 wood-panelled chalets, with kitchenettes and views of the bay. May–Oct only. Studios $105; chalets $135
National park camping Reservations ☏ 877 737 3783, ⓦ reservation.pc.gc.ca. The park's three campgrounds all offer unserviced campsites ($15.70–25.50), while *Chignecto North* (mid-May to early Oct) and *Headquarters* (late June to Aug) also offer serviced ($23.50–35.30) sites and the posh oTENTik cabins ($100). Both serviced campgrounds are located near the east entrance (close to Alma) along with most of the park's tourist facilities. For greater isolation, take the 10km-long by-road southwest from the visitor centre to *Point Wolfe*, where the medium-sized, unserviced campground (late June to Aug) is tucked in among the wooded hills above the coast – and near the starting point of the Point Wolfe Beach and Coppermine trails (see above). There are also thirteen backcountry campgrounds ($9.80), which require registration with the visitor centre. $15.70

St Martins

The fishing village of **ST MARTINS** winds along the Bay of Fundy shoreline about 40km to the east of Saint John, a pretty ensemble of neat gardens and clapboard houses culminating (after 3km) at the **harbour**, a compact affair of lobster pots and skiffs set within a ring of hills. Be sure to get a photo of the **twin covered bridges** over the Irish River (the Vaughan Creek Bridge was built in 1935; upriver is the Hardscrabble Bridge of 1946) along with the lighthouse (the information centre), built in 1983 and actually a replica of the old Quaco Head Lighthouse.

Quaco Museum

236 Main St · Late June to Aug Tues–Sat 10am–5pm; Sept to mid-Nov Tues–Sat 10am–4.30pm · Free (donation requested) · ☏ 506 833 4740, ⓦ quaco.ca

St Martins was settled by Loyalists in 1783 (it was originally known as Quaco), and from 1803 to 1919 was a major shipbuilding centre. Learn about this surprising history at the tiny **Quaco Museum**, staffed by devoted volunteers.

INFORMATION   ST MARTINS

Tourist information centre 424 Main St, in the lighthouse at the harbour (July–Sept daily 9am–5pm; ☏ 506 833 2006, ⓦ stmartinscanada.com).

ACCOMMODATION

St Martins Country Inn 303 Main St ☏ 506 833 4534, ⓦ stmartinscountryinn.ca. Built around 1857, this luxurious option features high Victorian gables and fancy gingerbread scrollwork; the inn has seventeen en-suite rooms decorated in broadly period style. April–Dec. $139
Tidal Watch Inn 16 Beach St ☏ 506 833 4772 ⓦ tidalwatchinn.ca. An elegant option is this nineteenth-century clapboard property down by the water, with fifteen cosy rooms blending antiques with whirlpool spa tubs and TV. Breakfast included. $125

5

EATING

Caves Restaurant 82 Big Salmon River Rd (Orange Hill) ☎ 506 833 4698, ⊛ cavesrestaurant.com. Just beyond St Martins harbour (drive across the covered bridge), *Caves* is justly praised for its seafood-crammed chowder ($13.99), fresh lobster dinners ($30), burgers (from $10) and waterside deck. May Sat & Sun 11am–7pm; June & Sept to mid-Oct daily 11am–7pm; July & Aug daily 11am–8pm.

Coastal Tides 7 Beach St ☎ 506 833 1103. Mingle with the locals over strong coffee at this friendly diner just off Main St; it offers burgers, scallop and chips, lobster rolls,

chowder and a small Chinese menu (dinner mains $15–17). June–Sept Tues–Sat 11am–7pm, Sun 9am–6pm; Oct–Dec & March–May Fri 4–7pm, Sat 11am–7pm, Sun 9am–6pm).

St Martin's Ice Cream Parlour 30 Main St (just off Rte-111) ☎ 506 833 9892. Small shack that doles out scrumptious home-made ice cream in summer; think black raspberry cheesecake, maple sugar and peanut butter mudslide (from $2.45). Also does lobster rolls ($11.95–19.95) and burgers (from $4.95). May–Sept daily 11am–8pm.

The Fundy Trail Parkway

3 Fundy Trail Parkway, Salmon River • Daily: mid-May to mid-June & early Sept to mid-Oct 9am–5pm; mid-June to late Aug 8am–8pm; late Aug to early Sept 9am–7pm • $9 • ☎ 506 833 2019, ⊛ fundytrail.ca

From St Martin's harbour it's 8km east along Big Salmon River Rd to the **Fundy Trail Parkway**, one of the province's most magical destinations. The 30km parkway threads past craggy headlands, dense forest and stupendous viewpoints at almost every turn; you might see moose, porcupine and deer along the way. The road is also shadowed by a multi-use **trail** offering fine and comparatively easy hiking and biking, as well as access to several gorgeous beaches and falls. The parkway passes the **Big Salmon River Interpretive Centre**, whose exhibits give the historical lowdown on the former lumber town of Big Salmon River (the inhabitants packed up shop in the 1940s). The nearby **Cookhouse** offers more exhibits on the lumber industry. From the centre, you can stroll down the hillside and cross the suspension bridge to the river below or continue on to **Long Beach Interpretive Centre** with spectacular views across Tufts' Point. At the time of research, **Hearst Lodge** was closed, but may be re-opened in future. The Hearst family – of newspaper fame and owners of the lumber mill – built the hunting and fishing lodge here in 1968.

The final stretch of parkway to the **McCumber Brook/Walton Glen Gorge/Falls area** was completed in 2018, ending at a second entry kiosk on McCumber Brook Rd; the connector road to Sussex is due to open in 2020 and the road to Alma is scheduled to open in 2021 (ultimately linking to Fundy National Park, see page 370); until then you must return to St Martins to move on.

Saint John

The largest city in New Brunswick (pop. 129,000), **SAINT JOHN** is better known for its industrial prowess than its tourist attractions, home to iconic products such **Moosehead beer**, the mighty **Irving group** of companies and a booming oil and gas sector. Yet the surprisingly compact downtown area is crammed with diverting sights, from resplendent Victorian architecture to the absorbing **New Brunswick Museum** and the **Reversing Falls Rapids** on the St John River, a dramatic spot to see the effects of the Fundy tides.

THE FUNDY FOOTPATH

Experienced hikers can tackle the 50km between Fundy National Park (see page 371) and the Fundy Trail Parkway (see page 370) via the spectacular coastal **Fundy Footpath** (⊛ fundyhikingtrails.com), accessible from the end of Goose River Path (7.9km; 2hr 30min) from Point Wolfe in Fundy National Park. The challenging trail ends near the Big Salmon River Interpretive Centre on the Parkway. Most people take four days and camp along the way; all hikers are required to register by calling ☎ 866 386 3987.

5

The French established a trading post here in 1631, but the city proper was founded by Loyalist refugees from America in 1783. In the nineteenth century Saint John thrived on the lumber and shipbuilding industries, and despite a devastating fire in 1877, it was sufficiently wealthy to withstand the costs of immediate reconstruction. Consequently, almost all the city's older buildings – at their finest in the **Trinity Royal Historic Preservation Area** – are late Victorian.

Most of the action in Saint John takes place in the downtown area, known here as **Uptown** – the part of the city across the harbour is dubbed **West Side**.

Market Slip

The tiny rectangular dock at the foot of King Street, known as the **Market Slip**, is where the three thousand Loyalists disembarked in 1783. The Slip no longer functions as a port, but is still at the heart of Saint John, with warehouses converted into wine bars, restaurants and boutiques that front the modern Market Square shopping mall behind. Opposite is **Barbour's General Store** (10 Market Slip; late June to late Sept Thurs–Sat 10am–6pm, Sun noon–6pm; free; ☎506 642 2242), an emporium that operated between 1860 and 1940 in Sheffield, New Brunswick, and is now stuffed with Victorian paraphernalia from formidable-looking sweets to an old barber's chair. At the back you can enjoy various teas in the tearoom.

New Brunswick Museum

1 Market Square (Market Square shopping mall) • Mon–Wed & Fri 9am–5pm, Thurs 9am–9pm, Sat 10am–5pm, Sun noon–5pm; Nov to mid-May closed Mon • $10 • ☎506 643 2300, ⓦnbm-mnb.ca

Inside the Market Square shopping mall, the **New Brunswick Museum** has an especially revealing section on the province's lumber, industrial and shipbuilding traditions as well as a fine collection of Chinese decorative and applied art. There's also much on the region's marine life, including the skeleton of a rare North Atlantic Right whale, and a 13m-high tidal tube constructed to illustrate the rise and fall of the Bay of Fundy tides.

Loyalist House

120 Union St • Mid-May to Oct Mon–Sat 10am–5pm • $5 • ☎506 652 3590, ⓦfacebook.com/merritthome

Completed in 1817 for merchant David Merritt – who fled colonial New York after the American Revolution – the white clapboard **Loyalist House** boasts an attractive Georgian interior and is one of the oldest homes in the city. Thanks to Merritt's ancestors, who lived here until 1958 and never threw anything away, it's kitted out with a remarkable ensemble of original furnishings. Enthusiastic guides bring these pieces to life and provide a good introduction to the Loyalist story (see page 329); favourites include the disguised water closet, a clock made in London around 1780 and a bed once slept in by the future Edward VII.

City Market

47 Charlotte St • Mon–Fri 7.30am–6pm, Sat 7.30am–5pm • ☎506 658 2820, ⓦsjcitymarket.ca

In operation since 1876, the cheery **City Market** is heaped with fresh fruits and the characteristic foods of New Brunswick – **fiddleheads**, a succulent fern tip that tastes rather like asparagus, and **dulse**, dried seaweed. This is also a great place for **lunch** (see page 377).

Prince William Street

After the fire of 1877, the city's merchant class funded an ambitious rebuilding programme, epitomized by the brimmingly self-confident structures that grace the **Trinity Royal Historic Preservation Area**, especially along **Prince William Street**, south of the Market Slip. Note especially the grandiose Second Empire sandstone facades of the 1881 **Old Post Office** at no. 115 (offices today), the 1879 **Old City Hall** at no. 116 and Bank of Nova Scotia's 1878 **Palatine Building** at no. 124. **Postal Station A** at no. 126

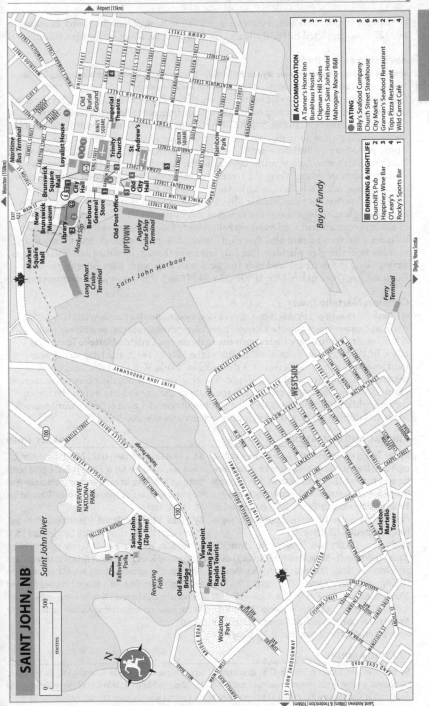

SAINT JOHN, NB

Airport (15km)

Saint John River

Moncton (150km)

Bay of Fundy

Saint John Harbour

Digby, Nova Scotia

Saint Andrews (98km) & Fredericton (106km)

ACCOMMODATION
A Tanner's Home Inn	4
BunkHaus Hostel	3
Chipman Hill Suites	1
Hilton Saint John Hotel	2
Mahogany Manor B&B	5

EATING
Billy's Seafood Company	5
Church Street Steakhouse	6
City Market	3
Grannan's Seafood Restaurant	2
Tops Pizza Restaurant	1
Wild Carrot Café	4

DRINKING & NIGHTLIFE
Churchill's Pub	2
Happinez Wine Bar	3
O'Leary's	4
Rocky's Sports Bar	1

Map labels

Maritime Bus Terminal
New Brunswick Museum
Market Square Mall
Library
Market Slip
Long Wharf Cruise Terminal
Barbour's General Store
City Hall
Old Post Office
Old City Hall
Loyalist House
Old Burial Ground
Imperial Theatre
Trinity Church
King's Square
St Andrew's
Rainbow Park
Queen Square
Pugsley Cruise Ship Terminal
UPTOWN
Ferry Terminal
WESTSIDE
Carleton Martello Tower
RIVERVIEW NATIONAL PARK
Saint John Adventures (Zip line)
Fallsview Park
Reversing Falls
Old Railway Bridge
Viewpoint
Reversing Falls Rapids Tourist Centre
Wolastoq Park

SAINT JOHN THROUGHWAY

0   500
metres

N

5

(1915) displays the later Beaux-Arts style, while the **Bank of New Brunswick Building** at no. 125 was completed in 1879 with a Greek Revival facade of Corinthian columns.

Reversing Falls Rapids

Reversing Falls Rapids Tourist Centre and **Skywalk** 200 Bridge Rd • Late May to Oct daily 9am–sunset; Nov to late May Tues–Sun 11am–sunset • $15 late May to Oct, otherwise $7 • ☎ 506 642 4400 • ⓦ skywalksaintjohn.com

Like just about everywhere else on the shores of the Bay of Fundy, Saint John is proud of its explosive tides. What you have here are the impressive **Reversing Falls Rapids**, created by a sharp bend in the St John River about 3km west of the centre. At low tide, the rapids flow quite normally, but the incoming tide forces them into reverse, causing a brief period of equilibrium when the surface of the water is totally calm, before a churning, often tumultuous, surge upstream; the visitor centres post **tide times**. Several vantage points are posted along the river, with **Fallsview Park** the closest to the fiercest cascades (best reached by taxi or car). Another way to reach the falls is by walking the 2km **Harbour Passage** from Market Slip, a pedestrian trail that hugs the river. This ends at a viewing station high above the rapids at the bridge on Rte-100. On the other side of the bridge you'll find the **Reversing Falls Rapids Tourist Centre** and **Skywalk**, which includes a thirteen-minute film that explains the falls phenomenon, restaurant, and a stainless steel and glass platform that juts out from the cliff over the river. You can also **zipline** along the riverbank and over the local seals with Saint John Adventures at 50 Fallsview Ave (June to late Oct; ☎ 506 634 9477; $65–75; ⓦsaintjohnadventures.ca).

Carleton Martello Tower

454 Whipple St • Late June to early Sept daily 10am–5.30pm; early Sept to early Nov Mon–Fri 8.30am–4pm • $3.90 • ☎ 506 636 4011, ⓦ pc.gc.ca/carletonmartellotower • Beyond the falls viewing station, take the first left along Lancaster Ave and follow the signs

A stub of circular masonry high above the harbour, the **Carleton Martello Tower** was raised in 1815, too late to be of much use in the War of 1812, and later served as a local museum, a detention centre for deserters in World War I and the focal point of the coastal defence system during World War II – hence the ungainly concrete structure plonked on top. The **visitor centre** tells the story of the site and lays out the historical context, while inside the tower there's a reconstruction of a nineteenth-century barrack room and displays on World War II, plus stellar views over town and bay.

ARRIVAL AND DEPARTURE

SAINT JOHN

By car Driving into uptown Saint John can be a baffling experience; the best strategy is to keep on Rte-1 and follow the signs from Exit 122. Parking by meter or in municipal lots (Mon–Fri 7am–6pm; $2/hr) is usually easy to find.

By bus Maritime Bus (☎ 506 672 2055, ⓦ maritimebus. com) runs long-distance bus services throughout the region from the terminal at 125 Station St.

Destinations Charlottetown (3 daily; 5hr 20min–6hr 10min); Fredericton (2–3 daily; 1hr 20min); Halifax (3 daily; 5hr 55min–7hr 20min); Miramichi (1 daily; 5hr); Moncton (4 daily; 2hr 10min); Montréal (1–2 daily; 13hr–13hr 30min); Québec City (1–2 daily; 10hr 15min–11hr); St Andrews (1 daily; 2hr); St Stephen (US Border; 2hr 30min).

By ferry Saint John's ferry terminal, 5km west of the centre across the mouth of the St John River at 170 Digby Ferry

Rd, is served by Bay Ferries (☎ 888 249 7245, ⓦ ferries.ca), which sails across the Bay of Fundy to Digby, Nova Scotia (see page 349). There are no buses direct to the centre from the terminal – take a cab (around $15) or call Diamond Taxi (☎ 506 648 8888).

By plane Saint John Airport (ⓦ saintjohnairport.com), 15km east of the city centre at 4180 Loch Lomond Rd, is a small affair, with flights on Air Canada to/from Halifax, Montréal and Toronto, and Porter Airlines to Ottawa. Saint John Transit (ⓦ saintjohn.ca) city bus #32 runs from the airport into town (Mon–Fri 8 daily; $2.75), and Diamond Taxi operates taxis (around $40 to the centre on the meter). All the major car rental companies have counters at the airport.

GETTING AROUND

By bus Saint John Transit (☎ 506 658 4700, ⓦ saintjohn. ca) operates a range of bus services; most start and finish downtown at King's Square. Bus #1 and #2 run from King's Square along King St to the Reversing Falls Rapids (every 15–20min), while bus #15A and #15B (every 30min) run to the Carleton Martello Tower (25min). Fares are $2.75.

By taxi Saint John taxis should all have meters: anywhere in the centre (including the falls) is likely to be $10–15, with downtown to the airport around $40.

INFORMATION

Visitor centre The main visitor information centre is in the centre of town inside the Shoppes of City Hall mall off King St (Mon–Sat 9am–5.30pm; ☎ 506 658 2855, ⊚ discoversaintjohn.com). This is the best place to get the latest on local boat trips and bus tours.

Internet Free internet and wi-fi is available at the Saint John Free Public Library (June to early Sept Mon–Tues & Fri 10am–5pm, Wed & Thurs 10am–9pm; early Sept to May Mon, Tues & Fri–Sun 10am–5pm, Wed & Thurs 10am–9pm) inside Market Square mall.

ACCOMMODATION

A Tanner's Home Inn 190 King St East ☎ 506 634 8917, ⊚ tannershomeinn.com; map p.375. Just a short stroll from the city centre, this beautiful old house was built by a local tanner in 1878, with five charming bedrooms decked out in Victorian period style. Breakfast, satellite TV and off-street parking included. $130

BunkHaus Hostel 36 Water St ☎ 506 646 9895, ⊚ bunkhaushostel.com; map p.375. Best of the budget accommodation, with centrally located dorms (with immaculate wood bunks) and cozy basic doubles, excellent shared kitchen and stylish common areas. No parking. Dorms $45; doubles $90

★ **Chipman Hill Suites** 9 Chipman Hill ☎ 506 693 1171, ⊚ chipmanhill.com; map p.375. Centrally located suites in twelve historic properties (circa 1860s), all with fully equipped kitchenettes or kitchens and cable TV (all buildings have laundries) – a fabulous deal. $126

Hilton Saint John Hotel 1 Market Square ☎ 506 693 8484, ⊚ 3.hilton.com; map p.375. Most rooms have waterfront views at this plush, modern tower block right beside Market Slip. Location and amenities (it has an indoor pool) are top-class, though you'll pay extra for parking ($20/day) and wi-fi ($6.95/day, free in public areas). $206

Mahogany Manor B&B 220 Germain St, at Queen St ☎ 506 636 8000, ⊚ sjnow.com/mm; map p.375. This is the pick of uptown's B&Bs, with five en-suite guest rooms in an elegant Edwardian villa (1905) with high gables and wraparound veranda. Located in a quiet, leafy part of town, a 10min walk southeast of Market Slip. Free parking. $110

EATING

★ **Billy's Seafood Company** 49–51 Charlotte St, in City Market ☎ 506 672 3474, ⊚ billysseafood.com; map p.375. Facing Charlotte St inside City Market and also open in the evenings, this market restaurant serves up fine fresh seafood such as lobster by the pound, clams ($22), beer battered haddock and chips ($18) and crab cakes ($17), and there's an excellent oyster bar (Thurs & Fri). Mon–Fri 11am–10pm, Sat 9am–10pm, Sun 4–10pm (closed Sun Jan–March).

Church Street Steakhouse 10 Grannan St, off Prince William St ☎ 506 648 2373, ⊚ grannangroup.com; map p.375. Best steaks in the city, using prime Angus beef and starting at $26 for the 8oz Baseball Sirloin. Mon, Tues & Sun 4–10pm, Wed 11.30am–10pm, Thurs 11.30am–11pm, Fri & Sat 11.30am–1.30pm & 4pm–midnight.

City Market 47 Charlotte St ☎ 506 658 2820, ⊚ sjcitymarket.ca; map p.375. Enticing food stalls here include the aromatic meat kebabs at *Shawarma Hut*, *Jeremiah's Deli* sandwiches and "Dave's Famous Chili" ($5.50) at *Slocum & Ferris*, in business since 1895. Mon–Fri 7.30am–6pm, Sat 7.30am–5pm.

Grannan's Seafood Restaurant Level 1, Market Square (on Market Slip) ☎ 506 634 1555, ⊚ grannangroup.com; map p.375. Among the string of pricey bars and cafés on Market Slip this is the best, where the catch of the day and fresh lobster is a treat and you get everything from haddock and chips ($16.50) and mussels ($17), to maritime fish pie ($18) and maple curry chicken pasta ($25). Mon–Thurs 11.30am–11pm, Fri & Sat 11.30am–midnight (bar till 2am), Sun noon–10pm.

Tops Pizza Restaurant 215 Union St, at Sydney St ☎ 506 634 0505; map p.375. This old-school diner and local favourite knocks out decent pizzas but also great lasagne, coleslaw and home-made soups – you can have a filling lunch for under $10. Booths and bar stools. Cash only. Daily 7am–9pm.

Wild Carrot Café 47 Charlotte St, in City Market ☎ 506 632 1900, ⊚ wildcarrotcafe.com; map p.375. Small café stall inside the market dishing up wholesome and vegetarian snacks and light meals; huge variety of soup pots ($5.10), wraps ($7–8) and quiches (from $5). Mon–Fri 8am–6pm, Sat 8am–5pm.

DRINKING

Churchill's Pub 8 Grannan St ☎ 506 648 2373, ⊚ grannangroup.com; map p.375. Congenial place next to the *Church Street Steakhouse* (see above) that offers 24 draughts on tap, tangy Martinis and delicious burgers (from $14). Mon–Wed 11.30am–1am, Thurs–Sat 11.30am–2am, Sun 11.30am–midnight.

5

Happinez Wine Bar 42 Princess St ☎ 506 634 7340, ⓦ happinezwinebar.com; map p.375. To take a break from Saint John's beer-heavy pub scene, try this intimate wine bar, with exposed brick walls and exceptional wine list. Enjoy the compact "hapito" patio outside in summer. Wed & Thurs 4pm–midnight, Fri 4pm–1am, Sat 5pm–1am.

O'Leary's 46 Princess St ☎ 506 634 7135, ⓦ olearyspub. com; map p.375. This local stalwart, an Irish pub with plenty of imported and domestic draught beers, has live music Fri & Sat, mostly folk, Irish or Maritime. Mon & Tues 11.30am–11pm, Wed–Fri 11.30am–2am, Sat 3pm–2am.

Rocky's Sports Bar 2/F, Shoppes of City Hall (take the footbridge from Market Square) ☎ 506 652 5452, ⓦ rockyssportsbar.com; map p.375. This friendly place attracts locals as well as tourists, regularly earning the title Best Sports Bar in Canada. Over 35 TVs cover all manner of sporting events, and there's plenty of snack food to accompany the beers. Daily 7.30am–1am.

St Andrews

Founded by Loyalists fleeing an independent America in 1783, **ST ANDREWS** was transformed into an affluent resort town in the late nineteenth century, with manicured gardens and neat rows of pastel-coloured clapboard houses more reminiscent of New England than the rougher fishing villages further north. Montréal-based architect **Edward Maxwell** (1867–1923) built many of the houses that now grace the main drag, **Water Street**, lining the Passamaquoddy Bay waterfront with cafés and craft shops, and the enchanting clapboard houses of **King Street**, which leads up the hill from the pier. Maxwell's "American shingle style" owes much to Henry Hobson Richardson (1838–86), creator of the Romanesque Revival style in North America.

Sheriff Andrews House

63 King St • Early June to early Oct Tues–Sat 9.30–4.30pm • Free, donation suggested • ☎ 506 529 5080

Elisha Andrews (1772–1833) was just 9 years old when his father – a Loyalist minister – fled Connecticut to the region that would become St Andrews. The family first lived on Minister's Island (see opposite), but in 1820 Elisha (who was now county sheriff) moved into his newly built red-brick Georgian home, now the **Sheriff Andrews House**. The rooms have been restocked with period furniture (1700s–1840) and enthusiastic costumed guides fill you in on the family history (ask for a free guided tour – there are no labels to tell you what you're looking at). Be sure to time your visit for the tea and home-made ginger cookies (free), served from 2 to 3.30pm.

Ross Memorial Museum

188 Montague St, at King St • Early June to early Oct Tues–Sat 10am–4.30pm (also Mon 10am–4.30pm July & Aug) • Donation suggested • ☎ 506 529 5124, ⓦ rossmemorialmuseum.ca

The **Ross Memorial Museum** is housed in the stately red-brick Georgian mansion built by Loyalist Harris Hatch in 1824, but stands today as a memorial to fascinating American couple **Henry and Sarah Ross**, world travellers and art collectors. Independently wealthy, they purchased the house in 1938 with the express purpose of gifting it to the town loaded with their treasures (the couple died childless in 1945). The two had been living in St Andrews since 1902 (see page 380). Inside you'll find nine immaculately preserved period rooms crammed with antique furniture, carpets and art; seascapes by Scot **George Horne Russell**, work of cabinet-maker **Thomas Nisbet**, and American "traitor" **Benedict Arnold's chair**, auctioned from his Saint John home in 1791. An absorbing exhibit about the Ross family exploits is upstairs.

Kingsbrae Garden

220 King St, at Prince of Wales St • Mid-May to mid-Oct daily 9am–6pm (till 7pm July & Aug) • $16, family $38 • ☎ 506 529 3335, ⓦ kingsbraegarden.com

Kingsbrae Garden overflows with flowers, shrubs and trees, but also local fauna, always a big hit with the kids: goats, ducks and the more exotic peacocks and alpacas, and

ST CROIX ISLAND

In August 1604, **St Croix Island**, in the middle of the St Croix estuary near modern-day St Andrews, became the first European/French settlement in Canada. The colony established by Pierre Dugua, Sieur de Mons (with Samuel de Champlain taking notes), only survived one grim winter (half the men died), with the post relocating to Port Royal in Nova Scotia (see page 353), but its symbolic significance remains. Today the island is managed by the US Parks Service and is off-limits, though there is an interpretive trail on the US mainland, 13km south of Calais on US-1. On the **Canadian side**, around 7km north of St Andrews on Rte-127, a series of interpretive boards provides context along with a viewpoint of the island itself.

even a ladybug release at 10.30am. A mini-Dutch windmill, woodland trail, cedar maze and treasure hunts round off the family-friendly attractions.

St Andrews Blockhouse

23 Joe's Point Rd, at the end of Water St • June–Aug daily 10am–6pm • $0.90 • ☎ 506 529 4270, ⓦ pc.gc.ca/en/lhn-nhs/nb/standrews

The squat, shingled **St Andrews Blockhouse** is the original wooden tower built in 1813 to protect the area from the Americans during the **War of 1812** – boards provide information on the conflict, while the cramped interior has been filled with replicas from the period (the wooden frame is original, but the shingle was added in the 1880s when it was used as a summer home).

Fundy Discovery Aquarium

1 Lower Campus Rd • Mid-May to mid-Oct daily 10am–5pm • $14.25, children 4–17 $10 • ☎ 506 529 1200, ⓦ huntsmanmarine.ca

A major family-friendly attraction, just north of the town centre, **Fundy Discovery Aquarium** is home to Loki and Snorkel, a couple of playful harbour seals (feedings 11am & 4pm), as well as several viewing tanks of various Bay of Fundy fish, seahorses, rare lobsters and monstrously big sturgeon.

Minister's Island

Bar Rd • Mid-May to mid-Oct 1–2 tours daily (2hr); open-access late June–Aug (daily 8am–8pm, depending on tides) • $10 (including tour) • ☎ 506 529 5081, ⓦ ministersisland.net

Connected to the mainland by a tidal causeway, the two-square-kilometre **Minister's Island** was the home of Passamaquoddy people for thousands of years before being purchased by railway tycoon **Sir William Van Horne** in the early 1890s. Today the grand edifices that architect Edward Maxwell created for him remain frozen in a state of benign neglect, atmospheric testimony to the wealth of the Gilded Age. The first European home on the island (known as the Blue House), was built by Anglican minister (thus the island's name) Reverend Samuel Andrews in 1790; his son became the sheriff. Van Horne – actually an American – made his fortune building the Canadian Pacific Railroad in the 1880s, and used the island as a summer home until his death in 1915.

Unless it's an open-access month (when you can visit independently), the only way to visit the island is via a guided tour – you pay the guide at the mainland side of the causeway before driving across as a group (boats shuttle across at high tide).

Covenhoven

The main feature of the island is Van Horne's grand fifty-room sandstone and shingle mansion, **Covenhoven**, containing a trove of his own vaguely Impressionist paintings, and small exhibits on the Passamaquoddy. The peeling paint, empty, haunting rooms and exposed wood make it especially atmospheric (most of the contents were auctioned off in the 1970s), but the giant billiard table and an Italian cabinet from 1642 remain. The upstairs rooms are especially dilapidated, though some still contain the original, fading wallpaper painted by Van Horne himself. Outside is the distinctive windmill

5

CANADA'S CHOCOLATE TOWN

Just across the St Croix River from Calais (pronounced 'kal-us'), Maine, New Brunswick's **St Stephen** has been dubbed Canada's Chocolate Town (it's a "sweet experience" etc) thanks to the presence of confectioner (and the town's major employer) **Ganong Chocolates**, founded here back in 1873. Today the absorbing **Chocolate Museum** (March & April Wed–Sun 11am–4pm; May Wed–Sun 11am–5pm; June Mon–Fri 10am–4pm, Sat & Sun noon–4pm; July & Aug Mon–Sat 10am–6pm, Sun 11am–5pm; Sept & Oct Mon–Sat 10am–5pm, Sun 11am–5pm; Nov Wed–Sat 10am–4pm, Sun noon–4pm; $10; ☎ 506 466 7848, ⓦ chocolatemuseum.ca), 73 Milltown Blvd, tells the story of chocolate-making in the town, with plenty of free samples. St Stephen has three border crossings with the US, all open 24hr.

(actually just a water tank), the circular **Bath House** overlooking the beach and, further away, the enormous wooden **Barn**.

INFORMATION

ST ANDREWS

St Andrews Visitor Information Centre 24 Reed Ave, on Rte-127 as you enter town (daily: early May to June 9am–5pm; July & Aug 9am–7pm; Sept to early Oct 9.30am–5.30pm; ☎ 506 529 3556, ⓦ standrewsbythesea.ca). It issues free tide tables and town maps, supplies information on local bike rental, has the schedule for visits to Minister's Island, and will help you with accommodation.

TOURS AND ACTIVITIES

The main pier is packed with **boat-tour** companies: trips run 3–4 times a day in peak season, but usually require a minimum of six people. Whales are the main attraction (minke and finback June–Oct, humpback July–Oct), but you'll also see harbour seals and porpoises year-round. Prices range $60–70, and trips usually run 2–3hr.

Eastern Outdoors 165 Water St ☎ 506 529 4662, ⓦ easternoutdoors.com. Runs kayak tours of Passamaquoddy Bay from $145 for a full day, and historic Navy Island for $69 for a half-day.

Fundy Tide Runners 16 King St (wharf) ☎ 506 529 4481, ⓦ fundytiderunners.com. Operates 7.5m Zodiac boat that zips up close to the whales ($70).

Quoddy Link Marine ☎ 506 529 2600, ⓦ quoddylinkmarine.com. Operates first-class whale-watching cruises (late June to mid-Oct 1–3 daily; 3hr; $60), each of which has a naturalist on board.

ACCOMMODATION

Algonquin Resort 184 Adolphus St ☎ 506 529 8823, ⓦ algonquinresort.com. The largest hotel in town is a sprawling and well-equipped resort complex whose mock-Tudor turrets and gables, dating from 1915 (the 1889 original burnt down in 1914), dominate St Andrews. Indoor and outdoor pools, spa, free parking and free shuttle to the wharf. **$220**

Kingsbrae Arms 219 King St ☎ 506 529 1897, ⓦ kingsbrae.com. The most illustrious hotel in town, this sumptuous, immaculately maintained mansion overlooks the botanical gardens. There are just eight guest rooms here, six of them suites with balconies offering wide views of the gardens and the bay, and each is decorated in lavish modern style. **$250**

★ **Montague Rose** 258 Montague St ☎ 506 529 8963, ⓦ themontaguerose.com. This inviting B&B is housed in a striking Second Empire-style home built in 1859, with three spacious rooms all with whirlpool or claw-foot tubs, satellite TV and DVD players. **$110**

Picket Fence Motel 102 Reed Ave ☎ 506 529 8985, ⓦ picketfencenb.com. Great budget option (at least by St Andrews standards), with seventeen basic motel units equipped with cable TV, just beyond Rte-127 (Mowat Drive), and a short drive from Water St. **$85**

Rossmount Inn 4599 Rte-127 ☎ 506 529 3351, ⓦ rossmountinn.com. Henry and Sarah Ross (see page 381) bought this gorgeous estate in 1902, and though the original burnt down in 1961, the current incarnation has been faithfully furnished with antiques and replica Queen Anne style, with modern amenities: cable TV, pool and the town's top restaurant (see page 381). **$135**

EATING AND DRINKING

The Gables 143 Water St ☎ 506 529 3440. Stylish little restaurant housed in a gabled, clapboard home built in 1870, serving fresh lobster, Bay of Fundy scallops ($21.50), chowders ($9) and tasty burgers ($14.50) from its bayshore location – seating overlooks the water. May–Aug daily 11am–10pm; Sept to early Oct Mon & Wed–Sun noon–8pm.

Garden Café Kingsbrae Garden, 220 King St ☎ 506 529

3335, ⓦkingsbraegarden.com. Famed for its afternoon tea ($15.95) from 2.30pm, chowder ($8.95) and fresh garden salads ($7.50–9.50). Mid-May to early Oct 11am–4pm (July & Aug to 8pm).

Red Herring Pub 211 Water St ☎506 529 8455, ⓦredherringpub.ca. This old clapboard and shingle pub with small outdoor deck serves good beer, tasty haddock and chips ($15), and is the best place in town for live music. Mon–Fri noon–2am, Sat & Sun 11.30am–2am (food till 9pm).

Rossmount Inn 4599 Rte-127 ☎506 529 3351, ⓦrossmountinn.com. This inn is justly praised for its quality cuisine, served up nightly by chef Chris Aerni. After being entertained with *amuse bouche*, expect the freshest local produce and seafood: lobster-celery rolls, Bay of Fundy haddock fillet and ginger-hoisin glazed duck breast (mains $24–30). Daily 6–11pm.

Campobello Island

US president Franklin D. Roosevelt loved **Campobello Island** for its quiet wooded coves, rocky headlands and excellent fishing – though he rarely returned after contracting polio here in 1921. The island, which is just 16km long by 5km wide, is now sprinkled with second homes and busy with day-trippers, though the southern half is protected as the **Roosevelt Campobello International Park**. Here, mixed forests, marshes, tidal flats, beaches and gullies are crossed by 24km of gravel road, which give access to a variety of gentle **hiking trails**.

Roosevelt Cottage

459 Rte-774, Welshpool • Late May to mid-Oct daily 10am–6pm • Free • ☎ 506 752 2922, ⓦfdr.net

Several hiking trails – including the refreshing 1.5km-long walk over to Friar's Head – begin beside the Campobello's star turn, the red-and-green **Roosevelt Cottage** built in 1897, set among the woods by the seashore about 3km south of the ferry dock. One look at the place and you'll see that "cottage" is an understatement – it's a 35-room mansion built in a Dutch colonial style and packed with memorabilia, from FDR's childhood potty and the Christmas list he made when he was knee-high, to the megaphone with which the Roosevelt children were summoned to dinner.

ARRIVAL AND DEPARTURE
CAMPOBELLO ISLAND

Most visitors still come to Campobello Island **over the bridge** from Lubec in Maine (USA). The only way to reach the island directly from mainland Canada is the seasonal ferry via **Deer Island**.

By ferry To Deer Island (daily every 30min 6.30am–7.30pm, then hourly till 10.30pm; 20min; free; first-come first-served; ☎506 642 0520, ☎855 882 1978, ⓦcoastaltransport. ca); ferries leave from Letete on the southeast shore of Passamaquoddy Bay, 14km south of Rte-1 (and the village of St George) on Rte-172. They dock at the island's northern shore, from where it's a 16km drive south to the Deer Island–Campobello ferry (mid-June to Sept hourly 8.30am–6.30pm; 35min; car & driver $20, foot passenger $4; ☎506 747 2159, ⓦeastcoastferriesltd.com; first-come first-served) – look for the signs to Deer Island Point. Ferries also sail from this jetty to Eastport in Maine (late June to mid-Sept hourly 9am–6pm; 20min; car & driver $17, foot passenger $4; same contact details). Both ferries are quite small, so get there early.

ACCOMMODATION AND EATING

Family Fisheries 1977 Rte-774, Wilson's Beach ☎506 752 2470, ⓦfamilyfisheries.com. Of the handful of small diners on the island, the pick is *Family Fisheries*, where lobster, lobster stews and lobster rolls top a tasty menu of shellfish, fish and chips and grills (seafood served spring and summer only). Leave room for the home-made blueberry pie. Main $7–15. July & Aug Mon–Sat 11.30am–8pm, Sun 11.30am–7.30pm; May–June, Sept to early Oct & Nov–Dec Mon, Tues & Thurs–Sun 11.30am–8pm (closed early to end Oct).

Owen House 11 Welshpool St ☎506 752 2977, ⓦowenhouse.ca. Just south of the ferry, this lovely B&B dates from 1835 and occupies a leafy spit overlooking the bay, with six attractive en-suite rooms (and three with shared bath), two tranquil lounges and superb breakfasts (no wi-fi and no TV in rooms). Late May to mid-Oct. Shared bath **$104**; en suite **$115**

Grand Manan Island

At the mouth of the Bay of Fundy lies **Grand Manan Island**, a rugged nature hot-spot some 30km long that has remained remarkably undeveloped, at least compared to

5

islands off the US coast further south. While day-trips can give you a decent taster, staying a couple of nights will allow a greater appreciation of the island's languid charm. **Hiking** trails cover the island, and Grand Manan is an ideal place to go **bird**- and **whale-watching**. The naturalist and painter James John Audubon first documented the island's assembly of puffins, gannets, guillemots, stormy petrels and kittiwakes during his visit in 1831. The best birdwatching times are in the spring migratory period (early April to early June), the summer nesting season and the autumn migration (late Aug to Sept).

North Head

The ferry arrives at the north end of the island at Grand Manan's largest settlement, **NORTH HEAD**, just opposite the tiny **Whale and Seabird Research Station**. Turning right at the ferry takes you towards the dramatically sited 1860 **Swallows Tail Lightstation**, perched on a small outcrop connected to the main island by a wooden bridge.

Whale & Seabird Research Station

24 Rte-776 • Early June to early Oct daily 9am–5pm • Donation suggested • ☎ 506 662 3804, ⓦ gmwsrs.org

The **Whale & Seabird Research Station** provides a thoughtful introduction to the several species of whale hereabouts via the tiny Gaskin Museum of Marine Life, but to get a look at the real thing, take a trip with Whales-n-Sails Adventures (see opposite), on the wharf.

Hole in the Wall Park

42 Old Airport Rd, North Head • Open 24hr • $4 mid-May to mid-Oct; free other times • ☎ 506 662 3152, ⓦ grandmanancamping.com

The rocky coast on the north end of the island provides some of the Grand Manan's best **hiking**, with trails leading to Fish Head and the **Hole in the Wall** rock formation, just over a kilometre away. Paths are narrow and quite rugged (marked with red disks), and if you don't fancy the hike, you can drive 2km up to **Hole in the Wall Park**, where you can park within a few metres of the coast. Alternatively, you can take a **sea-kayak** tour or rent a **bike** from Adventure High (see page 383).

Grand Harbour

Heading south from North Head, the main road hugs the coast to **GRAND HARBOUR**, the commercial and educational centre of the island, where the **Grand Manan Museum** (1141 Rte-776; early June to mid-Sept Mon–Fri 9am–5pm; also Sat 9am–5pm & Sun 1–5pm July & Aug; $7; ☎ 506 662 3524, ⓦ grandmananmuseum.ca) houses all sorts of locally procured curios, as well as a small display recounting the history of the island and its inextricable link with the fisheries: special attention is paid to wrecks, the island's unusual geology and **Willa Cather**, the American author who spent her summers here from the 1920s to the 1940s.

Seal Cove and Southwest Head

It's a brief drive southwest from Grand Harbour to **SEAL COVE**, a fishing village that still bears the signs of the once-thriving smoked herring industry. Restored smokehouses and rickety wharves crowd the small harbour, where the prize catch now is lobster. The village is also home to the dependable Sea Watch Tours (see page 383). From Seal Cove the road winds on to **Southwest Head**, where a small 1880 lighthouse guards some oddly shaped cliffs, rock formations and more trails with stupendous views across the sea.

White Head Island

Some 3.5km south of Grand Harbour is **Ingalls Head**, from where a toll-free **ferry** (4–10 daily; 25min) scuttles over to **White Head Island**, a tiny islet whose blissfully untrammelled beach makes for a pleasant day-trip.

ARRIVAL AND DEPARTURE

GRAND MANAN ISLAND

By ferry To get to Grand Manan Island, catch the car ferry from Blacks Harbour, located 10km south of Rte-1 between St Andrews and Saint John (late June to mid-Sept 6–7 daily; mid-Sept to late June 3–4 daily; 1hr 30min–2hr; cars $35.80 return, passengers $12 return; ☏ 506 662 3724, ⓦ coastaltransport.ca). Spaces are allocated on a first-come, first-served basis so arrive at least an hour before the departure time, and be prepared to queue, especially in July and Aug; no fares are collected on the outward journey – you pay the whole deal on the way back (cash or credit card; you can also book with credit cards online in advance).

INFORMATION AND TOURS

Visitor centre North Head, in the business centre next to the old village hall (July & Aug daily 9am–5pm; ☏ 506 662 3442, ⓦ grandmanannb.com).

Internet The visitor centre has free wi-fi, as does the library in Grand Harbour.

TOURS

Adventure High 83 Rte-776 ☏ 506 662 3563, ⓦ adventurehigh.com. Runs half-day guided kayak tours (3hr; May–Oct) for $60; also offers 6hr day-trips ($110) and even 2hr moonlight paddle tours ($75).

Sea Watch Tours 2476 Rte-776, Seal Cove (turn down SC Breakwater Rd) ☏ 506 662 8552, ⓦ seawatchtours.com. Runs whale-watching trips ($69) July–Sept; whales are guaranteed or the tour is free. It also offers birdwatching tours ($130; 5hr 30min) from late June to July to Machias Seal Island (18km south), the best place to see puffins.

ACCOMMODATION

Hole-in-the-Wall Park Campground 42 Old Airport Rd, North Head ☏ 506 662 3152, ⓦ grandmanancamping.com. Offers some spectacular cliff-top pitches, but they are popular, so arrive early or book ahead. Hook-ups are an extra $9/day. Mid-May to mid Oct. Sites $29; cabins $44

★ **The Inn at Whale Cove Cottages** 26 Whale Cove Cottage Rd, North Head ☏ 506 662 3181, ⓦ whalecovecottages.ca. Tranquil property comprising three cosy, Shaker-furnished en-suite rooms in the main shingle house dating from 1816, a spacious one-bedroom bungalow and two other larger properties with two or four bedrooms; the Willa Cather Cottage was built by the renowned author in the 1920s. All cottages come with kitchens and radios but no TVs or phones. To get there, turn off the main road in North Head and head 700m up Whistle Rd. Rooms $150; bungalow $160; cottages $1000 (per week); Willa Cather Cottage $1300 (per week)

McLaughlin's Wharf Inn 1863 Rte-776, Seal Cove ☏ 506 662 8760, ⓦ mclaughlinswharfinn.ca. To stay at the opposite end of the island try this simple inn that began life as a hardware store in 1885, and now occupies a prime position on the harbour. It features six plain but comfy rooms, two shared bathrooms and one TV lounge. Self-serve breakfast, lunch and dinner available at the convenience store (open year-round daily 5am–10pm). June–Sept. $115

EATING

Local seafood – particularly lobster (May–July) and shellfish – take centre stage at the island's crop of cafés and restaurants. Don't forget to sample another Grand Manan treat – **dulse** (dried, edible seaweed). It grows on the western shore, in the shade of the cliffs, and is sold all over the island.

★ **Inn at Whale Cove** 26 Whale Cove Cottage Rd ☏ 506 662 3181. The seasonal dining room here is the best place for dinner on the island – reservations required. Menus change daily, but offer two or three choices for each course and feature an abundance of local and seasonal produce such as juicy scallops and lobster (mains $25–28). May to late June Sat & Sun 6–8pm; late June to mid-Oct daily 6–8pm.

North Head Bakery 199 Rte-776, North Head ☏ 506 662 8862, ⓦ northheadbakery.ca. Bakes French artisan bread and pastries, making it a great place to stock up for a picnic; it's marked with just a "Bakery" sign. Must-eats include the flaky croissants, small doughnuts and crumbly date slices. May–Sept Tues–Sat 6.30am–5.30pm.

Fredericton

Situated 100km or so inland from the Bay of Fundy on the banks of the St John River, **FREDERICTON**, the capital of New Brunswick, has a well-padded air, the streets of its tiny centre graced by elms and genteel villas. There's scarcely any industry here and the metro population of 105,000 mostly work for the government or the university. Founded by Loyalists in 1783, the city has retained several intriguing reminders of the British army in the **Historic Garrison District**, while the **Beaverbrook Art Gallery** is simply outstanding.

5

City Hall

397 Queen St, at York St • Tours only (30min): mid-May to mid-Oct daily 3.30pm • Free • ☎ 506 460 2129

Fredericton's **City Hall**, with its distinctive 35m clock tower, was completed in 1876. It's worth taking the tours to get beyond the visitor information centre at the entrance, mainly to see the elaborate workings of the clock, built in 1878 by Croydon-based Gillett & Bland, and the **Council Chamber**, still in use today. The chamber is circled by 27 **tapestries** produced by local artists in 1985, depicting the city's history.

The Garrison District

West of City Hall the old British military base, occupied 1784 to 1869 to counter the threat of American attack, is preserved today as the **Historic Garrison District**. Walk along Queen Street to the **Soldiers' Barracks** in front of the New Brunswick College of Craft & Design, a sturdy three-storey block that at one time accommodated more than two hundred squaddies. Built in 1826, the building's lower floor is home to **craft shops** (June–Sept daily 10am–5pm), while the upper levels belong to the college. The **Garrison Night Market** (featuring local produce, craft beers and arts and crafts) runs on Carleton Street every Thursday night (4.30–9pm) between late June and early Sept.

Guard House

15 Carleton St • July & Aug daily 10am–6pm • Free • ☎ 506 460 2129

Behind the Soldiers' Barracks, a few metres down Carleton Street, the **Guard House** is an 1828 sandstone, wood and slate-roofed structure where guides in period British uniforms show you round a restored orderly room, a guardroom and detention cells that create a fearsome picture of military life in the middle of the nineteenth century: the guardroom is little different from the airless cells where villains were locked up waiting to be flogged, branded and/or transported.

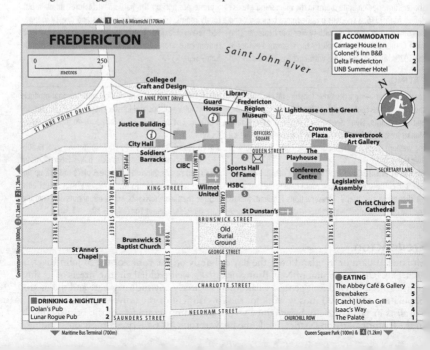

CHANGING OF THE GUARD

Officers' Square, at the foot of Regent Street and Queen Street, is the location of Fredericton's **Changing of the Guard** (July & Aug daily 11am & 4pm, also Tues & Thurs at 7pm; ☎ 506 460 2041), a crowd-pleasing re-enactment of Canadian Infantry School Corps drill circa 1883, replete with scarlet tunics and skirling bagpipes.

Fredericton Region Museum

571 Queen St • April–June & Sept–Nov Tues–Sat 1–4pm; July & Aug daily 10am–5pm • $6 • ☎ 506 455 6041, ⓦ frederictonregionmuseum.com

The elegant three-storey British Officers' Quarters, with its symmetrical columns and stone arches completed in 1853, is now the **Fredericton Region Museum**. Inside you'll find seven permanent exhibits, covering aspects of regional history from the Acadians and the Loyalists to the "cow nuisance" that plagued Fredericton for decades and the stuffed remains of the 20kg "**Coleman Frog**", a giant-sized amphibian of dubious origin. The local innkeeper, who found it in the 1880s, claimed to have fed it on beer and buttermilk.

Lighthouse on the Green

Regent Street Wharf, Regent St • Café late June to Aug daily 10am–10pm; tower free to climb • ☎ 506 460 2939

On the river-side of grassy Officers' Square, the **Lighthouse on the Green** contains a small café (known for its ice cream in summer), gift shop and an upper-floor viewing deck accessible via the outdoor stairs on the side. Exhibits inside (mostly black-and-white photos) highlight the history of the St John River, including some of the devastating floods that have hit the city – ironically, the massive flooding of 2018 did substantial damage to the café and exhibit (ask the tourist office about current opening times).

Beaverbrook Art Gallery

703 Queen St • Mon–Sat 10am–5pm, Thurs till 9pm, Sun noon–5pm (closed Mon mid-Oct to May) • $10, Thurs 5–9pm pay as you wish • ⓦ beaverbrookartgallery.org

Lord Beaverbrook (1879–1964), the newspaper tycoon, was raised in New Brunswick's Newcastle and moved to England in 1910 – becoming a close friend of Churchill and a key member of his war cabinet. In Fredericton his largesse was extended to the university, the Playhouse Theatre and the **Beaverbrook Art Gallery**, where an eclectic and regularly rotated collection of mostly British and Canadian art shares space with an imaginative programme of temporary exhibitions. A large gallery extension opened in 2017, the East Wing has been renovated, and there is also a sculpture garden leading to and along the riverside path behind the gallery.

Of the permanent work on display, Salvador Dalí's monumental *Santiago El Grande*, depicting St James being borne up towards a vaulted firmament on a white charger, resides in a purpose-designed space in the **High Gallery**. The **Vaulted Gallery** contains some real gems: *Leda* (1945), a crayon drawing from Matisse, a classic mill scene from Lowry (1956), and a dark, brooding study by Constable, *Scenes of Wood & Water* (1830). The **Sir Max Aitken Gallery** features portraits by Gainsborough and Joshua Reynolds, while the **Vaughan Gallery** contains a mix of Flemish tapestries, porcelain, a couple of Ford Madox Brown pencil-and-ink drawings and *"HMS Terror" Iced-in off Cape Comfort* by early nineteenth-century artist George Chambers, a wonderfully melodramatic canvas, the creaking ship crushed by the ice underneath a dark and forbidding sky. On the lower level are galleries dedicated to modern art from New Brunswick with some Andy Warhol prints thrown in (including his *Liz Taylor*) and a selection of the Christmas-card works of the prolific **Cornelius Krieghoff** (see page 73), including two of his finest, *Merrymaking* and *Coming Storm at the Portage*. Look out also for a couple of Winston Churchill's own paintings.

5

Legislative Assembly Building

706 Queen St, at John St • Mon–Thurs 8.30am–5pm, Fri 8.30am–4.30pm • Free • ☎ 506 453 2527, ⓦ gnb.ca/legis/index-e.asp

The **Legislative Assembly Building**, the home of New Brunswick's parliament, stands opposite the Beaverbrook Art Gallery, its robust and imposing sandstone-and-granite exterior topped by a ponderous tower and cupola. Completed in 1882, the interior holds a sumptuously decorated **Assembly Chamber**, adorned with portraits of George III and Queen Charlotte by Joshua Reynolds, as well as a splendid oak-and-cherry spiral staircase leading to the chamber's visitors' gallery.

Christ Church Cathedral

168 Church St • Tours (free) July & Aug Mon–Fri 9am–6pm, Sat 10am–6pm, Sun 1.30–4pm; Sept–June Mon–Fri 9am–4pm • Free • ☎ 506 450 8500, ⓦ cccath.ca

Built between 1845 and 1853 in Gothic Revival style, **Christ Church Cathedral** is rather modest, despite its status. Its most distinguishing features are its elegant tapering 60m spire, and the intricate grace of its red-pine hammerbeam ceiling.

Government House

51 Woodstock Rd (Rte-102) • Guided tours only: mid-May to Aug Mon–Sat 10am–4pm, Sun noon–4pm (on the hour) • Free • ☎ 506 453 2505, ⓦ gnb.ca/lg/ogh/index-e.asp

A short drive or stroll west along the river from downtown lies **Government House**, the official residence of the Lieutenant-Governor of New Brunswick. Completed in 1828, the elegant Georgian mansion was abandoned and its contents auctioned off in the 1890s (it was deemed too expensive to maintain), and it wasn't until 1999 that the governors returned. Illuminating tours (45min) visit all the lavishly restored main rooms and exhibit galleries on the first two floors (the third floor is reserved for the governor). There's free parking on-site.

ARRIVAL AND DEPARTURE   FREDERICTON

By car You should find plenty of parking – try behind City Hall, off Queen St ($1/hr Mon–Fri 8am–5pm; free other times). **By bus** Maritime Bus (☎ 505 455 2049, ⓦ maritimebus.com) runs long-distance bus services to/from Fredericton from the terminal at 105 Dundonald St at Smythe St, on the edge of downtown.

Destinations Charlottetown (1 daily; 6hr); Halifax (2 daily; 6hr 55min–7hr 15min); Moncton (2–3 daily; 2hr 15min–3hr 30min); Québec City via Rivière-du-Loup (7hr 50min);

Saint John (2–3 daily; 1hr 20min).

By plane Air Canada provides domestic flights from Toronto, Montréal and Halifax into Fredericton Airport (☎ 506 460 0920, ⓦ yfcfredericton.ca), 16km southeast of town on Rte-102; Porter Airlines runs flights to/from Ottawa. The fixed-rate taxi fare into the centre costs around $24 (Checker Cab ☎ 506 450 8294). Avis, Budget, Enterprise and National have counters at the airport, and there's free wi-fi.

INFORMATION

Downtown visitor centre City Hall, 397 Queen St at York St (daily: mid-May to late June & Sept to early Oct 10am–5pm; late June to Sept 10am–8pm; early Oct to end-Oct Mon–Fri 10am–4.30pm ☎ 506 460 2129, ⓦ tourismfredericton.ca).

Internet Free wi-fi is available in most of the city.

ACCOMMODATION

Carriage House Inn 230 University Ave, at George St ☎ 506 452 9924, ⓦ carriagehouse-inn.net; map p.384. This ten-room B&B, on the east side of the city centre and in one of the older residential areas, occupies a grand Queen Anne-style house built in 1875. It comes complete with antique furnishings, ballroom, and capacious veranda, though it's starting to show its age. The rate includes breakfast. **$132**

Colonel's Inn B&B 843 Union St ☎ 506 452 2802, ⓦ thecolonelsin.com; map p.384. On the north side of the St John River, this enjoyable B&B has three en-suite guest rooms decorated in appealing pastel shades. The breakfasts are great and the house itself, dating from 1894, offers splendid views back across to Fredericton's downtown, a 15min walk away via the old railway bridge. **$112.50**

Delta Fredericton 225 Woodstock Rd ☎ 506 457 7000, ⓦ marriott.com; map p.384. Modern high-rise hotel, now part of the Marriott stable with rooms in a plush, contemporary style. Luxurious suites and posh doubles

5

PICAROONS

One of Fredericton's best microbreweries, **Picaroons**, has crafted some exceptional beers since it opened in 1995. Visit their downtown store at 422 Queen St (Mon–Wed 11am–10pm, Thurs & Fri 11am–11pm, Sat 10am–11pm, Sun noon–5pm; ☎506 457 9082, ⌨picaroons.ca) or visit the website for brewery tours.

with views of the river, with indoor and outdoor pools. Free parking. **$210**

UNB Summer Hotel (front desk in Sir James Dunn Residence) ☎506 447 3227, ⌨unb.ca; map p.384. Budget doubles in a sparse, but well-kept Queen Anne mansion (1895) on the University of New Brunswick campus (it serves as student dorms during the school year). Continental breakfast included, parking ($4/day) and one-day gym pass. Self-service laundry is $1.75. Late May to Aug only. **$75**

EATING

★ **The Abbey Café & Gallery** 546 Queen St ☎506 455 6368, ⌨facebook.com/abbeycafegallery; map p.384. Casual restaurant set in a colourful gallery of local artists, specializing in excellent vegan and vegetarian meals (including vegan desserts), plus locally roasted Whitney coffee. Mon–Fri 9am–9pm, Sat 11am–9pm, Sun noon–6pm.

Brewbakers 546 King St, between Regent and Carleton streets ☎506 459 0067, ⌨brewbakers.ca; map p.384. First-rate fish cakes ($14), seared haddock sandwich ($14), maple curry penne ($16) and PEI mussels ($14). Often packed at the weekend. Mon 11.30am–9pm, Tues–Thurs 11.30am–10pm, Fri 11.30am–11pm, Sat 5–11pm, Sun 5–9pm.

[Catch] Urban Grill Delta Hotel, 225 Woodstock Rd ☎506 451 7935; map p.384. Café-restaurant noted for its seafood (Atlantic salmon from $28.95; Graystone Ale and garlic mussels $11.95) and a popular Sunday brunch. Mon–Sat 7am–2pm & 5–9pm, Sun 7am–2pm.

★ **Isaac's Way** 649 Queen St ☎506 474 7222, ⌨isaacsway.ca; map p.384. One of the town's most popular restaurants, offering a consistently high-quality menu of salads, seafood, vegetarian dishes and pasta (think sun-dried tomato cod and maple curry salmon). Mains $18–27. Mon & Tues 11.30am–9pm, Wed–Fri 11.30am–10pm, Sat 10am–10pm, Sun 10am–9pm.

The Palate 462 Queen St ☎506 450 7911, ⌨thepalate.com; map p.384. Bright and breezy café-cum-restaurant with a lively, inventive menu featuring everything from Digby scallops to porcini and *escargot* Brie. In the evening, main courses range $18–30, there are pizzas ($11), paninis ($11–13) for lunch and special brunch deals on Sat ($11–12). Mon–Fri 11am–3pm & 5–9pm, Sat 10am–3pm & 5–9pm.

DRINKING

Dolan's Pub Pipers Lane, 349 King St ☎506 454 7474, ⌨dolanspub.ca; map p.384. Bustling bar with imported and domestic beers on draught and regular live rock music. Also does decent steak sandwiches and long happy hours. Mon & Tues 11.30am–midnight, Wed–Sat 11.30am–2am.

Lunar Rogue Pub 625 King St ☎506 450 2065, ⌨lunarrogue.com; map p.384. Busy bar serving British and Maritime ales as well as an extensive range of malt whiskies. Live music on most weekends. Summer patio. Mon–Fri 11am–1am, Sat 10am–1am, Sun 11am–10pm.

ENTERTAINMENT

The Playhouse ☎506 458 8344, ⌨theplayhouse.ca. Another gift from the Beaverbrooks, this theatre puts on a good variety of shows and is home to the province's only professional English-speaking theatre company, Theatre New Brunswick (Sept–April season; ⌨tnb.nb.ca).

Gagetown

Travelling between Fredericton and Saint John along leisurely Rte-102, be sure to spend an hour or two in **GAGETOWN** (⌨villageofgagetown.ca), a pretty village whose graceful clapboard houses are sprinkled along the St John River about 60km from Fredericton (and 100km from Saint John). There are several engrossing craft and pottery shops here, the prim and proper **St John's Anglican Church**, and the grand old Queens County Court House of 1836, 16 Court House Rd, now the **Court House Museum** (mid-June to mid-Sept daily 9am–5pm; $3; ☎506 488 2483,

5

ⓦqueenscountyheritage.com). **Tilley House**, 69 Front St (same details; combined ticket $5), dates back to 1786 and was the birthplace of Samuel Tilley in 1818, one of the province's "Fathers of Confederation" – today it serves as the county museum and **visitor information centre**.

ACCOMMODATION AND EATING　　　　　　　　　　　　　　　　　　GAGETOWN

Old Boot Pub & Dockside Bar 48 Front St ☎506 488 3441. Check out the 6.8m-long bar (actually a sailboat) or waterside deck at this old pub, offering decent beer, meals and live music at the weekends. Sept–May Mon–Thurs noon–9pm, Fri noon–1am, Sat 10am–1am, Sun 10am–9pm.

Lang House B&B 58 Front St ☎506 488 1808, ⓦlanghousebandb.com. The best of the area's accommodation, with five well-kept guest rooms in an 1880s white clapboard house down by the river. May–Dec. $130

King's Landing

5804 Rte-102, Prince William • Early June to mid-Oct daily 10am–5pm • $18, children 6–15 $12.41 • ⓦkingslanding.nb.ca

Some 35km west of Fredericton on Rte-102 lies **King's Landing Historical Settlement**, a collection of historic buildings carefully relocated here in the 1960s to form the nucleus of an open-air museum of nineteenth-century rural life. Since then, further judicious purchases have added to the housing stock and, supplemented by a handful of replicas, there are now seventy buildings spread out amid tranquil waterside woods and fields. King's Landing aims to provide an immersive experience to its visitors, and plans to reinstate its popular role-playing "inhabitants" engaged in bread-making, horseshoeing, logging, milling, weaving and cattle-driving. Themed villages are not to everyone's taste, but this one works very well and several of the buildings are fascinating in their own right – particularly the **Jones House**, a stone dwelling built into the hillside in a manner typical of this area, the **Ingraham House**, once the property of a well-to-do farmer, and the fully operational sawmill.

Hartland

Surrounded by forest, **HARTLAND**, some 90km beyond King's Landing via Rte-2, advertises itself exclusively on the size of its **wooden bridge** (open to both vehicles and pedestrians), which at 391m is by far the longest covered bridge in the world. It was completed in 1921 (replacing the 1901 original), the idea being to protect the timbers of the bridge from the elements by means of a long shed-like affair built in the manner of a barn. You can park on the Hartland side of the river, next to the local **information centre** at 365 Main St (late May to early Oct daily 9am–6pm; ☎506 375 4075).

Grand Falls

North of Hartland, the scenery changes as the maples give way to a great undulating belt of potato fields. There's a surprise in store here at **GRAND FALLS**, 105km from Hartland, where, right in the centre of what is otherwise a nondescript town, a spectacular weight of water squeezes through hydroelectric barriers to crash down a 23m pitch. Even if the diversion of the St John River through nearby turbines has deprived the falls of their original vigour, they're still impressive, as is the 2km-long gorge they've carved downstream, a steep-sided ravine encircling half the town. There's a 1.6km **trail** along the gorge (free; tours $10) and a 400-step **stairway** (July & Aug daily 10am–6pm; $5) that leads down into the gorge from the **La Rochelle Tourist Center** at 1 Chapel St. The trail can be accessed across the bridge from the **Malabeam Information Centre** at 25 Madawaska Rd (daily: June 10am–6pm; July & Aug 9.30am–7.30pm; Sept to mid-Oct 10am–5pm; ☎506 475 7769, ⓦgrandfallsnb.com), which perches on the bridge above the actual falls. This being Canada, you can also **zipline** across the falls via **Zip Zag** (May–Sept Sat & Sun noon–5pm; ☎506 473 4924; $40;

ⓦzipzag.ca) or **Open Sky Adventures** (June–Oct 10am–6pm; $50; ☎506 477 9799, ⓦopenskyadventures.com), further downstream

ARRIVAL AND DEPARTURE   GRAND FALLS

By car From Grand Falls it's a further 58km north along Rte-2 to Edmundston, then just 18km to the Québec border – it's a still a long drive to Rivière-du-Loup (108km) and Québec City (around 200km) from here, however.

By bus The Maritime Bus (☎506 473 4862, ⓦmaritimebus.

com) stop is at 555 Madawaska Rd (Ultramar gas station). **Destinations** Fredericton (2 daily; 2hr 40min); Moncton (2 daily; 5hr 25min); Rivière-du-Loup (2 daily; 2hr); Saint John (2 daily; 6hr 40min).

ACCOMMODATION AND EATING

Hill Top Motel 131 Madawaska Rd ☎506 473 2684, ⓦhilltopgrandfalls.ca. There's nothing much else to see in Grand Falls, but straightforward accommodation and

a restaurant (Mon–Sat 5.30am–9pm, Sun 7am–9pm) is available right by the waterfall at this simple but comfy motel. Breakfast included. <u>$121</u>

The Acadian Coast

From Moncton, Rte-15 cuts across to the Northumberland Strait at **SHEDIAC**, the province's lobster capital, where Rte-11 heads north along what's been dubbed the **Acadian Coast** all the way to Miramichi (see page 390). Settled in the years after the deportations of the 1750s, the string of pretty villages here are all French-speaking and proud of their Acadian roots. **BOUCTOUCHE**, 35km north of Shediac (55km from Moncton), was founded by Acadians in 1785 and is the birthplace of Canadian business legend **K.C. Irving** in 1899 – he opened his first petrol station here in 1924.

Le Pays de la Sagouine

57 Acadie St, Bouctouche (off Rte-134) • Late June to Aug daily 10am–5.30pm • $20; students 13 and over $15, children 12 and under free • ☎506 743 1400, ⓦsagouine.com

The highlight of the Acadian Coast is **Le Pays de la Sagouine**, a sort of Acadian fantasy village set on the Île-aux-Puces and connected to the mainland by a 325m wooden footbridge. Conceived by acclaimed local Acadian writer Antonine Maillet (the name comes from her 1971 novel **La Sagouine**) and opened in 1992, costumed actors show off traditional Acadian crafts, cuisine and trades such as fishing, all enhanced with humorous tales and period costume (including the eponymous heroine of *La Sagouine*, an uneducated washerwoman, considered the voice of the Acadian people). Actors also take part in musical performances throughout the day: the excellent dinner theatre is around $60, but check the website for performances in English (it's generally French only). You'll probably enjoy this more if you speak at least some French (skits and performances are in French, but it's easy to understand what's going on), but the site is bilingual and daily tours run in English.

Irving Eco-Centre, La Dune de Bouctouche

1932 Rte-475, St-Édouard de Kent • **Boardwalk** Daily 24hr • **Interpretation centre** Daily: June & Sept 10am–5pm; July & Aug 10am–6pm • Free • ☎888 640 3300

Some 9km north of Bouctouche, the **Irving Eco-Centre, La Dune de Bouctouche**, is the gateway to a 12km stretch of sparkling white sands. The "dune" is more like a long sandbank topped with marram grass and with a **boardwalk** that snakes along the coast for 800m. Soak up the sea views (you can just see PEI on the horizon) or find a secluded stretch of beach. The small **interpretation centre** at the boardwalk entrance contains exhibits and touchscreens about the ecology of the area.

ACCOMMODATION   THE ACADIAN COAST

Auberge Bouctouche 50 Industrielle St, Bouctouche ☎506 743 5003, ⓦaubergebouctoucheinn.ca. If you

need somewhere to stay, try the modern and motel-like *Auberge Bouctouche* in the centre of Bouctouche, with

5

spacious doubles and suites (breakfast included). **$135**
★ **Maison Tait House** 293 Main St, Shediac ☎ 506 532
4233, ⓦ maisontaithouse.com. Gorgeous Queen-Anne
style home dating from 1911 converted into an atmospheric

hotel (breakfast is $5 extra), with elegant rooms and
wonderful restaurant – the oak interior was beautifully
restored in 2007. **$109**

EATING

Black Rabbit 310 Main St, Shediac ☎ 506 870 0336,
ⓦ baroloandco.com/blackrabbit. This lovely old house
with veranda re-opened as a stylish gourmet restaurant
in 2018, but check the website to make sure their run
continues. Think fresh oysters, lobster rolls, short rib and
home-made mushroom tagliatelle. Mid-May to Sept daily
5–10pm.

Shediac Lobster Shop 261 Main St, Shediac ☎ 506
533 1437, ⓦ shediaclobster.ca. It would be a shame to
visit this region without trying the succulent lobster – this
is the cheapest place to buy them ready cooked (takeaway
only – you'll need the tools to eat them). May–Aug daily
10am–7pm, Sept–Dec Thurs–Sun 10am–6pm (closed
Jan–April).

Kouchibouguac National Park

186 Rte-117 • **Information Centre** Daily: mid-May to mid-June & early Sept to mid-Oct 9am–5pm; mid-June to early Sept 8am–8pm •
July, Aug & Dec–March $7.80; April–June & Sept–Nov $3.90 • ☎ 506 876 2443, ⓦ pc.gc.ca/en/pn-np/nb/kouchibouguac

Around 45km north of Bouctouche, Rte-11 skirts the coastal forests, salt marshes,
lagoons and sandy beaches of the **Kouchibouguac** ("Koo-she-boo-gwack") **National
Park**, an untrammelled forest wilderness perfect for cycling, kayaking or just lazing on
the beach.

Near the park's main **entrance** is the **Information Centre**, where you can pick up maps
and view displays on the area's complex ecology and human history (some 1200 people
were relocated when the park was created in 1969). From here, it's a few kilometres'
drive to the sandy expanse of **Kellys Beach** – the park's main attraction, with a sheltered
lagoon ideal for kids and a puppet theatre in the summer. You can also rent canoes or
kayaks at **Ryans Rental Centre**, or rent bikes to explore 60km of some of the best (and
level) trails in Canada. The **hiking trails** in the park range from 1km to the 11.3km
Kouchibouguac River Trail, which wriggles west along the river bank (allow at least six
hours). In the winter the park opens for skiing.

ACCOMMODATION   KOUCHIBOUGUAC NATIONAL PARK

National Park camping The park has one fully serviced
campsite, *South Kouchibouguac* (mid-May to mid-Oct;
$27.40–38.30) also with posher oTENTiks, and one
unserviced campsite, *Côte-à-Fabien* (June to early Sept;
$15.70). Reservations (☎ 877 737 3783, ⓦ reservation.
pc.gc.ca) are advised for *South Kouchibouguac*, but *Cote-à-*

Fabien is first-come, first-served. In addition there are three
backcountry sites accessible on bike or foot: *Petit-Large*,
Pointe-à-Maxime and *Sipu* ($9.80; reservations ☎ 506 876
2443). If you're not camping, the park is easily visited on a
day-trip from Bouctouche or Miramichi, 50km north (see
page 390). Sites **$27.40**; oTENTiks **$100**

Miramichi

Sprawling along the banks of the salmon-rich Miramichi River, **MIRAMICHI** ("mira-
mishee") is home to the absorbing cultural and historic sights of Beaubears Island
and Metepenagiag Heritage Park, though there's little else to see in the city itself.
Miramichi City was only created in 1995 through the amalgamation of two towns and
several villages; notably the humdrum commercial centre of **Newcastle** (Miramichi
West), **Chatham** (Miramichi East), the best place to stay, and historic **Nelson**, the most
attractive village in the valley. Today the whole area has a population of around 18,000.

Beaubears Island

Interpretive Centre 35 St Patrick's Drive, Nelson • Mid-June to June 30 & Sept 1 to mid-Sept Mon–Sat 10am–4pm, Sun noon–4pm; July
& Aug Mon–Sat 10am–6pm, Sun noon–8pm • $5 • **Island tours** July & Aug Tues–Sat 2pm • $15–25 ; self-guided tour $10 (both include
centre admission and boat transport) • ☎ 506 622 8526, ⓦ beaubearsisland.com

5

MIRAMICHI FOLKSONG FESTIVAL

The **Miramichi Folksong Festival** (☎ 506 622 1780, ⊛ miramichifolksongfestival.com) is held over five days in early August and generally reckoned to be one of the best of its kind, with vocal performances its forte. Passes for the whole festival are around $100 (individual concerts $16–42), with most events held at the Beaverbrook Kin Centre, 100 Newcastle Blvd.

Hard to believe today, but the pristine, pine-smothered **Beaubears Island**, in the middle of the Miramichi River, has a turbulent history going back to the 1700s. The island contains the **Boishébert National Historic Site**, monument to the thousands of Acadians who hid and died here between 1755 and 1758, and the **Beaubears Island Shipbuilding National Historic Site**, location of what was once a thriving nineteenth-century shipbuilding yard 1840 to 1866. Nothing now remains above ground on the island, but tours are enhanced by enthusiastic guides and costumed interpreters. Start at the **interpretive centre** on shore, which has an absorbing series of exhibits explaining the sites' complex history, and arranges boats across.

Metepenagiag Heritage Park

2156 Micmac Rd (Rte-420), Red Bank (Metepenagiag) • Mid-May to mid-Oct daily 10am–5pm • $8 • ☎ 506 836 6118, ⊛ metpark.ca

It's worth driving out to the beautifully designed **Metepenagiag Heritage Park** in Red Bank ("Metepenagiag" in Mi'kmaq), 28km along the Northwest Miramichi River via routes 425 and 420, where the local **Mi'kmaq** tribe enthusiastically showcases their culture and history through thought-provoking multimedia presentations and displays. Also inside are rare archeological finds from two nearby historic sites uncovered in the 1970s, the 3000-year-old Oxbow village and Augustine Mound.

ARRIVAL AND INFORMATION

MIRAMICHI

By car Miramichi is 165km north of Fredericton via Rte-8.

By bus The Maritime Bus (☎ 506 773 5515, ⊛ maritimebus. com) terminal is at the Irving petrol station (186 King St), Rte-11, on the outskirts of Chatham).

Destinations Campbelltown, for connections with Orléans Express buses (⊛ orleansexpress.com) to Québec (1 daily; 2hr 40min); Fredericton (1 daily; 4hr 50min); Moncton, for connections throughout the Maritimes (1 daily; 2hr); Saint John (1 daily; 5hr).

By train Miramichi is served by VIA Rail (⊛ viarail.ca), with the station at 251 Station St in Newcastle. There are just six trains in each direction per week, west to Montréal and south to Halifax via Moncton.

Visitor centre 21 Cove Rd, between Newcastle and Nelson on the north bank of the river (late June to Aug daily 9am–9pm; ☎ 506 778 8444, ⊛ miramichi.org and ⊛ discovermiramichi.com).

ACCOMMODATION

Governor's Mansion Inn 62 St Patrick's Drive, Nelson ☎ 506 622 3036, ⊛ governorsmansion.ca. This B&B occupies a handsome 1880 villa that was once the residence of Lieutenant-Governor J. Leonard O'Brien (last private owner of Beaubears Island). The house is graced by antique furnishings and holds eight guest rooms on the two upper floors; there are four additional rooms in a second old house,

Beaubear Manor. **$99**

Rodd Miramichi River Hotel 1809 Water St, Chatham ☎ 506 773 3111, ⊛ roddvacations.com. Set right on the river in the heart of Chatham's historic downtown, this is a luxury option, with spacious, modern rooms featuring pine wood, old-lodge-style decor, flat-screens and river views (there's even an indoor swimming pool). **$170**

EATING AND DRINKING

1809 Restaurant & Bar Rodd Miramichi River Hotel, 1809 Water St, Chatham ☎ 506 773 5651, ⊛ roddvacations.com. The best place to eat in town, specializing in the local salmon ($25) cooked five different ways: try the classic Miramichi boiled mayonnaise. Also does pastas ($2124), burgers ($15) and fish and chips ($15). Mon–Thurs & Sun 7am–10pm, Fri & Sat 7am–11pm.

O'Donaghue's Irish Pub 1696 Water St, Chatham ☎ 506 778 1066. Largely thanks to immigration in the 1840s, Miramichi is known as Canada's "Irish Capital". This authentic Irish boozer is the best place to soak up that heritage, with great pub food (amazing fish and chips for $16) and craft beers on tap. Mon–Wed 11am–10pm, Thurs 11am–midnight, Fri 11am–2am, Sat 10am–2am, Sun 10am–10pm.

5

MAKING NOISE

Caraquet is the setting for the region's most important **Acadian Festival** (☎ 506 727 2787, ⓦ festivalacadien.ca), a two-week programme of music and theatre held August 1–15, which begins with the blessing of the fishing fleet by a local bishop. One of the highlights is the **Tintamarre** (on Aug 15, National Acadian Day), where revellers are invited to make as much noise as possible for one hour – the resulting cacophony is quite a sound (and sight).

Caraquet and the Acadian Peninsula

The **Acadian Peninsula**, which protrudes some 130km into the Gulf of St Lawrence in the northeast corner of New Brunswick, is another part of the province where Acadian culture has flourished since the 1760s. The best place to get a sense of the region's roots is **CARAQUET**, on the north shore, a fishing port founded by Acadian refugees in 1758 and now home to some 4000 people. The town straggles along the seafront for some 13km of Rte-11, making an excellent base for the local **beaches**, some French-inspired culinary gems and the region's pride and joy, the phenomenal **Village Historique Acadien**.

Village Historique Acadien

14311 Rte-11, Rivière-du-Nord • Early June to early Oct daily 10am–6pm • $20 (two days); late Sept to early Oct $9.50 • ☎ 877 721 2200, ⓦ vhanb.ca

Around 16km west of Caraquet is the illuminating **Village Historique Acadien**, a living museum containing 63 old Acadian buildings relocated from other parts of New Brunswick. It's by far the best evocation of Acadian life anywhere in the Maritimes, with costumed interpreters adding context and demonstrating traditional agricultural techniques as well as old methods of spinning, cooking and so on – all in a gorgeous rustic setting surrounded by woodland. The main trail passes through sections focusing on rural life in the eighteenth, then nineteenth centuries (the oldest building is the **Martin House** of 1773), before crossing a covered bridge into the twentieth-century area: the highlight here is the grand **Hôtel Château Albert**, a replica of a local hotel from 1910 (in the summer you can actually spend the night here; from $99.95). French is obviously the main lingua franca here, but everyone is happy to speak English.

ACCOMMODATION AND EATING | CARAQUET AND THE ACADIAN PENINSULA

Boulangerie Grains de Folie 171 blvd St-Pierre West ☎ 506 727 4001, ⓦ grainsdefolie.ca. Wonderful French-inspired modern café, with a range of tempting pastries, cakes ($3.50–5) and light meals, as well as wine and beer and a selection of fresh cheese. Librairie Pélagie (bookshop) on site and free wi-fi. Wed–Fri 7am–5pm, Sat & Sun 8.30am–5pm.

Hotel Paulin 143 blvd St-Pierre West ☎ 506 727 9981, ⓦ hotelpaulin.com. Among a bevy of additional Caraquet accommodation options, the pick is this smart and comfortable hotel, a family-operated inn with eight guest rooms in an attractive Victorian building built in 1891. The restaurant here is first-rate, featuring traditional Acadian cuisine. **$215**

La Table de Ancêtres 14311 Rte-11, Rivière-du-Nord ☎ 877 721 2200, ⓦ vhanb.ca. If you visit the Village Historique Acadien you can sample traditional Acadian food at this restaurant; think chicken *fricot*, dried codfish and lard and molasses cake (mains from $10–15). Daily 11.30am–4pm.

Les Blancs d'Arcadie (Fromagerie) 488 blvd St-Pierre West ☎ 506 727 5952, ⓦ lesblancsdarcadie.ca. Buy (takeaway only) cheddar cheese made on the premises in a variety of flavours (smoked, pesto, herbs) – or try the justly popular bag of curds with BBQ flavour ($3.50). Mon 8am–5pm, Tues–Fri 8am–5.30pm, Sat 10am–5pm.

Prince Edward Island

After the dense forests and rugged, misty coastlines of Nova Scotia and New Brunswick, **PRINCE EDWARD ISLAND (PEI)** is a real surprise, a land of rich, red earth,

COVEHEAD LIGHTHOUSE, PRINCE EDWARD ISLAND

5

gently rolling farmland and neat villages of Victorian homes. Visit in the summer and it really does seems like a rustic oasis, little changed since local-born novelist Lucy Maud Montgomery described the island floating "on the waves of the blue gulf, a green seclusion and haunt of ancient peace". Even today, Canada's smallest province remains thoroughly agricultural, with Islanders remarkably successful in controlling the pace of change. Fish and lobsters are still sold off fishing boats, doors remain unlocked and everyone seems to know everyone else; laws ban large billboards and there are no freeways. The French settled what they called **Île-St-Jean** in the 1720s, but the British turned them out in the 1760s and renamed the island in 1799.

Charlottetown, the graceful capital, sits on the south coast, its tree-lined streets, wide range of accommodation and fine restaurants making it the best **base** for exploring the island. On the north coast, **Prince Edward Island National Park** is the island's busiest tourist attraction, with kilometres of magnificent sandy beach and a profusion of sights associated with **Anne of Green Gables**. PEI also has a well-deserved reputation for **cuisine**; the island is home to organic farms, fine oysters, mussels and artisan producers of all kinds, from potato vodka and gouda cheese, to ice cream and home-made pickles. It remains best known for the excellence of its **lobsters**, which are trapped during May and June and again in late August and September; the catch is kept fresh in saltwater tanks to supply the peak tourist season (this careful management is one of the reasons the lobster population is flourishing). Look out for posters advertising **lobster suppers**, inexpensive set meals served in several church and community halls during the lobster season.

ARRIVAL AND DEPARTURE
PRINCE EDWARD ISLAND

By plane There are regular flights to Charlottetown Airport (⊛ flypei.com) from several cities in eastern Canada, primarily Halifax, Montréal and Toronto, with the principal carriers being WestJet and Air Canada. Taxis (☎ 902 566 6666) run into the city for a fixed-fare of $16 (plus $5 per additional person). T3 Transit (see page 396) buses run to Charlottetown Mall (Mon–Fri only; $2.25) where you'll have to transfer for downtown. All the major car rental chains have desks at the airport.

By car The majority of drivers arrive via the 13km-long Confederation Bridge (☎ 902 437 7300, ⊛ confederation bridge.com) spanning the Northumberland Strait between New Brunswick's Cape Tormentine and Borden, 60km west of Charlottetown. A toll of $47 is levied on each standard-size vehicle, but this is only collected as you leave the island.

Cycling is a popular pastime on PEI, but cyclists aren't allowed on the bridge; instead, they are transported across in a shuttle bus ($8.75 per cyclist; $4.50 pedestrians), which operates 24/7; advance reservations are not accepted.

By bus Maritime Bus (☎ 902 566 1567, ⊛ maritimebus. com) runs to/from 7 Mt Edward Rd in Charlottetown (2km north of the wharfside), and also serves Summerside (Irving petrol station, 96 Water St). T3 Transit (see page 396) buses link the bus station at 7 Mt Edward Rd with Charlottetown Mall (Mon–Fri only; $2.25) where you'll have to transfer for downtown.

Destinations Halifax (3 daily; 5hr via transfer in Amherst); Moncton (3 daily; 3hr 20min); Saint John (3 daily; 6hr 25min, via transfer in Moncton); Summerside (3 daily; 1hr 30min, transfer at Borden).

CYCLING AND HIKING THE CONFEDERATION TRAIL

Prince Edward Island's quiet roads and gentle terrain make it a great place for **cycling**, but although there are several **cycle-tour operators**, it's much less expensive (and entirely straightforward) to plan your own route: in Charlottetown, both Outer Limit Sports, 330 University Ave (Mon–Fri 9am–6pm, Sat 9am–5pm; ☎ 902 569 5690, ⊛ ols.ca; from $35/day, $226/week), and MacQueen's, 430 Queen St (Mon–Thurs & Sat 8.30am–5.30pm, Fri 8.30am–7pm, July & Aug also Sun 10am–2pm; ☎ 902 368 2453, ⊛ macqueens.com; from $40/day, $210/week), rent out all the necessary gear, offer shuttles and will advise on trails. The most popular of these is the 273km **Confederation Trail** (⊛ tourismpei.com/pei-confederation-trail), a combined **hiking and cycling trail** (gravel surface) that weaves its way across the bucolic heart of the island from east to west, partly following the route of PEI's old railway, which was closed in the 1980s. You won't see much of the coast from the trail, but you won't see any cars either, and it's a wonderful way to take in the idyllic countryside.

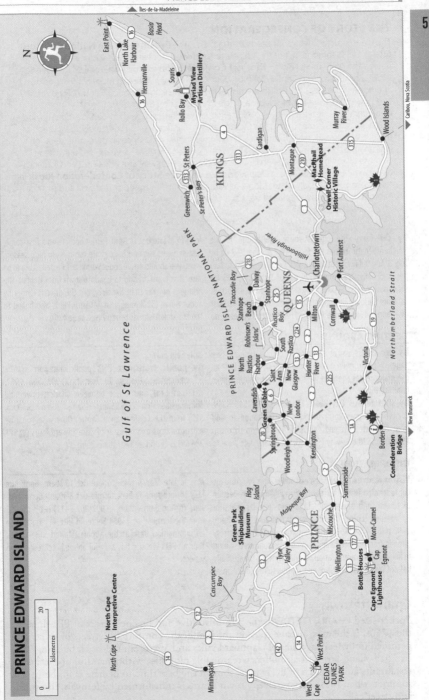

PRINCE EDWARD ISLAND

Gulf of St Lawrence

Îles-de-la-Madeleine

East Point
North Lake Harbour
Hermanville
Souris
Basin Head
Myriad View Artisan Distillery
Rollo Bay

KINGS

Cardigan
St Peters
Greenwich
St Peter's Bay
Murray River
Wood Islands
Montague
MacPhail Homestead
Orwell Corner Historic Village

Caribou, Nova Scotia

PRINCE EDWARD ISLAND NATIONAL PARK

Hillsborough River

Charlottetown
Fort Amherst

QUEENS

Tracadie Bay
Dalvay
Stanhope
Stanhope Beach
Rustico
Robinson's Island
Rustico Bay
North Rustico
Harbour
South Rustico
Milton
Cornwall
Northumberland Strait

Saint Ann
New Glasgow
Hunter River
Victoria

Cavendish
Green Gables
New London
Springbrook
Woodleigh
Kensington
Confederation Bridge
Borden

New Brunswick

Malpeque Bay
Hog Island
Summerside

PRINCE

Green Park Shipbuilding Museum
Tyne Valley
Miscouche
Mont-Carmel
Bottle Houses
Cap Egmont
Cape Egmont Lighthouse
Wellington

Cascumpec Bay

North Cape
North Cape Interpretive Centre

Miminegash

West Cape
West Point
CEDAR DUNES PARK

N

0   20
kilometres

THE STORY OF CONFEDERATION

The island's most significant historical attraction is the **Province House National Historic Site** at 165 Richmond St, but this is likely to be **closed** until at least 2021 for a massive renovation. Until then, visit the **Story of Confederation** exhibit (Jan–April & Nov–Dec Sat 10am–3pm; May, June, Sept & Oct Mon–Sat 10am–3pm; July & Aug Mon–Sat 9am–5pm, Sun noon–5pm; free), housed in the upper foyer of the Confederation Centre of the Arts (see page 397). Here there's a replica of the Confederation Chamber where the Fathers of Confederation – representatives of Nova Scotia, New Brunswick, then-Canada (Ontario and Québec) and PEI – met during the Charlottetown Conference in 1864, to discuss a union of the British colonies in North America. It took two more conferences before confederation was finally achieved in 1867, though PEI didn't join for a further six years, and only then because it was bankrupt after an ill-advised splurge on railway construction. Parks Canada's twenty-minute film *Building of Destiny* adds context. The **Story of Confederation Kiosk** in the house gardens (July & Aug Mon–Sat 9am–5pm, Sun 11am–4pm; free) will also provide information and guided tours of the city.

By car ferry The alternative to the bridge is the Northumberland Ferries car ferry (May & June 5–7 daily; July & Aug 9 daily; Sept to mid-Oct 7 daily; mid-Oct to late Dec 3–5 daily; 1hr 15min; $20 passenger return, $78 for car & passengers; bicycles $20; ☏ 902 566 3838, ⬤ ferries.ca) from Caribou, Nova Scotia, to Wood Islands, 61km east of – and a 45min drive from – Charlottetown. There's no ferry from late Dec to April. Ferries operate on a first-come, first-served basis and queues are common in high season, when you should arrive about 90min before departure to be safe. If you are driving to Charlottetown from Halifax, the bridge is quicker than the ferry, but the drive is longer by about 80km (320km against 240km). PEI is also linked to the Magdalen Islands by ferry (see page 405).

GETTING AROUND

By car Unless you're planning a cycling holiday (see page 394), you need a car to make the most of PEI – all the major rental agencies have offices at the airport or in Charlottetown.

By shuttle bus City Beach Express (☏ 902 566 5259, ⬤ citybeachexpress.com) provides transportation to and from Charlottetown and Cavendish (on the north coast; 45min) for $20 one-way ($29 return); 4 daily, late June to early Sept only.

By public transport PEI's public transport system is rudimentary, though T3 Transit (☏ 902 566 9962, ⬤ t3transit.ca) runs buses between Charlottetown and Summerside (Mon–Fri 6.25am, 7.45am, 4.20pm & 5.30pm; $10) from the Confederation Centre. Otherwise you'll be reliant on taxis and tours: see Prince Edward Tours (☏ 877 286 6532, ⬤ princeedwardtours.com).

INFORMATION

Visitor centres Take the first exit on PEI after you cross the Confederation Bridge for the Gateway Village, a collection of touristy gift shops but also home to a large visitor information centre (100 Abegweit Drive; daily 9am–8pm; ☏ 800 463 4734, ⬤ tourismpei.com). You'll find courtesy phones, free internet, heaps of information and staff willing to help book accommodation. Arriving by ferry, the similarly helpful Wood Islands visitor information centre (daily: mid-May to late May & mid- to late Oct 10.30am–6pm; late May to mid-June & Sept to mid-Oct 8.30am–6pm; mid-June to Aug 8am–10pm; ☏ 902 962 7411) is up the hill from the terminal at 13054 Shore Rd (Rte-4). There's also an information desk at the airport (staffed June–Sept). Tourism PEI's website has a useful online hotel reservation service.

Charlottetown

Pocket-sized **CHARLOTTETOWN**, the administrative and business heart of PEI since the 1760s, is the most urbane spot on the island, the comfortable streets of its centre hemmed in by leafy avenues of clapboard villas and Victorian red-brick buildings. In small-island terms, it also offers a reasonable **nightlife**, with a handful of excellent restaurants and a clutch of lively bars, though the best time to be here is in the summer, when the otherwise sleepy town centre is transformed by festivals, live music and street cafés.

5

Confederation Centre of the Arts

145 Richmond St • Daily: June–Sept 9am–8pm; Oct–May 9am–5pm • Free • ☎ 902 628 1864, ⓦ confederationcentre.com

Built in 1964, the **Confederation Centre of the Arts** may be housed in a glass-and-concrete monstrosity, but it's the home of the Charlottetown Festival and *Anne of Green Gables* musical (see page 399), the island's main library, a couple of theatres, the **Story of Confederation exhibit** (see page 396) and an eclectic **art gallery** (mid-May to mid-Oct daily 9am–5pm; mid-Oct to mid-May Wed–Sat 11am–5pm, Sun 1–5pm; donation suggested), whose changing exhibitions always have a Canadian emphasis and often include a variety of nineteenth-century artefacts.

St Dunstan's Catholic Basilica

45 Great George St • Daily 8am–5pm • Free • ☎ 902 894 3486, ⓦ stdunstanspei.com

A couple of hundred metres south of the Confederation Centre lie the pretty terraced houses of Great George Street, which face the twin spires and imposing facade of **St Dunstan's Catholic Basilica**. Finished in 1919, the church has all the neo-Gothic trimmings, from lancet windows to heavy-duty columns and a mighty vaulted ceiling. Some of Charlottetown's most historic clapboard and brick buildings are concentrated on and around **King Street** to either side of Great George Street; while **Victoria Row**, also near the church, has the city's finest example of commercial architecture, a long and impressive facade that now holds a series of restaurants and bars; in the summer the whole street is pedestrianized and smothered with alfresco diners.

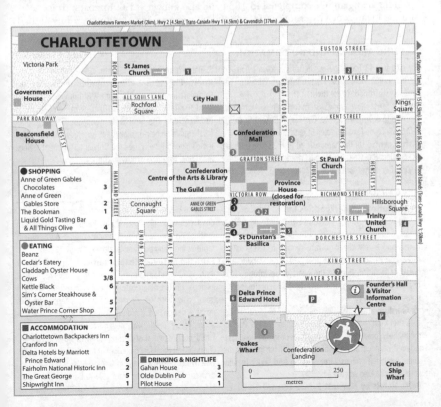

FOUNDERS' HALL MARKET

Plans are tabled to turn *Founders' Hall* (6 Prince St), facing Charlottetown's harbourfront, into a daily urban market. The hope is to fill the hall with a combination of local produce and artisanal food stalls, plus local arts and crafts, with the market open year-round. The market should be up and running sometime in 2019, but check at the Charlottetown Visitor Information Centre, which shares the same premises (see below). The market would be independent of the excellent *Charlottetown Farmers Market* at 100 Belvedere Ave (Sat 9am–2pm; also mid-June to early Oct Wed 9am–2pm; ⓦ charlottetownfarmersmarket.com), 3km north of the waterfront.

Beaconsfield House

2 Kent St • May, June, Sept & Oct Mon–Fri noon–4pm; July & Aug daily 10am–4pm;; Nov–April Mon–Fri noon–4pm • $5 • ☎ 902 368 6603, ⓦ peimuseum.com

Northwest of the town centre, **Beaconsfield House** is a resplendent, late Victorian mansion, built in 1877 for James Peake, one of Charlottetown's leading shipbuilders (he went bust five years after its completion). The house changed owners and roles several times thereafter, until a local conservation society returned it to its former glory in the 1970s.

Government House

1 Government Drive • July & Aug Mon–Fri 10am–3.30pm • Free • ☎ 902 368 5480, ⓦ gov.pe.ca/olg

The assorted greenery of **Victoria Park** edges the grandiose **Government House**, a splendid Georgian pile completed in 1834 and also known as Fanningbank. It is still the Lieutenant-Governor's residence and only open for guided tours in July and August.

GETTING AROUND AND INFORMATION   CHARLOTTETOWN

By city bus T3 Transit buses zip around town (Mon–Fri; $2.25; ☎ 902 566 9962, ⓦ t3transit.ca), though you probably won't need to use them.

By taxi Taxis follow a zone system (no meters), with most journeys in downtown $6–10. City Taxi, 193 Kent St ☎ 902 892 6567; Co-op Taxi, 305 Allen St ☎ 902 892 1111.

Visitor centre On the harbourfront in the same building as Founders' Hall (see above), at 6 Prince St (daily: Jan–May & Oct–Dec 9am–4pm; June 8.30am–6pm; July & Aug

8.30am–7pm; Sept 8.30am–5pm; ☎ 902 368 4444).

Internet Free at the harbourfront visitor centre and at the Confederation Centre Public Library, Richmond St (Mon, Fri & Sat 10am–5pm, Tues–Thurs 10am–9pm, Sun 1–5pm).

Publications The local daily newspaper, *The Guardian* (ⓦ theguardian.pe.ca), makes for an enjoyable read, and there's a good-quality, free monthly entertainment listings magazine, *The Buzz* (ⓦ buzzon.com).

ACCOMMODATION

★ **Charlottetown Backpackers Inn** 60 Hillsborough St ☎ 902 367 5749, ⓦ charlottetownbackpackers. com; map p.397. Excellent HI-affiliated hostel with dorms and a few cheap private rooms in a renovated, three-storey house. There's a pool table, free parking and breakfast included, right in the heart of downtown. May to early Oct. Dorms $31, non-members $35; doubles $99, non-members $110

★ **Cranford Inn** 177 Fitzroy St ☎ 888 573 5022, ⓦ fairholminn.com/cranford-house; map p.397. Part of the Fairholm properties' stable (with check-in and breakfast, included, next door at the Hillhurst Inn), with ten immaculate, suites (with flat-screens), free parking and super-friendly hosts – book a long way ahead. $199

Delta Hotels by Marriott Prince Edward 18 Queen

St ☎ 902 566 2222, ⓦ marriott.com; map p.397. Charlottetown's plushest chain hotel, in a high-rise overlooking the harbour; luxurious rooms with superb facilities including pool and health centre. $275

Fairholm National Historic Inn 230 Prince St ☎ 902 892 5022, ⓦ fairholminn.com; map p.397. A fine example of mid-nineteenth-century architecture, this inn from 1838, with its elegant red-brick exterior, doubles up as a designated National Historic Site. The interior is appropriately plush with seven capacious guest rooms kitted out in period style and all with open fireplaces. Check-in and breakfast next door at the Hillhurst Inn. $249

The Great George 58 Great George St ☎ 902 892 0606, ⓦ thegreatgeorge.com; map p.397. Bang in the centre of town, opposite St Dunstan's, a cluster of fifteen old timber houses has been carefully renovated to hold this immaculate and atmospheric hotel. All the rooms are comfortable and tastefully decorated – the most appealing overlook the church. A continental breakfast is included. $\underline{\$233}$

★ **Shipwright Inn** 51 Fitzroy St ☎902 368 1905, ⓦshipwrightinn.com; map p.397. Crammed with antiques, this rambling 1865 timber mansion (with a more recent extension) has nine individually decorated guest rooms managed by a couple of affable British expats. Very appealing – especially with its thoughtful additions (like popcorn, afternoon tea and muffins, videos and CDs), and its superlative breakfasts. $\underline{\$169}$

EATING

Beanz 138 Great George St ☎902 892 8797, ⓦbeanz espressobar.com; map p.397. Great coffee and a range of tasty sandwiches and salads from around $6–9 at this agreeable little café. Especially popular at lunch times with the town's office workers. Mon–Fri 7am–5pm, Sat 8am–4pm.

Cedar's Eatery 181 Great George St ☎902 892 7377; map p.397. Charlottetown has had a relatively large Lebanese population since the 1880s, and this is one of their favourite haunts; think hummus, fragrant *kafta* and stuffed vine leaves (most mains $14–20). Mon–Thurs 11am–10pm, Fri & Sat 11am–11pm, Sun 4–10pm.

Claddagh Oyster House 131 Sydney St at Queen St (beneath the Olde Dublin Pub) ☎902 892 9661, ⓦcladdaghoysterhouse.com; map p.397. Attractive modern restaurant set in a red-brick Victorian, specializing in delicious PEI oysters ($2.95 each); a 12-piece tasting plate costs $35. Otherwise, the menu offers a competent selection of seafood and PEI beef dishes with mains $22–40. Mon–Thurs 5–9pm, Fri & Sat 5–10pm (open Sun 5–10pm May–Sept).

Cows 150 Queen St, at Grafton St ☎902 892 6969, ⓦcows.ca (also on Peake's Wharf May–Oct 10am–5pm); map p.397. Island institution, serving totally addictive ice cream in creative flavours like Wowie Cowie (vanilla, toffee, crunch and choc flakes) and Gooey Mooey. You can also tour the factory (Mon–Thurs 10am–7pm, Fri–Sun 10am–8pm; free; ☎902 370 3155) on the outskirts of town at 12 Milky Way, on the North River Causeway (Rte-1). June–Aug daily 10am–11pm; Sept–May Mon–Thurs 10am–5.30pm, Fri 10am–8pm, Sat 10am–6pm, Sun noon–5pm.

★ **Kettle Black** 45 Queen St ☎902 370 0776; map p.397. Hip café managed by a couple of Ottawa transplants, serving the best coffee (in real mugs) and desserts in town. They also do breakfast bagels and yoghurt bowls ($5–9), and sandwiches and wraps ($7–9). Mon–Fri 7am–6pm, Sat & Sun 8am–6pm.

★ **Sim's Corner Steakhouse & Oyster Bar** 86 Queen St ☎902 894 7467, ⓦsimscorner.ca; map p.397. The town's top restaurant, with delectable local oysters ($3 each), a huge wine list and prime Canadian aged steaks – try the secret pepper sauce (steaks $39–65). Features outdoor terrace and barbecues in summer. Mon–Thurs 11am–10pm, Fri 11am–10.30pm, Sat 10am–10.30pm, Sun 10am–9.30pm.

Water Prince Corner Shop 141 Water St ☎902 368 3212, ⓦwaterprincelobster.ca; map p.397. It may look like a corner shop, but many locals swear by the seafood here – even if they are usually outnumbered by the tourists. The lobster dinners and chowders are perhaps the best on the island, but the scallop burger is superb too. You can also buy fresh lobsters to go. Moderately priced with mains from as little as $10. Daily: May, June & Sept to Oct 10am–8pm; July & Aug 10am–10pm; Nov to mid-Dec noon–8pm.

DRINKING

★ **Gahan House** 126 Sydney St ☎902 626 2337, ⓦcharlottetown.gahan.ca; map p.397. PEI's microbrewery produces seven crisp handcrafted ales on-site, from the potent Sydney Street Stout to the lighter Harvest Gold Pale Ale. The pub food is equally comforting – try the signature Brown Bag Fish & Chips, ale-battered haddock (yes, served in a brown bag; $16). Mon–Wed & Sun 11am–midnight, Thurs–Sat 11am–1am.

Olde Dublin Pub 131 Sydney St ☎902 892 6992, ⓦoldedublinpub.com; map p.397. Intimate and justifiably popular spot with imported and domestic ales, Guinness and Kilkenny included. Live folk music – mostly Irish – nightly from May to Sept. Mon–Wed 11am–10pm, Thurs 11am–midnight, Fri & Sat 11am–2am, Sun noon–9pm.

Pilot House 70 Grafton St ☎902 894 4800, ⓦthepilothouse.ca; map p.397. Traditional pub-cum-diner in a fine nineteenth-century building, with booths to sit in and fish and chips (from its bar menu; $16) to devour. Daily 11.30am–11.30pm.

ENTERTAINMENT

Confederation Centre of the Arts 145 Richmond St ☎902 566 1267, ⓦconfederationcentre.com. Hosts an extensive variety of acts, from rock and jazz through to comedians, magicians, theatre, opera and ballet. The centre is also the home of the main show of the annual Charlottetown Festival (mid-June to Sept), which is a musical adaptation of *Anne of Green Gables* (mid-June to Aug; tickets from $30) running since 1965.

SHOPPING

Anne of Green Gables Chocolates 100 Queen St ☎ 902 368 3131, ⓦ annechocolates.com; map p.397. The Anne brand was inevitably applied to chocolate in 1999, and this store is chock-full of old-fashioned sweets and handmade chocs (try the Cow Chips). Mon–Sat 9.30am–6pm, Sun noon–6pm.

Anne of Green Gables Store 110 Queen St ☎ 902 368 2663, ⓦ annestore.ca; map p.397. Indulge your Anne obsession in the definitive Green Gables shop. Mon–Fri 9am–8pm, Sat 9am–6pm, Sun 11am–6pm (winter hours Mon–Sat 10am–6pm, Sun noon–5pm).

The Bookman 177 Queen St ☎ 902 892 8872, ⓦ bookmanpei.com; map p.397. The best of several secondhand bookstores along this stretch of Queen St. Mon–Sat 9am–9pm, Sun 11am–5pm.

Liquid Gold Tasting Bar & All Things Olive 72 Queen St ☎ 902 370 8809, ⓦ allthingsolive.ca; map p.397. This little homage to the Mediterranean invites you to sample its selection of fresh, extra virgin olive oil before buying – rich liquids that taste like bottled olive juice. They also sell balsamic vinegars from Modena, Italy. Mon–Sat 10am–5pm.

Prince Edward Island National Park and around

Open year-round, but facilities (toilets, beach boardwalks, visitor centres, picnic areas and campgrounds) close from Oct through to mid-May • Entrance fee per adult per day $3.90 in June; $7.80 July & Aug; at other times entry free • ☎ 902 672 6350, ⓦ pc.gc.ca/en/pn-np/pe/pei-ipe

Pulling in thousands of visitors every summer, the gorgeous sandy beaches of **Prince Edward Island National Park** extend along the Gulf of St Lawrence shore for some 40km. Rarely more than a couple of hundred metres wide, the main body of the park incorporates both the beaches and the sliver of low red cliff and marram grass-covered sand dune that runs behind – a barrier which is occasionally interrupted by slender inlets connecting the ocean with a quartet of chubby little bays. A narrow road runs behind the shoreline for most of its length, but **Rustico Bay** effectively divides the main body of the park into two: the smaller, more **westerly portion** (see page 402) runs from Cavendish – home of **Green Gables** – to North Rustico Harbour; the **easterly section**, which is wilder and more untrammelled, goes from Robinson's Island to Tracadie Bay, with a third, smaller section lying further east still at **Greenwich**, at the mouth of St Peter's Bay. The park has fifteen short **hiking trails**, easy strolls that take in different aspects of the coast from its tidal marshes and farmland to its woodlands and dunes.

Robinson's Island and Stanhope Beach

The fastest route from Charlottetown to the easterly section of the national park is the half-hour, 23km thump along Rte-15, which branches off Rte-2 on the north side of town. This takes you past the delightful **Dunes Studio Gallery and Café**, located just 600m beyond the Rte-6 and Rte-15 junction (see page 401), a pottery shop and art gallery (daily: May & Oct 9am–6pm; June & Sept 9am–9pm; July & Aug 9am–10pm).

Inside the national park, at the end of Rte-15, turn left along the coast for the causeway over to wooded **Robinson's Island** (home of RITS, or Robinsons Island Trail System, designed for mountain-bikers), or right for the 5km trip along the seashore to **Stanhope Beach**, the setting for a string of perfectly placed beachside cottage complexes (see page 401).

Dalvay to Greenwich

About 6km east of Stanhope Beach, the Gulf Shore Parkway passes **Dalvay-by-the-Sea National Historic Site of Canada**, whose most conspicuous asset is the **Dalvay-by-the-Sea Inn** (see page 401), built in 1896 for Scottish-American oil tycoon Alexander McDonald – Prince William and Kate spent time here on their 2011 tour of Canada. Further along the coast to the east of Dalvay is the slender sand spit that shelters much of **Tracadie Bay** from the ocean. There are no roads to this part of the park – just hiking trails; this also applies to the most easterly segment at **GREENWICH**, the partly wooded headland at the mouth of **St Peter's Bay**. Make a pit stop at the village of St Peter's for **Rick's Fish & Chips** (see page 402) before following Rte-313 west to the park interpretation centre. From here, the scenic and partly boardwalked 4.8km-long **Greenwich Dunes Trail** drifts across the headland, exploring its wild and especially beautiful beaches, dunes and wetlands.

To Prince Edward Island National Park via New Glasgow

The 40km-long journey from Charlottetown to Cavendish and the western portion of the National Park covers some of PEI's most alluring scenery. Take Rte-2 west from the capital and after about 23km turn north along Rte-13 to **NEW GLASGOW**, whose matching pair of black-and-white clapboard churches sit on opposite sides of an arm of Rustico Bay.

Prince Edward Island Preserve Company

2841 New Glasgow Rd • Jan–April & mid-Oct to Dec Mon–Fri 9am–5pm, Sat 10am–4pm; May daily 9am–5pm; June to late Sept daily 8.30am–8.30pm; late Sept to mid-Oct daily 8.30am–5pm • ☎ 902 964 4300, ⓦ preservecompany.com

In the centre of New Glasgow, the **Prince Edward Island Preserve Company** is a great place to buy local jams, mustards and maple syrups, and the attached **restaurant** (daily late May to late Oct) serves first-rate breakfasts, lunches and – in the summer – evening meals: try the cedar-planked salmon. From New Glasgow, it's 10km to Cavendish along Rte-13.

INFORMATION	PRINCE EDWARD ISLAND NATIONAL PARK

Visitor centres and kiosks The Greenwich Interpretation Centre (mid-June to mid-Sept daily 9am–5pm); acts as the main visitor centre for the park, though the Cavendish Visitor Information Centre, at Rte-6 and Rte-13 (mid-Oct to Dec Mon–Fri 11am–2pm; mid-May to late June & Sept to mid-Oct daily 9am–5pm; late June–Aug daily 8am–9pm; ⓦ cavendishbeachpei.com), is more convenient for the western side. Seasonal information kiosks at every entrance to the park (mid-June to late June 11am–5pm; late June to Aug 10am–6pm) levy the entrance fee.

ACCOMMODATION

Brackley Beach Hostel 37 Britain Shore Rd, Brackley Beach ☎ 902 672 1900, ⓦ brackleybeachhostel.com. A welcome budget option with shared and private rooms, very popular with families – extras include a tranquil outdoor deck, pool table, table tennis, big TVs and shared computers. Mid-June to mid-Sept. Dorms **$30**; doubles **$65**
Dalvay-by-the-Sea Inn 16 Cottage Crescent (Rte-6) ☎ 902 672 2048, ⓦ dalvaybythesea.com. This 1895 Queen Anne Revival-style mansion features high gables, rough-hewn stonework, a magnificent wraparound veranda and a croquet lawn. The inn holds 25 tastefully decorated rooms (no TVs) and has an ideal location inside the park close to the beach. It's also worth stopping for high tea (July & Aug Sat & Sun 2–4pm; $40), an elaborate affair involving sticky date pudding, fine china and pots of exotic teas. June–Sept. **$209**
Del Mar Cottages 1235 Gulf Shore Parkway, Stanhope ☎ 902 672 2582, ⓦ delmarcottages.com. Little red-and-white cottages that sleep up to four, located midway between the Brackley and Dalvay beaches, all with cable TV, DVD players and barbecues. Discounts available for weekly rentals plus early June and late Sept to Oct rentals. Open June–Oct. **$160**
Prince Edward Island National Park camping ☎ 877 737 3783, ⓦ reservation.pc.gc.ca. The park has two campsites; the larger is the well-equipped, fully serviced *Cavendish Campground* (mid-June to mid-Sept), where there's a supervised sandy beach that's great for swimming. The quieter *Stanhope Campground* (mid-July to early Sept), a short walk from the beach near the hamlet of Stanhope, is similarly well equipped. Both offer plush oTENTiks (with water and electricity). A few sites are allocated on a first-come, first-served basis, but most can be reserved; reservations are strongly advised. Unserviced site **$27**; serviced site **$32**; oTENTik **$120**
Shaw's Hotel & Cottages 99 Apple Tree Rd, Brackley Beach ☎ 902 672 2022, ⓦ shawshotel.ca. A short drive from Robinson's Island and Stanhope Beach on Rte-15, this is the pick of the resort and cottage complexes hereabouts, with charmingly rustic rooms and year-round chalets occupying extensive grounds about 10min walk from the beach; *Shaw's* also does canoe, kayak and bike rental for guests and non-guests. June to mid-Oct. Cottages **$194**; doubles **$157**

EATING

Dunes Studio Gallery and Café 3622 Brackley Point Rd (Rte-15), Brackley Beach ☎ 902 672 2586, ⓦ dunesgallery.com. Pottery shop and art gallery, which serves mouthwatering snacks and meals from an imaginative menu (brie and pear pizza $16; banana bread crumb-crusted halibut $42) that includes plenty of

5

vegetarian dishes. Daily: June & Sept 11.30am–9pm; July & Aug 11.30am–10pm; Oct 1 to mid-Oct 11.30am–4.30pm.

New Glasgow Lobster Suppers 604 Rte-258, New Glasgow ☎ 902 964 2870, ⊚ peilobstersuppers.com. These famed lobster suppers have been running since 1958, with the usual gut-busting line-up of home-made rolls, seafood chowder, mussels and salad before the main event and ending with the "mile-high" lemon meringue pie

(it's a set-price menu; pay at the door). Sets with a 500g (1lb) lobster from $36.95. Daily: June & Sept to mid-Oct 4–8pm; July & Aug 4–8.30pm.

Rick's Fish & Chips 5544 Rte-2, St Peter's ☎ 902 961 3438 ⊚ ricksfishnchips.com. Situated just back from the bay on Rte-2, step in for some of the best fried haddock and seafood on the island (big portions from $18). Mid-May to June & Sept to early Oct Mon–Thurs & Sun 11am–7pm, Fri & Sat 11am–9pm; July & Aug daily 11am–9pm.

Anne Country: Cavendish and around

Straggling **CAVENDISH**, clumped around the junction of Rte-6 and Rte-13, lies behind another stretch of fabulous PEI National Park **beach**. The west and east sections of the beach are not connected by road (both are signposted from Rte-6), but you can walk between them: the west side is better for swimming, while the east is noted chiefly for its crumbling red sandstone headlands. Yet the reason so many people come to Cavendish – indeed, this is the most congested part of the island in July and August, and definitely the most commercialized – is because it lays claim to the key sights associated with the ubiquitous **Anne of Green Gables** (see page 403). Real fans will want to spend at least a day soaking up the attractions, but even the uninitiated will appreciate the old houses (and the genuine enthusiasm of the local guides).

Lucy Maud Montgomery's Cavendish Home

8521 Cavendish Rd (Rte-6, just east of Rte-13) • Daily: late May to June & Sept to late Oct 10am–5pm; July & Aug 9.30am–5.30pm • $6 • ☎ 902 963 2969, ⊚ lmmontgomerycavendishhome.com

The best place to start in Cavendish is the site of **Lucy Maud Montgomery's Cavendish Home**, where the author of *Anne of Green Gables* lived, on and off, between 1876 to 1911, and where she wrote her most famous novels; it's been combined with the Green Gables Heritage Place to form **L. M. Montgomery's Cavendish National Historic Site**. The farmhouse belonged to her grandparents, the Macneills, who raised Lucy after her mother died. Though it's the most historically significant site in town, there's not much to see, as the main buildings were knocked down in the 1920s; but the site has been beautifully maintained by the descendants of the family (John and Jennie Macneill), and enhanced with signs pointing out important features and quotes from the author.

Green Gables Heritage Place

8619 Cavendish Rd (Rte-6) • May–Oct daily 9am–5pm • $7.80, ages 6–16 free; May, June, Sept & Oct $6.30, children 6–16 free • ☎ 902 963 7871, ⊚ pc.gc.ca/en/lhn-nhs/pe/greengables

From the back of the Lucy Maud Montgomery's Cavendish Home you can walk along the old homestead lane, across Rte-13 and along the Haunted Wood Trail into the back of **Green Gables Heritage Place**, the primary Anne pilgrimage site. The main entrance is on Rte-6, just 500m west of Rte-13. The two-storey timber house was built in 1831 and was once owned by the Macneill cousins of Montgomery, serving as her inspiration for the fictional **Green Gables** farm in the novel. The house has been modified several times since then, and the rooms have been decked out in authentic period furnishings, though few pieces are original to the house – the main aim was to faithfully match descriptions in the book, and Matthew's bedroom, the parlour and Anne's room are littered with items fans will recognize from the story. You can also explore the replica outhouses, and the **visitor centre**, which contains Lucy's original typewriter and scrapbooks.

On the corner of routes 6 and 13, the old cemetery contains the **grave** of Montgomery, her husband and her mother. Lucy died in Toronto, but according to her last wish, was buried back on the island – the ceremony held here in 1942 is said to have been the closest thing to a state funeral PEI has ever had.

ANNE, LUCY AND PEI

PEI may be the home of Confederation, juicy oysters, beaches and tasty lobsters, but even the most jaded travellers spend a couple of hours paying homage to **Anne of Green Gables**. The heart-warming tale of a red-haired, pigtailed orphan girl who Mark Twain dubbed the "most lovable childhood heroine since the immortal Alice" has become a phenomenal worldwide sensation since it was published in 1908, and the vivid descriptions of rural PEI, handsomely captured in the 1985 TV miniseries, has undeniably inspired many a trip here. Thousands of Japanese tourists visit every year; the book has been on school curricula there since the 1950s and remains extremely popular.

Many visitors find it hard to separate the fictional life of Anne Shirley and the real life of her creator **Lucy Maud Montgomery**, one of Canada's best-selling authors. In 1876, when Montgomery was just 2, her mother died and her father migrated to Saskatchewan, leaving her in the care of her grandparents in Cavendish. Here she developed a deep love for her native island and its people, and although she spent the last half of her life in Ontario, PEI remained the main inspiration for her work. Completed in 1905 and published three years later (after being rejected five times), *Anne of Green Gables* remains her most popular book. Today, many Islanders remain conflicted over her legacy, troubled by the commercialization of the novel but deeply proud of the author's success.

Avonlea Village

8779 Cavendish Rd (Rte-6) • Daily: July & Aug 10am–8pm; Mid-June to end-June & Sept 3 to mid-Sept to 10am–5pm (Anne Of Green Gables Store also open late May to mid-June & mid-Sept to late Oct 10am–5pm • Free • ☎ 902 963 3050, ⊛ avonlea.ca

Families may well want to check out **Avonlea Village**, a mock nineteenth-century village based on Anne of Green Gables' fictitious home, stocked with shops, *Cows* ice cream and cafés – sadly, the role-playing actors, animals and period theme were cut in 2014. Artisan studios still enhance the experience for little ones. The village does contain three originals: the Belmont School, where Montgomery taught in 1896; the Long River Church (where the live shows take place); and the Clifton Manse from New London, now a tearoom.

Lucy Maud Montgomery Birthplace

6461 Rte-6, New London • Mid-May to early Oct daily 9am–5pm • $5 • ☎ 902 886 2099, ⊛ lmmontgomerybirthplace.ca

Serious Anne aficionados should check out the **Lucy Maud Montgomery Birthplace** in New London, 13km west of Cavendish on Rte-6, a lovely old clapboard house where the author was born in 1874. The house has been decked out with period furniture, personal scrapbooks and a replica of Montgomery's wedding dress.

Anne of Green Gables Museum

4542 Rte-20, Park Corner • Daily: May & Oct 11am–4pm; June & Sept 10am–4pm; July & Aug 9am–5pm • $6 • ☎ 800 665 2663, Sat & Sun ☎ 902 886 2884, ⊛ annemuseum.com

The 1872 home of Montgomery's aunt Annie and uncle John Campbell in Park Corner, 8km west of New London on Rte-20, is now the **Anne of Green Gables Museum** (still owned by the Campbells). Montgomery spent much of her childhood playing here, and went on to base at least four novels on the house (including *Story Girl*). She was even married in the tiny parlour in 1911, and marriages still take place in exactly the same spot. All the rooms are littered with Montgomery memorabilia, and you can also take a **horse and carriage ride** around the premises (max five people; $75/30min, $125/1hr).

ACCOMMODATION

CAVENDISH

Barachois Inn 2193 Church Rd, Rte-243, North Rustico ☎ 902 963 2194, ⊛ barachoisinn.com. Dripping with historic character, this inn features two gorgeous

nineteenth-century properties with luxurious, Victorian-themed rooms. Open year-round. $180

Cavendish Maples Cottages 73 Avonlea blvd (off

5

Rte-6) ☎ 888 662 7537, ⓦ cavendishmaples.com. An appealing option, offering 22 beautifully finished one- to three-bedroom wood cabins, with kitchens, a/c, barbecues and cable TV. Mid-May to mid-Oct. **$195**

Kindred Spirits Country Inn & Cottages 46 Memory Lane (off Rte-6) ☎ 902 963 2434, ⓦ kindredspirits.ca. Centrally located complex (next to Green Gables) offering cosy Victorian-style rooms in the main inn with TVs, DVD players and a/c, and larger self-catering cottages. Mid-May to late Oct. **$120**; cottages **$175**

EATING

Chez Yvonne's 8947 Cavendish Rd (Rte-6) ☎ 902 963 2070, ⓦ chezyvonnes.com. The pick of the otherwise lacklustre Cavendish restaurants, this solid family-friendly place serving steaks and seafood (mains $15–32). Daily: June & Sept 8am–8.30pm; July & Aug 7.30am–9pm.

Fisherman's Wharf Lobster Suppers 7230 Rustico Rd (Rte-6), North Rustico ☎ 902 963 2669, ⓦ fishermans

wharf.ca. In the centre of nearby North Rustico with an unlimited salad bar including mussels and chowder ($23.99), this is a tempting place to sample the island's lobster suppers ($34.50), though it's popular with tour buses. Daily: May, June & Sept to early Oct 11am–9pm; July & Aug 8am–9pm; lobster suppers May & June 4–9pm; July to early Oct noon–9pm.

Points East Coastal Drive

The attractions on the eastern half of PEI are linked by what the tourism authorities have dubbed the **Points East Coastal Drive** (ⓦ pointseastcoastaldrive.com), which essentially follows the main roads that hug the coast between Charlottetown and rugged **East Point** – you'll need one or two days to do it justice, even if you take shortcuts to the highlights, listed below.

Orwell Corner Historic Village

98 Macphail Park Rd (just off Rte-1), Orwell • June & Sept to mid-Oct Mon–Fri 8.30am–4.30pm; July & Aug daily 8.30am–4.30pm • $10.30 • ☎ 902 651 8515, ⓦ peimuseum.ca/orwell

Some 30km east of Charlottetown, just off the Trans-Canada Highway in the village of **ORWELL**, rustic **Orwell Corner Historic Village** was originally settled by Scottish and Irish pioneers in the early nineteenth century but abandoned in the 1950s. The historic graveyard and a handful of buildings remained and in recent years these have been restored and supplemented by replicas of some of the early buildings, like the blacksmith's shop, barns and shingle mill. Care has been taken to give the interiors the authentic flavour of Orwell's past, from the farmhouse's darkened, cluttered living rooms and the austerity of the Presbyterian church to the cheeky graffiti carved into the schoolhouse desks. The gardens are splendidly maintained in period style, farm animals root around purposefully and the village hosts a wide variety of special events, including ploughing contests and ceilidhs.

Souris

Around 81km northeast of Charlottetown lies **SOURIS**, a busy fishing port and harbour, which curves round the shore of Colville Bay and has a regular car ferry service to the **Magdalens** (see page 405). There's not much to see here, but it makes a logical overnight stop.

ACCOMMODATION AND EATING   SOURIS

21 Breakwater Restaurant 21 Breakwater St ☎ 902 687 2556. Gorgeous little restaurant overlooking the bay, with a small but carefully crafted menu (excellent braised beef, Portuguese-style fish and chips) and especially good desserts – try the chocolate banana bread pudding (mains average $16–28). Jan–March Thurs–Sat 11.30am–9pm; July & Aug daily 11.30am–9pm; Sept & May Mon–Sat 11.30am–9pm; Oct 1 to late Oct, Dec & April Wed & Thurs 11.30am–8pm, Fri & Sat 11.30am–9pm (closed

late Oct to Nov); drinks only 3–5pm.

★ **FireWorks** Inn at Bay Fortune, 758 Rte-310, Bay Fortune ☎ 902 687 3745, ⓦ innatbayfortune.com. For a real treat, head to the innovative restaurant of chef Michael Smith, a 10min drive west of Souris, internationally lauded for its eight-course set menus of organic and foraged local dishes, cooked over a wood-burning fire and served family style at butcher's-block tables ("feasts" are $145/person, includes tips; drinks are extra). Oyster Hour runs 6–7pm.

FERRY TO THE MAGDALEN ISLANDS

Operated by CTMA, a **car ferry** (☎ 418 986 3278, ☜ traversierctma.ca/en) makes the five-hour hop between **Cap-aux-Meules** on the Îles-de-la-Madeleine (see page 295) and **Souris** year-round (Dec–March 3 weekly; April 5 weekly; May, June & Sept 6 weekly; July & Aug 7–11 weekly; Oct & Nov 4 weekly). A one-way adult fare is $53.25 ($34.40 mid-Sept to mid-June), plus $99.25 ($69.80) per car and $15.30 per bike.

Late May to early Oct daily 6pm; early Oct to mid-Dec Fri–Sun 6pm.

★ **The Lobster Shack** 8 Main St ☎ 902 743 3347, ☜ colvillebayoysterco.com. The retail outlet for Colville Bay Oyster Co, this small shack on the beach sells some of the island's best oysters ($1.25 each), fresh from the bay, plus fresh and cooked island lobster from $16 (take-out only – eat on the picnic tables on the boardwalk). Mid-June to mid-Sept daily 10am–7pm.

Myriad View Artisan Distillery 1336 Rte-2, Rollo Bay ☎ 902 687 1281, ☜ straitshine.com. This acclaimed distillery produces its unique brands of "moonshine", gin and vodka, all of which can be bought on site. May Mon–Fri 10am–6pm; June to mid-Sept Mon–Sat 10am–6pm, Sun 11am–5pm; second half of Sept Mon–Sat 10am–6pm.

Singing Sands Inn 2518 East Point Rd (Rte-16), Kingsboro ☎ 800 667 2371, ☜ singingsandsinn.ca. A short drive 11km east of Souris, close to "Singing Sands" beach and the beach at Basin Head, this is a simple but good-value option, with all rooms equipped with cable TV and some with a/c. Mid-May to mid-Oct. $139

East Point

You can drive round the island's northeast corner along Rte-16 from Souris, ending at the remote **East Point**. You can climb to the top of the 19.5m **East Point Lighthouse** (404 Lighthouse Rd; late May to early Oct daily 10am–6pm; $6; ☎ 902 357 2106, ☜ eastpointlighthouse.ca), built in 1867, and there's a craft shop on-site (same hours). Nearby **North Lake Harbour** is a raw fishing port, where freshly caught tuna are snapped up by Japanese buyers, and the rows of fishing shacks make for a more authentic PEI picture.

Victoria

The most diverting settlement on the **South Coast** is the old seaport of **VICTORIA**, overlooking the Northumberland Strait about 35km west of Charlottetown along the Trans-Canada Highway. Though short on traditional sights, its gridiron of nineteenth-century clapboard houses is exceptionally picturesque – in July and August it can get packed with day-trippers, so go early.

EATING
VICTORIA

Island Chocolates 7 Main St ☎ 902 658 2320, ☜ island chocolates.ca. Producer of Belgian-style handmade chocolates (you can see them making it) and a fine coffee, as well as a wicked hot chocolate. July–Sept daily 9am–5pm.

Landmark Café 12 Main St ☎ 902 658 2286, ☜ landmarkcafe.ca. Serves excellent and moderately priced home-cooked meals ($16–32), pastas, wholesome sandwiches ($8–12) and chunky lobster rolls ($19). Daily 11.30am–2.45pm & 5–9pm.

ENTERTAINMENT

★ **Victoria Playhouse** Main St, at Howard St ☎ 902 658 2025, ☜ victoriaplayhouse.com. Historic 1915 theatre offers a good range of modern plays and musical evenings, performed from late June to late Sept. Tickets from $35.

Summerside

Some 37km west of Victoria, **SUMMERSIDE** is PEI's second largest settlement, a sprawling bayside town of fifteen thousand people that was once the island's main port. The historic downtown is a leafy, beautifully restored area of clapboard houses centred

5

on the graceful nineteenth-century Trinity United Church on Spring Street and the nearby **Wyatt Heritage Properties**, while the waterfront features the **Spinnakers Landing** development of gift shops and restaurants (daily: June & Sept 9.30am–5.30pm; July & Aug 9.30am–9pm; ⓦ spinnakerslanding.com).

Wyatt Historic House Museum

85 Spring St • Late June to Aug tours Mon–Sat 10am–4pm (hourly) • $10 • ☎ 902 432 1296, ⓦ culturesummerside.com

Of several historic buildings here, the **Wyatt Historic House Museum** is one of the most absorbing, built in 1867 and crammed with ornate furnishings and antiques ranging from the 1890s to the 1950s. **Tours** (45min) are the only way to visit.

International Fox Museum

33 Summer St • Late June to Aug Mon–Sat 10am–5pm • Donation suggested • ☎ 902 432 1296, ⓦ culturesummerside.com

Housed in the old 1911 armoury, the grandly titled **International Fox Museum** is a homage to the extraordinary boom-bust history of fox-ranching on the island, from its beginnings in 1894 to its collapse in the 1930s. It was here that the rare silver fox – a mutation of the red fox in the wild – was farmed for the first time, reaping huge profits for those involved in the fur trade. The small exhibit room contains examples of the fox pelts and an entertaining 45-minute video. Upstairs, **Gallery 33** (same hours) houses temporary art exhibitions.

INFORMATION SUMMERSIDE

Visitor centre Inside Harbourfront Theatre on the waterfront at 124 Heather Moyse Drive (June daily 9am–7pm; July & Aug daily 9am–9pm; Sept daily 10am– 6pm; Oct–May Mon–Fri 11am–4pm (☎ 902 888 8364, ⓦ exploresummerside.com).

ACCOMMODATION AND EATING

Cairns Motel 721 Water St East ☎ 877 224 7676, ⓦ cairnsmotel.net. Summerside offers plenty of B&B and motel accommodation but this little gem is the best deal in town, with friendly owners and spacious, modern rooms equipped with microwaves and flat-screen TVs. **$89.95**

Samuel's Coffee House 4 Queen St ☎ 902 724 2300, ⓦ samuelscoffeehouse.ca. Cosy café housed in the old Summerside Bank building (you can even sit in the old vault), serving superb coffee, pastries, Montréal-style bagels ($2.75) and breakfast "sammies" (stuffed with egg, spinach, cheese and tomato; $6). Mon–Thurs 7.30am– 5pm, Fri 7.30am–9pm, Sat & Sun 8am–5pm.

★ **Skip's Fish n' Chips** 561 Notre Dame St ☎ 902 436 5151, ⓦ skipsfishnchips.com. Justly acclaimed for its sumptuous main dish, a huge haddock fillet embedded in delicious batter served with tasty chips ($9.50–17.45); the eat-in special ($12.95) comes with drink and ice cream sundae. April–Dec Tues–Sat 11.30am–7pm.

La Région Évangéline

The most traditionally French part of the island, a short drive west of Summerside, was settled by Acadians (see page 354) in the eighteenth century and is known as **La Région Évangéline** (ⓦ regionevangeline.com).

Acadian Museum

23 Main Drive (Rte-2), Miscouche • July & Aug daily 9.30am–5pm; Sept–June Mon–Fri 9.30am–5pm, Sun 1–4pm • $4.50 • ☎ 902 432 2880, ⓦ museeacadien.org.

Just 8km from Summerside, the village of **Miscouche** is home to the bright and informative **Acadian Museum**, a solid introduction to the island's French-speaking community and the traumatic deportations of 1755.

Mont-Carmel

Continuing west from Miscouche, the **Cap Egmont headland** is a major centre of Acadian settlement, with tiny **MONT-CARMEL** dominated by the incongruous red-brick mass of the **Église Notre-Dame** (July & Aug daily 9.30am–6pm; free; ☎ 902 854 2208).

5

Built in 1898, this is the most important Acadian religious site in PEI, its stern lines and neat cemetery enhanced by a stunning location overlooking the sea.

Bottle Houses

6891 Rte-11, Cap-Egmont • Daily: mid-May to June & Sept to mid-Oct 9am–6pm; July & Aug 9am–8pm • $8 • ☎ 902 854 2987, ⓦ bottlehouses.com

The Acadian village of **Cap-Egmont** is home to the island's quirkiest sight, the **Bottle Houses**. Édouard Arsenault built the three curious-looking buildings (one is a chapel) in the early 1980s from around thirty thousand bottles; the houses were reconstructed in the 1990s and are now nestled within pleasant, blossom-strewn gardens.

ACCOMMODATION AND EATING	LA RÉGION ÉVANGÉLINE
Chez Yvette 1154 Rte-124, Urbainville • ☎ 902 854 2966, ⓦ chezyvette.ca. The best place to stay is in nearby Urbainville, a clapboard home dating from 1930, with three neat bedrooms and two shared bathrooms. **$100**	cultural centre runs a family restaurant serving delicious Acadian favourites such as the potato-pie-like *râpure* ($8), clam pie ($10), fish cakes ($12) and fresh mussels ($11). You can buy cakes and pastries at *La Galette Blanche Bakery* on-site (same hours). Mid-June to mid-Sept daily
★ **Resto-bar La Trappe** 1745 Rte-124, Abram-Village ☎ 902 854 3300, ⓦ villagemusical.com. This Acadian	11am–7pm.

Up West

The far northwest of PEI, or just **Up West** to the locals, is a long winding drive from Summerside, starting with the slightly hillier scenery along the northwest shore of **Malpeque Bay**, home of the famed and eponymous **oyster** variety (listed on many PEI menus), the bulk of which are shipped overseas.

Green Park Shipbuilding Museum

Green Park Provincial Park, 364 Green Park Rd (off Rte-12), Port Hill • June Mon–Fri 9am–4.30pm; July & Aug daily 9am–4.30pm • $5.75 • ☎ 902 831 7947, ⓦ peimuseum.com

Malpeque Bay's reedy waters were once fringed by tiny shipbuilding yards, and the scant remains of one of them have been conserved as part of the **Green Park Shipbuilding Museum**. The museum also incorporates an interpretive centre, focusing on PEI's shipbuilding industry, and the restored **Yeo House**, built in the 1860s.

West Point Lighthouse Museum

364 Cedar Dunes Park Rd (off Rte-14) • June–Sept daily 9am–8.30pm • $5 • ☎ 902 859 3605, ⓦ westpointharmony.ca

It's about 50km from Green Park to the western tip of the island, where the remote and windswept **West Point Lighthouse Museum** holds a small collection of photographs and memorabilia portraying the lives of the lighthouse keepers. Built in 1875, the 20m-tall lighthouse primarily functions as an unusual **hotel** today (see below), but nonguests can climb to the top.

North Cape Wind Energy Interpretive Centre

21817 Rte-12 • Mid-May to June & Sept to mid-Oct daily 10am–6pm; July & Aug daily 9am–8pm • $5 • ☎ 902 882 2991, ⓦ northcape.ca

Right at the end of Rte-12, isolated **North Cape Wind Energy Interpretive Centre** really is the end of the road some 167km from Charlottetown. Inside are rather outdated exhibits on the nearby wind turbines and the history of the North Cape, as well as a small aquarium. The (still-working) **North Cape Lighthouse** nearby dates back to 1865, with spectacular views and a shoreline littered with stone *inukshuks*.

ACCOMMODATION	UP WEST
West Point Lighthouse Inn ☎ 902 859 3605, ⓦ west pointharmony.ca. One room in the lighthouse and twelve more in the adjoining building, all en suite and	decorated in cheery modern style, making the most of a great seaside location, overlooking a long sandy beach. June–Sept. **$179**

Newfoundland and Labrador

ICEBERG OFF THE COAST OF TRINITY

Newfoundland and Labrador

The province of Newfoundland and Labrador only joined Canada in 1949, a controversial move supported by just 52.3 percent of the population at the time. Even now, parts of Newfoundland seem like an entirely different country. The island's remarkable family of dialects, in essence an eclectic mix of old Irish and English, developed because the outports – ancient fishing settlements that were home to the first Europeans – could only be reached by boat. Today almost all are connected to the skein of side roads that plugs into the Trans-Canada Highway, but most of the interior remains an untouched wonderland of snow-capped mountains, fish-filled rivers and mesmerizing fjords.

Newfoundland's natural and historic charms are considerable, yet, astonishingly, the island rarely seems busy or crowded. Most visitors fly straight to **St John's**, which provides the best introduction to island life, not least for its museums, enticing restaurants, bars and flourishing folk music scene. The city is also within easy striking distance of the whale-watching at **Bay Bulls**, the lighthouses of **Cape Spear** and the **East Coast Trail**, providing opportunities for everything from a short ramble to a full-scale expedition.

Newfoundland's attractions don't end on the Avalon Peninsula though. Tiny **Trinity**, on the Bonavista Peninsula, is perhaps the most beguiling of all the old outports, though **Twillingate** comes a close second and **Fogo Island** remains one of the most traditional. **Gros Morne National Park**, 700km west of St John's, features wondrous mountains and glacier-gouged lakes, while another 350km north of the park, at **L'Anse aux Meadows**, lie the scant but evocative remains of an eleventh-century Norse colony, as well as a remarkable hotel in the old lighthouse on **Quirpon** island. The southern coast of Newfoundland chips in with the wild and windswept Burin Peninsula, which is a quick ferry ride from French-speaking **St-Pierre et Miquelon**, a tiny archipelago that is – as an imperial oddity – a *département* of France.

Labrador, though part of mainland Canada, has been tied to the island of Newfoundland since the 1760s, yet here too you'll find a strong sense of identity, one that blends recent arrivals with ancient Inuit and Innu traditions. Iron-ore mines and hydroelectric schemes drive the economy, but these industrial blemishes are mere pinpricks in the barely explored **wilderness** that defines this part of the province. Unimaginably vast, Labrador boasts some of Canada's highest mountains, a jaw-dropping national park, a spectacular shoreline and a forested hinterland teeming with wildlife. A trip here is a true adventure.

GETTING AROUND AND INFORMATION   NEWFOUNDLAND

By plane Newfoundland has two international airports – St John's and Gander – as well as domestic airports at Deer Lake, Stephenville and St Anthony.

By ferry Ferries connect Newfoundland with Nova Scotia (see page 324), Labrador (see page 452) and St-Pierre et Miquelon (see page 429). If arriving at the port of Argentia, contact Newhook's Transportation (☏ 709 682 4877, ✆ griffinevlynn@hotmail.com), which charges $40 for the trip to St John's (daily departures depend on ferry times; 2hr). If arriving at Channel-Port aux Basques try to connect with DRL Coachlines.

By bus You need a car to make the most of Newfoundland, though it is possible to travel by bus or taxi. The only long-distance bus on Newfoundland is operated by DRL Coachlines (☏ 709 263 2171, ✆ drl-lr.com), a once-daily service running between Channel-Port aux Basques to St John's via the Trans-Canada Hwy, stopping at over twenty points on the way. The one-way fare costs $126 (from Channel-Port aux Basques, Grand Falls is $79, Deer Lake $50 and Corner Brook $42), and the whole trip takes 13hr 35min; confirm bus tickets and departure details before you set out. The westbound coach departs St John's at 7.30am; the eastbound coach departs

Highlights

❶ St John's This lively port city, with its fine coastal setting and raucous nightlife, provides the best introduction to Newfoundland culture, history and culinary traditions. See page 412

❷ Cape St Mary's Jaw-dropping cliff-side seabird sanctuary, one of the most incredible wildlife spectacles in the world. See page 427

❸ St-Pierre et Miquelon Tiny French enclave of fine restaurants, cosy B&Bs and rich marine life. See page 429

❹ Fogo Island Weathered fish huts, traditional outports and a community of artists occupy one

of the most beautifully preserved islands in the province. See page 438

❺ Icebergs and whale-watching The east coast can be studded with vast, shimmering lumps of ice in summer, and dozens of whales frolic just offshore. See page 441

❻ Gros Morne National Park Plunging fjords, rearing mountains and the dazzling waters of Western Brook Pond. See page 445

❼ Battle Harbour Wonderfully evocative and isolated fishing village off the coast of southern Labrador, a magical place to spend the night. See page 456

HIGHLIGHTS ARE MARKED ON THE MAP ON PAGE 412

Channel-Port aux Basques at 8am.

By taxi/minibus A patchy transport network is provided by a string of minibus/taxi companies, most of which are based in St John's or Corner Brook on the west coast – see

relevant sections for details.
Newfoundland and Labrador Tourism ☎800 563 6353 inside North America, ☎709 729 2830 elsewhere; Ⓦ newfoundlandlabrador.com.

St John's

For centuries life in **ST JOHN'S** has focused on its **harbour**, a dramatic jaw-shaped inlet approached through the 200m-wide channel of **The Narrows**. In its heyday, the port

NEWFOUNDLAND AND LABRADOR

HIGHLIGHTS

1. St John's
2. Cape St Mary's
3. St-Pierre et Miquelon
4. Fogo Island
5. Icebergs and whale-watching
6. Gros Morne National Park
7. Battle Harbour

> ### NEWFOUNDLAND TIME ZONES
>
> All of Newfoundland, as well as the Labrador coastal communities south of Cartwright (from L'Anse-au-Claire, on the Québec border, to Norman Bay), is on **Newfoundland Standard Time** (3hr 30min behind GMT, and 1hr 30min ahead of Eastern Standard Time). Most of Labrador (Cartwright, Happy Valley-Goose Bay and Labrador West), as well as the Maritime Provinces, is on **Atlantic Time**, half-an-hour behind Newfoundland time. St-Pierre et Miquelon also has its own time zone – half-an-hour ahead of Newfoundland Time.

was crammed with ships from a score of nations; today, although traffic is not as brisk, it draws a mixed maritime bag of trawlers, container ships and oil construction barges. It still possesses a boisterous nightlife too, but the rough houses of the waterfront have been replaced by shops, slick office buildings and chic restaurants, and its inhabitants – of whom there are about 200,000 – are less likely to be seafarers than white-collar workers, artists and students from all over Canada. Yet the waterfront remains the social hub, sprinkled with lively **bars** that showcase the best of Newfoundland **folk music** – one good reason for visiting in itself – as well as providing the backdrop for hit Canadian TV show *Republic of Doyle* (2010–2014).

With the exception of Signal Hill, all the main downtown attractions are within easy walking distance of each other. Note that the appellation "cove", commonplace here, means a short side street, not a bay.

Harbourside Park

Tiny **Harbourside Park**, on Water Street, is the logical place to start a visit to the city: it was here – or at least hereabouts – that Sir Humphrey Gilbert landed in 1583 to claim the island for England. A series of historical plaques in the park gives all the background, and behind are two bronze **dogs**, a **Newfoundland** and a **Labrador**. The early settlers were very reliant on their dogs and the Newfoundland breed, with its double-layered waterproof coat and webbed feet, was perfect for their requirements, though the Labrador – a cross between a Newfoundland and a Pointer – proved better for hunting.

Anglican Cathedral of St John the Baptist

16 Church Hill (entrance on Gower St) • Mid-June to Sept Mon–Fri 10am–4pm, Sat 10am–noon • Free • ☎ 709 726 5677, ⓦ stjohnsanglicancathedral.org

Perched on the hillside, a short but steep walk from Water Street, the blue stone **Anglican Cathedral of St John the Baptist** was designed in Gothic Revival style by the English architect Sir George Gilbert Scott. Begun in 1847, much of the church burnt down in 1892, but Scott's son rebuilt it to the original plans.

In summer you can enjoy tea and home-made cakes in the **Crypt Tea Room** (July & Aug Wed–Sat 2–4pm; $10, cash only), reached by the west door on the south side of the cathedral. **Organ recitals** (free) take place on Wednesdays from 1.15 to 1.45pm. The cathedral backs onto **Gower Street**, one of the city's most charming residential thoroughfares, its long line of brightly painted clapboard (or vinyl imitation) houses known locally as **Jellybean Row**.

Commissariat House Provincial Historic Site

11 King's Bridge Rd, at Military Rd • Mid-May to June & Sept to early Oct Wed–Sun 9.30am–5pm; July & Aug daily 9.30am–5pm • $6 • ☎ 709 729 6730

From the north end of Gower Street it's a short stroll over to the robust Georgian clapboard of the **Commissariat House Provincial Historic Site**. Completed in 1820, this was the home and offices of the assistant commissary general, who was responsible for keeping the British garrison in St John's paid, fed and clothed. Though all the rooms have been faithfully restored in austere 1830s style and you can wander around on your own, it's far better to be shown around by one of the knowledgeable guides (free), who will add the context; balancing the demands of spendthrift commanders with a penny-pinching Treasury back in London wasn't easy.

Government House

50 Military Rd • Tours by appointment Mon–Fri 9am–4pm • Free • ☎ 709 729 2669, ⊕ govhouse.nl.ca/visit-us

A very brief walk from Commissariat House is the elegant red sandstone **Government House**, completed at great expense in 1831. It has since served as the residence of the Lieutenant-Governor, the Queen's representative on the island. The only way to get inside to see the wonderfully preserved Main Foyer, Ballroom, Drawing Room, Dining Room and Billiards Room is to call in advance to arrange a **free tour** (1hr), but you're free to stroll around the leafy grounds any time.

Basilica-Cathedral of St John the Baptist

200 Military Rd • Mon–Fri & Sun 8am–4pm, Sat 9am–5pm • Free • ☎ 709 754 2170, ⊕ thebasilica.ca

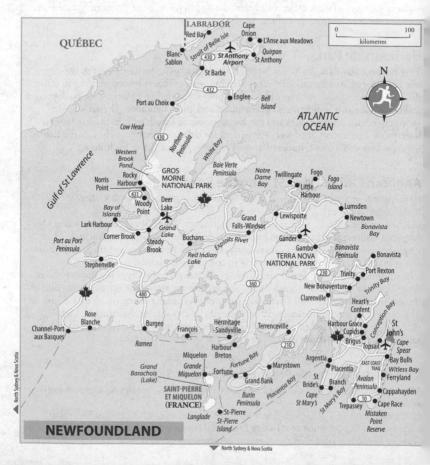

MOOSE DANGER

A word about the **moose**: Newfoundland has thousands of them and they present a real danger to the motorist at dawn and dusk and to a lesser extent at night – so much so that many locals prefer not to drive at these times. The problem is that this large and powerful animal is drawn to vehicle headlights as if hypnotized and the results of a collision can be devastating for beast and human alike: on impact, cars typically knock the moose's legs away, leaving the animal's body to come barrelling through the windscreen.

By far the grandest of the city's churches, the twin-towered limestone and granite mass of the **Basilica-Cathedral of St John the Baptist** overlooks the harbour from the crest of a hill. The church was completed in 1855, with the facade modelled on the great Romanesque churches of Italy. The interior is even better, the 65 stained glass windows illuminating a delightfully ornate and embossed gold, maroon and deep-green ceiling. Look out for Irish sculptor John Hogan's *The Redeemer in Death*, at the altar, a moving statue created in Carrara marble in 1854.

Basilica Museum

Cathedral Square • Early June to Aug Mon–Fri 10am–noon & 1–4pm • $2

On the left side of the Basilica, in what used to be the old Bishop's Palace, the **Basilica Museum** includes the Mullock Episcopal Library completed in 1860, with many of the ancient tomes still on display. Panels explain the history of the Basilica and the Library, enhanced with old vestments, reliquaries and religious artefacts – look out for the 1861 Gaelic Bible from Dublin.

The Veiled Virgin

Cathedral Square, 170 Military Rd • June–Oct daily 1–4pm; Nov–May Mon–Fri 1–4pm • Free

On the right side of the Basilica lies the **Presentation Convent**, home of the revered, marble **Veiled Virgin**, carved in Rome by sculptor Giovanni Strazza and delivered here in 1856. It's a stunning work of art, the marble creases perfectly mimicking a silk veil delicately draped across Mary's face.

The Rooms

9 Bonaventure Ave • June to mid-Oct Mon–Sat 10am–5pm (Wed till 9pm), Sun noon–5pm; mid-Oct to May Tues–Sat 10am–5pm (Wed till 9pm), Sun noon–5pm • $10 • ☏ 709 757 8000, ⓦ therooms.ca

Housed in stylish modern premises, **The Rooms** exhibits Newfoundland's best historical, ethnographic and fine art collections. A rolling programme of temporary exhibitions occupies every nook and cranny, though **Floor 3** has a permanent display that zips through the island's history beginning with its earliest inhabitants, the Maritime Archaic Peoples, and their successors, the Dorset Inuit and the Beothuks. Perhaps most interesting of all, and stored in the drawer of a small wooden cabinet, are the crude but particularly poignant drawings made by **Shanawdithit**, the last of the Beothuks (see page 417).

Signal Hill

On the northeast side of central St John's and rearing up above The Narrows, **Signal Hill National Historic Site** (open access) is a huge, grass-covered chunk of rock with views dramatic enough to warrant the strenuous half-hour (2km) walk up from the northern end of Duckworth Street (there's no city bus). Originally known as The Lookout, Signal Hill took its present name in 1704, when it became common practice for flags to be hoisted here to notify the city of impending arrivals. The hill was also an obvious line of defence, and the simple fortifications established after the last French

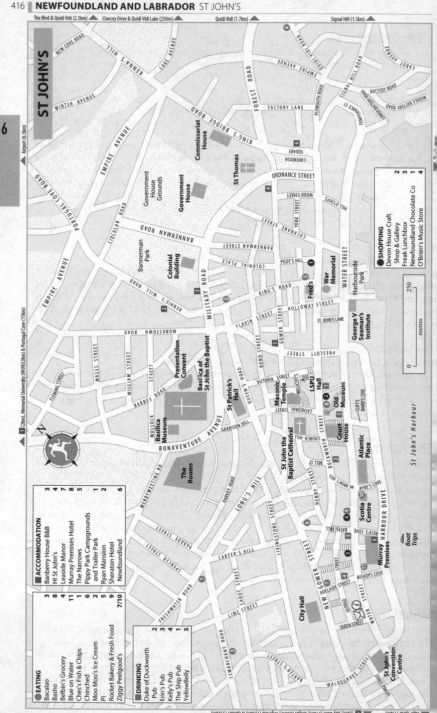

ST JOHN'S

● SHOPPING

Devon House Craft	
Shop & Gallery	2
Freak Lunchbox	3
Newfoundland Chocolate Co	1
O'Brien's Music Store	4

■ ACCOMMODATION

Banberry House B&B	3
HI St John's	4
Leaside Manor	7
Murray Premises Hotel	11
The Narrows	5
Pippy Park Campgrounds	
and Trailer Park	8
Ryan Mansion	6
Sheraton Hotel	
Newfoundland	9

● EATING

Bacalao	3
Basho	8
Belbin's Grocery	4
Blue on Water	11
Chess's Fish & Chips	1
Chinched	6
Moo Moo's Ice Cream	2
Pi	5
Rocket Bakery & Fresh Food	9
Ziggy Peelgood's	7/10

■ DRINKING

Duke of Duckworth	
Pub	2
Erin's Pub	3
Kelly's Pub	4
The Ship Pub	1
YellowBelly	5

THE LAST OF THE BEOTHUKS

The Algonquian-speaking **Beothuks**, who reached Newfoundland in about 200 AD, were seminomadic, spending the summer on the coast and moving inland during the winter. They were the first North American Aboriginal peoples to be contacted by English explorers, who came to describe them as "Red Indians" from their habit of covering themselves with red ochre, perhaps as some sort of fertility ritual or simply to keep the flies off. Neither side seemed to need or want anything from the other, and even after three hundred years of coexistence, hardly anything was known about the Beothuks. As settlers spread north from the Avalon Peninsula in the eighteenth century, they began to encroach on the Beothuks' ancient hunting grounds, pushing them inland. By the early 1800s, settlers' attitudes had hardened and the Beothuks who hadn't succumbed to European diseases were casually slaughtered. Some white settlers organized expeditions into the interior to catch one or two alive, but the last seen member of the tribe, a young woman named **Shanawdithit**, died of tuberculosis aged 29 in 1829. She spent the last years of her life in the protective custody of the attorney general in St John's, and it was here that she built a small model of a Beothuk canoe and made ten simple drawings of her people and their customs. No other Beothuks were ever found; she is considered the last of her people.

occupation in 1762 were embellished every time there was a military emergency, right up until World War II.

Johnson Geo Centre

175 Signal Hill Rd • Daily 9.30am–5pm (closed Mon Jan to mid-March) • $12; 3D movie $5 extra • ☎ 709 737 7880, ⊕ geocentre.ca

The road to the summit of Signal Hill is dotted with a string of attractions, beginning with the flashy **Johnson Geo Centre**, devoted to earth sciences. An introductory film illustrates various natural phenomena, followed by a section each on the Earth, Newfoundland and Labrador's geology, and the Earth's peoples. Special exhibits also focus on the *Titanic* and oil and gas, and there's a 3D Theatre for special movie presentations.

Signal Hill Visitor Centre

230 Signal Hill Rd • Mid-May to May 31 Wed–Sun 10am–6pm; June to early Sept daily 10am–6pm; early Sept to mid-Oct Sat–Wed 10am–6pm • $3.90 • ☎ 709 772 5367, ⊕ pc.gc.ca/signalhill

Halfway up Signal Hill Road lies **Signal Hill Visitor Centre**, whose well-chosen displays and dramatic twenty-minute multimedia presentation explore the military and civilian history of the site, particularly the bitter struggle for the city between France and England in the eighteenth century. Ask here about firing the **Noon Day Gun** (July & Aug daily noon; $49; reserve 48hr in advance).

Queen's Battery and Signal Hill Tattoo

Signal Hill Tattoo July to mid-Aug Wed, Thurs, Sat & Sun at 11am & 3pm (1hr) • $10 • ☎ 709 772 5367, ⊕ signalhilltattoo.org

A short walk from Signal Hill Visitor Centre is the **Queen's Battery**, whose antiquated cannons peer over the entrance to the harbour. The plot of ground beside the battery is occupied every summer by the authentic guns and drums of the **Signal Hill Tattoo**, a re-enactment of military exercises by the Royal Newfoundland Regiment of Foot circa 1795.

Cabot Tower

Signal Hill Rd • Mid-May to May 31 Wed–Sun 10.30am–5.30pm; June to early Sept daily 10.30am–5.30pm; early Sept to mid-Oct Sat–Wed 10.30am–5.30pm • $3.90 • ☎ 709 772 5367, ⊕ pc.gc.ca/signalhill

Plonked on top of Signal Hill is **Cabot Tower**, a short and stout stone structure completed in 1900 to commemorate John Cabot's voyage of 1497 and Queen Victoria's Diamond Jubilee. The tower holds a small display on electronic signalling, and outside in the car park there's a **plaque** honouring Guglielmo **Marconi**, who confirmed the reception of the first transatlantic radio signal here in December 1901. The views over the city and out to sea are jaw-dropping, and half a dozen **hiking trails** fan out across the peak.

Quidi Vidi

Tiny **QUIDI VIDI** ("kiddy-viddy"), a couple of kilometres north of the city centre, is a well-known beauty spot, where a handful of old fishing shacks are backdropped by sharp-edged cliffs and set beside the deep-blue waters of a slender inlet. To get to Quidi Vidi from the city centre, take Forest Road from beside the *Sheraton Newfoundland* hotel and keep going – or take Metrobus service #15 from Plymouth Road on the harbourside of the same hotel. En route, you'll travel the length of **Quidi Vidi Lake**, the site of the **Royal St John's Regatta** (ⓦstjohnsregatta.ca), held every August. This is one of the oldest sporting events in North America, featuring fixed-seat rowing races and a huge garden party.

Quidi Vidi Village Plantation

10 Maple View Place • Wed–Sun 11am–5pm • Free • ☏ 709 570 2038, ⓦ qvvplantation.com

Quidi Vidi Village Plantation doubles as local information desk and working art gallery, with studio space upstairs for up to ten locally based artists. The aim is to nurture new and emerging talent – you might see jewellery, prints, ceramics or glassware, and artists can also sell their work to visitors on-site. The centre – built in the style of the old fish loft that once stood here – offers the best views of the village from its outdoor deck.

Quidi Vidi Brewery

35 Barrows Rd • Hop Shop Daily 10am–6pm • Tap Room Sun–Wed noon–8pm, Thurs noon–10pm, Fri & Sat noon–midnight • Tours Mon–Fri 11am, Sat & Sun every 30min noon–6pm • $12 • ☏ 709 738 4040, ⓦ quidividibrewery.ca

Lovers of real beer should not miss the exceptional **Quidi Vidi Brewery**, set in an old fish plant right on the harbour. Tastings (Mon–Fri noon, 1pm, 2pm, 3pm & 4pm; 45min; $10) of their craft beers include the best-selling **Iceberg Beer**, made with real iceberg water, while tours take in a video and a quick stroll through the bottling and brewing operations. Their legendary summer **Kitchen Party Fridays** (beer, live music and food from 4.30pm on Fridays) are extremely popular – folks often line up before 4pm.

ARRIVAL AND DEPARTURE   **ST JOHN'S**

By plane St John's International Airport (ⓦstjohnsairport. com) is about 6km north of the city centre at 100 World Pkwy (just off Rte-40 to Portugal Cove); inside the terminal are two CIBC ATMs, free wi-fi zones and a large tourist information desk (daily 8am–12.30am; ☏ 709 758 8515). You'll find all the major car rental firms at the airport. Metrobus #14 ($2.50; see below) runs from the airport to Memorial University of Newfoundland, where you'll have to change to Metrobus #10 for downtown. Otherwise, City Wide (☏ 709 722 7777) has a monopoly on taxis with fares based on a zone system; most of downtown is $25, plus $3 for each additional passenger (coming back, taxis use the meter).

By bus DRL Coachlines (see page 410) buses from Channel-Port aux Basques ($126) terminate at the St John's campus of Memorial University, outside the University Centre on Prince Philip Drive, about 3km northwest of the city centre. Westbound buses depart from here daily at 7.30am. To get to the centre, take a taxi or Metrobus #10 to City Hall ($2.50).

Destinations (DRL) Channel-Port aux Basques (1 daily; 13hr 35min); Corner Brook (1 daily; 10hr 25min); Deer Lake (1 daily; 9hr 42min); Grand Falls (1 daily; 6hr 44min).

By taxi/minibus All these services require advance booking; prices are per person; and they will usually pick you up at your hotel. Newhook's Transportation (☏ 709 682 4877) charges $40 for the trip to the Argentia ferry (daily departures depend on ferry times). Foote's Taxi (☏ 709 832 0491, ✉ shirleyb832@gmail.com) operates a once-daily service to Grand Bank and the St-Pierre ferry terminal at Fortune for $50; it starts picking up from Fortune at around 6.30am, arriving in St John's 4–5hr later, and departure from St John's is at around 2pm. Marsh's Taxi (☏ 709 468 7715, ⓦ marshstaxi@hotmail.com) runs out to Bonavista (4hr) via Trinity (3hr 30min) for $45 (cash only). The shuttle departs daily from Bonavista around 6.30am (arriving St John's around 10–10.30am), and leaves St John's for the return trip at 1.30pm (arriving Bonavista around 5.30–6pm).

GETTING AROUND AND INFORMATION

By bus The best way to explore St John's is on foot, but for more outlying attractions you might want to catch a bus. Metrobus (single fare $2.50, ten-ride pass $22.50; timetable information at ☎709 722 9400, ⓦmetrobus.com) has about a dozen routes serving most parts of the city.

By taxi Bugden's ☎709 722 4400; Casino ☎709 579 5999.

There's a rank outside the *Sheraton Newfoundland* and on George St. Meters usually start at $3.75.

Tourist office The city tourist office is one block up from the harbour at 348 Water St (Mon–Fri 9am–4.30pm; late May to Sept also Sat & Sun 9am–4.30pm; ☎709 576 8106, ⓦstjohns.ca).

TOURS AND BOAT TRIPS

Iceberg Quest ☎709 722 1888, ⓦicebergquest.com. Runs four daily trips in summer ($70; 2hr) from Pier 6, 135 Harbour Drive in St John's out to Cape Spear, where you might spy whales (July & Aug), puffins and big chunks of ice (June).

Legend Tours ☎709 753 1497, ⓦlegendtours.ca. Provides entertaining 3hr bus trips round the city centre, Signal Hill, Quidi Vidi and Cape Spear for $69; they operate year-round, weather permitting (daily 10am & 2pm).

Ocean Quest Adventure 17 Stanley's Rd, Conception

Bay South (around 20km west of St John's) ☎866 623 2664, ⓦoceanquestadventures.com. Runs boat trips and half-day wreck dives (from $170) around Bell Island in Conception Bay.

St John's Haunted Hike ☎709 685 3444, ⓦhaunted hike.com. Offers some of the most enjoyable guided tours of the city (June to late Sept Mon–Thurs & Sun 9.30pm; $10; 1hr 15min), intriguingly spooky walking tours delve into the city's dishevelled past, which start at the west entrance to the Anglican Cathedral.

ACCOMMODATION

Banberry House B&B 112 Military Rd ☎709 579 8006, ⓦbanberryhouse.com; map p.416. This gorgeous old clapboard house, dating back to 1892, has been intelligently restored with all modern conveniences grafted onto all manner of period detail, from the wide wooden staircase to the expansive bay windows. Rooms come with cable TV and DVD player, while the handy location is a 5min walk from the town centre. **$159**

HI St John's 8 Gower St ☎709 754 4789, ⓦhihostels.ca; map p.416. Solid backpacker option offering dorms and private rooms, all within stumbling distance of George St. You get lockers, a decent shared kitchen and very laidback staff. Dorms **$34**, non-members **$39**; doubles with shared bathroom **$80**, non-members **$90**

★**Leaside Manor** 39 Topsail Rd ☎709 722 0387, ⓦleasidemanor.com; map p.416. Wonderful, luxurious suites in *Leaside Manor* and nearby *Compton House*, ranging from the hip (open-plan with jacuzzis) to traditional (nineteenth-century decor with four-poster canopy beds). Opt for the Jellybean Suite if you like leopard pattern prints. **$160**

Murray Premises Hotel 5 Beck's Cove ☎709 738 7773, ⓦmurraypremiseshotel.com; map p.416. Perfect location for nightlife, one block from George St, featuring smart, boutique-like rooms carved out of an 1840s warehouse; the second-floor executive rooms are much nicer, with hot-tub, flat-screen TVs and jet showers. The thin floors mean it can get a bit noisy. **$209**

The Narrows 146 Gower St ☎709 739 4850, ⓦthe

narrowsbb.com; map p.416. Infinitely cosy B&B in an old terrace house a short walk from the centre, with four en-suite guest rooms decorated in a neat and trim version of period style. **$175**

Pippy Park Campgrounds and Trailer Park Nagle's place, Pippy Park ☎709 737 3669, ⓦpippypark.com; map p.416. Around 216 sites, about 4km west of the city centre, near the Confederation Building. To get there, proceed west along Allandale Rd; Nagle's Place is on the left, just beyond Prince Philip Drive. There are clean, accessible washrooms and a convenience store –wi-fi only at fully serviced sites. Mid-May to mid-Oct. Sites **$24**; serviced RV sites **$45**; unserviced RV sites **$29**

★**Ryan Mansion** 21 Rennies Mill Rd ☎709 753 7926, ⓦryanmansion.com; map p.416. Lavishly maintained 1911 Edwardian property, with utterly luxurious suites (home to Prince Charles and Camilla in 2009); bathrooms come with steam rooms, heated marble floors, "therapeutic tubs", while the beds are comfortable hardwood four-posters. **$395**

Sheraton Hotel Newfoundland 115 Cavendish Square ☎709 726 4980, ⓦmarriott.com; map p.416. The exterior of this chain hotel is all modern clunkiness, but the interior has a real sense of itself – as befits the city's most famous hotel, whose earliest incarnation dates back to 1926. All the rooms are kitted out in top-whack chain style and most have great views over the harbour. Indoor pool and fitness facilities included. **$210**

EATING

★**Bacalao** 65 Lemarchant Rd ☎709 579 6565, ⓦbacalaocuisine.ca; map p.416. Giving traditional home-cooked Newfoundland food a contemporary twist,

chef Mike Barsley might serve "jiggs dinner" as a cabbage roll appetizer, delicate cod tongues, local mussels, caribou, lobster in season and *bacalao* (cod) *du jour* (most mains

6

average $24–33). Free parking on site. Tues 6–10pm, Wed–Fri noon–2.30pm & 6–10pm, Sat 11am–2.30pm & 6–11pm, Sun 11am–2.30pm.

Basho 283 Duckworth St ☎709 576 4600; map p.416. Shrine to Japanese fusion cuisine by Tak Ishiwata, a student of New York-based maestro Nobu Matsuhisa. The food is exceptional: think pan-seared caribou steak, sushi rolls and iceberg Martinis made with real chunks of Greenland bergs. Mains $29–37. Mon–Sat 6–11pm.

Belbin's Grocery 85 Quidi Vidi Rd ☎709 576 7640, ⓦbelbins.com; map p.416. Traditional Newfoundland cuisine can be purchased at this old-fashioned store, open since 1943; especially good for local fruit pies and seal flipper pie. Mon–Fri 8.30am–8pm, Sat 8.30am–6pm, Sun 10am–6pm.

Blue on Water 319 Water St ☎709 574 2583, ⓦblueonwater.com; map p.416. Chic restaurant (and boutique hotel) decorated in sharp modern style and featuring local ingredients on its pricey but inventive menu – try the delicious red wine chicken stew. Mains $18–38. Mon–Fri 7.30am–10pm, Sat 9am–10pm, Sun 9am–9pm.

Ches's Fish & Chips 9 Freshwater Rd ☎709 726 2373, ⓦchessfishandchips.ca; map p.416. Legendary fish and chips since 1951 ("chesses"), with several locations in the city (Freshwater is closest to downtown); the main event is two pieces of crisp cod served with hand-cut chips ($13.99), though the menu also offers cod bites ($12.49), chicken wings ($9.49), burgers ($4.99) and shellfish (shrimp from $10.99). Mon–Thurs & Sun 9am–2am, Fri & Sat 9am–3am.

★ **Chinched** 5 Bates Hill ☎709 722 3100, ⓦchinched. com; map p.416. Superbly crafted cuisine from chefs/ owners Shaun Hussey and Michelle LeBlanc – amazing cheese, charcuterie boards, local mussels, pan-seared cod, crispy pig ears and sandwiches made with artisanal meats,. Mains $12–25. Tues–Fri 11am–2pm & 5.30–10pm, Sat 5.30–10pm.

★ **Moo Moo's Ice Cream** 88 Kings Rd ☎709 753 3046; map p.416. Much loved ice-cream counter inside *The Market* convenience store, serving sorbets and luscious ice cream with local flavours like partridgeberry (loganberry) and bakeapple (cloudberry). June–Sept daily noon–10pm; Oct–May Mon–Thurs noon–6pm, Fri–Sun noon–10pm (seasonal changes possible).

Pi 10 Kings Rd ☎709 726 2000, ⓦpinl.ca; map p.416. Best pizza in Newfoundland, thin-crusted delights made with vegan-friendly dough and innovative toppings from $14 ($21 large); the "pi" ($19–30) offers shaved steak, roasted red peppers, mushrooms, avocado slices and leeks. Mon & Wed–Sat noon–3pm & 5–9pm, Sun 4–9pm.

Rocket Bakery & Fresh Food 272 Water St ☎709 738 2011, ⓦrocketfood.ca; map p.416. Café and bakery selling exquisite *pain au chocolat*, partridgeberry macaroons ($2.25), croissants, fresh bread, salads ($5–7.95), fish cakes ($3.95) and filling sandwiches ($8.95). Seating area or takeaway. Mon–Fri 7.30am–10pm, Sat 8am–10pm, Sun 8am–6pm.

★ **Ziggy Peelgood's** 235 Water St (outside Scotia Centre); Churchill Square; Adelaide St, at New Gower St ☎709 738 3788, ⓦfacebook.com/ziggypeelgoods; map p.416. This chip van has cult status in St John's, and now has three locations. The perfectly cooked fries ($4–6; add cheese or gravy for $1) and poutine ($6–8) have provided comfort food to pub-goers since 1986. Churchill Square and Water St branches daily 11am–6pm; Adelaide St Thurs–Sat 10pm–4am.

DRINKING AND NIGHTLIFE

St John's is said to have more drinking places per square kilometre than any other city in the country. Most of the more popular joints are on Water and adjoining George streets and they can get mighty crowded (and boisterous) at weekends. At some point you're likely to be invited to be **screeched in**, a touristy but fun ritual for all newcomers – routines vary, but it usually involves kissing a stuffed cod, reading something written in Newfoundland slang, and downing the local brand of Screech Rum.

Duke of Duckworth Pub 325 Duckworth St (McMurdo's Lane) ☎709 739 6344, ⓦdukeofduckworth.com; map p.416. Popular bar and *Republic of Doyle* location, just down the steps off Duckworth St. Serves a wide range of Newfoundland ales (including Quidi Vidi and its own tasty brew, Duke's Own), but its speciality is English pints and fish and chips. Mon–Thurs & Sun noon–2am, Fri & Sat noon–3am.

Erin's Pub 186 Water St ☎709 722 1916, ⓦfacebook. com/erinspubnl; map p.416. Popular and well-established no-frills Irish pub, showcasing the best of folk acts Wed–Sun night. It also has the best Guinness in town. Daily noon–3am.

Kelly's Pub 25 George St, at Adelaide St ☎709 753 5300; map p.416. Lively spot with a youthful (drunken) clientele. Good range of beers and pub food (yet more lip-smacking fish and chips), with frequent live folk music from the likes of Ray (Blacky) O'Leary. Daily 11am–2am.

The Ship Pub Solomon's Lane, at 265 Duckworth St ☎709 753 3870, ⓦfacebook.com/theshippubkitchen; map p.416. Down the steps from Duckworth St, this dark, earthy pub showcases an eclectic mix of live music that attracts everyone from grizzled old-timers who love their folk music to arty, black-clad students. Mon–Tues 3pm–1am, Wed noon–1am, Thurs noon–2am, Fri–Sun noon–3am.

YellowBelly 288 Water St ☎709 757 3784, ⓦyellow bellybrewery.com; map p.416. Visit this gastropub for top microbrews and the basement "Underbelly" dining room, dating from 1725 (the oldest room in the city) where you can see a crossbeam charred by the great fire of 1892. Mon–Thurs 11.30am–2am, Fri–Sun 11am–3am.

6

REELS, FIDDLES AND FOLK

The English and Irish settlers who first colonized Newfoundland brought their music with them: step dances and square sets performed to the accompaniment of the **fiddle** and the **button accordion**, followed by the unaccompanied **singing** of locally composed and "old country" songs. The music was never written down, so as it passed from one generation to the next a distinctive Newfoundland style evolved, whose rhymes and rhythms varied from outport to outport – though its Irish and English roots always remained pronounced.

This traditional style of folk music has lingered on, as exemplified by the island's most famous fiddlers, **Rufus Guinchard** and **Émile Benoit**. The two died in the 1980s, but their approach was adopted by younger artists like singer-songwriters Jim Payne and Ron Hynes, musician-producer Kelly Russell and groups such as **Figgy Duff** (named after the traditional Newfoundland pudding). Currently, Celtic music is the big deal in the bars of St John's (**Shanneyganock** is one of the biggest bands on the scene), but local musicians regularly perform in a more traditional idiom. In particular, look out for one of the most popular bands since the 1990s, the **Irish Descendants**, who still occasionally perform here. Other artists to watch out for include **Duane Andrews**, who blends traditional Newfoundland folk with Gypsy Jazz; and local girl **Amelia Curran**, who has scored big since her 2000 debut. The best of the island's dozen folk festivals, the Newfoundland and Labrador Folk Festival (☎ 709 576 8508, ⓦ nlfolk.com), is held in Bannerman Park in St John's in early August.

ENTERTAINMENT

Spirit of Newfoundland 6 Cathedral St ☎ 709 579 3023, ⓦ spiritofnewfoundland.com. The old Masonic Temple, completed in 1897, is now home to the Spirit of Newfoundland theatre company – performances usually feature a Newfoundland theme, and are often combined with dinner (tickets around $72 plus tax and $4 building restoration fee). June–Sept Tues–Sat 6.30pm; Oct–May usually Fri–Sun only.

SHOPPING

Devon House Craft Shop & Gallery 275 Duckworth St ☎ 709 753 2749, ⓦ craftcouncil.nl.ca; map p.416. Good place to purchase handicrafts, knitwear and jewellery. Mon–Sat 10am–6pm, Sun 1–5pm.

Freak Lunchbox 308 Water St ☎ 709 726 7521, ⓦ freaklunchbox.com; map p.416. The bizarre world of the Halifax-based sweet shop (see page 335) comes to St John's. Late May to early Sept Mon–Sat 9am–10pm, Sun 11am–7pm; early Sept to late May Mon–Sat 10am–9pm, Sun noon–6pm.

Newfoundland Chocolate Co 166 Duckworth St ☎ 709 579 0099, ⓦ newfoundlandchocolatecompany.com; map p.416. Chocolates handmade here in St John's, from white hot chocolate and chocolate roses to cocoa nibs and chocolate "puffin eggs". Mon–Wed & Sat 10am–6pm, Thurs & Fri 10am–9pm, Sun 10am–5pm.

O'Brien's Music Store 278 Water St ☎ 709 753 8135, ⓦ obriens.ca; map p.416. Newfoundland's best traditional music store since 1939, reopened in 2015 after closing briefly due to bankruptcy. Mon–Sat 10am–6pm, Sun noon–5pm.

DIRECTORY

Laundry Mighty White's, 152 Duckworth St (Tues–Thurs 8am–9pm, Mon & Fri–Sun 8am–7pm; ☎ 709 753 7947) has coin-operated machines for around $2.50 per wash.

Police ☎ 709 729 8333.
Post office 354 Water St, at Queen St (Mon–Fri 8am–4pm).

Cape Spear National Historic Site

1914–1930 Black Head Rd (Cape Spear Drive) • Lighthouse mid-May to May 31 Wed–Sun 10am–6pm; June to early Sept daily 10am–6pm; early Sept to mid-Oct Sat–Wed 10am–6pm • $3.90 • ☎ 709 772 5367, ⓦ pc.gc.ca/lhn-nhs/nl/spear

From St John's it's a 15km drive via Rte-11 to **Cape Spear National Historic Site** (open access), a rocky, windblown headland that is nearer to Europe than any other part of mainland North America. The cape is crisscrossed by boardwalks, the most obvious of which leads up from the car park past the Heritage Shop (mid-May to mid-Oct daily 10am–5.30pm), CCG Alumni Association Art Gallery (July to early Sept daily 10am–5pm) and the modern lighthouse to the squat and rectangular Victorian **lighthouse**, the oldest in the province. Built in 1836, the lighthouse's interior has been pleasantly decked out in nineteenth-century style, down to imitation barrels of sperm whale oil and the neatly made bed. The other specific attraction is the substantial remains of the World War II **gun emplacement** at the tip of the cape, but the views are really the main event, right along the coast and up to St John's. In spring and early summer, the waters off the cape are a great place to spy blue-tinged **icebergs**, and there's a reasonable chance of spotting **whales**.

6

The Avalon Peninsula

St John's sits on the northeast corner of the **Avalon Peninsula**, a jagged, roughly rectangular slab of land divided into four arms and connected to the rest of Newfoundland by a narrow, tapering isthmus. Highlights include the varied attractions along the **Irish Loop**; **Heart's Content**, with its antique cable station; **Castle Hill**, from where there are panoramic views over Placentia Bay; and the sea-bird colonies of **Cape St Mary's**. With the exception of the cape, which is a tad too far away for comfort, all make good day-tripping destinations from St John's.

Southeast Avalon: The Irish Loop

The **Irish Loop** (a 312km combination of highways 10 and 90) covers the southeastern arm of the Avalon Peninsula, the road snaking from one rock-bound cove to another. Don't skip the wildest section of the loop, from Portugal Cove South to St Mary's, which runs from high moorland where you might see the dwindling **Avalon woodland caribou herd**, down to the stunning vistas of 21km-long **Holyrood Pond**.

Witless Bay Ecological Reserve

Straggling around the head of a deep and pointed inlet, 25km south of St John's on Rte-10, the village of **Bay Bulls** makes much of its living from **boat tours** to the four tiny offshore islets comprising the **Witless Bay Ecological Reserve**. The best time to visit is between mid-June and mid-July, when over 800,000 birds gather here – the reserve has the largest **puffin** colony in eastern Canada and there are also thousands of storm

---

THE EAST COAST TRAIL

Negotiating much of the length of the Avalon Peninsula, the **East Coast Trail** is a long-distance **hiking trail** that passes through fishing communities, provincial parks, national historic sites and a couple of ecological reserves. The 300km stretch from Portugal Cove to Cape St Francis and down to Cappahayden has been completed, but there are many undeveloped trails: to Topsail, on Conception Bay in the north, Trepassey in the south and across to Placentia in the west (from Ferryland). It's an extraordinarily ambitious enterprise (the Topsail section will be developed first, depending on funding), and largely reliant on volunteer labour. The **East Coast Trail Association** (☎ 709 738 4453, ⓦ eastcoasttrail.com) sells first-rate 1:25,000 waterproof topographical maps covering the whole trail ($37 per set of 24), and guidebooks covering different sections of it. Only one – from Petty Harbour to Bay Bulls ($28.95) – is currently available.

The East Coast Trail is linear, which means that if you're after a day's hiking you really need two cars and at least two people, but there are places to stay along the trail and it is possible to arrange to be picked up (and/or taken out) by taxi. The Association is glad to help and advise, and also organizes free group hikes. The 3.7km hike from the former fishing village of **Blackhead to Cape Spear** is one of the easier and more accessible portions of the trail and it covers a handsomely rugged stretch of coastline; allow one and a half to two hours. The trailhead is clearly signed.

LIGHTHOUSE PICNICS

From the Colony of Avalon a bumpy gravel road leads 2km up to Ferryland Head, towards the lighthouse and one of Newfoundland's most pleasurable experiences: **Lighthouse Picnics** (late May to Sept Wed–Sun 11.30am–4.30pm; ☎ 709 363 7456, ⊚ lighthousepicnics. ca). Halfway along you must park your car – part of the attraction is the walk along the final section (allow 25min each way), studded with jaw-dropping views of Ferryland Harbour and Bois Island. Inside the lighthouse itself you pick up your picnic (usually a choice of sandwiches, all with salad, dessert and lemonade; around $26/person) and blanket, then just pick a spot on the headland, high above the rocky point and the waves. Reservations highly recommended.

6

petrels, common murres, kittiwakes, razorbills, guillemots and cormorants. In addition, the area is home to the largest population of **humpback whales** in the world, and finback and minke whales are often spotted between June and August.

TOURS

Gatherall's 90 Northside Rd, Bay Bulls ☎ 709 334 2887, ⊚ gatheralls.com. Run 2hr trips May–Sept ($62), usually four times daily in peak season (July & Aug); reservations are advised.

O'Brien's Whale & Bird Tours Lower Rd ☎ 709 753

WITLESS BAY ECOLOGICAL RESERVE

4850, ⊚ obriensboattours.com. Similar tours in a slightly bigger boat for $60. They'll provide transport to and from major hotels in St John's, though this has to be arranged in advance ($29.95 return).

Ferryland

George Calvert, the first Baron Baltimore (named after Baltimore Manor in Ireland), was a favourite of King James I of England, who gave him a slab of land in Newfoundland to settle as a colony. Calvert dispatched a band of prospective colonists under **Captain Edward Wynne** to what is now **FERRYLAND** in 1621. Baltimore himself stayed here briefly 1628 to 1629, before fleeing south to lay the foundation for Maryland (the city of Baltimore was named after his son). Ferryland was totally destroyed by the French in 1696; in subsequent years a few hardy settlers returned to found the modern village, but the ruins of the first colony were rediscovered only in 1980. Today the site is preserved as the fascinating **Colony of Avalon**, some 45km south of Bay Bulls.

Colony of Avalon

1 The Pool, Ferryland (Rte-10) · Mid-June to mid-Sept daily 10am–6pm · $15 · ☎ 709 432 3200, ⊚ colonyofavalon.ca

Visits to the **Colony of Avalon** begin at the **Visitor Centre**, which gives the historical background to Calvert's venture through panels, videos and some of the artefacts actually found here, from grape seeds to cannon balls. Evidence of the decidedly wealthy backgrounds of some of the inhabitants include gold rings, a 1601 gold coin and a gold seal. You can then explore (or take a **tour**, included) of the site itself, some 400m along the headland; reconstructed gardens, sections of a cobblestone road, slate walls (denoting Calvert's "mansion house"), hearths, a forge and the original sea wall have been unearthed and preserved, but as you'll see, this is very much a work in progress (archeologists are usually at work mid-June to Sept Mon–Fri 8am–4.30pm). Tours end at the reconstruction of a kitchen of the time, with examples of hearth-baked bread to taste.

Mistaken Point Ecological Reserve

Rte-10, Portugal Cove South · **Edge of Avalon Interpretive Centre** Mid-May to late Oct daily 10am–6pm (closes at 5pm Sept to late Oct) · $5 · **Tours** mid-May to early Oct daily 1pm (3hr 30min, including a 45min walk each way) · $20 (includes Edge of Avalon Interpretive Centre; $25 ticket also includes Myrick Wireless Interpretive Centre) · ☎ 709 438 1100, ⊚ edgeofavalon.ca

It's another 58km south on Rte-10 from Ferryland to **PORTUGAL COVE SOUTH** and the gravel road for Cape Race and **Mistaken Point Ecological Reserve**, home to over 6000 incredibly well preserved Precambrian fossil remains *in situ*. Discovered in 1969, it is

6

considered one of the most important fossil sites in the world (the fossils range from 575 to 542 million years old), but what makes it particularly special is that visitors are free to clamber all over the great slabs of tilted rock to see them up close. Visitors must be accompanied by an **official tour guide**. Tours (book ahead) start at the **Edge of Avalon Interpretive Centre**, just at the turning to the reserve in Portugal Cove South, and involve a short hike; a free minibus covers the first section. Inside the centre you can watch ten-minute videos about the site, and also learn about the mind-blowing project to make casts of the whole thing (a sample is on display).

Cape Race Lighthouse National Historic Site

Off Rte-10, Cape Race • Interpretive Centre June–Aug daily 11am–5.30pm; Sept 1 to mid-Sept Fri–Mon noon–5.30pm • $10 (includes Edge of Avalon Interpretive Centre) • ☎ 709 438 1100

The isolated 32m-high **Cape Race Lighthouse**, built from reinforced concrete in 1907 (interior closed to the public), lies at the end of the gravel Mistaken Point road (20km from Rte-10), but you can visit this site without a guide. Hard to believe today, but in the 1940s and 1950s, there were over eighty people living out here, with 35 children attending school. Learn more at the adjacent **Myrick Wireless Interpretive Centre**, a replica of the Marconi Marine Radio Station built here in 1904 (famous for receiving the *Titanic* distress call in 1912).

ACCOMMODATION AND EATING	THE IRISH LOOP

Claddagh Inn 459–463 Main Rd (Rte-90), St Mary's • ☎ 709 525 2229, ⊛ thecladdaghinn.ca. If seeing the Irish Loop in a day-trip from St John's seems too rushed, a good overnight option is this friendly B&B overlooking St Mary's Harbour, halfway round. Boasts six comfy en-suite doubles with satellite TV and an excellent on-site pub and restaurant (featuring local snow crab), serving dinner and breakfast. __$165__

Northwest Avalon: the Baccalieu Trail

The **Baccalieu Trail** (230km, primarily along routes 80 and 70) covers the northwestern section of the Avalon Peninsula (known as the **Bay de Verde Peninsula**), starting with Brigus and historic Cupids at the southern end of Conception Bay.

Brigus

More like an affluent New England village than a typical Newfoundland port, **BRIGUS**, about 80km from St John's, is one of the prettiest towns in the region. Founded as an offshoot of Cupids in 1612, it was destroyed by French raids in 1697 but boomed in the nineteenth century thanks to the Labrador seal fishery. Today the old centre is a pint-sized pocket of handsome Victorian houses and slate-lined streams that backs onto the bay.

Hawthorne Cottage National Historic Site

1 South St, at Irishtown Rd • Usually open mid-May to Aug; check website for latest time and fees • ☎ 709 753 9262, ⊛ pc.gc.ca/en/lhn-nhs/nl/hawthorne

The town's most famous son is **Captain Robert Bartlett** (1875–1946), whose memory is preserved at the **Hawthorne Cottage National Historic Site**. The seemingly inexhaustible Bartlett was a much-sought-after Arctic explorer – he helped get Robert Peary to the North Pole in 1909, and led a heroic Shackleton-esque escape from the ice-bound *Karluk* in 1914. His birthplace in Brigus was his nominal home from 1886, though the Captain spent more time at sea and in New York – his mother and then his sisters lived here until the 1970s.

Built in 1830 in the romantic "picturesque" style (rare in Newfoundland), the house is adorned with a trellised, wrought-iron, wraparound veranda, while the small, tiny rooms (a bit like ship cabins) have been atmospherically preserved and crammed with family belongings. Make sure you listen to the recordings in each room (based on family diaries) and watch the videos upstairs of Captain Bob in action. In July and August

> **SUMMER SHAKESPEARE**
>
> In the summer you can watch entertaining versions of Shakespeare plays by Perchance Theatre at Cupids (☎ 709 771 2930, ⊚ perchancetheatre.com) in the grounds of *Cupids Haven* (see below). The theatre looks like a mini-version of the Globe in London – an outdoor wood-and-sail edifice with tickets ranging $15–40.

catch one of the "**Live! On the Lawn Theatre**" productions in the garden. Note that most of the **house was closed** in 2019 for a massive rehabilitation project that may take several years – check the website for the latest (guides will still be on site throughout).

Cupids

Tiny **CUPIDS**, a few kilometres north of Brigus, was the unlikely site of **Canada's first English settlement**, a venture established by Bristol merchant John Guy and 38 colonists in 1610 that acted as a catalyst for the colonization of the rest of Newfoundland. Today it's a pretty village straggled along the shore of the harbour and dominated by the jagged cliffs of **Spectacle Head** on the other side.

Cupids Legacy Centre

368 Seaforest Drive · Early June to early Oct daily 9.30am–5pm · $8.65 ($14.75 with the Plantation) · ☎ 709 528 1610, ⊚ cupidslegacycentre.ca

The original settlement of "Cupers Cove" (now Cupids) was all but abandoned after it was burned in 1665, probably during a Dutch raid, and it wasn't until the 1990s that the site was rediscovered by archeologists. Today the absorbing **Cupids Legacy Centre** chronicles the history of the site with multimedia displays and some of the 160,000 artefacts recovered since 1995: thimbles, clay pipes, jugs and coins, among them an Elizabethan fourpenny piece minted in 1561. You can also visit the Archeology Lab, where artefacts are cleaned and catalogued, and the rooftop viewing deck.

Cove Plantation Provincial Historic Site

467 Seaforest Drive · Mid-May to early Oct daily 9.15am–5pm · $6 ($14.75 with Cupids Legacy Centre) · ☎ 709 528 1413, ⊚ baccalieudigs.ca

At the location of the original English colony, **Cupids Cove Plantation Provincial Historic Site** is still very much an active dig, with experts uncovering more remains each year. You can wander the site on your own but you'll get more out of it by taking a guided tour (30min; included with entry). Only the base of walls and cobblestones are visible, but a wooden "ghost structure" (outline) of the original 1610 storehouse has been erected to get a sense of what it would have looked like. More recent discoveries have included an outer gun battery and a small cemetery.

ACCOMMODATION AND EATING   CUPIDS

★ **Cupids Haven B&B & Tea Room** 169 Burnt Head Rd ☎ 729 528 1555, ⊚ cupidshaven.ca. Superb accommodation in a beautifully converted Anglican chapel built in 1910; rooms feature original Gothic windows and wooden fittings (with cable TV). Just outside you can hike the Burnt Head Trails, visit the theatre in the garden (see box below) and the on-site *Tea Room* (late May to Sept Sat & Sun 8am–7pm) serving great pots of tea, pan-fried cod and classic treats such as *toutons* (pancakes) with molasses. **$119**

Harbour Grace

Founded in 1614 by the same Bristol merchants who had established Cupids, **HARBOUR GRACE** stretches out along **Water Street**, most attractive near its northern end, where a handful of elegant clapboard houses flank a slender inlet and are overseen by three **churches**: the handsome, twin-towered Catholic Church of the Immaculate Conception; the modest clapboard Coughlan United Methodist effort nearby; and the pretty neo-Gothic stonework of St Paul's Anglican Church further up the road. As you enter the town (off Rte-70, at the southern end of the harbour) look out for the **SS Kyle**, a 1913 steamship that ran aground here and has been in elegant decay since 1967.

Conception Bay Museum

1 Water St East • Late May to mid-Sept Mon–Fri 10am–noon & 1–4pm, Sat noon–4pm • $3 • ☎ 709 596 5465

The 1870 red-brick Customs House has been turned into the three-storey **Conception Bay Museum**, featuring special sections on **Peter Easton**, the so-called "Pirate Admiral", **Amelia Earhart**, and the history of the fishery in Harbour Grace. Easton, who was based here between 1610 and 1614, ran a phenomenally successful pirate fleet, manned by five thousand sailors who made their leader rich enough to retire to a life of luxury in the south of France. Next door to the museum, the tiny park contains a **wing-shaped monument** honouring the early aviators who flew across the Atlantic from Harbour Grace between 1919 and 1937. The most famous was Amelia Earhart, the first woman to complete the journey solo in 1932. Earhart is also commemorated with a plaque on the grassy airstrip above the town – this was Canada's **first airfield** when it opened in 1927 (signs lead the way from town via a bone-shaking dirt track).

Heart's Content

It might be hard to believe in the age of 5G and satellites, but the advent of the long-distance telegraph in the nineteenth century – the transmission of Morse code through electric wires – changed the world. In 1858, little **HEART'S CONTENT**, 30km northwest of Harbour Grace on the shores of Trinity Bay, was the scene of the audacious attempt to connect North America with Britain by telegraph cable. Soon after Queen Victoria and US President James Buchanan had swapped inaugural jokes the cable broke. It was eight years before an improved version, running from Valentia in Ireland, was successfully laid by Brunel's *Great Eastern* – the cable revolutionized communications, standardized ship schedules and prices on the New York and London stock markets, and vastly improved weather forecasting on both sides of the Atlantic. Thereafter Heart's Content became an important relay station to New York, a role it performed until technological advances made it obsolete in the 1960s.

Cable Station Provincial Historic Site

Hwy-80 • Late May to early Oct daily 9.30am–5pm • $6 • ☎ 709 583 2160

Tight against the waterfront in Heart's Content, the **Cable Station Provincial Historic Site** contains the old cable operating room from 1918, preserved with all the archaic equipment in pristine condition. The main displays are in the adjacent 1876 building, covering the history of telecommunications and details of the problems encountered during the laying of the first telegraph lines – a twenty-minute video tells the whole dramatic story. It also chronicles how the town was transformed after 1866, noting the social divisions between the relatively wealthy cable operators and local fishing families.

Wooden Boat Museum of Newfoundland & Labrador

Hwy-80, Winterton • Early June to late Sept daily 10am–5pm • $8 • ☎ 709 583 2044, ⚓ woodenboatmuseum.com

Around 12km north of Heart's Content, the village of **WINTERTON** contains the enlightening **Wooden Boat Museum of Newfoundland & Labrador**, where traditional boat-building techniques are preserved by skilled craftsmen in a special workshop at the back. The surprisingly large museum itself tells the story of the wooden boat from Inuit kayaks to modern punts and dorys.

ACCOMMODATION   **THE BACCALIEU TRAIL**

★ **Ocean Delight Cottages** Hwy-80, Whiteway ☎ 877 588 2026, ⚓ oceandelightcottages.net. Halfway between the Trans-Canada and Heart's Content, this water-side accommodation comes with jaw-dropping sunset views across the water to Shag Rock (owners Laurelyn Berry and Jerry Byrne will usually be able to take you out in their boat). The luxurious self-catering cottages feature two bedrooms, kitchens and barbecues on the shore. April–Oct. **$135**

Southwest Avalon: the Cape Shore

The thumb-shaped promontory filling out the southwest corner of the Avalon Peninsula is dubbed the **Cape Shore**, a foggy wilderness of cranberry bogs and spruce-smothered headlands, whose coast is negotiated by **Hwy-92** and **Hwy-100**, branching off the Trans-Canada some 80km from St John's.

Castle Hill National Historic Site

Hwy-100, Placentia • 24hr • Free • Visitor centre June–Aug daily 10am–6pm • $3.90 • ☎ 709 227 2401, ⓦ pc.gc.ca/en/lhn-nhs/nl/castlehill

6

Just north of Newfoundland's old French capital at **PLACENTIA** lies **Castle Hill National Historic Site**, magnificently located above Placentia Harbour, one of Newfoundland's finest anchorages. The harbour's sheltered waters attracted the French, who established their regional headquarters, "Plaisance", here in 1662, with Fort Royale (now Castle Hill) up above as the key defensive position completed in 1703. As the fortunes of war changed, the harbour and fort were successively occupied and refortified by the British in 1713, who maintained a garrison here until 1811. This history, as well as the process of cod fishing in the eighteenth century, is skilfully explored at the **visitor centre**. Little remains of the fort today – just a few stone walls and ditches – but it's worth making the trip for the views.

Cape St Mary's Ecological Reserve

13km off Hwy-100 • Dr Leslie M. Tuck Centre daily: May & Oct 9am–5pm; June–Sept 8am–7pm • Free • ☎ 709 277 1666

Immortalized in the much-loved ballad *Let Me Fish Off Cape St Mary's*, these days the wild, isolated headland, some 65km southwest of Placentia, is more famous for its mesmerizing sea-bird colony, protected within **Cape St Mary's Ecological Reserve**. It's one of the few places in the world where 24,000 gannets, 20,000 kittiwakes and 20,000 murres (guillemots) congregate to nest on easily accessible sea cliffs and stumpy sea stacks, 140–150m above the waves; you can get exceptionally close via paths overlooking the shore (littered with blue-flag irises in summer), the rocks so smothered with birds they look like snow-covered peaks – you'll smell them before you see them. The main gannet colony, and the most dazzling spectacle, is generally considered to be 90m-high **Bird Rock**, just a few metres from the cliffs and a twenty-minute (1.4km) walk away from the car park, **lighthouse** and **Dr Leslie M. Tuck Centre**. Inside the latter you can watch a video about the site and view an exhibition on the local birds and ecology – you can also pick up one of the reserve's **guided walks** (free). Make sure you wear sturdy **footwear** and prepare for **fog**, even in midsummer.

ACCOMMODATION AND EATING   CAPE ST MARY'S

Cape St Mary's is just over 200km from St John's, making it too far away for a comfortable day-trip, but there are several places to **stay** in the fishing village of St Bride's (16km northwest of the reserve) and Branch (32km northeast), a much prettier village on St Mary's Bay.

Capeway Motel 11 Hwy-100, St Bride's ☎ 709 337 2163, ⓦ thecapeway.ca. Former Presentation Convent, now a spick-and-span motel with seven unassuming en-suite rooms with cable TV and microwaves. **$109**

Da Bird's Eye 5 Main St, St Bride's ☎ 709 337 2860. This no-frills canteen knocks out super-fresh seafood, usually caught that morning; the cod and chips is excellent ($9.75–14.95), but it also does chowders ($8.75) and home-made fruit pies. May–Sept daily 11am–7pm.

The Burin Peninsula

The wild, wind-blown moorlands of the **Burin Peninsula** are way off the beaten path for most visitors, though it harbours some of the most enticing destinations on the island. A lonely 200km from the Trans-Canada Highway on Hwy-210 lies the edge-of-the-world fishing village of **Grand Bank**; a few kilometres on is **Fortune**, the departure point for **passenger ferries** over to **St-Pierre et Miquelon** (see page 429).

6

Grand Bank

Perched on the edge of Fortune Bay, the weathered streets of **GRAND BANK** maintain an isolated, end-of-the-road air, with most of the houses sturdy white bungalows and a fierce wind blowing off the water. A French fishing station in the 1600s, Grand Bank was permanently settled by the English in 1763 (Captain Cook visited two years later), and it's one of the most intriguing settlements on the island thanks to its links with France and Lunenburg (see page 340) in Nova Scotia through its assortment of late nineteenth-century clapboard and shingle houses – a few are Queen-Anne beauties equipped with the so-called "widow's walks", rooftop galleries from where the women watched for their menfolk returning from the sea. The boom years of the Grand Banks fishery were 1880 to 1940 but today shellfish, particularly **surf clams**, provide the village of around 2500 with a modest income.

Provincial Seamen's Museum

54 Marine Drive • Late April to Sept Mon–Sat 9am–4.30pm, Sun noon–4.30pm • $2.50 • ☎ 709 832 1484, ⓦ therooms.ca/museums

It's something of a surprise to see the **Provincial Seamen's Museum** on the edge of Grand Bank, housed in what was the Yugoslav pavilion at Montréal Expo '67, moved here in 1971 and shaped like the sails of a schooner – look out for Atlantic Canada's **largest mural** on the exterior, a scene depicting the nineteenth-century wharf. The museum is essentially a repository for a vast collection of historic artefacts, all beautifully presented but without much labelling. Downstairs the focus is on the sea – old dorys, scale models of boats, ship lanterns, antique engines and giant ship's wheels – while the upstairs gallery contains old carriages, agricultural tools, archaic ploughs and the like.

George C. Harris House

16 Water St • Late June to mid-Oct Mon–Sat 9am–4.45pm, Sun noon–4.45pm • $3 • ☎ 709 832 1574, ⓦ grandbankheritagesociety.ca

The grandest home in Grand Bank is the **George C. Harris House**, now a museum of local history with special emphasis on the period 1881 to 1954. Built in 1908 by successful merchant Samuel Harris for his son George, in a classic Queen Anne style, it's topped by a "widow's walk" (which you can stroll out on), and contains period rooms crammed with furniture, toys, photos, books and other bits and pieces.

ACCOMMODATION AND EATING   GRAND BANK

Sharon's Nook & Tea Room 12 Water St ☎ 709 832 0618. Best of several local diners in Grand Bank, with folk music piped in, and a massive, deadly menu of baked desserts and cheesecakes. Cash only. Mon, Tues & Sat 7.30am–9pm, Wed–Fri 7.30am–10pm, Sun 11am–7.30pm.

★ **The Thorndyke** 33 Water St ☎ 709 832 0820, ⓦ thethorndyke.ca. Grand Bank's best digs is this magical B&B, an especially well-maintained sea captain's house built in 1917 with four en-suite period rooms, replete with grand beds, wood floors, cable TV and antiques – the widow's walk looks out over the sea and frolicking whales in summer. May–Sept. $130

Fortune

From Grand Bank, it's 5km or so to **FORTUNE**, a slightly smaller village of around 1400 people, and the departure point for the foot passenger ferries over to **St-Pierre et Miquelon** (see page 429).

Fortune Head Geology Centre

49–51 Bunkerhill Rd (opposite the ferry terminal, Hwy-420) • Late May to early Oct Mon–Sat 8am–8pm, Sun 10am–6pm • $7.50; guided tours mid-July to Aug Mon, Fri & Sun 11am, 2pm & 4pm; Tues & Thurs 2pm & 4pm; $20 with centre entry • ☎ 709 832 3031, ⓦ fortunehead.com

The **Fortune Head Geology Centre** celebrates the Cambrian Explosion, the evolutionary event when the first creatures with skeletons and shells burrowed into the sea floor a mind-bending 543 million years ago. The enlightening, family-friendly exhibit explains how the fossils were created and puts the whole thing into context, as well as charting the geology of the Burin Peninsula in general. The "Golden Spike" at the **Fortune Head Ecological Reserve** itself is the best place on the planet to see fossils from this period; it's another 2.5km east along Hwy-210, then 3km along a gravel road to the **Fortune Head Lighthouse**. Here you can scramble down to the jagged shale below, though to the untrained eye the squiggles across the rocks can seem a little underwhelming. **Guided tours** are much more rewarding, with transport included from the Geology Centre.

ARRIVAL AND DEPARTURE   FORTUNE

By taxi/minibus Foote's Taxi (☎ 709 832 0491) operates a once-daily service between Grand Bank and the St-Pierre ferry terminal (see page 431) at Fortune and St John's for $50/person. It starts picking up from Fortune at around 6.30am, arriving in St John's 4–5hr later; departure from St John's is at around 2pm – check ferry times in advance if you intend to reach St Pierre in one day.

St-Pierre et Miquelon

In 1760 the French surrendered Montréal and Québec to the British, signalling the end of their North American empire. Sort of. Unbeknown to millions of North Americans and Europeans, the tiny archipelago of **St-Pierre et Miquelon**, 20km off the coast of the Burin, has remained a self-governing overseas **territory of France** (officially a *collectivité d'outre-mer* since 2003). French law applies, French is the official language and despite its location, the **euro** is the official currency – government entities cannot accept Canadian (or US) dollars for payment (which includes museums). The French connection pulls in several thousand visitors each year, especially charmed by the high-quality French **cuisine** on offer (aided by duty-free imports from the motherland – forget Canadian wines here), the exuberant celebrations on **Bastille Day** (*la Fête nationale*, July 14), and the sheer novelty of a European enclave in North America. The main settlement, **Ville de St-Pierre**, is crammed with fine restaurants and simple guesthouses with a genuinely Gallic flavour, and all but seven hundred of the seven thousand islanders live here, with the remainder on **Grande Miquelon** island to the north. The third and middle island, **Langlade**, or **Petite Miquelon**, has just a scattering of houses and is only inhabited in summer. When planning your trip, note that everything **closes** between noon and 2pm every day, and all day Sunday (much is closed on Saturday also).

Brief history

The Portuguese stumbled across the archipelago in 1520, but it was **Jacques Cartier** who claimed it for the French in 1536. Subsequently settled by fishermen from the

---

ST-PIERRE CURRENCY AND IMMIGRATION

Since St-Pierre is literally part of France, local currency is the **euro** (€), made up of 100 cents. Canadian and US dollars are widely accepted in shops and some restaurants, but you'll usually get change in euros. Note however, that museums, local ferries and any government-run service will **only accept euros** (and may not accept credit cards) – you'll need to get at least some euros in cash before or when you arrive. There is only one bank, Banque de St-Pierre et Miquelon (Mon–Fri 8.30am–noon & 1.30–5pm), on the harbourfront, near L'Arche Musée, which can change money and has an ATM; there is also an ATM next to *Bar Rustique* on rue Albert in the centre.

To clear St-Pierre et Miquelon's **immigration** and **customs control**, EU and US nationals need a **passport** (providing visa-free entry for up to thirty days); Canadians just need photo ID. Entry requirements are essentially the same as visiting France for other nationals, so check the latest requirements. For **medical emergencies**, dial ☎ 15, police ☎ 17.

Basque provinces, Normandy and Brittany, the islands were alternately occupied by Britain and France until the British ceded them to the French in 1763. The Brits continued to invade the islands however (and deport the locals), whenever war with France loomed, until Napoleon was beaten in 1815 – the following year the French returned to St-Pierre and were left alone thereafter.

After World War I, the French colonial authorities wanted to expand the local fishing industry, but their efforts became irrelevant with US **Prohibition** in 1920. Quite suddenly, St-Pierre was transformed from a maritime backwater into a giant transit centre for smuggling booze, thanks to Al Capone and Bill McCoy. It was an immensely lucrative business, but when Prohibition ended thirteen years later the St-Pierre economy collapsed. More misery followed during World War II, when the islands' governor remained controversially loyal to the collaborationist **Vichy regime**. Both the Canadians and the Americans considered invading, but it was a **Free French** naval squadron that got there first, crossing over from their base in Halifax and occupying the islands in late 1941 without a shot being fired.

Since then, the St-Pierrais have remained largely loyal to France, and they certainly needed the support of Paris when the Canadians extended the limit of their territorial waters to two hundred nautical miles in 1977. The ensuing wrangle between Canada and France over the islands' claim to a similar exclusion zone was finally resolved in 1994, although the tightening of controls on foreign vessels has largely ended St-Pierre's role as a supply centre. Today the island is slowly diversifying its economy into tourism and crab fishing, with the assistance of vast amounts of cash from the French government. The permanent population is mostly of Basque, Breton, Norman and Acadian descent.

Ville de St-Pierre

The tidy streets of **VILLE DE ST-PIERRE** nudge back from the harbour, a pleasant ensemble of plain stone and brightly painted clapboard buildings with a quintessentially French demeanour. **Fires** have actually levelled the town numerous times (the last in 1972), with the great fire of 1867 destroying 177 buildings. There's little sign of that today, and the central area makes for an enjoyable stroll, though there's nothing special to aim for, with the possible exception of the 1907 **Cathédrale de Saint-Pierre**, on place Maurier, with its Romanesque, stone bell tower and rich array of modern stained glass inside (enter through the chapel at the back Mon–Sat 8am–5pm).

L'Arche Musée et Archives

Rue du 11 Novembre • Daily: May, June, Sept & Oct 9.30am–noon & 1.30–4.30pm; July & Aug 9am–5pm; Nov–April by appointment only • €7 • ☎ 0508 41 04 35, ⓦ arche-musee-et-archives.net

It's about 700m southwest of **place du Général de Gaulle** along the harbourfront to the impressive bulk of **L'Arche Musée et Archives**, which features displays on local history and culture with old photos, artefacts and some labelling in English. Look out for the guillotine downstairs, and the small display of Maritime Archaic artefacts dating back to 3000 BC, some from the **L'Anse à Henry** site (guided tours of the latter are €25). The museum also arranges **themed walking tours** of the town (€15–25).

Musée Héritage

1 bis, rue Maître Georges Lefèvre • Mid-June to mid-Sept Mon–Fri 2–8pm, Sat 10am–noon & 2–5pm • €7 • ☎ 0508 41 39 80, ⓦ musee-heritage.fr

Just off place du Général de Gaulle, the **Musée Héritage** offers a cheerful look at the islands' history, with ten rooms crammed with antique bric-a-brac, including exhibits on the local Nuns of St Joseph, nineteenth-century schoolrooms and the fisheries.

Île aux Marins

Ferries daily 8.30am–6pm (hourly) from St-Pierre • €6 return; tickets at 12 rue Pierre Perrin • ☎ 0508 41 70 70

Just ten minutes across St-Pierre's harbour lies the minuscule **Île aux Marins** (Sailor's Island), where the barren, treeless rocks were once strewn with thousands of drying cod fish on stone platforms known as "*graves*". After centuries of use, the islet was abandoned in 1964, its assorted buildings now preserved as an open-air museum – five buildings serve as the **Musée Archipélitude** (July to mid-Sept daily 2–5.30pm; €5; ☎ 0508 41 25 76). You can visit the town hall, the old school, the lighthouse and a garish Stations of the Cross trail that leads to a small cemetery perched on a windy promontory. The church, **Notre-Dame des Marins**, is the islet's most intriguing building, a large and handsome structure whose original furnishings, dating from 1874, have survived, including a large black-wrapped catafalque, used for carrying coffins. Labels are in French only, but **guided tours** in English are available (see page 432).

Grande Miquelon

At the north end of the archipelago, the stubby little island of **Grande Miquelon** comprises peat bog, marsh and a couple of hills which slope away from the only village, **MIQUELON**. The village has a couple of sights of some modest interest, beginning with **l'Église Notre-Dame-des-Ardilliers** of 1865, whose sombre exterior hides a folksy interior filled with faux-marble columns and containing a good copy of a Murillo *Virgin* donated by Napoléon III – it's above the altar.

Just down the street from the church at 5 rue Sourdeval is the cramped **Musée de Miquelon** (mid-June to mid-Sept daily 8.30am–noon & 1.30–5.30pm; €2; ☎ 0508 41 67 07), displaying all manner of items salvaged from local shipwrecks.

Langlade

The archipelago's most unusual feature is the **Isthme de Langlade**, a sweeping 12km sandy isthmus linking Grande Miquelon with **LANGLADE**. The isthmus began to surface above the ocean two hundred years ago as a result of sand collecting around a shipwreck and is now anything up to 2500m wide. There's a road along the length of the dune, but heavy seas can swamp parts of it, so be sure to stick to the guided tours. These stop at the **Grand Barachois**, a large saltwater pool at the northern end of the isthmus that's a favourite haunt of breeding seals. Langlade itself has a more varied landscape than the other islands – high hills, deciduous forests and rushing brooks – and is at its liveliest in summer, when the St-Pierrais arrive in droves to open up their summer homes.

ARRIVAL AND DEPARTURE   **ST-PIERRE ET MIQUELON**

By plane Air St-Pierre (☎ 0508 41 00 00, ☎ 877 277 7765, ⓦ airsaintpierre.com) flies to St-Pierre et Miquelon from Montréal (3hr 15min); Paris, France (5hr; July & Aug only); Halifax in Nova Scotia (1hr 30min); Îles-de-la-Madeleine (1hr; July & Aug only); and St John's, Newfoundland. The least expensive flights are from St John's (3–5 weekly; 45min; €224/$260 one way), where the company has a desk at the airport (☎ 709 726 9700). St-Pierre airport is 1.9km south of the town of St-Pierre; taxis run into the centre (€6).

By ferry With two new ferries introduced between St-Pierre et Miquelon and Newfoundland in 2018, it's now possible to bring your car across – in theory. In practice, the wharf at Fortune would need extensive upgrades to handle cars, a project that seems unlikely to gain government funding in the near future. SPM Ferries has mooted a move to Grand Bank instead, which can handle cars, but with no agreement at the time of writing – check the website for the latest. For now, two ferries, the *Suroît* and *Nordet* (Newfoundland ☎ 709 832 3455, ⓦ spm-ferries.fr/en/home; April to Dec 1–2 daily; check website for latest times; €48 one way, €80 return; bikes are permitted for €10 each way), run from Fortune in Newfoundland to the town of St-Pierre in 1hr 30min (it can be a little bouncy). You can pay for secure car parking at Fortune ferry terminal ($10/day). You can now also take these ferries direct from Fortune to Miquelon (1hr 30min), but only during the peak summer months (see website for details).

6

TOURING ST-PIERRE ET MIQUELON

By far the easiest way of venturing beyond Ville de St-Pierre is to join a **guided tour**, and from mid-June to late September there are several **day-trips** to choose from. You can buy tickets at the tourism office in St-Pierre.

St-Pierre island Bilingual minivan tours from Le Caillou Blanc, 2 rue du Maine (☎ 0508 55 74 22, ⓦ lecailloublanc.fr) for €20.

Île aux Marins Guided tours (1hr 30min) run May to mid-Oct from L'Arche Musée et Archives (1–2 daily; €30 including boat trip; reservations ☎ 0508 41 04 35).

Miquelon and Langlade The Miquelon Tourist Information Centre in Place des Ardilliers (see page 432) offers guided tours of Miquelon and Langlade on foot and by bus (€15–45).

Tour agency Atlas Voyages, 18 rue Albert Briand, St-Pierre (☎ 508 41 76 7, ⓦ atlasspm.com).

GETTING AROUND

Ville de St-Pierre and Miquelon village are small enough to explore on foot, but to see the rest of St-Pierre and Miquelon islands you'll need to take a tour (see above), or rent a bike or car.

By ferry Ferries link Ville de St-Pierre with Miquelon village (€16 one-way, €24 return; bikes €4 each way; 1hr 30min; 1–2 daily); Langlade (€10 one-way, €17 return; bikes €2 each way; 1hr 15min; 1–3 daily), and Île aux Marins (see page 431). Buy tickets in the SPM Ferries/visitor information centre at 20 place du Général de Gaulle; Mon & Wed 8.30am–noon & 1.30–5pm, Tues 6.30am–noon & 1.30–4.45pm, Thurs 7.30am–noon & 1.30–5pm, Fri 6.30am–noon & 1.30–5.15pm, Sat normally closed, Sun 10am–noon & 1.30–4.15pm; ☎ 0508 41 08 75, ⓦ spm-ferries.fr).

By plane Air St-Pierre flies between St-Pierre and Miquelon (2–4 daily; 15min; €17.50 one way, €29 return).

By car On St-Pierre you can rent cars from Garage Norbert Marie, 24 rue Albert Briand (☎ 508 41 29 00); on Miquelon contact Max Girardin, 10 rte du Cap Blanc (Mon–Fri 8.30am–noon & 1.30–6pm, Sat 9am–noon; ☎ 508 41 65 03).

By taxi Taxis run around St-Pierre; figure on €6 for most destinations, but you'll need to call them (try Taxi Bechet ☎ 508 41 70 90). There are no conventional taxis on Miquelon or Langlade, but Lucas Transport Service (☎ 508 55 65 78, ⓔ lucastransportsservices@yahoo.fr) can arrange lifts and tours.

By bike You can rent bikes (from €13 per day) at X Sports SPM at 1 rue des Français libres in St-Pierre (Mon 2–6.30pm, Tues–Fri 10am–noon & 2–6.30pm, Sat 10am–noon & 2–5pm; ☎ 508 41 33 00, ⓦ facebook.com/xsports.spm).

INFORMATION

St-Pierre Tourist Information Center in the centre of Ville de St-Pierre, just metres from the ferry dock at 20 place du Général de Gaulle (June–Sept daily 8am–6pm; Oct–May Mon–Fri 8.30am–noon & 1.30–5.30pm, Sat 8.30am–noon, Sun 6–8pm; ☎ 0508 41 02 00, ⓦ spm-tourisme.fr). It supplies all sorts of information about the archipelago, issues free maps, and also has the timetable of the local passenger ferry.

Miquelon Tourist Information Centre is inside the Nature Interpretation Centre at Place des Ardilliers (Mon, Wed, Thurs & Sat 10am–noon & 1.30–5pm, Tues & Fri 9am–noon & 2–6.30pm, Sun 10am–noon & 2–6pm; ☎ 0508 41 02 01, ⓦ spm-tourisme.fr).

Electricity Electrical appliances run on 220 volts here, so US/Canadian appliances won't work unless they are compatible (most phone and laptop adapters can take both currents). You'll also need an adapter as plugs use the round-pin French style (most hotels can supply these).

Phones The islands' area telephone code is ☎ 508; if calling from elsewhere, dial the international access code before this (☎ 011 from Canada or the US). To call Canada or the US from the island, dial ☎ 001 before the area code (dial ☎ 00 plus country code for other places).

Post office Next to the ferry dock (Mon–Fri 8am–noon & 1.30–4.15pm, Sat 8am–noon).

ACCOMMODATION

Hôtel Robert 2 rue du 11 Novembre ☎ 0508 41 24 19, ⓦ hotelrobert.com. Where Al Capone stayed during Prohibition; a small museum off the foyer has one of his straw hats and other memorabilia. The superior rooms are a bit more expensive (€118) but a huge step-up from the workaday standards. **€90**

L'Auberge Saint-Pierre 16 rue Georges Daguerre ☎ 0508 41 40 86, ⓦ aubergesaint-pierre.com. One of the best places to stay, compact but stylish modern rooms with cable TV, big breakfast and friendly staff eager to help. Also offers summer tastings of liqueurs made from local berries. Rates drop to €98 Oct–May. **€136**

Nuits Saint-Pierre 10 rue du Général Leclerc ☎ 0508 41 20 27, ⓦ nuitssaintpierre.com. Gorgeous boutique above *Délices de Joséphine* (see below), with one suite and four luxurious bedrooms, all equipped with extra-comfy beds, linens and bathrobes and flat-screen TVs. No children under 14. **€160**

EATING

St-Pierre's **restaurants** are good, combining the best of French cuisine with local delicacies such as *tiaude*, a highly seasoned cod stew, though most ingredients are imported. Prices are fairly high – reckon on about €25–30 for a main course. Reservations are essential in summer.

★ **Chez Janot** Langlade ☎ 0508 55 01 09. Restaurant that's legendary on the islands, run by the indomitable Annick Boissel. Offers snacks and drinks throughout the day, and often a merry gathering of locals and musicians in the evenings. Daily 8am–1am (closed Dec–May).

La crêperie du "Vieux port" Hotel Robert, 2 rue du 11 Novembre ☎ 0508 41 27 00. The place for classic Breton *galettes*, from "La forestière" (mushrooms, onions, egg and Emmental cheese) to "La pêcheur" (cheesy "St Jacques"

seafood sauce, shrimps and leeks). Mains €6–25. Daily 7am–10pm (Oct–April noon–1.30pm & 7–9.30pm).

Les Délices de Josephine 12 rue Général-Leclerc ☎ 0508 41 20 27. Chic tearoom serving a huge range of teas (€3–5), coffees (€3.50) and hot chocolate (€5.50). Add a slice of the house *gâteau* (€6); it also does wonderful quiches and baguette sandwiches. May–Sept Mon–Sat 10am–2pm & 3–6pm, Sun 10am–2pm; Oct–April Wed–Sat 3–5pm.

Les P'tits Graviers 2 rue Amiral Muselier ☎ 0508 41 75 28, ⓦ lateliergourmandspm.com. Top-notch French and local seafood, but also burgers, sandwiches, wood-fired pizzas and fish and chips (€9.50–11.50). Lunch set menus (€12.50–19, mains €15–26). Mon–Sat noon–2pm & 7–10pm, Sun noon–2pm (seasonal hours).

The Bonavista Peninsula

The thickly wooded **Bonavista Peninsula** pokes out into the ocean for some 120km, its shredded shoreline confettied with bays, coves and islands. The English settled here in numbers during the seventeenth century, establishing dozens of tiny outports and one administrative centre, **Trinity**, with a gorgeous headland setting and medley of fine old buildings.

Trinity

Situated about 70km from the Trans-Canada Highway via Hwy-230 and 270km north of St John's, tiny **TRINITY** has narrow lanes edged by a delightful ensemble of white and pastel-painted clapboard houses, all set between a ring of hills and the deep and intricate Trinity Bight.

St Paul's Anglican Church

Church Rd • ☎ 709 464 3658

The architectural high point of the village is **St Paul's Anglican Church**, completed in 1894, whose perfectly proportioned Gothic Revival exterior is adorned by elaborate scrollwork. Inside, the graceful and dignified nave is divided into three, the side aisles entered through arches carved to resemble whale bones and the ceiling up above fashioned in the shape of an upturned boat.

Trinity Historical Society sites

Mid-May to mid-Oct daily 9.30am–5pm • Combined admission ticket $20 (includes provincial sites; see page 435); Trinity Museum only, donation suggested • ☎ 709 464 3599, ⓦ trinityhistoricalsociety.com

The Trinity Historical Society manages several historic sites in the village, giving a flavour of what life was like here in the nineteenth century. Opposite the church is the modest but entertaining **Trinity Museum**, a classic saltbox home from the 1880s, which crowds together an eccentric collection of bygones arranged by theme: an old shoemaker's kit in the washroom and a fire engine of 1811 in the shed next door, the oldest on the island.

The **Green Family Forge** on the corner of West Street and Dandy Lane, displays artefacts associated with the town's blacksmiths between 1750 and 1955, including two fully-operational forges. The nearby **Lester-Garland House** on West Street is a three-storey Georgian-style brick home with expertly reproduced period rooms (the 1819 original was demolished in the 1960s, and the current building is a modern reconstruction).

Trinity Provincial Historic Sites

Mid-May to early Oct daily 9.30am–5pm • $6 for all three sites ($20 with Trinity Historical Society sites; see page 434) • ☎ 709 464 2042

The three **Trinity Provincial Historic Sites** include the yellow-and-green **Hiscock House** (1881) on Church Road, where guides in period costume explain the intricacies of early twentieth-century merchant life in the outports. The **Mercantile Premises** on West Street commemorate the establishment of merchant Benjamin Lester of Poole, England, here in 1748; today the building comprises an 1820s counting house and the early twentieth-century **Ryan General Store**, restored to its 1910 appearance. The final property is the **Trinity Visitor Centre**, also on West Street, with general exhibits and information about Trinity and the surrounding area.

ACCOMMODATION AND EATING   TRINITY

★ **Campbell House (Artisan Inn)** 49 High St ☎ 709 464 3377, ⓦ trinityvacations.com. Trinity boasts several appealing rental homes and rooms in handsome Victorian buildings managed by the Artisan Inn, foremost of which is the *Campbell House* of 1840. It has two double rooms, both en suite, with TV and DVD. Mid-May to mid-Oct; register first at the *Twine Loft*, where breakfast is included. $159

Eriksen Premises B&B 8 West St ☎ 709 464 3698, ⓦ mytrinityexperience.com. A good choice, in a late Victorian property, is the *Eriksen Premises*, which has seven en-suite rooms, mostly with sea views. May–Oct. $119

★ **Twine Loft** 57 High St ☎ 709 464 3377, ⓦ trinity vacations.com. The best place to eat in town (breakfast and dinner only) is this waterside restaurant, just off the High St and part of the Artisan Inn stable; local seafood (especially fresh cod) is the speciality, along with the delicious rhubarb custard tartlets. Dinner (without wine) averages $40/person. May–Oct daily 8–10am; dinner sittings daily 5.30pm & 7.45pm June–Sept (May & Oct 7pm only).

New Bonaventure

About 15km southwest of Trinity, Hwy-239 slips into **NEW BONAVENTURE**, a haphazard assortment of clapboard houses edging a rocky bay. On a rainy day it seems like the end of the world, but a side road pushes on even further – fork right over the hill as you descend into the village and continue for another 500m until you reach **St John's Anglican Church** at the end of the road, constructed in 1923.

Random Passage Site

Hwy-239 • Late May to late Sept daily 9.30am–5.30pm • $10 • ☎ 709 464 2233, ⓦ randompassagesite.com

Beginning at St John's church, a gravel road leads 600m down to the **Random Passage Site**, a replica, early nineteenth-century outport with fishing stages, roughly hewn wooden shacks, a church and a school. The site was built in 2000 for the miniseries dramatizations of *Random Passage* and *Waiting for Time*, two romantic novels written by Newfoundland's Bernice Morgan, telling the tale of the fictional Andrews family, who settled at a spot called Cape Random in the 1820s. Enthusiastic local guides are on hand to explain the basic plot if required – some of them are real characters themselves, and a few appeared in the series as extras. The whole project is run as a not-for-profit organization by the local community. The location is stunning, but the authentic mud and stone hovels emphasize the harsh nature of life here, and how everything revolved around the fishery.

Cape Bonavista

Some 50km north of Trinity, **Cape Bonavista** is witheringly beautiful, a desolate headland of dark-grey rock and pounding sea inhabited by hundreds of puffins. Explorer **John Cabot** is supposed to have first clapped eyes on the Americas here in

6

> **ROOT CELLARS AND PUFFINS**
>
> The straggling community of **Elliston**, 5.6km from Bonavista, is known as the "root cellar capital of the world" for good reason, with around 135 hobbit-like cellars for storing produce through the winter dug into the hillside since 1839 (you can visit some of them). The village also boasts the closest viewing of **puffins** from land in North America, a colony of over 80,000 spread over the cliffs – you'll be able to get very close to the more curious birds.

1497, exclaiming – or so it's claimed – "O buona vista!" ("O, happy sight") and, true or not, a statue has been erected in his honour. The cape is 5km from the sprawling fishing village of **Bonavista**, which spreads out across the flattish headlands surrounding its double harbour. Settled by the English in the seventeenth century, this was once a successful trading centre and fishing station.

Ryan Premises National Historic Site

10 Ryan's Hill Rd • June–Sept daily 10am–6pm • $3.90 • ☎ 709 468 1600, ⓦ pc.gc.ca/en/lhn-nhs/nl/ryan

The history of Bonavista is explored at the **Ryan Premises National Historic Site**, a nineteenth-century fish-processing complex on the harbour. Inside you'll find the Bonavista Museum of local history, a multimedia exhibit on Labrador's seal fisheries, and the restored Ryan offices, circa 1900.

Ye Matthew Legacy

15 Roper St • Mid-June to mid-Sept daily 9.30am–5pm • $7.25, children (6–16) $3 • ☎ 709 468 1493

Bonavista's nautical heritage is celebrated at the **Ye Matthew Legacy**, which features a full-scale replica of **Cabot's ship** of 1497, the 28m-long *Matthew*, with tours below deck; the attached interpretation centre charts the history of the boat, as told through the eyes of a young cabin boy. Note that the ship is now a little worse for wear, and has been moved indoors.

Mockbeggar Plantation Provincial Historic Site

Roper St • Mid-May to early Oct daily 9.30am–5pm • $6 (includes entry to lighthouse) • ☎ 709 468 7300

Bonavista's other noteworthy sight is the plain white clapboard **Mockbeggar Plantation Provincial Historic Site**, once the home of F. Gordon Bradley, a lawyer-turned-politician who met here with Joe Smallwood throughout the 1940s to mastermind the island's bid for confederation. Though it was built around 1871 by a local merchant, the house has been returned to its appearance in 1939 when Bradley was on the brink of victory, and comes complete with a full set of heavy-duty Victorian and Edwardian furniture, much of it made by Bradley's father. Enthusiastic guides provide background and descriptions. The saltbox **Big Store** outside may date from 1733, which would make it the oldest building on Newfoundland.

Cape Bonavista lighthouse

Cape Shore Rd • Mid-May to early Oct daily 9.30am–5pm • $6 (includes entry to Mockbeggar Plantation) • ☎ 709 468 7444

Cape Bonavista has always been hazardous to shipping and it's still overseen by the 10m-tall red-and-white-striped **Cape Bonavista lighthouse** built in 1843, attractively restored to its appearance in 1870 when it was occupied by an 80-year-old lighthouse keeper, Jeremiah White, and his family; costumed guides give the background and the adjacent interpretive centre gives an overview of the island's crucial lighthouse system.

ARRIVAL AND DEPARTURE   CAPE BONAVISTA

By taxi/minibus Marsh's Taxi (☎ 709 468 7715, ⓦ marshstaxi@hotmail.com) runs out to Bonavista (4hr) via Trinity (3hr 30min) for $45. The shuttle departs daily from Bonavista around 6.30am, and leaves St John's for the return trip at 1.30pm.

ACCOMMODATION AND EATING

★ **Bonavista Social Club** 2 Longshore Rd, Upper Amherst Cove ☎ 709 445 5556, ⓦ bonavistasocialclub. com. You'll smell the goodness from the only wood-fired pizza and bread oven in Newfoundland here, with breads baked daily, fine pizzas, tomato cod soup, famed moose burgers and sandwiches. Try the rhubarb lemonade. Mains $12–30. Mid-May to early Oct Tues–Sun noon–8pm.

Butler's by the Sea 15 Butler Crescent ☎ 709 468 2445, ⓦ bbcanada.com/1412.html. One of the better B&Bs in town, with two well-appointed, en-suite rooms overlooking the water in a home dating back to 1915. May–Sept. $145

★ **Harbour Quarters Inn** 42 Campbell St ☎ 866 468 7982, ⓦ harbourquarters.com. In the centre of the village, on the waterfront, this plush option is open year-round with cosy rooms (and cable TV) in a converted 1920s general store. $159

Mifflin's Tea Room 21 Church St ☎ 709 468 2636. Serves refreshing afternoon tea, veggie dishes, local specialities and outstanding desserts – everything is made from scratch, so check the wi-fi (free) while you wait (most dishes $9–14). June–Oct Mon–Sat 8am–9pm, Sun noon–9pm.

Central Newfoundland

The Trans-Canada Highway cuts a long and lonely course across **central Newfoundland** on its way from Clarenville, at the base of the Bonavista Peninsula, to Deer Lake, a distance of 450km. There's little to see amid this vast forested wilderness beyond the **Terra Nova National Park**, and to make the most of this region you need to get off the highway and head to the isolated outports along the coast. Some 100km north lie the old fishing port of **Twillingate** and the wonderfully preserved **Fogo Island**, each on a craggy broken coastline that attracts icebergs by the score from April to June.

Terra Nova National Park

Trans-Canada Hwy (Hwy-1) • Daily 24hr • $5.80 mid-May to early Oct • ☎ 709 533 2801, ⓦ pc.gc.ca/terranova

Heading north from Clarenville along the Trans-Canada Highway, it's about 40km to the southern edge of **Terra Nova National Park**, whose coniferous forests, ponds and marshes border a deeply indented slice of rugged coastline. The road slices right through the park, giving clearly signed access to its various facilities, most of which are concentrated about 35km in, at the head of **Newman Sound**.

Salton's Brook Visitor Centre

Mid-May to mid-June & early Sept to early Oct Mon & Thurs–Sun 10am–4pm; mid-June to early Sept daily 10am–6pm • ☎ 709 533 2942

Located on Newman Sound (clearly signposted off the Trans-Canada), **Salton's Brook Visitor Centre** contains excellent displays explaining and illustrating the park's flora and fauna – child-friendly touch tanks contain crabs and starfish. The centre also supplies oodles of information about guided walks, boat trips, safe swimming areas, diving, canoeing and sea-kayaking.

Blue Hill and the trails

Highlights at Terra Nova include the observation point at **Blue Hill** (199m), the park's highest point, the gentle 3km loop of **Sandy Pond Trail** (watch for caribou and pitcher plants) and the **Coastal Trail** (9.5km return) from the visitor centre, which offers scintillating views across Newman Sound. You might see **moose** anywhere in the park, usually ambling through the undergrowth.

ACCOMMODATION AND EATING

TERRA NOVA NATIONAL PARK

Clode Sound Motel & Restaurant 8 Main St, Charlottetown, about 15km south of Newman Sound on Hwy-1 ☎ 709 664 3146, ⓦ clodesound.com. If camping seems too daunting, aim for here, where you'll find reasonably priced motel rooms and a restaurant (daily:

May, June & Sept 11am–2pm & 4.30–7.30pm; July & Aug 8am–10pm) known for its fruit pies and crumbles, and lots of fresh seafood ($10–20). May–Oct. $120

★ **Inn at Happy Adventure** 8 Harbour View Rd, Happy Adventure ☎ 709 677 2233, ⓦ innathappyadventure.

6

6

com. By far the best place to stay in the region is this modern hotel in the fishing village of Happy Adventure, about 15km from the park's northern entrance via Hwy-310. The spacious suites come with stunning balconies overlooking the harbour and flat-screen TVs, with *Chucky's Seafood & Wildgame Restaurant* downstairs knocking out tasty moose dishes and fish and chips (May to late Sept Wed–Sun noon–2.30pm & 4.30–8pm). $199

National Park camping ☎ 905 426 4648, ⓦ pccamping. ca. In addition to several primitive campgrounds ($15.70), permits for which must be arranged at the centre before you set out, the National Park also has two serviced campgrounds, the largest being *Newman Sound Campground* (mid-May to early Oct; reservations advised). Luxurious oTENTik tents are also available (from $100). Serviced (electricity) $29.40; unserviced (but including bathrooms) $25.50

Smallwood Interpretation Centre

13 Station Rd (off Riverside Drive), Gambo • June–Sept daily 9am–6pm • $3 • ☎ 709 674 4342

Around 32km north of Terra Nova National Park, the Trans-Canada reaches the logging town of **GAMBO**, where signposted off Hwy-320 is the **Smallwood Interpretation Centre**, celebrating the life and times of its most famous son, **Joe Smallwood**. The larger-than-life Newfoundland premier dominated the political scene from 1949 to 1972, and remains a controversial figure. Most islanders would now agree that his main contribution was in squeezing through the vote for confederation in the referendum of 1948, but his attempts to diversify the economy by attracting industry were often ill considered and very costly. The centre contains documents, artefacts, portraits and memorabilia from the Smallwood era, as well as a replica of Smallwood's study.

Barbour Living Heritage Village

Village Newtown • Late June to early Sept daily 10am–5pm • $10 • ☎ 709 536 3220, ⓦ barbour-site.com

North of Gambo, Hwy-320 aka "Road to the Capes" makes a loop through the small villages of the Kittiwake Coast, best known for their wide sandy beaches, especially at Lumsden. The major cultural diversion is in **NEWTOWN** (83km from Gambo), where the **Barbour Living Heritage Village** is a collection of clapboard houses, wharves and a **tearoom** preserved as a living museum – locals dressed in period costume enliven the experience with skits and demonstrations. Special galleries on **sealing** and the numerous disasters that occurred at sea emphasize just how grim and dangerous the industry was, right up to World War II.

Newtown itself is extremely picturesque, the "Venice" of Newfoundland, its clapboard homes and pretty **St Luke's Church** set on seventeen barren, gale-whipped islands linked by bridges.

Fogo Island

In 2006 Canadian millionaire **Zita Cobb** decided that she wanted to return to her childhood home on **Fogo Island**, an isolated place devastated by the cod moratorium, and help to revive the economy. Locals reacted cautiously at first, but since then the island has become the envy of many an outport community: grants and loans have improved infrastructure, and an innovative arts programme (see ⓦ fogoislandarts. ca) has boosted tourism. Yet all of this has simply highlighted what the locals knew all along – that the air here is cleaner, the ocean saltier, the people friendlier and the scenery more enchanting than anywhere else on the planet.

Fogo Island Marine Interpretation Centre

79 Harbour Drive, Seldom (off Hwy-333) • June–Sept daily 10am–4pm • $2 • ☎ 709 627 3366

Just a short ride from the ferry in the village of **SELDOM**, **Fogo Island Marine Interpretation Centre** occupies the old Fisherman's Union (FU) Trading Company premises, with the 1913 White Retail Store next door now a fishing museum. Learn about the **"Fogo Process"**, the establishment of a Fogo Island Co-operative in 1967 that revitalized the local fishing industry (crab, fish and shrimp are still caught and processed on the island).

Fogo

The town of **FOGO** was the first part of the island to be settled, around 1720, by Poole-based merchant John Slade. It's an extremely picturesque place, surrounded by rocky hills and containing several historic churches, notably **St Andrews**, dating from 1841. Nearby is craggy **Brimstone Head**, renowned locally for the dubious distinction of being proclaimed one of the "four corners of the world" by the now defunct Flat Earth Society – it's a chilling, nerve-tingling spot regardless, with an easy **trail** to the 90m summit for the best views on the island.

Fogo Wireless Interpretation Centre

15 Pickett's Rd Extension • June–Sept daily 9.30am–6pm • Free • ☎ 709 266 3543

The Marconi Company operated a wireless station above Fogo between 1912 and 1931, and the **Fogo Wireless Interpretation Centre** contains exhibits about their work and the history of the town, including some Beothuk remains. The views are worth the drive up alone, and you can hike to the actual station site (though little remains).

Experience Fogo

5–7 North Shore Rd • June–Sept daily 10am–6pm • Free • ☎ 709 266 3543

The **Experience Fogo** site is a small but atmospheric collection of wooden buildings preserved to give a sense of the town's fishing heritage: a trap store, stable, carpenter's store and a fish flake leading out to a fishing stage on the harbour.

Tilting

Visit in the early morning, or just before the sun goes down, and you may not want to leave the bewitching village of **TILTING**. Gorgeous clapboard cottages, saltboxes, creaky wharves and boathouses cling to the rocks around the placid harbour. The village is proud of its Irish heritage, and the best way to soak it up is to just wander the streets; though if the sun is out, you should also make a trip to **Sandy Cove Beach**, one of Canada's best stretches of sand.

ARRIVAL AND DEPARTURE
FOGO ISLAND

By ferry Fogo Island is connected to the mainland by a scheduled ferry service (4–5 daily 8.30am–8pm; 45min direct or 1hr 15min via Change Islands; ☎ 709 535 6244), from the tiny port of Farewell, some 86km north of Gander and Hwy-1. Times change seasonally, with most departures stopping at Change Islands (20min; $10) along the way. For one person with a normal car the cost is $25.50, plus $8.50 per additional adult (you don't pay coming back). Try to get to the port 1hr before departure to ensure you get on – if it's full you'll have to wait for the next one (no reservations).

ACCOMMODATION AND EATING

Brimstone Head RV Park Banks Cove Rd ☎ 709 266 2402, ⓦ brimstoneheadrvpark.com. You can camp on the grassy field at *Brimstone Head RV Park*, with showers and toilets available. Tent sites $15; serviced RV sites $25

★ **Fogo Island Inn** 210 Main Rd (Hwy-334), Joe Batt's Arm ☎ 709 658 3444, ⓦ fogoislandinn.ca. The culmination of Cobb's vision for the island, this five-star, stilt-raised edifice dominates the horizon, featuring floor-to-ceiling windows, ocean views, infinity pool and luxurious contemporary rooms and personalized island tours available. It's a spectacular but exclusive experience, with rooms priced accordingly. Full board only. Non-guests can make reservations at the on-site restaurant for lunch ($50 set) and dinner, or take a short tour of the hotel. $1975

Growlers 125 Main Rd, Joe Batt's Arm ☎ 709 266 7982. Superb ice cream utilizing local flavours; think bakeapple, custard and "O Canada Maple" to celebrate Canada Day. Cash only. July & Aug daily 11am–9pm; June & Sept Thurs–Sun 12.30–8pm.

Quintal House 153 Main Rd (Hwy-334), Joe Batt's Arm ☎ 709 658 7829, ⓦ quintalhouse.ca. Beautifully restored merchant's home from the 1800s, with three cosy en-suite rooms and the downstairs kitchen, dining room and living room shared among the guests – cakes and cereals (but no TV). $140

The Scoff 159 Main Rd, Joe Batt's Arm ☎ 709 658 3663, ⓦ facebook.com/scoffrestaurant. Best eating on the island, with finely crafted local dishes including crab cakes, beer-battered fish and chips and seafood stew – always ask about local specials such as *toutons* and beans or jiggs dinner (see page 40). Mains $12–18. Late May to mid-Oct Wed–Sat 5.30–9.30pm (longer hours July & Aug).

Twillingate and around

The outport of **TWILLINGATE** is one of the largest towns in northern Newfoundland, with over three thousand inhabitants and a rich history that goes back to the 1700s. Twillingate Island became the year-round headquarters of Poole-based merchant John Slade in 1750, after several decades of use by itinerant French fishermen, who gave the place its original name, "Toulinguet", from an island back home in Brittany. Though it remains an old fishing village at heart, it's far more developed than Fogo Island – several boat operators compete for tours of frolicking whales in summer and parades of towering icebergs in the spring. If you visit the town in September, you'll be able to go **berry-picking**; thousands of bakeapples (cloudberries), partridgeberries (lingonberries) and blueberries smother the slopes around the town.

Twillingate Museum

1 St Peter's Church Rd (off Main St) • Mid-May to early Oct daily 9am–5pm • Free (donation) • ☎ 709 884 2825, ⓦ tmacs.ca

Housed in the old rectory, built in 1915 behind St Peter's Anglican Church, the **Twillingate Museum** contains several period rooms crammed with historic bric-a-brac from the area, mostly from the nineteenth century. The most intriguing rooms lie upstairs, where there's a small display of **Maritime Archaic** artefacts dug up from the nearby **Curtis Site** (1500 BC) and an exhibit dedicated to chanteuse **Georgina Stirling** (the "Nightingale of the North"), who was born in Twillingate in 1867. Her sensational opera-singing career was cut tragically short in 1901 after an illness, and she struggled with depression for years afterwards.

Long Point Lighthouse

262 Main St, Crow Head • May, June & Sept daily noon–5pm; July & Aug daily 10am–5.30pm • $7 • ☎ 709 884 5651

Landlubbers still stand a good chance of spotting an iceberg from the bright red and white **Long Point Lighthouse**, which occupies a commanding position on a high rocky cliff at the tip of Twillingate North Island. Viewpoints and trails lace the headland, and you can now climb up the narrow passage to the top of the lighthouse. The old keeper's cottage, built in 1876, has been turned into a gallery for travelling exhibits and a permanent display on *Titanic*.

Boyd's Cove Beothuk Site Interpretive Centre

Off Hwy-340, Boyd's Cove • Mid-May to early Oct daily 9.30am–5pm • $6 • ☎ 709 729 0592

A short drive south of Twillingate, **Boyd's Cove Beothuk Site Interpretive Centre** commemorates a small village inhabited by Beothuks between 1650 and 1720 – eleven house pits have been identified, with four excavated so far. Visits begin with an enlightening twenty-minute video about the quest to find and excavate the site in the 1980s. Some of the 41,000 artefacts dug up are on display, including iron nails stolen from European fishing stations, ingeniously modified by the Beothuks into arrowheads. The actual village site is a 1.5km hike (one way) from the centre, though nothing remains above ground.

ACCOMMODATION AND EATING   TWILLINGATE

Captain's Legacy B&B 14 Ocher Pit Rd ☎ 709 884 5648, ⓦ captainslegacy.com. Charmingly renovated, two-storey 1881 Gothic Revival home, rooms featuring DVDs and flat-screen TVs, gorgeous views of the bay, outstanding breakfasts and friendly hosts. Mid-May to Oct. $115

Crow's Nest Café 127 Main St, Crow's Head ☎ 709 893 2029, ⓦ facebook.com/crowsnestcafe. You'll find plenty of fish-and-chips-type canteens in Twillingate, but try this

TWILLINGATE ICEBERG-SPOTTING

Between **late May and July**, the myriad inlets near Twillingate can ensnare dozens of **icebergs** as they float down from the Arctic, though in these days of climate change it can be hard to predict their appearance. You won't forget the experience if you do encounter one: tinted in shades of aquamarine and white by reflections from the sea and sun, they seem like otherworldly cathedrals of ice, which stand out brilliantly from the blue-green ocean and, if you're particularly lucky, you might witness the moment when one of them rolls over and breaks apart, accompanied by a tremendous grating and wheezing and then an ear-ringing bang. You should also check out ⓦ icebergfinder.com for a heads-up on the latest berg activity. Several local companies offer **iceberg-watching boat tours**:

Iceberg Quest Pier 52, Main St ⓣ709 884 1888, ⓦ icebergquest.com. Daily departures at 9.30am, 1pm, 4pm and 7pm in peak season (2hr; $60). May to Oct.

Twillingate Adventure Tours ⓣ709 884 5999, ⓦ twillingateadventuretours.com. Mid-May to mid-Sept 3–4 daily; 2hr; $55.

Twillingate Island Boat Tours (Iceberg Man Tours) 50 Main St ⓣ709 884 2242, ⓦ icebergtours. ca. Mid-May to Sept daily 9.30am, 1pm & 4pm; 2hr; $60.

---

cosy café for quality fair-trade coffee, cinnamon buns and light meals, from cod chowder to veggie wraps. June to mid-Oct daily 8am–8pm (Wed, Fri & Sat till 10pm); mid-Oct to May seasonal hours (see website).

★ **Hillside B&B** 14 Blanford's Lane ⓣ709 884 1666, ⓦ bbcanada.com/nfhillside. One of the best places to stay in Twillingate, an attractive, well-kept B&B in an 1870s clapboard house overlooking the harbour; it has three en-suite rooms, each decorated in simple modern style, and a spacious cottage with its own veranda. May–Sept. $118

Toulinguet Inn 56 Main St ⓣ709 884 2080, ⓦ toulinguetinn.com. Three cosy, en-suite rooms down on the waterfront, in a 1920s saltbox, with balconies overlooking Twillingate harbour and continental style breakfast served in room. Mid-May to mid-Oct. $122

SHOPPING

★ **Auk Island Winery** 29 Durrell St ⓣ877 639 4637, ⓦ aukislandwinery.com. Visit this local winery for an introduction to the island's growing number of eminently drinkable fruit wines, made with local blueberries, partridgeberries, bakeapples, raspberries and crowberries. Winery tours (May–Sept every 30min; $6, $10 with tastings) and tastings ($6) are also available. Daily 9.30am–6.30pm

(Oct–April Mon–Fri 10am–4pm).

Iceberg Shop 50 Main St ⓣ709 884 2242, ⓦ iceberg tours.ca. Arts and crafts shop in a 160-year-old building once owned by Georgina Stirling (see page 440), with a vast range of clothing, jewellery, paintings and souvenirs (you can also book boat tours here). Daily 8.30am–8.30pm.

Grand Falls-Windsor

Some 140km west of Gambo along the Trans-Canada Highway, **GRAND FALLS-WINDSOR** sits among some of the island's most valuable strands of timber, an expanse of **forest** that's been intensively exploited ever since Alfred Harmsworth, later Lord Northcliffe, opened a paper mill here in 1909. Grand Falls is an unprepossessing place today (the AbitibiBowater paper mill closed in 2009 leaving hundreds out of work), though the **falls** themselves retain a certain rugged charm, hemmed in by jagged rocks and rapids.

Salmonid Interpretation Center

100 Taylor Rd • Mid-June to mid-Sept daily 8am–8pm • $9 • ⓣ709 489 7350, ⓦ erma.ca

The best place to see the falls is at the **Salmonid Interpretation Center**, on the south bank of the Exploits River 2km from the centre. The main attraction here is the 150m fishway or fish ladder, where thousands of **Atlantic salmon** leap and fight upstream to spawning grounds at Red Indian Lake – since a fishing moratorium in 2003 stocks have soared to well over 30,000. Exhibits in the interpretation centre highlight the history, biology and habitat of salmon, while the observation level provides an underwater view of the migrating fish.

Mary March Provincial Museum

24 St Catherine St (take exit 18, Cromer Ave, from Hwy-1) • Late April to Sept Mon–Sat 9am–4.30pm, Sun noon–4.30pm • $2.50 • ☎ 709 292 4522

Focusing on the early history of Newfoundland, the **Mary March Provincial Museum** serves up a thought-provoking series of displays on the region's prehistoric cultures and especially the **Beothuks**.

ACCOMMODATION AND EATING

GRAND FALLS-WINDSOR

Hill Road Manor B&B 1 Hill Rd ☎ 709 489 5451, ⓦ hillroadmanor.com. The most enticing B&B in Grand Falls, a large 1930s clapboard mansion with four spacious rooms enhanced with cable TV. Take exit 18A off the highway (see website for directions). **$124**

Hotel Robin Hood 78 Lincoln Rd ☎ 709 489 5324, ⓦ hotelrobinhood.com. Comfortable motel-style accommodation not far from the main highway. Free

breakfast and spacious, modern rooms. The owners are from Nottingham (England), hence the name. **$139**

Juniper Kitchen & Bistro 48 High St ☎ 709 393 3663. The best restaurant in town – you won't find better quality: the seafood chowder ($11.50) and Atlantic salmon fillet ($21.95) are excellent, but it's always worth asking about the nightly specials. Lunch sandwiches and salads are much cheaper. Daily 10am–2pm & 5–10pm.

The Humber Valley

As it nears the west coast of Newfoundland, the Trans-Canada Highway cuts through the magnificent **Humber Valley**, beginning with mountain-rimmed **Deer Lake** and dropping into an increasingly steep and rugged gorge bristling with rocky outcrops and mountains rolling away on each side. From here you can head south on the Trans-Canada to the Nova Scotia ferry at **Channel-Port aux Basques**, or cut north to the **Gros Morne National Park** and Labrador.

Deer Lake

About 210km west of Grand Falls, **DEER LAKE** is a logging community that dates back to the 1860s, and today it's a convenient pit stop, this time at the junction of the Trans-Canada Highway and Hwy-430, the road to the Northern Peninsula.

Newfoundland Insectarium

2 Bonne Bay Rd (Hwy-430), Reidville • Mid-May to early Oct Mon–Fri 9am–5pm, Sat & Sun 10am–5pm (July & Aug daily 9am–6pm) • $13, children (5–14) $9 • ☎ 709 635 4545, ⓦ nlinsectarium.com

The only real attraction in Deer Lake is the **Newfoundland Insectarium**, which features a tranquil pavilion of around one thousand dazzling butterflies, as well as a fascinating colony of leaf-cutter ants, an observation bee hive and tarantula section upstairs.

ARRIVAL AND INFORMATION

DEER LAKE

By plane If you fly into Deer Lake Regional Airport (5.5km northeast of the centre), metered taxis (☎ 709 635 2521) are around $7–9 into town, but realistically you'll need a car to get around: there are several car-rental offices at the terminal: Avis/Budget (☎ 709 635 5010), Enterprise (☎ 709 635 4667), National (☎ 709 635 3282) and Hertz (☎ 877 283 0898). Star Taxi (☎ 709 634 4343) provides a shuttle bus service to Corner Brook for $22/person (call in advance). Air Canada runs daily flights to St John's, Halifax, Toronto and Wabush; WestJet flies to Toronto in the summer; PAL Airlines flies to St John's and Goose Bay.

By bus DRL Coachlines (see page 410) runs once daily

to St John's (depart 12.33pm; $97) and Channel-Port aux Basques (depart 5.12pm; $50) from the Circle K store on Hwy-1 just outside town.

By taxi/minibus Martin's (☎ 709 453 2207) shuttles operate Mon–Fri between Deer Lake (departing around 4.30–5pm) and Woody Point in Gros Morne ($15–25).

Information centres The well-stocked information centre at the airport (☎ 709 635 1003) is open year-round 9am–2pm. The main visitor information centre (daily June–Oct 9am–5pm; ☎ 709 635 2202) is on Trans-Canada Hwy, just south of junction 16 (for Hwy-430) and the Irving petrol station.

ACCOMMODATION AND EATING

Big Stop 62 Trans-Canada Hwy ☎709 635 2130. For meals in Deer Lake, most travellers stick to this convenient option, at the Irving petrol station. Service can be hit-and-miss, but it serves a full menu of classic dishes (turkey dinners, grilled salmon), the obligatory fish and chips and hefty lemon meringue pies (mains $15–18). *Big Stop* is a chain, but in Newfoundland the cooks are usually locals who tend to knock out superb home-made dishes in addition to the standard menu. Daily 6am–11pm.

Holiday Inn Express Deer Lake 38 Bennett Ave (Hwy-1, exit 15) ☎888 465 4329, ⓦ hiexpress.com. Not actually at the airport, but Deer Lake's most modern and inviting hotel nonetheless, with spacious rooms, indoor pool, and buffet breakfast included. **$196**

Humberview B&B 11 Humberview Drive (Hwy-1, exit 15) ☎709 635 4818, ⓦ humberviewbandb.com. If you prefer B&Bs to motels, this is your best bet in Deer Lake; it occupies a large and well-appointed, modern, two-storey brick house on the north side of the highway (exit 15), with seven comfy rooms. **$130**

Steady Brook

The most dramatic section of the Humber Valley lies between exits 7 and 8 of the Trans-Canada in **STEADY BROOK**, an area offering plenty of attractions in summer and winter. It's a short but steep hike up to majestic **Steady Brook Falls**, a 60m cascade that plunges through a jagged gap in the rocks and down into the valley (take exit 8 and follow the signs behind George's Mountain Village).

Marble Mountain Ski Resort

Exit 8, Trans-Canada Hwy · Day-pass $45 · ☎888 462 7253, ⓦ skimarble.com

Steady Brook's premier attraction is **Marble Mountain Ski Resort**, offering some of the best **skiing** east of the Rockies, and plenty of scenic hiking trails in summer. Buy your pass at the lodge first before renting equipment. Look out for the **Heritage Tree** at the entrance to the resort, a 17m, 300-year-old cedar trunk (a bit like a totem pole), with sixty scenes of Newfoundland history carved into it.

ACTIVITIES

★ Marble Zip Tours ☎709 632 5463, ⓦ marble ziptours.com. Just off the Trans-Canada Hwy (exit 8), Marble Mountain Ski Resort is also the home of one of Newfoundland's most adrenaline-pumping attractions, a series of nine exhilarating zip-lines zigzagging across the falls and gorge, 86m above the ground. Daily 9am–5pm; tours 9am, 11am, 1pm, 3pm & 5pm; $109.

Corner Brook

CORNER BROOK, some 50km from Deer Lake and 10km from Steady Brook, is magnificently sited, surrounded by steep wooded hills dropping down to the blue waters of the **Humber Arm**. The city is Newfoundland's second biggest, a workaday pulp-and-paper town of around 40,000, supplying newsprint to much of the world.

Captain James Cook National Historic Site

Crow Hill Rd, off Atlantic Ave · Daily 24hr · Free · ☎709 639 9792

The coast hereabouts was charted by Captain Cook in 1767, who now accounts for the city's most absorbing attraction, the **Captain James Cook National Historic Site**, to the west of the centre in a small park at the top of Crow Hill with fabulous views of the valley. Copies of the charts mapped by Cook are on display.

ARRIVAL AND INFORMATION

CORNER BROOK

By bus DRL Coachlines (see page 410) runs a once-daily service from Corner Brook south to Channel-Port aux Basques (5.55pm; $42) and east to St John's (11.25am; $103), from the Circle K on Confederation Drive.

By taxi Taxis to Marble Mountain in Steady Brook will cost around $20, or $60 to Deer Lake Airport; Star Taxi (☎709 634 4343) runs a shuttle bus from *Greenwood Inn* at 48 West St to the airport for $22.

6

BAY OF ISLANDS BY BOAT

The Humber flows into the **Bay of Islands**, a mesmerizing blend of mountain-topped islands and soaring fjords. To best appreciate the bay and the isolated inlets to the north, contact **True North Tours** (☎ 709 688 2718, ⓦ truenorthtours.ca). Tony and Joan Oxford run 2hr 30min tours along Middle and Goose Arms from **Cox's Cove** (at the end of Rte-440, 40km from Corner Brook), passing resettled villages, a Dorset Paleo-Eskimo site and plenty of wildlife, including whales, ospreys and bald eagles. During the journey they regale their passengers with folk songs and stories of Newfoundland history – you might also catch a cod or two. Tours run daily between July and September (from $40).

By minibus Martin's (☎ 709 453 2207) shuttles operate Mon–Fri, departing Corner Brook at around 4pm to Woody Point (1hr 30min) via Deer Lake – rates range $15–25. Burgeo Bus Lines runs from Corner Brook to Burgeo (Mon–Fri 3pm; $40, cash only; ☎ 709 886 2700, ⓔ burgeobus@hotmail.com). Buses usually depart from the bus stop adjacent to the Millbrook Mall, but always call ahead.

Corner Brook Visitor Information Centre 15 Confederation Drive, just off the highway (exit 6; June–Sept daily 9am–6pm; ☎ 709 639 9792, ⓦ cornerbrook.com).

ACCOMMODATION AND EATING

Comfort Inn 41 Maple Valley Rd (Hwy-1, exit 5) ☎ 709 639 1980, ⓦ choicehotels.ca. Accommodation in Corner Brook tends to fill up fast, especially the popular *Comfort Inn* just off the highway; book ahead. Rooms come with free local calls, *Jungle Jim's Restaurant* on-site and all the usual chain amenities. **$199**

Glynmill Inn 1B Cobb Lane ☎ 709 634 5181, ⓦ steele hotels.com. Right in the heart of town, this hotel has heaps of character, built in mock-Tudor style in 1924 to house pulp-mill managers. Today the spacious suites still retain a classical feel, but with all modern appliances. Enjoy some fine dining in the *Carriage Room* restaurant (daily 7am–2pm & 5–9pm). **$145**

Newfound Sushi 117 Broadway ☎ 709 634 6666, ⓦ newfoundsushi.com. Small (six tables) but top-notch sushi restaurant (think Atlantic salmon, crab and shrimp) with salads, stir-fry and grilled seafood also on the menu (sushi samplers $17–20; teriyaki $12–18). Tues–Sat 11am–2.30pm & 4–9pm.

Lark Harbour and around

The Humber empties into the fjord-like expanse of **Humber Arm** at Corner Brook, a gorgeous inlet that becomes more spectacular the further west you travel. Hwy-450 follows the south shore for 47km to **LARK HARBOUR**, a small fishing village overlooking a bay visited by whales and hemmed in by craggy mountains. Along the way you'll have plenty of opportunities to hike: along the massive **Blow-Me-Down Mountains** (643m), or up into **Blow Me Down Provincial Park** (cars $10), the long, peak-studded peninsula that separates Lark Harbour from York Harbour. Beyond Lark Harbour the road continues to **Bottle Cove**, a protected lagoon banked with magnificent outcrops of rock – the **Bottle Cove Hiking Trail** (take the dirt road to the car park) cuts a short but scintillating path to the edge of the bay. Hwy-450 ends at **Little Port**, a tiny working fishing harbour with another trail to Cedar Cove.

EATING

LARK HARBOUR AND AROUND

★ **C&E Takeout** 68 Main St, Mount Moriah (Rte-450) ☎ 709 785 2358. This unassuming takeaway shack (7km west of Corner Brook, 40km from Lark Harbour) knocks out the best fish and chips on the west coast ($12.50). It also does scallop, shrimp and clam with chips ($8–10), hot turkey sandwiches ($9.50) and excellent burgers *poutine* (from $5). April–Oct daily 11am–9pm.

★ **Myrtles On The Bay** 23 Main St, Lark Harbour (off Rte-450) ☎ 709 681 2103, ⓦ myrtlesonthebay.ca. Village pub and restaurant right on the water offering wide range of tasty meals, from pizzas and chilli nachos, to fried chicken ($9.50) and poutine ($5.75), morphing into locals bar at night. Late May to early Sept Tues–Thurs noon–1am, Fri & Sat noon–2am, Sun noon–midnight.

Burgeo and the southwest coast

From the Trans-Canada, some 50km south of Corner Brook, it's another winding 150km via Rte-480 to **BURGEO**, best known for its pristine, white-sand **beaches**. Indeed, the main attraction in summer is **Sandbanks Provincial Park**, 7km of bone-white beaches facing the Cabot Strait. From Burgeo it's still possible to travel by boat along the southwest coast to isolated fjords and villages such as **Ramea** and **Francois** – a real journey back to the nineteenth century.

6

Ramea and Francois

Just a short ferry ride from Burgeo, the island community of **RAMEA** is one of the most dramatic of the coast's outports, best explored via hiking or mountain-bike trails.

From Ramea ferries continue 26km to picturesque **Grey River** before making another 36km jump to **FRANCOIS** ("franz-way"), one of the most isolated and stunning villages on the island. The village, officially home to 89 people, perches on the coast beneath a giant cliff. Like many remote Newfoundland villages, it may be resettled at some point in the future (it last rejected resettlement in 2013), so visit while you can.

ARRIVAL AND DEPARTURE | BURGEO AND THE SOUTHWEST COAST

By minibus Burgeo Bus Lines runs between Corner Brook to Burgeo (Mon–Fri 3pm; $40; 2hr; ☎709 886 2700, ✉burgeobus@hotmail.com). Return trips depart Burgeo Mon–Fri 8am–9.15am.

By ferry Car ferries (☎709 292 4302, ⓦtw.gov.nl.ca/ferryservices) depart from Burgeo (mid-May to mid-Oct Mon–Fri 1–3 daily; one-way rates: passenger $6, car and driver $17; 1hr 15min) to Ramea. From Ramea ferries continue to Grey River (Tues & Thurs 2 daily; 1hr 20min; $6.25; cars $19), where you can pick up passenger-only ferries to Francois (1 daily 4.45pm except Thurs; $7.50; 1hr 45min). Ferries from Francois back to Burgeo (3hr 45min) via Grey River depart daily (except Thurs) at 7.30am ($11.75). On Thursdays, you can also take the passenger ferry from Francois to McCallum ($7.50; 2hr 15min) and then to Hermitage ($10.50) at the end of Hwy-360.

ACCOMMODATION

Gillett's Motel 1 Inspiration Rd, Burgeo ☎888 333 1284, ⓦgillettsmotel.ca. A good bet in Burgeo, with modern rooms (cable TV) and also a decent restaurant, the *Galley*. **$129**

Ramea Retreat 2 Main St, Ramea ☎709 625 2522, ⓦeasternoutdoors.com. Offers a range of accommodation on the island, from hostel-like dorms to four traditional Newfoundland houses with wi-fi and cable TV. Dorms **$39**; rooms **$89**; houses **$195**

Gros Morne National Park

Park entry mid-May to Oct $9.80/person, ages 6–17 free (pay at kiosks at the entrance, 9am–5pm); Nov to mid-May $7.80 (kids free) • ⓦpc.gc.ca/en/pn-np/nl/grosmorne

Some of Newfoundland's most mesmerizing scenery is contained within **GROS MORNE NATIONAL PARK**, its bays, wild beaches, straggling villages and wizened sea stacks with a backcloth of bare-topped, fjord-cut mountains. The park's forested lower slopes are home to thousands of moose, woodland caribou and snowshoe hare, and **minke whales** regularly feed in Bonne Bay. Gros Morne has also attracted its fair share of artists and musicians, highlighted at the **Trails, Tales and Tunes festival** (ⓦtrailstalestunes.ca) held in Norris Point each May.

Most visitors come here during the short summer season (June–Sept), and other times you'll find many services shut – the exception is the peak **winter season** (Feb–April), when the park experiences another mini-boom in snowmobiling and cross-country skiing.

Rocky Harbour

Some 70km northwest of Deer Lake, **ROCKY HARBOUR** is Gros Morne's largest village, curving around a long and sweeping bay with the mountains lurking in the background.

6

Gros Morne Wildlife Museum

76 Main St North • July & Aug daily 9am–9pm (also open May, June, Sept & Oct at reduced hours, call ahead) • $8 • ☎ 709 458 3396, ⓦ grosmornewildlife.com

If you haven't had much luck seeing the local fauna up close, visit the **Gros Morne Wildlife Museum**, an artfully presented gallery of all the crowd-pleasers in natural scenes: caribou, moose, fox, sea birds, beaver, black bear and even a giant polar bear (the latter was acquired in Nunavut). All the animals were acquired humanely from the Parks Service, found having died naturally or having been killed in accidents before being preserved using modern techniques (not stuffed).

Lobster Cove Head Lighthouse

Off Main St North • Mid-May to early Oct daily 10am–5.30pm • Free with park entry • ☎ 709 458 2417

Completed in 1897, **Lobster Cove Head Lighthouse** offers stunning panoramas across the bay and a small exhibition on the history of the region (the upper section of the lighthouse is still in use and off-limits to the public).

Norris Point

From Rocky Harbour it's 6km south to **NORRIS POINT** on the north shore of **Bonne Bay**, at the point where this deep and mountainous fjord divides into two inlets – East Arm and South Arm. The village was established in 1833 by a family from Dorset (England), and today is a thriving community of around seven hundred.

Bonne Bay Marine Station

Norris Point Waterfront • Mid-May to early Sept daily 9am–5pm • $6.25 • ☎ 709 458 2874, ⓦ bonnebay.ca

Right on the waterfront, the **Bonne Bay Marine Station**, a unit of Memorial University, offers guided tours (every 30min) of its research facilities and aquarium; tanks feature local lobsters, cod, skate, and even a furry sea mouse.

Jenniex House and Lookout

104 Main St • Late June to mid-Sept daily 9am–7pm • Free • ☎ 709 458 2257, ⓦ norrispoint.ca

On the from Rocky Harbour to Norris Point, stop at the **Jenniex House and Lookout**, a 1926 saltbox home high above the bay. It was moved to this spot in 1995, one of the most jaw-dropping locations in the park. Inside you'll find a craft shop, a small museum of local historic bits and pieces upstairs and a traditional "mug up" – tea and muffins with molasses.

Western Brook Pond

The remote **Western Brook Pond**, reached by just one access point, 25km north of Rocky Harbour beside Rte-430, is one of eastern Canada's most enchanting landscapes 16km of deep, dark-blue water framed by mighty mountains and huge waterfalls. From the car park it's a forty-minute (3km) walk on a well-maintained trail through forest

---

BONNE BAY BOAT AND KAYAK TOURS

The best way to experience Bonne Bay is by guided **boat tour** with Bontours (July & Aug daily 10am & 2pm; June & Sept daily 2pm; $46/2hr; ☎ 709 458 2016 ⓦ bontours.ca), departing from **Norris Point Waterfront**. You can also tour the bay by **kayak** with nearby Gros Morne Adventures (rentals $39/2hr, add $10 for each additional hour; 2hr guided tours $59–69; ☎ 709 458 2722, ⓦ grosmorneadventures.com). On a clear day the bay serves up some rich sights, with whales, otters, seals and bald eagles sometimes spotted. The company also arranges serious hikes around Western Brook Pond (three nights; $1395).

> **WOODY POINT HERITAGE THEATRE**
>
> If you're staying the night in Woody Point (see below), check out the **Heritage Theatre** (☎ 709 453 2304) in the centre of the village, which hosts an impressive roster of folk musicians and performers throughout the summer, including the **Writers at Woody Point** festival (☎ 709 458 3388, ⓦ writersatwoodypoint.com), which attracts the best Canadian literary talent every August.

and over bog to the edge of the lake. When you get to the end, don't skimp on the two-hour **boat trip** (reservations required; July & Aug daily 10am, 11am, 12.30pm, 1.30pm, 3pm, 4pm & 5pm; June & Sept daily 12.30pm; $65) operated by Bontours (see page 446). The boat inches its way between the cliffs right to the extreme eastern end of the lake, past several huge rockslides, dramatic hanging valleys and former sea caves now marooned high above the water.

Broom Point

Rte-430 • June to mid-Sept daily 10am–5.30pm • Admission with park ticket

Around 6km north of Western Brook Pond, **Broom Point** is a desolate, windswept promontory crowned with a picturesque smattering of fishing shacks, one of which has been turned into a small fishing museum – guides tell the story of the Mudge family fishing operation here (1941–75), and also the nearby Paleo-Eskimo site.

Cow Head

The village of **COW HEAD**, 11km north of Broom Point, is perched at the most northerly end of the park, and is noted chiefly for its **Gros Morne Theatre Festival** (June to early Sept; ☎ 877 243 2899, ⓦ theatrenewfoundland.com), based at the Warehouse Theatre in the centre of the village. Its programme of drama, music and cabaret, such as the much-loved *Neddy's Norris Nights*, always has a local slant and is thoroughly entertaining (tickets from $32).

Woody Point and the southern section

The **southern section** of the park is just as rewarding as the northern side, with plenty to keep you occupied for several days. Route 431 eventually rolls into minuscule **WOODY POINT**, a sleepy fishing village that was once the main port on Bonne Bay, established by the English fishing merchants Bird & Co around 1800. Nothing much survived a devastating fire in 1922, but the clapboard buildings built in subsequent years form an attractive heritage district near the waterfront.

Discovery Centre

Rte-431 • Daily: mid-May to late June and early Sept to mid-Oct 9am–5pm; late June to early Sept 9am–6pm • Free with park entry ($9.80) • ☎ 709 453 2490

Start your national park activities in this section with a visit to the **Discovery Centre**, just outside Woody Point on the road to Trout River. Interactive exhibits inside examine the area's geology, plant and animal life, with special focus on climate change – there's also an introductory film (18min).

The Tablelands

The Discovery Centre runs guided tours of the nearby **Tablelands**, a Mars-like landscape of reddish, barren flat-topped rock – at 450 million years old, this is an extremely significant geological site, one of the few places on Earth where this mantle pokes above ground. If you can't make a tour, grab an Explorer hand-held device (providing video commentary) at the centre and hike the easy **Tablelands Trail** (4km return), which cuts along the base of the main section.

Trout River

Rte-431 • All museums late July to Sept daily 11am–6pm • $4, $10 for all three • ☎709 451 5376

Route 431 comes to an end at **TROUT RIVER**, another fishing village founded by settlers from Dorset in the 1820s. Lobster and crab fishing remain the staples, but you can visit several historic buildings on the bayfront (Main St). The **Interpretation Centre** contains historic curios and artefacts, old photos and videos on the village, while the **Jacob A. Crocker Heritage House** is a picture-perfect yellow saltbox from 1898. The **Fishermen's Museum** at the far end of the harbour commemorates the main activity of the village – prepare for photos of monstrous halibut.

Trout River Pond

Just south of Trout River lies **Trout River Pond**, a truly spectacular body of water sandwiched by the rusty bareness of the Tablelands and the massive, greyish 500m cliffs bordering the Gregory Plateau. Here, in dramatic profile, you can see the extraordinary force of the uplift created by the collision of the North American and European continents 450 million years ago. Hiking the **Trout River Pond Trail** (14km return) takes around four to five hours, but check at the park visitor centre to see if any boat tours are operating on the lake.

ARRIVAL AND INFORMATION
GROS MORNE NATIONAL PARK

By taxi/minibus Martin's (☎709 453 2207) shuttle buses operate Mon–Fri between Corner Brook, Deer Lake and Woody Point (1hr 30min) in Gros Morne; they usually leave Woody Point at 9.30am, departing Corner Brook for the return trip at 4pm and Deer Lake between 4.30 and 5pm ($15–25). Private taxis from Corner Brook or Deer Lake to Woody Point cost $100–200.

Visitor centre The main visitor information centre (daily: late June to early Sept 8am–8pm; mid-May to late June & early Sept to late Oct 9am–5pm; ☎709 458 2066) is situated beside Rte-430 as it approaches Rocky Harbour,

70km from Deer Lake. There are displays on the natural and human history of the park, as well as an introductory film; also free maps, brochures on the park's key hiking trails and details of local boat excursions.

Shuttle service You'll need a car to make the most of the park, as public transport is non-existent. Bon Tours runs a 20min shuttle ferry service between Norris Point (mid-June to early Sept 9am, 12.30pm & 5pm) and Woody Point (returning 9.30am, 1.15pm & 5.30pm). The service is $8 one way or $14 return.

ACCOMMODATION

Rocky Harbour is the best **place to stay** in the park, not least because it's relatively compact and has a reasonable range of tourist facilities, but there are also some choice options in the **southern section**. Reserving in advance for all accommodation is a good idea anytime, but crucial in July and August and also in winter, when many places are closed. The park runs five **campgrounds** (☎877 737 3783, ⓦpccamping.ca), as well as a number of backcountry primitive campsites dotted along the longer trails ($9.80); you can reserve spaces in advance at the main campsites, but for backcountry ones you just have to register at the park visitor centre before heading out.

NORTH SIDE

Berry Hill Campground Rte-430, Rocky Harbour ☎877 737 3783, ⓦreservation.pc.gc.ca. Of all the park-run campsites, this is the best, with 152 shaded, serviced and unserviced sites (with toilets and showers), 5km

north of Rocky Harbour. Mid-June to mid-Sept. Unserviced **$25.50**; serviced **$32.30**

Gros Morne/Norris Point KOA Campground 5 Shearakin Lane (Norris Point access road from Rte-430) ☎709 458 2229, ⓦkoa.com/campgrounds/gros-morne. Secluded campsite in a wooded valley, overlooking the water; laundry, games room, store and kayaks. Mid-May to mid-Oct. Sites **$26**; cabins **$77**

★**Neddies Harbour Inn** 7 Beach Rd, Neddies Harbour, Norris Point ☎709 458 3089, ⓦtheinn.ca. The spectacular view from the sun deck and bar across Bonne Bay is the real highlight here, while the stylish rooms are decked out with local beechwood in a crisp, contemporary design reflecting the sensibilities of the Swiss owners; you also get fine dining on-site and plenty of ecofriendly touches. Mid-May to mid-Oct. **$195**

Ocean View Motel 38–42 Main St, Rocky Harbour ☎709 458 2730, ⓦtheoceanview.ca. Fabulous location in the heart of the village, overlooking the waterfront, with 53 modern a/c rooms with cable TV and a decent restaurant with sea views. $\overline{\$189}$

★ **Tides Inn** 263 Main St, Norris Point ☎ 709 458 3310, ⓦ thetidesinn.ca. Five spacious, modern suites offering sensational sunset views overlooking the harbour, along with kitchenettes and healthy breakfasts. $\overline{\$205}$

WOODY POINT (SOUTH SIDE)

Aunt Jane's Place B&B 1 Water St, Woody Point ☎ 709

453 2485, ⓦ grosmorneescapes.com. Antique-laden B&B built in the early 1900s, offering five great-value rooms (three with shared bathrooms), with common living room (containing the only TV) and shared kitchen. Mid-May to mid-Oct. Shared bathroom $\overline{\$75}$; private bathroom $\overline{\$95}$

★ **Bonne Bay Inn** 145 Main Rd, Woody Point ☎ 709 453 2223, ⓦ woodypointmagic.com. This modern, cosy hotel offers sensational views across the bay, comfy beds and the congenial *Elements* pub. Breakfast is included. May to early Oct. $\overline{\$199}$

6

EATING AND DRINKING

ROCKY HARBOUR

Earle's 111 Main St South ☎ 709 458 2577. This no-frills groceries store and bakery sells a tempting array of breads and cakes but also has a restaurant with outdoor deck serving a vast range of Newfoundland dishes, including fish and brewis (a traditional fish and hard bread dish), juicy moose burgers and giant moose pizza – the pizzas here are the best in the region and most dishes average around $10–15. Daily 9am–11pm.

★ **Java Jack's** 88 Main St North ☎ 709 458 2710, ⓦ javajacks.ca. Fabulous café and B&B, serving hearty breakfasts (lobster benny $18), well-priced lunches (salt cod fish cakes $12) and dinners such as seared salmon with peach ($28), veggie lasagne ($28) and rabbit pie ($27), much of the produce coming from the organic garden. Late May to Sept daily 8.30am–8.30pm.

NORRIS POINT

★ **The Black Spruce** 7 Beach Rd, Neddies Harbour ☎ 709 458 3405, ⓦ theblackspruce.ca. This hotel restaurant serves superb gourmet dinners, featuring

such delights as slow roasted sweet potato soup ($12), Newfoundland mussels ($12), rack of lamb ($38) and local desserts like steamed carrot pudding ($12). Tues–Sun 5–9pm.

Cat Stop 2–4 Stones Lane, Norris Point Waterfront ☎ 709 458 3343. Pub and café with a sun-drenched upper deck, perfect for early drinks and light snacks ($5–10) after a kayak or boat trip. Also hosts live folk music in the evenings, and has free wi-fi. June–Sept daily 8.30am–8pm (Fri–Sun until 1am).

WOODY POINT

Granite Coffee House 2 Water St ☎ 709 453 2047. Cosy cabin café on the bay, serving potent espresso, cakes, ice cream and light meals ($8–17). Cash only. Also has laundry and free wi-fi. June–Sept daily 7am–5pm.

Old Loft Restaurant 8 Water St ☎ 709 453 2294, ⓦ theoldloft.com. Fine dining in the southern section of the park, where tasty seafood and traditional island dishes ($15–28) are served up in a 1936 clapboard fishing loft near the water. Late May to Sept daily 11.30am–9pm.

The Northern Peninsula

Stretching between Gros Morne and the township of St Anthony, a distance of about 350km, the **Northern Peninsula** is a rugged, sparsely populated finger of land separating the Gulf of St Lawrence from the Atlantic. Its interior is dominated by the spectacular **Long Range Mountains**, a chain of flat-topped peaks that are some of the oldest on Earth. **Route 430** trails along the western edge of the peninsula, connecting the small fishing villages of the narrow coastal plain, but the region's most remarkable sight is the remains of the Norse colony at **L'Anse aux Meadows**, at the tip of the peninsula some 50km beyond St Anthony.

Port au Choix

Mysterious bone, stone and ivory artefacts were being discovered by locals in the small fishing village of **PORT AU CHOIX**, about 160km north of Rocky Harbour, as far back as 1904, but it wasn't until the 1960s that professional archeologists uncovered some astonishing finds: a mass of prehistoric bones, tools and weapons and several ancient cemeteries, ultimately yielding 117 skeletons from the Neolithic period.

Port au Choix National Historic Site

Point Riche Rd • Early June to early Sept daily 9am–5pm • $3.90 • ☎ 709 861 3522, ⓦ pc.gc.ca/en/lhn-nhs/nl/portauchoix

Port au Choix's archeological heritage is preserved within the **Port au Choix National Historic Site**, with a **visitor centre** set halfway along a bleak headland 2.5km from the village. Films, touch-screen presentations and artefacts dug up from Neolithic cemeteries introduce the various cultures that existed here, while **trails** lead out across the headland to the sites themselves – there's really not much left to see, but you'll probably spy plenty of caribou. The primary discovery, right in the middle of the village, is a cemetery belonging to the **Maritime Archaic Indians**, hunter-gatherers who lived here between 3500 and 1200 BC.

St Anthony

Northeast of Port au Choix, Rte-430 slips through a handful of fishing villages and then cuts east across the peninsula, passing the road to L'Anse aux Meadows (see page 451) before carrying on to the fishing and supply centre of **ST ANTHONY**. This is the area's largest settlement, a humdrum port stretched around the wide sweep of its harbour. The best place to **view icebergs** (and eat) is **Fishing Point** and the squat lighthouse at the head of the harbour, where the small Fishing Point Emporium (June–Oct daily 9am–9pm; free; ☎ 877 661 2500) sells local arts and crafts, Labradorite and bakeapple ice cream, and has a small exhibition of local flora and fauna. From here you can climb the steep path to the viewing deck at Fishing Point Head.

Grenfell Historic Properties

1 Maraval Rd • June–Sept daily 8am–5pm; Oct–May interpretation centre only Mon–Fri 9am–5pm • Combined admission $10 • ☎ 709 454 4010, ⓦ grenfell-properties.com

St Anthony's primary land-based attraction is a group of memorials collectively dubbed the **Grenfell Historic Properties**, dedicated to the pioneering missionary doctor, Sir Wilfred Grenfell, an Englishman who first came here on behalf of the Royal National Mission to Deep Sea Fishermen in 1892. He never returned home and, during his forty-year stay, he established the region's first proper hospitals, nursing stations, schools and co-operative stores.

Start at the **Grenfell Interpretation Centre**, which introduces the subject with a film and two floors on Grenfell's life and times, before moving on to the **Grenfell House Museum**, completed in 1910 and the actual Grenfell home. Behind the museum, there's a pleasant woodland path leading – in twenty minutes – to the top of **Tea House Hill**, where Grenfell and his wife were buried.

You should also see the remarkable ceramic murals depicting the culture and the history of Newfoundland inside the nearby **Rotunda** (the main entrance of the Charles S. Curtis Memorial Hospital), created by Montréal artist Jordi Bonet in 1967.

ARRIVAL AND TOURS
ST ANTHONY

By plane Served by PAL Airlines (regular flights to Blanc-Sablon, Goose Bay and St John's), St Anthony Airport is near Seal Bay, a rather distant 55km west of town on Rte-430 – and 72km from L'Anse aux Meadows. Onward transport is by Danny's Airbus shuttle (☎ 709 454 2630, ✉ dannysairbus@nf.aibn.com; it's $30 to St Anthony; 40min).

Boat tours You can get closer to the bergs (and whales) with Northland Discovery Boat Tours (☎ 709 454 3092, ⓦ discovernorthland.com), which runs 2hr 30min cruises (mid-May to late Sept; 1–3 daily; $60.90) from the waterfront behind the Grenfell Interpretation Centre.

ACCOMMODATION AND EATING

Crows Nest Inn B&B 1 Spruce Lane ☎ 709 454 3402, ⓦ crowsnestinn.ca. For comfortable accommodation, try this sensitively renovated B&B, with eight spacious rooms equipped with cable TV, most offering fine views of the harbour. $109

Lightkeepers Seafood/Great Viking Feast Fishing Point Rd ☎ 709 454 4900, ⓦ lightkeepersvikingfeast.com. Located in the former home of the Fishing Point lighthouse keeper, dine on tasty Newfoundland seafood – lobster, crab, mussels and cod – while enjoying the views of ocean, whales and icebergs (most mains $20–32). The Great Viking Feast Dinner Theater (where staff dressed as Vikings entertain and serve traditional Scandinavian food; set buffet meals from $75) takes place in the adjacent replica sod hut – call ahead to check feast dates. May–Sept daily 11.30am–9pm.

L'Anse aux Meadows

Rte-436 (36km north of Rte-430) • Daily: early to mid-June & late Sept to early Oct 9am–5pm; mid-June to late Sept 9am–6pm • $11.70 • ☎ 709 458 2417, ⓦ pc.gc.ca/en/lhn-nhs/nl/meadows

In 1960 on the far northern tip of Newfoundland, a local named George Decker took Helge Ingstad, a Norwegian writer and explorer, to a group of grassed-over bumps and ridges beside Epaves Bay; the place was **L'Anse aux Meadows** and the bumps turned out to contain the remnants of the only **Norse village** ever to have been discovered in North America. Ingstad dug up the foundations of eight turf and timber buildings and a ragbag of archeological finds, including a bronze cloak pin (which provided the crucial carbon dating for the site), a stone anvil, nails, pieces of bog iron, an oil lamp and a small spindle whorl. The Norwegian concluded that the remains were left behind by a group of about a hundred Viking sailors, carpenters and blacksmiths who probably remained at the site for just one or maybe two years, using it as a base for further explorations.

Begin at the **visitor centre**, where the Norse artefacts appear alongside exhibitions on the background to the site as well as Viking life and culture. From here it's a few minutes' walk to the cluster of gentle mounds that make up what's left of the original village, and another short stroll to a group of full-scale replicas centred around a **longhouse** – costumed role-playing interpreters enhance the experience with demonstrations of traditional activities such as cooking, weaving and boat building.

Norstead

Norstead Rd, Rte-436 (38km north of Rte-430) • Early June to mid-Sept daily 9.30am–5.30pm • $10 • ☎ 709 623 2828, ⓦ norstead.com

Just 2km from the original Viking settlement at L'Anse aux Meadows, **Norstead** is an impressive replica of a Norse port replete with full-scale Viking ships, a touristy but extremely entertaining glimpse into Viking life a thousand years ago. Costumed interpreters lead hands-on activities, tell stories in the chieftain's hall and demonstrate ancient crafts like spinning and pot making.

VINLAND AND THE VIKINGS

By 870 AD the **Vikings** had settled on the shores of Iceland, and by the start of the eleventh century there were about three thousand Norse colonists established in Greenland. The two **Vinland sagas** – Eirik's Saga and the Graenlendinga – give us the only extant account of further explorations west, recounting the exploits of Leif Eiriksson and Thorfinn Karlsefni, his merchant brother-in-law, who founded a colony they called **Vinland** in North America around 1000 AD. Crucially, the Norse settlers failed to establish reasonable relations with their Aboriginal neighbours – whom they called skraelings, literally "wretches" – and the perennial skirmishing that ensued eventually drove them out of Vinland, though they did return to secure raw materials for the next few decades; it seems likely that **L'Anse aux Meadows** is the result of one of these foragings.

The Norse carried on collecting timber from Labrador up until the fourteenth century, when a dramatic deterioration in the climate made the trip from Greenland too dangerous. Attacks from the Inuit and the difficulties of maintaining trading links with Scandinavia then took their toll on the main Greenland colonies. All contact between Greenland and the outside world was lost around 1410 and the last of the half-starved, disease-ridden survivors died out towards the end of the fifteenth century – just as Christopher Columbus was eyeing up his "New World".

6

ACCOMMODATION
L'ANSE AUX MEADOWS

★ **Quirpon Lighthouse Inn** ☎ 709 634 2285, ⓦ linkumtours.com. One of the region's most alluring hotels, out on isolated Quirpon Island ("kar-poon"), featuring ten rooms in the two old lighthouse keeper's houses from 1922. The inn boasts a spectacular location, standing next to the lighthouse with the cliffs jagging down below. Rates include the boat trip over (15min) and all meals; the dock in Quirpon village is 8km from L'Anse aux Meadows along a short gravel turning off Rte-436. Once here you can go whale- and iceberg-watching, rent kayaks and hike all over the island. May–Oct. **$425**

★ **Valhalla Lodge** Rte-436, Gunner's Cove ☎ 709 754 3105, ⓦ valhalla-lodge.com. The folks at the *Norsemen* (see below) also run this excellent B&B, with five en-suite rooms sharing a cosy TV room and sauna. The site also includes *Quoyle's House*, the luxurious cottage once owned by Annie Proulx, author of *The Shipping News*. Late May to late Sept. **$125**; *Quoyle's House* **$270**

Viking Village B&B Rte-436, Hay Cove ☎ 709 623 2238, ⓦ vikingvillage.ca. An inexpensive and accessible option is the all-year, five-room *Viking Village*, in a modern wood chalet 1km from L'Anse aux Meadows. **$88**

EATING

Dark Tickle St Lunaire-Griquet, Rte-436 (19km north of Rte-430) ☎ 709 623 2354, ⓦ darktickle.com. Shop selling all sorts of home-made products made from local berries, including bakeapples and partridgeberries. June–Sept daily 9am–6pm; Oct–May Mon–Fri 9am–5pm.

★ **The Norseman** Rte-436, L'Anse aux Meadows ☎ 709 754 3105, ⓦ valhalla-lodge.com. The best place to eat near the Viking site, serving fabulous locally inspired dishes such as fish chowder, baked cod, bakeapple cheesecake and caribou tenderloin. Mains $19–39. Late May to mid-Sept daily noon–9pm.

Labrador

One of the last great unspoiled adventure destinations, **Labrador** is home to the planet's largest herd of caribou, wandering polar bears, awe-inspiring waterfalls and a string of pristine coastal communities that have preserved a raw, nineteenth-century quality despite the onset of wi-fi and SUVs. Travel here takes some planning and can be expensive, but the rewards are considerable; you can still hike or point your kayak anywhere into the interior (most of which is Crown land), and camp, fish or meditate for a couple of days, totally cut off from civilization.

Labrador also has a rich cultural heritage, with two of the most important historic sights in Canada, **Red Bay** and **Battle Harbour**, on the coast. Around one third of the population of 29,000 lives here, while the remainder inhabit the towns of the interior: **Happy Valley-Goose Bay**, **Churchill Falls** and **Labrador City**, each offering quite different experiences. Labrador has a distinct identity to that of Newfoundland, with a diverse ethnic mix of white settlers, Métis, Innu and Inuit; the **Labrador flag** is flown everywhere with pride. Summer is the most pleasant time to visit, though winter can be fun – especially if you travel by snowmobile – and has the added bonus of seeing the spectacular **Northern Lights** (see page 797).

ARRIVAL AND DEPARTURE
LABRADOR

By plane Flights from Newfoundland, Nova Scotia and Québec connect Labrador to the rest of the world. Air Canada flies to Goose Bay from Halifax and to Wabush from Montréal, via Québec City and Sept-Îles. PAL Airlines flies from St John's, Deer Lake, Wabush and Lourdes de Blanc-Sablon to Goose Bay; flights from the latter are always listed as Blanc-Sablon local time, which is 30min behind the neighbouring Labrador coastal communities in winter and 1hr 30min behind in summer.

By ferry Labrador has ferry links from St Barbe on Newfoundland to Blanc-Sablon (May to early Jan 1–3 daily; 1hr 45min; ☎ 866 535 2567, ⓦ labradormarine.com;

$11.75 passengers, car and driver $35.25) on the Québec–Labrador border; reservations are recommended and all traffic must check in 1hr before departure. Departures from Blanc-Sablon are listed in Newfoundland time, not local time (unlike the airport; see above), so be careful if you plan to take the ferry and a flight on the same day. Relais Nordik (see page 320) runs less frequent ferries taking several days to find their way to Blanc-Sablon from Rimouski via numerous communities on the Québec north shore of the St Lawrence River.

By train The Québec North Shore & Labrador Railway runs an exhilarating 416km from Sept-Îles on Québec's North

Shore to Schefferville, primarily serving the iron ore mines of Labrador West and First Nations communities. Tshiuetin Rail Transportation Inc, a First Nations venture, operates passenger trains (reservations Mon–Fri 8am–noon & 1–4.30pm; ☎ 418 962 5530, ⓦ tshiuetin.net). Travelling all the way to the Innu/Naskapi settlement at Schefferville in Québec is somewhat pointless; it's better to get off at Emeril

Junction on the Trans-Labrador Hwy, 63km from Labrador City. Trains leave Sept-Îles for Emeril Junction Mon and Thurs at 7am (7hr) and arrive around 3pm; they depart on Tues and Fri at around noon and arrive at Sept-Îles around 7pm (around $80 one way). A taxi is required to get back and forth from Labrador City (CJ Cabs ☎ 709 944 7757); expect to pay at least $125 one way.

GETTING AROUND AND INFORMATION

By public transport There is no land-based public transport in Labrador. The passenger-only *Northern Ranger* ferry sails weekly from Happy Valley-Goose Bay, and is the main lifeline for the northern coast (see page 458).

By plane If you want to reach the distant outposts quickly, the only choice is by internal flights with Air Borealis (operated by PAL Airlines). It serves six coastal communities, most with daily flights.

By car If you want to explore the south coast but don't have your own transport, you can rent a car from Eagle

River Rent-a-Car in Forteau (☎ 709 931 3300). Unless you have an SUV it's probably a good idea to rent one here – note, though, petrol is more expensive here than in Newfoundland. Exploring the coast road is easily done in a couple of days – most rental firms allow you to drive to Cartwright, but no further along the Trans-Labrador Hwy (see page 457).

General information The best source of tourist information is ⓦ newfoundlandlabrador.com.

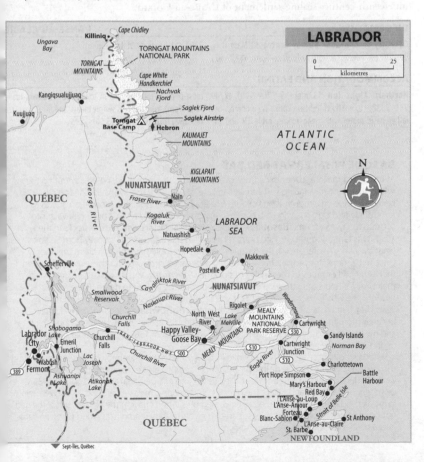

The Labrador Straits

Thanks to a regular ferry link from St Barbe in Newfoundland (see page 452), the **Labrador Straits** region (southern Labrador) is the most accessible part of the mainland and easily explored by car. The history of the area is at its most evocative in some of the old settlements along the **southern coast**, particularly so at **Red Bay** and the rebuilt fishing centre of **Battle Harbour** further north.

Blanc-Sablon

From tiny **BLANC-SABLON** in Québec most travellers head east into Labrador along **Rte-510**, which connects a string of former fishing camps that are now modest little places huddling against the coastal cliffs. There's nothing to see in Blanc-Sablon itself: the ferry terminal (see page 452) is 2km west of town, while the airport (see page 452) is a further 7km west, beyond **Lourdes de Blanc-Sablon**, the primary service centre in the area.

L'Anse-au-Claire

The first community heading into Labrador on Rte-510 is **L'ANSE-AU-CLAIRE**, 8km east of the Blanc-Sablon ferry terminal, which has the area's main source of information, the **Gateway to Labrador Visitor Centre**, housed in a 1909 church. From here you can follow the 3.4km trail along the coast to the **Jersey Rooms**, the ruins of the abandoned nineteenth-century sealing settlement of L'Anse-au-Cotard.

INFORMATION L'ANSE-AU-CLAIRE

Gateway to Labrador Visitor Centre 38 Main Hwy, Rte-510 (mid-June to Sept daily 9am–6pm; ☎ 709 931 2360, ⍟ labradorcoastaldrive.com).

ACCOMMODATION AND EATING

Northern Light Inn 58 Main St (Rte-510) ☎ 709 931 2332, ⍟ northernlightinn.com. A modern, but rather basic motel with clean rooms, cable TV and the most popular food options in town: the restaurant (daily 7am–9pm), which serves simple meals, and the *Greco* pizza takeaway (pizzas $10.50–25.50). $135

BASQUE WHALERS AT RED BAY

At its peak in the late sixteenth century, over two thousand men lived in Red Bay during the **whaling** season, producing half a million gallons of whale oil that was subsequently shipped back to Europe on a month-long voyage. Whale oil was used for light, lubrication and as an additive to drugs, soap and pitch; one 55-gallon barrel could fetch a price equivalent to $10,000 today – so for the **Basques** the discovery of Labrador's right-whale stocks in the 1530s was tantamount to striking gold. Yet as well as the treacherous journey from Spain to what they knew as Terranova, the Basques withstood terrible hardships to claim their booty. Once in Labrador, they rowed fragile wooden craft called *chalupas* into these rough seas and then attached drogues to the whales to slow them down. It was then a matter of following their prey for hours until the whale surfaced and could be lanced to death. Three factors brought the whale boom to an end: first, the Basques were so successful that within thirty years they had killed off more than fifteen thousand **right whales**; second, the industry became more hazardous with early freeze-ups in the 1580s; and, finally, many Basque ships and men were absorbed into the ill-fated Spanish Armada of 1588 – by the 1620s the annual migration was over.

Serious study of the Red Bay area began in 1977, when marine archeologists discovered the remains of three Basque **galleons** and four *chalupas*. Land excavations uncovered try-works (where the whale blubber was boiled down into oil), personal artefacts and, in 1982, a cemetery on Saddle Island where the remains of 140 young men were found. Many were lying in groups, indicating that they died as crew members when chasing the whales, but some had not been buried – suggesting at least part of the community died of starvation when an early freeze dashed their chances of getting home.

Forteau

Some 10km northeast along Rte-510 from L'Anse-au-Claire is **FORTEAU**, at its liveliest during the annual three-day **Bakeapple Festival** in mid-August. A worthwhile hike out of Forteau is the **Overfall Brook Trail**, which leads 1.3km from the village along the coast to a 30m-high waterfall.

ACCOMMODATION AND EATING FORTEAU

Grenfell Louie A. Hall B&B 3 Willow Ave ☎ 709 931 2916, ⊛ grenfellbandb.ca. In a 1946 nursing station, this B&B has simple, pleasant rooms – each named after a former staff member – and a common room. May–Sept. **$120**

Sea View Cottages & Restaurant 33 Main St (Rte-510) ☎ 709 931 2840, ⊛ labradorseaview.ca. The motel-like cabins are large and basic, but the restaurant (daily: Jan–April 11am–8pm; May–Dec 11am–9pm) is known for its caribou, seafood and home-baked goods. **$149**

Point Amour Lighthouse

L'Anse-Amour Rd (off Rte-510, between Forteau and L'Anse-au-Loup) • Mid-May to early Oct daily 9.30am–5pm • $6 • ☎ 709 927 5825, ⊛ pointamourlighthouse.ca

Drive 2km east of the village of **L'Anse-Amour** (which is 11km east of Forteau) on gravel roads and you'll reach the 36m-high **Point Amour Lighthouse**, which provides fabulous 360-degree views from the top of its 128-step tower. Completed in 1857 and still in use, its history and that of the whole straits region is laid out in the adjacent lightkeeper's quarters, staffed by costumed guides.

Labrador Straits Museum

11 Branch Rd (just off Rte-510), L'Anse-au-Loup • July to mid-Sept Mon–Sat 9.30am–5.30pm, Sun 1–5.30pm • $5 • ☎ 709 927 5077, ⊛ labradorstraitsmuseum.ca

Some 13km east of Forteau, in **L'ANSE-AU-LOUP**, the tiny **Labrador Straits Museum** is an endearing collection of local relics and curios, mainly from the 1920s and 1930s, though there are a few real gems: a wooden needle for mending codfish nets, a traditional *komatik* (sledge), bits from the 1922 wreck of HMS *Raleigh* and Labradorite from Nain. The story of the nearby 7500-year-old **burial mound** of a 12-year-old Archaic-Indian boy (the oldest-known funeral monument in North America), is also told in detail. You can see the mound itself – a well-defined heap of rocks – on the side road to Point Amour Lighthouse (see above), a few kilometres back.

Red Bay

It seems inconceivable today, but the sleepy village of **RED BAY** – 75km northeast of L'Anse-au-Claire on Rte-510 – was once the world's largest whaling port, occupied by Basque fishermen years before the arrival of the Pilgrims in New England. Despite the abundance of broken red tiles on the beaches, their presence here was eventually forgotten, and only rediscovered in the 1970s after obscure documents in Spain led to the astounding discovery of the remains of a Basque ship buried in the harbour.

Red Bay National Historic Site

11 Main Hwy (Rte-510) • Early June to early Oct daily 9am–5.30pm • $7.80 • ☎ 709 920 2142, ⊛ pc.gc.ca/redbay

Artefacts from the Basque archeological digs here can be viewed at the **Red Bay National Historic Site**. Start at the **reception centre**, where the discoveries are introduced with a twenty-minute film and the most impressive relic is displayed: one of the small *chalupas* (see page 454) actually used by the whalers in the 1580s. In all, seven ships have been found – academics speculate that the largest vessel was the *San Juan*, which is known to have sunk here in 1565, but this has never been proven. Down the road, the **interpretation centre** contains two floors of artefacts recovered from the wrecks and nearby **Saddle Island**, including astonishingly well-preserved clothing worn by sixteenth-century sailors. You can take a **boat trip** to Saddle Island itself (hourly departures from the interpretation centre daily 9am–4pm July–Sept;

6

DRIVING THE TRANS-LABRADOR HIGHWAY

As of 2019, much of the monumental 1208km Trans-Labrador Highway (TLH), from the Québec border near Labrador City to Blanc-Sablon on the south coast via Happy Valley-Goose Bay and Red Bay, was paved; even the remaining gravel sections can be passed in a normal car, but it's best to only attempt the trip in high summer. If you're renting, another problem might be your **rental policy**: most firms try to bar drivers from the roughest sections of the highway (between Cartwright Junction and Happy Valley). They can't physically stop you ignoring this rule but if you have an accident, insurance may not cover you. Check the latest situation for the current extent of paving. A greater barrier to renting is sheer distance; returning a car to Blanc-Sablon or anywhere in Newfoundland means driving a massive loop of almost 3000km through Québec (via Québec Rte-389) and the Maritimes via at least two ferries, while one-way drop-off fees are exorbitant.

$3), where you can roam around the eerie whalers' cemetery and other labelled sites on a self-guided tour.

ACCOMMODATION AND EATING   RED BAY

Whaler's Station 72–76 West Harbour Drive ☎ 709 920 2156, ⊛ redbaywhalers.ca. The main restaurant in town, offering simple but hearty meals (stick with the classic "chalupa" fish and chips) for $10–17. For accommodation, your best bet is the attached cabins, offering en-suite rooms with cable TV, some with kitchenettes. May–Oct. $115

Mary's Harbour

Northeast of Red Bay, gravel Rte-510 is gradually being paved all the way to Happy Valley – by 2018 the paved section had reached 85km up the coast to **MARY'S HARBOUR**, a settlement founded in 1930 by a handful of families after the hospital fire at Battle Harbour began an exodus to the mainland. Today it's a surprisingly vibrant little town, living primarily on the seasonal crab fishery and tourism. It's also a sensible place to spend the night, though if you can afford it, the main attraction here is **Battle Harbour** 9km offshore – signs lead through the village to the ferry dock.

ACCOMMODATION AND EATING   MARY'S HARBOUR

Riverlodge Hotel 6163 Main Rd (Rte-510) ☎ 709 921 6948, ⊛ riverlodgehotel.ca. Stay and eat at the comfortable hotel (with satellite TV) overlooking the river, where locals cook up hearty meals of roast beef, fried chicken, turkey and sometimes fresh fish and scallops in its restaurant (mains $14–23). Old Pete's Pub, also on the premises, is a good place to share stories with fellow travellers and locals. $130

Battle Harbour

Mid-June to mid-Sept • ☎ 709 921 6325, ⊛ battleharbour.com

Spending a night or two on the island of **BATTLE HARBOUR** is one of the most memorable experiences in Canada. This beautifully restored fishing port is visited by towering icebergs in spring and humpback whales in summer; killer whales often cruise right off the dock. Established in the 1770s, Battle Harbour became one of the world's busiest saltfish, salmon and sealing ports in the nineteenth century; Wilfred Grenfell opened a hospital here in 1893, it was home to a Marconi wireless station from 1904 and was the scene of Robert E. Peary's first news conference after he conquered the North Pole in 1909. A devastating fire in 1930 exacerbated long-term decline, and by the late 1960s most residents had been relocated to Mary's Harbour on the mainland – the last fish merchant was closed in the wake of the 1992 cod moratorium. Since then an epic restoration project by the Battle Harbour Historic Trust has resulted in a clutch of wonderfully evocative old wooden buildings opening to the public, a **visitor centre** and several walking trails; you can also **stay** in some of the old houses (see page 457). Many of the former residents of the town serve as guides and are as equally absorbing as the site itself – prepare for seriously traditional Labrador accents.

The best way to experience the island is to buy an overnight package, which includes all meals and the ferry across, but pricey **day-trips** can be arranged through **Cloud 9 Boat Charters and Tours** (see below).

ARRIVAL AND DEPARTURE

BATTLE HARBOUR

By ferry Daily ferry sailings (11am, return at 9am; 1hr) from Mary's Harbour to Battle Harbour, depart from the Grenfell Mission wharf and visitor centre on Main St; the cost is included in all accommodation packages.

Day trips Cloud 9 Boat Charters and Tours (15 Barney's Pond Rd; ☎ 709 921 6250, ⓦ cloud9boattours.ca) departs the wharf and visitor centre at 11am daily (mid-June to early Sept) heading back at 4pm, for a 5pm arrival at Mary's Harbour; day-trip rates range from $105–135.

ACCOMMODATION AND EATING

Package rates below include full board for two people, the ferry and a guided tour (extra guests and children aged 5–12 cost extra); after the first night, subsequent nights are cheaper (in parentheses below).

★ **Battle Harbour Inn** ☎ 709 921 6325, ⓦ battle harbour.com. Accommodation options include the doubles with shared bath in this antique-laden merchant house. $545 ($355)

★ **Cookhouse-Bunkhouse** ☎ 709 921 6325, ⓦ battle harbour.com. The old cookhouse now offers clean, hostel-like accommodation, with one dorm room and eleven berth-style beds. $225 ($130)

Grenfell Doctor's Cottage ☎ 709 921 6325, ⓦ battle harbour.com. You can stay in one of four cottages on the island, including the self-catering *Grenfell Doctor's Cottage*, with one bedroom on the ground floor and two bedrooms on the second, plus full kitchen. $495 plus $175 ($80) per person

Isaac Smith House ☎ 709 921 6325, ⓦ battleharbour. com. This rustic, three-bedroom cottage (the oldest on the island) has only oil lamps and wood fires, plus a modern kitchen and bath. Only rented as a single unit. $365 plus $175 per person first night (then $80 per night)

Port Hope Simpson

Heading northwest on Rte-510 from Mary's Harbour, it's 55km to **PORT HOPE SIMPSON**, another isolated fishing community and your last chance for petrol and provisions before the long haul up to Cartwright.

ACCOMMODATION AND EATING

PORT HOPE SIMPSON

Alexis Hotel 2 Alexis Drive (Rte-510) ☎ 709 960 0228, ⓦ alexishotel.ca. Right on the water, this is a decent place to stay, with satellite TV, meals (daily 7am–10pm), laundry and kayak rentals. $155

Cartwright

With the completion of the Trans-Labrador Highway in 2009, tiny **CARTWRIGHT**, around 200km from Port Hope Simpson, was left stranded 90km north of the main road via Rte-530. It remains a useful pit-stop on the drive to Happy Valley-Goose Bay nevertheless, with several attractions to justify the detour. The settlement is named after Captain George Cartwright, one of the first European traders to coexist with the Aboriginal peoples when he established a post here in 1775. All that remains of his former shack, grandly titled **Caribou Castle**, is a large rock marking the boundary of his land, right at the end of Main Street facing the water. Nearby you'll find a small **memorial** to Cartwright in the old cemetery.

Today, Cartwright is best known for two things: some of the finest **salmon fishing** in the world (along the **Eagle River**; July only) and **Wonderstrand**, a 56km-long sandy beach that can only be visited by boat or ATV (12km from Cartwright). The Vikings almost certainly visited the latter – their descriptions of the "Wunderstrand" are too precise to be anywhere else. Experience Labrador (☎ 709 938 7444, ⓦ experiencelabrador.ca) can arrange fishing trips and excursions to the beach (July & Aug; from $240 for 2hr 30min; $520 for two people for 5hr), where you can spend a day – or longer – hiking the beach, stumbling across historical remains, the odd moose and virtually no one else; it rates as one of Canada's great adventures. Its office is at

6

the **Mealy Mountain Gallery**, 20 Lethbridge Lane. Note that the **Cartwright Hotel** was destroyed by fire in 2013 – contact Experience Labrador for accommodation tips.

Happy Valley-Goose Bay

Sandwiched between the mighty Churchill River and the westernmost tip of sprawling Lake Melville, the town of **HAPPY VALLEY-GOOSE BAY** is the principal transport and administrative hub of Labrador, as well as its largest settlement (with around 8100 people).

The town is a relatively recent creation, established when US forces built the **Goose Bay** airfield in 1941; this eventually became a sprawling NATO military base, housing up to twelve thousand military personnel. **Happy Valley**, where most of the shops and restaurants are located a few kilometres from the airfield, is a fairly quiet, laidback sort of place, originally developed to house the workers for the base. In 2006 NATO left, leaving the base managed by a handful of Canadian Air Force personnel, and the town struggling to adjust to potentially devastating social and economic changes. Against all the odds, it's done incredibly well since then: jobs related to the creation of **Nunatsiavut** (see page 461), Labrador Health Authority and the mining sector have led to a mini-housing boom, and the base is being converted into a major business park.

The distinctions between the Goose Bay and Happy Valley sections of the town (around 4km apart) have largely disappeared since 2006, and new housing projects have effectively linked the two along the main drag, **Hamilton River Road**. There's no real centre, and you'll need a car to get around.

Northern Lights Military Museum

170 Hamilton River Rd • Tues–Sat 10am–5.30pm • Free • ☎ 709 896 5939

The town's two museums largely focus on its military heritage – the **Northern Lights Military Museum** occupies a room in the basement of a general store and is stuffed with military memorabilia, primarily weapons and uniforms.

Labrador Military Museum

Canex building, 381 Banshee Blvd • July & Aug Mon, Tues, Thurs & Fri 9am–noon & 1–4pm, Sat & Sun 1–4pm • Free • Call ☎ 709 896 6900 ext 2177 to confirm times.

The **Labrador Military Museum** (which relocated to swish new premises on the old air force base in 2019), documents the history of the Canadian, British, American, Dutch and German military presence with displays of flags, insignia and radar apparatus. Particularly poignant are the references to the all-too-frequent fatal air crashes that have occurred here in past decades.

Dome Mountain

Don't leave town without driving up to 227m-high **Dome Mountain** (aka Pine Tree Lookout) around 16km from the visitor centre; there are no signs and the road becomes a potholed, jarring gravel track barely passable in a regular vehicle, but the views of the town, Churchill River, Lake Melville and the mountains are stupendous. To get there, drive towards the airport on Loring Drive, then take a left along Lahr Boulevard; take another left on River Road and follow this to the end – you'll need to turn left two more times before the dirt road rises up towards the old radar tower on the summit.

ARRIVAL AND INFORMATION

HAPPY VALLEY-GOOSE BAY

By plane Goose Bay Airport (ⓦ goosebayairport.com) is located on the former NATO base, in the old Goose Bay area of town. Its sole ATM is unreliable, so make sure you bring cash. There's no public transport, so you'll have to rely on taxis (Cooney's Taxi; ☎ 709 896 3311). National (Mon–Fri & Sun 8am–11pm, Sat 8am–8.30pm; ☎ 709 896 5575) and Budget (daily 8am–10pm; ☎ 709 896 2973) have booths at the airport. To get to town, head along Loring Drive and

6

turn right at the traffic lights (the only ones in town) onto Hamilton River Rd.

By ferry The ferry terminal is 5km north of the visitor centre on the shores of Lake Melville: the *Northern Ranger* docks here (see page 461). You won't find much at the wharf: taxis into Goose Bay should be around $20, and $25 into Happy Valley.

Visitor centre Happy Valley-Goose Bay's Visitor Information Centre is at 6 Hillcrest Rd (June–Aug Mon–Fri 8.30am–8pm, Sat & Sun 9am–5pm; Sept–May Mon–Fri 8.30am–noon & 1–4.30pm; ☎ 709 896 3489, ⓦ tourismlabrador.com); it provides brochures, free wi-fi and helps plan trips out of town.

ACCOMMODATION

Big Land Bed & Breakfast 34 Palliser Crescent ☎ 709 896 2082, ⓦ biglandbedandbreakfast.com. Centrally located B&B with three rooms with private bathrooms and satellite TV; there's a choice of breakfast options. **$90**

★ **Royal Inn** 5 Royal Ave ☎ 709 896 2456, ⓦ royalinn

andsuites.ca. This centrally located, plush motel-like option is the best value in town; continental breakfast is included, rooms are new and comfy and it has self-service laundry and decent satellite TV. It's popular and can get very busy and noisy at times. **$140**

EATING AND DRINKING

Mariner's Galley 25 Loring Drive ☎ 709 896 9301. Excellent option for breakfast, lunch and dinner, specializing in steaks and fine seafood (mains $15–24); most popular joint for out-of-towners. The nautical theme is enhanced by the wooden ship centrepiece. Daily 6am–9pm.

★ **Maxwell's & Bentley's** 97 Hamilton River Rd ☎ 709 896 3565, ⓦ maxwellsandbentleys.ca. Located right on

the waterfront, *Bentley's* restaurant is the main spot for a night out, featuring a sports bar showing all the big events. Lunch specials are also good, as well as pastas, salmon, cod dishes, steaks and grills (mains $15–22). The other side of the building morphs into *Maxwell's* nightclub Thurs–Sat nights. Daily happy hour 4–7pm. Restaurant Mon–Sat 11am–9.30pm; club Thurs–Sat 11.30am–3am.

North West River

From the visitor centre in Happy Valley-Goose Bay paved Rte-520 heads north 38km to **NORTH WEST RIVER**, one of the oldest settlements in Labrador and picturesquely surrounded by three vast bodies of water: Grand Lake, Little Lake and the briny Lake Melville. In summer you'll see several makeshift camps along the road – these belong to local **Innu** from the community of **Sheshatshiu**. You'll pass their village just before crossing the bridge into North West River, but there's little point in stopping here.

North West River itself was a fur-trading post established by the French in 1743 and subsequently developed by Métis and English trappers. The **Hudson's Bay Company** arrived in 1836 and dominated the fur trade and life in the village until the construction of Goose Bay airbase started to draw the trappers away – today most of the 550 or so inhabitants work in Happy Valley-Goose Bay.

Labrador Heritage Museum

3 River Rd • Mid-June to mid-Sept daily 9am–5pm • $3 • ☎ 709 497 8858, ⓦ labradorheritagemuseum.ca

The Hudson's Bay trading post in North West River closed in the 1970s, but the **Labrador Heritage Museum** incorporates the old Hudson's Bay store, restored to its 1930 appearance. Inside exhibits cover the history of the area, enhanced with a life-size reconstruction of a trapper's "tilt" (cabin) and a curious assortment of artefacts; look out for the disturbing "tonsil snare", and a portable steel incubator – the guides know one of the babies transported in it (he's now in his 60s). The museum also has an intriguing account of the ill-fated 1903 **Wallace-Hubbard expedition** into the Labrador interior.

Labrador Interpretation Centre

2 Portage Rd • May to Sept Mon–Sat 9am–4.30pm, Sun noon–4.30pm • Free • ☎ 709 497 8566, ⓦ therooms.ca/labrador-interpretation-centre

The **Labrador Interpretation Centre** has a temporary gallery (usually displaying local art) and an enlightening permanent display introducing the four main cultural groups

6

THE NORTHERN RANGER

Labrador North is the region at its most remote, yet the coast is fairly easy to explore, thanks to the weekly, summer-only **ferry service** of the **MV Northern Ranger**, which is becoming popular as a budget cruise. The foot-passenger-only ship, run by Nunatsiavut Marine (☎855 896 2262, ⓦlabradorferry.ca), leaves once a week from Goose Bay to Nain (usually Mon 1pm, arrives Nain 12.30pm Weds; departs Nain 4.30pm Weds), with stops at Rigolet (6hr 30min), Makkovik (18hr 30min), Postville (23hr), Hopedale (30hr) and the Innu community of Natuashish (35hr). In most cases the hour or so the ferry spends at every stop is plenty for a look around. Should you decide to stop for longer, you'll have to stay for several days until the ferry docks in again, and will have to ask around for somewhere to stay, though it's generally not too hard to find accommodation. The ferries run from mid-June to late November; soon after this, the Arctic ice pack closes in to seal up the area for the rest of the year. The late-season schedule is notoriously unreliable since storms can delay sailings, sometimes for days.

Fares are based on the number of nautical miles travelled, with supplements for cabin space, which you should reserve well in advance, otherwise it's likely you'll have no option but to make yourself as comfortable as possible on the aircraft-style seats. A single trip from Happy Valley-Goose Bay to Nain costs around $219 and $489 for a standard cabin. Prices at the **onboard canteen** are reasonable but choice is limited and the meals are reminiscent of overcooked school dinners, so it's worth stocking up on provisions beforehand.

---

of Labrador (Innu, Inuit, Métis and Settlers). The guides are extremely knowledgeable and are happy to explain the significance of the most intriguing artefacts on show: Innu tea dolls, the Innu shaking tent and a chunky sculpture made of serpentine (a dark green mineral) by Inuit artist Gilbert Hay.

Labrador North

The **north** is the most untouched and least visited part of Labrador. Up here, **Inuit** culture begins to assert itself; polar bears are common; there are no cars in most of the settlements; and arctic char are still hung in the street to dry. In 2005 most of the coast became part of autonomous **Nunatsiavut** (not to be confused with Nunavut; ⓦtourismnunatsiavut.com), giving the Inuit special rights and ownership of 15,800 square kilometres. Based in Hopedale and Nain, the Nunatsiavut government (which remains nominally part of Labrador) has authority over local health, education and justice, with an elected president every four years. North of Nain, the hauntingly beautiful **Torngat Mountains National Park**, Canada's most isolated national park, beckons the adventurous.

The *Northern Ranger* (see above) from Happy Valley-Goose Bay takes three days to reach **Nain** – and a sudden storm can leave you stranded for days in one of the tinier midway settlements. Travelling only by plane and passenger ferry certainly creates lots of opportunity to spy whales, seals and all manner of northern wildlife, plus **icebergs** – around three thousand drift over from Greenland every year.

Nain

Labrador's most northern settlement, **NAIN** has a population of just under 1500, despite being the capital of Nunatsiavut. Founded as a Moravian mission in 1771, fishing is the primary activity here, though the town is also known for its adroit Inuit **carvers** and nearby **Labradorite** quarry at Ten Mile Bay (most of the stone is processed in Italy and used for floor tiles).

ACCOMMODATION **NAIN**

Atsanik Lodge Sand Banks Rd ☎709 922 2910, ⓔatsaniklabrador@msn.com. This is the dependable place to stay in town, and has satellite TV, en-suite rooms, wi-fi and restaurant. **$175**

6

Torngat Mountains National Park

Nain is as far north as you can get using public transport in Labrador, and to travel another 200km to the awe-inspiring wilderness of the **Torngat Mountains National Park** you need to take a tour, rent a boat or charter a plane – all very expensive options (see box, below). If you can afford it, you'll have the utterly intoxicating experience of hiking in the highest range east of the Rockies, spot loads of polar bears and truly spectacular fjords. The **Torngat Mountains Base Camp** operates from mid-July to August at St John's Harbour in Saglek Bay (the southern boundary of the park). Here you'll find tent accommodation and excursions via speedboat, longliner, helicopter and fixed-wing charters.

Labrador West

A vast expanse of forested mountains, lakes and tracts of tundra, **Labrador West** is punctuated by towns that live to serve the phenomenal mining and engineering projects that have sprouted up here since the 1960s. Tours of these mind-blowing facilities are the area's most obvious attractions, but **Labrador City** is also an important stop on the Trans-Labrador Highway.

Churchill Falls Generating Station

Tours daily 9am, 1.30pm & 7.30pm • Free • Make reservations in advance by calling ☎ 709 925 3335 (Mon–Fri 8am–noon & 1–5pm), Ⓦ nalcorenergy.com

Few people would normally get excited about touring a power station, but the **Churchill Falls Generating Station**, 288km west from Happy Valley-Goose Bay on Rte-500, is not your average public utility. The sheer size of this mammoth project is overwhelming. The only way to appreciate its scale is to take a two-and-a-half-hour **tour**.

The facility exploits the raw power of the **Churchill River** as it plunges 75m into McLean Canyon. Around 6700 square kilometres – an area three and a half times the size of Lake Ontario – was dammed for the development, a project conceived by the then premier, Joe Smallwood, to boost Newfoundland's economy. Wrangling with financial backers, and then with the Québec government, delayed its completion until 1971. Québec came out tops: it reserved the right to buy all the electricity for 65 years at a low fixed rate – Hydro Québec has since been selling this power on to the US at ten or twenty times what it pays Newfoundland and Labrador. The most infamous contract in Canadian history, it's been a source of deep bitterness for Labradorians ever since.

Labrador City and Wabush

Some 238km west of Churchill Falls and something of a shock to come across, **LABRADOR CITY** and neighbouring **WABUSH** are two lively communities of wide streets, shopping malls and fast-food joints in the middle of nowhere. Both were established in the 1960s to serve the nearby **iron ore mines** which still dominate the local economy and, with a combined population of around ten thousand, they make up the largest concentration of people in Labrador. Don't expect grimy mining towns – both are modern and tidy places with plenty of families, lakeside parks, services and schools.

TOURING THE TORNGAT

The Torngat Mountains Base Camp (☎ 709 896 8582, Ⓦ thetorngats.com) offers packaged **excursions to Torngat Mountains National Park** (late July to Aug) that include charter flights with PAL Airlines from Goose Bay to Saglek airstrip (it's 1hr 30min to Nain for a brief stop, then 40min to Saglek), and onward zodiac and boat transport to the Torngat Base Camp (15–20min) at St John's Harbour in Saglek Bay. Packages also include all meals, tent accommodation, and guided excursions (with Inuit "bear guards") – prices start at $5648 for two nights/three days.

LABRADOR MINE TOURS

Despite falling global demand, half of Canada's iron ore output is produced in Labrador West, from canyon-like open pit mines that are serviced by oversized 20m-long dump trucks. The only way to appreciate the superhuman scale of what goes on here is to take a **mine tour**, which you can arrange at Gateway Labrador (see page 463). The biggest and most mind-boggling facility belongs to **Iron Ore Company of Canada** in Labrador City; it normally offers regular tours from July to August (Wed & Sun 1.30pm) for $10. Call Gateway in advance to check the current situation. Arcelor Mittal also offers free tours of its **Mont-Wright mine**, the largest open-pit mine in Quebec near the town of Fermont, 25km from Labrador City (mid-June to mid-Aug; ☎ 418 287 5339).

6

Wabush is the smaller of the two, located off the Trans-Labrador Highway (Rte-500) on Rte-503, and you're better off focusing on Labrador City, just 4km away on the main highway.

Gateway Labrador

1365 Rte-500 • Late June to Aug Mon–Wed 9am–6pm, Thurs & Fri 9am–8pm, Sat & Sun noon–8pm • Museum $5 • ☎ 709 944 5399, Ⓦ gatewaylabrador.ca

Gateway Labrador, on the main highway on the edge of Labrador City, doubles as the local visitor centre. Inside you'll find a well-presented **museum** outlining the history of Labrador West, from the early days of the fur trappers to the recent boom in mining and energy.

ARRIVAL AND DEPARTURE   LABRADOR WEST

By plane Wabush Airport lies midway between the two towns on Rte-503. Budget (☎ 709 282 1234) and National (☎ 709 282 3059) have desks at the terminal and taxis (CJ Cabs ☎ 709 944 7757) meet most flights.

ACCOMMODATION AND EATING

Two Seasons Inn 96 Avalon Drive ☎ 709 944 2661, Ⓦ twoseasonsinn.ca. This comfy, centrally located hotel features modern rooms with fridges, a/c and cable TV, plus a restaurant open daily 6.30am–10pm (think cod "O gratin" and chowder). **$150**

Wabush Hotel 9 Grenfell Drive, Wabush ☎ 709 282 3221, Ⓦ wabushhotel.com. Giant chalet-style hotel dating from 1960, with aging motel-style rooms and the *Grenfell Restaurant* offering all-you-can-eat buffets featuring Canadian and (somewhat bizarrely) Chinese dishes (call ahead for times). **$160**

The Prairie Provinces

CALGARY STAMPEDE

The Prairie Provinces

Spreading over the provinces of Manitoba, Saskatchewan and Alberta, the vast lands between Ontario in the east and the Rocky Mountains in the west are commonly called "the Prairies". This is certainly not Canada's glamour region, with the main cities caricatured as dull and the scenery monotonous. In truth, this image is unfair and comes mainly from the fact that most cross-country journeys follow Trans-Canada 1 through generally flat and treeless plains. Here isolated farms guard thousands of acres of swaying wheat or immense grasslands with giant cattle herds. But these landscapes only typify the region's southernmost part, and even then they're broken up by the occasional river valley and range of low-lying hills. The prairie's other major cross-country route – Hwy-16 or the Yellowhead Route – lies to the north and travels through a more diverse landscape of low hills and sporadic Aspen Parkland forests.

7

Further north again, this transitional zone gives way to the vast and sparsely inhabited boreal forest. Here conifers, rivers and myriad lakes cover the rocky outcrops of the Canadian Shield and well over half the entire region – stretching north to the Northwest Territories and the hostile, treeless tundra around the Hudson Bay. These northerly climes are characterized by deep, cold winters that alternate with brief, bright summers, when the top few centimetres of topsoil thaw to create millions of stagnant pools of water where mosquitoes thrive. Yet the region remains captivating for its sense of desolate wilderness; a staggering number of first-rate backcountry canoe routes and wildlife that includes caribou, polar bear, bison and many migratory birds.

The eastern gateway to the prairies is **Winnipeg**, which rewards a stopover, with some interesting historical sights, restaurants and nightlife. The city can also provide a base for exploring the varied lakes and plains of **Southeastern Manitoba** and, if you've got the time, Northern Manitoba, where the biggest draw is the desolate town of **Churchill**, on the southern shore of Hudson Bay, one of the world's best places to see **beluga whales** and **polar bears**.

The more varied scenery makes **Yellowhead Route** (Hwy-16) from Winnipeg to Edmonton (1310km away) the best route west. It takes its name from a light-haired Iroquois guide nicknamed *Tête Jaune* ("yellow head") by the *voyageurs*, French-speaking boatmen who plied the waterways transporting people, furs and supplies. The culture of original settlers is preserved today in small towns like **Dauphin**, but the route is most rewarding for its easy side-trips to two national parks, **Riding Mountain** in Manitoba and **Prince Albert** in Saskatchewan, both with good hiking and canoeing. The Yellowhead Route also runs through **Saskatoon**, Saskatchewan's largest city, an ordinary but likeable place thanks to an attractive riverside setting and good restaurants. Nearby are important Métis and Plains

---

TIME ZONES

Manitoba and Saskatchewan are both on **Central Time**. In winter, both provinces run one hour behind Ontario and one hour ahead of Alberta, which is on **Mountain Time**. In summer, Manitoba adopts daylight saving time but Saskatchewan does not: so between April and October, Saskatchewan runs on the same time as Alberta and one hour behind Manitoba.

POLAR BEARS IN CHURCHILL

Highlights

❶ Canoeing in Whiteshell Provincial Park
Easily organized canoe adventures get you deep
into the wilderness; Prince Albert National Park is
a similarly jaw-dropping choice. See page 485

❷ Churchill Make this once-in-a-lifetime trip
north to witness polar bears in the wild, snorkel
with beluga whales or see the Northern Lights.
See page 490

❸ Little Manitou Lake Float your way to better
health in lake or spa waters that are three times
saltier than the Dead Sea. See page 499

❹ Grasslands National Park Strike out off

the beaten track to this beautiful – and under-
visited – expanse of prairie landscape. See
page 529

❺ Drumheller Go back to Jurassic times at the
Royal Tyrrell Museum and explore Alberta's arid
and unforgiving, but beautiful, Badlands. See
page 538

❻ Calgary Stampede The best-known
Canadian rodeo celebrates plains cowboy
culture, with everything from bull-riding and
blacksmith competitions, to live country music
and line dancing. See page 541

HIGHLIGHTS ARE MARKED ON THE MAP ON PAGE 468

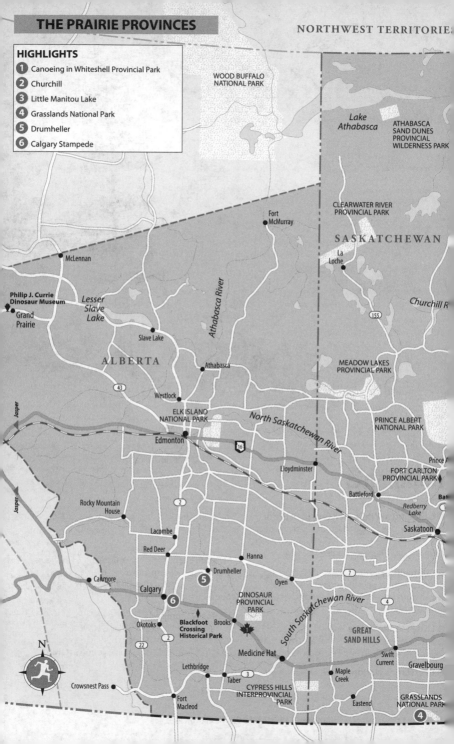

Indians sites. Once in Alberta, the Yellowhead continues to **Edmonton**, a slightly bleak but bustling city that's a gateway to an immense expanse of low hills and boreal forest to the north.

However, the quickest route west from Winnipeg is **Trans-Canada Hwy-1**, which briskly slices through 1500km of bland and productive prairie on its way to the Rockies. Once the novelty of all the hypnotically swaying wheat, oceans of dazzling yellow rapeseed and the big skies with their ever-changing clouds wears off, you can preserve your sanity with a series of diverting side-trips. These include old farmsteads, lush **provincial parks**, the easy-going city and Mountie-capital of **Regina**, the gritty little atmospheric town of **Moose Jaw**, with its worthwhile Tunnels of Moose Jaw attraction, and restored **Fort Walsh**. With more time, strike out further to the attractive coulees and buttes of the pristine and wonderfully empty **Grasslands National Park**. The first big town in Alberta is **Medicine Hat**, where **Hwy-3** begins – the most direct route to Vancouver. Otherwise, continuing on Hwy-1, the ranching belt is interrupted by the intriguing and arid **Badlands** around **Drumheller** where dinosaurs left abundant traces. The region is within the catchment of **Calgary**, the oil town and self-styled cowboy city famous for the is **Calgary Stampede** and for being the main gateway to the Canadian Rockies (see page 552).

INFORMATION AND GETTING AROUND THE PRAIRIE PROVINCES

GETTING AROUND

By train VIA Rail operates just two passenger trains in the region: the main east–west line between Toronto and Vancouver, via Winnipeg, Saskatoon and Jasper, while a northern line runs from Winnipeg to Churchill, beyond the reach of the road.

INFORMATION

Provincial tourism organizations for the prairie region are:

Travel Manitoba ☎204 927 7800, ☎800 665 0040, ⓦtravelmanitoba.com.

Tourism Saskatchewan ☎306 787 9600, ☎877 237 2273, ⓦtourismsaskatchewan.com.

Travel Alberta ☎780 427 4321, ☎800 252 3782, ⓦtravelalberta.com.

PROVINCIAL PARKS

While the National Parks of Manitoba, Saskatchewan and Alberta probably contain the finest landscapes, all these provinces also have worthwhile Provincial Parks, with thousands of acres of wilderness, lakes, rivers and forests, great hikes and hundreds of kilometres of canoe routes. Many draw local campers in droves on summer weekends and each province has its own park regulations.

MANITOBA

Entry to **Manitoba**'s provincial parks (ⓦmanitobaparks.com) costs $5/vehicle/day (multi-day passes available), while entry by boat, foot or bike is free. Park campsites ($11.55–28.35) can be reserved from April to September via the Parks Reservation Service ($10/reservation; ☎204 948 3333, ☎888 482 2267; ⓦprspub.gov.mb.ca).

SASKATCHEWAN

Entry to **Saskatchewan**'s provincial parks (ⓦsaskparks.net) is $10/vehicle/day, $24 for three days. Between mid-May and August you can reserve all park campsites ($18–40; ☎855 737 7275, ⓦsaskparks.goingtocamp.com) for a $12 fee, which is a better bet than simply turning up – particularly at weekends.

ALBERTA

Entry to **Alberta**'s provincial parks (ⓦalbertaparks.ca is free, but camping costs $5–26. At peak times the most popular campgrounds are largely reservation-only ($12/reservation; ⓦreserve. albertaparks.ca).

Brief history

If you're in the Prairie Provinces in the winter, when Artic winds can bring temperatures below -30°C, it's hard to imagine how the European pioneers survived, huddled together in remote log cabins. Yet they did, and went on to cultivate, between about 1895 and 1914, the great swath of land making up the wheat belt and the Aspen Parkland, turning it into one of the world's most productive wheat-growing areas. This development came with a high price: the nomadic culture of the **Plains Indians** was almost entirely destroyed and the disease-ravaged, half-starved survivors were dumped into a string of meagre reservations. Similarly, the **Métis** – descendants of white fur traders and Aboriginal women – who for over two centuries had acted as intermediaries between the two cultures, found themselves overwhelmed, their desperate attempts to maintain their independence leading to a brace of futile rebellions (see page 505).

With the Métis and the First Nations out of the way, thousands of European immigrants concentrated on wheat yields. But with prosperity so dependent on grain prices and railroad charges, the region's farmers experienced alarming booms and busts throughout the twentieth century. This situation continues to affect the prairie economies, although Saskatchewan in particular has diversified, exploiting its supplies of potash (fertilizer) and some of the same vast oil and gas reserves that underpin Alberta's economy. Even so, prairie farmers often struggle to make ends meet when wheat prices fall and so formed **wheat pools**, which attempt to control freight charges and sell the grain at the best possible time. The political spin-off was the evolution of a strong socialist tradition, built on the farmers' mistrust of markets. For many years Saskatchewan was a stronghold of the **Co-operative Commonwealth Federation (CCF)**, the forerunner of the New Democratic Party; in 1944 the CCF formed the country's first leftist provincial government, pushing through bills to set up provincially-run medical and social security schemes, which the rest of Canada eventually adopted.

Winnipeg

With around 700,000 inhabitants, **WINNIPEG** accounts for more than half of Manitoba's population, and lies at Canada's centre, sandwiched between the US border to the south and the infertile Canadian Shield to the north and east. The city's been the gateway to the prairies since 1873, and a major transcontinental hub when the railroad arrived twelve years later. From the very beginning Winnipeg was described as the city where "the West began", and it still has something of that gateway feel. Certainly, Winnipeg makes for an enjoyable stopover, with all the main attractions a reasonable walk from each other. **The Forks**, a riverside development of shops, cafés and attractions, is the obvious visitor hub and buzzes with tourists and locals alike all summer. Next door, the eye-catching **Canadian Museum for Human Rights** gives the area a heavyweight attraction, while just across the Red River, the francophone neighbourhood of **St Boniface** has a delightful museum in the house and chapel of the Grey Nuns, who canoed here from Montréal in 1844. Then, five minutes' walk north of the forks, the happening **Exchange District** showcases early twentieth-century Canadian architecture and is noted for its restaurants and performing-arts scene. A block away, the **Manitoba Museum**, uses engaging reconstructions and dioramas to explore provincial history. Winnipeg's commercial downtown stretches southwest of the Exchange District along its main drag, Portage Avenue, where the **Winnipeg Art Gallery** boasts the world's largest Inuit art collection. Winnipeg also makes a useful base for day-trips to pioneer sites, beaches and canoeing of southeastern Manitoba (see page 482).

Brief history

Named after the **Cree** word for murky water ("*win-nipuy*"), Winnipeg owes much of its history to the Red and Assiniboine rivers, which meet close to its centre at **The Forks**. Fort Rouge was founded nearby in 1738 in an attempt to extend French influence west – and prospered from good connections north to Lake Winnipeg and the Hudson Bay, and west across the plains along the Assiniboine.

After the defeat of New France in 1763, local trading was absorbed and dominated by the Montréal-based **North West Company (NWC)**, until Thomas Douglas, the **Earl of Selkirk**, bought a controlling interest in the rival **Hudson's Bay Company (HBC)**, in 1809. Douglas resettled many of his own impoverished Scottish crofters in farmland around The Forks, which he named the Red River Colony, or Assiniboia. For the next thirty years, the colony sustained both farmers and Métis hunters, and trade was established along the Red River to Minnesota. But with the decline of buffalo herds in the 1860s

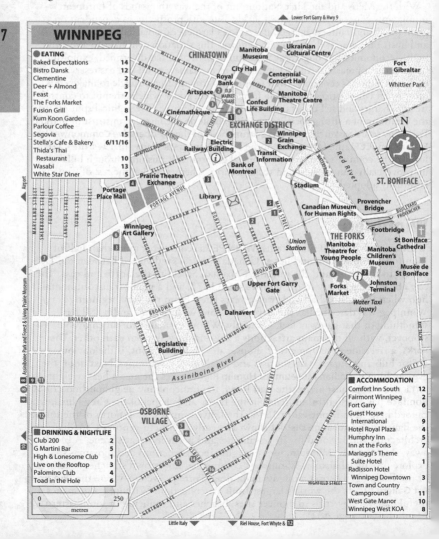

7

WINNIPEG

● EATING

Baked Expectations	14
Bistro Dansk	12
Clementine	2
Deer + Almond	3
Feast	7
The Forks Market	9
Fusion Grill	8
Kum Koon Garden	1
Parlour Coffee	4
Segovia	15
Stella's Cafe & Bakery	6/11/16
Thida's Thai Restaurant	10
Wasabi	13
White Star Diner	5

■ DRINKING & NIGHTLIFE

Club 200	2
G Martini Bar	5
High & Lonesome Club	1
Live on the Rooftop	3
Palomino Club	4
Toad in the Hole	6

■ ACCOMMODATION

Comfort Inn South	12
Fairmont Winnipeg	2
Fort Garry	6
Guest House International	9
Hotel Royal Plaza	4
Humphry Inn	5
Inn at the Forks	7
Mariaggi's Theme Suite Hotel	1
Radisson Hotel Winnipeg Downtown	3
Town and Country Campground	11
West Gate Manor	10
Winnipeg West KOA	8

Lower Fort Garry & Hwy 9

CHINATOWN

Manitoba Museum

Ukrainian Cultural Centre

Fort Gibraltar

Whittier Park

WILLIAM AVENUE
BANNATYNE AVENUE
MCDERMOT AVE

City Hall

Royal Bank

Artspace

OLD MARKET SQUARE

Centennial Concert Hall

MARKET AVE

NOTRE DAME AVENUE

Cinémathèque

Confed Life Building

Manitoba Theatre Centre

CUMBERLAND AVENUE

EXCHANGE DISTRICT

Winnipeg Grain Exchange

Red River

ST. BONIFACE

QU'APPELLE AVENUE

Electric Railway Building

Transit Information

WATER AVE. TACHE

Bank of Montreal

ELLICE AVENUE

Prairie Theatre Exchange

Stadium

Portage Place Mall

PORTAGE AVENUE

Library

Canadian Museum for Human Rights

Provencher Bridge

BOULEVARD PROVENCHER

Footbridge

St Boniface Cathedral

GRAHAM AVE

THE FORKS

Winnipeg Art Gallery

ST. MARY AVENUE

Union Station

Manitoba Theatre for Young People

Manitoba Children's Museum

Musée de St Boniface

YORK AVENUE

BROADWAY

Upper Fort Garry Gate

Forks Market

Johnston Terminal

Dalnavert

Water Taxi (quay)

BROADWAY

ASSINIBOINE AVENUE

ST. MARY'S ROAD

GOULET ST

Legislative Building

Assiniboine River

RIVER AVE

OSBORNE VILLAGE

ROSLYN ROAD

STRAND BROOK AVE

DONALD STREET

LYNDALE DRIVE

HIGHFIELD STREET

RIVER AVE

WARDLAW AVE

GERTRUDE AVE

WARD LAW AVE

GERTRUDE AVE

0 ——— 250
metres

Little Italy

Riel House, Fort Whyte & **12**

Airport

Assiniboine Park and Forest & Living Prairie Museum

N

WINNIPEG FESTIVALS

Festival du Voyageur Ten days in Feb ⓦfestivalvoyageur.mb.ca. St Boniface's French-Canadian heritage is honoured annually in the Festival du Voyageur, ten days of February fun, whose events lead up to a torchlit procession and the Governor's Ball, where everyone dresses in period costume.

Manito Ahbee Mid-May ⓦmanitoahbee.com. One of North America's largest pow wows, which celebrates Aboriginal culture in music, dance, arts and crafts.

Pride Winnipeg Late May ⓦpridewinnipeg.com. Large LGBTQ festival with a colourful parade and dozens of associated events and performances over nine days.

Winnipeg International Jazz Festival Mid-June ⓦjazzwinnipeg.com. The biggest of Winnipeg's ambitious summer programme of open-air concerts is this nine-day jazz festival.

Winnipeg Folk Festival Early July ⓦwinnipegfolkfestival.ca. A three-day extravaganza featuring over a hundred concerts, held at Birds Hill Provincial Park, 25km northeast of the city.

Winnipeg Fringe Festival Late July ⓦwinnipegfringe.com. A ten-day event of theatrical productions, held in the Exchange District.

Folklorama Early Aug ⓦfolklorama.ca. Apart from the music festivals, the biggest festival in Manitoba celebrates Winnipeg's multiethnic population. The festival has over forty pavilions spread across town, each devoted to a particular country or region.

this collapsed, and the Métis faced extreme hardship while the Hudson's Bay Company lost effective territorial control.

At this time, politicians in eastern Canada agreed the **federal union** of 1867, opening the way for the transfer of the Red River from British to Canadian control. The Métis majority – roughly six thousand compared to some one thousand – were fearful of the consequences and their resistance took shape around **Louis Riel** (see page 505), under whose impetuous leadership they captured the HBC's Upper Fort Garry and created a provisional government. A delegation went to Ottawa to negotiate terms of admission into the Dominion, but their efforts were handicapped when the Métis **executed** an English settler from Ontario, Thomas Scott. The subsequent furore pushed prime minister John A. Macdonald into dispatching a military force to restore "law and order" and precipitated the 1870 Manitoba Act which brought the Red River into the Dominion, renaming it Winnipeg.

The eclipse of the Métis and the security of Winnipeg were both assured by the arrival of the transcontinental **Canadian Pacific Railway** in 1885. With the town handling the expanding grain trade and local industries supplying the vast rural hinterland, its population was swelled by thousands of **immigrants**, particularly from Ukraine, Germany and Poland, who were attracted by the fertile soils. By World War I, Winnipeg had become Canada's third-largest city and North America's largest grain centre. Since then, the development of other prairie cities, such as Regina and Saskatoon, has lessened Winnipeg's pre-eminence, but it's still central Canada's transport hub.

The Forks

With plenty of parking and something always going on, **The Forks**, the chunk of land where the Red and Assiniboine rivers meet, is an ideal place to start exploring the city. Long an Aboriginal peoples campsite, this confluence later became the start of the main Métis cart tracks west across the prairies (the Portage Trail), and up to Lake Winnipeg past riverside farm lots and Lower and Upper Fort Garry. Later still it became Canada's largest rail yard, as the CNR freight cars and cabooses still dotting the grounds remind, but commercial redevelopment of various warehouses has since turned The Forks into Winnipeg's premier social space. Its **Explore Manitoba Centre** has reasonably interesting themed displays on the province and an outdoor stage hosts regular events. Meanwhile a riverside path leads up to the Exchange District, passing the big bold **Canadian Museum of Human Rights** and the **Provencher Pedestrian Bridge** with its striking white cables and precariously overhanging restaurant. Its loos were locally dubbed "the million-dollar-toilets" for their extraordinarily expensive plumbing.

The Forks Market

1 Forks Market Rd • Forks Market: daily 7am–11pm; Johnston Terminal Fridays 10am to 9pm Sat–Thurs 10am to 6pm • ⓦ theforks.com

At the centre of The Forks are two old railway buildings: **The Forks Market** and the **Johnston Terminal**. Both house food stalls, bars and restaurants and acres of handicraft and souvenir shops. Don't miss climbing the tower of the former for free city views. Outdoors, restaurant seating and street performers vie for space on the plaza between the two buildings and overlook boats you can hop on to explore the river (see page 480).

Manitoba Children's Museum

45 Forks Market Rd • Mon–Thurs 9.30am–4.30pm, Fri & Sat 9.30am–6pm • $11 • ☎ 204 924 4000, ⓦ childrensmuseum.com

An 1889 Forks rail maintenance shed houses the **Manitoba Children's Museum**, a hands-on, state-of-the-art enterprise whose star exhibit is a vintage steam-engine with Pullman carriage. A dozen other interactive and often high-tech displays, aimed at kids aged one to nine, encourage crafts and creative learning. There's a giant playground in the shape of a lasagne, digital paint to play with, and a dairy farm.

Union Station and around

Winnipeg Railway Museum Mon & Thurs 10am–4pm; Tues, Wed & Fri 11am–4pm; Sat 10am–5pm; Sun 11am–5pm • $7 • ☎ 204 942 4632, ⓦ wpgrailwaymuseum.com

Though its back door is rather hidden behind the large Forks parking lots, the ponderous **Union Station South** is worth a peek for its Beaux Arts-style design, a throwback to the time of relaxed journeying on iron rails. Designed by New York's Grand Central Station architects, its antique interiors also contain the **Winnipeg Railway Museum**. Across the street in a small park is a stone gate that's the sole remnant of **Upper Fort Garry**, a Hudson's Bay Company fort from 1837 to 1870 and thereafter the residence of Manitoba's lieutenant governors until 1883, when it was dismantled. The pointed dormers and turrets behind belong to *Hotel Fort Garry*, a château-like structure built for the Grand Trunk Railroad.

Canadian Museum for Human Rights

400-269 Main St • Tues & Thurs–Sun 10am–5pm, Wed 10am–9pm • $21 • ☎ 204 289 2000, ⓦ humanrightsmuseum.ca

Some whizz-bang modern architecture on the banks of the Red River announces the **Canadian Museum for Human Rights** and rightly suggests the scale of its task. Assessing this nebulous yet vital concept was always going to broach uncomfortable and controversial subjects, but with the help of the latest multimedia and presentation techniques the museum makes an intelligent stab at it. All this adds up to an engaging and world-class attraction that would be a pity to miss if you're in town.

The giant building is by American architect Antoine Predock who took inspiration from Canada's landscape. The lobby floor resembles cracked earth while the building above bursts from its Manitoban limestone shell in a mass of swirling glass that celebrates ice and light and soars into a single pinnacle. Inside, the first exhibition reflects on global events that paved the way for today's human rights, then immediately moves on to a second gallery detailing Canada's Aboriginal interpretation. This seems rather unfocussed, but at least underlines how subjective things can be: the right "to hunt, trap and fish" is certainly not the stuff of UN charters. The third gallery is the museum's strongest – a huge chamber of smaller rooms that look self-critically at Canada's past human rights breaches of ethnic minorities and other marginalized groups. The exhibits are brisk and commendably frank. Canada's role remains the starting point for most subsequent galleries too, though the context becomes global: at the time of the Nazi Holocaust, for example, anti-Semitism was virtually institutionalized in Canada.

The final elevator ride up the museum tower provides an airy antidote with fine city views. Orientation is helped by the museum's free smartphone app, which is in any case worth downloading for its self-guided tour; the museum has free wi-fi, but bring headphones for the audio. For most this is better than the museum tour ($5), which adds nothing and forces your pace. Should you start to flag during your visit, then bear in mind that your ticket is good for the whole day and that the nearby Forks (see opposite) makes a good spot for lunch.

St Boniface

The suburb of **St Boniface** lies east of downtown over the Red River. An early French-Canadian and Métis settlement, it was founded by two French-Canadian Catholic priests in 1818 and still retains a distinctive character – a quarter of its population still speaks French as a first language. St Boniface's main historic sights line the river along **Avenue Taché**.

The cathedral and around

A massive white-stone façade is all that remains of **St Boniface Cathedral**, a huge neo-Romanesque structure built in 1908 and largely destroyed by fire in 1968. Its replacement, just behind, was designed with an interior in the style of a giant teepee. The large silver-domed building immediately east is the **Collège Universitaire de Saint-Boniface**, a former Jesuit college and now the French-speaking campus of the University of Manitoba. Here a controversial statue of Manitoba founder Louis Riel portrays him naked and deformed. Its original location was in the Legislative Building's grounds, but it caused such protest that it was moved here in 1994. In front of the cathedral lies the cemetery containing **Riel's grave**, whose modest tombstone gives no hint of the furore surrounding his execution in Regina in 1885. Only after three weeks did the authorities feel safe enough to move the body, which was then sent secretly by rail to St Boniface. The casket lay overnight in Riel's family home in the suburb of St Vital (see page 478) before its transfer to the cathedral, where most of the Métis population attended the funeral Mass. That same evening, across the river, Riel's enemies burnt his effigy on a street corner, a symptom of a bitter divide that lasted well into the twentieth century.

Musée de Saint-Boniface

494 Taché Ave • Mon–Wed & Fri 10am–4pm, Thurs 9am–9pm, Sat noon–4pm • $7 • ☎ 204 237 4500, ⓦ msbm.mb.ca

The **Musée de Saint-Boniface** is housed in an attractive whitewashed building across from the cathedral. The oldest building in Winnipeg and largest squared-oak log building in North America, it was built between 1846 and 1851 as a convent for Grey Nuns, a missionary order whose four-woman advance party had arrived by canoe from Montréal in 1844. The building was subsequently used as a hospital, school and orphanage. Inside, a series of cosy rooms are devoted to the Red River Colony, notably an intriguing collection of Métis memorabilia that includes colourful sashes – the most distinctive feature of Métis dress. You can also see the battered wooden casket used to transport Riel's body from Regina to St Boniface. There's a lovely little chapel, whose papier-mâché Virgin was made from an old newspaper that one of the original Grey Nuns found outside Upper Fort Garry when she walked across the frozen river to buy food.

Fort Gibraltar

866 rue St-Joseph • Tours Wed & Thurs 10am–6pm, Fri & Sat 10am–4pm • $10 • ☎ 204 237 7692, ⓦ fortgibraltar.com

A ten-minute walk north through riverfront parkland from the Provencher Bridge leads to Fort Gibraltar whose wooden stockade seems entirely out of kilter with the neighbouring residential district. This 1809 fur-trade fort was first built at The Forks but has been carefully re-created here – down to the furnishings in the bunkhouse, smithy and general store. Access is by tour in the company of enthusiastic costumed guides who help bring the era alive.

The Exchange District

A roughly rectangular neighbourhood of well-preserved old warehouses, commodity exchanges and commercial buildings, the Exchange District has, since the late 1970s, attracted art galleries, boutiques, antique shops and restaurants creating a faintly bohemian area centred on **Old Market Square** with its weekend produce market, flea markets and buskers.

This part of town was built during Winnipeg's boom, a period that peaked in 1882, but lasted only until World War I. The standard architectural design was simple and symmetrical, with plain brick walls topped off by decorative stone cornices. However, one or two companies financed extravagant variations – notably the **Electric Railway Chambers Building** at 213 Notre Dame Ave, an imaginative blend of Italian Renaissance and early twentieth-century motifs, its terracotta facade lined with six thousand electric lights. Possibly the most gracious building in the district is the former **Winnipeg Grain Exchange** on Lombard Avenue. Completed in 1908, it was the largest of its type in Canada and grain offices still occupy some floors. Also imposing is the ten-storey **Confederation Life Building**, at 457 Main St, with its curved white terracotta facade, and the massive **Royal Bank Building** at Main Street and William Avenue.

Artspace

100 Arthur St • T 204 947 0984, W art-space.ca

Artspace, in a warehouse building at the corner of Arthur Street and Bannatyne Avenue, is a large artist-run centre with a cinema and several galleries; it's a great place to see contemporary Canadian art, photography and wacky multimedia installations.

Manitoba Museum

190 Rupert Ave • Mid-May to early Sept daily 10am–5pm; early Sept to mid-May Tues–Fri 10am–4pm, Sat & Sun 11am–5pm • Museum $16, Planetarium $16, Science Gallery $16; two $24.40; all three $29.20 • W manitobamuseum.ca

The hulking **Manitoba Museum** is packed with provincial geography and history and, though new exhibits are regularly added, the place feels charmingly dated. Dense, dry and almost scholarly information boards sit alongside its many old-fashioned but highly effective dioramas (polar bears, moose, Aboriginal peoples), painstaking reconstructions (cabins, ships and streets) and more recent high-tech exhibits. It's easy to spend a day here, particularly with a visit to the **Planetarium** and the interactive and child-friendly **Science Gallery**.

The museum's highlights include a mesmerizing giant animation of northern Manitoba 450 million years ago – when it was equatorial and life on Earth had not yet moved from the seas; a re-created 1920s Winnipeg street; and, best of all, an impressive full-scale replica of the **Nonsuch**, the ship whose 1668 fur-collecting voyage to the Hudson Bay led to the creation of the Hudson's Bay Company. It's "moored" in a reproduction seventeenth-century dockside and an adjacent room shows relics from the company. Also in the museum is a good brief introduction to the Métis, the marginalized mixed-race population that briefly contested power in the province.

Chinatown

Just northwest of the Exchange District lies **Chinatown**, originally settled in the 1920s by immigrant railway-workers. The area has many good restaurants and groceries, as well as shops selling silk fabrics and exotic herbs and spices – but no real sights. On the eastern edge of Chinatown at 184 Alexander Ave E, the **Ukrainian Cultural and Educational Centre** (Mon–Sat 10am–4pm; $2; ☎ 204 942 0218, ⓦoseredok.ca) occupies a 1930s office building and has some interesting displays on culture and folk art. The gift shop sells fine embroidery, weaving, woodcarving and exquisite examples of *pysanky*, Easter egg painting.

Downtown

The traditional centre of Winnipeg's generally bleak and business-like **downtown** is the intersection of **Portage Avenue** and **Main Street**. Here the grand Neoclassical **Bank of Montreal**, with its fussily carved capitals, contrasts starkly with the clean lines of neighbouring skyscrapers; the intersection is also known as Canada's **windiest**.

Portage Avenue

Underground passageways and glass-enclosed overhead walkways link malls along **Portage Avenue**, the city's main shopping street, providing relief from summer heat and winter cold. The largest complex is the ugly **Portage Place** mall, with its 160 shops. More architecturally attractive buildings on Portage include the Paris Building (no. 259), which boasts a splendid tiered facade and delicate cornice, and the Boyd Building (no. 388), with its cream and bronze terracotta decoration.

7

Winnipeg Art Gallery

300 Memorial blvd • Tues–Thurs, Sat & Sun 11am–5pm, Fri 11am–9pm • $12 • ☎ 204 786 6641, ⓦ wag.ca

The star attraction of the uncompromisingly modern **Winnipeg Art Gallery** at the western end of Portage Avenue is the world's largest public Inuit art collection. Many of these galleries are devoted to particular themes – from the symbolic significance of different animals, to the role of women sculptors in isolated communities. There's also a decent selection of Gothic and Renaissance paintings and European modern art – including works by Joan Miró, Marc Chagall and Henry Moore – though this is often in storage to allow for hit-or-miss temporary exhibitions of modern Canadian art.

Dalnavert

61 Carlton St • Wed–Sun noon–4pm; tours every 30min • $6 • ⓦ dalnavertmuseum.ca

On the southern edge of downtown, **Dalnavert** was once home to Hugh John Macdonald, the son of Canada's first prime minister; he was briefly, premier of Manitoba. Built in 1895 in Queen Anne Revival style, the house has been painstakingly restored, its simple red-brick exterior engulfed by a fanciful wooden veranda and the interior all heavy, dark-stained woods. Macdonald's conservatism, reflected in the decor, was mellowed by a philanthropic disposition – he even reserved part of his basement for some of the city's destitute.

Legislative Building

450 Broadway • Daily 8am–8pm; Tours: July & Aug hourly 9am–6pm; Sept–June by appointment • Free • ☎ 204 945 5813, ⓦ gov.mb.ca/legislature

Surrounded by trim lawns and flower borders, the **Manitoba Legislative Building** lies five minutes' walk southeast of Portage Avenue. The building, made of local Tyndall stone embedded with fossils, has a central pediment decorated with splendidly pompous sculptures representing ideals of Canadian nationhood. A half-kneeling figure, symbolizing progress, beckons his lazy neighbour to come to the land of promise, while a muscular man, with a team of powerful horses, idealizes pioneer spirit. High above, a central square tower rises to a copper-green dome topped by the **Golden Boy**, a 4m-high gold-plated bronze figure that's supposed to embody the spirit of enterprise and eternal youth. Inside, the foyer's balconies house two magnificent life-size bronze buffalo sculptures. The mural over the entrance to the legislative chamber depicting World War I scenes is by Anglo-Welsh artist Frank Brangwyn.

The official tour covers much of this elegantly, but an even more rewarding insight – including into hieroglyphic inscriptions, numerological codes, and hidden Freemasonic symbols – is provided by Heartland Tours (see page 480).

The grounds are also worth exploring, in particular for the group of polar bear sculptures painted by local artists, and a giant, statesmanlike statue of Louis Riel; here to replace the controversial one moved to St Boniface (see page 475).

Riel House

330 River Rd • Late May to June Mon–Fri 10am–5pm; July & Aug Fri–Wed 10am–5pm, Thurs 1–8pm • $4 • ☎ 204 785 6050, ⓦ pc.gc.ca/en/lhn-nhs/mb/riel • Bus #16 from Portage Ave & Main St

The tiny clapboard **Riel House** in the suburb of **ST VITAL**, 10km south of downtown, was built by the Riels in 1880–81 and stayed in the family until 1968. Louis Riel never actually lived here, but his body was brought here after his 1885 execution, and the house has been restored to its appearance at that time, complete with black-bordered photographs and a few artefacts left by his wife, Marguerite. Other period furnishings and fittings give a good idea of the life of a prosperous Métis family in the 1880s. Costumed guides provide an enjoyable twenty-minute tour of the house and garden, the sole remnant of the once sizeable Riel landholdings.

Fort Whyte

1961 McCreary Rd • Mon–Tues 9am–5pm, Wed–Fri 9am–7pm, Sat & Sun 10am–7pm • $7 • ⓦ fortwhyte.org

Across the Red River from St Vital the **Fort Whyte Centre** is an environmental education complex that explores the diversity of the prairie ecosystem's flora and fauna. There's a wildlife observation tower, herd of bison, deer enclosure and a maze of self-guided trails through woodlands and marsh, plus an interpretive centre, all providing a taste of the outdoors in the city.

Royal Canadian Mint

520 Lagimodière blvd, on the edge of town around 10km southeast of Portage and Main • May–Sept daily 9am–4pm, Oct–Apr Tues–Sat 9am–5pm; 45min tours every 30min until 4pm • $8 • ☎ 204 983 6429, ⓦ mint.ca • Bus #50 from the east end of Portage Ave

An estimated one-in-four of the world's adults have a coin from the Winnipeg mint jangling in their pocket. Its presses thunder out the coinage for 72 countries, as the mint's upbeat tours inform. These talk you through the intricacies of the techniques involved – punching, rimming, plating, annealing, crushing, checking and packing – while you look in on the hypnotically twinkling conveyor belts on the factory floor (operational Mon–Fri). Without a tour you can only visit a gift shop and a small exhibition, where you can step on scales that calculate how much you'd be worth if you were made of Loonies (the nickname for Canada's one-dollar coin).

Assiniboine Park

Free • Bus #21 to Overdale

Some 8km west of the city centre and south of Portage Avenue, a great chunk of land has been set aside as **Assiniboine Park**, whose wooded lawns, gardens, cycling paths, playing fields and zoo attract hundreds of visitors every summer weekend. There's even more of the great outdoors to enjoy beyond it too, in the 700-acre nature reserve of **Assiniboine Forest**, which adjoins the park to the south and is home to deer, ruffled grouse and waterfowl.

Leo Mol Sculpture Garden

The park's English gardens of daisies, marigolds, roses and begonias bloom beneath columns of spruce trees and blend into the excellent **Leo Mol Sculpture Garden**, which contains the works of Ukrainian artist Leo Mol (1915–2009). Dozens of graceful sculptures – deer, bears, nude bathers and other whimsical figures – are featured here, reflecting in ponds and in a glass-walled **gallery**. Mol's studio is also on view just behind the gallery.

Pavilion Gallery Museum and the Lyric Theatre

Pavilion: Daily 9am–5pm (until 4pm mid-Oct to mid-Mar)Tues–Sun 10am–8pm • Free

The park's best-known feature is a large, half-timbered, mock-Tudor building, home to the **Pavilion Gallery Museum** with works by local artists Ivan Eyre, Walter J. Phillips and Clarence Tillenius as well as a small collection of Winnie the Pooh art and memorabilia. Their link with the city comes from an orphaned cub purchased and named Winnie by local man Lieutenant Harry Colebourn on his way to World War I. The bear later became his regimental mascot before being gifted to London Zoo at the end of the war, where it became a favourite of A.A. Milne's son, Christopher Robin.

Outside the pavilion, the similarly Tudor-esque bandshell of the **Lyric Theatre** has free performances by the Royal Winnipeg Ballet and the Winnipeg Symphony Orchestra, and hosts jazz, folk and drama festivals.

7

Zoo

Daily: Mid-Mar to mid-Oct 9am–5pm; Mid-Oct to mid-Mar 10am–4pm • $20 • ☎ 204 982 0660, ⓦ assiniboineparkzoo.ca

Winnipeg's sizeable **zoo** has over fifteen hundred animals, a giant tropical conservatory and a steamy Palm House, but its main attraction is its "Journey to Churchill". This set of enclosures and exhibits celebrates the natural history of this Northern Manitoban town (see page 490) and is the best place to get a sense of its wonders short of going there. It's full of snazzy and thoughtful multimedia exhibits on the region and its bears, who ultimately steal the show of course. The zoo has seven polar bears – all orphaned, injured or problem bears – who are particularly stunning when viewed from glass tunnels that enable you to watch them swimming from below. That said, the bears are loath to swim except during what the zoo describes as "positive reinforcement times" – a daily feeding ritual at 11am that shouldn't be missed.

ARRIVAL AND DEPARTURE

WINNIPEG

By plane Winnipeg International Airport (ⓦ waa.ca) is 8km west of downtown. There's a tourist information desk inside the concourse and a free hotel-booking phone nearby. Winnipeg Transit bus #15 (daily every 30min 6am–2am; $2.95) runs downtown, dropping passengers at or near most large hotels; taxis charge around $20.

Destinations Chicago (2 daily; 2hr); Churchill (1 daily; 2hr); Regina (3 daily; 1hr 10min); Saskatoon (3 daily; 1hr 39min); Toronto (14 daily; 2hr 20min); Vancouver (6 daily; 3hr).

By Bus Rider Express (☎ 1 833 583 3636, ⓦ riderexpress.ca) buses pick up at the Flying J Travel Center, 4100 Portage Ave,

a truck stop that lies 25 min west of Downtown on Hwy 1. The terminus of the frequent bus #22 from Portage Place is about a 20-minute walk away.

Destinations Calgary Regina (1 daily; 8hr); Saskatoon (1 daily; 11hr); Edmonton (1 daily; 18hrs).

By train Union Station is on Main St, just south of Portage Ave.

Destinations Churchill (2 weekly; 36hr); Edmonton (3 weekly; 23hr); Jasper (3 weekly; 30hr); Saskatoon (3 weekly; 15hr); Toronto (3 weekly; 33hr); Vancouver (3 weekly; 49hr).

INFORMATION

Travel Manitoba Centre 25 Forks Market Rd (Daily 9am–5pm;   ☎ 204 927 7838, ☎ 800 665 0040, ⓦ travelmanitoba.com).

GETTING AROUND

Local buses The free Downtown Spirit Bus, which circles between The Forks, Portage Avenue and Memorial Boulevard, is operated by Winnipeg Transit (☎ 204 986 5700, ⓦ winnipegtransit.com), who also run buses to the suburbs. Tickets cost $2.95 per journey; ask the driver for a transfer for trips involving more than one bus.

Bike rental Natural Cycle, 91 Albert St ☎ 204 957 5762, ⓦ naturalcycle.ca; $25/24hr.

By car Driving around Winnipeg is straightforward and traffic jams rarely a problem. For convenient and central parking try the lots beisde Forks Market ($2/hr).

By taxi Duffy's ☎ 204 925 0101.

7

WINNIPEG TOURS

You can find a good selection of self-guided walking, cycling, driving and paddling tours on Tourism Winnipeg website (Ⓦ tourismwinnipeg.com/play/tours).

Heartland Tours ⓣ 204 989 9630, Ⓦ heartland travel.ca. Interesting and offbeat tours of Winnipeg look at its rock'n'roll era, its dancehall history, hauntings and, most rewardingly of all, the hidden meanings behind the architecture of the Legislative Building by the author of a best-seller on the subject.

Historic Exchange District Walking Tours ⓣ 204 942 6716, Ⓦ exchangedistrict.org. Interesting guided tours of the Exchange District leave from the Old Market Square between June and August. The choice is between standard 1hr 30min district tours and themed 1hr offerings. Advance phone reservations required.

Parks Canada Walking Tours ⓣ 204 983 6757, Ⓦ parks canada.ca/forks. A "6000 Years in 60 Minutes" walking tour (late May–Aug Mon–Fri 11am & 1pm; $4) sees costumed guides tell six thousand years of history in an hour and offers a geocaching kit to help you unearth the past for yourself ($6). For both enquire at the Explore Manitoba Centre.

Splash Dash ⓣ 204 783 6633, Ⓦ splashdash.ca. River boat tours (daily every 15min: mid-May to Aug 10am–sunset; Sept–mid-Oct noon–sunset; 30min; $11.50) from a quay by The Forks; water buses ($4 one way) between eight different spots along the river; canoe rental (daily 10am–9pm; $20/hr or $40/day).

ACCOMMODATION

Most Winnipeg **hotels** are central, rarely full and often offer weekend sizeable discounts. Major approach roads are dotted with **motels**, particularly Rte-42 and the Trans-Canada Highway. Destination Winnipeg lists some twenty **B&Bs**.

HOTELS AND MOTELS

Comfort Inn South 3109 Pembina Hwy ⓣ 204 269 7390, Ⓦ choicehotels.ca; map p.472. One of several no-frills motels around the junction of the Trans-Canada and Pembina highways, 11km south of downtown. With restaurant, free wi-fi and continental breakfast included. $139

Fairmont Winnipeg 2 Lombard Pl ⓣ 204 957 1350 Ⓦ fairmont.com; map p.472. Pleasant, large and modern 4-star business hotel in a useful location close to the Exchange District, yet far from the scrappier areas that lie on the other side of it. Indoor pool and a good quality restaurant and cocktail lounge. $249

Fort Garry 222 Broadway ⓣ 204 942 8251, Ⓦ fortgarry hotel.com; map p.472. Built in neo-Gothic style between 1911 and 1914 and near the train station, this lavish hotel has an elegant, balconied foyer leading to 250 rooms. Rates include a breakfast buffet and wi-fi. $135

Hotel Royal Plaza 330 Kennedy St, ⓣ 204 783 3000, Ⓦ hotelroyalplaza.ca; map p.472. Modern, central place that seems undecided if it's a hostel or hotel, but perhaps all the better for it: the basic but cheerful rooms are private, while the sociable common room offers billiards and ping-pong. The location behind Portage Place Mall also puts lots on your doorstep. Free wi-fi. $105

Humphry Inn 260 Main St ⓣ 204 942 4222, Ⓦ humphry inn.com; map p.472. There's a dozen different varieties of beige in the fittings and furnishings of this comfortable and fairly bland mid-sized hotel. But definitely worth

considering for its killer sightseeing-and-nightlife location between Downtown and the Forks, plus its indoor pool. The reasonable rates include basic breakfast. $153

★ **Inn at the Forks** 75 Forks Market Rd ⓣ 204 942 6555, Ⓦ innforks.com; map p.472. Self-consciously hip boutique hotel in a tremendous central location at the confluence of the Assiniboine and Red rivers. Rooms feature local art and also have internet access; there's also a stylish spa and innovative restaurant. $264

★ **Mariaggi's Theme Suite Hotel** 231 McDermot Ave ⓣ 204 947 9447, ⓣ 866 947 9190, Ⓦ mariaggis.com; map p.472. You'll pay through the nose, but it's all to enjoy sumptuous Hawaiian, Mexican, Moroccan or African themed suites or a tropical penthouse. Most have hot tubs and fireplaces, some even have pool tables. Free wi-fi. $345

Radisson Hotel Winnipeg Downtown 288 Portage Ave ⓣ 204 956 0410, ⓣ 800 395 7046, Ⓦ radisson.com/ winnipegca; map p.472. Large and smart hotel with fine top-floor views, as well as a gym, saunas, whirlpool and swimming pool. Free wi-fi and big weekend discounts. $220

B&BS

West Gate Manor 71 West Gate ⓣ 204 772 9788, Ⓦ westgatemanor.ca; map p.472. Six pleasant rooms with Victorian period furnishings in Armstrong Point, within walking distance of downtown. $85

HOSTELS

Guest House International 168 Maryland St ⓣ 204 772 1272, ⓣ 800 743 4423, Ⓦ backpackerswinnipeg. com; map p.472. Sociable hostel in a Victorian house with dorms, private rooms and living room walls decorated with Aboriginal art. Facilities include a laundry, kitchen, game room, and free wi-fi. To get there take bus #29 from Broadway to Sherbrook. Dorms $30; doubles $60

CAMPGROUNDS

Town and Country Campground 56001 Murdock Rd ☎ 204 256 2186, ⊛ townandcountrycamping.com; map p.472. Beyond the fringes of the city and surrounded by blooming sunflowers in season. There's a mix of sites and all the usual basic facilities, but there's also a waterslide and an amusement park a couple of minutes' drive away. Tents $32; RVs $41

Winnipeg West KOA Trans-Canada Hwy, St François Xavier ☎ 204 864 2201, ☎ 888 562 0378, ⊛ winnipeg westkoa.com; map p.472. Attractively located in a small town on the Assiniboine River, 15km west of Winnipeg, this campground has a variety of sites, most with water and electricity, as well as a pool and free wi-fi. May–Sept. Sites $30

EATING

Winnipeg's dynamic dining scene boasts dozens of good, inexpensive places and a great selection of world cuisines. Most interesting options cluster in the hip Exchange District and studenty Osborne Village.

Baked Expectations 161 Osborne St ☎ 204 452 5176, ⊛ bakedexpectations.ca; map p.472. Delicious burgers and salads, but especially known for its cheesecakes. Mains $6–11. Mon–Thurs 11.30am–midnight, Fri & Sat 11.30am–1am, Sun 11am–midnight.

★ **Bistro Dansk** 63 Sherbrook St ☎ 204 775 5662, ⊛ bistrodansk.com; map p.472. Small family-owned bistro serving a range of northern and central European dishes; from delicious schnitzel to first-class borscht and crab salad. Mains average about $13 at lunch, $20 at dinner. It's fiercely popular, so reserve ahead if you can. Tues–Sat 11am–2.30pm & 5–9pm.

★ **Clementine** 123 Princess St ☎ 204 942 9497 ⊛ clementinewinnipeg.com; map p.472. Hip Exchange District restaurant with raw beams, tiled counters, an open kitchen and lots of chatter. Brunch specialist with a short menu innovative egg dishes and light lunches (mains around $12), all immaculately presented and very tasty, which means the wait for a table can be close to an hour at peak times (no reservations). Pick-me-up breakfast cocktails are also a specialty. Mon–Fri 7am–3pm, Sat & un 8am–4pm.

★ **Deer + Almond** 85 Princess St ☎ 204 504 8562, ⊛ deerandalmond.com; map p.472. Hip, creative bistro with exposed brick, wooden tables and chalkboards listing daily specials. These often defy categorization, yet the unique taste combinations – sirloin with curry kohlrabi; fried chicken with caramelized onion and gruyere biscuits generally work well. Mains run $16–21; reservations are recommended. Mon–Sat 11am–3pm & 5–11pm.

Feast 587 Ellice Ave ☎ 204 691 5979, ⊛ feastcafe bistro.com; map p.472. Smart little modern bistro that's owned by a local First Nations lady and serves food touched by that tradition., including bannock bison burgers and "Indian" tacos. The emphasis is on high-quality fresh ingredients yet the prices are reasonable with most mains around $11. Good cooked breakfasts too. Mon & Tues 11am–4pm; Wed–Sat 9am–9pm.

The Forks Market 1 Forks Market Road ⊛ theforks. com; map p.472. This converted railway shed with a food court where booths sell a variety of dishes from Caribbean to Greek, from Chilean to Ukrainian. The *Tall Grass Prairie Bakery* is worth seeking out for organic local fare and good coffee. Daily 10am–10pm.

Fusion Grill 550 Academy Rd ☎ 204 489 6963, ⊛ fusion grill.mb.ca; map p.472. Though in a shopping district midway between downtown and the airport it's worth the trek for the expert handiwork of a local celebrity chef who uses regional ingredients to craft fine gourmet dishes like pan-roasted pike or white truffle *pierogies*. Mains $25–39. Tues–Sat 11.30am–2.30pm & 5.30pm–late.

Kum Koon Garden 257 King St ☎ 204 943 4655, ⊛ kumkoongarden.com; map p.472. Much-loved Cantonese place among a clutch of authentic Chinatown places. The dim sum is first-class and great value – even large portions are under $5. Otherwise most lunch and dinner dishes are around $15, but sizeable. Mon–Thurs 11am–3pm & 4.30–11pm, Fri 11am–3pm & 4.30–noon, Sat 10.30am–3pm & 4.30–noon, Sun 10.30am–3pm & 4.30–10pm.

Parlour Coffee 468 Main St ⊛ parlourcoffee.ca; map p.472. Hip and minimalist Exchange District coffee shop that's as proud of its brew as it is of having no phone or wi-fi to distract. Features baked goods from the *Tall Grass Prairie Bakery*. Mon–Fri 7am–5pm, Sat 9am–5pm.

★ **Segovia** 484 Stradbrook Ave ☎ 204 477 6500, ⊛ segoviatapasbar.com; map p.472. Top-notch tapas bar with tasty and imaginative dishes such as spicy lamb dumplings, Thai cauliflower and pork belly with grapefruit. Expensive – with most plates around the top end of their $6–22 range – but also fiercely popular. Turn up early, or be prepared to wait, since you can't reserve. Mon, Wed, Thurs & Sun 5–11pm, Fri & Sat 5pm–midnight.

★ **Stella's Cafe & Bakery** 166 Osborne St ☎ 204 453 8562, ⊛ stellas.ca; map p.472. Breakfast specialist with all the trusty stand-bys, plus delicious home-made jam. Lunchtime soups and quiche are also great. There are seven other locations including at 116 Sherbrook St; 460 Portage Ave; 1895 Grant Ave; and at the airport. Daily 7am–11pm.

Thida's Thai Restaurant 72 Donald St ☎ 204 942 2639, ⊛ thidas.com; map p.472. Authentic, family-run Thai place with tidy oriental decor and food that's made regulars of many locals and put the restaurant's highly rated peanut sauce on Winnipeg supermarket shelves. Most mains are around the $11 mark. Mon–Thurs 11am–9pm, Fri 11am–

7

10pm, Sat 4–10pm, Sun 4–9pm.

Wasabi 105–121 Osborne St ☎204 474 2332; map p.472. Buzzing, trendy sushi bar in Osborne Village. Sushi from $2, $23 for a combo platter. Mon–Thurs 3pm–midnight, Fri–Sat 12.30am–1am, Sun 12.30–midnight.

★ **White Star Diner** 58 Albert St ☎204 947 6930, ⓦwhitestardiner.ca; map p.472. Tiny diner with bar-stool seating and a 1930s ocean liner theme, that eschews fast-food ingredients in favour of quality seasonal produce and seasonings. The results are good ol' fashioned burgers, succulent and washed down with a milkshake, the way God intended. Mon–Fri 11am–6.30pm & Sat noon–3pm.

NIGHTLIFE AND ENTERTAINMENT

Winnipeg supports a good range of theatre, ballet, opera and classical music and has some lively **nightlife**, in which live music also plays a big part. For listings, consult the *Winnipeg Free Press* (ⓦwinnipegfreepress.com).

BARS, CLUBS AND LIVE MUSIC

Club 200 190 Garry St ☎204 943 6045, ⓦclub200. ca; map p.472. Prime gay and lesbian club with a busy dancefloor, karaoke nights and other weekly events. Mon–Sat 4pm–2am, Sun 6pm–midnight.

★ **G Martini Bar** 454 River Ave ☎204 284 3996, ⓦmeijisushi.ca; map p.472. Small, swank and lively Martini bar that shares space with a sushi place. Tues–Sun 7pm–2am.

★ **High & Lonesome Club** 234 Main St ☎204 957 0982, ⓦhighandlonesomeclub.ca; map p.472. Rough-and-ready country, rock, jazz and blues place. Regular live bands keep this old-fashioned honky-tonk ticking over. Times vary; usually Thurs–Sun 6pm–2am.

Live on the Rooftop Winnipeg Art Gallery ☎204 786 6641, ⓦwinnipegarts.com; map p.472. Showcases frequent summer performances by some of Canada's best-known jazz musicians; with regular live folk and world music too. Cash-only bar. Opening times depend on performances.

Palomino Club 1133 Portage Ave ☎204 722 0454, ⓦpalominoclub.ca; map p.472. Winnipeg's key nightclub, with regular live music that's also the best place for a good boot-scoot (that's line dancing, if you're wondering). Mon–Fri 9pm–2am, Sat 8pm–2am.

Toad in the Hole 112 Osborne St ☎204 284 7201, ⓦtoadinthehole.ca; map p.472. Gregarious wood-panelled pub with British beer that packs out with sociable twenty- and thirty-somethings; pool, darts and regular live music. Daily 2pm–2am.

THEATRES AND CINEMAS

Centennial Concert Hall 555 Main St ☎204 956 1360, ⓦcentennialconcerthall.com. Large stage in the Exchange District for performances by the Winnipeg Symphony Orchestra (Sept–May; ⓦwso.ca); the Manitoba Opera (Nov–April; ⓦmanitobaopera.mb.ca); and the Royal Winnipeg Ballet (ⓦrwb.org) – Canada's finest dance company.

Cinémathèque 100 Arthur St ☎204 925 3456, ⓦwinnipegcinematheque.com. Winnipeg's best downtown cinema concentrates on art-house and Canadian releases.

Manitoba Theatre Centre 174 Market Ave ⓦroyalmtc. ca. Well-organized nonprofit company that runs two stages with some 250 annual performances. Often something interesting going on.

Manitoba Theatre for Young People 2 Forks Market Rd ☎204 942 8898, ⓦmtyp.ca. Offers a full programme of child-oriented (ages 3–12 depending on the show) but adult-friendly performances with tickets around $13.

Prairie Theatre Exchange 393 Portage Ave ☎204 942 5483, ⓦpte.mb.ca. Community-based company that puts on some offbeat and experimental theatre productions in the Portage Place Mall.

DIRECTORY

Internet Millennium Library, 251 Donald St ☎204 986 6450; Mon–Thurs 10am–9pm, Fri & Sat 10am–6pm, Sun 1–5pm.

Medical Health Sciences Centre, 820 Sherbrook St ☎20 787 3661 ⓦhsc.mb.ca.

Post office 1000-266 Graham Ave ☎800 267 1177.

Southeastern Manitoba

Southeastern Manitoba offers several tempting day-trips from Winnipeg, with a mix of cultural, historic and natural attractions. Highlights include Steinbach's interesting **Mennonite Heritage Village** to the south, and the **Whiteshell and Nopiming provincial parks** to the east. Accessible gateway communities in both serve to open up a sparsely inhabited region of lakes, rivers and forests on the granite Canadian Shield landscapes. Particularly noteworthy is the superb network of canoe routes between backcountry campsites.

THE MANITOBA STAMPEDE

During the third week of July, be sure to pack up your spurs (or maybe just your camera) and head to the pleasant small town of **MORRIS**, 61km south of Winnipeg via Hwy-75, for the annual **Manitoba Stampede** and Exhibition. It's one of Canada's largest rodeos, yet still small enough to retain the feel of an authentic small-town hoedown.

Relying on **public transport** to explore this region is awkward but just about workable, since most key places have at least one or two bus services per day.

Steinbach and Mennonite Heritage Village

231 Hwy-12N • May, June & Sept Mon–Sat 9am–5pm, Sun 11.30am–5pm; July & Aug Mon–Sat 9am–6pm, Sun 11.30am–6pm; Oct–April Mon–Fri 9am–5pm, outdoor buildings closed • $10 • ☎ 204 326 9661, ⓦ mhv.ca

The sprawling workaday prairie town of **STEINBACH**, 63km southeast of Winnipeg, is worth visiting for its **Mennonite Heritage Village**. It reconstructs a nineteenth-century pioneer settlement on the north edge of town, which includes a church, a windmill and a couple of stores and farmhouses, but it's the general flavour of the place that appeals most. Costumed guides provide intriguing accounts of Mennonite history, as do displays in a tiny museum.

7

EATING STEINBACH

Livery Barn 231 Hwy-12N ☎ 204 326 9661. For a Mennonite meal, try the inexpensive cafeteria-style *Livery Barn*, within the museum. Serves items like borscht, stone-ground bread, smoked sausages and other rustic delights. Mon–Sat 10am–4pm, Sun 11.30am–4pm.

Whiteshell Provincial Park

With its fairly extensive road system dotted with holiday homes, lodges and campgrounds, **Whiteshell Provincial Park** is not a place where wilderness is readily found but it does offer the great outdoors for the minimum preparation and fuss. Summer weekends can get busy, but the crowds are quickly left behind and the canoeing is superb, with interesting overnight or multi-day trips easily organized.

The park takes its name from *megis*, a small, white shell sacred to the Ojibwa, who believe the creator blew through it to breathe life into the first human. These shells, left behind when the prehistoric lake that covered the entire region disappeared, are concentrated along the park's two main rivers, the Whiteshell to the south and the Winnipeg to the north; the latter waterway was an important canoe route for the *voyageurs* of the North West Company on their way from Montréal to the Red River.

Falcon Lake and West Hawk Lake

Most park visitors head for **FALCON LAKE** and **WEST HAWK LAKE**, two well-developed but unexciting tourist townships either side of Hwy-1, near the Ontario border. Crowded throughout the summer, each has facilities such as serviced campsites, resort motels, fuel stations, grocery stores and miniature golf, as well as boat and watersports equipment rental. Falcon Lake has the better supermarket, but West Hawk Lake is more modest and sympathetic.

West Hawk Lake itself was formed by a meteorite and is the deepest lake in Manitoba, making it popular with scuba-divers. On its south side the 13km **Hunt Lake Hiking Trail** passes through forests, across sticky, aromatic bogs and over rocky outcrops, to Little Indian Bay and back (8hr).

Caddy Lake

From West Hawk Lake, Hwy-44 cuts north towards **CADDY LAKE**, the starting point for one of the area's most beautiful **canoe routes**, the 160km journey along the

7

CANADA'S MENNONITES

There are about 100,000 **Mennonites** in Canada today, almost all descendants of those who joined a Dutch Protestant sect in the early sixteenth century under the leadership of Menno Symons. The movement eventually divided into two broad factions: one group refused contact with the secular state and sustained a hostile attitude to private property; the more "liberal" clans were inclined to compromise. Many of the former – the Ammanites – moved to the US and then Ontario, settling around Kitchener-Waterloo, while the more liberal population migrated to Russia and then Manitoba in the 1870s. The **Steinbach area** remains a Mennonite stronghold, and though few adherents wear the traditional black and white clothes or live on communal farms, most are pacifist.

Whiteshell River to Lone Island Lake, in the centre of the park. The *Caddy Lake Resort* (see opposite) rents out canoes for $60 per day.

Experienced walkers could tackle the 60km (3–6 day) **Mantario Hiking Trail** just to the east of Caddy Lake along Provincial Road 312. Shorter options are the **Bear Lake** (2hr; 6km) and **McGillivray Falls trails** (2–3hr; 4km) – clearly signposted from Hwy-44 west of Caddy Lake. Both cover a good sample of the park, including jack pine dry ridges, black spruce bogs and two shallow lakes brown with algae and humic acid. Opposite the start of the Bear Lake Trail, the **Frances Lake** canoe route makes for a pleasant overnight excursion: a 20km trip south to the Frances Lake campsite, with three portages past rapids and twelve hauls round beaver dams.

Rennie and Hwy-307

Some 32km west of West Hawk, the unremarkable village of **RENNIE** is home to the **Alf Hole Goose Sanctuary** (late May to mid-Oct daily 10.30am–6pm). It's best visited in spring or autumn, when Canada geese pass through on their migration, but even in summer a couple of hundred are in residence. Also in Rennie are the park headquarters (see opposite), while its western edge is the start of the 80km stretch of Hwy-307 that passes through the northwest section of the park. It links a string of lonely campgrounds, lodges, trails and canoe routes, some good hikes and a few interesting sites, particularly the **Bannock Point Petroforms**: Aboriginal designs made by placing stones on the ground. Free tours of Bannock Point are offered (1hr 30min; June–late Aug Thurs 7.30pm & Sun 10.30am; ☏204 369 3157), with no need to book in advance.

INFORMATION AND ACTIVITIES

WHITESHELL PROVINCIAL PARK

Park headquarters In Rennie (Mon–Fri 8.30am–noon & 12.45–4.30pm; ☏204 369 3153, ⓦgov.mb.ca). It has a comprehensive range of local information including trails and canoe routes.

Canoe trips The Manitoba Naturalists' Society (ⓦnature manitoba.ca) runs excellent guided canoe trips in the Whiteshell wilderness in July and August. The trips last for five days, cost $415 and are based at a cabin on secluded Lake Mantario. All equipment is provided, as are the services of fully experienced guides, who teach canoeing and survival skills.

ACCOMMODATION AND EATING

Caddy Lake Resort Hwy-44, Caddy Lake ☏204 349 2596, ⓦcaddylakeresort.com. Modest resort with a small sandy beach, canoe rentals and a range of cabins from basic to quite smart, all with kitchen and bedding – though you'll need to bring towels. May–Aug. $100

★**Pinewood Lodge** Dorothy Lake ☏204 348 7549, ⓦmypinewood.com. Lovely ecofriendly choice beside Dorothy Lake, 51km from Rennie, with pretty, luxurious rooms (and suites with hot-tubs and fireplaces) at fair prices. The location is hard to beat and rates include canoe use plus an indoor pool, hot tub and fitness centre. $149

Hi-Point Restaurant on 44 Hwy-44 West Hawk Lake ☏204 349 2269, ⓦhi-pointrestaurant.ca. The best place to eat in West Hawk Lake is this family-oriented place specializing in juicy steaks ($23–29) and prime ribs ($26), though the lunchtime soups, sandwiches and wraps are also good. Mon–Wed 9am–8pm, Thurs–Sat 9am–10pm, Sun 9am–3pm.

Nopiming Provincial Park

Some 100km north of Whiteshell Provincial Park, via Hwy-11 and provincial roads 502, 313, 315 and 314, **Nopiming Provincial Park** is a more remote, near-wilderness experience: *nopiming* is Ojibwa for "entrance to the wilderness". The park's main arteries are two gravel roads: Rte-314, which meanders across the 80km of its western edge, and the shorter Rte-315, a 30km track that cuts east south of Bird Lake to the Ontario border. This is a rocky area with granite shoreline cliffs above black-spruce bogs and tiny sandy beaches. In the south of the park, **BIRD LAKE** is a useful base, with a main settlement on the south shore that's equipped with a campsite, grocery store and cabins. There's also motorboat rental, canoe and guide rental for excursions to Snowshoe Lake, around falls and over rapids. Nopiming Park is crossed by the Oiseau and Manigotagan waterways, whose creeks and rivers trickle or rush from lake to lake, forming no less than 1200km of possible canoe routes.

ACCOMMODATION   NOPIMING PROVINCIAL PARK

Campgrounds Some four lakeside campgrounds dot the park's two routes; camping is only allowed at these designated grounds and backcountry campsites reached by boat. They have no services save water and fire pits; wood can be purchased nearby. Campgrounds all May–Sept. **$11.55**

Nopiming Lodge Bird Lake ☎ 204 884 2281, Ⓦ nopiminglodge.com. Family-run business, which incorporates a general store, restaurant and seven basic self-catering cabins. Wild moose are regular visitors, and there's plentiful fishing and miles of trails and canoe routes through a pristine landscape on the doorstep. Canoe and kayak rentals are offered for $25/day. **$100**

7

The Red River and Lake Winnipeg

As Main Street becomes Hwy-9 north of Winnipeg dreary suburbs fade into seamless prairies and the only major interruption is the **Red River** as it pushes its way towards **Lake Winnipeg**, the vast 400km-long finger of water which feeds the Nelson River and the Hudson Bay.

The main sight along the Red River corridor is **Lower Fort Garry**, a well-preserved former trading post. From here, birdwatchers should make a beeline to the marshlands of the **Oak Hammock Marsh Wildlife Area**, while most recreational traffic heads to beaches around the lake itself at **Grand Beach Provincial Park**, where waves lap onto

---

BACKCOUNTRY CANOEING IN MANITOBA

If you've already explored the superb canoeing in Whiteshell and Nopiming provincial parks or want real wilderness, then you're spoilt for choice in Manitoba. Much of the best water is in the eastern and remote **Atikaki Provincial Wilderness Park**, which has impressive stands of thick forest, several ancient pictograph sites as well as moose, timber wolves, coyotes and black bears. Its dramatic **Bloodvein River** to Lake Winnipeg is particularly outstanding, with rapids, falls and wild water balanced by peaceful drifts through quiet lakes and wild-rice marshes. In the far north the Hayes, Seal and Deer rivers all drain into Hudson Bay, home to easily spotted beluga whales, which makes for outstanding subarctic trips.

All the above are only for experienced, skilled and self-reliant backcountry canoeists. You'll need to organize floatplane transportation and plan carefully using information from Paddle Manitoba (Ⓦ paddle.mb.ca) and Manitoba Conservation (Ⓦ gov.mb.ca/conservation) and purchase topographic maps – available from Canada Map Sales, Land Information Centre, 1007 Century St, Winnipeg (☎ 204 945 6666, ☎ 877 627 7226, Ⓦ canadamapsales.com). Several outfitters offer trips that can spare you some preparation. Northern Soul (☎ 204 878 3570, ☎ 866 425 9430, Ⓦ northernsoul.ca) and Wilderness Spirit (☎ 204 452 7049, ☎ 866 287 1591, Ⓦ wildernessspirit.com) both run trips to Hudson Bay and on several Atikaki rivers. These start at $400 for three days, but cost up to $4500 for a full-blown two-week adventure on the Seal River, the most remote of all.

sand dunes that stretch as far as the eye can see. The beaches of the lake's west shore have less of a seaside atmosphere; its fishing and farming villages are of little interest, except for **Gimli**, which has its own windblown charm and an intriguing Icelandic history. Visiting the nearby **Narcisse Wildlife Management Area** is a must in April and May, when thousands of red-sided garter snakes gather to mate. Otherwise, head north along the lake's western coast and you'll encounter the scattered islands, unspoilt marshes and forests of the **Hecla/Grindstone Provincial Park**.

Lower Fort Garry

5925 Hwy-9 • Early May to June daily 9.30am–5pm; July–early Sept Fri–Wed 9.30–5pm, Thurs noon–8pm; early Sept to early May grounds only until sunset • $7.80 (Oct–May free) • ☎ 204 785 6050, ⓦ pc.gc.ca • Exclusive Bus Lines from Winnipeg (Mon–Fri 10 daily, Sat 5 daily, Sun 4 daily; $6 one way; ☎ 204 888 4411, ⓦ exclusivebuslines.com)

If you drive north out of Winnipeg along Main Street, which becomes Hwy-9, it's about 32km to **Lower Fort Garry National Historic Site**. Built on the banks of the Red River, it was the Hudson's Bay Company headquarters between 1830 and 1847, and the brainchild of George Simpson, governor of the company's "northern department", an area bounded by the Arctic and Pacific oceans, Hudson Bay and the Missouri River Valley. Nicknamed "Little Emperor" for his autocratic style, Simpson selected the site because it was downriver of the treacherous St Andrew's rapids but not prone to flooding as Upper Fort Garry had been. The visitor centre presents a comprehensive history of the fort and the local fur trade, while beyond it several low, thick limestone walls protect reconstructed company buildings, including the retail store, where a small museum is devoted to Inuit and Aboriginal crafts, including exquisite decorated pouches and an extraordinary necklace fringed by thin strips of sardine can. Next door, the combined shop and clerk's quarters has a fur loft packed with pelts, while the middle of the compound is dominated by the Big House, built for Governor Simpson in 1832. Guides in 1850s costume stroll the grounds, ensuring a period atmosphere. The **restaurant** sells good *tourtière* – a Québécois meat pie – and bannock (freshly baked bread).

Oak Hammock Marsh

Daily: Sept & Oct 10am–dusk; Nov–Aug 10am–4.30pm • $8 • ☎ 204 467 3300, ⓦ oakhammockmarsh.ca

The **Oak Hammock Marsh Wildlife Management Area** is all that remains of a far greater wetland that once almost stretched as far as the Red River. Most was drained and farmed around the start of the twentieth century, but since the 1960s some wetlands were restored and protected by dykes and islands built to provide marshland birds a safe nesting place. An excellent interpretive centre explains all this, as well as providing observation decks and information on the local trail network.

The best time to visit is spring or autumn, when the grebes, coots and other resident are joined by thousands of migrating birds, including snow and Canada geese. But summer is also worthwhile, since between mid-June to August the area of the reserve that has been returned to tall-grass prairie is carpeted with wildflowers, including the purple blazing star and the speckled red prairie lily.

Grand Beach Provincial Park

Its long stretch of powdery white sand, high grass-crowned dunes and shallow waters have made **Grand Beach Provincial Park** a favourite swimming spot with Winnipeggers since the 1920s; it can get very crowded at summer weekends. The beach divides into two distinct parts, separated by a narrow channel and spanned by a tiny footbridge: to the west are privately owned cottages, sports facilities, boat rental, grocery stores and a restaurant; to the east the beach is less developed, bar the large campground. From the campsite office, the **Ancient Beach Trail** is a pleasant hour-long lakeshore walk.

SLITHERING AT NARCISSE

If you're in the Winnipeg area in late April or early May and have a strong stomach, don't miss the chance to watch thousands of **red-sided garter snakes** gather to mate in slithering heaps at the **Narcisse Wildlife Management Area**. It (ⓦgov.mb.ca) lies 25km west of Gimli on Hwy-231 or 90km north of Winnipeg on Hwy-17.

ACCOMMODATION   **GRAND BEACH PROVINCIAL PARK**

Grand Beach Campground ⓞ204 945 6784. Though Grand Maris, on the western edge of the park has a motel, your best bet is to camp in the park at this busy, large campsite nestling in the dunes. May–Sept. $11.55

Gimli

The most interesting town on the western shores of Lake Winnipeg is **GIMLI**, or "paradise" in Icelandic, the language of its key ethnic group. Its harbour, complete with a massive wharf and a fibreglass Viking statue, is modestly attractive, but the real reason to visit is the **New Iceland Heritage Museum** (94 1st Ave; Mon–Fri 10am–4pm; Sat & Sun 1–4pm; $7; ⓞ204 642 4001, ⓦnihm.ca). It chronicles the history of the **Republic of New Iceland** which began in 1875 when some two hundred Icelanders moved to a block of land between today's Winnipeg Beach and Hecla Island, to which they had secured exclusive rights. Here they founded a large self-governing and self-sufficient settlement with its own Icelandic-language school, churches and newspaper. But their independence would, however, only last until 1897, when they acquiesced to the federal government's decision to allow other ethnic groups, and by the 1920s, an identifiable Icelandic community ceased to exist. Nevertheless, Manitoba still has the largest number of Icelandic descendants outside Iceland, and this heritage is celebrated during the rather commercial Islendingadagurinn (Icelanders' Day) festival, on the first weekend in August, when locals wear Viking helmets and organize beauty pageants, concerts and firework displays.

INFORMATION   **GIMLI**

Lake Winnipeg Visitor Centre Downtown at 97 1st Ave (May–Sept daily 10am–6pm; ⓞ204 642 7974).

ACCOMMODATION AND EATING

★ **Lakeview Resort** 10 Centre St ⓞ204 642 8565, ⓦlakeviewhotels.com. One of Gimli's few places to stay, with comfortable suites and rooms, each with a balcony overlooking either the town or the lake. $190

Reykjavik Bakery Lighthouse Mall, Centre St ⓞ204 642 7598. Icelandic bakery with a great range of unusual goodies from the home country. Great for picnic items. Daily 9am–6pm.

Ship & Plough 42 Centre St ⓞ204 642 5276, ⓦshipandplough.ca. Friendly neighbourhood joint with Western saloon frontage that serves quality gastro-pub fare (fantastic Lake Winnipeg pickerel fish tacos, $16) and entertains with live music, comedy and trivia nights. Good Manitoban craft beers too. Mon–Thurs 4pm–1am, Fri–Sun noon–2am.

Hecla/Grindstone Provincial Park

There's more Icelandic heritage, along with gentle rural charms and hiking trails through forest and marsh to be enjoyed some 70km north of Gimli in the **Hecla/Grindstone Provincial Park**. The park consists of several islands and a slender peninsula that just out into Lake Winnipeg, almost touching the eastern shore and is approached along Hwy-8, which runs across a narrow causeway to the largest of the islands, **HECLA**. **Hecla Village** lies close to its centre and has a number of old houses, a church and a school dating from the early years of Icelandic settlement; a short heritage trail covers the highlights (guided tours available in summer). The tourist village of **Gull Harbour** is at the end of Hwy-8.

Gull Harbour Campground ☎ 204 279 2369, ☎ 888 482 2267. On the neck of land between Gull Harbour and the lake and with beach access. Offers around 200 sites, some with electricity, most unserviced. May–Sept. <u>$11.55</u>

Solmundson Gesta Hus Hecla Village ☎ 204 279 2088, ⓦ hecla.ca. Bed and breakfast accommodation with hot tub, immaculate gardens and various health and beauty treatments available. <u>$105</u>

Northern Manitoba

With lakes Winnipeg and Winnipegosis creating a vast natural barrier between it and the southern province, Northern Manitoba is a world apart. Distances are vast, the population thin and the largest towns, **Flin Flon** and **The Pas**, only worthwhile as bases for the region's two main provincial parks: **Clearwater Lake** and **Grass River**. Even further north is **Thompson**, the penultimate stop on the remote railway line to the windswept town of **Churchill** on the Hudson Bay. Though far beyond the reach of the road network, this is the region's key tourist centre since, depending on the season, it's easy to see **beluga whales**, **polar bears** and the **Northern Lights**.

With distances so vast and the population so thin, public transport in Northern Manitoba is understandably poor, yet Greyhound services go to all main towns – except Churchill – and the **Saskatchewan Transportation Company** provides an additional bus service between Flin Flon and Saskatoon.

The Pas

Situated on the southern bank of the Saskatchewan River 400km north of Dauphin (see page 497) via Hwy-10, **THE PAS** is a former fur-trading and missionary centre founded in 1750. It's also a town with no major sights, though it does host the annual **Northern Manitoba Trappers' Festival** over four days in late February; competitions include pioneer skills like tree felling, trap setting, ice-fishing and muskrat skinning, with the highlight being the World Championship Sled Dog Races and its 50km mushes. If you're in town in mid-August, you can join First Nations celebrations honouring the Cree people during **Opasquiak Indian Days**.

Tourist office 81 Edwards Ave, beside the tiny Devon Park (Mon–Thurs noon–4.30pm; ☎ 204 623 6459).

Wescana Inn 439 Fischer Ave ☎ 204 623 5446, ☎ 1800 665 9468, ⓦ wescanainn.com. Comfortable lodgings in the centre, near the train station, with bright modern rooms, free wi-fi and a reasonable restaurant – as well a a sports bar and nightclub. <u>$119</u>

Clearwater Lake Provincial Park

Just 19km north of The Pas, the square-shaped lake and adjoining strip of coniferous forest that constitute **Clearwater Lake Park** are a favourite haunt of the region's anglers, who come here for northern pike, whitefish and highly prized trout. Park amenities are concentrated along Rte-287, off Hwy-10, which follows the lake's southern shore past The Pas airport.

Carpenter's Clearwater Lodge ☎ 204 624 5467, ⓦ carpenterslodge.com. Offers beautiful cabins which sleep up to four and have access to a games room and hot-tub. Fishing boat rental offered too. <u>$340</u>

Provincial Park Campgrounds ☎ 204 948 3333. Choo from two summer campgrounds, with basic and electrica serviced sites and showers at Campers Cove and at Pioneer B where all sites have lake views. Mid-May to mid-Sept. <u>$11.</u>

Grass River Provincial Park

A 75km drive north along Hwy-10 from Clearwater Lake Provincial Park brings you to **Grass River Provincial Park**: several thousand square kilometres of evergreen forest, lake and river interspersed by the granite outcrops of the Canadian Shield. Its channels and lakes were first charted in the 1770s by Hudson's Bay Company employee Samuel Hearne and still noted as excellent **canoe routes**. The most popular route begins close to **Cranberry Portage**, a straggling township along Hwy-10, on the western edge of the park, and runs 180km to **Tramping Lake** and Hwy-39 near the park's eastern boundary. It's about a ten-day trip – all the route's portages are short and fairly easy and there are lots of basic campsites on the way.

There are other access points to Grass River Park along Hwy-39, which runs along its southern boundary, from where circular canoe trips can be accomplished in one day.

ACCOMMODATION   **GRASS RIVER PROVINCIAL PARK**

CRANBERRY PORTAGE
Cranberry Portage Park Hwy-10 and Portage Rd ☎ 204 687 0278; ⓦ mckenziesrvpark.ca. Small campground 1km west of Cranberry Portage with its own beach, good fishing and some hiking trails. Some sites have electricity; basic 2-person bunkhouses available. Mid-May to Sept. Sites $20; bunkhouses $75

Viking Lodge 35 Public Rd NE ☎ 204 472 3337, ⓦ vikinglodge.ca. One of a handful of holiday lodges along the lakeshore which also offer canoe rentals along with hunting and fishing packages. Mid-May to early Oct. RV and tent campsites $29; lodges $100

GRASS RIVER PROVINCIAL PARK
Grass River Provincial Park campgrounds Hwy-39 passes three small and absolutely basic summer campsites – *Gyles* (24km east of Hwy-10), *Iskwasum* (40km) and *Reed Lake* (56km). $11.55

Wekusko Falls Provincial Park

About 35km east of the park's boundary in the separate **Wekusko Falls Provincial Park**, the falls of the same name make for a worthwhile side-trip. It requires a drive south along a short stretch of gravel road (Hwy-596) to where the Mitishto River drops dramatically in a series of falls and rapids. You can view the spectacle from two suspension footbridges or along the walking trails below.

ACCOMMODATION   **WEKUSKO FALLS PROVINCIAL PARK**

Wekusko Falls Campground Hwy-596. River and lakeside campground with showers and an area for tents that's separate from the rest of the drive-through sites. May–Sept. $11.55

Flin Flon

The mining township of **FLIN FLON** – 138km from The Pas on Hwy-10, or 409km from Prince Albert on Saskatchewan's Hwy-106 – gouges copper, gold, lead and zinc from a massive seam discovered in 1914. Straddling the Manitoba–Saskatchewan border, it's a stark, rough-looking town, full of steep streets, where the houses are built on sheer rock in a barren landscape. Flin Flon takes its unusual name from the hero of an obscure dime-novel entitled *The Sunless City*, which one of the first prospectors was reading at the time of the discovery. In the book, Josiah Flintabbatey Flonatin builds a submarine and enters the bowels of the earth, where he discovers that everything is made of gold. There's not much to see in town, except in July, when the town hosts the **Trout Festival**, with a parade, a Queen Mermaid Pageant, the Great Northern Duck Race – and the tantalizing smell of frying fish.

INFORMATION   **FLIN FLON**

Tourist office About 4km east of the centre along Hwy-10A (May–Sept daily 8am–8pm; ☎ 204 687 7674, ⓦ cityofflinflon.ca).

ACCOMMODATION AND EATING

Flin Flon Friendship Centre Hostel 57 Church St ☎ 204 687 3900. Hostel in a modern multi-complex building with communal lounge and shared bathrooms. Also encompasses a restaurant and handicraft outlet. **$35**

Flin Flon Tourist Park & Campground Hwy-10 and Hwy-10A ☎ 204 687 7674. The tourist office runs the main campsite opposite a large statue of the intrepid Flintabbatey Flonatin and offers a mix of electrical and nonelectrical sites. May–Sept. **$19**

★ **Orange Toad Café** 115 Main St. The best place to mooch around in, with an imaginative choice of lattes such as London Fogs (Earl Grey with vanilla and milk), good muffins and a selection of used books. Mon–Fri 7am–5pm, Sat 10am–5pm.

Victoria Inn 160 Hwy-10A ☎ 204 687 7555, ⓦ vicinn. com. Quality motel along the main highway, with small pool, and large TVs. Also has three different restaurants and bars on site, so much of Flin Flon's nightlife. **$138**

Thompson

The sprawling nickel-mining town of **THOMPSON** at the end of Hwy-6 and 399km from The Pas is as far north as you can go on Manitoba's network of sealed highways and a long haul from anywhere. Driving here you'll pass through hundreds of kilometres of boreal forest, with barely another vehicle in sight – there's little reason to come here other than to catch the overnight train to Churchill, thereby cutting the cost and journey time of picking up the service in Winnipeg.

Thompson's Visitor Information Centre (see below) incorporates the **Heritage North Museum** ($3.25), which bursts with stuffed local wildlife and history. They can also organize tours of local mines and suggest other ways in which to kill a few hours before your train leaves, if you're not busy stocking up on groceries in the large downtown malls.

ARRIVAL AND INFORMATION

By train The station is just southeast of the town centre – take Station Rd, just south of Wal Mart but this desolate spot is prone to vandalism. If leaving your car here, your better option is to park at City Hall, 226 Mystery Lake Rd (just off the main drag), for free and take a taxi with Thompson Cab (☎ 204 677 6262), or leave your car at the *McReedy Campground* (see below).

Destinations Churchill (3 weekly; 16hr); Winnipeg (2 weekly; 24hr).

Visitor Information Centre 162 Princeton Drive, on the southeastern edge of town beside the highway (June–Sept 10am–5pm; Sept–May Mon–Sat 1pm–5pm; ☎ 204 677 2216, ⓦ heritagenorthmuseum.ca).

ACCOMMODATION

Best Western Thompson Hotel 205 Mystery Lake Rd ☎ 204 778 8887, ⓦ bestwestern.com. There's not much to choose between the main hotels in Thompson, making this standard higher-end motel as good a choice as any. With a sauna and reasonable breakfast included. **$120**

McCreedy Campground 17 Jasper Dr (off Hwy 391 N) ☎ 204 679 6315. Pleasantly wooded lakeside campground on the northern fringes of town. Offers car storage for $1 per day, including courtesy shuttle service to and from the railway station. May–Sept. Tent and RV sites **$20**

Churchill

Sitting on the east bank of the Churchill River where it empties into Hudson Bay, **CHURCHILL** has the neglected look of many remote northern settlements, its unkempt open spaces dotted with the houses of its mixed Inuit, Cree and white population. These grim buildings are fortified against the biting cold of winter and the voracious insects of summer. Like York Factory (see page 494), Churchill began life as a fur trading post, with the Hudson's Bay Company building its first fort here in 1717 and using it for shipments to Britain until the 1870s when better trade routes through the USA took over. The development of agriculture on the prairies then brought a reprieve and in 1929 the Canadian National Railway completed a line. Unfortunately, the port has never been very successful, largely because the bay is ice-free for only about three

months a year. So, with its grain-handling facilities underused, the visitors who flock here for the wildlife (particularly the **polar bears**) – or the aurora borealis (Northern Lights) common in the skies between late August and April – have thrown the town a real lifeline.

Kelsey Boulevard and the Town Centre Complex

Lying beside the train station and adjacent Parks Canada Visitor Centre (see page 493), **Kelsey Boulevard** is the town's main street. Crossing it, a quick walk northeast brings you to the large and rather forlorn **Town Centre Complex** overlooking Hudson Bay. The town's administrative offices are here, as are its library (free internet) and various recreational facilities, including curling and hockey rinks, swimming pool, bowling alley and a cinema.

The Eskimo Museum

242 La Vérendrye Ave • June–Oct Mon 1–5pm, Tues–Sat 9am–5pm; Nov–May Mon & Sat 1–4.30pm • Donation • ☎ 204 675 2030

A block southeast of the Town Centre Complex, the **Eskimo Museum** houses the Inuit collection of the Oblate Fathers of Mary Immaculate, who began missionary work here around 1900. Animal-hide canoes and stuffed Arctic animals dominate the museum's one large room, which has Inuit art arranged in cases round the walls. It's a fine range of material, from caribou-antler pictographs and highly stylized soapstone figurines through to walrus-tooth scrimshaw and detailed ivory and stone carvings. The sculptures fall into two distinct periods. Up until the 1940s, the work of the local Inuit was essentially limited to carving figurines in walrus ivory, modelled on traditional designs. However, in 1949 Canadian painter James Houston travelled the Hudson Bay encouraging the Inuit to vary their designs and experiment with different materials – which led, in particular, to larger and more naturalistic soapstone sculptures. One corner of the museum functions as a **gift shop** selling prints and carvings, plus a good collection of books on the North.

CHURCHILL TOUR OPERATORS

Local wildlife **tour operators** have proliferated in Churchill, and are all listed in the indispensable *Guide to Churchill* pamphlet, available at all major Manitoban tourist offices, and at Churchill's Parks Canada Visitor Centre.

Churchill Wild ☎ 204 377 5090, ☎ 866 846 9453, ⓦ churchillwild.com. Top-end tour company with wildlife tours year-round from around $12,000 per week.

Frontiers North Adventures ☎ 204 949 2051, ☎ 800 663 9832, ⓦ tundrabuggy.com. An excellent option if you've $5000; four days to spare and can book months in advance. Uses vehicles specially designed to avoid damaging the tundra.

Great White Bear Tours ☎ 204 675 2781, ☎ 866 765 8344, ⓦ greatwhitebeartours.com. Runs day-trips ($473/person) to find polar bears in October and November, using huge custom-built buses.

Hudson Bay Helicopters ☎ 204 675 2576, ⓦ hudsonbayheli.com. Outside the main polar-bear season, consider splashing out on a flight with this company, who can all but guarantee polar bear sightings, for $1500/hr.

Lazy Bear Lodge (see page 494). Runs a number of tours including five days for around $5500 including airfare; and 3-hour kayaking trips ($175).

North Star Tours Bayport Plaza, Munck St ☎ 204 675 2356, ☎ 800 665 0690 ⓦ northstartours.net. A good first stop to get a feel for what's on offer at any time of year. The outfit is headed up by a jolly third-generation local who runs an excellent minibus tour of local sites ($110; 3hr) – which includes a good look for polar bears – but they won't hesitate to suggest, and even call, other companies for you if you have particular activities in mind.

Sea North Tours 39 Franklin St ☎ 204 675 2195, ☎ 888 348 7591, ⓦ seanorthtours.com. Offers Zodiac trips ($115; 2hr 30min) that allow you to listen in on the belugas using stereo hydrophones and visit Prince of Wales' Fort (see above). For the more active there are also kayak (no experience necessary; $160; 2hr 30min) and snorkelling trips ($295; 3hr), when visibility in the bay is good enough. Mid-June to late Aug.

CHURCHILL'S FLORA AND FAUNA

Churchill occupies a transitional zone where stunted taiga trees (subarctic conifers) meet tundra mosses. Blanketed with snow in winter and covered by thousands of bogs and lakes in summer, the terrain is completely flat until it reaches the sloping Churchill River banks and the ridge around Hudson Bay, whose grey-quartzite boulders have been rubbed smooth by ice, wind and water.

Once spring starts to melt the winter snows in April, the tundra reveals a colourful sheet of moss, lichens, flowers and miniature shrubs and trees, including dwarf birch, spruce and cranberry. In June the Churchill River ice beings to break, creating a spreading patch of open water that attracts up to three thousand white **beluga whales**. These intelligent, inquisitive and vocal mammals spend July and August around the mouth of the river, joining the **seals**, who arrive in late March for five months.

Polar bears also start to arrive in June, forced ashore until the ice re-forms enough to support their weight, allowing them to hunt seals; a polar bear can detect a scent from 32km away and can pick up the presence of seals under a metre of snow and ice. The best months to spot bears are September, October and early November, just before the ice re-forms completely.

The area around Churchill is also a major migration route for **birds** heading north between April and June and returning south in August or early September. Nesting and hatching take place from early June until early July. A couple of hundred species are involved, including gulls, terns, loons, Lapland longspurs, ducks and geese. The star visitor is the rare Ross's gull, a native of Siberia, which has nested in Churchill for some years. The *Birder's Guide to Churchill* by Bonnie Chartier lists them all and is sold at the Eskimo Museum.

Cape Merry National Historic Site

About a 30min walk from town • Check with Parks Canada for guided tour times (see below)

A couple of minutes' walk north from the town centre, Churchill's grain elevators and silos stand at the base of a narrow peninsula that sticks out into the mouth of the Churchill River. Beyond it a track leads to the tip, where **Cape Merry National Historic Site** has the remains of an eighteenth-century gun emplacement and a cairn commemorating Danish explorer Jens Munck, who led an expedition forced to winter here in 1619; most of the crew died from cold and hunger. At high tide the cape is a brilliant spot from which to watch belugas in the bay, but take local advice before setting out as polar bears often potter among the rocks here making the area unsafe.

Prince of Wales' Fort National Historic Site

July & Aug; only accessible as part of a $115 guided tour of the Churchill River by Sea North Tours (see page 492) • Site entry costs an extra $7.80 • ☎ 204 675 8863

On the opposite side of the estuary from Cape Merry, **Prince of Wales' Fort National Historic Site** is a partly restored eighteenth-century stone fortress built to protect the trading interests of the Hudson's Bay Company from the French. Finished in 1771, this massive structure took forty years to complete, but even then proved far from impregnable. When a squadron of the French fleet appeared in the bay in 1782 the fort's governor, Samuel Hearne, was forced to surrender without firing a shot because he didn't have enough men to form a garrison. The French spiked the cannon and undermined the walls, and after this fiasco the Company never bothered to repair the damage.

ARRIVAL AND INFORMATION   CHURCHILL

By plane Flights from Winnipeg are operated by Calm Air (☎ 204 778 6471, ☎ 800 839 2256, ⊛ calmair.com), Kivalliq Air (☎ 204 888 0100, ☎ 877 855 1500, ⊛ kivalliqair.com) and First Air (☎ 800 267 1247, ⊛ firstair.ca) and cost around $1000 for a return ticket. Churchill's airport is 7km from the centre; a taxi to town costs around $30 (Churchill Taxi ☎ 204 675 2345),

but many accommodations offer a free shuttle service.

By train Churchill is well beyond the reach of Manitoba's highways, but connected by train, with VIA Rail running services to Thompson (3 weekly; 16hr), The Pas (2 weekly; 9hr 30min) and Winnipeg (2 weekly; 40hr).

Parks Canada Visitor Centre (Daily: June–Nov Mon–Sat

10am–8.30pm; Dec–May 10am–5pm; ☎204 675 8836, ⓦpc.gc.ca). Part of the train station and has displays on artic wildlife and other Churchill attractions. Free evening

lectures cover archeological history and climate change. More useful before you go is Travel Manitoba's dedicated website: ⓦeverythingchurchill.com.

ACCOMMODATION AND EATING

The polar bear presence means you can't camp in Churchill, but otherwise the town's reasonable range of accommodation is an easy walk from the train station and should be booked in advance, even outside peak bear-season when the prices below double.

Lazy Bear Lodge 313 Kelsey blvd ☎204 675 2969, ☎866 687 2327, ⓦlazybearlodge.com. Its log cabin-style gives it more character than elsewhere in town and its restaurant, with its mixed international menu, is reasonable too: there's usually musk ox and other game on the menu here (mains around $29; daily noon–10pm). With free wi-fi and a shuttle service from station or airport. $160

Polar Bear Bed & Breakfast 87 Hearne St ☎204 675 2819, ⓦpolarbearbandb.com. A modest family home some 5min walk from the town centre with single, double and four-bed family rooms. Lends out bikes to guests for

free and has free wi-fi too. $160

Polar Inn 15 Kelsey blvd ☎204 675 8878, ⓦpolarinn. com. Basic motel-style units, albeit with a vaguely boutique feel – and some have kitchenettes. Self-service continental breakfast included. $190

Seaport Hotel 215 Kelsey Blvd ☎204 675 8807, ⓦseaporthotel.ca. Fairly standard motel-quality rooms but also a key locals' hangout with occasional live music and good bar food (mains average $14, serving 7am–10pm). $155

Tundra Inn 34 Franklin St ☎204 675 8831, ⓦtundrainn. com. Another of Churchill's basic but pricey hotels, offering dorm accommodation as well as some private and hotel-quality rooms, and free wi-fi. Frequent live entertainment in the bustling pub, which serves reasonable food (bison burger $19). $175

York Factory

In 1682, the Hudson's Bay Company established a fur-trading post at **York Factory** (see page 494), a marshy peninsula some 240km southeast of today's Churchill. From here the direct sea route to England was roughly 1500km shorter than the old route via the St Lawrence River, while the Hayes and Nelson rivers gave access to the region's greatest waterways. Within a few years, a regular cycle of trade became established, with the company's Cree and Assiniboine go-betweens heading south in the autumn to **hunt and trade** for skins and returning in the spring laden with pelts to exchange for the company's manufactured goods. This made York Factory the central storehouse of the northwestern fur trade throughout the eighteenth century, its wooden palisades housing soldiers, explorers, travellers, traders and settlers bound for present-day Winnipeg. In its heyday, there were some fifty buildings within the stockade, including a guesthouse, fur stores, trading rooms, living quarters and shops, but all were destroyed in the 1930s, with the exception of the **main warehouse** (1832), a sturdy wooden building that remains the only hint of the fort's earlier significance. Parks Canada Visitor Centre in Churchill (see opposite) has information on camping at the site and can arrange guided tours between mid-June and mid-September.

ARRIVAL AND DEPARTURE   YORK FACTORY

By plane This remote spot can only be reached by charter plane. Try Calm Air (☎204 778 6471, ⓦcalmair.com), from

Thompson or Churchill.

Hwy-16: Winnipeg to Saskatoon

Hwy-16 (nicknamed the **Yellowhead Route**) follows the Trans-Canada Highway (Hwy-1) west out of Winnipeg but soon cuts northwest for a more attractive journey across the prairies. It goes through the pretty little town of **Neepawa** before passing south of the attractive forests, lakes and grasslands of **Riding Mountain National Park**, 250km from Winnipeg. Just north of the park the small town of **Dauphin** and its surroundings have a Ukrainian past that's still in evidence, particularly in the Doukhobor settlement of **Veregin** and the functional prairie town of **Yorkton**. From here, the highway embarks on one of its dullest stretches across the prairies towards Saskatoon, but don't miss **Little Manitou Lake** – Saskatchewan's Dead Sea.

Neepawa

Elms and cottonwoods line the streets of tiny, pleasant **NEEPAWA**, some 90km west along Hwy-16 from Portage la Prairie. Its oldest buildings dot the principal drag, Mountain Avenue, and include the neo-Romanesque Knox Presbyterian Church at Mill Street and 1st Avenue, with its unusual thick, turreted bell tower, and the tidy, late Victorian, County Court House, close to Hamilton Street.

The old CNR station at the west end of Hamilton Street contains the **Beautiful Plains Museum** (91 Hamilton St West; May & June Mon–Fri 9am–5pm; July & Aug Mon–Fri 9am–5pm, Sat & Sun 1–5pm; donation; ☎204 476 3896), with diverting displays on the district's pioneers. Margaret Laurence (1926–87), one of Canada's best-known writers, lived in Neepawa in her early years and used the town (renamed Manawaka) as a setting for many of her novels, which portray strong women struggling against small-town life. Her former home at 312 1st Ave North is now a museum of her life (mid-May to Sept daily 10am–5pm; $5; ☎204 476 3612).

ACCOMMODATION AND EATING NEEPAWA

★ **Brews Brothers Bistro** 376b Mountain Ave ☎204 841 0439. Neepawa has several unexciting places to eat downtown and along the main highway, but this is the only place that stands out. A lovely café for home-made soups, salads and sandwiches ($8–11) using premium ingredients. Tues–Fri 8.30am–7pm.

Westway Inn Motel 153 Main St W ☎204 476 2355, ⓦwestwayinnneepawa.com. The pick of a basic trio of motels designed catch the passing trade along Hwy-16 and useful if you can't make Winnipeg or Riding Mountain before dark. $99

Riding Mountain National Park

A 45km detour from Hwy-16 near the sleepy but likeable town of Minnedosa, **Riding Mountain National Park** is a vast expanse of wilderness, roughly 50km by 100km, that provides some of Manitoba's finest hiking, biking and scenery. Its name comes from fur trappers who changed from canoe to horseback to travel its wooded highlands, and it's also known as the place where **Grey Owl** (see page 878) spent six months or so living with his wife and their pet beavers in 1931.

The park

The park's eastern edge is marked by a 400m-high ridge studded with a dense evergreen forest which soon gives way to a highland plateau whose mixed forests and lakes form the core of the park and surround its only significant settlement, the resort village of **WASAGAMING**, on Clear Lake on the park's southern edge. There's a scrawny beach here that gets overcrowded in July and August (beaches on the southwest and northern edge of the lake are quieter with shallower and warmer water). Some 4km to the south of the park the straggly community of **ONANOLE** provides additional basic services, particularly groceries and a couple of budget motels. To the west, forests give way to aspen woodlands, meadow and open grassland.

However you explore, the **wildlife** rather than the landscape will be the likely highlight. Dawn and dusk are the optimal viewing times and some of the best spots readily accessible: elk and a carefully tended **buffalo** herd graze near Lake Audy, a 45-minute drive northwest of Wasagaming; for **moose**, try the Moon Lake Trail, just off Hwy-10 or the nearby Boreal Trail which, though only 1km, is usually a good bet.

Bears are often spotted alongside all the park highways and trails, so make plenty of noise to avoid bumping into them while hiking or biking.

Most **hiking** trails in or near Wasagaming are short and easy. The best is the 8km **Grey Owl Trail**, leading to the man's old cabin. This trail connects with the nearest overnight routes, the **Cowan Lake Trail**, which branches off through a region of dense forest, small lakes and meadows; all the overnight trails have primitive campsites. If you have your own transport, the best trail for a half-day hike is the 6.4km **Gorge Creek Trail** near the East Park Gate. Dense with tree roots, this trail descends through thick woodland, continually re-crossing the tiny creek and delivering good views from the Riding Mountain escarpment along the way; the hike is frequently offered as an organized trip by the **visitor centre** as part of its summer events programme.

Also near the East Gate are some challenging **mountain bike** routes: the J.E.T. and Bald Hill trails have been developed to offer an alternative to the very gentle Wasagaming options.

INFORMATION AND ACTIVITIES — RIDING MOUNTAIN NATIONAL PARK

Entry fees Park entry costs $7.80 per person per day, though family and annual packages are available.

Riding Mountain Park Visitor Centre (mid-May to late June & Sept to mid-Oct Thurs–Mon 9.30am–5pm; July & Aug daily 9.30am–8pm; ☎ 204 848 7275, ☎ 1866 787 6221, ⓦ parkscanada.gc.ca/riding). At the centre of Wasagaming; sells fishing licences ($9.80) and backcountry camping permits ($15.70). From early Oct to mid-May, the centre closes and the administration office opposite (Mon–Fri 8am–noon & 12.30–4pm) provides these services.

Bike rental Tempo petrol station at the centre of town rents bicycles (☎ 240 848 2535; $18/hr, $85/day).

Canoe and boat rental Rent canoes and powerboats ($20/hr) from the jetty on Clear Lake.

ACCOMMODATION

HOTELS AND MOTELS

Elk Horn Resort ☎ 204 848 2802, ⓦ elkhornresort.mb.ca. The only year-round possibility and barely more expensive than the park's basic motels, this four-star resort on the edge of Wasagaming has smart modern rooms, a slick spa, golf course and horseriding, a steakhouse and a pizzeria. **$180**

Lakehouse 128 Wasagaming Drive ☎ 204 848 7366, ⓦ staylakehouse.ca. A 1930s motel has been successfully refurbished here to give it a more rustic and boutique look across its one- or two-bedroom suites. Most have kitchenettes and free wi-fi. There's a sundeck, barbecues and a hot tub too. May–Oct. **$159**

Mooswa Resort Mooswa Drive ☎ 204 848 2533, ⓦ mooswa.com. Modern A-frames and battered but clean motel rooms, but mostly two-bedroom "chalets", surrounding an outdoor pool and close to tennis courts and a beach. May to early Oct. **$195**

CAMPSITES

★ **Moon Lake Campground** 35km north of Wasagaming on Hwy-10. Quiet spot away from all the hubbub of Wasagaming, with 29 sites for RVs or tents by a lake. With a good lakeside hiking trail, toilets and fire wood. Sites can't be reserved. **$16**

Wasagaming Campground ☎ 204 848 7275, ☎ 877 737 3783, ⓦ pccamping.ca. The main park-run campground has some 600 sites, close to the action with an innovative selection of ways in which to bed down, including yurts or large static tents (each $90) for up to six people (you need your own bedding and gear for either). **$27**

Whirlpool Lake Campground 15km from Wasagaming on Hwy-19. Small tent-only campground with lake views and some fifteen sites – all first-come, first-served – a kitchen shelter and toilet. **$16**

EATING AND DRINKING

★ **Poor Michael's Bookshop & Café** Onanole ☎ 204 848 0336, ⓦ poormichaels.ca. Tempting for lengthy lingering thanks to many secondhand books, crafty items, occasional musical events and readings, and good café food. Pretty much an essential stop-off on grocery runs to Onanole. May–Oct daily 9am–8pm.

★ **TR McKoys** 117 Wasagaming Drive ☎ 204 848 2217, ⓦ trmckoys.ca. The best of Wasagaming's restaurants, with quality Italian food served in a vintage log building. Thin-crust pizza and pasta dishes from $18, as well as decent curries and steak. Reservations recommended. May–Oct daily for lunch and dinner (hours vary).

★ **Whitehouse Bakery** 104 Buffalo Drive ☎ 204 848 7700. Excellent but generally overcrowded bakery selling superb cinnamon buns to take away, plus a little restaurant for standard but satisfying breakfasts and lunches. Daily mid-May to Oct 7am–4pm.

NATIONAL UKRAINIAN FESTIVAL

The **National Ukrainian Festival** (Ⓦcnuf.ca) celebrates Dauphin's ancestry on the first weekend of August at a purpose-built complex on the edge of Riding Mountain Park. The complex has a splendid thousand-seat hillside amphitheatre, ideal for music and dance performances, and a tiny heritage village dedicated to early Ukrainian settlers. You can visit its shop for Ukrainian handicrafts year-round beside *Corinna's on Main* (see below).

Dauphin and around

Heading north out of Riding Mountain National Park on Hwy-10, you'll soon hit **DAUPHIN**. Founded as a French fur-trading post in 1739, it's now a pleasant prairie town that would be unremarkable, if it weren't for the preservation of its **Ukrainian** ancestry. Those who cleared and settled this part of Manitoba between 1896 and 1925 assimilated rather more slowly into local culture, leaving the onion domes of Ukrainian Orthodox churches scattered throughout the region. Dauphin's only real attraction is **Fort Dauphin Museum** by the river at 4th Ave SW (May, June & Sept Mon–Fri 9am–5pm; July & Aug Tues–Sun 9am–5pm; Oct–April by appointment; $5; ☎204 638 6630, Ⓦfortdauphinmuseum.wordpress.com). This tidy wooden replica North West Company stockade holds reconstructions of several sorts of pioneer building, including a trapper's cabin.

7

Wasyl Negrych Pioneer Farmstead

Gilbert Plains · July & Aug daily 10am–5pm · $5 · ☎204 548 2326, Ⓦnegrychpioneerhomestead.blogspot.com

A near-complete example of what life was like for Ukrainian immigrants can be seen at the **Wasyl Negrych Pioneer Farmstead**, near the village of Gilbert Plains, 30km west of Dauphin. Wasyl and Anna Negrych and their seven children arrived here from the Carpathian Mountains in 1897 to build their farmstead. It ended up with ten buildings, including an 1899 home that replaced their first log house after it burnt down, three granaries, barns, a chicken coop, pigsty, garages and a bunkhouse with a fully-preserved working *peech* (the log and clay cookstove once the heart of every Ukrainian household). Amazingly, two of Wasyl and Anna's children ran the farmstead according to traditional practices until their deaths in the 1980s, never introducing electricity, sewers or phones.

INFORMATION   **DAUPHIN**

Tourist office 100 Main St South (May–Aug Mon–Fri 9am–4.30pm, Sat 10am–3pm; Sept–April Mon–Fri 9am– 4.30pm; ☎204 622 3216 , Ⓦtourismdauphin.ca).

ACCOMMODATION AND EATING

Canway Inn and Suites 1601 Main St ☎204 638 5102, ☎888 325 3335, Ⓦcanwayinnandsuites.com. An okay, pretty standard motel option, though at 4km south of town near the junction of highways 5 and 10, it's not central. Some rooms have en-suite jacuzzis – plus there's an indoor pool and sauna. Connected to a branch of diner-chain *Smitty's*. **$144**

Corinna's on Main 1430 Main St ☎204 638 7040. The dining scene in downtown Dauphin is fairly desperate,

while fast-food abounds around the edges of town where this diner – with its solid cooked all-day breakfasts, hearty sandwiches and juicy burgers – provides a pleasant surprise. Mains average a modest $12. Daily 7am–8pm.

Vermilion Park Campground 21 2nd Ave NW ☎204 622 3125. Lies a 10min walk north of Main Street and has some 200 shaded campsites, a wading pool, picnic sites, playground and 3km of trails. May–Oct. **$15**

Yorkton and around

As Hwy-16 heads west into Saskatchewan, **YORKTON** is the first and last sizeable place you reach until Saskatoon, 333km away. Though founded in the 1880s by Ontarian farmers, its **Ukrainian** heritage has left the strongest mark – like many places

GRAIN ELEVATORS

Though a US invention, there's hardly anything more distinctively Canadian Prairie than the **grain elevator**. These tall and traditionally wooden grain warehouses were utilitarian in design and built simply to store wheat before its transport by rail. Yet with their clean, functional lines rising high above the plains, they've been likened to cathedrals, earned nicknames like "castles of the New World" and "prairie sentinels", and found their way into many a prairie heart.

The first Canadian grain elevators were built in the 1880s and by 1938 some 5800 dotted the region, each emblazoned with the names of the small towns they marked. But as grain transport switched from rail to road their numbers dwindled to the present seven hundred. In 2000, the Canadian Wheat Board decided to build massive central concrete terminals at main transit points, to which grain now travels by truck, making old-style elevators even more redundant. Some have already been dismantled, threatening to change the prairie landscape irrevocably, but many still hold out; while in **Inglis**, a tiny town just to the west of Riding Mountain National Park, a row of 1920s wooden elevators beside an abandoned railway line have been preserved as a National Historic Site (Ⓦ ingliselevators.com).

hereabouts. The town's most prestigious attraction is the late-May **Yorkton Short Film and Video Festival** (Ⓦ yorktonfilm.com), the oldest of its kind in North America, started in 1947.

Western Development Museum

Hwy-16 • Jan–March Tues–Fri 9am–5pm Sat & Sun noon–5pm; April–June & mid-Aug to Dec Mon–Fri 9am–5pm, Sat & Sun noon–5pm; July to mid-Aug Tues–Sun 9am–5pm • $10 • Ⓦ wdm.ca

The Ukrainian community features strongly in Yorkton's branch of the **Western Development Museum**, which is devoted to the various ethnic groups who have settled the region. You'll also find a replica of the interior of a 1902 Catholic church and a superb collection of early twentieth-century Fords and Buicks. The most startling sights are the bright-red, huge-wheeled early fire trucks, looking entirely too fragile to function. To see farmworkers and their fierce-looking machines in action, along with a number of other pioneering skills – bread baking, grain grinding, threshing, sawmill operation, blacksmithing, quilting and ice cream making – attend the **Threshermen's Show**, held here in early August.

Godfrey Dean Art Gallery

49 Smith St • Mon–Fri 11am–5pm, Sat & Sun 1–4pm • Free • ☎ 306 786 2992, Ⓦ deangallery.ca

Home to a small but striking permanent collection of Saskatchewan art, plus several galleries with temporary exhibitions, the **Godfrey Dean Art Gallery** tends to be strong on applied and contemporary art, but is always worth a look for the local flavour.

Good Spirit Lake Provincial Park

About 48km northwest of Yorkton off Hwy-16 • $10/vehicle/day • ☎ 306 792 4750, Ⓦ saskparks.net/goodspiritlake

The attractive **Good Spirit Lake Provincial Park** is noted for its ecologically fragile sand dunes and its warm, shallow lake, which has exceptionally clear water. The south shore has fine beaches, a fuel station, mini-golf, tennis courts, riding stables, dining and snacking facilities.

Veregin and the National Doukhobor Heritage Village

70km northeast of Yorkton • Mid-May to mid-Sept daily 10am–6pm; rest of year by appointment • $5 • ☎ 306 542 4441, Ⓦ ndhv.ca

The tiny settlement of **VEREGIN** takes its name from **Peter Veregin**, the leader of the pacifist Doukhobor sect (see page 653) whose seven thousand members migrated to Saskatchewan at the end of the nineteenth century. His large, square and refurbished two-storey prayer home, complete with many original furnishings, is part of the

National Doukhobor Heritage Village, where a modest museum traces the history of the sect. The building, with its encircling veranda and wrought-iron adornment on both levels, dominates a large green lawn and faces the other village buildings, which were mostly moved here from other Doukhobor colonies in Saskatchewan. Lined in a neat row are a farmhouse, blacksmith's shop, granary, bakery and bathhouse, the latter equipped with fragrant dried oak leaves used to cleanse the skin. Another, smaller prayer home features a Russian library and a display on Tolstoy, whose financial support helped the Doukhobors migrate. The imposing bronze statue of the writer was donated by the Soviet Union.

ACCOMMODATION AND EATING	YORKTON AND AROUND

Good Spirit Lake Provincial Park Campground 48km northwest of Yorkton off Hwy-16 ☎ 306 792 4750. The best spot to camp in the Yorkton area is a 30min drive from town and beside the lake – and its excellent beach. Facilities for this 214-site campground include hot showers, tennis courts, mini-golf and a grocery store. __$18__

Tapps Brewing Company 69 Broadway ☎ 306 783 2522. In Yorkton's drab dining scene the *Tapps Brewing Company* stands out as a lively brewpub with good bar food and its own line of interesting beers. Daily 11am–2am.

Windy Acres RR3 Yorkton ☎ 306 786 5050, ⓦ windy acresinn.ca. 111 Darlington St West ☎ 306 783 7078. Several reasonably priced but bland hotels gather along Broadway Street, but a more interesting choice is this sprawling wood-clad lodge some 6km west of downtown via Hwy-52. Its pleasant bearskin-decorated common room has a ping-pong table. Rates include a good hot buffet breakfast. __$105__

7

Little Manitou Lake

An hour's drive south of Hwy-16 – some 120km east of Saskatoon and 260km west of Yorkton – lies **Little Manitou Lake**. Set in a rather arid landscape it looks just like any other lake, until you submerge yourself in its murky waters – or try to, for its salt content is three times that of ocean water, and denser than Jordan's and Israel's Dead Sea. You'll inevitably find yourself floating on the surface, feet up. The lake has also long been known for its healing properties among Aboriginal peoples who camped on its shores. Today, most people head to the tiny, rather ramshackle, resort town of **Manitou Beach** on the lake's south shore and bathe in heated indoor mineral pools (see box below).

Saskatoon

Set on the wide South Saskatchewan River at the heart of a vast wheat-growing area, **SASKATOON** is a commercial centre with a population of around 260,000 – making it Saskatchewan's largest city. All the same it's an easy-going place, with pleasant riverside paths and a nice-enough stop on any prairie itinerary. Most of the worthwhile sites, such as the Plains Indian **Wanuskewin** complex (see page 504), are outside town.

Brief history

Ontario Methodists founded Saskatoon as a temperance colony in 1883 and named it after a local berry, but in spite of their enthusiasm the new settlement made an

---

MANITOU SPRINGS MINERAL SPA

To experience near-weightlessness and soothe any rheumatic or arthritic pains in heated comfort, try **Manitou Springs Mineral Spa** (daily 9am–10pm; $16; ☎ 306 946 2233, ☎ 800 667 7672, ⓦ manitousprings.ca), one of Canada's largest and oldest. You can also stay and eat in their hotel, whose rates ($156) include a dip in the spa and a hot buffet breakfast.

extremely slow start, partly because the semi-arid farming conditions were unfamiliar and partly because the 1885 Northwest Rebellion raised fears of Aboriginal hostility. Although the railroad reached Saskatoon in 1890, there were still only 113 inhabitants at the start of the twentieth century. But the next decade saw a sudden influx of European and American settlers and, as the regional agricultural economy expanded, a group of entrepreneurs, nicknamed **boomers**, dominated and made Saskatoon the provincial economic hub. This success was underpinned by particularly sharp municipal loyalty: people who dared criticize any aspect of the city – from poor water quality to tyrannical labour practices – were dubbed **knockers**, and their opinions rubbished by the press. Even so the boomers established a pleasant, well-groomed city where solidarity overwhelmed differences in income and occupation.

Meewasin Valley Trail

Ideal for a pleasant riverside walk and useful to get your bearings, the **Meewasin Valley Trail** is a circular, 20km walking and cycle route that follows a narrow strip of park along both banks of the river. Usefully, it connects most of Saskatoon's principal sights. Walking the loop from the Remai Modern past Downtown stretch and up to the University and back on the other side of the river takes about an hour.

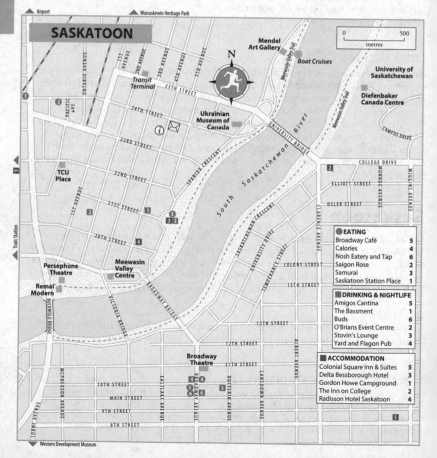

SASKATOON'S FESTIVALS

Saskatchewan Jazz Festival Late June or early July ⓦ saskjazz.com. Saskatoon's biggest and best shindig with over five hundred musicians performing jazz, gospel and blues across the city, mostly for free.

Shakespeare on the Saskatchewan Festival July & Aug ⓦ shakespearesask.com. Sees plays performed in tents on the river bank by the Mendel Art Gallery.

Nutrien Fringe Festival Early Aug ⓦ 25thstreettheatre.org. A week of alternative performances featuring comedy and theatre from all over the world.

Folkfest Mid-Aug ⓦ saskatoonfolkfest.com. Large three-day festival that celebrates the town's multiethnic roots in a number of nationally or regionally themed pavilions, with cultural performances, cuisines and crafts.

Remai Modern

100 Spadina Crescent E • Tues & Fri 10am–10pm, Wed,Thurs, Sat & Sun 10am–5pm • $12 • ☎ 306 975 7610, ⓦ remaimodern.org

Said to be inspired by the prairie landscape, the avant-garde Remai Modern looks like a number of giant building blocks that have been balanced on top of one another on the banks of the South Saskatchewan River. Opened in 2017, it's Saskatoon's great cultural jewel and provides an airy home for the city's premier art collection which numbers almost eight-thousand pieces. Only a portion's on display at any one time, but look out for pieces by some of Canada's most renowned artists: Emily Carr, Lawren Harris and David Milne among them. On top of this there's an impressive collection of linocuts and ceramics by Picasso.

Ukrainian Museum of Canada

910 Spadina Crescent E • Tues–Sat 10am–5pm, Sun 1–5pm • $7 • ⓦ umc.sk.ca

A few minutes' walk north from the centre, along the west bank, the **Ukrainian Museum of Canada** is the more interesting of the city's two Ukrainian museums, representing the Orthodox as distinct from the Catholic tradition. Displays cover the history of Ukrainian migration, traditional textile design, festivals and Easter-egg painting.

University of Saskatchewan

Museum of Antiquities Mon–Fri 9am–4pm, Sat noon–4.30pm • Free **Kenderdine Gallery** Tues–Fri 11.30am–4pm • Free • **Diefenbaker Canada Centre** Mon–Thurs 9.30am–8pm, Fri 9.30am–4.30pm, Sat & Sun noon–4.30pm • Free • ☎ 306 966 8384, ⓦ usask.ca

Over University Bridge from downtown is the campus of the **University of Saskatchewan**, on a prime riverbank site just north of College Drive – one of the finest **views** of the city is from the centre's grounds. Departmental collections include a **Museum of Antiquities** in the Murray Building, and the small **Kenderdine Gallery**. Neither draw as many visitors as the **Diefenbaker Canada Centre**, a museum, archive and research centre at the west end of the campus, beside the river. Graduating here in 1915, John Diefenbaker served as prime minister from 1957 to 1963. With his large flat face, protruding teeth and wavy white hair he was a caricaturist's dream and the museum's high point is its assortment of newspaper cartoons.

Western Development Museum

2610 Lorne Ave S • Jan–March Tues–Sun 9am–5pm, Apr–Dec daily 9am–5pm • $12 • ⓦ wdm.ca • Bus #1 from 3rd Ave downtown

South of both the river and downtown, the Saskatoon **Western Development Museum** has as its highlight "Boomtown". It's an ambitious reconstruction of a typical Saskatchewan small-town main street circa 1910, complete with boardwalk sidewalks and parked vehicles. More like a film set than a museum, its mixture of replica and original buildings includes a school, general store, church, train station and a combined pool hall and barbershop.

ARRIVAL AND INFORMATION

By plane Saskatoon airport (ⓦyxe.ca), 5km northwest of downtown, is linked by bus #11. Some hotels operate their own shuttle service, otherwise a taxi downtown will cost about $18.

Destinations Calgary (12 daily; 1hr 20min); Toronto (6 daily; 3hr); Vancouver (2 daily; 2hr).

By train The station lies on Chappell Drive, 8km southwest of downtown and a 5min walk from bus #3 on Dieppe St; a taxi downtown costs about $20.

Destinations Edmonton (3 weekly; 8hr); Jasper (3 weekly; 15hr); Toronto (3 weekly; 48hr); Vancouver (3 weekly; 34hr);

Winnipeg (3 weekly; 15hr).

By bus The city's bus station (ⓉⓉ306 933 8000) lies at 23rd St East and Pacific Ave in the centre. Rider Express buses (ⓉⓉ1 833 583 3636, ⓦriderexpress.ca) pick up at 1736 Quebec Ave, a ten-minute walk east of Downtown, a 7 min ride on the #14 bus from the Downtown Transit terminal.

Destinations Edmonton (1 daily; 7hrs); Regina (3 daily; 3hr); Winnipeg (1 daily; 9hr 30min).

Visitor information office 202 4th Ave North (Mon–Fri 8.15am–5.30pm, Sat & Sun 8.30am–5.30pm; Ⓣ306 242 1206, Ⓣ800 567 2444, ⓦtourismsaskatoon.com).

GETTING AROUND AND TOURS

By bus Saskatoon Transit (ⓉⓉ306 975 3100; ⓦtransit. saskatoon.ca) operates a good bus system ($3 one way; pay driver, no change).

River cruise Cruises along the South Saskatchewan River, with its weir, sandbars and fast-flowing currents, are

offered by the *Prairie Lily* (May–Sept Mon–Fri 3.30pm & 6pm; Sat & Sun 1.30pm, 3.30pm & 6pm; $20; Ⓣ888 747 7572, ⓦtheprairielily.com); the one-hour trip departs from the dock by the Remai Modern.

ACCOMMODATION

Complementing the central choices below, are a good number of chain motels on Hwy-11 south of town and Hwy-16 going east.

HOTELS, MOTELS AND B&BS

Colonial Square Inn & Suites 1301 8th St East Ⓣ306 343 1676, Ⓣ800 667 3939, ⓦcolonialsquareinn.com; map p.500. Eighty simple singles and doubles, all with cable TV & free wi-fi. Close to the Broadway Ave area. $104

★ **Delta Bessborough Hotel** 601 Spadina Crescent Ⓣ306 244 5521, Ⓣ800 890 3222, ⓦmarriott.com; map p.500. Built for the CNR in 1931, the *Bessborough* is an enormous turreted and gabled affair, set in Kiwanis Memorial Park, beside the river. It's been tastefully refurbished in a French château style, which makes it the city's most striking building; some claim it's haunted. $143

The Inn on College 1020 College Dr Ⓣ306 665 9111 ⓦinnoncollege.com; map p.500. With snug rooms

that sport minimalist and light-wood and furnishings, this looks a little like a modern budget European hotel. Spotless, good-value, close to the university and with a comfortable communal lounge. Basic breakfast included. $85

Radisson Hotel Saskatoon 405 20th St East Ⓣ306 665 3322, Ⓣ800 967 9033, ⓦradisson.com; map p.500. Well-kept tower-block hotel with plush rooms appointed with granite and marble bathrooms and good views. Free wi-fi and weekend rates are often very good. $148

CAMPGROUNDS

Gordon Howe Campground 1640 Ave P South, off 11th St Ⓣ306 975 3328, Ⓣ866 855 6655; map p.500. Most comfortable and central of the three city campsites, with over 130 serviced sites, with barbecue, picnic area and laundry. It's located near the South Saskatchewan River, 6km southwest of the centre; take 22nd St out of town, then follow Ave P south. Mid-April to mid-Oct. $23

EATING

Many Saskatoon **restaurants** cluster downtown and along Broadway Ave – the city's modest cultural strip with its handful of more alternative shops and cafés. Many city bars (see below) serve good food too.

Broadway Café 814 Broadway Ave Ⓣ306 652 8244, ⓦbroadwaycafesaskatoon.ca; map p.500. Straightforward greasy spoon loved for its breakfasts but also perfect to satisfy simple sandwich, burger and crispy onion-ring cravings. A vague 1950s nostalgia abounds, even if the decor is all much newer. Most dishes below $10. Daily 8am–9pm.

Calories 721 Broadway Ave Ⓣ306 655 7991, ⓦcalories restaurants.ca; map p.500. Atmospheric French-style bistro (the chef grew up in Provence so, yes, it's the real

deal), with great wine list. Mains from $23. Mon–Thurs 11am–10pm, Fri & Sat 10am–11pm, Sun 10am–4pm.

Nosh Eatery and Tap 820 Broadway Ave 306 Ⓣ933 3355, ⓦnosheateryandtap.com; map p.500. Sleek, primarily vegetarian, bistro with beet chips, yam sandwiches, and halloumi crostini among its delights. Mains run $11–27. Mon–Thurs 11am–11pm, Fri & Sat 11am–1am, Sun 10.30am–10pm.

Saigon Rose 69 24th St East Ⓣ306 242 1351; map p.500. Simple place with plastic tablecloths and fantastically cheap and filling Vietnamese and Chinese food; most dishes are $7–10. Mon–Sat 11am–9pm, Sun 4–9pm.

SASKATOON BERRY PIE

The thing to try while in town is **Saskatoon berry pie**, made with berries grown on the outskirts of the city. One popular place is the *Berry Barn*, 830 Valley Rd (April to mid-Dec Mon–Fri 11am–8pm, Sat & Sun 9am–8pm; ☎306 978 9797, ⓦberrybarn.ca), a good restaurant serving hearty home-made food, 11km southwest of town on Hwy-11. It's one of a number of places along this road that allow you to pick your own fruit.

Samurai At the Delta Bessborough Hotel (see above), 601 Spadina Crescent ☎306 683 6926; map p.500. Good but pricey Japanese sushi and *teppanyaki* restaurant. Mains $24–39. Daily 4–10pm.

Saskatoon Station Place 221 Idylwyld Drive North ☎306 244 7777, ⓦsaskatoonstationplace.com; map p.500. Dine on steak and prime rib in Pullman cars in a converted train station. Lunch dishes average $13 for wraps, burgers and salads; dinner entrées are around $25. The Sunday brunches are great. Daily 11am–10pm.

DRINKING AND NIGHTLIFE

Nightlife is a little slow, but a few pubs and clubs in the old warehouse district at 24th St and Pacific Ave can reward the determined. Otherwise consult the weekend listings of the *Star Phoenix* (ⓦthestarphoenix.com) newspaper. While you're in town try a bottle of the local **Great Western Beer**, whose future was threatened by a merger of Canada's two brewing giants, Molson and Carling O'Keefe. The workers bought the factory and can now barely keep up with demand.

★ **Amigos Cantina** 806 Dufferin Ave ☎306 652 4912, ⓦamigoscantina.com; map p.500. Hip and casual Mexican restaurant that becomes a club at night with local bands often playing. Mains $14–17. Daily 11.30am–2am.

★ **The Bassment** B3 202 4th Ave North ☎306 683 2277, ⓦthebassment.ca; map p.500. Great jazz venue attracting international performers. Live jazz Fri & Sat eve (Oct–April), usually starting at 8pm.

Buds 817 Broadway Ave ☎306 244 4155, ⓦbuds.

dudaone.com; map p.500. Rough-and-ready bar with nightly R&B acts, plus jam sessions on Saturday afternoon. Cover around $5. Mon–Fri 4pm–2am, Sat 3pm–2am, Sun 5pm–midnight.

O'Brians Event Centre 241 2nd Ave South ☎306 651 1000, ⓦobrianseventcentre.ca; map p.500. One of Saskatoon's key midsize concert venues with great lighting and sound systems; the programme is always worth a look. Hours vary according to events.

Stovin's Lounge At the Delta Bessborough Hotel (see page 502); map p.500. A quiet and comfortable lounge, ideal for chatting and unwinding when all the other options sound like too much effort. Daily 2.30–11pm.

Yard and Flagon Pub 718 Broadway Ave ☎306 653 8883; map p.500. Broadway bar with a lively rooftop that pulls in the university crowd. Also has good bar food but is particularly loved for its chicken curry soup. Mains average $15. Daily 11am–2am.

ENTERTAINMENT

Broadway Theatre 715 Broadway Ave ☎306 652 6556, ⓦbroadwaytheatre.ca. Screens many of the best foreign, art-house and domestic films. Adult tickets cost $15.

Persephone Theatre 100 Spadina Crescent ☎306 384 7727, ⓦpersephonetheatre.org. The city's best-known professional theatre company, within a swank new arts

centre and a season that runs from October to May.

TCU Place 35 22nd St E ☎306 975 7777, ⓦtcuplace. com. This is where visiting ballet, theatre and opera companies will appear and also the regular venue for the Saskatoon Symphony Orchestra (tickets $34–73; ☎306 665 6414, ⓦsaskatoonsymphony.org).

DIRECTORY

Hospitals Saskatoon City Hospital, 701 Queen St ☎306 655 8000.

Library Frances Morrison Library, 311 23rd St E (Mon–Thurs

10am–9pm, Fri & Sat 10am–6pm). Free internet access.

Post office 309 4th Ave N; Mon–Fri 8am–5pm.

Taxi Comfort Cabs ☎306 664 6464.

Around Saskatoon

North of Saskatoon, Hwy-11 cuts through a narrow slice of prairie between the final stretches of the North and South Saskatchewan rivers, before they flow together in the northeast. There's nothing to see on the road itself, but a brief detour will take you to the atmospheric Plains Indian site of **Wanuskewin** and the informative **Batoche**

National Historic Site, where the Métis rebellion of 1885 reached its disastrous climax. Setting out early and with your own transport you can combine these with visits to a museum at **Duck Lake** and the reconstructed **Fort Carlton** where you can camp. With longer to spare, consider heading to the healing waters of Little Manitou Lake (see page 499) or up into the wilds of Prince Albert National Park (see page 506).

Wanuskewin Heritage Park

RR #4, Penner Rd • Daily: 9am–4.30pm • $8.50 • ⓦ wanuskewin.com

Wanuskewin Heritage Park, 14km north of downtown via Hwy-11, is Saskatoon's principal attraction and a lavish tribute to the culture of Northern Plains First Nations. It's well worth the trip out here, as the commercial aspect is played down in favour of a sensitive interpretation of the First Nations' spiritual relationship to the land and to living creatures.

Bordering the South Saskatchewan River in the attractive wooded Opamihaw Valley, the park embraces a string of marshy creeks and wooded ridges that have been used by Aboriginal peoples for more than six thousand years. All along the trails are ecologically fragile plants and flowers that must not be picked. Its nineteen sites are connected by trails to a visitor centre featuring reconstructions of teepees, a buffalo pound and a buffalo jump, as well as displays of traditional skills as diverse as tool making and storytelling. The attached **restaurant** specializes in indigenous foods such as buffalo meat and bannock bread, and a gift shop has a range of beautiful arts and crafts. Wanuskewin has been developed with the cooperation of local Aboriginal peoples, who provide most of the interpretive staff. There is no public transport, though the park is connected by the Meewasin hiking and cycling trail (see page 500); a **taxi** from downtown costs around $20.

Batoche National Historic Site

Mid-May to June & early Sept to Oct Mon–Fri 9am–5pm; July to early Sept daily 9am–5pm • $7.80 • ☎ 306 423 6227, ⓦ pc.gc.ca

North of Saskatoon on Hwy-11, the briefest of detours takes you to the site of the Métis' last stand – and the last place where Canadians fought Canadians. **Batoche National Historic Site** occupies a splendid site on the east bank of the South Saskatchewan River, just off Hwy-225. A **visitor centre** provides an insight into the Métis way of life and a blow-by-blow account of the battle, in part using an exceptional 45-minute film. But it all rather glosses over the cause of the conflict; the displays are perhaps too sympathetic to the Métis, instead of appreciating the government's concern over Canada being split in half – the West was still very much an open territory at the time.

Behind the centre, the main footpath leads to a refurbished Catholic church and adjacent rectory: all that is left of the original village. A few minutes' walk away, in the cemetery perched above the river bank, memorials inscribed with the hoary commendation "a credit to his race" contrast with the rough chunk of rock that commemorates Riel's commander-in-chief, **Gabriel Dumont**. A stern and ferocious man, Dumont insisted he be buried standing up – so he could enjoy a good view of the river. The church and cemetery are at the centre of the park's **walking trails**, which extend along the river bank in both directions joining military graveyards, a Métis farmhouse, the remains of rifle pits, and the site of the old ferry crossing.

Duck Lake

On the west side of the South Saskatchewan River on Hwy-11, the tiny farming community of **DUCK LAKE** – where many buildings have outdoor murals depicting local history – is home to a regional **interpretive centre** (late May to early Sept daily 10am–5.30pm; $4.50; ⓦ ducklakemuseum.com) with displays on Aboriginal, Métis

THE MÉTIS AND THE NORTHWEST REBELLION

As the offspring of Aboriginal women and white fur traders, the Métis were for centuries Canada's most marginalized group. Recognized neither as Canadians nor Aboriginals, they were denied rights and often forced to wander the country in poverty with nowhere to settle. The 1869–70 Red River rebellion in Manitoba, led by **Louis Riel**, won significant concessions from the Canadian government but failed to protect the Métis' way of life against the effects of increasing white settlement. Consequently, many Métis moved west to farm the banks of the **South Saskatchewan River**, where the men acted as intermediaries between Aboriginals and the whites. Yet when government surveyors arrived in 1878 the Métis realized – as they had on the Red River twenty years before – their claim to the land they farmed was far from secure.

Beginning with the Métis, a general sense of instability spread across the region in the early 1880s, fuelled by the increasingly restless and hungry **Cree** peoples, as well as by the discontent of white settlers angry at high freight charges for their produce. The leaders of the Métis decided to act and in June 1884 sent a delegation to Montana, where Riel was in exile. Convinced the Métis were chosen by God to purify the human race – and that he was their Messiah – Riel was easily persuaded to return.

In March 1885, Riel declared a provisional government at **Batoche** and demanded the surrender of **Fort Carlton**, the nearest Mountie outpost, 35km to their west on the North Saskatchewan River. The police superintendent refused and the force he dispatched to re-establish order was badly mauled at **Duck Lake**. When news of the uprising reached the Cree, some 300km away, they attacked the local Hudson's Bay Company store, killing its nine occupants in the so-called **Frog Lake Massacre**. Within two weeks, three columns of militia were converging on Big Bear's Cree and the meagre Métis forces at Batoche. The total number of casualties – about fifty – does not indicate the full significance of the engagement, which ended the Métis' brief independence. Riel's execution in Regina on November 16, 1885, was bitterly denounced in Québec and remains a symbol of the divide between English- and French-speaking Canada.

For more information on the events and sights relating to 1885, look at the excellent website ⓦ trailsof1885.com.

7

and pioneer society from 1870 to 1905. Prize exhibits include elaborate Cree costumes, an old outfit of Sioux chief Little Fox (adviser to Sitting Bull) and Gabriel Dumont's gold watch, presented to him in New York where he appeared in Buffalo Bill's Wild West Show. The building's huge tower makes the centre easy to find and provides views a long way over the prairies.

Fort Carlton Provincial Park

Late May to late June Mon–Fri 10am–6pm; late June Thurs–Mon 10am–6pm • $10 • ⓦ saskparks.net/fortcarlton

Fort Carlton Provincial Park lies 25km west along Hwy-212 from Duck Lake and celebrates a reconstruction of a Hudson's Bay Company trading post circa 1860. Founded in 1810, the river-bank station was fortified in successive decades and became an important centre of the fur and pemmican trades, until the demise of the buffalo brought an end to its success. Reduced to a warehouse in the early 1880s, the fort was garrisoned by the Mounties during the Northwest Rebellion (see page 505), but was finally burnt down and abandoned in 1885. The **visitor centre** provides an introduction to the fort, whose stockade shelters replicas of the clerk's quarters, a sail and harness shop, a fur and provisions store with piles of colourfully striped Hudson's Bay Company blankets and bottles of bright trading beads and a shop, whose merchandise included gunpowder – which meant the clerks were forbidden to light a stove here, no matter the temperature. There's an on-site **campground** (mid-May to Aug; $18), but with no facilities. Take care when camping or hiking here, as the wooded gullies of the North Saskatchewan River are home to a number of **black bears**.

Northern Saskatchewan

Some 230km north of Saskatoon the aspen parkland of the south meets the boreal forest of the north and is protected **Prince Albert National Park**. This great tract of wilderness is a landscape of rivers and creeks, deep lakes, tiny meadows and spruce bogs. The shift in vegetation is mirrored by the **wildlife**, with prairie species such as coyote and wild bison giving way to black bear, moose, wolf, caribou, osprey and eagle further north.

Prince Albert National Park is about as far north as most casual visitors go, but travel another 150km north to **Lac La Ronge Provincial Park** or even another 430km further to **Clearwater River Provincial Park** and you'll find an even greater wilderness with some of Canada's premier canoeing routes (see page 507). Both are also a big draw for the hook-and-bullet brigade, but the province's greatest lure for backcountry enthusiasts of all stripes is the extremely remote **Athabasca Sand Dunes Provincial Wilderness Park**.

Prince Albert National Park

The only settlement in the wilds of **Prince Albert National Park** is the tourist village of **WASKESIU**, which is approached from the south by Hwy-263 and from the east by highways 2 and 264. Spread out along the southern shore of Waskesiu Lake, it has all the usual facilities, plus a narrow sandy beach that gets ridiculously overcrowded in summer.

Several of the park's easier **hiking trails** begin in or near Waskesiu, most notably the 13km **Kingfisher Trail**, which loops through the forest just to the west. The best trails and **canoe routes** begin roughly 15km further north at **Kingsmere Lake**, accessible by boat or car from Waskesiu. They include a delightful week-long canoe trip along the western shore of Kingsmere Lake before heading through a series of remote lakes amid dense boreal forest. There's also a 20km hike or canoe (a good overnight trip) to the idyllic **Grey Owl's Cabin** (May–Sept), beside tiny Ajawaan Lake, near the northern shore of Kingsmere. Grey Owl (see page 878) lived here from 1931 until 1937, the year before his death, writing one of his better books, *Pilgrims of the Wild*; this is also where he, his wife and daughter are buried.

Whatever you do in the park, remember **insect repellent**.

ARRIVAL AND INFORMATION PRINCE ALBERT NATIONAL PARK

Visitor centre 969 Lakeview Drive (mid-May to early Oct daily 8am–8pm; early Oct to mid-May Mon–Fri 8am–4pm;, Sat & Sun 10am–5pm; ☎ 306 663 4522, ⓦ parkscanada.ca/princealbert). They sell park passes, if you didn't already buy one ($7.80/day) at the gate; provide advice on wildlife, hiking and weather; and issue backcountry camping permits ($10) for the campsites dotted along many remote trails.

ACTIVITIES

Canoe rental Canoe and kayak rentals (from $20/hr; $60/day; ☎ 306 663 1999, ⓦ waskesiumarina.com) are available at three marinas within the park, while Canoeski Discovery (☎ 306 653 5693, ⓦ canoeski.com) offers multi-day paddling trips for around $200 per day.

ACCOMMODATION AND EATING

Waskesiu's main street, Waskesiu Drive, roughly follows the southern lakeshore and has most of the park's **hotels**, **restaurants** and **snack bars**.

All Season Waskesiu Lake Lodge Lakeview Drive ☎ 306 663 6161, ⓦ waskesiulakelodge.com. Roomy lodge with a mix of smart and floral one- and two-bedroom suites. Units all have lakeside decks and barbecues. With wi-fi. May to mid-Oct. **$245**

Beaver Glen Campground Waskesiu ☎ 877 737 3783, ⓦ pccamping.ca. Wooded campground near Waskesiu Lake is central and popular with RVs, but for tents the unserviced campsites ($10) along Hwy-263 and on Kingsmere Lake are quieter options. Mid-May to Sept. **$29**

Hawood Inn 851 Lakeview Drive ☎ 306 663 5911, ⓦ hawood.com. Good motel accommodation with the bonus of rooftop hot tubs and a higher-end dining option

CANOEING IN NORTHERN SASKATCHEWAN

A seemingly endless web of canoe routes connects Northern Saskatchewan's thousands of lakes, but the key places for extended adventures are the turbulent white waters of the **Clearwater River** in **Clearwater River Provincial Park** and on the **Churchill River** in **Lac La Ronge Provincial Park**. The Churchill was once part of the main route into the northwest for the *voyageurs*: the river swerves across the width of the province, from west to east, before heading into Manitoba.

For most canoeists the best bet is a guided trip but independent and experienced wilderness travellers should start at the provincial parks' dedicated webpage: ⓦ saskparks.net/canoeing.

OPERATOR
Churchill River Canoe Outfitters ☎ 877 511 2726, ⓦ churchillrivercanoe.com. This excellent company is based in Missinipe, 80km north of the workaday uranium-mining town of La Ronge. It offers rentals, courses and accommodation in cabins and a hostel.

on site. Mains start at around $18 and include excellent local steak. **$140**
Kapasiwin Bungalows ☎ 306 663 5225, ☎ 877 963 5225, ⓦ kapasiwin.com. The best place for bungalow accommodation with rustic cabins in immaculately kept grounds, some 2km around the lake east of Waskesiu. With wandering elk, nesting loons and a private beach. May to mid-Oct. **$149**

Athabasca Sand Dunes Provincial Wilderness Park

Lying in Saskatchewan's extreme northwest corner, **Athabasca Sand Dunes Provincial Wilderness Park** protects the world's most northerly (and probably most incongruous) sand dunes. They provide a unique getaway for well-heeled wilderness fans: since the area can only be reached by private floatplane, it's expensive. One outfitter is Athabasca Eco Adventures (☎ 800 922 0957, ⓦ athabascalake.com/ecoindex.htm), who offer a week in the dunes with flights, food, accommodation and gear for around $4000.

Hwy-16: Saskatoon to Edmonton

From Saskatoon it's 275km to the Albertan border which is straddled by the service town of **Lloydminster**. En-route **Redberry Lake** is a must for keen birdwatchers, while the **Battlefords** make another good short stop to see a refurbished Mountie stockade. In Alberta, the run up to Edmonton brings rippling hills, rivers, lakes, lonely farms and open prairie, but also **Elk Island National Park**, where bison roam, and the interesting **Ukrainian Cultural Village**.

Redberry Lake

Interpretive centre Mid-May to mid-Sept daily 9am–5pm • Free • ☎ 306 549 2360, ⓦ redberrylake.ca

The **Redberry Lake Biosphere Reserve**, about 100km northwest of Saskatoon via highways 16, 340 and then 40, is one of the province's best areas to view over two hundred species of bird. Rarities include the piping plover and white pelican. There are lakeshore trails and an interpretive centre on the lake's fragile ecosystem, with information on a regional driving tour. Within the reserve, Redberry Lake Regional Park (May–Sept; $10) has **camping** ($18–40).

The Battlefords

Following the Yellowhead Highway towards Edmonton, you'll come to the **Battlefords**, 140km from Saskatoon. Sedate little **BATTLEFORD**, with its trim riverside streets, lost its pre-eminence when the Canadian Pacific Railway routed its transcontinental line through Regina in 1883. Twenty years later, its prospects were further damaged as the Canadian Northern Railway laid tracks on the opposite bank of the North Saskatchewan River, some 5km away, where grimy rival **NORTH BATTLEFORD** became a moderately successful industrial centre. Both towns have interesting museums and Battleford's **Saskatchewan Handcraft Festival**, in mid-July, is one of the largest and best of its kind.

Fort Battleford National Historic Site

Battleford · Mid-May to June Mon–Fri 10am–4pm; July to early Sept daily 10am–4pm · $7.80 · ⊛ parkscanada.gc.ca/battleford

Overlooking the river valley from the top of a steep bluff, **Fort Battleford National Historic Site** preserves a late nineteenth-century Northwestern Mounted Police base. An information centre provides an introduction while displays and costumed guides in the restored barracks explain more. Within the replica stockade stand four original buildings, including the **Sick Horse Stable**, where the Mounties' horses – most of which came from Ontario – were coaxed into accepting unfamiliar prairie grasses. The centrepiece of the park is the **Commanding Officer's Residence**. The hewn-log house contains an enormous carved bed-head and a couple of magnificent black and chrome oven ranges, which must have been a nightmare to transport this far west. The house was not as comfortable as it seems today, principally because the high ceilings made it almost impossible to heat.

Western Development Museum

North Battleford · Jan–March Tues–Sun 9am–5pm; April–Dec daily 9am–5pm · $10 · ⊛ wdm.ca

On Hwy-16, just east of **North Battleford**, a branch of the **Western Development Museum** covers local farming history. Inside, vintage vehicles and a "Jolly Life of the Farmer's Wife" exhibit of old ranges and laundry equipment recall older, harder, times. Outside, the heritage farm and village contains 36 buildings from around the province, including tiny churches and homesteads, banks, a general store, creaky barns and a 1928 grain elevator. The museum is an excellent introduction to prairie history and most fun on the second weekend in August when costumed locals bake bread and make crafts.

Allen Sapp Gallery

Railway Ave East, North Battleford · June–Sept daily 11am–5pm; Oct–May Wed–Sun noon–4pm · Donation · ⊛ allensapp.com

At the northwestern edge of North Battleford's depressed downtown, the old municipal library now houses the **Allen Sapp Gallery**. It showcases the work of local Cree Allen Sapp, one of the best-known Canadian contemporary First Nations artists, who trawls his childhood recollections of life on the Red Pheasant reserve in the 1930s for most of his material. His simply drawn figures are characteristically cast in wide prairie spaces, whose delicately blended colours hint at a nostalgia for a time when his people had a greater sense of community.

INFORMATION
THE BATTLEFORDS

Battleford Visitor Centre In the Fred Light Museum, 11 20th St East (mid-May to Sept daily 9am–8pm, Sept to mid-May 9am–4pm; free), along with firearms, military uniforms and a replica of an old general store.

North Battleford Visitor Centre (Mon–Fri 9am–5pm; ☎ 306 445 2000, ⊛ battlefords.ca) is on Hwy-16, 2km from downtown.

ACCOMMODATION AND EATING

BATTLEFORD

Eiling Kramer ☎ 306 937 6212. Quiet campground in a pretty location overlooking the river valley beside Fort Battleford with all the usual facilities, firewood and some sites with electric hook-ups. May–Sept. $20

Pennydale Junction 92 22nd St and Main St ☎ 306 937 3544. Best of a poor bunch of Battleford's restaurants, with a broad range of North American standards that start around $15 per main. The setting – a converted 1908 CNR train station – is much more memorable. Mon–Fri 11am–9pm, Sat 4–10pm, Sun 4–9pm.

NORTH BATTLEFORD
Tropical Inn 1001 Hwy-16 Bypass ☎ 306 446 4700, ☎ 800 219 5244, ☷ tropicalinns.com. Most downtown "hotels" tend to be dispiriting haunts of the drunk and the dispossessed, so stick to motels like this along Hwy-16. This cheerful place also has an upbeat sports bar and a *Smitty's* chain diner on site. Rooms are smart, with free wi-fi and there's an indoor pool with waterslides and hot tub too. **$124**

Elk Island National Park

Interpretive centre May–Sept daily 10am–6pm • Park $7.80 • ☎ 780 922 5790, ☷ parkscanada.gc.ca/elk

The rolling aspen parklands of **Elk Island National Park**, 45km east of Edmonton (344km from Battleford) along Hwy-16 draw visitors in numbers, thanks to their eight-hundred-strong herd of plains and wood bison. Viewing these animals is often easy, and the chances of seeing free-roaming bison at close quarters from your vehicle very good. If you don't see them there, you almost certainly will along some of the 16km of hiking paths crisscrossing the park where you may well also see moose, deer, beaver and coyote. The park's interpretive centre by the south gate has information on the animals, along with information on hiking, cycling, canoeing, skiing and snowshoeing. They can also advise on **camping** (☎ 905 566 4321, ☎ 877 737 3783, ☷ pccamping.ca; $15.70–25.50), with most sites in the north of the park at Astotln Lake where there's a beach and most park facilities: playgrounds, showers and the like. Tours of Elk Island National Park are offered from Edmonton (see below).

Ukrainian Cultural Village

Mid-May to early Sept daily 10am–5pm • $15 • ☎ 780 662 3640, ☷ history.alberta.ca/ukrainianvillage

A good side-trip from Elk Island National Park is the **Ukrainian Cultural Heritage Village**, 5km east of Edmonton on Hwy-16. This reconstructed village celebrates the culture of the 250,000 Ukrainians who migrated here in the late nineteenth and early twentieth centuries, attracted by a familiar landscape and climate. The centrepiece is an impressive Ukrainian Orthodox Church, surrounded by many seemingly authentic pioneer homes and businesses with costumed guides.

Edmonton

Alberta's provincial capital, **EDMONTON**, is among Canada's most northerly cities and at times – particularly in the teeth of its bitter winters – can seem a little too far north for comfort. It straddles the North Saskatchewan River, whose leafy banks contrast strikingly with the high-rises of downtown, and is a proud and bustling city that tries hard with its restaurants, urban-renewal projects and festivals – which include August's world-class **Folk Music Festival**.

For years the **downtown** core on the north side of the river had a somewhat bleak feel to it, but with vast construction projects going on around the new Royal Albert Museum and Rodgers Place, the giant new stadium for the Edmonton Oilers ice hockey team;– things should be better very soon. Meanwhile, the core district on the southern side of the river is **Old Strathcona**, a rejuvenated, late nineteenth-century area, whose main strip is filled with heritage buildings, low-key museums and a booming restaurant, bar and **nightlife** scene – all fuelled by a huge recent injection of oil money (and young workers) into the city. Several other attractions dot the outskirts, including the impressive **TELUS World of Science** museum, but none is more famous than the **West Edmonton Mall**, a gigantic shopping centre, which for long was the main attraction for visitors and is still an essential outlet in the dead of winter even if it feels a little dated. Attractions that are an easy day-trip from town – if you have your own

7

EDMONTON FESTIVALS

International Jazz City Festival End June Ⓦedmontonjazz.com. Runs for ten days at three different venues and offers a great-value $99 ticket which gives access to all shows.
International Street Performers Festival Early July Ⓦedmontonstreetfest.com. Well-regarded festival, which attracts over one thousand street performers.
K-Days Ten days in late July Ⓦk-days.com. The more contrived and commercial K-Days is a giant funfair, which tries to steal some of Calgary's Stampede thunder.
Edmonton Folk Music Festival Early Aug Ⓦedmontonfolkfest.org. Edmonton's finest event, held over four days at Gallagher Park near the Muttart Conservatory, where six stages draw artists from all around the world.
Fringe Theatre Festival Mid-Aug Ⓦfringetheatreadventures.ca. Increasingly popular ten-day theatrical jamboree that's turned into one of the largest festivals of its kind in North America.

transport – include **Elk Island National Park** (see page 509) and the **Ukrainian Cultural Village** (see page 509).

Brief history

Edmonton began life in 1795 as Fort Edmonton, the burly log stockade of the Hudson's Bay Company, in some of Canada's richest fur country. A century later the town became a staging point for those heading north, particularly during the 1897 Yukon Gold Rush. Then in 1947, things boomed again when an oil strike caused some three thousand wells to sprout within 100km of the city in a decade. Oil money flooded in again in recent decades as rising prices made difficult-to-extract oil in Alberta's north economically viable, helping keep Edmonton's population around a million.

Downtown and around

For the longest time Edmonton's six-block **downtown** area around Sir Winston Churchill Square only really came alive on sunny days when office workers pour out for lunch, or during a city festival. Two ongoing initiatives promise to change all that with the construction of an Arts District, focused around the Royal Alberta Museum and the Winspear Centre . An adjacent "Ice District" will centre on the Edmonton Oilers ice-hockey team's new stadium, Rogers Place. While the major pieces of the puzzle are now in place, it will take some years to completely revitalise downtown. In the meantime, there's certainly enough to keep you occupied here for the best part of a day.

Art Gallery of Alberta

2 Sir Winston Churchill Square • Tues & Wed 11am–8pm, Thurs & Fri 11am–5pm, Sat & Sun 10am–5pm• $12.50 • ☏780 425 5379, Ⓦ youraga.ca

A swirl of metal and glass on the northern edge of Sir Winston Churchill Square contains the **Art Gallery of Alberta**, which shows mainly modern Canadian artists, but continuously hosts varied visiting exhibitions. Despite having over six thousand works in its collection, the galleries can be very hit or miss and often the building itself steals the show. It's the product of an $88 million "renovation" completed in 2010 after having demolished vast chunks of the existing 1960s brutalist building. The impressive work was carried out by Los Angeles architect Randall Stout.

Royal Alberta Museum

9824 103a Ave NW • $19 • ☏780 453 9100, Ⓦ royalalbertamuseum.ca

Re-opening to much fanfare in 2018, the $375 million Royal Alberta Museum showcases many great treasures from the province and beyond. Natural history is understandably a strong point: dinosaur skeletons compete for attention with mammoth replicas and modern wildlife dioramas. Some intriguing First Nations exhibits are here too – including a 1700-year-old roasting pit from Head-Smashed-In Buffalo Jump (see page 537) – and the Manitou Stone, a spiritually significant meteorite. Some of these and many other exhibits in the museum are made even more remarkable by the light that pours in through its giant swirling windows. Other features of the building's architecture are also worth a look: particularly the section

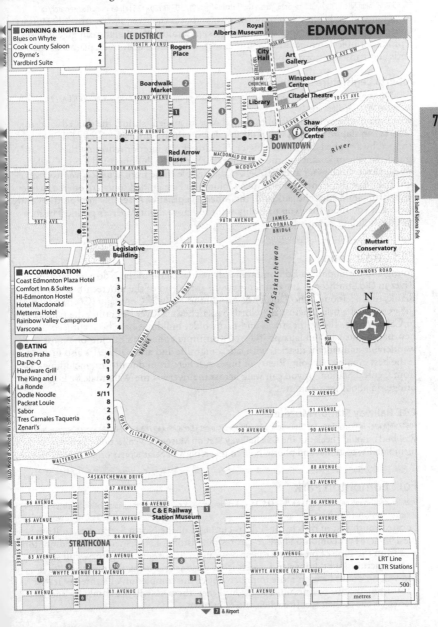

DRINKING & NIGHTLIFE
Blues on Whyte	3
Cook County Saloon	4
O'Byrne's	2
Yardbird Suite	1

ACCOMMODATION
Coast Edmonton Plaza Hotel	1
Comfort Inn & Suites	3
HI-Edmonton Hostel	6
Hotel Macdonald	2
Metterra Hotel	5
Rainbow Valley Campground	7
Varscona	4

EATING
Bistro Praha	4
Da-De-O	10
Hardware Grill	1
The King and I	9
La Ronde	7
Oodle Noodle	5/11
Packrat Louie	8
Sabor	2
Tres Carnales Taqueria	6
Zenari's	3

ICE DISTRICT
EDMONTON
Royal Alberta Museum
Rogers Place
City Hall
Art Gallery
Winspear Centre
Citadel Theatre
SIR W CHURCHILL SQUARE
Library
Boardwalk Market
JASPER AVENUE
Shaw Conference Centre
DOWNTOWN
Red Arrow Buses
River
Legislative Building
Muttart Conservatory
CONNORS ROAD
North Saskatchewan
OLD STRATHCONA
C & E Railway Station Museum
WHYTE AVENUE (82 AVENUE)

- - - - LRT Line
● LTR Stations

0   500
metres

7

Elk Island Nations Park

& Airport

where a giant metal sash has been wrapped around a glass cylinder. This and other design elements were intended to blur the distinction between indoors and outdoors. Look out too for the intriguing mosaics from a 1960s post office that previously occupied the site and have been worked into the building.

Muttart Conservatory

9626 96A St • Mon,Tues & Fri–Sun 10am–5pm, Wed & Thurs 10am–5pm • $12.50 • ☎ 780 442 5311, ⓦ muttartconservatory.ca

In a chunk of parkland south of downtown and over the river, the worthwhile **Muttart Conservatory** consists of four distinctive glass pyramids. These high-tech greenhouses reproduce tropical, temperate and arid climates, complete with trees, plants, exotic birds and natural history displays.

Alberta Legislature Building

10800 97th Ave NW • Jun–Aug daily 10am–5pm; Sept–May Mon–Fri 9am–5pm, Sat & Sun noon–5pm • Free • ☎ 780 427 7362, ⓦ assembly.ab.ca • LRT station Grandin

Set in the manner of a medieval cathedral over an ancient shrine, the domed sandstone **Alberta Legislature Building** was built in 1912 on the original site of Fort Edmonton. Topped by a vaulted dome, it's a big city landmark, its interior reflecting the grandiose self-importance of the province's early rulers, who imported wood for their headquarters from as far afield as Belize; the marble came from Québec, Pennsylvania and Italy, and the granite from British Columbia. Free guided tours are offered, while just north, amid adjacent parkland, the **Alberta Legislative Assembly Interpretive Centre** can teach you more than you probably want to know about Alberta's political history and the building (same hours).

Old Strathcona

Young and cosmopolitan Edmonton mostly resides south of the North Saskatchewan River in **Old Strathcona**. The district grew up at the end of the nineteenth century, thanks to a decision by the Calgary & Edmonton Railway Company (C&E) to avoid the expense of a bridge across the North Saskatchewan River by ending the railway to Calgary here. Today, the streets and many older buildings have been spruced up, new pavements laid and faux period street furniture added. It's Edmonton's most wanderable and vibrant district, with cafés, nightlife and alternative arts also making it the best evening hangout. Plenty of buses run here from downtown, including #57 from Central Station, or you can walk across the river via the Walterdale or High Level bridges in about forty minutes.

C&E Railway Station Museum

10447 86th Ave • June–Aug Tues–Sat 10am–4pm; winter by appointment • Donation • ☎ 780 433 9739, ⓦ canderailway.museum.com

Rail buffs should check out the **C&E Railway Station Museum**, a collection of railway memorabilia, costumes and photos housed in a replica of Strathcona's original 1891 station.

Fort Edmonton Park

Open for special events only until 2021 • ☎ 780 442 5311, ⓦ fortedmontonpark.ca • LRT to South Campus Station, then bus #595 (every 20min) or #596 to Fort Edmonton Park

Located southwest of the city on a deep-cut bend of the North Saskatchewan River, the 158-acre **Fort Edmonton Park** re-creates the history of settlement in the Edmonton area from the time of pre-contact First Nations to the twentieth century. Full size reconstructions of buildings and streets from various eras bring the things to life and will no doubt be even more impressive after the completion of a three-year refurbishment, due to finish in 2021. Until then the park will open only for special events, so check their website when you're in town.

OLD STRATHCONA FARMERS' MARKET

The neighbourhood centres on **Whyte Avenue** (82nd Ave) between 109th and 103rd streets. Just to the north, on 83rd Avenue, is the **Old Strathcona Farmers' Market** (Sat 8am–3pm; ⓦosfm.ca; free), a happy hunting ground for picnic supplies and craft goods.

TELUS World of Science

11211 142nd St • Sun–Thurs 9am–5pm, Fri & Sat 9am–6pm • $23 or $34 with IMAX • ☎ 780 451 3344, ⓦ edmontonscience.com • Bus #5 (to Westmount) from Jasper Avenue in downtown

The splendid **TELUS World of Science** in Coronation Park features a range of temporary exhibitions on scientific and technological themes from dinosaur digs to living in a spacecraft. There are also assorted displays on advanced communications technology and a selection of science demonstrations – all of it best suited for the kids or families. Also here is Canada's largest planetarium, and an **IMAX** screen.

7

West Edmonton Mall

8882 Edmonton • **Mall** Mon–Sat 10am–9pm, Sun 11am–6pm • **World Waterpark** Times vary; minimum: daily 11am–5pm • Day-pass $45 • **Galaxyland** Times vary; minimum: daily noon–6pm • Day-pass $45 • **Marine Life Centre** Mon–Thurs 11am–6pm, Fri–Sun10am–6pm • $12 • **Ice Palace** Times vary; usually: daily 11am–4pm • $12 (skate rental $6) • ☎ 780 444 5200, ⓦ wem.ca • Bus #100 from downtown

"The greatest indoor show on earth" is the claim of **West Edmonton Mall** – a deliberate snipe at Calgary's "greatest outdoor show", the Stampede – and so worded to tempt you to become one of 28 million annual visitors to North America's largest shopping mall. The complex extends over the equivalent of 48 city blocks, boasts eight hundred-plus shops and has room for twenty thousand cars. There's also an on-site hotel and countless places to eat, though none are remarkable. The mall's effect on Edmonton has been double-edged: it crippled downtown shopping but employs 23,000 people and provides a lifeline during Edmonton's long, bleak winters.

It's not the shops that make the mall, but the clutch of **attractions**, including the world's largest indoor lake (122m long), which harbours a **Marine Life Centre** with two hundred different species, sharks, sea turtles and penguins among them; along with sea lions that perform in a twice daily show.

Continuing with the water theme, the **World Waterpark** is a superb collection of vast swimming pools, immense water slides and wave pools. Tack on to these attractions **Galaxyland**, a huge indoor amusement park, the **Ice Palace**, with its NHL-sized rink, or several other lesser amusements and you've filled a day – or been driven mad by the rampant consumerism of it all.

ARRIVAL AND INFORMATION   EDMONTON

By plane The international airport (ⓦflyeia.com) lies 29km south of downtown off Hwy-2. The Sky Shuttle bus daily every hour 6am–7.30pm; $18 one way; ☎780 465 8515, ⓦedmontonskyshuttle.com) services a large number of central locations by request and leaves from outside Arrivals; buy tickets from the driver. A taxi or Uber downtown costs around $50. Sun Dog Tours links Edmonton airport with Jasper (daily at 3.25pm; $99 one way; ☎780 852 4056, ☎888 789 3641, ⓦsundogtours.com).
Destinations Montréal (2 daily; 4hr); Toronto (13 daily; 3hr 10min); Vancouver (14 daily; 1hr 40min).
By train The station is 3km northwest of downtown at 2360 121st St. To get there on public transport it's best

to take the #3 or #5 bus (frequent; 20min) to 124 Street & 114 Avenue then walk 25min north from there. A taxi from downtown costs around $15.
Destinations Jasper (2–3 weekly; 7hr); Saskatoon (2–3 weekly; 8hr); Toronto (2–3 weekly; 56hr); Vancouver (2–3 weekly; 26hr); Winnipeg (2–3 weekly; 23hr).
By bus Red Arrow buses serving Calgary (☎403 531 0350, ☎800 232 1958, ⓦredarrow.ca) use Holiday Inn Express Plaza, 10014 - 104th St, as their station. Northern Express Buses (☎780 983 8225, ⓦnorthernexpress.ca) depart from the *Continental Inn & Suites*, 16625 Stony Plain Road NW. Rider Express (☎1 833 583 3636, ⓦriderexpress.ca) buses pickup at the train station.

Destinations Calgary (Red Arrow: 15 daily; 4hr); Peace River (Northern Express: 1 daily; 6hr 30min); Regina (Rider Express: 1 daily; 10hr); Saskatoon (Rider Express: 1 daily; 7hr); Winnipeg (Rider Express: 1 daily; 18hr).

Edmonton Visitor Centre 9797 Jasper Ave (Mon–Fri 8am–4pm; ☎780 401 7696, ⊚ exploreedmonton.com). There's also a small information desk (Mon–Fri 9am–5pm) in the airport arrivals area.

GETTING AROUND AND TOURS

Edmonton Transit The downtown area is easily negotiated on foot. For longer journeys use Edmonton Transit Service (ETS; ☎780 496 1611, ⊚ edmonton.ca), an integrated bus and light-rail (LRT) system. Single tickets, valid for 1hr 30min, cost $3.25; day-passes $9.75 and can be bought from bus drivers or at LRT station machines.

Walking tours Ask at the Visitor Centre about free downtown walking tours (usually July & Aug Mon–Fri at 1pm from 104th St and 101st Ave) or explore Old Strathcona's paranormal side with Edmonton Ghost Tours Walking Tour (July & Aug Mon–Thurs (9.30pm; ⊚ edmontonghosttours.com; from 10322 83rd Ave; $15).

ACCOMMODATION

Edmonton has no shortage of central accommodation, while many more **motels** dot the arterial roads on the unlovely city outskirts, particularly the Stony Plain Road (northwest of downtown) and on the Calgary Trail (south). Most **B&Bs** (⊚ bbcanada.com) are outside the centre and more expensive than many hotels; while searching Airbnb (⊚ airbnb.ca) should reveal several choices close to downtown or Old Strathcona for around $70 per night.

HOTELS AND MOTELS

Coast Edmonton Plaza Hotel 10155 105th St ☎780 423 4811, ⊚ coasthotels.com; map p.511. Large, smart and modern choice in a downtown high-rise where many of the 299 rooms have good views. There's also an indoor pool, hot tub and fitness centre. **$126**

Comfort Inn & Suites 10425 100th Ave ☎780 423 5611, ☎800 613 7043, ⊚ choicehotels.ca; map p.511. Reliable downtown motel with parking and a heated indoor pool. Light breakfast included in the rates. **$114**

Hotel Macdonald 10065 100th Ave ☎780 424 5181, ☎800 257 7544, ⊚ fairmont.com/macdonald; map p.511. One of the big historic railway hotels once run by the CPR, and undoubtedly the first choice if you want to overnight in traditional style. Some rooms are a little small for the price, but there are lots of facilities, including pool and health club. **$299**

Metterra Hotel 10454 Whyte Ave ☎780 465 8150, ⊚ metterra.com; map p.511. Well-located modern boutique choice near all the Whyte Avenue action; also has its own library with fireplace, a gym, wi-fi and free parking, with a good hot breakfast buffet included in the rate. **$199**

Varscona 8208 106th St ☎780 434 6111, ☎866 465 8150, ⊚ varscona.com; map p.511. Plush Old Strathcona boutique hotel, with every thinkable business amenity and many luxuries, including a fitness centre and nightly wine and cheese tastings, served by attentive staff. Extensive breakfast buffet included. **$189**

HOSTELS AND CAMPGROUNDS

HI-Edmonton Hostel 10647 81st Ave ☎780 988 6836, ☎877 467 8336, ⊚ hihostels.ca; map p.511. This 104-bed hostel is in a former convent in the Old Strathcona district and has plenty of facilities, including laundry, library, bike rental, free wi-fi and roomy kitchen. Dorms **$35**, non-members **$40**; private rooms **$78**, non-members **$85**

Rainbow Valley Campground 13204 45th Ave NW ☎780 434 5531, ⊚ rainbow-valley.com; map p.511. Within the city limits and off the Whitemud Freeway at 119th St and 45th Ave, in Whitemud Park. It's full by afternoon in summer, so arrive early or be sure to book in advance. May to early Oct. Sites **$36**

EATING

★ **Bistro Praha** 10117 101 St ☎780 424 4218, ⊚ bistropraha.com; map p.511. A good opportunity to sample Eastern European cuisine, Edmonton-style, in the city's oldest European-style restaurant. Slightly highbrow and expensive, though, with most mains over $20. Mon–Thurs 11am–11pm, Fri 11am–1am, Sat noon–1am, Sun 4–11pm.

★ **Da-De-O** 10548A Whyte Avenue ☎780 443 0903, ⊚ dadeo.ca; map p.511. Upbeat Cajun diner with chrome-rimmed tables and great Southern food. All the old favourites – oysters, gumbo, jambalaya and Southern fried chicken – are very good and reasonably priced (mains

from $17); as are the sweet potato fries. Mon, Tues & Thurs 11.30am–10pm, Fri & Sat 11.30am–11pm, Sun noon–10pm.

★ **Hardware Grill** 9698 Jasper Ave NW ☎780 423 0969, ⊚ hardwaregrill.com; map p.511. The seasonally inspired Canadian cuisine in the best restaurant in Edmonton is served in a chic modern environment with dark hardwood floors, simple lines, elegant linen and prices to match (mains run $35–50). Book ahead. Mon–Thur 5–9.30pm, Fri & Sat 5–10pm.

The King and I 8208 107th St ☎780 433 2222, ⊚ thekingandi.ca; map p.511. Superb Thai restaurant where prices are nonetheless moderate. One good choice is the *galanga* cashew chicken ($19): chicken fillets in a sweet dark tamarind sauce with asparagus, ginger and cashews. Mon–Thurs 11am–10pm, Fri & Sat 11am–10.30pm, Sun 4–8pm.

La Ronde 10111 Bellamy Hill ☎780 420 8366, ⓦchateaulacombe.com; map p.511. Stunning views of Edmonton from the city's only revolving dining room (atop the *Château Lacombe*). The expensive (mains from $25) Albertan cooking – steaks, bison, berries – is good too. Dancing nightly and live entertainment Friday till Sunday. Tues–Sat 5.30pm–11pm, Sun 10.30am–2pm & 5.30–9.30pm.

★ **Oodle Noodle** 10803 82nd Ave ☎780 988 7808, ⓦoodlenoodle.ca; map p.511. Excellent, inexpensive Asian noodle house, where the food's speedily cooked to order and boxed for a quick chow-down on the premises or a takeaway. Cash only. Several other Edmonton locations too, including downtown at 10842 Jasper Ave. Fri & Sat 11am–11pm, Sun–Thurs 11am–10pm.

Packrat Louie 10335 83rd Ave ☎780 433 0123, ⓦpackratlouie.com; map p.511. Bright, young and welcoming bistro in Old Strathcona with generous portions

of steaks, salads, chicken and other more sophisticated international dishes. Mains $16–41. Fri & Sat 11am–11pm, Sun–Thurs 11am–10pm.

Sabor 10220 103 St NW ☎780 757 1114, ⓦsabor.ca; map p.511. Top-quality Spanish restaurant and seafood specialist with prices to match: dinner mains range $20–40, though a three-course daily menu is offered for $50. There's also an impressive wine list, live entertainment (Wed–Sat) and a tapas bar below the restaurant. Mon–Fri 11.30am–2pm & 5–10pm, Sat 5pm–10pm, Sun 5–9pm.

★ **Tres Carnales Taqueria** 10119 100A St ☎780 429 0911, ⓦtrescarnales.com; map p.511. Delicious and authentic Mexican food assembled from fresh and largely local produce. Choose from delights such as *carnitas torta*, a slow, braised pork shoulder or near-unbeatable fish tacos. Large portions with reasonable prices, with many mains around $11. Mon–Fri 11am–10pm.

Zenari's 10180 101st St NW ☎780 423 5409, ⓦzenaris.ca; map p.511. Great Italian deli/houseware shop with a tremendous lunch counter for soups, salads, sandwiches and Italian staples, including gnocchi with tomato sauce ($10). Mon–Wed 7am–6.30pm, Thurs & Fri 7am–8pm, Sat 8.30am–6pm.

DRINKING AND NIGHTLIFE

The key nightlife focus is Old Strathcona, though if you're staying in that part of town you might try bars along the up-and-coming stretch of Jasper Ave – the ten blocks west of 108th Street. For **listings** check the free *Vue Weekly* (ⓦvueweekly.com), widely available across town.

Blues on Whyte 10329 82nd Ave ☎780 439 3981, ⓦbluesonwhyte.ca; map p.511. At the *Commercial Hotel*, this is one of the city's better live music clubs, with bands most nights and jam sessions on Saturdays. Times vary; often 7pm–2am.

Cook County Saloon 8010 Gateway blvd ☎780 432 2665, ⓦcookcountysaloon.com; map p.511. Deservedly popular Old Strathcona country & western venue, cited many times as Canada's best country nightclub,

attracting twentysomethings in droves and packing out on weekend nights. Cover $7. Fri & Sat 9pm until late.

O'Byrne's 10616 82nd Ave NW ☎780 414 6766, ⓦobyrnes.com; map p.511. Old Strathcona's popular version of an Irish pub has good food, live music, drink and reasonably authentic atmosphere. If this doesn't take your fancy, there are a dozen or so other bars an easy stagger away along Whyte Ave. Daily 11am–2am.

★ **Yardbird Suite** 11 Tommy Banks Way, corner 102nd St and 86th Ave ☎780 432 0428, ⓦyardbirdsuite.com; map p.511. The city's top live jazz venue; the Tuesday-night jam session features impressive local talent. Daily 10pm–2am.

ENTERTAINMENT

Citadel Theatre 9828 101A Ave ☎780 425 1820, ☎888 425 1820, ⓦcitadeltheatre.com. Venue with five stages for high-quality and generally fairly mainstream theatre productions and films; always worth a look.

Jubilee Auditorium 11455 87th Ave ⓦjubilee auditorium.com. Top performing-arts venue that's also home to the Edmonton Opera (Oct–April; ☎780 424 4040,

ⓦedmontonopera.com).

Winspear Centre 4 Sir Winston Churchill Square ☎780 428 1414, ☎800 563 5081, ⓦwinspearcentre.com. Downtown performing-arts centre that's best known as the home of the Edmonton Symphony Orchestra (ⓦedmontonsymphony.com).

DIRECTORY

Medical Royal Alexandra Hospital, 10240 Kingsway ☎780 477 4111.

Police ☎780 423 4567.

Post office 11808 104 Ave (9am–5pm Mon–Fri).

Taxis Alberta Co-op ☎780 425 2525.

North and west of Edmonton

The region north and west of Edmonton acts as a vast corridor for traffic pushing not only towards the Rockies but also up towards Alaska, Wood Buffalo National Park (see page 853) and Yellowknife (see page 855). The scenery and scattered service towns are pretty dull though, with only the occasional attraction brightening the long journeys up.

The busiest route is the westbound **Hwy-16**, which is 357km to Jasper (see page 591), though the scenery only really picks up around the lumber town of **HINTON**, 79km from Jasper. Hinton is a decent place to stop as it has a stock of budget motels and a well-designed mountain bike trail system.

The start of **Hwy-43** lies 50km west along Hwy-16 from Edmonton, from where it rolls through unexceptional towns, hills and prairie scenery for 602km west to Dawson Creek, mile-zero of the **Alaska Highway** (see page 813). It's a mind-numbing journey, making the unfocused sprawl of **Grande Prairie**, 463km from Edmonton, a relative highlight.

Northbound travellers doing the 501km trek along **Hwy-2** from Edmonton to Peace River and the start of the Mackenzie Highway (see page 850) can look forward to a day of watching the slow transition from prairie to boreal forest. A scattering of settlements along the way offer places to soak up small-town life, stretch legs and do some excellent birdwatching.

GETTING AROUND

By public transport A VIA Rail train service runs between   Edmonton and Jasper (and on to Vancouver or Prince Rupert).

Grand Prairie and around

Philip J. Currie Dinosaur Museum 22km west of town on Hwy-43 · June Aug Tues Fri 10am–8pm, Sat–Mon 10am–6pm; Sept–May Tues–Sun 10am–5pm· $14 · ☎ 587 771 0662, ⊛ dinomuseum.ca

The only real attraction in **GRAND PRARIE** is the collection of reconstructed pioneer buildings with local history exhibits in Muskoseepi Park, just west of downtown. Far more spectacular is the flashy **Philip J. Currie Dinosaur Museum**, where – well off the beaten track, much like the Royal Tyrrell Museum (see page 539) – vast numbers of dinosaur bones were found in area the size of several football fields. Seemingly a kind of mass grave in the wake of a disaster, many species were involved, some previously unknown to science.

INFORMATION   HWY-43: GRANDE PRAIRIE

Grand Prairie Visitor Centre 11330 106 St (mid-May–Aug daily 8.30am–7pm; Sept–mid-May Mon–Fri 8.30am–4.30pm, Sat & Sun 10am–4.30pm; ☎ 780 539 7688, ☎ 866 202 2202, ⊛ gptourism.ca). On Hwy-43, on the northwestern edge of the town.

Slave Lake and Lesser Slave Lake Provincial Park

Boreal Centre for Bird Conservation: May–Aug Mon–Fri 8.30am–4.30pm, Sat & Sun 10am–5pm, Sept–Dec Mon–Fri 10am–4pm, Jan–Mar Mon–Sat 10am–4pm, Apr Mon–Fri 8.30am–4.30pm · Free · ☎ 780 849 8240, ⊛ borealbirdcentre.ca

Another 165km northwest of Westlock on Hwy-2 brings you to the 100km-long **Lesser Slave Lake** and its gateway community **Slave Lake**, which takes its name from the Slavey people, the dominant First Nations group hereabouts. Its **Lesser Slave Lake Provincial Park**, strung out along the lake and Hwy-88 to the north, is really the only attraction, where you can join locals on its long white-sand Devonshire Beach or explore inland parts of the park.

Highlights include the excellent **Boreal Centre for Bird Conservation**, which introduces the area's extraordinarily rich birdlife. The **Marten Mountain Lookout**, some 30km north of Slave Lake along Hwy-88, has grand views spread over an otherwise relatively flat region. From the lookout you can also **hike** out to the pretty little **Lily Lake** – ideal for swimming and trout fishing – along a rough 6km trail (allow at least 2hr for the return trip). Another good active option is **kayaking** on Lesser Slave Lake, with the bird refuge of **Dog Island**, 5km from the shore, the most tempting destination.

INFORMATION   **SLAVE LAKE**

Slave Lake Visitor Centre The helpful and well-stocked tourist office (Fri 9am–9pm, Sat–Mon 10am–6pm; ☎ 780 805 0066 ⓦ slavelakeregion.ca) lies beside Hwy-2 on the southern side of town.

ACCOMMODATION AND EATING

Marten River Campground Hwy-88 ☎ 780 849 7100, ⓦ reserve.albertaparks.ca. Campers should head 38km north along Hwy-88 from Slave Lake to this provincial park campsite. It offers heavily shaded sites and its own narrow sand beach on the shores of the Lesser Slave Lake. Most sites are serviced with electricity. **$26**
Slave Lake Inn 1200 Main St S ☎ 780 849 4101, ☎ 855 843 4101, ⓦ slavelakeinn.ca. The best of Slave Lake's slew of pricey highway motels, with a sauna and exercise room; fishing and kayaking packages are also available. **$125**

TA's 109 2nd Ave NW ☎ 780 849 6658, ⓦ tasasiangrill. com. Asian place that's head-and-shoulders above all the very average local restaurants and fast-food chains. Though the menu dares to run the gauntlet between several cuisines – samosas to chop suey to teriyaki chicken to filet mignon – the results are consistently spot-on and prices average a reasonable $13/main. Service can be a bit laidback but there are big-screen sports to keep you occupied. Mon–Fri 10am–10pm, Sat & Sun 11am–11pm.

McLennan and the Kimiwan Lake Bird Sanctuary

Kimiwan Lake Centre: May–Aug 10am–5.30pm • ☎ 780 324 2004

If the bird observatory in the Lesser Slave Lake Provincial Park whetted your appetite, then stop in tiny **MCLENNAN**, 166km west of Slave Lake. It's not an overstatement to say that its **Kimiwan Lake Bird Sanctuary** is of international importance, with white pelican among the hundreds of species – some 300,000 birds – that stop here on their migration routes. The sanctuary and visitor centre are easily found by the highway just east of downtown.

Hwy-1: Winnipeg to Regina

West of Winnipeg, the Trans-Canada Highway steers west to **Brandon**, Manitoba's second largest city, with its handful of Victorian mansions and lively events calendar. Between them, **Spruce Woods Provincial Park** contains an exceptional dune landscape, while **Turtle Mountain Provincial Park** on the US border contains attractive turtles and good canoeing. West, over the provincial border in Saskatchewan, **Cannington Manor Provincial Historic Park** offers a quirky quick diversion, while the **Qu'appelle River Valley** offers an attractive alternative to the straight, flat Trans-Canada.

The Manitoba Agricultural Museum

Mid-May to Sept daily 9am–5pm, Oct to mid-May daily 10am–4pm • $10 • ⓦ ag-museum.mb.ca

Some 137km west of Winnipeg in **AUSTIN**, the **Manitoba Agricultural Museum** has Canada's largest collection of early twentieth-century farm machinery, from gigantic steam tractors through to threshing machines and balers. The site also includes a homesteaders' village, which simulates late nineteenth-century life and has the province's largest collection of pioneer household articles. The immensely popular **Manitoba Threshermen's Reunion and Stampede** (ⓦ threshermensmb.ca) is held here every year in late July – four days of rodeo riding, threshing displays, ploughing competitions, square dancing, jigging and Central Canada's Fiddle Festival. You can camp in the museum grounds on a mix of serviced and unserviced sites (mid-May to Oct; $20).

Spruce Woods Provincial Park

Some 26km south of Hwy-1 at the tiny and unassuming community of **CARBERRY**, **Spruce Woods Provincial Park** is a unique and rewarding place with Manitoba's only **desert**, a whole host of strange, bluish-green ponds formed by underground streams and rare species such as the hognose snake and the prairie skink (a lizard). It straddles both the slowly meandering Assiniboine River and Hwy-5 and its two key groups of walking trails begin near the road.

The **Epinette Creek Trails** to the north run through woodland and marsh and are open to mountain bikes, while the more popular and rewarding **Spirit Sands Trails** lie roughly 5km to the south. These cross mixed-grass prairie before entering shifting sand dunes and pots of quicksand. These "Spirit Sands" were of great religious significance to the Ojibwa who, according to one of the earliest fur traders Alexander Henry, told "of the strange noises heard in its bowels, and its nightly apparitions". There's lots of poison ivy about, so take care. If it's too hot to walk the 7km loop, try a ninety-minute horse-drawn **wagon tour** along the trail (see below).

Off Hwy-5, around 1km south of the Spirit Sands trailhead, a scatter of buildings known as **KICHE MANITOU LAKE** has a visitor centre, campground, grocery store, restaurant, beach, and canoe rental.

INFORMATION AND ACTIVITIES   SPRUCE WOODS PROVINCIAL PARK

Visitor centre At the entrance to Kiche Manitou Lake off Hwy-5 (daily mid-May to early Sept 9am–5pm; ☎ 204 827 8850).

Wagon tours Generally May, June & Sept Sat & Sun & 2pm; July & Aug daily 10am, noon & 2pm, but times vary; $17; ☎ 204 827 8851.

ACCOMMODATION

Epinette Trail Camping For free camping in five primitive campgrounds along the Epinette Trail you can register at the trailhead.
Kiche Manitou Lake Camping ☎ 204 948 3333, ☎ 888

482 2267, ⊛ prspub.gov.mb.ca. You can book campsites or yurts at Kiche Manitou Lake. May–Sept, $10/reservation. Sites $12; yurts $57

Brandon

Brought to life in the 1880s as a refuelling depot for the transcontinental railroad, **BRANDON** is now a major agricultural centre and host to Manitoba's largest livestock show – the **Royal Manitoba Winter Fair** – in late March, and a sizeable rodeo, the **Wheat City Stampede**, in late October. At other times it's a reasonable enough place to break a journey, 215km from Winnipeg, with plenty of accommodation beside the Trans-Canada Highway. And you might venture downtown to view some of the late nineteenth-century brick downtown core where most of the best of the city's restaurants and cafés are.

ARRIVAL AND INFORMATION   BRANDON

Riverbank Discovery Centre (May–Sept Mon–Fri 8.30am–8pm, Sat & Sun 11am–8pm; Oct–April Mon–Fri 8.30am–5pm, Sat & Sun noon–5pm; ☎ 204 729 2141, ☎ 888 799 1111, ⊛ brandontourism.com). A short drive south of Hwy-1 along 18th St North and the starting point of several trails along the Assiniboine River; self-guided tour leaflets are available, including the one covering downtown ($3).

ACCOMMODATION AND EATING

Barney's Motel 105 Middleton Ave ☎ 204 725 1540, ☎ 866 825 8166. Slightly eccentric establishment: a place so scrupulously clean it'll cut your bill by ten cents for every dead fly you find; some rooms have kitchenettes. Basic continental breakfast included, and wi-fi. $85

Chilly Chutney 935 Rosser Ave ☎204 573 9310, ⓦthechillichutney.ca. Excellent East-Indian bistro which serves a full range of curries (around $13) and offers daily buffets ($13–17) which allow you to try a wide range of dishes. Mon–Fri 11.30am–9.30pm, Sat noon–9.30pm, Sun 4–9.30pm.

Double Decker Tavern & Restaurant 943 Rosser Ave ☎204 727 4343, ⓦdoubledeckertavern.com.

Happening bar with regular live music and a good line in bar food; great home-made burgers and wings are the headline acts. Tues 4–11pm, Wed–Sat 4pm–1am.

Super 8 Motel 1570 Highland Ave ☎204 729 8024, ☎800 800 8000, ⓦsuper8.com. One of several chain hotels beside the highway. Good value by Brandon's fairly pricey standards. With a free continental breakfast, plus pool and hot tub. $130

Turtle Mountain Provincial Park

Heading 97km south of Brandon along Hwy-10 will bring you to **Turtle Mountain Provincial Park**, a mixed area of marsh, rolling hills and deciduous forest, whose four hundred shallow lakes form an ideal habitat for the western painted turtle, the park's namesake; there's also a substantial moose population, most visible in late September. All the main facilities congregate at the small hub of **ADAM LAKE**, including a beach, a store, and a number of walking and cross-country skiing trailheads.

Oskar Lake Canoe Route

The key park attraction, other than lazing on lakesides, is the **Oskar Lake Canoe Route**, a 19km paddle and portage excursion across ten of the park's lakes that starts from **Max Lake**. Best done in the spring or autumn, the route should be tackled in an anticlockwise direction to avoid climbing steep hills. It's generally done in a couple of days, with an overnight stay at one of several backcountry campsites that dot the lakeshores; there are no canoe-rental facilities.

INFORMATION	TURTLE MOUNTAIN PROVINCIAL PARK
Visitor centre The park office (Mon–Thurs 10am–noon & 1–6pm, Fri & Sat 10am–10pm, Sun 1–4pm; ☎204 534	2028, ⓦgov.mb.ca) is at Adam Lake.

ACCOMMODATION	
Adam Lake Campground ☎204 948 3333, ☎888 482 2267. The park's principal campground has both electric and unserviced sites, showers and free firewood. Mid-May to mid-Sept. $16	**Max Lake** Provincial Rd 446 ☎204 948 3333, ☎888 482 2267. The smaller, prettier and much quieter park campground lies in the western portion of the park on its largest lake and is well positioned for canoeing. May–Sept. Sites $14

Cannington Manor

Mid-May to early Sept Wed–Mon 10am–5pm • $10

A short-lived experiment in transplanting English social customs to the prairies is the subject of the **Cannington Manor Provincial Historic Park**, a partly reconstructed Victorian village about 52km west of Brandon. Founded in 1882 by Edward Pierce, the would-be squire, the village attracted a number of British middle-class families determined to live as "gentlemen farmers", running small agricultural businesses, organizing tea and croquet evenings and even importing a pack of hounds to stage hunts. Their efforts failed when the branch rail line was routed well to the south, and by 1900 the settlement was abandoned.

The Qu'Appelle River Valley

The slow-moving **Qu'Appelle River** flows 350km from Lake Diefenbaker (160km west of Regina) to Manitoba. Its lush, deep and wide lake-filled valley provides a welcome scenic break from the prairies and a prettier alternative to Hwy-1, if you've a couple of hours to spare. To take it from the east, leave Hwy-1 at Hwy-9, then follow Hwy-247 west past the pleasantly quiet Round and Crooked lakes (both have good campgrounds). From the west follow signs up Hwy-10 to Fort Qu'Appelle.

Motherwell Homestead National Historic Site

3km south of Abernethy, Saskatchewan • May to late June 10am–4pm; late June to Sept daily 10am–4pm • $7.80 • ☎ 306 333 2116, Ⓦ pc.gc.ca

From Crooked Lake, a 68km drive along Hwy-22 brings you to the **Motherwell Homestead National Historic Site**, 3km south of Abernethy and 32km from Fort Qu'Appelle. This large, square house, with its odd assortment of multicoloured fieldstones embedded in the exterior walls and wrought-iron "widow's walk" on the roof, was built in 1898 for local farmer and politician W.R. Motherwell, who moved himself – and this style of architecture – here from Southern Ontario.

Fort Qu'Appelle

FORT QU'APPELLE, 32km from the Motherwell Homestead, centres on Broadway Street, whose most attractive building is the 1897 red-brick **Hudson's Bay Company store**, Canada's oldest. A five-minute walk south and two blocks east of the store, lies the town **museum**, 198 Bay Ave (June–Aug daily 1–5pm; $3), on the site of the original trading post and fort, with its small display on the area's European pioneers and North West Mounted Police. A further three blocks south, a stone **obelisk** at Fifth Street and Company Avenue commemorates the 1874 Treaty Number 4 between the Ojibwa, Cree, Assiniboine and Lieutenant-Governor Alexander Morris. It was a fractious process. The Ojibwa insisted the HBC had stolen "the earth, trees, grass, stones, all that we see with our eyes", hectoring Morris until he confined the more militant leaders to their tents, undermining the unity of the bands and getting the treaty signed in return for land grants, pensions and equipment.

Fort Qu'Appelle's location at the foot of the grooved escarpments puts it amid a chain of eight little lakes known collectively as the **Fishing Lakes**. All are attractive and accessible by road. The nearest, **Echo Lake**, has camping.

INFORMATION   FORT QU'APPELLE

Tourist office 160 Company Ave S (Mon–Fri 8am–noon &   1–4pm; ☎ 306 332 5266, Ⓦ fortquappelle.com).

ACCOMMODATION

Echo Valley Provincial Park Campground 8km west of Fort Qu'Appelle via Hwy-56 Ⓦ saskparks.goingtocamp.com. Pretty provincial park between Pasqua and Echo lakes, with two beaches, several hiking trails, barbecues, mini-golf and volleyball, showers, laundry and a nearby convenience store. Online reservations accepted. $18

Regina

REGINA, 575km west of Winnipeg, is Saskatchewan's capital, as well as a commercial and administrative centre that anchors a vast network of agricultural towns and villages. Yet despite its status, brash shopping malls and 193,000 citizens, Regina feels like a small and unremarkable prairie town. Still, it's a comfortable place to spend a couple of days (it gets more sunshine than any other major Canadian city) and is an essential stop if you're keen on the Royal Canadian Mounted Police (RCMP), or **Mounties** (see page 524).

Brief history

Regina stems from the 1881 decision of Edward Dewdney, lieutenant-governor of the Northwest Territories (which then spread west from Ontario to the Arctic and Pacific oceans) to move his capital south from Battleford (see page 507) to **Pile**

o'Bones – an inconsequential place named for the heaps of bleached buffalo bones left by generations of Aboriginal hunters – after the Canadian Pacific Railway was routed across the southern plains. The city was renamed Regina (Latin for "queen"), after Queen Victoria, but the site was far from being fit for royalty, let alone anyone else: the sluggish creek provided a poor water supply, the clay soil was muddy in wet weather and dusty in summer and there was no timber for building. Accordingly, the railway

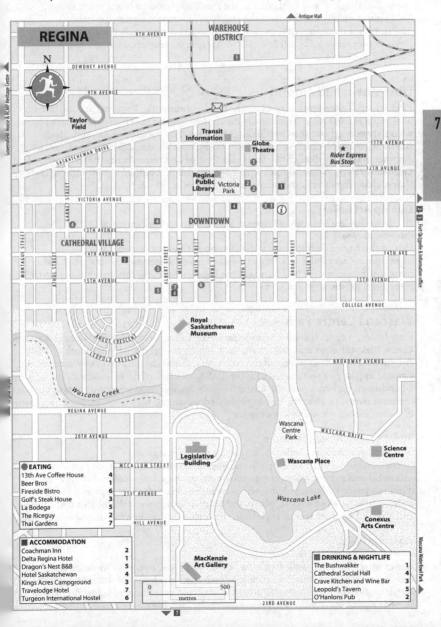

REGINA

N

▲ Antique Mall

WAREHOUSE DISTRICT

8TH AVENUE

DEWDNEY AVENUE

9TH AVENUE

Taylor Field

SASKATCHEWAN DRIVE

Transit Information

Globe Theatre

11TH AVENUE

Rider Express Bus Stop

12TH AVENUE

Regina Public Library

Victoria Park

VICTORIA AVENUE

DOWNTOWN

13TH AVENUE

CATHEDRAL VILLAGE

14TH AVENUE

14TH AVE

15TH AVENUE

15TH AVENUE

COLLEGE AVENUE

GARNET STREET
MONTAGUE STREET
ATHOL STREET
ALBERT STREET
McINTYRE ST
SMITH STREET
LORNE ST
SCARTH ST
ROSE ST
BROAD STREET
OSLER ST

Royal Saskatchewan Museum

ANGUS CRESCENT
LEOPOLD CRESCENT

BROADWAY AVENUE

Wascana Creek

REGINA AVENUE

20TH AVENUE

Wascana Centre Park

WASCANA DRIVE

Science Centre

Legislative Building

MCCALLUM STREET

Wascana Place

21ST AVENUE

Wascana Lake

HILL AVENUE

Conexus Arts Centre

MacKenzie Art Gallery

0   500
metres

23RD AVENUE

● EATING
13th Ave Coffee House	4
Beer Bros	1
Fireside Bistro	6
Golf's Steak House	3
La Bodega	5
The Riceguy	2
Thai Gardens	7

■ ACCOMMODATION
Coachman Inn	2
Delta Regina Hotel	1
Dragon's Nest B&B	5
Hotel Saskatchewan	4
Kings Acres Campground	3
Travelodge Hotel	7
Turgeon International Hostel	6

■ DRINKING & NIGHTLIFE
The Bushwakker	1
Cathedral Social Hall	4
Crave Kitchen and Wine Bar	3
Leopold's Tavern	5
O'Hanlons Pub	2

Government House & RCMP Heritage Centre

Fort Qu'Appelle & Information office

Wascana Waterfowl Park

7

board refused to oblige and the end result was farcical: Government House and the Mounted Police barracks were built where Dewdney wanted them, but the train station was a three-kilometre trek south.

Regina became the capital of the newly created province of **Saskatchewan** in 1905 and settlers flocked here from the US and Central Europe. The city soon overcame its natural disadvantages by extensive tree-planting, which provided shade and controlled the dust, and by damming the creek to provide a better water source. Yet Regina's success was based on the fragile prosperity of a one-crop (wheat) economy and throughout the twentieth century boom alternated with bust. Today, Regina's prosperity looks solid, thanks to sizeable oil reserves, uranium mines and its administrative role.

Downtown and around

Regina's small **downtown** centres on the leafy, symmetrical Victoria Park and a cluster of skyscrapers and malls immediately north. Just north again is the **Warehouse District**, where abandoned commercial buildings have become bars and clubs, and, along Broad Street to the east, less mainstream businesses; antique dealers among them. Another alternative district flourishes just west of downtown across Albert Street. Here **Cathedral Village** gathers around 13th Avenue with its boutiques, coffee shops, craft shops, classy restaurants and occasional hemp store.

Dunlop Art Gallery

2311 12th Ave • Mon–Thurs 9.30am–9pm, Fri 9.30am–6pm, Sat 9.30am–5pm, Sun noon–5pm • Free • ☎ 306 777 604, ⓦ dunlopartgallery.org

Part of the Regina Public Library, the **Dunlop Art Gallery** is always worth a stop for its temporary art exhibitions, often innovative, and sometimes controversial. Its permanent collection of Saskatchewan art is generally more conservative, but certainly gives a feel for the province.

Wascana Centre Park

Roughly eight times the size of downtown, Regina's most distinctive feature is **Wascana Centre Park**, the city's main recreation area, which begins three blocks south of 13th Avenue and extends southeast to the city limits, following the curves of **Wascana Lake**. Created as part of a work project for the 1930s' unemployed, the park is equipped with a bandstand, barbecue pits, snack bars, boating facilities and waterfowl ponds, but for the most part it's a cheerless mix of reed-filled water and bare lawn. However, a number of its attractions are worth stopping for.

Royal Saskatchewan Museum

2445 Albert St • Daily 9.30am–5pm • Donation • ☎ 306 787 2815, ⓦ royalsaskmuseum.ca

In the northwest corner of the park, the **Royal Saskatchewan Museum** provides a successful and engaging insight into provincial geology and wildlife. Informative dioramas portray Aboriginal life, while the Life Sciences Gallery explores the relationships between habitat, plants and animals using many skilfully stuffed animals and artificial flora set against backdrops that evoke Saskatchewan's diverse ecoregions.

Wascana Place

Mon–Fri 8am–4.30pm • ☎ 306 522 3661, ⓦ wascana.sk.ca

About fifteen minutes' walk southeast of the Royal Saskatchewan Museum along the lakeshore is **Wascana Place**, the park headquarters, which has information on lake activities. **Boat rentals** (canoes $20/hr) are available over the road below the *Willow on Wasana* restaurant, a short stroll south along the lakeshore.

Saskatchewan Science Centre

2903 Powerhouse Drive • **Science Centre** Mid-May to early Sept Mon–Fri 9am–6pm, Sat & Sun 11am–6pm; early Sept to mid-May Tues–Fri 10am–5pm, Sat & Sun noon–6pm • $12 • **IMAX** opens for shows • $10, joint ticket with centre $20 • ☎ 306 791 7914, ⓦ sasksciencecentre.com

On winding Wascana Drive east of the lake lies the open-plan, airy **Saskatchewan Science Centre**, with hundreds of interactive scientific exhibits. Many are quite entertaining – try scoring goals against a virtual keeper – but a display on uranium mining and on the soils and weather and running a farm in Saskatchewan are of particular regional interest. There's also an **IMAX cinema**.

The Legislative Building

2405 Legislative Drive • Daily: mid-May to early Sept 8am–9pm; early Sept to mid-May 8am–5pm; 1hr tours every 30min • Free • ⓦ legassembly.sk.ca

On the west side of the lake, accessible from Albert Street, is the grand **Legislative Building**, a self-confident cross-shaped structure of Manitoba limestone with an impressive central domed tower. Tours take in the oak-and-marble-panelled legislative chamber and six small art galleries, highlights of which include Edmund Morris's portraits of local Aboriginal leaders, presented to the province in 1911, and thirty-odd canvases by contemporary Métis and Aboriginal artists, notably Allen Sapp (see page 508).

MacKenzie Art Gallery and the Shumiatcher Theatre

3475 Albert St • Mon–Wed, Fri & Sat 10am–5.30pm, Thurs 10am–9pm, Sun noon–5.30pm • Free • ⓦ mackenzieartgallery.ca

A few minutes' walk south of the Legislative Building is the **MacKenzie Art Gallery**. Its spacious, modern galleries are devoted to temporary exhibitions by modern Canadian artists, plus there's a good permanent collection. Part of the building holds the **Shumiatcher Theatre**, the venue each year for *The Trial of Louis Riel* (late July Wed–Fri; $25; ⓦ rielcoproductions.com), a play based on transcripts of the September 1885 trial, which took place in Regina. The trial was *the* controversial event of the time in Canada: most anglophones were determined Riel – who had returned from US exile to lead his second rebellion in fifteen years (see page 505) – should hang as a rebel, whereas French-Canadians saw him as a patriot and champion of justice. Though Riel was subject to visions and delusions, the court rejected the defence of insanity on the grounds he knew what he was doing and found him guilty.

RCMP Heritage Centre

5907 Dewdney Ave West • Daily: Sept–June 11am–5pm; July & Aug 10am–6pm; driving tour June–early Sept daily • $10 • ☎ 306 522 7333, ⓦ rcmphc.com • Bus #1 from 11th Ave

All Mounties do their basic training at the **RCMP Heritage Centre**, 4km west of downtown Regina, but the centre also holds a wealth of information on the history of this famous police force (see box above), from its early contacts with the Plains Indians and Métis through to its present role as an intelligence-gathering and crime-fighting organization. Exhibits illustrate the **Long March** that first took the Mounties from Ontario to the West in 1874 and relations with **Sitting Bull** (see box above). To reinforce the romantic Hollywood image of the Mounties, an on-site cinema has continuous free showings of such glorified interpretations as the 1936 film *Rose Marie*.

In the summer, a driving **tour** of the grounds is included in the price of a ticket to the Heritage Centre. It involves being driven between various buildings, including mock-up houses where arrests and surveillance techniques are practised, the drill hall and the 1883 chapel – Regina's oldest building – a splendid structure furnished in dark, polished oak where you can escape the intense training activity outside.

If possible, try to time your arrival for either the closely choreographed **Sergeant Major's parade** (Mon–Fri noon) or the **Sunset Retreat Ceremony** (mid-July to mid-Aug Tues 6.30pm).

7

THE MOUNTIES

The heroes of a hundred adventure stories and eccentric, epic films, including such classics as *Canadian Mounties versus the Atomic Invaders*, the **Mounties** have been the continent's most charismatic good guys since the mid-1870s. The **North West Mounted Police**, as they were originally called, were established in Ottawa in 1873 and given the task of restoring law and order in Saskatchewan and Alberta's "Whoop-up Country" in the aftermath of the Cypress Hills Massacre (see page 533). But there was no long-term strategy: the force's areas of responsibility were undecided and even their uniforms had been slung together from a surplus supply of British army tunics. Yet they did a brilliant job, controlling whisky traders who had created pandemonium by selling liquor to the Plains Indians. The force's future was secured after they successfully defused a very delicate situation in 1876. Fearing reprisals after his victory over General Custer at the Battle of the Little Bighorn, **Chief Sitting Bull** and five thousand Sioux moved north, establishing a camp at Wood Mountain, 350km east of Fort Walsh. Aware of the danger, Inspector James Walsh rode into the camp with just four other constables to insist the Sioux obey Canadian law. Walsh's bravery helped establish a rough rapport with Sitting Bull and greatly enhanced the force's reputation.

The Mounties became vital in administering the West, acting as law enforcement officers and justices of the peace. From the 1880s onwards their patrols crisscrossed the territory, their influence reinforced by their knowledge of local conditions accumulated in the exercise of a great range of duties – including delivering the mail and providing crop reports. Despite this level of autonomy, the Mounties saw themselves as an integral, if remote, part of the **British Empire**, their actions and decisions sanctioned by the weight of its authority. They despised the individualism of the US sheriff and marshal; Mounties expected obedience because of the dignity of their office, not their speed with a firearm. Officers became respected for an even-handedness that extended, remarkably for the period, to dealings with the Plains Indians. Yet the force's conservative class prejudice was less positive in their approach to policing "lower orders".

After 1920, when the force became the **Royal Canadian Mounted Police**, this conservative undertow became more problematic. The RCMP consistently supported politicians – Prime Minister Richard Bennet among them – who used them to break strikes. They have also often been accused of bias in their dealings with the Québécois. In recent years their reputation has taken a further hit: accusations of widespread corruption, making errors that led to the rendition of Canadian citizen Maher Arar to Syria and the Taser-related death of a man at Vancouver airport in 2007. The coverage of these incidents showed, though, that the Mounties remain a potent national symbol.

Government House

4607 Dewdney Ave • May–Aug Tues–Sun 9am–5pm; Sept–April Tues–Sun 9am–4pm • Donation • ☎ 306 787 5773, ⓦ governmenthouse.gov.sk.ca • Bus #1 from 11th Ave

A couple of kilometres west of the city centre, the stolid yellow-brick **Government House** was the residence of the lieutenant governors of the Northwest Territories and subsequently Saskatchewan from 1891 to 1945. Restored to its late nineteenth-century appearance, the offices and reception areas downstairs are splendid, as is the balconied staircase leading up to the bedrooms. The men's billiards room is decorated with an enormous bison head and there are also mementoes of Amédée Forget, a more eccentric governor, whose specially designed "salesman's chair", beside the entrance, was meant to be uncomfortable, with protruding gargoyles sticking into the visitor's spine, legs shorter at the front than the back and a flesh-pinching crack cut across the middle of the seat. The rocking horse in the office was for Forget's pet monkey. **High tea** is usually served in the ballroom one weekend each month from 1 till 4pm.

ARRIVAL AND DEPARTURE
REGINA

By plane Regina's airport (306 761 7555, ⓦ yqr.ca) is 5km west of the city centre, from which the taxi trip downtown costs about $11, or you can take the Hobo Express Shuttle bus (☎ 306 533 3862) to Regina's downtown hotels. A

15min walk east of the airport brings you to the junction of Regina Ave and Pasqua St, from where Regina Transit's bus #8 heads for the city centre.

Destinations Toronto (4 daily; 3hr); Vancouver (2 daily; 2hr 15min).

By bus Rider Express (☎ 1 833 583 3636, ⓦ riderexpress. ca) buses pick up at 1517 11th Ave, a ten-minute walk east of Downtown.

Destinations Edmonton (1 daily; 10hrs); Saskatoon (3 daily; 3 hr); Winnipeg (1 daily; 6hr 30min) Saskatoon (3 daily; 3hr).

INFORMATION AND GETTING AROUND

Regina Visitor Centre 2900 Wascana Drive Regina (Mon–Fri 8.30am–noon 1–5pm; ☎ 306 789 5099, ☎ 800 661 5099, ⓦ tourismregina.com).

By bus Regina Transit (ⓦ regina.ca/) runs good bus services

to outlying attractions; a one-way fare is $3.25 and most lines cross downtown on 11th or 12th Avenue, depending on the direction of travel.

ACCOMMODATION

Regina has plenty of central options, but many of the best budget options are **motels** that lie a little way out, clustering east of the centre along Victoria Avenue East (Hwy-1) and south, along Albert St.

HOTELS, MOTELS AND B&BS

Coachman Inn 835 Victoria Avenue ☎ 306 522 8525 ☎ 888 522 8525, ⓦ coachmaninnregina.weebly.com; map p.521. Budget motel among several on the Victoria Avenue strip; very basic rooms with cheap plasticky furniture and bathrooms but clean and good value considering the presence of fridges, microwaves and free wi-fi. **$77**

Delta Regina Hotel 1919 Saskatchewan Drive ☎ 306 525 5255, ☎ 800 209 3555, ⓦ deltahotels.com; map p.521. One of Regina's best hotels and with a good central location, albeit in a dowdy part of town. Amenities include restaurant, bar, coffee shop, wi-fi, gym, spa, pool and three-storey waterslide. **$159**

Dragon's Nest B&B 2200 Angus St ☎ 306 525 2109, ⓦ dragonsnestbb.com; map p.521. Boutique-style B&B with six individually decorated rooms and a hearty cooked breakfast included. There's also access to a couple of common rooms and a hot tub. **$85**

Hotel Saskatchewan 2125 Victoria Ave ☎ 306 522 7691, ☎ 800 333 3333, ⓦ hotelsask.com; map p.521.

Large, luxurious old-fashioned hotel – think chandeliers and doormen – overlooking Victoria Park. The full range of facilities includes a fitness centre with whirlpool. Complimentary airport pick-up. **$163**

Travelodge Hotel 4177 Albert St S ☎ 306 586 344, ⓦ travelodgeregina.com; map p.521. Modern chain hotel with large, comfortable, clean rooms and with family restaurant; a big hit with kids who tend to take over the pool and waterslide: ask for a room away from the pool to avoid the noise. **$170**

HOSTELS AND CAMPSITES

Kings Acres Campground Hwy-1 East ☎ 306 522 1619, ⓦ kingsacrescampground.com; map p.521. A full range of serviced and unserviced sites on a spacious property 1km east of town. With store, phone, pool, laundry, TV and games room and wi-fi. Tents welcome. April–Oct. Sites **$27**

Turgeon International Hostel 2310 McIntyre St ☎ 306 791 8165, ☎ 800 467 8357, ⓦ hihostels.ca; map p.521. Extremely clean HI hostel in a restored heritage house, immediately south of the downtown core, with cooking and laundry facilities, small library and free wi-fi. Dorms **$32**, non-members **$37**; private rooms **$63**, non-members **$73**

EATING

In recent years food trucks have become a big deal in Regina – they congregate downtown around Victoria Park.

★ **13th Ave Coffee House** 3136 13th Ave ☎ 306 522 3111, ⓦ 13thavecoffee.com; map p.521. Long-standing

---

REGINA FESTIVALS

First Nations Pow Wow Mid-April ⓦ fnuniv.ca/powwow. For something a little different, attend this First Nations gathering featuring crafts, music and dancing.

Country Thunder Mid-July ⓦ countrythunder.com. A good live music event, this four-day country music festival is held in Craven, a twenty-minute drive north of town.

Queen City Ex Late July ⓦ thequeencityex.com. Regina's biggest bash, a week-long festival with a lot of livestock exhibitions, plus rides and music shows, which all ends in a massive fireworks display.

Regina Folk Festival Early Aug ⓦ reginafolkfestival.com. Held in Victoria Park, this is another big musical deal.

7

vegetarian restaurant whose healthy helpings of Asian tofu dishes and great veggie burgers (mains around $11) keep the place packed with happy chatter. Mon–Fri 7.30am–8pm, Sat 8.30am–8pm, Sun 10am–7pm.

Beer Bros 1801 Scarth St ☎306 586 2337, ⓦbeerbros.ca; map p.521. Sociable brick-and-beam place that not only loves its beer, but is delightfully obsessed with pairing it with the right food. Enter a gastro-pub menu that's been designed to accompany various brews. All the usual favourites, but the *pierogies* ($22) a firm Saskatchewan favourite, are particularly good. Otherwise be sure to try their innovative beet ketchup with your fries. Mon & Tues 11.30am–11pm, Wed & Thurs 11.30am–midnight, Fri & Sat 11.30am–1am.

Fireside Bistro 2305 Smith St ☎306 761 2305, ⓦfiresidebistro.ca; map p.521. Great bistro tucked in a leafy residential neighbourhood by Wascana Park with a sunny summer terrace. A reliable mix of burgers, sandwiches, salads and wraps (around $12) emerge for lunch; later on the range broadens, with some great seafood dishes – teriyaki salmon with wasabi cream ($19) and snapper and tiger prawns in chilli ($20) among the options. Mon–Fri 11am–late, Sat & Sun 10am–late.

Golf's Steak House 1945 Victoria Ave ☎519 579 4050, ⓦgolfsteakhouse.com; map p.521. Special-occasion steakhouse with a quiet atmosphere, top-notch prime rib and charbroiled steaks along with high-end seafood offerings like swordfish and lobster. Book ahead for the excellent $25 Sunday brunch. Mon–Fri 4pm–9pm, Sat 4–11pm, Sun 10.30–9pm.

La Bodega 2228 Albert St ☎306 546 3660, ⓦlabodegaregina.ca; map p.521. Hip restaurant with great patio where movies are screened on a neighbouring wall and adventurous tapas dishes are served. The Thai mango and palm salads are particularly good, while odd bedfellows like sushi and bannock bruschetta are more an acquired taste. But the execution and presentation are always good though prices fairly steep: many of the hot dishes are over $15. Mon–Thurs 4pm–2am, Fri 11am–2am, Sat & Sun 10am–2am.

The Riceguy 1950 Hamilton St ☎306 352 7687 ⓦthericeguy.com; map p.521. Basic bistro that's ideal for a quick bite. The Szechuan-inspired food's light and tasty with no hint of that glutinous "western Chinese" treatment. Mon–Fri 11am–9pm, Sat 11am–8pm.

Thai Gardens 2317 Albert St ☎306 584 0347, ⓦthaigardenfamilyrestaurant.com; map p.521. Huge portions of tasty Thai and pan-Asian food –with most items around $12 – and located on the same block as the hostel on the south side of town. Takeout available. Mon–Fri 11.30am–10pm, Sat & Sun 5–10pm.

NIGHTLIFE AND ENTERTAINMENT

City **nightlife** focuses on a strip of clubs and brewpubs along Dewdney Ave just north of downtown.

★ **The Bushwakker** 2206 Dewdney Ave ☎306 359 7276, ⓦbushwakker.com; map p.521. Successful chain brewpub with twelve types of beer and a large selection of single-malt scotches; excellent hearty bar food including *pierogies* and buffalo steaks. Live music frequently livens things up later on, or follow the crowds to a number of basic clubs lined up in the old warehouses along the road here. Mon–Thurs 11am–midnight, Fri & Sat 11am–1am, Sun noon–9pm.

Cathedral Social Hall 2062 Albert St ☎306 359 1661, ⓦthefreehouse.com; map p.521. Busy bar and restaurant with locally brewed beers and good wood-fired pizzas, sandwiches and burritos as well as an excellent bouillabaisse that combines halibut, salmon, scallops, shrimp, walleye and tiger prawns. Mon–Thurs 11am–midnight, Fri & Sat 11am–2am, Sun 10am–11pm.

Crave Kitchen and Wine Bar 1925 Victoria Ave ☎306 525 8777, ⓦcravekwb.com; map p.521. Slick wine bar with more than a hundred excellent tapas to choose from. Mon–Wed 11am–11pm, Thurs 11am–midnight, Fri 11am–1am, Sat 4pm–1am.

Leopold's Tavern 2330 Albert St ☎306 525 5367 ⓦleopoldstavern.com; map p.521. A bit of a miserable concrete bunker on the outside, but inside it's a convivial neighbourhood bar that bursts with a miscellany of bright memorabilia and offers a good pub-grub menu. Choose from burgers, poutine, nachos, wings, tacos (most around $15) with a wide range of craft beers too. Mon–Fri 11am–2am, Sat & Sun 10am–2am.

O'Hanlons Pub 1947 Scarth St ☎306 566 4094; map p.521. Dependably happening Irish theme pub which shares a patio with the *Copper Kettle* and offers live music on Fridays, dancing on Saturdays and pub trivia on Sundays. Respectable pub food too: nachos, burgers and the like. Mon 1pm–1am, Tues 3–10pm, Wed–Sun 3pm–2am.

ENTERTAINMENT AND SPECTATOR SPORTS

Conexus Arts Centre 200B Lakeshore Drive ☎306 525 9999, ☎800 667 8497, ⓦconexusartscentre.ca. As the home to its Symphony Orchestra (ⓦreginasymphony.com), this is Regina's premier venue for high culture, and attracts scores of touring musicians, though it tends to have a busier programme in winter.

Globe Theatre 1801 Scarth St ☎306 525 6400, ☎866 954 5623, ⓦglobetheatrelive.com. Premier local theatre hub with a stage that allows productions in the round, and which rarely puts on a production that doesn't get rave reviews.

Saskatchewan Roughriders ☎306 525 2181,

Ⓦ riderville.com. Regina has the fanatically supported CFL (Canadian Football League) team, who are well worth catching; they play between June and November in Mosaic Stadium, 2940 10th Ave, a 20min walk northwest of downtown.

DIRECTORY

Internet Central Library, 2311 12th Ave ☎ 306 777 6000; downtown and the 13th Ave district have a giant free wi-fi hot-spot.
Medical Regina General Hospital, 1440 14th Ave ☎ 306

766 4444.
Police ☎ 306 777 6500.
Post office 2200 Saskatchewan Drive.
Taxis Capital Cab ☎ 306 791 2222.

Southern Saskatchewan

From Regina the 400km drive west across **Southern Saskatchewan** on Hwy-1 is monotonous, with **Moose Jaw**, the 1920s Prohibition hangout of American gangsters, the only really worthwhile stop. Away from Hwy-1 things get more interesting: undulating farmland is broken up by lake-dotted valleys, lakes, pockets of badlands and the odd range of wooded hills. A trio of minor attractions – a steam railway at **Ogema**, the **Big Muddy Badlands** and the unusually francophone prairie town of **Gravelbourg** might tempt you to lengthen your journey. But the biggest attraction lies near the US border: here **Grasslands National Park** protects the sort of wild prairie landscape that the region's first white settlers encountered. The town of **Swift Current** documents a little of these settlers' lives in two reconstructed villages, but these are no more impressive than the beautiful landscapes in striking distance of the cowboy town of **Maple Creek**; among them the starkly beautiful **Great Sand Hills** and the forested hills and ridges of **Cypress Hills Interprovincial Park** with its restored Mountie outpost, **Fort Walsh**.

Moose Jaw

MOOSE JAW, 70km west of Regina, was founded as a railway depot in 1882. Its name comes from a Cree word for "warm place by the river", although some believe it was named for the repairs done to a cartwheel by an early pioneer using a moose's jawbone.

The city achieved notoriety during the 1920s US Prohibition, when liquor was smuggled south to Chicago. For most locals this period of bootleggers, gangsters and gamblers was not a happy one, and for years various schemes to attract tourists by developing the "Roaring Twenties" theme met with considerable opposition from those who'd experienced them. Despite this, the **Tunnels of Moose Jaw** (see below) became the most interesting attraction in town.

Today, the city is a quiet sort of place with plenty of reminders of its 1920s which amply reward pulling off the Trans-Canada.

Downtown

Until very recently **downtown** was a fairly dispiriting place, and traces of these economically slender years remain in the battered empty shopfronts a block or so away from Main Street. But rejuvenation is afoot, with cafés springing up along a strip that's livened up by pioneer-day **murals** concentrated on 1st Avenue NW. The city's stagnation has also ensured that much remained unchanged since the 1920s: wide treeless avenues are still framed by solemn brick warehouses, hotels and porticoed banks. **River Street**, at the southern end of the strip, is particularly atmospheric, with its rough-and-ready *Royal* and *Brunswick* hotels once the favourite haunts of gangsters.

The Tunnels of Moose Jaw

18 Main St North • Hours vary, roughly: June–Sept Mon–Fri 10am–7pm, Sat & Sun 10am–8pm; Oct–May daily noon–5.30pm; tours every 20min • One tour $15, two tours $25 • ☎ 306 693 5261, Ⓦ tunnelsofmoosejaw.com

A network of **tunnels** runs underneath River Street from the basements of some of the city's oldest buildings. No one knows who built these passageways – or why – but what is known is that Chinese railway workers extended and used them in the early 1900s, hoping to escape the $500 "head tax", a measure designed to force them to return to famine-stricken China after their railway work was done. Later, during Prohibition, Chicago gangsters used the tunnels to negotiate deals for Canada's liquor supplies and to hide out in when things got too hot in Chicago.

The **Tunnels of Moose Jaw** tells this history in two entertaining fifty-minute theatrical tours: the **Chicago Connection** tour is a light-hearted look at the capers of Al Capone's men, complete with speakeasy, police bust and slimy Chief of Police. The more serious **Passage to Fortune** tour tells the horrific Chinese story, with re-creations of a laundry, sweatshops, a herbalist and an opium den. Costumed guides ham it up along the way, helped by old movies and state-of-the-art animatronics.

Moose Jaw Trolley

Visitor centre departures: May & June call for times; July & Aug 1pm, 2.15pm & 3.30pm; 1hr • $14.50 • ☎ 306 693 8097

A replica of one of Moose Jaw's original electric trams, the **Moose Jaw Trolley** travels local sights with a guide who dwells on the town's shady past. It leaves from the visitor centre or at a changing downtown location (ask at the visitor centre). Fun ghost-tours are also offered (May & June Sat 9.30pm & 10.45pm; July & Aug Fri & Sat 9.30pm & 10.45pm; $17).

Western Development Museum

50 Diefenbaker Drive. • Jan–March Tues–Sun 9am–5pm; April–Dec daily 9am–5pm • $10 • ☎ 306 693 5989, ⊛ wdm.ca

Moose Jaw's branch of the **Western Development Museum** lies about 2km from the centre, beside the Trans-Canada Highway on the northern edge of town. Divided into sections covering air, land, water and rail transport, exhibits include a replica steamship, several CPR coaches, fragile old planes and a 1934 Buick converted to carry the chief superintendent along the rail line.

ARRIVAL AND INFORMATION   MOOSE JAW

By Plane The Hobo Express Shuttle bus (☎ 306 533 3862) runs from Regina's airport.

Tourist office East of town by the Trans-Canada Hwy (daily: mid-May to Aug 9am–6pm; Sept to mid-May 10am–4pm; ☎ 306 693 8097, ☎ 866 693 8097, ⊛ tourismmoosejaw.ca).

ACCOMMODATION

Capone's Hideaway Motel 1 Main St North ☎ 306 692 6422, ☎ 877 443 3003, ⊛ caponeshideawaymotel.com. One of the town's several central budget hotels and motels, located opposite the defunct train station. $79

The Redland Cottage B&B 1122 Redland Ave ☎ 306 694 5563, ⊛ redlandcottage.com. This B&B in a tree-lined residential area has comfortable bedrooms with floral quilts, hardwood floors, internet access and full breakfasts – but requires a two-night minimum stay. $119

Temple Gardens Mineral Spa 24 Fairford St East ☎ 306 694 5055, ☎ 800 718 7727, ⊛ templegardens. sk.ca. Book well in advance for the four-star *Temple Gardens Mineral Spa*, which has luxurious rooms (with jacuzzi), geothermal pools and facilities for massage, facials, reflexology and hydrotherapy treatments. $189

EATING AND DRINKING

Bobby's Place 63 High St East ☎ 306 692 3058. Bustling pub with a fine range of whiskies and regular live music; also serves good ribs and huge burgers and other pub fare, with dishes mostly in the $11–16 range. Mon–Thurs 11am–11pm, Fri & Sat 11am–2am.

★**The Gallery Café** 76 Fairford St West ☎ 306 693 7600, ⊛ yvettemoore.com. Part of the Yvette Moore Gallery in the 1910 Land Titles building, with a good range of home-made salads, soups, ciabattas and delicious bread-pudding with vanilla ice cream. The prairie art is worth a look too. Mon–Sat 10am–3pm.

Nit's Thai Food 124 Main St ☎ 306 694 6404, ⊛ nitsthaifood.ca. Steer away from the menu's interloping Chinese dishes in favour of authentic Thai food that bursts with flavour. However, with many mains well over $20, it's not a cheap option. Daily 11am–8pm.

Prairie Oasis Hwy-1 and Thatcher Drive ☎ 306 693 4334, ⓦ prairie-oasis.com. The restaurant of a huge truckstop and tourist complex (motel, camping, waterslide) beside the Trans-Canada and close to the visitor centre; serving good inexpensive breakfasts and freshly baked pies. Free wi-fi. Daily 6.30am–9pm.

Veroba's Family Restaurant 28 Fairford St West ☎ 306 693 5943. Take the hospital cafeteria ambience in your stride to enjoy this top-notch family-run diner with excellent and inexpensive home-cooked standards: full breakfasts, burgers and lovely soups. Mon–Fri 7am–8pm, Sat & Sun 8am–8pm.

Ogema

115km south of Regina · **Southern Prairie Railway** May–Sept Sat & Sun 10am & 1.30pm · $47 · ☎ 306 459 1200, ⓦ southernprairierailway.com · **Deep South Pioneer Museum** 10am–5pm Sat & Sun · ☎ 306 459 2904

The tiny town of **OGEMA** is best visited when its steam-driven **Southern Prairie Railway** runs. The trips along an old CPR branch line aims to present the region as 1920s settlers would have seen them; included is a guided tour of a grain elevator. Also offered are separate star-gazing train tours – check online for dates. Also in Ogema is the **Deep South Pioneer Museum**, a lovingly preserved collection of some thirty old prairie buildings furnished with objects and equipment from bygone days.

The Big Muddy Valley

Big Muddy Badland Tours July & Aug daily 9.30am; May, June & Sept by appointment · $65 · ☎ 306 267 3312

Southwest of Ogema the **Big Muddy Valley** is the epicentre of an area of Badlands where dramatic sandstone butte and caves resemble the landscapes of Westerns, and were indeed where American outlaws including Butch Cassidy and his Wild Bunch often hid out until their antics were curtailed by the arrival of a detachment of Mounties in 1904. They were led by Corporal Bird, known ruefully as the "man who never sleeps". To explore, take Hwy-34 towards the village of Big Beaver – looking out for the dramatic 70m-high Castle Butte en route – then follow signs towards the dreary little town of Coronach – about 158km south of Moose Jaw. Here you can join a Big Muddy Badland tour for a more detailed look at the area including some First Nations burial cairns.

Gravelbourg

117km southwest of Moose Jaw via Hwy-2 · **Gravelbourg Visitor Information** 209 Main St ☎ 306 648 3301, ⓦ gravelbourg.ca · **Gravelbourg and District Museum** 300 Main St · Mon–Sat 9am–6pm, Sun noon–6pm · $5 · ☎ 306 648 2332 **Our Lady of the Assumption** Call for hours · ☎ 306 648 3322, ⓦ gravelbourgcocathedral.com

GRAVELBOURG carries the name of its founder Reverend Louis-Pierre Gravel who in 1906 called upon francophones in Canada and the US to settle here. Today a third of its population still speaks French and most inhabitants are bilingual. This unusual history is revealed at the **Gravelbourg museum**, otherwise the town's key sight is its impressive Our Lady of the Assumption cathedral built in 1919; though its ornate Romanesque interiors were added a decade later.

Grasslands National Park

Directly west of the Big Muddy Valley, and around 250km southwest of Moose Jaw, **Grasslands National Park** is predominantly mixed-grass prairie, a flat, bare badlands broken up by splendid coulees, buttes and river valleys – notably the wide ravine edging the Frenchman River. Far from the moderating influence of the oceans, the area has a savage climate, with an average low in January of -22°C and temperatures that soar to 40°C in summer. Even so, this terrain is inhabited by many species adapted to cope with the shortage of water: prairie grasses, rabbit brush and different types of cacti, as well as the graceful pronghorn antelope and rattlesnakes. Prairie dogs, ferrets and bison also all thrive here as they did before white settlers arrived in the region.

7

The park

The park consists of east and west "blocks" separated by private ranches and farms, which the federal government eventually intends to buy, creating a single park stretching from Hwy-4 in the west to highways 2 and 18 in the east. The **western** section is more scenic and accessible, its limited system of gravel tracks and roads cutting in from highways 8 and 4, south and east of the tiny community of **VAL MARIE**.

Driving tours

The easiest introduction to the park for most is to follow the 80km "Ecotour" driving loop from the visitor centre in Val Marie. Here, you can pick up a free guide to the route; along it are a series of stops with short walks from the roadside to info boards about the flora and fauna. Take your time – around three hours is suggested – as there's a lot of landscape to soak in as well as prairie dogs to watch. Be sure too, to get fuel before you strike out as there's nothing en-route.

Hiking

Unlike most national parks you're free to roam almost everywhere and there are relatively few marked trails, though a couple of signposted suggestions are made in each block.

One of the best **hikes** leads to **70 Mile Butte** in the west block. This massive flat-topped promontory is the highest point of land in the region, rising 100m above the valley floor with wonderful views of the waving prairie grasslands. To get there, drive south of Val Marie on Hwy-4, turn east at Butte Road and continue to the end of the road. Though barely marked, the way becomes obvious as you begin walking over the hills from the end of the road. Even just a couple of hours' walk will take you through exceptional country.

Wherever you go remember a good supply of water, a stout pair of walking shoes and a stick to sweep in front of you in tall grass or brush as a warning to **rattlesnakes**. Animal activity is at its height at dawn and dusk and during spring and autumn; a pair of binoculars is always useful.

INFORMATION

GRASSLANDS NATIONAL PARK

Grasslands National Park Reception Centre In Val Marie, at Hwy-4 and Centre St (late-May to June Thurs–Mon 9am–5pm; July & Aug daily 9am–5pm; Sept to mid-Oct Fri–Sun 8am–5pm; ☎ 306 298 2257, ⓦ parkscanada. gc.ca/grasslands). Park rangers provide advice on weather and roads, hand out maps, arrange for guided or self-guided ecotours, issue camping permits and give tips on animal-spotting and hiking.

ACCOMMODATION

★ **Convent Country Inn** 4515 Hwy-4 ☎ 306 289 4515, ⓦ convent.ca. Attractive 1939 convent with lots of character that's been converted into a B&B with sleek and simple rooms. Also the best place to eat, though you need to reserve in advance. Continental breakfast included. **$109**
National Park campgrounds The *Frenchman Valley Campground* in the West Block has twenty sites, including some with electricity and drinking water. The *Rock Creek Campground* in the East Block has no electricity or water. You can also camp anywhere you like in the park so long as you do so 1km from a road and have a $9.80 backcountry permit from the visitor centre. Sites at either campground **$16**
Village of Val Marie Campground Just off Hwy-18/4. Well-worn grassy area close to the southern edge of Val Marie, but with plenty of shade and an easy walk from the centre. Some sites have electricity and hot showers are available – even non-campers can use them for $3. May–Oct. **$165**

Swift Current

Mennonite Heritage Village 17th Ave & South Railway St East • July & Aug Fri–Sun 1–5pm • Free • ☎ 306 773 7685, ⓦ mennoniteheritagevillage.ca **Doc's Town** Late June–early Sept Sat & Sun 1–5pm • $3 • ☎ 306 773 2944, ⓦ swiftcurrentex.com

West from Moose Jaw along the Trans-Canada Highway, it's about 180km to **SWIFT CURRENT**, a small industrial city and farm-research centre whose central

Kinetic Park contains two early twentieth-century reconstructed villages. The **Mennonite Heritage Village** consists of a long, rectangular house and adjoining barn, while **Doc's Town** reconstructs a prairie village using nine buildings and thousands of period artefacts. These include a fully functioning windmill, one-room schoolhouse and an old dancehall (now a tearoom), all transported here from rural Saskatchewan. For a natural stopoff in the area, try **Saskatchewan Landing Provincial Park**, some 40km north on Hwy-4. It centres on the large, artificial **Lake Diefenbaker** and offers camping.

INFORMATION
SWIFT CURRENT

Visitor centre 44 Robert St West, at the junction of highways 1 and 4 (Mon–Fri 9am–5pm; ☎ 306 778 9174, ⓦ tourismswiftcurrent.ca). Includes a good little free exhibition on the region.

ACCOMMODATION AND EATING

Best Western Inn 105 George St ☎ 306 773 4660, ☎ 800 773 8818, ⓦ bestwestern.sk.ca. One of several chain motels strung out along the Trans-Canada with pool and light self-service breakfast. **$124**

Miso House 285 North Service Rd West ☎ 306 778 4411. Delicious fresh Korean hotpots, Japanese sushi, bento boxes and the like served a few doors west of the visitor centre; with $15 lunch specials. Tues–Sat 11am–9pm, Sun 11am–8pm.

★ **Russell Up Some Grub** 12a 1081 Central Ave N ☎ 306 778 4782. For gigantic portions of home-cooked food – including Mennonite dishes like cheese *pierogies* in sausage gravy – head to this cheerful diner. The breakfasts are the best in town, with sandwiches, burgers and salads (most mains around $13) offered later on. Mon–Fri 6am–2pm.

Safari Inn Motel 810 South Service Rd East ☎ 866 773 4608, ⓦ safariinn.ca. Trans-Canada-side motel where average-looking, but spotless, rooms come with fridge, microwave, movie channels and wi-fi. **$79**

Eastend: T-Rex Discovery Centre

Mid-May to early Sept daily 10am–6pm • $6 • ☎ 306 295 4009, ⓦ royalsaskmuseum.ca/trex

In 1994, one of only thirteen Tyrannosaurus Rex skeletons in the world was discovered near **EASTEND**, a tiny town 140km southwest of Swift Current. The T-Rex was named Scotty (after the bottle of Scotch its discoverers consumed in celebration) and there is now a swish **T-Rex Discovery Centre** about 1km north of town, which is definitely worth a visit if you're travelling with children. After seeing a film on the difficulties involved in excavating Scotty, there's a small hands-on museum with replica bones of various dinosaurs, along with Scotty's impressive skull.

ACCOMMODATION
EASTEND

Riverside Motel ☎ 306 295 3630, ⓦ eastendvacations. net. Small motel among the rolling hills just west of Eastend on Hwy-13. With clean, basic rooms and free wi-fi. Also offers camping for both tents and RVs, with full hook-ups available. Sites **$15**; rooms **$100**

Maple Creek

From Swift Current it's 130km west along the Trans-Canada to **MAPLE CREEK**, 8km south of the highway. This is ranching country, and its streets are full of pick-up trucks, cowboy boots and Stetsons and even cowboy churches. Everything reaches wild heights in late September during the **Cowboy Poetry Gathering**, a literary celebration of wranglers that draws cowboys from across North America. Some of the late nineteenth-century brick storefronts have survived, and the trim and tidy **Old Timers' Museum**, 222 Jasper St (May–Sept Tues–Sat 9am–5.30pm; by donation), has good displays on pioneer life and the Mounties. The place is also the market town for a number of **Hutterite colonies**, whose women stand out with their floral dresses and headscarves (see box below). However, Maple Creek's biggest selling point is its proximity to the **Cypress Hills** and the **Great Sand Hills**.

7

7

THE HUTTERITES

The Hutterites, the only prairie community to have maintained its communal ideal, are members of an Anabaptist sect named after its first leader, Jacob Hutter. Originating in sixteenth-century Central Europe (Tyrol and Moravia), they gradually moved east, ending up in Russia, which they abandoned for South Dakota in the 1870s. It was fifty years before they felt obliged to move again, when during World War I the community's pacifism was in direct opposition to the military fervour that gripped the US. They moved north between 1918 and 1922, and established a series of colonies where they were allowed to educate their children, speak their own language and avoid military service. In these largely self-sufficient communities tasks are still divided according to ability and skill, property is owned communally, and social life organized around a common dining room and dormitories. Economically prosperous, they continue to grow, and a new branch community is founded whenever the old one reaches a secure population of between one and two hundred. Apart from the occasional disagreement with the outside world when they buy new land, the Hutterites have been left in peace and have resisted assimilation pressures more staunchly than their kindred spirits, the Mennonites (see page 484) and the Doukhobors (see page 653).

ACCOMMODATION AND EATING   **MAPLE CREEK**

Ghostown Blues Hwy 271, 2km west of Maple Creek. ☏ 306 661 8481 ⓦ ghostownblues.com. A wonderful opportunity to sleep on the range in a piece of prairie history, within one of these lovingly-refurbished cabins and wagons. Choose between the likes of cowboy cabins, 1870s sheep wagons and a converted 1940s grain truck. **$105**

Jimmy's Kitchen 21 Hwy N ☏ 306 661 8989, ⓦ jimmys kitchen.business.site. Maple Creek is a town that's big on burgers, pizza and fried chicken and short on variety. This is as good as any of the similar basic joints that line the main street through town and does what it does well (most mains $11–16). Daily 11.30am–9pm.

Great Sand Hills

Some 40km north of the Trans-Canada Highway a vast area of giant sand dunes, where kangaroo rats hop and mule deer and antelope graze, is known as the **Great Sand Hills**. The best place to view them is from the village of **LIEBENTHAL**: follow Hwy-21 for 77km north of the Trans-Canada then turn east in the direction of Fitters Ranch for 17.6km before turning off north for the final 2km to the dunes parking lot.

You can also get here from **SCEPTRE**, 18.4km to the north of the dunes, where the small **Great Sandhills Museum** on Hwy-32 (mid-May to early Sept Mon–Sat 10am–noon & 12.30–4.30pm, Sun 1–5pm; $5; ⓦ greatsandhillsmuseum.com) has displays on the ecology of the hills and can provide printed directions.

Cypress Hills

South of the Trans-Canada Highway, the wooded ridges of the **Cypress Hills** rise above the plains in a 130km-long plateau that in places reaches a height of 1400m – the highest point in Canada between Labrador and the Rockies. This elevation meant the area was untouched by glaciers as they moved south during the Ice Age, scouring the land bare of vegetation. The Cypress Hills also have a wetter and milder climate than the treeless surrounding plains, creating a rich variety of woodland, wetland and grassland. This comparatively lush vegetation supports a wealth of wildlife, including elk, lynx, bobcat, coyote, plus about two hundred species of bird; keep an eye out for colonies of long-necked wild turkey, as well as the sage grouse, whose bizarre courting rituals involve the male swelling out his chest and discharging air with a sound like a gunshot. One surprise – considering the name – is the absence of cypress trees. The early French *voyageurs* seem to have confused the area's predominant lodgepole pines with the jack pines of Québec, a species they called *cyprès*. Literal-minded translation did the rest.

Two sections of the hills, known as **Centre Block** and **West Block** (which is joined to adjacent lands in Alberta), have been set aside to form the **Cypress Hills Interprovincial Park** (ⓦcypresshills.com). Driving between them is difficult, since the **Gap Road** between the two are only suitable for high-clearance four-wheel-drive vehicles in dry weather. Call ☏306 662 5411 to check road conditions.

Centre Block

Teeosix • May–Oct • ☏306 663 1221, ⓦtreeosix.com

The lodgepole-pine dominated **Centre Block** lies 31km south of Maple Creek along Hwy-21 and is by far the busier area, with many parts having more the feel of a resort than a park. The big draw here is **Cypress Hills Eco-Adventures**, an operation that offers exciting zip-line rides ($89) and various other aerial assault courses and treetop adventures for kids and adults alike. Advance booking is necessary and available online.

West Block

The much larger **West Block**, accessible from Maple Creek along Hwy-271 in the east and via Alberta's Hwy-41 in the west, spans the Saskatchewan–Alberta border. It alternates between thick forest and open grassland and is broken up by steep hills and deep, sheltered ravines. The West Block is also attached to **Fort Walsh**, a partly refurbished Mountie station and replica trading post.

Fort Walsh National Historic Park

May to Sept daily 9.30am–5.30pm • $9.80 • ☏306 662 3590, off-season ☏306 662 2645, ⓦparkscanada.ca/walsh

A five-minute walk behind the park's information centre, and accessed from the eastern entrance of the park by the increasingly bumpy Hwy-271, **Fort Walsh National Historic Park** has excellent displays on the Plains Indians, fort history and the development of the RCMP. Built in 1875, the fort sits in a wide, low-lying valley, its trim stockade framed by pine forests. It was abandoned in favour of Maple Creek

---

THE CYPRESS HILLS MASSACRE AND THE MOUNTIES

Though by the 1870s it had become illegal to supply Aboriginal peoples with booze, **whisky traders** had nevertheless spread out across Canada's southwestern plains, which were aptly nicknamed **Whoop-up Country**. These traders were mostly from the US and brought their liquor north in the autumn, returning south in late spring laden with furs and buffalo robes. They established dozens of posts, such as that at Lethbridge (see page 536), where they could trade while being protected from their disorderly customers by log stockades.

In the spring of 1873, there were two such outposts beside **Battle Creek**, deep in the Cypress Hills. For reasons that remain obscure, though drunkenness no doubt played a part, this was the scene of a violent confrontation between a group of white wolf-hunters, whisky traders and a band of Assiniboine. Equipped with the latest fast-action rifles, the hunters and traders riddled the Assiniboine camp with bullets, killing up to seventy before packing up and heading back across the US border. News of the incident, known as the **Cypress Hills Massacre**, filtered back to Ottawa and helped speed up the recruitment of the newly formed **North West Mounted Police**, or Mounties, who received their first posting west that autumn (see page 524).

The Mounties attempted to have eight of the participants in the massacre extradited from the US, but failed. Three of these men were later arrested in Canada and a trial was held in Winnipeg in 1876, but because of conflicting testimonies and a lack of evidence, all three were acquitted; no one was ever punished.

Nevertheless, First Nations people appreciated the Mounties' efforts and were heartened by the thought that everyone was going to be seen as equal in the eyes of this new police force. The Mounties may have kept the peace, but they were also a major part of a policy of containment and control of Aboriginal peoples, spearheading a determined push that forced them onto reservations to open the area to European settlers.

just eight years later; in 1942 the RCMP acquired the land, and returned the site to its original appearance. Guides in period costumes take you on a tour of whitewashed log buildings, the whole site having returned to its original appearance. Close by, a cemetery contains the tombstones of several North West Mounted Police officers. Every 45 minutes a minibus makes the trip from the information centre over the hills to Battle Creek, where Abel Farwell's whisky trading post has been reconstructed to commemorate the 1873 Cypress Hills Massacre (see box above), and guides will also take you to the site of the massacre.

The Conglomerate Cliffs

Near Adams Lake, 10km northeast of Fort Walsh via Hwy-271, the **Conglomerate Cliffs** are worth a look if you're passing through. These strange-looking walls of rock some 150m high consist of multicoloured cobblestones that have been pressed together over time. You can drive to their base.

7

ACCOMMODATION   **CYPRESS HILLS**

CENTRE BLOCK
Campgrounds ☎855 737 7275, ⓦsaskparks.net/reserve-a-site. Several busy summer campgrounds gather around a central resort hub and can be booked at the campground office on Pine Ave, west of the centre (mid-May to Aug daily 8.30am–10pm). Sites $20
Cypress Park Resort Inn Pine Ave ☎306 662 4477, ⓦresortatcypresshills.ca. The only hotel near Centre Block has a range of lodgings from rooms to cabins and apartments. There's a reasonable higher-end restaurant

on-site too (dinner mains $19–29; daily 8am–10pm). $160

WEST BLOCK
West Block Campground ☎800 737 7275, ⓦsaskparks.net/reserve-a-site. The main option in Saskatchewan's West Block is this basic campground in an isolated spot 5km north of Fort Walsh. It's in dense forest with a stream running through it but you'll need your own supplies. May–Sept. $18

Southern Alberta

The most travelled route across Southern Alberta is Hwy-1, past the Alberta Badlands (see page 537), and on to Calgary, but **Hwy-3** branches off at **Medicine Hat** for a more southerly course across the plains to the Rockies at Crowsnest Pass (see page 624). Though a quieter and less spectacular route into the mountains, it's the quicker way to Vancouver, and a couple of diversions may hold you in the prairies for longer than you expected, particularly the **Head-Smashed-In Buffalo Jump** heritage site near Fort Macleod.

Medicine Hat

The first major Albertan town west of the Saskatchewan border along Hwy-1 is **MEDICINE HAT**. Although little more than one hundred years old, the origin of its wonderful name has already been confused. The most likely story has to do with a Cree medicine man who lost his headdress fleeing a battle with the Blackfoot; his followers lost heart at the omen, surrendered, and were promptly massacred. These days you rarely see the town mentioned without the adage that it "has all hell for a basement", a quotation Rudyard Kipling coined in response to the huge reserves of natural gas below the town. The gas fields feed a flourishing petrochemical industry which blots the otherwise park-studded downtown area on the banks of the South Saskatchewan River.

The town's main landmark is the world's **tallest teepee** beside the Trans-Canada Highway, a metal structure of twenty storeys, close to the town's **visitor centre**.

Medalta

713 Medalta Ave SE • Mid-May to early Sept daily 9.30am–5pm; early Sept to mid-May Tues–Sat 10am–4pm • $12 • ☏ 403 529 1070, ⊛ medalta.org

Medicine Hat's most rewarding attraction is **Medalta**, one of a series of old pottery factories that clustered here in the early 1900s, drawn by cheap natural gas. To get there from the visitor centre drive towards downtown, then follow signs for the "Historic Clay District". The factory once specialized in turning out sturdy tableware, or "war ware" as the simple cream-coloured pieces with their clean lines were dubbed, before mismanagement and a series of crippling strikes led to the factory's 1954 closure. It lay idle for half a century, until its reincarnation as an industrial heritage site. Partial refurbishment has helped provide spaces for exhibits, but it's the untouched parts, left in their original battered state at the time of closure, that give the best feel for the place, as does the chance to watch replicas being made by hand. Other museum highlights include samples of pottery personally commissioned by Haile Selassie for the Ethiopian court.

ARRIVAL AND INFORMATION

MEDICINE HAT

Visitor centre 8 Gehring Road SW beside Hwy-1 near the giant teepee (Sept to mid-May 9am–4.30pm; mid-May to Aug 9am–7pm; ☏ 403 527 6422, ⊛ tourismmedicinehat. com).

ACCOMMODATION AND EATING

Local Public Eatery 579 3rd St SE ☏ 430 487 5600, ⊛ localmedhat.com. "Common food done uncommonly well" is the claim and it's not far from the truth. Eggs Benedict, burgers, salads and sandwiches (most around $16) all make the menu and are reliable enough, at this busy, popular bar with outdoor patio. Mon–Thurs 11am–midnight, Fri & Sat 11am–2am, Sun 11am–9pm.

Medicine Hat Lodge 1051 Ross Glen Drive ☏ 403 529 2222, ☏ 800 661 8095, ⊛ medhatlodge.com. A little pricier than most highway motels, but worth it for the spa, pool, waterslides, four-star facilities and casino. With breakfast and wi-fi. $169

Sun Dek Motel 855 Gershaw Drive SW ☏ 403 526 1122, ⊛ sundekmotel.ca. Well-priced Trans-Canada-side motel with an almost quaint, vaguely 1970s feel, as well as a laundry, barbecue area, free local calls and wi-fi and clean and simple rooms. $65

★**Thai Orchid** 3–36 Strachan Court SE ☏ 403 580 8210, ⊛ thaiorchidroom.ca. Don't be put off by the ordinary location hidden beside a huge Trans-Canada shopping centre at the eastern edge of town: this is a first-class Thai restaurant that's one of the best bets for ethnic food in town. Most mains are $19. Tues–Thurs 11am–9pm, Fri 11am–10pm, Sat 4.30–10pm, Sun noon–9pm.

Lethbridge and Fort Whoop-Up

Fort Whoop-Up 200 Indian Battle Park Rd • June–Sept daily 10am–5pm; Oct–May Wed–Sun noon–4pm • $10 • ☏ 403 329 0444, ⊛ fortwhoopup.com

LETHBRIDGE thrives on the back of oil, gas and some of Alberta's most productive agricultural land, none of which is of much consequence to visitors, though you might be tempted by **Fort Whoop-Up**, a reconstruction of the wild whisky-trading post set up in 1869 by American desperadoes from Montana. It became the largest and most lucrative of the many similar illegal forts on the Canadian prairies and led to the arrival of the North West Mounted Police in 1874. Aboriginal peoples came from miles around to trade anything – including the clothes off their backs – for lethal hooch and rifles. The fort was also the scene of the last armed battle between Aboriginal peoples in North America (Cree and Blackfoot in 1870).

INFORMATION

LETHBRIDGE

Tourist office 2805 Scenic Drive (summer daily 9am–8pm; winter Mon–Sat 9am–5pm; ☏ 403 320 1222, ⊛ explore southwestalberta.ca). At the corner of highways 4 and 5.

Fort Macleod

Fort Museum 219 25th St • May & June daily 9am–5pm; July to early Sept daily 9am–6pm; early Sept to Oct Wed–Sun 10am–4pm • $10 • ⊛ nwmpmuseum.com

FORT MACLEOD, 50km west of Lethbridge, catches traffic travelling between the US and Calgary on Hwy-2, which eases around the town centre past the largely rebuilt wooden palisade of the **Fort Museum**. This fort was the first to be established in Canada's Wild West by the North West Mounted Police, who got lost after being dispatched to raid Fort Whoop-Up in Lethbridge, allowing the whisky traders to flee; finding Whoop-Up empty, they continued west under Colonel James Macleod to establish a permanent barracks here on Oldman Island on the river in 1874. The RCMP "musical ride" ($5), a display of precision riding, is performed four times daily by students in replica dress.

ACCOMMODATION	FORT MACLEOD

Sunset Motel Main St ☎ 403 553 4448, ⓦ sunset-motel.ca. Probably the pick of the town's five similarly priced motels which all fill quickly in summer. It's on Hwy-3 at the western entrance to town and, though a bit dated and with thin walls, is certainly clean and friendly enough. **$82**

Head-Smashed-In Buffalo Jump

Hwy-785 18km west of Fort Macleod • Daily: July to early Sept 9am–5pm; rest of year 10am–5pm • $15 • ☎ 403 553 2731, ⓦ headsmashedin.ca• No public transport; taxis from Fort Macleod cost about $25

The image of Indians trailing a lone buffalo with bow and arrow may be Hollywood's idea of how Aboriginal peoples secured food, but the truth, while less romantic, was often far more effective and spectacular. Over a period of ten thousand years, Blackfoot hunters perfected a technique of luring buffalo herds into a shallow basin and stampeding them to their deaths over a broad cliff, where they were then butchered for meat (dried to make pemmican, a cake of pounded meat, berries and lard), bone (for tools) and hide (for clothes and shelter). Such "jumps" existed all over North America, but **Head-Smashed-In Buffalo Jump** is the best preserved; its name is a literal description of how a nineteenth-century Blackfoot met his end after deciding the best spot to watch was at the base of the cliff. The modern **interpretive centre** delves deep into the history of the jump and First Nation culture in general. Its highlight, a film entitled *In Search of the Buffalo*, re-creates the thunderous death plunge using a herd of buffalo which were slaughtered, frozen and then somehow made to look like live animals hurtling to their deaths. Below the multilevel facility, a10m-deep bed of ash and bones accumulated over millennia is protected by the threat of a $50,000 fine for anyone foolish enough to rummage for souvenirs. All manner of artefacts and objects have been discovered amid the debris, including knives, scrapers and sharpened stones used to skin bison. Metal arrowheads in the topmost layers, traded with white settlers, suggest the jump was used until the early nineteenth century. Around the centre are a couple of kilometres of **trails**.

The Alberta Badlands

Formed by the meltwaters of the last Ice Age, the Red Deer River valley cuts a deep gash through the prairie – about 240km northwest of Medicine Hat and 140km east of Calgary – creating a surreal landscape of bare, sunbaked hills and eerie lunar flats dotted with sagebrush and scrubby, tufted grass. On their own, the **Alberta Badlands** justify a visit, but what makes them an essential detour is the **Royal Tyrrell Museum of Paleontology**, one of North America's greatest natural history museums, located 8km outside **Drumheller**, a dreary but obvious base. You'll need your own transport to explore and get to **Dinosaur Provincial Park**, home to the Tyrrell Museum Field Station and the source of many of its fossils.

Dinosaur Provincial Park
ⓦ albertaparks.ca/dinosaur

A 130km drive west of Medicine Hat on Hwy-1 and Hwy-876 leads to **Dinosaur Provincial Park**. Nestled among some of the baddest of the badlands, the park's landscape is not only one of Canada's most otherworldly, but also one of the world's richest fossil beds. Over three hundred complete skeletons have been found and dispatched to museums across the world, representing 35 (or ten percent) of all known dinosaur species.

Royal Tyrrell Museum Field Station

April to late June daily 9am–4pm, late June to Aug daily 9am–5pm; Sept to early Nov Tues–Fri 9am–4pm, Sat 10am–5pm, Dec–Mar Mon–Fri 9am–4pm• $6• ☎ 403 378 4344

The **Royal Tyrrell Museum Field Station** is the park's obvious hub and a starting point for five self-guided trails, the **Badlands Trail** and the **Cottonwood Flats Trail** being the most worthwhile. The centre also houses a small museum, but the real meat of a visit is the excellent ninety-minute **bus tour** (April to mid-Oct several daily; $15), to an otherwise out-of-bounds dinosaur dig near the centre of the park. A few exposed skeletons have been left *in situ*, with panels providing information. The station also organizes a variety of guided **hikes**, most notably the three-hour Centrosaurus Quarry Hike (daily, times vary; $18), which visits a restricted area where hundreds of Centrosaurus skeletons have been uncovered. All tours fill up quickly, so book ahead.

ACCOMMODATION	**DINOSAUR PROVINCIAL PARK**
Dinosaur Provincial Park Campground ☎ 877 537 2757. Open year-round but only serviced May–Sept, this is an excellent spot with quiet shaded sites close to the Field	Station and beside Little Sandhill Creek. Sites $26; canvas cabins $10

Blackfoot Crossing Historical Park

Hwy 842, 10km south of Hwy 1 • May–Oct daily 9am–5pm, Nov–Apr Mon–Fri 9am–5pm • $12 • ⊕ blackfootcrossing.ca

Some 120km west of Dinosaur Provincial, and about the same distance east of Calgary, Blackfoot Crossing Historical Park is centred on a vast, flat and round modern building, which looks as though it's been flattened by the big prairie skies. Inside, exhibits tell the story of the Siksika (ie Blackfoot) who held sway in these lands until 1877 when Chief Crowfoot signed the infamous Treaty 7 here, creating this reserve and ceding much of his homelands to the British crown. With massacres, small pox and abusive residential schools, theirs is not an easy history, but there's plenty of detail on Siksika culture and its revival to add an uplifting note. A tipi village outside regularly plays host to craft demonstrations, though their timetable is unreliable – and, like much of the centre, seems a little neglected and haphazardly run. It's worth calling ahead to arrange a free tour with a Siksika guide. Short walking trails around the centre lead to prairie viewpoints.

Drumheller and around

A downbeat town in an extraordinary setting, **DRUMHELLER** lies roughly ninety minutes' drive northeast of Calgary or two hours on dirt roads from Dinosaur Provincial Park. Nestled at the bottom of a parched canyon and surrounded by the detritus and spoil heaps from its mining past, the otherworldliness of Drumheller's immediate surroundings is heightened by the contrast to the vivid colours of the wheat and grasslands above. Its Red Deer River once exposed not only dinosaur fossils but also coal seams, which attracted the likes of Samuel. Drumheller, after whom the town is named. The first mine opened in 1911, but within fifty years it was all over and today Drumheller is sustained by agriculture, oil and tourism. There's not much to do in its tiny hardscrabble downtown, but the **Royal Tyrrell Museum** ensures visitors pass through in droves. The town has gone out of its way to try to tempt them in, with dino-mania at every turn. Though the museum is clearly the major local draw, the rest of the semi-arid Red Deer Valley is dotted with viewpoints and minor sights.

Royal Tyrrell Museum

Daily: May to Aug 9am–9pm; Sept 10am–5pm; Oct to mid-May Tues–Sun 10am–5pm • $19 • ⓦ tyrrellmuseum.com

A sleek building packed with high-tech displays and blended skilfully into desolate surroundings, the **Royal Tyrrell Museum**, 6km outside Drumheller, will appeal to anyone with even a hint of scientific or natural curiosity. Although the world's largest collection of complete dinosaur skeletons (120,000 specimens), the museum is far more than a load of old bones. As well as skilfully and entertainingly tracing the earth's natural history, it's also a leading research centre and you can watch scientists painstakingly scratch, blow and vacuum dirt from fossils. Hands-on activities include fossil casting or the chance to dig in a realistic quarry; book ahead for both. There's also a cafeteria, while outside you can spend the best part of an hour exploring a 1.4km hiking trail dotted with information boards.

The Dinosaur Trail and Horseshoe Canyon

For a **scenic drive** from Drumheller take the 48km **Dinosaur Trail**; maps are available from the visitor centre. Highlights include the Little Church (capacity six) and **Horsethief Canyon** and **Orkney Viewpoint**, both of which offer spectacular panoramas of the wildly eroded valley and are connected by a small car ferry at Bleriot (daily 10am–8.45pm; free).

For easy badland **hikes**, try **Horseshoe Canyon**, 19km southwest of Drumheller on Hwy-9, where a multitude of good trails snake around the canyon floor.

Wayne and the hoodoos

A couple of sights are an easy drive southwest of town. First is the near-ghost town (population 28) of **Wayne**, 14km from Drumheller, with its atmospheric Wild West-style *Last Chance Saloon* (see page 540). Another 9km southeast on Hwy-10 a series of **hoodoos** – slender columns of wind-sculpted sandstone topped with mushroom-like caps – makes for a good photo.

Atlas Coal Mine and Dorothy

Tours daily: May–June 9.30am–5pm; July & Aug 9.45am–7.30pm; Sept & Oct 9.30am–5pm • $10 admission, $25 extra for tour• ☎ 403 822 2220, ⓦ atlascoalmine.ab.ca

Some 23km south of Drumheller on Hwy-10, the **Atlas Coal Mine** offers tours that not only go underground but also examine the teetering wooden "tipple" dominating the site: once used to sort ore, it's now a beautiful and rather wistful piece of industrial archeology. There's also a 90-year-old train to ride on. As wistful are the ruins of near-ghost town **Dorothy**, 14km further south on Hwy-10.

ARRIVAL AND INFORMATION	DRUMHELLER AND AROUND

Visitor centre 60 1st Ave West (daily: May–June 9.30am–7.30pm; July & Aug 9am–9pm; Sept–April 10am–5.30pm; ☎ 403 823 1331, ☎ 866 823 8100) is attached to a 26.2m

T-Rex mock-up – about four times bigger than real life – which you can climb ($3).

ACCOMMODATION AND EATING

DRUMHELLER

Badlands Motel 801 North Dinosaur Trail ☎ 403 823 5155. Old-fashioned and well-kept no-frills motel on the fringes of town en route to the Tyrell Museum. Attached is *Whif's Flapjack House*, one of the town's best and long-standing dining options, a good place to breakfast or grab

a burger later on. $82

Bernie and the Boys Bistro 305 4th St W ☎ 403 823 3318, ⓦ bernieandtheboys.com. Reliable burger place that serves crinkle-cut fries and a huge variety of good shakes. Portions are large but you can make them gigantic by ordering triple patties or even the mind-blowing $30 mammoth burger. Tues–Sat 11am–8.30pm.

Pinters Campground 6km southwest of town along Hwy-10 in Rosedale ☎403 823 5810, ⊛pinters campground.ca. All campgrounds fill quickly on summer weekends so arrive early for these primitive sites by a river with plenty of shade. May–Oct. $20

Ramada Hotel 680 2nd St SE ☎403 823 2028, ⊛wyndhamhotels.com. Pretty standard upper-end chain motel with hot tub, indoor pool, and free wi-fi, but book well ahead, since accommodation in Drumheller is limited and often hard to find. $199

River Grove Campground and Cabins 25 Poplar St ☎403 823 6655, ⊛camprivergrove.com. The best central camping option has well-shaded campsites, basic cabin and lies a short walk northwest of downtown. May–Sept. Sites $38; cabins $104

Sizzling House 160 Centre St ☎403 823 8098. Despite a dowdy exterior, this is a better-than-average Chinese restaurant, which also has good Thai dishes from $9. Wed–Mon 11am–9pm.

WAYNE

★ **Last Chance Saloon & Rosedeer Hotel** ☎403 823 9189, ⊛visitlastchancesaloon.com. Wild West-style place where miners used to drink and brawl and still great for a bison burger and beer; pleasant tree-encircled tent sites and rooms are also offered. Wed & Thurs 11am–7pm, Fri & Sat 11am–9pm, Sun noon–7pm. Sites $20; doubles $65

Calgary

Southern Alberta's likeable main city, **CALGARY** is a mere hour's drive east of where the prairies buckle into the **Rockies** to form some of the continent's most magnificent scenery. So it takes self-restraint to give this city at the confluence of the Bow and Elbow rivers the day or two it deserves. It's best known as the home of the **Calgary Stampede**, a veritable cowboy carnival which takes place over ten days every July. It inspires most of the city and plenty of tourists to indulge in a boots-and-Stetson image that's still a way of life in the region. As such, Calgary's "Cowtown" nickname still has resonance – but a lot less relevance, given the wealth the oil and gas industry has brought to the city in recent decades. These riches have seen the city's population grow to over one million, many of whom live in an ever-expanding cookie-cutter suburban sprawl. Despite this Calgary is still an energetic place, harbouring a burgeoning **arts** scene, excellent **restaurants** and cafés, splendid parks and some lively neighbourhoods that are good for strolling.

Compact, high-rise **downtown** Calgary, loosely centred on the largely pedestrianized Stephen Avenue Mall (8th Avenue between 1st Street SE and 3rd Street SW), is a cluster of mirrored glass and polished granite. A monument to oil money, the area is sleek as can be, but short on sights, other than the prestigious **Glenbow Museum**, where any city tour should start. A jaunt up the **Calgary Tower**, across the street, will help you get your bearings. Much of the rest of the central city lends itself to wandering on foot; Eau Claire offers a riverfront focus opposite **Prince's Island**, the nearest of many parks and something of an epicentre for Calgary's excellent 210km system of **walking and bike paths**. A twenty-minute stroll west leads to **Kensington**, a gentrified, faintly bohemian shopping and café district north of the Bow River. A similar walk south of downtown, 17th Avenue SW, is packed with more shops, restaurants and cafés. The appeal of attractions further afield – **Fort Calgary**, **Heritage Park**, **Telus Spark** and **Calgary Zoo** – will depend on your inclinations. These and other sights can be easily reached by bus or light railway (C-Train). The city is also a great hub for day-trips to the dinosaur remains in the strange **Badlands** around **Drumheller** to the east (see page 538) and to **Head-Smashed-In Buffalo Jump** (see page 537).

Brief history

Calgary is one of Canada's youngest large cities. It was once the domain of the **Blackfoot**, who ranged over the whole area for several thousand years. About three hundred years ago, they were joined by the **Sarcee**, forced south by war from their northern heartlands, and the **Stoney**, who migrated north with Sitting Bull.

Europeans first gathered here in the late 1700s; explorer **David Thompson** wintered here during his travels, while the **Palliser expedition** spent time nearby en route to the

THE CALGARY STAMPEDE

The annual **Calgary Stampede** brings around 1.25 million spectators and participants to the city for ten days in early July. This is far more than a carefully engineered gift to Calgary's tourist industry, however, for the event is one of the world's biggest rodeos and comes close to living up to its "greatest outdoor show on earth" billing.

The competition end of things is taken very seriously and the combined prize money exceeds $2 million. The first show in 1912 put up $100,000 and attracted sixty thousand people to the opening parade, with a line-up that included two thousand Aboriginal people in full ceremonial garb and some of Pancho Villa's Mexican revolutionary bandits in an event billed as "The Last and Best Great West Frontier Days".

STAMPEDE EVENTS

Things officially kick off on the first Friday of the Stampede with a 9am **parade**, though many spectators are in place along the route at 6am. The two-hour march involves around 170 entries, 4000 participants and 750 horses. For the duration of Stampede, downtown's **Olympic Plaza** (temporarily renamed Rope Square) offers free pancake breakfasts (8.15–11.30am) and entertainment every morning; events include live music, mock gunfights and Aboriginal dancing, and square dancing also fills parts of Stephen Avenue Mall at 10am. To really experience how the city celebrates Stampede, move outside this central area, where you'll find entire neighbourhoods, shops, bars, churches and even local luminaries organizing their own festivities (usually a pancake breakfast). **Nightlife** is a world unto itself, with Stampede locations giving way to music, dancing, mega-cabarets, plus lots of drinking, eating (it's barbecue heaven), fireworks and general partying into the small hours.

The Stampede's real action – the rodeo and allied events – takes place in **Stampede Park**, southeast of downtown, by the C-Train Victoria Park–Stampede Station. This vast, open area contains an amusement park, concert and show venues, bars, restaurants and a huge range of stalls and shows that take the best part of a day to see. Entrance is $18, which gives you entry into everything except the rodeo and chuck-wagon races. **Entertainments** include: Indian Village, where members of the Blackfoot, Blood, Sarcee, Stoney and Piegan First Nations set up a teepee village; the World Blacksmith Competition; the Centennial Fair, which hosts events for children; the Agricultural Building, home to displays of cattle and other livestock; the outdoor Coca-Cola Stage, used for evening concerts; and Nashville North, an indoor country music venue.

To see the daily **rodeo** competition – bronco and bull riding, calf roping, steer wrestling, barrel racing and the rest – you'll need another ticket and unless you've bought these in advance it's hardly worth it: you'll likely be in poor seats and miles from the action or have to stand. You'll also need a ticket (also best bought in advance) to watch the other big event, the ludicrously dangerous but hugely exciting **chuck-wagon** races. Both events are held in the Stampede Park grandstand.

STAMPEDE PRACTICALITIES

If you're coming to see the Stampede, plan ahead. **Accommodation** is stretched and prices can skyrocket for the duration. **Tickets** for the rodeo and chuck-wagon races range from $20–400; tickets for the finals of both events are a few dollars more; all tickets include park admission. For ticket and all other general information, check ⓦcalgarystampede.com.

Rockies. Settlers started arriving around 1870, when hunters moved into the region from the United States, where they had hunted buffalo to the edge of extinction. In 1876 a fort was built here by the North West Mounted Police and christened **Fort Calgary**, after the Scottish birthplace of its assistant commissioner. The word *calgary* is Gaelic for "clear running water"; which seemed appropriate given the ice-clear waters of the Bow and Elbow rivers.

By 1883 a station had been built close to the fort, part of the new trans-Canadian **railway**. The township laid out nearby quickly attracted **ranchers** and British gentlemen farmers, cementing an enduring Anglo-Saxon cultural bias. By 1886, fires had wiped out most of the town's temporary wooden buildings and tents, leading to an edict declaring all new buildings should be constructed in sandstone and, for a while,

7

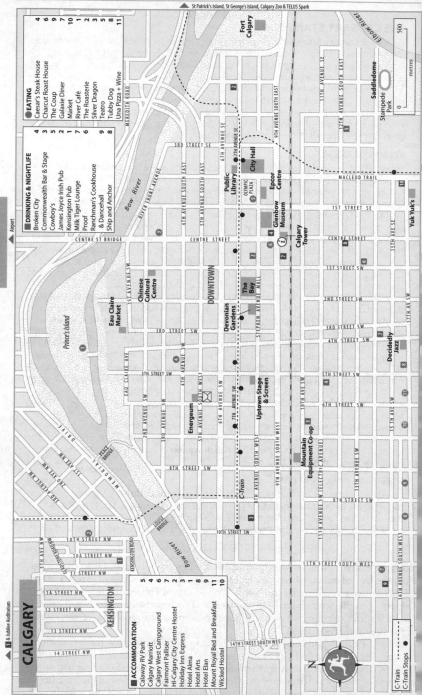

CALGARY

▲ T1 & Jubilee Auditorium

KENSINGTON

ACCOMMODATION

Calaway RV Park	5
Calgary Marriott	4
Calgary West Campground	6
Fairmont Palliser	2
Hi-Calgary City Centre Hostel	3
Holiday Inn Express	7
Hotel Alma	1
Hotel Arts	8
Hotel Elan	9
Mount Royal Bed and Breakfast	11
Wicked Hostel	10

DOWNTOWN

Eau Claire Market

Chinese Cultural Centre

Prince's Island

Devonian Gardens

The Bay

Energeum

Uptown Stage & Screen

Mountain Equipment Co-op

Decidedly Jazz

C-Train

DRINKING & NIGHTLIFE

Broken City	4
Commonwealth Bar & Stage	3
Cowboy's	5
James Joyce Irish Pub	1
Kensington Pub	7
Milk Tiger Lounge	6
Proof	2
Ranchman's Cookhouse & Dancehall	9
Ship and Anchor	8

EATING

Caesar's Steak House	4
Charcut Roast House	6
The Coup	9
Galaxie Diner	7
Market	10
River Café	1
The Roasterie	2
Silver Dragon	3
Teatro	5
Tubby Dog	8
Una Pizza + Wine	11

St Patrick's Island, St George's Island, Calgary Zoo & TELUS Spark

Fort Calgary

Elbow River

Saddledome

Stampede Park

City Hall

Public Library

OLYMPIC PLAZA

Epcor Centre

Glenbow Museum

Calgary Tower

Yuk Yuk's

Bow River

MACLEOD TRAIL

MEREDITH ROAD

Centre St Bridge

Louise Bridge

Peace Bridge

Memorial Drive

▲ Airport

▼ 5, 6, Bow Trail & Trans-Canada Highway (Canada Olympic Park)

C-Train
C-Train Stops

N

500
metres
0

CALGARY'S FESTIVALS

Calgary has a good number of festivals and events, though all are dwarfed by the Stampede (see page 541). Visit Calgary maintains an up-to-date what's-on list at Ⓦvisitcalgary.com/things-to-do/events-calendar.

Carifest Early June Ⓦcarifest.ca. Caribbean-themed celebrations, with food and music on Prince's Island.

Calgary Stampede Second week of July Ⓦcalgarystampede.com. Rodeo and agricultural show that's grown into a giant homage to the "West".

Calgary Folk Music Festival Late July Ⓦcalgaryfolkfest.com. Laidback festival on Prince's Island featuring four days of live folk music from around the world.

Calgary was nicknamed "Sandstone City". It achieved official city status in 1894, something it had taken rival Edmonton over a hundred years to achieve.

Cattle and the railway generated exceptional growth, though this was nothing compared with the prosperity that followed the discovery of **oil**. The first strike took place in 1914 in nearby Turner Valley. An oil refinery opened in 1923 and since then Calgary has rarely looked back. When prices soared during the oil crisis of the 1970s, the city exploded, becoming a world energy and financial centre – headquarters for some four hundred oil-related businesses. Crucially though, Calgary has diversified into light manufacturing, high-tech, film, transportation and tourism, with 4.6 million visitors to the city every year.

Glenbow Museum

130 9th Ave SE • Tues–Sat 9am–5pm, Sun noon–5pm • $16 • ☎ 403 268 4100, Ⓦ glenbow.org

The richly endowed **Glenbow Museum** is a testament to the cultural benefits of booming oil revenues and its three floors of displays make a fine introduction to the heritage of the Canadian West and its Aboriginal peoples. The permanent collection starts with **sacred art** from around the world, which dovetails with western Canadian **Indigenous art** and **European art** that depicted Aboriginal peoples. **Native crafts** are also explored, with stunning carvings, costumes and jewellery; the emphasis is on local Plains tribes such as the Blackfoot – though the collection also examines the Inuit and the Métis. Also on display are the original documents many chiefs were tricked into signing, believing they were peace treaties, when in fact they gave away land rights in deliberately incomprehensible legalese.

Otherwise the museum runs the gamut of western Canadian history with exhibits on the fur trade, the Northwest Rebellion, the Canadian Pacific Railway, pioneer life, ranching, cowboys, the Calgary Stampede, oil and wheat. It all adds up to a glut of period paraphernalia, including a terrifying exhibit on frontier dentistry, an absurdly comprehensive display of washing machines and a solitary 1938 bra. Finally, the museum's dazzling display of **gems and minerals** is said to be among the world's best.

Calgary Tower

101 9th Ave SW • Daily: July & Aug 9am–10pm; Sept–June 9am–9pm • $18 • ☎ 403 266 7171, Ⓦ calgarytower.com

The **Calgary Tower**, the city's favourite folly, is shorter and less imposing than tourist material suggests and at 190m tall (762 steps or a one-minute elevator) stands somewhat overshadowed by downtown's more recent buildings. Yet its unusual shape has made it a long-term landmark and it offers outstanding views, especially on clear days, when the snowcapped Rockies fill the western horizon, with the ski-jump towers of Canada Olympic Park in the middle distance. On the observation platform you'll also find a snack bar with reasonable food, a cocktail bar and an expensive revolving restaurant.

Core Shopping Centre and the Devonian Gardens

8th Ave & 2nd St SW • Daily 9am–9pm • Free

Any number of shopping malls lurk within the soaring high-rises, but **Core Shopping Centre** is the city's main indoor retail area and the unlikely site of the **Devonian Gardens**. Like something out of an idyllic urban utopia, this is the largest indoor park in North America, with 10,000 shrubs and 500 trees growing in a space the size of two football fields. This lush sanctuary for local and tropical species is particularly impressive, since it's on the fourth floor. Benches beside the garden's paths are perfect for picnicking on food bought in the mall below, while small concerts are often held here too.

Eau Claire Market and Prince's Island Park

North of downtown a refurbished warehouse houses the faintly alternative but dowdy **Eau Claire Market** mall; beyond it a footbridge connects **Prince's Island Park**, a popular but peaceful park on the Bow River with plenty of trees, flowers and a kids' playground. A five-minute wander to the northern end of the island provides a look at the impressive Peace Bridge, a pedestrian and cyclists' bridge based on the double helix design of Spanish architect Santiago Calatrava.

Calgary Chinese Cultural Centre

197 1st St SW • Museum daily 11am–5pm • $5 • ☎ 403 262 5071, ⊛ culturalcentre.ca

Just north of downtown lies the **Calgary Chinese Cultural Centre**, its big central dome modelled on the Temple of Heaven in Beijing. It forms the focus for Calgary's modest Chinatown and its large Chinese–Canadian population, most of whom descend from immigrant railway workers who arrived in the 1880s. It contains a small museum of Chinese artefacts, a gallery, gift shop and a restaurant.

Fort Calgary

750 9th Ave SE • Daily 9am–5pm • $12 • ☎ 403 290 1875, ⊛ fortcalgary.com • C-Train stop City Hall

Fort Calgary, the city's historical nexus, an easy five-block walk from the C-Train, was built in under six weeks by the North West Mounted Police in 1875. The fort was the germ of the present city, and remained operative as a police post until 1914, when it was sold to the Canadian Pacific Railway. The whole area remained buried under railway tracks and derelict warehouses until 1974 when the city bought back the land and rebuilt the log stockade as part of a pleasant forty-acre park at the confluence of the Bow and Elbow rivers. An adjoining **interpretive centre** traces Calgary's development with period photographs showing how wild Calgary still was in 1876. Kids will enjoy the chance to dress up as a Mountie.

Calgary Zoo

1300 Zoo Rd • Daily 9am–6pm, last admission 5pm • $30 • ☎ 403 232 9300, ☎ 800 588 9993, ⊛ calgaryzoo.org • C-Train to Zoo Station

Founded in 1920, **Calgary Zoo** is Calgary's most popular attraction and one of North America's best zoos, with some 1000 animals and 290 species in reasonably "natural" enclosures. Among them are underwater viewing areas for polar bears and sea creatures, dark rooms for nocturnal animals, greenhouses for tropical birds and butterflies and many classic big draws like gorillas, tigers and giraffes. Check out the extended North American and Canadian Wilds, Aspen Woodlands and Rocky Mountains sections for a taste of local fauna. Also here is **Prehistoric Park**, where sixteen life-size animatronic dinosaur models are a real hit with kids. Gardens and picnic areas are dotted throughout the zoo.

TELUS Spark

220 St George's Drive NE • Sun–Fri 10am–4pm, Sat 10am–5pm • $26, parking $5 • ☎ 403 817 6800, ⓦ sparkscience.ca • C-Train to Zoo Station

The bold, airy and modern **TELUS Spark** is an impressively slick, hands-on science centre and the best place in town to entertain kids on a rainy day. But with the emphasis on stimulating rather than informing, adults may well find the content a bit thin. The centre divides into four main areas: the ground-floor **Earth and Sky** and **Energy and Innovation** almost blend into one another and look at both the natural and man-made regional environments, particularly the locally all-important physics of energy. The focus is much looser in **Being Human**, which explores human psychology through activities such as pinning up notes with your aspirations, but at least a machine teaches you how to flirt. **Open Studio** is similarly loose, but perhaps the most engrossing for kids as it offers the chance to take apart circuit boards, build sea creatures and, most impressively, create video animations to email to yourself.

All this is probably best appreciated by the over-8s; for younger kids zero in on the indoor play area which includes crafts to try, experiments with magnets, water pipes to design. Entrance tickets also include admission to several daily shows at the three-storey-high IMAX that's in the round and state-of-the-art. The movies here mesmerize whatever the topic – sit high for best effect – but the screens are at their best during planetarium shows. Finally, be sure to check the website for daily events which can include demonstrations and astronomy sessions.

Inglewood Bird Sanctuary

2425 9th Ave SE • Park Dawn–dusk; Visitor centre May–Sept daily 10am–4pm; Oct–April Tues–Fri 10am–4pm, Sat noon–4pm • Free • Bus #411 or #31

Natural-history enthusiasts might want to visit the **Inglewood Bird Sanctuary**, on the Bow River's forested flats, 3km downstream of the zoo east of downtown. Some 230 species are present year-round and more during migratory cycles. You might see bald eagles, Swainson's hawks, ring-necked pheasants, warblers, grey partridge and great horned owls. Numerous duck, geese and other waterfowl are also present, as are muskrats, beavers, white-tailed and mule deer, foxes and long-tailed weasels.

Heritage Park Historical Village

Mid-May to early Sept daily 9.30am–5pm; early Sept–early Oct Sat & Sun 9.30am–5pm • $26.50 • ☎ 403 268 8500, ⓦ heritagepark.ca • Heritage C-Train station then bus #502

A sixty-acre theme park centred on a reconstructed frontier village 16km southwest of downtown, **Heritage Park** replicates life on the Canadian prairies before 1914 and panders relentlessly to the myth of the "Wild West". Full of family-oriented presentations and original costumes, the museum comprises more than 150 restored buildings, all transported from small-town locations. Each has been assigned to one of several communities – fur post, Aboriginal village, homestead, farm – and most fulfil their original function; thus you can see a working blacksmith, buy fresh bread, go to church and even get married. Transport is period appropriate, with steam trains, trams, a horse-drawn bus and stagecoaches. If you're here for the day you can pick up cakes and snacks from the traditional Alberta Bakery, or sit down to a full meal in the old-style *Wainwright Hotel*.

Canada Olympic Park

88 Canada Olympic Rd SW • Olympic Hall of Fame Daily: July & Aug 10am–5pm; Sept–June Wed–Sun 10am–5pm • $12 • ⓦ sportshall.ca

The focal point of the 1988 Winter Olympics, **Canada Olympic Park** lies beside Hwy-1 on the western edge of Calgary, where its striking ski jumps make it easy to find. A glass-elevator ride ($7) to their summit produces fine views over town and the Rocky

Mountain foothills. The other real sight here is the **Olympic Hall of Fame**, which records the feats of many great Canadian athletes and tells the story of the Calgary games, Eddie the Eagle and all. In winter you can use its lifts to **ski** or **snowboard** modest slopes or a superb half-pipe ($52/day). There's also **cross-country skiing, luge rides** and sixty-second, 120kmph tandem **bobsleigh rides** with a pro ($159). In summer the lifts access a handful of good, short **mountain-bike trails** ($38/day) and white-knuckle zip-line rides run from the top of the ski-jump towers ($60).

ARRIVAL AND DEPARTURE
CALGARY

By plane Calgary International Airport (ⓦ yyc.com) is about 15km northeast of downtown. There's a small information centre (daily 6am–11pm) in arrivals, along with courtesy phones for hotels and car rental. The cheapest way downtown is with Calgary Transit bus #300 (daily 5am–midnight; every 30min; around 30min; $10.50). A taxi costs $45. Several airport hotels offer shuttles from arrivals. Otherwise, the Allied Downtown Shuttle Service (daily 8am–midnight; every 30min; ☏ 403 299 9555, ⓦ airportshuttlecalgary.ca; $15) provides transport to downtown pick up points; their counter is near arrivals gate "C". Shuttles only pickup at downtown locations if you have a booking.

Destinations Edmonton (16 daily; 50min); Montréal (5 daily; 4hr); Regina (8 daily; 1hr 30min); Saskatoon (9 daily; 1hr 15min); Toronto (12 daily; 3hr 45min); Vancouver (23 daily; 1hr 30min); Winnipeg (9 daily; 2hr).

By train The only passenger service runs from Calgary to Vancouver with private Rocky Mountaineer Railtours (see page 706).

By bus Red Arrow buses serving Edmonton (☏ 403 531 0350, ☏ 800 232 1958, ⓦ redarrow.ca) use Downtown Fording Place, 101 205 9th Ave SE as their station; services also stop at the airport. Brewster Transportation (☏ 1 877 625 4372, ⓦ brewstertransportation.com) shuttle buses will pick you up from a number of Downtown hotels. Rider Express (☏ 1 833 583 3636, ⓦ riderexpress.ca) buses pick up at the 4949 Barlow Trail SE, 30mins on bus #24 from the Downtown Transit centre. Destinations Banff (Brewster: 5 daily; 2hr 30min); Canmore (Rider Express: 1 daily; 1hr) Edmonton (Red Arrow: 4–6 daily; 3hr 30min); Golden (1 daily; 3hrs); Lake Louise (Brewster: 5 daily; 3hr 30min); Kamloops (Rider Express: 1 daily; 7hrs); Revelstoke (Rider Express: 1 daily; 4hr 15min); Vancouver (Rider Express: 1 daily; 11hr 15min).

INFORMATION

Visitor Information Centre 101 9th Ave SW, in the base of the Calgary Tower (May–Sept 9am–7pm; Oct–April 9am–5pm; ☏ 403 750 2362, ⓦ visitcalgary.com).

GETTING AROUND AND TOURS

Most attractions are a comfortable walk from the centre. In winter, when temperatures can make it an ordeal, the city's much-vaunted **Plus-15** system (named for its height above ground in feet) helps out: it's a labyrinthine network of enclosed walkways that enable you to walk downtown without setting foot outside.

Public transport Calgary's cheap, clean and efficient public transport system (ⓦ calgarytransit.com) comprises a network of buses and the C-Train (every 15–30min; no late-night service), a tram that's free for its downtown stretch along the length of 7th Avenue SW between 10th Street and City Hall at 3rd Street SE. An on-board announcement tells you when the free section ends. Tickets valid for both buses and C-Train – and for 1hr 30min of travel in any direction – are available from C-Train station machines or on a bus (no change given at either). The one-way fare is $3.30, a day-pass $10.50.

By taxi Checker ☏ 403 299 9999; United Cab ☏ 403 777 1111.

Tours Calgary Walks (☏ 855 620 6520 ⓦ calgarywalks.com) offer downtown walking tours led by long-term residents; 2hr tours cost $18 and run April to October. Hammerhead Tours (☏ 403 590 6930, ⓦ hammerheadtours.com) run year-round van tours of the city that take around 3hr and cost $65; includes brief stops at Calgary's outlying attractions.

SHUTTLES TO BANFF AND LAKE LOUISE

Direct **buses** from the airport to **Banff** and **Lake Louise** mean you can be in Banff National Park a couple of hours after collecting your baggage. Services include: Banff Airporter (10 daily to Banff, $67; ☏ 403 762 3330, ☏ 888 449 2901, ⓦ banffairporter.com); Brewster Transportation (8 daily to Banff, $71; 6 to Lake Louise, $98; ☏ 403 760 6934, ☏ 877 625 4372, ⓦ brewster.ca). **Tickets** are available from desks in airport arrivals.

CALGARY ADDRESSES

When tracking down Calgary addresses, remember the city is divided into **quadrants** (NW, NE, SE and SW). The quadrant is always tagged after a house number in an address and easily overlooked, though essential: without it there can be four otherwise identical addresses in town.

ACCOMMODATION

Budget and mid-priced downtown **accommodation**, while not plentiful, is rarely full except during Stampede (mid-July) when prepaid reservations are essential months in advance. Otherwise, many hotels offer vastly reduced weekend rates. **Motels** also abound outside the centre, with "Motel Village" a cluster of a dozen or so motels in the $70–80 a night bracket, around the intersection of 16th Ave NW and Crowchild Trail; a taxi ride here costs about $15 from the centre. For B&Bs, try the Bed and Breakfast Association of Calgary (bbcalgary.com).

HOTELS, MOTELS AND B&BS

Hotel Alma 169 University Gate NW 403 220 3203, hotelalma.ca; map p.542. Smart, cheerful and compact rooms, with vaguely 1970s-style decor, on the university campus. Way out in the northwest suburbs, but with all the student facilities – including a great sports complex – on hand. Take the C-Train or bus #9. By car, head west from downtown along Hwy-1, then northwest on University Drive. **$130**

Hotel Arts 119 12th Ave SW 403 266 461, 800 661 9378, hotelarts.ca; map p.542. Stylish modern boutique hotel, three blocks from the centre of town. Room options – all quite plush – include pool, jacuzzi and luxury suites, and the on-site *Raw Bar* serves up some tasty fish and seafood. **$323**

★ **Hotel Elan** 1122 16th Avenue SW 403 229 2040, hotelelan.ca; map p.542. Smart boutique choice and one of the few options close to the buzzing 17th Ave restaurant and nightlife strip. Rooms are bold and bright and feature touches like heated toilet seats and L'Occitaine bathroom toiletries. Wi-fi and a good continental or cooked breakfast included. **$154**

Calgary Marriott 110 9th Ave SE 403 266 7331, 800 896 6878, calgarymarriott.com; map p.542. Central, upmarket hotel with very helpful staff and excellent facilities. Request a higher, east-side room for the best views. Parking can be a hassle, which makes the hotel's $35 per day on-site parking worthwhile. **$237**

Fairmont Palliser 133 9th Ave SW 403 262 1234, 800 257 7544, fairmont.com/palliser; map p.542. Built in 1914, this is the granddaddy of Calgary hotels and is where visiting dignitaries and celebrities stay. If you're after traditional style, superb service and excellent facilities, it's all here – just avoid the rooms overlooking the rail tracks. **$229**

Holiday Inn Express Calgary Downtown 1020 8th Ave SW 403 269 8262, 800 661 6017, hiexpress. com; map p.542. A ten-storey modern but slightly faded building just a block from the free C-Train. The rooms are more functional than flash, but bright and clean and some come with microwave and fridge. Rate includes a self-service breakfast. **$132**

Mount Royal Bed and Breakfast 809 18 Ave SW 403 245 9371, 800 556 1436, mountroyalbb. com; map p.542. A 1912 Edwardian house with two rooms, both with clawfoot tubs. The gourmet breakfasts are superb, and you're within walking distance of downtown, Stampede Park and trendy 17th Ave. **$143**

HOSTELS

HI-Calgary City Centre Hostel 520 7th Ave SE 403 269 8239, hihostels.ca; map p.542. Sociable hostel in a slightly seedy area close to downtown, two blocks east of City Hall and the free section of the C-Train. Rates fluctuate seasonally, but there are dorms and private rooms. Facilities include laundry, kitchen, bike storage, library and free wi-fi. Basic continental breakfast included. Dorms **$22**, non-members **$25**; en suite private rooms **$106**, non-members **$117**

Wicked Hostel 1505 Macleod Trail SE 403 265 8777, wickedhostel.com; map p.542. Clean, modern and fairly spartan hostel close to the Stampede grounds and an easy walk from both downtown and the 17th Ave scene. Rates include breakfast, parking, wi-fi, movie nights in the common room and use of a reading area. Bike rentals extra. Dorms **$38**; doubles **$95**

CAMPSITES

Calaway RV Park 245033 Range Rd 33 403 240 3822, calawaypark.com; map p.542. About 10km west of the city on the Trans-Canada Hwy towards Banff. It's also within walking distance of the Calaway Park amusement park – western Canada's largest. Full facilities, including showers and Stampede shuttle to downtown. Late May–early Sept. Tent sites **$29**; RVs **$35**

Calgary West Campground 221 101 St SW 403 288 0411, 888 562 0842, calgarycampground.com; map p.542. South of Hwy-1 on the western side of the city, close to Canada Olympic Park: 400 sites, laundry, store, golf course, outdoor pool and wi-fi. Mid-April to mid-Oct. Tents & RVs **$37**

7

EATING

In addition to Calgary's large and varied number of **cafés** and **restaurants** most bars and even live-music venues invariably serve good, and often well-priced, food.

Caesar's Steak House 512 4th Ave SW ☎ 403 264 1222, ⓦ caesarssteakhouse.com; map p.542. Best place for a huge, perfect steak ($35–50) in the sort of wonderfully cheesy steakhouse – think dimly-lit 1970s "Roman" decor – that's been around for decades. The ribeye is considered by many to be the finest slab of meat in town. Mon–Fri 11am–2pm & 4.30pm–midnight, Sat 4.30pm–midnight.

Charcut Roast House 899 Centre St South ☎ 403 984 2180, ⓦ charcut.com; map p.542. Despite pretensions as a "gathering place... serving urban-rustic cuisine", this local foodie favourite by the Calgary Tower excels in its use of fresh local ingredients. The menu changes daily, but always includes interesting meats from the rotisserie; dinner mains range $21–50. Mon & Tues 11am–11pm, Wed–Fri 11am–1am, Sat 5pm–1am, Sun 5–10pm.

The Coup 924 17th Ave SW ☎ 403 541 1041, ⓦ thecoup.ca; map p.542. Bohemian bistro serving creative vegetarian food using home-grown or local organic ingredients. Options include sa superb yam, tofu and cashew burger (dinner mains around $19). Its relaxed lounge bar is a pleasant place for an urbane tipple. Mon–Thurs 11am–3pm & 5–10pm, Fri 11am–3pm & 5–11pm, Sat 9am–3pm & 5–11pm, Sun 9am–3pm & 5–9pm.

★ **Galaxie Diner** 1413 11th St SW ☎ 403 228 0001, ⓦ galaxiediner.com; map p.542. Popular place with authentic 1940s diner decor where cooks grill up great breakfasts behind the counter (try the burrito). Mon–Fri 7am–3pm, Sat & Sun till 4pm.

Market 718 17th Ave SW ☎ 403 474 4414, ⓦ marketcalgary.ca; map p.542. If you're a serious locavore, then this farm-to-table place is a must. They not only grow innumerable ingredients, they bake their own bread, butcher their own meat and make their own cheese. The results are fresh and appealing gourmet dishes served in a bright modern restaurant. Seasonal international menu (mains around $32). Thurs–Sat 11.30am–midnight, Sun–Thurs 11.30am–11pm.

River Café Prince's Island Park ☎ 403 261 7670, ⓦ rivercafe.com; map p.542. Innovative Canadian cuisine – including game, smoked fish, roasted beet and crab apple borscht – an informal atmosphere and wonderful park setting. Mains from $29. Book ahead. Mon–Fri 11am–10pm, Sat & Sun 10am–10pm.

The Roasterie 314 10th St NW ☎ 403 270 3304; map p.542. There are no meals, but with twenty kinds of coffee – you'll smell it well before you see it – snacks and newspapers, this artsy coffee shop is a great place to take a load off and people-watch. Daily 7am–late.

Silver Dragon 106 3rd Ave SE ☎ 403 264 5326, ⓦ silverdragoncalgary.ca; map p.542. Long-standing and excellent Chinese restaurant with a team of Hong Kong-trained chefs, some two hundred dishes and moderate prices. Dim sum served 9.30am–2.45pm. Mon–Thurs 10am–11.30pm, Fri & Sat 9.30am–1am, Sun 9.30am–10pm.

Teatro 200 8th Ave SE ☎ 403 290 1012, ⓦ teatro.ca; map p.542. Ideal if you want to dress up and drop some money – perhaps appropriate, as it's in the old Dominion Bank building. The fine Italian-influenced food (mains from $28) rivals the *River Café*. Booking essential. Mon–Wed 11.30am–10pm, Thurs 11.30am–10.30pm, Fri 11.30am–11pm, Sat 5–11pm, Sun 5–10pm.

Tubby Dog 1022 17th Ave SW ☎ 403 244 0694, ⓦ tubbydog.com; map p.542. Small upbeat diner and virtual shrine to hot dogs and old-fashioned North American fast-food culture. Its stellar local reputation is built on excellent, huge and imaginative dogs – bacon wrapped, smothered in pizza sauce and the like (mostly around $7) – and its late-night hours. Mon–Thurs 11.30am–10pm, Fri & Sat 11.30am–midnight, Sun 11.30am–8pm.

Una Pizza + Wine 618 17th Ave SW ☎ 403 453 1183, ⓦ unapizzeria.com; map p.542. Trendy thin-crust pizza place ($17–24) with many wines and great desserts. Despite closely packed tables the place struggles to meet demand and there's often a wait, so arrive early. Daily 11.30am–1am.

DRINKING AND NIGHTLIFE

Calgary is liveliest during the Stampede, but **bars** are plentiful and mostly in three distinct areas: **Kensington** (10th St NW and along Kensington Rd); **Electric Avenue** (11th Ave SW between 5th and 6th streets) and **17th Avenue SW**, which has the most variety. The **live music** scene is good – especially jazz, blues and the genre closest to Calgary's heart, country. Check listings in Calgary's main dailies, the *Herald* (ⓦ calgaryherald.com) and the *Sun* (ⓦ calgarysun.com).

Broken City 613 11th Ave SW ☎ 403 262 9976, ⓦ brokencity.ca; map p.542. Alternative rock pub with a packed calendar of live music, a thriving rooftop patio and some good, simple pub grub – including veggie and vegan options. Daily 11am–2am.

★ **Commonwealth Bar & Stage** 733 10th Ave SW ☎ 403 232 6975, ⓦ commonwealthbar.ca; map p.542. Premier see-and-be-seen venue in an old warehouse; choose between a relaxed and self-consciously hip lounge or a buzzing dance club. DJs mostly spin retro and niche – from Motown and classic rap to dubstep – but live rock also features regularly. The broad appeal means the crowd is very mixed and the club fiercely popular; arrive by 9pm or expect a wait. Wed, Fri & Sat 9pm–2am, regular extra nights for events.

★ **Cowboy's** 421 12th Ave SE ⓦcowboysniteclub.com; map p.542. Legendary – and often raunchy – bar that holds over 3500 people on two levels, with nightly live entertainment. It's usually heaving, thanks to drinks promotions and the club's policy of financing breast implants for female employees. Wed–Sat 9pm–2 am.

James Joyce Irish Pub 114 8 Ave SW ⓣ403 262 0708, ⓦjamesjoycepub.com; map p.542. Calgary's downtown pedestrian precinct should be much livelier than it is in the evenings, but thankfully this authentic Irish place is an exception. Full of antiques and *craic* as well as solid bar food. Mon 11am–1am, Tues–Sat 11am–2am, Sun 11am–midnight.

Kensington Pub 207 10A St NW ⓣ403 270 4505, ⓦkensingtonpub.com; map p.542. A delightful unpretentious neighbourhood pub tucked away down a side street off Kensington Rd. The grub is good (try the chicken wings) and best accompanied by a pint or two of the local, UK or Irish brews on tap. Mon–Thurs 11am–1am, Fri–Sat 11am–2am, Sun 10.30am–midnight.

Milk Tiger Lounge 4th St SW ⓣ403 261 5009; map p.542. Narrow and cramped hole-in-the-wall cocktail bar, a little off the beaten track, and all the more desirable for it. A hipster favourite for its old soul music, creative cocktails (around $10) and mostly gluten-free menu, which includes a great meatball sandwich, tacos and risotto. Mon 5pm–1am, Tues–Sat 5pm–2am, Fri & Sat 5pm–2am; Sun 8pm–1am.

★ **Proof** 1302 1 St SW ⓣ403 246-2414, ⓦproofyyc.com; map p.542. Quirky small downtown cocktail bar with a seriously large variety of drinks (so many bottles they need a sliding ladder to access them) and lovely tapas-style accompaniments. The hip staff are passionate about what they do and there's always a buzz about the place. Daily 4pm–1am.

Ranchman's Cookhouse & Dancehall 9615 Macleod Trail South ⓣ403 253 1100, ⓦranchmans.com; map p.542. A classic honky-tonk and restaurant, 8km south of downtown. The food is hit-or-miss, but it's known throughout Canada for live country and western. Country dance lessons cost $10 but include two drinks – check website for dates. Tues–Sat 4pm–2am.

Ship and Anchor 534 17th Ave SW 403 245 3333, ⓦshipandanchor.com; map p.542. Long-established, friendly and laidback pub that heaves at weekends. Darts, upbeat music and excellent pub food make this a good place to start a big night out, or simply while away an evening. Mon–Fri 11am–2am, Sat & Sun 10am–2am.

ENTERTAINMENT

Arts Commons 205 8th Ave SE ⓣ403 294 7455, ⓦartscommons.ca. Much of the city's highbrow cultural life takes place on one of four stages or in the premier concert hall here. Several professional theatre companies including One Yellow Rabbit (ⓦoyr.org), Alberta Theatre Projects (ⓦatplive.com) and Theatre Calgary (ⓦtheatrecalgary.com) perform here, as do the Calgary Philharmonic Orchestra (ⓦcalgaryphil.com) and the excellent Alberta Ballet Company (ⓦalbertaballet.com).

Decidedly Jazz Danceworks 1514 4th St SW ⓣ403 245 3533, ⓦdecidedlyjazz.com. Exciting dance company with eclectic high-energy productions and often live music thrown in for good measure. The schedule is always worth a look.

Jubilee Auditorium 1415 14th Ave NW ⓦjubilee auditorium.com. Public event space for school productions and the like but also a popular venue for touring musicians and the main stage for the Calgary Opera (ⓦcalgaryopera.com).

Yuk Yuk's Calgary 218 18th Ave SE ⓣ403 258 2028, ⓦyukyuks.com. Comedy club in a very ordinary venue above the Elbow River Casino just southeast of downtown, but with a full programme of talented touring comedians nonetheless.

DIRECTORY

Internet Central Library, 616 Macleod Trail SE. Has both terminals and free wi-fi.

Medical Foothills Hospital, 1403 29th Ave ⓣ403 944 1110.

Outdoor gear Mountain Equipment Co-op (MEC), 830 10th Ave SW (ⓣ403 269 2420). Large camping and outdoor store that also rents out all manner of equipment.

Police 133 6th Ave SE ⓣ403 266 1234.

Post office 639 5th Ave SW ⓣ800 267 1177.

7

The Canadian Rockies

CASCADE MOUNTAIN, BANFF NATIONAL PARK

The Canadian Rockies

Rising with overwhelming majesty from Alberta's rippling plains, the Canadian Rockies are one of the main reasons people come to Canada, and few North American landscapes come loaded with such high expectations. So it's a relief to find the superlatives scarcely exaggerate the splendour or immensity of the region's forests, lakes, rivers and snow-topped mountains. Many of the best bits have been hived off into several impressive national parks, but be warned that planning an itinerary that neatly fits them all in is just about impossible. It's also unnecessary: the parks are equally sensational so it's best to put as much effort getting deep into the backcountry in one or two spots as it is to tour the most accessible highlights and main hubs.

Joined to their smaller US cousins, the Canadian Rockies extend north of the US border almost 1500km to Canada's far north, where they merge with ranges in the Yukon and Alaska, forming the Continental Divide in the process – a vast watershed which separates rivers flowing to the Pacific and Arctic oceans from those flowing into the Atlantic. But the range is best known for its virtually unbroken north–south chain of national and provincial parks, and for its world-class ski resorts (see page 567).

Almost immediately west of Calgary (see page 540), the region's main gateway city, lies **Kananaskis Country**. This series of less restrictively managed provincial parks exists in part to take the pressure off the adjacent **Banff National Park**, the region's best known and busiest park. Just north the range is protected by the less visited **Jasper National Park**, by far the largest park in the region. The western boundary of both Banff and Jasper parks is also the provincial border, so adjacent areas are protected in a separate set of BC parks: **Mount Robson Provincial Park**, just west of Jasper – which protects Mount Robson, the highest and most dramatic peak in the Canadian Rockies – while **Yoho** and **Kootenay** national parks lie just west of Banff National Park. At the southern end of Canada's Rockies, and coupled with Glacier National Park in the US, is small but impressive **Waterton Lakes National Park**.

To see as many of the highlights as possible in a couple of weeks, start with Banff National Park, then head north along the otherworldly Icefields Parkway to Jasper and Mount Robson before doubling back – no hardship, given the scenery – to take in as much of the Yoho–Golden–Radium–Kootenay loop as your time allows. With another week to play with, you might try to miss some of Kootenay in favour of a bigger loop south through Kimberley, Fernie and Waterton Lakes – the latter particularly tempting if you are on your way to or from the US.

You can get to all the parks except Waterton by **bus**, but travelling by **car** is the obvious way to get the most out of the region. Once here, you'd be foolish not to tackle some of the 3000km of **hiking and biking trails** that crisscross the mountains, the vast majority of which are well worn and well signed. We've highlighted the best short walks and day-hikes in each area, and you can get more details from the excellent park **visitor centres**, which sell 1:50,000 topographical maps and usually offer reference libraries of trail books. Other **activities** – fishing, skiing, canoeing, whitewater rafting, cycling, riding, rock climbing and so on – are comprehensively dealt with in visitor centres, and you can easily rent equipment or sign up for organized tours in the bigger towns.

Finally, don't **underestimate** the Rockies. Despite the impression created by the summer throngs in centres like Banff and Lake Louise, with their excellent roads and sleek park facilities, the vast proportion of parkland is wilderness and should be respected and treated as such.

ELK IN JASPER NATIONAL PARK

Highlights

❶ Banff National Park A hugely popular region at the heart of the Rockies, with sublime scenery and numerous outdoor activities. See page 561

❷ Lake Louise Hit the slopes to enjoy the winning combination of impressive scenery and challenging skiing. See page 579

❸ Jasper National Park Strike out on an epic, multi-day backcountry trail in the largest and wildest of the Rockies parks. See page 590

❹ Yoho Experience the awe-inspiring grandeur and outstanding hikes of this compact national park. See page 602

❺ Raft the Kicking Horse Make a splash rafting the bucking and roaring Kicking Horse River. See page 610

❻ Mountain biking in Fernie Explore the Rockies' most comprehensive system of mountain-bike trails around the fun-loving ski town of Fernie. See page 623

❼ Waterton Lakes National Park Superb hiking and stunning landscapes abound at this small park on the US border. See page 626

HIGHLIGHTS ARE MARKED ON THE MAP ON PAGE 554

Kananaskis Country

Most first-time visitors race straight from Calgary to Banff, ignoring **Kananaskis Country**, a dramatic foothill area that spreads along the eastern edge of Banff National Park. Cobbled together out of existing provincial parks to take pressure off Banff, Kananaskis remains almost the exclusive preserve of locals, who come to ski in winter and to hike, bike and camp in summer. The mountain scenery rivals that of the national parks, and the scope for outdoor activities is often better, thanks to more liberal protection policies. The town of **Canmore** is the region's natural focus and has a fair number of natural attractions that are accessible on foot or by bike, but to properly enjoy the adjacent **provincial parks** you'll need your own vehicle.

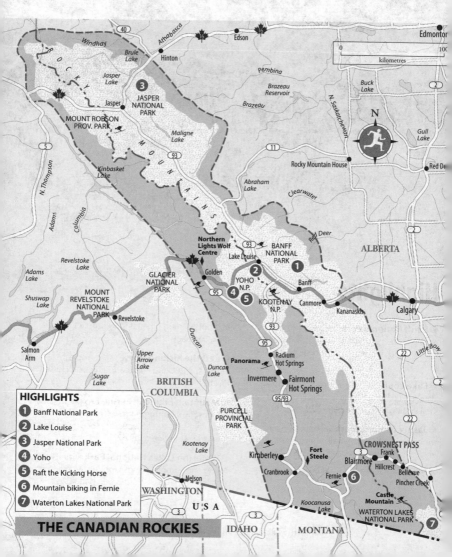

HIGHLIGHTS

1. Banff National Park
2. Lake Louise
3. Jasper National Park
4. Yoho
5. Raft the Kicking Horse
6. Mountain biking in Fernie
7. Waterton Lakes National Park

THE CANADIAN ROCKIES

THE CREATION OF THE CANADIAN ROCKIES

About four hundred million years ago, eroded debris from the mountains of the **Canadian Shield** (which covered North America from Greenland to Guatemala) was washed west by rivers and deposited as mud, shale and limestone on a "continental slope". Then, about two hundred million years ago, two strings of volcanic Pacific islands began to move eastward on the Pacific Continental Plate towards the North American coast. When the first string arrived off the coast, the heavier Pacific Plate slid beneath the edge of the North American Plate. The lighter rock of the islands stayed above, detaching itself from the plate as they crashed into the continent. The orderly deposits on the continental slope were crumpled and uplifted, their layers riding over each other to produce the coast's present-day interior and Columbia Mountains. Over the next 75 million years, the aftershock of the collision moved inland, bulldozing the ancient sedimentary layers still further to create the Rockies' **Western Main Ranges** (in Yoho and Kootenay national parks), and then moving east, where 4km of uplift created the **Eastern Main Ranges** (the mountains on a line with Lake Louise).

Following the first islands, the second archipelago also crashed into the continent, striking the debris of the earlier collision and creating more folding, rupturing and uplifting of the earlier ranges. About sixty million years ago, the aftershock from this encounter created the Rockies' easternmost **Front Ranges** (the line of mountains that rears up from the prairies). Three ice ages over the last 240,000 years applied the final touches, carving sharp profiles and dumping further debris.

Canmore and around

CANMORE competes with Banff, 28km away, for visitors, and, though a little less attractive, it's a decent alternative if you'd rather be in a less busy place and can live without Banff's variety of restaurants and shops.

Canmore began life in 1883 as a supply point for the Canadian Pacific Railway, before booming as a mining centre after the company discovered coal in surrounding hills. The last mine closed in 1979 and things looked bleak until Canmore hosted Nordic skiing for the 1988 Calgary Olympics, which gave the town its impressive **Nordic Centre**. On the back of this and thanks to its location outside national park restrictions, the town grew. Occasional references to it as the "Aspen of Alberta" overstate the case, but certainly many adventurous types and artists have relocated here, drawn by the hiking, climbing, biking, skiing and fishing on the fringes of town – and opportunities for many more activities, including caving and rafting, not far away. Canmore straddles the Trans-Canada Hwy, though its downtown area is entirely south of the road, and centred on relaxed **Main Street** (8th St), with its galleries, shops, cafés and restaurants. At its western end lies a spur of the extensive local **bike path** network.

Canmore Museum and Geoscience Centre

902 7th Ave • Mid-May to early Oct Mon–Thurs noon–4.30pm, Fri–Sun 10am–4.30pm; early Sept to mid-May Mon–Fri noon–4.30pm, Sat & Sun 11am–4.30pm • $7 • ⓦ cmags.org

In poor weather the **Canmore Museum and Geoscience Centre** is a good option and does a fine job of rooting around the town's past from its geological and First Nation origins to its Olympic glory days. There's quite a bit too about the incredible floods suffered by Canmore in 2013, when roads were ripped apart and much of the town was filled with debris.

North-West Mounted Police Barracks

609 Main Street • May–Sept Wed–Sun 10am–4.30pm, Mon & Tues 1–4pm, Oct Sat & Sun 1–4pm, Nov–Apr Fri–Sun 1–4pm • by donation • ☏ 403 678 1955, ⓦ cmags.org

Back in 1893 a small wooden cabin was built on Canmore's main street to house the local law enforcement. Here the North-West Mounted operated an office and jail as well as lodgings for the head of the local force. And that's the remarkable bit – one

Corporal Clarke, his wife Dora, and their five children dwelt in part of this tiny house from 1917 to 1929, with the modest extension only being added in 1923. Marvel at this and some Mountie memorabilia while listening to the volunteer staff's knowledgeable insights.

Canmore Nordic Centre

1988 Olympic Way • ☎ 403 678 2400, ⓦ canmorenordiccentre.ca

West of downtown and the Bow River the land begins to rise and the town starts to thin out, so that by the time Spray Lakes Road has climbed to the **Canmore Nordic Centre**, you're only left with views of the urban area. This state-of-the-art former Olympic facility is as popular in summer as in winter, since 70km of its extensive and well-balanced 300km cross-country-ski trail network is maintained for **mountain biking** and suitable for every level of rider. Free trail maps are available, as are bike rentals.

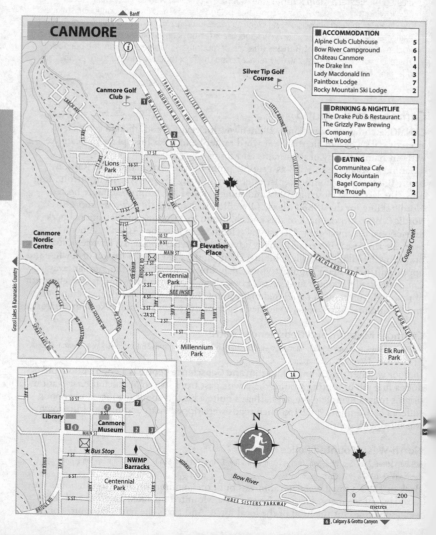

Grassi Lakes

This series of small picture-book emerald lakes high above Canmore is accessible from the scenic dirt road – the Smith Dorrien Spray Trail – 2km past the Canmore Nordic Centre. From a car park and trailhead just off the road, a rough and steep 2km trail leads up to **Grassi Lakes**. On reaching the upper lake, be sure to take an easy scramble up the scree slope to four **pictographs** of human figures painted onto the first large boulder of the gorge.

Spray Valley Provincial Park

High above Grassi Lakes, the Smith Dorrien Spray Trail climbs out of view of Canmore to enter **Spray Valley Provincial Park**, the most accessible part of high-mountain Kananaskis Country. The park's main feature is its 16km-long Spray Lakes Reservoir, which is used to generate electricity. Despite the industrial links the lake is a tranquil spot and surrounded by huge, impressively contorted mountains. A trail (4km; 4hr round-trip) from the *Spray Lakes West* provincial campground (see page 558) climbs to the small **Jakeroy Glacier**, perched high up in the Goat Range. The trail begins opposite campsite no. 17 and climbs steeply through pine, willow, spruce and larch forests to a narrow hanging valley. It's fairly well marked, but at the only river crossing be sure to head straight on up the scree slope rather than right up to the waterfall.

Cougar Creek and Grotto Canyon

The east side of Canmore is well set up for shorter hikes. An easy informal trail with good views follows the course of **Cougar Creek**, and it's possible to follow this all the way to the boundary of Banff National Park. An even better trail starts from Grotto Pond, 12km east of Canmore on Hwy-1A. It starts fairly unpromisingly, following a road below an overhead powerline, but soon cuts into the woods to **Grotto Canyon**. There's no formal trail but the way up the steep-sided canyon is clear enough; look out for **pictographs** around 300m into the canyon – on the left at about head-height at one of its narrowest points. Another 100m or so into the canyon is an impressive little waterfall, beyond which the valley opens up, passing a cave and some strangely shaped rock formations, called **hoodoos**.

ARRIVAL AND DEPARTURE
CANMORE AND AROUND

By bus Frequent shuttle bus services connect Calgary Airport (see page 546) with Canmore.

By car Canmore is a 1hr 15min drive from Calgary along the Trans-Canada Hwy.

GETTING AROUND AND INFORMATION

By bike Gear Up, 1302 Bow Valley Trail (☎ 403 678 1636, ⓦ gearupsport.com), is one of several places offering bike rental ($60/day for full-suspension). Bike rental is also offered at the Nordic Centre (see page 556).
By taxi Canmore Cabs (☎ 403 996 2229, ⓦ canmorecab.com).

Travel Alberta Visitor Centre 2801 Bow Valley Trail (June–Aug 8am–8pm; Sept–May 9am–6pm; ☎ 403 678 5277, ☎ 800 668888, ⓦ travelalberta.com), on the western edge of town just off the Trans-Canada. With small exhibition hall.

ACTIVITIES

Elevation Place, a huge recreation centre at 700 Railway Ave, offers a large, modern pool with a fun kids' area, including water slides and a gym with climbing wall. The fine city library is also here.

SUMMER

Cycling A bike is useful on the extensive trail network in and around town. Road-bikers will enjoy the largely traffic-free paths to Banff; mountain-bikers should pick up a free map of local trails from the visitor centre or head up to the Nordic Centre

(see page 556). Several places offer bike rental (see above).
Fishing Parts of Canmore's Bow River offer reasonable fishing for bull trout, brown trout and whitefish; Wapiti Sports, 1506 Railway Ave (☎ 403 678 5550, ⓦ wapitisports. com), can provide tackle and advice, and offer custom trips and lessons.
Rafting Among the companies rafting local rivers are Inside Out (☎ 403 949 3305, ☎ 877 999 7238, ⓦ insideout experience.com), which runs easy float and whitewater rafting trips on the Kananaskis River from $75/2hr; and

8

Canadian Rockies Rafting (701 Bow Valley Trail, Canmore; ☎403 678 6535, ☎877 226 7625, rafting.ca), offering everything from gentle trips on the Bow River ($55/2hr) to white-knuckle riverboarding on the Kananaskis ($98/day), as well as trips on the Kicking Horse in Yoho (see page 608).

Rock climbing Aside from the excellent climbing wall at Elevation Place, Canmore has many climbing crags – including at Grassi Lakes and Grotto Canyon – along with full-scale, multi-pitch climbs on the likes of Mount Rundle. In winter ice-climbing takes over. Contact Yamuska Adventures (☎403 678 4164, yamnuska.com) for details of courses.

WINTER

Cross-country skiing The main focus is the Canmore Nordic Centre where you can pick up all the rentals, accessories and advice you need at Trail Sports (☎403 678 6764, trailsports.ab.ca).

ACCOMMODATION

The bulk of Canmore's accommodation lies in modern **hotels and motels** beside the Trans-Canada and the parallel Bow Valley Trail. In summer prices are a little steep, but still much saner than in Banff. In winter rates are typically at least a third lower. For a less anonymous experience, check the listings of the Canmore Valley Bed and Breakfast Association (bbcanmore.com).

HOTELS, MOTELS AND B&BS

Château Canmore 1718 Bow Valley Trail ☎403 678 6699, ☎800 261 8551, chateaucanmore.com; map p.556. Choose between "deluxe" and "loft" suites, both of which have kitchenettes, gas fireplaces and pull-out sofas. There's also a fitness centre with indoor pool and outdoor hot-tub an on-site spa and restaurant. $227

The Drake Inn 909 Railway Ave ☎403 678 5131, drakeinn.com; map p.556. There's not much that isn't standard about this motel, which covers the basics well enough. But the location is spot-on, just yards away from the lively downtown strip, and some rooms have beautiful mountain views. Usually among the cheapest deals in town. $137

Lady Macdonald Inn 1201 Bow Valley Trail ☎403 678 3665, ☎800 567 3919, ladymacdonald.com; map p.556. Friendly B&B where all nine rooms – including the two with family-friendly lofts – have fireplaces and en-suite bathrooms. Breakfasts are superb. $215

★ **Paintbox Lodge** 629 10 St ☎403 609 0482, paintboxlodge.com map p.556. This central riverside lodge does smart rustic really well. Exposed wood and stone hearths feature in lofts and cabins that sleep up to four. Included are quality continental breakfasts, use of town bikes and cosy communal areas with board games. $275

Rocky Mountain Ski Lodge 1711 Bow Valley Trail ☎403 678 5445, rockyski.ca; map p.556. Sprawling motel with a mix of rooms and modern suites that make up in spaciousness and cleanliness what they lack in style. Some come with basic kitchens too. Avoid the highway-side units to minimize road noise. Also has a hot-tub, laundry facilities and free wi-fi. $199

HOSTELS AND CAMPGROUNDS

★ **Alpine Club Clubhouse** Indian Flats Rd, 5km northeast of downtown ☎403 678 3200, alpineclubofcanada.ca; map p.556. HI-affiliated hostel run by the Alpine Club of Canada in a fine modern wooden building at the base of Grotto Mountain. It has a wonderful mountaineering feel, exceptional valley views, plus a library and sauna. Dorms $30, non-members $40

Bow River Campground Trans-Canada Hwy, 1km east of Canmore ☎403 673 2163, bowvalleycampgrounds.com; map p.556. The closest of several sites run by Bow Valley Campgrounds, with tables, fire pit, wood and non-flush toilets. RVs welcome but no hook-ups. May–Oct. Sites $26

Spray Lakes West Campground 23km from Canmore via Smith Dorrien Trail ☎866 427 3582, albertaparks.ca; map p.556. Provincial park campground strung out along the western shore of Spray Lakes, and an exceptionally attractive spot to pitch a tent. Facilities are basic, however, so bring all you need except firewood. No reservations. May–Sept. Sites $26

EATING

★ **Communitea Cafe** 1001 6 Ave ☎403 678 6818, thecommunitea.com; map p.556. Friendly, bright and busy café with light wood decor and wholesome (often vegan or gluten-free) soups, sandwiches and such, with several great Asian dishes offered at lunch: the tofu, spinach and rice Buddha Bowl ($12.95) has a tasty tahini and garlic dressing. Mon–Thurs 8am–5pm, Fri–Sun 8am–6pm.

★ **Rocky Mountain Bagel Company** 830 Main St ☎403 678 9968, thebagel.ca; map p.556. One of several decent cafés on Main St that's ideal for a simple breakfast, light lunch or just hanging out. They make everything from scratch and specialize in – you guessed it – bagels, which form the basis for a good range of sandwiches. Daily 6am–6pm.

★ **The Trough** 725 9 St ☎403 678 2820, thetrough.ca; map p.556. Smart gourmet bistro tucked down a Canmore back alley where a mother-and-son team seems to do everything right. The menu is short, seasonal, built around flagship ingredients like wild red snapper, Quebec duck or Albertan ribs (most mains around $35) and above all, a labour of love. Best reserve. Tues–Sun 5pm–late.

DRINKING AND NIGHTLIFE

The Drake Pub & Restaurant 909 Railway Ave ☎ 403 678 5131, ⓦ thedrakepub.com; map p.556. Busy locals' pub with two large, heated outdoor decks, two fireplaces and occasional live music. It serves fairly standard pub food; most mains cost $18. Mon–Fri 11am–2am, Sat & Sun 10am–2am.

The Grizzly Paw Brewing Company 622 Main St ☎ 403 678 9983, ⓦ thegrizzlypaw.com; map p.556. The Rockies' only microbrewery, with excellent pub grub and reasonable beers; the Grumpy Bear Honey Wheat Ale is most refreshing after a day outdoors. Live music on Tues nights. Sun–Thurs 11am–11pm, Fri & Sat 11am–midnight.

The Wood 838 Main St ☎ 403 678 3404, ⓦ thewood.ca; map p.556. Long-standing local favourite in a log cabin with lots of Rocky Mountain charm. The huge patio-cum-beer-garden catches the sun and there's plenty of choice on the menu, with steak, fish, pizza, ribs and other North American staples for lunch (burgers and curries $12), but rather more in the evening, when mains start at around $21. Mon–Fri 7.30am–11pm, Sat & Sun 8am–11pm.

Kananaskis Valley

The broad **Kananaskis Valley** is the main focus of Kananaskis Country. Hwy-40, which intersects with the Trans-Canada Hwy 30km east of Canmore, travels south along its length, bisecting the high-mountain country, linking its main provincial parks, and providing a ribbon to which most of the trails, campgrounds and scattered service centres cling.

Kananaskis Village

The only real settlement in the valley is **Kananaskis Village**, a rather soulless resort-village that lies 25km south of the Trans-Canada Highway, around an hour's drive from either Calgary or Banff. It's beside a golf course and the Nakiska ski area, the major attractions, though a number of good hiking and biking trails radiate from here too. Of the former, the 9km hike to **Ribbon Falls** is deservedly popular and arrives at the eponymous campground (see page 561). From here you can either head back, or with basic rock-climbing skills head on and complete a loop by following the Galetea Creek trail below the hulking Mount Kidd. If you're fit and want to bag a peak, **Mount Allan** (2990m), just north of Kananaskis Village, beckons: it's one of the few maintained trails in the Rockies that leads to a summit.

Nakiska

Oct–April daily 9am–4pm • Day-passes $90 • ☎ 403 591 7777, ⓦ skinakiska.com

Developed for the 1988 Winter Olympics, the ski area of **Nakiska** has a vertical drop of 735m (2412ft) and includes all the usual rental, instruction and childcare facilities. Intended for downhill racers, runs are mostly smooth and steep, making it a great intermediate mountain for cruising – seventy percent of the runs are well-groomed and graded blue – and good for beginner boarders. Though only attracting 250cm of snow annually, lack of snow is rarely a problem, since snowmaking is possible on 85 percent of the mountain. The area also maintains two competition-standard half-pipes and a terrain park.

Peter Lougheed Provincial Park

Around 40km south of Kananaskis Village on Hwy-40, a short spur leads to Upper Kananaskis Lake, the head of the valley and the main focus of **Peter Lougheed Provincial Park**. The biggest concentration of accessible boating, fishing, camping and hiking possibilities in the region are on offer here; top trails include the rewarding half-day jaunt to Rawson Lake and the magnificent multi-day backcountry hiking adventure over Burstall Pass to Banff, easily one of the best in the region. This hike is well detailed, along with many others in the Kananaskis area, in the definitive and widely available *Where Locals Hike in the Canadian Rockies* by Kathy and Craig Copeland.

8

INFORMATION

Barrier Lake Visitor Centre 8km south of Hwy-1 on Hwy-40 (daily 9am–12.30pm & 1.15–4pm; ☎403 678 0760); provides a full breakdown of outdoor activities.

Elbow Valley Visitor Centre Beside Hwy-66 near Bragg Creek on the eastern side of the park (Fri–Sun 9.30– 12.30pm & 1.30–4.30pm).

Peter Lougheed Provincial Park Visitor Centre 4km

off Hwy-40 en route to Upper Kananaskis Lake (9.30am– 4.30pm; ☎403 678 0760).

Sheep River Visitor Centre Small info centre (Mid-May to mid-Oct Fri–Tues 8.30am–4.30pm, mid-Oct to mid-May Mon–Fri 8.30am–4.30pm; ☎403 933 7172) beside Hwy-546 near Turner Valley in the southeast of the park.

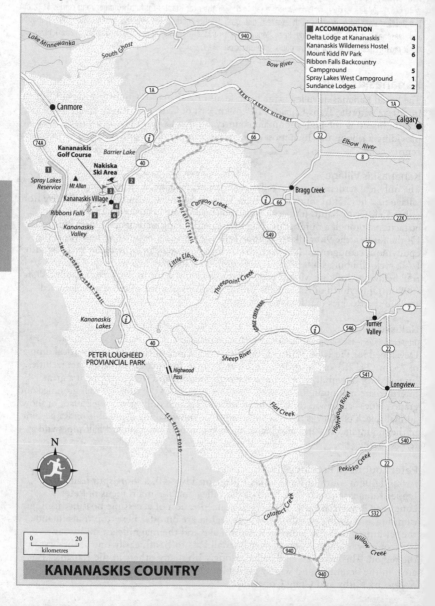

ACCOMMODATION	
Delta Lodge at Kananaskis	4
Kananaskis Wilderness Hostel	3
Mount Kidd RV Park	6
Ribbon Falls Backcountry Campground	5
Spray Lakes West Campground	1
Sundance Lodges	2

KANANASKIS COUNTRY

ACTIVITIES

Summer hiking, mountain biking and canoeing
Kananaskis Outfitters (☏ 403 591 7000, ⊛ kanana
skisoutfitters.com), based in the tiny village mall, organizes
hiking tours (from $90) and rents out a range of gear
including-hiking poles and packs, mountain bikes (front-
suspension $50/day) and canoes ($70/day), and will
happily point you in the right direction for any of the related
activities. The Kananaskis Course (☏ 403 591 7272, ☏ 877

591 2525, ⊛ kananaskisgolf.com) is rated highly for golf, as
much for its mountain views as its holes.
Winter Cross-country skiing and snowshoeing
Kananaskis Country has four good cross-country ski
areas and a huge number of snowshoeing possibilities.
Kananaskis Outfitters will rent you all the necessary gear
and can advise.

ACCOMMODATION

Delta Lodge at Kananaskis 1 Centennial Drive,
Kananaskis Village ☏ 403 591 771, ☏ 888 890 3222,
⊛ deltahotels.com; map p.560. Smart resort hotel with
huge, comfortable rooms, and great mountain views and
facilities (gym, spa, pool and outdoor hot tub). The hotel
organizes a range of activities for kids, as well as offering an
adult-only section for those who want a bit of peace. $465
★ **Kananaskis Wilderness Hostel** 1 Ribbon Creek
Rd ☏ 403 591 7333, ☏ 866 762 4122, ⊛ hihostels.ca;
map p.560. Cosy log-chalet hostel just off the Kananaskis
Village access road with kitchen, laundry, common room,
and free coffee and snowshoe use. Closed in late Oct and
late May. Dorms $31, non-members $34; doubles $71,
non-members $78
Mount Kidd RV Park Off Hwy-40, 8km south of
Kananaskis Village ☏ 403 591 7700, ⊛ mountkiddrv.
com; map p.560. Impressive – and with 229 sites, pretty
huge – RV resort with facilities including saunas and tennis

courts. Sites $35; full RV hook-ups $51
Ribbon Falls Backcountry Campground 9km from
Kananaskis Village on Ribbon Falls Trail ☏ 403 678
3136; map p.560. The smallest and quietest of the Spray
Valley Backcountry Campgrounds, near the pretty Ribbon
Falls. Permits by phone or from Barrier Lake Visitor Centre
(see page 560). June–Nov. Sites (per person, plus $12
reservation fee). $12
★ **Sundance Lodges** Off Hwy-40, 3km north of
Kananaskis Village ☏ 403 591 7122, ⊛ sundancelodges.
com; map p.560. Family-run campground with a range
of pleasant tent and RVs (unserviced) tucked in the woods
with a good amount of privacy. But its real claim to fame
is its teepees – some of which sleep four – containing
beds and mattresses. You'll need to bring or rent bedding,
cooking kit and towels (rental available on-site), plus all
the other camping gear. Mid-May to mid-Sept. Sites $32;
tipis $95

Banff National Park

BANFF NATIONAL PARK is the most famous Canadian Rockies park and Canada's
leading tourist attraction – so be prepared for the crowds in its key centres, Banff and
Lake Louise, as well as the most accessible of its 1500km of trails, many of which suffer
a continual pounding during the summer months. That said, it's worth putting up with
the crowds to enjoy the sublime scenery – and if you're camping or prepared to walk,
the worst park excesses are fairly easily left behind.

The actual town of **Banff** is a busy and commercial place where you can pause for a
couple of days to soak up the action and handful of sights – or stock up on supplies
and make for somewhere quieter as quickly as possible. Some 58km north along
Hwy-1, **Lake Louise**,is a much smaller but equally busy centre with some unmissable
landscapes, plus readily accessible short trails and day-hikes offering a quick taste of
the scenery.

Two popular roads within the park offer magnificent vistas: the **Bow Valley Parkway**
from Banff to Lake Louise is far preferable to the parallel Trans-Canada Highway,
and the much longer **Icefields Parkway** leads from Lake Louise to Jasper. Both are
lined with trails long and short, waterfalls, lakes, canyons, viewpoints, pull-offs and a
seemingly unending procession of majestic mountain, river, glacier and forest scenery.

Brief history

Modern road routes into the park provide transport links that have superseded the
railway that first brought the park into being. The arrival of the **Canadian Pacific**

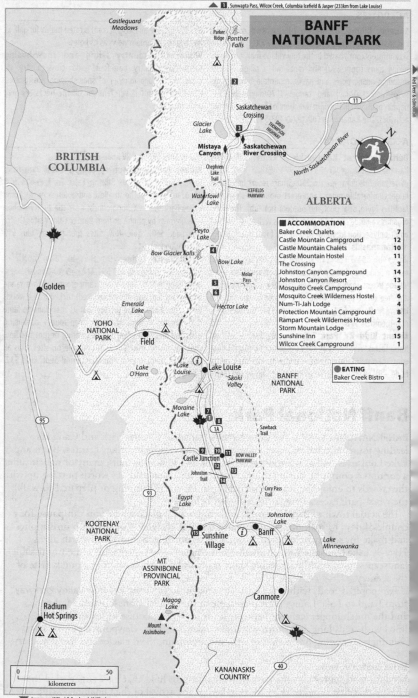

8

BANFF NATIONAL PARK

BRITISH COLUMBIA

ALBERTA

ACCOMMODATION

Baker Creek Chalets	7
Castle Mountain Campground	12
Castle Mountain Chalets	10
Castle Mountain Hostel	11
The Crossing	3
Johnston Canyon Campground	14
Johnston Canyon Resort	13
Mosquito Creek Campground	5
Mosquito Creek Wilderness Hostel	6
Num-Ti-Jah Lodge	4
Protection Mountain Campground	8
Rampart Creek Wilderness Hostel	2
Storm Mountain Lodge	9
Sunshine Inn	15
Wilcox Creek Campground	1

EATING

Baker Creek Bistro	1

NATIONAL PARK PASSES AND PERMITS

Anyone entering one of the Rockies national parks must buy a **permit** – $9.80/day or $67.70 for an annual pass – available at the road entrances to parks and at park visitor centres. Park centres are also the place to pick up the separate **Backcountry Permit** ($9.80/night, or $68.70/annual pass, plus $11.70 reservation fee), to stay overnight in the backcountry. All backcountry areas in all parks have a quota, so it's vital to make **bookings** well in advance (up to three months) if you wish to walk – and camp – on the most popular trails requiring overnight stops. Reservations can be made at ☎877 737 3783 or ⊛pccamping.ca.

Railway at the end of the nineteenth century brought to an end some ten thousand years of exclusive Aboriginal presence in the region. This area had previously been disturbed only by trappers and the prodigious exploits of explorers like Mackenzie, Thompson and Fraser, who had sought to breach the Rockies with the help of Aboriginal guides earlier in the century. Banff itself sprang to life in 1883 after three railway workers stumbled on the present town's Cave and Basin Hot Springs, its name coined in honour of Banffshire, the Scottish birthplace of two of the Canadian Pacific's early financiers and directors.

Within two years the government had set aside the Hot Springs Reserve as a protected area, and in 1887 enlarged it to form the **Rocky Mountains Park**, Canada's first national park. Yet the purpose was not entirely philanthropic: the new government-sponsored railway desperately needed passengers and profit, and spectacular scenery backed up by luxurious hotels was seen – rightly – as the best way to lure the punters. Cars were banned from the park until 1916.

Today Banff National Park attracts some five million annual visitors, putting inevitable pressure on the **environment**. Park authorities try to manage this, with measures including a 10,000-person ceiling on Banff's population, strict building controls and regular closures of some roads during wildlife migration seasons and certain trails during berry season. But many experts agree that Banff's ecosystem is on a knife-edge: more restrictions may save it, but they're in constant conflict with the park's recreational role.

Banff and around

BANFF is the unquestioned capital of the Canadian Rockies, and with its intense summer buzz it can be a fun, busy and likeable base – but if you've come to commune with nature, you'll quickly want to leave. For a small town, it handles an immense amount of tourist traffic, much of it of the RV and coach-tour variety: up to fifty thousand daily visitors arrive in high season.

However you feel about this, some contact with the town is probably inevitable, as it contains essential services and a range of restaurants and nightlife absent elsewhere in the park and even much of the region. And while many of the best local **walks** are some way from the town – you'll need a car or bike to explore properly – some surprisingly good strolls start just minutes from the main street.

With some of the world's most spectacular mountains on your doorstep, sightseeing in Banff might seem absurd, but it's good to have some rainy-day options. Among these are a couple of small museums on **Banff Avenue**, a thoroughfare lined with outdoor-clothing and souvenir stores, perfect for people-watching.

Banff Park Museum

93 Banff Ave • Daily mid-May to mid-Oct 10am–5pm • $3.90

The downtown **Banff Park Museum**, near the Bow River bridge, not only has the distinction of being Canada's oldest National Park building (1903), but also bulges with two floors of taxidermy, including many animals which are indigenous to the

8

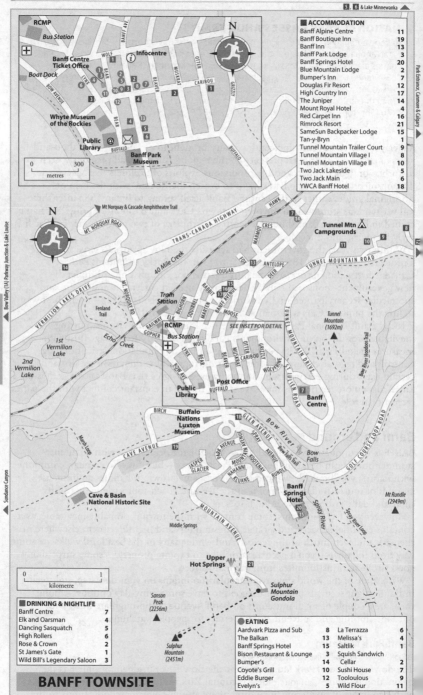

ACCOMMODATION

Banff Alpine Centre	11
Banff Boutique Inn	19
Banff Inn	13
Banff Park Lodge	3
Banff Springs Hotel	20
Blue Mountain Lodge	2
Bumper's Inn	7
Douglas Fir Resort	12
High Country Inn	17
The Juniper	14
Mount Royal Hotel	4
Red Carpet Inn	16
Rimrock Resort	21
SameSun Backpacker Lodge	15
Tan-y-Bryn	1
Tunnel Mountain Trailer Court	9
Tunnel Mountain Village I	8
Tunnel Mountain Village II	10
Two Jack Lakeside	5
Two Jack Main	6
YWCA Banff Hotel	18

DRINKING & NIGHTLIFE

Banff Centre	7
Elk and Oarsman	4
Dancing Sasquatch	5
High Rollers	6
Rose & Crown	2
St James's Gate	1
Wild Bill's Legendary Saloon	3

EATING

Aardvark Pizza and Sub	8	La Terrazza	6
The Balkan	13	Melissa's	4
Banff Springs Hotel	15	Saltlik	1
Bison Restaurant & Lounge	3	Squish Sandwich	
Bumper's	14	Cellar	2
Coyote's Grill	10	Sushi House	7
Eddie Burger	12	Tooloulous	9
Evelyn's	5	Wild Flour	11

BANFF TOWNSITE

park. In many ways the museum chronicles changing attitudes to **wildlife** over the years; many Victorians wanted to see the park's animals without the tiresome business of having to venture into the backcountry – so they killed and stuffed the beasts for permanent display. The hunting of game animals in the park was banned in 1890, but not before populations of moose, elk, sheep, goats and grizzlies had been severely depleted. Game wardens only arrived to enforce the injunction in 1913, and even then they didn't protect the "bad" animals – wolves, coyotes, foxes, cougars, lynx, eagles, owls and hawks – which were hunted until the 1930s as part of the park's "predator-control programme". Many of the stuffed victims in the museum date from this period. In summer the beautiful riverside **park** behind the museum is ideal for a snooze or picnic.

Whyte Museum of the Canadian Rockies

111 Bear St • Daily 10am–5pm • $10 • ⓦ whyte.org

The excellent **Whyte Museum of the Canadian Rockies** looks at the Rockies' emergence as a tourist destination through paintings and photographs, and at the early expeditions to explore and conquer the interior peaks. Pictures of bears foraging in Banff rubbish bins and of park rangers grinning over a magnificent lynx they've just shot give some idea of how times have changed.

Buffalo Nations Luxton Museum

1 Birch Ave • Daily: May to Sept 10am–7pm; Oct to Apr 11am–5pm • $10 • ⓦ buffalonationsmuseum.ca

Across the river, dated displays of Aboriginal history, birds and animals fill the **Buffalo Nations Luxton Museum**, an Aboriginal peoples-run enterprise attractively housed in a huge wooden stockade. The museum takes its name from Norman Luxton, a local who ran a trading post here and forged a close relationship with Banff's Stoney population over the course of sixty years. The exhibits aren't exciting, but the museum shop has some good Aboriginal crafts.

Banff Springs Hotel

405 Spray Ave • ☎ 403 762 2211, ⓦ fairmont.com/banff-springs • Either walk along the south bank of the Bow River (taking in Bow Falls) or pick up the Banff Transit bus from downtown

Even if the **Banff Springs Hotel** is out of your league, you can't spend much time in town without coming across at least one mention of the place, and it's hard to miss its landmark Gothic superstructure. Initiated in 1888, it got off to a bad start when the architect arrived to find the place being built 180 degrees out of kilter: while the kitchens enjoyed magnificent views over the river the guest rooms looked into thick forest. When it finally opened, with 250 rooms and a rotunda to improve the views, it was the world's largest hotel.

Don't bother with the hotel's guided tours: a voyeuristic hour or so can be spent looking around the hotel's first three floors on your own (pick up a map in reception) or taking a coffee, beer or afternoon tea in the second-floor café and **Sunroom** off the main reception. It's also worth walking out onto the terrace beyond the Sunroom for some spectacular views.

Banff Gondola

Mountain Ave, 5km south of Banff • April to mid-May & early Sept to mid-Oct daily 8am–8.30pm; mid-May to early Sept daily 8am–8.30pm; mid-Oct to mid-April Wed–Sun 10am–8.30pm, Mon & Tues 10am–4.30pm • $58 • ⓦ explorerockies.com/banff-gondola • The walk to the station is dull and tiring; take a taxi from downtown or book a free shuttle (☎ 403 760 6934)

Banff is rightly proud of the **Banff Mountain Gondola.** In spite of the crowds and the commercialization of the upper station (2281m) on Sulphur Mountain, it offers great views and the chance to do some high-level hiking without the slog of an early-morning climb – a glimpse of the remote high country if you're short of time or unable to walk the trails. The best times to take a ride are early morning or evening, when

8

wildlife sightings are more likely, and when the play of light gives an added dimension to the views.

The gondola trundles 700m skywards at a stomach-churning 51 degrees to immense panoramas from two observation terraces. It takes just eight minutes for the glass-enclosed four-passenger cars to reach the high point, where there are two restaurants.

From the restaurants, a 1km path, the **Summit Ridge Trail**, has been blazed to take you a bit higher, while the short **Vista Trail** leads to the restored weather station and viewpoint on **Sanson Peak**. Norman Betheune "N.B." Sanson was the first curator of the Banff Park Museum, and between 1903 and 1931 made around a thousand ascents of the mountain – that's before the gondola was built – to take his weather readings. If, like him, you slog the 5.5km switchback trail up from the car park you can ride the gondola down for half-price.

Cave and Basin National Historic Site

Cave Ave • Mid-May to June Tues–Sun 10am–5pm; July–early Sept daily 10am–5pm; early Sept to mid-Oct Wed–Sun 10am–5pm; mid-Oct to mid-May Wed–Sun 11am–5pm • $4 • ☎ 403 762 1566, ⓦ pc.gc.ca

Banff's first hot spring – now the Cave and Basin National Historic Site – was discovered on November 8, 1883 by three railway navvies prospecting for gold on their day off. The government soon bought them out, promoting travel to the springs as a means of contributing to the cost of the railway's construction. It became a small reserve in 1885, from which the present park eventually evolved.

Today, the historic site explores this history via multimedia exhibitions, explaining how Banff soon boasted eight hot springs, and how a plunge into the waters for their great reputed therapeutic effects was for a long time the next stop after the gondola ride on the standard itinerary of the Victorian gentry. This spring operated as a bathhouse until 1993 when it closed because of corrosion and low visitor numbers. Today you can't touch the waters for fear of damaging the unique local ecosystem, yet access to the original sulphurous cave where a shaft of light illuminates iridescent waters remains the highlight of a visit.

Upper Hot Springs

Mid-May to mid-Oct daily 10am–11pm; rest of year Fri & Sat 10am–11pm, Mon–Thurs & Sun 10am–10pm • $8, towel ($1.90) and swimsuit ($1.90) rental available • ☎ 403 762 1515, ⓦ hotsprings.ca

Originally developed in 1901, the **Upper Hot Springs** now offer a soak at 38°C in a large outdoor pool, along with a day-spa. Sadly, since 1998 the flow of natural spring water has dwindled so that from time to time the pool has to be topped up using tap water. Other attractions include a steam room, cold plunge and a good poolside restaurant with outside terrace, fresh juice bar and hot and cold snacks.

Lake Minnewanka

Boat trips Mid-May to early Oct; 3–9 daily • $56 • ☎ 403 762 3473, ⓦ banffjaspercollection.com • Easily accessed by bike or car from the Trans-Canada at the northern end of Banff Ave

Lake Minnewanka, a few kilometres north of Banff, is the largest area of water in the national park. Its name means "Lake of the Water Spirit", and with the peaks of the Fairholme Range as a backdrop it provides a suitably scenic antidote to the bustle of downtown. Various dams have augmented the lake to provide Banff with hydroelectric power, though they've done little to spoil the views, most of which are best enjoyed on a **boat trip**.

Mount Norquay

Mt Norquay Access Road • Dec to mid-April daily 9am–4pm • Winter day-pass $89; snow tubing $35/day; summer chairlift $35; Via Ferrata $149 • ☎ 403 762 4421, ⓦ banffnorquay.com

The closest ski resort to Banff, **Mount Norquay** lies just 6km and ten minutes' drive from downtown. The mountain (the first in Canada to get a chairlift, in 1948) is as renowned for its uncrowded beginners' slopes as for its expert runs, with five lifts serving 28 runs. And with artificial snow covering 85 percent of the area, reasonable conditions are almost guaranteed. Amenities include a visitor centre, ski school, rental shop, day-care, snow tubing and – on Wednesdays and Fridays – night skiing.

In summer chairlift rides offer excellent park views, but the more unique draw is the Via Ferrata, an easy climbing route made relatively safe using fixed cables.

Hiking in and around Banff

Banff is an obvious base for **walks** in the park, and trails around the town cater to all. Short walks can provide an opportunity to see a remarkably wide range of **wildlife** and are particularly good for **birdwatching**; many can be walked with "Friends of Banff" (see page 569). Longer day-hikes from the town are limited – you need transport and usually have to head a few kilometres up the Trans-Canada or Bow Valley Parkway (see page 576) to reach trailheads for hikes that leave the flat valley floor for the mountains.

Fenland Trail

The quickest and easiest way to get among local flora and fauna is along the **Fenland Trail**, a 1.5km loop west of town through the montane wetlands near the First Vermilion Lake (there are three; all can be accessed off Vermilion Lakes Drive). Marsh in this area is slowly becoming forest, creating habitats whose rushes and grasses provide a haven for wildlife, birds in particular, and the lakes are the single most important **birdwatching** area in the entire park. Ospreys and bald eagles nest around the lake, together with a wide range of other birds and waterfowl, including tundra

8

WINTER SPORTS IN THE ROCKIES

With terrific terrain, reliable snow cover, uncrowded slopes and relatively low prices, the Rockies are perfect for a **ski or snowboard holiday**. The region is also ideal for many other **winter sports** like cross-country skiing, snowshoeing, dog-sledding and snowmobiling (though the last is forbidden in national parks). The **season** runs from mid-December until the end of May, with the best conditions often in March, when the days get warmer and the snowpack is deepest. Arrive earlier in the year and be prepared for the possibility of bitterly **cold** conditions – with temperatures below -20°C not uncommon.

The best known, busiest and most expensive resorts are in **Banff National Park** and within easy reach of the town of Banff. These include the small and steep **Mount Norquay** (see page 566); the well-rounded, intermediate-friendly **Sunshine Village** (see page 576); and the vast, varied and challenging **Lake Louise** (see page 579). The three have a joint lift-ticket system: a **Tri-Area Pass** (Ⓦ skibig3.com) valid for up to fourteen days' skiing; a one-day pass is $119, a three-day pass is $372, six days $544, fourteen days $1666.

Locals make up a sizeable chunk of the business, so weekends are peak times, leaving weekdays particularly quiet. A glorious three-hour drive north of Banff through craggy montane scenery along the Icefields Parkway lies **Marmot Basin** (see page 593). Though far more modest than the Banff resorts, it is quieter and less expensive and has a truly vast system of cross-country ski trails on its doorstep.

In BC's Rockies, several less accessible resorts are often blessed with even better snow and milder temperatures. And with much of the surrounding land outside strictly regulated national park boundaries, there's plenty of heli-skiing nearby too. The closest to Banff is **Kicking Horse** (see page 608), which bristles with high-alpine expert terrain and awesome views. The grand vistas have provided the name of mellower **Panorama** (see page 617) to the south, while another couple of hours' drive south is the cheerful, family-oriented ski hill **Kimberley** (see page 618). Its multi-day tickets are valid at **Fernie** (see page 620), whose bountiful mountain bowls and ridges can take weeks to fully explore. With each of these BC resorts no more than a couple of hours' drive from the next, they make for an ideal multi-resort trip that includes Banff and can be tackled as a loop from Calgary.

BEST HIKES IN AND AROUND BANFF

Cory Pass Trail Serious day-hike. See below
Fenland Trail Easy hike for wildlife-spotting. See page 567
Sawback Trail Multi-day backcountry hike between Banff and Lake Louise. See page 577
Sunshine Meadows Quick access to high-alpine terrain. See page 576
Tunnel Mountain Easy access and spectacular Banff views. See below

---

swan, hooded merganser and northern shoveler. You may also see beaver and muskrat, perhaps even coyote, elk and other deer.

Discovery Trail and Marsh Loop

From the Cave and Basin interpretive centre (see page 566), a short trail (15min) heads up the hill for a view over the historic site. Just below, on Cave Avenue, is the start of the boardwalk **Marsh Loop** (2.8km; 45min return); in winter, Banff's wolves have been known to hunt within sight of this trail. It's a treat for birdwatching enthusiasts: low-elevation wetlands teem with waterfowl during the winter and spring migrations, with the chance to see – among others – Barrow's goldeneye and all three species of teal (cinnamon, blue-winged and green-winged). The warm microclimate produced here by the springs' warm waters supports mallards over the winter, as well as attracting seasonal rarities such as killdeer, common snipe and rusty blackbird. During the summer you might see belted kingfisher, common yellowthroat, willow flycatcher and red-winged blackbird.

Sundance Canyon Trail

Off Cave Avenue, the excellent **Sundance Canyon Trail** is an easy and deservedly popular stroll along a paved path (4.3 km; watch for cyclists and in-line skaters) to the picnic area at the canyon mouth; you can extend your walk along the 1.2km loop path up through the canyon, past waterfalls and back down a peaceful wooded trail. Hiking the whole lot should take about three hours.

Bow Falls, Spray River and the Hoodoos

For a short walk, and a burst of spectacular whitewater, stroll the level and very easy **Bow Falls Trail** (1km) from beneath the bridge on the south side of the river. It follows the river bank east to a powerful set of waterfalls and rapids just below the *Banff Springs Hotel*. If you fancy a longer hike, consider extending this by crossing the river beyond Bow Falls and following the **Spray River Loop**, which will extend your hike a flat, 13km up the Spray River and return to the *Banff Springs Hotel*.

Alternatively, stay on the downtown side of the Bow River and follow Buffalo Street east to another lookout over Bow Falls and the start of the **Hoodoos Trail**, only lightly used, which makes its attractive and easy way along the river to the tall, thin rock spires known as hoodoos (4.6km). You can pick up a bus back into town by the nearby *Tunnel Mountain* campgrounds (see page 572) if you'd rather not walk.

Tunnel Mountain

The most strenuous but scenically rewarding walk near town is to the summit of **Tunnel Mountain** (5km; 2hr return). It's approached on a winding track (300m ascent) from the southwest from Tunnel Mountain Drive, culminating in great views over the town, Bow River and flanking mountains.

Cory Pass and Edith Pass trails

Though arduous, the best day-hike close to Banff is the **Cory Pass Trail**, which, combined with the **Edith Pass Trail**, makes a 13km loop (4hr return). The trailhead lies 6km west of town, at the start of the Bow Valley Parkway (see page 576). The stiff climbing involved, and a couple of scree passages, means it's not for the inexperienced or faint-hearted. But the rewards are fantastic, with varied walking, a high-mountain environment and spine-tingling views. From the 2350m pass itself you can return on the Edith Pass Trail – whose start you pass 1km into the Cory Pass walk – to loop back.

Cascade Amphitheatre

Another popular local day-hike, the trail to **Cascade Amphitheatre** (2195m), starts at Mount Norquay Ski Area, 6km north of the Trans-Canada. This offers a medley of landscapes, ranging from alpine meadows to deep, ice-scoured valleys, and a close view of the knife-edged mountains that loom so tantalizingly above town. Allow about three hours for the walk (7.7km; 610m ascent).

ARRIVAL AND DEPARTURE   BANFF

By train The town can be reached from Calgary and Vancouver on a tour with Rocky Mountaineer Railtours (see page 706).

By bus Several operators offer efficient shuttle services from Calgary Airport (see page 546). Brewster (ⓦ brewster transportation.com) need to be booked in advance in Banff

(ⓣ 1 877 625 4372) and will pick you up from any address in town. The Parks Canada Shuttle to Lake Louise (mid-May to early-Oct) departs from Banff Train Station.

Destinations Calgary (5 daily; 2hr 30min); Calgary Airport (8 daily; 2hr); Lake Louise (6–13 daily; 1hr).

GETTING AROUND AND INFORMATION

By bus While central Banff is easy to navigate on foot, a frequent town bus service, called Roam ($2; ⓣ 403 760 8294, ⓦ roamtransit.com), provides transport from Banff Avenue to outlying areas, including the *Tunnel Mountain* campgrounds and Banff gondola.

By taxi Banff Taxi (ⓣ 403 762 0000).

Banff Information Centre The showpiece visitor centre is at 224 Banff Ave (daily: late June to early Sept 9am–5pm; early Sept to late June 9am–7pm; ⓣ 403 762 8421, ⓦ banfflakelouise.com; park information ⓦ pc.gc.ca/banff). The centre issues park permits (see page 577) and has many

free handouts. Make a point of asking for the *Banff and Vicinity Drives and Walks* and *The Icefields Parkway* for maps of park facilities. The *Backcountry Visitors' Guide* is invaluable for details on backcountry hiking trails and campgrounds, while *Biking Trails in the Banff Area* details all mountain-bike trails. The centre also has a selection of maps and guides to consult for free and sells topographical maps at the "Friends of Banff National Park" shop, but all the more popular trails are so well-signed and -trodden that detailed maps are generally unnecessary. The Friends also offer various guided walking tours (some free), for which you can register here.

ACTIVITIES

SUMMER

Canoeing To rent canoes for paddling on the Vermilion Lakes or quiet stretches of the Bow River, contact The Banff Canoe Club ($20/boat and $20/hr; ⓣ 403 762 5005, ⓦ banffcanoeclub.com); the dock is on the river at Wolf St.

Climbing The Sally Borden Recreation Centre, 107 Tunnel Mountain Drive (Mon–Fri 6am–10pm, Sat & Sun 7am–10pm; $15; ⓣ 403 762 6450, ⓦ banffcentre.ca/sbb) in the Banff Centre, has climbing walls and gear rentals.

Cycling The visitor centre (see page 569) has free maps and guides to cycling in Banff. The town's most convenient and rewarding mountain-bike trails loop around the northeast of town and are reasonably well-marked and graded for difficulty; most are intermediate-level, though the trails on east side of Tunnel Mountain are great for experts. For road biking try the loop road south of Lake Minnewanka, the cycle path that runs parallel to the highway to Canmore or the punishing climb to Mt Norquay. For an easy family ride try the paved trail to Sundance

Canyon (see page 568). Bactrax Bike Rentals, 225 Bear St (ⓣ 403 762 8177, ⓦ snowtips-bactrax.com), rents out full suspension mountain bikes for $60/day, touring bikes for $42/day, road bikes for $42/day and town bike for $35/day. If you'd rather pootle about on a beach cruiser bike, rent one from The Banff Canoe Club (see above) at the Banff Adventures Activities Centre, 211 Bear St for $12/hr.

Fishing Lake Minnewanka Boat Tours (ⓣ 403 762 3473, ⓦ explorerockies.com) offers guided fishing trips from $182/3hr. For longer, more personalized trips for around $525/person you could take an all-day drift-boat fishing trip along the Bow River or a walk-and-wade trip with outfitters such as Tightline Adventures (ⓣ 403 762 4548, ⓦ tightlineadventures.com) or Banff Fishing Unlimited (ⓣ 403 678 2486, ⓣ 866 678 2486, ⓦ banff-fishing.com).

Hiking and camping There are plenty of good hikes locally (see opposite). If you need to buy or rent hiking or camping gear you'll find a glut of places in Banff, including Bactrax, 225 Bear St (ⓣ 403 762 8177, ⓦ snowtips-bactrax.com).

ROOM-AND-SKI PACKAGE OPERATORS

If you're booking last-minute in peak season, you might try one of the dedicated booking services for accommodation in Banff. These are worth a look well in advance too, since various promotions and packages can produce sizeable savings.

Enjoy Banff ☎403 313 6161, ☎888 313 6161, ☜ enjoybanff.com.

Ski Banff–Lake Louise (winter only) ☎403 762 4561, ☎800 754 7080, ☜ skibig3.com.

Horseriding Outfitters include Banff Trail Riders, 132 Banff Ave (☎403 762 4551, ☜ horseback.com), and the local choice of riding trips ranges from one-hour treks to two-week backcountry expeditions. A one-hour ride will cost around $62, three hours $162, a six-day trip around $2049.

Rafting Much of the best whitewater in the region is on the Kicking Horse River in Yoho National Park, so companies in Banff and Lake Louise head there for their wilder trips. Gentler "float" trips are generally run on the Kananaskis, Kootenay and Bow rivers. One long-established, quality outfitter is Hydra River Guides (211 Bear St; ☎403 762 4554, ☎800 644 8888, ☜ raftbanff.com), whose range of float and whitewater trips start at $75. Other operators are based in Canmore (see page 557), Golden (see page 610) and Radium (see page 612).

Swimming The *Douglas Fir Resort* (see page 571) on Tunnel Mountain Drive (Mon–Fri 4–10pm, Sat & Sun 9am–10pm; $12) has two large indoor waterslides and a pool. The Sally Borden Recreation Centre, 107 Tunnel Mountain Drive (Mon–Fri 6am–10pm, Sat & Sun 7am–10pm; $5.50), in the Banff Centre, has a 25m swimming pool, whirlpool, steam rooms and an outdoor sun deck. The only swimmable lake in the park is Johnson Lake, northeast of town off Lake Minnewanka Rd: others are generally glacier-fed and so too cold.

WINTER

Cross-country skiing A number of groomed summer walking trails offer the chance to enjoy the park from a pair of Nordic skis. Details of the full network are in the *Winter Trails in Banff National Park* pamphlet available from the town's visitor centre (see page 569) or online. Popular areas include Spray River and Sundance Canyon, around Lake Louise (see page 579), and Canmore's wonderful Nordic Centre (see page 556). To ski Banff's backcountry it's best to have the company of an experienced guide; try Banff Mountain Guides (☎403 762 2591, ☜ banffmountainguides.com).

Dog-sledding and sleigh rides Being pulled through the snow by man's best friend is a popular and easily organized activity. Expect to pay around $200 for two hours of mushing or about $38/45min in the lee of a couple of horses. Trips of both kinds can be booked with Discover Banff Tours (☎403 760 5007, ☎877 565 9372, ☜ banfftours.com), or contact operators direct: Snowy Owl Sled Dog Tours (☎403 678 4369, ☜ snowyowltours. com) for sledding, and Holiday on Horseback, 132 Banff Ave (☎403 762 4551, ☜ horseback.com), for sleigh rides.

Downhill skiing Ski equipment is available from a number of operators; Bactrax, 225 Bear St (☎403 762 8177, ☜ snowtips-bactrax.com), has a particularly good range, which includes touring skis.

Ice-climbing Johnston (see page 578) and Grotto (see page 557) canyons are both ice-climbing hot-spots; for information contact Banff's visitor centre (see page 569), where climbers should also register.

Ice-fishing Contact Banff Fishing Unlimited (☎403 678 2486, ☎866 678 2486, ☜ banff-fishing.com).

Ice-skating and tobogganing Head to the *Banff Springs Hotel* (see p.571), where the outdoor rink is made particularly appealing by a fire beside it. Ice skates can be rented from The Ski Shop in the hotel; you can also rent sleds here for use on the unofficial run beside the rink.

Snowshoeing and winter hiking To appreciate the quiet, snowy serenity of the park in winter, head out on snowshoes. The easy trails outlined in the hiking section (see opposite) are usually ideal, and the visitor centre (see page 569) can advise on more ambitious jaunts. Generally snowshoes are best on fresh snow, winter hiking boots best on trampled snow. One of the nicest winter walks is through the fairytale scenery of Johnston Canyon (see page 578) on boardwalks suspended from its limestone walls to impressive pillars of glassy ice. Though icy, the boardwalks are navigable in winter with the right gear and knowledge. White Mountain Adventures (☎403 760 4403, ☎800 408 0005, ☜ whitemountainadventures.com) and Discover Banff Tours (☎403 760 5007, ☎877 565 9372, ☜ banfftours.com) offer trips down the canyon, as well as to the slightly less spectacular Grotto Canyon (see page 557) near Canmore. A highlight of either trip is watching ice-climbers scale the frozen columns.

ACCOMMODATION

Don't expect to visit Banff in July or August and find reasonably-priced **accommodation**. Preplanning is essential too; the visitor centre (see page 569) maintains a constantly updated vacancies board and has a list of 40-plus local **private rooms** and **B&Bs**. They're usually fairly cheap by Banff standards (typically around $150) and among the first places to go each day. Most Banff **motels** are on the busy spur of the Trans-Canada into town, probably the town's least attractive area. Off-season (Oct–May), rates are usually considerably lower, and even halve in the depths of winter. **Campgrounds** are not quite as hard to find (the town offers over a thousand pitches), but even these often fill up by 2pm, so reserve ahead or turn up early. In addition to campgrounds listed here, there are lovely, less-developed park-run sites along the Bow Parkway to the north (see page 576).

HOTELS AND MOTELS

Banff Boutique Inn 121 Cave Ave ☎403 762 4636, ⓦbanffboutiqueinn.com; map p.564. Comfortable accommodation that defies categorisation: smart as a hotel but with just three bedrooms; not a B&B as the breakfast is basic and staff very much in the background; not a hostel, though there's a shared kitchen and lounge. But certainly, it's ideal for several nights stay for those keen to self-cater. **$245**

Banff Inn 501 Banff Ave ☎403 762 8844, ☎800 667 1464, ⓦbanffinn.com; map p.564. Fancy-looking 99-room hotel, a 5min walk from town, whose gables, loft windows, stucco and stone-clad walls make it stand out from neighbouring complexes. The smart and spacious rooms are much more ordinary, though some come with a fireplace and bath-tubs. Facilities include a steam room, jacuzzi, free wi-fi and underground parking. **$278**

Banff Park Lodge 222 Lynx St ☎403 762 4433, ☎800 661 9266, ⓦbanffparklodge.com; map p.564. Quietly sophisticated, low-slung cedar and oak hotel, a block from the town centre. Scandinavian-style rooms are simple and airy; some come with jacuzzi and fireplace. Facilities include two restaurants, lounge, hot tub, steam room, indoor pool, laundry and dry-cleaning service. **$334**

★ **Banff Springs Hotel** 405 Spray Ave ☎403 762 2211, ☎866 540 4406, ⓦfairmont.com/banff-springs; map p.564. One of the continent's most famous hotels – built in Scots Baronial style with turrets and cornices towering above its thick, nine-storey granite walls – offering luxurious service that borders on pageantry. The glut of facilities, which include a world-class fitness and spa complex, several stores and restaurants, make the hotel almost entirely self-contained. Rates are extravagant but winter prices are almost halved. **$889**

Bumper's Inn 603 Banff Ave ☎403 762 3386, ☎800 661 3518, ⓦbestofbanff.com; map p.564. Small, 1970s motel on the northeastern fringe of town, but only 50m from the nearest ski-shuttle stop. Facilities are basic, but there is an on-site steakhouse (see page 574). Usefully shares an online booking system with several other local properties. **$219**

Douglas Fir Resort Tunnel Mountain Rd ☎403 762 5591, ☎800 661 9267, ⓦdouglasfir.com; map p.564. Collection of low-rise, wood-clad condo blocks in a secluded wooded area on Tunnel Mountain, a 15min walk from the town centre. Ideal for families or groups, units have a kitchen and lounge with fireplace as well as access to a host of leisure facilities, a huge indoor kids' play area and a pool with waterslides. There's also a laundry and small convenience store. **$197**

High Country Inn 419 Banff Ave ☎403 762 2236, ☎800 293 5142, ⓦbanffhighcountryinn.com; map p.564. Mid-range motel with some luxury suites in a great central location. Facilities include a sauna, two hot tubs, an indoor pool and a Swiss-Italian restaurant, *Ticino*. **$249**

★ **The Juniper** 1 Juniper Way ☎403 762 2281, ☎866 551 2281, ⓦthejuniper.com; map p.564. Boutique hotel that breaks the predictable mould of most mid-range Banff offerings with its chic, simple and contemporary interiors in a series of chalets (the larger two- and three-bedroom ones offer kitchenettes). The mountain views are among the best from any Banff hotel, but at 2km from the town centre at the foot of Mount Norquay, it's not central. **$269**

Mount Royal Hotel 138 Banff Ave ☎403 762 3331, ☎877 442 2623, ⓦmountroyalhotel.com; map p.564. The bland, three-storey exterior of this building amid downtown shops at the centre of town belies the perfectly acceptable interior – near-luxurious in the more expensive suites. Most rooms have mountain views, and there's a large health club with whirlpool. **$349**

Red Carpet Inn 425 Banff Ave ☎403 762 4184, ☎800 563 4609, ⓦbanffredcarpet.com; map p.564. Pastel-shaded inside and out, this no-frills establishment is a clean, central and decent-value option. Wi-fi and continental breakfast are included, and guests can use the pool, sauna and hot tubs at the *High Country Inn*. **$269**

Rimrock Resort 300 Mountain Ave ☎403 762 3356, ☎888 746 7625, ⓦrimrockresort.com; map p.564. Elegant and richly furnished hotel in an imposing, ten-storey, angular building that nestles alone among thick stands of trees on the lower slopes of Sulphur Mountain, 3km south of town. The smart, modern rooms come with Bow Valley views, but they can't match the views from its superb French restaurant, *Eden*. Extensive fitness facilities and a free shuttle into town. **$358**

B&BS

★ **Blue Mountain Lodge** 137 Muskrat St ☎403 762 5134, ⓦbluemtnlodge.com; map p.564. Friendly and central budget place with ten small rooms, all with private bathroom and spectacular mountain views. Facilities include a guest kitchen, lounge and laundry facilities. **$179**

★ **Tan-y-Bryn** 118 Otter St ☎403 762 3696, ⓦtanybryninbanff.com; map p.564. Set in a quiet residential district three blocks from downtown, these

8

eight simple and extremely reasonable B&B rooms come with private or shared bathroom and in-room continental breakfast. No credit cards. **$67**

HOSTELS

Banff Alpine Centre 801 Hidden Ridge Way, off Tunnel Mountain Rd ☎ 403 762 4123, ☎ 866 762 4122, Ⓦ hihostels.ca; map p.564. Friendly, modern, 216-bed hostel in a great setting, but 3km from downtown and a $9 cab ride from the bus depot. Great facilities include a large kitchen, laundry, lounge with fireplace, ski workshop and an adjoining inexpensive restaurant that can save trips downtown. Dorms **$47**, non-members **$52**; doubles **$159**, non-members **$175**

SameSun Backpacker Lodge 449 Banff Ave ☎ 403 762 4499, ☎ 877 972 6378, Ⓦ banffhostel.com; map p.564. Cheerful, busy and sociable hostel on the strip just north of town, with dorm beds as well as en-suite private doubles, plus a bar and all the usual hostel facilities. Dorms **$58**; doubles **$199**

★ **YWCA Banff Hotel** 102 Spray Ave ☎ 403 762 3560, ☎ 800 813 4138, Ⓦ ywcabanff.ca/hotel; map p.564. Quiet and tidy hostel a short walk from downtown. In addition to a huge living room with gigantic stone fireplace, the hostel has a café with reasonable food, as well as a guest kitchen and lounge, laundry facilities and showers. Shared dorms as well as large, somewhat clinical private rooms are available, both with and without en-suite bathroom. Dorms **$45**; doubles **$195**

CAMPGROUNDS

Tunnel Mountain Trailer Court Tunnel Mountain Rd ☎ 450 505 8302, ☎ 877 737 3783, Ⓦ pccamping.ca; map p.564. A large park-run campground off Tunnel Mountain Road, but RV-only with full hook-ups at each of the 320 sites. Mid-May to Sept. RVs **$38.20**

Tunnel Mountain Village I Tunnel Mountain Rd ☎ 450 505 8302, ☎ 877 737 3783, Ⓦ pccamping.ca; map p.564. A giant, 618-site, park-run campground with flush toilets, showers and fire pits, 4.3km from town but on the Banff public bus route. Reservations are accepted for some sites; others are first-come, first-served, and it fills up quickly. Alcohol possession and consumption bans are regularly in effect. Mid-May to Sept. Sites **$27.40**

Tunnel Mountain Village II Tunnel Mountain Rd ☎ 450 505 8302, ☎ 877 737 3783, Ⓦ pccamping.ca; map p.564. Beside *Village I* but a bit closer to downtown (2.4km), this offers otherwise much the same deal, except that electric hook-ups are available but fire pits aren't. It's set amid trees, with good views, plenty of space and short trails close at hand; bighorn sheep, elk and even the odd bear may drop in. Open year-round. Sites **$32.30**

Two Jack Lakeside 12km northeast of Banff on Lake Minnewanka Rd; map p.564. No reservations are taken at this 74-pitch, park-run campground, with flush toilets, showers and fire pits. June to mid-Sept. Sites **$27.40**

Two Jack Main 13km northeast of Banff on Lake Minnewanka Rd; map p.564. The largest non-reservable park-run site, with 380 sites, running water and flush toilets, but no showers. June to mid-Sept. Sites **$21.50**

EATING

Banff's hundred-plus **restaurants** run the gamut from Japanese to nouvelle-frontier grub. For cheap eats you're best off sticking to hostel cafés, though Banff Avenue is lined with good spots for **coffee and snacks**, and many bars (see page 574) also do good food. For groceries try the big Safeway **supermarket** at 318 Marten St.

CAFÉS AND SNACKS

★ **Aardvark Pizza and Sub** 304a Caribou St ☎ 403 762 5500; map p.564. Tiny takeaway place with subs, wings, tacos, nachos, *poutine* (French fries with cheese curd, the favourite Québécois comfort food) and fantastic thick-crust pizzas (available by the slice). There's almost nowhere to sit, but with the best takeaway food in town, and open until 4am, popularity's assured. Daily 10am–4am.

Eddie Burger 137 Banff Ave ☎ 403 762 2230, Ⓦ eddieburgerbar.ca; map p.564. Hip and tiny burger bar with an upbeat and busy vibe that's enhanced by televised sport. The menu is a fair encyclopedia of patties (beef, lamb, bison, veggie), buns and fries (the sweet potato variety is good). All very tasty, as they should be for $19 a burger. Mon–Fri 11am–10pm, Sat & Sun 8am–11pm.

Evelyn's 215 Banff Ave ☎ 403 762 0352, Ⓦ evelynscoffeebar.com; map p.564. A superb range of coffees wash down pastries and muffins in a café that's popular enough to justify two other outlets, *Evelyn's Too*, at 229 Bear Ave, and *Evelyn's Again*, at 119 Banff Ave. All put together deli sandwiches (around $8) that make ideal picnic food. Daily 7am–11pm.

★ **Squish Sandwich Cellar** 211 Banff Ave ☎ 403 985 5000; map p.564. Basement café with simple decor and extremely good, fresh and often creative sandwiches: the Reuben (corned beef, Swiss cheese) is excellent, as is the Montréal smoked-meat offering. Not a budget choice though, with most options well above $10. Free wi-fi. Mon–Thurs 11am–4pm, Fri–Sun 11am–4pm.

★ **Sushi House** 304 Caribou St ☎ 403 762 4353; map p.564. Sushi delivered by train – a toy train that is – that circulates around the counter. Take what you fancy; you'll be charged for the number of your dirty plates (around $5/plate). Fresh and good fun for a quick and inexpensive bite – if you don't mind being elbow-to-elbow with other diners

Banff's other budget dining options line the same street. Daily 11.30am–10pm.

Wild Flour 211 Bear St ☎403 760 5074, ⓦwildflour bakery.ca; map p.564. Large, airy and fairly minimalist bakery and coffee house with organic, local and natural aspirations. It's nicely away from Banff's main drag and crowds, so maintains a relaxed atmosphere – including out on the pleasant patio. Good for sandwiches; better still for muffins, cakes and brownies. Daily 7am–4pm.

RESTAURANTS

★**The Balkan** 120 Banff Ave ☎403 762 3454, ⓦbanffbalkan.ca; map p.564. Cheerful restaurant best known for its large portions of decent Greek food and bellydancing shows on Tuesdays and Thursdays. Avoid non-Greek menu items in favour of dishes like lamb *souvlaki* ($26) or *spanakopita* ($15) – a spinach and filo dish that's an excellent vegetarian choice. Daily 11.30am–3.30pm & 4–10pm.

Banff Springs Hotel 405 Spray Ave ☎403 762 6860, ⓦfairmont.com/banff-springs; map p.564. With around fifteen dining options under one roof, all open to non-guests, Banff's grandest hotel has plenty of variety. The *Vermillion Room* is the largest restaurant, with its seafood and rotisserie-grilled meats menu. Other places include the super-luxurious *1888 Chophouse*, *Castello Ristorante*, a top-class Italian, and *Samurai*, which serves excellent sushi. *Grapes Wine Bar* is great for light snacks such as salads, pâtés, cheeses or excellent fondue. Hours vary; something is always open.

★**Bison Restaurant & Lounge** Bison Courtyard, 211 Bear St ☎403 762 5550, ⓦthebison.ca; map p.564. Banff's best bistro, with a chic, contemporary, light-wood interior, large windows and splashy modern art: the perfect setting for modern, creative Canadian cookery (mains $24–48). The rooftop patio isn't bad either, and there's a hip downstairs lounge if you want to make a night of it. Mon–Sat 5–11pm, Sun 10am–2pm.

Bumper's 603 Banff Ave ☎403 762 2622, ⓦbumpers thebeefhouse.com; map p.564. Busy, good-value steakhouse with adjoining laidback bar in an off-puttingly ugly building that's part of the *Bumper's Inn* on the edge of town. Mains start at around $22; vegetarians can console themselves with a decent salad bar. Daily 7am–10am &

5–10pm.

Coyote's Grill 206 Caribou St ☎403 762 3963 ⓦcoyotesbanff.com; map p.564. Small, simple café just off the main drag, serving top-notch breakfasts. One of the best is the cream-cheese-filled French toast with fruit ($14), but the hungry should try the huge Mountain Man Breakfast ($16.50), which includes two eggs, two pancakes, bacon or sausage and roast potatoes. Evenings see fine renditions of pizza, pasta and Southwestern Tex-Mex mains ($17–34). Daily 7.30am–10pm.

★**La Terrazza** 222 Lynx St in Banff Park Lodge ☎403 762 4433; map p.564. Fine-dining, special-occasion restaurant that's inauspiciously tucked behind a lounge bar and a hotel lobby. But the food is excellent, with many locally inspired dishes, such as elk medallions with coffee mashed potato ($37). Daily 5.30–11.30pm.

Melissa's 218 Lynx St ☎403 762 5511 ⓦmelissas missteak.com; map p.564. Probably Banff's most popular daytime destination: big breakfasts, superb steaks, salads and burgers, plus a good upstairs bar, *Mel's*, for a leisurely drink, and a summer patio for food and beer in the sun. Prices are moderate, with most mains in the $15–25 range. Recommended, particularly for lunch. Daily 7.30am–9.30pm.

Saltlik 221 Bear St ☎403 762 2467, ⓦsaltlik.com; map p.564. Swanky nouvelle steakhouse with wacky lamps and loud art in an otherwise understated interior. It prides itself on its near-finicky preparation of sirloin (around $20); most main courses, such as rotisserie chicken, smoked cod or sea bass, are under the $25 mark. Sides cost extra, however, so budget an extra $10 and don't miss the crisp, seasoned shoestring fries. The happening ground-floor bar is a good place for a drink before or after dinner, and has a good bar menu, too. Fri & Sat 11am–1am, Sun–Thurs 11.30am–midnight.

★**Tooloulous** 204 Caribou St ☎403 762 2633 ⓦtooloulous.ca; map p.564. The swamps meet in the mountains at this cheerful Louisianan bistro with its red-check table-cloths and Cajun flavours. The crispy fried alligator or frog's legs with barbeque sauce may not be for everyone, but there's plenty of more conventional seafood and burgers (most mains $16–25) to be had without missing out on the great Southern flavours – grits and all. Great for breakfast too. Daily 7.30am–9.30pm.

DRINKING AND NIGHTLIFE

With huge numbers of summer travellers and a large, young seasonal workforce, Banff has no shortage of **bars** a short walk from one another, and a few late-night **clubs** to stagger to afterwards. Less boozy entertainments include **ten-pin bowling** at the *Banff Springs Hotel*, **films** at the Lux Cinema, 229 Bear St (☎403 762 8595), and the Banff Centre arts programme.

BARS

Elk and Oarsman 119 Banff Ave ☎403 762 4616 ⓦelkandoarsman.com; map p.564. Refined pub with a fine roof terrace, with excellent food – pizza, steaks, burgers and salads – albeit with a "gourmet" twist at around $16–21 for most mains. There's also a good range of beers on tap, many local. Mon–Wed midnight–11pm, Thurs–Sat noon–midnight, Sun 11am–midnight.

Rose & Crown 202 Banff Ave ☎403 762 2121, ⓦroseandcrown.ca; map p.564. Victorian-style pub with a family-oriented restaurant serving decent bar food (mains around $19). There's pool here and live music every night, making it a cornerstone of town nightlife. Daily 11am–2am.

St James's Gate 207 Wolf St ☎403 762 9355, ⓦstjamesgatebanff.com; map p.564. Genuinely dingy dark-wood pub, originally built in Ireland then reassembled here to become hugely popular with locals and visitors alike. The thirty beers on tap include Guinness, as do many dishes on the satisfying bar menu, which includes the likes of Guinness, crab and asparagus soup ($7), and Guinness, steak and mushroom pie ($18). Other options are equally earthy, like the tasty beefy barley soup ($6), juicy cod and chips ($18), and decent Irish lamb stew ($18). Regular live music. Daily 11am–1am or later.

★ **Wild Bill's Legendary Saloon** 203 Banff Ave ☎403 762 0333, ⓦwildbillsbanff.com; map p.564. Busy second-floor country-and-western bar with live bands and line-dancing lessons. There's also a pool hall and games room, and before 8pm good Tex-Mex and vegetarian food is served in a more family-oriented atmosphere. Daily 11am–midnight or later.

CLUBS AND MUSIC VENUES

Banff Centre 107 Tunnel Mountain Drive ☎403 762 6100, ⓦbanffcentre.ca; map p.564. Banff's bastion of high culture lies in a sprawling arts and conference centre at the foot of Tunnel Mountain. A number of arts festivals take place here, and there's a full programme of music and opera performances by visiting artists. Box office Tues–Sat noon–5pm.

Dancing Sasquatch 120 Banff Ave ☎403 762 4002, ⓦbanffnightclubs.ca; map p.564. Banff's busiest dance club yet nothing extra-ordinary and a bit hit-and-miss depending on the crowd. Regular events though and yes, there's someone is a Sasquatch outfit on the dance floor – but Fridays only. Wed, Thurs & Sun 9pm–midnight, Fri & Sat 9pm–3am.

High Rollers 110 Banff Ave, ☎ 403 762 2695, ⓦhighrollersbanff.com; map p.564. Retro fun's on offer at this small upbeat ten-pin bowling alley ($45/hour), with good pizza ($13–28) and a couple of dozen craft beers to complete the experience. Mon–Thurs 3pm–2am, Fri–Sun noon–2am.

DIRECTORY

Hospital Mineral Springs Hospital, 301 Lynx St (☎403 762 2222, ⓦbanffmineralspringshospital.com).

Internet Banff Public library, 101 Bear St (Mon–Thurs 10am–8pm, Fri 10am–6pm, Sat 11am–6pm, Sun 11–6pm; ☎403 762 2661, ⓦbanfflibrary.ab.ca), offers free wi fi and terminals.

Laundry Cascade Coin Laundry, Lower Level, Cascade Plaza, 317 Banff Ave (☎403 762 3444).

Pharmacy Gourlay's Pharmacy, 229 Bear St (☎403 762 2516).

Police ☎403 762 2228.

Post office 204 Buffalo St (☎403 762 2586).

8

Hwy-1 and the Bow Valley Parkway

Two roads run parallel through the Bow Valley from Banff to Lake Louise (58km) - the fast **Hwy-1** (the Trans-Canada); and the **Bow Valley Parkway** (Hwy-1A), a quieter scenic route. The two are only linked at one point en-route: at Castle Junction, 30km from Lake Louise. Both routes are impressively beautiful as the mountains start to creep closer to the road, and for the entire run, the mighty Bow River, broad and emerald green, crashes through rocks and forest. Despite the tarmac and heavy summer traffic, the surroundings are pristine, giving a sense of the immensity of the wilderness to come. Sightings of elk and deer are common, particularly around dawn and sundown, and occasionally you'll spot moose too.

Both roads offer some good **trails** (see page 578): one of the best day-hikes in Banff National Park is the Bourgeau Lake Trail off Hwy-1; Johnston Canyon, off the Parkway, is a classic short hike.

Hwy-1

Most people tend either to cruise **Hwy-1**'s rapid stretch of the Trans-Canada without stopping and certainly on Greyhound or Brewster **buses** you're whisked through to Lake Louise in about forty minutes. The vast fences that hug this section of the road are designed to protect animals from traffic but necessitated the construction of a series of landscaped bridges to allow wildlife to cross the road.

BEARS AND OTHER WILD ANIMALS

Two types of **bear** roam the Rockies – black bear and grizzly – and you don't want to meet either. They're not hugely common and risks are pretty low on heavily tramped trails, but if you're camping or walking it's still essential to be vigilant, obey basic rules, know the difference between a black bear and a grizzly (the latter are bigger and have a humped neck) and how to avoid dangerous encounters, and understand what to do if confronted or attacked. Popular misconceptions about bears abound – that they can't climb trees, for example (they can, and very quickly) – so it's worth picking up the park service's **pamphlet** *You are in Bear Country*, which cuts through the confusion and advises on how to behave to avoid attacks. Cardinal **rules** include storing food and rubbish properly, making sure bears know you're there, not approaching or feeding them, and, if you meet one, not screaming or running away.

Other wild animals can also be dangerous, and while you would be unlucky to encounter cougars, which are relatively rare, the chances of meeting **elk** are much higher. Generally, these are benign creatures, often seen grazing at roadsides, but can become aggressive if approached or if they are with young; don't clamber out of your car, or cross the highway, to poke a camera in their faces.

Sunshine Meadows and Village

18km southwest of Banff off Hwy-1 • **Sunshine Village** (ski resort) Late Nov to late May daily 9am–4pm • Day-passes $114 • ☎ 403 705 4000, ⓦ skibanff.com • **Sunshine Meadows (summer hiking)** Shuttle/gondola mid-June to late Sept 8am–4.45pm; hourly from valley car park, daily from Banff • $42 return • Free bus from Banff to shuttle mid-June to late Sept 7am–5pm • ☎ 403 762 7889, ⓦ sunshinemeadowsbanff.com

A beautiful and unusually large tract of alpine grassland straddling the Continental Divide at 2160m, **Sunshine Meadows** is a stunning spot for both summer hiking and winter skiing and boarding. Its focus is a collection of resort buildings known as **Sunshine Village**, which includes the only slope-side accommodation in the national park (see opposite). Even better, though, is the 10m of generally soft and light annual snow that lands on 107 runs and 3358 acres of terrain. Half of this is intermediate-level; the rest is split between beginner and expert runs, the latter some of the most stunning and challenging in North America. Amenities include thirteen lifts, a day-lodge, day-care, ski school and rental shop.

In winter a **gondola** carries skiers up to the ski area from a valley car park; in summer a **bus** does the run for hikers keen to explore wildflower meadows and high-alpine hiking on a few connecting trails. A free sketch map from the Sunshine Meadows Nature Centre in the ski village shows two major **trails** – to Healy Pass and to Mount Assiniboine (both serious ventures) – and a superb little loop that uses the first sections of each to connect four viewpoints and three lakes for a 9–14km hike. You can also access the area by walking up from the valley car park, but it's an arduous 6km gravel road.

Bow Valley Parkway

The **Bow Valley Parkway** boasts more scenic splendour than Hwy-1 – which is saying something – and offers more distractions: several trails, campgrounds, plus plenty of accommodation choices and one excellent eating option. This makes the Parkway the preferable route if you have the time, and you should try to fit in at least one of the **trails** en route, in particular the easy but impressive Johnston Canyon Trail (see box below).

The largest concentration of sightseers is likely to be found at the Merrent turn-off, enjoying fantastic views of the Bow Valley and the railway winding through the mountains. Be aware before you set off though that the southern end of the Bow Valley Parkway – south of Johnston Canyon – is usually closed every day from early March to late June between 8pm and 8am to give the wildlife some peace. Closures are clearly posted – or consult a park visitor centre in advance for the current arrangements.

Backswamp Viewpoint and the Mule Shoe Picnic Area

Around 8km down the highway, look out for the **Backswamp Viewpoint**, where the panorama extends to the mountains and across a river swamp area where you might see beaver, muskrat, osprey and other birds, as well as the common butterwort, a purple-flowered carnivorous plant whose diet consists largely of marsh insects. In winter, the viewpoint is also one of the most likely areas to spot wolves; at other times of the year you might also see bighorn sheep or mountain goats on the slopes above. About 3km beyond Backswamp Viewpoint you come to **Mule Shoe Picnic Area**, a spot noted for its good birdwatching.

Pilot Lake and around

Some 11km on from Mule Shoe Picnic Area, a 400m trail takes you to a lovely little lake once known as Lizard Lake after the long-toed salamanders that thrived here. These were eaten when the lake was stocked with trout, so it was renamed **Pilot Lake**. About 3km beyond is the trailhead for the **Johnston Canyon Trail**, deservedly the most popular in the area (see box opposite); 3km beyond that is **Moose Meadows**, where you'll be mighty lucky to see any moose: habitat changes have forced them out.

ACCOMMODATION   **HWY-1 AND THE BOW VALLEY PARKWAY**

LODGES AND HOTELS

★ **Baker Creek Chalets** Hwy-1A,12km southeast of Lake Louise, 60km northwest of Banff ☎403 522 3761, ⓦbakercreek.com; map p.562. Log-cabin complex with a mix of one- and two-room options that sleep up to six, as well as suites in the main lodge. The range in style and price is fairly broad, but all interiors share much the same rustic feel, a vibe helped by the absence of TVs and phones – and slow wi-fi. Facilities include a sauna, gym and a cosy guest lounge. There's also an excellent restaurant, the *Baker Creek Bistro* (see page 579). $515

Castle Mountain Chalets Castle Junction, 32km from Banff on Hwy-1A ☎403 762 3868, ☎877 762 2281, ⓦcastlemountain.com; map p.562. The individual log cabins and chalets here might seem a bit too polished, but they provide plenty of creature comforts. The chalets for four with kitchenettes and fireplaces are more expensive, but the best option is the delightful deluxe cabins for four, five or six people, with full kitchen, dishwasher and hot-tub. $265

Johnston Canyon Resort Hwy-1A, 26km west of Banff ☎403 762 2971, ☎888 378 1720, ⓦjohnstoncanyon.

8

BACKCOUNTRY HIKING IN BANFF NATIONAL PARK

Some of the best **backcountry hiking** options lie in the Egypt Lake area, accessible from the Sunshine Village (see page 576) car park, with good side-trails radiating from the lake's campground. Elsewhere in the backcountry around Banff the choice of trails is huge. Classics include routes that lead from Banff to Lake Louise – the Sawback Trail and the Bow Valley Highline – or the tracks in the Upper Spray and Bryant Creek Valley south of town. You'll need topographic maps to tackle any of these.

   Wherever you choose to hike in the backcountry, your first step should be to read the "Backpacking" section of the **Banff National Park** website (ⓦpc.gc.ca). Then you'll need to come up with a planned hike with dates and **book** the relevant backcountry campgrounds ($11.70 booking fee, plus $9.80/night) up to six months in advance either online, by phone (☎403 762 1556), or in person at the Banff (see page 569) or Lake Louise visitor centres (see page 582). This per-night fee is variously called a Backcountry Permit but also covers camping at a particular backcountry campground. You should check online or with a visitor centre just before your hike for very latest on trail conditions and closures. The sooner you book your spot, the better, as the most popular of the fifty-odd backcountry campgrounds fill up well in advance. Reserve ahead in particular for Marvel Lake, Egypt Lake, Luellen Lake, Aylmer Pass, Mystic Meadow, Fish Lakes, Paradise Valley, Hidden Lake, Baker Lake, Merlin Meadows, Red Deer Lakes and Mount Rundle.

TOP TRAILS OFF THE BOW VALLEY PARKWAY AND HWY-1

Five major **trails** branch off the Bow Valley Parkway, while there are two outstanding options along Hwy-1.

BOW VALLEY PARKWAY

The best short walk is the **Johnston Canyon Trail** (2.7km each way), 25km from Banff, an incredibly engineered path to a series of spray-veiled waterfalls. The Lower Falls are 1.1km, the Upper Falls 2.7km from the trailhead on the Parkway. From the Upper Falls you can continue on to the seven cold-water springs of the Ink Pots, which emerge in pretty open meadows, to make a total distance of 5.8km (215m ascent; 4hr return).

Another short possibility is the **Castle Crags Trail** (3.7km each way; 520m ascent from the signed turn-off 5km west of Castle Junction). Short but steep, and above the tree-line, this walk offers superb views across the Bow Valley and the mountains beyond. Allow ninety minutes one-way to take account of the stiff climb.

The best day-hike is to **Rockbound Lake** (8.4km each way), a steepish climb to 2210m with wild lakeland scenery at the end; allow at least two and a half hours one-way, due to the 760m ascent. Another fifteen minutes' walk beyond Rockbound and Tower lakes at the end of the trail lies the beautiful Silverton waterfall. The other Parkway trails – **Baker Creek** (20.3km) and **Pulsatilla Pass** (17.1km) – serve to link backcountry hikers with the dense network of paths in the Slate Range northeast of Lake Louise.

HWY-1

The trek to **Bourgeau Lake** (7.5km one way) is considered by many to be among the top five day-hikes in Banff; it starts from a parking area 10km west of Banff – allow two and a half to three hours for the 725m ascent. The second is the long day-hike to **Shadow Lake** (14.3km each way), where the lakeside campground (at 1840m), in an impressive subalpine basin, gives access to assorted onward trails; the main trail starts from the **Redearth Creek** parking area 20km west of Banff – allow four hours for the 440m ascent.

com; map p.562. Smart creekside wood cabins – some with fireplaces, some with kitchenettes – that retain a sense of tranquillity despite the hubbub in the neighbouring Johnston Canyon car park and the on-site restaurant, shop, garage, tennis court and barbecue area. Mid-May to early Oct. $250

★ **Storm Mountain Lodge** Hwy-93, 27km from Banff via Hwy-1 ☎ 403 762 4155, ⓦ stormmountainlodge. com; map p.562. A collection of fourteen authentically rustic 1920s log cabins with immaculate interiors that include wood-burning stone fireplaces, clawfoot tubs and hand-crafted log bed-frames. There's a good restaurant and lounge, and hikers' picnic lunches can be ordered. $354

Sunshine Inn Sunshine Village, 15km west of Banff via Hwy-1 ☎ 403 277 7669, ☎ 877 542 2633, ⓦ sunshinemountainlodge.com; map p.562. The only ski-in, ski-out option in Banff National Park, this modest 84-room hotel is accessed by gondola (other transport available outside gondola operating times) and lies remote from Banff services. You're guaranteed first tracks, but options when the lifts close are more limited, though there is a restaurant, two bars and small convenience store. A huge hot tub, sauna, exercise and games room, and a children's programme every evening are added bonuses. Early Dec to early April. $245

HOSTELS AND CAMPGROUNDS

Castle Mountain Campground Castle Junction, 32km from Banff on Hwy-1A; map p.562. Set in a beautiful wooded area near Castle Junction, this 43-pitch, first-come, first-served site has no facilities beyond hot and cold running water, flush toilets, kitchen shelters and fire pits – but is close to a small store and restaurant. Mid-June to early Sept. Sites $21.50

Castle Mountain Hostel Castle Junction, 32km from Banff on Hwy-1A; ☎ 403 762 2367, ☎ 866 762 4122, ⓦ hihostels.ca; map p.562. This is a basic but atmospheric hostel, thanks largely to a wood-burning stove and large bay windows in its common room, but its real strong point is its closeness to cross-country skiing, hiking and biking trails. July–Sept. Dorms $17, non-members $24

Johnston Canyon Campground Hwy-1A, 22km from Banff; map p.562. As the best-equipped and closest Bow Valley Parkway site to Banff and with reservable sites in a prime location at the Johnston Canyon trailhead. Facilities include hot and cold running water, showers, flush toilets and fire pits. June to mid-Sept. Sites $27.40

Protection Mountain Campground Hwy-1A, 48km from Banff; map p.562. Just north of Castle Junction, this primitive park-run campground has 72 pitches, none of which are reservable. With flush toilets, piped cold water, kitchen shelters and fire pits. Late June to early Sept. Sites $21.50

EATING

★ **Baker Creek Bistro** In the Baker Creek Chalets (see page 577), Hwy-1A, 12km east of Lake Louise ☎ 403 522 2182, ⓦ bakercreek.com; map p.562. Romantic dining in a softly lit log cabin outfitted with deer-antler chandeliers. The menu offers innovative steaks, pastas and good game dishes, and everything is home-made: apple cake is the house speciality. Mains $30–41. June–Sept daily 7.30–10am, 11.30am–2.30pm & 5–9pm; Oct–May hours vary.

Lake Louise and around

Banff National Park's other main centre, **LAKE LOUISE**, is very different from Banff – less a town than two distinct artificial resorts. The first is a small mall of shops and hotels just off the Trans-Canada known as **Lake Louise Village**. The second is the **lake** itself, 4.5km from the village (and 200m higher) on the winding Lake Louise Drive, the self-proclaimed "gem of the Rockies" and – despite its crowds and monster hotel – a sight you must see. A third area, **Moraine Lake**, 13km south of the village, has almost equally staggering scenery and almost unparalleled **hiking country**. All three areas are packed in summer; in winter, things slow down considerably, though plenty still turn up for some of Canada's best **downhill skiing** at the nearby ski area as well as the hundreds of kilometres of **cross-country** skiing trails and numerous other winter activities.

Lake Louise Village

Lake Louise Village doesn't amount to much, but it's an essential supply stop, with more or less everything you need in terms of food, accommodation, information and equipment rental. The village centres on the Samson Mall and car park, with a smart hostel and a couple of hotels dotted along the service road to the north.

Lake Louise Ski Area

3km east of Lake Louise Village • Daily: mid-May to mid-June, late Sept & early Nov to mid-May 9am–4.30pm; mid-June to early Sept 9am–5pm • Winter day-pass $114; summer gondola $38 • ☎ 877 956 8473, ⓦ skilouise.com • Free shuttle buses run from Lake Louise hotels

Lake Louise is among the finest North American **ski** areas, with some of the best powder snow on the continent and stunning landscapes to boot. It also offers something for everyone, with its 139 runs and 4200 acres divided fairly evenly between every ability level and served by eight lifts at which short lines are usual. Glorious, groomed green and blue runs cover the front of the mountain, while behind, a series of **back bowls** are flecked with some really taxing black-diamond terrain. The ski area also offers the full range of facilities, from nurseries and ski schools to restaurants and bars. The only real drawback is the potential for phenomenally low January and February **temperatures**.

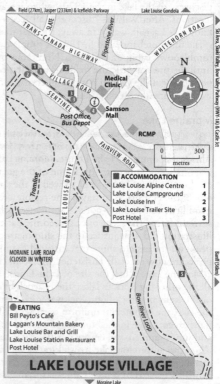

8

ACCOMMODATION

Lake Louise Alpine Centre	1
Lake Louise Campground	4
Lake Louise Inn	2
Lake Louise Trailer Site	5
Post Hotel	3

EATING

Bill Peyto's Café	1
Laggan's Mountain Bakery	4
Lake Louise Bar and Grill	4
Lake Louise Station Restaurant	2
Post Hotel	3

LAKE LOUISE VILLAGE

In summer the **Lake Louise Gondola** takes thirteen minutes to whisk visitors to 2088m for sensational views from the side of Mount Whitehorn. There's also a self-service restaurant here, along with sun decks, picnic areas, souvenir shops and trailheads through the woods and meadows, one leading to the summit of Mount Whitehorn (2669m).

Lake Louise

You can walk between the village and the lake (the uphill hike is 2.7km on the Louise Creek Trail or 4.5km along the Tramline Trail), but you're better off saving the walking for around the lake and taking a free shuttle bus from the Lake Louise Overflow parking lot 6km south of Lake Louise village via Hwy 1 (mid-May to early Oct; every 15min; 8am–4.30pm).

Before you see **Lake Louise** you see the hotel: *Château Lake Louise*, a grandiose monstrosity that would surely never get planning permission today. Yet even so intrusive an eyesore fades into insignificance beside the immense beauty of its surroundings. The lake is brilliant turquoise, the mountains sheer, the glaciers vast; the whole ensemble is perfection. Outfitter Tom Wilson, the first white Canadian to see Lake Louise when he was led here by a local Aboriginal in 1882, wrote: "I never, in all my explorations of these five chains of mountains throughout western Canada, saw such a matchless scene... I felt puny in body, but glorified in spirit and soul."

You can't help wishing you could have been Tom Wilson, and seen the spot unsullied by the hotel and before the arrival of the tourists and general clutter. In peak season, around ten thousand visitors daily come here to gawp, while noticeboards on the waterfront seem obsessed with the profoundly dull account of how the lake came by its name (in honour of the fourth daughter of Queen Victoria). The Aboriginal name translates as the "Lake of the Little Fishes". Wilson, showing precious little wit, originally called it Emerald Lake. More interesting is the account of Hollywood's discovery of the lake in the 1920s, when it was used to suggest exotic European locations. After Wilson's "discovery" all access was by rail or trail – the station, then known as Laggan, was 6km away; the first road was built in 1926.

The first hotel appeared in 1890, a simple two-bedroom affair which replaced a tumbledown cabin on the shore. Numerous fires, false starts and additions followed until the present structure made its appearance. Be sure to have a walk here, despite the popularity of the various paths, and consider **canoeing**; gliding through the turquoise waters seems almost magical.

Moraine Lake

If you're without your own transport, you'll have to rely on a bike or take the free shuttle bus from Lake Louise Overflow parking lot (6km south of Lake Louise village via Hwy 1; mid-May to early-Oct every 15mins: 8 am–4.15pm).

Almost as popular as Lake Louise, **Moraine Lake** is its smaller neighbour and in many ways its scenic superior. This is one of the great landscapes of the region, offering some cracking trails (see page 582), as well as the splendid yet discreet *Moraine Lake Lodge*, one of the best places to stay in the region (see page 584). Bar the lodge, with its good little café and top-notch restaurant, nothing disturbs the lake and its matchless surroundings. The scene once graced the back of Canadian $20 notes, though the illustration did little justice to the shimmering water and the jagged, snow-covered peaks on the eastern shore that inspired the nickname "Valley of the Ten Peaks". The peaks are now officially christened the Wenkchemna, after the Stoney word for "ten".

Moraine Lake is half the size of Lake Louise but an even more vivid turquoise. As with all the other big Rockies lakes, the peacock blue is caused by fine particles of glacial silt, or till, known as rock flour. Meltwater in June and July washes this powdered rock into the lake, the minute but uniform particles of flour absorbing all colours of incoming light except those in the blue–green spectrum. When the lakes have just melted in May and June – and are still empty of silt – their colour is a more normal sky-blue.

You can admire the lake by walking along the east shore, or from above by clambering over the great glacial moraine dam near the lodge (though the lake was probably created by a rock fall rather than glaciation); alternatively, rent a **canoe** from just beyond the lodge and car park. For the best overall perspective, tackle the Larch Valley–Sentinel Pass trail through the forest on the east shore (see page 582).

ARRIVAL AND DEPARTURE

By bus Parks Canada Shuttles to Lake Louise (mid-May to early-Oct) Brewster (May–Oct; ⓦ brewstertransportation.

LAKE LOUISE AND AROUND

com) buses stop several locations around Lake Louise including at the Samson Mall and the lake itself.

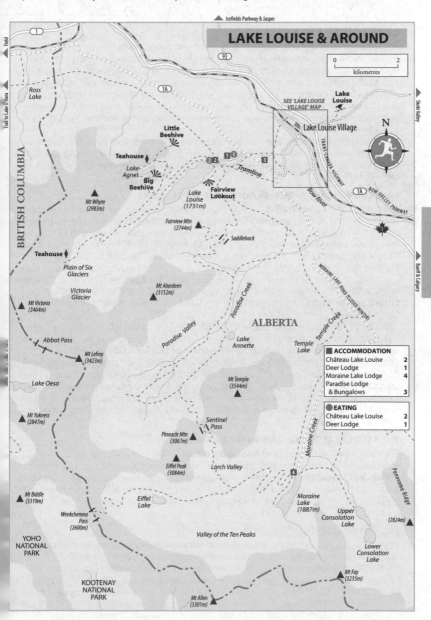

Destinations Banff (6-13 daily; 1hr); Calgary (5 daily; 3hr 30min); Calgary Airport (8 daily; 3hr).

GETTING AROUND AND INFORMATION

Lake Louise Visitor Centre Samson Mall (May to mid-June & Sept to mid-Oct daily 9am–5pm; mid-June to Aug daily 9am–7pm; mid-Oct to April Thurs–Sun 9am–4.30pm, ☏ 403 522 3833 ⓦ pc.gc.ca). As well as information, there are a few good natural-history exhibits.

LAKE LOUISE AREA HIKES

The Lake Louise Ski Area has some of the most heavily used **trails** on the continent, trodden by fifty thousand-plus people in summer. All the trails are well worn and well marked, and don't require you to be a seasoned hiker or skilled map-reader. A couple even pass **teahouses** – mountain chalets selling welcome, if pricey, snacks. Before hiking, check with the **visitor centre** in Lake Louise (see page 582) on the latest restrictions imposed due to **bear activity**. Sometimes you need to walk in groups of at least four, but with people often waiting to join a group at trailheads, making up the numbers shouldn't be a problem.

Shorter strolls alongside Lake Louise and Moraine Lake are doable by all. If you're after a more strenuous, but relatively short day-hike the top choices are the Lake Agnes–Plain of the Six Glaciers loop from Lake Louise and the Larch Valley–Sentinel Pass hike from Moraine Lake.

LAKE LOUISE–LAKE AGNES–PLAIN OF THE SIX GLACIERS

The signed **Lake Agnes Trail** (3.4km), said to be the most-walked path in the Rockies (but don't let that put you off), strikes off from the right (north) shore of the lake immediately past the hotel. It's a gradual 400m climb, relieved by ever more magnificent views and a teahouse beautifully situated beside mountain-cradled Lake Agnes (2135m); allow one to two hours. If you want more of a walk, things quieten down considerably beyond the teahouse. You can continue on the right side of the lake and curve left around its head to climb to an easily reached pass. Here a 200m stroll to the left brings you to **Big Beehive** (2255m), an incredible eyrie, 1km from the teahouse. Almost as rewarding is the trail, also 1km from the teahouse, to **Little Beehive**, a mite lower, but still privy to full-blown panoramas over the broad sweep of the Bow Valley.

Keener walkers can return to the pass from Big Beehive and turn left to follow the steep trail down to intersect another trail; turning right leads west through rugged and increasingly barren scenery to the second teahouse at the **Plain of the Six Glaciers** (2100m). Alternatively, the more monotonous Six Glaciers Trail (leaving out the whole Lake Agnes–Big Beehive section) leads from the hotel along the lakeshore to the same point (5.3km to the teahouse; 365m ascent). However, a better option is to follow the Lake Agnes and Big Beehive route to the Plain, then use the Six Glaciers Trail for the return to *Château Lake Louise*, which neatly ends the day's loop with a downhill stroll and an easy but glorious finale along the shore of Lake Louise.

THE SADDLEBACK TRAIL AND FAIRVIEW MOUNTAIN

The main appeal of the less-used **Saddleback Trail** (3.7km one way), that starts on the southern side of the Lake Louise parking lot, is that it provides access to the superb viewpoint of **Fairview Mountain**. Allow one to two hours to Saddleback itself (2330m; 595m ascent); the trail to the summit of Fairview (2744m) strikes off right from here. Even if you don't make the last push, the Saddleback views – across to the 1200m wall of Mount Temple (3544m) – are staggering.

PARADISE VALLEY

In 1894, the mountaineer Walter Wilcox deemed **Paradise Valley** an appropriate name for "a valley of surpassing beauty, wide and beautiful, with alternating open meadows and rich forests". North of Moraine Lake, it's accessed via Moraine Lake Road, about 3km from its junction with Lake Louise Drive. The walk is a fairly straightforward hike up one side of the valley and down the other, a loop of 18km (7–8hr) with 385m of vertical gain. Along the way Lake Annette provides an

ACTIVITIES

SUMMER

Canoeing June–Sept daily 11am–7pm; $105/30min from lakeside boathouses at both Lake Louise and Moraine Lake.

Cycling You can rent mountain and road bikes from Wilson

Mountain Sports (☎ 403 522 3511, ⓦ wmsll.com) in Lake Louise Village. Prices start at $39/day.

Fishing For trout fishing on the Bow River get advice from *Castle Mountain Chalets* (see page 577). Rental equipment

unmatched view of Mount Temple's 1200m north face. You can stay overnight at the Horseshoe Meadow backcountry campground at the head of the valley (9km from the trailhead), though this is popular and often full. A stiff climb over loose rock up to Sentinel Pass on the south side of the valley allows you to connect with the Moraine Lake trails.

THE SKOKI VALLEY

The **Skoki Valley** region east of Lake Louise offers fewer day-hikes; to enjoy it you'll need a tent to stay overnight at any of the six backcountry campgrounds. The trailhead begins off a gravel road that runs behind the Lake Louise Ski Area, off Hwy-1. Many people hike out-and-back to Boulder Pass (2345m), an 8.6km trek and 640m ascent from the trailhead (6–7hr round trip). *Skoki Lodge* lies 8km beyond; various well-signposted long and short trails running from here and the backc.0ountry campgrounds are detailed in leaflets available from the visitor centre.

MORAINE LAKE AND CONSOLATION LAKE

The easiest Moraine Lake area walks are the 1km amble along its shores, followed by the 3km stroll to **Consolation Lake**, an hour's trip that may be busy but can provide some respite from the frenzy at Moraine Lake itself. This almost level walk ends with lovely views of a small, mountain-circled lake, its name coined by an early explorer who thought it a reward and "consolation" for the desolation of the valley that led to it. If you're happy to camp overnight, are fairly fit, or can arrange a pick-up, you could take the highline **Panorama Ridge Trail** (2255m), which branches off the trail (signed "Taylor Lake") to run 22km to the Banff–Radium Hwy 7km west of Castle Junction.

MORAINE LAKE–LARCH VALLEY–SENTINEL PASS TRAIL

One of the Rockies' premier hikes, the popular **Larch Valley–Sentinel Pass Trail** sets off from the lake's north shore, 100m beyond the lodge, and takes around four hours for the return trip. A fairly stiff climb through forest on a broad track, with breathtaking views of the lake through the trees, brings you to a trail junction after 2.4km and some 300m of ascent. Most hikers branch right – left goes to Eiffel Lake (see below) – where the track levels into Larch Valley, broad, alpine upland with stands of larch and majestic views of the encircling peaks. If you have the energy, push on to Sentinel Pass, in all some two hours' walk and 720m above Moraine Lake. At 2611m, this is the highest trail over a pass in the Canadian Rockies. You can take much of the view from the vantage point of the meadows, but the airy vistas over Paradise Valley are reserved for the crest of the pass itself. You could even continue down into Paradise Valley, a tough, scree-filled descent, and complete an exceptional day's walk by dropping down into Lake Louise Village, or circling back on trails that parallel the Moraine Lake Road.

MORAINE LAKE–EIFFEL LAKE–WENCHEMNA PASS TRAIL

This third Moraine Lake option, the less-walked **Moraine Lake–Eiffel Lake–Wenchemna Pass Trail**, follows the same climb from the lake as for the Larch Valley path before branching off left instead of right at the 2.4km junction. It's equally sound, virtually level and if anything has the better scenery, taking in the stark, glaciated grandeur at the head of the **Valley of the Ten Peaks**. At 2255m, Eiffel Lake is a 5.6km hike and 370m climb (allow 2–3hr) from Moraine Lake, and you don't need to go much further than the rock pile and clump of trees beyond the lake to get the best out of the walk. Ahead of you, a slightly rougher track continues through bleak terrain to Wenchemna Pass (2600m), clearly visible 4km beyond, which offers still broader views of the Valley of the Ten Peaks as well as into Yoho and Kootenay parks.

8

is on offer at Wilson Mountain Sports (see page 583). Compulsory fishing permits ($9.80/day) are available from the visitor centre (see page 582).

Hiking For a guided hike contact Great Divide (☎403 522 2733, ⊚greatdivide.ca), which offers several full- and half-day hikes in the area from $94/person. Wilson Mountain Sports (see above) rents out a range of hiking and mountaineering gear.

Horseriding Brewster Lake Louise Stables at *Château Lake Louise* (☎403 762 5454, ⊚brewsteradventures.com) and the similar but slightly cheaper Timberline Tours (☎403 522 3743, ⊚timberlinetours.ca), behind the *Deer Lodge*, organize rides to many local destinations, including the shores of Lake Louise, Lake Agnes, Plain of the Six Glaciers, Paradise Valley, Horseshoe Glacier and the Skoki Valley – Timberline offers pick-ups and drop-offs at the *Skoki Lodge*. Rides range from around $80/1hr 30min to $199 for a full-day ride with lunch. Timberline also organizes overnight trips for up to ten nights.

Rafting Wild Water Adventures (☎888 647 6444, ⊚wildwater.com) runs gentle trips and whitewater rafting adventures on the Kicking Horse River in Yoho National Park. Half-day trips cost from $105, including transport from Lake Louise.

WINTER

Cross-country skiing There are plenty of options around Lake Louise itself, on Moraine Lake Rd and in the Skoki Valley north of the village. Wilson Mountain Sports (see above) has gear to buy or rent.

Dog-sledding Kingmik Dog Sled Tours (☎403 763 8887, ☎877 919 7779, ⊚kingmikdogsledtours.com) runs tours – from 30min romps ($199 for two people) to trips to Yoho (1hr 30min) for $270.

Ice-skating Ice-skating on the floodlit lake in front of *Château Lake Louise* is a spine-tingling experience; hire skates from inside the hotel at Chateau Mountain Sports (daily 8am–8pm; $16/day; ☎403 522 3837, ⊚chateaumountainsports.com).

Sleigh rides Brewster (☎403 762 5454, ⊚brewster adventures.com) offers 45min rides for $37/person from *Château Lake Louise*; reservations are necessary.

Snowmobiling White N Wild adventures in Golden (☎250 344 6546, ☎800 668 9119, ⊚whitenwild.ca) organizes all-inclusive snowmobiling trips from $195/person for half a day.

8 | ACCOMMODATION

Hotel **accommodation** in or near Lake Louise is always pricey and often full in summer; when reservations six months in advance are not unusual. Bow Valley Parkway (see page 576) options, including the *Castle Mountain Hostel* and *Baker Creek Chalets*, are within easy driving distance.

HOTELS

★**Château Lake Louise** Lake Louise Drive, 4km west of Lake Louise Village ☎403 522 3511, ☎800 257 7544, ⊚fairmont.com/lake-louise; map p.581. Imposing landmark hotel with commanding views over Lake Louise from its 511 grand rooms and suites. The hotel is worth a look alone for its bizarre fusion of alpine and neocolonial furnishings. Its battery of five-star facilities includes several bars and restaurants. Rates are slashed in the off-season (Oct–Dec), when good-value ski packages are offered too. $849

★**Deer Lodge** Lake Louise Drive, 3.5km west of Lake Louise Village ☎403 522 3991, ⊚crmr.com; map p.581. The labyrinthine lodgings in this 1920s log teahouse contrast with the pomp of its neighbour, *Château Lake Louise*, a short walk away. This is far more relaxed and focused on getting away from it all; rooms come with phones, but no TV. The rooftop hot tub has fantastic views, and there's a sauna, restaurant and lounge. $289

Lake Louise Inn 210 Village Rd ☎403 522 3791, ☎800 661 9237, ⊚lakelouiseinn.com; map p.579. The least expensive village hotel, with nine varieties of room, some with kitchens, balconies and gas or wood fireplaces.

Facilities include a heated indoor pool, hot tub and sauna. $175

★**Moraine Lake Lodge** Moraine Lake, 14km south of Lake Louise Village ☎403 522 3733, ☎877 522 2777, ⊚morainelake.com; map p.581. One of the most enticing and magnificent hotels in the Rockies, with high-quality cabins and lodge rooms designed by architect Arthur Erickson (also behind the Vancouver's UBC Museum of Anthropology). Open fires give the cabins edge. June–Sept. $714

★**Paradise Lodge and Bungalows** Lake Louise Drive, 2.3km west of Lake Louise Village ☎403 522 3595, ⊚paradiselodge.com; map p.581. A 10min walk from *Château Lake Louise*, with 21 self-contained bungalows and 24 one- and two-bedroom suites (some with kitchens) and reasonable off-season rates. Mid-May to mid-Oct. $310

★**Post Hotel** Village Rd ☎403 522 3989, ☎800 661 1586, ⊚posthotel.com; map p.579. Grand log chalet-hotel that is the top spot in the village, with a noted restaurant and bar (see page 585), pretty riverside setting, a good pool and fitness facilities. $445

HOSTEL AND CAMPGROUNDS

★**Lake Louise Alpine Centre** 203 Village Rd ☎403 522 2201, ⊚hihostels.ca; map p.579. Excellent, mountain chalet-style hostel an easy walk from Lake Louise Village. Its sparkling facilities include a communal kitchen, laundry, mountaineering library and a handy restaurant; there's also internet access and free wi-fi. Reservations are virtually essential, up to six months in advance for summer and for winter ski weekends. Dorms $47.50, non-members $53; doubles $144, non-members $159

Lake Louise Campground Fairview Rd, 1km from Lake Louise Village ☎877 737 3783, ⓦpccamping.ca; map p.579. Attractive and convenient but busy park-run site with 206 pitches, hot and cold water, showers, flush toilets and kitchen shelters. Its trees offer some privacy, but with sites close together and the railway line nearby, the place is generally noisy. Late June to late Sept, but in early spring

and late autumn tents are not permitted due to bears – check with park authorities before booking. Sites $27.40

Lake Louise Trailer Site 1km south of Lake Louise Village on Fairview Rd ☎450 505 8302, ☎877 737 3783, ⓦpccamping.ca; map p.579. RV-only area adjacent to *Lake Louise Campground* with 189 sites available in summer, 30 in winter. Facilities include hook-ups, hot and cold running water and showers. Late June to late Sept. RVs $32.30

EATING

★ **Bill Peyto's Café** 203 Village Rd ☎403 522 2201; map p.579. This relaxed hostel café open to non-guests serves great snacks and reasonably priced full meals. The menu includes sandwiches, burgers, mountainous nachos, salads and pasta, along with more unusual items like a *souvlaki* platter – all in the $8–20 range. The huge all-day breakfast costs $12. Daily 7am–4pm.

Château Lake Louise Lake Louise Drive, 4km west of Lake Louise Village ☎403 522 351; map p.581. The grand hotel has several bars and restaurants. The *Poppy Brasserie* is the family option, with a buffet breakfast ($34), extensive Sunday brunch ($40), and evening pizza and pasta buffet ($35). The *Walliser Stube* is the fine-dining option, specializing in Swiss food, with an excellent fondue selection (basic two-person cheese fondue $48) and raclette, along with some local fish and game dishes; main courses cost $38–55. Hours vary, but there is always something open 8am–11pm.

Deer Lodge Lake Louise Drive, 3.5km west of Lake Louise Village ☎403 522 3991; map p.581. This venerable hotel has a couple of dining options. The *Mount Fairview Dining Room* (reservations ☎403 522 4202) oozes rustic charm and has a great menu based around dishes prepared by early local mountain guides. These are strong on game and include a chance to sample elk from the lodge's own ranch ($45). More casual is the *Caribou Lounge*, the lodge's original log teahouse with a magnificent view of the Victoria Glacier. Perfect for afternoon tea or an evening cognac. Daily: restaurant 7–11am & 6–9pm; lounge 11am–10pm.

Laggan's Mountain Bakery Samson Mall ☎403 522

2017; map p.579. Despite its cafeteria vibe, this is a great place for a quick breakfast and a useful place to stock up on superb basic picnic items, such as cookies, pies, sandwiches, quiche and delicious, sweet poppy-seed bread. All are baked in-house and without any artificial additives. The coffee's good too. Daily 6am–6pm.

Lake Louise Bar and Grill Samson Mall ☎403 522 3879; map p.579. The only dedicated drinking den and family diner in the Lake Louise area is upstairs in the mall, and suffers from a stairwell that looks like the entry to an old-fashioned public lavatory. Good for boozing and billiards but don't expect much from the food. Daily 7am–11pm.

Lake Louise Station Restaurant 200 Sentinel Road ☎403 522 2600, ⓦlakelouisestation.com; map p.579. Unusual restaurant in a restored 1909 station building; choose between hearty Canadian food in the informal station building and the more formal and expensive menu in the restored railway dining carriages. Mains $22–52. Daily 11.30am–9.30pm.

★ **Post Hotel** Village Rd ☎403 522 3989, ☎800 661 1586, ⓦposthotel.com; map p.579. The gourmet restaurant at this high-end hotel has a cosy atmosphere thanks to its low ceilings and crackling wood fire. The rich meat and fish mains (average $60) are served with phenomenal sauces, while the list of accompanying wines has a strong French bias. Their fondues are the real deal: the chef is Swiss. Dinner reservations are advised. Also here is the *Outpost Pub*, a sports bar with good pub food (mains $18–28). Daily: restaurant 7am–2pm & 5–10pm; bar from late afternoon.

Icefields Parkway

The splendour of the **Icefields Parkway** (Hwy-93) can hardly be overstated: a 230km road from Lake Louise to Jasper through the heart of the Rockies, it ranks as one of the world's best drives. Its unending succession of huge peaks, immense glaciers, iridescent lakes, wildflower meadows, wildlife and forests – capped by the stark grandeur of the Columbia Icefield – can be almost overwhelming. Although about a million people a year take this route, for the most part you can go your own way in relative serenity.

You could drive the whole highway in about four hours, but to do so would be to miss out on the panoply of short (and long) **trails**, **viewpoints** and the chance to soak up the incredible **scenery**. If you want to make a day-trip of the Icefields Parkway, your best bet is to go just as far as the **Columbia Icefield**, the highlight for many, then turn back, since the landscape is a touch less dramatic along the northern half of the road. A free pamphlet from Parks Canada visitor centres provides a detailed map and summary of all sights and trailheads, and bus tours along the route are available (see page 588).

Brief history

Fur traders and Aboriginal people who used the route as far back as 1800 reputedly christened it the "Wonder Trail", though they tended to prefer the Pipestone River Valley to the east as it avoided the swamps and other hazards of the Bow Valley. The present highway was only completed in 1939 and opened in 1940 as part of a Depression-era public-works programme.

Bow Lake and Bow Glacier Falls

A great short trail sets off from beside the *Num-Ti-Jah Lodge* (see page 589), 37km from Lake Louise, to **Bow Lake** and **Bow Glacier Falls** (4.3km; 155m ascent; 1–2hr one way), taking in the flats around Bow Lake – one of the Rockies' most beautiful – and climbing to some immense cliffs and several huge waterfalls beyond (the trail proper ends at the edge of a moraine after 3.4km, but it's possible to pick your way through the boulders to reach the foot of the falls 900m beyond). There's also a pleasant waterfront picnic area at the southeast end of the lake.

Bow Summit and Peyto Lake

Three kilometres up the Parkway from *Num-Ti-Jah Lodge* comes the pass at **Bow Summit** (40km from Lake Louise), source of the Bow River, the waterway that flows through Banff, Lake Louise and Calgary. At 2069m this is the highest point crossed by any Canadian highway. Just beyond is the unmissable twenty-minute stroll to **Peyto Lake Lookout** (1.4km; 100m), one of the finest vistas in the Rockies. The beautiful panorama only unfolds in the last seconds, giving a breathtaking view of the vivid emerald lake far below; mountains and forest stretch away as far as you can see. Another 3km along the Parkway lies a viewpoint for the **Peyto Glacier**, part of the much larger Wapta Icefield.

Chephren Lake and Mistaya Canyon

Some 57km from Lake Louise you reach the *Waterfowl Lakes Campground* and the **Chephren Lake Trail** (3.5km; 80m ascent; 1hr one way), which leads to quietly spectacular scenery with a minimum of effort. The next pause, 14km further along the Parkway, is the **Mistaya Canyon Trail**, a short but interesting 300m stroll along a river-gouged "slot" canyon.

Saskatchewan Crossing

The hamlet of **Saskatchewan Crossing** (77km from Lake Louise) is the lowest point on the road before the icefields; the 700m descent from Bow Summit brings you from the high subalpine region into a montane environment with its own vegetation and wildlife. Largely free of snow, the area is a winter favourite for mountain goats, bighorn sheep and deer and is one of the best black bear habitats close to the road anywhere in the park. The bleak settlement itself offers expensive food (restaurant and cafeteria), petrol, a tacky gift shop and *The Crossing* motel and pub (see page 589).

Big Hill to Sunwapta Pass

Shortly before the spectacular **Panther Falls** (113.5km from Lake Louise), the road makes a huge hairpin climb (the so-called "Big Hill"), to open up yet more panoramic angles on the vast mountain spine stretching back towards Lake Louise. The unmarked and often slippery 1km trail to the falls starts from the lower end of the second of two car parks on the right.

Further down the road (117km from Lake Louise) is the trailhead to **Parker Ridge** (2.4km one way; ascent 210m; 1hr30min return), which, at 2130m, commands fantastic views from the summit ridge of the Saskatchewan Glacier (at 9km, the Rockies' longest). If you're only going to do one walk after the Peyto Lake Lookout, make it this one; it gets cold and windy up here, so bring extra clothing.

Nearby **Sunwapta Pass** (122km; 2023m) marks the border between Banff and Jasper national parks and the watershed of the North Saskatchewan and Sunwapta rivers: the former flows into the Atlantic, the latter into the Arctic Ocean. From here it's another 108km to Jasper.

Wilcox Pass trail

The *Wilcox Creek Campground* (see page 589), 130km from Lake Louise, is also the trailhead for one of the finest hikes in the national park, never mind the highway: the **Wilcox Pass trail** (4km one way; 335m ascent; 2hr round trip). The path takes you steeply through thick spruce and alpine fir forest before emerging suddenly onto a ridge that offers vast views over the Parkway and the high peaks of the Icefield, including Mount Athabasca. Beyond, the trail enters a beautiful spread of meadows, tarns and creeks, an area many people choose to halt at or wander all day without bothering to reach the pass itself. You could extend the walk to 11km (one way) by dropping from the pass to Tangle Falls further along the parkway.

Columbia Icefield

Just beyond Sunwapta Pass (133km from Lake Louise) and covering an area of 325 square kilometres, the **Columbia Icefield** is the largest collection of ice and snow in the entire Rockies, and the biggest glacial area in the northern hemisphere outside the Arctic Circle. It's also the most accessible of some seventeen glacial areas along the Parkway. Meltwater flows from the Icefield into the Arctic, Atlantic and Pacific oceans, forming a so-called "hydrological apex" – the only other one in the world is in Siberia. This is fed by six major glaciers, three of which – the Athabasca, Dome and Stutfield – are partially visible from the highway.

Icefield Centre and the Glacier Skywalk

Icefield Centre Daily May to Sept 9am–5pm • Free **Glacier Skywalk** Daily: Late Apr, May & Sept 10am–5pm; June to early Aug 9am–6pm; early Aug to early Sept 9am–7pm; Oct 10am–4pm • $32 • ☎ 780 852 6550, ☎ 877 423 7433; Parks Canada ☎ 780 852 6288, ⓦ banffjaspercollection.com

---

TOP 5 ICEFIELDS PARKWAY HIKES

Peyto Lake Lookout Spectacular views reward little effort. See above
Bow Lake Idyllic lakeside walk to dramatic cliffs and waterfalls. See page 586
Mistaya Canyon A short walk into a slot canyon. See page 586
Parker Ridge Quick access to fantastic views above a glacier. See above
Wilcox Pass Best walk of all: straightforward, varied and with expansive, high-alpine views. See above

8

GLACIER TOURS

Brewster's Ice Explorers run 1hr 30min, 5km **rides over the glacier** in custom buses, with a chance to get out and walk safely on the ice (daily every 15–30min: April & Oct 10am–4pm, depending on the weather; May & Sept 9am–5pm; June–Aug 9am–6pm; $99; book at the Icefield Centre or call ☎ 780 852 6550, ⓦ banffjaspercollection.com). They're heavily subscribed, so aim to avoid the peak midday rush by taking a tour before 10.30am or after 3pm.

More dedicated types can sign up for the two Athabasca Glacier **ice walks** (mid-June to early Sept daily at 9.40am; $105–175; ☎ 780 852 5595, ⓦ icewalks.com), led by licensed guides. Sign up online or at the front desk of the Icefield Centre – be sure to bring warm clothes, boots and provisions.

The busy **Icefield Centre** embellishes the background information and sheds light on both the Columbia Icefield and Canada's most extensive cave system – the **Castleguard Caves**, which honeycomb the ice but are inaccessible to the public. Above all, the centre provides a **viewpoint** for the most prominent part of the icefields: the Athabasca Glacier, which has substantially shrunk since the centre's construction – as photos there show. Crowds and tour buses, however, make this not a place to linger, unless you are here to pick-up tickets or the five-minute shuttle rides to either Brewster's Ice Explorer tours (see box below) or the somewhat over-rated **Glacier Skywalk**, a horseshoe-shaped, glass-floored walkway that elevates visitors 280 metres above the mountain goats and crashing waterfalls of the Sunwapta Valley.

Athabasca Glacier

You can walk up to the toe of the **Athabasca Glacier** from the Sunwapta Lake parking area opposite the Icefields Centre. Note the date-markers, which show just how far the glacier has retreated (1.5km in the last hundred years). It's also possible to walk onto the glacier – but not a good idea, as it's riddled with dangerous crevasses; people are injured or killed here every year. Full-scale expeditions are the preserve of experts, but you can join an **organized trip** (see box).

Sunwapta Falls

A 1km gravel spur leads off the highway to **Sunwapta Falls** (181km from Lake Louise, 54km from Jasper), fifteen minutes' walk through the woods from the road: they're not terribly dramatic unless in spate, but are interesting for the deep canyon they've cut through the surrounding valley. A short river-bank trail leads to more rapids and small falls downstream.

Athabasca Falls and Hwy-93A

The last main stop before you're in striking distance of Jasper, **Athabasca Falls** (30km from Jasper), is impressive enough, but the platforms and paths show the strain caused by thousands of tramping feet, making it hard to feel you're any longer in wilderness.

Hwy-93A, the route of the old Parkway, branches off the Icefields Parkway at Athabasca Falls and runs parallel to it for 30km. This alternative route has less dramatic views than the Parkway, as dense trees line the road, but the chances of spotting wildlife are higher. There's also the chance to peel off on the 14km drive to Cavell Meadows (see page 593).

ARRIVAL AND GETTING AROUND   ICEFIELDS PARKWAY

By bus Brewster Transportation (☎ 403 762 6710, ⓦ brewstertransportation.com) runs several tours and a single scheduled bus daily in both directions between Banff, Lake Louise and Jasper from late May to mid-October.

A word with the driver will usually get you dropped off at hostels and trailheads en route. Brewster also organizes 7hr bus tours on the Icefields Parkway (late April to late Oct daily; $221; ☎ 403 760 6934,) that include a ride on an Ice Explorer (see box).

By car Tourist literature often misleadingly gives the impression that the Parkway is highly developed. In fact, the wilderness is fairly extreme, with snow often closing the road from October onwards, and there are only two points for services, at Saskatchewan Crossing (the one place campers can stock up with groceries, 77km from Lake Louise) and at the Columbia Icefield (133km).

ACCOMMODATION

There are several accommodation options dotted along the Parkway. Book hostels and hotels as far in advance as you can and arrive early for first-come, first-served front-country campgrounds.

MOTELS, LODGES AND INNS

The Crossing Saskatchewan Crossing ☎ 403 761 7000, ⓦ thecrossingresort.com; map p.562. The tacky highway-service-station feel of the rest of Saskatchewan Crossing doesn't quite extend to this 66-room motel. Though the peeling paint on the exterior of the low-slung cabins is off-putting, the interiors are better, with furnishings that range from standard to boutique. Early April to Oct. **$229**

Glacier View Inn Icefield Centre ☎ 780 852 6550, ⓦ banffjaspercollection.com; map p.590. This 32-room inn provides airy modern rooms on the top floor of the Icefield Centre; some rooms even have glacier views. Room rates almost halve before mid-June and after mid-September. Late-April to late Oct. **$289**

★ **Num-Ti-Jah Lodge** Hwy-93 ☎ 403 522 2167, ⓦ sntj. ca; map p.562. With its dazzling red roofs and magnificent Bow Lake views, this is one of the most famous old lodges in the Rockies. It was built in 1920 by legendary guide and outfitter Jimmy Simpson (who lived here until 1972); he wanted a large building and ended up with a strange octagonal structure as he only had access to short timbers. Also has a coffee shop and restaurant. May–Oct. **$375**

HOSTELS

Athabasca Falls Wilderness Hostel Hwy-93, 32km south of Jasper ☎ 778 328 2220, ⓦ hihostels.ca; map p.590. Basic hostel accommodation (with an outdoor cold-water shower) in five cabins within earshot of the Athabasca Falls. There's a great kitchen and common room. May–Sept daily. Check-in after 5pm. Dorms **$30**, non-members **$33**; doubles **$67**, non-members **$74**

Beauty Creek Wilderness Hostel Hwy-93, 17km north of the Columbia Icefield ☎ 778 328 2220, ⓦ hihostels. ca; map p.590. Cheerful hostel beside the placid Beauty Creek and with a trail to the impressive Stanley Falls from the back door. With kitchen, common room and fire pit but no running water or flush toilets. Check-in after 5pm. Dorms **$30**, non-members **$33**

Mosquito Creek Wilderness Hostel Hwy-93, 25km from Lake Louise ☎ 778 328 2220, ⓦ hihostels.ca; map p.562. Minimalist set-up of four log cabins that sleep 32,

a kitchen, large common room and a wood-fired sauna; there's no telephone, electricity or showers, but some wi-fi. Early May to early Oct & late Nov to early April. Check-in after 5pm. Dorms **$30**, non-members **$33**; doubles **$67**, non-members **$74**

Rampart Creek Wilderness Hostel Hwy-93, 12km north of Saskatchewan Crossing ☎ 778 328 2220, ⓦ hihostels.ca; map p.562. 24 beds in two cabins, a functional kitchen, a small common room and a fantastically rustic little sauna beside the Creek. Check-in after 5pm. Dorms **$30**, non-members **$33**

CAMPGROUNDS

Columbia Icefield Campground Hwy-93, 2km south of the Icefield Centre; map p.590. Unserviced but very popular tent-only campground with glacier views from most sites. With outhouses, picnic tables and cookhouses. RVs should park at the unserviced campground beside the Icefield Centre. Mid-May to early Oct. Sites **$15.70**

Honeymoon Lake Campground Hwy-93, 53km south of Jasper; map p.590. A 35-pitch campground for tents and motorhomes under 25 feet. Near *Sunwapta Falls Restaurant*, it has kitchen shelters, swimming in the lake and dry toilets. Mid-May to mid-Sept. Sites **$15.70**

Jonas Creek Campground Hwy-93, 78km south of Jasper; map p.590. Unserviced 25-site campground in earshot of a gurgling creek and with a quiet backcountry feel. For tents and motorhomes under 27 feet. Mid-May to early Sept. Sites **$15.70**

Kerkeslin Campground Hwy-93, 36km south of Jasper; map p.590. A 42-pitch site spread over a tranquil riverside tract with cooking shelters, dry toilets, and swimming and paddling on the doorstep. For tents and motorhomes under 25 feet. Mid-May to early Sept. Sites **$15.70**

Mosquito Creek Campground Hwy-93, 25km from Lake Louise; map p.562. These 32 non-reservable riverside sites have access to hand-pumped well water, fire rings and wood, and dry toilets. You're near the Bow River flats here, and the mosquitoes, as the name suggests, can be a torment. June–early Oct. Sites **$17.60**

Wilcox Creek Campground Hwy-93, 3km south of the Icefield Centre; map p.562. Pleasant and pretty basic campground where some of the very popular 46 wooded sites have views of the Sunwapta Pass. Takes both tents and RVs, and supplies running water and fire wood. June to mid-Sept. Sites **$15.70**

8

Jasper National Park

Although traditionally viewed as the "other" big Rockies park after Banff, **JASPER NATIONAL PARK** covers an area greater than Banff, Yoho and Kootenay combined, and looks and feels far wilder and less commercialized than the rest. Its backcountry is more extensive and less travelled, and **Jasper**, its only settlement, is more relaxed and far less of a resort than Banff, with just half its population. Most pursuits centre on Jasper and the **Maligne Lake** area about 50km southeast. Other key zones are **Maligne Canyon**, on the way to the lake; the Icefields Parkway (see page 585); and the **Miette Hot Springs** region, an area well to the east of Jasper renowned for its springs and trails.

The park's **backcountry** is a vast hinterland scattered with countless rough campgrounds and a thousand-kilometre **trail** system considered among the best in the world. Opportunities for day- and half-day hikes are more limited and scattered than in other parks. Most of the shorter strolls from Jasper are just low-level walks to forest-circled lakes; the best of the more exciting day-hikes start from more remote points off the Maligne Lake road, Icefields Parkway (Hwy-93) and Yellowhead Highway (Hwy-16).

Brief history

Permanent settlement first came to the Jasper in the winter of 1810–11. The great explorer and trader **David Thompson** left **William Henry** at Old Fire Point (just outside the present town), while he and his companions pushed up the valley to blaze a trail over the Athabasca Pass that would be used for more than fifty years by traders crossing the Rockies. In the meantime, Henry established **Henry House**, the first permanent European presence in the Rockies. In 1813 the North West Company established

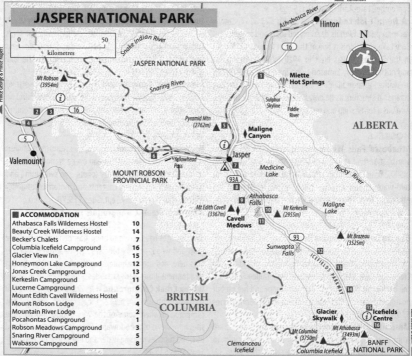

JASPER NATIONAL PARK

ACCOMMODATION	
Athabasca Falls Wilderness Hostel	10
Beauty Creek Wilderness Hostel	14
Becker's Chalets	7
Columbia Icefield Campground	16
Glacier View Inn	15
Honeymoon Lake Campground	12
Jonas Creek Campground	13
Kerkeslin Campground	11
Lucerne Campground	6
Mount Edith Cavell Wilderness Hostel	9
Mount Robson Lodge	4
Mountain River Lodge	2
Pocahontas Campground	1
Robson Meadows Campground	3
Snaring River Campground	5
Wabasso Campground	8

Jasper House at the eastern edge of the park's present boundary. Named after Jasper Hawes, a long-time company clerk there, it moved closer to Jasper Lake in 1829. By 1884, and the collapse of the fur trade, the post had closed. By 1900, the entire region boasted just seven homesteads.

Jasper's true origins date back to the coming of the railway in the late nineteenth century. The Canadian Pacific had made Banff and Yoho boom in 1885, and the **Grand Trunk Pacific Railway** hoped for similar success when in 1902 it started to push its own route west. Jasper Forest Park was duly created in 1908, and Jasper became a centre for railway operations in 1924, greatly boosting its population and importance. The first road link from Edmonton was completed in 1928 and official national-park designation came in 1930.

Jasper and around

JASPER's small-town feel comes as a relief after the razzmatazz of Banff: its streets still have the windswept, open look of a frontier town and, though the mountains don't ring with quite the same majesty as Banff, you'll probably feel the town better suits its wild surroundings. Situated at the confluence of the Miette and Athabasca rivers, its core centres on just two streets: **Connaught Drive**, which contains the bus and train terminals, restaurants, motels and park information centre, and – a block to the west – the parallel **Patricia Steet**, lined with more shops, restaurants and the odd hotel. With very few tourist attractions of its own, Jasper is more a place to sleep, eat and stock up. If you want to know a little more about the town or park from the locals, contact the Friends of Jasper National Park (see page 596).

Jasper Yellowhead Museum

400 Bonhomme St · Mid-May to early Sept daily 10am–5pm; early Sept to mid-May Thurs–Sun 10am–5pm · $7 · ☎ 780 852 3013, Ⓦ jaspermuseum.org

The smart and engaging little **Jasper Yellowhead Museum** is one of the town's best rainy-day options. It tells Jasper's story, starting with the settlement of the Athabasca Valley ten thousand years ago – as early tools here prove – but largely concentrates on the better-documented era after settlers arrived. Excerpts from the diaries of governor George Simpson help paint a picture of frontier life, as do the paintings of Paul Kane.

As the town laid down proper roots, a cast of local adventurers became involved in the race to bag local summits for the first time as climbers from all over the world converged; the last peak to be conquered was Mount Alberta in 1925. The coming of the railway is given particularly extensive treatment, while another exhibit looks at the early national park and the backcountry lives of early wardens, with a charming old uniform on display. Also intriguing are details of the top-secret Project Habakkuk, an eccentric World War II-era quest to build a ship out of ice that would resist torpedos. The museum ends its coverage in the 1960s when the local ski industry started in earnest, and bears still roamed Jasper's streets.

Patricia and Pyramid lakes

A winding road heads 5km north from Jasper to **Patricia and Pyramid lakes**, pretty, moraine-dammed lakes full of rental facilities for riding, boating and canoeing ($32/hr). Short **trails**, generally accessible from the approach road, include the Patricia Lake Circle, a 4.8km loop by the Cottonwood slough and creek offering good opportunities for seeing birds and beavers in the early morning and late evening. The island on Pyramid Lake, connected by a bridge to the shore, is an especially popular destination for a day out; continue on the lake road to the end of the lake and you'll find everything a little quieter.

8

Lake Edith and Lake Annette

On the east side of the Athabasca River from Jasper, **Lake Edith** and **Lake Annette** – both similarly busy during the day – are the remains of a larger lake that once extended across the valley floor. Their waters are the warmest in the park, thanks to the lakes' shallow depth, and in summer you can lie out on sandy beaches or grassy areas. A clutch of picnic sites are the only development,

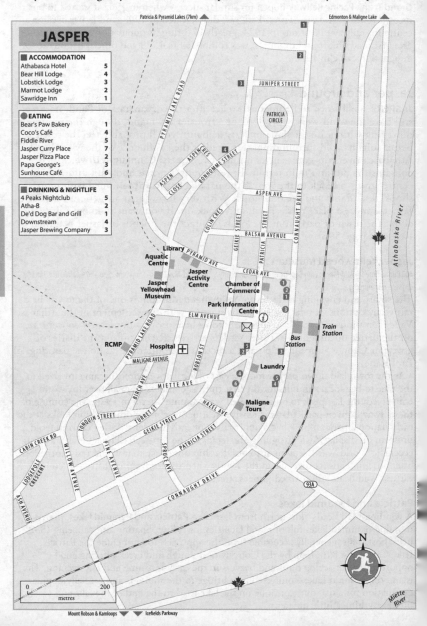

JASPER

ACCOMMODATION
Athabasca Hotel	5
Bear Hill Lodge	4
Lobstick Lodge	3
Marmot Lodge	2
Sawridge Inn	1

EATING
Bear's Paw Bakery	1
Coco's Café	4
Fiddle River	5
Jasper Curry Place	7
Jasper Pizza Place	2
Papa George's	3
Sunhouse Café	6

DRINKING & NIGHTLIFE
4 Peaks Nightclub	5
Atha-B	2
De'd Dog Bar and Grill	1
Downstream	4
Jasper Brewing Company	3

Patricia & Pyramid Lakes (7km)

Edmonton & Maligne Lake

Mount Robson & Kamloops   Icefields Parkway

JASPER'S TOP 5 HIKES

The range of **hiking trails** in Jasper National Park is vast, and well beyond the scope of this book, but the best are below; more great options lie along the Icefields Parkway (see page 587).

Cavell Meadows Easy day-hike featuring meadows, glaciers and waterfalls. See below
Maligne Canyon Stroll alongside twisted cliffs and pounding waters. See page 594
Opal Hills Moderate day-hike with splendid Maligne Lake views. See page 595
Skyline Trail The classic multi-day backcountry hike. See page 595
Sulphur Skyline Hard day-hike with glorious, craggy views and nearby hot springs. See page 596

and the wheelchair-accessible Lee Foundation Trail meanders around Lake Annette (2.4km).

Old Fort Point

The **Old Fort Point** viewpoint, 1.6km or a pleasant thirty minutes' walk east of town, is well worth visiting for its vistas of the valley and the milky Athabasca as it surges under an impressive iron access bridge. The moderate-to-hard 6.5km hiking loop from the adjacent car park is remarkably scenic, with panoramic views and plenty of quiet corners.

Jasper Tramway

Whistlers Mountain Rd, 8km from Jasper via Hwy-93 • Daily: April to mid-May & Sept to Oct 10am–5pm; mid-May to late June 9am–8pm; late June to Aug 8am–9pm • $47 return, $18.50 one way • ☎ 780 852 3093, ⓦ jaspertramway.com • Shuttle from 611 Patricia St (6 daily May–Oct); $12 return; ☎ 780 852 4056)

The two thirty-person cable cars of the **Jasper Tramway**, Canada's longest and highest cable car, take turns in climbing 1000m in seven minutes to provide splendid views (at 2285m) over Jasper. The summit also has an interpretive centre and an expensive restaurant; but best of all is the moderate hike (2.8km return; 1hr) to the top of **Whistlers Mountain** (2470m), for even better views and a bit of high-alpine exercise. Bring warm clothes year-round. In peak season there may well be a long wait for the Tramway, in which case you could just take the hard, four-hour hiking trail up from *Jasper International Hostel* (7.7km one way), then ride the tram down.

Marmot Basin

Marmot Rd, 22km from Jasper via Hwy-93 • Mid-Nov to early May daily 9am–4pm • Day-pass $102 • ☎ 780 852 3816, ⓦ skimarmot.com

Although more modest and basic than most Canadian Rockies resorts, **Marmot Basin** is the only ski area in Jasper National Park, and as such it's the scenic match of any, usually with excellent snow. Over 1675 acres of terrain, the 86 runs are largely beginner and intermediate; the difficulty of almost all expert terrain is exaggerated. But if that suits, and you're looking for a well-rounded winter-sports holiday, this is a destination to consider. The local snowshoeing and cross-country skiing (see page 597) are particularly good, and there's also spectacular heli-skiing not far away (see page 597).

Cavell Meadows

The trailhead lies 27km south of Jasper via the Icefields Parkway, Hwy-93A and Mount Edith Cavell Rd

Cavell Meadows (3.8km one way; 370m ascent) is one of Jasper's finest hikes thanks to its lovely alpine meadows and outstanding views of Angel Glacier and the dizzying north wall of Mount Edith Cavell. Named after a British nurse who was executed during World War I, the full round-trip hike requires about two hours and reaches a breathless 2135m. But be warned, the hike is popular, so don't expect solitude – hike before 10am or after 3pm to avoid the crowds.

Maligne Lake Road

Bumper to bumper with cars, campers and tour buses in the summer, the **Maligne Lake Road** runs east from Jasper for 48km, taking in a number of beautiful but rather busy and overdeveloped sights before reaching the sublime Maligne Lake (pronounced *ma-leen*). If you have time to spare, and the transport, you could set aside a day for the trip, whitewater rafting the Maligne River or walking one of the trails above the lake.

Joint tickets are offered for the lake shuttle bus and other activities organized by Maligne Tours, notably cruises, raft trips and horse rides (see page 597).

Maligne Canyon

The often rather crowded **Maligne Canyon** is 11km out of Jasper, with an oversized car park and a tacky café/souvenir shop. This heavily sold excursion promises one of the Rockies' most spectacular gorges: the canyon is deep (50m), but almost narrow enough

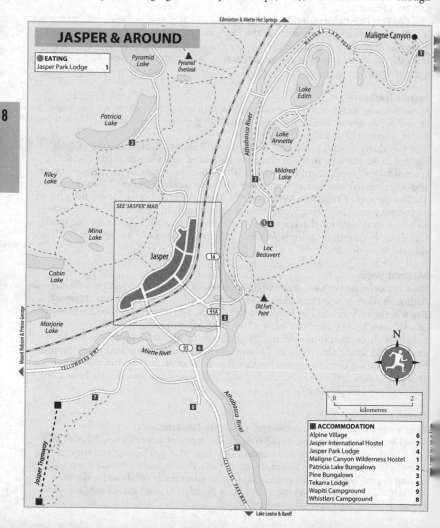

JASPER & AROUND

EATING
Jasper Park Lodge 1

Edmonton & Miette Hot Springs

Maligne Canyon

Pyramid Lake
Pyramid Overlook

Lake Edith

Patricia Lake

Lake Annette

Riley Lake

Mildred Lake

Athabasca River

SEE 'JASPER' MAP

Mina Lake

Jasper

Lac Beauvert

Cabin Lake

Old Fort Point

Marjorie Lake

Miette River

Jasper Tramway

Mount Robison & Prince George

Yellowhead Hwy

Icefield Parkway

Athabasca River

Lake Louise & Banff

N

0   2
kilometres

ACCOMMODATION
Alpine Village	6
Jasper International Hostel	7
Jasper Park Lodge	4
Maligne Canyon Wilderness Hostel	1
Patricia Lake Bungalows	2
Pine Bungalows	3
Tekarra Lodge	5
Wapiti Campground	9
Whistlers Campground	8

BACKCOUNTRY HIKING IN JASPER

Jasper's system of **backcountry hiking trails** and 111 backcountry campgrounds makes it one of the leading areas for backcountry hiking in North America. All **backcountry campgrounds** operate a **quota system**; contact the park information office for details and book as soon as you can (reservations $11.70). Trails remain busy even into September; the busiest are Skyline, Maligne Lake, Brazeau and Tonquin Valley.

The park information office offers invaluable advice, and excellent, cheap maps of several trails. For overnight hikes, talk to staff or get hold of a copy of *The Canadian Rockies Trail Guide* – but by general consent the finest long-distance trails are the **Skyline** (44km; 820m ascent) and **Jonas Pass** (19km; 555m ascent), the latter often combined with the **Nigel** and **Poboktan** passes (total 36km; 750m ascent) to make a truly outstanding walk. Not far behind come two hikes in the Tonquin Valley – **Astoria River** (19km; 445m ascent) and **Maccarib Pass** (21km; 730m ascent) – and the **Fryat Valley** (3–4 days). Others to consider are Maligne Pass and the long-distance North and South Boundary trails (the latter two both over 160km).

---

to jump across – many have tried and most have died in the attempt. In the end the geology is more interesting than the scenery; the violent erosive forces that created the canyon are explained on the main trail loop, an easy twenty-minute amble that can be extended to 45 minutes (few people do, so the latter part of the trail is often quiet), or even turned into a hike back to Jasper. In winter, licensed guides lead tours (more like crawls) through the frozen canyon.

Medicine Lake

Next stop is picture-perfect **Medicine Lake**, 32km from Jasper, whose levels fluctuate intriguingly. With no surface outlet, the lake fills and empties through lake-bed sink holes into the world's largest limestone cave system. Its waters then re-emerge some 17km away towards Jasper (and may feed some of the lakes around it). When the springs freeze in winter, the lake drains and sometimes disappears altogether, only to be replenished in the spring. The lake's strange behaviour captivated local Aboriginal peoples, who believed spirits were responsible, hence the name. Few people spend much time here, preferring to press on to Maligne Lake, so it's a fairly quiet spot.

Maligne Lake

Maligne Lake Cruise Late May–Oct hourly 10am–4pm; 1hr 30min • $79 • ☏ 780 852 3370, ☏ 866 625 4463, ⓦ malignelake.com

The Maligne Lake Road ends 48km east of Jasper at stunning **Maligne Lake**, surrounded by snow-covered mountains. At 22km long, this is the largest lake in the Rockies, its name deriving from the French for "wicked", coined by Jesuit missionary Father de Smet, in memory of his difficult 1846 crossing of the river below the lake. The road peters out at a warden station, three car parks and a restaurant flanked by a picnic area and the start of the short Lake Trail along the lake's east side to the **Schäffer Viewpoint** (3.2km loop; from Car Park 2; 1hr).

Glass-enclosed boats run from the small waterfront area on narrated **cruises** to Spirit Island; the views are sensational. The company also rents canoes ($30/hr) and other vessels; reservations are advisable in summer (see above).

The Opal and Bald hills

For a longer walk from Maligne Lake try the **Opal Hills Circuit** (8.2km round trip; 460m vertical ascent) from the picnic area to the left of the uppermost Maligne Lake car park. After a heart-pumping haul up the first steep slopes, the trail negotiates alpine meadows and offers sweeping lake views before reaching an elevation of 2160m. The trip takes about four hours, but you could easily spend all day loafing around the meadows.

Meanwhile, the **Bald Hills Trail** (5.2km one way; 480m ascent) starts with a monotonous fire-road plod from the same car park, but ends with excellent views at 2170m; allow four hours for the round trip.

Miette Hot Springs and around

58km northeast of Jasper via Hwy-16 • Mid-May to mid-June & early Sept to mid-Oct daily 10.30am–9pm; May to early Oct daily 9am–11pm • $7, day-pass $10 • ☎ 780 866 3939, ⓦ hotsprings.ca

Signed from Hwy-16 some 41km east of Jasper, the **Miette Hot Springs** are one of the most popular excursions in the park, rain or shine. They're the hottest in the Rockies and have to be cooled for swimming and soaking in two separate pools. Bathing suits, towel and locker rentals cost extra, as do massages.

Sulphur Skyline Trail

Maligne Adventures (ⓦ maligneadventures.com) run a shuttle service (daily; $35) with stops at both ends of the Skyline Trail. Book online in advance.

If you need a good reason for a soak, you'll find none better than the **Sulphur Skyline Trail** (4km one way; 700m ascent), a hike that starts by the springs and offers exceptional views of knife-edged ridges, deep gorges, crags and remote valleys; allow two hours each way for the steep slopes to 2070m. Other trails from the springs make for **Fiddle River** (4.3km one way; 275m ascent) and **Mystery Lake** (10.5km one way; 475m ascent).

ARRIVAL AND GETTING AROUND

JASPER AND AROUND

By train Jasper lies on the line between Toronto and Vancouver; its VIA Rail ticket office (☎ 780 852 4102, ⓦ viarail.ca) is open only on days when trains arrive. Summer seats are hard to come by but otherwise there's little need to book. Destinations Edmonton (2–3 weekly; 5hr 30min); Kamloops (2–3 weekly; 8hr 30min); Prince George (2–3 weekly; 6hr); Prince Rupert (2–3 weekly; 32hr); Toronto (2–3 weekly; 57hr); Vancouver (2–3 weekly; 19hr); Winnipeg (2–3 weekly; 25hr).

By bus Brewster (ⓦ brewstertransportation.com) use bus station in the train station building at 607 Connaught Drive. Destinations Banff (1 daily; 4hr 45min); Calgary (1 daily; 6hr 30min); Calgary Airport (1 daily; 7hr); Lake Louise (1 daily; 3hr 30min).

By taxi Caribou Cabs (☎ 780 931 2334).

INFORMATION

Jasper National Park Visitor Centre The superb visitor centre at 500 Connaught Drive (daily: Jan to mid-May & mid-Oct to Mar 9am–5pm; mid-May to mid-Jun & Oct 9am–7pm; mid-Jun–Sept 8am–8pm; ☎ 780 852 6176), lies at the centre of town by an open grassy area. It offers park and campground information, national park passes ($9.80/day), backcountry camping/wilderness permits ($9.80) and trail registration, and also has a shop (good for maps) run by the Friends of Jasper (☎ 780 852 4767, ⓦ friendsofjasper.com), who offer guided walks and other summer activities. A Jasper Chamber of Commerce desk (☎ 780 852 3858, ⓦ jasperparkchamber.ca) deals with accommodation and town information.

ACTIVITIES

RECREATION CENTRES

Activity Centre 303 Pyramid Ave ☎ 780 852 3381. With racquetball and squash courts, climbing wall, curling lanes and an indoor ice rink.

Aquatic Centre 305 Bonhomme St ☎ 780 852 3663. Includes large swimming pool, whirlpool and steam room.

SUMMER

Cycling Parks Canada produces a free map and trail guide for mountain-bikers, and there are plenty of good trails around town, most beginner or intermediate level. Rent bikes from On-Line Sport & Tackle, or Source for Sports (☎ 780 852 3654, ⓦ jaspersports.com). Rates are between $40–50/day for quality mountain bikes.

Climbing Rockaboo Mountain Adventures 807 Toquin St (☎ 780 820 0092, ⓦ rockaboo.ca) offer climbing courses ($125 for 4hr) and trips exploring the Athabasca Glacier ($225 for 7hr; see page 588).

Fishing On-Line Sport & Tackle (600 Patricia St ☎ 780 852 3630, ⓦ fishonlinejasper.com) and Currie's Guiding, 414 Connaught Drive (April–Oct; ☎ 780 852 5650, ⓦ curriesguiding.com), in Source for Sports (see above)

HELI-SKIING IN THE NORTHERN ROCKIES

Backcountry helicopter-accessed downhill skiing, or **heli-skiing**, is a big deal in the northern Rockies thanks to plentiful terrain and great snow. The longest-established operator in the area is **Mike Wiegele Helicopter Skiing** (☎ 250 673 8381, ☎ 800 661 9170, ⌨ wiegele.com), an operator based in a Bavarian-style village roughly midway between Kamloops and Jasper. With 3000 square kilometres of terrain in the idyllic Monashee and Cariboo mountains to choose from, the skiing is magnificent, and places are booked up far in advance. Also in the area is one of the **CMH** (☎ 403 762 7100, ⌨ cmhheli.com) lodges in Valemount, 135km west of Jasper. Some 132km north of Valemount at Crescent Spur, **Crescent Spur Heli-skiing** (☎ 250 553 2300, ☎ 800 715 5532, ⌨ crescentspurheliski.com) is the northernmost operator in the region, a small set-up accommodating only sixteen guests and offering some of the finest snow anywhere. All three charge a sizeable whack – the norm for heli-skiing – for the pleasure of pristine snow. For three days you'll have to budget at least $5000, more like $10000 for a week – though prices vary by thousands over the season.

offers trout- and pike-fishing trips, mostly on Maligne and Medicine lakes (half-day from $199). Source for Sports also rents out fishing gear.

Hiking Walks and Talks (☎ 780 852 4994, ⌨ walksntalks. com) offers a number of different daily hikes, from 4–7hr treks, for $65–90; they vary what's available according to where they think the best conditions are. For hiking-gear rentals try Source for Sports (see above) who rent out everything from bear spray to tents.

Horseriding Jasper Riding Stables (☎ 780 852 7433, ⌨ jasperstables.com), 4km from Jasper on Pyramid Lake Rd, organizes trail rides in that area; Skyline Trail Rides (☎ 780 852 4215, ☎ 888 852 7787, ⌨ skylinetrail.com) offers three-day backcountry packages for $1200.

Rafting Maligne Rafting Adventures, 616 Patricia St (☎ 780 852 3370, ☎ 866 625 4463, ⌨ raftjasper.com), has the biggest selection of trips and competitive prices. Similar trips are offered by Jasper Raft Tours (☎ 780 852 2665, ☎ 888 553 5628, ⌨ jasperrafttours.com) and Jasper's White Water Rafting (☎ 780 852 7238, ☎ 800 557 7238, ⌨ whitewaterraftingjasper.com). Expect to pay around $70 for 2hr of family-friendly Class II water on the Athabasca to $100 for 2hr on a Class III stretch of the Sunwapta, both including transport from Jasper.

WINTER

Jasper is surrounded by fine winter trails and stunning natural wonders like Maligne Canyon, but it's also fairly handy for activities that are banned in the park lands: Valemount, 116km to the west in BC, is a hub for snowmobiling and heli-skiing (see box).

Cross-country skiing and snowshoeing As good as anywhere in the Rockies, since many of the summer trails are ideal for winter grooming or easily accessible. Pick up the park's excellent *Cross-Country Skiing* leaflet at the visitor centre or download it from ⌨ pc.gc.ca. To buy or rent gear, try Totem Ski Shop 408 Connaught Drive (☎ 780 852 3078, ⌨ totemskishop.com).

Hiking From late December the torrential river through Maligne Canyon freezes into attractive waterfalls and ice caves, shining with magically translucent colours. Icy conditions – and the clambering and squeezing required – make this a hike that's best done guided. Sundog Tours (see page 596) organizes 3hr tours three times per day, with one at night, led by the light of headlamps ($60/person).

Ice Climbing Rockaboo Mountain Adventures (see page 596) run daily 6hr ice climbing trips for $225.

Ice-skating Parts of Pyramid Lake and Lac Beauvert are cleared for skating; Source for Sports (see page 596) offers skate rentals.

ACCOMMODATION

Beds in Jasper are not as expensive or elusive as in Banff, but still near unobtainable in late July and August. The *Jasper Home Accommodation Association* (⌨ stayinjasper. com) has rooms in around 120 **private homes**, at $75–150 for a double – contact the visitor centre or check the website for availability. Most **motels** dot Connaught Drive on the eastern edge of town; prices drop sharply in the off-season. Often cheaper and more pleasant are **cabins**, a few kilometres out of town. The four park-run **campgrounds** close to town and three local **hostels** all fill up promptly in summer, so bear in mind Icefields Parkway options (see page

589). There are no accommodation or camping facilities at Maligne Lake, but two backcountry campgrounds ($14) on the lakeshore can be reached by canoe (get details from Jasper's visitor centre).

HOTELS, MOTELS, CHALETS AND B&BS

★ **Alpine Village** 2.5km south of town on Hwy-93A ☎ 780 852 3285, ⌨ alpinevillagejasper.com; map p.594. Assortment of serene one- and two-room cabins, including twelve deluxe versions and lodge suites, most with great mountain views, and some with wood-burning fireplaces. There's a big outdoor heated pool too. May–Oct. $230

Athabasca Hotel 510 Patricia St ☎780 852 3386, ☎877 542 8422, ⓦathabascahotel.com; map p.592. Despite the grand lobby adorned with taxidermy, rooms (some without private bathroom) are plain, functional and cramped – but the downtown location is fantastic. Try to get a room higher in the building if the hotel's noisy bar is likely to disturb. $139

Bear Hill Lodge 100 Bonhomme St ☎780 852 3209, ⓦbearhilllodge.com; map p.592. Simple but comfortable bungalows, suites, chalet and lodge units on the northwest edge of town in a pleasant wooded setting (wildlife sometimes wanders through). With a lovely spa, including jacuzzi and sauna. $238

Becker's Chalets 5km south of Jasper on Hwy-93 ☎780 852 3779, ⓦbeckerschalets.com; map p.590. With 96 one-, two-, three- and four-bedroom log cabins – the best in the area – most with wood-burning stoves or fireplaces and full kitchens or kitchenettes. May to mid-Oct. $155

Jasper Park Lodge Lac Beauvert ☎780 852 3301, ☎866 540 4454, ⓦfairmont.com/jasper; map p.594. With a layout reminiscent of a summer camp, this collection of luxurious log cabins blends in well with its surroundings on the secluded shores of Lac Beauvert, 6km northeast of Jasper. The vast main lodge is replete with large lounges and restaurants (see page 599), and boasts an outdoor heated pool, on-site spa and an underground mall. $729

Lobstick Lodge 94 Geikie St ☎780 852 4431, ☎888 852 7737, ⓦmpljasper.com; map p.592. Reliable east-end motel, with large, simply furnished and clean rooms – though the dingy basement is to be avoided – some with kitchenettes. There's also an indoor pool and three outdoor jacuzzis. $293

Marmot Lodge 86 Connaught Drive ☎780 852 4471, ☎888 852 7737, ⓦmpljasper.com; map p.592. This large motel spreads over three separate buildings, with rooms of varying sizes all decorated with Aboriginal art and crafts. Some units have kitchens, fireplaces and fine mountain views. Common amenities include a hot tub and sauna. $296

Patricia Lake Bungalows 5km northwest of downtown on Pyramid Lake Rd ☎780 852 3560, ☎888 499 6848, ⓦpatricialakebungalows.com; map p.594. This complex of cabins, cottages and bungalows makes for a pleasant out-of-town base. Some of the 38 units have fine views over Patricia Lake, and several come equipped with kitchens. There are more secluded (and expensive) options, all with full kitchens and fireplaces, alongside the main complex. Fishing, boat, canoe and paddle boat rentals are available. May to mid-Oct. $235

Pine Bungalows 2km east of Jasper on the Athabasca River at 2 Cottonwood Creek ☎780 852 3491, ⓦpine bungalows.com; map p.594. The 72 wooden cabins here sleep two to six people and have no telephones or TVs, allowing you to make the most of the peaceful forested and riverside setting. Most of the cabins have kitchens, and more than half come with fireplaces; motel-style rooms available too. May to mid-Oct. $210

Sawridge Inn 82 Connaught Drive ☎780 852 6590, ☎888 729 7343, ⓦsawridgejasper.com; map p.592. Plush hotel on the eastern edge of town. Some rooms look onto an atrium, while others have balconies to take advantage of the mountain views. There's also an on-site day-spa. $345

★ **Tekarra Lodge** 1km south of town on the Athabasca River, off Hwy-93A ☎780 852 3058, ☎800 709 1827, ⓦtekarralodge.com; map p.594. These 42 quiet, wooden cabins, with hardwood floors, stone fireplaces and fully equipped kitchens have a sense of old-fashioned style. The views over the Athabasca River are fantastic, and there's a fairly high-end restaurant too. B&B rooms also available. May–Oct. $299

HOSTELS

Jasper International Hostel 1 Skytram Rd, 7km south of town via Hwy-93 ☎780 852 3205, ☎866 762 4122, ⓦhihostels.ca; map p.594. The biggest of three HI hostels near Jasper. Some dorms are pretty large and institutional so request a smaller dorm if possible. Facilities include kitchen, lounge and free wi-fi, but with no services in the vicinity, be sure to pick up supplies before you get here. The hostel is located 7km south of town via the Icefields Parkway (Hwy-93) and linked by a shuttle from 611 Patricia St; May–Oct 7 daily; $8 return); taxis cost around $20. Check-in noon–midnight. Dorms $35, non-members $38; doubles $77, non-members $86

Maligne Canyon Wilderness Hostel Maligne Lake Rd, 11km east of town ☎778 328 2220, ☎866 762 4122, ⓦhihostels.ca; map p.594. Basic hostel in two cabins in a lovely setting, sleeping up to 24 in six-bed rooms; there's no running water, showers or flush toilets, but purified water is available for cooking. The Maligne Adventures shuttle from downtown will drop you here (see page 596). Dorms $30, non-members $33

Mount Edith Cavell Wilderness Hostel Edith Cavell Rd, 13km off Hwy-93A, 23km south of town ☎778 328 2220, ☎866 762 4122, ⓦhihostels.ca; map p.590. Sleeps 32 in two cabins with great views of the Angel Glacier. Also has an outdoor wood-burning sauna and requires a 12km ski-in in winter. Dorms $30, non-members $33

CAMPGROUNDS

Pocahontas Campground Miette Rd, 45km northeast of Jasper, via Hwy-16 ☎877 737 3783, ⓦpccamping.ca; map p.590. This secluded spot on the eastern boundary of the park is one of two campgrounds to the northeast of

Jasper on this road. It has 140 spacious sites, hot and cold water and flush toilets but no showers. There's a café up Miette Rd. Mid-May to Aug. Sites $21.50

Snaring River Campground 13km northeast of Jasper on Hwy-16; map p.590. Simple, first-come first-served, park-run facility with 66 sites on the beautiful Snaring River with lovely mountain views. There's tap water and kitchen shelter, with dry toilets only and no showers. With overflow camping ($10.80), so a good bet when others are full. Mid-May to late-Sept. Sites $15.70

Wabasso Campground 16.5km south of Jasper on Hwy-93A; map p.590. A 228-pitch, park-run riverside site with flush toilets, hot water but no showers. Takes tents and RVs under 27 feet; serviced sites are available. Mid-May to mid-Sept. Sites $21.50

Wapiti Campground 5.4km south of Jasper and 2km south of Whistlers on Hwy-93 ☎877 737 3783, ⓦpccamping.ca; map p.594. 362-pitch, park-run place with flush toilets and coin showers; takes both tents and RVs. Some 90 sites remain open for winter camping from October (with water and flush toilets; $17.60). Open year-round. Sites $27.40

Whistlers Campground 3.5km south of Jasper, off Hwy-93 ☎877 737 3783, ⓦpccamping.ca; map p.594. Jasper's main 781-site, park-run campground is the largest in the Rockies, with three sections, and prices depending on facilities, which include showers. It also has smart "cottage tents" ($120/night) that sleep up to four adults and two kids, but other than shelter and mattresses, you supply the rest of the camping gear. Early May to early Oct. Sites $27; RVs $38

EATING

★ **Bear's Paw Bakery** 4 Cedar Ave ☎780 852 3233, ⓦbearspawbakery.com; map p.592. Off the main drag, but always busy. Freshly baked buns, cakes and pastries, plus big sandwiches, snacks and great trail food such as date squares and carrot cake. Good coffee, but with few tables so most people take their loot to go. There's a newer and larger offshoot, *The Other Paw*, opposite the station at 610 Connaught Drive. Daily 6am–6pm.

Coco's Café 608 Patricia St ☎780 852 4550, ⓦcocoscafe. ca; map p.592. Tiny, earthy and fun café with a glut of fabulous home-made items including tasty egg breakfasts, wraps, sandwiches, cakes and smoothies, most available to take away – great for picnics. Daily June–Aug 6am–6pm; Sept–May 6am–4pm.

★ **Fiddle River** 620 Connaught Drive ☎780 852 3032, ⓦfiddleriverrestaurant.com; map p.592. Stylish restaurant with dried-flower and oil-lamp decor, mountain panoramas and excellent fresh seafood at prices that reflect its distance from the sea; expect to pay $60/person for three courses. Mains range from the basic (beer-battered cod and chips) to the exotic (seafood jambalaya, or green curry grilled swordfish). Daily 5–9.30pm or later.

Jasper Curry Place 632 Connaught Dr ☎780 852 2737 ⓦjaspercurry.ca; map p.592. Business is brisk at this large curry house thanks to its well-priced buffet – which really hits the spot after a long day in the mountains. Despite the high volume of diners the curries are still very good and the prices reasonable (lunch $15; dinner $20 per person). Daily 11am–9pm.

Jasper Park Lodge Lac Beauvert ☎780 852 3301, ⓦfairmont.com/jasper; map p.594. The area's most prestigious lodging (see opposite) has several restaurants.

Choices include the sleek and small *Oka Sushi* and *ORSO Trattoria* where western Canadian produce becomes Northern Italian fare. A clear notch above either, the *Moose's Nook* serves local mountain fare, including excellent whisky-soaked salmon dishes and, occasionally, musk ox (main courses around $34). Daily 6–10pm.

Jasper Pizza Place 402 Connaught Drive ☎780 852 3225, ⓦjasperpizza.ca; map p.592. Despite the open kitchen and everyday bar furnishings that provide a chain-restaurant ambience, the wood-fired pizzas (from $17) come with toppings such as Dijon mustard, *escargot*, smoked oysters and palm hearts. Salads like the spinach and beet with goat's cheese and pecans ($17) are equally adventurous and tasty. Other options include a gargantuan lasagne ($17), burgers (from $16) and pita-pizzas that are ideal for a quick snack. Pool tables in the basement invite you to hang out after your meal, plus there's a rooftop patio. Mon–Thurs noon–10pm, Fri–Sun noon–11pm.

Papa George's 404 Connaught Drive ☎780 852 3351, ⓦpapageorgesjasper.com; map p.592. Locals' favourite in the *Astoria Hotel*, and one of the town's oldest restaurants (opened in 1924). Plain, but serves giant portions of excellent and varied food – ravioli, risotto, game burgers, fish and chips, meatballs and so on. Dinner mains are $21–38; breakfasts and lunches $7–11. Daily 7.30am–2pm & 5–10pm.

★ **Sunhouse Café** 610 Patricia St ☎780 852-4742, ⓦsunhousejasper.com; map p.592. Blessed with huge windows looking out to splendid mountain views (and a lovely patio), this elegant café is also efficiently run and its sandwiches, salads, coffees and cakes (fabulous cheesecake) are all exceptionally good, with ingredients locally sourced. Daily 8am–4pm.

DRINKING AND NIGHTLIFE

Jasper's few down-to-earth bars are short on style but long on enthusiasm; but anyway, with many hostels and campgrounds far out of town, much of the fun is of the make-your-own variety. For other evening entertainment – which can include theatre, cinema, music or dance – consult the town guide available from the tourist office (see page 596).

> ### PACIFIC TIME IN THE MOUNTAINS
> The Yellowhead Pass marks the boundary between Jasper National Park (on **Mountain time**) and the Mount Robson Provincial Park (on **Pacific time**, one hour behind). Mount Robson park is the only place in this chapter on Pacific time.

4 Peaks Nightclub 612 Patricia St ☎780 852-8393 ⓦ4peaksnightclub.com; map p.592. If you'd expect Jasper to be too small to support a club, this second-floor joint sets out to prove you wrong. It's a modest affair, but that doesn't stop it rocking until the small hours. Hosts regular events; busiest when the ski crowd's in town. Tues–Sun 9pm–2am.

Atha-B 510 Patricia St ☎780 852 3386; map p.592. This uninspired, large and occasionally rowdy bar in the *Athabasca Hotel* (see page 598) is Jasper's most reliably busy, with nightly dancing – mostly to mainstream chart hits – and regular live music. Small cover charge. Daily 11am–2am.

De'd Dog Bar and Grill 404 Connaught Drive ☎780 852 3351, ⓦdeddog.com; map p.592. Often unruly sports bar in the *Astoria Hotel* that's almost invariably full of sociable, thirtysomething locals. Diversions include pool, darts, big-screen sports and a bar menu with great burgers (from $9.50). The generous happy hour runs from 5 to 7pm. Daily noon–1am.

★ **Downstream** 620 Connaught Drive ☎780 852 9449, ⓦdownstreamjasper.ca; map p.592. Funky and spacious bar with several sofas below the *Fiddle River* restaurant (see page 599). Particularly great for imaginative sandwiches, with ingredients like marinated tofu, smoked meat and sauerkraut (priced $18–26) including salad, fries or soup); burgers; and snacks like *pierogi* and yam fries, as well as mean steaks. Daily 5pm–2am.

Jasper Brewing Company 624 Connaught Drive ☎780 852 4111, ⓦjasperbrewingco.ca; map p.592. Brewpub with smart, wood-beamed interior and imaginative, well-cooked, but somewhat pricey food; try the Bison Brisket ($29) or walnut and arugula rigatoni ($19). Choose from seven of their own beers, plus many others. Daily 11 am–2am.

DIRECTORY

Hospital Seton General, 518 Robson St (☎780 852 3344).
Internet In the library, 500 Robson St (Mon–Thurs 10am–8pm, Fri & Sat 10am–5pm).
Laundry Coin Clean (607 Patricia St; ☎780 852 3852).

Police ☎780 852 4848.
Post office 502 Patricia St (Mon–Fri 9am–5pm; ☎780 852 3041).

Mount Robson Provincial Park

The impressive **MOUNT ROBSON PROVINCIAL PARK** borders Jasper National Park and protects Mount Robson (3954m), the highest peak in the Canadian Rockies and surrounded by scenery that equals anything in the region. Mount Robson is one of the most staggering peaks you'll ever see, thanks mainly to its colossal south face – a sheer rise of 3100m – and to the view from the road, which frames the mountain as a single mass isolated from other peaks. A spectacular glacier system, concealed on the mountain's north side, is visible if you make the popular backcountry hike to Berg Lake (see opposite). Local Aboriginal peoples called the peak Yuh-hai-has-hun (the "Mountain of the Spiral Road"), an allusion to the clearly visible layers of rock, which resemble a road winding to the summit. It was first climbed in 1913, and is still considered a dangerous challenge.

The park begins 24km west of Jasper at **Yellowhead Pass** (1131m). Long a vital Aboriginal and fur-trading route across the Rockies, today it's a railway with regular hundred-car freight trains, that meanders alongside Hwy-16 for much of its length. Otherwise the park loosely divides into two parts: an eastern hub around Yellowhead Lake and a western hub around the park visitor centre some 50km away on Hwy-16.

Park **facilities** are minimal, so stock up on food beforehand; otherwise most of the few amenities, including a café and a garage, are near the visitor centre.

Yellowhead Lake Trails

Yellowhead Lake, at the eastern end of the park, has the trailheads for two main hikes. **Yellowhead Mountain** (4.5km one way; 715m ascent) is an excellent day-hike involving a two-hour climb through forest before the trail levels out in open country at 1830m for sweeping views of the Yellowhead Pass area. The trailhead lies 1km north along a gravel road from Hwy-16 just south of Yellowhead Lake.

About 1km east along Hwy-16 lies the trailhead for the **Mount Fitzwilliam Trail** (13km one way; 945m ascent; 8hr return): a more demanding walk, especially over its last half, but well worth it for the spectacular basin of lakes and peaks at the end. A couple of backcountry campgrounds are en route to break the journey.

The Berg Lake Trail

Starting 2km north of the park visitor centre, the **Berg Lake Trail** (22km one way; 795m ascent) is perhaps the most popular short backcountry hiking trip in the Rockies, and the only trail near Mount Robson. You can comfortably do the first third as a rewarding day-walk, passing through forest to the lovely glacier-fed **Kinney Lake** (6.7km; campground at the lake's northeast corner). Trek the whole length and you'll traverse the stupendous **Valley of a Thousand Waterfalls** – including the thundering 60m Emperor Falls (14.3km; campgrounds 500m north and 2km south) – and eventually enjoy the phenomenal area around **Berg Lake** itself (17.4km to its nearest, western shore). Mount Robson rises an almost sheer 2400m from the lakeshore, its huge cliffs cradling two creaking rivers of ice, Mist Glacier and Berg Glacier. The latter is one of the Rockies' few "living" or advancing glaciers, 1800m long by 800m wide and the source of the great icebergs that give the lake its name.

Beyond the lake you can pursue the trail 2km further to Robson Pass (21.9km; 1652m ascent; campground) and another 1km to Adolphus Lake in Jasper National Park. The most popular campgrounds are the *Berg Lake* (19.6km) and *Rearguard* (20.1km), both on Berg Lake itself; but if you've got a Jasper backcountry permit you could press on to *Adolphus* where there's a less-frequented site.

Toboggan Falls and Robson Glacier

Once you're camped at Berg Lake, a popular day-trip is to **Toboggan Falls**, which starts from the southerly Berg Lake campground and climbs the northeast (left) side of Toboggan Creek past a series of cascades and meadows to eventual panoramas over the lake's entire hinterland. The trail peters out after 2km, but you can easily walk on and up through open meadows for still better views.

The second trail in the immediate vicinity is **Robson Glacier** (2km), a level walk that peels off south from the main trail 1km west of Robson Pass near the park rangers' cabin. It runs across an outwash plain to culminate in a small lake at the foot of the glacier; a rougher track then follows the lateral moraine on the glacier's east side, branching east after 3km to follow a small stream to the summit of Snowbird Pass (9km from the rangers' cabin).

8

PROVINCIAL CAMPGROUNDS IN BC

Tent and RVs at many BC provincial park **campgrounds** can be **reserved** through Discover Camping (☎519 826 6850, ☎800 689 9025, ⊛discovercamping.ca) up to three months in advance but no later than 48 hours before the first day of arrival. A non-refundable booking fee of $6 per night, for up to a maximum of three nights, is charged. For general information on the parks, see ⊛env.gov.bc.ca/bcparks.

INFORMATION

MOUNT ROBSON PROVINCIAL PARK

Mount Robson Visitor Centre The visitor centre (daily: early May to mid-June & mid- to late Sept 8am–5pm; mid-June to early Sept 8am–7pm; first week of Oct 9am–4pm; ☏ 800 435 5622, ⓦ env.gov.bc.ca) is at the Mount Robson viewpoint near the western entrance to the park.

ACCOMMODATION

Lucerne Campground Hwy-16, 10km west of the Alberta–BC border; map p.590. 36 sites at the east end of Mount Robson Park that are available on a first-come, first-served basis. Facilities include dry toilets, pumped well water but no showers. Mid-May to mid-Sept. Sites $28

Mountain River Lodge 13990 Swift Current River Rd ☏ 250 566 9899, ☏ 888 566 9899, ⓦ mtrobson.com; map p.590. Bed and breakfast in a spectacular setting, overlooking the Fraser River and Mt Robson on the western edge of the park and 36km west of its headquarters along Hwy-16. Choose from rooms in the main lodge or a private, self-catering cabin, the latter with barbecue and fireplace (wood provided). Twins $189; cabins $229

Mount Robson Lodge 5km west of the park on Hwy-16 ☏ 250 566 4821, ☏ 888 566 4821, ⓦ mountrobsonlodge.

com; map p.590. The eighteen log-sided riverfront cabins here sleep two to six people, have electricity, heating and private bathrooms, and most come with kitchenettes, but there are no telephones or TVs – the idea is to soak up the views and disconnect from the world. Organizes rafting, helicopter and riding tours and offers camping in its *Robson Shadows Campground*. Showers are included in the price. Mid-May to mid-Oct. Sites $28; cabins $189

Robson Meadows Campground Just west of the visitor centre on Hwy-16 ☏ 519 826 6850, ☏ 800 689 9025, ⓦ discovercamping.ca; map p.590. With 125 reservable sites and the same facilities as *Robson River*, but families may find it more appealing for the playground and an amphitheatre that hosts interpretive programmes. Reserve at least two days in advance. Mid-May to Sept. Sites $28

Yoho National Park and around

Wholly in BC on the western side of the Continental Divide from Lake Louise, **YOHO NATIONAL PARK**'s name derives from a Cree word meaning "wonder" – a fitting testament to the awesome grandeur of its mountains, lakes and waterfalls. Yet it's a small park, whose intimate scale makes it the one favoured by Rockies' connoisseurs. As in other national parks, it was the railway that spawned tourism in the area: the first hotel in Field was built by the Canadian Pacific Railway in 1886 and within a few months sixteen square kilometres at the foot of Mount Stephen (the peak to Field's east) had been set aside as a special reserve. By 1911, Yoho had become Canada's second national park.

The Trans-Canada Highway divides Yoho neatly in half, climbing from Lake Louise over the **Kicking Horse Pass** to share the broad, glaciated valley bottom of the Kicking Horse River with the old Canadian Pacific Railway. The only settlement, **Field**, has the park visitor centre, some services and limited accommodation (the nearest towns are Lake Louise, 28km east, and **Golden**, 54km west). Other accommodation is available at trail hubs – **Lake O'Hara**, the **Yoho Valley** and **Emerald Lake** – the start of stunning and well-maintained **hiking** routes (see page 606) and the main focal points of the park.

Field

No more than a few wooden houses backed by an amphitheatre of sheer-drop mountains, **Field** looks like an old-world pioneer settlement, little changed from its 1884 origins as a railroad-construction camp, named after Cyrus Field, sponsor of the first transatlantic communication cable, who visited Yoho that year. Field has a few interesting attractions nearby – the Burgess Shale and the Spiral Tunnels – but it's mostly a base for **hikers**.

The Burgess Shale

Guided hikes July–Sept Mon–Fri • Parks Canada hikes from $55, Burgess Shale Geoscience Foundation hikes $95 • Burgess Shale Geoscience Foundation ☏ 250 343 3006, ⓦ burgess-shale.bc.ca; Parks Canada ☏ 250 343 6783, ☏ 800 737 3783, ⓦ reservations. parkscanada.gc.ca

Yoho today ranks as highly among geologists as it does among hikers and railway buffs, thanks to the world-renowned **Burgess Shale**, a unique geological formation near Field. The shale – layers of sedimentary rock – lie on the upper slopes of Mount Field and consist of the fossils of some 120 types of soft-bodied marine creatures from the Middle Cambrian period (515–530 million years ago), one of only three places in the world where these unusual remains are found. Soft-bodied creatures usually proved ill-suited to the fossilization process, but here they are so well preserved and detailed that in some cases scientists can identify what they were eating before they died.

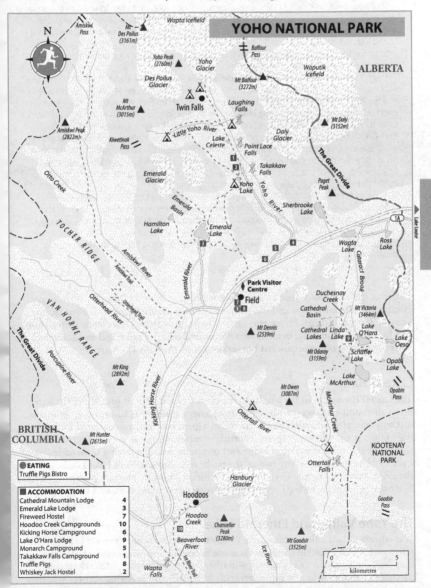

YOHO NATIONAL PARK

8

FIELD'S RAILWAY AND THE SPIRAL TUNNELS

Regular passenger services no longer come through Field, but the **railway** is still one of the park's "sights", and among the first things you see whether you enter from east or west. That it came this way at all was the result of desperate political and economic horse-trading. The Canadian Pacific's chief surveyor, Sandford Fleming, wrote of his journey over the proposed Kicking Horse Pass route in 1883: "I do not think I can forget that terrible walk; it was the greatest trial I ever experienced." Like many in the company he was convinced the railway should take the much lower and more amenable Yellowhead route to the north.

The railway was as much a political as a transportation tool, designed to unite the country and encourage settlement. A northerly route would have ignored great tracts of valuable prairie near the US border (around Calgary), and allowed much of the area and its resources to slip into the hands of the US. So, against all engineering advice, the railway was cajoled into taking the Kicking Horse route, and thus obliged to negotiate four-percent grades, the greatest of any commercial railway of the time.

The result was the famed **Spiral Tunnels**, two vast figure-of-eight galleries within the mountains; from a popular viewpoint about 7km east of Field on Hwy-1, you can watch the front of goods trains emerge from the tunnels before the rear wagons have even entered. More notorious was **Big Hill**, where the line drops 330m in just 6km from Wapta Lake to the flats east of Field. The first train to attempt the descent plunged into the canyon, killing three railway workers. Runaways became so common that four blasts on a whistle became the standard warning for trains careering out of control (the wreck of an engine can still be seen near the main Kicking Horse Park campground). Lady Agnes Macdonald, wife of the Canadian prime minister, rode down Big Hill on the cowcatcher (a metal frame in front of the locomotive to scoop animals off the track) in 1886, remarking that it presented a "delightful opportunity for a new sensation". She'd already travelled around 1000km on her unusual perch; her husband, with whom she was sharing the symbolic trans-Canada journey to commemorate the opening of the railway, managed just 40km on the cowcatcher. Trains climbing the hill required four locomotives to pull fifteen coaches; the ascent took over an hour, and exploding boilers (and resulting deaths) were frequent.

To visit the area you'll need to join a **guided hike** to **Walcott Quarry** (760m ascent; 20km or 11hr round-trip) and the trilobite beds on **Mount Stephen** (780m ascent; 6km or 7hr round-trip). Hikes are run by the Burgess Shale Geoscience Foundation and by Parks Canada; the latter's hikes are around half the price and less academic. The Foundation also offers occasional **horseriding** trips to Walcott Quarry.

Lake O'Hara

The **Lake O'Hara** area, in the southeastern corner of the park, is one of the Rockies' finest all-round enclaves – with staggering scenery, numerous lakes and an immense diversity of alpine and subalpine terrain. It's a great base for concentrated hiking (see page 606): you could easily spend a fortnight exploring the well-constructed trails that strike out from the central lodge and campground. The setting is matchless, with Lake O'Hara itself framed by two of the peaks that also overlook Lake Louise across the ridge – mounts Lefroy (3429m) and Victoria (3464m). The one problem is **access** (see below), which is severely restricted to protect mountain flora and fauna.

The Yoho Valley and Emerald Lake

Less compact than Lake O'Hara, the **Yoho Valley** and adjacent **Emerald Lake** spread north of the Trans-Canada and are far more accessible for casual visitors. Though they lack the magic of O'Hara, they still offer some great sights – **Takakkaw Falls** in particular – and a variety of top-rated trails in equally mesmerizing scenery (see page

606). The lake and valley combine to form one of the Rockies' most important backcountry zones, and the web of interlocking trails allows you to tailor walks to suit your schedule or level of fitness. Equally, if you're simply after a good day- or half-day hike, or even an easy stroll, there's plenty here too.

ARRIVAL AND DEPARTURE   YOHO NATIONAL PARK

LAKE O'HARA

On foot The simplest but also physically the hardest way to get to Lake O'Hara is hiking from a trailhead 1km off the Trans-Canada 3.2km west of the Continental Divide. From here you can follow a gravel road or the more picturesque Cataract Brook Trail for 11km to the Lake O'Hara region.

By bus If you don't walk, the only other option up to the lake is by bus (all other vehicles, including bikes, are banned), but a quota system applies and priority is given to those staying in the 30-site backcountry campground

or those with bookings at the *Lake O'Hara Lodge* (see page 605) or Alpine Club huts. Bus reservations can be made with Parks Canada up to three months in advance by phone only (April–Sept; $15; ☎ 250 343 6433, ⊕ pc.gc.ca), though last-minute seats, the results of cancellations, are worth trying for if you're in the area. Baggage restrictions mean you are allowed only one large or two small bags per person; maximum weight 25kg; maximum length 97cm. The maximum party number is six.

INFORMATION

Yoho Park Visitor Centre Yoho's visitor centre (daily: Apr, May & early Oct 9am–5pm; June to Sept 8.30am–7pm; ☎ 250 343 6783, ⊕ pc.gc.ca/yoho), marked by a distinctive blue roof about 1km east of Field, sells park passes ($9.80/ day) and backcountry permits ($9.80/night, reservations $11.70), and takes bookings for Lake O'Hara (see page

606). It also has displays, lectures and slide shows – notably on the famous Burgess Shale (see box) – and provides extensive trail information, including current conditions. The centre also has details of walking tours of Field offered by the non-profit Friends of Yoho (☎ 250 343 6393, ⊕ friendsofyoho.ca).

8

ACCOMMODATION

Yoho experiences high demand on limited **accommodation**. If you're having trouble finding somewhere, trawl the list at the visitor centre of the twenty or so small guesthouses and rooms in **private homes** (⊕ field.ca/accommodations) in Field. Most are priced between $100 in low season and about $200 in high, and lie within a few minutes' walk of each other in Field's small grid of streets. If you're really stuck, make for Golden (see page 608). The most central and popular **campgrounds**, listed below, are first-come, first-served, so arrive early at peak times. There are also quite a number of backcountry campgrounds in the park, including at Lake O'Hara, that are accessible only on foot. The visitor centre can advise, sell you a permit and take reservations up to three months in advance (see page 577).

HOTELS

★**Cathedral Mountain Lodge** 3km off Hwy-1 on Yoho Valley Rd ☎ 250 343 6442, ☎ 866 619 6442, ⊕ cathedralmountain.com; map p.603. This fabulous collection of luxury log cabins is beautifully situated in the lee of Cathedral Mountain, 4km east of Field and 15min drive from Lake Louise. Ideally placed for exploring the Yoho Valley, with no phones or TVs to distract. Late May to early Oct. $477
Emerald Lake Lodge 1km west of Field, off Hwy-1 ☎ 250 343 6321, ☎ 800 663 6336, ⊕ crmr.com; map p.603. Historic "railway hotel" built to compete with the likes of *Banff Springs* and *Château Lake Louise* and with

style, grandeur and prices to match. $459
★**Lake O'Hara Lodge** Lake O'Hara ☎ 250 343 6418, ☎ 250 678 4110 in winter, ⊕ lakeohara.com; map p.603. You need to reserve weeks in advance and part with plenty of cash to stay at this stunning 1920s mountain lodge. There are eight rooms in the main lodge, eleven two-person cabins along the lakeshore and eleven four-person cabins overlooking the lake. In winter, access is by ski or snowshoe only. Feb to mid-April & mid-June to late Sept. $730
Truffle Pigs 100 Center St, Field ☎ 250 343 6303, ⊕ trufflepigs.com; map p.603. Elegant, midsize hotel whose rooms have a contemporary boutique feel and sweeping views of the Kicking Horse Valley. Some have kitchens and sleep up to six, but one big bonus is that only lodge guests can reserve a table at *Truffle Pigs Bistro* (see page 608). Winter rates start from $89. $189

HOSTELS

Fireweed Hostel 313 Stephen Ave, Field ☎ 250 343 6999, ☎ 877 343 6999, ⊕ fireweedhostel.com; map p.603. This smart little hostel has room for 16 in four- and six-bunk rooms, as well as a couple of private rooms. The bunk beds are solid but comfy, the showers excellent, and there's a big, well-equipped kitchen, lounge and dining room, plus a deck with valley views. Dorms $45; doubles $155
★**Whiskey Jack Hostel** Just beyond the end of Yoho Valley Rd ☎ 778 328 2220, ⊕ hihostels.ca; map p.603.

An appealing option, thanks largely to its proximity to Takakkaw Falls. There are 27 beds in three nine-bed dorms, plus a common room and kitchen. June–Sept. Dorms $32, non-members $35

CAMPGROUNDS

Hoodoo Creek Campgrounds 22km west of Field, off Hwy-1; map p.603. Basic thirty-pitch campground with a cold-water hand pump and dry toilets but no showers or fires. Mid-May to Aug. Sites $15.70

Kicking Horse Campground 3km east of Field, off Hwy-1, near the junction with Yoho Valley Rd for Takakkaw Falls; map p.603. The largest (88 sites) and most central of the five park-run campgrounds, and pleasantly forested (riverside sites are best), though the rumble of trains echoes day and night. All the basic facilities, with flush toilets,

---

HIKES IN YOHO NATIONAL PARK

Hiking in Yoho is magnificent. If you have time for just a single day-walk, make it the Iceline–Whaleback–Twin Falls Trail, rated among the top five day-hikes in the Rockies. If you're really short on time, get a quick taste of the park on the Trans-Canada side roads to Emerald Lake and the Yoho Valley.

LAKE O'HARA

The **Lake O'Hara region** divides into five basic zones, each of which deserves a full day of exploration: Lake Oesa, the Opabin Plateau (this area and others are often closed to protect their grizzlies), Lake McArthur, the Odaray Plateau and the Duchesnay Basin.

If you only have time for one day-hike, the classic trails are the **Wiwaxy Gap** (12km one way; 495m ascent), or the **Opabin Plateau Trail** (3.2km one way; 250m ascent; 2hr), from the *Lake O'Hara Lodge* to Opabin Lake. Despite the latter's brevity, you could spend hours wandering the plateau's tiny lakes and alpine meadows on the secondary trails that crisscross the area. Most people return to Lake O'Hara via the **East Circuit Trail**, but a still more exhilarating hike – and a good day's outing – is to walk the **Yukness Ledge**, a section of the Alpine Circuit (see below) that cuts up from the East Circuit just 400m after leaving Opabin Lake. This spectacular high-level route leads to the beautiful Lake Oesa, from where it's just 3.2km down to Lake O'Hara. Oesa is one of many beautiful lakes in the region, and the **Lake Oesa Trail** (3.2km one way; 240m ascent 2hr) from Lake O'Hara is the single most walked path in the Lake O'Hara area. Close behind comes the **Lake McArthur Trail** (3.5km one way; 310m ascent; 2hr), leading to the largest and most photographed of the lakes in the area. The **Odaray Plateau Trail** (2.6km one way; 280m ascent; 2hr) is another highly rated, but rather over-popular hike.

The longest and least-walked path is the **Linda Lake–Cathedral Basin** trip, past several lakes to a great viewpoint at Cathedral Platform Prospect (7.4km one way; 305m ascent; 3hr). The most challenging hike is the high-level **Alpine Circuit** (11.8km), taking in Oesa, Opabin and Schaffer lakes. This is straightforward in fine weather and when all the snow has melted; very fit and experienced walkers should have little trouble, though there's considerable exposure and some scrambling. At other times it's best left to climbers, or left alone completely.

YOHO VALLEY

Most trails in the **Yoho Valley area** start from a car park at the end of the Yoho Valley Road by the *Takakkaw Falls Campground* and the *Whiskey Jack Hostel* (see page 605). The 14km road here leaves the Trans-Canada about 5km east of Field and is a narrow, switchbacking, summer-only affair that's unsuitable for trailers and RVs.

The shortest hikes in the valley all strike out to waterfalls. **Takakkaw Falls** lie an easy twenty-minute hike away and drop some 254m, making them among the most spectacular road-accessible falls in the mountains. Other, less busy, options are **Point Lace Falls** (1.9km one way; minimum ascent; 90min return) or **Laughing Falls** (3.8km one way; 60m gain; 1hr).

Another shortish, extremely popular walk from the same car park is the **Yoho Pass** (10.9km one way; 310m ascent, 510m height loss; 3hr), which links to Emerald Lake and its eponymous lodge (though you'll need transport arranged at the lake). A southern branch from this hike will take you over the Burgess Pass and down into Field, another manageable day-trip with fine overviews of the entire area.

The most trampled path in the Yoho Valley is the **Twin Falls Trail** (8.5km one way; 290m ascent 3hr) from the Takakkaw Falls car park. This easy six-hour return journey passes the Laughing Falls and has the reward of the Twin Falls cataract at the end, plus fine scenery and other, lesser

showers and fire pits. Aim to arrive extremely early to bag a spot. Late July to early Oct. Sites $27.40

Monarch Campground 3km east of Field, within walking distance of the Kicking Horse site; map p.603. Some 44 basic sites in a big meadow, with pumped well water and dry toilets. There's a kitchen shelter with a wood stove but no fire pits. May to early Sept. Sites $17.60

Takakkaw Falls Campground 17km east of Field, at the top of Takakkaw Falls Rd; map p.603. Only 300m from Takakkaw Falls' day-use car park and with great views of the falls from most of the 35 sites, this is one of the best bases for local hikes (see page 606). It's first-come, first-served and for walk-in, tent camping only. With pumped well water, dry toilets and a kitchen shelter with stove, fire pits and wood. Late June to early Oct. Sites $17.60

waterfalls en route. Stronger walkers could continue over the highly recommended **Whaleback Trail** (4.5km one way; 1hr 30min) for some incredible views of the glaciers at the valley head. A complete circuit returning to Takakkaw Falls with the Whaleback is 20.1km.

If you're allowing yourself just one big walk in Yoho it's a hard choice between the Takakkaw Falls–Twin Falls–Whaleback Trail above or the **Iceline–Little Yoho Valley–(Whaleback)–Twin Falls** combination. The Iceline (695m vertical gain) starts close to the Takakkaw Falls car park, climbing west through a large avalanche path onto a level bench with jaw-dropping views of the Emerald Glacier above and the Daly Glacier across the valley. It contours above Lake Celeste (a trail drops to this lake, making a shorter 17km circuit in all back to the car park) and then drops to the Little Yoho Valley and back to Takakkaw Falls for a 19.8km circuit. If you're very fit (or can camp overnight to break the trip), tagging on the Whaleback before returning to Takakkaw Falls makes a sensational 27km walk with 1000m of ascent. Most choose to do this as a backcountry hiking option (there are four backcountry campgrounds up here) – though the Iceline–Little Yoho walk coupled with the trek west to the **Kiwetinok Pass** (30km; 1070m) is also on many people's lists of top five day/overnight Rocky Mountain hikes. Juggling further with the permutations brings the Whaleback into this last combination to make one of the best backcountry hiking routes in the Rockies: Iceline–Little Yoho Valley–Kiwetinok Pass–Whaleback (35.5km; 1375m ascent), a route up there with the Rockwall Trail in Kootenay, Skyline in Jasper and Berg Lake in Mount Robson Provincial Park.

EMERALD LAKE

The Emerald Lake Road leaves the highway about 2km west of Field and ends, 8km on, at *Emerald Lake Lodge* (see opposite). Like the Yoho Valley Road, this route offers access both to easy strolls and longer jaunts.

For a stroll from Emerald Lake, follow the self-guided and wheelchair-accessible **nature trail** (4.6km circuit; minimal ascent; 2hr) around the lake from the car park to the bridge at the far end of the lake. Even shorter is the trail from the car-park entrance to **Hamilton Falls** (1.6km return; minimal ascent; 1hr).

The best day-trip is the **Hamilton Lake Trail** (5.5km one way; 850m vertical; 2–3hr), also starting from the car park at the end of Emerald Lake Road. It's demanding and steep in places and forested for the first hour or so – but thereafter it's magnificent, culminating in a classic alpine lake. The more modest climb to **Emerald Basin** (4.3km one way; 300m vertical; 1–2hr) follows the lakeshore before climbing through forest and ending in a small, rocky amphitheatre of hanging glaciers and avalanche paths.

THE TRANS-CANADA

Several short walks can be accessed off the **Trans-Canada Highway** as it passes through Yoho. From east to west, these are: **Ross Lake** (1.3km one way), a stunning little walk for the loveliness of the lake and the ease with which you reach it (accessed 1km south of the Great Divide picnic area); **Sherbrooke Lake** (3.1km one way; 1hr), a peaceful subalpine lake accessible from the Wapta Lake picnic area (5km west of the Great Divide), where stronger walkers can peel off after 1.4km to Paget Lookout for huge views of the Kicking Horse Valley (3.5km; 520m ascent; 3hr); **Hoodoo Creek** (3.1km one way; 1hr), on the western edge of the park (22km west of Field), accessed from the 600m gravel road from the *Hoodoo Creek Campground* (the steep path, starting 1km along the first campground access road, leads to the weirdly eroded hoodoos themselves, pillars of glacial debris topped by protective capping stones); and finally **Wapta Falls** (2.4km one way), an excellent and almost level forty-minute walk on a good trail to Yoho's largest waterfalls (by volume of water), accessed via a 1.6km dirt road 25km west of Field.

8

EATING

★ **Truffle Pigs Bistro** 100 Center St, Field ☎ 250 343 6303, ⊕ trufflepigs.com; map p.603. Hip gourmet bistro with dishes made from fresh local ingredients and decor featuring flying pigs. For all its range of snacks, home-baked breads and cakes, the dinner menu is the highlight, including creative seasonal dishes like beef *bourguignon*

($22), Brome Lake duck confit ($26), along with the offbeat likes of black truffle *pierogies* ($30). Great valley views and an unpretentiousness that extends to welcoming muddy boots and kids are further pluses. Daily 11am–9pm, bar until 11pm; open from 7.30am in July & Aug.

Golden

Some 54km west of Field and midway between Yoho and Glacier national parks, **GOLDEN** is the nearest town to either. Despite its name and mountain backdrop, the Golden most people see is little more than an ugly ribbon of motels and garages at the junction of Hwy-1 and Hwy-95. The modest little town itself straddles the Columbia River, below the highway; here you'll find an up-and-coming place that's beginning to make its mark as a **ski** town and **mountain-biking** destination. **Rafting** on nearby stretches of the Kicking Horse River provide a big draw too.

Kicking Horse Mountain Resort

1500 Kicking Horse Trail, 13km from Golden • Winter: day-pass $110; Summer: gondola ride $41; Via Ferrata $85–175/2hr mountain biking $55/day; bear refuge tours $30 • Lifts: early Dec to early April & June–Sept 10am–3pm (closing later at peak times) • ☎ 250 439 5425, ☎ 888 706 1117, ⊕ kickinghorseresort.com

Step out of the Golden Eagle Gondola, the main lift at **Kicking Horse Mountain Resort**, at the top of its 1245m vertical ascent, and it's hard not to stop and gape at the lofty wonderland of clouds and peaks that stretch ahead. The **ski area** below is just as seductive to skilled skiers and boarders, since it encompasses many untamed, backcountry-style open bowls, steep chutes, glades and gullies. The ski area spreads over 2800 acres, with its 120 runs overwhelmingly geared towards expert skiers; beginners and intermediates tend to find themselves confined to the lower slopes.

From June to September its gondola is also well worth riding for the views along with the option of some good, fairly easy ridge hiking and a harder three-hour loop. Further temptations include three daily trips along three fairly easy Via Ferrata climbing routes, a world-class, lift-accessed **mountain-biking park**, and a **grizzly bear refuge** with interesting tours. Otherwise the resort also offers the usual mix of accommodation, gear rental, bars, restaurants and childcare.

Northern Lights Wolf Centre

1745 Short Rd • Daily: May–June 10am–6pm; July & Aug 9am–7pm; Sept 10am–6pm; Oct–April noon–5pm; $12 • ☎ 250 344 6798, ⊕ northernlightswildlife.com

If you enjoyed the grizzly bear refuge at Kicking Horse (see above) then make a beeline for the Northern Lights Wolf Centre, some 16km north of Golden via Hwy 1. Here a small pack of grey wolves – all animals rescued from the wild or born in captivity – are housed in a cage for visitors to view. Regular interpretive talks shed light on this oft-misunderstood animal, but real photography or wolf nuts should book a tour that allows you to become part of the pack and roam with them through the bush ($380 for two people). There's some basic accommodation here too if you fancy waking to the howl of wolves ($82/night).

ARRIVAL AND INFORMATION

Golden Visitor Centre Golden's visitor centre, 1000 Trans Canada Highway (June–Aug Mon–Sat 10am–4pm; Sept–May Mon–Fri 10am–4pm; ☎ 250 439 7290, ☎ 800 622 4653, ⊕ tourismgolden.com), lies opposite the highway slip-road into town.

RAFTING IN THE ROCKIES

Rafting in the Canadian Rockies has become very popular, with a range of experiences on offer, from mellow, relaxing float trips to whitewater odysseys that require you to be a strong swimmer. Either way, no previous experience is generally required, but it's handy to know how rivers are **graded**: Class 1 water is gentle, Class 6 basically a waterfall. The **season** runs from May to mid-September, with the "biggest" water generally in June when snowmelt swells rivers. Operators should supply you with everything you need, and will probably also provide a shuttle from the main regional towns. On any trip it's a good idea to have a change of clothes, wear shoes you don't mind getting wet, bring a towel and have a bag for valuables.

BANFF REGION

In the Banff region, the main whitewater river is the **Kicking Horse**, on the edge of Yoho National Park, an hour from Banff. Its Class 4 sections (including one called "Man Eater Hole") in the upper sections and stretches of the Lower Kicking Horse Canyon give even seasoned rafters pause for thought. More tranquil is the **Kootenay River**, in Kootenay National Park (see page 611), two hours from Banff, a Class 2–3 river; meanwhile, Banff's stretch of the Bow River is a haven for mellow float trips through pretty scenery.

JASPER NATIONAL PARK

In **Jasper National Park**, the Class 2 **Athabasca River** (from Athabasca Falls, 35km south of the town) is scenic and provides gentle rafting, with one or two harmless whitewater sections, from May to October. The Class 3 **Sunwapta River**, 55km south of Jasper, offers some thrilling stretches of water, magnificent landscapes and good chances to spot wildlife. The Class 2–3+ **Maligne River**, 45km from town, includes a lively 1.6km stretch of rapids and is used for a variety of trips from July to September. The **Fraser River**, an hour west of Jasper in Mount Robson Provincial Park, is Class 4 in places but also has some gentle sections where the chance to watch salmon spawning at close quarters from mid-August to September provides an added attraction.

   Operators can be found in Banff (see page 570), Lake Louise (see page 584), Canmore (see page 557), Golden (see page 608), Radium (see page 612) and Jasper (see page 597).

SUMMER ACTIVITIES

Mountain biking Golden has an extensive, purpose-built mountain-bike trail network called the Moonraker trails, just west of town. Either visitor centre can provide an essential free map for this area as well as for Mt Seven, the location of more extreme trails on the opposite side of town. **Rafting** One of the best whitewater rivers in the Rockies, the Kicking Horse, runs through Golden, though the put-in for the best sections is up the road in Yoho (see page 602). Wet 'n' Wild Adventures (☎ 250 344 6546, ☎ 800 668 9119, ⓦ wetnwild.bc.ca/rafting), offers a range of full-day and half-day trips (from $89), in the wilder, lower part of the canyon for more advanced rafters, as well as easier, child-friendly trips and two-day trips.

ACCOMMODATION

★ **Country Comfort B&B** 1001 10th Ave S ☎ 250 344 6200, ⓦ countrycomfortbandb.com. Central, family-run bed and breakfast with seven rooms decked out in floral Laura Ashley-style decor, and a wood-burning fireplace in the guest lounge. A hearty breakfast's included, and the friendly hosts provide discounts at local restaurants. $155

★ **Dreamcatcher Hostel** 528 9th Ave N ☎ 250 439 1090, ⓦ dreamcatcherhostel.com. You wouldn't have come here for a good night's sleep a few years ago, but today this refurbished former strip joint provides luxurious hostel accommodation. The dorms and private rooms are immaculate and en suite, and the vast, sociable common room has a roaring fire, great kitchen and free wi-fi. Dorms $32; doubles $90

Golden Municipal Campground 1407 9th St S ☎ 250 344 5412, ☎ 866 538 6625, ⓦ goldenmunicipalcampground. com. Riverside sites three blocks east of the main street with flush toilets, hot showers and firewood, and the added bonus of being adjacent to a swimming pool and tennis courts. Free wi-fi. May to mid-Oct. Sites $35; RVs $38

Ponderosa Motor Inn 1206 Trans-Canada Hwy ☎ 250 344 2205, ⓦ ponderosamotorinn.bc.ca. Spick-and-span, family-run motel with pretty rooms, though some suites have surprisingly boutique-style furnishings. Some units have mountain views, some kitchenettes, and there's a hot tub for all. $110

EATING

★ **Bacchus Books & Café** 409 9th Ave N ☎ 250 344 5600, ⓦ bacchusbooks.ca. Relaxed café where you can combine browsing thousands of new and used books with a coffee in the upstairs café or on the pretty little riverfront patio. The home-made food is delicious and includes breakfast bagels or wraps, and burgers and panini for lunch (all around $8). Mon–Sat 9am–5.30pm, Sun 10am–4pm.

★ **Eleven 22 Grill** 1122 10th Ave S ☎ 250 344 2443 ⓦ eleven22restaurant.com. Hip and popular restaurant with an oft-changing but always eclectic menu (from pasta to curry and fondue; mains $18–208), but whose great strength is Asian food. The Dragon Boat ($27) –scallops, prawns and mussels in a smoky paprika red wine sauce – is delicious. With a lovely outdoor patio. Daily 5–11pm or later.

Nagomi Sushi 519 9th Ave N ☎ 250 344 4550. Basic little eatery whose authentic rice bowls, noodles and soups ($8–10) and fresh delicious sushi (rolls $5–10) – to eat in or take out – makes it Golden's best lunchtime option. Mon–Fri noon–5pm.

Kootenay National Park and around

Lying across the Continental Divide from Banff in BC, **KOOTENAY NATIONAL PARK** is the least known Rockies' park, and the easiest to miss out – many people prefer to follow the Trans-Canada Highway through Yoho. Yet the park's scenery is still impressive and if you're not determined to head west you could drive a neat 378km loop from Banff through Kootenay on Hwy-93 to **Radium Hot Springs** (the western gateway to the park), head north on Hwy-95 to Golden, then return on the Trans-Canada through Yoho to Lake Louise and Banff. With an early start you could drive this in a day and still have time for a few short walks and a dip in Radium's hot springs.

Kootenay lends itself to admiration from a car, bus or bike, mainly because it's little more than a 16km-wide ribbon of land running either side of Hwy-93 for around 100km. All its numerous and easy **short walks** start immediately off the highway. Options for **day-hikes** are more limited, though the best longer walks are as good as anything in the Rockies and can be extended into outstanding multi-day backcountry options. Whichever hike you choose, check first with the visitor centre for the latest trail conditions and to pick up the *Kootenay National Park Backcountry Guide* (downloadable at ⓦpc.gc.ca).

Radium Hot Springs

RADIUM HOT SPRINGS is a far less attractive town than its evocative name suggests but, as the service centre for Kootenay National Park, you may well have need of its tacky motels, garages, grocery stores and middling restaurants. The town spreads across the flats of the Columbia Valley, 3km from the southern/western entrance of the park at the junction of Hwy-93 and Hwy-95.

The hot springs

2km north of Radium Hot Springs via Hwy-93 • Hours vary, usually daily: mid-May to mid-Oct 9am–11pm; mid-Oct to mid-May noon–9pm • $7.30; swimsuit rental $1.90; towel rental $1.90; lockers $1 • ☎ 250 347 9485, ☎ 800 767 1611, ⓦ hotsprings.ca

Radium's **hot springs** – large outdoor pools with odourless 45°C waters below hulking cliffs – are serviced by a large, modern centre and see up to four thousand people per day take the plunge in summer. It's not really the place for a quiet swim, but in the late evening or off-season you can escape the madness and pretend more easily that the water is having some sort of soothing effect. The supposedly therapeutic traces of radium may sound a bit worrying, but this was what first turned the springs, used by First Nations peoples for centuries, into a recreational gold mine in the 1890s.

ARRIVAL AND INFORMATION

RADIUM HOT SPRINGS

Visitor Centre Radium shares its visitor centre with Kootenay National Park at 7556 Main St East (daily: mid-May to mid-Oct 9am–7pm, mid-Oct to mid-May 9am–5pm; ☎ 250 347 9331, ☎ 888 347 9331, ⓦ radiumhotsprings.com).

ACTIVITIES

Rafting The fairly mellow Kootenay River and Toby Creek near Radium can be rafted or canoed with family-friendly specialist Kootenay River Runners (4987 Hwy-93, Radium; ☎250 347 9210, ☎800 599 4399, ⊛raftingtherockies. com). Half-day trips cost from $67.

ACCOMMODATION

Alpen Motel 5022 Hwy-93 ☎250 347 9823, ⊛alpen motel.com. Bursts of colour from its window boxes distinguish this place from the many other standard motels along this stretch of Hwy-93, injecting a bit of the Alps into a motel that's otherwise pretty standard, though spotlessly clean and with friendly management. Like most Radium motels, rates include free passes to the hot springs. $139

★**Misty River Lodge** 5036 Hwy-93 ☎250 347 9912, ⊛mistyriverlodge.ca. Cheerful hostel on the edge of Kootenay National Park, run by keen travellers and with fairly bare-bones dorms and private rooms (some en suite) sleeping up to six. There's also a guest kitchen, small common room, huge deck with great valley views and bicycle rental. Continental breakfast is offered for $10. Dorms $46; doubles $97

Vermilion Pass

Vermilion Pass (1637m) marks the northern entrance to the park, the Continental Divide's watershed and the border between Alberta and BC. Little fanfare accompanies the transition – only the barren legacy of huge forest fires that ravaged the area in 1968 and again in 2003 leaving a 24-square-kilometre blanket of stark, blackened trunks. Take the **Fireweed Trail** (0.5km one way) through the desolation from the car park at the pass to see how nature deals with such disasters and seems to invite fires to promote phoenix-like regeneration. The ubiquitous lodgepole pine, for example, specifically requires the heat of a forest fire to crack open its resin-sealed cones and release its seeds.

At Vermilion Pass a broad carpet of lodgepole pine has taken root among the blasted remnants of the earlier forest, while young plants and shrubs are pushing up into the new clearings. Birds, small mammals and deer, elk and moose are being attracted to new food sources and, more significantly, **black and grizzly bears** have gradually returned to the area. Burning takes place in the park, and some trails may be closed as a result; details are posted at the park centre or at ⊛pc.gc.ca.

Stanley Glacier

About 3km south of Vermilion Pass, the small, well-defined **Stanley Glacier Trail** (4.2km; 365m ascent; 1hr 30min one way) climbs Stanley Creek from a highway-side parking area. The first 2km provides a hike through the Vermilion Pass Burn (see above), before pushing into a beautiful hanging valley below Stanley Peak (3155m) where the path effectively ends at a sign warning that the rest of the path is unmanaged (smaller onward paths abound but are difficult to follow). Here you can enjoy close-up views of the Stanley Glacier and its surrounding, recently glaciated landscapes. The area is also known for its fossils, and for the chance to see marmots, pikas and white-tailed ptarmigan.

Marble Canyon

Marble Canyon, 8km south of Vermilion Pass, the site of a park-run campground (see page 616), has an easy trail (800m) that's probably the most heavily trafficked Kootenay hike. It crosses a series of log bridges over Tokumm Creek, which has carved a fault in the limestone for eight thousand years to produce a 600m-long and 37m-deep gorge. In cold weather this is a fantastic medley of ice and snow, but in summer the climax is the viewpoint from the top of the path onto a thundering waterfall, with the creek pounding its way through the narrowest section of the gorge. The rock here was once mistakenly identified as marble – hence the canyon's name; the white rock is actually dolomite limestone.

Kaufmann Lake

One of the park's better long hikes, the **Kaufmann Lake Trail** (15km one way; 570m ascent; 4–6hr one way), also starts from the Marble Canyon car park. It climbs along Tokumm Creek to a campground on one of the park's loveliest high-mountain lakes. The first few kilometres of the trail – easy valley and meadow walking – make an appealing hour's stroll.

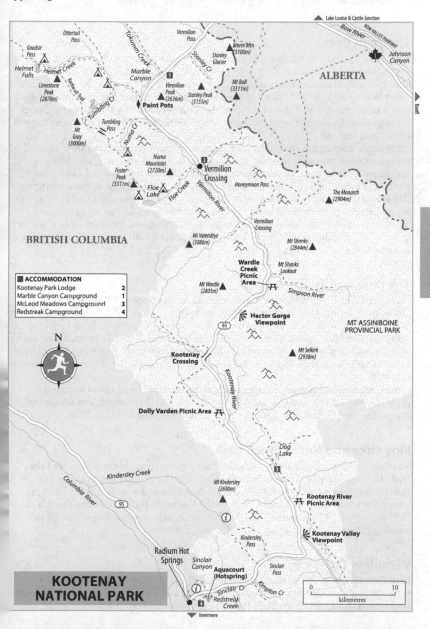

■ ACCOMMODATION	
Kootenay Park Lodge	2
Marble Canyon Campground	1
McLeod Meadows Campground	3
Redstreak Campground	4

> **TOP 5 KOOTENAY NATIONAL PARK HIKES**
> **Marble Canyon and Paint Pots** Rewarding easy strolls. See page 612
> **Stanley Glacier** Half-day hike with glacier views. See page 612
> **Kindersley Pass Trail** Top day-hike with great views See page 615
> **Floe Lake Trail** Ideal for overnight backpacking. See below
> **Rockwall Trail** One of the Rockies' finest multi-day routes. See below

The Paint Pots

You could extend the Marble Canyon walk by picking up the Paint Pots Trail south, which adds another 2.7km to your walk, or drive 2km south and stroll 1km to reach the same destination. Either way you come first to the Ochre Beds (after 800m) and then (1.5km) to the **Paint Pots**, one of the Rockies' more magical spots: red-, orange- and mustard-coloured pools preceded by damp, moss-clung forest and views across the white water of the Vermilion River to the snow-capped mountains beyond.

The pools' **colours** are created by iron-laden water bubbling up from three mineral springs through clay sediments deposited on the bed of an ancient glacial lake. Aboriginal peoples from all over North America collected the coloured clays from the ponds and ochre beds to make into small cakes, which they baked in embers. The fired clay was then ground into powder – **ochre** – and added to animal fat or fish oil to use in rock, teepee or ceremonial body painting. The Stoney and Ktunaxa peoples saw these oxide-stained pools and their surroundings as inhabited by animal and thunder spirits – which didn't stop European speculators in the 1920s from mining the ochre to manufacture paint in Calgary.

The Rockwall Trail

From the Paint Pots, two longer trails strike out for the **Rockwall Trail**, an incredible 30km, high-level backcountry trail (55km including approach trails; 1450m ascent). It follows the line of the mountains on the west side of Hwy-93, and can be joined using the Tumbling Creek, Helmet Creek, Floe Lake and Numa Lake trails. You could hike the trail in about two days, making one 55km loop, or do a series of shorter loops using the adjoining trails listed above. The entire trail usually doesn't open until early to mid-July.

There are five backcountry campgrounds along the trail, but a quota system is in place, so **reservations** are required. You can do so up to three months in advance by contacting the Radium Hot Springs visitor centre (see page 611).

Floe Lake and Numa Creek trails

The best of the day-hikes after Kindersley Pass (see opposite) is the easier **Floe Lake Trail** (10.5km one way; 715m ascent; 4hr) in the park's northern section, up to a spellbinding lake edged by a 1000m sheer escarpment and a small glacier. There are campgrounds on the route, and a tie-in to the Rockwall Trail. The **Numa Creek Trail** (6.4km one way; 115m ascent; 2hr), further north, is less enthralling – though you could use it as a downhill leg to add to the Floe Lake Trail.

Vermilion Crossing

Vermilion Crossing, 20km south of the Paint Pots Trail, is gone in a flash, but it's the only place, in summer at least, to find petrol and food in the park. You can also stop here to walk the **Verendrye Creek Trail** (2.1km one way; 30min), accessed west off the highway: an easy stroll, but forest-enclosed, and with only limited views of Mount Verendrye as a reward. One of the Rockies' tougher walks heads east from the Crossing, up over Honeymoon Pass and Redearth Pass to Egypt Lake and the Trans-Canada Highway in Banff National Park, while to the south, equally demanding trails provide the only west-side access to the wilderness of Mount Assiniboine Provincial Park.

Mount Assiniboine Provincial Park

Sandwiched between Kootenay and Banff national parks, the **Mount Assiniboine Provincial Park** was created in honour of Mount Assiniboine (3618m), a dramatic, sabre-tooth-shaped mountain, whose Stoney name means "those who cook by placing hot rocks in water". The **Simpson Road Trail** (8.2km) leads to the park boundary, and then divides into two paths (20km and 32km) to Lake Magog in the heart of Assiniboine. Some 8.5km beyond Vermilion Crossing look out for the **animal lick**, a spot where animals come to lick nutrients from a natural mineral source: with luck you may see elk, mule deer and even moose. Over the next few kilometres, for similar reasons, you might also see mountain goats by banks at the side of the road.

Kootenay Crossing and around

Kootenay Crossing is no more than a ceremonial spot – it was where the ribbon was cut to open Hwy-93 in 1923 – though a clutch of short trails fan out from its park warden station, and the nearby *Dolly Varden Campground*, the park's only winter campground. **Wardle Creek** nearby is a good place to unpack a picnic if you want to stick to the road.

Around 11km south of the Kootenay Crossing is the **McLeod Meadows** campground (see page 616), and immediately behind it to the east, the easy **Dog Lake Trail** (2.5km), much-tramped as an after-dinner leg-stretcher by campers (the trail can also be accessed from the highway at the picnic area 500m south). The path offers glimpses of the Kootenay Valley through the trees, and ends in a marsh-edged lake whose temperate microclimate makes it ideal for nature study. You may see deer, elk and coyotes, and – if you're lucky – bears and moose. Several types of orchid also bloom here in June and July. About 11km further on, the **Kootenay Valley Viewpoint** offers one of the broadest views on the highway, with great vistas of the Mitchell and Vermilion mountain ranges, as well as the inevitable hordes in search of a photo opportunity.

Sinclair Pass and Kindersley Pass Trail

For its final run down out of the park, the highway doglegs west through **Sinclair Pass**, a red-cliff gorge filled with the falling waters of Sinclair Creek and the start of the **Kindersley Pass Trail** – if you have time and energy for only one long walk in Kootenay, make it this one (allow about 7hr). The strenuous 9.8km trail climbs to Kindersley Pass and then cuts northeast for the steep final push to Kindersley Summit (2690m). Here you can enjoy the sublime prospect of an endless succession of peaks fading away to the horizon to the northeast. Rather than double-back down through the open tundra, many people push on another 2km (trail indistinct) and contour around the head of the Sinclair Creek valley before descending off the ridge (the Kindersley–Sinclair Col) to follow the well-defined **Sinclair Creek Trail** (6.4km) down to meet the highway 1km from the starting point (do the hike this way round – the Sinclair Creek Trail is a long, dull climb).

If this seems too much of a slog, Sinclair Pass offers three far easier short trails, all marked off the highway to the west. The best is the **Juniper Trail** (3.2km one way; 1hr), accessed just 300m inside the park's West Gate. The trail drops to Sinclair

Creek and over the next couple of kilometres touches dry canyon, arid forest slopes of juniper and Douglas fir and thick woods of western red cedar before emerging at the hot springs, or Aquacourt, 1.4km up the road from the start. The **Redstreak Creek Trail** (2.7km one way; 1hr), 4.5km east of the West Gate, starts off as a good forest walk, but becomes progressively less interesting, as does the **Kimpton Creek Trail** (4.8km one way; 1hr 30min), also on the south side of the road and canyon, 7.5km east of the West Gate.

ARRIVAL AND INFORMATION   KOOTENAY NATIONAL PARK

Visitor centre The main park visitor centre shares an address with the Radium Hot Springs visitor centre (see page 611, ⓦ pc.gc.ca/kootenay) and sells all kinds of park permits, including basic entrance ($9.80) which can also be picked up at the park gate. The visitor centre has information on most hikes and can take bookings for the free guided walks and other activities organized by the Friends of Kootenay (ⓦ friendsofkootenay.ca).

ACCOMMODATION

Radium (see page 612) offers the only practical accommodation options, bar a trio of park-run campgrounds and a handful of cabins at Vermilion Crossing. A further dozen or so **backcountry sites** with pit toilets and firewood are scattered within easy range of the highway; you'll need a **permit** ($9.80) from the visitor centre (see above).

Kootenay Park Lodge Vermilion Crossing, Hwy-93 ☎ 403 762 9196, ⓦ kootenayparklodge.com; map p.613. The only indoor option in the heart of the park, so book your spot in one of its ten rustic cabins well in advance. Most have fireplaces and several come with a hotplate or microwave; one cabin has a full kitchen. There's also an on-site restaurant, a small library and a shop selling coffee, sandwiches, gifts and clothing. Mid-May to Sept. **$220**

Marble Canyon Campground 7km south of the Banff–Kootenay boundary; map p.613. High-altitude campground by the Marble Canyon Gorge interpretive trail. There are 61 sites, and amenities include flush toilets, water

and kitchen shelters with stoves. Late June to early Sept. Sites **$21.50**

McLeod Meadows Campground 27km north of Radium Hot Springs village; map p.613. Situated on the Kootenay River, the 98 sites here are spacious, and the scenic Dog Lake (see page 615) is a 2.5km stroll away. Facilities include flush toilets, piped cold water and kitchen shelters. mid-June to mid-Sept. Sites **$21.50**

Redstreak Campground 2.5km above Radium Hot Springs village, off Redstreak Rd ☎ 877 737 3783, ☎ 250 347 9567, ⓦ pccamping.ca; map p.613. The largest (242 sites) and most luxurious of the park-run campgrounds, and the only one that accepts reservations. Its proximity to Radium village and its hot springs (easy trails link the campground to both), as well as its amenities – flush toilets, hot showers, playgrounds and partial or full RV hook-ups – make this campground justifiably popular. May to early Oct. Sites **$27.40**; RVs **$32.30**

The Columbia and Kootenay valleys

Heading south from Radium Hot Springs and Kootenay National Park, Hwy-93/95 travels through scenery that rivals the big Rockies parks to the north. The route follows the bottom of the broad **Columbia River Valley**, which becomes the **Kootenay River Valley** in the south and is bordered to the east by the soaring, craggy Rockies and to the west by the more rolling **Purcell Mountains**. At **Cranbrook** these highways meet Hwy-3, which heads east to **Fernie**, **Crowsnest Pass** and **Alberta**, or west towards Vancouver along the US border – over which there are numerous crossings. Greyhound **buses** ply all these routes.

Invermere and around

About 16km south of Radium Hot Springs, on the western shore of Windermere Lake, **INVERMERE** is a feel-good summer resort with the usual range of aquatic temptations. However, droves of anglers, boaters and beach bums mean summer vacancies may be in short supply; call the main visitor centre (see below) for B&B information.

INFORMATION

INVERMERE

Invermere Visitor Centre The visitor centre (July & Aug daily 9am–5pm; Sept–June Mon–Fri 9am–5pm; ☎ 250 342 2844, ⓦ cvchamber.ca) is located near the junction of Hwy-93 and Hwy-95.

ACCOMMODATION AND EATING

Best Western Invermere Inn 1310 7th Ave ☎ 250 342 9246, ☎ 800 661 8911, ⓦ invermereinn.com. Smart, upper-end motel in a handy downtown location, with an outdoor hot tub and fitness room. Rates include a reasonable cooked breakfast. $160

★ **Blue Dog Café** 1213 7th Ave ☎ 250 342 3814. Popular, bohemian wholefood café whose soups ($6) are a particular strong point and change every day. You might find curried red lentil and apple, tomato corn chowder or Canadian split pea. It's also particularly good for vegetarians; the lentil burgers and falafels ($13.50) are

delicious. Mon–Sat 10am–5pm, Sun 10–1pm.

The Canterbury Inn 747 12th St ☎ 250 342 6618, ☎ 877 442 6618, ⓦ thecanterburyinn.com. Many of the rooms at this longstanding town motel have been given a recent boutique-style facelift – neutral tones, flat screen TVs, slate tile washrooms and soft bedding – with little in the way of a price hike. Some units have kitchenettes. $149

Dry Gulch Provincial Park Campground Hwy-93/95, 11.5km north of Invermere. A 26-site campground with both RV and tent sites, set in a small park. Non-reservable but with drinking water, flush toilet and fire pits. May to Sept. Sites $25

Panorama

Skiing: Early Dec to mid April Mon–Wed 9am–4pm, Thurs–Sun 9am–9pm; Summer activities: Late June to early Sept • Skiing day-pass $106; mountain-biking day-pass $55 • Central reservations ☎ 250 342 6941, ☎ 800 663 2929, ⓦ panoramaresort.com • 10 daily shuttles from Invermere run in winter

From Invermere the minor Toby Creek Road climbs 18km west to **Panorama Mountain Village**, a **ski resort** with nine lifts and over 120 runs, whose slick resort-village accommodation also provides summer lodgings for **golfers** visiting the highly rated Greywolf course, and downhill **mountain-bikers** hurtling down lift-accessed routes.

Purcell Wilderness Conservancy Provincial Park

The chief appeal of the area in summer is **hiking**, particularly towards the **Purcell Wilderness Conservancy Provincial Park** (the road stops 9km short of the park), one of the few easily accessible parts of the Purcell Mountains. If you have a tent and want a robust hiking experience, you could tackle the 61km **trail** through the area to Argenta (see page 647) at the northern end of Kootenay Lake, an excellent cross-country route that largely follows undemanding valleys, except when crossing the Purcell watershed at Earl Grey Pass (2256m). See ⓦ env.gov.bc.ca/bcparks for trail information.

Fairmont Hot Springs and around

Back in the Columbia Valley, Hwy-93/95 heads south following the shores of Lake Windermere en route to the modern, upmarket resort of **Fairmont Hot Springs** which feeds off the appeal of the hot springs themselves. The pools were commandeered from the Ktunaxa (Kootenay) peoples in 1922 for exploitation as a tourist resource; the calcium **springs** (daily 7am–10pm; $12) were particularly prized by Europeans because they lack the sulphurous stench of many BC hot dips.

The resort also offers a range of other **activities** including golf, tennis, a spa, guided nature hikes, bike rental and horseriding. In winter its family-oriented **ski area** runs two lifts serving 12 runs over 300 acres; also on hand are 6km track-set cross-country ski trails, an ice-skating rink, snowmobile tours and sleigh rides.

The Dutch Creek Hoodoos

Just 4km south of Fairmont Hot Springs, **Hwy-93/95** curves around the **Dutch Creek Hoodoos**, fantastically eroded river bluffs created (according to Ktunaxa legend) when a vast wounded fish crawling up the valley expired at this point; as its flesh rotted, the bones fell apart, creating the hoodoos.

Whiteswan Lake Provincial Park

Some 23km south of the Dutch Creek Hoodoos on Hwy-93/95 lies the turn-off for **Whiteswan Lake Provincial Park**, a handkerchief-sized piece of unbeatable scenery at the end of a 20km gravel logging road; the park has five campgrounds but few trails, as its main emphasis is on boating and trout fishing. Also keep an eye open for the undeveloped **Lussier Hot Springs** at the entrance of the park (17.5km from the main road). The same access road (called the Lussier River Rd after it passes the park) continues another 30km from Alces Lake to **Top of the World Provincial Park**, a far wilder and gorgeous alpine region with good hiking trails, where you need to be completely self-sufficient.

Wasa Lake Provincial Park

South along Hwy-93/95 from the Whiteswan Lake turn-off, a blanket of trees begins to encroach upon the Columbia Valley. One worthwhile stop along the way is **Wasa Lake Provincial Park**, 30km north of Kimberley; the lake is warm enough for summer swimming and you can camp here.

ACCOMMODATION

Fairmont Hot Springs Resort ☎ 250 345 6000, ☎ 800 663 4979, ⓦ fairmonthotsprings.com. The resort centres on a vaguely rustic, but modern and fairly high-end lodge with a range of lofts, suites, standard rooms, summer cabins and an RV-only campground, one minute from the pools. The resort's *Spruce Grove Campground*, 2km south of the lodge on the banks of the Columbia River has its only tent sites, as well as another outdoor pool. Sites $\overline{\underline{\$33}}$; doubles $\overline{\underline{\$205}}$

Wasa Lake Provincial Park Campground Hwy-93/95, 35km northeast of Kimberley ☎ 519 826 6850, ☎ 800 689 9025, ⓦ discovercamping.ca. Reservations are accepted at least two days in advance for this campground. With water and fire pits, but no showers. Sites $\overline{\underline{\$30}}$

Whiteswan Lake Provincial Park campgrounds There are five campgrounds in the park, three of which are at Whiteswan Lake itself, the other two at Alces Lake. May–Sept. Sites $\overline{\underline{\$20}}$

Kimberley

Some 94km south of Fairmont Hot Springs and 30km north of Cranbrook, **KIMBERLEY** is Canada's second highest city (1117m), but probably its silliest, thanks to a 1970s tourist-tempting ruse to transform itself into a Bavarian village. The resulting kitsch was almost irresistible: buildings got a plywood-thin veneer of authenticity; Bavarian music was piped from shops with names like The Yodelling Woodcarver; and even the fire hydrants were painted to look like miniature replicas of Happy Hans, Kimberley's *lederhosen*ed mascot. The subsequent influx of tourists and European immigrants – Germans included – who supported numerous cafés and restaurants and a variety of family-oriented activities long rewarded the ploy; but these days much of the Teutonic gloss has faded and the town's become more mainstream in its approach. Nevertheless **Canada's Biggest Cuckoo Clock** remains the significant centrepiece in the pleasant pedestrianized downtown – even if it's a fraudulent affair and little more than a large wooden box twittering inane music.

Kimberley Alpine Resort

301 North Star blvd, 2km west of Kimberley • Early Dec to mid-April: daily 9am–4pm; night-skiing Thurs, Fri, Sat & some hols 5.30–8.30pm • Skiing day-pass $90 • ☎ 250 427 4881, ☎ 800 258 7669, ⓦ skikimberley.com

Technically, **Kimberley Alpine Resort** lies in the Purcell Mountains, though the squat foothills around this small family ski resort are a far cry from their hulking cousins further north. Nevertheless, the terrain is ideal for learning on wide green runs, and intermediate cruising and carving on rollercoaster blues. Expert skiers, meanwhile, can content themselves with a collection of incredible bump runs tucked around the back of the resort. In all, there are five lifts serving eighty runs, the longest of which extends more than 6km. Several runs are regularly lit for night-skiing.

INFORMATION   KIMBERLEY

Kimberley Visitor Centre 270 Kimberley Ave (July & Aug daily 10am–6pm; Sept–June Mon–Sat 10am–5pm; ☎ 250 427 3666, ☎ 866 913 3666, ⓦ kimberleychamber.com), in a car park beside the pedestrianized centre.

ACCOMMODATION AND EATING

★ **Alpenglow B&B** 3 Alpenglow Court ☎ 250 427 0273, ⓦ alpenglowbb.com. Rustic bed and breakfast whose hardwood floors and simple wood furnishings match the aesthetic of the *Old Bauernhaus* opposite. Breakfasts are superb, with plenty of fresh fruit, home-made breads and jams and cooked items. Facilities include a hot tub, infrared sauna and lounge. Ski packages are offered for the nearby resort. $120

★ **Château Kimberley** 78 Howard St ☎ 250 427 1500, ☎ 866 488 8886, ⓦ chateaukimberleyhotel. com. Refurbished industrial administration building that now provides classy central lodgings with almost no trace of their past. The bright and airy, country-style rooms are dotted with local art, and there are pleasant common rooms too. Continental breakfast included. $110

Kimberley Riverside Campground St Mary Lake Rd, 7km south of Kimberley via Hwy-95A ☎ 877 999 2929, ⓦ kimberleycampground.com. The nearest campground to town is this tidy and well-managed place. Some sites have river views and most are separated by a few trees. Facilities include a laundry, a heated outdoor pool and wi-fi. Mid-April to Oct. Sites $30; full-service RVs $40

★ **Old Bauernhaus** 280 Norton Ave ☎ 250 427 5133. Halfway up the road to the ski area lies a surprise in the form of this 350-year-old post-and-beam farmhouse, dismantled and brought here from southern Bavaria. True to its appearance, it serves excellent, traditional Alpine food: Swiss raclette, schnitzel, potato dumplings and apple strudel. Mains average $20. Thurs–Mon 5–9pm.

★ **Snowdrift Café** 110 Spokane St ☎ 250 427 2001. Small and earthy café that's great for a filling breakfast bagel and a quality coffee, or a lunchtime soup or sandwich on home-made bread for around $10. Daily 9am–4pm.

Cranbrook and around

The regional service town of **CRANBROOK**, 96km from Fernie, is one of the most uninspiring in the province, its overwhelming strip of motels, giant retailers and marshalling yards distracting from a small, woebegone historic downtown. The only real sight is the **Canadian Museum of Rail Travel**, 57 Van Horne St (July & Aug daily 10am–5pm; Sept–June Tues–Sat 10am–5pm; tours $21; ☎ 250 489 3918, ⓦ trainsdeluxe.com), which preserves restored luxury passenger cars that chugged between Montréal and Vancouver in the 1920s.

Fort Steele Heritage Town

Daily: May–June & Sept–Apr 10am–4pm; July & Aug 10am–5pm • $12–17 depending on season • ☎ 250 417 6000, ⓦ fortsteele.ca

Some 16km northeast of Cranbrook on Hwy-93/95 in a superb mountain-ringed setting lies **Fort Steele Heritage Town**, an impressive village of some 55 buildings c.1900. Compared to many other similar ventures in western Canada, Fort Steele has the distinct advantage of authentic roots – this was a settlement that grew on the back of a mining boom and was rescued from becoming a ghost town by funding in the 1960s. It's a pleasure to wander around and absorb the atmosphere, and there are plenty of **activities** such as gold-panning and stagecoach rides to keep kids entertained too.

INFORMATION   CRANBROOK

Visitor centre 2279 Cranbrook St N (Mon–Fri 8.30am– 5pm, Sat & Sun 9am–5pm; ☎ 250 426 5914, ☎ 800 222 6174, ⓦ cranbrookchamber.com).

ACCOMMODATION

Avoid Cranbrook's dreary chain motels in favour of accommodation in more attractive Kimberley (see above), unless you're camping. Then, two local provincial park campgrounds are worth seeking out; if you reserve, do so at least two days in advance at either.

Kikomun Creek Provincial Park Campground 8km south of Elko via Hwy-3/93 (turn-off 3km west of Elko) ☎ 519 826 6850, ☎ 800 689 9025, ⦾ discovercamping. ca. This lovely provincial park is beside the huge artificial Lake Koocanusa and near several pretty lakes where painted turtles are easily spotted. Good swimming is available off tiny beaches. Only a handful of the 171 sites have hook-ups; the vast majority are reservable. May–Sept. Sites $\overline{\$35}$

Moyie Lake Provincial Park Campground 20km west of Cranbrook on Hwy-3 ☎ 519 826 6850, ☎ 800 689 9025, ⦾ discovercamping.ca. Moyie Lake Provincial Park has a few good short trails, decent fishing, a sandy swimming beach and an excellent campground. Only half the sites are reservable; hot showers cost extra. May–Sept. Sites $\overline{\$33}$

Fernie

Straddling the ice-clear Elk River among knife-edged mountains, the hip ski-town of **FERNIE** is one place where first impressions should be ignored. Look beyond the lacklustre condo-, motel- and mall-lined highway and you'll find pleasant, leafy streets lined with small, wooden houses that pave the way to an attractively low-slung brick downtown along 2nd Avenue. Here it's immediately obvious that though Fernie has long depended on logging and open-pit coal mining, its outdoorsy appeal – primarily to skiers and mountain-bikers – has brought in a more liberal demographic. Art galleries, gift shops, coffee shops, outdoor-gear stores and health-food shops thrive in this upbeat little town.

Fernie Museum and visitor centre

491 2nd Ave · Daily 10am–5.30pm · $5 · ☎ 250 423 7016, ⦾ ferniemuseum.com

The modest **Fernie Museum** gives a disarmingly quick and cheerful rundown of the evolution of the town – from coal mining to winter sports – and provides a space for temporary displays of local and regional art. It's housed in one of the town's oldest buildings, one of a string on 2nd Avenue that date back to 1908, when the town rebuilt itself after a fire (the second in four years). The visitor centre (see page 622) maintains a desk at the museum and has details of a self-guided **heritage walking tour**.

Fernie hikes

Unlike in the region's national and provincial parks, **hikes** in Fernie are barely marked, with trailheads tricky to find, so before you head out pick up a map and directions from the visitor centre (see page 622). The hikes around Mount Fernie Provicial Park (see page 621), *Island Lake Lodge* and *Fernie Alpine Resort* (both page 622) are the most clearly marked, but several other rewarding options exist around the town itself.

Castle Mountain

The rock stud that watches over town, known as **Castle Mountain**, is the most rewarding half-day hike from downtown and one of the best mountain-bike rides too – if you have the legs. The trail is interesting and varied, the views are spectacular, and there's a satisfying summit too. Hikers should park on Coal Creek Road (the next turn-off beyond the Aquatic Centre on Cokato Road) at the unmarked car park by a bridge at the junction with River Road about 1km east of town. From here cross the bridge and soon turn left up a steep dirt road to an overhead powerline, where you can pick up a trail opposite (Hyper Extension) to a saddle and another (Castle Rocks) to the summit. Take the Hyper Ventilation and Roots trails on the way back down, returning to the start by turning right along River Road. All this makes for a 7.5km loop that should take four hours, but be on the lookout for bears and bikes along the way. Fit bikers will find the loop is best ridden in reverse in about half the time.

Mount Fernie

Mount Fernie, the huge flat-top mountain just west of town, rewards with great views in every direction as you climb above the tree-line into the high-alpine zone, including west over the Lizard Range. Two main routes lead to the summit, both of which should take three to four hours return. One follows the Moccasin Trail from Burma Road opposite a helipad and requires a bit of a scramble towards the end. The other, longer and gentler option starts at the overhead powerline above the Alpine Trails neighbourhood and climbs up the ridge.

Fairy Creek and the Mount Proctor Trail

The challenging, full-day **Mount Proctor Trail** climbs the mountain that lies just southeast of the distinctive Three Sisters (see below), providing a closer look at the mountain's dramatic forms along with superb views down the Elk Valley. The trail starts from the main visitor centre on Hwy-3 (see opposite), heads up the valley along **Fairy Creek**, climbs around the back of Mount Proctor and onto its summit, then drops down the front to form a loop that takes about seven hours. The beginning section up Fairy Creek is popular as a gentle and scenic out-and-back hike, for as long as you feel like.

The Three Sisters and Heiko's trails

Fernie's two most epic and rewarding trails leave from a trailhead on Hartley Lake Road northwest of town. Both the eight-hour return trip to the top of the colossal **Three Sisters** and the ten-hour hike to *Island Lake Lodge* (see page 622) along **Heiko's Trail** (also called the Mountain Lakes Trail) provide plenty of high-alpine drama, with waterfalls, caves and canyons to explore along the way. Both are pretty serious undertakings, however, and the trail is only lightly used, so you need to know what you're doing. To get to the trailhead follow Hwy-3 north out of town, turn onto Dicken Road, then almost immediately onto Hartley Lake Road, a rough gravel forestry road. The trailhead lies some 9km along its length, past Hartley Lake: look for a very short and unmarked spur road on your left leading to a large clearing and a large wooden trailhead sign.

Mount Fernie Provincial Park and Island Lake Road

The turn-off to **Mount Fernie Provincial Park** lies some 2km south of town along Hwy-3, where Island Lake Road quickly brings you to the park picnic area and campground (see page 623), from which several **hiking** and **biking** trails radiate. For an easy hour or two's hike through the forest and past a good viewpoint, cross the river by the picnic area and follow the Sherwoody Trail to Gorbie Road, a dirt track, onto which a right turn brings you back over the river and Island Lake Road. Follow it back to the picnic area – or take any of the trails on its right along the way for a more pleasant but slightly longer route. The circuit is relatively flat and a popular snowshoeing option in winter.

Island Lake Lodge and around

A full 9km from Hwy-3, Island Lake Road arrives at **Island Lake Lodge**, a high-end outfit that specializes in winter catskiing trips (see opposite) in the attractive bowl of mountains that surrounds it. In summer it's Fernie's premier **hiking** hub. A pleasant thirty-minute walk around the placid little lake (2km) is the easiest option from the lodge and the most popular, followed by a spell on the restaurant patio for lunch or a drink (see opposite). You can also rent **canoes** at the lodge ($20/hr). For a longer hike, park midway along Island Lake Road at the "Old Growth Forest" sign then follow the hike up to the resort through ancient cedar trees (1hr 30min).

A range of other trails start at the lodge and the staff will happily advise; the Tamarack Trail or Mount Baldy Trails are hard, each taking about five hours; the three-hour return hike to Lizard Lake is a much easier option.

8

Fernie Alpine Resort

2km from Hwy-3, 5km west of town • Skiing Nov–May; hiking and mountain biking late June to early Sept Wed–Sun • Ski day-pass $110; hiking day pass $27; mountain-biking day-pass $55 • ☎ 250 423 4655, ☎ 866 633 7643, skifernie.com

Fernie's population doubles in the winter, when ski bums gather to roost at **Fernie Alpine Resort**, one of Canada's finest ski hills. It can claim the longest ski season in the BC Rockies, and a whopping 9m of annual snowfall on its 107 trails and 2500 acres.

Generally only busy at weekends, the **ski hill** spreads across five adjacent mountain bowls which have so many hidden corners that they can take a whole season to explore. The resort tends to attract experienced skiers and riders, so beginners will find plenty of quiet terrain effectively set aside for them. Intermediate-level skiers tend to come up a bit short, since many blues are harder than they should be, but generally conditions encourage mastering harder terrain. The resort maintains a number of slope-side lodging options and all the usual ski-school, childcare, restaurant, bar and café facilities – though the après is a bit weak, so you'll soon want to head into town.

Between late June and early September the resort opens its lifts to **hikers** and **mountain-bikers**, and maintains a sizeable network of trails. Many of the biking trails off the Elk lift are approachable with a regular mountain bike and good basic skills, but for those off the Timber Chair you'll want a solid downhill bike and some experience. For hikers, the Timber lift provides access to a couple of easy viewpoints and a superb circuit along a high-alpine ridge to Polar Peak and back that takes around four hours to complete.

8

INFORMATION — FERNIE

Visitor Centre 102 Commerce Rd (late May to Oct daily 9.30am–5.30pm; Sept–Nov Mon–Fri 9.30am–5pm; Dec to April Tues–Sat 9.30am–5pm; ☎ 778 519 0748, tourismfernie.com), 2km north of town on Hwy-3 by a reconstructed wooden oil derrick. There's also an information desk in the museum (see page 620).

ACTIVITIES

Catskiing Both *Island Lake Lodge* (see opposite) and Fernie Wilderness Adventures (☎ 250 423 6704, ferniewildernessadventures.com), who have a desk in the *Park Place Lodge* (see below), offer top-notch catskiing: downhill skiing using snowcats rather than lifts to get to the terrain. It's heli-skiing on the cheap – well, about $550 per day, but still half the price.

Fishing The Fernie region has some of North America's best fly-fishing. An ideal place for local tips, licensing information, gear and guiding is the Kootenay Fly Shop, 821 7th Ave (☎ 250 423 4483, kootenayflyshop.com). Fernie Wilderness Adventures (see above) also runs trips, and has superb knowledge of many hidden backcountry spots.

Mountain biking Fernie is a hub for mountain biking (see page 623). For rentals call in at one of the three bike stores on 2nd Ave, including Straightline at no. 461b (☎ 250 423 3532, straightlinefernie.com). Expect to pay around $60/day for a full-suspension bike, more for a downhill bike for use at the resort – which also offers bike rentals.

Rafting Canyon Raft Company (☎ 250 423 7226, ☎ 888 423 7226, canyonraft.com) will take you on day- or overnight whitewater rafting trips down the Elk or Bull rivers, which both have some sustained stretches of Class IV water – the wildest rafted by any Rockies operator (day-trips $135). Mild float-trips are available for $65.

ACCOMMODATION

In addition to the places below, *Fernie Alpine Resort* (skifernie.com) has lots of accommodation. If you want to camp but fail to find a spot at the provincial park campground, consider camping wild, which is tolerated up Coal Creek Rd – fork left when the road crosses the first bridge.

HOTELS, MOTELS AND B&BS

★ **Island Lake Lodge** Island Lake Rd ☎ 250 423 3700, islandlakecatskiing.com. Upscale lodge and catskiing operation with a huge amount of astounding terrain. In winter three-day packages start at $2301, but in summer the lodge offers B&B accommodation from $169, and there's a high-end restaurant too (see page 623). $169

★ **The Old Nurses Residence** 802 4th Ave ☎ 250 423 3091, oldnurse.com. Downtown B&B in a former nurses' residence, which has been restored to its original Victorian elegance with the help of period antiques, quilts and furnishings. The immensely congenial hosts provide wholesome cooked breakfasts. $149

Park Place Lodge 742 Hwy-3 ☎ 250 423 6871, ☎ 800

MOUNTAIN BIKING IN FERNIE

If you're in the Rockies to **mountain bike** then Fernie's where you should end up. It boasts its biggest trail network, most lenient landowners and most active trail-builders. If you're in town for any length of time, pick up the excellent *Fernie Mountain Bike Guide* ($20) from any downtown sports shop. Even with this in hand a few pointers are useful:

- The season runs from May to October, but snow can cause problems at either end, so late June to early September is best; that's also when Fernie Alpine Resort opens its lifts to bikers (see page 622).
- The best central spot to park is the Aquatic Centre on Cokato Rd. There's a trail map posted beside a good little dirt park, pump track and trials area.
- The best easier trails (graded intermediate or blue) are in the Ridgemont area, easily accessed from beside the cemetery above the Aquatic Centre.
- Trail combinations not to miss include Swine Flu–Mad Cow; Dem Bones–Mushroom Head–Phat Bastard; and Project 9.
- After snow and wet weather Castle Mountain trails and Project 9 dry out first.
- The best longer rides (2–3hr) are Castle Mountain, Slunt and Big Money.
- The most challenging ride in terms of length and backcountry exposure is the 44km Porky Blue.
- The most technically difficult trails are Three Kings and Dirt Diggler.

381 7275, ⊚ parkplacelodge.com. Comfortable but fairly nondescript hotel, whose large and clean rooms cluster around an indoor atrium, location of a pool and hot tub. Also here is a restaurant and happening bar. $154

Powder Mountain Lodge 891 Hwy-3 ⊕250 423 4492, ⊕877 562 2783, ⊚ powdermountainlodge.com. Reasonable mid-range motel with an unusual number of facilities, including Fernie's only outdoor pool, a hot tub, a guest kitchen, a lounge and free wi-fi. $89

Stanford Inn 100 Riverside Way ⊕250 423 5000, ⊚ ferniestanfordresort.com. Upper-end motel midway between downtown Fernie and the ski hill, whose facilities include a pool with water-slide. It also offers free wi-fi and continental breakfast, plus there's a fantastic Indian restaurant (see page 624). $189

HOSTEL AND CAMPGROUND

Mount Fernie Provincial Park Campground Mt Fernie Park Rd ⊕519 826 6850, ⊕800 689 9025, ⊚ discovercamping.ca. Reserve at least two days in advance for this campground at the epicentre of the small provincial park, with forty superb pitches surrounded by dense foliage. With dry toilets, drinking water and fire pits but no showers. Mid-May to Sept. Sites $30

★ **Raging Elk Hostel** 892 6th Ave ⊕250 423 6811, ⊚ ragingelk.com. Cheerful hostel with a slightly ragged bohemian feel, but clean dorm and private rooms (some en suite). Facilities include a huge and well-equipped kitchen and common room, a laundry and a bar with cheap drinks and basic pub food. Dorms $27, non-members $30; doubles $76, non-members $84

EATING AND DRINKING

★ **Big Bang Bagels** 502 2nd Ave ⊕250 423 7778. This bagel specialist marries a wide range of home-made bagels with a broad selection of fillings, to create great breakfasts and lunches (filled bagels $5–8). Best pass on the watery coffee though. A second branch in the resort – halfway up the Mighty Moose lift – offers the best-value slope-side food. Daily 7am–5pm.

★ **Blue Toque Diner** 601 1st Ave ⊕250 423 4637, ⊚ bluetoquediner.com. The Fernie Arts Station, the town's main arts venue, is an appropriate spot for this creative bistro. Pick from various eggy breakfasts, soups, sandwiches, salads, burgers (the excellent bison burgers cost $16) and the like. But expect some offbeat combos: the Andean burrito ($12) includes quinoa, black beans, dried apricots, pumpkin seeds and coconut curry. Thurs–Mon 9am–3pm; closed holidays.

Curry Bowl 931 7th Ave ⊕250 423 2695. Small and friendly place that serves a range of good pan-Asian dishes, from rice bowls to udon noodles (mains average $13), and has a wide selection of beers, including the locally brewed Fernie Griz. Daily 5–10pm.

The Fernie Hotel & Pub 691 1st Ave ⊕250 423 6444. Workaday sports bar with pub grub that's well above average; the fish and chips ($18) is particularly good. As in most Fernie bars, live music is a regular part of the programme. Daily 11am–1am.

Island Lake Lodge Island Lake Rd ⊕250 423 3700. The local gourmet option offers top-quality food – think foie gras and game (dinner mains around $30). Lunches ($15) are plainer and lighter, and there's a lovely deck with mountain views. Daily 11am–10pm.

The Northern Bar and Stage 561 2nd Ave ⊕250 423 3075. The smartest of Fernie's collection of main street bars – more urban-chic sports bar than the ski-bum

Western style common elsewhere – but as good as any for live music. The food quality's a notch above the usual bar offerings: great burgers and the like for about $14. Mon–Thurs 4pm–2am, Fri noon–2am, Sat & Sun 10am–2am.

★ **The Tandoor & Grill** 100 Riverside Way ☎ 250 423 5000. A great Indian restaurant whose presence in the bland *Stanford Inn* (see page 623) amid lacklustre condo developments could hardly be more incongruous. Never-theless, it dishes up Fernie's best ethnic cuisine by far, charging around $15 for mains, including rice or *naan* bread. Wed–Mon 11am–10pm, Tues 4–10pm.

DIRECTORY

Hospital Elk Valley Hospital, 1501 5th Ave (☎ 250 423 4453).

Internet At Fernie Public Library, 492 3rd Ave (Tues, Wed & Fri 11am–6pm, Thurs 11am–8pm, Sat 1pm–5pm; ☎ 250 423 4458).

Post office 491 3rd Ave (☎ 250 423 7555).

Crowsnest Pass

In rounding **Crowsnest Pass** (1382m), Hwy-3 connects BC with Alberta in mountain surroundings largely shaped by mining. On the BC side of the pass the service town of **Sparwood**, 31km from Fernie, provides no real reason to stop other than to look at the "World's Largest Truck", a vast mining vehicle, and pick up provincial information in the visitor centre beside it (see page 625).

On the Alberta side of the pass, Crowsnest Pass also becomes the collective name for a scatter of ragged old **mining communities** crouching between steep-sided mountains. These date back a hundred years to when Crowsnest's vast coal deposits were to make it the "Pittsburgh of Canada". Such hopes were dashed by disasters, poor-quality coal, complicated seams and competition from oil and gas, but at least the bust that followed the boom preserved several atmospheric settlements. They've since been declared historic districts and provide a revealing snapshot of the recent past. But the greatest draw is a fascinating museum on the area's heritage and biggest mining disaster: the Frank Slide (see box opposite).

The Frank Slide Interpretive Centre

1.5km off Hwy-3 · July to early Sept 9am–6pm; early Sept to June 10am–5pm · $13 · ⓦ frankslide.com

The slick **Frank Slide Interpretive Centre**, 1km east of what's left of the village of Frank, presents the history of the slide (see box opposite) from several points of view – geological, social and industrial – and in so doing looks more broadly at Crowsnest Pass history too. It's full of unexpected drama, including Marxist rallies, shootings, train robberies and smuggling. Films provide a potted history of mining – explaining how mines were "only as safe as the stupidest man in the mine" – and a dramatized version of the slide. The centre also conveys engaging snippets of survival and loss, inadvertently providing a charming snapshot of the era. Insights are also offered into Turtle Mountain's still-crumbling south peak thanks to interactive digital summit views and examples of modern seismic metering technology that are sensitive enough to register you leaning on a block of stone. Some sixty of these devices on the mountain should ensure several weeks' notice of the next slide. A 1.5km **trail** from the car park reveals good views of the vast scale of the earth movement.

Bellevue

Bellevue Mine 21814 28th Ave · May & Jun daily 9am–5pm; July & Aug 10am–6pm, Sept & Oct Mon–Fri 9am–5pm; tours every 30min · $21 · ☎ 403 564 4700, ⓦ bellevuemine.com

The Crowsnest Pass trail of destruction, death and disaster continues at the sleepy village of **BELLEVUE**, the most westerly of the Crowsnest communities where the main draw is the chance to explore – complete with hard hat and miner's lamp – the wonderfully dark and dank old **Bellevue Mine**. The only local mine open to the public, it ceased production in 1962, but remains infamous for a 1910 explosion that

---

THE FRANK SLIDE

On April 29, 1903, a good portion of Turtle Mountain tumbled down onto the little mining town of **Frank**. The term "slide" doesn't do it justice: nineteen million tonnes of limestone crashed down with enough ferocity to trap air and allow some rocks to effectively "surf" across the valley. This is Canada's deadliest rockslide, with well over a hundred people buried under the rubble, but amazingly no miners were killed – they dug themselves out after fourteen hours of toil.

The legacy of the disaster lies in a vast, rocky wasteland on either side of the highway and railway line and below Turtle Mountain, whose contours were once riddled with the galleries of local mines.

---

destroyed the ventilator fan, killing thirty men, not from the blast, but by breathing so-called "afterdamp", the lethal mix of carbon dioxide and monoxide left after a fire has burnt oxygen from the atmosphere.

Hillcrest

In spite of the tragedies at Frank and Bellevue, Canada's worst ever mining disaster occurred beneath the scattered village of **HILLCREST** in 1905. It lies immediately south of Bellevue (over Hwy-3), and its cemetery on 8th Avenue holds the mass grave of many of the 189 men who were killed by the explosion and the afterdamp.

Leitch Collieries Provincial Historic Site

Hwy-3, 3km east of Bellevue • Mid-May to early Sept daily 10am–5pm; site unstaffed in winter • Donation • ⓦ leitchcollieries.ca

Once the region's largest mining and coking concern, the **Leitch Collieries** site was also the first to close (in 1915). Today a boardwalk trail weaves between a few old buildings past interpretive signs that fill you in on mining techniques.

Castle Mountain

Hwy-774, 45km southwest of Pincher Creek • Dec–April daily 9am–3/3.30pm • Day-pass $95; catskiing $399/day • ☏ 403 627 5101, ⓦ skicastle.ca

Castle Mountain is the least known Canadian Rockies resort, probably because there's no mountain town nearby, which makes it something of a hidden gem: there's a lot of great terrain here and remarkably few people to compete with for fresh snow, of which it gets about as much as any other Rockies resort. The only real snags are its remoteness – it's at the end of a fairly minor road some 40km from Hillcrest – and that its winds can be fierce, often making life pretty unpleasant and sometimes even shutting down its six lifts. Pick a good day, though, and it's skiing paradise, with 78 runs, 3500 acres and 863m vertical. The terrain is overwhelmingly graded intermediate and expert, and there's the chance to go catskiing too.

ARRIVAL AND INFORMATION	CROWSNEST PASS

Visitor centre Hwy-3, 8km west of Coleman (May–Sept Mon–Fri 9am–5pm; longer hours and Sat & Sun Jan–Oct; ☏ 250 425 2423, ⓦ travelalberta.com). There's also a small, summer-only tourist office by Bellevue campground.

ACCOMMODATION

Bellecrest Community Association Campground Hwy-3, on eastern edge of Bellevue. Directly beside busy Hwy-3, but a nice little campground all the same, with toilets, tap water, a picnic shelter and its own tiny, ten-seat wooden church where you can pray for the traffic to die down. May–Oct. Sites $10

Chinook Provincial Recreation Area Campground Coleman. From a signpost a couple of kilometres east of the Crowsnest visitor centre (see above) on Hwy-3, a back road shoots off to a pleasant lakeside campground below the striking Crowsnest Mountain. There's water and dry toilets, but little else. Sites $23

8

Waterton Lakes National Park

With an isolated location 264km from Calgary and well south of other Canadian Rockies parks, **WATERTON LAKES NATIONAL PARK** appears on maps to be simply an extension of the much larger Glacier National Park, across the US border. Yet, despite its modest size, the park's 255km of trails are among the best made and most scenic in the Canadian Rockies. Because the park is compact and easily accessed from the only settlement, **Waterton**, it's particularly superb for day-hikes, with most walks climaxing at small alpine lakes cradled in spectacular hanging valleys; a few hikes, like the Tamarack Trail, head over or along ridges to offer multi-day backcountry options.

There's plenty for those not mad about hiking too, with attractive drives along two wonderfully scenic access roads, **Akamina Parkway** and **Red Rock Parkway**. Both probe west into the interior from Waterton and are dotted with viewpoints as well as spots to picnic, camp and rent boats.

Brief history

Up to nine thousand years ago the region provided a hunting ground for Aboriginal peoples such as the **Ktunaxa** (Kootenay), from present-day BC, who crossed the mountains to fish and hunt bison on the prairie grasslands around Waterton. By about 1700, rival Blackfoot peoples had extended their sphere of influence here from central Alberta, pushing out the Ktunaxa, but by the mid-nineteenth century they had retreated eastwards, leaving the region virtually uninhabited.

It was the Waterton area's first permanent white resident, John George Brown (see page 630), who first noticed globules of oil on Cameron Creek, a local river, a discovery that would bring entrepreneurs to ravage the region. Ironically, given Brown's environmental zeal, he even helped start the local industry by skimming oil from the river, bottling it, and selling it to nearby settlements. In 1901 the Rocky Mountain Development Company struck oil, leading to western Canada's first commercial oil well, which soon dried up; a monument on the Akamina Parkway (see page 628) now marks its original location.

Only in the 1920s, when the Great Northern Railway introduced a bus link from its Montana-to-Jasper railway, did **tourists** arrive in any numbers, and it was for them that the venerable *Prince of Wales Hotel* was built (see page 630). In 1995 UNESCO

THE NATURAL ENVIRONMENT OF WATERTON LAKES

The unique **geological history** of Waterton becomes clear when you compare it with the strikingly different landscapes of Banff and Jasper national parks. Rock and mountains in Waterton moved east during the Rockies' formation, travelling as a single vast mass known as the Lewis Thrust. Some 6km thick, this monolith moved over 70km along a 300km front, the result being that rocks over 1.5 billion years old from the Rockies' "sedimentary basement" came to rest undisturbed on top of the prairies' far more recent sixty-million-year-old shales. Scarcely any zone of transition exists between the two, which is why the park is often known as the place where the **"peaks meet the prairies"**, and its landscapes as "upside-down mountains". The effect was to produce not only slightly lower peaks than to the north, but also mountains whose summits are irregular in shape and very different from the distinctive sawtooth ridges of Banff National Park.

The huge variety of altitude, habitats and climate within the park means that plants and wildlife from prairie habitats co-mingle with the species of the purely montane, subalpine and alpine regions. The result is the greatest diversity of **flora and fauna** of any western national park: 1200 plant species and 250 species of bird.

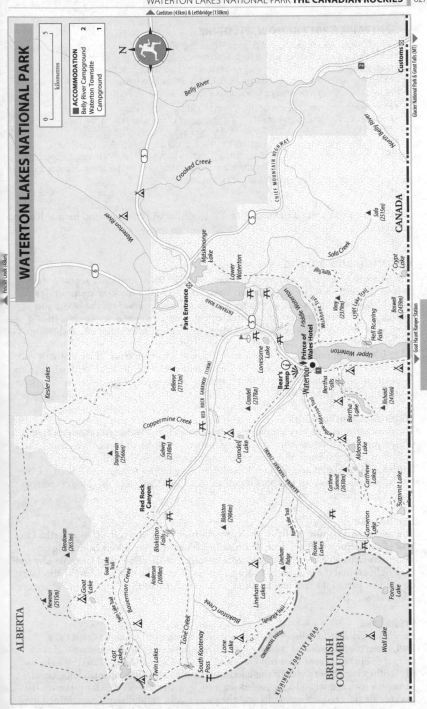

WATERTON LAKES NATIONAL PARK

▲ Cardston (43km) & Lethbridge (130km)

■ ACCOMMODATION
Belly River Campground 2
Waterton Townsite Campground 1

N

0 ─── 5
kilometres

Pincher Creek (49km) ►

ALBERTA

Kesler Lakes

Newman (2515m)

Glendown (2653m)

Lost Lakes

Goat Lake
Goat Lake Trail

Twin Lakes

Anderson (2698m)

Bauerman Creek

Lone Lake

South Kootenay Pass

CONTINENTAL DIVIDE

KISHINENA FORESTRY ROAD

BRITISH COLUMBIA

Wall Lake

Forum Lake

Lineham Lakes

Lineham Ridge

Tamarack Trail

Blakiston Creek

Lone Creek

Dungarvan (2566m)

Golwey (2345m)

Coppermine Creek

Bellevue (2112m)

RED ROCK PARKWAY (15km)

Red Rock Canyon

Blakiston Falls

Blakiston (2904m)

Rowe Lake Trail

Rowe Lakes

Cameron Lake

Carthew Summit (2630m)

Carthew Lakes

Summit Lake

Alderson Lake

Carthew-Alderson Trail

AKAMINA PARKWAY (16km)

Crandell Lake

Crandell (2378m)

Lonesome Lake

Park Entrance

ENTRANCE ROAD

Belly River

Crooked Creek

6

5

5

Waterton River

Maskinonge Lake

Lower Waterton

CHIEF MOUNTAIN HIGHWAY

Sofa Creek

Sofa (2515m)

CANADA

North Belly River

5

Vimy Trail

Prince of Wales Hotel

Bear's Hump

Waterton

Upper Waterton

Middle Waterton

Wishbone Trail

Vimy (2379m)

CRYPT Lake Trail

Hell Roaring Falls

Crypt Lake

Boswell (2435m)

Bertha Falls

Bertha Lake

Richards (2416m)

Goat Haunt Ranger Station ►

Glacier National Park & Great Falls (MT) ►

Customs ⊠

8

SEPTEMBER 2017 KENOW WILDFIRE

Fuelled by hot weather, strong winds and extremely dry conditions, the Kenow Wildfire made its way into Waterton Lakes National Park in September 2017. Despite to the efforts of 148 firefighters and 11 helicopters some 38 percent of the park went up in flames. It left much of the western half of the park closed to visitors. Portions have been reopened, but the process will take years. Key re-openings to look out for include:

- Bears Hump – the parks best short walk with incredible valley views
- Red Rock Parkway – a couple of easy walks at the end of this road explore the water-gouged Red Rock Canyon, while wildlife sightings are common along the road.
- The Akamina Parkway – provides access to several good day hikes, including Lineham Ridge and Carthew Summit, but is particularly known as the trailhead for the park's best two overnight backpacking adventures: the difficult but terrific Tamrack Trail and the glorious Carthew–Alderson Trail, arguably the park's best hike.

---

declared Waterton a **World Heritage Site**, for its distinctive environment, natural history and scenery.

Waterton and around

The park's only real base and service centre, **WATERTON** is idyllically set on a shelf of land that juts into Upper Waterton Lake (at 150m, the Rockies' deepest). It's a lovely, laidback little place with an easy-going air; deer graze on the lawns and holidaymakers stroll around the assortment of shops, cafés and restaurants in the tiny centre, to Cameron Falls, the town's own tame little waterfall, and along the lakefront.

The lakefront promenade leads to a trio of classic Waterton **trails**: at its southern end it becomes the Waterton Lakeshore Trail and leads to the Bertha Lake Trail, while from its northern end **boats** from the quay cruise the lake (see page 629) and provide a shuttle to the Crypt Lake Trail.

Waterton Lakeshore Trail

The most obvious, and very simple, walk from town is the **Waterton Lakeshore Trail** (13km one way; 100m ascent; 4hr), along the western shore of Upper Waterton Lake. Take it as far as you fancy and then return, or take a boat to the end across the US border to Goat Haunt and then walk back (see page 629) – though you'll need a US visa or visa waiver in your passport if you are not Canadian, since this border crossing doesn't issue them.

Bertha Lake

The single most popular half-day or day's walk from Waterton is the classic **Bertha Lake Trail** (12km return; 460m ascent; 4hr 30min). It's a short, steep hike beginning on Evergreen Drive to a busy but remarkably unsullied mountain-ringed lake. An easy trail runs right around the lakeshore (adding another 5km to the trip); you could also just do the first part of the trail and break off at Lower Bertha Falls (2.9km from Waterton; 150m ascent; 1hr).

Crypt Lake

Another excellent, if challenging, walk out of Waterton is the unique **Crypt Lake Trail**, often touted as one of the best in Canada. The 8.6km hike (one way; 675m ascent; 6–8hr) involves a boat trip (see box opposite) across Upper Waterton Lake to the trailhead on the east side of the lake, a (perfectly safe) climb up a ladder, a crawl through a rock tunnel and a section along a rocky ledge with a cable for support. The rewards are the crashing waterfalls and the great glacial amphitheatre containing Crypt

Lake (1955m); rock walls tower to 600m on three sides, casting a chill shadow that preserves small icebergs on the lake's surface throughout the summer. Be sure to allow time to catch a return boat.

Chief Mountain Highway

The 32km **Chief Mountain Highway** (open mid-May to Oct), runs along the park's eastern border from the park entrance. After 7km it reaches a fine **viewpoint** over the mountain-backed Waterton Valley and then passes the *Belly River Campground* (see opposite), before reaching the Chief Mountain US–Canadian **border crossing** (June–Oct 7am–10pm) at 25km. This is the place to sort visas you might need for hikes across the border. When the Chief Mountain crossing is closed, the nearest border crossing is at Carway, Alberta (daily 7am–11pm), a 140km round-trip from the park gates.

INFORMATION

Entry fee A National Park pass ($9.80) is required to enter Waterton Lakes; though the park is run in tandem with the USA's Glacier National Park, the two remain distinct, with separate entry fees.

Visitor centre The main centre is on Entrance Rd, opposite the *Prince of Wales Hotel* on the way into Waterton but is closed due to fire damage. Until it re-opens, there's

WATERTON LAKES NATIONAL PARK

a temporary center in the Lion's Hall, Fountain Avenue (Mon–Fri 8am–4pm) in Waterton. Otherwise the staff at the park gate can help. The Canadian Parks Service 1:50,000 map of Waterton Lakes National Park, useful if you're doing any serious walking, is available from the visitor centre.

ACTIVITIES

Cycling Bikes, including mountain bikes (with front suspension $15/hr), can be hired from Pat's Convenience Store, 224 Mountain View Rd (☎ 403 859 2266), and there are a few good mountain trails in the park. The best option for the fit and experienced is to ride on the road up to the *Crandell Campground* (12km), climb the broad but rocky trail up to Crandell Lake and then follow the single-track trail back to town. The total route is about 20km and will probably take around three hours – bear encounters are likely.

Fishing There's good fishing on the lakes, but pick up a compulsory national park permit ($9.80/day) from the visitor centre.

Golf 4km north of town on the main highway, Waterton Lakes Golf Course (☎ 403 859 2114, ⓦ golfwaterton.com) is an eighteen-hole course.

Horseriding Alpine Stables (☎ 403 859 2462, ⓦ alpinestables.com) is just east of the highway, about 1km north of the visitor centre. Rides start at $45/hr.

ACCOMMODATION

Waterton Lakes is popular enough to warrant **advance booking** for much of July and August. All of the accommodation is in or around Waterton with the exception of some backcountry campgrounds. The main town campground fills to capacity in summer, when park staff will direct you to an RV park a short drive outside the park gates,

or the primitive *Belly River Campground* (technically in the park but a long way from anywhere you'd want to be). There are nine designated **backcountry campgrounds**, where you'll find dry toilets and a water supply; a few of them also have shelters and cooking facilities. To use a backcountry site you need a camping permit ($9.80 per person, plus

---

UPPER WATERTON LAKE CRUISES

Waterton Shoreline Cruises at the marina (☎ 403 859 2362, ⓦ watertoncruise.com) runs scenic two-hour **cruises** (May to early Oct 2–4 daily; $51) up and down the lake across the US–Canadian border to Goat Haunt in Montana, little more than a quayside and park ranger station, where there is a scheduled thirty-minute stop before the return to Waterton. You could also take an early boat to Goat Haunt and then return on foot along the **Waterton Lakeshore Trail** (see page 628) – though you'll need a passport and pre-register with the US border controls (links on ⓦ watertoncruise.com). Or use the same company's ferry to Crypt Lake (Late June to early Oct 2 daily; $26).

KOOTENAI BROWN

John George Brown – or **"Kootenai Brown"** – was a character straight out of a Wild West fantasy. Born in Ireland and allegedly educated at Eton, he spent time with the British Army in India, decamped to San Francisco, laboured in the gold fields of BC and worked as a Pony Express rider with the US Army. While travelling to the Waterton region he was attacked by Blackfoot natives, and supposedly wrenched an arrow from his back with his own hands. He was then captured by Chief Sitting Bull and tied naked to a stake, but managed to escape in the dead of night to join the rival Ktunaxa, with whom he spent years hunting and trapping, until their retreat from the prairies. Brown was later spared the hangman's noose, acquitted of murder following an altercation in which he killed a man.

Marriage proved a calming influence, and encouraged Brown to build a cabin (the region's first) alongside Waterton Lake. In 1895 a reserve was established, with Brown as its first warden. In 1911 it was designated a **national park**, the fourth in Canada. Brown, then aged 71, was made its superintendent, but died five years later, still lobbying hard to extend the park's borders. His grave lies alongside the main road into Waterton Village.

$11.70 reservation fee; ☎ 877 737 3783), issued on a first-come, first-served basis by the visitor centre (see opposite).

HOTELS AND MOTELS

Bayshore Inn 111 Waterton Ave ☎ 403 859 2211, ☎ 888 527 9555, ⓦ bayshoreinn.com. This very comfortable hotel is just south of the marina, and 49 of its seventy units are on the lakefront. Choose from the "romantic", "deluxe" or "family" suites, and lakefront or mountain-view rooms. It also has an on-site spa, restaurant, bistro and bar. May to mid-Oct. **$299**

Crandell Mountain Lodge 102 Mountview Rd ☎ 403 859 2288, ☎ 866 859 2288, ⓦ crandellmountainlodge. com. The seventeen nicely finished rooms in this pretty lodge are more intimate than in some town hotels; rooms with kitchenettes or gas fireplaces are available. **$199**

★ **Northland Lodge** 408 Evergreen Ave ☎ 403 859 2353, ⓦ northlandlodgecanada.com. These nine cosy rooms (seven with private bathroom) are set in a 1928 lodge south of town in the lee of the mountains and one block south of Cameron Falls. A two-night minimum booking applies Jun–Aug. Mid-May to mid-Oct. **$139**

Prince of Wales Hotel Waterton Lake, off Hwy-5 ☎ 403 892 2525, ⓦ glacierparkinc.com. Famous and popular old hotel – the best in town if you want a place with a sense of history and in an unbeatable position – and one whose 1927 Gothic outline is in almost every picture of Waterton. It's worth it if you can afford the pricier lakeside rooms (around $25 more) with views. The "standard" rooms are rather small. Early June to mid-Sept. **$280**

CAMPGROUNDS

Belly River Campground Chief Mountain Highway, 26km from Waterton; map p.627. A basic, park-run, overflow camp-ground (bring your own water). Mid-May to mid-Sept. Sites **$15.70**

Waterton Townsite Campground Off Vimy Ave ☎ 877 737 3783, ⓦ pccamping.ca; map p.627. On the southern side of Waterton village, this busy 238-site park-run campground is the only one that can be booked in advance. Facilities include hot showers, flush toilets, kitchen shelters, food storage and full RV hook-ups; no open fires allowed. Mid-April to mid-Oct. Sites **$22.50**; RVs **$27.40**

EATING AND DRINKING

Bayshore Lakeside Chophouse Waterton Ave ☎ 403 859 2211, ☎ 888 527 9555, ⓦ bayshoreinn.com. This hotel restaurant is one of the more elegant spots in town, with a dining room overlooking the lake. The food is North American – ribs, spaghetti and meatballs – but most dishes come with a gourmet twist. Mains $18–46. Daily 7am–10pm.

Pearl's 305 Windflower Ave ☎ 403 859 2284. Bustling and upbeat wholefood café with a good range of breakfast options, excellent coffee and some huge, healthy and delicious speciality wraps, including an excellent crab and avocado option ($9.95). The hiker lunches – packs to take

with you for the trail – are highly recommended; call a day ahead. At the height of summer the place stays open until 9pm with a range of good world-food options like curries and a satisfying pasta bar. Daily 7am–2pm; until 9pm in July & Aug.

Pizza of Waterton 303 Windflower Ave ☎ 403 859 2660. The dough for the tasty pizzas served up here ($15–30) is made daily on the premises; they also have soups and salads, and are licensed to serve alcohol. Daily noon–10pm.

★ **Prince of Wales Hotel** Waterton Lake, off Hwy-5 ☎ 403 859 2231. This luxury hotel offers a number of dining choices, all open to non-guests. The *Windsor Lounge* is the more casual bar; the *Royal Stewart Dining Room* is the fanciest option, offering near-gourmet breakfast, lunches and dinners; but the hotel is best known for its refined afternoon tea (1–5pm daily; $33) in front of glorious lake views – a real throwback to colonial times. Dress up, as the place is fairly smart. Daily 11.30am–10pm.

The BC Interior

VINEYARDS IN THE OKANAGAN VALLEY

9

The BC Interior

Home to Canada's only semi-arid desert, an award-winning wine region and boasting some of North America's best backcountry skiing and epic glaciers, British Columbia's magnificent interior offers a thrilling range of landscapes to explore and all the wide-open space to enjoy the outdoor adventure lifestyle that its locals adore. It says something about the relentlessly jaw-clanging beauty of the interior that you can approach it from the Rockies or Vancouver and find landscapes every bit as spectacular as those you've left behind. However, in this case, the road less travelled really offers up the best sights: both major east–west routes across the region – Trans-Canada (Hwy-1) and Hwy-3 along the US border – skirt the real highlights. More rewarding are the two north–south routes: the easternmost snakes through the Kootenay region – an idyllic assortment of mountains, lakes and peaceful towns and its vast Glacier and Revelstoke national parks – all the way south to the US border near the quaint old mining town and skiing and biking haven of Rossland. Roughly parallel to the west, Hwy-97 travels through the arid Okanagan: a California-like enclave of orchards, vineyards, lakes and resort towns, whose beaches and scorching summers draw hordes of holiday-makers from all over the world.

The regional transport hub of **Kamloops** effectively forms the Okanagan's northern gateway. It's also on the doorstep of the laidback **Shuswap** region – a medley of lakes and rivers loved by houseboaters and spawning salmon – and the magnificent **Wells Gray Provincial Park**, a remote collection of exceptional waterfalls and perfect canoeing lakes. And it's from Kamloops too that the most spectacular portion of the Trans-Canada begins: along the awesome **Fraser Canyon** to Vancouver, which is as scenically spectacular as anything in this incredible region.

Glacier National Park

GLACIER NATIONAL PARK protects a representative example of the Selkirk Mountains in the Columbia Mountain Range adjacent to the Rockies. Canada's second oldest national park, its mountains are older than those to the east, with harder rock and sharper peaks; these glacier-clad mountains are credited with being the birthplace of sport mountaineering in Canada. Here weather systems from the Pacific meet the mountains making for highly variable conditions – you can set off in blazing sunshine and meet a blizzard by lunchtime – but despite this, the soaring alpine scenery and vast wilderness attracts **climbers**, **backcountry skiers** and **hikers** from across the world. There are 147 glacier masses in the park with 8.3 percent of the park permanently blanketed with ice. The most famous of these glaciers, the **Illecillewaet Glacier**, is easily seen from the Trans-Canada Highway and is the birthplace of glaciology in North America. It was first photographed in 1887 and is still monitored today.

The park's highest point, **Mount Hasler**, in the Dawson Range, is 3399m tall – and historically it and its neighbours have presented as much of a barrier as their Rocky Mountain cousins. The "impenetrable peaks" of the Selkirk Mountains were the

HELMCKEN FALLS, WELLS GRAY PROVINCIAL PARK

Highlights

❶ Glacier and Revelstoke national parks
Breathtakingly beautiful mountain scenery that rivals the Rockies – and Canada's backcountry-ski capital, Revelstoke. See pages 634 and 638

❷ The Kootenays A pristine region of lakes, mountains, forests, natural hot springs and charming old-world villages. See page 642

❸ Nelson British Columbia's most compelling interior town, thanks to hundreds of vintage buildings and a thriving cultural scene. See page 653

❹ The Okanagan Award-winning wineries, lush fruit orchards and the surreal, scrub-covered landscape of Canada's only semi-arid

desert, complete with slithering rattlesnakes and cacti. See page 659

❺ The Kettle Valley Railway Scenic cycle along an old rail-bed over dramatic trestles with glorious Okanagan lake and mountain views. See page 664

❻ Roderick Haig-Brown Provincial Park Enjoy the captivating sight of thousands of salmon struggling upstream to spawn. See page 669

❼ Wells Gray Provincial Park Vast tract of wilderness with several tremendous waterfalls and lakes that are perfect for overnight canoe trips. See page 674

HIGHLIGHTS ARE MARKED ON THE MAP ON PAGE 636

9

last great obstacle to the completion of the great transcontinental railway. In 1881, Major A.B. Rogers, an American railway surveyor, made his place in history when he discovered **Rogers Pass** (1321m) for the Canadian Pacific Railway, the final link that brought Canada together as a nation.

Despite the railway's best efforts, its pounding by repeated avalanches eventually forced the company to bore a tunnel through the mountain, but the 1962 completion of the Trans-Canada Highway along the pass once again made the area accessible. This time huge snowsheds were built, backed by the world's largest **mobile avalanche-control system**.

Hiking in Glacier National Park

Some of the park's twenty trails (140km of walking in all) push close to glaciers for casual views of the ice – though only two spots are now safe at the toe

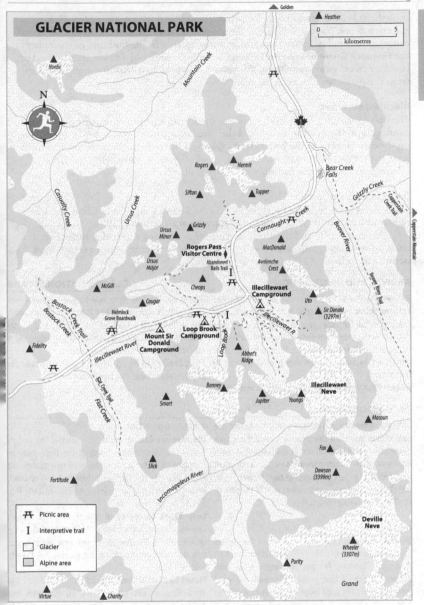

GLACIER NATIONAL PARK

of the Illecillewaet – and the backcountry is noticeably less busy than in the Rockies parks.

Short trails off Hwy-1

The easiest short strolls off the Trans-Canada are: the **Abandoned Rails Trail** (2.8km round trip; 1hr; suitable for wheelchairs), along old rail-beds to abandoned

9

snowsheds between the Rogers Pass visitor centre and the Summit Monument; the **Loop Brook Trail** (1.6km) from the viewpoint just east of the *Loop Brook* campground, full of viewpoints and features relating to the building of the railway; the **Hemlock Grove Boardwalk** (350m), a stroll through old-growth stands of cedar hemlock trees, some more than 350 years old (wheelchair-friendly; trailhead 5km from the park's western boundary).

Illecillewaet trails

The hub for most of Glacier's day-hikes is the *Illecillewaet* campground near the confluence of the Asulkan Brook and the Illecillewaet River, which can be appreciated on the easy **Meeting of the Waters Trail** (30min). Otherwise six manageable day-hikes leave the campground to provide superb views of glaciers, particularly the Great Glacier, Avalanche Crest and Abbott's Ridge trails.

Backcountry options

The longest Glacier backcountry option is the **Beaver Valley Trail** (42km one way); this can be combined with a trail up **Copperstain Mountain** (2595m) to form a loop through forests and meadows and alpine tundra for a four-day hike. Two backcountry campgrounds are available en route; contact the visitor centre for a permit (see below).

ARRIVAL AND INFORMATION

By car There are no services on the Trans-Canada between Golden and Revelstoke. Note that Park Canada experts monitor the slopes year-round, and at dangerous times they close the Trans-Canada Hwy and call in the Canadian Armed Forces, who use 105mm howitzers to bring down avalanches before they become a threat to motorists.

Rogers Pass visitor centre (Daily: May to mid-June &

GLACIER NATIONAL PARK

Sept to mid-Nov 9am–5pm; mid-June to Aug 8am–7pm; Nov–Apr 7am–4pm; ☎ 250 837 7500, ⌨ pc.gc.ca/glacier), 1km west of Rogers Pass, sells the nightly backcountry camping permit ($9.80), has good walking maps and a variety of excellent natural history displays.

Entry fee The park fee is $7.80 and is valid on the same day at Revelstoke National Park (see below) as well.

ACCOMMODATION

Hotel **accommodation** is often best sought in Golden (see page 610) or Revelstoke (see page 641), since the options below both tend to be full in season. If all three first-come, first-served, park-run **campgrounds** are full – or you want more facilities (no park campgrounds have showers) – try one of three commercial campgrounds west of the park on the Trans-Canada Hwy towards Revelstoke.

HOTELS

Heather Mountain Lodge 24km east of the Rogers Pass visitor centre ☎ 866 344 7490, ⌨ heathermountain lodge.com. Spacious, fir- and larch-beam lodge with 22 rooms which all have private bathrooms and good mountain views. The main lodge has two large fireplaces, a deck with a hot-tub, a dining room and a more relaxed second-floor lounge. $139

CAMPGROUNDS

Illecillewaet Campground 3km west of the Rogers Pass visitor centre. The closest of the three park-run campgrounds to the visitor centre, with sixty pitches and lots of hiking nearby. Facilities include flush toilets, water, kitchen shelters and fire wood. Late June to early Oct. $21.50

Loop Brook Campground 5km west of the Rogers Pass visitor centre. The twenty sites here have the same facilities as the Illecillewaet. It's self-serve check-in, but park staff will register visitors in the evening. July to early Sept. $21.50

Mount Sir Donald Campground 1km west of the Loop Brook Campground. Offers fifteen primitive sites and nothing more than a dry toilet. Fires are not permitted. July to early Sept. $15.70

Mount Revelstoke National Park

The smallest national park in the region, **MOUNT REVELSTOKE NATIONAL PARK** is a somewhat arbitrary creation, put together at the request of local people in

1914 to protect the Clachnacudainn Range of the Columbia Mountains. The lines on the map mean little, for the thrilling scenery in the 16km of no-man's-land between Glacier and Revelstoke is largely the same as that within the parks. The mountains here are especially steep, their slopes often scythed clear of trees by avalanches. The views from the Trans-Canada Highway, as it peeks out of countless tunnels, are of forests and snow-capped peaks aplenty and, far below, the railway and the Illecillewaet River crashing through a twisting, steep-sided gorge.

The Meadows-in-the-Sky-Parkway

The main access point to the park interior is the easily accessed **Meadows-in-the-Sky-Parkway** to the 26km-distant summit of Mount Revelstoke (1938m). It opens when the road is snow free, usually May to early October, though it may not be fully open until mid-July. It strikes north from the Trans-Canada Highway at Revelstoke and winds up sixteen switchbacks through forest and alpine meadows noted for glorious displays of wildflowers, which are best enjoyed from half a dozen roadside viewpoints. A gate lies on the road 1km shy of the summit at **Balsam Lake** where you can park your car and take a regular shuttle bus (daily 10am–4.30pm) to the summit or do the 1km hike.

Summit hikes

At the summit the 1km **First Footsteps Trail** is a quick paved loop through alpine meadows with First Nations art along the way. Look out for the so-called Icebox, a shaded rock cleft that contains what is reputedly the world's smallest glacier. Other short and obvious trails fan out, while the most popular day-hikes head to **Miller or Eva lakes**, both around 12km (5hr) return over gently rolling subalpine terrain. You can easily double that time by extending this hike over treeless tundra **Jade Lakes**, where you'd probably want to make use of its backcountry campground, for which you'll need a permit (see below), before returning.

Short hikes off Hwy-1

A couple of good, very short and easily overlooked trails lie at the far eastern edge of the park off Hwy-1. Some 26km east of Revelstoke, the **Skunk Cabbage Boardwalk Trail** (1.2km) snakes through a rare wetland habitat which harbours muskrat, beaver and numerous birds. Another 4km east, the **Giant Cedars Boardwalk Trail** is a 0.5km jaunt with informative panels through old-growth forest crammed with 500-year-old cedars.

INFORMATION

MOUNT REVELSTOKE NATIONAL PARK

Visitor kiosk A park welcome station kiosk (mid-May to early June & Sept to early Oct 9am–5pm, mid-June to Aug 8am–5pm) is at the start of the Meadows-in-the-Sky-Parkway, but when it's closed you have to visit the park administration office.

Administration office Revelstoke post office, 301b 3rd St West (Mon–Fri 8 am–noon & 1–4.30pm; ☎ 250 837 7500).
Entry fee The park fee is $7.80 and is valid on the same day at Glacier National Park (see page 634) as well.

ACCOMMODATION

Camping Backcountry camping in the park – with tent-pads, outhouses and food-storage poles provided – at Eva and Jade lakes (it's not possible to drive in) needs to be paid for at the Parkway welcome station kiosk or at the Revelstoke office (see opposite). $9.80
Canyon Hot Springs Resort Campground Halfway between Mount Revelstoke and Glacier national parks, 35km east of Revelstoke ☎ 250 837 2420, ⓦ canyonhotsprings.com. Commercial campground close to the park's borders, with about two hundred secluded sites for tents and RVs, as well as cabins for two and chalets for four. The on-site hot springs – piped from two miles away to an outdoor pool – cost $11.50 extra. May to late Sept. Tent sites $35; RVs $45; cabins $95; chalets (for four) $245

9

Revelstoke

Like many BC mountain towns, **REVELSTOKE** is divided between a motel-and-garage strip along the highway and a dispersed collection of frontier-type houses in a downtown area some distance away. As you drive into town you are welcomed by a pair of carved bears. If you want to relax close to town, try warm-watered **Williamson Lake**, a favourite swimming spot for locals which also has a campground (see page 641).

Revelstoke Railway Museum

719 Track St West • Wed–Sat noon–5pm • $10 • ☎ 250 837 6060, ⓦ railwaymuseum.com

Downtown, the small but polished **Revelstoke Railway Museum** has a steam engine, snowploughs and assorted memorabilia relating to the building of the stretch of the Canadian Pacific Railway between Field and Kamloops.

Revelstoke Dam

Hwy-23, 5km north of Revelstoke • Mid-May to Sept daily 10am–4pm • $6 • ☎ 250 814 6697

A trip to a dam may sound dull, but the **Revelstoke Dam** makes a surprisingly interesting outing and receives thousands of visitors each year. This 175m-tall barrier holds back the waters of the Columbia River, around 500km from its source, and its sleek, space-age **visitor centre** has over a dozen interactive displays.

Revelstoke Mountain Resort

2950 Camozzi Rd, 6km southeast of town past the airport • Dec to mid-April • Day-pass $109 • ☎ 250 814 0087, ☎ 888 837 2188, ⓦ revelstokemountainresort.com

Though only opening in 2008, Revelstoke's **ski hill** has already developed a solid national reputation as a superb skiing spot thanks to its rugged terrain and huge

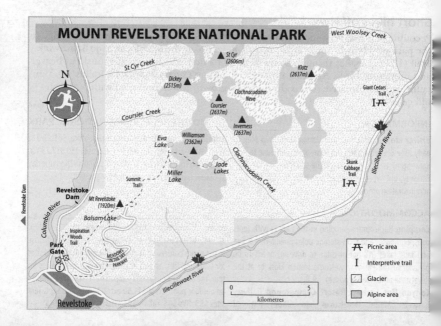

MOUNT REVELSTOKE NATIONAL PARK

West Woolsey Creek

St Cyr Creek

▲ St Cyr (2606m)

Klotz (2637m) ▲

Giant Cedars Trail I⛱

Dickey (2515m) ▲

Clachnacudainn Neve

Coursier Creek

Coursier (2637m) ▲

Inverness (2637m) ▲

Eva Lake

Williamson (2362m) ▲

Jade Lakes

Clachnacudainn Creek

Illecillewaet River

Skunk Cabbage Trail I⛱

Summit Trail

Miller Lake

Revelstoke Dam

Columbia River

Revelstoke Dam

Mt Revelstoke (1920m) ▲

Balsam Lake

Inspiration Woods Trail

Park Gate

MEADOWS IN THE SKY PARKWAY

Illecillewaet River

Revelstoke

0 — 5 kilometres

⛱ Picnic area
I Interpretive trail
Glacier
Alpine area

N

HELI- AND CATSKIING NEAR REVELSTOKE

The only way to get up into the deep powder is via snowcat or helicopter, but neither are especially cheap; expect to pay around $550 for a day cat skiing and $1000 for heli-skiing. Daypackages are available but multiday lodge-based options are best if you want to explore untouched terrain and experience backcountry skiing at its best.

K-3 Cat Skiing ⓣ250 837 5100, ⓦk3catski.com. One of Revelstoke's newest outfits offers day- and multi-day catskiing on K3 in the Monashee Mountains.

Revelstoke Mountain Resort (see below). The least expensive option for backcountry skiing without the climb is the resort's own catskiing operation.

Selkirk Tangiers Heli-skiing ⓣ250 837 5378, ⓦselkirk-tangiers.com. Revelstoke Mountain Resort-owned operation that uses the town as its base so a good choice if you're not staying in a lodge.

Selkirk Wilderness Skiing ⓣ250 366 4424, ⓦselkirkwilderness.com. Operates from a lodge located high above the valley in the Selkirk Mountains.

White Grizzly Adventures ⓣ250 366 4306, ⓦwhitegrizzly.com. Runs trips in the region from a small lodge that only holds twelve guests.

1713m vertical drop – North America's highest. About half of the hill is geared to experts, and only a couple of the 52 runs are beginner-level, so it's one resort where it's really worth knowing what you're doing. If you don't, you may be more tempted by its **snowtubing** and **snowshoeing**. Snow conditions in Revelstoke are dependably good, with the resort averaging around 11m of snow annually, but if you happen on conditions that don't provide much lovely untracked snow then you can always treat yourself to cat- or heli-skiing (see box).

ARRIVAL AND INFORMATION — REVELSTOKE

By bus Stoke Shuttle buses provide transport from Kelowna International Airport to accommodation in Revelstoke (4 daily; ⓣ888 569 1969).

Downtown visitor centre 301 Victoria Rd W (Mon–Fri 8.30–4.30pm, Sat & Sun 9am–4.30pm; ⓣ250 837 5345, ⓦseerevelstoke.com). Offers basic park information.

Mount Revelstoke National Park Office 301b 3rd St West in the post office building (Mon–Fri 8.30am–noon & 1–4.30pm). Sells maps and guides with staff on hand to give advice.

ACCOMMODATION

HOTELS AND MOTELS

The Cube Hotel 311 Campbell Ave ⓣ250 837 4086, ⓦcubehotel.ca. Pleasingly modern boutique hostel-style hotel with spotlessly clean accommodation ranging from singles to four-person family rooms with double bunks. Complimentary breakfast and shuttle pass to resort included; individual showers are located in the hallway adjacent to rooms. **$94**

Regent Hotel 112 First St East ⓣ250 837 2107, ⓦregenthotel.ca. Smart hotel whose rooms have "standard" and "premium" town or mountain views, massive beds and large bathtubs. For more privacy or group accommodation, choose a one- or two-bedroom unit in the "the Annex", just across the street. Amenities include a restaurant and pub, nightclub and a breakfast café. **$171**

Revelstoke Gateway Inn 1500 1st St West ⓣ250 837 2164, ⓣ877 837 8337, ⓦrevelstokegatewayinn.com. Smart and simple motel where some rooms have kitchenettes and the more roomy two- and three-bedroom family suites have full kitchens. Rates include continental breakfast and free wi-fi and there's a hot tub, too. **$109**

HOSTELS AND CAMPGROUNDS

Lamplighter Campground 1760 Nixon Rd ⓣ250 837 3385, ⓦrevelstokecc.bc.ca/lamplighter. Peaceful, fully serviced fifty-site tent and RV campground within walking distance of downtown. To get here from town, cross the Columbia River bridge; take Hwy-23 south towards Nakusp, then take the first left onto Nixon Rd. Free wi-fi. May–Sept. Sites **$31**; RVs **$37**

Revelstoke Backpacker Hostel 400 2nd St West ⓣ250 837 4050, ⓦsamesun.com/Revelstoke. Central house that's convenient for downtown and offers private rooms and dorm beds. The communal area, which includes a full kitchen, patio and barbecue deck, has free wi-fi. Dorms **$30**; doubles **$65**

Williamson Lake Campground 1818 Williamson Lake Rd ⓣ250 837 5512, ⓦwilliamsonlakecampground.com. Pleasant, fifty-site lakeside campground 3km south of the town centre near the airport. There are free hot showers, flush toilets, laundry, a beach, canoe and rowing boat rentals and a mini-golf course. Sites **$30**, RVs **$35**

9

EATING

112 Restaurant & Lounge 112 First St East ☎ 250 837 2107, ⓦ 112restaurant.ca. Dependably good local spot in the *Regent Hotel* with good food like rack of lamb with *spätzle* (German noodles). Mains cost $16–32, and there's a lively pub and dancefloor too. Daily 5.30am–10pm.

The Modern Bakeshop & Café 212 Mackenzie Ave ☎ 250 837 6886, ⓦ themodernbakeshopandcafe.com. Simple café serving tasty inexpensive meals such as salads and open sandwiches, washed down with excellent home-made iced tea or lemonade. Mon–Sat 8am–3pm.

Paramjit's Kitchen 116 First St West ☎ 250 837 2112, ⓦ paramjitskitchen.com. Exceptional downtown Indian diner that also specializes in German food. The chef combines the two cuisines with far more success than you'd expect – saffron prawn *spätzle* ($20) anyone? Mon–Fri 11am–9pm, Sat 4–9pm.

★ **Village Idiot** 306 MacKenzie Ave ☎ 250 837 6240, ⓦ thevillageidiot.ca. Locals' favourite hangout year-round, which attracts a big ski-season crowd too. The suntrap patio gets packed, so come early to bag a table. Excellent pizzas ($13), sandwiches, burgers and customizable piled-high *poutines*. Daily 11am–midnight.

The Kootenays

The Kootenays are one of the most attractive and lightly visited parts of BC, and centre on two major north–south valleys which harbour **Kootenay Lake**, the **Upper and Lower Arrow lakes** and three adjacent mountain ranges – the Purcells, Selkirks and Monashees – whose once-rich mineral deposits formed the kernel of the province's early mining industry. **Nelson** (see page 653) is the key spot, slightly peripheral to the Kootenays' rugged core, but a lovely place, and one of the few provincial towns with real attractions in its own right. Smaller, more relaxed, lakeside towns, notably **Kaslo** and **Nakusp**, make excellent bases for excursions into mountain scenery that has a pristine quality rarely found elsewhere. **Creston** offers a glimpse into the region's rich agricultural bounty with Canada's juiciest cherries, and **Rossland** has bags of small town charm and was the site of Canada's first downhill ski race. Water-based activities – **canoeing** and **fishing** in particular – are excellent, and you can also explore the ramshackle mining heritage of near-ghost towns like **Sandon** and **New Denver**. Many of these towns and villages also have more than their fair share of artists, painters, writers and artisan foodies, lending the region considerable cultural lustre. **Castlegar** also offers a fascinating immigrant history through the story of the **Doukhobors** who settled here from Russia.

Getting around the region without **private transport** is tricky, which is a shame because the roads here are among the most beautiful in the province, especially Hwy-31A from Kaslo to New Denver, and the pleasingly dramatic Hwy-6, which leads south of Nakusplong along the Slocan Valley and west to Vernon, setting you up nicely for the Okanagan.

Nakusp

Some 58km south of the Galena Bay–Shelter Bay ferry (see page 643) – and 105km from Revelstoke on Hwy-23 – **NAKUSP** has a wonderful, typically Kootenays lakefront setting, beside the huge **Upper Arrow Lake** with the snowcapped Selkirk Mountains to the east providing a majestic backdrop. You can happily wander around the town for an hour along the main street, Broadway, and the lakefront promenade, then go boating or swimming at the public **beach**. There's also plenty of fishing and hiking – ask for details at the visitor centre.

Nakusp Hot Springs

Daily 9.30am–9.30pm • $10.50, day-pass $16.50 • ☎ 250 265 4528, ☎ 866 999 4528, ⓦ nakusphotsprings.com

The main attraction in Nakusp is the excellent **Nakusp Hot Springs**, a well-signposted 13km northeast of town. The complex consists of a couple of midsize tiled pools in a lovely mountain setting with chalets and a campground.

THE GALENA BAY–SHELTER BAY FERRY

Travellers heading along Hwy-23 between **Revelstoke** and **Nakusp** need to interrupt their 105km journey to take the **Galena Bay–Shelter Bay ferry**. This free and superbly scenic service usually runs hourly from 5am to midnight – with half-hourly sailings at peak times in summer. The latest times are posted on the highway as you leave both Revelstoke and Nakusp.

ARRIVAL AND INFORMATION   NAKUSP

By bus BC Transit (ⓦ bctransit.com) provides buses to and from Nelson and many other local destinations, but only a couple of times a week. The full schedule is posted on the wall of the helpful visitor centre.

Visitor centre 92 6th Ave, beside the post office on Broadway (May to mid-Sept Mon–Sat 9am–5pm, Sun 10am–5pm; mid-Sept to April Tues–Fri 11am–3pm; ☎ 250 265 4234, ☎ 800 909 8819, ⓦ nakusparrowlakes.com).

ACCOMMODATION

Casa Mandala 206 Broadway ☎ 250 265 3288, ⓦ casamandala.ca. Funky, self-contained guesthouse with sweeping views over Arrow Lake and Saddleback Mountain just around the corner from Nakusp's main drag. Ideal for families, the guesthouse offers a full kitchen with a patio deck and barbecue. **$150**

Leland Hotel 96 4th Ave SW ☎ 250 265 4221, ⓦ leland hotelnakusp.com. Right on the lake, the *Leland* has been operating as a hotel since 1892 and so claims to be BC's oldest. Don't expect large or modern rooms, but they have free wi-fi, a/c, fridges and microwaves – and the views from many of them are great. The hotel also has a cheerful locals' pub and restaurant with a lovely lakeside patio. **$99**

The Lodge at Arrow Lakes 515 Broadway ☎ 250 265 3618, ☎ 800 663 0100, ⓦ arrowlakeslodge.com. Bland but clean, tidy and modern downtown motel with its own sports bar and restaurant specializing in good-value North American favourites – great for full breakfasts. A block from the lake and opposite a good little café. **$100**

Nakusp Hot Springs Chalet and Camping Ground 8500 Nakusp Hot Springs Rd ☎ 250 265 4528, ⓦ nakusp hotsprings.com. Very simple but clean and comfortable A-frame cabins, with en-suite bathtubs (no showers). Close to the hot springs. Also has riverside camping beside the babbling Kuskanax. May to mid-Oct. Sites **$20**; RVs **$31.50**; cabins **$94**

EATING

Broadway Deli Bistro 408 Broadway ☎ 250 265 3767. Laidback café with good all-day breakfasts, sandwiches, baked goods, and some Mexican food for $6–10, including *huevos rancheros* and *quesadillas* served with spicy home-made salsa. Free wi-fi. Wed–Mon 6am–3pm.

Karl's Pizza n' More 314 Broadway ☎ 250 265 0060. A good spot with a nice patio, which serves generous portions of German favourites like schnitzel ($15) as well as baked salmon ($19) and of course pizzas, plus German beers. Mon–Sat 11am–9pm.

Hwy-6: Nakusp to Vernon

South of Nakusp, Hwy-6 runs alongside **Upper Arrow Lake** and past a series of cabins, resorts and campgrounds on its way to Vernon, 194km away (see page 666). Some 58km from Nakusp the free **Needles Cable Ferry** (usually every 30min 5am–10pm, latest times posted on highway at edge of Nakusp) crosses the lake at the hamlet of **FAUQUIER**, with its handful of buildings including a garage, store, campground and motel.

On the western side of the lake Hwy-6 becomes a gloriously empty ribbon as it burrows through the staggering **Monashee Mountains**. Some 21km beyond **Monashee Pass** (1198m), the scattered town of **CHERRYVILLE** (47km from Vernon) provides one of the route's very few accommodation options, along with the nearest access to **Monashee Provincial Park** – 62km to the north – which provides experienced backcountry enthusiasts with some real wilderness to explore.

Beyond Cherryville, the highway begins its long descent through the **Coldstream Valley** towards the Okanagan. Snow dusts the mountains here almost year-round and crags loom above beautiful flower-filled valleys that break the forest cover to wind down to the highway.

Gold Panner Campground and Historic Village Cherryville ☎ 250 308 4780, ⓦ goldpannercampground. com. Offers pretty campsites, chalets and cabins but is most unusual for the chance to pan for gold in the grounds – and you don't have to be a guest to rent the $10/day kit. April–

Oct. Sites $29; RVs $38; cabins $85
Tukaluk Fauquier ☎ 250 269 7355. Located off Hwy-6 at the northern entrance to the hamlet, *Tukaluk* offers twenty sites for both tents and RVs and has shower facilities too. April–Oct. Sites $20

Hwy-6: Nakusp to New Denver

Another scenic gem, Hwy-6 east of Nakusp takes 46km to reach New Denver. At the 15km mark it reaches **Summit Lake**, a perfect jewel of water amid mountain and forest, served by the Summit Lake Provincial Park **campground** (see opposite). A road south from here goes into the mountains and to the small Summit Lake **ski** area (Dec–March Wed–Sun 10.30am–3.30pm; day-pass $32; ☎ 250 265 3312, ⓦ skisummitlake.com, cash only), which only boasts a single T-bar, but does have night skiing and big plans.

New Denver

NEW DENVER was once known as Eldorado for its mineral riches, and, like many settlements in the area, was born of the 1890s silver-mining boom. All that has gone, but something of the rough-and-ready pioneering feel remains. Its pretty setting on Slocan Lake and the **Nikkei centre** are its main (albeit minor) draws, but New Denver can also be a launch point for boat access to Valhalla Provincial Park (see page 645), and an abandoned railroad that offers easy cycling to Sandon (see page 646); the visitor centre can provide details of rentals and point you to the trailhead.

Nikkei Internment Memorial Centre

306 Josephine St • May–Sept daily 10am–5pm; Oct–April by appointment • $9 • ☎ 250 358 7288

Well signposted from Hwy-6, the moving **Nikkei Internment Memorial Centre** is dedicated to the 22,000 Nikkei (Canadians of Japanese ancestry) who, in 1942, were forcibly relocated from the West Coast to remote internment camps in the BC Interior after Pearl Harbor. Beautiful Japanese gardens now surround the wooden shacks and outhouses the Nikkei were forced to build. Although the majority of Nikkei were Canadian citizens, they were all labelled "enemy aliens" and stripped of their possessions, homes and businesses. It wasn't until 1988 that the Canadian government formally apologized to Japanese-Canadians and awarded them token monetary compensation.

Visitor centre 202 6th Ave, on the main street by the lakefront (May to June Sat & Sun 10am–2pm; July to early Sept daily 9am–5pm; ☎ 250 358 2719, ⓦ slocanlake.com).

Bike rental Wilds of Canada Cycle (Main St at 6th Ave; ☎ 250 358 7941, wildsofcanadacycles.blogspot.com).

ACCOMMODATION AND EATING

★**Apple Tree Sandwich Shop** 210 6th Ave ☎ 250 358 2691. Relaxed, local community cornerstone that specializes in sandwiches made from locally made bread – from lowly (and inexpensive) peanut butter and jam combos ($4) to exotic delights like the Bermudian (ham and pineapple on honey garlic bread; $8). Mon–Fri 7am–3pm.
★**The Domes** 602 6th Ave ☎ 250 358 7242, ⓦ thedomes.ca. This ecologically sound, domed lodge with twelve spotless rooms and four self-contained cabins provides the area's most exotic accommodation and a

chance to contemplate whether round rooms really are healthier, as the management claims. With communal kitchen, hot tub, sauna and wi-fi. $145
Glacier View Cabins 8th Ave and Hwy-6 ☎ 250 358 7277, ⓦ glaciercabins.com. Located just off Hwy-6, these are simple, bright, clean, quiet and central cabins, with kitchens. The owners also run boat trips and a water taxi to Valhalla Provincial Park. $95
Rosebery Provincial Park Campground Hwy-6, 4km north of New Denver ⓦ westkootenayparks.com/

rosebury-provincial-park. The best local campsites are on the lightly forested banks of Wilson Creek, with lake and mountain views, flush toilets and cold pumped water; campfires permitted. No reservations. May to mid-Sept. $\overline{20}$

Summit Lake Provincial Park Campground Hwy-6, 18km south of Nakusp or 26km southwest of New Denver

ⓦ westkootenayparks.com/summit-lake-provincial-park. A large site with waterfront access for 17 of the park's 34 campsites. Ideal for canoeing, fishing or swimming. Goats can often be seen grazing on the mountain, and in late summer thousands of toads hop from the lake to the forest to hibernate for winter. May 13 to Sept 21. $\overline{26}$

Slocan and around

Southbound out of New Denver, Hwy-6 winds through the tight confines of the Slocan Valley offering up gasp-inducing mountain and lake landscapes on both sides. Be certain to stop at the **Slocan Lake Viewpoint**, 6km out of New Denver, where a short path up a small cliff provides stupendous views.

At the southern end of Slocan Lake, you'll hit sprawling **SLOCAN**, another former mining village. Though with staggeringly few shops and services, it does provide one of the best access points for trips into the 506-square-kilometre **Valhalla Provincial Park**, a wilderness area with very few developed facilities, on the western side of Slocan Lake. Try **floating in a tube** down the Slocan River, a lazy way to spend a summer's day – or riding some of the Slocan Rail Trail, a popular 50km cycling route from Slocan, south to Crescent Valley.

Gravel roads from Slocan also lead east from Hwy-6 to **Kokanee Glacier Provincial Park** (see page 648). Pick up detailed directions and further information about either park at the New Denver or Slocan visitor centres.

Valhalla Provincial Park

A popular wildflower-lined trail leads 7.2km from Slocan past many good fishing and swimming spots along the western shore of the lake to **Evans Beach**, the most accessible part of the park. From the small campground here the Evans Creek trail leads to equally attractive spots beside lakes en route to **Beatrice Lake**, where the fishing is excellent. Most other park trailheads need to be accessed by kayak or canoe (see page 645), or take a water taxi from the *Glacier View Cabins* (see above). Among the park's premier trails are the steep and difficult 8.8km **Sharp Creek Trail** to the **New Denver Glacier** – the park's real scenic highlight – and the easy 4km **Nemo Creek Trail**, which passes **Nemo Falls**, spectacular rock formations, an old cabin and a massive ageing cedar and hemlock forest. Much of the upper valleys in the park are prime grizzly bear habitat, so extreme care should be taken if backcountry camping, which is possible in many good spots around the park.

ARRIVAL AND INFORMATION
SLOCAN

By bus There's a bus service to Nelson (2–3 daily; 1hr; ☏ 855 993 3100, ⓦ bctransit.com/west-kootenay).

Visitor centre 1020 Griffin Rd at the *Springer Creek*

Campground (July & Aug daily 8am–11am & 3–6pm; ☏ 250 355 2266, ⓦ slocancity.com). It has up-to-date timetables for buses.

ACTIVITIES

Bike rental For bike rental and a shuttle service, contact the *Spoke 'n' Dog B&B* (see below).

Watersports For kayak or canoe rentals, as well as guided

whitewater rafting trips, contact Smiling Otter Wilderness Adventures (☏ 250 355 2373, ⓦ smilingotter.com).

ACCOMMODATION AND EATING

Lemon Creek Lodge 7680 Kennedy Rd, 7km south of Slocan ☏ 250 355 2403, ⓦ lemoncreeklodge.com. Rustic post-and-beam lodge with mountain views, that offers lodge rooms, cabins and campsites as well as great locally grown food, a sauna and bike and kayak rental. Sites $\overline{20}$;

doubles $\overline{95}$; cabins $\overline{125}$

Spoke 'n' Dog B&B and Cycling 6285 McKean Rd, Winlaw ☏ 250 226 6752, ⓦ spokendog.com. Smart bed and breakfast halfway along the Slocan Rail Trail (see page 645) which offers an airy, modern two-bedroom suite,

9

with its own kitchen, laundry and free wi-fi. $90
Springer Creek Campground 1020 Giffin Rd ☎250 355 2266, ✉springr@telus.net. The office doubles as the town's visitor information, but otherwise manages a number of pleasant wooded campsites for tents. Facilities include showers ($1) and easy nearby trails strike out to waterfalls. Mid-May to Sept. Sites $20; RVs $25

Hwy-31A: New Denver to Kaslo

Hwy-31A runs for 46km from New Denver to **Kaslo**, allowing for a longer but far more scenic and interesting journey to Nelson than on Hwy-6 via Slocan (see page 645). From New Denver the road climbs past exits to the interesting near-ghost town of **Sandon** and the unmissable dirt road up Idaho Peak before nearing its high point beside some stunningly picturesque lakes: **Fish Lake** is deep green and has a nice picnic spot: **Bear Lake** is equally pretty; and **Beaver Pond** is an amazing testament to that animal's energy and ingenuity. Beyond the lakes the road descends alongside the Kaslo River, a crashing torrent choked with branches and fallen trees, and hemmed in by the cliffs and dark rock of the Selkirk Mountains. **Cycling** is also popular in this area, especially along the 17km **Galena Trail**; get information and rent a bike in New Denver (see page 644) or Slocan.

Sandon

SANDON, one of five ghost towns in the area, lies 13km east of New Denver via Hwy-31A and a gravel side road that climbs through scenery of utmost grandeur. The ragtag remains of Sandon form quite the contrast to its lovely surroundings, since a number of its current population (around a dozen) run a haulage company and are keen renovators of old machinery, and collectors of vintage BC Transit buses and 1900s steam locomotives.

Otherwise there are few relics of Sandon's silver-mining heyday, when the town had 24 hotels, 23 saloons, an opera house, a thriving red-light district and five thousand inhabitants – it even had electric light, well before Victoria or Vancouver. Still, you can pop into old City Hall and pick up a walking tour pamphlet ($1) from the **visitor centre** (usually July–Sept daily 10am–5pm), which vividly documents the area's Wild West mining history, harking back to an era when Slocan produced the lion's share of Canada's silver. Then head for the **museum** (June to mid-Oct daily 10am–5pm; $5; ⊛sandonmuseum.ca) in the old general store, with photos and domestic and commercial artefacts.

Idaho Peak

From Sandon, don't miss the hike up **Idaho Peak** (2280m), one of the most accessible and spectacular walks in the area. A 12km gravel access road from behind the museum leads into alpine pastures and a car park, from where it's a steep 3km to the summit of Mount Idaho and back, with views emerging all the way up to the spectacular panorama at the Forest Service lookout point.

ACCOMMODATION   **SANDON**

Camping There's no accommodation in Sandon, but RVers can use an electric hook-up beside the visitor centre, which can also advise on the many free Crown-land camping spots along the creek. $10

Kaslo

KASLO, 46km east of New Denver along glorious Hwy-31A or 70km north of Nelson along the pretty shores of Kootenay Lake (see page 642), must rate as one of British Columbia's most attractive and friendliest little villages. Huddled at the edge of Kootenay Lake and dwarfed by towering mountains, its half-dozen streets are lined with picture-perfect wooden homes and flower-filled gardens. It started life as a sawmill in 1889 and turned into a boom town – there were 27 bars, compared with a handful today – with the discovery of silver in 1893; diversification, and the steamers that plied the lakes, saved it from the cycle of boom and bust that ripped the heart out of so many similar towns. Today, Kaslo remains an urbane and civilized community whose thousand or so citizens work hard at keeping it that way, supporting a cultural centre, art galleries and a concert society. The **Kaslo Jazz Festival** (ⓦkaslojazzfest.com) in early August has some top-notch acts that perform on a floating stage on Kootenay Lake.

The SS Moyie

324 Front St • Mid-May to mid-Oct Daily 10am–5pm • $12 • ☎ 250 35 2525, ⓦ klhs.bc.ca

Kaslo's main attraction is the SS *Moyie*, the oldest surviving **steamwheeler** in North America, which ferried people, ore and supplies along the mining routes from 1898 until the advent of reliable roads in 1957. Similar steamers were the key to the Kootenays' early prosperity, their shallow draught and featherweight construction allowing them to nose into the lakes' shallowest waters. Inside is a collection of antiques, artefacts and photographs from the steamer's heyday.

The Langham

447 A Ave **Gallery** Thurs–Sun 1–4pm **Museum** Tues–Thurs 10am–5pm, Fri–Sun 1–4pm • ☎ 250 353 2661, ⓦ thelangham.ca

Kaslo's thriving arts centre, **The Langham**, stands opposite the post office and specializes in theatrical performances and art exhibitions. The 1893 building began life as a hotel for silver miners and was also used as an internment centre for Japanese-Canadians during World War II; a **museum** display commemorates this.

Argenta and the Purcell Wilderness

Kaslo makes an ideal base for pottering around charming local lakeshore communities such as tiny **Argenta**, 35km to the north – get directions from the visitor centre. Founded in 1952 as a refugee settlement for Californian Quakers alienated by the United States' growing militarism, Argenta is also the western trailhead for the difficult 61km **Earl Grey Pass Trail** through the **Purcell Wilderness Conservancy** (see page 617) to Invermere (see page 616). The area also offers a good chance of seeing **ospreys**: the Kootenays' hundred or so breeding pairs represent the largest concentration of the species in North America.

ARRIVAL AND INFORMATION   **KASLO**

By bus Weekly shuttle buses connect Nelson to Kaslo (ⓣ855 993 3100, ⓦbctransit.com/west-kootenay).
Visitor centre 324 Front St, beside the steamwheeler (mid-May to mid-Oct daily 9am–4pm; ☎250 353 2525, ⓦvisitkaslo.com).

TOURS AND ACTIVITIES

Kaslo Kayaking 315 A Ave ⓣ855 505 2925, ☎250 353 1925, ⓦkaslokayaking.ca. Rents out kayaks and offers lessons and guided tours to view Aboriginal petroglyphs on lakeside cliffs on half-day tours that cost $149, min 2 people.

ACCOMMODATION

★ **Beach Gables** 243 Front St ☎250 353 2111, ⓦbeachgables.ca. The best central accommodation in town, near the visitor centre, with uninterrupted lake views and three themed rooms. Free wi-fi. **$120**

Kaslo Municipal Campground Foot of Ave A, by the lake ☎250 353 2662, ⓦkaslo.ca. A pleasant location, with serviced and unserviced sites, picnic area and shelter, a children's playground and hot showers. May–Sept. **$25–35**

Lakewood Inn 6km north of Kaslo on Kohle Rd ☎250 353 2395, ⓦlakewoodinn.com. Fully equipped lakeside log cabins, trailers and tent and RV sites with private beach, boat rentals and sauna. Sites **$30–50**; cabins **$120**

Mirror Lake Campground 5777 Arcola Lake Rd ☎250 353 7102, ⓦmirrorlakecampground.com. Beautifully situated 5km south of town on the main road to Ainsworth, this campground's facilities include fire-pits, washrooms, showers, a laundry and store, games room, playground and sandy beach. Mid-April–mid-Oct. Sites **$25**; RVs **$30**

EATING

Blue Belle Bistro and Beanery 347 Front St ☎ 250 353 7361. Friendly coffee shop and bistro with healthy contemporary food such as rice bowls, salads, pizza, falafel and a superb apple raspberry pie. With regular live music and a patio. Mon–Fri 8.30am–8pm, Sat–Sun 9am–8pm.

Kaslo Hotel 430 Front St ☎ 250 353 7714, ⓦ kaslohotel. com. Historic hotel, whose pub has an appealing lakefront terrace and a good range of standard bar food. Its restaurant offers fancier dishes like the delicious seafood lasagne (mains around $22). Free wi-fi. Mon–Thurs 4–9pm, Fri–Sun 11.30am–9pm. $165

★ **Teresa's Coffee Shop** 402 Front St ☎ 250 353 2115,

ⓦ ilovekaslo.com. Welcoming café with sandwiches made with home-baked bread (all named after local mines, try the Lucky Jim!), wonderful pies and, rather unexpectedly, a mining and logging museum in the basement packed with fascinating artefacts (museum entry by donation). Open daily 7am till late.

Treehouse Restaurant 419 Front St ☎ 250 353 2955, ⓦ kaslotreehouse.com. For food and small-town hospitality, try the town's social hub, an unpretentious diner with big breakfasts and mains that average $12. Fri 6.30am–7pm, Sat–Thurs 6.30am–3pm.

Balfour and around

From Kaslo the delightful lakeshore **Hwy-31** twists its way 36km south to **BALFOUR** and the ferry crossing before turning into the much brisker Hwy-3A that heads 33km west to Nelson. Balfour itself is a fairly uneventful collection of motels, garages and cafés – albeit in verdant surroundings – gathered to catch the traffic rolling on and off the ferry. There's really not much to do, so you may want to time your ferry journey carefully, especially in the off-season.

Ainsworth Hot Springs

3609 Balfour-Kaslo-Galena Bay Hwy ☎ 800 668 1171, ⓦ hotnaturally.com • Springs daily 10am–9pm • single visit $13

A better place to stay than Balfour itself is **Ainsworth Hot Springs**, about 16km north on Hwy-31. Soaking in the large outdoor naturally-heated pool looking out over the mountains, or wading inside the resort's small network of underground caves is the main attraction.

Cody Caves Provincial Park

South Slocan ☎ 250 359 2283, ⓦ codycavetours.com • Check website for tour times • 2hr family tours from $45, 5hr adventure tours from $125

Cave and bat enthusiasts might want to take a guided tour through **Cody Caves Provincial Park**. It lies 12km up a rough gravel side-road off Hwy-3, some 3km north of Ainsworth, then a twenty-minute hike from the parking area. Check the website for details on what you need to bring to join the tours; appropriate clothing and footwear is required.

Kokanee Glacier Provincial Park

From Kokanee Creek Provincial Park (see opposite), 11km west of Balfour, Kokanee Glacier Road climbs north for 16km; other approaches to the park are from Hwy-31, 10km north of Ainsworth, driving 13km up Woodbury Creek into the park; from Hwy-6, 14km north of Slocan, where you drive 13km up Enterprise Creek; and from Hwy-6, 8km south of Slocan, up Lemon Creek for 16km

Kokanee Glacier Provincial Park straddles the Slocan Range of the Selkirk Mountains, and at the Gibson Lake park entrance there's a trailhead for a 2.5km jaunt around the lake. Another trail leads 4km uphill to lovely Kokanee Lake, where it levels out and continues another 3km to Kaslo Lake. Backcountry campgrounds and the *Kokanee*

THE KOOTENAY LAKE FERRY

The **Balfour-to-Kootenay Bay ferry** (daily 6.30am–9.40pm; free; ☎ 250 229 4215) is the longest free ferry in North America for car and foot passengers, and leaves every fifty minutes from Kootenay Bay (see page 649) from June to September, and every one hour, forty minutes the rest of the year. The 9km, forty-minute **crossing** is beautiful.

Glacier Cabin (see below) lie 2km further on. This is a wilderness area with no supplies or equipment available, so bring everything you need.

ACCOMMODATION AND EATING   **BALFOUR AND AROUND**

BALFOUR

Dock & Duck 7924 Hwy-3A ☎250 229 4244, ⓦdockn duck.ca. This pub with spotlessly clean suite-style rooms complete with full kitchens and a deck patio is right next to Balfour's jetty. The family-friendly pub below the rooms serves decent pizzas, ribs and sandwiches. Burgers (around $16) come in several unusual versions (guacamole and bacon; teriyaki and pineapple) and can be served with *pierogies* on request. Daily 11.30am–9.30pm. $159

AINSWORTH HOT SPRINGS

Ainsworth Hot Springs Resort 3609 Balfour-Kaslo-Galena Bay Hwy ☎1800 668 1171, ⓦhotnaturally.com. Though a tasteful resort, the mineral springs here are its main draw (see page 648), and it's a real luxury not to have to go far after your soak. Spa treatments cost extra. There's an on-site restaurant too. $159
Ainsworth Motel ☎250 229 4711, ☎888 848 4463, ⓦainsworthmotel.com. Dated but clean motel steps away from the springs and pools overlooking the lake, all suites have a kitchenette and the owners are friendly and helpful. $95

KOKANEE CREEK PROVINCIAL PARK

Kokanee Creek Provincial Park Hwy-3A, 11km west of Balfour and 19km northeast of Nelson ☎519 826 6850, ☎800 689 9025, ⓦdiscovercamping.ca. Campgrounds line Hwy-3A from Balfour to Nelson, but this provincial park is the most attractive spot, with a sandy beach, interpretive centre with trail advice, and a mosquito problem. Reserve at least two days in advance. May–Sept. $32

KOKANEE GLACIER PROVINCIAL PARK

Kokanee Glacier Cabin ☎403 678 3200, ⓦalpine clubofcanada.ca. Attractive alpine-chalet-style hut with full kitchen, but bring your own bedding for the dorm accommodation. Advance reservations essential. Per person $25

Southern Kootenay Lake: Kootenay Bay to Creston

The ferry from Balfour (see box) arrives at **KOOTENAY BAY**, the most fleeting of settlements, after which Hwy-3 bends south along the shores of Kootenay Lake for the rest of its winding 80km journey to Creston. The quiet road winds past a multitude of pretty inlets and beaches, with many tempting stops along the way, though none of the villages marked on maps are more than scattered houses hidden in the woods.

Crawford Bay and around

The tiny community of **CRAWFORD BAY**, 3.5km from the ferry, boasts the Kootenay Forge (ⓦkootenayforge.com), where in summer you can watch blacksmiths working, and visit a number of other artisan shops, from traditional broom-makers to weavers. In keeping with the general vibe is the **Yasodhara Ashram**, at 527 Walkers Landing Rd to the north on the lakeshore (☎250 227 9224, ☎800 661 8711, ⓦyasodhara. org), a spiritual centre offering a range of multi-day courses and retreats. Thirty-five kilometres south, just further than **Boswell**, a curious (and rather overpriced) attraction is **Glass House** (daily: May, June, Sept to mid-Oct 9am–4pm; July & Aug 8am–7pm; $10; ☎250 223 8372), constructed in 1952 entirely from embalming bottles by David Brown, after 35 years in the funeral business.

ACCOMMODATION AND EATING   **CRAWFORD BAY AND AROUND**

Kokanee Chalets RV Park & Campground Hwy-3A, Crawford Bay ☎250 227 9292, ☎800 448 9292, ⓦkokaneechalets.com. Nicely wooded campground with tent and RV sites as well as motel and chalet rooms a short walk from the beach. Mid-April to Oct. Sites $24; RVs $30; doubles $85
Kokanee Lake Lodge Resort 12622 Hwy-3A, Boswell ☎250 223 8181, ☎877 610 6960, ⓦkootenaylakelodge. com. Rustic waterfront log lodge and cabins with private beach, wood-fired cedar baths and canoes for rent. Four-night min rental for summer chalet stays. $325
Lockhart Beach Provincial Park Campground Hwy-3A, 25km south of Gray Creek. The closest and easiest-to-reach campground on the southern portion of Kootenay Lake lies 40km north of Creston (see below) and has RV and tent sites. May–Sept. No reservations. $23

9

Wedgwood Manor Country Inn 16002 Crawford Creek Rd, Crawford Bay ☏ 250 227 9233, ☏ 800 862 0022, ⓦ wedgwoodretreat.ca. Pleasant 1910 heritage manor house built for the daughter of British pottery magnate Josiah Wedgewood, with tasteful, antique-furnished rooms, that's set amid fifty acres of gardens and estate with cabins dotted around the grounds. Book well in advance. June–Sept. $130

Creston

Prosperous little **CRESTON** offers plenty of diversions from wine tasting to birdwatching with hiking and biking trails for the summer, and snowshoeing, snowmobiling and cross country skiing in the winter. An agricultural community, Creston boasts Canada's largest asparagus farm and award-winning black cherries – look out for a bottle of "Tabletree" juice to buy. Creston overlooks a broad mountain-flanked valley that's home to the idly meandering Kootenay River. Over the years the river has repeatedly burst its banks, creating a rich alluvial plain beloved by farmers, and producing the lush medley of orchards and verdant fields. The flood plain and its wetlands – the so-called "Valley of the Swans" – is a haven for birds and waterfowl.

Creston Valley Wildlife Management Area

10km northwest of town off Hwy-3 • Wildlife Interpretation Centre: early May to June & Sept Mon–Sat 9am–4pm; July & Aug daily 9am–4pm; Sept to early Oct Tue–Sat • Free • ☏ 250 402 6908, ⓦ discovery-centre.ca

The 7000-hectare **Creston Valley Wildlife Management Area** offers bountiful birdwatching. It has one of the world's largest nesting **osprey** populations, while some 250 other species have been recorded in the area (not to mention otters, moose and other animals). The sanctuary's **Wildlife Centre** has full details and plenty of advice on what's around and where to go.

The Stone House Museum and Columbia Brewery

Stone House Museum 219 Devon St • Mid-May to Oct daily 10am–3.30pm • $3 • ☏ 250 428 9262 **Columbia Brewery** 1220 Erickson St • Mid-May to mid-Oct Mon–Fri 4 tours daily • $5 • ☏ 250 428 9344, ⓦ columbiabrewery.ca

If you do end up in downtown Creston, you might pause at the **Stone House Museum**, known for its replica Kootenay (Ktunaxa) canoe. Similar canoes, with their down-pointed ends, are only found in parts of eastern Russia, underlining the fact that millennia ago, migrations took place across the Bering Strait into North America. If you're not driving, another temptation is the **Columbia Brewery**, whose Kokanee beers you'll find in most of the region's bars and restaurants.

INFORMATION
CRESTON

Visitor centre 121 NW Boulevard (daily July & Aug 9am–5pm; Mon–Fri Sept–June 9am–5pm; ☏ 866 528 4342, ⓦ crestonbc.com). Provides local accommodation listings.

EATING AND DRINKING

★ **Chatka** 2808 Hwy-3 ☏ 250 428 7200, ⓦ chatka.ca. Family-orientated restaurant and purveyor of top-notch Polish favourites such as schnitzel, *pierogies*, cabbage rolls and borscht. Tues–Sat 11am–8pm.

Skimmerhorn Winery 1218 27 Ave S ☏ 250 428 4911 ⓦ skimmerhorn.ca. One of the many wineries that have sprung up in the region, Skimmerhorn has a tasting room and wine shop with superb views across the Skimmerhorn Mountains where you can sample their award-winning Devil's Chair or Kootenay Crush White. April to late-June & early Sept to Dec Fri–Sun 11am–5pm, end June to early Sept daily 11am–5pm.

Kootenay Pass

A classic stretch of scenic road, Hwy-3 climbs west from the fruit-growing plains around Creston then over **Kootenay Pass** (1774m), making it one of the highest main roads in the country. It's frequently closed by bad weather and there are no services for 70km, so check your petrol before setting out. If cycling, brace yourself for a 46km

SHAMBHALA MUSIC FESTIVAL

Tiny **SALMO** transforms every August when the **Shambhala Music Festival** comes to town for five days and four nights of electronic music and art in glorious natural surroundings (tickets go on sale in November, see ⓦshambhalamusicfestival.com). Free of corporate sponsorship, the festival runs entirely thanks to volunteers. Acts such as Skrillex and Bonobo whip up the alcohol-free (no booze is allowed on-site) crowd into a natural-high frenzy. Over-19s only.

uphill slog and beware the extreme weather changes – but the reward is an unexpected and pretty lake at the pass, where there's a pull-off picnic area and views of distant high peaks.

Rossland

Picturesque **ROSSLAND** is an attractive enough place to poke around for a few days and certainly well worth the trip in winter for the skiing at **Red Mountain Resort**. Rossland held Canada's first recorded downhill ski race in 1896, organized by Olaf Jeldness – there's a statue of him in the main street. It's also the childhood home of Olympian Nancy Greene. In summer locals switch skis for mountain bikes (see below) and there's some good hiking and golf to be had at the **Redstone Resort** (ⓦredstoneresort.com) too. The town was founded on gold mining, with some $125 million-worth ($7.5 billion at today's prices) gouged from the surrounding hills in the early 1900s. To learn about the town's gold-mining heritage, local heritage and skiing, visit the **Rossland Museum**, junction of Hwy-3B and 22 (mid-May to mid-Oct Tues–Sun 10am–5pm; July & Aug daily 10am–6pm; winter hours noon–5pm; $10; ☎250 362 7722, ⓦrosslandmuseum.ca).

Red Mountain Resort

3km west of Rossland on Hwy 3 · Mid-Dec to April · Day-pass $96 · ☎250 362 7384, ☎800 663 0105, ⓦredresort.com

The town's major draw is the **Red Mountain Resort**, which offers six lifts and some of the biggest ski areas in BC with around 7.5m snowfall per year. It offers an incredibly diverse terrain with gladed tree skiing, groomed runs and easy access to side country.

ARRIVAL AND INFORMATION   ROSSLAND

By bus Rossland's Mountain Shuttle company (☎250 231 4305, ⓦmountainshuttle.ca) runs regular airport transfers to Trail, Castlegar, Kelowna and Cranbrook and also offers an on-demand shuttle bus.

Visitor centre 2185 Columbia Ave (May–Sept daily 9am–5pm; ☎250 362 5666, ☎888 725 0599, ⓦtourismrossland. com). It shares the museum building at the junction of the town's two main roads (Hwy-3B & Hwy-22).

ACTIVITIES

Mountain biking From April to October the area around Rossland offers excellent mountain biking. The Seven Summits Trail is an International Mountain Biking Association "Epic Trail". All local trails are detailed on a useful free map available from the visitor centre or from Revolution Cycles and Service, 1990 Columbia Ave (☎250 362 5688, ⓦrevolutioncycles.ca), which rents out bikes and arranges daily trailhead shuttles.

ACCOMMODATION

Mountain Shadow Hostel 2125 Columbia Ave ☎250 362 7160, ⓦmshostel.com. Shabby but spotlessly clean downtown hostel accommodation, with kitchens, TV room, reading room, lounge and laundry. Dorms $30; doubles $70
Nancy Greene Provincial Park Junction of Hwy-3 & Hwy-3B, 26km northeast of Rossland. A basic ten-pitch campground (no showers) nestled in the Monashee Mountains on a pristine alpine lake; not all pitches have shade. Mid-May to mid-Sept. No reservations. $13
Prestige Inn Review 1919 Columbia Ave ☎250 362 7375, ⓦprestigehotelsandresorts.com. Sizeable downtown motel which has the same up-to-date boutique feel as the other hotels in this good regional chain. Facilities include a sauna and hot tub, as well as a dependably busy

bar and lounge with good pub food. Ski packages offered. **$180**

Red Mountain Resort Lodging 4310 Red Mountain Rd ☎ 877 969 766, ☎ 250 362 5553, ⓦ redreservations.com. An expensive – but worth splurging – option is the high-end rental units at the resort, complete with ski in/out accessibility and all mod cons including gas fireplace, hot tub, full kitchen and washer/dryer facilities en suite. **$235**

EATING

★ **Alpine Grind** 2104 Columbia Ave ☎ 250 362 2280, ⓦ alpinegrindcoffee.com. *The* place for freshly ground coffee in town with the wildly popular Oso Negro beans from nearby Nelson, regularly changing guest roasts, and tasty baked goods. Mon–Fri 7am–5pm, Sat & Sun 8am–4pm.

Idgies 1999 2nd Ave ☎ 250 362 0078, ⓦ idgies restaurant.com. Friendly locals' spot tucked away from the main drag serving delicious pasta dishes ($21), grills and juicy, fresh, wild, local sockeye salmon ($26). Daily 5–9.30pm.

Misty Mountain Pizza 1999 2nd Ave ☎ 250 362 5266, ⓦ mistymountainpizza.ca. Adjoins Idgies (see above); delivers excellent pizzas, and serves pies by the slice ($3.50). 3–9.30pm.

Castlegar

CASTLEGAR, 44km west of Nelson on Hwy-3, is a diffuse place with no obvious centre, probably because the meeting of roads and rivers – Hwy-22 from Rossland (see page 651) ends here and the Kootenay joins the Columbia – make it more a transport hub than a community. In the early 1900s it was famous for its immigrant **Doukhobors** (see box).

Doukhobor Village Museum

112 Heritage Way • May–Sept Mon–Sat 10am–5pm, Sun noon–5pm • $10 • ☎ 250 365 5327, ⓦ doukhobor-museum.org

Much of the local Doukhobor community's heritage has been collected in the **Doukhobor Village Museum**, on the east bank of the Columbia close to Hwy-3. A Doukhobor descendant is on hand to take you through the reconstructed village, which houses farm machinery, handmade tools, superb archive photographs and traditional Russian clothing.

Zuckerberg Island Heritage Park

Off 7th Ave & 9th St south of downtown • May–Oct Wed–Sat 10am–5pm • By donation • ☎ 250 365 6440

An ideal spot for a picnic, **Zuckerberg Island Heritage Park** can be accessed by a 90m pedestrian suspension bridge made from locally donated materials. You can learn about the Lakes Salish First Nations who fished the area and built their winter pit houses here hundreds of years ago, and the Estonian teacher Alexander Zuckerberg who, after leaving Russia, settled in Castlegar to teach the Doukhobor community. In 1951 he bought the island and built a log Russian Orthodox chapel and other buildings and memorials here – which include some extraordinary wood sculptures, such as a woman carved out of a stump.

ARRIVAL AND INFORMATION   CASTLEGAR

By bus BC Transit Buses (ⓦ bctransit.com) leave from the Greyhound Station at 601 23rd St.
Destinations Nelson (hourly; 50 min); Trail (2 daily; 25min).
By plane West Kootenay Regional Airport lies east of the Columbia River, alongside Hwy-3A.
Destinations Calgary (1 daily; 1hr); Vancouver (2–3 daily;

1hr 15min).
Visitor centre 1995 6th Ave, off Hwy-3 just west of the Columbia River (July & Aug daily 8am–7pm; rest of year Mon–Fri 9am–5pm; ☎ 250 365 6313, ☎ 888 365 6313, ⓦ castlegar.com).

ACCOMMODATION AND EATING

Castlegar RV Park, Cabins and Campground 1725 Hwy-3 ☎ 250 365 2337, ⓦ castlegarrvpark.com. Wooded place about 3km west of town with good campsites and smart cabins that sleep four. Has wi-fi, hot showers, laundry and restaurant. Sites **$25**; RVs **$36**; cabins **$85**

Chamelon Hotel 330 Columbia Ave, ☎ 250 365 4981, ⓦ chameleonhotel.com. Immigrant culture lives on at this central hotel whose simple restaurant serves up a

THE DOUKHOBORS

The **Doukhobors** were a sect who fled southern Russian in 1899 after being persecuted for their religious and political views. Fiercely pacifist, they rejected secular government and ignored the liturgy and procedures of the organized church, believing God resided in each individual rather than in a building or institution. Their proto-communist views made them unpopular with the tsars, with their leader, **Peter Veregin**, a keen advocate of communal labour and collective property ownership.

The flight from Russia was aided by Quakers and novelist Leo Tolstoy, both of whom identified and supported the Doukhobors' pacifist and other ideals. Around 7500 left in the first wave, travelling to western Canada, and to **Saskatchewan** in particular. Initially, authorities were sympathetic to their beliefs and granted religious, educational and housing concessions. In 1905 members refused to swear an oath of allegiance to the dominion government and then, in 1907, when the Canadian government insisted all Doukhobor homesteads be registered as private property, things fell apart and the colonists were divided. Over a third accepted government proposals, despite bitter opposition from the collectivists, who showed their contempt for worldly possessions by destroying their belongings; some even burnt their clothes and organized Canada's first naked demonstrations. Irretrievably divided, some stayed in the prairies to create a prosperous, pacifist and Russian-speaking community, which remained separate and distinct until the 1940s, while Veregin and his supporters left for southern BC.

By the 1920s BC had around ninety Doukhobor settlements, each with a population of around sixty. They had arrived in **Castlegar** in 1908, establishing at least 24 villages in the area, each with Russian names meaning things like "the beautiful", "the blessed" or "consolation". Accomplished farmers, they laboured under the motto "Toil and a Peaceful Life", creating highly successful orchards, farms, sawmills and packing plants. Although their way of life waned after Veregin's death in 1924 (he was killed by a bomb planted in his railway carriage), the Doukhobors' considerable industry and agricultural expertise transformed the Castlegar area. Today, the Doukhobors number around fifteen thousand across the region (those with Doukhobor roots about thirty thousand) and Russian is still spoken. There's also a breakaway radical sect, the **Freedomites**, or **Sons of Freedom**, infamous for their eye-catching demonstrations (including fires and naked parades) against materialism and other morally dubious values.

---

good mix of German and Eastern European food: Schnitzels to Blinchinky, via Borsch and Bratwurst, with most mains under $20. The owners speak languages from these regions too. Hotel room décor is a bit of a hodgepodge – more a homestay than motel – but sparkly clean and great value. Restaurant Apr–Oct 11.30am–2pm & 4.30–8.30pm. $70

Fireside Motor Inn 1810 8th Ave ☎ 250 365 2128, ⓦ firesideinn.ca. Modern motel beside the noisy junction of highways 3 and 22 whose spacious rooms have ugly standard-issue decor. But it's clean and friendly and rates include wi-fi, a good breakfast and use of the *Super 8* pool

and waterslide over the road. $98

Pass Creek Regional Park 2km west off Hwy-3A at the Kootenay River Bridge ☎ 250 304 4602. One of several regional and provincial park campgrounds in the vicinity, 30min walk from Castlegar, which has a nice, sandy beach and hot showers. No reservations. April–Oct. $17

The Wandering Greek Oven 400 Columbia Ave ☎ 250 365 2311, ⓦ thewanderinggreekoven.com. Consistently good little Greek place with great salads, generous portions of dishes like *souvlaki* ($19.95) and dependable pizza. Tues–Sat 11.30am–8.30pm.

Nelson

With its idyllic lakeside setting and 350-plus heritage buildings dating from the late nineteenth to the early twentieth century, **NELSON** is one of BC's best towns, and one of the few interior settlements in which you could happily spend two or three days, longer if you use it as a base for touring **the Kootenays** (see page 642) by car. The elegant town is famed – and often slightly ridiculed – for having more than its fair share of hipsters and dreadlocked refugees from the mainstream, but they've certainly helped to nurture a young, friendly, civilized and close-knit community with a healthy

NELSON ARTWALK

In July and August a dozen or so of Nelson's shops, studios and galleries display the works of local artists to create a self-guided walking tour called **Artwalk** (the visitor centre has details). At other times **Craft Connection** (441 Baker St; ☎ 250 352 3006, ⓦ craftconnection.org) is a particularly good gallery to seek out.

cultural scene. The liberal liveliness manifests itself in wholefood cafés, hemp stores and secondhand shops. There's also a high concentration of artists and craftspeople, and the town's Chinese-medicine school and its Kootenay School of the Arts attract students from all over North America. The town's claim to cinematic fame is as the location of *Roxanne*, Steve Martin's spoof of *Cyrano de Bergerac*.

Downtown

Nelson forms a tree-shaded grid of streets laid over the hilly slopes that edge down to the westernmost shores of Kootenay Lake. Most of the heritage buildings are immaculately kept and vividly painted, and even the commercial **buildings** along the parallel main east–west streets – Baker and Vernon – owe more to the vintage architecture of Seattle and San Francisco than to the Victoriana of western Canada. To add purpose to your wanderings, pick up the *Heritage Walking Tour* pamphlet from the visitor centre (see opposite). Highlights of the route are the **courthouse** on Ward Street and **City Hall** at the corner of Ward and Vernon streets, both designed by F.M. Rattenbury, also responsible for *Victoria's Empress Hotel* and BC's Legislature building. Also check out the old railway station and the *Hume Hotel*.

The Mining Museum

215 Hall St • Daily 9am–3pm • Free • ☎ 250 352 5242

The region owes its development to the discovery of copper and silver on nearby Toad Mountain in the late nineteenth century and the **Mining Museum**, next to the visitor centre, sheds light on some of this. Nelson's mines declined fairly quickly, but its diversification into gold and lumber, along with its roads, railway and waterways, saved it.

Touchstones Nelson: Museum of Art and History

502 Vernon St • Jun–Sept Mon–Sat 10am–5pm, Thurs till 8pm, Sun 10am–4pm; Oct to mid-May Wed–Sat 10am–5pm, Thurs till 8pm, Tues & Sun 10am–4pm • $8, Thurs 5–8pm by donation • ☎ 250 352 9813, ⓦ nelsonmuseum.ca

Housed in the former Postal, Customs and City Hall building, **Touchstones Nelson** hosts changing, but always good, art exhibitions and uses materials from the city archives to present snapshots of Nelson's past.

The farmers' market

May to mid-Oct Sat 9.30am–3pm

If you're in town in summer on a Saturday, make a point of stopping by the Cottonwood Falls **farmers' market**, near the old railway station in Cottonwood Falls Park, with organic fruit, vegetables, delicious breads and local arts and crafts. Otherwise, the town's premier organic food store is the Kootenay Co-op at 295 Baker St.

Lakeside Park

A pleasant twenty-minute walk east from downtown along the lakefront paths, **Lakeside Park** near the Nelson Bridge has a thriving beach scene on sunny days. Aside from the sandy beaches, there are also picnic areas, playgrounds, tennis courts and often live music around the park. If you don't want to walk from town, take the restored **Streetcar 23** (May to mid-June & early Oct Sat & Sun; mid-June to Sept daily; times can change but usually hourly 11am–5pm; $3), from the *Prestige Lakeside Resort*.

Pulpit Rock

From the north shores of Kootenay Lake opposite Nelson, an hour's steady climbing on the 3km-long **Pulpit Rock** trail ends with an eagle's-eye view of the city. The trailhead lies 2.3km west of the Hwy-3 bridge, close to the *North Shore Motor Inn*.

Whitewater Ski Resort

22km south of Nelson via Hwy-6 • Dec–April • Day-pass $89 • ☎ 250 354 4944, ☎ 800 666 9420, ⓦ skiwhitewater.com

The local ski hill, **Whitewater Winter Resort**, may be fairly small by regional standards – with only three lifts – but its mountains have some of the best powder in North America. Half its 4.8 square kilometres are reserved for black diamond runs. There's also 25km of cross-country trails ($8/day) and a daily ski shuttle from Nelson – the resort has the latest details.

INFORMATION   NELSON

Visitor centre 91 Baker St (June–Aug Mon–Fri 8.30am–5.30pm, Sat 9am–6pm, Sun 10am–5pm; Sept–May Mon–Fri 8.30am–5pm; ☎ 250 352 3433, ☎ 877 663 5706, ⓦ discovernelson.com).

ACTIVITIES

Mountain biking Gerick Cycle and Ski, 702 Baker St (☎ 250 354 4622), and The Sacred Ride, 213 Baker St (☎ 250 354 3831), rent out bikes and have trail maps of the many local mountain-biking routes. Beware the difficulty of local trails though – even blue-rated trails would get black diamonds elsewhere. The best place for first-timers to strike out from is Morning Mountain, on Granite Road, 3km west of the town centre on well-signposted trails with washrooms along the way.

Watersports In the *Prestige Lakeside Resort*, Captain Erik's Watertoys (☎ 250 551 5502) rents boats and canoes and offers wakeboarding lessons.

Hiking Surrounded by mountains cut through with old mining and logging roads, and an abandoned railway line, Nelson is a hiker's paradise. The Nelson Salmo Great Northern Trail is a multipurpose trail shared by runners and cyclists that takes in some exciting trestles from its days as Canadian Pacific Railway tracks. Iron-thighed hikers get a workout up along Elephant Mountain on the other side of West Arm, hiking the popular Pulpit Rock trail through the forest. The visitor centre can help with trail maps and advice.

ACCOMMODATION

Nelson has a reasonable spread of **accommodation**; central choices include hostels, charming boutique hotels and a wide range of B&B options. Most motels are on Hwy-31A at the north end of town or over the Nelson Bridge on the north side of the lake. Nelson's campgrounds are cramped and unexciting; you're much better off at **Kokanee Creek Provincial Park**.

Adventure Hotel 616 Vernon St ☎ 250 352 7211, ☎ 888 722 2258, ⓦ adventurehotel.ca. Boutique hotel a block from the main strip that offers simple and snug, but modern, rooms – including some well-priced bunk-style rooms ($69). With light breakfast included. **$95**

★ **Cloudside Inn** 408 Victoria St ☎ 250 352 3226, ☎ 800 596 2337, ⓦ cloudside.ca. Spotlessly clean B&B in a heritage house from 1900 with eight rooms of varying size, where the decor reflects the well-travelled hosts Chris and Sally's backpacking adventures. Parking and large home-style breakfast included. **$119**

Dancing Bear Inn 171 Baker St ☎ 250 352 7573, ☎ 877 352 7573, ⓦ dancingbearinn.com. A beautifully renovated hostel on the main street between Kootenay St and Hwy-3A. There's a kitchen, resource library, plus free wi-fi. Dorms **$28**; non-members **$30**; doubles **$68**, non-members **$76**

★ **Hume Hotel** 422 Vernon St ☎ 250 352 5331, ☎ 877 568 0888, ⓦ humehotel.com. This charming, 1898 four-storey hotel is the best central, mid-range choice. It has cosy, old-world rooms (some with views) and complimentary hot breakfast in the downstairs restaurant. **$139**

North Shore Inn 687 Hwy-3A ☎ 250 352 6606, ☎ 800 593 6636, ⓦ nshoreinn.com. On the north side of town, this thirty-unit motel is simple, clean and offers good value and views over the lake, with ample free parking and breakfast included. **$84**

Prestige Lakeside Resort 701 Lakeshore Drive ☎ 250 352 7222, ☎ 877 737 8443, ⓦ prestigehotelsandresorts.com. The most luxurious hotel in town, this is part of Nelson's lakefront redevelopment; it has a spa, gym, marina, shops and all the other resort trimmings. **$171**

9

EATING

★ **All Seasons Café** 620 Herridge Lane ☎ 250 352 0101, ⊛ allseasonscafe.com. In a restored heritage home, this top-flight restaurant is one of the Kootenays' best dining experiences. Tucked away between Josephine and Hall streets, it serves superb West Coast (or what it calls "left-coast") food and boasts a wine list that has won a prestigious *Wine Spectator* Award of Excellence. Mains from $28. Daily 5pm–late.

★ **Bite** 700 Block Baker St ☎ 250 551 2483, ⊛ bitetruck. com. Check out the fun *poutine* bar at this gourmet food truck with toppings such as The Great Canadian with maple syrup and bacon heaped on fries, gravy and "squeaky" cheese curds ($7). The burgers ($10), made from hormone-free beef are excellent and there are gluten-free and veggie options too. May–Oct Mon–Sat 11.30am–7pm.

★ **Cantina del Centro** 561 Baker St ☎ 250 352 3737, ⊛ cantinadelcentro.ca. Outstanding tacos, tostadas, wraps and other Mexican standards made with delicious local ingredients. Soak up the local flavour on the suntrap patio and work your way through the tequila-spiked cocktails. Daily 11am–late.

The Full Circle 402 Baker St ☎ 250 354 4458. For superb breakfasts ($12) follow the locals to this busy little coffee shop with vegan, vegetarian and gluten-free choices. Lunches are also good with the Portobello burger and pulled-pork sandwich both excellent. Mon–Sat 6.30am–2.30pm, Sun 7am–2pm.

★ **Kootenay Bakery Café** 377 Baker St ☎ 250 352 2274. Organic, from-scratch bakery with a busy cafeteria – great for wholesome salads, burritos, quiches and cakes. Fast service and good, hot, daily specials too. Mon–Sat 7.30am–6pm.

Mike's Place At the Hume Hotel (see page 655). This usually packed spot sells good pub food along with the full range of Nelson Brewing Company beers (founded 1893); top tipple is the flagship Old Brewery Ale. There's usually dancing from 9pm (Fri & Sat) at the adjoining *Spirit Bar* nightclub. The *Hume's* more elegant bar, *The Library*, as its name suggests, offers a quieter drinking experience. Mike's: Mon–Thurs 11am–1am, Fri & Sat 11.30–1.30am, Sun 11.30am–midnight.

Outer Clove 353 Stanley St ☎ 250 354 1667. For novelty value head to this restaurant where virtually everything from the decor to dessert features garlic (it's better than it sounds). Mains $16–24. Mon–Sat 11.30am–9pm.

★ **Pitchfork Eatery** 518 Hall St ☎ 250 352 2744 ⊛ pitchforkeatery.ca. Taking locally-sourced to the next level, this farm-owned restaurant grows and forages for many of its ingredients. The menu may be short and unadventurous – burgers, steak, fresh-fish (mains average $22) – but its quality and look matches the place's appealing smart rustic-boutique decor. With a great line in cocktails ($13) and weekend brunches. Mon–Fri noon until late, Sat & Sun 10am until late.

Hwy-3: Osoyoos to Hope

Beyond **Osoyoos** (see page 659), Hwy-3, also known as the Crowsnest Highway, climbs out of the US border zone to an ear-popping mountain pass, then swoops down into the beautiful and fertile rural landscape around the fruit-growing centre of **Keremeos**, then follows the serene Similkameen Valley to quietly attractive **Hedley** before descending to Hope through the gripping mountain scenery of the Coastal Ranges and **E.C. Manning Provincial Park**. Hwy-3A, a mostly two-lane winding road, which cuts through the sloping hills covered with tenacious Ponderosa pines and past dozens of tempting side-roads leading to the Okanagan's award-winning wineries, loops past Oliver to the bottom of Skaha Lake before heading west again to **Keremeos.**

Keremeos

Pretty little **KEREMEOS** is a rustic, two-street affair that's almost unspoilt by neon or other urban clutter and spreads over a dried-up lakebed from which hills and mountains rise on all sides. It's all very attractive and made even more so by a local climate that blesses it with Canada's longest growing season. Lush, irrigated orchards surround the town, and in spring huge swaths of flowers appear across the valley floor. You can pick up fruit and vegetables – including cherries, apricots, peaches, pears, apples, plums and grapes – from stands on the road through town and dotted more or less everywhere, and also try wine tasting at the cluster of wineries between Keremeos and Cawston, in the **Similkameen Wineries Association** (⊛ similkameenwine.com)

9

including **Orofino** (ⓦorofinovineyards.com), Canada's only straw-bale winery with a tasting room run on solar panels.

Hedley

West from Keremeos, Hwy-3 travels 29km along the extremely picturesque and ever-widening Similkameen Valley to **HEDLEY**. This old gold-mining hamlet is today little more than a single street with great scenery. The **visitor centre**, 712 Daly St (mid-May to Aug daily 9am–5pm; rest of year Thurs–Mon 9am–4pm; ☎250 292 8787, ⓦhedleybc.ca), is part of a small but interesting **museum** (same hours; donation requested) with archive photos and mining memorabilia. Pick up details of the self-guided walking tour around the village's period buildings. For years the big local lure was touring Mascot Gold Mine (ⓦmascotmine.com), a small group of buildings perched daringly above the town. Closed for safety reasons, these may re-open in time. Check the same website to see if the Snaza'ist Discovery Centre, a local First Nations heritage centre has re-opened. It recounts the history of Upper Similkameen Indian Band, who still own much of the valley, and is well worth a look for its striking re-creations of ancient local cave pictographs.

ACCOMMODATION AND EATING HEDLEY

Bromley Rock Provincial Park Campground Off Hwy-3 about 17km west of Hedley. This lovely picnic stop looks down on the whitewater of the Similkameen River and offers seventeen basic campsites – with water, toilets and fire pits; no reservations. $23

★ **The Hitching Post** 916 Scott Ave ☎ 250 292 8413, ⓦhitchingpostrestaurant.ca. Stylish restaurant, in another downtown heritage building, that serves generous portions of seafood, steak and ribs; mains $15–24. Wed–Sun 11am–8pm.

Stemwinder Provincial Park Campground 5km west of Hedley on Hwy-3. Tiny, pine-tree-dotted park with campground with 26 first-come, first-served basic sites. With cold water, toilets and fire pits. Mid-April to Sept. $18

E.C. Manning Provincial Park

E.C. Manning Provincial Park, hard on the US border 147km from Hedley and 64km east of Hope, is one of the few parks in the Coast and Cascade mountain ranges and so is always quite busy. It parcels up a typical assortment of mountain, lake and forest scenery, so even if you're just passing through, it's time well spent walking at least one of the short **trails** off the road, including the accessible-to-all 700m Sumallo Grove interpretive trail, 10km east of the park's western entrance. The most popular drive within the park is the 15km side road to **Cascade Lookout**, which overlooks an amphitheatre of mountains. A gravel road carries on another 6km from there to **Blackwall Peak**, the starting point for the **Heather Trail** (10km one way), renowned for its summer wildflowers. Other manageable day-hikes leave the south side of the main highway, the majority accessed from the Lightning Lake Road. In the winter, some 160km of trails are available for backcountry skiing and snowshoeing, while *Manning Park Resort* (see below) has downhill skiing (day-pass $52) and grooms 30km of trails for cross-country skiing.

INFORMATION E.C. MANNING PROVINCIAL PARK

Park visitor centre 30km inside its western boundary (June–Sept daily 9am–6pm).

ACCOMMODATION

Manning Park Resort ☎ 250 840 8822, ☎ 800 330 3321, ⓦmanningpark.com. The park's only indoor lodging option consists of hotel rooms and cabins and chalets that sleep eight to fourteen people. Facilities also include a pool complex with hot tubs, sauna and exercise room, a restaurant, bar, laundry and convenience store. Doubles $114; cabins $209; chalets (min 2 nights) $309

Provincial park campgrounds ☎ 519 826 6850, ☎ 800 689 9025, ⓦdiscovercamping.ca. There are four provincial park campgrounds on and off the highway, those close to the road being *Coldspring*, *Hampton* (each $23) and *Mule* ($25). A fourth, *Lightning Lake* ($35), has free hot showers and flush toilets, and is the only reservable campground (reserve at least two days in advance). In addition the park has ten backcountry campgrounds (sites $5) for backpacking hikers. **$23**

The Okanagan

The vine- and orchard-covered hills and warm-water lakes of the **Okanagan**, located in south-central BC, are in marked contrast to the rugged beauty of the region's more mountainous interior, making the region not only one of Canada's finest fruit-growing areas but also one of its most popular holiday destinations. Unless you want a resort beach holiday, you may want to avoid the crowds and bypass the area in summer. Three main centres – **Kelowna**, **Penticton** and **Osoyoos**, ranging from north to south along the hundred-kilometre-long **Okanagan Lake** – together contain the lion's share of BC's interior population. All have pretty ordinary downtown cores with an array of accommodation and attractions. Things get more picturesque if you can slip away from the towns to the hills or lakeshore to quieter spots like **Summerland**.

The almost year-round lushness that makes this "the land of beaches, peaches, sunshine and wine" means that, in the relative peace of **off-season**, you can begin to experience the region's considerable charms: fruit trees in blossom, quiet lakeside villages and wine tastings in local vineyards. You can also expect room rates to halve. Kelowna is the biggest and probably best base at any time of the year, but smaller Penticton arguably has the edge in summer when it has much more of a relaxed beach-resort vibe.

Osoyoos

Surrounded by half-bare, scrub-covered, ochre hills, **OSOYOOS** (which comes from the Syilx'tsn word *suius* for "narrowing of the waters") has one of Canada's most curious landscapes. With a mere 25cm of rain per year, this is a bona fide **desert**, with lizards, cacti and snakes: 23 types of invertebrate are endemic. Temperatures are regularly 10°C higher than in Nelson, less than a morning's drive away, which means exotic fruit like bananas and pomegranates can be grown, with the temperature also inspiring the odd adobe building around town. Its other great feature is **Lake Osoyoos**, Canada's warmest freshwater lake, with an average summer temperature of 24°C. In summer it comes alive with swimmers and boaters while streams of RVs slow-tail their way northwards.

The relative lack of crowds and strange scenery might persuade you to do your beach-bumming in Osoyoos, though you may be pushed to find space in any of the town's twenty or so **hotels** and **motels** during high season.

Desert Centre

14580 146 Ave • Daily: late April to mid-May & Sept 10am–2pm; mid-May to mid-Sept 9.30am–4.30pm • $7 • ☎ 250 495 2470, ☎ 877 899 0897, Ⓦ desert.org

A visit to the **Desert Centre**, on Hwy-97 just north of town, is a good way to learn a little more about the region's desert environment. There are tours over a 1.5km boardwalk through a small area of desert, a fascinating ecosystem of some one hundred rare plants, including tiny cacti and sage, as well as three hundred animals from rattlesnakes to pocket gophers, now all under serious threat.

Nk'Mip Desert Culture Centre

1000 Rancher Creek Rd • **Desert Culture Centre** March & April Tues–Sat 9.30am–4pm; May to mid-June daily 9.30am–4.30pm; mid-June to Aug daily 9.30am–8pm • $12 • ☎ 250 495 7901, ☎ 888 495 8555, Ⓦ nkmipdesert.com • **Nk'Mip Cellars** Tours Apr–Oct 2pm daily • $15 • ☎ 250 495 2985, Ⓦ nkmipcellars.com •

The Osoyoos Indian Band's **Nk'Mip Desert Culture Centre** is next door to Spirit Ridge and the Nk'Mip (pronounced ink-A-meep) winery, Canada's first Aboriginal-owned

9

winery. The centre offers a well-run programme of cultural events including two multi-sensory theatres on-site showing short films, traditional dancing, drumming and singing, guided desert walks, 2km of trails and craft workshops.

INFORMATION OSOYOOS

Visitor centre 9912 Hwy-3 near the junction of Hwy-97 and the bus stop (June daily 9am–5pm; July & Aug daily 8am–6pm; Sept–May Mon–Fri 9am–5pm; ☎ 250 495 5070, ⓦ destinationosoyoos.com).

ACCOMMODATION

Best Western Sunrise Inn 5506 Main St ☎ 250 495 4000, ☎ 877 878 2200, ⓦ bestwesternosoyoos.com. Upper-end motel chain with its usual array of modern rooms as well as an indoor pool, spa and restaurant. Rates include a cooked breakfast and high-speed wi-fi. **$152**

Swiẃs (previously Haynes Point) Provincial Park Campground Hwy-97 & 32nd Ave, 2km south of Osoyoos ☎ 519 826 6850, ☎ 800 689 9025, ⓦ discovercamping. ca. Reservations can be made three months in advance at this popular and picturesque campground with basic facilities, but with sandy beaches and a warm-water lake for swimming. April to early Oct. **$32**

★ **Spirit Ridge** 1200 Rancher Creek Rd ☎ 250 495 5545, ⓦ spiritridge.ca. Luxurious resort with a top-notch spa, pool and nine-hole golf course. There's plenty of Indiginous art and sculpture dotted around, as well as a first-class restaurant where you can pair food with the truly ambrosial wine grown on the vines below. **$275**

★ **Watermark Beach Resort** 15 Park place ☎ 250 495 5500, ☎ 888 755 3480, ⓦ watermarkbeachresort.com. Excellent, modern, bright suites directly on the lake with kitchens, dining room space; many rooms offer washer/ dryers too, perfect for longer stays. Family-friendly pool, hot tubs and award-winning restaurant. Check online for special rates. **$239**

EATING

Ambrosia Western & Indian Cuisine 6910 Main St ☎ 250 495 2227, ⓦ ambrosiarestaurant.ca. Excellent Indian food in a basic diner at reasonable prices, since the $12 dishes include rice and naan bread. Daily 7am–8pm.

Jojo's Café 8316 Main St ☎ 250 495 6652, ⓦ jojoscafe. ca. Excellent coffee house specializing in large, healthy sandwiches on freshly baked bread. Most are around $8 and both the fresh turkey and shrimp fillings are tasty. The $5 breakfast sandwich is superb. Daily 7am–4pm.

★ **Roberto's Gelato** Suite 227, 15 Park place ☎ 250 495 5425. The searingly hot temperatures Osoyoos often experiences make this top-notch ice-cream bar an essential stop-off. Home-made using all natural ingredients. May–Oct daily noon–10pm.

★ **Sonora Room** 500 Burrowing Owl place ☎ 877 498 0620, ⓦ okwineshuttle.com. Treat yourself to a world-class dining experience in the gorgeous room at the Burrowing Owl winery where wonderful locally sourced cuisine showcases the best of the Okanagan (mains around $30). May to mid-Oct daily for lunch, tapas & dinner; April Thurs–Mon lunch & dinner; late Oct to mid-Dec Fri–Sun lunch, Thurs–Sun dinner.

Penticton

PENTICTON is a corruption of the Salish phrase *pen tak tin* – "a place to stay forever"; while this may overstate the town's appeal, in summer it is a laidback option compared to the buzz of Kelowna, 68km to the north. Its summer daily average of ten hours of sunshine ranks it higher than Honolulu, making tourism its biggest industry after fruit (this is "Peach City"). That, along with Penticton's proximity to Vancouver and the US, ensures the town and beaches are thronged with watersports enthusiasts, cyclists and hikers exploring the Kettle Valley Railway (see page 664), rock climbers and, like the rest of the Okanagan, plenty of food and wine fans. Away from the beaches, there's some festival or other playing virtually every day of the year to keep the punters entertained, the key ones being the Okanagan-wide **Wine Festival** in May and late October, and the **Peach Festival** in August.

Downtown

Penticton's **downtown** – focused on Main Street a block or so south of Lake Okanagan – is upbeat enough with quirky local stores and a thriving restaurant and bar scene. The **Penticton Museum**, 785 Main St (Tues–Sat 10am–5pm; donation; ☎ 250 490 2451), is worth a visit to see the eclectic collection of everything from dinosaur bones to a model First Nations village. **Penticton Art Gallery**, 199 Marina Way (Tues–Fri 10am–5pm, Sat & Sun 11am–4pm; by donation; ☎ 250 493 2928, ⍟ pentictonartgallery.com), often has high-quality shows. Make time to visit the lovely Penticton-Ikeda Japanese gardens behind the gallery. The gallery lies at the end of Front Street, a diagonal street that crosses Main a block from the lake and gives the town a tiny bohemian quarter with cheap eateries and independent cafés.

Beaches and Skaha Bluffs

Most leisure time in Penticton is undoubtedly spent on its two beaches, with **Okanagan Beach** the closest sand to downtown and usually busy for most of its one-kilometre length. Lakefront bars and restaurants provide inviting people-watching spots, and you can take tours around the paddlewheeler **SS Sicamous** (May–Sept Mon & Thurs 11am–5.30pm, Tues 1–9pm, Fri 11am–7pm, Sat & Sun 10am–5.30pm, Oct–Apr Sat & Sun 10am–4pm; $6, ⍟ sssicamous.ca) at its western end, which has a good little museum of local marine history on board. At Riverside Park beside the steamer, Coyote Cruises (see page 661) rents inflatable tubes to allow you to spend a couple of relaxing hours floating 4km south down the adjacent Okanagan River Channel to Skaha Lake, and the slightly quieter and trendier **Skaha Beach**. Beside the beach the famed **Skaha Bluffs** offer one of North America's premier **rock-climbing** spots.

Apex Mountain Resort

Nov–April · Day-pass $85 · ☎ 250 292 8222, ☎ 877 777 2739, ⍟ apexresort.com

Winters in Penticton centre on **Apex Mountain Resort**, 33km west of town, with its four lifts, 67 runs and 6m of annual snowfall. Almost half its terrain is intermediate level, though the resort is famed for its black diamond mogul runs.

ARRIVAL AND INFORMATION
PENTICTON

By plane Penticton airport lies 8km south of downtown. Destinations Vancouver (3 daily; 1hr).

Wine Country and Visitor Centre 553 Vees Drive (June–Sept daily 8am–7pm; Oct–May Mon–Fri 9am–5pm; ☎ 250 276 2170, ☎ 800 663 5052, ⍟ tourismpenticton.com), off Hwy-97 on the north side of town. Helpfully staffed modern info point, which also includes a Wine Country advice centre with hundreds of wines available at winery prices with daily tastings.

ACTIVITIES

Mountain biking Bike Barn at 200 Westminster Ave West (☎ 250 492 4140) and Freedom Bike Shop at 533 Main St (☎ 250 493 0686, ⍟ freedombikeshop.com) rent bikes and offer a wealth of trail info and advice.

River floating Coyote Cruises, 215 Riverside Drive (☎ 250 492 2115, ⍟ coyotecruises.ca). Rates include a return

---

VINEYARD TOURS NEAR PENTICTON

Penticton has some 60 wineries within 20 minutes' drive of downtown. The best way to explore is on a wine tour so you are free to sip and sample the award-winning grapes on offer. Try the cool-climate white varietals such as Riesling and Gewürztraminer or juicy red Pinot Noir or Cabernet Franc. With any luck you might visit the **Red Rooster Winery** which boasts an on-site art gallery whose work includes a replica of *The Baggage Handler*, a controversial sculpture known to locals as "Frank"; it was banished from its original home in a downtown Penticton traffic circle after its nudity offended locals – one incensed vandal even hacked off Frank's privates.

TOUR OPERATORS
Grape Escape (☎ 250 493 3238, ⍟ grapeescapes. ca) run small tours daily to five wineries around the Naramata Bench with Penticton hotel pick-ups and snacks included from $95.

Top Cat Tours (☎ 250 493 7385, ⍟ topcattours.com) offer half- ($60) and full-day tours to three or four vineyards; full-day tours ($129) include lunch.

9

shuttle. Bus and flotation tube $12.
Rock climbing Skaha Rock Adventures, 113–437 Martin St (☎ 250 493 1765, ⓦ skaharockclimbing.com). Runs tours for beginners for $155/day.
Watersports Castaways, 21 Lakeshore Drive (☎ 250 490

2033, ⓦ castawayswatersports.com). Offering parasailing from $85, and rental of every possible craft to set sail on the water from paddleboards ($20/hr) and peddleboats ($20/hr) to Sea-Doos ($100/hr).

ACCOMMODATION

Penticton brims with all kinds of accommodation from luxurious resorts to B&Bs, campsites and RV parks.
★ **Barefoot Beach Resort** 4145 Skaha Lake Rd ☎ 778 476 0484, ⓦ barefootresort.ca. Set directly on the shores of Skaha Lake with spacious pristine camp sites, RV hook-ups, and beautifully equipped yurts on-site. The resort boasts a licensed restaurant, market, ice cream and taco shop, beachwear store, plus a beachfront coffee and juice bar and Canada's only on-beach Crossfit gym. Sites $40; yurts $159
Camp-Along RV Resort 6km south of town off Hwy-97 ☎ 250 497 5584, ☎ 800 968 5267, ⓦ campalong.com. Campground with pool, internet café and shaded sites, in an apricot orchard overlooking Skaha Lake – 5min drive from the beach. April–Sept. $33
Cormier Studio 495 Vancouver Ave ☎ 250 493 3273, ⓦ cormierstudio.com. Welcoming B&B with three rooms,

each with their own patio and kitchenette, based in the home of a local artist, who has created a delightful sculpture garden. Direct beach access from the backyard and the Kettle Valley Railway can be reached from the top of the hill. Full breakfast $16 extra. $199
HI hostel 464 Ellis St ☎ 250 492 3992, ☎ 866 782 9736, ⓦ hihostels.ca. The HI hostel is in an old bunkhouse downtown, one block south from the bus station, with dorms and private rooms. Dorms $30, nonmembers $33; twin $60, nonmembers $66
Penticton Lakeside Resort 21 Lakeshore Drive West ☎ 250 493 8221, ☎ 800 663 9400, ⓦ penticton lakesideresort.com. Mammoth modern hotel that dominates the waterfront skyline and provides a good amount of luxury. With three restaurants, a bar, casino, spa and wi-fi. $216

EATING

★ **Bad Tattoo Brewing** 169 Estabrook Ave ☎ 250 493 8686, ⓦ badtattoobrewing.com. Bright, airy, wood-panelled brewpub that does a great range of weird and wonderful pizzas from their brick oven. Be bold: try the quirkier options like the Sriracha chicken with yoghurt and balsamic ($18), which is wonderful washed down with their Los Muertos Cerveza Negra. Beer samples for $1.50. Daily 11am–11pm.
Bench Market 368 Vancouver Ave ☎ 250 492 2222, ⓦ thebenchmarket.com. Locals' favourite spot for breakfast, lunch and weekend brunch, serving up fresh, local, mostly BC produce, and with a gloriously sunny patio. Perfect for stocking up on BC foodie gifts or packing a picnic. The smoked salmon eggwich ($11) is a must-have. Mon–Fri 7am–4pm, Sat & Sun 8am–4pm.
★ **Brodo Kitchen** 483 Main St ☎ 250 476 1275, ⓦ tastebrodo.com. Simple food made with locally sourced ingredients, changed seasonally to reflect what's freshly

harvested. Basic soups, salads and sandwiches are the order of the day, but oh, so very well done. The albacore tuna melt is a thing of beauty ($9) and the soups are addictive; ordering a flight of three is highly recommended ($8). Mon–Sat 11am–8pm.
Burger55 52 Front St ☎ 778 476 5529, ⓦ burger55. com. Upbeat local burger joint with exceptionally delicious burgers, an easy walk from the beach behind the Front St strip. The choice of combos is bewildering but there's always a good burger of the month and several signature burgers (around $10) to make deciding easier. Fri & Sat 11am–8pm, Sun–Thurs 11am–7pm.
Tacos del Norte 86 Backstreet blvd ☎ 250 689 2453, ⓦ tacosdelnorte.ca. Delicious made-from-scratch authentic Baja-style tacos with local ingredients including organic cheese, house-made sauces and salsas. Perfect spot to laze on the patio with a locally brewed beer. Daily 11am–7pm.

Summerland

The agricultural community of **SUMMERLAND** is tucked away above the west side of Okanagan Lake, with hills gently rolling on either side and an extinct volcano, **Giant's Head Mountain**, dominating the skyline. The only one of the Okanagan's towns which is not bisected by Hwy-97, Summerland makes for a pedestrian-friendly stopover to explore bakeries and brunch spots along its curious mock-Tudor-style Main Street. Summerland is blessed with an unspoiled beachfront which offers plenty for the bucket-and-spade brigade as well as those looking for paddling or boating adventures, and the surrounding hills are a haven for hikers and bikers. Food and wine fans are well served by the popular **Bottleneck Drive** (Ⓦbottleneckdrive.com), which showcases 16 of the area's wineries including the excellent Okanagan Crush Pad and Sumac Ridge.

Kettle Valley Steam Railway

18404 Bathville Rd • Mid-May to late-June, early Sept to early Oct Sat, Sun, Mon 10.30am, 1.30pm; late-June to early Sept Thurs–Mon 10.30am, 1.30pm • $25• Ⓣ 250 494 8422, Ⓦ kettlevalleyrail.org

Jump aboard a pristinely renovated 1912 steam locomotive which runs along ten miles of the only preserved section of the historic **Kettle Valley Railway** on a one-hour-thirty-minute scenic trip through Summerland and across Trout Creek Bridge over the Okanagan Lake and the canyon below. Special events include a Wild West-themed *Great Train Robbery* ride and barbecue, and Christmas and Easter trains.

ARRIVAL AND INFORMATION   SUMMERLAND

Downtown visitor centre 15600 Hwy-97 just north of downtown (mid-May to mid-Oct daily 9am–5pm; mid-Oct to mid-May Mon–Fri 9am–4pm; Ⓣ250 494 2686, Ⓦtourismsummerland.com).

ACCOMMODATION

Apples and Quails B&B 12014 Trayler place S Ⓣ778 516 6300, Ⓣ855 751 8220, Ⓦapplesandquails.com. Hosts Ming and Walter run a well-equipped B&B offering spotlessly clean rooms with a range of features from double baths to private decks. Perched on Giant's Head Mountain with panoramic views of the lake and valley below, each day starts with a lavish breakfast including home-made granola and organic coffee. $179

Peach Orchard Campground 6321 Peach Orchard Rd Ⓣ250 494 9649, Ⓦpeachorchard.ca. Spacious well-run campground on Okanagan Lake minutes away from the town centre and within easy walking distance of beaches. Community fire pits offer free fire wood, and there's also a shop, kids' playground and tennis courts on-site. Sites $30; RVs $40

Summerland Waterfront Resort and Spa Lakeshore Drive S Ⓣ 250 494 8180, Ⓣ877 494 8111, Ⓦsummerland resorthotel.com. Relaxing, lakeside all-suite hotel with direct beach access and well-stocked modern rooms boasting a full kitchen, fireplace and bath. Many suites offer suntrap balconies overlooking the hotel pool and lake. $199

EATING

Local On Lakeshore 12817 Lakeshore Drive Ⓣ250 494 8855, Ⓦlocalonlakeshore.com. One of the area's best, with a lovely patio and innovative menu featuring whatever's fresh, in season and local. The Okanagan cherry spare ribs ($26) are rightly considered a must-try. Mon–Fri 4pm–9pm, Sat & Sun 10am–9pm.

★ **True Grain** 10108 Main St Ⓣ250 494 4244, Ⓦtruegrain.ca. Excellent, European-inspired organic bakery using flour milled on-site from a range of different grains. The cheese pretzels are fantastic and the Copenhagen swirls are unmissable. Mon–Sat 8am–5pm.

Kelowna

If you want a summer suntan, big crowds, wineries, wonderful restaurants and nightlife then **KELOWNA** ("grizzly bear" in Salish) – is the place to come. Kelowna is also famous for its fruit, growing virtually all Canada's apricots, half its pears and plums and a third of its apples – making it eternally indebted to one Father Pandosy, a French priest who founded a mission here in 1859 and planted apple trees two years later. Today, Kelowna ranks as a metropolis compared with other Interior towns; pay no attention to the conglomeration of motels, garages and fast-food outlets on Hwy-97 on the way into town. Kelowna's downtown core is attractively developed along the lakefront and beaches, and there's a friendly vibe. Kelowna is home to the province's oldest vineyards and there are five wine trails in the area with plenty of wineries to explore (see box opposite). If wine's not your thing then you can check out microbreweries such as **Tree Brewing**, or **Okanagan Spirits** distillery, offering tours, tastings and the chance to buy locally made booze.

Beaches

One of Kelowna's main downtown attractions is its public beaches. Those off **City Park** and along Lakeshore Road to the south tend to attract a younger, trendier crowd:

9

Rotary Beach here is a windsurfers' and kite surfers' hangout, and **Gyro Park**, just north, is where the town's teenagers meet. Across the bridge **Bear Creek** and **Fintry provincial parks** are 7km and 30km up the lake's west bank, respectively; both are lovely spots with great beaches and campgrounds.

The cultural district

Kelowna has a growing arts scene, and is justifiably proud of its six-block **cultural district**, centred on Cawston Avenue and Water Street. Its main attractions are the **Rotary Centre for the Arts**, 421 Cawston Ave (☎250 717 5304, ⓦrotarycentreforthearts. com), with its gallery, theatre, studios and café, and the small but impressive **Kelowna Art Gallery**, 1315 Water St (Tues–Sat 10am–5pm, Thurs 10am–9pm, Sun 1–4pm; $5, free Thurs; ☎250 762 2226, ⓦkelownaartgallery.com).

On the same block as the arts centre and the gallery, and also worth a look, is the BC Wine and Orchard Museum, 1304 Ellis Street (Mon–Sat 10am–5pm & Sun 11am–4pm; by donation; ☎ 778 478 0325, ⓦkelownamsuems.com). Here old wine and fruit-processing paraphernalia – vibrantly painted fruit crates, live bee hives and cherry pitting equipment –provide a sense of the region's heritage and a feel for what still makes it tick behind the scenes.

Knox Mountain

Getting away from Kelowna's crowds isn't easy, but you can almost shake them off by climbing **Knox Mountain**, the high knoll overlooking the city to the north, just five minutes' drive (or a 30min walk) from downtown. It offers lovely views over the lake and town, particularly at sunset, and there's a wooden observation tower to make the most of the panorama.

Big White Ski Resort

5315 Big White Rd · Dec to mid-April · Day-pass $125 · ☎ 250 765 3101, ☎ 800 663 2772, ⓦ bigwhite.com

Come winter, Kelowna's recreation focal point moves 56km southeast (via Hwy 33) to **Big White Ski Resort**. Its dry winters make this something of a powder paradise, with sixteen lifts, 7355 skiable acres and 118 runs – over half of which cater to intermediate skiers. Since Big White is fairly remote, many choose to stay in its fairly extensive resort village: there's the full range of accommodation options – from a hostel up – and several restaurants and bars. Check the resort website for details, deals and the latest schedule of the ski-season Kelowna shuttle.

The Kettle Valley Steam Railway and Myra Canyon

To get to the eastern trailhead, drive 25km southeast from central Kelowna on Gordon Drive, KLO Road & McCulloch Road

The **Kettle Valley Railway** operated in the Thompson–Okanagan region from 1915 until the early 1960s, to be finally abandoned in 1989, apart from a 10-mile section, which is used by a working steam engine (see page 663). Since then great chunks of it have been part of a rails-to-trails programme which allows you to hike or cycle for hundreds of kilometres through the region, though the key stretch is the 215km section between Midway – on Hwy-3 near the US border – and Penticton (see page 660). However, its greatest spectacle is **Myra Canyon** above Kelowna. Here the series of gigantic wooden trestles which once allowed the railway to be routed between the Kettle Valley and Okanagan now provide an impressive testament to engineering. This was underlined by the spirited work involved in rebuilding the structures after 2003 wildfires ran riot, as interpretive boards along the route explain. From the eastern trailhead car park you can walk or cycle out and back along the trestles for an hour or two, or even cycle all the way to Penticton, an eight- to nine-hour ride which descends into the Okanagan Valley – with a series of tunnels and the gorgeous scenery below making it a memorable ride. You'll need someone to pick you up at the other end; Monashee Adventure Tours (see page 665) offers this service along with bike rentals.

KELOWNA'S VINEYARDS

When you're surrounded by some thirty or so wineries – many international gold medal award-winners – the best option is to take a **wine tour** (see page 661) and let someone else worry about driving. At one time wines in the area focused on crisp, fruity whites and dessert wines, but now successful reds and cold-climate whites are common. It's worth visiting a couple of vineyards, since the valley's microclimates and differing soil types allow neighbouring vintners to produce completely different wines. The wineries join together in early May and early October for annual spring and autumn **wine festivals** (w thewinefestivals. com) when free wine tastings, gourmet dinners, grape stomps and vineyard picnics lure the connoisseur and novice alike. More background can be found at Kelowna's **BC Wine Museum**, which reopened as a bigger and better enterprize in 2016. Below are a few recommended wineries to try if you strike out on your own.

VINEYARDS

Cedar Creek Estate Winery 5445 Lakeshore Rd ☎ 250 764 8866, w cedarcreek.bc.ca. Twice voted Canada's Winery of the Year and always a top contender with a terrific restaurant, *Vineyard Terrace*, open May–Sept. Daily May–Oct 11am, 1pm & 3pm; Nov–April by appointment; $7.

Mission Hill Family Estate 1730 Mission Hill Rd ☎ 250 768 6448, w missionhillwinery.com. Lying on the west side of the lake, its buildings wouldn't look out of place in Tuscany. Award-winning restaurant open June–Oct, check for hours. Tours daily: July & Aug hourly from 11am–5pm; Sept to mid-Oct 11am, 1pm, 3pm; $12.

Summerhill Pyramid Winery 4870 Chute Lake Rd ☎ 250 764 8000, ☎ 800 667 3538, w summerhill. bc.ca. Located in a beautiful spot with a top-notch restaurant and wines aged in a replica Egyptian pyramid – there's even organic sparkling wine. Tours daily noon, 2pm & 4pm; $10.

ARRIVAL AND INFORMATION

KELOWNA

By plane Kelowna has a major regional airport 12km north of town on Hwy-97; regular shuttles and local buses run to the centre.

Destinations Calgary (12 daily; 1hr 10min); Edmonton (7 daily; 1hr 20min); Prince George (1 daily; 1hr 20min); Seattle (1 daily; 1hr 10min); Toronto (2 daily; 4hr); Vancouver (18 daily; 1hr); Victoria (6 daily; 1hr).

Visitor centre 544 Harvey, five blocks back from the lake (Daily 8.30am–5pm; ☎ 250 861 1515, ☎ 800 663 4345, w tourismkelowna.com).

TOURS AND ACTIVITIES

Bike and boat rental Jet skis and boats can be rented from $90/hr from Kelowna Marina (☎ 250 861 8001, w kelownamarina.ca) at the end of Bernard Ave; or Lakefront Sports (☎ lakefrontsports.com) on the opposite side of the Marina which rents, among other things, jet skis ($119/hr), paddleboards ($25/hr) and kayaks ($25/hr). They also rent mountain bikes ($25/2hrs), as do **Monashee Adventure Tours** (see below).

Distinctly Kelowna Tours 1310 Water St ☎ 250 979 1211, ☎ 866 979 1211, w distinctlykelownatours.ca. Located in the *Delta Grand Okanagan Resort*. Offers a raft of wine tours such as the Westside Bench tasting experience, which takes in four wineries over 3hr 30min ($99).

Monashee Adventure Tours 1591 Highland Drive North ☎ 250 762 9253, ☎ 888 762 9253, w monashee adventuretours.com. Offers cycling tours to wineries and the Kettle Valley Railway (see page 664). The Myra Trestles plus wineries ($150) includes bike hire, snacks and water, and takes 6 hours.

ACCOMMODATION

There are a staggering number of motels and campgrounds in and around town, though accommodation of any kind can be a major headache in the height of summer so try to book well ahead. The **motels** on northbound Hwy-97 are a dependable option for vacancies, but they're well away from downtown and the lake and certainly less attractive than the more central places; prices drop the further out you go. Reservations are recommended for campsites throughout the summer.

HOTELS

Delta Grand Okanagan Lakeside Resort 1310 Water St ☎ 250 763 4500, ☎ 800 465 4651, w deltahotels.com. The top money-no-object choice in town, with a choice of spacious, modern rooms, villas and vacation homes. The complex includes a good spa, restaurant, fitness centre, casino and tour company. $332

Prestige Hotel 1675 Abbott St ☎ 250 860 7900, ☎ 877 737 8443, w prestigehotelsandresorts.com. Across

9

from City Park and close to the beach, this is one of the best options in town. Rooms have modern, country-style furnishings, and there's access to an indoor pool, hot-tub and fitness centre, plus a funky bar, 27, and a seafood restaurant. $210

HOSTELS

Kelowna International Hostel 2343 Pandosy St, near Guisachan Rd and the hospital ☎250 763 6024, ⓦkelowna-hostel.bc.ca. Charming, intimate hostel south of downtown. The owner will pick you up from the bus station, laundry and kitchen facilities are available, and a pancake breakfast and wi-fi use are included in the cost. Dorms $30; doubles $80

SameSun Hostel 245 Harvey Ave ☎250 763 9814, ☎877 972 6378, ⓦsamesun.com. Enormous custom-built hostel just across from the beach with thirty private rooms and one hundred dorm beds. Facilities include a

massive kitchen, ping-pong and a large outdoor area with patio and hot tub. From the station take bus #97 to Queensway downtown then walk south four blocks to Water St. Dorms $35; doubles $120

CAMPSITES

Bear Creek Provincial Park Westside Rd, 9km west of town via Hwy-97 ☎519 826 6850, ☎800 689 9025, ⓦdiscovercamping.ca. A good option if you want to be further away from the crowds, this campground has showers and most facilities, as well as 400m of sandy beach and 5km of hiking trails. All sites are reservable three months in advance. March–Nov. $35

Hiawatha RV Park 3795 Lakeshore Rd ☎250 861 4837, ☎888 784 7275, ⓦhiawatharvpark.com. Reasonably close to the action and backing onto Lakeshore Rd, with a separate tent area, laundry, heated pool and free hot showers. March–Oct. Sites $56; RVs $74

EATING

RauDZ 1560 Water St ☎250 868 8805, ⓦraudz.com. Much-loved bistro serving fresh, market-led, locally sourced Pacific Northwest food, with an all-BC wine list, plus cocktails. They have one of the best burgers in town ($17) but the more unusual offerings such as lamb prosciutto ($15) or chicken-leg confit *poutine* ($12) are well worth sampling. Daily 5pm until late.

Salt & Brick 243 Bernard Ave ☎250 484 3234, ⓦsaltandbrick.ca. Excellent casual spot serving boards of house-cured meats ($15) and artisan cheeses ($15) alongside wines from the Pacific Northwest. For something more filling try the salads or absurdly large – and very delicious – sandwiches ($13). Fri 11.30am–midnight, Sat 10.30am–midnight, Sun–Thurs 11.30am–10pm.

★**The Table at Codfathers Seafood Market** 2355 Gordon Drive ☎250 763 3474, ⓦthetableatcodfathers.com. Sustainable seafood market with a restaurant attached serving heaped-high plates of zingingly fresh seafood at decent prices (mains around $12), and beach-ready picnic packs to take away. Mon–Fri 11.30am–7.30pm, Sat & Sun 10.30am–7.30pm.

Waterfront Restaurant 104, 1180 Sunset Drive ☎250 979 1222, ⓦwaterfrontrestaurant.ca. One of the finest restaurants in the region serving elevated comfort food which combines the use of fresh, seasonal Okanagan produce with globally-inspired dishes and French technique. Think *kimchi* made with local apples served alongside velvety BC scallops ($15). Mains around $30 and absolutely worth splurging on. Daily 5pm–10pm.

DRINKING AND NIGHTLIFE

Doc Willoughby's 353 Bernard Ave ☎250 868 8388, ⓦdocwilloughbys.com. Kelowna's hub for live underground music, taking in an eclectic roster of sounds from hip-hop to ska, punk to rock 'n' roll. Daily 11am–2am.

Level 275 Leon Ave ☎250 861 5851, ⓦlevelclub.ca. Dance club spread across three levels with a thriving college night every Thursday. Thurs–Sat 9.30pm–2am.

Rose's Pub 1352 Water St ☎250 860 1141. If you're in town to sink a beer and people-watch, make for this lakeside terrace popular with party-goers. Daily 11am–2am.

Sapphire 238 Leon Ave ☎250 762 2007, ⓦsapphire kelowna.com. Three rooms offering Kelowna's hottest DJ nights and live shows with international DJs and recording artists. Thurs–Sat 9.30pm–4am, check listings for mid-week nights.

Vernon

The beach scene in **VERNON**, on the northern edge of Okanagan Lake, is less frenetic than elsewhere in the region and it's easier to find a place to stay than in Kelowna. But though the town attracts fewer of the bucket-and-spade brigade, the emphasis on fruit and the great outdoors is as strong as ever. It's a hub for golfers, with five courses in the area including one of Canada's best at **Predator Ridge** (see page 667). You'll also find one of the country's swankiest spas here, the Swarovski crystal-studded **Sparkling Hill** is at 888 Sparkling Place (☎250 2751556, ⓦsparklinghill.com).

9

CARRS LANDING ROAD

If you're travelling between **Kelowna** and **Vernon** with time on your hands, consider taking **Carrs Landing**, which turns into Commonage Rd in preference to Hwy-97. It's a quiet detour that offers something of the beauty for which the area is frequently praised and is part of the **Scenic Sip** (Ⓦscenicsip.ca) wine route. As the road weaves through woods and small bays, the views through to the lake are enchanting. To get to Carrs Landing Road from downtown Kelowna take Spall Rd from Hwy-97, which becomes Glenmore Drive and then winds along the lake as the two-lane Okanagan Centre Rd West; then take Carrs Landing which becomes Mission Road and Commonage Road.

Downtown Vernon centres on Main Street (30th Ave), a pretty tree-lined road with independent shops and ethnic eateries. At the southern entrance to town, sprawling **Polson Park** is a green sanctuary, but for **beaches** head 8km south of Vernon to **Kalamalka Provincial Park**, which sits on the stunning blue-green eponymous lake. The most popular strip of sand here is the tree-fringed Kal Beach, with convenient parking just across the railway, and *Alexander's Pub* offers a terrace at its eastern end.

Silver Star Mountain Resort

Silver Star Rd, 22km east of Vernon via 48th Ave • Nov–April • Day-pass $115 • ☏ 800 663 4431, Ⓦ skisilverstar.com • Winter shuttle from Vernon on Sat & Sun for $18

Year-round outdoor recreation is on hand at **Silver Star Mountain Resort**, where a local by-law requires all buildings to be painted in five colours, which gives the impression of a colourful gingerbread-house village. These frivolities are absent in the adjacent ski area, which has a 760m vertical drop, twelve square kilometres and 115 trails served by twelve lifts. Overall the resort favours the intermediate skier, but there's the full range of runs, with plenty of variety and a natural division of terrain that largely keeps different ability groups separate. Night skiing is also offered. In summer, a **ski lift** trundles to the top of Silver Star Mountain (1915m) for wide views and meadow-walking opportunities; the most-used trail wends from the summit back to the base area. This is also a very popular **mountain-biking** centre and chairlift uplift ($56 per day), and 60km of cross-country bike trails to explore; bike rental is available. There's a range of accommodation – including a hostel – at the resort and listed on its website.

The Historic O'Keefe Ranch

9380 Hwy-97 North • Daily: May, June & Sept to mid-Oct 10am–5pm; July & Aug 10am–6pm • $13.50 • ☏ 250 542 7868, Ⓦ okeeferanch.ca

Some 12km north of Vernon on Hwy-97, the **Historic O'Keefe Ranch** is a collection of early pioneer buildings and a tidy little museum that's well worth a half-hour's pause for its neat and engaging summary of nineteenth-century frontier life. A corn-maze provides an additional attraction between July and September.

ARRIVAL AND INFORMATION — VERNON

Visitor centre 3004 39th Ave (daily 9am–6pm; ☏ 250 542 1415, ☏ 800 665 0795, Ⓦ vernontourism.com). Just a few blocks from the downtown core and Main St.

ACTIVITIES

Golf Predator Ridge at 301 Village Centre Place (☏ 250 542 3436, ☏ 888 578 6688, Ⓦ predatorridge.com). One of Canada's best courses, Predator Ridge is open for public play for around $199 for the Ridge course and $189 for the Predator.

Paragliding On the western side of the valley Paraglide Canada offers an eagle's-eye view of the area with tandem rides from the top of Vernon Mountain (☏ 250 503 1962, Ⓦ paraglidecanada.com).

9

ACCOMMODATION

Ellison Provincial Park 16km southwest of Vernon ☎ 519 826 6850, ☎ 800 689 9025, ⓦ discovercamping. ca. Campgrounds near town all get busy during high season, making this rural one at Provincial Park Okanagan Lake with a beach and hiking trails a good option. Reserve at least two days in advance. Apr–Sept. $32

Super 8 Motel Vernon 4204 32nd St ☎ 250 542 4434, ⓦ wyndhamhotels.com. The high prices and very ordinary standard of most Vernon accommodation make this dependable chain the pick of the more budget-priced places. With pool, hot tub, and a modest breakfast included in the rate. $135

Vernon Lodge 3914 32nd St ☎ 250 545 3385, ☎ 800 663 9400, ⓦ vernonlodge.com. Pleasant high-end motel nine blocks from Main St on Hwy-97, with 127 a/c rooms, indoor pool and hot tub, a lounge and sports bar. $121

EATING

Bamboo Beach Fusion Grille 3313 30th Ave ☎ 250 542 7701, ⓦ bamboobeach.ca. Slick minimalist restaurant where both the menu and furnishings lean towards Japan, but the concept is fusion food. The fresh seafood is usually a good choice – such as the halibut in a peach white-wine sauce ($23). Reserve Friday and Saturday night. Tues–Thurs 11am–2pm & 5–8pm, Fri & Sat 5–8.30pm.

The Bean Scene 2923 30th Ave ☎ 250 558 1817. Smart but comfortable downtown coffee house with a good range of fair-trade and organic roasts, various baked goods and local art to enjoy. A regular venue for artsy events too. Mon–Thurs 6.30am–8pm, Fri & Sat 6am–8pm, Sun 7.30am–5pm.

Eclectic Med 2915 30th St ☎ 250 558 4646, ⓦ eclecticmedrestaurant.com. Correctly describing itself as "casual affordable fine dining", this restaurant's menu is eclectic indeed, with Mediterranean, North African and Asian mains from $18–40. Luckily the broad range doesn't compromise the quality, which is uniformly high. Mon–Fri 11.30am–1.30pm & 5–10pm, Sat & Sun 5–10pm.

Hwy-97: Vernon to Kamloops

Passing through landscapes of Eden-like clarity and beauty, **Hwy-97** is the best northern exit from (or entrance to) the Okanagan. The grass-green meadows, grazing cattle and low wooded hills here are the sort of scenery pioneers must have dreamed of and most of the little hamlets en route make charming spots to stay; if you have time and transport a number of minor roads lead off to small lakes. Hwy-97 branches off north of Vernon, joining the Trans-Canada 26km east of Kamloops. **FALKLAND**, 39km from Kamloops, is an unassuming place with a rustic village atmosphere from which country lanes lead to **Bolean Lake** (10km), **Pillar Lake** (13km) and to **Pinaus Lake** (10km).

ACCOMMODATION
HWY-97

Monte Lake RV Park 3973 Hwy-97, 21km south of Hwy-1 ☎ 250 375 2505, ⓦ montelakeresort.com. Lovely waterfront campground with a selection of serviced and unserviced lakeview tent and RV sites. With good spots for fishing, swimming and boating as well as hot showers, laundry and internet. April–Oct. Sites $25; RV full hook-up $40

The Shuswap

Some 60km north of Vernon along Hwy-97A, you arrive in the Shuswap, a photogenic region of gently sloping mountains, tranquil lakes and sandy beaches. The scenic lakeside city of **SALMON ARM**, the largest of the area's pretty resorts, is at the heart of the Shuswap region, whose centrepiece is **Shuswap Lake**. Taking its name from a mispronunciation of the Secwepemc Nation, who encompass 17 bands in BC's interior, the region and lake offer 1000km of shoreline and 32 provincial parks, making them ideal for **fishing**, swimming, waterskiing, paddling or **houseboating**. The area has a small but impressive wine-growing region specializing in cool-climate whites, especially Ortega. **Birdwatching** is another local draw, as the bay in Shuswap Lake is one of the world's last nesting areas of the western grebe. But the main attraction is the spectacle of the annual migrations of **spawning salmon** every October; Salmon Arm was named for an era when it was possible to spear salmon straight from the lake,

---

HOUSEBOATING ON SHUSWAP LAKE

Houseboating on Shuswap Lake is a hugely popular way to idle away a week or a long weekend and the pleasant waterfront village **SICAMOUS**, 31km east of Salmon Arm along Hwy-1, is known as the "houseboat capital of Canada". The season runs May to September with prices from around $4000 per week for eight people, but there are many larger (up to 22 people) and pricier options. **Agencies** include: Waterway Houseboats (☎250 836 2505, ☎877 928 3792, ⓦwaterwayhouseboats.com), Bluewater Houseboats (☎250 836 2255, ☎800 663 4024, ⓦbluewaterhouseboats.ca) and Twin Anchors Houseboat (☎250 836 2450, ☎800 663 4026, ⓦtwinanchors.com).

---

and fish were so plentiful that they were shovelled onto the land as fertilizer. Salmon spawn and die in four-year cycles; in dominant years (the next is 2022) up to two million fish brave the run from the Pacific up to their birthplace in the Adams River, a tributary of the mighty Fraser River, though there's a huge variability in numbers in other years. During spawning time, people also migrate here – around 250,000 visitors come during the peak week of a dominant year and there is a festival to celebrate: ⓦsalmonsociety.com has the full details.

Roderick Haig-Brown Provincial Park

The sleepy lakeside town of **CHASE** and the hamlet of **SQUALIX** gather around **Little Shuswap Lake**, 45km northwest of Salmon Arm on Hwy-1. Not only do they offer a couple of interesting overnight options but they're also the gateway communities for the **Roderick Haig-Brown Provincial Park**, which provides an easily accessible and superb view of the salmon migrations from signposted viewing platforms. Although the park offers no camping there is a 26-mile trail system used for hiking and mountain biking in summer and snowshoeing and cross-country skiing in winter. If you're thinking of dangling a line, pick up the *Fishing in Shuswap* leaflet from the visitor centre in Chase or Salmon Arm; don't forget to get a licence at the same time. The park is 5km north of Squalix on a signposted side road.

ARRIVAL AND INFORMATION

THE SHUSWAP

By plane Kamloops and Kelowna airports both have shuttle services to Salmon Arm (1hr 30min): Let's Go Transportation for Kelowna (☎844 877 0101, ⓦletsgotransportation. ca) and Sun Star for Kamloops (☎250 554 8005, ⓦsunstarshuttle.com).

Chase visitor centre 400 Shuswap Ave (July–Sept Mon–Fri 9am–5pm; Oct–March Mon–Wed 8.30am–4pm; April–June Mon–Fri 9am–5pm; ☎250 679 8432, ⓦchasechamber.com).

Salmon Arm visitor centre 20 Hudson Ave NE, Suite 101 (mid-May to Sept Mon–Fri 8.30am–4.30pm, Sat & Sun 10am–4pm; Sept to Oct 26 Mon–Fri 8.30am–4.30pm, Sat & Sun 9am–4pm; Oct 28–May Mon–Fri 8.30am–4.30pm; ☎250 832 2230, ⓦshuswaptourism.ca).

Sicamous visitor centre 3, 446 Main St (Early-May & June Mon–Sat 9am–5pm, Sept–June Tues–Sat 9am–4pm; July & Aug daily 9am–6pm; ☎250 836 3313, ⓦsicamouschamber.bc.ca).

ACCOMMODATION

There are plenty of options from hostels to ultra-luxe resorts in the Shuswap, and of course, houseboating.

Podollan Inn 1460 Trans-Canada Hwy NE, Salmon Arm ☎888 668 4180, ⓦpodollanhotels.com. Boutique hotel a few blocks from downtown with pools, excellent restaurant and cosy rooms – many with fireplaces and hot-tubs. They offer a seasonal "Salmon and Sommelie" overnight stay that includes a picnic lunch, viewing the salmon run, tastings at two of the area's wineries and a slap-up wine-paired salmon dinner ($255). $10 less for room-only. **$129**

Quaaout Lodge 1663 Little Shuswap Rd, Squalix ☎250 679 3090, ☎800 663 4303, ⓦquaaoutlodge.ca. 4km northwest of Squalix, the plush lakeside lodge is owned and run by the Little Shuswap Indian Band; it has a traditional sweat lodge, full service spa and a restaurant serving gamey dishes such as Elk and Bison (mains $24–$36). You can also book an excellent guided walk with First Nations interpreters around the grounds visiting their traditional "Kekuli" winter house. Also here is the highly rated Talking Rock golf course. **$189**

9

SPAWN TO BE WILD

At times it seems impossible to escape the **salmon** in BC. Whether on restaurant menus, in rivers or in photographs of grinning fishermen clutching their catch, the fish is almost as much a symbol of the region as the mountains and forests. Five different species inhabit the rivers and lakes of western Canada: **pink**, **coho**, **chum**, **chinook (or spring)** and **sockeye**.

Though they start and finish their lives in fresh water, salmon spend about four years in the open sea. Mature fish make their epic migrations from the Pacific to **spawn** in the BC rivers of their birth between June and November, swimming about 30km a day; some chinook travel more than 1400km up the Fraser beyond Prince George, which means almost fifty days' continuous upstream swimming. Though the female lays between 2000 and 6000 eggs, less than six percent of the offspring survive. On the Adams River near Salmon Arm, for example, it's estimated that of four billion sockeye eggs laid in a typical year, one billion survive to become fry (hatched fish about 2cm long), of which three-quarters are eaten by predators before becoming smolts (year-old fish) and only one-in-twenty makes it to the ocean. This means each pair of spawners effectively produce about ten mature fish; of these, eight are caught by commercial fisheries and only two return to reproduce.

These statistics clearly put the salmon's survival and BC's lucrative salmon **fishing industry** on a knife-edge. This suffered its first setback as long ago as 1913, when large rockslides at Hell's Gate in the Fraser Canyon disrupted many spawning runs. Although fish runs were constructed to bypass the slides, new pressures have since been heaped on the salmon, including fish farms, mining, logging, urban and agricultural development and the dumping of industrial and municipal wastes. Much of the concern surrounds farmed salmon: the incidence of disease among them is high, and a possible threat is that Atlantic salmon preferred by BC farms will escape in numbers that undermine wild populations through interbreeding and competition for resources.

An increasingly important line of defence, **hatcheries** have been built on rivers on the mainland and Vancouver Island to increase the percentage of eggs and fry that successfully mature. Meanwhile, overfishing remains a major concern, although various government measures have been implemented, including a moratorium on large-scale drift nets and the closure of the Fraser and Thompson rivers to all salmon fishing. Despite these measures, Greenpeace estimates hundreds of stocks of wild salmon in BC and Yukon are either extinct or at risk.

Squalix General Store 229 Trans-Canada Hwy, Chase ☎ 250 675 2977, ☎ 888 675 2977, ⓦ hihostels.ca. The HI-affiliated waterfront hostel offers dorm beds in converted railway carriages, and you can put up a tent. Sites $12; dorms $20, non-members $24; doubles $48, non-members $58

Kamloops

Almost any trip in southern BC brings you sooner or later to **KAMLOOPS**, a sprawling town 355km northeast of Vancouver and 110km west of Salmon Arm, which has been a transport hub from time immemorial. Its name derives from the Secwepemc word for "meeting of the rivers" and today it marks the meeting points of the Trans-Canada and Yellowhead (South) highways, the region's principal roads, and the Canadian Pacific and Canadian National railways. One of the region's largest towns, it's a bland, unobjectionable but determinedly functional place that's yet to completely shake off its rough-edged Wild West feel. Otherwise there's no particular need to stick around, but it makes a handy provisions stop, especially for those heading north on Highway-5 or south on the Coquihalla Highway, neither of which has much in the way of facilities.

With its distinctively small-town feel, Kamloops' downtown strip along Victoria Street is worth a ten-minute wander for its mix of shops, museum and gallery.

However, in summer the high temperatures will quickly encourage you to seek refuge in the pleasant, well-shaded **Riverside Park**, with its lakeside beach, at the northern end of 1st Avenue, over the railroad track from town.

The Kamloops Museum

207 Seymour St • Tues–Sat 9.30am–4.30pm • Donation • ☎ 250 828 3576

Though a local history museum like many others in the province, **Kamloops Museum** is worth a look, since plenty of love has obviously gone into the displays of illuminating archive photographs, artefacts, period set-pieces and a particularly well done section on the Shuswap.

Kamloops Art Gallery

465 Victoria St • Mon, Tues, Fri & Sat 10am–5pm, Wed & Thurs 10am–8pm • $5; free Thurs • ☎ 250 377 2400, ⓦ kag.bc.ca

Kamloops Art Gallery spreads over a couple of vast airy chambers within the town's architecturally impressive, modern central library building. The gallery has a huge collection and draws on different parts of it to showcase the contemporary art of Canadian artists, particularly those from BC.

Kamloops Heritage Railway

510 Lorne St • July & Aug Mon, Tues & Fri 7pm, Sat 11am; Sept Sat 11am; Oct Sat 7pm • $25 • ☎ 250 374 2141, ⓦ kamrail.com

A good way to see the scenery is to take a one-hour-ten-minute ride on the **Kamloops Heritage Railway,** a restored steam-powered heritage train that hisses and whistles its way through the countryside from just east of downtown. The October service is themed as a Ghost Train and there is a Spirit of Christmas service too.

Around Kamloops

Perhaps the most striking thing about Kamloops is its surroundings, dominated by the bare-earthed brown hills, which provide almost surreal touches of near-desert, which are particularly marked in the bare rock and clay outcrops above the bilious waters of the Thompson River and in the bleached scrub and failing stands of pines that spot the barren hills. The visitor centre (see opposite) has details of those diversions a short drive out of town (with a bias towards the dozen-plus golf courses).

Sunmore Ginseng Spa

925 McGill Place, 3km west of downtown • Daily 9am–5pm • ☎ 250 372 2814, ⓦ sunmore.com

North American ginseng has become one of the region's prime crops and the opulent **Sunmore Ginseng Spa** offers pampering sessions. Treatments such as the one-hour-thirty-minute ginseng body wrap are priced around $220, but massages start at $150 for an hour. Next door to the spa is a ginseng factory with a showroom where you can

---

KAMLOOPA POW WOW AND KAMLOOPS COWBOY FESTIVAL

Along with its excellent Secwepemc Museum, Kamloops offers a rare chance to learn more about First Nations history and modern culture at the annual **Kamloopa Pow Wow**, held each year around the end of July on the Tk'emlups Indian Band Pow Wow grounds ($10/day; ☎ 250 828 9782). One of Western Canada's largest First Nations celebrations, you can enjoy traditional storytelling, tap your toes to infectious drumbeats and watch dances in traditional beaded regalia. Celebrating an altogether different heritage, the **Kamloops Cowboy Festival** ($25/day; ⓦ bcchs.com) is held annually in mid-March and showcases cowboy poetry, Western art and music, and even has a cowboy church.

9

learn about medicinal qualities of the plants – North American varieties sedate, Asian varieties stimulate – and their cultivation.

Secwepemc Museum and Heritage Park

200–355 Hwy-5, just north of South Thompson River 3km from downtown • Mon–Fri 8am–4pm • $10 cash only • ☎ 250 828 9749, ⓦ secwepemcmuseum.com

For a fairly in-depth picture of local First Nations history and traditions, call at the **Secwepemc Museum**, a five-hectare heritage park which gives a fascinating insight into the lives and culture of the Secwepemc people. Visit archeological remains of a 2000-year-old Secwepemc winter village with reconstructed pit-houses and summer tule-mat lodges. The buildings here were first used as Residential Schools for First Nations children who were taken from their parents in an attempt to force them to "assimilate" into Canadian culture; some exhibits tell the tragic tale of this now-deplored government policy that's been labelled "cultural genocide" by a recent Truth and Reconciliation Commission. One of western Canada's largest pow wows is hosted on its grounds in the summer (see box above).

Paul Lake Provincial Park

Paul Lake Rd, 17km north of Kamloops via Hwy-5

The nearest and most popular lake of the two hundred or so trout-stuffed lakes that dot the hinterland, the 402-hectare **Paul Lake Provincial Park** northeast of town has beaches, swimming and a campground on the north side ($18). There's a 20km mountain-bike trail and a nature trail for a gentle hike to the summit of Gibraltar Rock (elevation 900m).

British Columbia Wildlife Park

9077 Dallas Drive • March, April, Sept 8 to Oct daily 9.30am–4pm; May–Sept 8 daily 9.30am–5pm; Nov–Feb Sat & Sun 9.30am–4pm • $12.45 • ☎ 250 573 3242, ⓦ bczoo.org

To get up close and personal with grizzly bears, wolves, moose and cougars – albeit with the animals languishing safely behind a fence – visit this zoo and animal rehabilitation centre 15km east of Kamloops.

ARRIVAL AND INFORMATION

KAMLOOPS

By plane Kamloops airport lies 7km northwest of the centre. Bus services are next to nonexistent, so you'll need to take a cab for about $20 or the Sun Star shuttle (see page 669).

Destinations Calgary (5 daily; 1hr 10min); Prince George (1 daily; 1hr 5min); Vancouver (5 daily; 1hr).

By train The station lies 11km north of Kamloops, off Hwy-5 on CNR Yard Access Road. With no public transport, you'll need to call a taxi firm, such as Kami Cabs (☎ 250 374 5151),

and pay $15 to get downtown.

Destinations Jasper (3 weekly; 8hr 30min); Vancouver (3 weekly; 10hr).

Visitor centre 1290 West Trans-Canada Hwy, 6km west of downtown (mid-May to Aug daily 8.30am–6pm; Sept Mon–Sat 9am–5pm, Sun 10am–3pm; Oct to mid-May Mon–Fri 9am–5pm; ☎ 250 374 3377, ☎ 800 662 1994 ⓦ tourismkamloops.com); has free wi-fi.

ACCOMMODATION

Kamloops' huge volume of accommodation is aimed at the motorist and consists of thick clusters of motels, most of which blanket the town's eastern margins on Hwy-1 or out on Columbia St West. For camping, Paul Lake Provincial Park (see above) is your best bet.

Sandman Signature Kamloops Hotel 225 Lorne St ☎ 250 377 7263, ⓦ sandmanhotels.com. This vast modern riverfront hotel is as good a bet as any central option. Downtown's an easy walk away and there's a lovely

waterfront park to hang out in. The 3-star rooms are smart boutique-style and there's an indoor pool, hot-tub and sundeck. $135

Plaza Heritage Hotel 405 Victoria St ☎ 250 377 8075 ☎ 877 977 5292, ⓦ theplazahotel.ca. Downtown hotel whose rooms have been restored to their original grandeur to provide a real sense of history. Club rooms include full hot breakfast and parking. $149

EATING

Brownstone 118 Victoria St ☎ 250 851 9939, ⓦ brownstone-restaurant.com. Fine-dining establishment in a 1904 heritage building that's entertained the likes of Harrison Ford and Jennifer Lopez. Mains $23–36. Mon–Fri 11am–2pm; daily 5pm–late.

Peter's Pasta 149 Victoria St ☎ 250 372 8514. Kamloops has plenty of eating options, with competition fierce along Victoria Street, but this place is always packed thanks to its

fresh and reliable Italian food (mains $11–19). Tues–Sat 5pm–late.

Swiss Pastries & Café 359 Victoria St ☎ 250 372 2625. Snack food is served in generous portions at this popular café, which really is run by Swiss people. It does good muesli, cappuccino, pastries and excellent sandwiches. Mon–Sat 8am–5pm.

DRINKING

Cactus Jacks 417 Seymour St ☎ 250 374 7289, ⓦ cactusjackssaloon.com. Down your beer with local cowboys and cowgirls at this bona fide Western bar a block

south of Victoria St. With attractions like mechanical bull riding or line dancing. Wed & Thurs 9.30pm–2am, Fri & Sat 9pm–2am.

Hwy-5 and Wells Gray Provincial Park

From Kamloops, northbound **Hwy-5** (the Yellowhead South) heads upstream along the North Thompson River, coursing through high hills and rolling pasture before carving through the Monashee Mountains. The results are scenically impressive, particularly along the latter half of the journey – beyond the main town of **Clearwater** – where the road skirts the immense **Wells Gray Provincial Park**, one of the finest protected areas in BC. The Thompson's source lies near the modest town of **Valemount** as does the road's junction with the main Yellowhead Hwy (Hwy-16) at Tête Jaune Cache, a total distance of 338km from Kamloops. From here it's 270km to Prince George (see page 794) and 77km east to Jasper National Park (see page 590) and the BC–Alberta border.

Sun Peaks Resort

53km northeast of Kamloops via Hwy 5 • Late Nov to mid-April • Day-pass $105 • ☎ 250 578 5474, ⓦ sunpeaksresort.com

It may not receive half the attention lavished on Whistler, but BC's second-largest winter destination with Canada's second-largest skiable terrain, **Sun Peaks Resort** has some pretty impressive statistics of its own: 4270 acres of terrain, 133 trails and glades, 11 lifts and 36.6km of cross-country trails, with the terrain mainly intermediate level. Come summer, Sun Peaks attracts mountain-bikers to its lift-accessed bike park (day-pass $47) as well as hikers and golfers. The ever-increasing accommodation options – all bookable through the resort – range from a hostel to a five-star hotel.

Clearwater

A dispersed logging and ranching community 125km north of Kamloops, **CLEARWATER** is invisible from Hwy-5 and unless you're planning to spend time exploring Wells Gray Provincial Park, there's no need to investigate: everything you need, apart from the supermarket, is on or just off the highway.

ARRIVAL AND INFORMATION CLEARWATER

By train The VIA Rail station is just south of North Thompson River, 2km south of Hwy-5; call Wells Gray Taxi (☎ 250 674 1542) for a pick-up.
Destinations Jasper (3 weekly; 6hr); Vancouver (3 weekly; 13hr).

Visitor centre 425 East Yellowhead Hwy (mid-May to mid-Oct daily 10am–6pm; ☎ 250 674 2646, ⓦ clearwater bcchamber.com).

9

ACCOMMODATION

Clearwater Lodge 331 Eden Rd ☎ 250 674 3080, Ⓦ clearwaterlodge.bcresorts.com. Smart motel with modern spacious rooms, pool, hot tub, sauna and the *Gateway Grill* (see opposite). **$155**

Clearwater Valley Resort & KOA Campground 373 Clearwater Valley Rd ☎ 250 674 3918, ☎ 800 562 3239, Ⓦ koa.com. One block from the visitor centre, this big resort and campground has a combination of cabins, camping and RV sites (March to mid-Oct), with a heated pool and a restaurant. Ssites **$36**; RVs **$44**; cabins **$83**

Dutch Lake Motel and Campground 333 Roy Rd ☎ 250 674 3325. Reasonable budget motel by Hwy-5 with dated, but clean, basic rooms. Also has some good camping

spots, but best of all is its private lake access for swimming. With laundry and free wi-fi. Sites **$32**; RVs **$42**; doubles **$125**

Dutch Lake Resort & RV Park 361 Ridge Drive ☎ 250 674 3351, ☎ 888 884 4424, Ⓦ dutchlake.com. The best of several campgrounds on Dutch Lake between Hwy-5 and downtown Clearwater. With cabins as well as tent and RV sites. April–Oct. Sites **$45**; RVs **$48**; cabins **$149**

Half Moon Guesthouse 625 Greer Rd ☎ 250 674 4199, Ⓦ halfmoonhostel.com. Small hostel, about 4km north of town and just off Clearwater Valley Rd, which offers private rooms (but no dorm beds), a full kitchen and common room. **$75**

EATING

★ **Hop "N" Hog Tap & Smokehouse** 424 Clearwater Valley Rd ☎ 250 674 3654 Ⓦ canadiansmokehouse.com. Log-cabin restaurant that's reliably packed thanks to its excellent barbeque meats. To get the best out of the menu order the smoked platter for two ($58); otherwise the smoky brisket burger ($23) is a class act – thanks to having spent 14 hours in the onsite smokehouse. The smoked veggie platter ($24) is a fine meat-free alternative. Various craft beers are on tap ready to complement the food. Wed–Sat 5pm until late.

Gateway Grill In Clearwater Lodge (see below). One of the best places to eat in town for the usual range of North American food, including burgers, pasta, steaks and the like; mains average $18. Daily 5–9pm.

Painted Turtle In Dutch Lake Resort (see above). Popular seasonal restaurant with a charming open-air covered patio offering spectacular views over the lake. On the menu is everything from steaks and pasta to salmon and sandwiches. Lunchtime often brings a bustling coach party trade. April to mid-Oct daily 8am–9pm.

Wells Gray Provincial Park

WELLS GRAY PROVINCIAL PARK is the equal of any Rocky Mountain parks: if anything, its wilderness is probably more extreme – so untamed that many of its peaks remain unclimbed and unnamed. **Wildlife** sightings are common – you may encounter black and grizzly bears, mountain goats, cougars, timber wolves, coyotes, weasels, martens, mink, wolverines and beavers.

Clearwater Valley Road

Even if you're not geared up for the backcountry, **Clearwater Valley Road**, the 63km **access road** to Clearwater Lake from Clearwater, opens up a medley of waterfalls, walks, viewpoints and picnic spots that make a detour extremely worthwhile. The road is paved for the first 42km into the park boundary, but the remaining 36km to **Clearwater Lake** is gravel. Most sights are well signed and you can see all obvious scenic landmarks in a day.

Spahats Falls and Wells Gray Recreation Area

About 10km north of Clearwater, a short walk from a well-signed car park brings you to the 61m **Spahats Falls**, the first of several mighty cascades along this route. You can watch the waters crashing down through layers of pinky-red volcanic rock from observation platforms, which also provide an impressive and unexpected view of the Clearwater Valley. A few hundred metres further up the road, a 15km gravel lane peels off into the **Wells Gray Recreation Area**; a single trail from the end of the road strikes off into alpine meadows.

9

ACTIVITIES IN WELLS GRAY PROVINCIAL PARK

With some 250km of maintained trails and dozens of other lesser routes, the 1.3 million-acre park is magnificent for **hiking**. We've outlined short walks and day-hikes from the park's access road (see above), but serious long-distance hikers can easily spend a week or more on backcountry hikes, most of which are in the southern third of the park and link together for days of hiking and wilderness camping. Pick up a free *BC Parks* map-pamphlet at the Clearwater visitor centre; if you're thinking of doing any backcountry exploration you'll want to invest in their more detailed maps and guides. Steep switchbacks, muddy conditions, thick brush and large deadfall as well as tramping across sharp lava flow and loose rock make the going slow on many of the more remote trails. The longest one-way trail connects **Clearwater Lake** to **Kostal Lake** (26km) and begins on the main Wells Gray Park Road, just across from *Clearwater Lake* campground.

Another of the park's big attractions is **canoeing** on Clearwater and Azure lakes. The former is at the end of the access road and can be linked with a short portage to make a fifty-plus-kilometre dream trip for paddlers; rent canoes ($60 day, $225 week) from Clearwater Lake Tours (☎250 674 2121, ⓦclearwaterlaketours.com; mid-May to Oct) on the south end of Clearwater Lake. Several local operators run **tours** featuring **whitewater rafting**, riding, fishing, boating and floatplane excursions around the park; the Clearwater visitor centre has details.

Battle Mountain and Green Mountain Lookout

About 25km up the main access road from Clearwater, a 4WD track branches east to reach the trailhead for **Battle Mountain** (19km), with the option of several shorter hikes like the Mount Philip Trail (5km) en route.

Some 10km further along the road and on the left just after the park entrance, a rough, winding road leads to **Green Mountain Lookout**. It offers one of the most enormous roadside panoramas in BC with nothing but an almighty emptiness of primal forest and mountains as far as you can see.

Dawson and Helmcken falls

The next essential stop, 6km beyond the park entrance, is **Dawson Falls**, a broad, powerful cascade (91m wide and 18m high) a five-minute walk from the access road, signed "Viewpoint". Beyond, the road crosses an ugly iron bridge and shortly after meets the start of the **Murtle River Trail** (14km one way), a particularly good walk that takes in the more spectacular Majerus and Horseshoe waterfalls.

Almost immediately beyond Dawson Falls the next turn-off leads to **Helmcken Falls**, the park's undisputed highlight which, at 137m, is two and a half times the height of Niagara Falls. The site is heavily visited, and it's not unknown for wedding parties to come here for dramatic matrimonial photos in front of the luminous arc of water that plunges into a black, carved bowl fringed with vivid carpets of lichen and splintered trees. The whole ensemble is framed by huge plumes of spray wafting up on all sides.

The Ray Farm, Bailey's Creek and Clearwater Lake

Attractions along the final 18km of the road to Clearwater Lake include **Ray Farm**, the former home of John Bunyon Ray, who arrived in 1912 to become the first homesteader in the area; it's now a group of picturesquely ruined, wooden shacks scattered in a lush clearing. Some 4km beyond is **Bailey's Creek** where, in August and September, the robust chinook salmon attempt to jump the rapids before giving up and spawning a kilometre downstream. The park road ends at the southern end of **Clearwater Lake**, location of some boat launches, a provincial campground and a series of short trails.

By car Without your own transport, you'd have to hitch from Clearwater along the park access road (see page 674) – feasible at the height of summer, but highly unlikely at any other time. There are also some less-travelled gravel roads into other sections of the park from Blue River, 112km north of Clearwater on Hwy-5, and from the village of 100 Mile House, on Hwy-97 west of the park.

Visitor centre ⓦ wellsgray.ca. The excellent Wells Gray Provincial Park visitor centre is in Clearwater (see page 673).

Clearwater Lake Tours Clearwater Lake Campground at the southern end of Clearwater Lake ☎ 250 674 2121, ⓦ clearwaterlaketours.com. This outfitter offers guided canoe trips and rentals, motorboat tours as well as camping and fishing gear rentals. They also run a water-taxi service, which drops you off at any site on Clearwater Lake, picking you up at a prearranged time.

ACCOMMODATION

Helmcken Falls Lodge 6664 Clearwater Valley Rd ☎ 250 674 3657, ⓦ helmckenfalls.com. Log cabin and standard motel-quality rooms beside the Wells Gray Golf Course and 35km from Hwy-5. There are tent and RV sites as well as a restaurant, and they can organize tours and arrange rentals for a wide range of park activities from horseriding to rafting to snowshoeing. May–Sept & Jan to mid-March. Sites $30; RVs $42; doubles $219

Wells Gray Guest Ranch 5565 Clearwater Valley Rd ☎ 250 674 2792, ⓦ wellsgrayranch.com. Friendly rustic resort with accommodation provided in log cabins just within the park entrance, 27km from Hwy-5 via Clearwater Valley Rd. Rates include continental breakfast. Activities such as horseriding, hiking and canoeing are offered for an extra charge. Cabins $155

Wells Gray Provincial Park campgrounds ☎ 519 826 6850, ☎ 800 689 9025, ⓦ discovercamping.ca. The park has three provincial campgrounds along the park access road with a mix of reservable and first-come, first-served sites. Many other backcountry campgrounds (with self-service registration facilities at trailheads; $5) dot the shores of the park's major lakes; Clearwater Lake Tours operates a water-taxi service. May–Sept. Reserve at least two days in advance. Sites $23

The Fraser Canyon

Travellers heading west from **Kamloops** can either take the brisker Coquihalla Highway to **Hope** or follow the **Trans-Canada Hwy** along the **Fraser Canyon**. This adds around 70km to the journey but the reward is seeing one of BC's grandest waterways squeezed between the high ridges of the Cascade and Coast mountain ranges. Long regarded as impassable, the canyon has forced the highway to pass through seven tunnels and along a series of perilous rock ledges hundreds of metres above the swirling waters. The Canadian Pacific Railway and Canadian National Railway also pass this way. Beyond the town of Hope all road and rail routes combine to roll west along the Fraser's lower reaches to Vancouver; before you enter its hinterland you might break your journey at the charming resort town of **Harrison Hot Springs**.

Cache Creek

Sleepy **CACHE CREEK**, 337km from Vancouver and 84km west of Kamloops, is sometimes known as the "Arizona of Canada" for its extraordinary rocky landscapes and baking summer climate, which settles a heat-wasted somnolence onto its dusty streets. The parched, windswept mountains here are anomalous volcanic intrusions in the regional geology, producing a legacy of hard rock and semiprecious stones – including jade – that attract climbers and rock hounds. You can watch semiprecious stones being worked at several places, or check out **Hat Creek Ranch**, ten minutes north of Cache Creek by the junction of highways 97 and 99 (May–Oct daily 9am–5pm; tours and stagecoach 10am–4.30pm; $15; ☎ 250 457 9722, ☎ 800 782 0922, ⓦ hatcreekranch.com), which preserves the feel of the 1870s with its collection of original buildings including a log stopping house and a reconstruction of a First Nations Shuswap village.

9

THE COQUIHALLA HIGHWAY

Anyone travelling east–west in any sort of hurry, travels the 207km between Hope and Kamloops on the **Coquihalla Highway** (Hwy-5). The scenery is unexceptional for the 68km west of the wind- and snow-whipped Coquihalla Pass (1244m) but things look up considerably to the east. Here, forests, mountains and crashing rivers add drama – despite being somewhat compromised by old mines, road-building scars, forest fire-ravaged landscapes and the devastating effects of the Pine beetle infestation, which has often necessitated large-scale clear-cuts.

ACCOMMODATION   CACHE CREEK

Bonaparte Motel 1395 Hwy-97 North ☎250 457 9693, ☎888 922 1333, ⓦbonaparteinn.ca. One of several highway motels, with standard rooms – some with kitchenettes – but also a heated outdoor pool, indoor hot tub and sauna. Celebrities including John Cusack and Woody Harrelson have stayed here while filming in the area. Free wi-fi. **$99**

Hat Creek Ranch Junction of highways 97 and 99, 11km north of Cache Creek ☎250 457 9722, ☎800 782 0922, ⓦhatcreekranch.com. This open-air museum also offers camping for tents and RVs with and without electrical hook-ups, but a greater draw is the mix of miners'

tents, teepees, covered wagons and the rare chance to rent a *kekuli* – an Aboriginal pit house (for up to ten people). Unless you want a cabin, you'll need your own bedding or you can rent some for $5. Amenities include showers, fire pits and a restaurant serving breakfast and lunch. Sites **$17**; RVs **$22**; miners' tents **$37**; tipis **$47**; covered wagons **$65**; cabins **$97**; *kekuli* **$105**

Hungry Herbie's Drive-In Hwy-97 ☎250 457 6644. A good place to put hunger pangs to rest is this old-fashioned diner and burger joint with home-made monster burgers ($6–9) and a full menu of cooked breakfasts. Daily 8am–10pm.

Lytton

LYTTON, 50km north of Hell's Gate, marks the start of BC's arid interior. Lying at the junction of the Fraser and Thompson rivers, it's a small lumber town and a main centre for **whitewater rafting**. The most notorious stretch is along the Thompson River from Spences Bridge to Lytton, home to rapids with intimidating names like Devil's Gorge and Witch's Cauldron. Various companies listed at the visitor centre run trips from May to August (starting at around $139 for half a day), including *Kumsheen Rafting Resort* (see below).

INFORMATION   LYTTON

Visitor centre 400 Fraser St (June to early Sept daily 9am–5pm; Oct–May call for times; ☎250 455 2523,   ⓦlyttonchamber.com).

ACCOMMODATION AND EATING

Kumsheen Rafting Resort 5km east of Lytton on Hwy-5 ☎250 455 2296, ☎800 663 6667, ⓦkumsheen.com. The resort offers lovely antique-furnished tent-cabins and tipis, camping (tent and sleeping bag rentals available) and RV sites. Also has an outdoor pool and restaurant. Tents

$52; RV sites **$55**; cabins and tipis **$162**

Skihist Provincial Park 6km east of town along Hwy-1. Campsites in a small park with views of the Thompson River canyon. With cold water, fire pits and sani-dump, but none of the 58 sites can be reserved. **$23**

Hell's Gate

Around 20km north of Yale on Hwy-1 is the famous **Hell's Gate**, where – in a gorge almost 152m deep – the huge swell of the Fraser River is squeezed into a 35m channel of foaming water that crashes through the rocks with awe-inspiring ferocity. The Fraser is one of the key runs for Pacific salmon, and every summer and autumn they fill it as they head for tributaries and upstream lakes to spawn (see page 670). For some startling panoramas of the canyon, travel 10km north of Yale on Hwy-1 to the **Alexandra Bridge Provincial Park**. Some 8km further

9

north, the **Air Tram cable car** (daily: late April to mid-May & early Sept to mid-Oct 10am–4pm; mid-May to early Sept 10am–5pm; $24; ☎604 867 9277, ⓦhellsgateairtram.com) offers more vertiginous views of the river, and there is a gift shop, café and gold panning experience on-site, along with an excellent fisheries exhibit. On a lighter note, the locals claim that the area is haunted and the Air Tram's owners have capitalized on this with various spooky surprises along the way.

Yale

YALE, about 25km north of Hope, marks the southern end of the Fraser Canyon with a ring of plunging cliffs. Sitting at the river's navigable limit, it was once a significant site for Canada's Aboriginal peoples, providing an important point of departure for the canoes of the Stó:lo ("River People"). A Hudson's Bay Company post, called the Falls, was established here in the 1840s, later renamed in honour of James Murray Yale, commander of the HBC post at Fort Langley. Within a decade it became the largest city in North America west of Chicago and north of San Francisco, though today Yale is a small town of about two hundred people. A visit to the **Yale Heritage Site** (mid-April to mid-Oct daily 10am–5pm; $10; ☎604 863 2324, ⓦhistoricyale.ca) on the corner of Hwy-1 and Douglas Street, offers an in-depth account of the town's golden age with interpretive guides and plenty of hands-on experiences including gold panning.

If large rocks impress you, have a peek at **Lady Franklin Rock**, the vast river boulder that blocked the passage of steamers beyond Yale – all goods heading north to the goldfields had to transfer to wagon trains bound for the Cariboo Wagon Road. It's a ten-minute walk from the museum (which can provide directions). For a longer jaunt, take Hwy-1 1km south out of the village to reach the trailhead of the **Spirit Cave Trail**, a three-hour walk with fine views of the mountains.

ACCOMMODATION   YALE

Emory Creek Provincial Park Campground Hwy-1, 10km south of Yale. A large, peaceful wooded site with   river walks. With water, toilets and fire pits. No reservations possible. May–Oct. **$21**

SIMON FRASER

The Fraser River is named after **Simon Fraser**, one of North America's most remarkable early explorers who, as an employee of the North West Company, helped established the first colonial trading posts west of the Rockies: Fort McLeod (1805), Fort St James (1806), Fort Fraser (1806) and Fort George (1807). Having traced the route taken by fellow explorer Alexander Mackenzie across the continent, he set out in 1808 to discover a practical route to the Pacific for transporting furs and supplies. Instead, he travelled some 840km of the Fraser – under the mistaken impression he was following the Columbia – from Fort George to the Pacific. "We had to pass where no human being should venture," he wrote, making most of the journey on foot guided by local First Nation people, pushing forward using ladders, ropes and improvised platforms to bypass rapids too treacherous to breach by boat. Reaching the river's mouth, where he would have glimpsed the site of present-day Vancouver, he realized his error and deemed the venture a commercial failure, despite the fact he had successfully navigated one of the continent's greatest rivers for the first time. Few people felt the need to follow Fraser's example until the discovery of **gold** near Yale in 1858; prospectors promptly waded in and panned every tributary of the lower Fraser until new strikes tempted them north to the Cariboo.

Teague House B&B ☎ 604 863 2336, ☎ 800 363 7238, ⓦ teaguehouse.com. Attractive 1864 heritage-listed bed and breakfast with many period pieces throughout and a communal kitchen. Also runs whitewater rafting trips down the Fraser River. $\overline{\$125}$

Hope

Reputedly christened by pioneers familiar with Dante, **HOPE** – as in "Abandon all hope..." – is a pleasant, mountain-ringed town 158km east of Vancouver, which achieved a certain fame as the place wasted in spectacular fashion by Sylvester Stallone at the end of *First Blood*, the first Rambo movie. Despite the number of roads converging here – the Trans-Canada Hwy, Hwy-3 and the Coquihalla Hwy – it remains remarkably unspoilt. In the past it was rivers, not roads that accounted for the town's growth: the Fraser River (Simon Fraser himself passed through in 1808; see box below) and two of its major tributaries, the Skagit and Coquihalla rivers, meet here. The original Aboriginal villages were forced to move when a Hudson's Bay post was established in 1848, the status quo being further disturbed when a gold rush hit in 1858.

The town **museum** (May–Sept Mon–Fri 10am–4pm, Sat & Sun 9am–5pm; donation) is in the same building as the visitor centre, and offers First Nations artefacts and a history of logging in the area. Time permitting, drop by **Memorial Park** downtown, where trees ravaged by rot have been given a new life by local chainsaw sculptors. Nearby, the **Christ Church National Historic Site**, built in 1861, is one of BC's oldest churches.

Hope hikes

Hiking, fishing, canoeing and even gold panning are all popular around the hundreds of local lakes and rivers; you can get details from the visitor centre. Of the hikes, the **Rotary Nature Trail** (2km) from the end of 7th Street to the confluence of the Fraser and Coquihalla rivers is popular, as is the more demanding **Mount Hope Loop and Lookout Trail** (4.8km), with a view worth the steep climb. Another popular walking expedition is the dark jaunt through the five colossal **Othello-Quintette Tunnels** (closed Nov–April) of the Hope-Midway Kettle Valley Railway, opened in 1916 but abandoned in 1959 after countless avalanches, mudslides and rock falls. The tunnels are reached by a short trail from the **Coquihalla Canyon Provincial Park** parking area, 6km northeast of town off the Coquihalla Hwy. Check for tunnel closures; a torch is recommended. One of the backcountry locations used during the filming of *First Blood*, it offers spectacular views over the cliffs and huge sandbars of the Coquihalla Gorge. **Kawkawa Lake**, 2.5km northeast of the Hope town centre, on Kawkawa Lake Road, is another popular mountain retreat, with plenty of relaxing and swimming opportunities.

ARRIVAL AND INFORMATION — HOPE

Visitor centre 919 Water Ave (Mon–Fri 10am–4pm, Sat & Sun 9am–5pm; ☎ 604 869 2021, ⓦ hopebc.ca).

ACCOMMODATION

Best Continental Motel 860 Fraser Ave ☎ 604 869 9726, ⓦ bestcontinentalmotel.com. Cheap motels proliferate along Old Hope Princeton Way – the business loop off Hwy-3 – but it's worth avoiding most of them in preference for this standard motel, a block back from the main highway: you'll save a few dollars and it's quieter too. $\overline{\$89}$

Othello Tunnels Campground & RV Park 67851 Othello Rd, 8km east of town ☎ 604 869 9448, ☎ 877 869 0543, ⓦ othellotunnels.com. Family-run campground with full hook-ups and fire pits at all sites and a rainbow-trout fishing pond that delights the kids. Free wi-fi. $\overline{\$36}$

9

EATING

Blue Moose Coffee House 322 Wallace St ☎604 869 0729. For snacks, try this buzzing café with its good line in wraps and soups. The coffee is outstanding and there's local art to ponder too. Daily 7am–9pm.

★ **Kimchi** 821a 6th Ave ☎604 869 0070. One of few downtown places to eat out, and a little away from most of the action further west down Wallace Street, *Kimchi* is well worth seeking out for the excellent Korean and Japanese cuisine with bento boxes from $10. Mon–Sat 11am–9pm.

Harrison Hot Springs and around

An easy 41km drive through pretty farmland on Hwy-7 from Hope, **HARRISON HOT SPRINGS** populates the southern edge of Harrison Lake, which Aboriginal peoples have visited for centuries for its healing properties, though the waters were then "discovered" in 1858 by gold prospectors who popularized it and, shortly after, the town became BC's first resort. Today, tourism remains the main industry, as you'll see from the number of motels lining the lake. It remains a scenic spot, reminiscent of an old-fashioned seaside community, ringed by beautiful mountain views, and you'll find plenty of Sasquatch statues and souvenirs here, as it's believed that Canada's mythical "Big Foot" has regularly been sighted here.

The lake itself is 60km long – making it one of BC's largest – and its waters are very clean, but chilly. The only swimming option is in the artificial lagoon on the lake's shore; to get on to the lake itself, you can rent boats, windsurfing equipment and jet skis from the town's marina by the town's main attraction, *Harrison Hot Springs Resort*. The **springs** are a short walk along the shore from the resort and a scalding 73ºC at source. To make the waters suitable for soaking, they're cooled and redirected to the **Harrison Hot Springs Public Pool** (Mon–Thurs 10am–8pm, Fri 10am–9pm, Sat 9am–9pm; Sun 9am–8pm; $9, day-pass $14) at the intersection of Hot Springs Road and the Esplanade in town.

Circle Farm Tour

Foodies should ask at the visitor centre for a map of the Agassiz-Harrison Mills **Circle Farm Tour** (ⓦcirclefarmtour.com), which takes you to several local farms, including a hazelnut orchard, a cheese-maker's, a chicken farm and a corn barn, all within a 25km radius.

Clear Creek Hot Springs

For free hot springs in a series of tubs in a remote setting be prepared to drive to **Clear Creek Hot Springs**, 56km north along the east side of Harrison via East Harrison Forestry Service Road (past Sasquatch Provincial Park). These can get very popular during weekends and holidays. If your car isn't up to the challenge, you'll have to journey the last 10km on foot. For detailed directions, ask at the **visitor centre**.

ARRIVAL AND INFORMATION
HARRISON HOT SPRINGS

By bus Local buses link Harrison Hot Springs with Chilliwack (11 daily; ⓦbctransit.com).

Visitor centre 499 Hot Springs Rd, in an old logging-camp bunkhouse (June–Sept Mon & Thurs–Sun 9.30am–5.30pm; Oct–May Sat & Sun 10am–4pm; ☎604 796 5581, ⓦtourismharrison.com).

ACCOMMODATION

★ **Harrison Heritage House and Cottages** 312 Lillooet Ave ☎604 796 9552, ☎800 331 8099, ⓦharrisoncottages.com. Beautiful riverside cottages alongside one of the village's few heritage buildings. Splurge on the jacuzzi suite which boasts "the biggest tub this side of the Rockies". $195

Harrison Hot Springs Resort & Spa ☎604 796 2244, ☎866 638 5075, ⓦharrisonresort.com. A 1950s favourite of Clark Gable's, this friendly updated resort has spacious bright rooms and five indoor and outdoor pools with water piped from the springs. For a treat, head to the

Resort's Copper Room – the smartest of four eating options – for the rack of lamb ($39). $209

Sasquatch Provincial Park campgrounds Hwy-7, 6km north of Harrison Hot Springs ☎519 826 6850, ☎800 689 9025, ⓦdiscovercamping.ca. There are several private campgrounds in and around the resort, but the nicest of all are the three campgrounds in Sasquatch Provincial Park, with canoeing (rentals available), swimming in warmish lakes and short hiking trails nearby, though none of the sites have showers. Reserve at least two days in advance. April to early Oct. $23

The Spa Motel 140 Esplanade ☎604 796 2828, ⓦharrisonspamotel.com. Charming and immaculately kept mid-range downtown motel across from the beach. Some two-bedroom units are offered, as are ones with kitchenettes. $119

EATING

Morgan's Bistro 160 Esplanade Ave ☎604 796 5563. One of the best of several eating options along the lakeside Esplanade. With a large patio, uncomplicated seasonal menus (mains $15–27) and largely local ingredients: great fish and chips and even better lamb. Save space for the superb Key Lime pie. Tues–Sun 11.30am–10pm.

Muddy Waters 328 Esplanade Ave ☎604 491 1696. Excellent coffee shop and café offering locally roasted beans, BC craft beers, and ice cream. Perfect for people-watching on their patio with sweeping lake and mountain views. Mon–Fri 9am–5pm, Sat & Sun 9am–6pm.

Village Pizzeria 160 Lilooet Ave ☎604 796 1170. Friendly locals' spot serving up delicious piled-high pizzas (from $15), fresh salads and good pasta basics just around the corner from the main drag. Takeaway and eat-in available. Mon–Thurs 4–10pm, Fri–Sun noon–10pm.

Vancouver and Vancouver Island

FALSE CREEK INLET

Vancouver and Vancouver Island

Vancouver and Vancouver Island stand apart from the rest of British Columbia, the big-city outlook and bustling, cosmopolitan streets of Vancouver, Canada's third-largest metropolis, and Victoria, the provincial capital, dramatically at odds with the interior's small towns, remote villages and vast tracts of wilderness. While Vancouver Island has scenery that occasionally matches that of the interior, its landscapes are generally more modest, the island's intimate and self-contained nature and relatively small extent creating a region that feels more sea-based than the rest of mainland BC.

10

Vancouver is one of the world's great scenic cities, its water and mountain-ringed setting equalling those of Sydney and Rio de Janeiro. Long after the many fine galleries and museums, and the even better restaurants, have faded, the memory of the Coast Mountains rearing above Burrard Inlet, or the beaches and semi-wilderness of Stanley Park, will linger. Vancouver is also a sophisticated and hedonistic city, having more in common with the West Coast ethos and outlook of San Francisco than, say, Toronto or Ottawa to the east.

With all its natural advantages, it is no wonder most of Vancouver is booming, the Downtown core growing rapidly in a wave of gleaming new condominiums; the city's eastern fringes, however, remain grittier and, in places, downright impoverished. The boom, and Vancouver's enhanced international profile, received an additional boost after the city hosted the 2010 Winter Olympics, the honour in no small part due to the proximity of **Whistler**, 125km north of Vancouver, a modern centre for winter sports, hiking, golf and, above all, mountain biking (the resort now has as many summer as winter visitors). Beyond Whistler stretch the endless forests and ranch country of the Fraser Valley and **Cariboo** region, a largely untamed wilderness whose remote towns sprang up in the fever of the 1860s Gold Rush.

The **Sea to Sky Highway** (Hwy-99) to Whistler is one of two tempting obvious road excursions from Vancouver. The other is the 150km **Sunshine Coast** (Hwy-101), distinguished by stretches of fine coastal scenery, but experienced by most travellers only as far as Horseshoe Bay, one of several points of embarkation for ferries to Vancouver Island.

The proximity of **Vancouver Island** to Vancouver makes it one of Canada's premier tourist destinations. The largest of North America's west-coast islands, it stretches almost 500km from north to south, but has a population of around 775,000, mostly concentrated around **Victoria**, whose small-town feel belies its role as BC's second metropolis and provincial capital. Today, the city is considerably smaller than Vancouver, a comfortable and easy-going place of small-town values, a pretty waterfront, excellent restaurants, one superb museum and, despite being home to BC's oldest Chinatown, a decidedly English ambience.

Most visitors to the island start in Victoria, easily reached by ferry or seaplane from Vancouver or nearby ferry terminals. Few break their journey en route, missing out on the **Gulf Islands**, an archipelago scattered across the Strait of Georgia between the mainland and Vancouver Island. If you have time, the islands' laidback vibe, numerous small galleries and attractive beaches make them great places in which to catch your breath for a few days.

Vancouver Island's main attraction is the outdoors and **whale-watching**, an activity which can be pursued from Victoria, **Tofino**, **Ucluelet**, **Telegraph Cove** and several other places on the island. The scenery is a mosaic of landscapes, principally defined by a central spine of snowcapped mountains that divide it between the rugged and sparsely

MUSUM OF ANTHROPOLOGY, UNIVERSITY OF BRITISH COLUMBIA

Highlights

❶ **Stanley Park** North America's largest urban park is an oasis of ancient forest, beaches, gardens and peaceful trails. See page 694

❷ **Granville Island** A superb market and specialist art and craft stores are the main attractions of this hugely popular enclave. See page 699

❸ **Museum of Anthropology** Vancouver's finest museum is a beautiful showcase for Canada's best collection of First Nations art and artefacts. See page 701

❹ **Richmond** The Far East meets the Pacific Northwest just 25 minutes from Downtown Vancouver, with North America's largest Buddhist temple and most acclaimed Asian dining scene. See page 703

❺ **Whistler** Come here for superlative outdoor activities in the summer or winter. See page 726

❻ **Whale-watching Victoria** British Columbia's anglophile capital is a great place to spot orcas and minke, as well as grays and humpbacks. See page 739

❼ **Pacific Rim National Park** Beautiful Long Beach makes this park Vancouver Island's scenic highlight. See page 767

❽ **The Inside Passage** Take this day-long ferry ride to enjoy the best of British Columbia's magnificent coastline. See page 786

HIGHLIGHTS ARE MARKED ON THE MAPS ON PAGES 686 AND 688

populated wilderness of the west coast and the more sheltered lowlands of the east. Rippling hills characterize the northern and southern tips, and few areas are free of the lush forest mantle that supports one of BC's most lucrative logging industries.

The beaches at **Parksville** and **Qualicum** lure locals and tourists alike, while the magnificent seascapes of Tofino and the unmissable **Pacific Rim National Park**, and the mountainous vastness of **Strathcona Provincial Park** are the main destinations for most visitors. Both parks offer a panoply of outdoor activities, with hikers being particularly

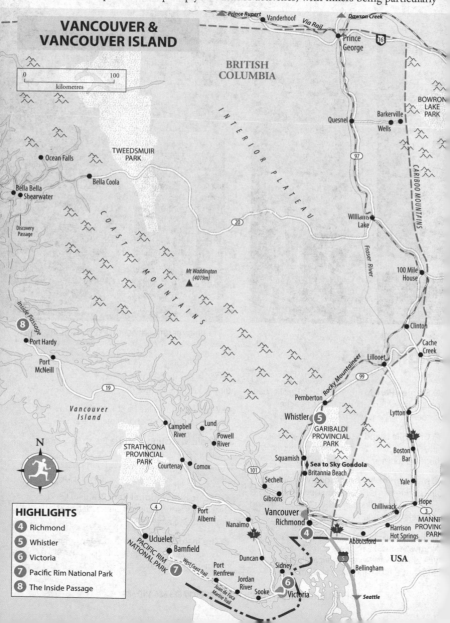

VANCOUVER & VANCOUVER ISLAND

BRITISH COLUMBIA

0   100
kilometres

BOWRON LAKE PARK

TWEEDSMUIR PARK

Ocean Falls

Bella Bella
Shearwater

Bella Coola

Discovery Passage

INTERIOR PLATEAU

Prince Rupert   Vanderhoof   Via Rail   Dawson Creek

Prince George

16

Quesnel   Barkerville
Wells

97

Williams Lake

Fraser River

CARIBOO MOUNTAINS

100 Mile House

Clinton

Cache Creek

C O A S T   M O U N T A I N S

Mt Waddington
(4019m)

20

Inside Passage

Port Hardy

Port McNeill

19

Vancouver Island

Campbell River   Lund
Powell River

STRATHCONA PROVINCIAL PARK

Courtenay   Comox

101

Sechelt

Gibsons

Lillooet

Pemberton

99

Whistler   5

GARIBALDI PROVINCIAL PARK

Rocky Mountaineer

Squamish
Britannia Beach   **Sea to Sky Gondola**

Lytton

Boston Bar

Yale

Hope

Chilliwack

MANNI PROVIN PARK

3

Vancouver
Richmond   4

Harrison Hot Springs

Abbotsford

USA

4

Port Alberni

Nanaimo

Ucluelet
Bamfield

PACIFIC RIM NATIONAL PARK

West Coast Trail

Port Renfrew

Duncan

Sidney

7

Jordan River

Juan de Fuca Marine Trail

Sooke

Victoria   6

5

Bellingham

Seattle

N

HIGHLIGHTS

4 Richmond
5 Whistler
6 Victoria
7 Pacific Rim National Park
8 The Inside Passage

RESERVING PROVINCIAL CAMPGROUNDS

Tent and RV sites at many public **campgrounds** in British Columbia's provincial parks can be reserved through Discover Camping (📞800 689 9025, 📞519 826 6850 from overseas, 🌐discovercamping.ca). Reservations can be made up to four months in advance. A nonrefundable booking fee of $6/night, up to a maximum of three nights, plus tax, is charged. Reservations made by phone have an additional $5 surcharge (avoided by online booking). General information on the parks is at 🌐env.gov.bc.ca/bcparks.

10

well served by the national park's **West Coast Trail**, a demanding and popular long-distance path. Of the visitors who venture farther north, most are either fishermen or whale-watchers, or those intending to catch a ferry from **Port Hardy**, linked by bus to Victoria, at the northern tip, along the **Inside Passage** or **Discovery Passage** to Prince Rupert or Bella Coola, two of western Canada's most memorable journeys.

Vancouver

Cradled between the ocean and mountains, **VANCOUVER** has a dazzling Downtown district that fills a narrow peninsula bounded by Burrard Inlet to the north, English Bay to the west and False Creek to the south. Greater Vancouver sprawls south to the Fraser River. Edged around its idyllic waterfront are fine beaches, a dynamic port and a magnificent swath of parkland, together with glass-fronted skyscrapers that look across Burrard Inlet and its bustling harbour to the residential districts of North and West Vancouver. Beyond these comfortable suburbs, the Coast Mountains rise in steep, forested slopes to form a dramatic counterpoint to the Downtown skyline and the most stunning of the city's many outdoor playgrounds. Small wonder, given Vancouver's surroundings, that Greenpeace was founded here.

Vancouver's 2.5 million or so residents exploit their spectacular natural setting to the hilt, and when they tire of the immediate region can travel a short distance to the vast wilderness of the BC Interior. Whether it's for sailing, swimming, paddling, fishing, hiking, skiing, golf or tennis, locals barely have to move to indulge in a plethora of **recreational whims**. Summer and winter the city oozes hedonism and healthy living, typically West Coast interests that spill over into its sophisticated **arts and culture** scene. Vancouver claims a world-class museum and symphony orchestra, as well as opera, theatre and dance companies at the cutting edge of contemporary arts. Festivals proliferate throughout its mild, if occasionally rain-soaked, summer while numerous music venues provide a hotbed of up-and-coming rock bands and a well-established jazz scene.

Vancouver is a new, multicultural city, and much of the area's earlier immigration focused on its **Chinatown**, just one of a number of ethnic enclaves – Italian, Greek, Indian and Japanese in particular – which lend the city its cosmopolitan vibe. Although a wealthy city, Vancouver's Downtown Eastside and parts of Chinatown have a highly visible population of homeless people and addicts – at odds with the glitz of its other residential neighbourhoods. The city is also grappling with a high cost of living that's pushing young people further into **East Vancouver** (an unofficial area generally considered everywhere east of Main Street) and Greater Vancouver.

Vancouver is not a city that requires relentless sightseeing, but it has a thriving **counterculture**, distinguished by varied restaurants, craft breweries, secondhand shops, avant-garde galleries, clubs and bars, and a handful of sights that make worthwhile viewing by any standards. You'll inevitably spend a good deal of time in the **Downtown** area and its Victorian-era equivalent, **Gastown**, a hip stretch of boutique shops and coffee houses. **Chinatown** could easily absorb a morning and contains more than its share of interesting shops and restaurants. The former warehouse district of **Yaletown**,

10

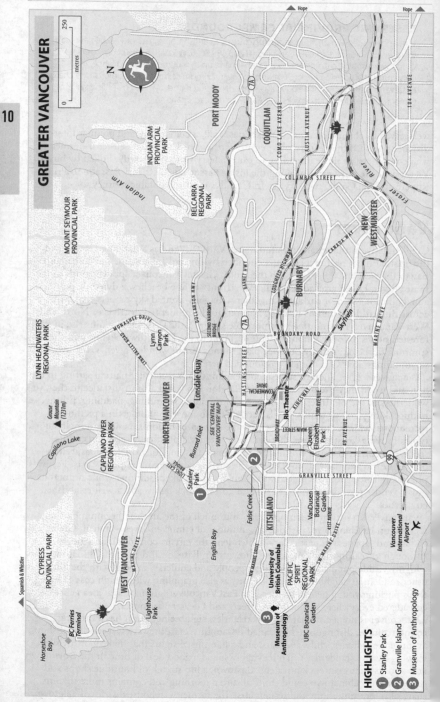

GREATER VANCOUVER

▲ Hope

▲ Hope

N

0 — 250
metres

▲ Squamish & Whistler

CYPRESS PROVINCIAL PARK

LYNN HEADWATERS REGIONAL PARK

Capilano Lake

Grouse Mountain (1231m)

CAPILANO RIVER REGIONAL PARK

MOUNT SEYMOUR PROVINCIAL PARK

Indian Arm

INDIAN ARM PROVINCIAL PARK

BELCARRA REGIONAL PARK

PORT MOODY

COQUITLAM

COMO LAKE AVENUE

AUSTIN AVENUE

104 AVENUE

COLUMBIA STREET

Fraser River

MONASHEE DRIVE

Lynn Canyon Park

LYNN VALLEY ROAD

DOLLARTON HWY

SECOND NARROWS BRIDGE

BARNET HWY

(7A)

COLQUHOUN HIGHWAY

CANADA WAY

NEW WESTMINSTER

BURNABY

WEST VANCOUVER

MARINE DRIVE

Lighthouse Park

Horseshoe Bay

BC Ferries Terminal

LIONS GATE BRIDGE

NORTH VANCOUVER

Lonsdale Quay ●

Burrard Inlet

Stanley Park

SEE CENTRAL VANCOUVER MAP

HASTINGS STREET

COMMERCIAL DRIVE

Rio Theatre

BOUNDARY ROAD

SkyTrain

MARINE DRIVE

❶

KINGSWAY

BROADWAY

MAIN STREET

33RD AVENUE

Queen Elizabeth Park

49 AVENUE

English Bay

False Creek

❷

KITSILANO

GRANVILLE STREET

VanDusen Botanical Garden

41ST AVENUE

99

NW MARINE DRIVE

University of British Columbia

❸

PACIFIC SPIRIT REGIONAL PARK

Museum of Anthropology

UBC Botanical Garden

SW MARINE DRIVE

Vancouver International Airport ✈

HIGHLIGHTS

❶ Stanley Park
❷ Granville Island
❸ Museum of Anthropology

on Downtown's southeast fringes, is also great for exploring: a compact grid full of chic cafés, galleries and contemporary restaurants and bars. For a taste of the city's greener side, hit **Stanley Park**, a huge area of semiwild parkland, forest and beaches that crowns the northern tip of the Downtown peninsula. Take a walk or a bike ride here and follow it up with a stroll to the **beach**. Be certain to spend a morning on **Granville Island**, the city's most tempting spot for wandering, eating and people-watching. If you prefer a cultural slant, hit the spectacular **Museum of Anthropology** or the museums of **Vanier Park**, the latter easily accessible from Granville Island.

At a push, you could cram the city's essentials into a couple of days. If you're here for a longer stay, you'll want to venture farther from Downtown: trips across Burrard Inlet to **Vancouver's North Shore**, worth making for the views from the SeaBus ferry alone, lend a different panoramic perspective of the city, and lead into the mountains and forests that give Vancouver its tremendous setting. The most popular sights here are the **Capilano Suspension Bridge**, tucked beside an old-growth forest, and the cable-car trip up **Grouse Mountain**, which affords staggering views of the city. Just a stone's throw away on the Canada Line, lies **Richmond**, a fascinating blend of Asian-Canadian culture, where the majority of the city's immigrants from mainland China and Hong Kong have settled and you'll find some of Canada's finest Asian cuisine tucked away in nondescript strip malls.

Brief history

Vancouver in the modern sense has existed for 130 years. Over the course of the previous nine millennia, the metropolitan Vancouver region was home to the Coast Salish peoples, who inhabited the Northwest Coastal region prior to European arrival. The Musqueam, Squamish and Tsleil-Waututh Nations lived along the mouth of the Fraser River and coastal inlets. The fish, particularly the salmon, were in abundance and a staple of local diets. Over the millennia these people created more permanent communities along the waterways – their highways – with little need to venture into the mountainous interior. With a special spiritual, cultural and economic connection to the land and water, they were skilled carpenters, canoe-makers, weavers and artists. Their strong culture and traditions carry on today and their work can be seen in galleries, experienced through local nature tours, or explored further with a stay at the city's Aboriginal-owned *Skwachàys Lodge* art boutique hotel (see page 710), or at a restaurant or food truck serving traditional and fusion cuisine.

The eighteenth century

Europeans appeared in notable numbers during the **eighteenth century**, when Spanish explorers charted the waters along what is now southwestern British Columbia. In 1778 **Captain James Cook** reached nearby Nootka Sound while searching for the Northwest Passage, sparking off British interest in the area. In 1791 José María Narváez, a Spanish pilot and surveyor, glimpsed the mouth of what would eventually be christened the Fraser River from his ship, the *Santa Saturnina*. This led to wrangles between the British and Spanish, disputes quickly settled in Britain's favour when Spain became domestically embroiled in the aftermath of the French Revolution. **Captain George Vancouver** officially claimed the land for Britain in 1792, but studying the river from a small boat decided that it seemed too shallow to be of practical use. Instead he rounded a headland to the north, sailing into a deep natural port – the future site of Vancouver – which he named "Burrard" after one of his companions. He then traded briefly with several of the Squamish Nation at X'ay'xi, a village on the inlet's forested headland (the future Stanley Park). Vancouver sailed on, having spent just a day in the region – scant homage to an area that was to be named after him a century later.

The nineteenth century

Vancouver's error over the river was uncovered in 1808, when Scottish-born **Simon Fraser** made an epic 1368km journey down it from the Rockies to the sea. In 1827

10

VANCOUVER'S SEAWALL

One of Vancouver's finest features, the **Seawall** wraps around the city's Downtown core with an uninterrupted 28km pathway which began as a loop around Stanley Park, and was then extended to take in the Convention Centre, False Creek and Kitsilano Beach Park. Taking in unspoiled views of the water and mountains, the scenic pathway is divided into two sections, the one nearest the water is for walkers and runners, and the inside path is for cyclists and inline skaters. If you're cycling, make sure you wear a helmet as the local police issue $29 fines. Interesting little sights dot the anticlockwise promenade around Stanley Park, all signed and explained, the most famous being the *Girl in a Wetsuit* statue, a sporty update of Copenhagen's *Little Mermaid*.

the Hudson's Bay Company set up a fur-trading post at **Fort Langley**, 48km east of the present city, bartering with First Nations hunters and fishermen for furs and salmon, the latter being salted and then packed off to company forts across Canada. Fort Langley was kept free of homesteaders, despite being the area's first major European settlement, their presence deemed detrimental to the fur trade. Major colonization of the area only came after the Fraser River and Cariboo gold rushes in 1858, when **New Westminster** bustled with the arrival of as many as 25,000 hopefuls, many of whom were refugees from the 1849 Californian rush. A number of residents drifted in from the US, underlining the fragility of the national border and the precarious nature of British claims to the region. These claims were consolidated when BC was declared a Crown colony with New Westminster as its capital. Both were superseded by Fort Victoria in 1868, by which time the gold rush had dwindled to almost nothing.

In 1860 three British prospectors, unable to find gold in the interior, bought a strip of land on the southern shore of Burrard Inlet and started a brickworks. This soon gave way to the Hastings Sawmill and a shantytown of bars that by 1867 had taken the name of **Gastown**, which two years later became incorporated as the town of **Granville** and prospered on the back of its timber and small coal deposits. The birth of the present city dates to 1884, when the **Canadian Pacific Railway** decided to make it the terminus of its transcontinental railway. In 1886, on a whim of the CPR president, Granville was renamed Vancouver, only to be destroyed on June 13 that year when fire razed all but half a dozen buildings. The setback proved short-lived, and since the arrival of the first train from Montréal in 1887 the city has never looked back.

Downtown

You soon get the hang of Vancouver's **Downtown** district, an arena of avenues and shopping malls centred on **Robson Street**. On hot summer evenings it's like a latter-day vision of *La Dolce Vita* – a buzzy meeting place crammed with bars, restaurants, late-night stores, and youths sucking down Bubble Tea or eating frozen yoghurt. At other times a more sedate class hangs out on the steps of the Vancouver Art Gallery or glides in and out of the three big department stores, Holt Renfrew, Nordstrom and The Bay. Downtown's other principal thoroughfares are **Burrard Street** – all smart shops, hotels and offices – and **Granville Street**, partly pedestrianized with plenty of shops, bars and music venues, but curiously seedy in places, especially at its southern end near the Granville Street Bridge. New development is taking Downtown's reach farther east, and at some point you should try to see the **public library** at 350 West Georgia St, a striking piece of modern architecture.

Canada Place and FlyOver Canada

Canada Place Walkways open 24hr • Free • ☎ 604 775 7200, ⓦ canadaplace.ca • **FlyOver Canada** Daily 10am–9pm • $33 • ☎ 604 620 8455, ⓦ flyovercanada.com

For the best possible introduction to Vancouver, walk down to its beautiful waterfront where you'll find excellent public art including the pixelated *Digital Orca* from local celeb Douglas Coupland, the Olympic Cauldron from 2010 – at Jack Poole Plaza – which is lit on special occasions, and **Canada Place**, the Canadian pavilion for Expo '86. An architectural tour de force at the time it was built, the Place houses a luxury hotel, cruise-ship terminal and a glitzy convention centre. It makes a superb viewpoint, buzzing with boats, helicopters and floatplanes, with sweeping vistas of the port, and the mountains. Canada Place's design, and the manner in which it juts into the port, is meant to suggest a ship, and you can walk the building's perimeter as if "on deck", stopping to read the boards that describe the immediate cityscape. **FlyOver Canada** is a more recent addition, a popular thirty-minute virtual flight experience that takes you "gliding" over the many natural and man-made marvels of Canada, complete with wind, scents and mists. Curiously exhilarating – and although the ride itself is only 8 minutes long, the rest of the time is a pre-show and boarding – it's certainly worth the entry fee.

Marine Building

355 Burrard St • Lobby Mon–Fri 8am–6pm • Free • ☎ 604 683 8604

If you're visiting Canada Place, take a moment to pop into the lobby of the nearby 22-storey **Marine Building**, an Art Deco marvel. Built in 1930, this landmark's terracotta facade is imprinted with ships, seahorses and bubble-blowing fish. Step through the massive doors, decorated with metallic turtles and scallops, for a glimpse of the interior's stained glass window and brass elevator, the latter swirled with a seaweed design. Note the marble floor, inlaid with signs of the zodiac, and the kooky hall clock, whose hands point to marine creatures instead of numbers.

Vancouver Lookout

555 West Hastings St • Daily: mid-May to Sept 8.30am–10.30pm; Oct–early May 9am–9pm • $17.50 • ☎ 604 689 0421, Ⓦ vancouverlookout.com

An alternative to Canada Place's vantage point (see above), the **Harbour Centre** is one of the city's tallest structures. On a fine day it's worth paying to ride the stomach-churning glass elevators that run up the side of the tower – 168.6m in 40 seconds – to the fortieth-floor observation deck, which has a staggering 360-degree view. Admission is valid all day so you can return and look out over the bright lights of Vancouver at night.

Bill Reid Gallery

639 Hornby St •Mid-May to early Sept daily 10am–5pm, early Sept to mid-May Wed–Sun 11am–5pm • $13 • ☎ 604 682 3455, Ⓦ billreidgallery.ca

If you can't visit the First Nations collection at the Museum of Anthropology, make a stop at the **Bill Reid Gallery**, which celebrates the life's work of one of Canada's foremost artists (you'll see his work on the $20 bill). Born to a Haida mother and a Scottish-German father, Reid (1920–98) shaped cedar logs, onyx and precious metals into majestic formations of West Coast animals such as wolves, bears and orcas. The small space displays sculptures, lithographs and jewellery; the latter, much of it based on traditional tattoos, is the most compelling. Temporary exhibits feature other First Nations artists and craftspeople.

The Vancouver Art Gallery

750 Hornby St • Daily 10am–5pm, Tues till 9pm • $24 • ☎ 604 662 4700, Ⓦ vanartgallery.bc.ca

For now, the **Vancouver Art Gallery** is centrally located in the handsome old city courthouse, but it's slated to move a few blocks to a stunning $350 million purpose built home on the corner of West Georgia and Cambie Streets. The permanent collection has over eight thousand works, but until the new gallery space is built, the only part you can be sure of seeing is the Emily Carr portion on the top floor. The other three floors are given over to (admittedly often excellent) touring shows and a rotating display of parts of the permanent collection. This features an international

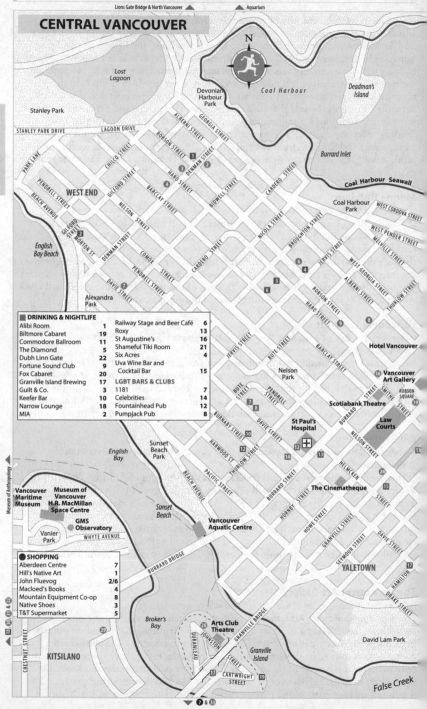

CENTRAL VANCOUVER

10

■ **DRINKING & NIGHTLIFE**

Alibi Room	1
Biltmore Cabaret	19
Commodore Ballroom	11
The Diamond	5
Dubh Linn Gate	22
Fortune Sound Club	9
Fox Cabaret	20
Granville Island Brewing	17
Guilt & Co.	3
Keefer Bar	10
Narrow Lounge	18
MIA	2

Railway Stage and Beer Café	6
Roxy	13
St Augustine's	16
Shameful Tiki Room	21
Six Acres	4
Uva Wine Bar and Cocktail Bar	15

LGBT BARS & CLUBS

1181	7
Celebrities	14
Fountainhead Pub	12
Pumpjack Pub	8

● **SHOPPING**

Aberdeen Centre	7
Hill's Native Art	1
John Fluevog	2/6
Macleod's Books	4
Mountain Equipment Co-op	3
Native Shoes	8
T&T Supermarket	5

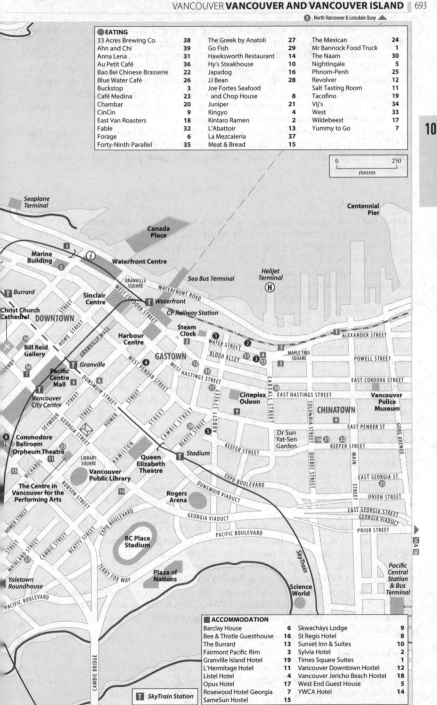

● EATING

33 Acres Brewing Co.	38	The Greek by Anatoli	27	The Mexican	24
Ahn and Chi	39	Go Fish	29	Mr Bannock Food Truck	1
Anna Lena	31	Hawksworth Restaurant	14	The Naam	30
Au Petit Café	36	Hy's Steakhouse	10	Nightingale	5
Bao Bei Chinese Brasserie	22	Japadog	16	Phnom-Penh	25
Blue Water Café	26	JJ Bean	28	Revolver	12
Buckstop	3	Joe Fortes Seafood		Salt Tasting Room	11
Café Medina	23	and Chop House	8	Tacofino	19
Chambar	20	Juniper	21	Vij's	34
CinCin	9	Kingyo	4	West	33
East Van Roasters	18	Kintaro Ramen	2	Wildebeest	17
Fable	32	L'Abattoir	13	Yummy to Go	7
Forage	6	La Mezcaleria	37		
Forty-Ninth Parallel	35	Meat & Bread	15		

■ ACCOMMODATION

Barclay House	6	Skwachàys Lodge	9
Bee & Thistle Guesthouse	16	St Regis Hotel	8
The Burrard	13	Sunset Inn & Suites	10
Fairmont Pacific Rim	3	Sylvia Hotel	2
Granville Island Hotel	19	Times Square Suites	1
L'Hermitage Hotel	11	Vancouver Downtown Hostel	12
Listel Hotel	17	Vancouver Jericho Beach Hostel	18
Opus Hotel	17	West End Guest House	5
Rosewood Hotel Georgia	7	YWCA Hotel	14
SameSun Hostel	15		

⊤ SkyTrain Station

assortment, with works by Warhol and Lichtenstein, and Italian, Flemish and British paintings spanning the sixteenth to twentieth centuries. In recent years the gallery has made a determined effort to concentrate on contemporary works – videos, sculptures, installations and, in particular, photo-based and photoconceptual art – especially from the Vancouver School. In the last area the gallery boasts the largest such collection in North America, including wonderful pieces by Cindy Sherman (famed for her "self" portraits), Vancouver artist Jeff Wall, Henri Cartier-Bresson, Ansel Adams and monumental photographs by Andreas Gursky.

A must-see are the powerful works of **Emily Carr**, who was born on Vancouver Island in 1871 and whose paintings – characterized by deep greens and blues – evoke the scale and intensity of the West Coast landscape. The **gallery café**, with its suntrap of a terrace, is also excellent.

Stanley Park

One of the world's great urban spaces, **Stanley Park** is Vancouver's green heart, helping lend the city its particular character. At nearly four square kilometres, it's one of the largest urban parks in North America – a semiwilderness of dense rainforest, marshland and three **beaches**: English Bay which has a waterslide during summer season, Second Beach with its pool and concession stands, and the quieter Third Beach which allows barbecues. Ocean surrounds the park on three sides, with a road and parallel cycleway/pedestrian promenade following the **Seawall** (see page 690) all the way round. A brisk walk of this coastal path takes two to three hours and you get exceptional views of the city and across the water to the mountains.

Away from the coastal trail network and main draw – the aquarium – the interior is lush scrub and forest, with leafy paths and few people. There are also plenty of open, wooded or flower-decorated spaces to picnic, snooze or watch the world go by. There's a café-restaurant at **Prospect Point**, a busy spot on the park's northern tip, popular for its outdoor deck and sweeping views. Southwest of here lies **Siwash Rock**, also known by its indigenous name Slhxi7lsh, an outcrop which has defied the weather for centuries, attracting numerous First Nations legends in the process, and which is distinguished by its solitary tree.

The peninsula was partially logged in the 1860s, but in 1886 the newly formed city council showed an admirable sense of priorities and moved to make what had become a military reserve into a permanent park. Thus its remaining first-growth forest of cedar, hemlock and Douglas fir, and the swamp now known as Lost Lagoon, were saved for posterity in the name of Lord Stanley, Canada's governor general from 1888 to 1893.

The Lost Lagoon

Exploring the park, especially on a busy Sunday, gives a good taste of what it means to live in Vancouver. The first thing you see is **The Lost Lagoon**, a tranquil lake that started life as a tidal inlet, and got its name because its water all but disappeared at low tide. Dozens of feathered species inhabit its shoreline from great blue herons to urban bald eagles. You can find out more at the **Stanley Park Ecology Society** (ⓦstanleyparkecology.ca) who have a small nature house on Lost Lagoon. To the northwest is the **Cathedral Trail**, which takes you through beautiful West Coast forest, and just east are the pretty Rose Garden and Vancouver Rowing Club, before which stands a statue of Scottish poet Rabbie Burns.

Brockton Point

If you're following the Seawall or taking a more modest loop of the most easterly point of Stanley Park, you'll pass Brockton Point Visitor Centre, where three carved red-cedar portals welcome visitors to the traditional land of the Coast Salish people, and you'll see the park's **totem poles**. The first poles were at Lumberman's Arch, and originally came from Vancouver Island's Alert Bay in the 1920s, and then more were added in 1936 from Haida Gwaii and BC's central coast Rivers inlet. In the mid-1960s they were moved to Brockton Point, and then sent to various museums for preservation. Some of the remaining poles are loaned replacements, others specially commissioned; the last, carved by Robert Yelton of the Squamish Nation, was added in 2009.

Vancouver Aquarium

845 Avison Way • Daily 10am–5pm; seasonal hours and statutory holidays 9.30am–6pm • $38, ages 4–12 $21 • ☏ 604 659 3400, Ⓦ vanaqua.org

Ranked among North America's best attractions of its kind, the **Vancouver Aquarium** is the park's most popular destination. Home to over 50,000 animals including penguins, sea otters and beluga whales, and with state-of-the-art exhibits, a recent renovation has added a new entranceway, indoor and outdoor cafés, and a two-level exhibition space that houses large temporary exhibitions.

The **Arctic** section concerns the fragile world of the Canadian North, offering a chance to see belugas face-to-face through glass and peer in at cod, char, sea cucumbers and hot-pink sea anemones, all indigenous to this icy domain. The steamy **Amazon** gallery displays the vegetation, fishes, marmosets, sloths and other creatures of the rainforest in a climate-controlled environment, which includes an open enclosure with flying macaws; while the **Wild Coast** habitat performs a similar role for otters, harbour porpoises and other animals of the waters of BC.

Annually, the aquarium sees more than a million visitors, and at times it seems like they're all stopping by at once. To avoid cramming in like a sardine, aim to visit on a weekday or during morning hours.

ARRIVAL AND DEPARTURE STANLEY PARK

By bus Catch a Stanley Park bus #19 ($2.75; ☏ 604 953 3333, Ⓦ translink.ca) from the corner of Burrard and Pender streets Downtown, which drops you just inside the park a 5min walk from the Aquarium. Other buses that will take you close to the park are the #C21 (Beach) to Davie St and Beach Ave, and the #5 (Robson) to Denman St.

On foot From Downtown, the most scenic approach to the park is along the Seawall from Coal Harbour, which begins at Canada Place and parallels West Cordova St. Alternatively, Beach Ave to the south and West Georgia St lead to either end of the Seawall.

INFORMATION AND ACTIVITIES

Information There are two information points in the park. The first is a booth just inside the Georgia Street entrance, which offers information on services in the park, snacks, brochures and toilet facilities. The Brockton Visitor Centre situated by the totem poles, has panels explaining the history and culture of the Coast Salish people as well as a gift shop, toilets and snack bar.

Bike rental The corner of Denman and W Georgia streets has a cluster of bike rental outlets; from Denman it's just a minute's pedalling to the park.

Swimming Though people do swim in the sea at beaches around the park's western fringes, many bathers prefer the swimming pool next to Second Beach, which is just west of Lost Lagoon.

Guided walks Nature walks are occasionally offered around the park; ask for details at the park's visitor centre, or explore the park on a 1hr 30min walk that focuses on First Nations culture, history, foraged foods and of course the forest, with Talking Trees Walk ($40; ☏ 800 605 4643, ☏ 604 628 8555, Ⓦ talaysay.com).

Gastown

An easy walk east of Downtown – five minutes from Canada Place and concentrated on Water Street – **Gastown** is a piece of city rejuvenation distinguished by cobblestone streets, twentieth-century brick buildings, stylish shops, and the city's hippest cafés, restaurants and bars. The name derives from "Gassy" (as in loquacious) Jack Leighton, a retired sailor turned publican and self-proclaimed "mayor", who arrived on site by canoe in 1867, quickly opening a bar to service the nearby lumber mills. Leighton's statue stands in **Maple Tree Square**, Gastown's heart, focus of its main streets and reputed site of this first tavern. Trade was brisk, and a second bar opened, soon followed by a village of sorts – "Gassy's Town" – which, though destroyed by fire in 1886, formed in effect the birthplace of modern Vancouver. Over the years, the Downtown focus moved west and something of Gastown's boozy beginnings returned to haunt it, as its cheap hotels and warehouses turned into a skid row for junkies and alcoholics. By the 1970s the area was declared a historic site – the buildings are the city's oldest – and an enthusiastic beautification programme was set in motion.

10

It's a Gastown rite of passage to snap photos with the **Steam Clock**, on the corner of Cambie and Water streets. Easily identified by the fog emanating from its frame, the two-tonne landmark sounds out the Westminster "chime" every fifteen minutes and was the first of its kind when built in 1977.

Vancouver Police Museum

240 East Cordova St • Tues–Sat 9am–5pm • $12, children $8 • ☎ 604 665 3346, ⓦ vancouverpolicemuseum.ca

One sight worth hunting out in the area between Gastown and Chinatown is Vancouver's **Police Museum**, an eclectic little museum housed in the city's old Coroner's Court Building.

Built in 1932, the building has its own place in Vancouver folklore, not least for the fact that it was here that the actor **Errol Flynn** was brought after he died in Vancouver in 1959. Flynn arrived in the city in October of that year and within two days had dropped dead in his rented West End apartment. The body was brought to the Coroner's Court, where the pathologist conducting the autopsy is said to have removed venereal warts from Flynn's penis and placed them in formaldehyde as a souvenir. After spotting this alteration, the horrified chief coroner reattached the missing pieces to the corpse with sticky tape. The body was then dispatched to Los Angeles for burial.

The **autopsy room** is still here, together with a suitably macabre selection of mangled and preserved body parts; check out the **morgue**, penultimate resting place of many over the years. Other rooms include a **forensics lab** and an imitation cell where you can dress up and take photos, in addition to displays on notorious local criminals, crime-scene reconstructions and a sizeable collection of firearms.

Chinatown

Vancouver's vibrant **Chinatown** – clustered mainly on Pender Street between Carrall and Gore streets and on Keefer Street from Main to Gore – is a city apart and expanding all the time. Vancouver's Chinatown is considered to be one of North America's largest and Chinese-Canadians are the city's oldest and largest ethnic group after the British-descended majority with a population of around 600,000. Many crossed the Pacific in 1858 to join the Fraser Valley gold rush; others followed under contract to help build the Canadian Pacific Railway. Most stayed, only to find themselves being treated appallingly. Denied citizenship and legal rights until as late as 1947, the Chinese community sought safety and familiarity in a ghetto of their own, where clan associations provided for new arrivals and the local poor, and helped build the distinctive buildings of recessed balconies and ornamental roofs that have made the area a protected historic site.

Vancouver's Chinatown is authentic and lively: shops, markets, tiny restaurants and dim alleys vie for attention amid a hustle of jammed pavements and the buzz of conversation. Virtually every building replicates an Eastern model, and written Chinese characters feature everywhere. Most people flock dutifully to the 1913 **Sam Kee Building**, at the corner of Carrall and Pender streets; at just 1.8m wide, it's registered with the *Guinness Book of Records* as the world's narrowest commercial building. Striking and unexpected after Downtown's high-rise glitz, the district brings you face to face with Vancouver's oft-touted multiculturalism, and helps explain why immigrants

10

SHOPPING IN CHINATOWN

Apart from the obvious culinary temptations (see page 713), Chinatown's main points of reference are its **shops**. Some of the best boast butchers with delicious roasted duck, barbecue pork with crispy skin and fragrant Chinese sausages. Keefer Street is bakery row and it's worth dropping in to one of the local herbalists to browse their panaceas and learn more of their passed-down ancient wisdom. **Ming Wo**, established in 1917 (23 East Pender St; ☎ 604 683 7268, ⓦ mingwo.com), is a fantastic cookware shop that probably carries every utensil ever devised and **Bamboo Village**, in its current location since 2000 (135 East Pender St; ☎ 604 662 3300, ⓦ bamboovillage.weebly.com), is a wonderfully kitsch collection of lanterns, cards, Chinese Folk Art and even antique furniture.

---

from China and Hong Kong continue to be attracted to the city. Yet it's a district with a distinct edge, and visitors should avoid the area's dingier streets at night, such as East Hastings near Main. Although Vancouver's historic Chinatown remains an excellent place to visit, newer Chinese immigrants now tend to settle in the nearby Greater Vancouver region, especially in the cities of Richmond and Burnaby.

Dr Sun Yat-Sen Classical Chinese Garden

578 Carrall St • Daily: May to mid–June & Sept 10am–6pm; late June to Aug 9.30am–7pm; Oct–April 10am–4.30pm; closed Mon Nov 1– April 30 • $14 • ⓦ 604 662 3207, ⓦ vancouverchinesegarden.com

Chinatown's chief cultural attraction is the **Dr Sun Yat-Sen Garden**, the first full-scale classical Chinese garden built outside of China. Constructed in 1985 using Ming Dynasty-era craftmanship, its courtyards, corridors and pavilions were pieced together without the use of nails or power tools. Emulating a Ming Dynasty (1368–1644) scholar's home, the garden achieves a subtle balance of *yin* and *yang*: small and large, soft and hard, flowing and immovable, light and dark. Every stone, pine and flower was carefully placed and has symbolic meaning, such as the zigzagging hallways, said to keep out evil spirits. Admission includes tea and a guided tour that explains the Taoist philosophy behind the carefully placed elements.

Science World at TELUS World of Science

1455 Quebec St • Mon–Fri 10am–5pm, weekends & school hols 10am–6pm (closed Mon Sept 8–Dec 18) • $25, ages 3–12 $17 • ☎ 604 443 7440, ⓦ scienceworld.ca

Although much of the 1986 **Expo site** around Canada Place, and at other points to the south and east, has been levelled or redeveloped, you can see one of the surviving structures just south of Chinatown. The geodesic dome is a striking city landmark and now home to **Science World**. Children reach a state of euphoria exploring its two floors of hands-on exhibits, which include a hippo-lifting machine and a set of instruments that Dr Seuss would appreciate: the "infrared harp", played without strings, and a "whapophone", whose tubes make a tune when thumped with a paddle. In the **Search: Sara Stern Gallery**, devoted to natural science, you can pat a raccoon or zebra pelt, or – if you're very brave – cradle a corn snake or Madagascar hissing cockroach. It's also home to the world's largest OMNIMAX theatre (a $6 upgrade to the main ticket price), a whopping five storeys high and 27m in diameter.

VanDusen Botanical Garden

5251 Oak St, 7km south of Downtown (off West 33rd Ave) • Daily: Jan, Feb, Nov & Dec 10am–3pm, March & Oct 10am–5pm, April & Sept 9am–6pm, May 9am–7pm, June–Aug 9am–8pm • $11.25 (April–Sept), $8 (Oct–March) • ☎ 604 257 8463, ⓦ vandusengarden.org

In addition to UBC's botanical garden (see page 702), Vancouver is home to a number of idyllic green spaces, the most noteworthy of which is the **VanDusen Botanical Garden**. This manicured retreat has over 7000 plants, a hedge labyrinth, rose garden, and intoxicating swaths of peonies, lilies and magnolias. Stop for tea at *Truffles Kitchen* in the architecturally impressive visitor centre building, and check listings as the VanDusen often hosts wine and musical evenings among the blooms.

Queen Elizabeth Park

4600 Cambie St **Park** Dawn to dusk • Free • ☎ 604 873 7000, Ⓦ vancouverparks.ca **Bloedel Conservatory** Daily: Jan–March, Nov & Dec 10am–5pm; April, Sept & Oct 10am–6pm, May–Aug 10am–8pm • $6.50, ages 4–12 $3.15 • ☎ 604 257 8584, Ⓦ vancouverparks.ca

Just 1km from the VanDusen Botanical Garden (as the crow flies), is the city's highest point, **Queen Elizabeth Park**, which is set on a long-extinct volcano and sports tremendous mountain views, framed in spring by blooming rhododendrons. Here, you'll also find fountains, gardened pathways and, at the top of the park, the **Bloedel Conservatory**, a 43m glass dome whose every centimetre is taken up by tropical palms and flowers, and teems with electric-coloured macaws.

Yaletown

A small, hip, captivating grid of shops, cafés and restaurants, **Yaletown** is centred on Homer, Hamilton and Mainland streets between Drake Street to the south and Smithe Street to the north. It takes its name from the many Canadian Pacific Railway workers who settled here in the 1880s, having followed the line west from the town of Yale 180km away in the BC Interior.

For most of the twentieth century it was a warehouse and packing district, but over the last decade or so has been transformed, helped by the spread of a booming Downtown south and east, and the ranks of condominiums that have sprouted on the north shore of False Creek. At street level, the broad, raised walkways provide the perfect stage for café terraces, while the narrow, lofty or otherwise unusual old warehouse spaces have become often dramatically designed bars and restaurants.

You can get here on the SkyTrain using the Yaletown-Roundhouse station, but it's an easy walk from central Downtown and you can take a pleasant walk along the **Seawall** to get there from Stanley Park.

Granville Island

Huddled under the Granville Street Bridge south of Downtown, **Granville Island** is an agreeable "people's place" – the title it likes for itself – and mostly lives up to its claim of being the heart of Vancouver. Friendly, easygoing and popular, its shops, markets, galleries, marina and open spaces are juxtaposed with a light-industrial setting whose warehouse past saves the area from any sense of pretentiousness.

The island, once a sandbar, was transformed in 1917 into an active ironworks and shipbuilding centre. By the 1960s the yards were derelict and the place had become a rat-infested depository. In 1972 the federal government agreed to bankroll a programme of residential, commercial and industrial redevelopment that retained the old false-fronted buildings, tin-shack homes, seawall and rail sidings. The best part of the job had been finished by 1979 – and was immediately successful – but work continues unobtrusively today, the various building projects only adding to the area's sense of change and dynamism. Most people come here during the day, but there are some good restaurants, bars and the Arts Club Theatre (see page 717), which keep the place buzzing at night.

Granville Island Public Market

Daily 9am–7pm • Ⓦ granvilleisland.com, ☎ 604 666 6477

Dominant among the maze of shops, galleries and businesses, the **Granville Island Public Market** is the undisputed highlight of the area. On summer weekends it's where

10

people go to see and be seen and it throngs with arts-and-crafts types. The quality and variety of **food** is staggering, with dozens of kiosks and cafés selling ready-made titbits and potential picnic ingredients. Parks, patios and walkways nearby provide lively areas to eat and take everything in. Other spots to look out for include Canada's first locally produced sake maker (1339 Railspur Alley; ☎604 685 7253, ☜artisansakemaker.com), who offers daily tastings from 11.30am to 6pm, Vancouver's first brewery, Granville Island Brewing (see page 716), and the Kids Market (a shopping mall for children and parents; it also has a water park).

ARRIVAL AND DEPARTURE
GRANVILLE ISLAND

By bus The most direct approach to Granville Island is to take bus #50 (☎604 953 3333, ☜translink.ca) from Gastown or Granville St.

On foot The walk down Granville St and across the bridge is deceptively long, and not terribly salubrious; it's faster to head for Burrard Street to cross Burrard Bridge towards Creekside Drive/Mariner Wharf instead. You can also walk from the island along the seawall back to the city (east) or to Vanier Park and Kitsilano Beach (west).

By ferry More fun, private ferries (from $3.75, day-pass $16 pay on board) ply the route almost continuously between the island and little quays at the foot of Hornby St or the Aquatic Centre at the foot of Thurlow St. They also connect from Granville Island to Science World and, more significantly, to Vanier Park.

Vanier Park museums

A little to the west of Granville Island, **Vanier Park** conveniently collects most of the city's main museums: the **Vancouver Museum**, the **H.R. MacMillan Space Centre** and the **Maritime Museum**. Vanier Park sits on the waterfront at the west end of the Burrard Bridge, near Kitsilano Beach and the residential shopping and dining centres of Kitsilano and West 4th Avenue; it's a fine spot to while away a summer afternoon. You could easily incorporate a visit to the museums with a trip to Granville Island using the **ferry** (see above). The park itself is pleasant, with a few nice patches of sandy beach on its fringes.

Museum of Vancouver

1100 Chestnut St • Mon–Wed 10am–5pm, Thurs 10am–8pm, Fri & Sat 10am–9pm, Sun 10am–5pm • $14 • ☜ museumofvancouver.ca

The **Museum of Vancouver** traces the history of the city and the lower British Columbian mainland, invoking the area's past in its very form: its shape is a nod to the conical cedar-bark woven hats of Coast Salish people. The fountain outside, which boasts a sharp-pincered giant crab statue, recalls the animal of First Nations legend that guarded the city's port. Keeping with the First Nations theme, the Musqueam gallery, "the city before the city", displays some 5000 years' worth of history that boldly seeks to ask the question: "whose home is Vancouver" and create a space for Musqueam to tell their stories, share their history and showcase the role they played in developing the modern City of Vancouver.

The museum's small, well-tailored galleries display ephemera from modern Vancouver's 1900s inception through to the 1970s. In the 1950s section, take a seat under an antique hairdryer to hear goings-on at the local salon. Take time to check out the excellent Neon Gallery, which records a time when Vancouver boasted some 19,000 neon signs, many of which have been rescued and lovingly restored, and see the temporary exhibitions that include "Haida Now" with work by Haida artists on view until April 2020.

H.R. MacMillan Space Centre

1100 Chestnut St • **Space Centre** Mon–Fri 10am–3pm, Sat 10am–5pm, Sun noon–5pm • $19.50, ages 5–11 $14; evening astronomy shows $14, kids $8.50 • **GMS Observatory** Sat 7.30–11.30pm • Admission by donation • ☎ 604 738 7827, ☜ spacecentre.ca

In the same building as the Museum of Vancouver, the **H.R. MacMillan Space Centre** incorporates the MacMillan Planetarium and a range of cosmos-related displays and shows. Its main draws are its forty-minute star shows – the standard planetarium fare, held several times daily – as well as live science demonstrations.

Many of the centre's exhibits are high-tech and hands-on, especially in the Cosmic Courtyard, where interactive displays allow you to battle an alien, design a spaceship, guide a lunar robot or plan a voyage to Mars. A number of displays also involve lots of impressive computer and other audiovisual effects. For star-gazing through a real telescope, head next door to the **GMS Observatory**.

Vancouver Maritime Museum

1905 Ogden Ave • Daily 10am–5pm, Thurs till 8pm • $13.50, children $10; Thurs night admission by donation 5–8pm • ⓦ vancouvermaritimemuseum.com

The **Vancouver Maritime Museum** features lovely early photographs evoking early twentieth-century Vancouver as well as nautical instruments, model ships, a 1915 lighthouse lens and original hand drawn charts from Captain Cook's exploration of the Pacific. That said, the presentation as a whole doesn't quite do justice to the status of the city as one of the world's leading ports. An exception is the renovated *St Roch*, a two-masted schooner once used by the RCMP in Canada's Arctic. The first vessel to navigate the famed Northwest Passage in a single season, and the first to make the trip from west to east, it now sits impressively in its own wing of the museum, where it can be boarded by guided tour. Outside, just below the museum on **Heritage Harbour**, the quay for ferries to and from Granville Island, you can admire (for free) more restored vessels, including the NASA undersea research vessel *Ben Franklin* and RCMP Nadon (aka *St Roch II*).

ARRIVAL AND INFORMATION

VANIER PARK MUSEUMS

By bus Coming from Downtown, take the #22 Macdonald bus south from anywhere on Burrard or West Pender streets – get off at the first stop after the bridge and walk down Chestnut Street to the park.
By ferry The ferry from Downtown via Granville Island

docks just below the Maritime Museum.
Vanier Park Explore Pass Valid for one visit to all three Vanier Park museums. Purchase at any of the Vanier Park attractions ($42.50).

Kitsilano

The leafy district (west from Burrard to Alma streets, and from the waterfront to about 16th Avenue) beyond Vanier Park is **Kitsilano**, or Kits. This former hippie and alternative-lifestyle neighbourhood, centred on West 4th Avenue, is now a des-res enclave of yoga pants-wearing, coconut water-drinking gentrification, but with shades of its past in its laidback cafés, independent shops, excellent restaurants and the easy-going charm of **Kitsilano Beach** and its wonderful, heated, saltwater outdoor **waterfront swimming pool** (2305 Cornwall Ave; end May to end Sept hours fluctuate, call for up-to-date information; $6.10; ☏604 731 0011, ⓦvancouver.ca). Both beach and streets are nice places to idle away a summer afternoon and evening, while the **shoreline path** is a lovely place for a stroll.

ARRIVAL AND DEPARTURE

KITSILANO

On foot Walk here from Vanier Park and the museums on the coast path (30min).
By bus From Downtown, take bus #2 southbound on Burrard Street.

The Museum of Anthropology and UBC campus

6393 NW Marine Drive • Daily 10am–5pm, Thurs till 9pm; mid-Oct to mid-May closed Mon • $18 • ☏604 822 5087, ⓦmoa.ubc.ca • #14 bus south (marked UBC) from Granville St to end of the line; turn right from the bus stop, walk along the tree-lined East Mall to the very bottom (10min), then turn left on NW Marine Drive; the museum is on the right after 5min • Paid parking at 6393 NW Marine Drive

Located twenty minutes from Downtown on the University of British Columbia campus, the **Museum of Anthropology** is Vancouver's most important museum. Emphasizing

10

the art and culture of the region's First Nations peoples, and the Haida in particular, its collection of carvings, totem poles and artefacts is unequalled in North America.

The museum's layout is a spacious collection of halls designed by Arthur Erickson, the eminent architect also responsible for converting the Vancouver Art Gallery. Particularly outstanding is the **Great Hall**, inspired by Aboriginal cedar houses, which makes as perfect an indoor setting for its thirty-odd **totem poles** as you could ask for. Huge windows look out to more poles and Haida houses, which you're free to wander around, backed by views of Burrard Inlet and the distant mountains. Most of the poles and monolithic carvings, indoors and out, are from the coastal tribes of the Haida, Salish, Tsimshian and Kwakiutl, all of which share cultural elements. One of the museum's great virtues is that few of its displays are hidden away in basements or back rooms, but are beautifully presented in the Great Hall and Multiversity Galleries close by: there's also a pleasant café.

Most of the permanent collection revolves around **Canadian Pacific** cultures, but the **Inuit** and **Far North** exhibits are also outstanding, as are the jewellery, masks and baskets of Northwest tribes, all markedly delicate after the blunt-nosed carvings of the Great Hall. Look out especially for the argillite sculptures, made from a jet-black slate found only on BC's Haida Gwaii islands.

Housed in a separate rotunda, **The Raven and the First Men**, a modern sculpture designed by Haida artist Bill Reid (see page 691), is the museum's pride and joy and has achieved almost iconic status in the city. Carved from a 4.5-tonne block of cedar by five people over three years, it describes the Haida legend of human evolution with admirable virtuosity, depicting terrified figures squirming from a half-open clam shell, overseen by an enormous and stern-faced raven.

Nitobe Memorial Garden

1895 Lower Mall • April–Oct daily 10am–4.30pm; call for winter hours • $7; joint ticket with Botanical Garden $13 • ☎ 604 822 6038, ⓦ botanicalgarden.ubc.ca/nitobe

A five-minute walk from the Museum of Anthropology leads to the **Nitobe Memorial Garden**, a compact Japanese garden good for a few minutes of peace and quiet. It's considered to be one of the world's most authentic Japanese gardens outside of Japan, and is full of gently curving paths, trickling streams and waterfalls, as well as numerous rocks, trees and shrubs placed with Zen precision. Cherry blossom season (April–May), is a particularly good time to visit.

UBC Botanical Garden

6804 SW Marine Drive • Daily 9.30am–5pm • $9; joint ticket with Greenheart Canopy Walkway $20; joint ticket with Nitobe $13 • ☎ 604 822 4208, ⓦ botanicalgarden.ubc.ca

The university's vast **Botanical Garden**, 2km southwest of the Beaty Biodiversity Museum, was established in 1916, making it Canada's oldest such garden. Even non-botanists will be intrigued by the poisonous plants of the Physic Garden, a re-created sixteenth-century monastic herb bed – though most plants here are actually medicinal rather than lethal. The Asian garden is another highlight, containing one of Canada's largest collections of rhododendrons, including many rare and endangered species. For an additional fee, you can also wander through the tree tops, thanks to the 308m **Greenheart TreeWalk** that winds its way between cedars, hemlocks and firs.

Beaty Biodiversity Museum

2212 Main Mall • Daily 10am–5pm; mid-Oct to mid-May closed Mon • $14, ages 5–12 $10 • ☎ 604 827 4955, ⓦ beatymuseum.ubc.ca

The **Beaty Biodiversity Museum** displays the university's vast natural history holdings, which comprise over two million specimens ranging from fossils, shells and fungi to amphibians and mammals. In the lobby, you'll find its *pièce de résistance*, a 25m blue whale skeleton. The museum posits that the living whale had a heart the size of a car and weighed 150 tonnes, as much as 33 elephants.

> **GULF OF GEORGIA CANNERY**
>
> Located 20km south of Downtown, the **Gulf of Georgia Cannery** (12138 4th Ave, Richmond; daily 10am–5pm; $11.70, children free; ☎ 604 664 9009, ⓦ gulfofgeorgiacannery. com) is a historic site that preserves what was once Canada's largest manufacturer of tinned salmon. In the early 1900s. Thanks to quick-fingered employees, the factory produced an astounding 178 cans of salmon a minute. Now a museum, the creaky property houses a mechanical canning line and displays on the building's history. Here, you'll learn about "slimers" – female employees responsible for salmon cleaning – and the butchers whose "singing knives" processed 15,000 fish per ten-hour shift.

10

Downstairs you can peruse the shell and pressed flower exhibits, alongside a somewhat creepy selection of preserved animals.

Richmond

Just 25 minutes south of Downtown Vancouver on the **Canada Line** lies the city of Richmond, which offers an unexpected voyage into the Far East; street signs and advertisements are in Chinese characters and you'll hear Cantonese spoken. More than 50 percent of Richmond residents identify as Chinese – many of them immigrated in the late 1980s from Hong Kong, Taiwan and Mainland China. The sweeping mountains that surround the city don't disguise the admittedly unlovely architecture of somewhat tatty strip malls, but what the city may lack in suburban beauty it more than makes up for with its dining scene, acknowledged as the Asian food capital of North America. **Food Street** (as Alexandra Road is called), makes up three blocks of some two hundred dining options of every kind of Asian cuisine from Cantonese to Korean and Thai. It's also a fun place to shop, with a trio of Asian malls: Parker Place, Yaohan Centre, and the Aberdeen Centre in **Golden Village**. You'll find both screamingly modern and traditional Asian goods at all of these; if you've time for only one, go to the shiny new Aberdeen Centre (see page 719). After the thrills of shopping, head for a peaceful retreat to No. 5 Rd, aka the **Highway to Heaven**, where you'll find some twenty different places of worship from global religions and just a little beyond that, North America's largest **Buddhist temple.**

Richmond Night Market

8700 McKim Way #3063 • Mid-May to mid-Oct Fri & Sat 7pm–midnight, Sun and holidays 7–11pm • $4.25 • ☎ 604 244 8448, ⓦ richmondnightmarket.com

One of the summer highlights for Vancouver foodies, the Richmond Night Market has some 20,000 visitors a night on busy weekends and is the only market of its kind in North America. The Night Market offers the chance to join the hordes snacking on fresh-cooked Asian street food as the sun sets over nearby YVR airport. On offer you'll find everything from "potato tornados" (deep-fried potatoes sliced wafer thin and wound around a stick) to *takoyaki* (octopus-stuffed creamy dough balls) and chocolate-filled Lucky Fish pancakes. It's de rigeur to overeat at the Night Market, most items are between $5–10 and it's generally cash only. As well as snacks and tempting Asian desserts, you'll also find toys, the latest must-have gadgets from Korea, cheap sunglasses and plenty of Hello Kitty merchandise.

International Buddhist Temple

9160 Steveston Hwy, between No. 3 and No. 4 Rds • Open daily 9.30am–5.30pm • Free • Tours are available pre-booked online for parties of 15 or more • ☎ 604 274 2882, ⓦ buddhisttemple.ca

Built to model the Forbidden City in Beijing, this vast Buddhist temple is North America's second largest and well worth a visit to stare in awe at the pitch-perfect Chinese Imperial architecture, intricate stonework and symbolic carvings. There are dozens of statues dotted through the grounds and halls; most impressive in the Gracious Hall is a 35ft-tall golden Buddha statue (the largest in North America) and out in the courtyard the Avalokitesvara Bodhisattva with Ten Thousand Hands and Ten Thousand Eyes. The on-site **Taste of Zen** restaurant offers a vegetarian lunch (suggested donation $15) from Thurs to Mon 11.30am to 3pm, made with produce grown on the grounds.

North and West Vancouver

10

Perhaps the most compelling reason to visit **North Vancouver** (known as North Van) is the trip itself by SeaBus which provides views of not only the Downtown skyline but also the teeming port area, a side of the city otherwise easily missed. Most of North Van itself is residential, as is neighbouring **West Vancouver**. You'll probably cross to the north shore less for these leafy suburbs than to sample the outstanding areas of natural beauty here: **Lynn Canyon**, **Grouse Mountain**, **Capilano River Regional Park** (the most popular excursion), **Mount Seymour** and **Lighthouse Park**. All are found in the mountains that rear up dramatically almost from the West Van waterfront, the proximity of Vancouver's residential areas to genuine wilderness being one of the city's most remarkable aspects.

Most of North Van is within a single bus ride of **Lonsdale Quay**, the north shore's SeaBus terminal. The **Lonsdale Quay Market**, 123 Carrie Cates Court (daily 9am–7pm; restaurants and brewery remain open later; ⓦ604 985 6261, ⓦlonsdalequay.com), to the right of the buses, is alone worth making the crossing. While not as vibrant as Granville Island Market, it's still an appealing place, with great food stalls and takeaways, plus walkways looking out over the port, tugs and moored fishing boats. Vancouver's main visitor centre (see page 709) has plenty of information and accommodation listings for North and West Van.

GETTING AROUND

NORTH AND WEST VANCOUVER

By bus Buses to all points leave from two parallel bays immediately in front of you as you leave the boat at Lonsdale Quay; blue West Van buses are run by an independent company but accept TransLink tickets. If you've bought a ticket to come over on the SeaBus (see page 707), you have 1hr 30min of transfer time to ride buses from the time of purchase, which should be long enough to get you to most of the destinations described below.

Grouse Mountain

6400 Nancy Greene Way • ☎ 604 980 9311, ⓦ grousemountain.com • **Cable cars** Daily 9am–10pm • $56 • To get directly to the base station of the cable car from Lonsdale Quay, take the special #236 Grouse Mountain bus from Bay 8 to the left of the SeaBus terminal; or #240 bus from West Georgia street and transfer to the #236 Grouse Mountain at Marine Drive and Fell Ave. May–Sept there is a free shuttle to Grouse from Canada Place, approx. 9am–5.30pm; purchase of mountain admission ticket needed

The trip to **Grouse Mountain**, named by hikers in 1894 who stumbled across a blue grouse, is a popular one. This is mainly due to the **cable cars** – it's North America's largest tramway – which run from the 290m base station to the mountain's 1231m summit. Local **skiers and snowboarders** like to head up here after work on winter evenings when 15 of the 33 runs are illuminated for night riding; the brightly lit mountain is a North Vancouver landmark. In summer, it's possible to walk up the aptly named Grouse Grind Trail, but it's a tough hike (known as "mother nature's stairmaster"), so unless you're feeling sporty, you'd do better to settle for the cable car.

After two lurches over the cables' twin towers you reach the summit, which despite its restaurants, wooden carvings and tourist paraphernalia, retains a sense of being immersed within nature. The views are astonishing, sometimes stretching as far as the San Juan Islands 160km away in Washington State.

Walk up the paved paths away from the centre in summer and you come to the scene of the "World Famous Lumberjack Show" (three daily; free), with a crowd-pleasing show of climbing, sawing and wood-chopping. Other attractions include a grizzly bear habitat where orphaned bears Coola and Grinder live, and an impressive birds of prey display. Also here is the **Peak Chairlift** (included in your ticket), which swings you high above the trees to the mountain's summit. There are plenty of add-ons to take your day to daredevil status, including aerial rope courses though the treetops ($39), zip lines which give a heart-pumping exploration of the old growth forest ($89), tandem paragliding which swoops you over the mountain to a 3300ft descent ($199), and the **Eye of the Wind** tour ($19.95), which heads to the top of the world's only glass-enclosed wind turbine with an observation deck, giving spectacular views. Check with the office at the lower cable-car base station for details of long **hikes** – many are down below rather than up at the summit proper. The best easy stroll is to **Blue Grouse Lake** (at the summit; 15min); the Goat Ridge Trail is for experienced hikers.

10

Lynn Canyon Park

3663 Park Rd **Park** Year-round 7am to dusk **Ecology Centre** June–Sept daily 10am–5pm; Oct–May Mon–Fri 10am–5pm, Sat & Sun noon–4pm • Donation requested • ☎ 604 990 3755, ⓦ lynncanyon.ca • Take bus #228 from the quay to Peters Rd, then a 10min walk to the gorge; or take the less frequent #229 West Lynn bus from Lonsdale Quay to Lynn Valley Centre and then transfer to #227 which takes you to the park entrance

Among the easiest targets for a quick taste of backwoods Vancouver is **Lynn Canyon Park**, a quiet, forested area with a modest ravine and suspension bridge which, unlike the more popular Capilano Suspension Bridge (see below), you don't have to pay to cross. Several walks of up to one and a half hours take you through fine scenery – cliffs, rapids, waterfalls and over the 50m-high bridge over Lynn Creek – all just twenty minutes from Lonsdale Quay. Before entering the gorge, it's worth popping into the **Ecology Centre**, where you can pick up maps and pamphlets on park trails and wildlife.

Capilano River Regional Park

3735 Capilano Rd • **Park** hours vary seasonally (see website) but roughly daily 9am–6pm • $46.95 • ☎ 604 985 7474, ⓦ capbridge.com
Salmon hatchery 4500 Capilano Park Rd • Daily: June & Aug 8am–8pm; May & Sept 8am–7pm; April & Oct 8am–6pm; Nov–March 8am–4pm • Free • ☎ 604 666 1790, ⓦ pac.dfo-mpo.gc.ca • Take bus #236 from the quay or ride the free shuttle bus from downtown (see website)

Lying just off the approach road to Grouse Mountain, **Capilano River Regional Park**'s most popular attraction is the 70m-high and 137m-long **suspension bridge** over the vertiginous Capilano Gorge. The first bridge here was built in 1889, though the present structure dates from 1956.

After traversing the wiggly-wobbly bridge, you'll come to **Treetops Adventure**, an idyllic boardwalk suspended 30m off the ground of a coastal temperate rainforest; one of the trees, dubbed "Big Doug", is 1300 years old, 63m tall and 6m wide. Back on the other side of the bridge, be sure to traverse the heart-thumping **Cliffwalk**, an elevated glass walkway attached to a granite cliff with sheer drops down to the Capilano River.

One kilometre upstream is the area's **salmon hatchery**, a federal operation designed to help salmon spawn and thus combat declining stocks. The building is well designed, and it's mesmerizing watching the coho and chinook flow through their underwater chambers.

Mount Seymour Provincial Park

Mount Seymour Rd, north of Mount Seymour Parkway, 16km north of Vancouver • Free • ☎ 604 986 9371, ☎ 604 986 2261, ⓦ env.gov.
bc.ca/bcparks • The road climbs to over 1000m and ends at a car park where boards indicate the trails and mountaineering options or you can take the #239 from Lonsdale Quay to Phibbs Exchange and then the #C15 to the Mount Seymour Parkway (1hr) – from there walk or cycle up the 13km road to the heart of the park (in winter, Mt Seymour run a shuttle bus from East and North Vancouver)

At 35 square kilometres, **Mount Seymour Provincial Park** is the biggest of the North Vancouver parks, with many **trails** that are manageable in a day. The easiest scenic (upper mountain) hikes go out to Goldie Lake, a thirty-minute stroll, and to Dog Mountain, an hour from the parking area (one way). Still better views, requiring more effort, can be had on the trails to First and Second Pump. The wildest and most demanding hike (7km) bypasses Mount Seymour's summit and runs by way of an intermittently marked trail to the forest- and mountain-circled Elsay Lake. There's also a café, toilets and picnic areas. In winter there are snowshoe and ski trails marked by BC parks, but families and learners flock to the designated **ski resort**, which is the biggest near Vancouver (⊛mtseymour.ca).

Cypress Provincial Park

Accessed via Cypress Bowl Rd off routes 1 and 99 • Free • ☎604 924 2200, ⊛env.gov.bc.ca/bcparks; for more information, ask at the Downtown visitor centre

10

Cypress Provincial Park is among BC's most visited day-use parks and probably the most popular of the north shore's protected areas. It takes its name from the huge old red and yellow cedars that proliferate here. Its trails can be rugged and muddy, but they're always well marked, and even just a few minutes from the parking area you can feel in the depths of the great outdoors.

Several good trails include the 2km wheelchair-accessible **Yew Lake Trail** and the **main park trail**, which climbs through forest and undergrowth, occasionally opening up to reveal views. The park also has two closely linked **ski** and **snowboard** areas: the alpine-skiing area at Cypress Bowl (⊛cypressmountain.com) and the cross-country ski area at Hollyburn just to the southwest.

Lighthouse Park

Head west along Marine Drive in West Vancouver, then left onto Beacon Lane • Free • ⊛lighthousepark.ca • The #250 bus makes the journey all the way to the park from West Georgia St in Downtown

Just southwest of Cypress Provincial Park, **Lighthouse Park** offers a seascape semi-wilderness at the extreme western tip of the north shore, 12km from the Lion's Gate Bridge. Smooth granite rocks and low cliffs line the coastline, backed by huge Douglas firs up to 500 years old, some of the best virgin forest in southern BC. A map at the car park shows trails to the 1912 Point Atkinson **lighthouse** itself; although the park has its secluded corners (no camping allowed), it can be busy during summer weekends.

ARRIVAL AND DEPARTURE
VANCOUVER

BY PLANE

Vancouver International Airport The airport (☎604 207 7077, ⊛yvr.ca) is 13km south of the city centre in Richmond. There's a 24hr tourist information desk as you exit customs and immigration. Close by are desks for direct bus services from the airport to Whistler (Pacific Coach Lines; ☎800 661 1725, ⊛pacificcoach.com) and Victoria (BC Ferries Connector; ☎888 788 8840, ⊛bcfconnector. com). There are also bus services (☎800 665 2122, ⊛quickcoach.com) for Bellingham Airport and Sea-Tac Airport (Seattle) in the US. Domestic passengers also have a tourist information desk (daily 8.30am–9.30pm) just before the terminal exit.

SkyTrain The best way to get into Vancouver from the airport is on SkyTrain (☎604 953 3333, ⊛translink.ca), the light rail system, on the Canada Line. Trains run from 5.07am to 12.56am, taking 26min to make the journey to Waterfront station close to Canada Place and the heart of Downtown. Change at Bridgeport Station for Richmond. Fares are $10.70 ($7.95 after 6.30pm weekdays and all day Sat and Sun and public holidays), which includes the $5 eastbound-only YVR AddFare.

By taxi Taxis to downtown cost about $35–39 (not including tip).

BY TRAIN

Pacific Central Station Skeletal VIA Rail services operate out of Pacific Central Station (1150 Station St; ☎888 842 7245, ⊛viarail.ca); they run to and from Jasper three times weekly (see page 591), where there are connections (also 3 weekly) for Prince George and Prince Rupert, and on to Edmonton and the east. There is a twice-daily train service run by Amtrak (☎800 872 7245, ⊛amtrakcascades.com) between Vancouver and Seattle (4hr 25min).

Train operators VIA Rail (☎888 842 7245, ⊛viarail. ca); Amtrak (☎800 872 7245, ⊛amtrak.com); Rocky Mountaineer (☎604 606 7200, ☎877 460 3200, ⊛rockymountaineer.com) for rail tours through the Rockies. Destinations Edmonton (3 weekly; 25hr); Jasper (3 weekly; 19hr); Toronto (3 weekly; 62hr), Winnipeg (3 weekly; 48hr).

BY BUS

Bus terminal Vancouver's main bus terminal is used by Pacific Coach Lines (☎604 662 7575, ☎800 661 1725, ⊛pacificcoach.com) to and from Victoria and Vancouver Island and Greyhound services (☎800 661 8747, ⊛greyhound.ca) to Seattle and the US. It is located alongside the VIA Rail Pacific Central train station at 1150 Station St. It's about a 30min walk to Downtown from the

ROUTES AND ITINERARIES

Vancouver is at the hub of transport links to many parts of western Canada. The basic alternative **routes and itineraries** are listed here together with cross-references to more detailed accounts of the various options.

THE YUKON AND ALASKA

You can **fly** to **Whitehorse** (see page 818) in the Yukon directly from Vancouver. Air Canada (ⓦaircanada.com) has nonstop flights from Vancouver to Anchorage, Alaska. For air travel to a greater variety of Alaskan destinations, head to the Seattle-Tacoma Airport in the US, which is fifty minutes by plane or around three hours by bus from Downtown or the Vancouver airport (see opposite). You can **drive** to Alaska through southern BC to **Dawson Creek**, where you can pick up the **Alaska Hwy** (see page 813), which runs through the Yukon to Fairbanks; allow at least three days. Alternatively, drive to Prince George, head west towards Prince Rupert and then strike north up the **Cassiar Hwy** (see page 810) to connect with the Alaska Hwy in the Yukon. By bus, things are more difficult since Greyhound pulled out of Northern BC and the Yukon. At the time of writing, the provincial government had stepped in to operate buses between Prince Rupert and Prince George, and from Prince George to Prince Nelson, but there's no replacement planned for the Yukon. Husky Bus (ⓦklondikeexperience. com) operates a summer service between Whitehorse and Dawson City, then you can ride the summer only Alaska Shuttle (ⓦalaskashuttle.com) from Dawson City to Anchorage. Buses link Whitehorse with other Yukon and Alaskan destinations. To travel to Alaska **by boat** from Vancouver you need to go via Bellingham (in the US), Prince Rupert (see page 799) or Port Hardy (see page 785) on Vancouver Island.

BC, CALGARY AND THE CANADIAN ROCKIES

Two main **roads** strike east from Vancouver towards Alberta and the Canadian Rockies – the **Trans-Canada Highway** and Hwy-3, both served by regular Greyhound buses (ⓣ800 661 8747, ⓦgreyhound.ca). Both give access to the **Okanagan** (see page 659), and the **Kootenays** (see page 642). VIA trains (ⓣ888 842 7245, ⓦviarail.ca) run three times weekly through the region via Kamloops to **Jasper** and **Edmonton**; there is no train service to Calgary. Buses serve the **Cariboo** region (see page 734), in the central part of the province. Several itineraries can be put together by combining car or public transport journeys in the **BC Interior** with BC Ferries connections from Port Hardy on Vancouver Island to either Bella Coola or Prince Rupert.

It takes about twelve hours to drive to **Calgary** on the Trans-Canada Hwy, and around one hour, thirty minutes less to reach **Banff**. Frequent one-hour flights connect Vancouver with Calgary or Kelowna.

bus terminal, so bear left from the station through a small park to the Science World–Main Street SkyTrain station, from where it's a couple of stops to Downtown ($2.95; take the train marked "Waterfront"). Alternatively, you can take a taxi Downtown from the station for about $10.
Bus companies BC Transit for city buses, SeaBus and SkyTrain (ⓣ604 953 3333, ⓦtranslink.ca); Greyhound (ⓣ800 661 8747, ⓦgreyhound.ca) for Seattle and the US; Pacific Coach Lines (ⓣ604 662 7575, ⓣ800 661 1725, ⓦpacificcoach.com) for Squamish and Whistler; Perimeter (ⓣ888 717 6606, ⓦperimeterbus.com) for services to Whistler and Squamish; Quick Shuttle (ⓣ604 940 4428, ⓣ800 665 2122, ⓦquickcoach.com) for Bellingham Airport, Downtown Seattle and Sea-Tac Airport.
Buses from the airport Pacific Coach Lines (ⓣ604 662 7575, ⓣ800 661 1725, ⓦpacificcoach.com) runs direct buses from the airport to Squamish and Whistler

(5 daily; $59). Other bus services from the airport are run by Perimeter (ⓣ888 717 6606, ⓦperimeterbus.com) to Whistler and Squamish, and Quick Shuttle (ⓣ604 940 4428, ⓣ800 665 2122, ⓦquickcoach.com) to Bellingham Airport, Downtown Seattle and Sea-Tac Airport. For Victoria on Vancouver Island, book with BC Ferries Connector (ⓣ888 788 8840, ⓦbcfconnector.com) who run 7 buses in spring/ summer (less off season). The fare is $59, which doesn't include the BC Ferries fare.
Destinations Banff (4 daily; 13hr 30min); Bellingham (11 daily; 2hr 5min); Cache Creek (3 daily; 5hr 35min); Calgary (5 daily; 15hr); Chilliwack, for Harrison Hot Springs (10 daily; 1hr 45min); Edmonton via Jasper (3 daily; 16hr 15min); Kamloops (6 daily; 5hr 5min); Kelowna (6 daily; 6hr 15min); Nanaimo (6 daily; 3hr 20); Pemberton (5 daily; 3hr 25min); Penticton (5 daily; 5hr 20min); Powell River (1 daily; 7hr 30min); Prince George via Cache Creek and

10

Williams Lake (3 daily; 12hr 35min); Salmon Arm (6 daily; 7hr 25min); Seattle, US (11–12 daily; 4hr 15min); Sea-Tac Airport, US (7 daily; 5hr 25min); Squamish (12 daily; 1hr 40min); Vernon (5 daily; 7hr 20min); Victoria (7 daily; 3hr); Whistler (12 daily; 2hr 30min).

BY FERRY

Ferries There are ferry sailings (☎888 223 3779, ⓦbcferries.com) between Vancouver and three points on Vancouver Island – Swartz Bay (for Victoria), Nanaimo and Comox. Most leave from Tsawwassen and Horseshoe Bay terminals, respectively a 45min and 30min drive south and west of Downtown. Foot passengers can buy inclusive bus and ferry tickets from Vancouver to Victoria or Nanaimo. Drivers should make advance reservations for all summer crossings. Public transport connects to the Pacific Rim National Park and to Port Hardy on the island's northern tip for ferry connections to Prince Rupert and Bella Coola.

Destinations Nanaimo from Horseshoe Bay Terminal (8 daily; 1hr 40min); Nanaimo from Tsawwassen Terminal (8 daily; 2hr); Victoria (Swartz Bay Terminal) from Tsawwassen (hourly summer 7am–9pm; rest of the year minimum 8 daily 7am–9pm; 1hr 35min).

GETTING AROUND

Vancouver's **public transport** system is an efficient, integrated network of bus, light rail (known as SkyTrain), SeaBus and ferry services that are operated by TransLink (daily 5.30am–midnight; ☎604 953 3333, ⓦtranslink.ca).
Tickets Public transport tickets are valid across the system on buses and the SkyTrain. Generally they cost $2.95 for journeys in the large, central Zone 1, and $4.20 or $5.70 for longer two- and three-zone journeys – though you're unlikely to go out of Zone 1 unless you're travelling to the airport from Downtown, which involves crossing from Zone 1 to 2; ditto for the SeaBus in North Vancouver. These regular fares apply in peak hours: Mon–Fri from start of service until 6.30pm. In off-peak hours – after 6.30pm and all day Saturday, Sunday and public holidays – a flat $2.95 fare applies across all three zones. Tickets are valid for transfers throughout the system for 1hr 30min from the time of issue. You can buy tickets individually (or in books of ten for $21 for Zone 1) at station offices or machines, 7-Eleven, Safeway and London Drugs stores, or any other shop or newsstand displaying a blue TransLink sticker. You must carry tickets with you as proof of payment. The simplest and cheapest deal if you're making three or more journeys in a day is a DayPass ($10.25), valid all day across all three zones (weekly passes are not available).
By bus You can buy tickets on the bus, but exact change is required; if the driver does not automatically give you one, ask for a transfer ticket if required. If you have a pass or transfer, simply show the driver. Buses are a one-zone fare all day, every day. Normal buses stop running around midnight, when a Night Bus service comes into effect on major routes until about 3.30am. Blue West Van buses (☎604 985 7777, ⓦwestvancouver.ca) also operate in the city (usually to North and West Vancouver destinations, including the BC Ferries terminal at Horseshoe Bay) – TransLink tickets are valid on these buses as well.
By SeaBus (☎604 953 3333, ⓦtranslink.ca). The Downtown terminal is Waterfront Station in the old Canadian Pacific station buildings at the foot of Granville St. Two 400-seat catamarans make the 12min crossing every 15–30min (6.30am–12.30am; $4.20 from Downtown). Arrival in North Vancouver is at Lonsdale Quay, where immediately to the left is a bus terminal for connections to Grouse Mountain and other North Vancouver destinations. Bicycles can be carried on board.
By ferry The city also has a variety of small ferries, run over similar routes at comparable prices by two companies: Aquabus (☎604 689 5858, ⓦtheaquabus.com) and False Creek Ferries (☎604 684 7781, ⓦgranvilleislandferries.bc.ca). These provide a useful, frequent and fun service (daily 7am–10.30pm, winter until 9pm). Aquabus runs boats in a continuous circular shuttle from the foot of Hornby St to Granville Island ($3.50) and to the Yaletown dock by the road loop at the east foot of Davie St ($5.50). False Creek Ferries also runs to Granville Island ($3.50) and to Vanier Park ($5.50) from Granville Island (and the Aquatic Centre). You buy tickets on board with both companies. They also run east up False Creek, with connections from Granville Island, to Yaletown, Science World and the Plaza of Nations (both $5.50).
By SkyTrain Vancouver's light-rail line – SkyTrain (☎604 953 3333, ⓦtranslink.ca) – links the Downtown Waterfront Station (housed in the CPR building with the SeaBus terminal) and the southeastern suburb of New Westminster. Only the first three or four stations – Waterfront, Burrard, Granville and Stadium-Chinatown – are likely to be of any practical use to the casual visitor. The Canada Line serves Richmond, including the airport.
By bike Bayshore Bicycles & Rollerblade Rentals, 745 Denman St (☎604 688 2453, ⓦbayshorebikerentals.ca); Spokes, 1798 West Georgia St, at Denman (☎604 688 5141, ⓦspokesbicyclerentals.com). To pick up downtown, visit Cycle City, 648 Hornby St (☎604 618 8626, ⓦcyclevancouver.com).
By car Main Downtown parking garages are at The Bay (Richards St, near Dunsmuir), Robson Square (Smithe St, at Howe) and the Pacific Centre (Howe St, at Dunsmuir). Metered spots are difficult (but not impossible) to come by in the city centre. Check EasyPark (ⓦeasypark.ca) to find more options.
By taxi Black Top and Checker Cabs (☎604 731 1111, ☎604 681 2181); Vancouver Taxi (☎604 871 1111); Yellow Cab (☎604 681 3311, ☎604 681 1111).

INFORMATION AND TOURS

Visitor centre Opposite Canada Place (see page 690) at the foot of Burrard St in the Waterfront Centre, 200 Burrard St at the corner of Canada Place Way (daily 9am–5pm ⓦ tourismvancouver.com). Besides information on the city and much of southern British Columbia, the centre provides information and tickets to sports and entertainment as well as transportation to Whistler, Tofino, Victoria and Seattle, as well as BC Ferries. Same-day tickets for events are often available for a 50 percent discount through community box office Tickets Tonight. It also has a comprehensive accommodation service.

Useful websites Tourism British Columbia ⓦ hellobc. com; Tourism Vancouver ⓦ tourismvancouver.com.

A Wok Around Chinatown (ⓣ 604 736 9508, ⓦ awokaround.com). Robert Sung leads daily cultural and culinary walking tours through the heart of Chinatown (2hr; $80 includes tastings).

Talking Trees Tour (ⓣ 604 628 8555, ⓦ talasay.com). Explore Stanley Park and its history on an in-depth and authentic First Nations walking tour (1hr 30min; $40).

Vancouver Foodie Tours (ⓣ 604 295 8844, ⓦ foodietours.ca). Foodie Tours began with Granville Island Market and it's still their most exciting tour. Wind your way in and out of the stalls while your guide skips the queues for tastings of cheese, charcuterie, coffee, donuts and more (2hr; $56.99).

10

ACCOMMODATION

Mid-range hotels that are reasonably priced are more likely to be outside the centre, but space everywhere can get tight in summer: you'll need to **book ahead**. Many of the nicer options are in the West End, a quiet residential area bordering Vancouver's wonderful Stanley Park, only a 5–10min walk from Downtown. Gastown, Chinatown and the area between them hold central Vancouver's cheapest hotels, but parts of these areas are somewhat shady at night, especially the Downtown Eastside. If you're on a low budget, you're better off in the **hostels** or the excellent **YWCA, or travel off season when rates are much more manageable**. Vancouver is not a camper's city: the majority of the in-city **campsites** are for RVs only. Prices below are high season (June–Sept) and include breakfast unless otherwise stated.

DOWNTOWN

The Burrard 1100 Burrard St ⓣ 604 681 2331, ⓣ 800 663 0366, ⓦ theburrard.com; map p.692. After a 2011 facelift, this traditional 1950s hotel has been transformed into a funky retro retreat. The smallish guest rooms, decorated in beach hues of white and turquoise, offer free calls to anywhere in North America, HDTVs with movie channels, and – best of all – complimentary bike use. The central courtyard is a lush square of plants and palms. $309

Fairmont Pacific Rim 1038 Canada place ⓣ 604 695 5300, ⓣ 877 900 5350, ⓦ fairmont.com/pacificrim; map p.692. Located on Canada Place and by the port, this modern 377-room hotel is the place to stay if money is no object and you're after a prime location. The property's sleek glass coat offers a major payoff to guests: many rooms have smashing views of the harbour, Stanley Park and the North Shore Mountains. Genteel quarters boast marble bathrooms with TVs, an evening turndown service and Bose sound systems. The hotel also runs two restaurants and a first-rate spa. $629

★ **L'Hermitage Hotel** 788 Richards St ⓣ 888 855 1050, ⓦ lhermitagevancouver; map p.692. The staff at this luxury hotel are famed for their warmth, helpfulness, and attention to detail; other perks include a heated saltwater pool, a stylish dining room and lounge and free bicycle use. Many of the suites come with fireplaces and stainless-steel kitchens. In the heart of Downtown, just a block from the city's main shopping stretch (Robson St). $522

Rosewood Hotel Georgia 801 West Georgia St ⓣ 604 682 5566, ⓣ 888 767 3963, ⓦ rosewoodhotels.com; map p.692. Established in 1927 and reopened in 2011, this is one of Vancouver's most historic hostelries, courting everyone from Ginger Rogers to the Rolling Stones. Inside the Georgian Revival building lies a 16m saltwater pool, a spa, and *Hawksworth Restaurant* (see page 712), one of the city's most celebrated places to dine. The attentive staff ensures your stay is first-rate, and you'd be hard-pressed to find fault with the luxurious guest rooms, which have refined decor and skyline views. $619

SameSun Hostel 1018 Granville St, at Nelson ⓣ 604 682 8226, ⓣ 877 972 6378, ⓦ samesun.com; map p.692. *Samesun* has popular hostels in Kelowna, Banff and elsewhere, and this zippy, bright hostel in Vancouver on Granville St – while central and away from the worst of this street's tawdriness – is not the quietest (earplugs are given out at check-in). The hostel has 250 beds in four-, six- and eight-bed rooms (the former have less street noise but the six-beds are now pod style), eleven private rooms, secure lockers, a modern kitchen with adjacent patio, common area, games room and computer access. There's also laundry facilities, wi-fi, a lively bar, and a free continental breakfast. Dorms from $65; private room with shared bath $170; en-suite private room $190

St Regis Hotel 602 Dunsmuir St ⓣ 604 681 1135, ⓣ 800 770 7929, ⓦ stregishotel.com; map p.692. They treat you right at this sophisticated, executive-class hotel: international phone calls, Steve Nash gym passes, and full cooked breakfasts are included in the rate. Other features include heated bathroom tiles and a striking collection of original art, displayed throughout the premises. The hotel

10

also runs a wine shop, a bar and the pre-eminent *Gotham Steakhouse*. **$419**

GASTOWN

★ **Skwachàys Lodge** 31 West Pender St ☎604 687 3589, ⓦskwachays.com; map p.692. You'll spot the soaring totem pole that sprouts from the rooftop before you arrive at Vancouver's only First Nations-run hotel and gallery, which offers an immersive chance to learn more about Aboriginal art, as each room is a unique installation created in partnership with Aboriginal artists and top Vancouver hotel designers. Pow Wow dancers, eagles, ravens and the sun and moon feature prominently but there are plenty of mod cons too, from high-thread-count sheets to in-room coffee and tea facilities. The location is within easy walking distance of Gastown and the rest of Downtown. **$259**

COMMERCIAL DRIVE

Bee & Thistle Guesthouse 1842 Parker St ☎604 669 0715, ☎877 669 7055, ⓦbeeandthistle.ca; map p.692. Just off Commercial Drive, Vancouver's Little Italy, this impeccable bed and breakfast is one of the city's best stays. Built in 1908, the proprietors have preserved the home's antique "bones", such as fireplaces and stained glass windows, and added modern extras like soft bathrobes, stocked mini-fridges, and iPod docking stations. Breakfast features healthy home-made granola, fresh muffins and home-made jam. The inn is a 12min drive from Downtown; alternatively, local buses stop close by. Two-night min. **$195**

WEST END

Barclay House 1351 Barclay St ☎604 605 1351, ☎800 971 1351, ⓦbarclayhouse.com; map p.692. Exquisitely furnished, six-room bed and breakfast in a canary-yellow home that dates to 1904. Free parking, and guest rooms come with wi-fi and DVD players (there's a movie library). Located in the heart of Vancouver, the *Barclay* is nicely situated for exploring the city; excellent breakfasts jump-start the day. **$170**

★ **Listel Hotel** 1300 Robson St ☎604 684 8461, ⓦthelistelhotel.com; map p.692. Boutique art hotel with an eco-friendly edge and lashings of originality with the popular *Forage* restaurant on-site (see page 714). The Museum floor showcases a collaboration with the Museum of Anthropology with original First Nations art on display; each room on the Gallery floor acts as its own mini art gallery with work from international and Canadian artists; and the Artist Series suites feature different artists and design movements. Doubles **$439**; suites **$538**

Sunset Inn & Suites 1111 Burnaby St, at Thurlow ☎604 688 2474, ☎800 786 1997, ⓦsunsetinn.com; map p.692. One of the best West End "apartment" hotels and a good spot for a longer stay – spacious studio and one-

bedroom suites (all with kitchens and balconies) with on-site laundry (soap available in the lobby vending machine), a jovial staff, free breakfast and many nearby cafés, restaurants and shops. A 10min walk to Downtown. **$377**

★ **Sylvia Hotel** 1154 Gilford St ☎604 681 9321, ⓦsylviahotel.com; map p.692. An ivy-wrapped landmark located in a heritage building, this popular place has an excellent reputation and unbeatable location, making reservations essential. It's at the beach two blocks from Stanley Park, and its snug bar, quiet, old-world charm and sea views make it one of Vancouver's best stays. Rooms are available at different prices depending on size, view and facilities. **$199**

★ **Times Square Suites** 1821 Robson St, at Denman ☎604 684 2223, ⓦtimessquaresuites.com; map p.692. Two short blocks from Stanley Park, *Times Square* offers inviting one- and two-bedroom suites that include full kitchens, wi-fi and a washer-dryer. The welcoming staff put your name on the front door, whether you're staying one night or one month. Be sure to spend some time on the rooftop deck, which has a barbecue set-up and views of Stanley Park. There are excellent restaurants, coffee shops, and a Whole Foods supermarket within close vicinity. Great for families. **$229**

Vancouver Downtown Hostel 1114 Burnaby St, at Thurlow ☎604 684 4565, ☎888 203 4302, ⓦhihostels. ca; map p.692. In a former nunnery on a quiet residential stretch in the West End one block from Davie St's restaurants and shops, this hostel has 222 beds split up between shared and private rooms (maximum four/room). Bike rental and storage are available, as well as laundry facilities, a kitchen, wi-fi, computer access, lockers and free breakfast. HI members get 10 percent discount. Dorms **$61.60**; private rooms **$140.80**

West End Guest House 1362 Haro St, at Jervis ☎604 681 2889, ☎888 546 3327, ⓦwestendguesthouse. com; map p.692. A wonderful, seven-room bed and breakfast with an old-time parlour and bright rooms, each with private bathroom. The proprietors have a great eye for design, and everywhere you look there's brilliant art, be it black-and-white photographs, oil paintings or Art Deco sculptures. Out back, there's a deck with striped seats and an enormous magnolia tree. Free parking, gourmet breakfast "sherry hour" and bicycle use included. two night min. **$420**

YALETOWN

Opus Hotel 322 Davie St ☎604 642 6787, ☎866 642 6787, ⓦopushotel.com; map p.692. Outside, the *Opus* gleams with Yaletown cool, but inside it screams sexy, decorative colours and materials (mosaic, marble and expensive fabrics). The 96 rooms are decadent – plush linens, personal iPads, big windows and sensuous bathrooms. The cool *Opus Bar* and *La Pentola* Italian restaurant mean you need never leave the hotel precinct for food, drink and evening relaxation – though with the temptations of Yaletown just seconds away, this would be a shame. $459

YWCA Hotel 733 Beatty St between Georgia and Robson ☎604 895 5830, ☎800 663 1424, ⓦywcavan. org/hotel; map p.692. Despite its name, Vancouver's main "Y" is open to all and is excellent, offering the city's best inexpensive accommodation. It was purpose-built in 1995 in a handy east Downtown location. Top-value rooms (especially for small groups) are spread over eleven floors with a choice of private, shared or hall bathrooms. There are no dorm beds. Most rooms have TVs, plus there are cooking facilities, wi-fi access, laundry, lounges, a/c, and rooms with mini-kitchens. Doubles $118; four-beds $275

GRANVILLE ISLAND

Granville Island Hotel 1253 Johnston St ☎604 683 7373, ☎800 663 1840, ⓦgranvilleislandhotel.com; map p.692. You're away from central Downtown in this polished, modern hotel, which has a good bar, restaurant, jacuzzi and sauna, and a spectacular waterfront setting, but you're in the heart of one of the city's most enjoyable little enclaves. Some of the rooms have water views. Breakfast $30/person. $469

KITSILANO

Vancouver Jericho Beach Hostel 1515 Discovery St, off NW Marine Drive ☎604 224 3208, ☎866 762 4122, ⓦhihostels.ca; map p.692. Canada's biggest HI hostel, located 20min southwest of Downtown, has a superb and safe position surrounded by Jericho Beach lawns. A former barracks, the 252-bed hostel fills up quickly. There are large dorms separated into smaller rooms by curtains and ten private rooms (sleeping up to four). Facilities include kitchen, café, bike rental and storage, lockers, free wi-fi, computer access and an excellent cafeteria. Opens seasonally from May to mid-Sept. HI members get 10 percent discount. Dorms $39.60; doubles $99

EATING

Vancouver's **restaurants** are some of Canada's finest and you'll be spoilt for choice. **Chinese** cuisine has a high profile (particularly in Richmond; see ⓦvisitrichmondbc.com for a delectable dumpling trail). **Japanese**, **Vietnamese** and **Thai** are also well represented, along with plenty of **Korean** options, and can often provide the best starting points if you're on a tight budget (sushi is a Vancouver mainstay and very affordable). One of the biggest trends in the Vancouver restaurant scene is for nose to tail, seed to stem dining and you'll find plenty of **"West Coast cuisine"** too, comprised of fresh local ingredients such as salmon, oysters, and sweet local spot prawns. Vegetarians, vegans and the gluten-intolerant are well served by a number of specialist places.

CAFÉS

Vancouver has plenty of café culture and the city takes coffee very seriously; look out for outposts of specialist roasters such as *Matchstick, Milano and Timbertrain* all across the Downtown core. Little Italy, the area around Commercial Drive (between Venables St and Broadway), is good for cheap, cheerful and trendy cafés.

33 Acres Brewing Co. 15 West 8th Ave, Mount Pleasant ☎604 620 4589, ⓦ33acresbrewing.com; map p.692. Yes, 33 Acres is a micro-brewery (an excellent one), but they also serve astonishingly good coffee and food in their minimalist and stylish space off Main Street. Weekday breakfast and weekend brunch includes avocado smash ($10) and an acai bowl ($12); cheese and charcuterie boards are served all day ($17) and there's wood fired pizza until 9pm. Mon–Fri 9am–11pm, Sat & Sun 10am–11pm.

★ **Au Petit Café** 4851 Main Street ☎604 873 3328; map p.692. Jump on the number #3 bus down Main Street to chomp down on one of the city's best *banh mi* Vietnamese sub sandwiches. You may have to queue to eat at this simple diner but it's always worth the wait thanks to the high-quality ham, pâté, meatballs and perfect bread ($5.25). Thurs–Tues 10am–7pm.

★ **Café Medina** 780 Richards St, Downtown ☎604 879 3114, ⓦmedinacafe.com; map p.692. Quite simply one of the best (and busiest) brunch spots in town with Mediterranean-inspired cuisine and delicious fresh-baked Belgian waffles. Menu highlights include the salmon fumé (a ciabatta sandwich with eggs and avocado; $14); lavender latte ($4.75); and waffles ($3.50). Avoid between 11am and 1.30pm or face waits of 30min and more. The cocktail menu is both delicious and innovative: try the Fez Hat ($12) with Mezcal and green apple. Mon–Fri 8am–3pm, Sat & Sun 9am–3pm.

★ **East Van Roasters** 319 Carrall St, Gastown ☎604 629 7562, ⓦeastvanroasters.com; map p.692. Inviting little coffee shop which specializes in coffee roasted on-site and also does a thriving trade in bean-to-bar artisan chocolate. As well as tasting delicious, *East Van Roasters* does good things too as the whole organization is a social enterprise that offers training and employment to the local female residents of the nearby *Rainier Hotel*. Mon–Fri 9am–5pm.

Forty-Ninth Parallel 2902 Main St, at East 13th Ave, Mount Pleasant ☎604 420 4900, ⓦ49thparallel roasters.com; map p.692. This spacious outpost of a pre-eminent Canadian coffee wholesaler roasts its own beans and takes espresso quality very seriously. There's often a queue, but with good reason – in this richly caffeinated town, *Forty-Ninth* still stands out as one of the best of the best. Beverages are sipped from Tiffany blue cups, and there

10

10

are fresh *Lucky's* donuts made on-site to complement your drink. Also Downtown and in Kits. Mon–Sat 7am–10pm, Sun 7.30am–9pm.

JJ Bean 1689 Johnston St, in the Granville Island Public Market ☎604 685 0613, ⌨jjbeancoffee.com; map p.692. With more than a dozen other outlets across the city, *JJ Bean* is a local success story. At their Granville Island outpost you'll find exceptional coffee (roasted in-house) and espresso drinks that rev you right for touring Vancouver's food market utopia. Scrunched between an exit door and a florist, there are no seats and no wi-fi, and often a queue. Daily 7.30am–7pm.

★ **Revolver** 325 Cambie St, Gastown ☎604 558 4444, ⌨revolvercoffee.ca; map p.692. In a city that's mad for coffee, *Revolver* reigns supreme for brewing ingenuity. French press, Chemex, aeropress and more, patrons choose their preferred drip method with the help of expert baristas, then watch their cup get painstakingly concocted. It's set in two beautiful rooms with exposed brick walls, wood floors, and huge windows perfect for indulging in Gastown people-watching. Free wi-fi, but seating can be tight. Mon–Fri 7.30am–6pm, Sat 9am–6pm.

RESTAURANTS

Vancouver's restaurant scene is a fast-paced delicious dazzle of new openings and chef switcheroos spread across the city. Gastown is the city's culinary hot-spot, its streets packed with fashionable restaurants boasting experimental cocktail bars. Neighbouring Chinatown offers a plethora of authentic and reasonably priced options. Downtown has plenty of chains and huge choice, particularly with top-dollar places and fast food: the local *White Spot* chain has some ten locations in Vancouver, offering good and glorified fast food. Superior chains like *Earl's*, *Milestones*, *Cactus Club Café* and *Joey's* are also highly commendable. Yaletown is also a key eating and nightlife area. Similar places line 4th Ave in Kitsilano and neighbouring West Broadway, and it's well worth venturing down Main Street and Commercial Drive (home of the city's Little Italy) to dip into the excellent dining options on offer, though these require a transit journey if you're based in or around Downtown. The heavily residential West End, notably around the 'U' of Robson, Denman and Davie streets – Vancouver's "gay village" – is also booming with a thriving pan-Asian, late-night scene, and it's always worth jumping on the Skytrain to Richmond for incredible Chinese food.

DOWNTOWN

★ **Chambar** 568 Beatty St ☎604 879 7119, ⌨chambar. com; map p.692. Reliable choice for breakfast, brunch, lunch or dinner: on the menu luscious heaped servings of *moules frites* ($29), delicately spiced tajines ($29) and from 8am to 3pm (11.30am weekdays), superb Belgian waffles with toppings like bacon-caramel and white chocolate

pistachio rosewater ($3.50). Also boasts a phenomenal wine list and convivial bar. Daily 8am–late.

★ **CinCin** 1154 Robson St, between Thurlow and Bute ☎604 688 7338, ⌨cincin.net; map p.692. This long-standing Italian gem has a refined, buzzy setting; try to book an outside table in summer. The food merits the prices (pastas from $24, mains around $34) and includes top-grade home-made pastas, superb wood-fire grilled meat and Ocean Wise fish options. The wine list is one of the best in the city and their cocktail-creating bartender one of Canada's finest. Daily 5pm–11pm, bar till midnight

★ **Hawksworth Restaurant** 801 West Georgia St, at the Rosewood Hotel Georgia ☎604 673 7000, ⌨hawksworthrestaurant.com; map p.692. Set in Vancouver's most distinguished hotel – the *Rosewood Hotel Georgia* (see page 709) – Hawksworth serves exquisite Canadian cuisine amid voguish chandeliers with an impressive wine cellar and one of the city's finest cocktail bars. The price of dinner mains, such as yarrow meadows duck breast, start around $42; at lunchtime you can soak up the culinary grandeur for a little less. Mon–Fri 6.30am–9.30pm, Sat & Sun 7am–9.30pm.

★ **Hy's Steakhouse** 637 Hornby St ☎604 683 7671, ⌨hyssteakhouse.com; map p.692. A Vancouver classic which got a $2million makeover in 2015. Hang the expense and dig into mouthwatering Alberta steaks ($43 and up), dry-aged for a month, paired with ambrosial sides like creamed spinach ($10.95), their legendary cheese toast for two ($7.95) or a classic Caesar salad made table-side ($13.95). Mon 11.30am–3pm & 5–10.30pm, Tues–Fri 11.30am–3pm & 5–11pm, Sat 5–11pm & Sun 5–10.30pm.

★ **Joe Fortes Seafood and Chop House** 777 Thurlow St, near Robson ☎604 669 1940, ⌨joefortes.ca; map p.692. This long-established oyster-bar-cum-chophouse and seafood restaurant is a city institution, with a lively summer patio upstairs on the roof garden and a draw year-round for the excellent service, lively atmosphere and irrepressible maître d', Frenchy. The restaurant plays the food straight and in generous portions. Mains cost from $24.95 but there are daily lunchtime $9.95 "Blue Plate specials" and a daily Happy Hour at the bar from 4–6. Daily 11am–11pm.

The Mexican 1049 Granville St ☎604 569 0955, ⌨themexican.ca; map p.692. Set in an unpromising section of Granville St this is probably one of the most underrated Mexican joints in the city serving up authentic cantina standards such as *chimichanga* ($12), vegetarian *tostadas* ($7) and an absurdly wonderful *queso fundido* which comes with a choice of mushroom or chorizo ($15). Mon–Thurs 11.30am–10pm, Fri & Sat 11.30am–midnight, Sun 11.30am–10pm.

Nightingale 1017 W Hastings St ⌨vhawknightingale. com; map p.692. Launched in 2016 from acclaimed chef David Hawksworth, this is his sister restaurant to

Hawksworth and offers a more casual and cosy experience. Open for lunch and dinner with 200 seats across two floors, everything on the menu works well as a share-plate option, hopping from Italy to Spain then California on the culinary map with charcuterie boards, oysters and beautiful seasonal salads. The pizzas (from $16) are superb – the dough recipe took two years to perfect – and the pork belly with apple, pistachio and bourbon glaze ($25) is a favourite too. Daily 11am–midnight.

★ **Vij's** 3106 Cambie St, 3km south of Downtown ☎ 604 872 3707, ⓦ vijs.ca; map p.692. One of Canada's best-known restaurants is on Cambie in a dazzling lantern-like building that's become a local landmark. All the usual much-loved internationally acclaimed *Vij's* favourites are on the menu, including the heavenly wine marinated lamb popsicles ($32); Indian street food snacks made with Pacific Northwest ingredients ($12) accompany craft cocktails with locally distilled spirits in the bar (where you might find yourself waiting, as there are no reservations). Daily 5.30pm–late.

GASTOWN

★ **L'Abattoir** 217 Carrall St ☎ 604 568 1701, ⓦ labattoir.ca; map p.692. Exceptional award-winning bar and restaurant serving up a thoughtful menu of West Coast seasonal delights with a decidedly French influence; mains like duck breast with salt-baked beetroot come in around $34 but their daily Happy Hour from 5.30–6.30pm has 50 percent off their appetizer menu giving a good chance to all to try this superb food. Killer brunch and dazzling cocktails complete the package. Mon–Fri 5.30–10pm, Sat & Sun 10am–2pm & 5.30–10.30pm.

★ **Meat & Bread** 370 Cambie St, also at 1033 West Pender St, Downtown ☎ 604 566 9003, ⓦ meatandbread.ca; map p.692. Hip, habit-forming sandwich shop famed for its *porchetta* sandwich ($10) – thick slices of slow-roasted, crispy pork doused with salsa verde, crammed into fresh bread, and served with fancy mustard. The tiny menu also includes a grilled cheese sandwich ($8), and daily soup or salad ($4.50). There is usually a line-up but it moves fast. Mon–Wed 11am–5pm, Thurs–Sat 11.30–7pm, Sun 11am–4pm.

★ **Salt Tasting Room** 45 Blood Alley ☎ 604 633 1912, ⓦ salttastingroom.com; map p.692. You can choose your own dining adventure at this charcuterie hideout where patrons pick three items from a rotating selection of 10 meats, 10 cheeses and 10 "condiments" – such as almonds or cornichons ($16). The servers are expert matchmakers, and quick to fix your comestibles up with the perfect wine (or mead) accompaniment (a three-taster wine flight is $15). Because of the small portion size, *Salt* is perhaps best for a romantic pre-dinner warm-up. Stylish, with exposed brick walls and communal tables this is the perfect place to taste award-winning BC wines. Daily 3.30pm–11pm.

★ **Wildebeest** 120 West Hastings St ☎ 604 687 6880, ⓦ wildebeest.ca; map p.692. Possibly the quintessential Gastown restaurant offering nose to tail dining, excellent brunch and decidedly moreish craft cocktails. Although this is an unashamedly meat-centric restaurant, vegetarians are well taken care of. Smoked Castelvetrano olives ($6) are a must, as is the house tartare ($17), roasted bone marrow with buttered leeks and oyster mushrooms and the monthly-changing "slushie" cocktails ($12). If you have the marrow ask for a "sherry luge" chaser ($3). Daily 5pm–midnight, brunch Sat & Sun 10am–2pm.

CHINATOWN

★ **Bao Bei Chinese Brasserie** 163 Keefer St, at Main ☎ 604 688 0876, ⓦ bao-bei.ca; map p.692. Wildly

---

FOOD TRUCK MANIA!

The food cart craze in Vancouver looks like it's here to stay: there are more than 100 trucks around the city and regular Food Truck events (see ⓦ yvrfoodfest.com) selling healthy, culturally diverse foods ranging from Korean-Mexican fusion to El Salvadorian pupusas. Check the StreetFoodApp ⓦ streetfoodapp.com/Vancouver to check opening times and locations.

Japadog Burrard at Smithe ⓦ japadog.com; map p.692. The spark that lit the food-cart fuse, this vendor (now with numerous local outposts) fires off Japanese riffs on traditional hot dogs. The "terimayo", topped with teriyaki sauce, mayo and seaweed, is the signature meal. It costs around $8 a dog. Sun–Thurs 11am–10pm, Fri & Sat till 11am–11pm.

Mr Bannock Food Truck 433 West 1st St, North Vancouver ⓦ mrbannock.com; map p.692. Fusion Indigenous cuisine by chef Paul Natrall of the Squamish Nation with the likes of bannock (fresh frybread, plain or dusted with sugar and cinnamon, $5) or juniper berry rubbed chicken and waffles ($10). See the Streetfood App for times and locations.

Tacofino Howe & Robson ⓦ tacofino.com; map p.692. Exceptional tacos ($5), gringas ($5) and burritos ($10) served up freshly-made with crunchy slaws, spicy salsas and sustainable Ocean Wise seafood. The chocolate Diablo cookies pack a delicious and hefty punch. "Blue" and "Pink" trucks at various Vancouver locations, but can often be found close to Vancouver Art Gallery. Mon–Fri 11.30am–3pm.

10

10

popular upscale Chinese fusion restaurant that packs in hungry diners every night. It's a gorgeous space: dim lighting, plenty of vintage design details like old lamps and armoires with friendly servers and delicious craft cocktails. Standout items include handmade dumplings ($10), beef tartare with taro chips ($18) and the "kick ass house fried rice" ($18). Mon–Sat 5.30pm–midnight, Sun 5.30–11pm.

★ **Juniper** 185 Keefer St ☎604 807 9199, ⓦjuniper vancouver.com; map p.692. Pacific Northwest-inspired, seasonally rotating food with rustic share-plates and tempting charcuterie and cheese board; try the Nordic-inspired fish board which really shows off the region's outstanding seafood. Mains from around $25. The bar focuses on small batch spirits, wines and beers from the region and they have an innovative G&T menu that teams different gins and tonics; try the barrel aged gin old fashioned with a blend of local gins ($16). Daily 4.30pm–late, Happy Hour 4–6pm, Sat & Sun brunch 10am–2pm.

Phnom-Penh 244 East Georgia St, near Gore ☎604 682 5777, ⓦphnompenhrestaurant.ca; map p.692. Excellent, cheap Vietnamese and Cambodian cuisine – legendary for their deep-fried chicken wings ($8.75), in a friendly, family-oriented restaurant. Most dishes cost around $9–14. Mon–Thurs 10am–9.30pm, Fri & Sun 10am–10pm.

SOUTH MAIN AND COMMERCIAL DRIVE

Ahn and Chi 3388 Main St ☎604 878 8883, ⓦahnandchi. com; map p.692. Bright and stylish diner serving up classic Vietnamese dishes cooked to perfection. Fresh spring rolls are scrumptious (tofu with soy sauce available for vegans $5) and "Land and Sea" mains include Caramalized Arctic Char ($23) or King Prawn tamarind soup ($22). Cocktails served after 5pm. No reservations, except for large groups choosing the tasting menu. Daily 11am–late.

★ **La Mezcaleria** 1622 Commercial Drive ☎604559 8226, ⓦlamezcaleria.ca; map p.692. Cheery neighbourhood joint, serving up authentic Mexican recipes using as much local produce as possible and sustainable Ocean Wise seafood. Taste some of BC's finest fish with the *Ceviche Callejero* ($13), or try *Hongos Con Kale* tacos ($6 each). Explore the vast Mezcal and Tequila list with a "flight" of three different varieties served up with grasshopper salt. Also at 68 East Cordova St, Gastown. Mon–Thurs 5pm–late, Fri 11am–late, Sat & Sun 10am–late.

TOP 5 BUDGET EATS

Au Petit Café See page 711
Buckstop See right
Kintaro Ramen See right
The Naam See page 715
Yummy To Go See right

WEST END

★ **Buckstop** 833 Denman St ☎604 428 2528, ⓦbuckstop.ca; map p.692. Decadent barbecue and small plates tavern offering up the West End's finest late-night eats and craft cocktails made with local spirits, fruits and herbs. Groups should order the Full Stop ($110) for a heaped-high meat-based festival of gluttony, but solo diners can find plenty of pocket-pleasing options too: the fried dill pickles are fantastic ($5) and the barbecue assortment for $16 offers three different meats to try. Mon–Sat 4.30pm–2am, Sat & Sun 10.30am–2.30pm brunch, Sun 4.30pm–midnight.

★ **Forage** 1300 Robson St ☎604 661 1400, ⓦforage vancouver.com; map p.692. Casual farm to table bistro with an outstanding eco-ethic and warm friendly service next to the *Listel Hotel*. The menu regularly changes to reflect the best seasonal, local ingredients available, but their award-winning sustainable seafood chowder is always on the menu ($8) and a must-have. Mains hover around $12–38, and are worth every cent. *Forage* brunch is a West End institution. Breakfast Mon–Fri 6.30–10am, Sat & Sun 7–10am, brunch Sat & Sun 10am–2pm, dinner daily 5pm–close.

Kingyo 8/1 Denman St ☎604 608 1677, ⓦkingyo izakaya.ca; map p.692. Legendary *izakaya* joint which offers the city's most elaborate lunch bento box ($22), which sells out every day. They only make 10, so arrive early and prepare to be amazed. The welcome is warm and loud at this boisterous restaurant with addictive Asian-influenced cocktails made with ingredients such as *shiso* leaves, *yuzu* and sake. Must-haves include the tuna *tataki* ($11.80), stone-grilled beef tongue ($9.80) and crunchy *ebi* (prawn) mayo ($11.80). Telephone reservations only. Sun–Thurs lunch 11.30am–2.30pm, dinner 5.30–11pm; Fri & Sat 11.30am–2.30pm, dinner 5.30pm–midnight.

Kintaro Ramen 788 Denman St, near Robson ☎604 682 7568; map p.692. Tiny, wildly popular Japanese soup joint with long queues and close-knit seating. Patrons choose light, medium or rich broth, which is accompanied by home-made noodles and either lean or fatty pork. Delicious and cheap (almost everything is under $10), it makes a great meal rain or shine. Cash or debit card only (no credit), $7 min per person. Tues–Sun 11.30am–11pm.

Yummy to Go 1711 Davie St ☎604 688 1870; map p.692. Absurdly cheap and surprisingly high quality hole-in-the-wall sushi bar a stone's throw from English Bay. Grab one (or two) of the combos and take to the beach to enjoy as the sun sets. There are a few tables but it's definitely not a salubrious place to dine. Eleven-piece sushi combos start from $6.75 with zingingly fresh fish. Skip the bubble tea; it's far better around the corner at *Che'Licious* (1120 Denman St). Mon–Thurs 11.30am–10pm, Fri–Sun 11.30am–11pm.

YALETOWN

★ **Blue Water Café** 1095 Hamilton St, at Helmcken ☎ 604 688 8078, ⓦ bluewatercafe.net; map p.692. One of Yaletown's most popular fixtures, thanks to its ground-breaking chef, Frank Pabst's passion for sustainable seafood (plus its attractive terrace and interior). There's an open kitchen, with mains beginning at $30 (great tuna dishes, BC sablefish or arctic char with leeks), plus a top-notch raw bar (for sushi, *ceviche* or oysters), and a cocktail bar, where you can explore one of Vancouver's longest whisk(e)y lists. Daily 5–11pm, bar 4.30pm–1am.

The Greek by Anatoli 1043 Mainland St ☎ 604 979 0700, ⓦ thegreekbyanatoli.com; map p.692. High-energy Greek meze restaurant with a great people-watching patio over Mainland Street. Service is fun and flirty and the food is fresh, bright and expertly presented. Classic Greek salad features feta flown in weekly from the motherland ($14), the lamb *youvetsi* mouthwatering ($17) and the house cocktails feature delights such as a white Negroni with a Campari dust rim ($12). Mon–Wed 11.30am–11pm, Thurs 11.30–midnight, Fri 11.30am–1am, Sat noon–1am, Sun noon–11pm.

GRANVILLE ISLAND

★ **Go Fish** 1505 West 1st Ave ☎ 604 730 5040; map p.692. Waiting in line for fish and chips at this waterfront stand (a short walk west of Granville Island proper) is a Vancouver rite of passage. On a beautiful Saturday, expect an hour wait to get to the counter, and an additional 30min till your food arrives (off-peak times have much shorter delays). The top-notch seafood is enhanced by a spectacular setting: the stand fronts bobbing boats and a skyline view of the city. A two-piece halibut meal will set you back $19.50, while fish "tacones" are $5.50. Tues–Fri 11.30am–6.30pm, Sat & Sun noon–6.30pm.

KITSILANO

★ **Anna Lena** 1809 W 1st Ave ☎ 778 379 4052, ⓦ annalena.ca; map p.692. Contemporary Canadian restaurant serving creative, locally sourced West Coast dishes in a geek-cool setting (look out for *Star Wars* tributes dotted all around, the best being the Storm Trooper campfire on the bar – which also serves up dazzling craft cocktails and a decent beer and wine selection). Dishes like the sockeye salmon tartare ($18) and buttermilk fried chicken ($15) are a dream; seven-course tasting menu available until 8.30pm ($74). Daily 5–9.45pm (bar till midnight).

Fable 1944 W 4th Ave ☎ 604 732 1322, ⓦ fablekitchen.ca; map p.692. Farm to table restaurant headed up by Top Chef Canada runner-up, Trevor Bird. The lunch burger is the stuff of local legend, served up plump and juicy ($15), but in the evening it's all about what's seasonal: charred beets with smoked almond cheese ($16), grilled flat iron 8oz with wild mushrooms ($34). The last Sunday of every month is "Boozy Brunch" with drinks half-price (no reservations for brunch).

Mon–Fri 11.30am–2.30pm & 5.30–10pm, Sat & Sun 10am–2pm & 5–10pm.

The Naam 2724 West 4th Ave, near Stephens ☎ 604 738 7151, ⓦ thenaam.com; map p.692. The oldest and most popular health-food and vegetarian restaurant in the city. Comfortable and friendly ambience with nightly live folk and other music and alfresco eating when the weather's nice. Choose right, and you can fill up for under $10. Daily 24hr (except Christmas Day).

★ **West** 2881 Granville St, near West 13th ☎ 604 738 8938, ⓦ westrestaurant.com; map p.692. *West's* emphasis is on exceptional, locally sourced ingredients, and a menu that changes according to what is seasonally available. Main courses cost from $35, but the steep prices bring consistently high-quality food. A vast wine list and talented bartenders make this a decent option for a pre-dinner drink if you'd like to try *West* on a budget. Mon–Fri 11.30am–2.30pm & 5.30–10.30pm, Sat & Sun 10.30am–2.30pm & 5.30–10.30pm.

RICHMOND

4 Stones Vegetarian Cuisine 7771 Westminster Hwy ☎ 604 278 0852, ⓦ fourstonesvegetarian.com. Casual vegetarian/vegan restaurant with mock meats and plenty of vegetable and tofu dishes. Steaming hot pots are around $15 and dim sum $6–8 (try the Taiwanese Cut Buns with peanut sauce). Reservations recommended (large tables only). Daily 11am–3pm & 5–8.30pm.

Chef Tony 4600 No. 3 Rd ☎ 604 279 0083, ⓦ cheftonycanada.com. This blinged-up Cantonese restaurant with chandeliers and a violet disco-like pillar in the centre of the room, opened in 2014 to a wave of rave reviews. This is modern *dim sum*, made with local sustainable ingredients and using less salt and oil; the results are delicious and surprisingly affordable with prices around the $5–15 mark. Must-haves include minced crab and diced scallop in a pearlike crisp croquette, baked lamb chops and black truffle, pork and shrimp dumplings. Daily 10.30am–3pm & 5–10pm.

Golden Paramount Seafood 8071 Park Rd ☎ 604 278 0873. In an insalubrious strip mall off No. 3 Rd – don't judge this restaurant by its outward appearance. *Dim sum* here is hand-made by the owner, showcasing Hong Kong classics such as crab and pork dumplings, deep-fried wontons and sweet and sour pork, with most items around $5–10. Wed–Mon 10.30am–3pm & 5–10pm.

Hong Kong BBQ Master 4651 No. 3 Rd ☎ 604 272 6568. Tucked away in the parking garage of the Real Canadian Superstore this is a real locals' joint and famed as the best barbecue in the city. Pork is roasted whole leaving the meat juicy and the crackling satisfyingly crisp. There are a few small tables in the store but most people get their order to take away. Get half-fat, half-lean, extra crispy for the best taste. A bargain at just $7.50 for two kinds of BBQ on rice. Thurs–Tues 11am–8pm.

10

10

DRINKING AND NIGHTLIFE

The city has a commendable assortment of **pubs** and **bars**; craft beer drinkers and fans of craft cocktails, in particular, will be well satisfied (South Main – the stretch of Main St between East 2nd and East 33rd avenues – is a hub for the latest craft brewery tasting rooms). **Clubs** are more adventurous than in many other Canadian cities, particularly those on and around Main St and Commercial Drive, and there's a varied and cosmopolitan blend of **live music**. Summer nightlife often takes to the streets, with outdoor bars and (to a certain extent) beaches becoming venues in their own right.

BARS AND BREWERIES

★ **Alibi Room** 157 Alexander St, Gastown ☎604 623 3383, ⓦalibi.ca; map p.692. Hip bar-restaurant filled with beer-loving locals and those who have travelled to pay homage to one of Vancouver's best spots for beer, with over fifty ever-changing craft varieties on tap. An excellent and eclectic food menu is served at surprisingly reasonable prices, and weekend brunch is a popular option. Mon–Thurs 5pm–11.30pm, Fri 5pm–12.30am, Sat 10am–12.30am, Sun 10am–11.30pm.

★ **The Diamond** 6 Powell St #2, Gastown ⓦdi6mond. com; map p.692. Tucked away on the first floor of a heritage building, this charming bar shakes up superlative cocktails for a thirsty crowd of regulars and visiting booze fans. The small space has bygone-era trappings like exposed brick and chandeliers, and windows boast bird's-eye views of the area. Step into the second bar to enjoy Happy Hour with retro favourites and a more high-spirited vibe. Mon–Thurs 5.30pm–1am, Fri & Sat 5.30pm–2am, Sun 5.30pm–midnight.

★ **Dubh Linn Gate** 1601 Main Street ☎604 449 1464, ⓦvancouver.dubhlinngate.com; map p.692. Newly opened Vancouver outpost of the popular Whistler institution that does everything you'd want a pub to do: warm welcome, live music, great drinks deals and tasty above-average pub food, all served up with a smile in a handy location across from the Main Street/Science World Skytrain and central train and bus station. Sun–Thurs 11am–midnight, Fri & Sat 11am–1am.

★ **Granville Island Brewing** 1441 Cartwright St ☎604 687 2739, ⓦgib.ca; map p.692. Virtually the first building you see on Granville Island if you enter by road (rather than ferry) is touted as Canada's first microbrewery (established 1984). This small daytime concern usually has a buzzing tap room and always has a huge variety of small batch beers. Daily tours and tastings (flight of three $9.75+tax). Daily noon–8pm.

★ **Keefer Bar** 135 Keefer St, Chinatown ☎604 688 1961, ⓦthekeeferbar.com; map p.692. Even die-hard beer drinkers have nothing but good words to say about this lively "apothecary" cocktail bar serving "prescriptions" made from house-made bitters, teas, syrups and infusions with herbs drawn from Traditional Chinese Medicine. Daily drinks deals make this an affordable option; try the duck sliders and don't miss burlesque Thursdays (9pm–1am; $10 cover). Mon–Thurs & Sun 5pm–1am, Fri & Sat 5pm–2am.

Narrow Lounge 1898 Main St at 3rd Ave, South Main ☎604 737 5206, ⓦnarrowlounge.com; map p.692. To find this slender hideout locate its facade's red light, which points to a secret staircase. Downstairs, the interior is endearingly quaint, brightened by peach wallpaper, oil paintings and a friendly ambience. There's a great rock soundtrack, nice beer and spirits selection, and delicious pub fare. It's sited 2.5km southeast of Downtown, in Vancouver's hipster neighbourhood. Mon–Thurs & Sun 5pm–1am, Fri & Sat 5pm–2am.

★ **Shameful Tiki Room** 4362 Main St ☎604 253 7141, ⓦshamefultikiroom.com; map p.692. Catch the #3 bus down Main St and get off after 26th St to escape to the South Pacific at this acclaimed Tiki lounge with a thatched bar, pufferfish lights and carvings on every wall. Cocktails are strong (the clue is on the menu which is divided into mild, moderate and yowza!) and painstakingly made with fresh-squeezed juices, house-made syrups and plenty of rum. Order a Mystery Bowl to hear the gong chime and the bar roar your order back at you, or thrill to the thunder and lightning effects of the "Volcano Bowl". Daily 5pm–late.

Six Acres 203 Carrall St, Gastown ☎604 488 0110, ⓦsixacres.ca; map p.692. Smack behind the Gassy Jack statue, this cosy bar (it looks like a refurbished barn) has a top-notch selection of beer, wine and spirits. Menus are bound in children's books, and the excellent bistro fare is surprisingly affordable (everything is under $13). In the upstairs loft you can challenge your friends to one of an array of board games. Mon–Thurs & Sun 11.30pm–11.30pm, Fri & Sat 11.30am–12.30am.

St Augustine's 2360 Commercial Drive ☎604 569 1911, ⓦstaugustinesvancouver.com; map p.692. Named for the patron saint of brewers, this agreeable pub honours its benefactor by stocking more than sixty beers on tap. Check the website before you go to see what's on draught – ingeniously, the percentage of beer left in kegs is shown in real time. A fun place to catch a Canucks game, drinks are complemented by delicious burgers, nachos and fish tacos. *Augustine's* is 7km from Downtown, but conveniently located next to the Broadway SkyTrain station. Mon–Thurs & Sun 11am–1am, Fri & Sat 11am–2am.

Uva Wine and Cocktail Bar 900 Seymour St, Downtown ☎604 632 9560, ⓦuvawinebar.ca; map p.692. Sleek but unpretentious cocktail lounge dressed up with cushy white armchairs and huge windows framing the Downtown parade. Running one of the city's best Happy Hour deals, from 2–6pm, this makes for an excellent spot for a perfectly made cocktail, glass of wine or craft beer paired with buck-a-shuck oysters or generously topped *bruschette* ($3). Daily 11.30am–2am.

LIVE MUSIC AND CLUBS

Biltmore Cabaret 2755 Prince Edward St, Mount Pleasant ☎ 604 676 0541, ⓦ biltmorecabaret.com; map p.692. Much-loved East Van stage that sees plenty of live indie rock and also hosts frequent DJs, Afro-Cuban bands and heavy metal. Lit by chandeliers, this has kitschy decor and red velvet booths lining the walls. Cover $5–15.

Commodore Ballroom 868 Granville St at Smithe St, Downtown ☎ 604 739 4550, ⓦ commodoreballroom.com; map p.692. The *Commodore* is the city's best midsize music venue. There is an adventurous music policy and both international and Canadian bands play.

★ **Fortune Sound Club** 147 East Pender St, Chinatown ☎ 604 569 1758, ⓦ fortunesoundclub.com; map p.692. If you're looking to cut a rug, this is the place: all types of Vancouverites mingle at this Chinatown dance club spinning old-school hip-hop, soul, house and others till the wee hours. Best sound system in the city, and the bouncers and staff are uniquely polite. Expect a $15 cover charge at weekends, and aim to get there before 11pm to avoid a long queue.

Fox Cabaret 2321 Main St, Mount Pleasant ⓦ foxcabaret.com; map p.692. Historic cinema transformed into multi-room live music, comedy and dance club venue.

Music policy ranges from classic Indie nights to Motown, rap and everything in between. Check listings for details but generally Wed–Sun 8pm–1 or 2am.

Guilt & Co. 1 Alexander St (downstairs), Gastown ☎ 604 288 1704, ⓦ guiltandcompany.com; map p.692. Dark and inviting Gastown bar with plenty of board games and nightly live acts – indie rock, jazz, burlesque, belly dancing and more. Daily 7pm–late.

MIA 350 Water St, Gastown ☎ 604 408 4321, ⓦ areyoumia.com; map p.692. Conveniently located in happening Gastown, *MIA* attracts some of the city's top DJs and live performances across two rooms. Decor tends to the dramatic with rich red and purple tones punctuated by flashy LED installations. Dress tends to be stylish.

Railway Stage & Beer Café 579 Dunsmuir St, at Seymour, Downtown ☎ 604 564 1430, ⓦ facebook.com/pg/railwaysbc; map p.692. Housed in the one-time *Railway Club* (which helped launch artists like k.d. Lang and the Barenaked Ladies), the *Railway Stage* continues the live music tradition with added DJs and chilled out tap room. Mon–Thurs & Sun 11am–2am, Fri & Sat 11am–3am.

Roxy 932 Granville St, at Nelson, Downtown ☎ 604 331 7999, ⓦ roxyvan.com; map p.692. Nightly events that include everything from country & western music to local bands to DJs spinning Top 40 hits. Casual and fun place for the college crowd and people in from the suburbs. Nightly 8pm–3am.

10

ENTERTAINMENT

The city hosts a range of **festivals**, from jazz to theatre, and the **performing arts** are as widely available as you'd expect in a city as culturally dynamic as Vancouver. Comprehensive **listings** appear in the *Georgia Straight* (ⓦ straight.com), a free weekly published on Thursday and available across the city. Half-price and last-minute same-day **tickets** are available via "Tickets Tonight" (ⓦ ticketstonight.ca) at the main visitor centre at 200 Burrard St (see page 709).

THEATRES AND MAJOR VENUES

Arts Club Theatre Main box office at 1585 Johnston St ☎ 604 687 1644, ⓦ artsclub.com. A leading light in the city's drama scene, performing at three venues: the Stanley Industrial Alliance Stage, 2750 Granville St, is the company's main venue and runs larger musicals, modern classics and acclaimed productions from around the world; the Granville Island stage offers mainstream drama, comedies and musicals; the next-door Revue Stage shows small-scale revues and cabaret.

Centre in Vancouver for the Performing Arts 777 Homer St ⓦ ticketmaster.ca. One of the city's largest cultural venues, hosting dance troupes and children's theatre. Located Downtown, opposite the central library.

Orpheum Theatre 884 Granville St, at Smithe St ☎ 604 665 3050, ⓦ vancouver.ca/theatres, ⓦ ticketmaster.ca. Vancouver's oldest theatre, this beautifully refurbished venue is headquarters of the Vancouver Symphony Orchestra.

Queen Elizabeth Theatre 630 Hamilton St, at Dunsmuir St ☎ 604 665 3050, ⓦ vancouver.ca/theatres. The main focus for the city's performing arts, this Downtown venue hosts visiting theatre, opera and dance troupes as well as the occasional rock concert.

Theatre Under the Stars (TUTS) Malkin Bowl, Stanley Park ☎ 877 840 0457, ☎ 604 734 1917, ⓦ tuts.ca. Summer productions here are fun and lightweight, but can suffer from being staged in one of Canada's rainiest cities.

CLASSICAL MUSIC

Music-in-the-Morning Vancouver Academy of Music, 1270 Chestnut St, Kitsilano ☎ 604 873 4612, ⓦ musicinthemorning.org. This began modestly in someone's front room 25 years ago; it has now grown past its morning moniker, organizing innovative and respected concerts of old and new music with local and visiting musicians. Coffee is served at 10am and the concerts begin at 10.30am.

10

LGBTQ VANCOUVER

Vancouver is a welcoming city for the LGBTQ community. **Davie Village**, which runs from Burrard St along Davie St to Denman St, is where the highest concentration of long-established gay clubs, pubs and stores are, while there's more of a lesbian scene on **Commercial Drive** ("The Drive"). For information on LGBTQ events, check ⓦ qmunity.ca ⓦ xtra.ca, ⓦ gayvancouver.net and ⓦ superdyke.com. The main draw in Vancouver's LGBTQ calendar is **Pride** (☎ 604 687 0955, ⓦ vancouverpride.ca), which usually takes place over three days during the first long weekend in August.

BARS AND CLUBS

1181 1181 Davie St, West End ☎ 604 787 7130, ⓦ 1181.ca; map p.692. Narrow, stylish bar with cork walls punctuated by slivers of mirror and movie classics projected in the back. Bartenders are easy on the eyes, and the place fills up quickly. Mon–Sun 6pm–3am.

Celebrities 1022 Davie St, West End ☎ 604 681 6180, ⓦ celebritiesnightclub.com; map p.692. High-profile and showcase club, with Davie St's largest dancefloor, the latest lighting and sound systems and a roster of the city's top DJs. Also numerous theme and one-off nights, plus excellent entertainers. Tues–Sat 9pm–3am.

Fountainhead Pub 1025 Davie St, West End ☎ 604 687 2222, ⓦ thefountainheadpub.com; map p.692. A popular and pleasantly buzzing place at the heart of Davie Village with good food, drink and a large, heated patio from which to spy on all the street action. Tends to attract a slightly older, more mellow crowd. Mon–Thurs & Sun 11am–midnight, Fri & Sat till 2am.

Pumpjack Pub 1167 Davie St, West End ☎ 604 685 3417, ⓦ pumpjackpub.com; map p.692. A spacious spot and Vancouver's leather and fetish bar of choice. Arrive early to guarantee a cruise-y window-side seat. There are pool tables and gogo nights. Expect queues at the weekends. Daily 1pm–late.

Vancouver Chamber Choir ☎ 604 738 6822, ⓦ vancouverchamberchoir.com. One of two professional, internationally renowned choirs in the city. They perform at the Orpheum and frequently at Ryerson United Church.

Vancouver Opera ☎ 604 683 0222, ⓦ vancouveropera. ca. Four operas are produced annually at the Queen Elizabeth Theatre Downtown – productions currently enjoy an excellent reputation.

Vancouver Recital Society 601 Cambie St, Downtown ☎ 604 602 0363, ⓦ vanrecital.com. Hosts one of the best and most popular cycles in the city: the main Vancouver Playhouse recitals (Oct–April). Catches up-and-coming performers plus a few major international names each year.

Vancouver Symphony Orchestra 601 Smithe St ☎ 604 876 3434, ⓦ vancouversymphony.ca. Presents most concerts at the Orpheum Theatre or Chan Centre for the Performing Arts on Crescent Rd off Northwest Drive, but also sometimes gives free recitals in the summer at beaches and parks, culminating in a concert on the summit of Whistler Mountain.

DANCE

Ballet British Columbia Sixth Floor, 677 Davie St, Yaletown ☎ 604 732 5003, ⓦ balletbc.com. The province's top company performs – along with visiting troupes – at the Queen Elizabeth Theatre.

Scotiabank Dance Centre 677 Davie St ☎ 604 606 6400, ⓦ thedancecentre.ca. This is a major source of information on dance in Vancouver and beyond, and provides studio and rehearsal space for around thirty companies; it's open to the public for workshops, classes, exhibitions and other events. Contact it for details on the primo Dancing on the Edge Festival (ⓦ dancingontheedge. org).

CINEMA

Cineplex Odeon 88 West Pender St, at Abbott, Gastown ☎ 604 806 0799, ⓦ cineplex.com. Just two blocks south of the heart of Gastown, this multi-screen in the International Village complex is the most modern of the city centre's first-run cinemas, with big screens, underground parking (free) and good seating.

The Cinémathèque 1131 Howe St, near Helmcken, Yaletown ☎ 604 688 8202, ⓦ thecinematheque. ca. Shows a good range of art-house, overseas and experimental films; the best non-mainstream cinema in the city. Any film buff will find something tempting here.

Rio Theatre 1660 E Broadway, East Vancouver ☎ 604 879 3456, ⓦ riotheatre.ca. Independent single-screen multidisciplinary art house with regular burlesque nights, first-run screenings, cult-classic movie marathons and fantasy film nights.

Scotiabank Theatre 900 Burrard St, Downtown ☎ 604 630 1407, ⓦ cineplex.com. Multiplex in the heart of the city with a range of screen sizes, excellent sound system and comfy seating.

SHOPPING

Most of Vancouver's smartest clothing stores and other **shops** – and several upmarket malls (notably the Pacific Centre) – are found on or around Burrard St and the central stretch of Robson St. Gastown has the city's best **clothing** boutiques, many located in beautiful heritage buildings. Yaletown boasts many **design** and **homeware** stores, along with plenty of interesting one-off shops. Edgier galleries, vintage and fashion stores are found on East Vancouver's Main St and Commercial Drive. Vancouver has launched two international brands of **footwear**, John Fluevog (see below), and Native Shoes (see below), and it was here in Kits that international yoga and sportswear brand Lululemon started out (their flagship store is 970 Robson Street).

Aberdeen Centre 4151 Hazelbridge Way, Richmond ⓦ aberdeencentre.com; map p.692. There's everything from high-tech toilet to aromatic herbal teas, beautiful chinaware and the budget "dollar store" chain, Daiso (ⓦ daisocanada.com) in this all-Asian mall right next to Aberdeen SkyTrain station in Richmond. Mon–Wed & Sun 11pm–7pm, Thurs–Sat 11am–9pm.

Hill's Native Art 165 Water St, Gastown ☎ 604 685 4249, ⓦ hills.ca; map p.692. North America's largest Northwest coastal art gallery takes in three floors of First Nations art from beautiful moccasins and Cowichan hand-knit jumpers to intricate masks, jewellery, totems and bentwood boxes. Daily 9am–9pm.

John Fluevog 65 Water St, Gastown, also 837 Granville St, Downtown ☎ 604 688 6228, ⓦ fluevog.com;

map p.692. Style maven John Fluevog has designed marvellously unconventional boots and heels for over thirty years and his flagship store is in Gastown. Mon–Wed & Sat 10am–7pm, Thurs & Fri till 8pm, Sun noon–6pm.

Macleod's Books 455 W Pender St, Gastown ☎ 604 681 7645; map p.692. A pleasingly chaotic floor-to-ceiling treasure trove of used and rare books with an incredibly knowledgeable staff who somehow manage to keep track of their vast inventory. Mon–Sat 10am–6pm, Sun 11am–6pm.

Mountain Equipment Co-op 130 West Broadway, SoMa ☎ 604 872 7858, ⓦ mec.ca; map p.692. Vancouver is an excellent place to shop for outdoor gear, most notably at this landmark shop, in business since 1971. You'll need to join the co-op at the checkout to shop here ($5). Mon–Wed 10am–7pm, Thurs & Fri till 9pm, Sat 9am–6pm, Sun 10am–5pm.

Native Shoes 14 Water St, Gastown ☎ 604 800 8630, ⓦ nativeshoes.com; map p.692. Fun, lightweight and certified vegan, Native's sandals, boots and shoes are stocked all over the city, but they opened their own physical store in 2017, which has a living and breathing moss wall. Daily 11am–7pm.

T&T Supermarket 179 Keefer place, Chinatown ☎ 604 899 8836, ⓦ tnt-supermarket.com; map p.692. Fascinating Asian supermarket with an irresistible selection of quirky snacks from durian-flavoured sweet wafers to Matcha green tea Kit Kats. Home to one of the

---

VANCOUVER'S MAJOR FESTIVALS

Dine Out Vancouver From mid-Jan to early Feb ⓦ dineoutvancouver.com. Canada's largest food and drink festival, with hundreds of restaurants across the city offering three course prix-fixe menus at three price points. Special culinary events also take place throughout the festival, such as guest chef lectures, street food markets and food photography urban safaris.

Vancouver International Wine Festival Mid-Feb to early March ☎ 604 873 3311, ⓦ vanwinefest.ca. One of Canada's best wine festivals with nine days of seminars, special winery dinners, galas and a grand tasting room with hundreds of wines on offer.

Bard on the Beach Shakespeare Festival June–Sept ☎ 604 739 0559, ☎ 877 739 0559, ⓦ bardonthebeach.org. Western Canada's largest not-for-profit Shakespeare festival offers plays and special events throughout the season in Vanier Park; the harbour and distant mountains help set the scene.

International Jazz Festival Late June to early July ☎ 604 872 5200, ⓦ coastaljazz.ca. Puts on 300 shows across the region (half of which are free), with names like The Avett Brothers and Jill Barber.

Vancouver International Folk Music Festival mid-July ☎ 604 602 9798, ⓦ thefestival.bc.ca. Three days of folk, food and festivities at Jericho Beach park.

The Fair at the PNE Late Aug to early Sept; gate passes from $16 ⓦ pne.ca. A 100-year-old Vancouver end-of-summer tradition with free concerts from crowd-pleasing artists such as the Beach Boys and Pointer Sisters, a host of entertaining shows and a heady mix of fairground rides and deep-fried foods.

Vancouver International Film Festival Late Sept to mid-Oct ☎ 604 685 0260, ⓦ viff.org. Many of the city's art-house cinemas join forces to host the annual showcase for more than 150 films.

10

city's best pan-Asian bakeries specializing in sticky buns and Japanese-style cakes. If you're on a budget, it's worth visiting on a Saturday to score free samples of everything

from fresh-cooked dumplings to spicy fish balls. Daily 8.30am–10pm.

DIRECTORY

Car rental Alamo, 180 West Georgia St (☎604 683 4357, ⓦalamo.ca); Avis, 757 Hornby St (☎604 606 2868, ⓦavis.ca); Budget, 416 West Georgia St (☎604 668 7000, ☎800 268 8900, ⓦbudget.ca); Hertz, 1270 Granville St (☎604 606 4711, ⓦhertz.com); Lo-Cost, 1835 Marine Drive, North Vancouver (☎604 986 1266, ⓦlocostrental.com).

Consulates Australia: Suite 2050, 1075 West Georgia St ☎604 694 6160; Germany: Suite 704, World Trade Centre, 999 Canada Place ☎604 684 8377; New Zealand: 1050 W Pender St ☎604 684 7388; Republic of Ireland: Suite 210, 837 Beatty St ☎604 683 9233; United Kingdom: Suite 800, 1111 Melville St ☎604 683 4421; United States: 1095 West Pender St ☎604 685 4311.

Currency exchange Vancouver Bullion & Currency Exchange, 800 West Pender St (☎604 685 1008, ⓦvbce.ca).

Directory enquiries ☎411.

Emergency services ☎911.

Hospitals St Paul's Hospital, 1081 Burrard St (☎604 682 2344); Vancouver General Hospital, 855 West 12th Ave (☎604 875 4111) or BC Children's Hospital, 4480 Oak St (☎604 875 2345). In North Van, Lions Gate Hospital, 231 East 15th St (☎604 988 3131).

Internet Free terminal use and wi-fi at the Vancouver Central Library, 350 West Georgia St (☎604 331 3600, ⓦvpl.ca); or from coffee shops and cafés (see page 711); Robson Internet Place, 1463 Robson St, at Nicola (☎604 558 3033), has terminals for $3/4hr.

Laundry Laundry Valet, 1238 Davie St (☎604 568 2020).

Pharmacies Shopper's Drug Mart, 1125 Davie St (☎604 669 2424, ⓦshoppersdrugmart.ca), is open 24hr and has numerous other outlets with long hours around town. London Drugs, 1650 Davie St (☎604 669 2884, ⓦlondondrugs.com), is open daily until 10pm.

Police Non-emergency 24hr (☎604 717 3321, ⓦvancouver.ca/police). Headquarters are located at 2120 Cambie St (open daily 8am–5pm). RCMP (☎604 264 3111, ⓦrcmp.ca).

Post office Main office at 349 West Georgia St (Mon–Fri 9am–5.30pm; ☎800 267 1177, ⓦcanadapost.ca). Outlets are also in many 7-Eleven and Shopper's Drug Mart stores.

The Sunshine Coast

A mild-weathered stretch of sandy beaches, rugged headlands and peaceful inlets running northwest of Vancouver, the **Sunshine Coast** offers some of western Canada's best diving, boating and fishing. A popular spot for soft adventure and hiking, the Sunshine Coast Trail offers Canada's longest hut-to-hut hike. The only tract of accessible coastline on mainland British Columbia, it's a possible springboard to Vancouver Island: ferries depart from Powell River, the coast's largest town, to Comox (on the Island). Most people on short trips make the run to Powell River and then turn back for Vancouver – there is no alternative route back to the city unless you fly, but there's plenty to see and do and the coastal journey offers beautiful scenery both ways. Although Hwy-101 ends in Lund, it's no end of the road, as it's a jumping-off point to access renowned Marine Park, Desolation Sound and Savary Island.

If you are just coming out from Vancouver for the day, note that you will need to make **ferry crossings** en route: the first is from Horseshoe Bay, from there, it's a short drive to Gibsons where you pick up Hwy-101 for the 79km run along the coast to Earl's Cove, and the beautiful (and slightly longer) crossing to Saltery Bay, where the boat provides views of some fine maritime landscapes. The road continues 35km to Powell River before ending 23km later at the picturesque village of Lund.

Gibsons

Selected in 2009 as the World's Most Liveable Community, the nicest area in **GIBSONS** is around the busy marina and public wharf – where you'll find jaw-dropping views of the coastal mountains. Clustered on Howe Sound and spread widely over a wooded hillside, the humble town has a claim to fame: from 1972 to 1990, it set the stage for *The Beachcombers*, one of Canada's most popular television shows. Grab lunch at **Molly's Reach** restaurant (647 School Rd; ☏604 886 9710, ⊕mollysreach.ca), a former set for the series (used as the home of character Molly Carmody).

Roberts Creek

Reached by turning off Hwy-101 (down Roberts Creek Rd; 12km west of Gibsons), the small, bohemian community of **ROBERTS CREEK**, known as the Gumboot Capital of the World, is an enjoyable place to while away an afternoon. Here you'll find a music store, a yoga studio, a handful of art galleries and a pier jutting into the Strait of Georgia.

10

Sechelt

With its attractive little commercial centre, **SECHELT** (12km west of Roberts Creek) has an array of galleries and shops that are boosted by exceptional surroundings. The village is circumscribed by coastal rainforest and a halcyon inlet, which means there's abundant scope for outdoor adventures – especially at Skookumchuck Narrows, a twice-daily natural wonder with a difference in water level that sometimes exceeds 9ft. Some 200 billion gallons of water flow through here and create the fast-moving **Sechelt Rapids**, a popular draw for extreme kayakers and surfers. Also worth seeing are the intricately carved totem poles of the Shíshálh nation.

Saltery Bay Provincial Park

Free • ☏ 800 689 9025, ⊕ env.gov.bc.ca/bcparks, ⊕ discovercamping.ca
From Saltery Bay (73km northwest by road and ferry from Sechelt), it's a couple of kilometres up the road to the most rewarding of all the provincial parks in this region, **Saltery Bay Provincial Park**. Everything here is discreetly hidden in the trees between the road and the coast, and the campsite ($16) – beautifully situated – is connected by short trails to a couple of swimming beaches.

Powell River

Established in 1910, **POWELL RIVER** was once the world's largest paper producer. The town has preserved four hundred of its early twentieth-century buildings, garnering it a National Historic District designation (one of just seven nationwide). Prominent among these historic properties is the buttercup-coloured, century-old **Patricia Theatre** (☏604 483 9345, ⊕patriciatheatre.com), which dates to 1913. Canada's longest-running cinema, this has had only four owners over the course of its lifetime. The interior sports its 1928 velvet drapes, and an organist frequently plays before films (check the website for show times). Note that if you're catching a ferry to Comox on Vancouver Island (4 daily; 75min), you might not see the historic part of the town, as the terminal is 2km to the east.

Lund

At the very northern end of Hwy-101 – which starts in Puerto Montt, Chile, making it one of the western hemisphere's longest continuous routes – lies the hamlet of **LUND**, 28km up the coast from Powell River. This little community is blessed with a breathtaking harbour and an edge-of-the-earth feel. A wooden boardwalk traverses the village, which has a tempting bakery and a handful of art galleries. It will only take you a few minutes to walk the length of Lund, which sees few visitors, its lonesome tranquillity only adding to its charm.

Desolation Sound Marine Provincial Park

Free, backcountry camping permit $5 • ⓦ env.gov.bc.ca/bcparks

Pristine and poetically named, **Desolation Sound Marine Provincial Park**, about 10km north of Lund, offers some of Canada's best boating and scuba diving, plus fishing, canoeing and kayaking. Oceanographer Jacques Cousteau called the Strait of Georgia "the best temperate water diving in the world, second only to the Red Sea", and touring the sound by boat you'll come across an eye-opening array of colourful sea stars, sea cucumbers and bull kelp, all in open water fringed by green mountains. There's no road access to the park, but a number of local outfitters run tours to it and can rent all the equipment you could possibly need.

ARRIVAL AND GETTING AROUND

By bus You can reach the ferry terminal at Horseshoe Bay in West Vancouver from the city by taking bus #250 or the #257 express westbound from points on West Georgia St Downtown. Take the crossing as a foot passenger and pick up the Sunshine Coast connector, which operates between Langdale Ferry Terminal and Powell River (ⓦ sunshinecoastconnector.ca).

By ferry There are regular sailings from Horseshoe Bay (in West Vancouver) to Langdale (near Gibsons) year-round

THE SUNSHINE COAST

(return tickets $13.70; cars $45.90; bikes $2). BC Ferries also head from Powell River to Comox on Vancouver Island and between Saltery Bay and Earl's Cove (ⓣ 250 386 3431, ⓣ 888 223 3779, ⓦ bcferries.com).

Destinations Horseshoe Bay–Bowen Island (15 round-trips daily; 20min); Horseshoe Bay–Langdale (8 round-trips daily; 40min); Powell River–Comox (4 daily; 75min); Sechelt–Powell River (8–9 round-trips daily; 50min).

INFORMATION

Gibsons visitor centre For more on the town and details of local trails, beaches and swimming areas, visit the information centre at 417 Marine Drive (July & Aug daily 9am–5pm; rest of year Wed–Sat 10am–4pm; ⓣ 604 886 2374, ⓣ 866 222 3806, ⓦ gibsonschamber.com).

Powell River visitor centre The information centre (mid-May to mid-Sept daily 9am–6pm; rest of year Mon–Sat 9am–5pm; ⓣ 604 485 4701, ⓦ powellriver.info) at 4760 Joyce Ave, has maps showing the many trails leading inland from the coast hereabouts; they can also advise on

boat trips on Powell Lake, immediately inland, and tours to Desolation Sound farther up the coast.

Sechelt visitor centre Find out more about attractions and a range of outdoor activities on land and sea at 5790 Teredo St (July & Aug daily 9am–5pm; June & Sept Mon–Sat 9am–5pm; rest of year Mon–Fri 10am–4pm, Sun 10am–2pm; ⓣ 604 885 1036, ⓣ 877 885 1036, ⓦ secheltvisitotrcentre.com).

Useful website ⓦ sunshinecoastcanada.com publishes a blog and loads of practical information.

ACTIVITIES

Alpha Adventures ⓣ 604 885 8838, ⓦ outdoor adventurestore.ca. If you'd like to get out on the water (or into the woods), contact this great local outfit in Sechelt that'll set you up for stand-up paddling, kayaking and canoeing; in winter, they run skiing and snowshoeing

groups. They have another location in Pender Harbour (ⓣ 604 741 1007; late June to early Sept only).

Powell River Sea Kayak ⓣ 866 617 4444, ⓦ bcsea kayak.com. An excellent kayaking and snorkelling operation; a 7hr combo tour costs $159.

ACCOMMODATION

★ **Deer Fern Bed and Breakfast** 120 Swallow Rd, 4km west of Gibsons ⓣ 604 886 6592, ⓣ 888 886 6511, ⓦ deerfern.com. Exceedingly comfortable, one-room B&B with magnificent views of the Strait of Georgia. Meander down the hill to beachcomb, then head back to relax on your tranquil deck, surrounded by woodlands and gardens. Amenities include heated bathroom floors, original art and Egyptian linens. The home-made breakfast (served in your suite) is exceptional. **$150**

Desolation Sound Resort 2694 Dawson Rd, 5km east of Lund ⓣ 604 483 3592, ⓣ 800 399 3592, ⓦ desolationresort. com. Ten hand-crafted wood chalets (four with hot tubs)

facing serene Desolation Sound. Accommodation is cosy and comes with full kitchens, barbecue grills and – best of all – access to the resort's oyster bed (guests are permitted five oysters a day). Note that only two units have TVs, and mobile phone service is spotty. Pet-friendly. **$169**

Sechelt Inlet Bed and Breakfast 5870 Skookumchuck Rd, Sechelt ⓣ 604 740 0776, ⓣ 877 740 0776, ⓦ secheltinletbandb.com. Three colourful suites decorated with lush oil paintings that depict the surrounding landscape. There are private decks (with ocean views), memorable breakfasts and an outdoor hot tub. The kindly innkeepers are consummate hosts. **$169**

Stillwater Bed and Breakfast 12417 Scotch Fir Point Rd, Powell River ☎604 487 2191, ⓦstillwater beachhousebnb.ca. You get the whole house to yourself at this designer cottage with incredible views and the waters of Frolander Bay lapping just outside. Guests glimpse sea lions and seals from the deck; inside you'll find a wood-burning fireplace and stylish decor. An eco-friendly property, *Stillwater* has solar roof panels and a composting toilet. $220

Up the Creek Backpacker's B&B 1261 Robert's Creek Rd, Robert's Creek ☎604 885 0384, ☎877 885 8100, ⓦupthecreek.ca. Friendly, well-tended hostel with hand-crafted dorm beds, spacious common areas and free bike use. Tent sites available if full (for travellers arriving by bike or bus only). Tent site per person $15; tent rental/sleeping bag per person $28; dorms $28; doubles $84

Willingdon Beach Municipal Campground 4845 Marine Ave, Powell River ☎604 485 2242, ⓦwillingdonbeach.ca. The most central of several campsites is the 81-site *Willingdon Beach*, on the seafront with laundry facilities, soft-sand beach and fishing pier. Sites $21; RVs $34.50

10

EATING

Costa del Sol 4578 Marine Ave, Powell River ☎604 414 7463. A huge wisteria plant welcomes guests to this compact and charming Latin restaurant with Baja style fish or prawn tacos (two for $14.75) and crunchy yam tacos (three singles $12.75). They're famed for their Key lime pie ($5). Wed–Mon 11.30am–late.

Gumboot Café 1053 Roberts Creek Rd, Roberts Creek ⓦthegumbootcafe.com, ☎604 885 4218. A healthy establishment and local institution that'll set you up right for a day of kayaking on the Strait of Georgia. Fresh home-cooking, with plenty of vegetarian and vegan options, this licensed café serves breakfast all day (try the breakfast burrito $12) and pizza by the slice and sandwiches/soup at lunchtime ($5–7). You'll also find sensational desserts and good coffee. Mon–Fri 7am–5pm, Sat & Sun 8am–5pm.

Lighthouse Pub 5764 Wharf Rd, Sechelt ☎604 885 9494, ⓦlighthousepub.ca. Boisterous pub with a big waterfront patio that's well-sited for watching the local seaplanes land and take off. Juicy burgers (from $16), mussels in cream sauce ($18.95) and seafood chowder ($7.95). Mon–Sat 10am–1am, Sun 10am–midnight.

SweetWater Bistro 280 Gower Pt Rd (top floor), Lower Gibsons ☎604 886 2024. Outstanding bistro with harbour views, deep blue walls and dark wood accents. Its excellent fare comes at a price – seared Atlantic scallops ($27), lamb sirloin with zucchini mint ($28) – but you're paying for some of the coast's best cooking. Tues–Sat 5.30pm–late.

The Sea to Sky Highway

One of the world's most picturesque drives, the **Sea to Sky Highway**, as Hwy-99 is rather lyrically known, takes you from Vancouver to Whistler along a mostly two-lane highway which scores in its coastal stretches, where the road clings perilously to an almost sheer cliff and mountains come dramatically into view on both sides of Howe Sound.

Throughout winter the section between Pemberton and Lillooet, the Duffy Lake Road, is nail-biting and often impassable, though the drive is a stunner, with wonderful views of lakes and glaciers.

GETTING AROUND AND TOURS

By bus Regular buses (see page 706) connect Vancouver and Whistler (Whistler Rides continues on to Pemberton), which you can easily manage as a day-trip.

Landsea Tours and Adventures ☎604 255 7272, ⓦvancouvertours.com. Offers an excellent all-day trip from Vancouver, which takes in the Britannia Mine Museum, Shannon Falls and the Gondola for $125.

Britannia Beach and around

Road and rail lines meet at tiny **BRITANNIA BEACH**, 53km from Vancouver, whose **Britannia Mine Museum** (Daily 9.30am–5pm tours Mon–Fri 3pm, Sat, Sun & hols 11am, 1pm & 3pm; $29.95, ages 5–12 $18.95; ☎800 896 4044, ⓦbritanniaminemuseum.ca) is the first reason to take time out from admiring the views. Centring on what was once one of the largest producers of copper in the British Empire – 56 million tonnes of ore were extracted here before the mine closed in 1974 – the museum is housed in a huge, twenty-storey building on the hillside and is chock-full of hands-on displays, original working machinery, a 235-tonne monster mine truck and archive photographs. You can also take guided underground tours (hourly) on small electric trains around about 350m of the mine's galleries. And if parts of the complex look familiar, it's because the mine has been used as a location in *The X-Files* and numerous other films and TV programmes.

Shannon Falls Provincial Park

Continuing north from Britannia Beach, you pass several small coastal reserves, the most striking of which is **Shannon Falls Provincial Park**, 7km from Britannia Beach, signed right off the road and worth a stop for its spectacular 335m **waterfall**, the third largest in BC. It's only five minutes' stroll to the viewing area at the base, but if you've got the time, there's a challenging 7km hike to Upper Shannon Falls (4–6hr round-trip; see ⓦ exploresquamish.com).

Squamish and around

The sea views and coastal drama end 11km beyond Britannia Beach at **SQUAMISH**, beautifully framed by snow-capped mountains, and known for its excellent climbing, windsurfing, biking, paddling and hiking – and for the displaced hippies and hipsters moving here from the big city. Sleepy Squamish (which can be a ghost town in the off season) is famed for the vast granite rock overshadowing it, "**The Stawamus Chief**", which looms into view to the east just beyond Shannon Falls. The Chief is the world's second-biggest free-standing rock (after Gibraltar). The town rates as one of Canada's top – if not *the* top – spot for **rock climbing**. Around 200,000 climbers from around the world come here annually, swarming to more than four hundred routes covering the 700m monolith: the University Wall and its culmination, the Dance Platform, is rated Canada's toughest climb.

The rock is sacred to the local Squamish Nation, whose ancient tribal name – which means "Mother of the wind" – gives a clue as to the town's second big activity: **windsurfing**. There are strong, consistent winds, but the water is cold, so a wet suit is a good idea (there are rental outlets around town). The area is run by the Squamish Windsports Society (see page 725) and is 3km from town.

Rounding out Squamish's outdoor activities is the tremendous **mountain-biking** terrain – there are over a hundred trails in the area ranging from gnarly single-track routes to readily accessible deactivated forestry roads. The best areas are the Valley Cliff Trails (stream-bed, single-track and woodland trails); Mamquam Forest Service roads (active logging roads with fine views of the Mamquam Glacier); the Cat Lake and Brohm Lake trails; and the Alice Lake trails, which include an abandoned railway for an easy ride.

Sea to Sky Gondola

2km south of Squamish on Hwy-99 • Daily: Jan to mid-May and Dec 10am–5pm, last ride down 6pm; mid-May to Oct 10am–4pm, last ride down 5pm; closed Nov (see website for exact dates) • $43.95 (online discount if purchased 24hr in advance) • ☎ 604 892 2550, ⓦ seatoskygondola.com

The fortunes of Squamish changed when the Sea to Sky Gondola launched in 2014. This superb attraction has opened up the scenic hiking trails around the alpine areas of Mount Habrich, Sky Pilot Mountain and Goat Ridge through numerous backcountry trails which were previously only accessible to iron-thighed individuals. The ten-minute gondola lifts you 885m above the jaw-clangingly beautiful Howe Sound up to a 100m suspension bridge, a rather good restaurant and café, plus a couple of easy all-level trails. Don't miss the Spirit Trail loop, which tells the story of the Squamish Nation and their relationship to the land through interpretive panels.

Brackendale

The area has one more unexpected treat: the Squamish River, and the tiny hamlet of **BRACKENDALE** in particular (10km north of Squamish on Hwy-99), is the world's best place to see **bald eagles**. Around three thousand congregate here in winter (mid-Nov to mid-Feb; Dec is the peak month), attracted by the migrating salmon. Although they can be spotted year-round, the coldest months yield the highest sightings. The best places to see them are the Eagle Run just south of the centre of Brackendale, and on the river in the Brackendale Eagles Provincial Park (ⓦ env.gov.bc.ca/bcparks).

INFORMATION AND GETTING AROUND   SQUAMISH AND AROUND

Visitor information centre On the other side of Hwy-99 from Cleveland Ave in Squamish, the Squamish Adventure Centre houses the visitor centre (ⓣ 604 815 4994, ⓣ 866 333 2010, ⓦ tourismsquamish.com), a café and shop. Mid-

May to Aug 8am–6pm, Sept to mid-May 8.30am–4.30pm.
By bus Public transport can be patchy here; check ⓦ bctransit.com for routes.

ACTIVITIES

Equipment rental Vertical Reality Sports Centre at 37835 2nd Ave (ⓣ 604 892 8248) has climbing shoes and mountain bikes. Tantalus (ⓣ 604 898 2588, ⓦ tantalusbikeshop.com), in the Garibaldi Village shopping centre at 40194 Glenalder Place, or Corsa Cycles (ⓣ 604 892 3331, ⓣ 855 892 2453, ⓦ corsacycles.com) at 38192 Cleveland Ave, also have mountain bikes for about $80/day.
Squamish Adventure A recommended local operator (ⓣ 866 923 8747, ⓦ squamishadventure.com) who'll

organize everything from horseriding to lessons in stand-up paddleboarding as well as rock climbing and mountain biking. **Squamish Windsports Society** (ⓦ squamishwindsports. com). Local non-profit outfit that hosts windsurfers and kite sailors on the southern tip of the Squamish River where it meets Howe Sound. On-site toilets and change rooms, retrieval sea-doo service and first aid. Non-members need to pay $20/day to launch at the spit (between mid-May and mid-Sept).

ACCOMMODATION

Howe Sound Inn 37801 Cleveland Ave ⓣ 604 892 2603, ⓦ howesoundinn.com. Stay at the top of town in one of the cosy rooms above the popular brewpub. Rooms look out over either the Chief or the Tantalus mountain range. Guests have access to the sauna and can take the daily brewery tour at 1pm. $89
Sunwolf 70002 Squamish Valley Rd, Brackendale ⓣ 604

898 1537, ⓣ 877 806 8046, ⓦ sunwolf.net. Ten three-person cabins on the shore of the Cheakamus River, boasting hardwood floors, gas fireplaces and en-suite shower rooms; many also have kitchenettes. Larger parties can book the luxurious Fisherman's Cottage. To see bald eagles from a raft costs $100/person, including lunch. *Sunwolf* also runs an excellent café, *Fergie's*. $100

EATING AND DRINKING

Howe Sound Brewing 37801 Cleveland Ave ⓣ 604 892 2603, ⓦ howesound.com. Central micro-brewery that pulls great pints in a cavernous lodge with pool table, big stone fireplace and spacious patio. The kitchen serves pub fare till 10pm, and there's takeaway beer for sale. Daily 11am–11pm.
Zephyr Café 38084 Cleveland Ave ⓣ 604 567 4568,

ⓦ zephyrcafe.ca. At the centre of town, this popular café serves up nutritious fare that will put you in good stead for a hike or a climb. Roaring fire when it's cold outside and sofas to get cosy. Organic brown rice bowls ($11), home-made veggie burgers ($15) and jazzy smoothies, including one made with ginger and spinach ($8). Free wi-fi, and a nice place to get a feel for the town. Daily 6.30am–7pm.

Garibaldi Provincial Park

Free • ⓦ env.gov.bc.ca/bcparks • For more information, including good advice on trails, visit ⓦ exploresquamish.com or get the dedicated *BC Parks* pamphlet from visitor centres

About 5km north of Squamish the road enters the classic river, mountain and forest country of the BC Interior, and the journey up to Whistler is a joy, with only the march of electricity pylons to take the edge off an idyllic drive. **Garibaldi Provincial Park** is a huge and unspoilt area that combines all the usual breathtaking ingredients of lakes, rivers, forests, glaciers and the peaks of the Coast Mountains (Wedge Mountain, at 2891m, is the park's highest point). Five rough roads access the park from points along Hwy-99 between Squamish and Whistler. There is very basic camping at Rampart Ponds and Elfin Lakes campgrounds, and at Elfin Lakes Shelter which has room for 33 people (reservations required; $15), but otherwise the only accommodation close to the park is at Whistler.

There are five main areas with trails, of which the **Black Tusk/Garibaldi Lake** region is the most popular and probably most beautiful, thanks to its high-mountain views. Outside these small, defined areas, the park is untrammelled wilderness (black bears are common).

Whistler

10

Located 56km beyond Squamish and 125km from Vancouver, **WHISTLER** is Canada's finest four-season resort, and frequently ranks as one of the world's top-five winter ski destinations. Skiing and snowboarding are the main activities, but all sorts of other winter sports are possible and in summer the lifts keep running to provide supreme mountain biking, highline hiking and other outdoor activities (as well as North America's best summer skiing). It is a busy place – over two million lift tickets are sold here every winter; fortunately, it also has one of the continent's largest ski areas, so the crowds are spread thinly over the resort's more than 50km of **trails** and 37 lifts.

The resort consists of two adjacent but separate mountains – **Whistler** (2182m) and **Blackcomb** (2284m) – each with their own extensive lift and chair systems (but a joint ticket scheme). The mountains can be accessed from a total of three bases, including lift systems to both mountains from the resort's heart, the purpose-built pedestrianized **Whistler Village**, the tight-clustered focus of many hotels, shops, restaurants and après-ski activity. Around this core are two other "village" complexes, **Upper Village** (for the gondola to Blackcomb Mountain), about a kilometre to the northeast, and Village North, about 700m to the north. Around 6km to the south of Whistler Village is **Whistler Creekside**, also with a gondola and lift base.

Whistler Village

The key to the resort is **WHISTLER VILLAGE**, a buzzing conglomeration of bars, boutiques, hotels, award-winning restaurants and mountain-gear shops. It's a far cry from February 1966 when what was then known as London Mountain (local population 25) first started skiing operations. Apparently the International Olympics Committee had let drop in the early 1960s that the region satisfied all the criteria for a successful Winter Olympic bid, and development began soon after. Over the years, Whistler would make no fewer than three failed bids, losing out to Sapporo in 1972, Innsbruck in 1976 and Lake Placid in 1980. But the fourth time was lucky, and Whistler secured the lion's share of the 2010 winter games.

The brouhaha that accompanied the awarding of the 2010 games led to a fury of investment, building and upgrading, especially in Whistler Village, which until the late 1970s had been the site of the community's rubbish tip. Whistler's name is said to derive either from the distinctive shriek of the marmot, or the sound of the wind whistling through Singing Pass up in the mountains. Whatever its origins, almost forty years' worth of investments, plus the money associated with the Olympics, have paid off; the resort's services, lifts and general overall polish are almost faultless. Winter-sports enthusiasts can argue long and late over the relative merits of **Whistler Mountain** and its neighbour, Blackcomb Mountain (see page 729), both accessed from lifts at Whistler Village. Both are great mountains, and both offer world-class skiing and boarding; if this makes the slopes sound big-scale and intimidating, they're not, and if you become lost, confused or just want advice, you can consult any of eighty or so green-jacketed "Mountain Hosts".

Squamish Lil'Wat Cultural Centre

4584 Blackcomb Way • Tues–Sun 10am–5pm • $18 • ☎ 604 964 0990, ⓦ slcc.ca

The superb **Squamish Lil'Wat Cultural Centre** which gives an insight into the history and culture of the Squamish and Lil'Wat First Nations. Explore with a First Nations ambassador on a tour which includes a welcome song, excellent short film and cedar-

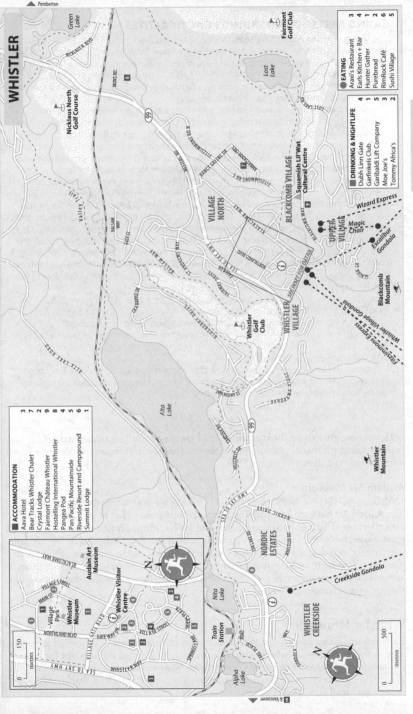

WHISTLER

10

● EATING	
Araxi's Restaurant	3
Earls Kitchen + Bar	4
Hunter Gather	1
Purebread	6
RimRock Café	5

■ DRINKING & NIGHTLIFE	
Dubh Linn Gate	4
Garfinkels Club	1
Garibaldi Lift Company	5
Moe Joe's	3
Tommy Africa's	2

■ ACCOMMODATION	
Aava Hotel	3
Bear Tracks Whistler Chalet	7
Crystal Lodge	2
Fairmont Chateau Whistler	9
Hostelling International Whistler	8
Pangea Pod	4
Pan Pacific Mountainside	5
Riverside Resort and Campground	6
Summit Lodge	1

10

SKIING AND SNOWBOARDING PRACTICALITIES

The **skiing and snowboarding season** for Whistler and Blackcomb is one of the longest in North America, often running for almost two hundred days from November to early June. The yearly average snowfall is an impressive 11.64m, while the average winter alpine temperature rarely falls below -5°C (compare this with a chillier -12°C in Banff). Whistler sits in an area of temperate rainforest, and rain can certainly be a problem at lower altitudes; but what falls as rain in the Village is often falling as snow higher up.

The mountains' winter ski season runs from mid-November to late May (Whistler Mountain closes at the end of May and Blackcomb closes end April). Lifts open at 8.30am and close at 3pm until late January (4pm Jan to late May). The family-friendly Tube Park on Blackcomb is open Mon–Fri 11am–6pm and 10am–6pm at weekends and holidays from mid-Dec to early April (times are weather dependent). Between mid-June and mid-July, Blackcomb Mountain opens for skiing and snowboarding on Horstman Glacier (advanced to expert skiers only; daily 11am–3pm).

Lift tickets give you full use of both Whistler and Blackcomb mountains, and it will take days for even the most advanced skier or snowboarder to cover all the terrain. A good plan is to pick one mountain and stick to it for the day, or use the PEAK 2 PEAK, a $50-million, 4.4km gondola suspended 436m above the valley floor that links the high alpine terrain mountains. Lift tickets include access to PEAK 2 PEAK and are available from the lift base in Whistler Village, the Upper Village on Blackcomb or at Creekside. Purchase tickets online ahead of time for the best rates and check lift times and other information at ⓦwhistlerblackcomb.com or book by phone on ☏800 744 0449 toll free in North America or ☏604 967 8950 internationally. **Prices** increase slightly in peak season – over Christmas and New Year and from mid-February to mid-March – and lift tickets are subject to a five percent tax.

You can rent equipment online or by phone ahead of time, or on-site at numerous rental shops in Whistler Village, Creekside and Upper Village. Rental gear can be picked up the morning of your ski day or after 4pm the evening before to save time. Visit ⓦwhistlerblackcomb.com for booking information, alternatively Summit Ski (☏604 932 6225, ☏866 608 6225, ⓦsummitsport.com) has several outlets around the Village, including the *Hilton Whistler Resort* (by the gondola).

Under-6s ski free. Daycare and full-day ski and snowboard lessons are available for children of all ages, as well as adults. Snow School lessons are all operated by Whistler Blackcomb and can be booked online at ⓦwhistlerblackcomb.com.

bark weaving. An exit on the mezzanine level takes you out to a traditional *istken* (underground pit house) and longhouse. Every Tuesday in summer the centre hosts a salmon barbecue dinner (5–8pm; $58).

Audain Art Museum

4350 Blackcomb Way • Mon & Wed–Sun 10am–5pm (till 9pm Fri) • $18, children free • ☏604 962 0413, ⓦaudainartmuseum.com

The **Audain Art Museum** is a stunning purpose-built gallery that houses the personal art collection of Vancouver home builder and philanthropist **Michael Audain** – the vast glass-walled lobby in the treetops is an architectural delight. Dedicated to BC art from pre-contact to today, the Northwest Coast First Nations masks are some of the finest you'll see, plus there are paintings by **Emily Carr** and modern art by the likes of **Brian Jungen** (don't miss his totem pole made of golf bags). The gallery also displays around three visiting exhibitions a year.

Whistler Mountain

Each mountain has its own distinctive character, and traditionally Whistler has been seen as the more approachable of the two, somewhere you can ski or board for days on end. One of Whistler's great advantages over Blackcomb is the sun, which the mountain catches much earlier: Seventh Heaven run aside, much of Blackcomb doesn't see the sun until after 11.30am.

Whistler Mountain's share of the ski area is 4757 acres and its breakdown of terrain is twenty percent beginner, fifty-five percent intermediate and twenty-five percent expert. Common consent has Whistler as the better mountain for beginners and intermediates – if you're attending ski school the beginners area is at mid-station.

Whistler's twenty **lifts** include two high-speed gondolas, one high-speed six-pack, six high-speed quads, two triple chairlifts and eight surface lifts. Helicopter drops make another one hundred runs and glacier runs available. If you want the fast track to the best skiing on a quality powder day, take the Harmony and Peak chairlifts. Total vertical drop is 1530m and the longest run is 11km.

10

Blackcomb Mountain

Blackcomb Mountain, the "Mile-High Mountain", is a ski area laden with superlatives: North America's finest summer skiing (on Horstman Glacier) and the continent's longest unbroken fall-line skiing.

Blackcomb is slightly smaller than Whistler, at 3414 acres, and has a similar breakdown of **terrain** (fifteen percent beginner, fifty-five percent intermediate and thirty percent expert). Blackcomb is steeper and has more narrow runs than Whistler, which can test beginners' stopping abilities to the limit.

The seventeen **lifts** include one high-speed gondola, seven high-speed quads, two triple chairlifts and seven surface lifts. There are over a hundred marked trails, two glaciers and five bowls along with one half-pipe, one skier-cross track and three terrain parks. Runs such as Ruby, Sapphire, Garnet and Diamond are some of the world's best steep and avalanche-controlled powder, as well as the legendary Couloir Extreme

---

MOUNTAIN BIKING

The phenomenal rise in the popularity of **mountain biking** in and around the resort sees an estimated 100,000 visitors annually coming to Whistler specifically to take to two wheels.

The resort's popularity is not all down to terrain and happy accident. It always did have hundreds of free trails, with endless options for single-track and double-track trails in and around the valley, plus around 200km of lift-serviced trails, the last factor vital: for there's nothing better than having a ski lift do all the hard work of carrying your bike up the mountain and letting gravity do the work – and provide the pleasure – coming down. What has made a big difference, however, is the deservedly celebrated **Whistler Mountain Bike Park** (☎800 766 0449, ⓦbike.whistlerblackcomb.com; daily mid-May to early or mid-Oct 10am–5pm, plus 5–8pm on some lifts mid-June to early Sept, depending on the light). This includes 85 trails, four bike park zones, six access lifts (Whistler Gondola, Fitzsimmons, Peak Chair, Garbanzo, Big Red and Creekside), expert staff on site, banked cruisers and dirt trails through canopied forest and self-guided rides over 4900 vertical feet of trails.

It'll **cost** you $73 for a day-pass in high season, purchase in advance online to get the best deal (from mid-June), there's also a discount for seniors and kids. Multi-day passes are available and all passes include riding and access to the lifts from 10am–5pm the twilight season pass is extra). You can also rent a high-quality "Park" bike from $112 for half a day (☎800 766 0449, ⓦwhistlerblackcomb.com/bike) from the park's Garbanzo outlet (beside the Whistler Gondola), or $140 for the whole day. Kids' downhill bike rentals cost approximately $65/95. Helmets are included and you can rent extra pieces of body armour (recommended) at an additional cost.

You can buy lift-only passes, rent equipment and do your own thing by visiting other rental outfits such as Cross Country Connection (☎604 905 0071, ⓦcrosscountryconnection.ca), which has bikes from $15 per hour, and also offers tours and lessons.

If you're a beginner, book Bike School 101 (ⓦwhistlerblackcomb.com/bike), which offers two-hour clinics to introduce newbies to elementary downhill bike control, technique and body position. Lessons are approximately $159 and include lift ticket, rental, helmet and pads. See online for trail maps and the latest trail status.

for those looking to get their hearts pumping. Even if you're not skiing, come up here (summer or winter) on the ski lifts to walk, enjoy the **view** from the top of the mountain, or to eat in the restaurants like the *Crystal Hut*, a cosy log cabin, famous for its all-day Belgian waffles.

Trails in and around Whistler

You can ride the ski lifts (roughly June to early Sept daily 10am–5pm, Fri–Sun till 8pm; late Sept to mid-Oct Sat & Sun only 10am–5pm; lift passes $58 bought online at ⓦwhistlerblackcomb.com) up both mountains for tremendous views and easy access to over 50km of lift-access high-alpine **hiking** trails suitable for all abilities. Along the way are stunning views over glaciers, alpine lakes, wildflowers and Whistler's wildlife.

Pick up the sheet of hiking trails from the information centres (see below), or buy the 1:50,000 *Whistler and Garibaldi Region* **map**. The two most popular high-level day-walks are the **Rainbow Falls** and **Singing Pass** trails (both five to six hours). Other good choices are the easy and mostly level 4km trail to Cheakamus Lake or any of the high-alpine hikes accessed from the Upper Gondola station (1837m) on Whistler Mountain or the Seventh Heaven lift on Blackcomb. Among the eight walks from Whistler Mountain Gondola station, consider the **Glacier Trail** (2.5km round-trip; 85m ascent; 1hr) for views of the snow and ice in Glacier Bowl. The slightly more challenging **Little Whistler Trail** (3.8km round-trip; 265m ascent; 1hr 30min–2hr) takes you to the summit of Little Whistler Peak (2115m) and gives grand views of Black Tusk in Garibaldi Provincial Park; time your hike to return to the gondola station for the last ride down (times vary according to season).

If high-level hiking seems too daunting (it shouldn't be – most are less than 5km, save the Musical Bumps-Singing Pass trail at 21km), you can opt for one of the plentiful trails for bikers, walkers and in-line skaters around the Village. The **Valley Trail** system starts on the west side of Hwy-99 by the Whistler Park Golf Course and takes you through parks, golf courses and peaceful residential areas: the 30km of trails on and around **Lost Lake**, entered by the northern end of the Day Skier car park at Blackcomb Mountain, wend through cedar forest and past lakes and creeks; the eponymous lake is just over a kilometre from the main trailhead. There are also numerous operators offering guided walks to suit all abilities.

ARRIVAL AND GETTING AROUND   WHISTLER

By bus Pacific Coach Lines (ⓣ800 661 1725, ⓣ604 662 7575, ⓦpacificcoach.com) runs a Whistler express bus from Vancouver airport and various Vancouver hotels to the Squamish Adventure Centre and Whistler Bus Loop. Reservations are required year-round for the service (free wi-fi onboard; 4–5 daily; 2hr 30min; $59 one way). Whistler Rides (ⓣ604 715 0196, ⓦwhistlerrides.ca) runs round trip shuttle buses between Burrard Station and Whistler Village, Creekside and HI-Hostel (free wi-fi onboard; 3–6 daily; 1hr 45min; round trip $31.98+tax). Winter schedules can be affected by bad weather on the Sea to Sky Hwy.

By car If you're driving from Vancouver, allow about two and a bit hours for the 125km drive. Note that there are no petrol stations between Squamish and Whistler.

Whistler Transit If you're staying in or near the Village, you probably won't need local transport, but Whistler Transit (ⓣ604 932 4020, ⓦbctransit.com/whistler) runs a free shuttle bus service around Whistler Village, Village North and Upper Village as well as paid service beyond the village to Whistler Creek and other destinations ($2.50 flat fare, day-pass $7, sheet of ten tickets $22.50). Buses have racks for skis and bikes.

By taxi ⓣ604 938 1515, ⓦresortcabs.com.

INFORMATION

Tourism Whistler (ⓣ800 944 7853, ⓦwhistler.com) is another source of information, including booking accommodation and activities, located in the visitor centre at 4230 Gateway Drive (daily 8am–10pm; ⓣ604 935 3357, ⓣ800 766 0449 toll free in North America and ⓣ0808 180 0606 toll free in the UK, ⓦwhistler.com), which can assist

with general information, tickets for events and last-minute accommodation.

Whistler Blackcomb For information on *Whistler Blackcomb* call ⓣ800 766 0449 (toll free in North America or ⓣ0800 587 1743 toll free in the UK, ⓦwhistlerblackcomb. com).

OTHER ACTIVITIES AT WHISTLER

In addition to skiing (see page 728), mountain biking (see page 729) and hiking (see page 730), Whistler offers a wealth of **outdoor activities** year-round. For further information, contact the visitor centres (see page 730) or visit ⓦ whistlerblackcomb.com, which can book and advise on most activities. Numerous **rental outlets** around the resort provide bikes, skis, snowshoes and other equipment.

TOURS AND ACTIVITIES

Scandinave Spa 8010 Mons Rd ☎ 604 935 2424, ⓦ scandinave.com. After any of these activities there are plenty of spas for massage, mud baths and treatments that soothe all aches and pains. For utter luxury, try Scandinave, whose outdoor hot pools come with incredible mountain vistas.

Wedge Rafting To the right of the Whistler Gondola ☎ 888 932 5899, ⓦ wedgerafting.com. From May through September, this outfit has a range of rafting trips priced from $119 for 2hr trips on the Green River (great for beginners), while experts can plump for the Class-IV thrills of the Elaho or Squamish river rapids (8hr; $169).

Whistler Core next to the Whistler Conference Centre ☎ 604 905 7625, ⓦ whistlercore.com; Mon–Fri 7am–10pm, Sat & Sun 8am–9pm. Year-round indoor rock-climbing facility and an outdoor summer climbing wall. A day's drop-in indoor climbing costs $18. A variety of guides and guided tours are available from $125 for a half-day climb.

The Adventure Group Near the base of Whistler Gondola, also inside Fairmont Château Whistler ☎ 855 824 9955, ⓦ tagwhistler.com. Comprehensive booking agency who offer tours year-round from 1hr 30min snowshoe tours through the ancient cedar forest for novices from $99, as well as ziplining, bungee jumping and axe throwing.

Blackcomb Snowmobile The lobby of the Hilton Resort Whistler ☎ 604 932 8484, ⓦ blackcomb snowmobile.com. You can ride snowmobiles (from $159) with this outfit, which also offers a range of dogsled rides: the "Mountain Mushing" tour (2 daily; 2hr 30min) costs $458 for 2 people. Canadian Wilderness Adventures (☎ 604 938 1616, ⓦ canadianwilderness. com) offers similar snowmobile tours and prices.

Heli-skiing ☎ 888 435 4754, ⓦ whistlerheliskiing. com. To take your experience to the next level, Whistler Heli-Skiing is available for helicopter drops to endless big mountain terrain that includes 173 glaciers and 475 runs outside of the *Whistler Blackcomb* resort. Three run packages start from $1050.

ACCOMMODATION

If you're here in summer and not on a package tour, all local **accommodation** can be booked through the excellent Whistler Central Reservations (☎ 604 932 2280, ☎ 877 932 2280 toll free in North America and ☎ 0808 101 3902 toll free in the UK, ⓦ whistlerreservations.com). In winter, reservations for those not on a package tour should be made well in advance (Sept at least), as many hotels have a thirty-day cancellation window and may insist on a minimum of two nights stay; prices are highest at this time. In winter there's no such thing as budget accommodation, unless you stay at the hostel; with ever greater numbers of visitors in the summer, prices – and availability – of beds are increasingly a problem outside the ski season too. Still, you don't have to stay in a "conventional" hotel, as there is a wide range of chalets, condos, apartments and houses to rent. These, as well as many hotels, often have kitchen facilities and are almost all spotlessly clean, modern and well-run.

Aava Hotel 4005 Whistler Way ☎ 604 932 2522, ☎ 800 663 5644, ⓦ aavawhistlerhotel.com; map p.727. Steps from the centre of the Village, this contemporary, mid-priced hotel offers good value (for Whistler) and has a hot tub, pool and sauna. Rooms come with wi-fi and flat-screen

TVs and are turned out in shades of caramel and apricot. **$170**

Bear Tracks Whistler Chalet 7461 Ambassador Crescent ☎ 604 932 4187, ⓦ beartrackswhistler.ca; map p.727. Eight rooms in a peaceful garden setting that is convenient for the Village, lifts and summer hiking trails. The owners pride themselves on providing big, home-made breakfasts. There's also a bike wash area, wi-fi and a hot tub. **$170**

Crystal Lodge 4154 Village Green ☎ 604 932 2211, ☎ 800 667 3363, ⓦ crystal-lodge.com; map p.727. If you're after central hotel accommodation (it's a snowball's throw to the gondolas for both Whistler and Blackcomb), you'd be hard-pressed to find a better deal than *Crystal Lodge*. There's free valet service for skis and bikes, a hot tub, sauna, underground car park, and a heated outdoor pool. Min two nights. **$294**

★ **Fairmont Château Whistler** 4599 Château blvd, Upper Village ☎ 604 938 8000, ☎ 800 257 7544, ⓦ fairmont.com/whistler; map p.727. Great facilities (including indoor and outdoor pools, fine spa, tennis and golf course) and ski-in/ski-out access to Blackcomb Mountain. The *Mallard Lounge* is one of the Village's best

10

hotel bars, with live music, honey cocktails from their rooftop hives and even a "chocolate bar" offering flights of single estate bean chocolates and other exotic treats. **$339**

★ **Hostelling International Whistler** 1035 Legacy Way, 7km south of the Village, on a bus route ☎ 604 962 0025, ☎ 866 762 4122, ⓦ hihostels.ca; map p.727. This sleek modern 188-bed hostel (32 four-bed dorm rooms and 14 double rooms) offers excellent access to bike trails and camping in the summer and is just 10 minutes to Creekside for lift access in winter. Spotlessly clean, it has a fireplace lounge, HDTV movie room and dining area. You'll also find a café, laundry facilities, and free bike and ski storage. HI members get 10 discount. Dorms **$38.50**; doubles **$99**

Pangea Pod 4333 Sunrise Alley ☎ 844 726 4329, ⓦ pangeapod.com; map p.727. Brand new boutique hostel with private pods, each with a double mattress and niceties like USB and charging points, a lockable cabinet and hangers and hooks (reserve a "side entry" pod for the most room). Couples can share, but it's no cheaper, as another pod will be kept empty (great for extra storage). The smart bar-restaurant serves great coffee and brunch, plus there's complimentary ski equipment storage (bikes for a fee). **$85.75**

Pan Pacific Mountainside 4320 Sundial Crescent ☎ 604 905 2999, ☎ 888 905 9995, ⓦ panpacific.com; map p.727. There's nowhere closer to the lifts than the older of Whistler's two *Pan Pacifics* – you can ski from the front door to the Whistler Mountain gondola station a few steps away. The contemporary lodge style is pleasant, and the 121 units include compact studios and one- and two-bedroom suites with kitchens. There's an outdoor pool, and the excellent *Dubh Linn Gate* Irish pub (see page 733) and lounge are popular après-ski locations. **$170**

Riverside Resort and Campground 8018 Mons Rd ☎ 604 905 5533, ⓦ parkbridge.com; map p.727. Whistler's only central campsite is 1.4km north of Whistler Village. There are 107 tent and RV sites (combined), as well as fourteen four-person log cabins and yurts tucked away in the forest on raised platforms with electricity and a fireplace. Sites **$43**; RVs **$70**; cabins (two-night min) **$210**; yurts (two-night min) **$105**

★ **Summit Lodge** 4359 Main St ☎ 604 932 2778, ⓦ summitlodge.com; map p.727. Funky independent boutique hotel with unique room designs, repurposed upcycled furniture and adorable sock puppets perched on each bed. Free winter ski shuttle and complimentary equipment and bike storage; the *Summit* also has a pool, hot tub, spa and restaurant. **$188**

EATING

Whistler Village and its satellites are loaded with **cafés** and around a hundred **restaurants**. Most hotels also have one or more places to eat, always open to nonguests. Look out for daily Happy Hour deals and *après* specials which give you the chance to dine for a fraction of the usual cost. If you're in town in the first two weekends in November, don't miss Whistler's annual festival of indulgence, **Cornucopia** (ⓦ whistlercornucopia.com), with its fun food and wine events, from spirited cocktail seminars and decadent Champagne parties to grand wine-tasting galas and cookery demos.

★ **Araxi's Restaurant** 4222 Village Square ☎ 604 932 4540, ⓦ araxi.com; map p.727. A top-rated restaurant of long standing that serves Italian and West Coast-style food, with inventive pasta, a high-quality raw bar and seafood dishes with outstanding service. The wine list runs to 27 pages and 9000 bottles, and there's a good choice of wines by the glass. A meal for two here will cost $100-plus, with mains from about $30 – expensive, but you're paying for what's possibly the best food in town. For a budget experience, head there for the daily oyster specials 3-5pm. Daily 3pm–midnight (food served from 5pm).

★ **Earls Kitchen + Bar** 4295 Blackcomb Way ☎ 604 935 3222, ⓦ earls.ca; map p.727. Popular Canadian casual dining chain with a killer patio, daily special drinks and food deals and a daily-changing happy hour (daily 3–5pm, 10pm–close) which make it ideal for diners on a budget. Portions are large; try the piled-high spicy Kung Pao Noodle Bowl ($14) or the Bigger Better Burger ($14.50). Mon–Thurs 11.30am–11pm, Fri 11.30am–midnight, Sat 10am–midnight, Sun 10am–10pm.

Hunter Gather 4368 Main St ☎ 604 966 2372, ⓦ huntergatherwhistler.com; map p.727. Casual self-service restaurant with an open kitchen and some outside seating. Local produce and large sizes: rustic sandwiches include beef brisket on brioche ($14.50), a lentil burger ($14) and smoked Steelhead Chowder ($12.50). Local craft beer to wash it down. Daily noon–late.

★ **Purebread** Olympic Plaza ☎ 604 962 1182, ⓦ purebread.ca; map p.727. Outstanding bakery with innovative sweet and savoury treats, serving up Portland's Stumptown Coffee. The queues can be long but it's absolutely worth it; you'll likely happen upon raspberry scones, salt caramel bars, caramel-frosted cinnamon buns and "pudgie pies" (roasted potato and goat's cheese tucked inside a plump pocket of puff pastry). They have a second location in Function Junction. Daily 8am–6pm.

★ **RimRock Café** 2117 Whistler Rd, 4km south of the Village ☎ 604 932 5565, ☎ 877 932 5589, ⓦ rimrock whistler.com; map p.727. This seafood restaurant with blazing fireplaces and exposed beams may be a little out of the way from the Village but it's a local institution for a reason. Dishes such as salmon with lobster mashed potatoes ($35) and rack of lamb ($46) come with steep price tags, but you'll dream about them long after you've left the mountain. Reservations recommended. Daily 5.45–9pm.

Sushi Village 4340 Sundial Cresc ☎604 932 3330 ⓦsushivillage.com; map p.727. Exceptional sushi restaurant and longtime locals' favourite spot in the heart of the village. Try the Super Hiro roll ($9.50) or dive into the affordable lunch combo platters such as chicken *karaage* with miso, tempura, salad and a sushi roll ($14). Lunch Fri– Sun noon–2.30pm; daily 5.30pm–10pm.

DRINKING AND NIGHTLIFE

Whistler enjoys year-round **nightlife** and après-ski activity, with visitors bolstered by the large seasonal workforce. Clubs come and go, but certain establishments have carved out well-defined niches, including *Moe Joe's* and *Tommy Africa's* for dancing. For peace and quiet, hit any of the bars and lounges in the luxury hotels such as the *Four Seasons* and *Fairmont Château Whistler*. Some clubs may charge a cover – anything from $10 to $30 – on busy nights, or for live music.

Dubh Linn Gate 170-4320 Sundial Crescent ☎604 905 4047, ⓦdubhlinngate.com; map p.727. Charming Irish pub with exceptional Happy Hour and one of the most lively patios in town. The Guinness is smooth, the crowd contented, and the nightly live music (Celtic-inspired, with plenty of sing-along rock songs thrown in) lifts the surliest spirits. Daily 7am–1am.

Garfinkels Club 1-4308 Main St, Village North ☎604 932 2323; map p.727. In your twenties and don't mind sports bars? Then *Garf's* is for you. It's a good dance place week round, Thursday is the longest running locals' night and Monday offers a fun ping-pong evening with an alt rock soundtrack. Daily 6pm–2am.

Garibaldi Lift Company 4165 Springs Lane ☎604 905 2220; map p.727. If it's a view you're after, this is the bar to hit: *GLC*'s patio looks out onto the Whistler lifts. Great for unwinding with a beer after a day on the slopes. Daily 11am–1am.

Moe Joe's 4115 Golfer's Approach ☎604 935 1152, ⓦmoejoes.com; map p.727. Fri nights are popular at *Moe Joe's*, one of the best places in Whistler for dancing. It's smaller and more intimate than *Garf's* but attracts a similar clientele and espouses a similar musical policy. Thurs–Sun 9.30pm–2am.

Tommy Africa's 4216 Gateway Drive ☎604 932 6090, ⓦtommyafricas.com; map p.727. This is the best-known dance club in the Village and usually the most musically adventurous. Closed for renovations at the time of research, but expected to reopen bigger and better. Nightly in winter, 9.30pm–2am; check online events calendar for off-season hours.

Lillooet and around

About 25km northeast of Whistler, Hwy-99 funnels down to two slow lanes at **Pemberton**, with beautiful mountain scenery that rivals anything you'll find at the ski resort. Beyond, you're treated to some wonderfully wild country. Patches of forest poke through rugged mountainsides and scree slopes, and a succession of glorious lakes culminate in Seton Lake, a startling turquoise colour which looks positively Photoshopped, and whose hydroelectric schemes feed power into the grid as far south as Arizona.

At the lumber town of **LILLOOET**, founded as Mile 0 of the 1858 Cariboo Wagon Road to the goldfields to the north (see opposite), the railway meets the Fraser River, which marks a turning point in the scenery as denuded crags and hillsides increasingly hint at *The Big Country*-type ranching country to come. In July and August, the rocky banks and bars of the sluggish, mud-coloured river immediately north of town are dotted with vivid orange and blue tarpaulins. These belong to Aboriginal peoples who still come to catch and dry salmon as the fish make their way upriver to spawn. It's one of the few places where this tradition continues and it's worth a stop to watch. The town's name, changed from Cayoosh Flat in the 1860s, is a rendering of "Leel-wat", one of the Aboriginal peoples who lived to the north.

From Lillooet, Hwy-99 heads east for 50km to Hwy-97; you can then either turn south towards Cache Creek (see page 676), or snake your way north to the goldfields of the Cariboo.

INFORMATION

Lillooet visitor centre The information centre/museum in the old church at 790 Main St (May & June Tues–Sat 10am–4pm; July & Aug daily 9am–5pm; Sept & Oct Tues–Sat 10am–4pm; Nov–April closed; ☎250 256 4308, ⓦlillooetbc.com).

10

ACCOMMODATION

Cayoosh Creek Campground 100 Cayoosh Park Rd ☎ 250 256 7527. The nearest campsite is the riverside *Cayoosh Creek* on Hwy-99 within walking distance of downtown (1km). Mid-April to mid-Oct. Hook up $40

Retasket Lodge & RV Park 1264 Bouvette Rd ☎ 250 256 2090, ☎ 866 456 2090, ⓦ retasketlodge. com. Twenty-room motel with a plain exterior but an extraordinary setting on a steep, mountain-ringed hill. Its updated rooms have microwaves, fridges, flat-screen TVs and wi-fi, there is a BBQ deck for guests to use. The

kindly owners make sure you're well taken care of, and a continental breakfast is included in the rate. There's room for eight RV's, too. $89

Reynolds Hotel 1237 Main St ☎ 250 256 4202, ☎ 877 655 5506, ⓦ reynoldshotel.com. Established in 1941, this central, compact hotel is the pick of the local inns with a shop, off-license and restaurant on-site. Rooms are all differently decorated; number 10 has an Asian theme with jade walls and raffia blinds; number 4 has a claw-foot bath and a bed on a raised platform. $179

EATING

★ **Fort Berens Estate Winery** 1881 Hwy-99 ☎ 250 256 7788. Modern winery ringed by the Fraser Bench and Coast Mountains with a tasting room and shop. The newly-opened *Ponderosa* restaurant offers the chance to sit on the

sun-soaked patio overlooking the vineyard and snack on charcuterie and cheese plates with plenty of by-the-glass wine options. Tasting room daily 10am–6pm, restaurant mid-May to mid-Sept daily noon–4pm.

The Cariboo

The Cariboo is the name given to the broad, rolling ranching country and immense forests of British Columbia's interior plateau, which extend north of Lillooet between the Fraser River to the west and Cariboo Mountains to the east. The region contains marvellous pastoral scenery, and much of the interest it offers – in addition to fishing and boating on thousands of remote lakes – comes from its **gold-mining** heritage. Initially exploited by fur traders to a small degree, the region was fully opened up following the discovery of gold in 1858 in the lower Fraser Valley. The building of the **Cariboo Wagon Road**, a stagecoach route north out of Lillooet, spread gold fever right up the Fraser watershed as men leapfrogged from creek to creek, culminating in the big finds at Williams Creek in Barkerville in 1861.

Much of the old Wagon Road is today retraced by **Hwy-97** (the Cariboo Hwy), which runs through pine forests and past the occasional ranch and small, marsh-edged lake.

Clinton

A compact little village surrounded by green pastures and tree-covered hills, **CLINTON** marks the beginning of the heart of Cariboo country. Right on the main drag, the **Clinton Emporium** (Hwy-97; daily 9am–6pm, closed Sun Nov–Jan; ☎ 250 459 0025) is a cowboy-style flea market packed with a glorious array of antique farming machinery and oddities, like care-worn signs and vintage perfume bottles.

The three tiny settlements beyond Clinton at 70, 100 and 150 Mile House are echoes of the old roadhouses built by men who were paid by the mile to blaze the Cariboo Wagon Road. Visit ⓦ southcaribootourism.com for details of the fishing, riding and other local outdoor pursuits.

ARRIVAL AND DEPARTURE

By bus Merritt Shuttle Bus services (☎ 604 414 7623) are planning a route between Prince George and Merritt, that will stop at Clinton and 100 Mile House.

ACCOMMODATION AND EATING

Cariboo Lodge 1414 Hwy-97 ☎ 250 459 7992. The dining room decor of this spruce log cabin is decidedly country & western, with wagon-wheel lamps, preserved

moose heads and saddles hung from ceiling beams. It's authentic and fun, with a solid menu offering wing ($8.50), burgers ($11) and steak sandwiches ($15). Th lodge also administers twenty simple, spotless motel-style rooms with cable TV and fridges. Restaurant July & Aug daily 7am–9pm; slightly reduced hours off-season. $99

★ **The Packing House** 3705 Riverview Ave, Spences Bridge, 88km south of Clinton ☎ 250 458 2256. About an hour's drive from Clinton, *The Packing House* is a foodie oasis on the long trip north to Cariboo or the return journey to Vancouver. At various times it has been an apple packing house, post office and country store, but the century-old structure now fires off great coffee, baked goods and home-made meals throughout the day. Daily 8am–7pm.

Williams Lake

WILLIAMS LAKE, 14km north of 150 Mile House and still 238km south of Prince George, is a busy transport centre huddled in the lee of a vast crag on terraces above the eponymous lake. The hub of the Cariboo and the gateway to the elusive Chilcotin region, its downtown is fairly unattractive, but the beautiful natural surroundings are ripe for outdoor activity. Mountain biking, in particular, is big here (Williams Lake boasts one of BC's largest bike trail networks; ⊛ ridethecariboo.ca), but there is also plenty of hiking, kayaking, fly-fishing and other activities. One of the best times to visit is the first weekend in July, when the town puts on its famous **rodeo** (⊛ williamslakestampede.com).

ARRIVAL AND INFORMATION
WILLIAMS LAKE

By bus At the time of writing Greyhound had suspended the bus route from Vancouver, so for the time being, there's no public transport between Vancouver and Williams Lake. Merritt Shuttle Bus services (☎ 604 414 7623) are planning a route between Prince George and Merritt, that will stop at Williams Lake.

By plane There are direct flights to Vancouver, Quesnel, Campbell River, Comox, Prince Rupert, Smithers and Terrace from the local airport (Central Mountain Air ☎ 888 865 8585, ⊛ flycma.com).

Williams Lake visitor centre The year-round information centre (which offers free wi-fi) is at 1660 South Broadway (May–Sept daily 9am–5pm; Oct–April Mon–Fri 9am–4pm; ☎ 250 392 5025, ☎ 877 967 5253, ⊛ tourism williamslake.com).

ACCOMMODATION

★ **Juniper Trails Bed and Breakfast** 2523 Dog Creek Rd ☎ 250 398 8296, ☎ 855 398 8926, ⊛ junipertrails. ca. A fantastic B&B at a great price, *Juniper Trails* has three modern suites with sleek and spacious bathrooms, luxury bedding, jazzy paintings by the owner, and a fresh look.

Home to five horses and three mini donkeys, the property faces mountains and a bucolic pasture. Its warm-hearted owners grew up in town and have extensive knowledge of the area. $129

EATING

Gecko Tree Café 54 North Mackenzie Ave ☎ 250 398 8983. Charming local favourite with mismatched chairs, a burgundy interior and rotating artwork. The all-day breakfast menu sports the "saucy Geck" (two eggs fried in green pepper rings and topped with feta, avocado and sprouts; $12.25); lunch sees big salads, wraps and quesadillas, all with an emphasis on organic ingredients.

Tues–Fri 7.30am–4pm, Sat 9am–3pm.

Red Tomato Pies 370 Proctor St ☎ 250 305 5555, ⊛ redtomatopies.com. Popular pizzeria with crust variations such as pan-fried and cornmeal and great pies like Crazy Canuck ($13) and veggie pesto ($13). Sun–Thurs 3–11pm, Fri & Sat 3pm–midnight.

Hwy-20: Williams Lake to Bella Coola

Hwy-20 branches west from Williams Lake, a part-paved, part-gravel road that runs 456km to **BELLA COOLA**, a wilderness-enveloped village in a superb setting. Most of the road ploughs through the forest or ranching country of the Chilcotin Plateau, but there are services, campsites and the odd hotel at regular intervals and the last very worthwhile 100km or so traverses the high and spectacular peaks of the Coast Mountains and **Tweedsmuir Provincial Park** (see page 736). Once you drive through the park you'll encounter the notorious "Hill", a winding and precipitous stretch of road

10

barely tamed by various upgradings over the years. No buses serve Bella Coola, and beyond the village there is no onward road route.

Bella Coola itself was formerly the domain of the Bella Coola, or Nuxalk, an Aboriginal people who prospered thanks to the surfeit of salmon in local rivers and were visited by Alexander Mackenzie as early as 1793; Mackenzie's arrival here on July 22 marked the conclusion of his successful attempt to become the first European man to cross North America. In 1869 the Hudson's Bay Company opened a trading post, though permanent European settlement only began in 1894. One house belonging to a company clerk is now all that remains of the post.

Besides the small museum in the old schoolhouse and surveyor's cabin (June to early Sept Sun–Sat 9am–5pm; $2.50; ☎ 250 799 5767, ⓦ bellacoolamuseum.ca) and glorious scenery, there's not much to see in Bella Coola. Language, heritage and buildings here – notably the square-logged barns – all show a Scandinavian touch. Norwegian settlers were early pioneers; many of today's inhabitants can trace their ancestry to 120 Norwegians led here from Minnesota in 1894 by a pastor determined to found a utopian society. **Hagensborg**, a village with accommodation (see page 737) 16km east of Bella Coola, preserves a particularly strong Nordic flavour. About 10km from the village, roughly midway to Bella Coola, are the **Thorsen Creek Petroglyphs**, a hundred or so rock drawings; the visitor centre should be able to provide a guide to explore the site.

ARRIVAL AND INFORMATION
BELLA COOLA

By plane There are direct flights from Vancouver to the small local airport (Pacific Coastal Airlines ☎ 250 982 2225, ⓦ pacific-coastal.com).

By ferry In spring/summer BC Ferries operates the scenic route to Bella Coola on the Discovery Coast Connector from Port Hardy via Bella Bella. From 2019, there will be a direct (also seasonal) service between Port Hardy and Bella Coola

on the *Northern Sea Wolf*.
Destinations Port Hardy (2–5 weekly; 21hr).

Bella Coola visitor centre In the Co-op grocery store at 450 Mackenzie St (late May to early Sept Mon–Sat 9am–5.30pm; Mon & Wed July & Aug 7am–5.30pm for early ferry arrivals; ☎ 250 799 5202, ☎ 866 799 5202, ⓦ bellacoola.ca).

ACCOMMODATION

Bella Coola Motel 1224 Clayton St ☎ 250 799 5323. At the base of the mountains, this friendly motel has clean rooms with kitchens and wi-fi. It also oversees a campground by the river with a fire pit and cooking area. Free shuttle from the ferry and airport. Tent $20; doubles $105

Bella Coola Mountain Lodge On Hwy-20 16km

east of Bella Coola ☎ 250 982 2298, ☎ 866 982 2298, ⓦ bcmountainlodge.com. In Hagensborg, this log cabin has fourteen colourful rooms with slate floors and is surrounded by a breathtaking landscape of gardens and snow-capped mountains. The lodge has an excellent restaurant, which features local produce (dinner only). $135

Tweedsmuir Provincial Park

Free • ⓦ env.gov.bc.ca/bcparks

If you want to explore the **Tweedsmuir Provincial Park**, which at 10,000 square kilometres is BC's largest, it's best to do so as a day- or multi-day trip from Bella Coola. One of the park's chief sights are the **Hunlen Falls**, 260m of plunging water, though it's a struggle to see them – you need to leave the road near Atnarko River (midway through the park) and take the rough road the 13km to the trailhead for the falls and Turner Lake. From here it's another 16km of walking, with an elevation gain of 2000m. This is typical of a trail system that is still relatively undeveloped, and there are few day-hikes or easy trails from the highway; an exception is the 8km round-trip to a series of pretty lakes from a trailhead 16km west of the Atnarko River campsites. An alternative is to take an expensive "flight-seeing" trip by helicopter or fixed-wing wheel plane; *Tweedsmuir Park Lodge* (see below) organizes one-hour trips.

ACCOMMODATION

Provincial campsites ⓦenv.gov.bc.ca/bcparks.com. There are two simple campgrounds on the north side of the Atnarko River. Both have running water and fire pits. $16
Tweedsmuir Park Lodge ⓣ604 905 4994, ⓣ877 982 2407, ⓦtweedsmuirparklodge.com. Established in 1929, this one-time hunting lodge is now a luxurious once-in-a-lifetime retreat with a guest fishing pond, spa and first-rate

TWEEDSMUIR PROVINCIAL PARK

gym. But its best amenity is its location on an expanse of mountain-strewn land within the provincial park – there are wildlife viewing platforms for guests' use. Rack rate overnight accommodation is only available in June, at all other times guests must book a multi night package that includes small group tours. Two nights $1790

10

Quesnel

North of Williams Lake on Hwy-97, the Fraser River re-enters the scenic picture and, after a dramatic stretch of canyon, reinstates bucolic hills and snatches of river meadows. Yet this also marks the start of some of the most concerted **logging operations** in all of BC. By **QUESNEL**, you're greeted with whole mountainsides of cleared trees and lumber mills surrounded by stacks of logs. The little downtown (centred on Reid St) is infinitely more quaint, with a vintage movie theatre and hardware stores, bookshops and restaurants, which all sport bright awnings.

INFORMATION

QUESNEL

Visitor centre 703 Carson Ave (Jan–May & Dec–Sept Tues–Sat 9am–4pm; June–Aug daily 9am–6pm; ⓣ250 992 8716, ⓣ800 992 4922, ⓦtourismquesnel.com).

EATING

Granville's Coffee 383 Reid St ⓣ250 992 3667. Popular locals' joint with eclectic decor: a lit-up antique petrol pump, a wall of licence plates, a papier-mâché toucan and a ceiling of flattened burlap coffee sacks. The menu has worthy comfort foods such as macaroni and cheese ($5.99) and "9 buck meals" including Shepherd's Pie or Fish and Chips ($9).

Free wi-fi. Mon–Sat 7am–9pm, Sun 8am–5pm.
Quesnel Bakery 468 Reid St ⓣ250 992 9604. A bakery that has been in business for over thirty years. Indulge your sweet tooth with their plump doughnuts, apple fritters and moose- and horse-shaped cookies (all less than a couple of dollars). Mon–Sat 6.30am–5.30pm.

Wells

Often mentioned in the same breath as Barkerville (see opposite), the modestly sized, artistically minded town of **WELLS** was settled in the 1930s during Canada's second gold rush. Sheltered by the Cariboo Mountains, Wells has preserved many of its original buildings, some painted bright hues. The **Amazing Space Gallery** (2338 Bowman Crescent; check for opening hours; ⓣ250 994 2332, ⓦclaireart.ca) has paintings, sculptures and silkscreens all displayed in a former church. Once a meat market, the **Island Mountain Arts** building (Pooley St; open June–Sept Wed–Sun 10am–6pm; ⓣ800 442 2787, ⓦimarts.com) is now the creative hub of Wells, with art classes and a small gallery. In late July/early August, the town's population swells for **ArtsWells** (ⓣ800 442 2787, ⓦartswells.com), a four-day festival of concerts, theatre performances, workshops and films.

ACCOMMODATION

Hubs Motel 12438 Barkerville Hwy ⓣ250 994 3313, ⓣ866 994 3313, ⓦhubsmotel.ca. Nothing fancy, but you'll find great service at this motel in the centre of town. The

movie library's well stocked, there's access to a barbecue and freshly baked cookies are a frequent phenomenon. The on-site fish and chips stand is open nightly (except Wed). $100

EATING AND DRINKING

★ **The Bear's Paw Café** Across from the Hubs Motel ⓣ250 994 3538, ⓦthebearspaw.ca. The neon arrow fronting *The Bear's Paw* is a beacon that draws diners from

all over. Wells' heart and soul, the café's *tchotchke*-laden interior is busy with plates of Thai noodles with prawns ($16), steak ($17) and mighty salads with grilled tomato

($9.50). Great wine and beer list, plus brunch till 1pm at weekends. The owners also run canoe and gold-mining tours (ⓦ whitegold.ca). May to early Oct Mon, Tues & Fri 10am–8pm, Wed & Thurs 10am–4pm, Sat & Sun 9am–8pm.

Wells Hotel 2341 Pooley St ⓣ 250 994 3427, ⓣ 800 860 2299, ⓦ wellshotel.com. The laidback pub at this restored 1933 country inn has a huge whisky selection, a piano, pool and a gang's-all-here vibe; there's also a café on-site serving burgers ($7.95). Daily 5pm–late; café: summer 7am–9pm, winter 8am–8pm.

10 Barkerville Historic Town

June–Sept daily 8am–8pm • $8 entry only, $23.50 for entry, theatre and stagecoach ride • ⓣ 250 994 3332, ⓦ barkerville.ca

Most people who take the trouble to drive Hwy-97 detour to the **Barkerville Historic Town**, 90km to the east of Quesnel in the heart of the Cariboo Mountains, the site of the Cariboo's biggest gold strike and an invigorating spot in its own right. In 1862 a Cornishman named Billy Barker idly staked a claim here and after digging down a metre or so was about to pack up and head north. Urged on by his mates, he dug another couple of spadefuls and turned up a cluster of nuggets worth $600,000. Within months, Barkerville, as it was later dubbed, had become the largest city in the region, and rode the boom for a decade until the gold finally ran out. Today, 107 buildings have been restored and 62 replicas built; costumed staff run demonstrations on gold mining and other aspects of frontier life.

ACCOMMODATION | BARKERVILLE

Barkerville Campgrounds ⓣ 250 994 3297, ⓦ barkervillecampgrounds.ca. You can camp at the linked 164-pitch *Government Hill*, *Forest Rose* and *Lowhee* sites of Barkerville Campgrounds, adjacent to the old town. There's firewood (for purchase), horse paddocks and a playground. Open mid-May to Sept. **$22**

St George Hotel ⓣ 888 246 7690, ⓦ stayinwells.ca. Restored 1890s heritage building that has seven hotel rooms done up in 19th-century style; some with shared bath. Breakfast is included. Shared bath **$135**; en suite **$145**

EATING

Lung Duck Tung On Barkerville's southwest side ⓦ barkerville.ca. Locals count down the days till this seasonal Chinese restaurant opens – it's that good. Superb "house special" tofu with pine nuts ($18.50), bean curd rolls ($5.50) and fried chicken wings ($7.50) served beneath glowing red lanterns. May, June & Sept daily 11am–6pm; July & Aug daily 11am–7pm.

Bowron Lake Provincial Park

Free • ⓦ env.gov.bc.ca/bcparks, ⓦ discovercamping.ca

Thirty kilometres east of Barkerville, the 116km canoe circuit (open mid-May to Sept) of **Bowron Lake Provincial Park** is considered one of the world's best. A pleasing rectangle of waterways and mountain-fringed lakes, the loop takes six to ten days to complete. If you're short on time, tackle the west side of the circuit, which requires only two to four days. Paddling the route requires a reservation (see website), and prior experience is recommended, as the water is challenging in parts. All provisions must be carried in and out.

Victoria

VICTORIA is BC's provincial capital and the region's second city after Vancouver. It's a popular excursion from Vancouver, and though it's possible to come here for the day, it's better to stay overnight and give the city the two or more days it richly deserves. Much of the waterfront area has an undeniably quaint and likeable English feel – "Brighton Pavilion with the Himalayas for a backdrop," said the writer Rudyard Kipling – and Victoria has more British-born residents than anywhere in Canada.

Despite the seasonal influx (some four million visitors per year), it's a small, relaxed and pleasantly sophisticated place. It also provides plenty of bars, restaurants (and the odd club) and serves as a base for a range of outdoor activities and slightly more far-flung attractions. Chief of these is **whale-watching**, with a plethora of companies offering trips. As a final lure, the weather – though often damp – is extremely mild; Victoria's meteorological station has the distinction of being the only one in Canada to record a winter in which the temperature never fell below freezing.

Victoria's heart is compact: the best shops, restaurants and attractions are within walking distance of the **Inner Harbour** area and the Old Town district behind it. On summer evenings this area is alive with strollers and buskers, and a pleasure to wander around as the sun drops over the water. Foremost among the daytime diversions are the **Royal British Columbia Museum** and the **Parliament Buildings**. Or you might drop by **Craigdarroch Castle** and think about a trip to the celebrated **Butchart Gardens**, some way out of town, but easily accessed by public transport or regular all-inclusive tours from the bus terminal. If you're around for a couple of days you should also find time to walk around **Beacon Hill Park**, a few minutes' walk from downtown to the south.

Brief history

Coast Salish peoples originally inhabited Victoria's site, in particular the Lekwungen (also called the Songhees), who were located in the Inner Harbour. Captain George Vancouver, when mapping the North American coast, described his feelings on first glimpsing this part of Vancouver Island: "The serenity of the climate, the innumerable pleasing landscapes, and the abundant fertility that unassisted nature puts forth, require only to be enriched by the industry of man with villages, mansions, cottages and other buildings, to render it the most lovely country that can be imagined."

The first step in this process began in 1843 when Victoria received some of its earliest **European visitors**, notably Hudson's Bay Company representative James Douglas, who disembarked at present-day Clover Point and built **Fort Camosun**, named after a First Nations landmark (the name was later changed to **Fort Victoria** to honour the British

---

WHALE-WATCHING FROM VICTORIA

The waters around Victoria offer different opportunities than those in Tofino (on the west coast of Vancouver Island) where you're more likely to spot grey whales. Throughout the season (May to Oct) transient and resident pods of orcas (**killer whales**) live in the seas around southern Vancouver Island, around a hundred animals in all, so you may see these, along with **minke**, occasional **greys** and **humpbacks**, with Dall's **porpoises**, harbour or elephant seals and California and Steller sea lions also present. Most outfits offer "guaranteed" whale sightings so if you don't see them on your first trip, you can return again for free.

While there are many outfits to choose from, they offer almost identical trips at the same prices, typically around $120 for a three-hour outing. The only real variables are the **boats** used, so you need to decide whether you want a rigid-hull cruiser (covered or uncovered), which is comfortable and sedate, a catamaran, or a high-speed aluminium-hull inflatable known as a "Zodiac", which is infinitely more exhilarating, but can offer a sometimes bumpy, chilly ride and lacks toilets. The two companies below are long standing; the visitor centre (see page 747) has details on others.

Five Star 645 Humboldt St ☎ 250 388 7223, ☎ 800 634 9617, ⊕ 5starwhales.com. Has been in business since 1985 and runs two daily 3hr trips from April to mid-October ($115). Trips are in forty-passenger catamarans.

Orca Spirit 146 Kingston St ☎ 250 383 8411, ☎ 888 672 6722, ⊕ orcaspirit.com. The folks behind Orca Spirit have been in the business for over two decades and offer between four and six 3hr Zodiac trips daily ($126) and two covered boat trips ($126). April to Oct only.

10

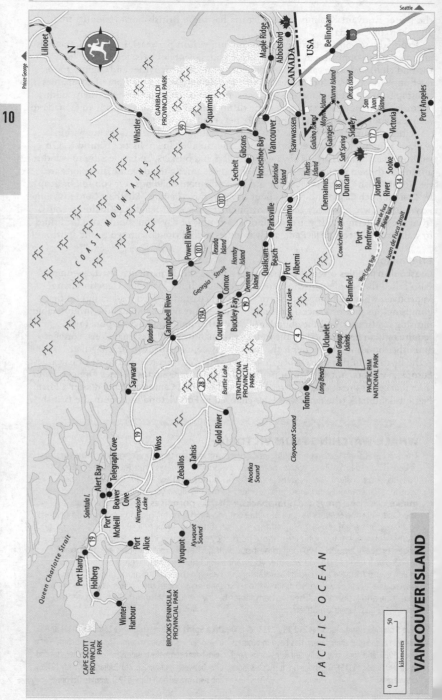

Seattle

Prince George

Lillooet

N

CANADA
USA

Bellingham

Port Angeles

Maple Ridge

Abbotsford

GARIBALDI
PROVINCIAL PARK

Whistler

Squamish

99

Orcas
Island

San
Juan
Island

Saturna Island

Mayne Island

Galiano Island

Vancouver

Tsawwassen

Sidney

Victoria

17

Sooke

Gibsons

Horseshoe Bay

Sechelt

Ganges

Salt Spring

Thetis
Island

Gabriola
Island

Chemainus

Duncan

18

Jordan
River

14

101

COAST MOUNTAINS

Powell River

Lund

Texada
Island

Hornby
Island

Georgia Strait

Denman
Island

Comox

101A

Parksville

Qualicum
Beach

Nanaimo

Port
Alberni

Cowichan Lake

Port
Renfrew

Juan de Fuca Trail

Marine Trail

West Coast Trail

Juan de Fuca Strait

Campbell River

Quadra

Courtenay

Buckley Bay

19

Sproat Lake

4

Bamfield

Sayward

28

Battle Lake

STRATHCONA
PROVINCIAL
PARK

Gold River

Ucluelet

Broken Group
Islands

PACIFIC RIM
NATIONAL PARK

19

Woss

Zeballos

Tahsis

Nootka
Sound

Tofino

Long Beach

Clayoquot Sound

Telegraph Cove

Alert Bay

Sointula I.

Beaver
Cove

Nimpkish Lake

Port
McNeill

Kyuquot

Kyuquot
Sound

PACIFIC OCEAN

19

Port Hardy

Holberg

Port
Alice

Queen Charlotte Strait

Winter
Harbour

BROOKS PENINSULA
PROVINCIAL PARK

CAPE SCOTT
PROVINCIAL PARK

VANCOUVER ISLAND

0 — 50
kilometres

queen). First Nations peoples from across the island settled near the fort, attracted by the new trading opportunities it offered. Soon they were joined by British pioneers and in time, the harbour became the busiest West Coast port north of San Francisco and a major base for the British navy's Pacific fleet.

Boom time came in the 1850s following the mainland gold strikes, when Victoria's port became an essential stop-off and supply depot for prospectors heading across the water and into the interior. Though the gold-rush bubble soon burst, Victoria carried on as a military, economic and political centre, becoming the capital of the newly created province in 1866 – years before the founding of Vancouver. But Victoria's planned role as Canada's western rail terminus was surrendered to Vancouver, and with it any chance of realistic growth or industrial development. Today, the town survives quite well almost entirely on the backs of visitors, the civil-service bureaucracy and retirees in search of a mild-weathered retreat.

10

The Royal British Columbia Museum

675 Belleville St • Daily 10am–5pm • Museum $26.95, IMAX 45min film and museum combined ticket $36.90 • ☎ 250 356 7226, ☎ 888 447 7977, ⓦ royalbcmuseum.bc.ca

The Royal British Columbia Museum, founded in 1886, is arguably the most compelling museum in BC. All conceivable aspects of the province are examined, and the First Nations section is probably the definitive collection of a much-covered genre. The natural history galleries – huge re-creations of ecosystems, complete with sights, sounds and smells – are mind-boggling in scope and imagination.

Second floor

The **second floor** contains full-scale reconstructions of some of the many natural habitats found in BC. The idea of re-creating shorelines, coastal rainforests and Fraser Delta landscapes may sound far-fetched, yet all are incredibly realistic, down to dripping water and cool, dank atmospheres. Audiovisual displays and a wealth of information accompany the exhibits, most of which focus on the province's 25,600km of coastline, a side of BC often overlooked in favour of its interior forests and mountains.

Third floor and mezzanine

The **third floor** houses an incredibly powerful collection of **First Nations Peoples** art, culture and history with intricately carved totem poles, black and white archive footage, and a fascinating languages section. It's presented in dim light, creating a solemn atmosphere in keeping with the tragic nature of many of the displays. The collection divides into two epochs – before and after the coming of Europeans. The whole collection takes a thoughtful and oblique approach, bringing you to the point where smallpox virtually wiped out in one year a culture that was eight millennia in the making. Alongside the First Nations exhibit is a collection of pioneer memorabilia; arranged from the present day backwards, it explores in detail every aspect of the province's social history over two centuries.

Parliament Buildings

501 Belleville St • Mon–Fri 9am–5pm for guided or self-guided tours; late May to early Sept Sat & Sun 9am–5pm guided tours only • Free • ☎ 250 387 3046, ⓦ leg.bc.ca

The **Parliament Buildings** are an imposing Victorian pile in the manner of a large and particularly grand British town hall. Beautifully lit at night by some 3300 tiny bulbs, the domed building is framed by the sea and well-kept gardens – take time out on the front lawns, distinguished by a perky statue of Queen Victoria and a giant sequoia, said to be a gift from the state of California.

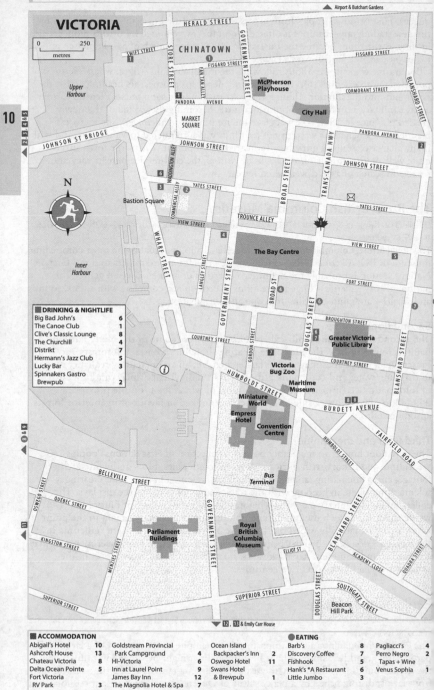

VICTORIA

0 250
metres

Airport & Butchart Gardens

HERALD STREET

GOVERNMENT STREET

SWIFT STREET

STORE STREET

CHINATOWN

FISGARD STREET

FISGARD STREET

FAN TAN ALLEY

McPherson Playhouse

CORMORANT STREET

BLANSHARD STREET

Upper Harbour

PANDORA AVENUE

MARKET SQUARE

City Hall

PANDORA AVENUE

JOHNSON ST BRIDGE

WADDINGTON ALLEY

JOHNSON STREET

BROAD STREET

TRANS-CANADA HWY

JOHNSON STREET

N

COMMERCIAL ALLEY

YATES STREET

YATES STREET

Bastion Square

VIEW STREET

TROUNCE ALLEY

WHARF STREET

The Bay Centre

VIEW STREET

Inner Harbour

LANGLEY STREET

BROAD ST

FORT STREET

GOVERNMENT STREET

DOUGLAS STREET

BROUGHTON STREET

DRINKING & NIGHTLIFE

Big Bad John's	6
The Canoe Club	1
Clive's Classic Lounge	8
The Churchill	4
Distrikt	7
Hermann's Jazz Club	5
Lucky Bar	3
Spinnakers Gastro Brewpub	2

COURTNEY STREET

GORDON STREET

Greater Victoria Public Library

COURTNEY STREET

BLANSHARD STREET

Victoria Bug Zoo

HUMBOLDT STREET

Maritime Museum

Miniature World

BURDETT AVENUE

Empress Hotel

Convention Centre

FAIRFIELD ROAD

HUMBOLDT STREET

BELLEVILLE STREET

Bus Terminal

OSWEGO STREET

QUÉBEC STREET

GOVERNMENT STREET

MENZIES STREET

Parliament Buildings

Royal British Columbia Museum

BLANSHARD STREET

KINGSTON STREET

ELLIOT ST

ACADEMY CLOSE

QUADRA STREET

SUPERIOR STREET

SUPERIOR STREET

DOUGLAS STREET

SOUTHGATE STREET

Beacon Hill Park

12 13 & Emily Carr House

Designed by the 25-year-old Francis Rattenbury, who was also responsible for the nearby *Empress Hotel*, the building was completed in 1898, at a cost of $923,000. Figures from Victoria's civic past are duly celebrated, the main door guarded by statues of Sir James Douglas, who chose the site of the city, and Sir Matthew Baillie Begbie (aka the "Hanging Judge"), responsible for law and order during the heady days of gold fever. Captain George Vancouver keeps an eye on proceedings from the top of the dome.

Beacon Hill Park

Bounded by the Juan de Fuca Strait and Douglas, Southgate and Cook streets

The best park within walking distance of the town centre is **Beacon Hill Park**, south of the Inner Harbour and a few minutes' walk up Douglas Street, behind the Royal British Columbia Museum. Victoria is sometimes known as the "City of Gardens", and Beacon Hill lives up to the sobriquet. The city's biggest green space, it has lots of paths, ponds, big trees and quiet corners, and plenty of views over the **Juan de Fuca Strait** to the distant Olympic Mountains of Washington State (especially on the park's southern side). The park was a favoured retreat of celebrated artist Emily Carr, who painted several of its scenes.

The gardens in the park are by turns well tended and wonderfully wild and unkempt, a far cry from its earliest days, when it was known by the local Salish as "Meeacan", their word for a belly, as the hill was thought to resemble the stomach of a large man lying on his back. They also claim one of the **world's tallest totem poles**, as well as the "Mile Zero" marker of the Trans-Canada Highway and – that ultimate emblem of Englishness – a cricket pitch. Some of the trees are massive old-growth timbers you'd normally only see on the island's unlogged west coast. In spring, there are swaths of daffodils and blue camas flowers, the latter a floral monument to Victoria's earliest First Nations inhabitants, who cultivated the flower for its edible bulb. Some 30,000 other flowers are planted in the gardens annually.

The Empress Hotel

721 Government St • ☎ 800 441 1414, ⓦ fairmont.com/empress-victoria

Most casual visitors come to the ivy-cloaked **Empress Hotel** to take tea in the *Tea Lobby* accompanied by a pianist in a gorgeous room overlooking the harbour – but you have to abide by the dress code and be prepared for an outlay of $78 plus tax and tip; a more affordable in-town option is *Venus Sophia Tea Room* (see page 749). For an alternative treat in the hotel, try an Empress 1908 cocktail ($19) in the fun **Q Bar**, with Queen Victoria looking down at you from the walls.

Victoria Bug Zoo

631 Courtney St • Mon–Fri 11am–4pm, Sat & Sun 11am–5pm • $12, kids $8 • ☎ 250 384 2847, ⓦ victoriabugzoo.ca

If you have little ones in tow, pay a visit to the small **Victoria Bug Zoo**, whose terrariums are alive with over forty insect and spider species, particularly tropical breeds of arachnids, scorpions and millipedes. Don't miss the colony of leaf-cutter ants, residing in what the museum believes is the world's largest ant farm. Knowledgeable guides assist in bug handling and are a font of insect expertise.

Maritime Museum

664 Humber St • Daily 10am–5pm (closed Mon in winter) • $12 • ☎ 250 385 4222, ⓦ mmbc.bc.ca

The modest **Maritime Museum** displays old charts, navigational devices, ships' bells, cannons and plenty of models. In all, the museum's collection has more than 35,000 artefacts, but since it relocated to a storefront building in 2015, most of these are in storage. The hope is that a new waterfront location can be found for the museum before 2021 – the 150th anniversary of BC joining the confederation.

Miniature World

649 Humboldt St • Daily: May–Sept 9am–9pm; Oct–April 9am–5pm • $16, ages 5–12 $8 • ☎ 250 385 9731, ⓦ miniatureworld.com

One of Victoria's oldest attractions, **Miniature World** has some 85 painstakingly hand-built dioramas which cover everything from the history of Canada by way of the railway (with plenty of buttons to press to make the trains whizz around the tracks), two of the world's largest dollhouses, a fun 2201AD space exhibit and even a diminutive Changing of the Guard at Buckingham Palace. The attention to detail is breathtaking at this pleasingly old-fashioned attraction and new exhibits are added each year.

The Old Town

The oldest part of Victoria focuses on **Bastion Square**, original site of Fort Victoria, from which it's a short walk to Market Square – a nice piece of old-town rejuvenation – and the main downtown shopping streets. Bastion Square's former saloons, brothels and warehouses have been spruced up and turned into offices, cafés and galleries, but sadly the prominent mocha-and-vanilla-coloured former courthouse has been empty since the Maritime Museum was forced to move out in 2015.

Market Square

Mon–Sat 10am–5pm, Sun 11am–4pm • ☎ 250 386 2441, ⓦ marketsquare.ca

Two blocks north of the Maritime Museum lies **Market Square**, the old heart of Victoria and now a collection of some 35 boutiques and cafés centred on a courtyard (bounded by Store, Pandora and Johnson streets). This area boomed in 1858 following the gold rush, providing houses, saloons, opium dens, stores and various salacious entertainments for thousands of chancers.

Chinatown

On the Pandora Avenue (dubbed the "Design District") side of the area was a ravine, marked by the current sunken courtyard, beyond which lay **Chinatown** (now centred one block north on Fisgard St), the oldest in Canada. Here, among other things, 23 factories processed 90,000 pounds of opium a year for what was then a legitimate trade and – until the twentieth century – one of BC's biggest industries.

Craigdarroch Castle

1050 Joan Crescent • Daily: mid-June to early Sept 9am–7pm; rest of year 10am–4.30pm • $14.25 • ☎ 250 592 5323, ⓦ thecastle.ca

Perched on a hilltop in Rockland, one of Victoria's more prestigious neighbourhoods, **Craigdarroch Castle** was built in 1890 as the opulent home of a robber baron. It was later transformed into a military hospital, college and music conservatory before reaching its current status as a historic house museum in 1994.

Aside from a brass telescope stashed in an upstairs hall, most of the castle's furniture is not original. What has been retained, however, is the superstructure's impressive collection of stained glass and woodwork, the latter culled from a panoply of cherry, Hawaiian koa, Spanish mahogany and maple.

The museum has plenty of enjoyable design quirks. Keep an eye out for "speaking tubes" on the second floor (an antiquated intercom system), and the stained glass window in the smoking room that depicts Sir Walter Raleigh chomping on a pipe (it's

said he popularized tobacco in Britain). Be sure to visit the tower, a perfect little circle (there's even a curved door), with panoramic views.

Art Gallery of Greater Victoria

1040 Moss St • Mon–Sat 10am–5pm, Thurs 10am–9pm, Sun noon–5pm; closed Mon early Sept–May • $13 • ☎ 250 384 4171, ⓦ aggv.ca

Just two blocks from Craigdarroch Castle, the **Art Gallery of Greater Victoria** has a small but beautifully presented collection of artworks housed in an 1890 mansion. Its offerings include a contemporary gallery filled with Emily Carr's (see page 694) work, an assembly of Japanese art, pastoral nineteenth-century oil paintings and a curious collection of snuff bottles. The museum boasts the only complete Shinto shrine in North America, installed in a garden with bluebells and Japanese maples.

Emily Carr House

207 Government St • May–Sept Tues–Sat 11am–4pm • $6.75 • ☎ 250 383 5843, ⓦ emilycarr.com

About four blocks from the Inner Harbour, th– e **Emily Carr House** reopened in May 2019 after renovations and restorations to its upper rooms; both floors of the early home of BC's best-known artist are now open to the public. The building was constructed in 1864 and Emily – the eighth of nine children – was born during a blizzard in 1871. Fans of Carr may want to pay homage, but note that there are no originals of her work here. Instead you'll find contemporary Canadian art and a wonderful gift shop with prints of her work (to see an ongoing exhibition of her paintings, head to the Art Gallery of Greater Victoria, or Vancouver's Art Gallery).

Butchart Gardens

800 Benvenuto Ave, on Hwy-17 towards the Swartz Bay ferry terminal; take bus #75 headed for "Central Saanich" from downtown • Daily: mid-June to Aug 9am–10pm; first two weeks of Sept & Dec 9am–9pm; rest of the year 9am–sunset • $18.75 in early Jan, then on a sliding scale through the year to $33.80 between mid-June and Sept • ☎ 250 652 4422, ☎ 250 652 5256 for recorded information, ⓦ butchartgardens.com

If you're into things horticultural, trek out to the celebrated **Butchart Gardens**, 23km north of Victoria. The gardens were started in 1904 by Jennie Butchart, wife of a mine-owner and pioneer of Portland Cement in Canada and the US, her initial aim being to landscape one of her husband's quarries. The garden now comprises rose, Japanese and Italian gardens and numerous decorative cameos. About half a million visitors a year tramp through the foliage, which includes over a million plants and seven hundred different species. The gardens are renowned for the **firework displays** that usually take place each Saturday evening from late June to early September, and are often followed by open-air concerts.

ARRIVAL AND DEPARTURE

VICTORIA

You can reach Victoria from Vancouver by **bus and ferry**, **car and ferry** or by **plane**. Most people travelling under their own steam from Vancouver use the first; just buy an all-inclusive through-ticket from Vancouver's bus terminal to Victoria's bus depot. There are also **ferries** from points in the US (see page 747).

BY PLANE

Flying into Victoria from Vancouver airport is expensive, with return fares typically running to around $200. It's more fun and more direct to fly from Vancouver harbour to Victoria harbour by floatplane (see opposite). Victoria International Airport (☎ 250 953 7500, ⓦ victoriaairport. com) is 26km north of downtown on Hwy-17 near the Sidney ferry terminal. The airport shuttle bus (☎ 250 386 2525, ☎ 877 386 2525, ⓦ yyjairportshuttle.com; $25) makes the 35min journey downtown (where it stops at major hotels) every 30min as long as there are flights, no reservations necessary.

Destinations Abbotsford (3 daily; 30min); Calgary (8 daily; 1hr 30min); Edmonton (3 daily; 1hr 40min); Kelowna (1 daily; 50min); Nanaimo (2 daily; 25min); San Francisco (4 daily; 1hr 40min); Seattle (5 daily; 40min); Toronto (4 daily; 5hr); Vancouver (25 daily; 25min).

BY HELICOPTER AND FLOATPLANE

Helijet (☎800 665 4354, ⓦhelijet.com) fly from Vancouver Harbour Airport (east of Canada Place accessed via the SeaBus terminal) to Victoria Harbour Heliport (near Ogden Point cruise ship terminal) in 35 minutes. Fares from $315 one way.

Harbour Air (☎800 665 0212, ⓦharbourair.com) flies in 35min from just west of Canada Place in Vancouver (from $139 one way).

BY BUS

The bus terminal is located downtown at 721 Douglas St, close to the Royal British Columbia Museum. Pacific Coach Lines buses (☎800 661 1725, ⓦpacificcoach.com) from Vancouver drop you here. It is the base for onward connections on Tofino Bus (☎866 986 3466, ⓦtofinobus.com).

Destinations Tofino Bus goes to Campbell River (4 daily; 5hr 15min); Nanaimo (4 daily; 2hr 10min); Port Alberni (2 daily; 4hr); Port Hardy (1 daily; 10hr); Qualicum Beach (4 daily; 3hr 30min); Tofino (1 daily; 6hr 40min). Pacific Coach Lines goes to Vancouver, and the fare includes the ferry crossing journeys and from ferry terminals at both ends. Journey time is approximately 3hr 50 min.

BY FERRY

Ferry reservations are essential in summer to avoid long waits. The route used by Vancouver–Victoria drivers is the Tsawwassen–Swartz Bay connection, also the route used by Pacific Coach Lines buses. Ferries ply the route almost continuously from 7am–9pm (14 sailings daily in summer, minimum of 8 daily in winter). Car tickets in high season (from late June to early Sept) cost $57.50. Bicycles cost $2 year-round. You need to add on per-person fares, which are $17.20.

BC Ferries operates four routes to Vancouver Island across the Georgia Strait from mainland BC (information on ☎888 223 3779 anywhere in North America, otherwise ☎250 386 3431, ⓦbcferries.com). From the US: Port Angeles to Victoria with Black Ball Ferry Line (☎250 386 2202, ☎360 457 4491, ⓦcohoferry.com; one way $18.50); Seattle to Victoria, with Victoria Clipper (☎250 382 8100, ☎206 448 5000, ☎800 888 2535, ⓦclippervacations.com/ferry; one way from $99); Anacortes to Sidney (27km north of Victoria), with Washington State Ferries (☎888 808 7977, ⓦwsdot.wa.gov/ferries; one way from $20.25).

Destinations Anacortes and San Juan Islands, US, from Victoria's Inner Harbour (1–2 daily; 2hr 30min); Seattle, US, from Inner Harbour (1–3 daily; 2hr 30min); Vancouver (Tsawwassen) from Swartz Bay (hourly summer 7am–10pm; rest of the year minimum 8 daily; 1hr 35min).

10

GETTING AROUND

By ferry The most enjoyable means of transport are the tiny Inner Harbour ferries (☎250 708 0201, ⓦvictoria harbourferry.com) that run around the harbour. Stops include Fisherman's Wharf, *Ocean Pointe Resort* and West Bay Marina, but they're worth taking just for the ride; try a 45min tour ($30, kids $20) around the harbour. Buy tickets (from $6, depending on route) on ferries in the Inner Harbour or book at the visitor centre.

By bus You're unlikely to need to use a local bus (☎250 382 6161, ⓦbusonline.ca) if you stick to the downtown area, but if you do venture out, most services run from the corner of Douglas and Yates streets. The fare within the large central zone is $2.50 – tickets and the DayPASS ($5) are sold at the visitor centre, 7-Eleven stores and other marked outlets, or you can pay on board (exact fare only).

By bike Cycle BC Rentals, at 685 Humboldt St (☎250 380 2453, ⓦcyclebc.ca) rents bikes (from $16/2 hr, $28 daily), scooters and motorbikes.

By taxi Blue Bird Line Taxi (☎250 382 2222); Yellow Cab (☎250 381 2222); Victoria Taxi (☎250 383 7111).

INFORMATION

Victoria visitor centre 812 Wharf St, in front of the *Empress Hotel* on the harbour (daily: May–Sept 8.30am–8.30pm; Oct–April 9am–5pm; ☎250 953 2033, ☎800 663 3883, ⓦtourismvictoria.com). The staff can help you book whale-watching and other tours (see page 739).

ACCOMMODATION

Victoria fills up quickly in the summer, and most of its limited budget accommodation is well known and heavily patronized. Top-price hotels cluster around the Inner Harbour area; hostels and more downmarket alternatives are scattered all over, though the largest concentration of cheap hotels and motels is around the Gorge Rd and Douglas St areas northwest of downtown. Reservations are virtually obligatory in all categories, though the accommodation service (☎800 663 3883, ⓦtourismvictoria.com) will root out a room if you're stuck. This will likely be in one of Victoria's vast selection of B&Bs, easily as inviting as the city's hotels. Victoria's commercial campsites are full to bursting in summer, with most space given over to RVs. Few of these are convenient for downtown – given that you'll have to travel, you might as well head for one of the more scenic provincial park sites. Most are on the Trans-Canada Highway to the north, or on Hwy-14 west of Victoria.

10

HOTELS

Abigail's Hotel 906 McClure St ☎ 250 388 5363, ☎ 800 561 6565, ⓦ abigailshotel.com; map p.742. Victoria's grandest adults-only accommodation, this 23-room Tudor mansion is filled with thick tapestries, wood-burning fireplaces and jet tubs. Three-course breakfasts, home-baked cookies and a shady patio are pleasing extras. A historic building (it dates to the 1930s), there are three floors but no elevator. $249

Chateau Victoria 740 Burdett Ave ☎ 250 382 4221, ☎ 800 663 5891, ⓦ chateauvictoria.com; map p.742. The main attraction at this independently-owned hotel is its rooftop restaurant with jaw-clanging views across the city, harbour and Olympic Mountains, with local produce on the menu (look out for the honey which comes from their rooftop hives). Suites offer spacious apartment-like rooms with full kitchens, balconies and mostly Canadian-made furniture. Their cocktail lounge *Clive's Classic* is a local favourite. $255

Delta Ocean Pointe 100 Harbour Rd ☎ 250 360 2999, ⓦ marriott.com; map p.742. Boasting one of the best patios in the city and unspoiled views across the harbour towards the parliament building, especially picturesque at night when it's lit up. Just five minutes' walk across the Johnson Street Bridge the *Delta* offers a peaceful retreat from the town centre with an award-winning spa, indoor pool and excellent restaurant as additional attractions. Rooms are spacious and bright in soothing beige tones; suites have dining rooms and plush living areas. $246

★ **Inn at Laurel Point** 680 Montréal St ☎ 250 386 8721, ☎ 800 663 7667, ⓦ laurelpoint.com; map p.742. Don't be put off by the size of this 200-room resort-style hotel. All the rooms have a balcony and good harbour view, thanks to a position on a landscaped promontory (with a Japanese garden) on the Inner Harbour. The contemporary aesthetic is simple and clean, and a far cry from the chintzy look of many of Victoria's hotels. There are two wings, north and south – you'll want to be in the southern one, designed by Arthur Erickson (see page 584). Here, the rooms are all pale wood and dark marble, with Japanese-style sliding doors, Asian works of art and airy, stylish bathrooms. $294

James Bay Inn 270 Government St, at Toronto ☎ 250 384 7151, ☎ 800 836 2649, ⓦ jamesbayinn.com; map p.742. This Edwardian building, just two blocks south of the BC Parliament, was where famed Canadian artist Emily Carr died as a patient when it was a priory. Today, it is – relatively speaking – one of Victoria's more reasonably priced options, with 45 simply furnished rooms, and a restaurant and pub in the basement. No elevator. $139

The Magnolia Hotel & Spa 623 Courtney St ☎ 250 381 0999, ☎ 877 624 6654, ⓦ magnoliahotel.com; map p.742. This 64-room boutique hotel lays on the character thick, the small lobby setting the period Edwardian tone, though the effect, especially in the high-quality rooms

(the best have harbour views and fireplaces) and superb bathrooms, is never stuffy. The on-site spa is one of the best in the city. $329

★ **Oswego Hotel** 500 Oswego St ☎ 250 294 7500, ☎ 877 767 9346, ⓦ oswegohotelvictoria.com; map p.742. This all-suite hotel has modish guest rooms plumped with designer furniture, stainless-steel kitchens and granite countertops. Coffee lovers enjoy the in-room French press, while weary travellers are happy to find a smart café and bistro with weekly live jazz, and a spa. $289

Swans Hotel & Brewpub 506 Pandora Ave ☎ 250 361 3310, ☎ 800 668 7926, ⓦ swanshotel.com; map p.742. Brewpub aside, the appeal of the thirty rooms here is the setting, a converted 1880s grain store that means many of the suites and larger rooms are quirky, loft-style spaces, often on a split level and with exposed beams and bold, original artwork. The one- and two-bedroom suites take up to six people, making them perfect for families, and there are fully equipped kitchens and dining and living rooms. $205

B&B

★ **Ashcroft House** 670 Battery St ☎ 250 385 4632, ☎ 866 385 4632, ⓦ ashcrofthousebandb.com; map p.742. Dating to 1898, this B&B is just a block from Beacon Hill Park and the Juan de Fuca Strait. Its five traditional guest rooms come with cushy robes and slippers and are blessed with a generous amount of sunlight. $139

HOSTELS

HI-Victoria 516 Yates St, at Wharf ☎ 250 385 4511, ☎ 866 762 4122, ⓦ hihostels.ca; map p.742. Large, welcoming and well-run place just a few blocks north of the Inner Harbour with free tea, coffee and toast at breakfast. The bunk rooms can be noisy but free earplugs are given at reception. The notice boards are packed with useful information on the city, and facilities include free wi-fi, laundry and bike storage. HI members get a 10 percent discount. Dorms $33; doubles $88

Ocean Island Backpacker's Inn 791 Pandora Ave, at Blanshard ☎ 250 385 1789, ☎ 888 888 4180, ⓦ ocean island.com; map p.742. This restored 1891 heritage building is in a reasonably central location and has a wide variety of dorms and rooms on a sliding scale depending on the time of year and the day of the week. Facilities include internet access, free wi-fi, a café and laundry. Weekly and monthly rates are available. Dorms $31; doubles $63; family rooms $99

CAMPSITES

Fort Victoria RV Park 340 Island Hwy-1A ☎ 250 479 8112, ⓦ fortvictoria.ca; map p.742. Closest site to downtown, located 9km west of Victoria off the Trans-Canada Hwy. Take bus #14 (for Craigflower) from the city centre; it stops right by the gate. Large 300-pitch site

mainly for RVs but with a few tent sites; free hot showers, plus laundromat. $2/person charged nightly. RV sites **$55**
Goldstream Provincial Park Campground 2930 Trans-Canada Hwy ☎ 800 689 9025, ⓦ goldstreampark. com; map p.742. Located 16km northwest of the city

off Hwy-1 (bus #50 from Douglas St downtown), this site is set in old-growth forests of cedar and Douglas fir and is Victoria's best camping option. Flush toilets and free hot showers, with plenty of hiking, swimming and fishing opportunities. **$40**

EATING

Coming out from Vancouver's culinary shadow, Victoria has a number of extremely good **restaurants** and offers greater variety than you'll find in most BC towns. Tempting snack and pastry shops abound, while at the other extreme there are budget-busting establishments if you want a one-off treat or a change from standard menus.

★ **Barb's** 1 Dallas Rd, Bastion Square ☎ 250 384 6515, ⓦ barbsfishandchips.com; map p.742. Superb floating fish and chips restaurant which knocks spots off all the other competition thanks to its excellent fast and friendly service, and the promise that "your meal will be perfect every time, if not we'll make it right". Pick from heaped portions of sustainable fish with crunchy crisp batter, shellfish suppers, burgers and other fried delights. Once you've polished that off, take a walk to see the harbour seals who play in the water around the wharf. Mid-March to Oct daily 11am–dusk.

Discovery Coffee 1011 Blanshard St ☎ 778 406 1111, ⓦ discoverycoffee.com; map p.742. Victoria has a thriving coffee culture and some of its best local brews can be found at any of the branches of *Discovery* dotted about downtown. Single-origin beans and blends are the order of the day along with carbonated nitro-cold brew coffee and other caffeinated innovations. Baked goods come from the delicious *Yonni's Doughnuts*; try the salt caramel variety. Daily 6.30am–6pm.

Fishhook 805 Fort St ☎ 250 477 0470, ⓦ fishhookvic. com; map p.742. A tasty blend of Indian flavours and French technique makes this small seafood restaurant with a suntrap backyard patio a locals' favourite. All the seafood is sustainable and the menu changes according to whatever is in season, but you'll always find piled-high tartines ($8) and delicately spiced curries (from $15). Daily 11am–9pm.

Hank's *A Restaurant Unit G2A 1001 Douglas St ☎ 778 433 4770, ⓦ hanksarestaurant.com; map p.742. Pull up a stool at the counter in this tiny blink-and-you'll-miss-it joint which started out as *Hanks Unconventional BBQ*. The rebrand enabled owners Andrew and Clark to branch out – they still only have ethically produced meat on the menu, including their own pigs and turkeys from the Comox Valley – but these days they might also serve mussels in a nduja

and wine sauce ($15) or pork hock with leek, apple and cabbage ($35). Tues–Sat 5–10pm.

Little Jumbo 506 Fort St ☎ 778 433 5535, ⓦ little jumbo.ca; map p.742. It's worth seeking out this hidden gem down a hallway at the end of Fort Street: you'll be rewarded with innovative Canadian cuisine showcasing whatever's fresh and in-season, and a killer bar programme from award-winning bartender, Nate Caudle. Think juicy local duck breast ($35), spice crusted albacore tuna ($28) and sublime desserts and dessert cocktails. Mon–Thurs & Sun 5–11pm, Sat & Sun 5pm–midnight.

Pagliacci's 1011 Broad St, between Fort and Broughton ☎ 250 386 1662, ⓦ pagliaccis.ca; map p.742. The best restaurant in Victoria if you want a fast, furious atmosphere, live music, good Italian food and excellent desserts. Prices are good, with mains from $14.50. A rowdy throng begins to queue almost from the moment the doors are open. Mon–Thurs & Sun 11.30am–11pm, Fri & Sat 11.30am–midnight.

★ **Perro Negro Tapas + Wine** 536 Yates St ☎ 250 382 2344, ⓦ ferrisoysterbar.com; map p.742. An extension to the popular *Ferris Upstairs Seafood and Oyster Bar*, *Perro Negro's* expertly prepared tapas and thoughtful wine list (ask for the *sidra* or *txacoli*) will take you on a delicious culinary journey through the very best that Spain has to offer along with the best West Coast ingredients. Must-haves are the *croquettas* of the day ($4), *charcuteria* with 17 month *jamón* ($14) and freshly shucked local oysters (a dozen for $27). No reservations. Thurs 5pm–10pm, Fri & Sat 5–11pm.

★ **Venus Sophia** 549 Fisgard St ☎ 250 590 3953, ⓦ venussophia.com; map p.742. Afternoon tea in Victoria can be a costly affair; however the *Venus Sophia* tearoom serves up a delicious and affordable vegetarian option, right in the heart of Chinatown. Chintzy sofas and comfy chairs combine with delightfully mismatched vintage china. Afternoon tea arrives on a triple-tiered tray with treats such as lapsang souchong-infused cheese pinwheel sandwiches, lavender flower scones and chocolate butter glitter cupcakes. Choose from 25 in-house tea blends to pair with each course. Reservations recommended. Tea is served from 11am–4.30pm; $39. Wed–Sun 11am–6pm.

DRINKING AND NIGHTLIFE

Victoria boasts a lively cocktail scene and even an annual **Art of the Cocktail** (ⓦ artofthecocktail.ca) festival, held each October. There is a smattering of brewpubs, **live music** venues and **clubs** to keep you happy. **Listings** appear in

the *Times-Colonist* (ⓦ timescolonist.com) newspaper and in a variety of free magazines distributed to shops, cafés and hotels, including the *Monday* magazine (ⓦ mondaymag. com). **Tickets** for most offerings are available from the

10

city's main performance space, the McPherson Playhouse, 3 Centennial Square, at Pandora and Government streets (☎ 250 386 6121, ☎ 888 717 6121, ⊛ rmts.bc.ca).

BARS AND PUBS

Big Bad John's 919 Douglas St ☎ 250 383 7137, ⊛ strathconahotel.com; map p.742. Next to the *Strathcona Hotel*, this is Victoria's most atmospheric bar, with bare boards and old banknotes and IOUs pasted to the walls. It also hosts occasional live bands and singers, usually of a country-music persuasion. Daily noon–2am.

★ **The Canoe Club** 450 Swift St ☎ 250 361 1940, ⊛ canoebrewpub.com; map p.742. One of the city's most popular places to eat and drink, with an impressive setting – this was once Victoria's power station, and the interior retains an old industrial feel, with sturdy walls and vast beams. The patio is superb, with views towards the harbour and the Johnson St bridge, and the beer, brewed on-site, is excellent. Sun–Wed 11.30am–11pm, Thurs 11.30am–midnight, Fri & Sat 11.30am–1am.

★ **Clive's Classic Lounge** 740 Burdett Ave ☎ 250 361 5684, ⊛ clivesclassiclounge.com; map p.742. Sublime cocktail bar shaking up some of Canada's best mixed drinks. The bitters are home-made, the juice freshly squeezed, and the lengthy drink list adventurous. Mon–Thurs & Sun 5pm–midnight, Fri & Sat 5pm–midnight.

The Churchill 1140 Government St ☎ 250 384 6835, ⊛ thechurchill.ca; map p.742. Dimly lit with a polished dark wood bar, The Churchill is a sophisticated and welcoming spot a few minutes' walk from Bastion Square.

Craft beer, cocktails, whiskey and wine are lovingly selected to represent the best of the Pacific Northwest (try the Old Fashioned with a maple syrup twist, $11). Mon–Sat 11am–1am, Sun 11am–midnight.

Spinnakers Gastro Brewpub 308 Catherine St, near Esquimalt Rd ☎ 250 386 2739, ⊛ spinnakers.com; map p.742. Thirty-eight beers, including several home-brewed options, a restaurant, live music, occasional tours of the brewery and good harbour views draw a mixed clientele. Catch bus #6 to Esquimalt Rd from Douglas St. Mon–Fri 11.30am–10.30pm, Sat & Sun 11am–10.30pm.

CLUBS AND LIVE MUSIC

Distrikt 919 Douglas St ☎ 250 220 8587, ⊛ distriktclub. ca; map p.742. Bumping, laser-lit dance club which is part of the *Strathcona Hotel*. Varied live bands, including the occasional big name, and nightly dancing. Sun–Thurs hours vary for live events, Fri & Sat 10pm–late.

Hermann's Jazz Club 753 View St, between Douglas and Blanshard ☎ 250 388 9166, ⊛ hermannsjazz.com; map p.742. Dimly lit club thick with 1950s atmosphere that specializes in Dixieland but has occasional excursions into fusion and blues. See the website for events. Weds–Sun till late.

Lucky Bar 517 Yates St ☎ 250 382 5825, ⊛ luckybar.ca; map p.742. For live local music, this is the place: all stripes of bands pack in here along with DJs, hip-hop karaoke and other fun nights. On Monday evenings, DJs get the crowd dancing with '90s tunes. Mon–Sat 10pm–2am.

DIRECTORY

Car rental Avis, 1001 Douglas St (☎ 250 386 8468) and Victoria Airport (☎ 250 656 6033, ⊛ avis.com); Budget, 757 Douglas St and Victoria Airport (☎ 250 953 5300, ☎ 800 668 9833, ⊛ budgetvictoria.com); National, 767 Douglas St (☎ 250 386 1213, ⊛ nationalcar.ca).

Doctor and dentist Cresta Dental Centre, Tillicum Centre, 3170 Tillicum Rd (☎ 250 384 7711, ⊛ crestadental.ca), and the Tillicum Medical Centre at the same address (☎ 250 381 8112, ⊛ tillicummedicalclinic.ca) both accept walk-in

patients.

Equipment rental Sports Rent, 1950 Government St, at Discovery (☎ 250 385 7368, ⊛ sportsrentbc.com), has a colossal range of equipment, including bikes, in-line skates, and camping, hiking, climbing and surfing gear.

Hospital Victoria General Hospital (☎ 250 727 4212, ⊛ islandhealth.ca), 1 Hospital Way (off Helmcken Rd).

Post office 706 Yates St (☎ 800 267 1177, ⊛ canadapost. ca). Mon–Fri 9am–5pm.

The Southern Gulf Islands

Scattered between Vancouver Island and the mainland lie several hundred tiny islands, most no more than lumps of rock, a few large enough to hold permanent populations and warrant a regular ferry service. Two main clusters are accessible from Victoria: the **Southern Gulf Islands** and the San Juan Islands, both part of the same archipelago, except that the San Juan group is in the United States.

You get a good look at the Southern Gulf Islands on the seaplanes from Vancouver or on the ferry from Tsawwassen, the coastline makes for superb **sailing**, and an armada of small boats crisscrosses between the islands for most of the year. Hikers and campers are also well served, and **fishing** is good, with the surrounding waters holding some of the world's biggest salmon. The climate is mild and the vegetation is particularly lush. There's also an abundance of marine wildlife (sea lions, orcas, seals, bald eagles, herons, cormorants). All this has made the Gulf Islands the dream idyll of many people from Washington State and BC, whether they're artists, writers, pensioners or dropouts from the mainstream. For full details of what's happening on the islands, grab a copy of the *Gulf Islander*, distributed at the island visitor centres and at ferry terminals.

ARRIVAL AND DEPARTURE
SOUTHERN GULF ISLANDS

10

By ferry BC Ferries (☎ 250 386 3431, ☎ 888 223 3779, ⓦ bcferries.com) sails to five of the Southern Gulf Islands – Salt Spring, Pender, Saturna, Mayne and Galiano – from Swartz Bay, 33km north of Victoria on Hwy-17 or Tsawwassen, south of Vancouver. A few other islands can be reached from Chemainus (Thetis and Penelakut islands) and from Nanaimo (Gabriola Island), plus there's a link to the north of Salt Spring from Crofton, just north of Duncan. Reckon on at least two crossings to each daily, but be prepared for all boats to be jammed solid during the summer. Visit the website or pick up the company's *Southern Gulf Islands* timetable, widely available on boats

and in the mainland visitor centres; it's invaluable if you aim to exploit the many interisland connections. Ferries take cars, bikes and motorbikes, though with a car you'll need to make a reservation.

Destinations from Vancouver Island Crofton (in the Cowichan Valley) to Salt Spring Island/Vesuvius Bay (14 round-trips daily; 20min); Victoria (Swartz Bay) to Salt Spring Island/Fulford Harbour (9 round-trips daily; 35min). Destinations from Vancouver Tsawwassen to Galiano Island/Sturdies Bay (2–3 round-trips daily; 55min); Tsawwassen to Mayne Island/Village Bay (2–3 round-trips daily; 1hr 30min).

GETTING AROUND AND INFORMATION

Except on Salt Spring, there's next to no public transport on the islands, so what few taxis there are can charge what they wish. Cycling can be a great way to see the islands: most are small (if hilly), with paved roads.

Gulf Islands Water Taxi The Gulf Islands Water Taxi (☎ 250 537 2510, ⓦ gulfislandswatertaxi.com) has been a feature of island life since 1978, complementing the BC Ferries service and carrying visitors, schoolchildren, fishermen and others on two scheduled routes from the Visitors' Dock below the *Oystercatcher Bar & Grill* in Ganges. The first route runs between Salt Spring (Ganges Harbour) to Galiano (Sturdies Bay) and Mayne (Miners Bay); the second runs between Salt Spring (Ganges Harbour), Pender (Port Washington)

and Saturna (Lyall Harbour); twice daily September to June school days only (students have priority); $20 one way, no extra charge for bicycles. Also operates on Saturdays in July and August; check online or call for latest schedule news.

Booking accommodation Have your accommodation worked out well in advance in summer. Campers should have few problems finding sites, most of which are in the islands' provincial parks, though at peak times you'll want to arrive before noon to ensure a pitch – there are reservations in some parks (see page 687).

Useful websites For help with planning, and booking accommodation, use the BC tourism website (see ⓦ hellobc. com) and ⓦ gulfislandstourism.com.

Salt Spring Island

SALT SPRING (pop. 10,000) is the biggest, most settled and most visited of the islands – its population triples in summer. Most enjoyment on Salt Spring, as with the other Gulf Islands, is to be had from sinking back into its laidback approach to life: grabbing a coffee at a café overlooking the water, browsing galleries, cycling the back roads or hiking the odd easy trail. There's a long-standing tradition of hitchhiking on the island and a public bus operates year-round.

Ganges

Ganges, the island's main village, on the east coast 5km from Long Harbour, has a rapidly proliferating assortment of galleries, shops and holiday homes, and is great for loafing about. Ganges has a number of inviting **beaches**; the best strips are on the more sheltered east side – Beddis Beach in particular, off the Fulford-to-Ganges road – as well as at Vesuvius Bay in the northwest and at Drummond Park near Fulford in the south. Between April and October, head for the **Saturday Market** (Sat 9am–4pm; **Tuesday Market** runs June–October 2–6pm; ⓦ saltspringmarket.com), in Ganges' Centennial Park, for food and crafts.

Ruckle Provincial Park

Free • ⓦ env.gov.bc.ca/bcparks • No public transport

One of the best parks in the Gulf Islands is **Ruckle Provincial Park**, a swath of lovely forest, field and maritime scenery tucked in the island's southeast corner 10km east of Fulford Harbour. It has 15km of trails, most leaving from trailheads at Beaver Point, the rocky headland that marks the end of the access road – the best path marches north from here along the coast of tiny coves and rocky headlands to Yeo Point.

10

Mount Maxwell Provincial Park

Free • ⓦ env.gov.bc.ca/bcparks • No public transport

Mount Maxwell Provincial Park lies midway up the west coast; the eponymous mountain provides a tremendous 588m viewpoint. The park is accessed on Cranberry Road, which strikes west midway down the island off the main Ganges-to-Fulford road and turns into Mount Maxwell Rd. Two caveats: the end part of the drive is a bit bumpy – it's pockmarked by potholes and rocks. There's also no potable water in the park, so bring what you need with you.

ARRIVAL AND INFORMATION   SALT SPRING ISLAND

By plane Salt Spring is served by Harbour Air seaplanes from Vancouver (☎800 665 0212, ⓦharbour-air.com) and Ganges-based Salt Spring Island Air (☎877 537 9880, ☎250 537 9880, ⓦsaltspringair.com).

By ferry The island has three ferry terminals (☎250 386 3431, ☎888 223 3779, ⓦbcferries.com): Fulford Harbour in the south, with sailings from Victoria's Swartz Bay (8 daily, more in summer; 35min; foot passengers $10.70, cars $31.35); Vesuvius Bay in the northwest, with sailings from Crofton, near Duncan, on Vancouver Island (13 daily;

20min; same fares); and Long Harbour, midway down the east coast, which points to points on the BC mainland, notably Tsawwassen, usually via other islands.

By bus The Salt Spring Island Transit System connects the ferry terminals with Ganges (☎250 537 6758, ⓦbctransit. com; $2).

Ganges visitor centre 121 Lower Ganges Rd (daily: April–Oct 10am–4pm; June–Aug 9am–5pm; Nov–March 11am–3pm; ☎250 537 8320, ⓦsaltspringtourism.com).

ACCOMMODATION

You can choose from the hundred or more charming but often rather expensive **B&B** options (whose owners can often arrange to pick you up from the ferry), or one of the simple "resorts" – usually a handful of woodland cottages. Each of the ferry terminals also has a range of mid-price **motels**, notably the *Salt Spring Inn*.

★ **Hastings House** 160 Upper Ganges Rd ☎250 537 2362, ⓦhastingshouse.com. The best accommodation on the island, this faux-Sussex country manor is a Relais & Chateaux property and has all the bells, whistles, luxe touches (and price tag) you'd expect including a spa and fine-dining restaurant. However, faultless service and beautiful harbour views coupled with cute cottages with real fireplaces and deluxe hillside suites, make this worth

splurging on. Closed winter. **$425**

Ruckle Provincial Park Campsite Beaver Point Rd ☎250 539 2115, ⓦenv.gov.bc.ca/bcparks. The island's best campsite is in Ruckle Provincial Park – a magnificent, waterfront, 78-pitch site at Beaver Point, reached by following Beaver Point Rd from the Fulford Harbour ferry terminal (10km). **$20**

Salt Spring Inn 132 Lower Ganges Rd ☎250 537 9339, ⓦsaltspringinn.com. Right in the heart of town, this delightful hotel is very well maintained (the building dates to 1937). Of the seven smallish rooms, all come with flat-screen TVs; four have shared bathrooms. There's a good family restaurant on the first floor (daily 9am–10pm, till 9pm on Sundays). **$135**

EATING AND DRINKING

★ **Auntie Pestos** 115 Fulford-Ganges Rd, Ganges ☎250 537 4181, ⓦauntiepestos.com. Excellent locals' favourite eatery a stone's throw from the market with a lovely water view. Locally sourced seasonal creations are the order of the day, with excellent pasta dishes (around $21), piled-high sandwiches at lunch (from $12) and delicious soup of the day served in a home-made bread cup ($6). Daily 11am–4pm & 5pm–close.

Moby's Pub 124a Upper Ganges Rd, Ganges ☎250 537 5559, ⓦmobyspub.ca. Housed in an angular, barn-like building, this sustainable seafood restaurant is walkable to downtown and boasts the island's best harbour views. The patio's a fun place to swig local craft beer and munch on 18 hour BBQ brisket ($17). Frequent live music. Mon–Thurs & Sun 11.30am–midnight, Fri & Sat 11.30am–1am.

Tree House Café 106 Purvis Lane, Ganges ☎250 537

TASTINGS ON SALT SPRING ISLAND

Salt Spring Island is blessed with two idyllic **vineyards, a brewery, a cider house** and a **fromagerie**. Garry Oaks Winery (1880 Fulford-Ganges Rd; ☎ 250 653 4687, ⓦgarryoakswinery. com) and Salt Spring Vineyards (151 Lee Rd; ☎ 250 653 9463, ⓦsaltspringvineyards.com) offer inexpensive tipples (April–Oct) amid well-tended grounds. Pair your Pinot gris with a fresh *chèvre* from the Salt Spring Cheese Company (285 Reynolds Rd; ☎ 250 653 2300, ⓦsaltspringcheese.com); quite simply one of the world's most beautiful cheese shops, set in the woods, with plenty of varieties to sample and buy. Salt Spring Wild (daily 11am–5pm, restricted hours in winter) near Ganges has flights and tastings available to try at their cider house (151 Sharp Rd; ☎ 250 538 8686, ⓦsaltspringwildcider) and Gulf Islands Brewing (Weds– Sun noon–6pm), makers of Salt Spring Island Ales, has a tasting "loft" above their brewery in the Fulford Valley (270 Furness Rd; ☎ 778 354 1121, ⓦsaltspringislandales.com).

10

5379, ⓦtreehousecafe.ca. Aptly named, this elf-sized house has a plum tree sprouting up through its centre, the branches overhanging the restaurant's wooden booths. There's healthy fare such as spinach salad with pumpkin seeds and feta ($10) and a tuna melt with purple onion ($12.50). Most nights, there is low-key live (often acoustic) music. Mon–Thurs & Sun 8am–7pm, Fri & Sat 8am–9pm.

Galiano Island

Long and finger-shaped, **Galiano** (pop. 1044) is just 27km from north to south and barely 5km wide. Unlike most of the other islands, it is easily reached from the mainland (regular ferries make direct crossings from Tsawwassen).

If you're **kayaking**, stick to the calmer waters, cliffs and coves off the west coast. **Hikers** can walk almost the entire length of the east coast, or climb Mount Sutil (323m) or Mount Galiano (341m) for views of the mainland mountains. To reach the trailhead for the latter, take Burrill Road south from the ferry at Sturdies Bay and along Bluff Road through the forest of Bluff Park. A left fork, Active Pass Drive, takes you to the trailhead (5km from the ferry).

The locals' favourite **beach** is at Coon Bay at the island's northern tip, but there are excellent marine landscapes and beaches elsewhere, notably at **Montague Harbour Provincial Marine Park** (ⓦenv.gov.bc.ca/bcparks), 10km from the Sturdies Bay ferry terminal on the west side of the island. It has stretches of shell and pebble foreshore, a café, shop, and a 3km waterfront trail to Gray Peninsula (though you can easily devise your own coastal walks).

ARRIVAL AND DEPARTURE

GALIANO ISLAND

By ferry There is one ferry terminal (☎ 250 386 3431, ☎ 888 223 3779, ⓦbcferries.com): Sturdies Bay in the southeast, which takes boats from Tsawwassen on the mainland (foot passengers $17.70, cars $67). You can also get here with the Gulf Islands Water Taxi (see page 751) and there are interisland BC Ferries connections (1–4 daily) from Salt Spring via Pender and Mayne.

ACCOMMODATION

Galiano Inn & Spa 134 Madrona Drive ☎ 250 539 3388, ☎ 877 530 3939, ⓦgalianoinn.com. Right on Sturdies Bay, each room at this posh inn has a wood-burning fireplace and front-row seats to the ocean spectacle. You'll also find a renowned spa, an upscale restaurant and wood-fired pizzas on the patio. **$269**

Montague Harbour Provincial Marine Park Campsite Montague Park Rd, 10km northwest of Sturdies Bay ☎ 800 689 9025, ⓦenv.gov.bc.ca/bcparks, ⓦdiscovercamping.ca (for reservations). The park has an idyllic provincial campsite, with 28 walk-in sites and 16 drive-in sites. Booking is essential in summer; see website. **$23**

EATING AND DRINKING

Hummingbird Pub 47 Sturdies Bay Rd ☎ 250 539 5472, ⓦhummingbirdpub.com. An island institution, the *Hummingbird* has good pub fare (two-piece fish and chips; $16.50), a blazing fireplace, board games, a laudable beer selection, darts and pool tables. From mid-June through to September it runs a nightly bus that transports customers to its door. Mon–Thurs & Sun 11am–midnight, Sat & Sun 11am–1am.

Max & Moritz Sturdies Bay Ferry Terminal ☎ 250 539 5888. Cheap, delectable Indonesian and German food served from a ketchup-coloured cart at the ferry terminal. The *nasi goreng* (stir-fried rice with vegetables; $8) is recommended, but if you're catching a ferry, be sure to allot enough time for your order (30min or so). April–Nov only; open for breakfast, lunch and dinner; hours fluctuate according to the ferry schedule.

Pilgrimme 2806 Montague Rd ☎ 250 539 5392, ⓦ pilgrimme.ca. Daily changing menu of shared plates blending locally harvested ingredients and modern techniques. Expect dishes like smoked blue barley, cauliflower, fermented corn and apple ($15) or Nass River sockeye salmon with Galiano herbs and sea vegetables ($24). *Pilgrimme* is a few minutes' walk from Montague Marina. Wed–Sun 5pm–close.

North and South Pender islands

The somnolent bridge-linked islands of **North and South Pender** muster about two thousand people between them, many of whom will try to entice you into their studios to buy local arts and crafts. Otherwise you can swim, snooze or walk on one of the many tiny **beaches** – there's public ocean access at some twenty points around the island. Two of the best are Hamilton Beach near Browning Beach on the east coast of North Pender, and Mortimer Spit, just north of the bridge that links the two islands. The latter is also the place to pick up trails to Mount Norman and Beaumont Provincial Marine Park.

ARRIVAL AND DEPARTURE   NORTH AND SOUTH PENDER

By ferry Ferries (☎ 250 386 3431, ☎ 888 223 3779, ⓦ bcferries.com) come to North Pender from Swartz Bay in Victoria (up to 8 daily; 40min direct or 2hr 15min via Galiano and/or Mayne; foot passengers $11.40, cars $35.60) and Tsawwassen (minimum of one island transfer – no direct service; foot passengers $17.70, cars $67).

ACCOMMODATION

Poets Cove Resort & Spa 9801 Spalding Rd, South Pender ☎ 250 629 2100, ☎ 888 512 7638, ⓦ poetscove.com. A plush resort which has a pool, marina, bistro-pub, restaurant, store, spa, tennis, harbour views, kayak, boat and bike rentals, and a choice of rooms or two-bedroom cottages and villas. Some of the only hotel-type rooms on the island. Pender's sunsets are oft-celebrated, and this inn has the perfect vantage point. **$275**

Prior Centennial Provincial Park Campsite ☎ 877 737 3783, ⓦ pccamping.ca. Small wooded campsite at Prior Centennial Provincial Park, 6km south of the Otter Bay ferry terminal. There are pit toilets and fire pits. Open mid-May to Sept. **$13.70**

WOODS on Pender 4709 Canal Rd, North Pender ☎ 250 629 3353, ☎ 800 550 0172, ⓦ woodsonpender.com. Luxury camp experience with Airstreams, retro-trailers, cabins and a lodge, complete with every thinkable campsite luxury, including coffee makers, hot tubs, bath robes, hammocks and fire pits. On-site restaurant *Coffee + Kitchen* features craft cocktails, locally sourced food and superb teas and coffees. Airstreams **$200**; lodge rooms **$99**

EATING

★ **Jo's Place** 4605 Bedwell Harbour Rd, North Pender ☎ 250 629 6033, ⓦ josplacepender.com. This modern café space in the Driftwood Centre dishes up an incredibly wide range of dishes, including outstanding skillets or bennies for breakfast ($15.25/$13.95) or burgers and salads for lunch (try Jon's Quinoa Green Salad, $15). Daily 8am–2pm.

Mayne Island

Mayne is the first island to your left (Galiano is on your right) if you're crossing from Tsawwassen to Swartz Bay – which is perhaps as close as you'll get, since it's the quietest of the islands served by ferries. It also has few places to stay, which may be as good a reason as any for heading out here – particularly if you have a bike to explore the island's quiet country roads.

Best of several **beaches** is Bennett Bay, a sheltered strip with warm water and good sand which offers excellent kayaking and stand-up paddleboarding

(ⓦbennettbaykayaking.com). It's reached by heading east from the island's principal community at Miner's Bay (five minutes from the ferry terminal at Village Bay on the west coast) to the end of Fernhill Road and then turning left onto Wilks Road. If you want a **walk**, try the 45-minute climb up Mount Parke in the eponymous regional park; it starts near the Fernhill Centre on Montrose Road.

ARRIVAL AND INFORMATION
MAYNE ISLAND

By ferry One-way tickets (ⓣ250 386 3431, ⓣ888 223 3779, ⓦbcferries.com) from Tsawwassen (via Galiano/ Montague Harbour) are $17.70 for foot passengers, $67 for cars. Victoria crossings from Swartz Bay also stop at Galiano first (foot passengers $11.40, cars $35.60).

Village Bay visitor centre (Don't be fooled by the name: there's no village) has a summer-only booth (daily 9am– 6pm; no phone, ⓦmayneislandchamber.ca) that should be able to fill you in on the limited hotel and B&B possibilities.

ACCOMMODATION

Blue Vista Cottage Resort 563 Arbutus Drive ⓣ250 539 2463, ⓣ877 535 2424, ⓦbluevistaresort.com. Wake up to deer munching on your lawn at one of these nine fully equipped cabins in a park-like setting, with ferry pick-up and bike rental. Located 6km from the ferry, it's a quick walk to sandy Bennett Bay beach. Very well maintained. $30 surcharge for one-night stays (when available). **$120**
Mayne Island Beach Resort & Spa 494 Arbutus Drive

ⓣ250 539 3122, ⓣ866 539 5399, ⓦmayneislandresort. com. In 2012, this 100-year-old hotel added eighteen designer cottages to its property, furnished with all-inclusive kitchens (microwave, dishwasher and washer/ dryer), and bathrooms with heated slate floors. Right on the water, each unit (in both inn and cottages) has an ocean view. Doubles **$159**; cottages **$299**

EATING

Bennett Bay Bistro 494 Arbutus Drive ⓣ250 539 3122 ext 2, ⓦbennettbaybistro.ca. Ocean Wise sustainable seafood is on the menu at this charming restaurant with dazzling views across the bay and Belle Chain Islets, that's part of the *Mayne Island Resort & Spa*. They keep it simple and fresh with burgers and sandwiches that are a cut above the rest; try the sesame-crusted tuna burger ($16.95)

Reservations recommended. Daily 11.30am–8pm.
★ **Farm Gate Store** 568 Fernhill Rd ⓣ250 539 3700, ⓦfarmgatestore.com. Bounteous little market purveying the robust veggies and herbs (as well as flour and meats) of Mayne Island and Victoria suppliers. They also have freshly cooked apple pies, freshly ground coffee and freshly baked bread on-site. Mon–Sat 10am–6pm, Sun 10am–5pm.

Saturna Island

To the south of Mayne Island, beautiful **Saturna Island** boasts some good **beaches**, the best being at Russell Reef and Winter Cove Marine Park on its northwest tip. There's walking, wildlife and good views to the mainland from Mount Warburton Pike (497m) and on Brown Ridge in the southwest of the island. On the former, it's likely you'll bump into the island's contented band of goats. Head to East Point, considered to be one of the best places in the province for on-shore whale-watching and you'll spot the little white Fog Alarm Building, built in 1938 and spared from demolition in 2003 by preservationists (you'll find an interpretive centre inside). Situated on a grassy bluff, the building overlooks smooth sandstone outcrops and the occasional river otter and seal.

ARRIVAL AND INFORMATION
SATURNA ISLAND

By ferry Saturna Island has daily ferries (ⓣ250 386 3431, ⓣ888 223 3779, ⓦbcferries.com) from Swartz Bay on Vancouver Island (2–3 daily; $11.40 for foot passengers, $35.60 for cars) and from Tsawwassen but only via Galiano

and Mayne.
Useful website For general information on Saturna, visit ⓦsaturnatourism.com.

ACCOMMODATION

Eastpoint Ocean Cottages 753 Tumbo Channel Rd ⓣ604 929 9829, ⓣ877 762 2073, ⓦeastpointresort.ca. in a park-like setting near a gradually sloping sandy beach,

Eastpoint's five cabins are fully equipped and you can choose between one- and two-bedroom units. In July and August there's a min stay of 2 nights to one week. **$200**

10

Saturna Lodge 130 Payne Rd ☎ 250 539 2254, ☎ 866 539 2254, ⓦ saturna.ca. Perched on a hill, this 1920s house has six colourful guest rooms and a deck with great views of Boot Cove. Its caring proprietors give good area advice and there's a manicured garden with roses, poppies and wisteria. $159

EATING

Saturna Café 101 Narvaez Bay Rd ☎ 250 539 5177. Located in the island's general store, this is one of only two official restaurants on Saturna (the second is the waterfront pub). Luckily, it's a wonderful place to dine, even if it is rarely open. If it's closed, you'll find hearty pre-made sandwiches in the grocery store. On the menu, plenty of Saturna-raised lamb, wild BC salmon and Salt Spring Island mussels (around $15 and a regular Friday pizza night). Wed 11.30am–1.30pm, Fri 6–9pm, Sat 9am–1.30pm 6–9pm & Sun 9am–1.30pm.

Hwy-14: Victoria to Port Renfrew

Hwy-14 runs west from **Victoria to Port Renfrew** and is lined with numerous beaches and provincial parks, most – especially those close to the city – crowded during the summer months. The 107km route is covered in summer by shuttles serving the West Coast Trail (see page 776) and Juan de Fuca Trail (see page 757) but also popular for the ride alone. West Coast Trail Express buses (see page 757) make stops at all these parks and beaches on request.

Sooke

Victoria city buses go as far as **SOOKE** (38km), and you can also cycle here on the Galloping Goose cycle trail (ⓦ gallopinggoosetrail.com). Sooke is the last place of any size, so stock up on supplies if you're continuing west. It's known for its excellent art galleries and a clutch of good restaurants. Check out the small **Sooke Region Museum** (Tues–Sun 9am–5pm; ☎ 250 642 6351, ⓦ sookeregionmuseum.com; donation), across the Sooke River Bridge at 2070 Phillips Rd, to bone up on local First Nations culture and the largely logging-dominated local history.

Sooke Potholes Provincial Park

Sooke River Rd, 8km northeast of Sooke • Free • ⓦ env.gov.bc.ca/parks

If you're in town on a hot day, be sure to take a dunk in one of the natural swimming pools of **Sooke Potholes Provincial Park**. During the last Ice Age, huge glaciers tore deep chunks from the Sooke River's bedrock, resulting in the smooth watering holes you'll see today.

INFORMATION

SOOKE

Visitor centre 2070 Phillips Rd (Tues–Sun 9am–5pm; ☎ 250 642 6351, ☎ 866 888 4748). In the same building as the Sooke Regional Museum.

ACCOMMODATION AND EATING

Sooke Harbour House 1528 Whiffen Spit Rd ☎ 250 642 3421, ⓦ sookeharbourhouse.com. Many make the trip to town just for a meal at this, one of the finest restaurants on the West Coast; it's expensive, but has a surprisingly casual atmosphere, its dining room centred on a grand stone fireplace. Four-course menu ($95) could include treats such as seared albacore tuna loin, or peashoot and potato gnocchi. It also has 28 rooms, sited on a spit that overlooks verdant gardens, the Juan de Fuca Strait and the distant mountains. $329

French Beach Provincial Park

Free • ⓦ env.gov.bc.ca/bcparks

The lonely beaches beyond Sooke are largely grey pebble and driftwood, but none the worse for that. The first key stop, 20km down the road, is **French Beach Provincial Park**. An information board here fills in the natural history background of the foreshore and rich Douglas fir and Sitka forest, and there are maps of trails and the highlights on the road farther west. There's good walking on the windswept beach. Sandy, signposted trails lead off the road to beaches over the next 9km, including **Jordan River**, a logging community known for its good surf. Just beyond is the best of the beaches on this coast, part of **China Beach Provincial Park**, reached after a fifteen-minute walk from the road through rainforest.

ACCOMMODATION | FRENCH BEACH PROVINCIAL PARK

French Beach Provincial Park Campsite Hwy-14 (20km west of Sooke) ☎ 800 689 9025, ⓦ discover camping.ca. A 69-pitch provincial park campsite on the grass immediately away from the shore. **$26**

Point No Point 10829 West Coast Rd ☎ 250 646

2020, ⓦ pointnopointresort.com. About 3km beyond the campsite, the 25 log cabins of *Point No Point* make a tremendous place to overnight near the water. All the units come with kitchens and fireplaces, and some have outdoor hot tubs. There's a great West Coast restaurant on-site. **$140**

Port Renfrew

The road is partly gravel from China Beach on – past Mystic and Sombrio beaches to the logging community of **PORT RENFREW**, which has gained from being the eastern starting point of the **West Coast Trail** (see page 776) and is becoming a destination in its own right, thanks to the surrounding "Big Trees". Accommodation in town is limited.

Juan de Fuca Marine Trail

As well as the West Coast Trail, the **Juan de Fuca Marine Trail** also starts from near Port Renfrew, 6km south of Juan de Fuca at **Botanical Beach** – a sandstone shelf and tidal-pool area that reveals a wealth of marine life at low tide. The 47km trail heads east towards Victoria, taking in the beaches and coastal rainforest strip of the **Juan de Fuca Provincial Park**.

Unlike the West Coast Trail, there's no complicated booking procedure, but the scenery is also less striking and the going far easier for the less experienced walker. If you don't have four days to spare to walk it all, car parks and highway access points are dotted along its length, allowing you to enjoy strolls or day-hikes. Alternatively, the West Coast Trail Express (see box) runs back and forth on **Hwy-14**.

Avatar Grove and Big Lonely Doug

Avatar Grove is a 20min drive from Port Renfrew: directions online or maps available at *Soule Creek Lodge* (see below) • ⓦ ancientforestalliance.org

Avatar Grove is a protected (since 2012) patch of old-growth forest north of Port Renfrew, and is home to Canada's "gnarliest tree". Continue 4.5km and take the first

---

WEST COAST TRAIL EXPRESS

The **West Coast Trail Express** bus service (☎ 250 477 8700, ☎ 888 999 2288, ⓦ trailbus. com) provides an invaluable complement to the relatively limited scheduled bus services on Vancouver Island. **Reservations** are recommended and if you book a return you get 20 percent off (reservations to or from Nanaimo are required at least 48hr in advance).

The Express offers a shuttle service (May–Sept only; leaves Victoria at 6.45am) from Victoria daily to and from **Port Renfrew** ($60), **Gordon River** ($60), **Pachena Bay** ($100) and **Bamfield** ($100), thus providing access to the trailheads of the West Coast Trail and to points in the Pacific Rim National Park, such as Bamfield, that would otherwise be difficult to reach without your own transport. It also provides **inter-town shuttles** between most combinations of these destinations – and a connection from **Nanaimo** (Nitinat $105; Pachena Bay and Bamfield $125). There's also a service for the **Juan de Fuca Trail**, which picks up and drops off passengers at Victoria, Sooke, Jordon River, China Beach, Sombrio Beach, Port Renfrew and Nanaimo (Port Renfrew to Victoria $55).

right-hand turn and you'll arrive at the trailhead for **Big Lonely Doug**, the second-largest Douglas fir tree in Canada, which stands alone in a logging clearcut. Set back in the woods, these trails are accessible only by gravel roads (for Big Lonely Doug especially, a 4WD is recommended). For a more accessible tree, visit the Harris Creek Spruce (a Giant Sitka, 4m in diameter), which is easily approached from the Circle Route, just off Harris Creek Main.

ACCOMMODATION   PORT RENFREW

Juan de Fuca Provincial Park Camping Hwy-14 ☎ 800 689 9025, ⓦ discovercamping.ca. Within the park, there is vehicle-accessible camping at China Beach (see page 757) and more rustic sites along the Juan de Fuca Trail. **$18**; wilderness camping **$10**

★ **Soule Creek Lodge** 6215 Powder Main Rd ☎ 250 647 0009, ☎ 866 277 6853, ⓦ soulecreeklodge.com.

Follow signs up a 2km gravel road and you'll arrive at this scenic hideaway with three designer yurts, one cabin and four suites. Run by two chef-brothers, *Soule's* serves a complimentary breakfast in a lodge-like dining room with striking First Nations art. Guests can glimpse Washington State, the West Coast Trail and the Juan de Fuca Strait from the front porch. Yurts **$180**; cabins **$190**; suites **$145**

EATING

★ **Coastal Kitchen Café** 17245 Parkinson Rd ☎ 250 647 5545. Just down the road from *Soule Creek* (see above), Port Renfrew is lucky to have this congenial café with mouthwatering fish and chips (two-piece halibut;

$17), salads tossed with fresh blackberry vinaigrette, and sandwiches crammed with chicken and pesto ($13). Summer only. Mon, Tues & Sun 8am–4pm, Weds–Sat 8am–4pm.

Hwy-1: Victoria to Nanaimo

The first leg of **Hwy-1** will come as a disappointing introduction to Vancouver Island's much-lauded scenery; however, after a lengthy sprawl of suburbs and billboards, the landscape becomes suddenly wooded and immensely lush, more than living up to its scenic reputation.

Thetis Lake Regional Park

Free • ⓦ crd.bc.ca/parks-recreation-culture/parks-trails

Situated 11km out of Victoria, **Thetis Lake Regional Park** is good for swimming, with forested trails and sandy beaches on two lakes backed by high cliffs. There's a busy beach near the car park, which is quieter round the shore, or beyond at the bottom of the hill at Prior Lake, where there's a clothing-optional beach.

Goldstream Provincial Park

Free • ⓦ env.gov.bc.ca/bcparks/

Twenty kilometres from Victoria is **Goldstream Provincial Park**, where you'll find an ancient forest of Douglas fir and western red cedar. There's also a network of marked **trails** to hilltops and waterfalls designed for anything between five minutes' and an hour's walking. Try the paths towards Mount Finlayson (3hr walk to the summit) for views of the ocean. Back on the main road, look out for the Malahat Summit (31km from Victoria) and Gulf Islands (33km) viewpoints. There are also camping facilities in the park (see page 687).

Duncan and around

Some 60km north of Victoria, **DUNCAN** has a little downtown area with a small-town feel and some interesting heritage buildings. Duncan calls itself the "City of Totems", based on the more than forty poles dotted around downtown; there's a map online for self-guided tours and in summer there are free one-hour guided tours. Don't miss the largest hockey stick in the world (designed for Vancouver's Expo 1986) displayed alongside the community centre at 2687 James St.

The local vineyards and cider houses are also worth visiting; one of the best is **Cherry Point** (840 Cherry Point Rd; open daily for tastings and sales 10am–5pm, call 48 hours in advance to book a tour; their bistro is open Wed–Sun 11.30am to 3pm; ☎ 250 743 1272, ⊛cherrypointestatewines.com).

British Columbia Forestry Discovery Centre

2892 Drinkwater Rd • June to early Sept daily 10am–4.30pm; check website for off season hours • $16, children $11 • ☎ 250 715 1113, ⊛ bcforestdiscoverycentre.com

A five-minute drive from Duncan, the **British Columbia Forest Discovery Centre** preserves logging industry-related artefacts. Spread over a spacious site next to a scenic lake, its narrow-gauge **steam train** is a good way to get around. Be sure to check out the temporary exhibitions, artefacts and archive material in the Main Exhibit Gallery. There's also an array of working blacksmiths, sawmill, a farmstead and an old logging camp.

Kinsol Trestle

Shelby Rd (off Glen Eagles Rd) in Shawnigan Lake, 25km southwest of Duncan; see website for directions and maps • Dawn–dusk • Free • ☎ 888 303 3337, ⊛ cvrd.bc.ca

At 44m high, this wooden crossing is one of the world's tallest railway trestles. Built so trains could transport lumber, the **Kinsol Trestle** was in use from 1920 to 1979, then lay dormant until 2011, when it opened to hikers and bikers following a multi-million-dollar restoration.

Ten minutes' walk away from the car park via a flat trail through the woods, the 188m-long trestle is a breathtaking sight, its height putting you at tree-top level, while below the bridge, the Koksilah River rushes.

The Raptors

1877 Herd Rd, 7km from Duncan • March to mid-May & Oct daily noon–3pm, mid-May to end Sept daily 10.30am–5pm (flying demos at 11.30am, 1.30pm & 3.30pm); check website for winter hours and demos • $16, ages 3–12 $8 • ☎ 250 746 0372, ⊛ pnwraptors.com

The Raptors is an educational facility that teaches falconry and the environmental importance of birds of prey. The centre has a hundred or so birds, such as owls, hawks, eagles and peregrines, all lovingly cared for in pens and on tethers. Some creatures have hit the big time, such as "Judge Dread", a turkey vulture seen in the film *Andromeda Strain*. Time your visit to attend one of the daily flying demos, where you'll learn how raptors fly, kill and eat.

ARRIVAL AND INFORMATION

DUNCAN AND AROUND

By bus Tofino Bus (☎ 866 986 3466, ⊛ tofinobus.com) stops here on its routes between Victoria and Tofino/Port Hardy. Destinations Campbell River (3 daily; 4hr); Nanaimo (4 daily; 1hr 10min); Port Hardy (1 daily; 8hr); Tofino (1 daily; 5hr 40min); Victoria (4 daily; 1hr 10min).

Cowichan Regional Visitor Centre 2896 Drinkwater Rd, opposite the Forestry Discovery Centre (early April–June Mon–Sat 9am–5pm; July–Sept daily 9am–5pm; Oct–March Tues–Sat 10am–4pm; ☎ 250 746 4636, ☎ 888 303 3337, ⊛ duncancc.bc.ca).

ACCOMMODATION AND EATING

Hudson's on First 163 First St ☎ 250 597 0066, ⊛ hudsons onfirst.ca. The award-winning *Hudson's* is housed in a 106-year-old building with plenty of fun detail like adjustable crank tables and a hammered tin ceiling, serving West Coast cuisine like pork piccata cassoulet ($24) and Salt Spring Island mussels ($25). In summer it boasts a lovely patio and is a popular weekend brunch spot. Tues 11am–2pm, Wed–Fri 11am–9pm, Sat 10am–9pm, Sun 10am–2pm.

★ **IslandSkye Bed and Breakfast** 1750 Map Bay Rd ☎ 250 746 4838, ⊛ islandskyebedandbreakfast.com. Six kilometres northeast of Duncan and surrounded by nature, this adorable B&B has just two perfectly appointed rooms (one is en suite).There's a large garden and a pergola for down time, plus incredibly friendly proprietors – Paul creates a seasonal breakfast, which might include pear and brie pancakes, muffins or French toast. **$140**

10

Cowichan Valley

Striking west into the hills from Hwy-1 north of Duncan, Hwy-18 enters the **Cowichan Valley** and fetches up at the 32km-long Lake Cowichan, the second largest freshwater lake on the island. The nicest way up the valley is to walk or cycle the **Cowichan Valley Trail**, following the river 18km from Glenora (a hamlet southwest of Duncan at the end of Robertson Road) to the town of Lake Cowichan on the lake's eastern shore. You could do the trip in a day, camp en route, or turn around at Skutz Falls and climb up to the Riverbottom Road to return to Duncan, which would be a half-day walk.

A road, rough in parts, circles **Lake Cowichan** (it's 75km round the lake by road – allow 2hr) and offers access to a gamut of outdoor pursuits, most notably fishing; the area is touted as the "Fly-Fishing Capital of the World". The water gets warm enough for summer swimming and there's also ample hiking in the wilder country above.

INFORMATION   COWICHAN VALLEY

Lake Cowichan visitor centre For details of the area's many tours, trails, wineries, artisan cheese makers and outfitters contact the information centre in town at 125c South Shore Rd (end May to early Sept Mon–Wed & Sun 9am–5pm, Thurs–Sat 9am–7pm; see website for hours rest of the year; ☎ 250 749 3244, ⓦ cowichanlake.ca).

ACCOMMODATION AND EATING

Gordon Bay Provincial Park Campsite Hwy-18 to Lake Cowichan, then 14km on South Shore Rd ☎ 800 689 9025, ⓦ discovercamping.ca. Good, cheap campsites line the shore of the lake, which despite minimal facilities can be quite busy in summer. The best is at Gordon Bay Provincial Park on the south shore, 14km from Lake Cowichan Village on South Shore Rd, a popular family place but with a quiet atmosphere and a good sandy beach. Reservations essential. **$35**

The Masthead 1705 Cowichan Bay Rd, in Cowichan Bay ☎ 250 748 3714, ⓦ themastheadrestaurant.com. This classy seafood restaurant with nautical decor is located on Cowichan Bay's main drag – a short, sweet stretch of cafés and gourmet food stores that overhangs a cove. Order the Dungeness crab (caught in town; $29) and pair it with a crisp Chardonnay. Daily 5pm–close.

Chemainus

CHEMAINUS calls itself the "Little Town That Did". After the 1982 closure of the local sawmill threatened the place with overnight extinction, the town created its own tourist attraction. In 1983 it commissioned an artist to paint a huge **mural**, *Steam Donkey at Work*, recording the area's local history. This proved so successful that 44 panels followed, drawing some 375,000 visitors annually to admire the artwork and tempting them to spend money in local businesses – seemingly mostly ice cream and home-made fudge stores. Ironically, the opening of a modern sawmill has done nothing to deter the welcome influx of resident painters and craftspeople attracted by the murals.

As murals go, these are quite good, and if you're driving it's worth the short, well-signed diversion off Hwy-1. You might also want to drop in on the **Chemainus Valley Museum**, 9799 Waterwheel Crescent (daily: June to early Oct 9am–4pm; mid-Oct to May 10am–3pm; donation; ☎ 250 246 2445, ⓦ chemainusvalleymuseum.ca), a community-run museum of local history with displays on logging, mills and pioneer life.

ARRIVAL AND INFORMATION   CHEMAINUS

By bus Cowichan Valley Regional Transit System (☎ 250 746 9899, ⓦ transitbc.com; $2) runs six daily connections between Chemainus and Duncan (Rte-6; 40min). Tofino Bus (☎ 866 986 3466, ⓦ tofinobus.com) stops at Coop gas station on the highway on its routes between Victoria and Tofino/Port Hardy (advance reservation only). Destinations Campbell River (3 daily; 3hr 50min); Nanaimo (4 daily; 1hr); Port Hardy (1 daily; 8hr 15min); Tofino (1 daily; 5hr 30min); Victoria (4 daily; 1hr 20min).

By ferry You can pick up a ferry here (☎ 250 386 3431 ☎ 888 223 3779, ⓦ bcferries.com) to the small islands of Penelakut and Thetis (10 round-trips daily; 35min; $9.25 for foot passengers, $21.80 for cars).

Visitor centre 9799 Waterwheel Crescent (June–Aug daily 9am–5pm; rest of year Mon–Fri 10am–4pm; ☎ 250 246 3944, ⓦ chemainus.bc.ca).

ACCOMMODATION AND EATING

Willow Street Café 9749 Willow St ☎ 250 246 2434, ⓦ willowstreetcafe.com. Burnished wood floors and wire chandeliers create a cosy ambience at this friendly café with just-like-mom's sandwiches, salads and soups. Very affordably priced, too. Daily 7am–4pm.

Nanaimo and around

With a population of about 89,000, **NANAIMO**, 111km from Victoria, is Vancouver Island's second biggest city, the terminal for **ferries** from Horseshoe Bay and Tsawwassen on the mainland, and a watershed between the island's populated southeastern tip and its wilder, more sparsely peopled countryside to the north and west. The town's setting is eye-catching – particularly around the harbour, which bobs with yachts and fishing boats and, if you've come from Victoria, allows the first views across to the big mountains on the mainland.

Coal first brought European settlers to the region, many of whom made their fortunes here, including the Victorian magnate **Robert Dunsmuir**, who was given £750,000 and almost half the island in return for building the Victoria–Nanaimo railway – an indication of the benefits that could accrue from the British government to those with the pioneering spirit. Five bands of Salish originally lived on the site, which they called *Snuneymuxw*, pronounced *Sney-ne-mous*, or "meeting place", from which the present name derives. It was they who innocently showed the local black rock to Hudson's Bay agents in 1852. The old mines are now closed, and the region is now a commercial hub for Vancouver Island with a strong retail sector and knowledge-based industries. The town's other claim to fame is the **Nanaimo bar**, a chocolate confection on sale everywhere (see page 763).

Nanaimo District Museum

100 Museum Way • Late May to early Sept daily 10am–5pm; Oct to mid-May Mon–Sat 10am–5pm • $2 • ⓦ nanaimomuseum.ca

Nanaimo District Museum houses a well-tailored collection of pioneer, logging, mining, First Nations and natural history displays. The museum also oversees the **Bastion**, two blocks north at the corner of Bastion and Front streets, a wood-planked tower built by the Hudson's Bay Company in 1853 as a store and a stronghold against native attack; it's the oldest (perhaps the only) such building in the West. It now contains a small **museum** of Hudson's Bay memorabilia (same hours as for the Nanaimo District Museum).

Petroglyph Provincial Park

Hwy-1, 3km south of Downtown • Free • ⓦ env.gov.bc.ca/bcparks

For the wildest of the local parks, head due west of Nanaimo to **Westwood Lake**, good for a couple of hours' peaceful hiking and some fine swimming. **Petroglyph Provincial Park** showcases First Nations carvings of the sort found all over BC (particularly along coastal waterways), many of them thousands of years old.

Wild Play

35 Nanaimo River Rd, 13km south of town • Mid-June to early Sept daily 10am–6pm; mid-May to mid-June, Sept–Nov Thurs–Mon 10am–4pm; hours vary according to activity, check website for specifics • First bungy jump $130; 40ft platform jumps from $20 • ☎ 250 716 7874, ☎ 888 716 7374, ⓦ wildplay.com

Nanaimo is also home to North America's first legal public bungee-jumping site, **Wild Play**; look out for the signed turn-off Hwy-1. Along with the standard 46m plunge off the bridge, you'll find five adrenaline-pumping aerial activities including ziplining and an aerial tree course.

Saysutshun (Newcastle Island)

Ferries (foot passengers only) April to end May & mid-Sept to mid-Oct generally daily 10am–4.30pm; end May to mid-Sept daily 9am–9pm; mid-Oct to early Nov Fri–Sun 10.30am–3.30pm • $8 return • ☎ 250 729 8738, ⓦ newcastleisland.ca, ⓦ nanaimoharbourferry.com

Barely a stone's throw offshore from Nanaimo lies Saysutshun (**Newcastle Island**), and beyond it the larger bulk of Gabriola Island, beneficiaries of what is said to be Canada's mildest climate. Ferries make the fifteen-minute crossing to Newcastle Island from Maffeo Sutton Park (the wharf behind the Civic Arena) to Saysutshun/**Newcastle Island,** which has a fine stretch of sand, no cars, and lots of walking (18km of trails in all) and picnic possibilities. It takes a couple of hours to walk the 7.5km trail that encircles the island.

Gabriola Island

10

Fifteen ferries daily; 20min • Foot passengers $9.70, cars $22.90 • ☎ 250 386 3431, ☎ 888 223 3779, ⓦ bcferries.com

Many of the two thousand residents of quiet **Gabriola Island** are artists and writers. Author Malcolm Lowry, of *Under the Volcano* fame, immortalized the island in a story entitled *October Ferry to Gabriola Island*. Like Newcastle Island, Gabriola has several **beaches** – the best are Gabriola Sands' Twin Beaches at the island's northwest end and **Drumbeg Provincial Park** (ⓦ env.gov.bc.ca/bcparks) – and lots of opportunities for scuba diving, birdwatching (eagles and sea birds), beachcombing and easy walking. Near Gabriola Sands is the curiosity of the **Malaspina Galleries**, a series of caves and bluffs sculpted by wind, frost and surf.

ARRIVAL AND DEPARTURE

NANAIMO AND AROUND

By plane Nanaimo's airport (ⓦ nanaimoairport.com) is 15km south of downtown on Hwy-1 and is connected by regular shuttle buses to the town centre. Seaplane connections to Vancouver with Harbour Air (see page 747) land close to downtown below Front St on the harbourfront.

By bus Nanaimo's bus terminal is located in the Departure Bay ferry terminal, and it is possible to be picked up from the airport, too (☎ 866 986 3466, ⓦ tofinobus.com).

Destinations Port Alberni (2 daily; 1hr 30min); Tofino (1 daily; 4hr 10min); Ucluelet (1 daily; 3hr 20min); Victoria (4 daily; 2hr).

By ferry BC Ferries (☎ 250 386 3431, ☎ 888 223 3779, ⓦ bcferries.com) sail from Departure Bay (☎ 250 753 1261), 2km north of downtown, to Horseshoe Bay on the mainland, 15min north of West Vancouver on Hwy-1 (summer 8 daily; foot passengers $17.20 one way, cars $57.50). The more convenient Duke Point terminal, just south of town, handles ferries to and from Tsawwassen (8 sailings daily; 2hr crossing; same prices).

Destinations Gabriola Island (11 daily; 20min); Vancouver/Horseshoe Bay terminal (8 daily; 1hr 40min); Vancouver/Tsawwassen terminal (5–8 daily; 2hr).

INFORMATION

Nanaimo visitor centre 2450 Northfield Rd, on inland Island Hwy-19 (daily 9am–5pm; ☎ 250 751 1556, ☎ 800 663 7337, ⓦ tourismnnanaimo.com). Can help with accommodation enquiries and provides details of the many boat rides and tours to local sawmills, canneries, nature reserves, craft breweries and local food tours.

ACCOMMODATION

Both Newcastle and Gabriola islands have several **campgrounds**; if you're thinking of staying the night, check availability with the Nanaimo visitor centre. Gabriola also has several **B&Bs**.

Buccaneer Inn 1577 Stewart Ave ☎ 250 753 1246, ☎ 877 282 6337, ⓦ thebuccaneerinn.com. Family-run motel with a convenient location three blocks south of the Departure Bay ferry terminal. Rooms are spotless and recently renovated; property perks include a barbecue, laundry facilities, and storage space for bikes and outdoor gear. Studios, suites and kitchenette rooms available. **$90**

Coast Bastion Hotel 11 Bastion St ☎ 250 753 6601, ☎ 800 716 6199, ⓦ coasthotels.com. Modern hotel perfectly sited between the inner harbour and Nanaimo's main drag – Commercial St – lined with art galleries, cafés and heritage buildings. Guest rooms sport water views and up-to-date amenities including flat-screen TVs. The hotel's seafood restaurant, *Minnoz*, does a mean salmon eggs Benedict ($15.45). **$165**

Saysutshun 11 Bastion St ☎ 250 754 7893, ⓦ newcastle island.ca, ⓦ discovercamping.ca. The Newcastle Island Marine Provincial Park (known as Saysutshun by the Snueymuxw First Nations) has eighteen idyllic camping pitches. Half can be reserved online, but the rest are first come, first-served. **$18**

Painted Turtle Guesthouse 121 Bastion St ☎ 250 753 4432, ☎ 866 309 4432, ⓦ paintedturtle.ca. Bright, central hostel with four-bed dorms, family rooms that sleep four, and traditional two-tops with a queen-sized bed. The attractive lounge has table football, wi-fi, a big kitchen, board games, couches and a small gas fireplace. Dorm rooms are done up in earth tones and have cool recharging stations where you can plug in a locked-up laptop. There are laundry facilities on-site. Dorms **$38**; doubles **$99**; family rooms **$121**

EATING AND DRINKING

Most of the town's **restaurants** are clustered around Commercial St, near the waterfront. Others are up the hill in the Old City Quarter (ⓦoldcityquarter.com), a quaint enclave of nineteenth-century buildings. While lip-smacking **Nanaimo bars** – a delicious multilayered cake-bar –are found all over town (the visitor centre has even put together a "Nanaimo Bar Trail"; ⓦnanaimo.ca), one of the best is the deep-fried variety at *Pirate Chips* (see below).

Gabriel's Café 39 Commercial St ☏250 714 0271. Café with delectable offerings like a pulled pork, coleslaw and brown rice wrap ($10.50) and a coconut curry rice bowl ($15). The menu is small but healthy, and the restaurant is right in the heart of things. Daily 8am–7pm.

Longwood Brewpub 5775 Turner Rd, 11km north of Downtown (off Island Hwy) ☏250 729 8225, ⓦlongwoodbrewpub.com. Atmospheric brewpub with fireplaces, pool tables, darts and views of the Vancouver Island mountains from the outdoor deck. The beer, lovingly brewed on-site, is excellent, and the sophisticated pub fare is nothing to sniff at either. There's now also an offshoot

brewery and tasting room at 2046 Boxwood Rd. Daily 11am–midnight.

★**Penny's Palapa** 10 Wharf St ☏250 753 2150, ⓦpennyspalapa.com. Floating Mexican restaurant filled with umbrella-topped tables, colourful flower pots and warm blankets for when the sea breeze blows. The menu (reckon on $25 for dinner) emphasizes organic produce, and the margaritas are made from scratch. Very popular – get there early to avoid a dinnertime queue (it's petite) – there's now a window for take-out tacos. April to Oct daily 11am–7.30pm.

Pirate Chips #1, 75 Front St ☏250 753 2447, ⓦpiratechips.ca. Almost everything is deep fried at this heart-stopping hangout with kooky maritime decor: chilli cheese fries ($12), *poutine* ($9.50) and fish and chips (two-piece haddock; $18.75). They also fire off the town's best Nanaimo bar, deep fried and served with ice cream ($8.50). Portion sizes are generous, gluten-free, vegan and vegetarian options available. Tues–Sat 11am–8pm, Sun 11am–9pm.

10

From Nanaimo to Port Alberni

North of Nanaimo Hwy-1 is replaced by **Hwy-19**, a stretch of road spotted with billboards. For sea and sand you have to hang on for **Parksville**, 37km north of Nanaimo, and its quieter next-door-neighbour **Qualicum Beach**. Parksville marks a major parting of the ways: while Hwy-19 continues up the eastern coast to Port Hardy, **Hwy-4**, the principal trans-island route, pushes west to **Port Alberni** and on through the tremendously scenic Mackenzie Mountains to the Pacific Rim National Park (see page 767). Greyhound runs up to three **buses** daily from Nanaimo to Port Alberni, where there are connecting services for Ucluelet and Tofino in the national park.

Parksville and around

Just beyond the bridge into **PARKSVILLE**, you'll find eight blocks of motels, strip malls and garages. Thankfully the promenade, which fronts **Parksville Beach**, is unspoiled; their annual **Beach Festival** (ⓦparksvillebeachfest.ca) draws one hundred and twenty-five thousand visitors between mid-July and mid-August. The beach offers lovely views across to the mainland's mountains and boasts some of Canada's warmest seawater – up to 21°C (70°F) in summer.

South of Parksville are lovely wooded dunes, with lanes striking off eastwards to hidden beaches and secluded **campsites**. The best of the out-of-town beaches is 4km away at **Rathtrevor Beach Provincial Park** (the tide goes out a kilometre here to reveal vast swaths of sand). The public beach is stretched along 2km and sports civilized facilities: cooking shelters, picnic spots and walking trails under the shady trees. Inland, in nearby Errington, is the **North Island Wildlife Rescue Association** (May–Aug daily 9am–4.30pm, call for hours rest of year; $12.50; ☏250 248 8534, ⓦniwra.org), who rehabilitate Vancouver Island wildlife such as raptors and black bears, and **Morningstar Farm** (ⓦmorningstarfarm.ca), home to the delicious Little Qualicum cheese works and MooBerry winery.

INFORMATION   **PARKSVILLE AND AROUND**

Parksville's Chamber of Commerce Clearly signed off the highway, downtown at 1275 East Island Hwy (May–Aug   daily 9am–5pm, call for hours rest of year; ☏250 248 3613, ⓦparksvillechamber.com).

10

ACCOMMODATION

If you'd like to stay, **camping** offers the best locations, with good provincial park sites (see page 687) reasonably close at Englishman River Falls and Little Qualicum Falls (see page 765). There are a multitude of cheapish generic **motels** in town and **resort complexes** out along the beaches.

Rathtrevor Beach Provincial Park camping ☎ 800 689 9025, ⓦ discovercamping.ca. In summer this area is madness; if you want to lay claim to some of the park's camping space (which was upgraded in 2013), you'll need to use the provincial park reservations service; however,

unclaimed or unreserved spots do come up, so check with the park operator. **$35**

★ **Tigh-Na-Mara** Seaside Spa Resort 1155 Resort Drive ☎ 800 663 7373, ⓦ tigh-na-mara.com. An idyllic resort comprised of 192 hand-crafted log cabins and bungalows set among 22 acres of arbutus and Douglas, with direct access to 3km of sandy beach overlooking the Strait of Georgia and the coastal mountains. The on-site award-winning Grotto spa has a mineral pool, as well as a full-service spa; there's also a separate pool with a sauna. **$217**

Qualicum Beach and around

Compared with Parksville 11km away, **QUALICUM BEACH** has more greenery and charm, and it's less commercialized (though probably has just as many summer visitors). More a collection of dispersed houses than a town, at least near the water, Qualicum's seafront is correspondingly wilder and more picturesque, skirted by the road and interrupted only by a **visitor centre**. A cluster of **motels** sits at its northern end, where the Island Highway swings inland. The road becomes quieter to the north and is edged with occasional **campsites**.

Old Country Market

2310 Alberni Hwy, Coombs (8km southwest of Qualicum Beach) • March–Nov Daily 9am–7pm, call to confirm winter hours • Free • ☎ 250 248 6272, ⓦ oldcountrymarket.com

It's a summertime tradition to visit Coombs' **Old Country Market** and its goats that munch on its grass-covered roof. Though the store sells an eclectic range of deli items and kitsch souvenirs, and there's a market restaurant with a much-loved jukebox, it's the height-defying animals that draw crowds of sightseers.

Milner Gardens and Woodland

2179 West Island Hwy • Late April to early Sept daily 10am–4.30pm • Entrance prices range from $6–12 depending on the season • ☎ 250 752 6153, ⓦ viu.ca/milnergardens

Spectacularly situated on a promontory that juts into the Strait of Georgia, the retreat of **Milner Gardens and Woodland** is dotted with rose, buttercup and honeysuckle flowerbeds. A particular highlight is the rhododendron garden, with its five hundred varieties. The property, overseen by Vancouver Island University, was a gift from its former residents, Veronica and Ray Milner, who lived in the wisteria-cloaked house that now serves tea to visitors. Veronica was born into British aristocracy, and in its heyday her home welcomed Queen Elizabeth, Prince Charles and Princess Diana.

INFORMATION
QUALICUM BEACH

Visitor centre 2711 West Island Hwy (Jan to mid-May & early Sept to Dec Mon–Sat 9am–4pm; mid-May to early Sept daily 9am–6pm; ☎ 250 752 9532, ☎ 866 887 7106,

ⓦ qualicum.bc.ca). The obvious building midway on the strand.

ACCOMMODATION

Crown Mansion 292 East Crescent Rd ☎ 250 752 5776, ☎ 800 378 6811, ⓦ crownmansion.com. Bordering a 300-year-old grove of Douglas firs, this 1912 mansion once courted actor John Wayne and the King of Siam. In 2009, it transformed into a small, refined hotel with antique wood panelling, clawfoot tubs and four-poster beds. **$179**

Free Spirit Spheres 420 Horne Lake Rd ☎ 250 757 9445,

ⓦ freespiritspheres.com. The unique accommodation here comprises three wooden spheres suspended from trees. Centred on a pond, the tidy little units sway gently in the breeze and have porthole windows, electricity and sinks. Composting toilets, a galley kitchen, sauna and barbecue are just outside. Guests must be 16 or over. **$299**

EATING

Bistro 694 694 Memorial Ave ☎ 250 752 0301, ⓦ bistrot694.com. Super little bistro with a relaxed vibe that doesn't mean less attention to detail. Owners Tony and Nancy Szeles opened up here after closing a successful restaurant in Vancouver's Kitsilano neighbourhood: locals here couldn't be happier about it. Mains include Kashmiri butter chicken ($24) and pan roasted wild salmon ($24). Reservations essential. Thurs–Sun 4–9pm.

Lefty's 710 Memorial Ave; also 101-280 East Island Hwy, Parksville ☎ 250 752 7530, ⓦ leftys.tv. All-day local favourite with oatmeal spice pancakes at breakfast ($12 for two large), soups, sandwiches and salads at lunch, and dressed-up dinner favourites like parmesan pesto chicken ($22) and burgers (wild salmon burger $16.50). Sun–Thurs 8am–8pm, Fri & Sat 8am–9pm.

10

Hwy-4: Parksville to Port Alberni

If you've not yet ventured off the coastal road from Victoria, the short stretch of **Hwy-4** to Port Alberni offers a real taste of the island's beauty. The first worthwhile stop is **Englishman River Falls Provincial Park** (ⓦ env.gov.bc.ca/bcparks/explore/parkpgs/englishman_rv/), 3km west of Parksville (exit at Errington Rd) and then another 8km south off the highway. Named after an early immigrant who drowned here, the park wraps around the Englishman River, which tumbles over two main sets of waterfalls. A thirty-minute trail takes in both falls, with plenty of swimming and fishing pools en route.

Back on the main highway, another 8km brings you to the **Little Qualicum Hatchery**, given over to chum, trout and chinook salmon, and just beyond it turn right for the beautiful **Little Qualicum Falls Provincial Park** (ⓦ env.gov.bc.ca/bcparks/explore/parkpgs/little_qualicum_falls/), on the north side of Hwy-4, 21km west of Parksville. A magnificent forest trail follows the river as it drops several hundred metres through a series of gorges and foaming waterfalls. A half-hour stroll gives you views of the main falls, but for a longer hike try the five-hour Wesley Ridge Trail. There's a swimming area on the river at the southern end of the campsite.

Midway to Port Alberni, the road passes **Cameron Lake** and then a belt of old-growth forest. At the lake's western end, walk ten minutes into **MacMillan Provincial Park** (ⓦ env.gov.bc.ca/bcparks; no campsite) to reach the famous **Cathedral Grove**, a beautiful group of huge Douglas firs, some of them reaching 70m tall, 2m thick; they are up to a thousand years old. Wandering the grove will take only a few minutes but, just to the east, at the Cameron Lake picnic site, is the start of the area's main **hike**. The well-maintained trail was marked out by railway crews in 1908 and climbs to the summit of **Mount Arrowsmith** (1817m), a long, gentle 20km pull through alpine meadows that takes between six and nine hours.

ACCOMMODATION HWY-4 FROM PARKSVILLE TO PORT ALBERNI

Englishman River Falls Provincial Park campsite ☎ 800 689 9025, ⓦ discovercamping.ca. This popular campsite is on the left off the approach road before the river, secreted among red cedars – BC's official tree – and lush ferns. **$23**

Little Qualicum Falls Provincial Park campsite ☎ 800 689 9025, ⓦ discovercamping.ca. In the park, there's a sheltered campsite by the river and a swimming area at the water's southern end. **$23**

Port Alberni

Self-proclaimed "Gateway to the Pacific", **PORT ALBERNI** is a lumber town and an increasingly popular site for exploring the centre and west coast of the island. It's also a busy fishing port, situated at the end of the impressive fjord-like Alberni Inlet, Vancouver Island's longest. Various logging and pulp-mill tours are available, but the town's main interest to travellers is as a forward base for the Pacific Rim National Park. Still, if you've ever wanted to hook a salmon, this is probably one of the easier places to do so and there are any number of boats and guides ready to help out.

ALL ABOARD MV FRANCES BARKLEY

One of the great boat trips in BC is aboard the **MV Frances Barkley**, a small Norwegian freighter that plies between Port Alberni, Bamfield, Ucluelet and the Broken Group Islands (see page 775). Primarily a conduit for freight and mail, it also takes up to two hundred passengers, many of whom use it as a drop-off for kayak and canoe trips or the West Coast Trail at Bamfield. You could easily ride it simply for the exceptional scenery – huge cliffs and tree-covered mountains – and for the abundant wildlife (depending on the time of year: sea lions, whales, eagles). Reservations are essential, and remember to dress warmly and wear comfortable shoes: this is still primarily a working boat with few creature comforts.

The basic year-round **schedule** is as follows: the boat leaves from the Argyle Pier, 5425 Argyle St at the Alberni Harbour Quay (Tues, Thurs & Sat 8am). After a stop to deliver mail to the floating post office at **Kildonan** it arrives in **Bamfield** ($42/84) at noon. You have an hour to explore the west coast of Bamfield before it starts its return journey at 1.30pm, reaching Port Alberni at 5pm.

From June to mid-September, there are additional sailings to the **Broken Group Islands** (Mon, Wed & Fri; departs Port Alberni 8am). At 11am, the boat docks at Sechart ($42/84), to drop off/pick up kayakers, site of the recommended *Sechart Lodge* (see page 776), the only place to stay on the archipelago if you're not wilderness camping. The Lodge is also the pick-up and drop-off point for those camping in the islands and bringing their own kayaks (see below). The boat continues to **Ucluelet** ($44/88), arriving at 1pm, giving you an hour to check out the aquarium or grab a Ukee Dog. The return journey starts from Ucluelet at 2pm, calling at Sechart (3.30pm) before arriving back at Port Alberni at 7.30pm.

In July and August there is an additional sailing (Sun only) on the route from Port Alberni (8am) to Bamfield (1.30pm) and back, with an outbound stop at Sechart at 11am. After a two-hour layover, the ship returns at 3pm, arriving in Port Alberni at 6pm.

Lady Rose Marine Services 5425 Argyle St, Port Alberni ☎ 250 723 8313, April–Sept ☎ 800 663 7192, ⓦ ladyrosemarine.com. The operator for MV *Frances Barkley* also administers the *Sechart Lodge* (see above) and the Sechart Water Taxi, which services Sechart, the Broken Islands, Toquaht Bay and Bamfield ($55–80 one way, min 2 people; ☎ 250 720 7358). Kayaks and canoes can be transported on the *Frances Barkley* (single $45, double $55) or rented from *Sechart Lodge* ($55/day, double kayak $70/day, includes safety gear and paddles).

McLean Steam Sawmill

5633 Smith Rd · Site open daily 10am–dusk year-round; mill building and steam train late June to early Sept Thurs –Sun 10am–5.15pm; check website for limited and occasional spring, autumn and winter opening and operations · Site donation; mill and theatre $15; mill, train and theatre $32.95 · ☎ 250 723 2118, ☎ 250 723 1376, ⓦ alberniheritage.com

From the colourful harbour quay, a small steam train (summer only) runs from the old train station at the corner of Kingsway Avenue and Argyle Street for about thirty minutes along the waterfront to the **McLean Steam Sawmill**, Canada's only commercial steam-operated mill, which you might also reach by bike or on foot on the 20km Log Trail from the visitor centre.

Sproat Lake Provincial Park

8km north of town on Hwy-4 · Free · ⓦ env.gov.bc.ca/bcparks

For hot-weather swimming, locals head out to **Sproat Lake Provincial Park**. It's hectic in summer, thanks to a fine beach, picnic area and a pair of good campsites (see page 767). At the park, you can follow the short trails that lead to a few ancient petroglyphs on its eastern tip. Go prepared, as there are no shops or fuel within two hours' driving.

ARRIVAL AND INFORMATION   PORT ALBERNI

By plane Pacific Seaplanes (☎ 855 933 5922, ⓦ pacific seaplanes.ca) operates between Port Alberni and Vancouver for $175 each way (1–3 daily; 35min).

By bus There are 2 daily buses (☎ 866 986 3466, ⓦ tofinobu com) from Port Alberni to Nanaimo; the terminal is at 454 Margaret St. Connections here continue to Ucluelet and Tofin

Destinations Nanaimo (2 daily; 1hr 30min); Tofino (1 daily; 2hr 20min); Ucluelet (1 daily; 1hr 30min).

Port Alberni visitor centre For help and information on fishing charters, hiking options, summer events, or tours of the local pulp mills, call in at the information centre (June–Nov Mon–Fri 9am–5pm, Sat & Sun 10am–2pm, 10am–4pm in June; Dec–May Mon–Fri 8am–4pm, Sat & Sun 10am–2pm, 10am–4pm in April & May; ☎ 250 724 6535, ⓦ avcoc.com), unmissable as you come into town, at 2533 Port Alberni Hwy – look out for the big yellow mural.

ACCOMMODATION

Given the early departure of the MV *Frances Barkley* (see page 766), there's a good chance you may have to stay overnight in Port Alberni. Most of the town's accommodation is budget or mid-range hotels.

Cedar Wood Lodge 5895 River Rd ☎ 250 724 6800, ☎ 877 314 6800, ⓦ cedarwood.bc.ca. Sweet eight-room inn off Hwy-4 a few minutes outside town. Rooms come with jacuzzis, gas fireplaces and HDTVs; the decor is a bit frilly. There are hanging plants and a swing on the long porch, and the well-maintained garden has bluebells and a huge rhododendron. Inside, the common area finds a pool table, library and fireplace. Continental breakfast included. $139

Somass Motel & RV 5279 River Rd ☎ 250 724 3236, ☎ 800 927 2217, ⓦ somass-motel.ca. A recommended choice, with one- and two-bedroom kitchen suites or standard rooms with fridge, microwave and HDTV. Guests can also make use of the barbecue, the on-site laundry or have staff arrange fishing charters. RV $40, doubles $109

CAMPSITES

China Creek Marina and Campground 2011 Bamfield Rd ☎ 250 723 9812, ⓦ campchinacreek.com. A big 250-site (tents & RVs) campground, 15km south of town on Alberni Inlet, which has a wooded, waterside location and sandy, log-strewn beach. $25.75

Sproat Lake Provincial Park 13km northeast of Port Alberni ☎ 800 689 9025, ⓦ discovercamping.ca. Two popular campsites, one on the lake, the other north of the highway about 1km away (only the latter is open in winter). $25

EATING AND DRINKING

All Mex'd Up 5440 Argyle St (booth #16) ☎ 250 723 8226, ⓦ allmexdup.ca. Cheerful Mexican café decked out with streamers, Zapatista photos and a handful of basic tables with colourful chairs. The small but satisfying menu consists of tacos (4.50), ensalada ($7.95), burritos ($9.95), enchiladas ($9.95) and *quesadillas* ($7.95). Tues–Fri & Sun 11am–5pm, Sat 9am–7pm.

Swale Rock Café 5328 Argyle St ☎ 250 723 0777. Much patronized by locals, this cosy joint has a big, affordable menu with salads, seafood, sandwiches and burgers. Nearly everything comes with a side of the hearty fisherman's bread. Daily 7.30am–3pm.

Pacific Rim National Park Reserve

Park entry fee $7.80/day, kids free, payable at the centres or at machines on the official trails • ☎ 250 726 3500, ⓦ pacificrimvisitor.ca, ⓦ pc.gc.ca

The **Pacific Rim National Park Reserve** is a magnificent amalgam of mountains, coastal rainforest, wild beaches and unspoiled marine landscapes stretching intermittently for 125km between the towns of Tofino in the north and Port Renfrew to the south. It divides into three distinct areas: **Long Beach**, which is the most popular; the **Broken Group Islands**, hundreds of islets only accessible to sailors and kayakers; and the **West Coast Trail**, a tough but popular long-distance hike. The whole area has also become a magnet for surfing and **whale-watching**. By taking the MV *Frances Barkley* from Port Alberni (see page 766) to Bamfield or Ucluelet and back, and combining this with shuttle buses or scheduled buses between Port Alberni, Ucluelet and Tofino, a wonderfully varied combination of itineraries is possible around the region.

Lying north of Long Beach, **Tofino**, once a fishing village, has been dramatically changed by tourism, but retained its natural charm and it still makes the best base for general exploration. **Ucluelet**, 40km to the southeast, is comparatively less touristy, but still able to provide tours and accommodate many of the park's 800,000 or so annual visitors. Unless you fly in, you'll enter the park on Hwy-4 from Port Alberni, which means the first part you'll see is **Long Beach** (see page 773), shadowed along its length to Tofino by Hwy-4. Note that the beautiful (105km) stretch of road from Port Alberni to the park's visitor centre requires careful driving – much of it is windy and adjoined

10

by sheer drops, although there's a significant upgrade underway at Hwy-4, near Kennedy Lake (see below). At "The Junction", where Hwy-4 forks east for Ucluelet and west for Tofino, you'll find the Pacific Rim National Park visitor information centre (see below). **Bamfield**, a tiny and picturesque community with a limited amount of accommodation, lies farther southeast (it's 190km from Ucluelet by road) and is known mainly as the northern trailhead of the West Coast Trail. The **weather** on this part of the island boasts short but sunny summers and a soaking rainy season (an average of 330cm of rain falls annually), but the motto for this part of the world is that there's no such thing as bad weather – just the wrong clothes; so bring boots and a rain coat and spend your time admiring crashing Pacific breakers, hiking the backcountry and surfing. In the off-season (Jan & Feb), **storm-watching** has become a popular pastime, and rates for accommodation tend to be cheaper.

ARRIVAL AND INFORMATION   **PACIFIC RIM NATIONAL PARK RESERVE**

By car The Pacific Rim Hwy-4 is the only road to the national park, Tofino and Ucluelet. A significant upgrade near Kennedy Lake is expected to cause delays until 2020 and 1hr traffic stoppages will be ongoing (check online or contact the visitor centre for information).
Pacific Rim Visitor Centre 2791 Pacific Rim Hwy, at the

T-junction of Tofino and Ucluelet (daily: Jan–June & Sept–Dec 10am–5pm, July & Aug 9am–7pm; ☎ 250 726 4600, ⓦ pacificrimvisitor.ca, ⓦ pc.gc.ca). Provides a wealth of material on all aspects of the park, plus information on the many whale-watching, fishing and other tours. You're in black bear country; pick up a Parks Canada leaflet for information.

Tofino

While **TOFINO** is showing the effects of its ever-increasing tourist influx, locals are keeping development to a minimum, clearly realizing they have a vested interest in preserving the salty, waterfront charm that brought them – and visitors – here in the first place. Sleepy in the off-season, the place erupts into a frenzy during the summer.

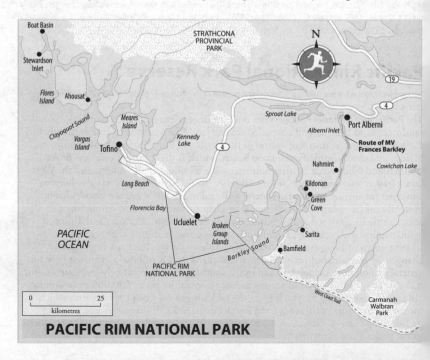

PACIFIC RIM NATIONAL PARK

WHALE-WATCHING IN PACIFIC RIM NATIONAL PARK RESERVE

The Pacific Rim National Park Reserve is one of the world's best areas for **whale-watching**, thanks to its location on the main migration routes, food-rich waters and numerous sheltered bays. It's easy to find a boat going out from Tofino (see page 771), Ucluelet or Bamfield, most charging around $100 a head for the trip depending on duration (usually 2–3hr).

Even if you don't take a boat trip, you stand a slim chance of seeing whales from the coast as they dive, when you can locate their tails, or during fluking, when the animals surface and "blow" three or four times.

10

Crowning a narrow spit, the fishing village is graced with magnificent views. There's an unexpectedly rich restaurant scene, as well as top-notch accommodation and a wide variety of boat and seaplane tours. Most of the latter have a **whale-watching**, surfing (Canada's best surf is close at hand) or fishing angle or provide a means to travel out to the nearby **islands and hot springs**.

There's an interesting arts and culture scene in Tofino, too. One particularly notable spot is the **Roy Henry Vickers Gallery**, 350 Campbell St (daily 10am–5pm; free; ☎250 725 3235, ⓦroyhenryvickers.com), a gallery housed in a traditional longhouse-style building with a cedar interior. Roy sometimes does storytelling here and the place gets packed out – see the homepage of the website for dates.

Three fine beaches lie southeast of town: **MacKenzie Beach**, **Chesterman Beach** and **Cox Bay**. The quietest beach around is **Tonquin**: ask at the visitor centre for directions.

ARRIVAL AND INFORMATION

TOFINO

By bus Tofino Bus (☎866 986 3466, ⓦtofinobus.com) runs a bus service with 1 daily departure/arrival between Tofino (346 Campbell St), Ucluelet (Murray's Grocery, 1738 Peninsula Rd), Port Alberni (4541 Margaret St), Nanaimo (departure bay BC Ferry Terminal) and Victoria (bus depot and hostels by arrangement), with connections to Vancouver and beyond. Seasonal schedules available online, booking recommended in advance. A free first-come-first-serve local transit service is available in July and August to visit local beaches in Tofino (ⓦtofinobus.com/transit).

By plane Pacific Coastal Airlines flies daily between Tofino/

Long Beach Airport (☎250 725 4454, ☎604 273 6864, ⓦpacificcoastal.com). **Harbour Air** (☎800 665 0212, ⓦharbourair.com) operates a seaplane between Vancouver Harbour and Nanaimo, with a connecting shuttle bus to Tofino.

Tofino visitor centre 1426 Pacific Rim Hwy (daily: Jan–May & Oct–Nov 10am–5pm; June–Sept 9am–5pm; ☎250 725 3414, ⓦtourismtofino.com). Offers the full lowdown on tour logistics. In summer, there's also a VW camper bus parked near the Municipal Hall at 121 Third St.

ACCOMMODATION

There are two main concentrations of accommodation options: in Tofino itself or a couple of kilometres south of town lining the beaches. Otherwise, try one of the near-town campsites. Reservations are a must in summer, when most places have a two- or three-night minimum.

HOTELS AND MOTELS

Ecolodge at Tofino Botanical Garden 1084 Pacific Rim Hwy ☎250 725 1220, ⓦtbgf.org. Eight of the eleven rooms at this eco-minded facility have shared baths, resulting in a pleasing price tag (by Tofino standards). There's also a bunk room for 4 ($159). The setting – at the heart of the town's botanical garden – is picturesque, the communal kitchen large and inviting, and the library (there are no TVs) well-stocked. All rooms include a copy of *On the Origin of Species*, and a continental breakfast and admission to the garden is included in the rate. **$149**

Ocean Village Beach Resort 555 Hellesen Drive ☎250 725 3755, ☎866 725 3755, ⓦoceanvillageresort. com. Right on Mackenzie Beach, 3.5km from town on the main road, with accommodation in single or duplex cedar cottages, all with ocean views and kitchen units. Also has a barbecue, laundry facilities and an indoor pool. If you can, spring for one of the single cottages (the soundproofing between floors is pretty thin). **$289**

★ **Pacific Sands** 1421 Pacific Rim Why, 7km south of town ☎250 725 3322, ☎800 565 2322, ⓦpacificsands. com. Designer beach houses and suites sandwiched between tall evergreens and the persistent surf of Cox Bay beach. Guest quarters come with full kitchens and gas fireplaces, and there are thoughtful extras like in-room raincoats and community "s'more roasts" of fire-toasted marshmallows sandwiched between chocolate biscuits (July and Aug). It's pricey, but breathtaking – worth it if you're looking to splurge. **$279**

10

Tofino Harbourview Motel 542 Campbell St ☎250 725 2055, ⓦislandvillagetofino.com. A thirteen-room motel on the eastern edge of town; rooms have balconies offering views of the sea and neighbouring islands. Family suites with kitchenettes available. $260

Wickaninnish Inn 500 Osprey Lane, at Chesterman Beach ☎250 725 3100, ☎800 333 4604, ⓦwickinn. com. If you're flush with cash (rooms start at $560, less off-season), shell out for this superb 75-room inn, situated on a rocky promontory at the western end of Chesterman Beach. All rooms are large and have ocean views, fireplaces and baths big enough for two. As well as the local attractions, storm-watching here is a popular wintertime activity and the spa is one of the best on the continent. $560

BED AND BREAKFASTS

Brimar 1375 Thorn berg Crescent ☎250 725 3410, ☎800 714 9373, ⓦbrimarbb.com. At the south end of Chesterman Beach, off Lynn Rd, these three immaculate rooms have good ocean views and come with an excellent breakfast. The proprietors go out of their way to ensure you have a pleasant stay. $385

★ **Chesterman Beach B&B** 1345 Chesterman Beach Rd ☎250 725 3726, ⓦchestermanbeach.net. Three luxurious oceanfront suites on the beach with private entrance, kitchenettes and bathrooms, one of which, the Garden Cottage, has a lovely private garden. Off season rates as low as $195. $355

HOSTELS

Tofino Trek Inn 371 Main St ☎250 725 2791, ⓦtofino trekinn.com. In the heart of town, this bright blue hostel

has two rooms with queen beds (both shared bath), and two three-bed dorms. Simply but cheerfully furnished – think kitchen cabinets painted a jazzy orange hue – the house, which dates to the 1920s, is tidy and secure. No TV, but there's a simple breakfast included and discounts on whale-watching (and other) tours. The best part of the experience is the kindly inn-keeper. Dorms $55; doubles $165

Whalers on the Point Guesthouse (HI) 81 West St ☎250 725 3443, ⓦtofinohostel.com. Excellent hostel, with a central downtown location and fabulous ocean views. Facilities include kitchen, games room, sauna, bike rental and storage, surf and wet-suit lockers. Reservations are essential. HI members get 10 percent discount. Dorms $55; doubles $142

CAMPGROUNDS

Bella Pacifica Campground 400 MacKenzie Beach Rd, 2km south of town ☎250 725 3400, ⓦbellapacifica. com. Offers both wilderness and oceanfront sites with hot showers, flush toilets, private nature trails to Templar Beach and walk-on access to Mackenzie Beach. Reservations recommended and there's a range of sites between $49 and $60 in peak season. Showers $2. Closed Nov–Feb. $49

Long Beach Campground ☎877 737 3783, ⓦpccamping.ca. This is the only Long Beach park campsite, on a lovely bluff overlooking the beach. It's likely to be full every day in July and August (reservations are taken up to three months in advance and are essential). 76 sites, each with a fire pit (firewood $8) and picnic table, plus washrooms and (free) showers. Closed Jan & Feb. Sites $40; RVs $60

EATING

Downtown has a lively café culture and there are plenty of first rate restaurants to choose from (reservations essential in summer). Industrial Way, just before town, is the place for start-ups with an East Van vibe – and don't miss the nearby *Crab Lady* at 900 Campbell St (fresh crab when the sign is out).

Common Loaf Bake Shop 180 1st St ☎250 725 3915. Come sunup, about everyone in town clusters around the heaving tables of the *Common Loaf*, a solid choice for breakfast, coffee and snacks (loafer breakfast with eggs, bacon and sausage $12.50, grilled sandwiches around $7.95); after lunch, the home-made dough is turned into pizzas instead of bread and rolls. Cash only. Daily 7am–6pm.

The Pointe Restaurant At the Wickaninnish Inn (see page 770) ☎250 725 3100, ⓦwickinn.com. If you fancy a big splurge, make a reservation at *The Pointe* – the area's most opulent restaurant. The views are wonderful, but be prepared to pay for them – you'll drop $105 for a four-course tasting menu ($75 for the veggie/vegan option),

and an extra $75 for wine pairings. More affordable (and still delicious) is the daily brunch menu, with eggs benedict ($22) and stuffed French toast ($21). Daily 7.30am–10pm.

★ **RedCan Gourmet** 700 Industrial Way ☎250 725 2525, ⓦredcangourmet.com. Set in an industrial part of town, the outwardly humble *RedCan* fires up extraordinary takes on Pacific Rim cuisine such as cumin-scented seafood chowder ($7) and their popular "Dirty" mac'n'cheese with bbq beef brisket ($17), as well as Tofino's best pizza. There are a handful of chairs, but most patrons head here for takeaway fare – perfect for a beach picnic. Menus change every Thursday. June–Aug daily 9am–9pm, call for off-season hours.

★ **Shelter** 601 Campbell St ☎250 725 3353, ⓦshelterrestaurant.com. A favourite for locals and visitors alike, this lodge-like hot-spot is where foodies, locavores, city slickers and surfers all rub elbows over "surf bowls" (wild salmon, teriyaki sauce and basmati rice; $15), warm *chèvre* salad with braised greens ($14) and mussels pulled up by town fishermen. Daily 11am–midnight.

TOFINO TOUR OPERATORS

Guided hikes and easy nature rambles in the forest and along the seashore are offered by several companies, and so are fishing charters; contact the visitor centre in Tofino (see page 769) for details.

WHALE-WATCHING AND BEAR-WATCHING

There are plenty of whale- and bear-watching operators in town (the season runs from March to late Oct), most offering similarly priced **excursions**. For whale tours all you need do is decide what sort of boat you want to go out on – Zodiacs (inflatables), which are bouncier, more thrilling and potentially wetter, or rigid-hull cruisers (covered or uncovered), which are more sedate (see page 769). If you take tours to Meares Islands and Hot Springs Cove, you stand a good chance of seeing whales en route – some operators try to combine whale-watching with excursions. Black bear watching happens at low tide on quieter vessels. Reckon on spending around $110 for a two- or three-hour trip in a Zodiac or rigid-hull. Operators in Tofino include:

Jamie's Whaling Station 606 Campbell St ☎ 250 725 3919, ☎ 800 667 9913, ⊛ jamies.com. Founded in 1982, this outfit offers a whale-watching choice of Zodiac boats ($125) or the 50ft *Chinook Princess*, which comes with a washroom and heated cabin ($125). If you don't see whales, Jamie's offers vouchers that can be used on another trip. Also runs the same themed tours as Ocean Outfitters (see below). Has another location in Ucluelet at 168 Fraser Lane (☎ 877 726 7444).

Ocean Outfitters 368 Main St ☎ 250 725 2866, ☎ 877 906 2326, ⊛ oceanoutfitters.bc.ca. Offers 2.5hr whale-watching tours (March to mid-Oct) on a 30ft covered vessel ($109) or zodiac ($109), as well as bear-watching (April–Oct; same price), hot springs (year-round; $109/$139) and Meares Island tours (year-round; self-guided $35, guided $125).

Remote Passages 51 Wharf St ☎ 250 725 3330, ☎ 800 666 9833, ⊛ remotepassages.com. Long-established (since 1986) Remote Passages is another laudable operation running whale-watching (Zodiacs $109; cabin $109), hot springs ($139) and bear-watching ($109).

West Coast Aquatic Safaris 101a Fourth St ☎ 250 725 9227, ⊛ whalesafaris.com. Offers whale-watching ($109), as well as bear-watching tours ($109) to inside passages on the northeast side of Meares Island and Fortune Channel or Tofino Inlet, as well as three daily trips to the Hot Springs Cove ($129).

SURFING AND KAYAKING

Tofino has established itself as the **surfing** capital of Canada thanks to reliable, enormous Pacific waves and the town is a springboard for Clayoquot Sound, which provides perfect sea kayaking conditions.

Paddle West Kayaking 606 Campbell St ☎ 250 725 3232, ⊛ paddlewestkayaking.com. For kayaks (no experience required), this operator offers 2hr 30min, 4hr and 6hr trips ($59/75/115). Also runs longer, customized tours with lodge accommodation or wilderness camping.

Surf Sister 625 Campbell St ☎ 250 725 4456, ⊛ surfsister.com. Learn to surf with a friendly local company founded in 1999, whose all-female instructors will have even the most timid novice up on their feet and catching their first wave by the end of a lesson. Wetsuits and boards are provided and they operate year-round. (group lesson $80).

T'ashii Paddle School ☎ 250 266 3787, ⊛ tofino paddle.com. This First Nations owned and operated company organises 2hr and 4hr dugout canoe tours (March–Sept; departing from Jamie's Whaling Station; $65/89) or a paddle board tour of Tofino Inlet (year-round; $65).

Sobo 311 Neill St ☎ 250 725 2341, ⊛ sobo.ca. This much-praised restaurant actually started out as a purple catering truck but has now become a hugely popular place to dine, thanks to its superb seasonal Pacific Rim cuisine – try the Killer Fish Tacos ($7.50). Daily 11.30am–9pm.

Summit Bread 681 Industrial Way ☎ 250 726 6767, ⊛ summitbreadco.com. In an industrial unit just outside own this simple bakery churns out sourdough, baguettes, iant muffins and delicious artisan pastries (try an almond croissant). Just next door is a small batch roastery, so you can get coffee with your baked goods. Tues–Sun 7am–4pm.

Tacofino 1184 Pacific Rim Hwy, 3.5km south of town ☎ 250 726 8288, ⊛ tacofino.com. Wildly popular food truck with long queues (expect a 30min wait in summer) and delectable fare like tempura fish tacos ($5.50), burritos ($11.50) and lime-mint "freshies" mixed with ice and sugar ($5). This is the original of the Tacofino west coast trucks. Daily 11am–6pm.

Wolf in the Fog 150 Fourth St ☎250 725 9653, ⓦ wolfinthefog.com. Winners of the prestigious *enRoute* "Best New Restaurant of the Year" award in 2014, the two-storey *Wolf* serves up a seasonally changing menu of fresh-foraged and locally caught and grown delights such as zingingly fresh olive oil poached cod ($28). Downstairs is a lively bar with a superb range of cocktails (try the cedar sour) and local beers. Daily 10am–late.

Clayoquot Sound

After wandering Tofino's handful of streets, most people head south to explore Long Beach (see opposite), or board one of the many boat and plane operators serving the stretch of ocean and landscapes around Tofino known as **Clayoquot Sound**. The name gained tremendous resonance in the 1980s and 1990s, when it became the focus for some of the most bitterly fought battles against loggers by environmentalists and First Nation campaigners.

The Sound stretches for some 65km from Kennedy Lake, to the south of Tofino, to the Hesquiat Peninsula 40km to the north, embracing three major islands – Meares, Vargas and Flores – and numerous smaller islets and coastal inlets. More importantly, it is the largest surviving area of low-altitude temperate **rainforest** in North America. Quite incredibly the BC government in 1993 gave permission to logging companies to fell two-thirds of this irreplaceable and age-old forest. The result was the largest outbreak of **civil disobedience** in Canadian history, causing eight hundred arrests, as vast numbers congregated at a peace camp in the area and made daily attempts to stop the logging trucks. The stand-off resulted in partial victory, with the designation of new protected areas and limited recognition of the Nuu-chah-nulth Band's moral and literal rights to the land through the establishment of tribal parks. There are five main destinations in this region for boat and floatplane trips from Tofino.

Meares Island

The shortest excursion from Tofino, and within Clayoquot Sound, is **Meares Island**, easily visible to the east of Tofino and just fifteen minutes away by boat tour (see page 771). A beautiful island swathed in lush temperate rainforest, its ancient cedars and hemlock are visible on the Meares Island Big Cedar Trail (4.2km), which meanders among some of the biggest trees you'll ever see, some of them more than a thousand years old and up to 6m across. Note that one kilometre of the trail is a wooden boardwalk of hand-split planks which can be uneven and slippery – the rest goes through the forest floor and can be very muddy).

Vargas Island

ⓦ env.gov.bc.ca/bcparks

Vargas Island lies just 5km north of Tofino and is visited for its beauty, beaches, kayaking and swimming possibilities. Highlights of the terrain here are exploratory mudflats, a craggy coastline and fragile bogs.

Flores Island

ⓦ env.gov.bc.ca/bcparks and ⓦ wildsidetrail.com

About 20km to the northwest of Tofino, **Flores Island** is accessed by boat or plane and, like Vargas Island, is partly protected by provincial park status. At the aboriginal peoples' community of Ahousaht you can pick up the Ahousaht Wild Side Heritage Trail ($25), which runs for 11km through idyllic beach and forest scenery to the Mount Flores viewpoint (886m). This is also a chance to encounter First Nations culture and people, with **tours** accompanied by local guides available; check with the Tofino visitor centre (see page 769).

Hot Springs Cove

One of the most popular trips from Tofino is the 37km boat or plane ride to **Hot Springs Cove**, site of one of only a handful of hot springs on Vancouver Island. This takes fifteen minutes by floatplane with the town's operator (☎250 725 2205, ☎866 662 8536, ⓦatleoair.com), though the most cost-effective way of reaching the steamy retreat is to take a day-tour with one of Tofino's many boat charters, who throw in whale-watching en route (see page 769). A thirty-minute trek from the landing stage brings you to the springs, which emerge at a piping 48°C and run, as a creek, to the sea via a small waterfall and four pools, becoming progressively cooler. Be prepared for crowds in summer – and note that swimming costumes are optional.

Long Beach

10

The most accessible of the park's treasures, **Long Beach** is just what it says: a long tract of wild sand and rocky points stretching for 30km south from Tofino to Ucluelet. Around 19km can be hiked unbroken from Schooner Cove in the west to Half Moon Bay in the east on trails through the woods and on the beach. The Coastal Mountain Range provides a scenic backdrop, while behind the beach lies a lush canopy of coastal rainforest. The white-packed sand is the sort of primal seascape that is all but extinct in much of the world, scattered with beautiful, sea-sculpted driftwood, smashed by surf, broken by crags and dotted with islets and rock pools oozing with marine life.

Long Beach, while a distinct beach in itself, also rather loosely refers to several other beaches to either side. If you haven't done so already, driving Hwy-4 along the beach area is the best time to call in at the Pacific Rim National Park **Visitor Centre** (see page 768).

Long Beach is noted for its **wildlife**, the BC coastline reputedly having more marine species than any other temperate area in the world. As well as the smaller stuff in tidal pools – starfish, anemones, sponges and more – there are large mammals like whales and sea lions, in addition to thousands of migrating birds (especially in May & Oct), notably pintails, black brants and Canada geese. Better weather brings out lots of beachcombers (Japanese glass fishing floats are highly coveted), anglers, surfers, kayakers, windsurfers and divers, though the water is too cold to venture in without a wetsuit, and rip currents and rogue lumps of driftwood crashed around by the waves can make swimming dangerous. And finally, resist the temptation to pick up shells or anything else as souvenirs – it's against park regulations.

As this is a national park, some of Long Beach and its flanking stretches of coastline have been very slightly tamed, but in a most discreet manner. The best way to get a taste

---

LONG BEACH WALKS

With an eye on the weather and tide, you can **walk** more or less anywhere on and around Long Beach. Various trails and roads drop to the beach from the main Hwy-4 road to Tofino, including nine official trails, most of them short and very easy – you could tackle a few in the course of a leisurely drive along the road. All the paths are clearly marked from Hwy-4, but it's worth picking up a guide from the visitor centre. Trail specifics are highlighted below.

1 & 2 Willowbrae and Halfmoon Bay (2.8km and 1km). Linked, level wooded trail that drops steeply onto tiny Half Moon Bay or the larger Florencia Bay to the north.

3 South Beach (1km). Runs above forest-fringed coves before reaching South Beach, famous for its rock-crashing breakers.

4 Nuu-chah-nulth (3.8km). Follows the South Beach trail, then passes through rainforest on a raised trail.

5 Shorepine Bog (800m). Wheelchair-accessible boardwalk trail that winds through fascinating stunted bog vegetation; trees which are just a metre or so tall here can be hundreds of years old.

6 Rainforest (2km each trail). Two small loops that follow a boardwalk through virgin temperate rainforest.

7 Combers Beach (500m). Idyllic walk along a sand beach.

8 Schooner Cove (2km). Leads through superb tranches of rainforest to an extremely scenic beach at Schooner Cove.

9 Radar Hill (200m). Steep viewpoint with peek-a-boo sea and mountain views through the forest.

of the area is to walk the beaches or forested shorelines themselves – there are plenty of hidden coves – or to follow any of nine very easy and well-maintained **hiking trails**.

Florencia Beach

West of Long Beach is the 5km **Florencia Beach** (1.5km from the hwy; access by trails 1, 2 and 4; see page 773), also known as Wreck Beach and formerly the home of hippie beach dwellers in driftwood shacks before the park's formation.

Kwisitis Visitor Centre

At the end of Wick Rd, 3.5km from Hwy-4 • Wed–Sun mid-March to late June 10am–4pm; daily July to early Sept 8am–7pm; daily mid-Sept to mid-Oct 10am–4pm; mid-Oct to mid-March Fri–Sun 10am–4pm

Located on a headland at the southeast end of Wickaninnish Beach, the **Kwisitis Visitor Centre** is the departure point for several trails (3, 4 and 5; see page 773). It has binoculars for whale-spotting and a variety of films, displays and exhibits relating to the park and the area's First Nations groups.

Cox Bay, Chesterman and MacKenzie beaches

About 4.5km northwest of Radar Hill (see page 773) – a couple of kilometres outside the park boundary – you come to **Cox Bay Beach**, **Chesterman Beach** and **MacKenzie Beach**, not part of the park but all accessed from Hwy-4. Cox and Chesterman are known for their breakers, and MacKenzie for its relative warmth.

Ucluelet

Located 8km south of the main Hwy-4 Port Alberni junction, **UCLUELET** (pronounced you-clue-let) means "safe harbour", from the aboriginal word *ucluth* – "wind blowing in from the bay". It was named by the Nuu-chah-nulth, who lived here for centuries before the arrival of Europeans. Today the port is still the third largest in BC by volume of fish landed; however it's no industrial hub. Instead, Ukee, as the locals call it, has become a destination in its own right, offering similar angling, kayaking, whale- and bear-watching opportunities as Tofino but with an even more laidback, friendly small-town vibe.

Wild Pacific Trail

Ⓦ wildpacifictrail.com

The town's biggest draw is its groomed 9km **Wild Pacific Trail**, which takes you through the rainforest alongside the ocean in two different sections: the Lighthouse Loop (plus the Terrace Beach Interpretive Trail) and the Big Beach to Rocky Bluffs section that takes in Browns Beach/Artist Loops and the Ancient Cedars trail. Much of the trail is accessible to all, including wheelchairs and strollers, and there are interactive children's sections along the way, painter's perches and astonishing views over the Broken Island group.

Ucluelet Aquarium

180 Main St, on the waterfront promenade • Daily 10am–5pm • $14, kids $7 • ☎ 250 726 2782, Ⓦ uclueletaquarium.org

This non-profit aquarium employs an ingenious "catch and release" system – all of its creatures come from, and get returned to, Ucluelet's waters. Kids will love inspecting the tanks (many of them hands-on), which are filled with fuchsia algae, a slinky Pacific octopus, fish, jellies, and bright corals and anemones.

ARRIVAL AND GETTING AROUND   UCLUELE⁻

By bus The Tofino bus running between Tofino and Victoria calls in at Ucluelet (see page 769).

By boat Boats from Port Alberni usually dock here three

days a week in the summer season (see page 766).

Getting around A car or bike is useful here, as there relatively little public transport in the central area.

ACTIVITIES

Subtidal Adventures 1950 Peninsula Rd, at the corner of Norah Rd ☎250 726 7336, ☎877 444 1134, ⓦsubtidaladventures.com. Many companies here offer whale-watching, fishing and sightseeing tours. The region's longest-established outfit is Subtidal Adventures, run by an ex-marine park warden, which offers whale-watching (mid-Feb to mid-Nov; $109) and bear-watching (May–Oct; $99) in a Zodiac or slower 12m former coastguard rescue vessel.

ACCOMMODATION

Black Rock Oceanfront Resort 596 Marine Drive ☎250 726 4800, ☎877 762 5011, ⓦblackrockresort. com. Luxurious, all-suite hotel whose guest room floor-to-ceiling windows – and balconies – overlook lanky pine trees and crashing surf. All studios and suites include a kitchenette. $249

Surfs Inn Guesthouse and Cottages 1874 Peninsula Rd ☎250 726 4426, ⓦsurfsinn.ca. Inviting, clean backpacker lodge with dorm beds, double-sized dorm beds and private rooms. The small lounge area has potted plants and a wood-burning fireplace; in summer, guests barbecue and drink beer on the front lawn. They also offer woodsy cottages that sleep four or six. Dorms $25; doubles $67; cottages $135

Surf Junction Campground 2650 Tofino–Ucluelet Hwy ☎250 726 7214, ☎877 922 6722, ⓦsurfjunction. com. A kilometre from the park and 500m south of the Tofino–Ucluelet junction, this campsite has 49 sites spread across a wide wooded area, with lots of space and privacy. Other perks include surf lessons and rentals, yoga classes, bocce ball, a hot tub and sauna. Open April–Oct. Sites $35

Wya Point 2695 Tofino Ucluelet Hwy ☎250 726 2625, ⓦwyapoint.com. Idyllic, peaceful First Nations-owned and run eco-retreat set on 600 acres of old-growth forest 5km from Ucluelet on a private beachfront accessed via a bumpy logging road through the forest. Options range from cosy yurts and well-equipped lodges with barbecue, fireplace and spectacular views to RV hook-ups and camping. Sites $35; RVs $30; yurts $150; lodges $349

EATING AND DRINKING

Hanks Ucluelet 1576 Imperial Lane ☎250 726 2225, ⓦhanksbbq.ca. Excellent barbecue shack offering take-out and eat-in options made with organic, free-range or hormone-free meat. Try the Gluttony Plate ($12) for a good selection of meaty snacks or dive into the Double Pork on Biscuits ($12) for rib-sticking fare. Daily 5–10pm.

Norwoods Restaurant 1714 Peninsula Rd ☎250 726 4001, ⓦnorwoods.ca. *Norwoods* serves the town's best cuisine – seasonal, sustainable Pacific Northwest dishes, such as Two Method Brome Lake Duck Breast ($39) – in a chic, wood-panelled building at the centre of town. Reservations recommended. Daily 6–10pm; call for off-season hours.

Ukee Dogs 1576 Imperial Lane ☎250 726 2103. Friendly and cheap hot-dog hut with innovative combinations such as a mac and cheese dog ($6.25), and the "whole hog", slathered with pulled pork, onions, barbecue sauce and cheddar ($8.50). Beer on tap, too. Daily 10am–4pm.

The Broken Group Islands

The only way for the ordinary traveller to approach the hundred or so **Broken Group Islands**, speckled across Barkley Sound between Ucluelet and Bamfield, is by seaplane, chartered boat or boat tours from Port Alberni or Ucluelet (see page 766); boats dock at Sechart, where you can stay at a former whaling station (see below).

Immensely wild and beautiful, the islands have the reputation for tremendous wildlife (seals, sea lions and whales especially), the best **kayaking** in North America, and some of the continent's finest **diving**; however, access to dive outfits is limited. You can rent kayaks and gear at Sechart – contact the Lady Rose Marine Services (see page 766) office in Port Alberni to check current arrangements. You need to know what you're doing – there's plenty of dangerous water – and you should pick up the relevant marine chart (*Canadian Hydrographic Service Chart: Broken Group 3670*) onboard the *Frances Barkley*, or it's available locally (try Pioneer Boat Works in Ucluelet, 166 Fraser Lane; ☎250 726 4382). Divers can choose from among fifty shipwrecks claimed by the reefs, rough waters and heavy fogs that beset the aptly named islands. Contact the Pacific Rim National Park information centre (see page 768) for latest details; (☎250 726 4212, ⓦpc.gc.ca).

| ACCOMMODATION | BROKEN GROUP ISLANDS |

Broken Group Islands Camping ☎250 726 4212, ⓦpc.gc.ca. Seven rough campsites serve the group, but water is hard to come by; pick up the park leaflet on camping and freshwater locations. Campfires permitted

along or below the high tide mark. $9.80
Sechart Lodge ☎ 250 723 8313, ☎ 800 663 7192,
ⓦ ladyrosemarine.com. The *Sechart Lodge* is a potentially
magical base for exploring the islands and the only place
to stay if you're not wilderness camping on the archipelago.
Access is via the MV *Frances Barkley*, which docks nearby
(see page 766). Rate includes meals. $357

Bamfield

A quaint, remote spot 190km southeast of Ucluelet, **BAMFIELD** is half-raised above the
ocean on a wooden boardwalk. The village is best known as the northern starting point
of the **West Coast Trail** (the trailhead is 5km away at Pachena Bay), but its population
jumps to well over two thousand in the summer with the arrival of divers, kayakers and
fishermen. Plenty of services have sprung up in the more downbeat part of the village
away from the boardwalk – tours, fishing charters, stores and galleries – but there's
relatively limited accommodation.

Despite the influx the village retains its charm, with the boardwalk accessing one side
of Bamfield Inlet (the open sea, the other), so that the bay below the boardwalk is a
constant hum of activity as boats ply the water. Trails lead down from the boardwalk
to a series of pleasant small beaches. The village is a good place to join the activities,
birdwatch, walk, beachcomb or sit in cafés. For a short stroll, wander to **Brady's Beach**
or the Cape Beale Lighthouse and Keeha and Tapaltos beaches some way beyond.
And if you just want to tackle the stage to the trailhead of the West Coast Trail and
return to Bamfield in a day, you can walk the 10km (round-trip) to the **Pachena
Point Lighthouse**, starting from the Ross Bible Camp on the *Huu-ay-aht First Nation*
campsite at Pachena Beach. After that, the route becomes the real thing.

ARRIVAL AND INFORMATION   BAMFIELD

By bus Make a reservation on the West Coast Trail Express
bus (see page 757; ☎ 250 477 8700, ⓦ trailbus.com),
which runs via Victoria, Port Renfrew and Nanaimo.
By boat Bamfield is accessible by the MV *Frances Barkley*
(see page 766).
By car Bamfield is accessible by a gravel logging road from

Port Alberni 76km to the north (note that there are no fuel
stations on this stretch), or gravel road from Lake Cowichan
113km to the east.
Bamfield visitor centre Centennial Park (☎ 250 728
3006, ⓦ bamfieldchamber.com). Open only in July and
August (daily 9am–7pm).

ACCOMMODATION

Pachena Beach camping 5km south of Bamfield
☎ 250 728 1287, ⓦ hfngroup.ca. The Huu-ay-aht First
Nation Pachena Bay band offers a beautiful campsite at
Pachena Beach, with sand-up paddleboards available
to rent. Note that a rough road leads up to the site.
Reservations are essential. April–Oct. Sites $36; RVs $45

Woods End Landing Cottages 168 Wild Duck Rd ☎ 250
728 3383, ☎ 877 828 3383, ⓦ bamfieldcottages.com
These feature four secluded log cottages that sleep four,
and two suites on a spacious waterfront site with great
opportunities for outdoor activities. Two-night min. $165

The West Coast Trail

One of North America's classic walks, the **West Coast Trail** (**WCT**) starts 5km south of
Bamfield and traverses exceptional coastal scenery for 75km to Port Renfrew. It's no
stroll, and requires expertise in backcountry camping, proper equipment and a fair
degree of fitness (and numbers are strictly limited). Many people do the first stage as a
day-trip from Bamfield. Reckon on six to eight days for the full trip; carry all your own
food and be prepared for rain, treacherous stretches, thick soaking forest and almost
utter isolation.

Mariners long ago dubbed this area of coastline the "graveyard of the Pacific", and when
the SS *Valencia* went down here with nearly all hands (a few of the crew survived) in 1906
the government was persuaded that constructing a trail would at least give stranded sailors
a chance to walk to safety along the coast. The path followed a basic telegraph route that

linked Victoria with outlying towns and lighthouses, and was kept open by linesmen and lighthouse keepers until the 1960s, when it fell into disrepair. Early backpackers reblazed the old trail, which now passes through the traditional territory of the Huu-ay-aht First Nation around Bamfield, Ditidaht First Nation country in the trail's middle section and ends in Pacheedaht First Nation traditional territory near Port Renfrew.

Weather is a key factor in planning any trip; the trail is only open May to September, July and August being the driest months; during that period it's patrolled by parks staff and First Nations guardians. Locals are on hand to ferry you (for a fee) across some of the wider rivers en route.

10

INFORMATION	THE WEST COAST TRAIL

Quota system Pre-planning is essential, as Parks Canada has a quota system and reservation-registration-orientation procedures to protect the environment. Numbers are limited to around 7000 a year while the path is open (May–Sept) and Port Renfrew (Gordon River trailhead is 5km north of the town; trailhead information centre daily in season 9am–5pm; ☎ 250 647 5434), Bamfield (Pachena Bay trailhead is 5km south of town; information centre daily in season 9am–5pm; ☎ 250 728 3234) and Nitinat Village are the *only* allowed entrance and exit points for the trail, except in exceptional circumstances.

Reservations You can make reservations from January of the year you wish to walk and you'll need to move fast. To make bookings, call ☎ 250 726 4453, ☎ 866 727 5722 (Daily 8am–4pm) or head online to ⓦ pc.gc.ca/pacificrim. Be ready to state the location from which you wish to start, the date of departure, two alternative start dates, credit card details and the number in your party (10 max). July and August are the most popular months.

Costs It costs $24.50 to make a reservation. Another $127.50/person is payable as a user fee, paid in person at the beginning of the trail. Allow $20 apiece for the two ferry crossings (at Gordon River and Nitinat Narrows) along the route (paid at the WCT centres at the orientation session – see page 776: the WCT Overnight Permit is your receipt for these crossings). The total you'll pay is $192. Take cash with you to pay nominal fees for camping on Aboriginal land.

Transport to and from the trail For the northern trailhead at Bamfield, the most exhilarating access is via the MV *Frances Barkley* from Port Alberni (see page 766). The West Coast Trail Express (see page 757) runs in each direction between Victoria and Pachena Bay/Bamfield via Nanaimo; to Port Renfrew and back from Victoria; and between Bamfield and Nanaimo. Reservations are essential.

Beginning the hike Before heading out, you must attend a compulsory 1hr orientation session at the trailhead information centre, where you will receive your permit and a briefing on conditions and safety issues.

Northern Vancouver Island

It's a moot point where the **north of Vancouver Island** starts, but if you're travelling on Hwy-19 the landscape's sudden lurch into more unspoilt wilderness after Qualicum Beach makes as good a watershed as any. From the road, the scenery is uneventful but restful on the eye, and graced with ever-improving views of the mainland. Along Hwy-19 lies the hamlet of Buckley Bay (43km north of Qualicum Beach), which consists of little more than a ferry terminal to **Denman and Hornby islands**.

Few of the towns along Hwy-19 require major sightseeing, and you could bus or drive the length of Vancouver Island to Port Hardy and take the **Inside Passage** or **Discovery Coast Passage** ferry, which are among the top experiences of any visit to BC. Both journeys are a great – and cheap – way of getting what people on the big cruise ships get: views of some of the grandest coastal scenery on the continent, including mountains, islands, waterfalls, glaciers, sea lions, whales and eagles. Alternatively, you could follow the main highway as far as **Courtenay**, and from there catch a ferry across to the mainland. Yet if you have the means, try to get into the wild, central interior, much of it contained within **Strathcona Provincial Park**.

Denman and Hornby islands

Denman and Hornby islands are two outposts that have been described, with some justification, as the "undiscovered Gulf Islands" with Hornby boasting some of the province's best beaches. The population is made up of a laidback medley of alternative types. Ferries drop you on the island's west coast a few moments' walk from Denman Village: to get to Hornby you need to head 11km across the island to another terminal at Gravelly Bay, where a fifteen-minute crossing drops you at the island's Shingle Spit dock. Most of what happens on Hornby happens at **Tribune Bay** on the far side of the island, 10km away. There's no public transport on either island, so you'll need a car or bike to explore.

Highlights on Denman are the beaches of the Sandy Island Provincial Marine Park (ⓦenv.gov.bc.ca/bcparks), an island accessed on foot at low tide from the northwest tip (take Northwest Rd from the village), and the 800m loop trail of Boyle Point Park at the southernmost tip (just beyond the Gravelly Bay ferry terminal) to the Chrome Island Lighthouse, and Fillongley Provincial Park (ⓦenv.gov.bc.ca/bcparks/explore/parkpgs/fillongley), where there's a campsite (see opposite), forest trails and a pretty stretch of coastline.

On Hornby, **Helliwell Bay Provincial Park** (ⓦenv.gov.bc.ca/bcparks/explore/parkpgs/helliwell/) at the island's southern tip (take Helliwell Road from Tribune Bay) and its trails are the highlight; the best is a 6km (1hr–1hr 30min) loop to Helliwell Bluffs, offering plenty of opportunities to see eagles, herons, spring wildflowers and lots of aquatic wildlife. Whaling Station Bay with its smooth sandstone rocks and Tribune Bay Provincial Park (ⓦenv.gov.bc.ca/bcparks) have exceptional beaches.

ARRIVAL AND DEPARTURE

BC Ferries (☎250 386 3431, ☎888 223 3779, ⓦbcferries.com) depart Vancouver Island (Buckley Bay) to Denman Island (10 round-trips daily; 10min) and from Denman Island to Hornby Island (10 round-trips daily; 10min). Note that you'll need to travel 11km between ports on Denman and there's no public transport on either island.

INFORMATION AND ACTIVITIES

Useful websites ⓦdenmanisland.com has a list of island accommodation and attractions. For further information on Hornby visit ⓦhornbyisland.com
Biking Mountain biking is popular on Hornby with 80km of well-maintained single track trails. Stop by Hornby Outdoo Sports bike shop at the Ringside Market (closed Dec–Feb) to pick up trail maps and advice.

ACCOMMODATION AND EATING
DENMAN AND HORNBY ISLANDS

Accommodation is in short supply on both islands, and it's essential in summer to have prebooked rooms. Hornby has far more **rooms** and **campsites**. At Tribune Bay on Hornby the Co-op (5875 Central Rd) at the Ringside Market is the hub of island life (Mon–Sat 9.30am–5.30pm; ☎250 335 1121, ⓦhornbyislandcoop.ca).

DENMAN
Earth Club Factory 3806 Denman Rd ☎250 335 2688, ⓦearthclubfactory.com. Friendly guesthouse in a 100-year old farmhouse, where deer trot through the garden nibbling on the grass, and its licensed bistro also hosts live music and performance nights. Rooms are basic but spotlessly clean and a DIY pancake breakfast is included. Dorms $\underline{\$24}$; private rooms $\underline{\$59}$
Fillongley Provincial Park Campsite Beadnell Rd ☎800 689 9025, ⓦenv.gov.bc.ca/bcparks, ⓦdiscover camping.ca. There's a small (ten-site), rural provincial park campsite here close to old-growth forest and pebbly beach, 4km across the island from the ferry on the east shore facing the Lambert Channel. $\underline{\$23}$

HORNBY
Bradsdadsland Waterfront Campsite 2105 Shingle Spit Rd ☎250 335 0757, ⓦbradsdadsland.com. You can camp at *Bradsdadsland*, a family-oriented campsite overlooking Lambert Channel, 3.3km from the ferry terminal. There's a small general store and beach access May–Oct. $\underline{\$41.50}$
Cardboard House Bakery 2205 Central Rd ☎250 335 0733, ⓦthecardboardhousebakery.com. Island hub housing a landmark summertime bakery: pizza served in the evening and live music on Wed and Sun. Plenty of vegetarian and vegan options, and there's a delightful garden where you can enjoy your meal. March–Sept Mon 8.30am–4pm, Tues–Sun 8.30am–9pm
Sea Breeze Lodge 5205 Fowler Rd ☎250 335 2321 ⓦseabreezelodge.com. Set on a picturesque and spacious property, *Sea Breeze* has sixteen family and pet-friendly waterfront cottages with sea views and an ocean-facing hot tub. Throughout July and August it becomes an all-meals-included resort with a smorgasbord of activities include bocce ball, tennis, boating and biking. $\underline{\$190}$

Comox Valley

On Hwy-19 north of Buckley Bay is a short stretch of wild, pebbly beach, and then the Comox Valley – open rural country. Of three settlements here – Comox, Cumberland and Courtenay – the last is of the most interest, with its quaint downtown area and small restaurant scene. Neighbouring Comox is notable for being a ferry link to Powell River (see page 721) on the mainland, and little Cumberland, thanks to its coal mining past, was once the second largest Chinatown on North America's west coast.

The Comox Valley scores higher inland, on the eastern fringes of Strathcona Provincial Park (see page 782) and the **skiing** area of Mount Washington (ⓦmountwashington.ca), 40km northwest of Comox. There's plenty of **hiking and mountain biking** in summer, especially on Forbidden Plateau, a former ski resort. For details of walks ask at the visitor centre (see below).

10

ARRIVAL AND INFORMATION   COMOX VALLEY

By ferry The terminal is located in Comox, a good 20min drive from town, down back roads (ⓣ250 386 3431, ⓣ888 223 3779, ⓦbcferries.com), with services to Powell River on the mainland (4 daily; 1hr 20min).

By bus Courtenay is connected to Nanaimo and Victoria by

3 daily buses (ⓣ866 986 3466, ⓦtofinobus.com).

Vancouver Island visitor centre 3607 Small Road, Cumberland (daily 9am–5pm; ⓣ855 400 2882, ⓦdiscover comoxvalley.com).

ACCOMMODATION

There are plenty of motels along the strip on the southern approach, close to Hwy-19A.

The Cona Hostel 440 Anderton Ave ⓣ250 331 0991, ⓣ877 490 CONA, ⓦconagetaways.com. Housed in a heritage building from 1894, in summertime you can jump straight into the Courtenay River from the hostel. Offering three dorms (two mixed and one women's) plus five private rooms, a fully equipped kitchen, barbecue and a winter shuttle bus to Mount Washington. Dorms $26; doubles $60

Miracle Beach Provincial Park Campsite Off Hwy-19A ⓣ800 689 9025, ⓦenv.gov.bc.ca/bcparks, ⓦdiscover

camping.ca. The best camping hereabouts is 22km north of Courtenay at Miracle Beach Provincial Park – a vast, but very popular, tract of sand. $28

Old House Village Hotel & Spa 1730 Riverside Lane ⓣ250 703 0202, ⓣ888 703 0202, ⓦoldhousevillage. com. Actually a delightful modern all-suite hotel located on the Courtenay River (which is shadowed by a pleasant bike path). Walkable to area restaurants, the guest rooms come with fireplaces and kitchenettes. You'll also find an outdoor heated pool and hot-tub. $170

EATING

Atlas Café 250 6th St ⓣ250 338 9838, ⓦatlascafe. ca. Aptly named, this café has a world-travelling menu that touches on everything from Italian (carbonara pasta; $18.50), Japanese (veggie nori rolls; $11) and Mediterranean flavours (platter; $17). Tues–Thurs 8.30am–9.30pm, Fri & Sat 8.30am–10pm, Sun 8.30am–3.30pm.

Wayward Distillery 2931 Moray Ave ⓣ250 871 0424, ⓦwaywarddistillationhouse.com. One of the many artisan craft distilleries that have popped up in BC, Wayward distills its "Unruly" gin and vodka from a pure BC honey base. Wayward's handsome tasting lounge is open daily from noon–6pm for tastings and tours.

Campbell River

Of the myriad Canadian towns that claim to be "Salmon Capital of the World", CAMPBELL RIVER is probably the one that comes closest to justifying the boast. The town grew to accommodate fishermen from the outset, centred around a hotel built in 1904 after word spread of the colossal fish that local Cape Mudge Aboriginal people were able to pluck from the sea. Today the majority of visitors come to dangle a line in the water. Others come for the diving, snorkelling with the salmon, and bear- and whale-watching, while for the casual visitor the place serves as the main road access to the wilds of Strathcona Provincial Park or an overnight stop en route for the morning departures of the MV *Uchuck III* from Gold River (see page 783).

Numerous shops and guides are on hand to help out and rent **fishing** equipment; you'll need a saltwater fishing licence that you can buy online in advance (ⓦfishing.

gov.bc.ca). Huge numbers of people fish (May–Oct 7am–dusk; $3/hr) from the 182m **Discovery Pier** (☎250 286 6199; 700 Block Island Hwy), Canada's first saltwater fishing pier. If you want to know more about salmon before it ends up on your plate, drop in at the **Quinsam Salmon Hatchery** (daily 8am–4pm; ☎250 287 9564), 5km west of town on Hwy-28 on the way to Gold River (see page 782).

10

Campbell River Museum

470 Island Hwy, at 5th Ave · Mid-May to Sept daily 10am–5pm; Oct to early May Tues–Sun noon–5pm · $8 · ☎250 287 3103, Ⓦ crmuseum.ca

A compelling little museum devoted to the region's fishing, logging and First Nation histories, the **Campbell River Museum** begins with a striking array of Kwakwaka'wakw masks, which, via a sound and light display, depict the mythical underwater voyage of Siwidi, a tribal ancestor. You'll also find incredible wood carvings, such as a "house post" with teeth-baring wolves, and a huge black and turquoise feast dish. Elsewhere are a re-created floathouse (complete with sounds of calling sea birds), and early settlement and salmon industry exhibits.

ARRIVAL AND INFORMATION
CAMPBELL RIVER

By plane Pacific Coastal Airlines (☎800 663 2872, Ⓦ pacificcoastal.com) and Central Mountain Air (☎888 865 8585, Ⓦ flycma.com) both fly to Campbell River from Vancouver.

By bus Three buses run daily to Victoria. The bus terminal is on the corner of Cedar and 13th near the Royal Bank (☎866 986 3466, Ⓦ tofinobus.com).

Campbell River visitor centre 1235 Shopper's Row (May–Oct daily 9am–6pm, call for hours rest of year; ☎877 286 5705, Ⓦ campbellriver.travel).

ACCOMMODATION

★**Painter's Lodge** 1625 McDonald Rd ☎250 287 3066, ☎800 663 7090, Ⓦ painterslodge.com. Legendary fishing lodge on the banks of Discovery Passage with a range of excellent accommodation from cabins in the woods to swish suites, with an on-site pub which offers live music, and a fine-dining restaurant overlooking the sea and mountains. *Painter's* has excellent adventure and fishing programmes. Twinned with the equally well equipped *April Point* on Quadra Island, there is a free shuttle boat between the two resorts. **$180**

Parkside Campground 6301 Gold River Hwy, 5km west of town ☎250 830 1428, Ⓦ parksidecampingrv. com. Well-tended, forested campground with laundry, wi-fi and fire pits. April–Oct. **$25**

EATING

Wasabiya Japanese Sushi Café 465 Merecroft Rd ☎250 287 7711, Ⓦ wasabiyasushicafe.com. Pre-eminent sushi spot with tempting menu divergences such as chilled noodles with fish cake ($11.50) and mixed tempura in a hot soup ($10.75). Reservations highly recommended. Tues–Thurs 11.30am–8pm, Fri 11.30am–9pm, Sat 4–9pm.

Quadra Island

Quadra Island and its fine beaches and museum are fifteen minutes away from Campbell River, the main excuse for the crossing is the **Nuyumbalees Cultural Centre** (May–Sept daily 10am–4pm; $10; ☎250 285 3733, Ⓦ museumatcapemudge.com) in Cape Mudge Village, south of the terminal near the island's southern tip (take Green Rd). The centre is home to one of the country's most noted sacred potlatch collections. As elsewhere in Canada, the regalia, masks and ritual objects of the community were confiscated by the government in 1884 in an attempt to stamp out one of the First Nations most potent ceremonies. The museum is involved in an ongoing repatriation project after the first items were returned after a 30-year negotiation. The museum offers tours if you call them at least two weeks in advance and throughout summer you can book a traditional salmon barbecue on Saturdays (reserve by Thursday) for $25 per person.

While on the island you can also laze on its beaches, walk its **trails** – Mortle Lake (5km loop) and Newton Lake from Granite Bay (8km round-trip) – or climb Chinese

Mountain (3km round-trip) for some cracking views. There's swimming in a warm, sheltered bay off a rocky beach at **Rebecca Spit Provincial Park** (ⓦenv.gov.bc.ca/bcparks), a 1.5km spit near Drew Harbour 8km east of the ferry terminal, but the water's warmer still at the more distant **Village Bay Lake**. The island's main community, Heriot Bay, is on the east coast with a store and coffee shop.

ARRIVAL AND DEPARTURE · QUADRA ISLAND

By ferry Ferries run roughly hourly from the well-signed terminal out of Campbell River to Quathiaski Cove on Quadra Island; the trip takes 10min ($8.90 return for foot passengers, $20.65 return for a car; ☎ 250 386 3431, ☎ 888 223 3779, ⓦ bcferries.com).

ACCOMMODATION

Taku Lodge 616 Taku Rd ☎ 250 285 3031, ⓦ takuresort.com. Idyllic wooden cabins, suites and houses sleeping 4–8, on Drew Harbour with unspoiled views across the sea and direct access to the pebble beach. Family and pet-friendly, the resort also offers kayaking and paddleboard rental and cookery classes. Sites __$35__; suites __$159__; cabins __$189__

Tsa-Kwa-Luten Lodge 1 Lighthouse Rd ☎ 250 285 2042, ☎ 800 665 7745, ⓦ capemudgeresort.bc.ca. A superb waterfront lodge by the Cape Mudge Lighthouse. Based on a longhouse, with a predominantly First Nations decorative scheme, there's a cottage and lodge units, restaurant, sauna, laundry, and access to tours and activities. __$129__

Cortes Island

If you've taken the trouble to see Quadra Island, then you should push on to the still quieter **Cortes Island** at the neck of Desolation Sound, one of North America's finest sailing and kayaking areas. Life here is relaxed and the main community is at **Manson's Landing**, 15km from the ferry terminal at Whaletown.

The island is also known for its superlative clams and oysters and for one of Canada's leading holistic centres, the *Hollyhock Retreat Centre* on Highland Road (☎250 935 6576, ☎800 933 6339, ⓦhollyhock.ca), where you can take all manner of body- and soul-refreshing courses. Places to make for around the island include the small **Smelt Bay Provincial Park** (ⓦenv.gov.bc.ca/bcparks), 25km south of the ferry, which has a campsite ($20) and opportunities to swim, fish, canoe and walk. Nearly adjacent is **Manson's Landing Provincial Park** (ⓦenv.gov.bc.ca/bcparks), with good beaches, and **Hague Lake Provincial Park** (ⓦenv.gov.bc.ca/bcparks), signed from Manson's Landing, with several looped trails such as Sutil Point, accessible from myriad turn-offs on the road. If you're in a canoe or boat then you can also make for a couple of marine parks (Von Donop and Manson's Landing), small bays, lagoons and beaches.

ARRIVAL AND INFORMATION · CORTES ISLAND

By ferry Cortes is 45min from Quadra on a second ferry (5 daily; foot passenger $10.45 return, car $24.10; ☎250 386 3431, ☎888 223 3779, ⓦ bcferries.com).

Useful website ⓦ ourcortes.com.

Elk Falls Provincial Park

Free · ⓦ env.gov.bc.ca/bcparks

The approach to Strathcona Provincial Park along Hwy-28 is worth taking for the scenery alone; numerous short trails and nature walks are accessed via a suspension bridge just a few minutes' walk through the forest away from the car park. **Elk Falls Provincial Park**, noted for its gorge and waterfall, is the first stop, ten minutes out of Campbell River. On the access road and lakeshore proper, good **shorter trails** include the 500m stroll to impressive Lupin Falls; the Karst Creek Trail (2km loop), which runs through a strange landscape of sinkholes and vanishing streams; Bedwell Lake at the lake's southern end, a steep (600m ascent) 10km round-trip trail to the eponymous lake and high meadows (allow 2hr each way); and Upper Myra Falls (3km each way), which climbs from near the end of the road to a viewpoint over the Myra waterfall.

ACCOMMODATION
ELK FALLS PROVINCIAL PARK

Elk Falls Provincial Park Campsite Hwy-28 towards Gold River ☎ 800 689 9025, ⓦ env.gov.bc.ca/bcparks, ⓦ discovercamping.ca (for reservations). Large campsite with sites split between the Quinsam River and a majestic forest. $20

Strathcona Provincial Park

Free • ⓦ env.gov.bc/bcparks

Established in 1911, **Strathcona Provincial Park** is Vancouver Island's largest protected area, and the oldest park in BC. It's also where the scenery approaches the grandeur of the mainland mountains. The island's highest point, Golden Hinde (2220m) is here, and there's a good chance of seeing rare indigenous wildlife such as the Roosevelt elk, marmot and black-tailed deer. Only two areas have any facilities for visitors – **Forbidden Plateau** on the park's eastern side, and the more popular **Buttle Lake** region, accessible from Campbell River via Hwy-28. The rest of the park is wilderness, but fully open to backpackers and hardier walkers.

You'll see numerous pictures of **Della Falls** around Campbell River which, at 440m, are Canada's highest, though it takes a two-day trek to see them via Port Alberni.

ACCOMMODATION
STRATHCONA PROVINCIAL PARK

Strathcona Park Lodge 41040 Gold River Hwy ☎ 250 286 3122, ⓦ strathconaparklodge.com. The park's only commercial accommodation is provided by this outfit just outside the Buttle Lake entrance, a blended hotel and outdoor-pursuits centre, where you can rent canoes, bikes and other outdoor equipment and sign up for organized tours and activities. $139

Strathcona Provincial Park camping Hwy-28 ☎ 800 689 9025, ⓦ env.gov.bc.ca/bcparks, ⓦ discovercamping.ca (for reservations). Buttle Lake has two provincial camp-sites with basic facilities – one alongside the park centre, the other at Ralph River on the extreme southern end of Buttle Lake. Both have good swimming areas nearby. Backcountry camping is allowed throughout the park, but no open fires. $20

Gold River

The tiny logging community of **GOLD RIVER**, 89km west of Campbell River was founded in 1965 in an isolated spot to service a big pulp mill 12km away at Muchalat Inlet (it closed in 1998). Its name dates from the 1860s, when gold panners flocked to the area; nowadays, it's a quiet spot with two motels, a golf course and a couple of shops – but the ride over on Hwy-28 is superb, and there's the chance to explore the

---

HIKING IN STRATHCONA PROVINCIAL PARK

Hiking is superb in Strathcona, with a jaw-dropping scenic combination of jagged mountains – including Golden Hinde (2220m) – lakes, rivers, waterfalls and forest. There are several shorter, **marked** trails accessible from the highway. All the longer trails can be tramped in a day, though the most popular, the **Elk River Trail** (10km), which starts from Drum Lake on Hwy-28, lends itself to an overnight stop; popular with backpackers because of its gentle grade, the path ends up at Landslide Lake, an idyllic camping spot. The other highly regarded trail is the **Flower Ridge** walk, a steep 14km round-trip (extendable by 10km) that starts at the southern end of Buttle Lake and involves a very stiff 1250m elevation gain. The same lung-busting ascent is called for on the **Crest Mountain Trail** (10km round-trip), a trail into high mountain country accessed from Hwy-28 at the park's western edge. The backpacking is great once you've hauled up onto the summit ridges above the tree-line.

In the Forbidden Plateau area, the most popular trek is the **Forbidden Plateau Skyride** to the summit of Wood Mountain where there's a 2km trail to a viewpoint over Boston Canyon.

BOATS FROM GOLD RIVER

Like the MV *Frances Barkley* out of Port Alberni, the **MV Uchuck III** Ltd (☎ 250 283 2515, ☎ 877 824 8253, ⓦ getwest.ca) boat trips started as a sideline. The operation is now far more of a commercial enterprise for kayakers and you can rent kayaks by the day ($45) or bring your own ($42 return). You'll need to book to reserve a place. There are **four basic routes**, (starting $38) all of them offering wonderful windows onto the wilderness and wildlife (bears, whales, bald eagles and more) of the region's inlets. The dock is at the end of Hwy-28, about 15km southwest of Gold River. Passengers on all trips should bring warm waterproof clothing; there's a coffee shop on board for drinks and hot snacks. Kayakers can be dropped off at most points en route by prior arrangement.

10

sublime coastline by boat and try sportfishing. Year-round, the **MV Uchuck III** (see box below), a converted World War II US minesweeper, takes mail, cargo and passengers to logging camps and settlements on a variety of routes.

Boat aside, one of the area's two minor attractions is **Upana Caves**, some of the deepest vertical caves in North America, parts of which are open to the public – for details ask at the visitor centre; the other is the **Big Drop**, a stretch of Gold River whitewater known to kayakers worldwide.

INFORMATION	GOLD RIVER

Gold River visitor centre Corner of Hwy-28 and Scout Lake Rd (mid-May to June Fri–Sun 10am–6pm; July to early Sept daily 10am–6pm; ☎ 250 283 2418, ⓦ goldriver.ca).

ACCOMMODATION

Critter Cove 395 Donner Court ☎ 250 412 6029, ☎ 250 283 7364 (off-season), ⓦ crittercove.com. You'll need to make boating arrangements (either through *Critter Cove* or the MV *Uchuck*) to reach this fishing hideaway, 33km across the water from Gold River. Accommodation ranges from floating lodge rooms to beach houses and cottages. Open mid-June to mid-Sept. **$161**

Campbell River to Port McNeill

The main highway north of Campbell River cuts inland and climbs through increasingly rugged and deserted country, particularly after Sayward, the one main community en route. With a car, you could strike off south from here to **Schoen Lake Provincial Park** (ⓦ env.gov.bc.ca/bcparks), located 77km south, off Hwy-19, which features a couple of forest trails. Tiny **TELEGRAPH COVE** is a likeable place 8km before you reach Port McNeill, accessed via a paved side road. One of BC's "boardwalk villages", the whole community – formerly a lone telegraph office, then a 1920s sawmill village – is raised on wooden stilts over the water. In summer, its historic character is somewhat diluted by a tourist influx. The enclave is one of the island's premier **whale-watching** spots, the main attraction being the pods of orcas that calve locally, and live at or visit Robson Bight, 20km down the Johnstone Strait, established as an ecological reserve in 1982 (the whales like the gravel beaches, where they come to rub). This is one of the world's most accessible and reliable spots to see the creatures, with around a ninety percent chance in season (mid-June to Oct).

PORT McNEILL, 195km north of Campbell River and the first major town along Hwy-19 has its roots based in logging, but nowadays offers more in the way of whale-watching and Aboriginal cultural tours.

INFORMATION AND TOURS	CAMPBELL RIVER TO PORT MCNEILL

Information The visitor centre is at 1594 Beach Drive (May–Sept daily 8.30am–5.30pm; rest of year hours variable; ☎ 250 956 3131, ⓦ town.portmcneill.bc.ca/ tourism).

Whale-watching Established in 1981, Mackay Whale Watching is an excellent local outfit in Port McNeill. The 4–5hr tours include lunch and run from late June to Oct. Offices are at 1514 Broughton blvd ($130; ☎ 877 663 6722,

10

Ⓦwhaletime.com). Stubbs Island Charters (☎250 928 3185, ☎800 665 3066, Ⓦstubbs-sightings.com), at the dock at the end of the boardwalk through the old village of Telegraph Cove, was the first whale-watching company in BC. It runs 3hr trips (mid-May to late Aug; $110). Call well in advance to be sure of a place onboard.

ACCOMMODATION

Black Bear Resort 1812 Campbell Way ☎250 956 4900, ☎866 956 4900, Ⓦport-mcneill-accommodation.com. Port McNeill's flashiest accommodation, rooms at this 40-room hotel have sharp decor, high-speed internet, fridges and microwaves. Cabins are now available, too. Doubles $176, cabins $216

★ **Hidden Cove Lodge** Lewis Point, a secluded cove on Johnstone Strait 14km from Telegraph Cove ☎250 956 3916, Ⓦhiddencovelodge.com. A stay here feels like you've moved to a nature reserve: sea lions, otters, grizzly bears and porpoises are all frequently spotted on the secluded property. The main building has nine units, and three cabins facing the Johnstone Strait. Breakfast and dinner served in the cavernous dining room. Open May–

Oct. Doubles $200; cabins $300

Schoen Lake Provincial Park camping Ⓦenv.gov. bc.ca/bcparks. The Provincial Park's sole accommodation option is this well-kept nine-pitch campsite; first-come, first-served. Mid-May to Sept. $11

Telegraph Cove Resorts ☎250 928 3131, ☎800 200 4665, Ⓦtelegraphcoveresort.com. This distinctive accommodation allows guests to stay in the wood-shingled cabins that make up Telegraph Cove, the one-time homes of 1920s-era sawmill workers. The resort also has the *Wastell Manor*, a five-bedroom renovated hotel where the linesmen used to live, and 120 campsites with showers and laundry facilities. Sites $35; cabins $250; doubles $220

EATING

Cable Cookhouse 1455 Sayward Rd, Sayward Ⓦcable cookhouse.com. If you're driving from Campbell River to Port McNeill, pay a visit to this long-established island landmark – a diner wrapped in 26 tonnes of old logging cable (from the outside, it looks like a woven steel basket). Great burgers, pie and ambience; the tables are huge tree slabs. Mains $9–17. Open three meals a day; hours

fluctuate.

Northern Lights Restaurant 1817 Campbell Way ☎250 956 3263, Ⓦnorthernlightsrestaurant.ca. In the heart of Port McNeill, *Northern Lights* serves toothsome, crowd-pleasing favourites such as wild salmon with maple butter glaze ($25), grilled chicken penne ($20) and marinated lamb chops ($24). Daily 5–9pm.

Alert Bay

The breezy fishing village of **ALERT BAY**, on Cormorant Island, is reached by frequent ferries from Port McNeill (8km away). The fifty-minute crossing in the migrating season (May–Sept) offers a good chance of spotting whales. Half the island population is Namgis First Nation and a day-visit here offers the opportunity to get a brief look into the history and to meet those who are keeping traditions alive. Off to the right from the terminal are the totems of a Namgis Burial Ground; you're asked to view from a respectful distance.

Bear left from the terminal, out of the main part of the village, to reach the excellent **U'Mista Cultural Centre** (mid-May to early Sept daily 9am–5pm; rest of the year Tues–Sat 9am–5pm; $10; ☎250 974 5403, Ⓦumista.ca) at 1 Front St, which houses a collection of masks, regalia and other sacred potlatch items which were confiscated by the government in 1921, and, after years of fighting, has mostly all been repatriated. It also shows a couple of films. You might come across local children being taught First Nations languages, songs and dances. More local artefacts are on show in the library and small museum, open most summer afternoons, at 118 Fir St. For years the village also claimed the world's tallest, fully carved **totem pole** (other contenders, say knowing villagers, are all pole and no carving), though much to local chagrin Victoria raised a pole in 1994 that the *Guinness Book of Records* has recognized as 2.1m taller. Also worth a look is the wildlife and swamp habitat at the Alert Bay Ecological Park behind the bay, accessible via several trails and boardwalks.

ARRIVAL AND INFORMATION   ALERT BAY

By ferry There are daily ferries (45min) from Port McNeill (foot passenger $10.45 return, car $24.10; ☎250 386 3431, ☎888 223 3779, Ⓦbcferries.com).

Visitor centre 116 Fir St, to your right as you come off

the ferry (July & Aug daily 9am–5pm; rest of year Mon–Fri 9am–5pm; ☎250 974 5024, Ⓦalertbay.ca).

Sointula

Located on Malcolm Island, accessible by ferry en route from Port McNeill to Alert Bay, **SOINTULA** village is a wonderful aberration. The fishing village would be a good place to wander at any time, thanks to its briney maritime appeal, but what gives added lustre is the fact that it contains a tiny Finnish settlement. An early utopian community, it was founded with Finnish pioneers as a model co-operative settlement in 1901 by Matti Kurrika, a curious mixture of guru, dramatist and philosopher. In 1905 the experiment collapsed, but one hundred Finns from the original settlement stayed on and you'll still hear Finnish being spoken on the streets. You can wander local beaches, explore the island interior by logging road, or spend a few minutes in the **Sointula Finnish Museum** (280 1st St; daily in summer; ⓦsointulamuseum.ca), just to the left after disembarking the ferry.

10

ARRIVAL AND DEPARTURE

SOINTULA

By ferry Ferries from Port McNeill take 25min (foot ☎888 223 3779, ⓦbcferries.com). passenger $10.45 return, car $24.10; ☎250 386 3431,

Port Hardy

Dominated by copper mining, a large fishing fleet and the usual logging concerns, **PORT HARDY**, 485km from Victoria and 230km from Campbell River, is best known as the departure point for ships plying one of the more spectacular stretches of the famous **Inside Passage** to Prince Rupert (and on to Alaska) and the **Discovery Coast Passage**.

If you have time to kill waiting for boats, you could visit the **Quatse Salmon Stewardship Centre** ($6 daily 10am–5pm; ☎250 902 0336, ⓦthesalmoncentre.org) at 8400 Byng Rd, just off Hwy-19 almost opposite the *Pioneer Inn*.

The visitor centre (see below) also has details on the immense wilderness of **Cape Scott Provincial Park** (ⓦenv.gov.bc.ca/bcparks), whose interior is accessible only by foot. As a short taster you could follow the one-hour hike from the small campsite and trailhead at San Josef River to some sandy beaches. Increasingly popular, but demanding and requiring between 4 to7 hours, is the historic **Cape Scott Trail**, part of a complex web of trails early Danish pioneers hacked from the forest. Around 28km has been reclaimed, opening a trail to the cape itself.

ARRIVAL AND INFORMATION

PORT HARDY

If possible, time your arrival in Port Hardy to coincide with one of the Inside Passage sailings (see page 786). If you stay overnight, there are shuttle services between the ferry and downtown for a fee, otherwise call a taxi (☎250 949 7877 or ☎250 230 7755).

By plane You can fly from Vancouver International Airport to Port Hardy (the airport is 12km south of the town) with Pacific Coastal Airlines (☎800 663 2872, ⓦpacific-coastal. com) from around $200 one way. Mount Waddington Transit has a stop near the airport that heads downtown (see ⓦbctransit.com for a map and schedule).

By bus Tofino Bus operates daily between Victoria and

Port Hardy arriving at the Port Hardy ferry terminal around 4.35pm.

By ferry The Port Hardy ferry terminal (☎888 223 3779, ⓦbcferries.com) is visible from town but is actually 10km away at Bear Cove. Leave plenty of time to reach the ferry terminal and double check your sailing time. In summer the Discovery Coast Connector leaves around 7am but in spring, autumn and winter the service to Prince Rupert is overnight.

Destinations Bella Coola (1 every two days; 15hr 30min or 22hr); Prince Rupert (1 every two days; 15hr).

Visitor centre 7250 Market St (year-round Mon–Fri 8.30am–4pm; ☎250 949 7622, ⓦvisitporthardy.com).

ACCOMMODATION

There's pressure on hotel accommodation in summer, so it's vital to call ahead if you're not camping or haven't worked your arrival to coincide with one of the ferry sailings. In summer, the ferry from Prince Rupert docks around

10.30pm, so you don't want to be hunting out rooms late at night with dozens of others. Contact the visitor centre for details on local B&B options.

10

HOTELS AND B&BS

★ **Ecoscape Cabins** 6305 Jensen Cove Rd ☎ 250 949 8524, ⊚ ecoscapecabins.com. Beautifully constructed, environmentally minded cabins built from salvaged cedar. All come with kitchenettes, flat-screen TVs, and access to barbecue grills and fire pits; the fanciest one has a washer-dryer and sleeping loft. Polished stones line the shower floors and there's a bubbling stream fronting the cabins. $200

Orange Tabby Bed & Breakfast 8755 Hastings St ☎ 250 949 8510, ⊚ orangetabbybb.com. Friendly, updated, three-room B&B that backs up onto a forest and garden. Guest quarters have access to a cushy common area and full kitchen with dishwasher. Nice central location near the bus station, and walkable to downtown and restaurants. Proprietors are very knowledgeable about the area. $160

Quarterdeck Inn 6555 Hardy Bay Rd ☎ 250 902 0455, ☎ 877 902 0459, ⊚ quarterdeckresort.net. The forty-room *Quarterdeck Inn* is the town's most comfortable hotel. There are views of the harbour and laundry facilities; some rooms have kitchenettes. $160

CAMPGROUNDS

Quatse River Campground 8400 Byng Rd ☎ 250 949 2395, ⊚ quatsecampground.ca. Sixty-two spruce-shaded sites partway between downtown and Bear Cove Ferry Terminal (7km). Sites $29; RVs $42

Wildwoods Campsite 8000 Clyde Creek Rd ☎ 250 949 6753, ⊚ wildwoodscampsite.com. Larger 75-site campsite (most of them secluded and fully serviced), 3km southwest of Bear Cove Ferry Terminal, on the water's edge. $30

EATING AND DRINKING

Café Guido and The Book Nook 7135 Market St ☎ 250 949 9808. Darling little café with colourful seating, good coffee and pastries and a subterranean bookstore. At breakfast and lunch, they stack up great sandwiches like the "gladiator": pesto, ham, havarti and mozzarella crammed between herbed flat bread ($7.50). Mon–Fri 7am–6pm, Sat 8am–6pm, Sun 8am–5pm.

The Inside Passage

One of Canada's great trips, between Port Hardy and Prince Rupert on the BC mainland, the **Inside Passage** makes a good leg in any number of convenient itineraries around BC, especially by linking up with Tofino Bus (☎ 866 986 3466, ⊚ tofinobus. com) or the VIA Rail terminal at Prince Rupert (☎ 888 842 7245, ⊚ viarail.ca). Some travellers will have come from Washington State, others will want to press on from Prince Rupert to Skagway by boat and then head north into Alaska and the Yukon on the Alaska Marine ferry (see page 802). Many simply treat it as a cruise, sailing north one day and south the next. It's vital to book accommodation at your final destination before starting your trip; Port Hardy and Prince Rupert hotels are very busy on days when the boat arrives.

INFORMATION   THE INSIDE PASSAGE

Schedules The *Northern Expedition* carries 600 passengers, 130 cars and runs every two days, departing at 7.30am on odd-numbered days in August, even-numbered days in June, July and Sept. The journey takes around 15hr, arriving in Prince Rupert about 10.30pm, sometimes with a stop at Bella Bella. From about Oct 15 to May 25 sailings are less frequent in both directions and are predominantly at night (leaving Port Hardy in the late afternoon), which defeats the sightseeing object of the trip.

Costs and reservations The cost in the peak mid-June to mid-Sept season is $202 one-way for foot passengers, $460.25 for cars; reservations are essential throughout the peak season if you're taking a car or want a cabin (☎ 250 386 3431, ☎ 888 223 3779, ⊚ bcferries.com). Full payment is required up front. Cabins range from $85 for two berths with basin, shower and toilet from Oct to April, $90 for the same in high season. Cabin accommodation is only available on overnight sailings. Bigger cabins with two berths, toilets and showers cost $95 in low season, $120 in high season. Luxury cabins are $250 in high season.

Car parking If you're making a return trip and want to leave your car behind, there are lock-ups in Port Hardy; you can leave vehicles at the ferry terminal, but this isn't recommended.

The Discovery Coast Passage

The **Discovery Coast Passage** (summer only) offers many of the scenic rewards of the Inside Passage, but over a shorter and more circuitous route between Port Hardy and **Bella Coola**, where you can pick up Hwy-20 through the Coast Mountains to Williams Lake (see page 735) – it goes nowhere else. En route, the boat stops at Bella Bella,

Shearwater, Klemtu and Ocean Falls. You can disembark at all of these places, but there are only a handful of accommodation options among them. Bella Coola is better equipped, and will probably become more so once the much-anticipated direct route from Port Hardy begins in 2019.

INFORMATION THE DISCOVERY COAST PASSAGE

Schedules There are departures roughly every couple of days between early June and mid-Sept, leaving Port Hardy at 10.15am on Tues and Thurs and at 9.30pm on Saturday, and returning from Bella Coola on Mon, Wed and Fri. There's a slight catch: while the morning departures offer great scenery, some arrive at Bella Coola at 6.30am, meaning the best bit of the trip – along the inlet to Bella Coola – is in the middle of the night. The Thursday departures are quicker and make Bella Coola the same day, arriving at 11pm, so the problem is lessened. Alternatively take the 9.30pm departure and wake at 7.30am with a further daylight trip towards Bella Coola, arriving at 6.30am the next morning; read the timetables carefully. Making the trip southbound from Bella Coola gets round the problem, though there are similar staggered departure and arrival times (services currently leave Mon, Wed and Fri at 8am, arriving Port Hardy at 9pm on the Mon departure, 7.45am on Wed sailing and 9am on the Fri boat), with overnight and same-day journeys and a variety of stopping points depending on the day you travel. In 2019, the *Northern Sea Wolf* will begin plying a direct (seasonal) route between Port Hardy and Bella Coola. At the time of writing it looked set to operate five days a week.

Costs and reservations Bookings can be made through BC Ferries (☎ 250 386 3431, ☎ 888 223 3779 toll-free in BC, ⊚ bcferries.com). Prices for foot passengers are $195.50 one-way to Bella Coola, $118.75 to all other destinations; cars cost $388.25, $237.25 to all other destinations. The fares between any two of Bella Bella, Ocean Falls and Klemtu are $42. There are no cabins: you sleep in reclining seats. Taking a canoe or kayak costs $10 from Port Hardy to Bella Coola; bicycles cost $5.

10

The North

DEMPSTER HIGHWAY, YUKON

The North

Although much of Canada still has the flavour of the "last frontier", it's only when you set off north to the Yukon, Northwest Territories or to Nunavut that you know for certain you've left mainstream North American life behind. In the popular imagination, the North figures as a perpetually frozen wasteland blasted by ferocious gloomy winters, inhabited – if at all – by hardened characters living outside the bounds of civilization. In truth, it's a region where months of summer sunshine offer almost limitless opportunities for outdoor activities and an incredible profusion of flora and fauna; a country within a country, the character of whose settlements has often been forged by the mingling of white settlers and Indigenous peoples. The indigenous hunters of the North are as varied as in the South, but two groups predominate: the Dene, people of the northern forests who traditionally occupied the Mackenzie River region from the Alberta border to the river's delta at the Beaufort Sea; and the Inuit (literally "the people") of Nunavut.

The North is as much a state of mind as a place. People "north of 60" – the 60th Parallel – claim the right to be called **Northerners**, and maintain a kinship with Alaskans, but those north of the **Arctic Circle** – the 66th Parallel – look with light-hearted disdain on these "Southerners". All mock the inhabitants of the northernmost corners of Alberta and such areas of the so-called Northwest, who, after all, live with the luxury of being able to get around their backcountry by road. Yet to any outsider – in terms of landscape and overall spirit – the North begins well south of the 60th Parallel. Accordingly, this chapter includes not just the territories of the "true North" – **Yukon**, the **Northwest Territories** and **Nunavut** – but also regions of both northern **British Columbia** and **Alberta** that are considerably starker and more remote than areas further south in those provinces.

The two roads into the Yukon strike through northern **British Columbia**: the **Alaska Highway** heads up from the eastern side of the province, connecting **Dawson Creek** to Fairbanks in Alaska, and to the west is the **Stewart-Cassiar Highway**, from near **Prince Rupert** through to **Watson Lake**, on the Yukon border. Though the Stewart-Cassiar's passage through the Coast Mountains offers perhaps the better landscapes, it's the Alaska Highway – serviced by plentiful motels and campgrounds – that is more travelled. While the scenery is superb, most towns on both roads are battered and perfunctory places built around lumber mills and mining camps, though increasingly they are spawning motels and restaurants to serve the surge of summer visitors out to capture the thrill of driving the frontier highways. Equally popular are the **sea journeys** offered along northern BC's coast, among the most breathtaking trips in Canada. Prince Rupert, linked by ferry to Vancouver Island, is the springboard for boats to the magnificent **Haida Gwaii** (formerly known as the Queen Charlotte Islands) and a vital way-station for boats plying the Inside Passage up to Alaska.

The Stewart-Cassiar and Alaska highways converge at Watson Lake, marking the entrance to the **Yukon Territory**. This exhilarating and varied region is truly bear country: 34,000 people live in the Yukon alongside ten thousand black bears and seven thousand grizzlies. It boasts the highest mountains in Canada, wild sweeps of boreal forest and tundra, and the fascinating nineteenth-century relic of **Dawson City**. The focus of the Klondike gold rush, Dawson City was also the territory's capital until 1952 when that role shifted south to **Whitehorse**, a city doing well on tourism, federal jobs

THE PALACE GRAND THEATRE, DAWSON CITY

Highlights

❶ **Skeena Valley** A glorious wildlife-rich river and estuary flanked by soaring mountains. See page 798

❷ **Haida Gwaii** The wild islands of "the Canadian Galapagos" are rich in flora and fauna and First Nations culture. See page 803

❸ **Alaska Highway** Some 2500km of stunning wilderness make this one of North America's great drives. See page 813

❹ **Dawson City** The focus of the Klondike gold rush is western Canada's most atmospheric and compelling historic town. See page 833

❺ **Dempster Highway** The only public road in North America to cross the Arctic Circle offers a fascinating insight into the tundra and chance encounters with wildlife. See page 839

❻ **Nahanni National Park** Magnificent gorges, waterfalls and mountain scenery are the chief attractions in one of Canada's finest national parks. See page 850

❼ **Auyuittuq National Park** Arctic scenery and culture are always compelling, but nowhere more so than in this largely glacial redoubt on Baffin Island. See page 867

HIGHLIGHTS ARE MARKED ON THE MAP ON PAGE 792

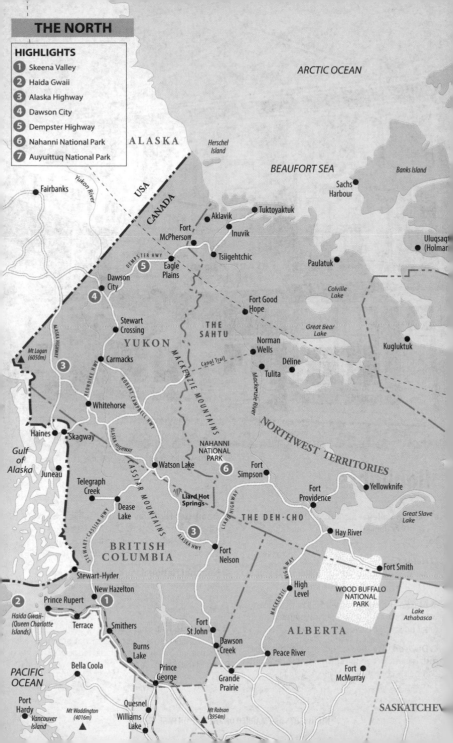

11

> **REGIONAL INFORMATION**
> **Haida Gwaii Tourism** ☎ 250 559 8316, ⓦ gohaidagwaii.ca
> **Nunavut Tourism** ☎ 866 686 2888 in North America, ☎ 800 491 7910 internationally,
> ⓦ nunavuttourism.com
> **Northwest Territories Tourism** ☎ 866 873 7200, ⓦ spectacularnwt.com
> **Tourism British Columbia** ☎ 800 663 6000, ⓦ hellobc.com
> **Tourism Yukon** ☎ 800 661 0494, ⓦ yukon.ca
> **Travel Alberta** ☎ 403 648 1000, ⓦ travelalberta.com

and the exploitation of the Yukon's vast mineral resources. From here, the **Klondike Highway** strikes north to link Whitehorse with Dawson City. North of Dawson City the **Dempster Highway** is the only road in Canada to cross the Arctic Circle, offering a direct approach to several remote communities in the Northwest Territories. The Yukon's other major road is the short spur linking the Alaskan port of Skagway to Whitehorse, which shadows the **Chilkoot Trail**, a popular long-distance footpath. If you're planning a backcountry trip in the Yukon, you can get wilderness information and emergency updates online at ⓦ yukon.ca. .

Combining coastal ferries with the Chilkoot Trail makes an especially fine itinerary. Following the old gold-rush trail, the route begins at Skagway – reached by ferry from Prince Rupert – then follows the Chilkoot to Whitehorse, before heading north to Dawson City. From there you could continue up the Dempster Highway, or travel on the equally majestic **Top of the World Highway** into the heart of Alaska. Alternatively, many people coming up from Skagway or plying the mainland routes from BC head to Alaska directly on the Alaska Highway to enjoy views of the extraordinary and largely inaccessible mountain vastness of **Kluane National Park**, which contains Canada's highest peaks and most extensive glacial wilderness.

If the Yukon is the far North at its most accessible, the **Northwest Territories** (**NWT**) is the region at its most uncompromising. Just three roads nibble at the edges of this almost unimaginably vast area, which occupies a third of Canada's landmass – about the size of India – but contains only forty-one thousand people, almost half of whom live in or around **Yellowknife**, the territories' colourful capital. Unless you're taking the adventurous and rewarding Dempster Highway from Dawson City across the tundra to **Inuvik**, Yellowknife will probably feature on any trip to the NWT, as it's the hub of the (expensive given the remoteness of the region) flight network servicing the area's widely dispersed communities.

Otherwise, most visitors come to the NWT to **fish**, **canoe**, **hunt**, **hike**, watch **wildlife** or to experience the Indigenous cultures and ethereal landscapes. After years of negotiations, the Inuit of the eastern NWT finally realized their dream of administering their land with the creation of **Nunavut** on April 1, 1999. This effectively split the former NWT into two distinct regions with the eastern half being renamed Nunavut (literally "Our Land"). Nunavut and the "old" western NWT issue their own tourist materials; pick up, or download, a copy of their respective *Explore Nunavut* and the Spectacular NWT *Explorers' Guide* brochures, which summarize accommodation options and airline connections, plus many of the available tours – costing anywhere from $50 to $5000-plus – and the plethora of outfitters who provide the equipment and backup essential for all but the most superficial trip to the region.

Prince George

Lying 780km north of Vancouver and 380km northwest of Jasper, rough-edged **PRINCE GEORGE** is the general area's services and transport centre. Forestry is at the core of its industrial landscape – if you ever wanted the inside story on the lumber business, this is where to find it.

Simon Fraser established a North West Trading Company post here in 1807, creating a commercial nexus that quickly altered the lives of the First Nations peoples, who abandoned their seminomadic migration from winter to summer villages in favour of a permanent settlement alongside the fort. Little changed until 1914 when the arrival of the Grand Trunk Railway spawned an influx of pioneers and loggers – the railway was laid on land bought from the Lheidli T'enneh local band, who were moved to a reserve at Shelley. The town was connected by road to Dawson Creek and the North as late as 1951, and saw the arrival of the Pacific Great Eastern Railway in 1958. From Prince George there are routes north and east to Dawson Creek, and on the Alaska Highway (see page 813).

Hikes and forests

Prince George offers a handful of attractions, many of which involve the city's surrounding forests. There are over 1600 lakes within a 150km radius of town, all offering beautiful settings for hiking, fishing and canoeing. A host of **hiking trails** exist, including an easy walk through the **Ancient Forest**, the world's furthest inland rainforest, while **Forests for the World** offers 15km of trails and a gorgeous lakeside picnic site. Just north of downtown the **Cottonwood Island Nature Park** has similar trails with interpretive signs and wood spirit carvings in the trees. The city's central **Connaught Hill Park** affords a 360-degree view over the city; check with the tourist office for trail details.

11

FLYING AROUND THE NORTH

The vast distances involved in seeing Canada's North can make driving difficult, tiring and expensive – although this really is the best way to see the region. However, many travellers will choose to fly to and between different northern destinations and use those as a base to explore from. Indeed, some places, the NWTs' fly-in communities (see page 845) and almost all of Nunavut (see page 858) will require flying to visit. We've listed below the major carriers that service the North, where they fly to and which larger, more southerly cities they can be reached from; smaller operators' and charter airlines' contact details are listed in the relevant account.

One option worth considering is the **Yukon Advantage Traveller Airpass**, offered by Air North (☎ 800 661 0407, ⊛ flyairnorth.com), which allows you ten segments to fly to or from seven destinations with Whitehorse as a hub (so all flights must begin or pass through that city). The pass covers up to two persons, and all segments must be flown within one year. It's also pretty flexible, with reservations possible up to one hour before flight and features low change/cancel fees. The cost is $3150, plus tax.

Air Canada and subsidiary Air Canada Jazz ☎ 888 247 2262, ⊛ aircanada.com. Prince George, Prince Rupert, Smithers, Haida Gwaii, Whitehorse and Yellowknife; flights can originate in Vancouver, Edmonton, Calgary or Ottawa.

Air North ☎ 867 668 2228, ☎ 800 661 0407, ⊛ flyair north.com. Whitehorse, Inuvik, Old Crow, Dawson City, Fairbanks (Alaska); flights can originate from Vancouver, Edmonton or Calgary.

Calm Air ☎ 800 839 2256, ⊛ calmair.com. Rankin Inlet, Baker Lake, Coral Harbour and other Nunavut communities; flights can originate from Winnipeg and Churchill, Manitoba.

Canadian North ☎ 800 661 1505, ⊛ canadiannorth. com. Yellowknife, Norman Wells, Inuvik, Iqaluit; flights can originate in Edmonton or Ottawa.

Central Mountain Air (CMA) ☎ 888 865 8585, ⊛ fly cma.com. BC and Alberta operator; from Vancouver, Kelowna, Kamloops and Edmonton to Prince George and connections to northern BC.

First Air ☎ 800 267 1247, ⊛ firstair.ca. Fort Simpson, Hay River, Yellowknife, Rankin Inlet, Iqaluit and several other Nunavut communities; flights can originate from Edmonton, Winnipeg, Ottawa and Montréal.

WestJet ☎ 888 937 8538, ⊛ westjet.com. Prince George, Yellowknife and Whitehorse (May–Oct); flights originate from Vancouver and Edmonton.

Railway & Forestry Museum

850 River Rd • June–Aug daily 10am–5pm; Sept–May Wed–Sun 11am–4pm • $8, children $5 • ☎ 250 563 7351, ⊛ pgrfm.bc.ca

Housing the largest vintage rail collection in BC, the **Railway and Forestry Museum** holds cars from the Cottonwood Railway, as well as many examples of rolling stock, heavy equipment, logging machinery and locomotives.

The Exploration Place

333 Becott Place (end of 20th Ave in Lheidli T'enneh Memorial Park) • Daily 9am–5pm • $11, children $8 • ☎ 250 562 1612, ☎ 866 562 1612, ⊛ theexplorationplace.com

The **Exploration Place Museum and Science Centre** features exhibits and activities touching on everything from dinosaur fossils to prisons to Terry Fox, who ran across Canada in 1980. Hodul'eh-a: A Place of Learning opened in 2017, and is dedicated to the Lheidli T'enneh band who have lived here for more than 9000 years. There's also a significant focus on programming for kids, who might like *The Little Prince* narrow gauge steam engine that rides around the park each summer.

ARRIVAL AND DEPARTURE

By plane Air Canada Jazz, CMA and WestJet fly to Prince George from Vancouver; the airport is 18km east of downtown and linked by regular shuttles.

By train The town is linked three times weekly by the Skeena, operated by VIA Rail (☎ 888 842 7245, ⊛ viarail. ca) to Jasper, and Prince Rupert (for the Haida Gwaii/Prince Charlotte Islands and Inside Passage ferries); the station is downtown at 1300 1st Ave (☎ 888 842 7245). It's possible to get to/from Vancouver with an overnight stay in Jasper, but it would be more than 2 days travel.

Destinations Jasper (3 weekly; 8hr 45min); Prince Rupert (3 weekly; 12hr 30min).

By bus Prince George is a staging post for routes to the north, and integral to the main road routes to Dawson Creek (for the Alaska Hwy) and Prince Rupert (for the Stewart-Cassiar Hwy). BC Transit (☎ 250 563 0011, ⊛ bctransit.com) now operates these routes; ask at the tourist office about buses replacing Greyhound on the Edmonton via Jasper and Vancouver routes. The bus stop is at 1566 12th Ave and close to a handful of hotels and motels.

Destinations Dawson Creek (2 weekly; 6hr 30min); Prince Rupert (2 weekly; 11hr).

INFORMATION AND GETTING AROUND

Tourist office 1300 First Ave, #101, near the downtown core (check online for hours, which vary by season); ☎ 250 562 3700, ☎ 800 668 7646, ⊛ tourismpg.com).

By taxi You can get a taxi with either Prince George Taxi (☎ 250 564 4444, ⊛ pgtaxi.ca) or Emerald Taxi Ltd (☎ 250 563 3333).

ACCOMMODATION

Blue Cedars RV & Campground 4433 Kimball Rd, 5km west of town on Hwy-16 ☎ 250 964 7272, ☎ 888 964 7271, ⊛ bluecedarsrvpark.com. Campground with a heated outdoor pool and free drinking water. April to mid-Oct. Sites $25; RVs $40; bunk house cabins $45

Coast Inn of the North 770 Brunswick St ☎ 250 563 0121, ☎ 800 716 6199, ⊛ coasthotels.com. One of the more luxurious hotels in town, with 155 rooms. Guests have access to a spa, hair salon, and a choice of fine dining at its three restaurants. $141

The Grateful Bed B&B 157 McKinley Crescent ☎ 866 618 4612, ⊛ gratefulbed.ca. A 10min drive west of the city centre and set in beautiful grounds, this homely B&B has just two rooms (one double, one twin – both comfortable)

and a shared bathroom. The hosts are fabulously friendly and serve a huge Irish breakfast. $100

Northern Experience RV 8km from town on Hwy-97 South ☎ 250 963 7577, ⊛ northernexperiencerv.com. The best option for camping near Prince George is at the *Northern Experience*, with back-in and pull through sites with tree screens for privacy. Coin operated showers and laundry. Sites $25; RVs $39

Spruceland Inn 1391 Central St W, junction of Hwy-97 & 15th Ave ☎ 250 563 0102, ☎ 800 663 3295, ⊛ sprucelandinn.com. A solid, cheap choice on the Hwy-97 strip, with eighty rooms, each equipped with a kitchenette and fridge. $79

EATING AND DRINKING

Cimo Mediterranean Grill 601 Victoria St ☎ 250 564 7975, ⊛ cimo.ca. For good Mediterranean dishes, *Cimo*

has an extensive choice of pasta (from $19) and mains including lamb *souvlaki* ($28) and sweet-pea risotto with

THE AURORA BOREALIS

The **aurora borealis**, or **Northern Lights**, is a beautiful and ethereal display in the upper atmosphere that can be seen over large areas of northern Canada. The night sky appears to shimmer with dancing curtains of colour, ranging from luminescent monotones – most commonly green or a dark red – to fantastic veils running the full spectrum. The display becomes more animated as it proceeds, twisting and turning in patterns called "rayed bands". As a finale, a corona sometimes appears, in which rays seem to flare in all directions from a central point.

The aurora was long thought to be produced by sunlight reflected from polar snow and ice, or refracted light produced in the manner of a rainbow. Certain Inuit believed the lights were the spirits of animals or ancestors; others thought they represented wicked forces. Research still continues into the phenomenon, and while the earth's geomagnetic field certainly plays some part in the creation of the aurora, its source would appear to lie with the sun – auroras become more distinct and are seen spread over a larger area two days after intense solar activity, the time it takes the "solar wind" to reach the Earth. This wind is composed of fast-moving electrically charged ions. When these hit the Earth's atmosphere they respond to the Earth's magnetic field and move towards the poles. En route, they strike atoms and molecules of gas in the upper atmosphere, causing them to become temporarily charged or ionized. These molecules then release the charge, or energy, usually in the form of light. Different colours are emitted depending on the gases involved: oxygen produces green hues (or orange at higher altitudes), nitrogen occasionally violet colours.

You should be able to see the Northern Lights as far south as Prince George in BC, over parts of northern Alberta (where on average they're visible some 160 nights a year) and over much of the NWT, the Yukon, Nunavut and northern Manitoba. (Check with the local tourist centres for information on viewing tours.) They are at their most dazzling **from December to March**, when nights are longest and the sky darkest, though they are potentially visible year-round. Look out for a faint glow on the northeastern horizon after dusk, and then – if you're lucky – for the full show as the night deepens.

BC Portabella mushrooms ($18). Artisan sandwiches and wraps at lunchtime, too. Reservations recommended. Mon–Sat 11.30am–2pm & 5–10pm.

Nancy O's 1261 3rd Ave ☎ 250 562 8066, ⓦ nancyos.ca. A local favourite offering a hearty menu of comfort foods and a good selection of beers. The owners pride themselves in showcasing the local arts community, plus there's live entertainment in the evenings. Mains start at $11. Mon–Fri 11am–11.30pm, Sat 10am–11.30pm, Sun 10am–3pm.

Ramen Ya Sendo Bon Voyage Plaza, 4488 Hwy-16 ☎ 250 964 6771. Previously *Sendo Sushi*, this much loved local spot now serves up slurp-able ramen ($13.50; gluten free and vegan also available) and freshly made gyoza (6 pcs $6). Tues–Sun 11.30am–8pm.

White Goose Bistro 1205 3rd Ave ☎ 250 561 1002, ⓦ whitegoosebistro.ca. For high-quality food, try *White Goose Bistro*, specializing in Italian and French cuisine – lobster ravioli ($22), ribeye steak ($30) and duo of duck ($32). They also have an express lunch menu with great fish tacos ($16). Mon–Sat 11am–2pm & 5pm–late, Sun 5pm–late.

Prince George to Prince Rupert

To make the 725km journey west from Prince George to **Prince Rupert**, you can travel either Hwy-16 (the Yellowhead Highway) or the parallel VIA Rail line; neither is terribly scenic by BC standards until you reach the glorious river and mountain landscapes of the **Skeena Valley** 150km before Prince Rupert. Most people make this trip as a link in a much longer journey, either connecting to **ferries** north to Alaska or south to Port Hardy on Vancouver Island, or to start the Stewart-Cassiar Highway en route to meet the Alaska Highway at Watson Lake over the Yukon border. The best place to pause during the journey is near **Hazelton**, approximately 450km from Prince George, where you can visit a cluster of First Nations villages.

Smithers and around

SMITHERS, the largest community after Prince George, is a picturesque outdoor-adventure hub. The sizeable Swiss population has made its mark on the alpine-themed downtown, focused on Main Street at the crossroads of Hwy-16.

There is mountain biking and hiking in the **Babine Mountains Provincial Park** and downhill and cross-country **skiing** 20km from town on Hudson Bay Mountain. For indoor attractions, try the **Bulkley Valley Museum** (Mon–Fri 9am–5pm, Sat noon–4pm; donation; ☏ 250 847 5322, ⊚ bvmuseum.org) at the corner of Main Street and Hwy-16, which has a permanent display on the history of flight in the area, and a lovingly tended exhibit on Smithers' brief brush with notoriety in 1911 – when a local invented the egg carton.

ARRIVAL AND DEPARTURE   SMITHERS AND AROUND

By plane Smithers Regional Airport is 5km west of town on Hwy-16, with regular Air Canada Jazz and CMA flights.

By train Smithers is serviced three times weekly by VIA Rail's "Skeena" train at 3815 Railway Ave.

By bus BC Transit (☏ 250 563 0011, ⊚ bctransit.com) buses run twice weekly in each direction along Hwy-16 – the station is just west of downtown at 4011 Hwy-16 (☏ 250 847 2204).

INFORMATION AND ACTIVITIES

Visitor centre 1411 Court St (June–Aug daily 9am–6pm; Sept to May Mon–Fri 9am–5pm; ☏ 250 847 5072, ☏ 800 542 6673, ⊚ tourismsmithers.com). Free wi-fi and information about activities nearby, including fishing, kayaking and horseriding.

Downhill skiing Dec to mid-April; day-pass $65 (☏ 250 847 2058, ☏ 866 665 4299, ⊚ hudsonbaymountain.ca).

Cross-country skiing Contact Bulkley Valley Nordic Centre (day pass $15; ☏ 250 847 5009, ⊚ bvnordic.ca).

ACCOMMODATION AND EATING

Prestige Hudson Bay Lodge Just east of downtown at 3521 Hwy-16 ☏ 250 847 4581, ☏ 877 737 8443, ⊚ prestigehotelsandresorts.com. Ignore the brace of motels on the road and opt for the big white-timbered *Prestige Hudson Bay Lodge* with its choice of comfy rooms, fitness centre and a great restaurant (*Fireside*) or pub, which serve mains from $20 to $30. During the day, take advantage of their jet-boat tours, heli-hiking or tubing options. **$130**

Riverside Municipal RV & Camping 3843 19th Ave, reserve at ☏ 778 210 0832 or ☏ 250 847 1649. The

campground occupies an idyllic spot northwest of Main St on the banks of the Bulkley River. Mid May to mid-Oct. Sites **$18**; RVs **$31**

Schimmel's Fine Pastries 1172 Main St ☏ 250 847 9044. Not to be missed – try their great coffee, artisan breads, soups, pizzas, tarts and home-made gelato all served with a European flare. Tues–Sat 7.30am–5pm.

Smithers Guesthouse 1766 Main St ☏ 250 847 4862, ⊚ smithersguesthouse.com. Five guest rooms complete with private bathrooms, and use of a fully equipped kitchen and guest living room. Breakfast an additional $15. **$75**

Skeena Valley

Just beyond Smithers, the **Skeena River** carves a beautiful valley through the Coast Mountains, an important trade route for First Nations peoples and stern-wheelers before the coming of the railway in 1912. For a couple of hours the road and railway run past an imposing backdrop of snow-capped peaks half-reflected in the estuary. Out on the water you might see seals or **bald eagles** perched on the river's logjams. Shortly after Hwy-16 meets the river crashing down from the north near **Hazelton** and **New Hazelton**, a couple of minor roads strike off to four nearby **villages**, where something of the culture of the indigenous **Gitxsan** peoples, consummate artists and carvers, has been preserved.

A few kilometres off Hwy-16, on the High Level Road out of New Hazelton, is **'Ksan Historical Village & Museum** (tours daily April–Sept 9am–5pm $15; museum $8, $2 if paid for tour; same summer hours plus Oct–Mar Mon–Fri 9.30am–4.30pm; ☏ 250 842 5544, ⊚ ksan.org), the most interesting of the four communities and the site of an entire reconstructed Gitxsan village. Guides take visitors around seven cedar longhouses and numerous totem poles, providing commentary on the carvings, buildings and masks on show. **Kispiox**, 13km north of Hazelton, is the ancient Gitxsan home of the Frog, Wolf and Fireweed clans and locals prefer the traditional village name, *Anspayaxw*, meaning "people of the hidden place". The highlights here are fifteen riverside totems, some of which can be spotted in Emily Carr's iconic paintings. To the west (500m north of the junction of highways 16 and 37) is **Gitwangak**, "the place of rabbits". It also has some impressive totems, as does **Gitanyow**, 21km north on Hwy-37, whose eighteen poles include the 140-year-old "Hole in the Sky" totem. You can sometimes watch poles being repaired at the village's two carving sheds.

INFORMATION   SKEENA VALLEY

Visitor centre The nearest is close to New Hazelton at the junction of highways 16 and 62 (mid-May to mid-Sept Thurs–Sun 9am–5pm; ☎ 250 842 6071, ⓦ hazletonstourism.ca).

ACCOMMODATION AND EATING

Bulkley Valley Motel 4444 Hwy-16 in New Hazelton ☎ 250 842 6817, ☎ 888 988 1144, ⓦ bvmotel.ca. Clean, cosy and quiet with newly renovated, air-conditioned rooms, each of which is equipped with a kitchen, TV and internet access. Laundry facilities, grocery and four restaurants are within easy walking distance. **$95**

River's Edge Campground Kispiox Valley Rd ☎ 250 842 5822. Popular with fishing enthusiasts, it's located 7km outside the village on the river. Sites **$22**; RVs **$28**

Trakehner Hof B&B 236 Glen Meadow Road ☎ 250 842 8077, ⓦ trakehnerhof.ca. Located close to the Skeena River, this three-room B&B offers modern and comfortable quarters with breathtaking views of the surrounding valley and mountains. Horseriding, totem-pole tours and fishing excursions are also on offer. **$100**

Terrace

Some 142km before Prince Rupert, Hwy-16 passes through **TERRACE**, the commercial centre of the Skeena Valley. You can **ski** 35km west off Hwy-16 at **Shames Mountain** (mid-Dec to mid-April; day-pass $55; ☎ 250 635 3773, ⓦ mymountaincoop.ca), which has 28 runs and trails.

Nisga'a Memorial Lava Bed Provincial Park

100km north of Terrace via Nisga'a Hwy (only first 70km is paved) • 4hr volcano tours 10am on Mon, Wed, Sat & Sun (book in advance); $45

Terrace is also a good jumping-off point for the 266-year-old lava flows at **Nisga'a Memorial Lava Bed Provincial Park**. There is a **campground** here with 16 sites (mid-May to mid-Sept; $18 per person) and the Nisga visitor centre (mid-June to Sept daily 9am–5pm; ☎ 250 641 4400) which can arrange volcano tours.

INFORMATION   TERRACE

Tourist office On the highway at 4511 Keith Ave (June–Aug daily 9am–5pm; rest of year Mon–Fri 8.30am–4.30pm; ☎ 250 635 4944, ⓦ visitterrace.com).

Prince Rupert

There's a bracing tang of salt and fish in the air in **PRINCE RUPERT**, a distinctive port on Kaien Island – linked by bridge to the mainland – that comes as an invigorating relief after the run out of Prince George. A stunning place when the mist lifts, it looks out over an archipelago of islands and is ringed by mountains that tumble to the sea along a beautiful fjord-cut coastline. A crowd of cars, backpackers and RVs washes daily through its streets off the Alaska, the Queen Charlotte and Port Hardy **ferries**, complementing the seafront's vibrant activity, and adding to the coffers of a town clearly on the up. In the summer, **cruise ships** make four-hour pit stops here, spewing up to two thousand passengers ashore at a time to gorge on fish and chips and sightsee.

11

GRIZZLY BEAR TOURS

Khutzeymateen Wilderness lodge ☎ 250 641 0957, ⓦ khutzlodge.com. A floating wilderness lodge hosting three-day tours, with a float plane transfer from Seal Cove in Prince Rupert. Accommodation is rustic but clean and cosy – just six bedrooms with shared bathrooms – and you can spend the day kayaking and stand-up paddleboarding. May–Sept, $2650.

★ **Ocean Light II Adventures** ☎ 604 328 5339, ⓦ oceanlight2.bc.ca. If you have the time, and plenty of spare change, the three-day tour on board the *Ocean Light II* offers a chance-of-a-lifetime opportunity to spot grizzlies in their natural habitat as you sail through the lush green Khutzeymateen Valley ($2525).

Prince Rupert Adventure Tours ☎ 250 627 9166, ☎ 800 201 8377, ⓦ adventuretours.net. Runs seven-hour boat tours to the sanctuary (mid-May to July) starting at $290.

There's plenty of outdoor and indoor attractions, and it's an amiable enough spot to while away a day while you're waiting for a boat. Some of the highlights include whale-watching, tours of the world-renowned Khutzeymateen Grizzly Bear Sanctuary, and a stop at the Museum of Northern British Columbia.

Museum of Northern British Columbia

1st Ave at McBride St • June–Sept daily 9am–5pm; Oct–May Tues–Sat 9am–5pm • $6 • ☎ 250 624 3207, ⓦ museumofnorthernbc.com

Prince Rupert's excellent **Museum of Northern British Columbia**, housed in an impressive reproduction First Nations cedar longhouse, is particularly strong on the culture and history of the local Tsimshian. The museum also boasts a clutch of wonderful silent archive films on topics ranging from fishing to the building of the railway – ideal ways to whittle away a wet afternoon, of which the city has plenty. There are also a variety of tours and performances throughout the summer, including visiting the town's totem poles ($2) and a one-hour tour through the rich history of the Northwest Coast Tsimshian First Nations (free with entrance ticket).

Khutzeymateen Grizzly Bear Sanctuary

A very popular trip from Prince Rupert is the 6hr boat tour to **Khutzeymateen Grizzly Bear Sanctuary** (best time mid-May to early Aug), a remote coastal valley 45km northeast of Prince Rupert created in 1994 to protect BC's largest-known coastal population of **grizzly bears** – the damage done to grizzly habitats by logging, mining, hunting and other concerns is one of the keenest environmental issues in the province. In the summer, several local tour operators run full-day and multi-day boat tours to view the grizzlies on the water's edge (see box above).

Mount Hays

Mount Hays gives a bird's-eye view of the harbour and the chance to spot bald eagles. To reach the steep track providing the only route to the top, take the Wantage Road turn-off on Hwy-16 just out of town. It's three hours to the top but you get fairly good views after clambering a short way up the track. For a less energetic **walk**, take the 5km interpretive loop trail through old-growth rainforest to **Butze Rapids** – reversing tidal rapids; the trailhead is about 5km east of town along Hwy-16.

ARRIVAL AND DEPARTURE   **PRINCE RUPER**

BY PLANE
The airport (☎ 250 624 6274) is on Digby Island just across the harbour, with ferry connections to the BC and Alaska

Marine ferry terminals and shuttle bus connections t downtown (☎ 250 622 2222), which leave and drop off a the *Prince Rupert Hotel* at 118 6 St.

To Vancouver Air Canada Jazz (see page 795) operates a daily service between Vancouver and Prince Rupert (2hr).
To Haida Gwaii Inland Air (☎ 250 624 2577, ☎ 888 624 2577, ⓦinlandair.bc.ca) runs a daily 50min flight to Masset on Haida Gwaii (see page 804) in summer, leaving east of town from the Seal Cove seaplane base on Bellis Road, plus on-demand flightseeing tours.

BY TRAIN

The train station is on the waterfront at Fairview Dock; the ticket office is in the BC Ferries building on Hwy-16 (open 2hr either side of departures and arrivals; ☎ 888 842 7245, ⓦviarail.ca). Trains to Prince George (3 weekly; 13hr) for connections to Edmonton via Jasper leave on Wednesday, Friday and Sunday at 8am, arriving in Prince George at 8.30pm. If you're taking the train right through, you'll have to overnight in either Prince George or Jasper, as there are no through-trains to Edmonton.

BY FERRY

Many people reach Prince Rupert by ferry, with several options from Vancouver or Vancouver Island (see page 708).

Ferry terminals for BC Ferries (for Port Hardy and the Haida Gwaii) and the Alaska Marine Hwy (for Skagway and Alaska Panhandle ports) are at Fairview Dock, 2km southwest of town at the end of Hwy-16. Walk-on tickets for foot passengers are rarely a problem at either terminal, but advance reservations are essential if you're taking a car or want a cabin for any summer crossing. Grab a taxi from downtown (☎ 250 624 2185) to get there.

To Haida Gwaii BC Ferries operates the MV *Northern Adventure* to Skidegate Landing on Haida Gwaii (early May to late Sept daily; rest of year three weekly; 6hr 30min–8hr, depending on weather) and costs $40.30 one-way for foot passengers ($32.90 late Sept to early May), plus $143/$117.70 for cars and $5 for bikes. Two-berth cabins cost $90. Return ferries from Skidegate sometimes provide a connection with the Inside Passage boat to Port Hardy on Vancouver Island (see page 785). For reservations or timetable information, contact BC Ferries on ☎ 250 386 3431, ☎ 888 223 3779 anywhere in BC, or in Prince Rupert on ☎ 250 624 9627; ⓦbcferries.com.

To Port Hardy Ferries to Port Hardy (see page 785; ☎ 800 686 0446, ⓦferrytravel.com) leave every other

11

THE "SPIRIT BEARS" OF PRINCESS ROYAL ISLAND

At first glance, you could easily mistake it for a polar or albino black bear. But the elusive **kermode** or "spirit bear" is actually a white-furred variation of the black bear; a recessive gene passed from both parents produces its white fur. The kermode is unique to the rugged temperate rainforest along BC's central coast, its habitat concentrated in the fifteen million acres stretching from Bella Coola to Prince Rupert (also known as the Great Bear Rainforest). Despite pressure from conservationists to preserve its habitat, the kermode remains under threat from logging, hunting and mining. The highest number of kermode bears can be found on **Princess Royal Island**, 200km south of Prince Rupert, where ten percent of black bears are born with white fur. No humans live on the island, and access is by boat or floatplane only, usually from **Hartley Bay**, a remote community of 180 Gitga'at people 140km south of Prince Rupert. The best viewing months are between August and October, when the bears gather around the creeks to feed on spawning salmon.

ARRIVAL AND INFORMATION

By plane or boat Hartley Bay is accessed by air or water from Prince Rupert: North Co Corp Ferry Service (ⓦmetlakatla.ca, ☎ 250 841 2522) runs a twice-weekly service (check for days), leaving from the terminal on Cow Bay Road (3hr 30min; $45 one way), while Harbour Air (☎ 800 665 0212, ⓦharbourair.com) operates a daily, one-hour flight ($200 round-trip).
Tourist office For current information regarding tours, transportation and accommodation in Hartley Bay, contact Gitga'at Tourism at 445 Hayimiisaxaa Way (☎ 250 841 2500, ⓦgitgaat.net/tourism).

ACCOMMODATION AND TOURS

Boat tours One day wildlife-viewing boat tours (☎ 250 841 2522, ⓦgitgaat.net) operate out of Hartley Bay.

Bluewater Adventures ☎ 888 877 1770, ⓦbluewateradventures.ca. A luxury tour from a boat plying the islands of the bay, Bluewater's eight-day Great Bear Rainforest excursion takes in water wildlife (whales and sea lions), hot springs, and hopefully some black and spirit bear sightings. There is usually a trip to a First Nations village and a day with a local guide as well. Boat departs/lands at either Terrace, Prince Rupert or Bella Bella; check schedule. $5885
Spirit Bear Lodge ☎ 250 339 5644, ⓦspiritbear. com. Lodge further down the coast in Klemtu, from where Spirit Bear Quest Tours operates several four- to seven-day bear- and wildlife-viewing tours starting at $2890/person for four days/three nights for two in low season (June and July) to $3460/person for same in high season (Sept to mid-Oct).

day in summer for a stunning day-long cruise, aboard the MV *Northern Expedition*, that lasts approximately 17hr, depending on the weather (overnight trip Oct to mid-Dec, three times every two weeks). One-way fares are $175 for passengers, $398 extra for a car, $5 extra for a bicycle (mid-May to Sept); Oct to Dec, discounts apply. Two-berth cabins cost $85 additional. To take a car on in the summer, you'll need to book at least two months in advance.

To Alaska Ferries run by Alaska Marine Highway (☎250 627 1744, ☎800 642 0066, ⓦdot.state.ak.us/amhs) go to Skagway in Alaska, via (some or all) Ketchikan, Wrangell, Petersburg, Sitka, Hyder, Stewart, Juneau, Haines, Hollis and other minor stops. Frequency is three times a week in the summer and twice a week in winter. Schedules and fares are complicated, given the many possible permutations of route and port, but can be sourced from the website or by calling the central reservations number. One-way adult fares from Prince Rupert to Skagway start at around US$179,

with US$34 extra to bring a bicycle and US$460 for a car. Two- or four-berth cabins can also be booked: reckon on a two-berth cabin from Prince Rupert to Haines or Skagway costing about US$187. Boats stop frequently en route, with the chance to go ashore for a short time, though longer stopovers must be arranged when buying a through-ticket. If you're a foot passenger arrive at least an hour before departure to go through US customs and immigration and three hours early if you have a car. Though the journey takes two days there are various restrictions on the fresh food you can take on board.

BY BUS

Since Greyhound pulled out of the region, BC Transit (☎250 563 0011, ⓦbctransit.com) handles twice weekly buses for the ten-hour ride to Prince George (around $50), with connections to Dawson Creek and Fort Nelson.

INFORMATION AND TOURS

Tourist office In the Atlin Terminal on Cow Bay Rd (☎250 624 5637, ⓦvisitprincerupert.com), a little to the north in an older part of town known as Cow Bay; it's a small and stylish waterfront enclave boasting attractive cafés, galleries and restaurants.

Tours While you're in town, check out some of the local tours or boat trips, many of which are inexpensive and

provide a good way to see the offshore islands and their wildlife. Prince Rupert Adventure Tours (☎250 627 9166, ☎800 201 8377, ⓦadventuretours.nct), with an office in Cow Bay, is perhaps your best bet for grizzly bear- (mid-May–July; 7hrs; $245) and whale-watching (mid-July–Oct; 4 hrs; $125) excursions.

ACCOMMODATION

With more ferry traffic and, consequently, visitors – many of whom, if coming off a later ferry, choose to stay the night before moving on – Prince Rupert's accommodation options have expanded, but it's still a good idea to book ahead.

HOTELS AND B&B

Black Rooster Guesthouse 501 6th Ave ☎250 627 5337, ☎866 371 5337, ⓦblackrooster.ca. A spacious affair that's half-apartments, half-hotel, and has the feel of an upmarket hostel. A choice of well-equipped twin, queen or family rooms (all with in-room phone and TV); groups might want to opt for the four-bed apartments (which also have a sofa bed). $85

Crest Hotel 222 1st Ave West ☎250 624 6771, ☎800 663 8150, ⓦcresthotel.bc.ca. This is the place to go if you want top-of-the-range accommodation with great views – it's set on a promontory overlooking the harbour. The more expensive suites have two-person soaking or jet-tubs (some with views), a fireplace and all the other standard amenities, while cheaper rooms are slightly less plush, but still very nice. $189

Enchanted Rainforest B&B 706 Ritchie St ☎250 624 9742, ⓦprincerupertbedandbreakfast.com. In a quiet and leafy residential area close to downtown, this B&B has three newly renovated and comfortable rooms (two are en

suite). There's a shared kitchen and living room, plus free parking. $140

Inn on the Harbour 720 1st Ave West ☎250 624 9107, ☎800 663 8155, ⓦinnontheharbour.com. Perhaps the best all-round central choice in town – especially if you can secure a room with a sea view (each room comes with binoculars). Nicely appointed (rain shower, Keurig coffee maker, mini-fridge) for the price. $139

Totem Lodge 1335 Park Ave ☎250 624 6761, ☎800 550 0178, ⓦtotemlodge.com. This is the nearest accommodation to the ferry terminals. The 31 rooms are very plain and most come with a kitchenette ($7/night fee) and have wi-fi. Continental breakfast included in rate. $99

HOSTELS AND CAMPGROUNDS

Pioneer Backpacker's Inn 167 3rd Ave E ☎250 624 2334, ☎888 794 9998, ⓦpioneerhostel.com. You'll have to be quick – or reserve in advance – to get a room here, as it fills up quickly in high season. The rooms are bright but basic, and all have shared bathrooms. The hostel also operates a free shuttle to and from the ferry terminals and train station, offers free wi-fi and holds a weekly barbecue. Dorms $35; doubles $80

Prince Rupert RV Campground 1750 Park Ave, 1km west of town ☎250 627 1000, ⓦprincerupertrv.com

This is the only local, big campground, and so a shame it's rather unattractive. Still, it's only 1km away from the ferry terminals so you're bound to be one of the first aboard. No need to book for a tent site. Sites $28; RVs $42

EATING AND DRINKING

Breakers Pub 117 George Hills Way ☎250 624 5990. A local hangout since 1986, *Breakers*, just across the bridge from Cow Bay, is a popular and inexpensive place to sink a beer (nightly specials) or to bite into tasty local seafood dishes. Mon–Thurs 11.30am–11pm, Fri & Sat 11.30am–12.30am, Sun noon–10pm.

Cow Bay Café 205 Cow Bay Rd ☎250 627 1212, ⓦcowbaycafe.com. For something more upmarket, locals flock to the *Cow Bay Café*, which does a roaring trade on the waterfront (mains $15–20). Also serves up tasty home-made baked goods. Tues–Fri 11.30am–2pm & 5–9pm, Sat 11.30–3pm & 5–9pm, Sun 1–8pm.

Cowpuccinos 25 Cow Bay Rd ☎250 627 1395. A cool café serving fair-trade coffee, fresh soups, sandwiches and home-made desserts. Daily Mon–Fri 7am–9pm, Sat & Sun 7am–6pm.

Waterfront Restaurant 222 1st Ave West at Crest Hotel ☎250 627 6771, ⓦcresthotel.bc.ca. Enjoy the region's finest northwest-coast cuisine with a tantalizing menu featuring local seafood, steaks and pasta while enjoying the view of the bald eagles soaring outside (mains from $15, from $28 for seafood and steak entrées). Mon–Fri 6.30am–9pm, Sat & Sun 7am–9pm.

11

Haida Gwaii

Arranged in a gentle arc some 150km off the Prince Rupert coast, **Haida Gwaii** (formerly known as the **Queen Charlotte Islands**) consists of a triangular-shaped archipelago of two major islands – **Graham** and **Moresby** – and two hundred islets that make an enticing diversion from the heavily travelled sea route up through BC's coast.

The islands are something of a cult destination among travellers and environmentalists – partly for their scenery, wildlife, and almost legendary remoteness from the mainstream – but also because they've achieved a high profile in the disagreement between the forestry industry and ecology activists. At the forefront of the disagreement were the **Haida**, who have made the islands their home for over ten thousand years (see page 805). After years of negotiations the **Gwaii Haanas National Park Reserve and Haida Heritage Site** was created, which protects large tracts of land, incredible biodiversity, traditional villages and numerous archeological sites. The Haida culture, and in particular the chance to visit their many **deserted villages**, forms an increasing part of the islands' attraction, but many also come here to sample the immensely rich flora and fauna, the profusion of which has earned the islands the title of the "**Canadian Galapagos**".

Some areas of Haida Gwaii were one of only two tracts in western Canada to escape the last Ice Age, which elsewhere altered evolutionary progress; this enabled the survival of many so-called **endemics**, species which aren't found anywhere else in the world. Those unique to the islands include a fine yellow daisy, the world's largest subspecies of black bear, a subspecies of pine marten, deer mouse, hairy woodpecker, saw-whet owl and Stellar's jay. There are also more **eagles** here than anywhere else in the region, as well as the world's largest population of Peale's peregrine falcons and the elusive black-footed albatross – whose wingspan exceeds that of the largest eagle. There's also a good chance of spotting several species of whale, otter, sea lion and other aquatic mammals, schools of fish and a host of colourful marine invertebrates.

ARRIVAL AND DEPARTURE

HAIDA GWAII

The islands can be accessed either by air from Vancouver or Prince Rupert, or by ferry from Prince Rupert. There is no public transport on the islands, but shuttle services are available.

By ferry Ferries from Prince Rupert (see page 801) dock at tiny Skidegate Landing between Queen Charlotte and Skidegate on Graham Island, the northernmost of

the group's two main collections of islands. BC Ferries (ⓦbcferries.com) also plies between Moresby (Alliford Bay) and Graham (Skidegate) with regular 20min crossings (10 daily; 7am–5.30pm; $8.90 foot passengers, $20.65 cars, $2 kayaks, canoes or bicycles); check online for current schedule and fares.

By plane Flights land at Sandspit (which has the islands' only airstrip) on Moresby Island. Air Canada Jazz flies to Sandspit daily from Vancouver, while Pacific Coastal Airlines (ⓦpacificcoastal.com) flies to Masset from Vancouver daily in the summer and six times weekly in the winter. You could also go from Prince Rupert with Inland Air (ⓣ250 624 2577, ⓣ888 624 2577, ⓦinlandair.bc.ca), which flies to Masset twice each weekday, and to Skidegate and Haida Gwaii on demand.

Eagle Transit (ⓣ250 559 4461, ⓣ877 747 4461, ⓦeagletransit.net) operates an airport shuttle (it meets all Air Canada flights) to and from the villages of Queen Charlotte and Skidegate.

GETTING AROUND AND INFORMATION

By car The easiest and cheapest way to get around the islands is by car – great if you've brought yours over on the ferry, but expensive to rent. Rates run about $50 a day plus mileage: Budget (ⓣ250 637 5688, ⓣ800 557 3228) with offices in Queen Charlotte and at Sandspit Airport, and National in Queen Charlotte and Massett (ⓣ250 626 3833); in summer you need to book in advance. Rates at Rustic Rentals (ⓣ250 559 4641) and Island Auto Rentals (ⓣ250 559 4118) on different ends of Oceanview Drive in Queen Charlotte may be a touch lower. If you're planning to drive logging roads (most of the roads are controlled by logging companies) ask at the visitor centres for latest access details.

By bike You can hire town bikes at Sandspit Visitor Centre close to the airport (1 Airport Rd; daily mid-May to mid-Sept; ⓣ250 637 5362); they have five bikes on a first-come first-served basis ($30/day). Masset Bikes (open year-round; ⓣ250 626 8939, ⓦmassetbikes.com) offer bikes and can organise pick up and drop off (town bike $25/day; fat tire $45/day; discount for longer term rentals).

By boat To see the Haida villages, virtually all of which are on inaccessible parts of Moresby, you'll need to take a boat. Enquire at the visitor centre for the latest information on outfitters.

By seaplane If you want to see SGang Gwaay in a day, you'll need to take a pricey tour by seaplane. For flights and tours around Haida Gwaii, contact Inland Air Charters in Queen Charlotte (ⓣ250 559 8136, ⓣ888 624 2577; in Prince Rupert ⓣ250 624 2577, ⓦinlandair.bc.ca), who'll take you out to the deepest backwoods, including Gwaii Haanas National Park Reserve.

Visitor centre In Queen Charlotte (see page 805).

Graham Island

Most casual visitors stick to **Graham Island**, where the bulk of the islands' roads and accommodation are concentrated along its eastern side, between **Queen Charlotte** in the south and **Masset** some 108km to the north. These settlements and the villages in between – **Skidegate**, **Tlell** and **Port Clements** – lie along Hwy-16, the principal road, and shelter in the lee of the islands, away from a mountainous and indented rocky west coast that boasts the highest combined seismic, wind and tidal energy of any west-coast North American coastline. Much of the east coast consists of beautiful half-moon, driftwood-strewn beaches and a provincial park where you can appreciate the milder climes produced by the Pacific's Japanese Current, a warming stream that contributes to the island's lush canopy of thousand-year-old spruce and cedar rainforests. On the downside, though, it drenches both sides of the island with frequent rainstorms, even in summer, so pack a raincoat.

Queen Charlotte

The island's second-largest settlement, **QUEEN CHARLOTTE**, is a fishing village and administrative centre spread out along the waterfront about 5km west of the Skidegate ferry terminal. The village takes its name from the ship of Captain George Dixon, the British explorer who sailed to Haida Gwaii in 1787, thirteen years after first European contact was probably made by the Spaniard Juan Perez. Until fairly recently, when the logging industry went into steep decline, most of its residents earned a living from the timber companies, whose felling exploits have cleared most of the hills around the port. For a fine overview of the place, try the hike (3–5hr) to the top of **Sleeping Beauty Mountain**; the trailhead is reached by a rough forest road accessible (ideally by a vehicle with high clearance) from Crown Forest Road near Honna Road. Farther afield you can drive to **Rennell Sound**, a west-coast inlet with shingle beaches: take the main logging road north from the town for 22km and then turn left and follow the steep

THE HAIDA

The **Haida** are widely considered to have the most highly developed culture and art tradition of BC's First Peoples. Extending from Haida Gwaii to southern Alaska, their lands included major stands of red cedar, the raw material for their huge dugout **canoes**, their traditional intricate **carvings** and their homes. The Haida were feared **warriors**, paddling into rival villages and returning with canoes laden with goods and slaves. Their skill on the open sea made them the "Vikings" of North America.

The Haida divided themselves into one of two main groups, or *moiety*: the **Eagles** and the **Ravens**, which were further divided into kin groups named after their original village location. Marriage within each *moiety* was considered incestuous, so Eagles would always seek Raven mates and vice versa. Descent was **matrilineal**, which meant a chief could not pass his property on to his sons because they would belong to a different group, so instead his inheritance passed to his sister's sons.

Haida **villages** were an impressive sight, their vast cedar-plank houses dominated by fifteen-metre totem poles displaying the kin group's unique animal crest or other mythical creatures, all carved in elegant, fluid lines. Entrance to each house was through the gaping mouth of a massive carved figure; inside, supporting posts were carved into the forms of the crest animals. Equal elaboration attended the many Haida ceremonies, one of the most important being the **memorial potlatch**, which served to mark the end of mourning for a dead chief and the validation of the heir's right to succession.

After **European contact** the Haida population was devastated by smallpox and other epidemics. In 1787, there were approximately ten thousand Haida scattered across the archipelago; by 1915, the population totalled just 588. They were then forced to leave many of their traditional villages, where homes and totems fell into disrepair and artefacts were appropriated by collectors. **SGang Gwaay**, a remote village at the southern tip of Haida Gwaii, remained relatively untouched. Today the remaining three thousand Haida live mostly in Old Massett and Skidegate.

Several Haida artists are highly regarded in the North American art world; Bill Reid, Freda Diesing and Robert Davidson are among the best known, and scores of others produce a mass of carvings and jewellery for the tourist market. They also play a powerful role in the islands' social, political and cultural life, and many have been key voices in the formation of sites such as the Gwaii Haanas National Park Reserve and Heritage Site (see page 809) and Duu Guusd Tribal Park (see page 807).

11

gravel road for 14km. The **Rennell Sound Recreation Site** offers paths through stands of primal rainforest to isolated sandy beaches and a couple of campgrounds with a number of popular beachfront wilderness pitches (free).

INFORMATION AND ACTIVITIES
QUEEN CHARLOTTE

Visitor centre 3220 Wharf St (May–Sept Mon–Sat 9am–8pm, Sun noon–8pm; reduced hours in winter; ☎ 250 559 8316, ⓦ qcinfo.ca, ⓦ gohaidagwaii.ca). The town is the major place to sign up for any number of outdoor activities; contact the office and be sure to pick up the invaluable and free *Guide to the Queen Charlotte Islands*. The centre is also the place to organize fishing, sailing, sightseeing and canoeing trips, plus they have information on the free, basic campgrounds on Graham and Moresby islands.

Kitgoro Kayaking Spruce Point (☎ 250 637 1412, ⓦ facebook.com/kitgoro). Brothers Luke and Kye are the people to talk to about kayaking the ocean, rivers and creeks around Haida Gwaii, and Skidegate Inlet in particular. They offer guided single or multi day trips or they can rent out all the outdoor gear that'll you'll need. Contact them for rates.

ACCOMMODATION

Accommodation is scarce and demand is high in summer; book early or enquire at the tourist office, whose website also has an extensive accommodation list.

Kagan Bay Campground Honna Forest Service Rd, 4km west of town. This BC Forest Recreation-run site has six lovely first-come, first-served beachfront pitches, with picnic tables. There are pit toilets but no running water. Free **Premier Creek Lodging** 3101 3rd Ave ☎ 250 559 8415, ☎ 888 322 3388, ⓦ haidagwaii.net/premier. The first-choice hotel in town is a restored 1910 heritage building overlooking the harbour and Bearskin Bay. Some single rooms available, with a shared bathroom. **$100**

Sea Raven Motel 3301 3rd Ave ☎ 250 559 4423, ☎ 800 665 9606, ⓦ searaven.com. Overlooking Bearskin Bay, the 30 rooms here are rather plain, but perfectly suitable (get a deluxe room with a balcony if you can). Kitchenette and family rooms are available, and some rooms are pet friendly. **$79**

Sword Fern Inn 3127 2nd Ave ☎ 250 626 9299, ⓦ swordferninn.com. An intimate inn (previously *Dorothy and Mike's*) that has a deck offering expansive views of the harbour from its hill vantage point). There's a fire pit and barbecue out in the lovely garden, and the place strives to be eco-friendly. Suites **$125**, doubles **$115**

EATING AND DRINKING

Ocean View Pub & Grill 3200 Oceanview Rd ☎ 250 559 8503. As lively a place as you'll find round here, the bar and grill has a respectable selection of brews and great menu with a seafood focus (fish and chips $18–$22). There are regular band performances and karaoke nights. Wed & Thurs 4pm–11pm, Fri 4pm–2am, Sat noon–2am, Sun noon–9pm.

Ocean View Restaurant 3200 Oceanview Rd ☎ 250 559 8503. Locals flock to the upstairs *Ocean View Restaurant*, which serves a wide selection of main courses ($15–25), including, naturally, plenty of fish and seafood. Mon, Tues, Thurs & Fri 11am–9pm, Sat & Sun 9am–9pm.

Queen B's 3208 Wharf St ☎ 250 559 4463. The welcoming *Queen B's* is a favourite hangout offering fine breakfasts, lunches and savoury snacks ($5–16). Serves dinner on Friday evenings. Mon–Sat 9am–5pm, & Fri eve.

Haida Heritage Centre at Kaay Llnagaay, Skidegate

Open year-round, call for times • $16 • ☎ 250 559 7885, ⓦ haidaheritagecentre.com

Ferries dock at Skidegate Landing, 2km to the south of **SKIDEGATE**. You can browse through the more accessible aspects of Haida culture at the **Haida Heritage Centre at Kaay Llnagaay**, located at Second Beach around 500m east of the ferry terminal. The centre – a series of longhouses fronted by totem poles – includes a canoe house, a restaurant, a performance space, an art and carving studio and a museum which, among other things, contains a comprehensive collection of the Haida's treasured argillite carvings. Argillite is a form of black slate-like rock found only on Haida Gwaii, and only in one site, whose location west of Queen Charlotte is kept a closely guarded secret. Also check out the platform here to view grey whales during their migrations (April–June), and ask at the museum about the **seafood feasts** sometimes held by the Haida Repatriation Committee in July and August and open to everyone for $50. At the canoe house you can view the famous *Loo Taas* ("Wave Eater") canoe, carved by Haida artist Bill Reid. It was made for the Expo '86 world fair in Vancouver and was the first Haida canoe carved since 1909.

Tlell

You really can't miss the ranching community of **TLELL**, 36km north of Skidegate, which is spread out over a 5–7km stretch of coastline. At the sea here you can stroll for hours on deserted wind-sculpted dunes; from here it is 90km along the unbroken beach to Rose Point, at the northeast tip of Graham Island.

Tlell is also at the southern border of the **Naikoon Provincial Park**, an enclave extending over Graham Island's northeast corner and designed to protect the fine beach, dune and dwarf-woodland habitats. The park offers numerous trails along the beach and through the forests. About 8km beyond the *Misty Meadows Campground* (see below), look out for the picnic site and trails at the southern tip of **Mayer Lake**. The most popular hike is to the **shipwreck of the Pesuta**, which ran aground here in 1928; the trail starts at the picnic site just north of the Tlell River Bridge.

ACCOMMODATION	TLELL

Cacilia's B&B ☎ 250 557 4664. Just north of Richardson Ranch on the main road is the rustic *Cacilia's B&B*, a renovated log house set behind the dunes on Hecate Strait. Meals and sea-kayak tours can be arranged. Living space is shared with the landlady. **$70**

Misty Meadows Campground ☎ 250 626 3337 ext 28. Campground in Naikoon Provincial Park just south of the Tlell River Bridge and 500m north of the park headquarters; backcountry camping is also allowed throughout the park. June–Sept. **$18**

Port Clements

The road cuts inland for **PORT CLEMENTS**, 21km northwest of Tlell. In the past it was famous for the **Golden Spruce**, a three-hundred-year-old bleached albino sitka spruce, sacred to the Haida; in 1997 a protestor chopped it down. A rare genetic mutation allowed the tree's needles to be bleached by sunlight; geneticists and foresters have reproduced a few of them, now on display at the University of British Columbia and in California. A twenty-minute trail along the banks of the Yakoun River leads to a viewpoint where you can see where the tree once stood; the trailhead is 6km south of town along unsealed Bayview Drive, and 10km further south, look out for the two-hundred-year-old partially carved, abandoned **Haida canoe** protruding from the bushes.

About 20km north of town on the road to Masset, watch for the signed **Pure Lake Provincial Park**, a good picnic stop along the lakeshore.

ACCOMMODATION AND EATING	PORT CLEMENTS

Sunset RV and Campground ☎ 250 557 4295. Campground at the south end of Bayview Drive close to the Golden Spruce Trail, it overlooks the Yakoun River estuary and gets stunning sunsets. May–Oct, no reservations. Sites **$10**; RVs **$15**

Yakoun River Inn 117 Bayview Drive ☎ 250 557 4440. For food and drink, the main option hereabouts is the *Yakoun River Inn*, with meals around $15. Daily for lunch and dinner.

Masset and around

MASSET, 40km north of Port Clements, is the biggest place on the islands, a scattered, rather ugly town – it's a former military base – of some one thousand people, most of whom are employed in the fishing industry.

Delkatla Wildlife Sanctuary

Many visitors are here to birdwatch at the **Delkatla Wildlife Sanctuary**, a saltwater marsh north of the village. The sanctuary is home to over 140 bird species, many of which stop over for a brief time while resting and refuelling before commencing their annual spring or fall migrations. Sightings include trumpeter swans, American coots and sandhill cranes. Visitors have access to viewing platforms and shoreline access viewpoints as well as a handful of short walking trails to the coastal beach. Contact Delkatla Bay Birding Tours (☎ 250 626 5015) for guided visits.

Old Massett

The neighbouring village of **Old Massett** – with an extra "t" – 2km to the west, is the administrative centre for the Council of the Haida First Nation and is where some eight hundred Haida live and work. Visitors should show respect when visiting totem sites, craft houses and community homes. Many locals are involved in producing crafts for tourists, or organizing wilderness tours, but some are restoring and adding to the dozen or so totems still standing locally (it's possible to visit various canoe and carving sheds). For more **information** on where to see carving and on the village in general, visit the Old Massett Council office at 348 Eagle Avenue (Mon–Fri 9am–5pm; ☎ 250 626 3337), where you should also enquire about permission to visit the **Duu Guusd Heritage Site and Conservancy**, established by the Haida to protect villages on the coast to the northwest. Two villages are still active, and the park is used as a base for the Haida Gwaii Rediscovery Centre, which offers courses to children on Haida culture and history.

Tow Hill

One of the more popular activities in Masset is to walk the trails around **Tow Hill**, 26km to the east of Old Massett along Tow Hill Road, in Naikoon Provincial Park. Three trails begin by the Hiellen River at the foot of Tow Hill itself. The easiest is the 1km **Blow Hole Trail**, which drops down to striking rock formations and basalt cliffs by the sea.

From here you can follow another path to the top of Tow Hill (109m) for superb views of deserted sandy beaches stretching into the hazy distance – on a clear day you can see Alaska approximately 75km away. The third track, the **Cape Fife Trail**, is a longer (10km one-way) hike to the east side of the island where there is a small, basic cabin (free).

ARRIVAL AND INFORMATION   MASSET

By plane The airport lies 3km east of town.
Tourist office 1455 Old Beach Rd (July & Aug daily 9am–5pm; ☎ 250 626 3995, ⓦ massetbc.com). Offers full details

of wildlife and birdwatching possibilities, as well as hiking trails and fishing.

ACCOMMODATION AND EATING

Agate Beach 26km east of Masset off the secondary road towards Tow Hill ⓔ park@mhtv.ca. A provincial park campground near trails and sandy beaches offering 43 basic sites, pit toilets and a rustic boat launch. June–Sept. $18
Haida Rose Café 415 Frog St ☎ 250 626 3311. A pleasant and popular place among locals in Old Massett, serving up coffee, pastries, soup and sandwiches. Daily for breakfast and lunch.
Hidden Island RV and Resort Tow Hill Rd, 2km north of town alongside the wildlife sanctuary ☎ 250 626 5286, ☎ 866 303 5286, ⓦ hidden-island-resort.com. The only nearby campground, with laundry facilities, showers and a fully licensed fish-and-chips restaurant. Popular with fishing enthusiasts. Sites $26; RVs $36
Island Sunrise Café 1645 Main St ☎ 250 626 9344. Another popular eatery among locals, which serves up delicious home-style cooking including hearty breakfasts.

Cash only. Daily 7am–3pm.
Masset Oceanview Lodge 1970 Harrison Ave ☎ 250 626 3388, ⓦ massethotel.ca. Eighteen standard rooms overlooking Masset Inlet. Breakfast is served in their waterside dining room. $135
Moon Over Naikoon Bakery Tow Hill Rd, 9km east of Masset ☎ 250 626 9344. Pizzas slices ($5), soup ($5) and their famous "cinny" cinnamon buns ($4), served on an old school bus in the sticks. There's a simple shelter outdoors (with hammocks) or you can eat in the cosily converted interior. Look out for the red barn and then take the second right. Cash only. Mid-May to Sept only, daily 10am–6pm.
Rapid Richie's Rustic Rentals 16km from Masset along Tow Hill Road ☎ 250 626 5472, ⓦ beachcabins.com. Four off-the-grid beach cabins nestled in the coastal rainforest of Naikoon Provincial Park. Three have wood stoves, all have decks, outhouses, and equipped kitchens. $80

Moresby Island

Moresby Island is all but free from human contact except for deserted Haida villages (one of which contains the world's largest stand of totems), forestry roads and the small logging community of **SANDSPIT**. The island's biggest draw is visiting the **Gwaii Haanas National Park Reserve and Haida Heritage Site**.

Most locals here and on Graham Island work in Moresby's forests and consequently, the transport system is almost limited to **logging roads**. If you're driving on these, take extreme care and check in with the visitor centre for updated logging activity before setting out. It is highly advisable to rent a 4WD to access these roads, but many rental agencies will have you sign a waiver stating you will not drive on the logging roads or beaches. Alternatively, you can sea-kayak, mountain bike or backpack through the interior of northern Moresby Island, but you need to know what you're doing and be prepared to lug plenty of supplies.

ARRIVAL AND INFORMATION   MORESBY ISLAND

By plane Seaplanes fly to Alliford Bay from Prince Rupert (see page 799) on demand.
By ferry Sandspit lies 15km from the Alliford Bay terminal for the inter-island ferry link with Skidegate on Graham Island.

Sandspit Visitor Centre In the airport terminal building (May–Sept daily 9am–5pm; ☎ 250 637 5362). Provides information for travel throughout Haida Gwaii and bike hire (see page 801).

ACCOMMODATION

501 RV/Tent Park 501 Beach Rd, Sandspit ☎ 250 637 5473, ⓔ 1rvpark@telus.net. For tenting, you can try the

501 RV/Tent Park; many people choose to sleep on the spit's beaches, which is not recommended due to the powerful tides. Public laundry and showers from 9am to 9pm. May–Sept. Sites $15; RVs $25

Bayview Garden 401 Alliford Bay Rd, Sandspit ☎ 250 637 5749, ☎ 866 306 6644, ⍟ bayviewgardenbandb.com. A waterfront heritage home with a separate three-bedroom cottage and hostel beds also available. You cook the complimentary breakfasts (not included for dorms) yourself. Dorms $28; doubles $95

Gray Bay Campgrounds Gray Bay, 21km southeast of Sandspit; contact the Teal Jones forestry offices on Beach Rd for details and road conditions ☎ 250 637 5323. Twenty primitive and peaceful campgrounds near gravel and sand beaches, inside Kunxalas Heritage Site and Conservancy. No reservations and no water. **Free**

Moresby Island Guest House 385 Beach Rd, Sandspit ☎ 250 637 5300, ☎ 877 874 1654, ⍟ moresbyislandguesthouse.com. Clean, comfortable accommodation with ocean views or a private patio at Shingle Bay. Bikes, laundry and kitchen facilities offered for guests. The family room sleeps five. $65

Gwaii Haanas National Park Reserve and Haida Heritage Site

Gwaii Haanas National Park Reserve and Haida Heritage Site, located on the southern portion of Haida Gwaii, is a 90km-long archipelago of 207 islands, some six hundred Haida archeological sites, five Haida Gwaii Watchmen village sites and 1750km of coastline. A 1993 agreement signed with the federal government gave the Haida joint control of this region and afforded protection to their ancient villages, traditional lands and resources, but some land claims to the region remain unresolved. You'll need to spend money and time, and expend a bit of effort, to see the park reserve; there are no roads and access is only by boat or chartered seaplane, although experienced sea-kayakers and boaters often travel here independently.

Visits to a variety of ancient **Haida village sites** and their totems and ruined dwellings are described here in order of distance (and therefore time and expense) from Sandspit. Closest is **K'uuna LInagaay (Skedans)**, accessible on day-trips by boat from Moresby Camp on the Cumshewa Inlet, 46km south of Sandspit; access to the camp is by logging road. Farther afield are **T'aanuu LInagaay, Hlk'yah GaawGa (Windy Bay)** and **Gandll K'in Gwaay-yaay (Hotspring Island)**, whose series of outdoor thermal pools make it one of the most popular destinations. These hot springs mysteriously dried up days after a 7.7 magnitude earthquake rocked the region in October 2012, but six years later they began flowing again. The finest site is the furthest away: **SGang Gwaay (Ninstints)** is close to the southern tip of the archipelago. Residents left around 1880 in the wake of smallpox epidemics and today it contains the most striking of the ruined Haida villages; the moss-covered depressions where longhouses once stood, and the many mouldering mortuary totems are a UNESCO World Heritage Site. In accordance with the wishes of the Haida, little attempt is made to preserve ancient village sites and, within decades, many of these decaying totem poles may have returned to nature.

INFORMATION AND TOURS   GWAII HAANAS

Tours The easiest way into the park reserve is with a tour; contact the Queen Charlotte visitor centre (see page 805). Archipelago Ventures (☎ 250 652 4913, ☎ 888 559 8317, ⍟ tourhaidagwaii.com) and Moresby Explorers (☎ 250 637 2215, ☎ 800 806 7633, ⍟ moresbyexplorers.com) offer good six-day kayak (Archipelago) or two- or four-day (Moresby) boat trips into the park. **Haida Style Expeditions** (☎ 250 637 1151, ⍟ haidastyle.com) takes visitors out on one-day expeditions from Queen Charlotte on an open-to-the-elements rigid hull zodiac (they kit you out with wet weather gear). If you want to see SGang Gwaay in one day, the only option is with Inland Air Charters (☎ 250 624 2577, ☎ 888 624 2577, ⍟ inlandair.bc.ca) whose full-day joint flight and boat tours start from $660/

person (5 passengers max.).

Independent travel To visit the reserve independently, you must make an advance reservation or obtain a stand-by space. Call ☎ 877 559 8818 between 8.30am and 4.30pm starting on the first business day in April, and check ⍟ pc.gc.ca/gwaiihaanas for the latest information. Six stand-by places daily are available on a first-come, first-served basis from the Parks Canada office at the Haida Heritage Centre at Kaay LInagaay in Skidegate. The fee to visit the park is $19.60 per person per day; $117.70 for a season pass.

Orientation An orientation session is mandatory for all independent visitors entering Gwaii Haanas (those on guided tours will receive the information as they travel with their guides). Sessions take place at the Haida Heritage

Centre at Kaay Llnagaay in Skidegate at 60 Second Beach Rd; contact Parks Canada for updated times and locations (☎ 250 559 8818). Sessions last around 1hr 30min and cover public safety, no-trace camping, natural and cultural heritage and the Haida Gwaii Watchmen Programme.

ACCOMMODATION

Apart from some restricted areas you can **camp** where you wish; fees for camping are included in the park's entrance fee. There are two rustic **accommodation** options just outside the park's southern boundary:

Gwaii Haanas Guest House 10km from SGang Gwaay ☎ 250 559 8689, ⓦ gwaiihaanas.com. Four rooms in a family homestead (boat or seaplane access only) that lies in ancient rainforest with ocean views, organic food, sea-kayak

rentals, guided boat tours, birdwatching and other outdoor activity possibilities. Shared bathroom and composting toilet. Meals (frequently Thai cuisine) included. **$320**

Rose Harbour Guest House 12km west of SGang Gwaay ☎ 250 559 2326, ☎ 604 757 3162, ⓦ roseharbour.com. The delightful and rustic *Rose Harbour Guest House* is on the site of an old whaling station (boat or seaplane access only). It offers guided boat tours, and meals are included. **$150**

11 Stewart-Cassiar Highway

The 733km stretch of the **Stewart-Cassiar Highway** (Hwy-37) – from the Skeena Valley east of Prince Rupert to Watson Lake just inside the Yukon – is one of the wildest and most beautiful of any road in BC. Though less famous than the Alaska Highway, the road provides a shorter route from Prince George to the Yukon, and is increasingly travelled by those in search of adventure. Some stretches are still gravel and the available petrol and repair facilities, let alone food and lodgings, are extremely patchy: don't contemplate the journey unless your vehicle's in top condition, with two spare tyres and spare fuel containers.

The highway has two main side-roads worth exploring. The first goes to **Stewart**, with its exceptional sea and mountain scenery, where you can branch off and cross into Alaska at **Hyder**. The second goes to **Telegraph Creek**, a tiny riverside town reminiscent of the early 1900s. There are two additional rough roads midway up that lead to the wilderness of **Mount Edziza Provincial Park** and the **Spatsizi Plateau Wilderness Park**.

In summer Stewart is added to the itinerary of certain sailings of the Alaska Marine Highway **ferry** service (see page 802) – albeit infrequently – so with careful planning you could travel over land to Stewart, or ride a boat to Ketchikan and then to either Skagway or Prince Rupert.

Gitwangak to Stewart

The Stewart-Cassiar Highway starts near Gitwangak (see page 799), off Hwy-16. A hint of the sense of adventure required comes when you hit a section (47km beyond **Cranberry Junction**), where the road doubles up as an airstrip – planes have right of way. The road pitches into the mesmerizing high scenery of the Coast Range, a medley of mountain, lake and forest that reaches a crescendo after 156km around **Meziadin Junction**, where Hwy-37A branches off.

Some 67km west of Meziadin Junction is **STEWART**, Canada's most northerly ice-free port. Here a series of immense glaciers culminates in the dramatic appearance of the unmissable **Bear Glacier**, a vast sky-blue mass of ice that comes down virtually to the highway and has the strange ability to glow in the dark. Stewart itself, 37km west of the glacier, is a shrivelled mining centre sitting at the end of the Portland Canal, the world's fourth longest fjord, a natural boundary between BC and Alaska that encircles the town with peaks (the ferry ride in from Prince Rupert through some of the west coast's wildest scenery is sensational); dominating its rocky amphitheatre is Mount Rainey.

The most interesting thing to do here is to take Salmon Glacier Road out 5km beyond Hyder in Alaska to Fish Creek, where from the viewing platform above the artificial spawning channel you may be lucky enough to see **black bears** catching some of the world's largest chum salmon.

INFORMATION

STEWART

Visitor centre 222 5th Ave near the entrance to the Portland Canal boardwalk (mid-May to Sept daily 9am–5pm; reduced hours May & Sept; ☎ 250 636 9224, ☎ 888 366 5999). Can also provide information about Hyder, just across the border in Alaska (see below).

ACCOMMODATION AND EATING

Bitter Creek Café 313 5th Ave ☎ 250 636 2166. Pleasantly polished and a popular spot for fine dining, this restaurant, part of the *Bay View Hotel*, offers an outside deck and a mouthwatering dinner menu that includes pistachio-crusted halibut ($20). For baked snacks, duck into the bakery and deli next door. Summer Sun–Wed 5–9pm, Thurs–Sat 12.30–9pm.

King Edward Hotel and Motel 405 5th Ave ☎ 250 636 2244, ☎ 800 663 3126, ⓦ kingedwardhotel.com. The hotel provides basic rooms, and the motel offers units with kitchenettes on the other side of the street. The *King's Table* and *Casey's Pub* operating here are also the town's main bar and dining room; the heaving king crab feast for $50 is enough for two people. Restaurant summer daily 7am–8pm; pub Mon–Sat 3–11pm. Hotel $109; motel $139

Rainey Creek Campground 8th Avenue ☎ 250 636 2537, ☎ 888 366 5999. This is the nearest campground, on the edge of town; the tent area is located across the pleasant little Rainey Creek. May–Sept. Sites $15; RV $25

Hyder

Most people come to **HYDER**, Stewart's oddball twin, simply to drink in one or both of its two bars. It's a ramshackle place, barely a settlement at all, just 3km from Stewart across the border in Alaska. You'll encounter none of the usual border formalities since there's nothing beyond the end of the road but 800km of wilderness. People use Canadian currency, the police are of the Mountie variety and the phone system (and ☎ 250 area code) are also Canadian. At the *Glacier Inn* the tradition is to pin a dollar to the wall (in case you return broke and need a drink) and then toss back a shot of hard liquor and receive an "I've Been Hyderized" card. The result is many thousands of tacked dollars. It sounds a bit of a tourist trap, but there's an amiability about the place that warrants its claims to be "The Friendliest Ghost Town in Alaska".

ACCOMMODATION AND EATING

HYDER

The town's two bars are often open 23 hours a day and a couple of **motels** are on hand if you literally can no longer stand. Only one is worth staying at, and as you're in Alaska, there's no room tax to pay.

Camp Run-A-Muck Premier Ave, off Main St ☎ 250 636 2486, ⓦ sealaskainn.com. The *Sealaska* (see below) runs a campground and RV park with fire pits, bathrooms/showers, free wi-fi, vending machines and laundry room. Sites $28; RVs $34

Sealaska Inn Premier Ave, off Main St ☎ 250 636 2486, ⓦ sealaskainn.com. This charming hotel and campground is the better option in town while you rest up and enjoy the breath-taking view of its surrounding mountains. Queen-sized beds, private bathrooms and free internet. Also home to one of the two bars in town. If you want something to soak up the alcohol, make for their restaurant for some artery-clogging deep-fried halibut ($18). $69

Iskut

For several hundred kilometres beyond the Stewart junction there's nothing along the Stewart-Cassiar other than the odd garage, rest area, campground, trailhead and patches of burnt or clear-cut forest etched into the Cassiar and Skeena mountains. Yet in places you can still see traces of the incredible 3060km Dominion Telegraph line that used to link the Dawson City goldfields with Vancouver, and glimpse a proposed railway extension out of Prince George that was abandoned in 1977.

ISKUT, a village 225km north of Meziadin Junction that's the home of the Iskut First Nation in the Tahltan territory, arranges tours into the adjacent wilderness parks, which are also accessible by floatplane from Dease Lake. For information, contact the Iskut Band Office (☎ 250 234 3331, ⓦ iskut.org) or local stores and garages.

11

ACCOMMODATION   ISKUT

Red Goat Lodge ☎ 250 234 3261, ⓦredgoatlodge.ca. Your best choice for local accommodation is the six-room *Red Goat Lodge* with a 26-pitch campground 3km south of the village – they also rent kayaks and canoes starting at $20. Late May to mid-Sept. Sites $20; RVs $25; doubles $109

Dease Lake and north

Some 65km north of Iskut is **DEASE LAKE** – it's best to stay here as the junction to the Alaska Highway is still 246km to the north. The road onwards to the Yukon border is wild and beautiful, passing through some miraculous scenery. Much of this area was swamped with gold-hungry pioneers during the **Cassiar gold rush** of 1872–80. In 1877 Alfred Freedman plucked one of the world's largest pure gold nuggets – a 72-ounce monster – from a creek east of present-day **CASSIAR** (133km from the junction with the Alaska Highway to the north). Today, the mining is focused on asbestos, 5km from the village.

ACCOMMODATION   DEASE LAKE AND NORTH

Arctic Divide Inn & Motel On the hwy, Dease Lake ☎ 250 771 3119, ⓦarcticdivide.ca. Comfortable digs with clean, spacious and warmly decorated rooms with pine accents. The hotel, along with its separate motel, offers private bathrooms, satellite TV, and access to kitchen facilities. Rooms at the inn include continental breakfast. $112

Boya Lake Provincial Park 150km north of Dease Lake. You can camp at the *Boya Lake Provincial Park*, a lovely 44-site lakeside campground (drinking water and pit toilets). Mid-May to mid-Sept. $20

Northway Motor Inn Boulder Ave, Dease Lake ☎ 250 771 5341, ☎ 866 888 2588, ⓦnorthwaymotorinn.com. Another pleasant place to spend the night with 44 clean rooms, complete with kitchenettes, private bathrooms and free internet. Pet friendly. $135

Telegraph Creek

For a taste of what may be a more remarkable landscape than along the Stewart-Cassiar Highway, it's worth driving the potentially treacherous 113km side road from Dease Lake to **TELEGRAPH CREEK** (allow 2hr in good conditions). This delightful river-bank town of city exiles, hunters and ranchers has a look and feel that harks back to the early twentieth century, when it was a major telegraph station and trading post for the gold-rush towns to the north. The road there navigates some incredible gradients and bends, twisting past canyons, old lava beds and touching on several **First Nations villages**, notably at Tahltan River, where salmon are caught and cured in traditional smokehouses and sold to passing tourists.

Much of the village revolves around the *General Store* – a combined café, grocery and garage. Enquire at the café for details of rafting and other trips into the backcountry.

ACCOMMODATION   TELEGRAPH CREEK

Up the Creek B&B 1261 Roberts Creek Road ☎ 250 235 3055, ⓦtelegraphcreek.com. All-season, private log cabin with large porch from which to enjoy views of the Stikine River. The backcountry cabin is solar powered and equipped with hot showers and kitchen facilities. $100

DRIVING THE ALASKA HIGHWAY

Food, fuel and lodgings are found at intervals of 40 to 80km, though cars still need to be in good shape. You should drive with **headlights on** at all times and take care when passing – or being passed by – heavy trucks. The wilderness – up to 800km of it on each side – begins at the highway's edge and unless you're very experienced, off-road exploration is not suggested. Free guides and pamphlets are available at **visitor centres** along the route through to Fairbanks, but **The Milepost** (ⓦthemilepost.com), the road's bible, is, for all its mind-numbing detail, the only one you need buy.

Alaska Highway: Dawson Creek to Whitehorse

Dawson Creek is the launching pad for the Alaska Highway. While it may not be somewhere you'd otherwise stop, it's almost impossible to avoid a night here whether you're approaching from Edmonton and the east or from Prince George (409km to Dawson Creek) on the scenically more uplifting **John Hart Highway** (Hwy-97). The route from Prince George leads you out of BC's upland interior to the so-called Peace River country, a region that belongs in look and spirit to the Albertan prairies.

The best part of the **Alaska Highway** – a span of about 1500km – winds through northern BC from Dawson Creek to Whitehorse, the capital of the Yukon; only 320km of the highway is actually in Alaska. Don't be fooled by the string of villages emblazoned across the area's maps – only **Fort Nelson** and a dip in the **Fort Liard Hot Springs** are worth stopping for; the rest are no more than a garage, a store and perhaps a motel. **Watson Lake**, on the Yukon border, is the largest of these lesser spots, and also marks the junction of the Alaska and Stewart-Cassiar highways. It's vital to book ahead for accommodation if travelling this stretch in July or August.

You need to adapt to a different notion of distance on a 2500km drive: points of interest on the Alaska Highway are a long way apart, and pleasure comes in broad changes in scenery, the sighting of a solitary moose, or in the passing excitement of discovering a lonely bar.

Dawson Creek to Pink Mountain

Except for a small museum next to the town's eye-catching red grain hopper, and the cairn marking Mile Zero of the Alaska Highway, there is one major attraction worth visiting in **DAWSON CREEK**. The **Alaska Highway House** (summer daily 9am–5pm; by donation; ☏250 782 4714), at 10201 10th St, showcases the history of the Alaska Highway with interpretive exhibits and audiovisual displays.

It takes forty minutes before the benign ridged prairies around Dawson Creek drop suddenly into the broad, flat-bottomed valley of the Peace River, a canyon whose walls are scalloped with creeks, gulches and deep muddy scars. **PINK MOUNTAIN**, 226km from Dawson, is a smart place to stop for coffee and basic groceries. Thereafter, the road offers immense **views** of utter wilderness in all directions, the trees as dense as ever, but noticeably more stunted than farther south. Look out for the bright "New Forest Planted" signs, usually a token riposte from loggers to the ecology lobby and invariably backed by a graveyard of sickly looking trees. This is good birdwatching country, but it's also good bear country, so be careful.

ARRIVAL AND INFORMATION

DAWSON CREEK

By bus Greyhound bus is no longer operating in BC, but BC Transit (☏250 563 0011, ⏴bctransit.com) is plugging some of the gaps. The bus terminal is at 1201 Alaska Ave (☏250 782 4275).
Destinations Fort Nelson (Tues only; 6hr 40min); Prince George (Wed & Thurs; 7hr 15min).

Tourist office 900 Alaska Ave (Jan to mid-May and Nov to mid-Dec Mon–Fri 10am–4.30pm; mid-May to early Sept daily 8am–6.30pm; early Sept to Oct Tues–Sat 10am–4.30pm; ☏250 782 9595, ☏866 645 3022, ⏴tourismdawsoncreek.com).

ACCOMMODATION AND EATING

DAWSON CREEK

George Dawson Inn 8th St ☏250 782 9151, ☏800 663 2745, ⏴thegeorgedawsoninn.com. Downtown inn with standard rooms complete with private bathrooms, fridges and microwaves, and free continental breakfast. Guests have access to fitness room. $119
Mile 0 RV Park and Campground ☏250 782 2590, ⏴mile0park.ca. The nearest campground to Dawson

11

HISTORY OF THE ALASKA HIGHWAY

The **Alaska Highway** runs northeast from Mile Zero at Dawson Creek through the Yukon to Mile 1520 in Fairbanks, Alaska. Originally a military road, it's now an all-weather highway travelled by bus services and thousands of tourists out to recapture the thrill of the days when it was known as the "junkyard of the American automobile". It no longer chews up cars, but the scenery and the sense of pushing through wilderness remain alluring.

In 1940 there was no direct land route to the Yukon or Alaska, other than trappers' trails. But with Japan attacking in the Pacific – threatening traditional sea routes north and seemingly ready to attack mainland Alaska – it prompted the US and Canadian governments to build a road north. A proposed coastal route from Hazelton, BC, was deemed susceptible to enemy attack, while an inland route bypassing Whitehorse and following the Rockies would have taken five years to build. This left the **Prairie Route**, which followed a line of air bases through Canada into Alaska.

Construction began in **March 1942**, the start of months of misery for the twenty thousand mainly US soldiers who had to ram a road through mountains, mosquito-ridden bogs and over icy rivers during harsh weather. Crews working on the eastern and western sections met at Contact Creek, BC, in September 1942 and completed the last leg to Fairbanks in October; this engineering triumph took less than a year but cost around $140 million.

By 1943 the road practically needed to be rebuilt. For seven years workers widened it, raised bridges, reduced gradients, bypassed swampy ground and began removing some of its vast bends – the reason why it's now only **1488 miles** (2394km) to the Mile 1520 post in Fairbanks. The highway was opened to civilian use in 1948, but within months so much traffic had broken down and failed to make the trip that it was closed for a year.

The road is now widely celebrated, as in August 2012 when a convoy of 97 historical military vehicles departed Dawson City and travelled south along the Alaska Highway in commemoration of its seventieth anniversary. But there are aspects of its story that are glossed over. Many of the toughest sections were assigned to African-American GIs to complete, few of whom received any credit. Indigenous peoples on the route were also affected; scores of them died from epidemics brought in by workers. The building of the controversial **Canol pipeline** at the same time left the area littered with poisonous waste and construction junk. Wildlife also suffered, with trigger-happy GIs taking pot shots as they worked.

Creek is the *Mile 0*, 1km west of the centre at the junction of highways 97 North and 97 South, on the Alaska Hwy. May to Oct. Sites $15; RVs $25

The Pantry At the George Dawson Inn ☎ 250 782 9151. Hotel restaurant offering full menu service featuring home-style classics. Daily 6.30am–10pm.

PINK MOUNTAIN

Pink Mountain Campground and RV Park ☎ 250 772 5133, ⊛ pinkmountaincampgroundrvpark.ca. One of the better places along the Alaska Hwy to spend the night.

Fuel, showers and laundry facilities available. Guests receive a discount on petrol. Open year-round. Sites $25, RVs $40

Rising Moon B&B 16066 RC Campground Rd (Tomslake) ☎ 250 786 0115, ⊛ risingmoonbb.com. There are three private cabins here with fireplaces, fine linens and access to a hot tub and lakeside cookhouse. $125

Sikanni River Campground & RV Park ☎ 250 772 5400, ⊛ sikannirivercampground.ca. 20km north of *Pink Mountain Campground*. Showers, wi-fi and coin laundry facilities available, along with a small store. Sites $20; RVs $40

Fort Nelson

One of the highway's key stops, **FORT NELSON**, is 253km on from Pink Mountain. This growing industrial town exudes the opportunity the North represents, which also means it's a town in transition, with older buildings standing side-by-side with new hotels, restaurants and commercial developments. Much of life here revolves around exploitation of the area's huge natural gas deposits – the town has the world's second-largest gas-processing plant. A small **museum** devoted to the highway's construction (5603 50th Ave South; mid-May to Aug daily 10am–7pm; $7; ☎ 250 774 3536,

@ fortnelsonmuseum.ca) does a good job illustrating the town's frontier past. From Fort Nelson you can take the Deh Cho Trail along Hwy-77 (see page 848).

INFORMATION
FORT NELSON

Visitor centre Regional Recreation Centre, 5500 Alaska Highway (mid-May to early Sept daily 8am–7pm, Oct to mid-May Mon–Fri 8.30am–4.30pm; ☎ 250 774 6400, @ tourism northernrockies.ca; @ visitorinfo@fortnelsonchamber.com).

ACCOMMODATION AND EATING

Fort Nelson has a large selection of hotels, motels and campgrounds, see the tourism website for a full list.
Woodlands Inn 3995 50th Ave South ☎ 250 774 6669, @ woodlandsinn.ca. On the town's southern approaches, this newish inn is better looking than many of the run-of-the-mill places and it's locally owned. There's a fitness centre, a good restaurant and an on-site liquor store. $152
Dan's Neighbourhood Pub 4204 50th Ave North ☎ 250 774 3929. For somewhere to eat and quaff a beer, try the popular *Dan's*. They serve pub grub, too. Daily 11am–midnight, Fri & Sat till 2am.

Fort Nelson to Liard Hot Springs

This stretch is the Alaska Highway at its best. Landscapes divide markedly around Fort Nelson, where the highway arches west from the flatter hills of Peace River country to meet the northern Rockies above the plains and plateau of the Liard River. Once the road has picked up the river's headwaters, you're soon in some of BC's most grandiose scenery. The area either side of the road amounts to some twenty million acres of wilderness – and experts say that only parts of Africa surpass the region for the variety of mammals present and the pristine state of its ecosystems. Services and motels are scarce, but those that exist – commonly beaten-up-looking places – make for atmospheric and often unforgettable stops. The first worthwhile one, 1km off the highway on a gravel road, is **Tetsa River Regional Park**, about 77km west of Fort Nelson, which has a campground and some appealing short hikes. The campground at **Stone Mountain Provincial Park**, 139km west of Fort Nelson, gives access to a short trail to two hoodoos (wind-sculpted rock columns); the longer Flower Springs Lake Trail (6km) leads to a delightful upland mountain lake. Some 260km from Fort Nelson, **Muncho Lake** sits at the heart of another large provincial park whose ranks of bare mountains provide a foretaste of the barren tundra of the far North.

ACCOMMODATION
FORT NELSON TO LIARD HOT SPRINGS

TETSA RIVER REGIONAL PARK
Tetsa River Lodge and Campground ☎ 250 774 1005, @ tetsariver.com. Just down the road from the Tetsa River Regional Park *Tetsa River Lodge* operates five cabins and a full service campground. May–Sept. Sites $20; RVs $30; cabins $95
Tetsa River Regional Park Campground A nice, secluded campground with appealing short hikes through the trees and along the river. May to mid-Sept. $20

STONE MOUNTAIN PROVINCIAL PARK AND AROUND
Stone Mountain Provincial Park Campground 139km west of Fort Nelson. In the summit Lake area of the park are 28 basic campgrounds with campfire rings. No reservations and no flush toilets. Open May to mid-Sept. $20
Toad River Lodge 195km from Fort Nelson ☎ 250 232 5401, ☎ 855 707 5407, @ toadriverlodge.com. Toad

River has perhaps the best motel on this stretch, the *Toad River Lodge,* with rooms and cabins offering superb views of thickly forested and deeply cleft mountains on all sides. It also has a gift shop, restaurant and petrol station. RVs $35; cabins $109

MUNCHO LAKE
There's a small motel and campground at the lake's southern end, but it's worth hanging on for these popular places.
Strawberry Flats or McDonald Campground Choice of two campgrounds located at Muncho Lake Provincial Park 11km further north. May–Sept. $20
Northern Rockies Lodge ☎ 250 776 3481, ☎ 800 663 5269, @ northern-rockies-lodge.com. A choice of log cabins or RV sites, plus an excellent on-site restaurant serving up European-style dining. Open year-round. RVs $47; doubles $135, cabins $155

11

Liard Hot Springs

$5 • ☎ 800 776 7000, ⓦ env.gov.bc.ca/bcparks

About 70km beyond Muncho Lake is one of the most popular spots on the entire Alaska Highway, the **Liard Hot Springs**, whose **two thermal pools** (Alpha and Beta) are among the hottest in BC. They're reached by a short wooden boardwalk across steaming marsh, and are otherwise unspoilt apart from a wooden changing room and the big high-season crowds. As the marsh never freezes, it attracts moose and grizzlies down to drink and graze, and some 250 plant species grow in the mild microhabitat nearby, including fourteen species of orchid.

ACCOMMODATION   LIARD HOT SPINGS

Liard River Hotsprings Provincial Park Campground ⓦ env.gov.bc.ca/bcparks. The nearby campground (53 sites) is one of the region's most popular, and can be booked through BC Parks (see page 687). **$26**

11 Watson Lake

Beyond the Liard Hot Springs the Alaska Highway follows the Liard River, settling into about 135km of unexceptional scenery before **WATSON LAKE**, just over the Yukon border. The town isn't big, but shops, motels and garages have sprung up here to service the traffic congregating off the Stewart-Cassiar and Robert Campbell highways to the south and north, respectively. There are also some peaceful hiking trails and plenty of fishing and boating opportunities.

Even if you're passing through it's worth taking a look at the **Alaska Highway Interpretive Centre** (May–Sept daily 8am–8pm; ☎ 867 536 7469), which provides information on the Yukon and has displays on the highway's construction. Situated on the highway behind the famous **Sign Post Forest**, it also acts as the local **tourist office**. The first tree in this "forest" was planted in 1942 by homesick GI Carl K. Lindley, who erected a sign pointing the way to his home in Danville, Illinois, and stating the mileage. Since then the signs have kept on coming, and at last count numbered around 72,000.

Northern Lights Centre

Mid-May to mid-Sept, six shows daily 1–8.30pm • $10; $1-off coupon from the visitor centre • ☎ 867 536 7827, ⓦ northernlightscentre.ca

In Watson Lake you might want to dip into the **Northern Lights Centre**, the only planetarium and science centre in North America dedicated to exploring the myths, folklore and science of the aurora borealis (see page 797). The price includes admission to the **SciDome** showcasing a space-related film that is projected on a High Definition 360° dome.

ACCOMMODATION   WATSON LAKE

Whitehorse is still 441km distant so many travellers wisely stop here overnight. There are a handful of hotels directly in town and two fabulous B&Bs located close to each other in the outskirts of town (10min drive) on the Robert Campbell Hwy. Countless small government-run campgrounds are dotted along the length of the highway beyond the village; the closest is a rustic place with sites for $12 4km west of the Sign Forest (May–Oct).

A Nice Motel 705 Frank Trail • ☎ 867 536 7222, ⓦ anice motel.com. Ten spacious rooms In a nonsmoking and pet-free environment; each room has a kitchenette, HDTV, full surround audio and internet. **$159**

Air Force Lodge ☎ 867 536 2890, ⓦ airforcelodge. com. The historic *Air Force Lodge* is one of the town's oldest buildings with a fascinating history: it was originally built as a barracks to house pilots during World War II. Today, the building has been fully renovated and has vintage touches in the shared areas and twelve standard rooms with shared bathrooms, wi-fi and satellite TV. April to mid-Oct. **$99**

Cozy Nest B&B 1175 Robert Campbell Hwy ☎ 867 536 2204, ⓦ cozynestbandb.com. Two queen-size rooms plus a lakeside cabin. Rooms at the B&B share a bath, living room and kitchen area. The cabin sleeps up to five, has basic services, but no running water and an outhouse (a true Canadian outdoor experience). Great dock with views of Watson Lake. Free wi-fi, and use of sauna (request when reserving). Cabins **$85**; doubles **$100**

Teslin

West of Watson Lake the road rambles through more fine mountain scenery, running for hour after hour past snowcapped peaks and thick forest. The **George Johnston Museum** (June–Aug daily 9am–6pm; $5; ☎867 390 2550, ⓦgjmuseum.yk.net), on the right on the way into the village of **TESLIN**, 263km west of Watson, has a good collection of Tlingit artefacts. The tiny **Teslin Tlingit Heritage Centre** (June–Aug; ☎867 390 2532, ⓦteslintlingitheritage.com), 3km west of town, is worth a visit for its fine displays of artefacts and masks which illustrate the last two hundred years of the Inland Tlingit culture. The centre also offers cultural programmes and sells authentic Tlingit crafts.

ACCOMMODATION AND EATING   TESLIN

Dawson Peaks Resort and RV Park ☎867 390 2244,   ☎866 402 2244, ⓦdawsonpeaks.ca. About 10km before

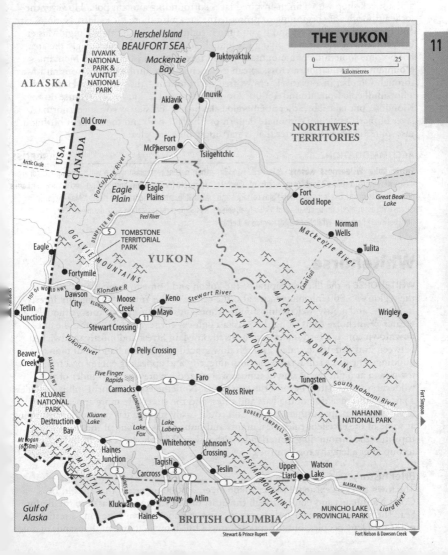

Teslin, 263km west of Watson, look out for this complex which houses an ageing motel, cabins and a campground. It boasts one of the region's better restaurants (pasta, steak and salmon mains $18–25); fishing and boat rentals also available as are guided river trips down the Nitsutlin River ($375). May–Sept. Sites $14; RVs $30; cabins $40; doubles $89

Tagish and Carcross

There are more gorgeous vistas on the Alaska Highway west of Teslin. After 73km turn onto the Tagish Road for **TAGISH** which serves as an entry into the Southern Lakes area for boating and fishing enthusiasts and wildlife-watching. At the end of Tagish Road, before connecting to the Klondike Highway North, you'll hit **CARCROSS**. At present it's little more than **Carcross Commons**, a collection of small retail buildings and a snack shop with Tlingit-inspired faces surrounding a totem pole. However the local authorities are beginning to promote the area a bit more for its First Nations and historical significance, and if you time it right you can also catch Tlingit Master Carver Keith Wolfe Smarch plying his trade here. And perhaps surprisingly the area has become something of a mountain-biking mecca: those who come to **Montana Mountain** (ⓦ destinationcarcross.ca) can experience some thrilling rides from mid-May through October in a relatively crowd-free environment – the Mountain Hero Trail is a downhill epic from around 4500ft. From here it's just 72km to Whitehorse on the Klondike, but take a breather at **Emerald Lake** on the left side as you speed north. A layer of marl, a calcium carbonate deposit on the lake bed, and the sunlight hitting it just so, result in shallow water that is startlingly blue and clear.

ACCOMMODATION

CARCROSS

Spirit Lake Wilderness Resort ☎ 867 821 4337, ⓦ spiritlakeyukon.com. About 6km north of Carcross proper you'll run into this log cabin motel plus cottages and cabins with associated campground – and It's likely all you'll find between here and Whitehorse. Adjacent is a better-than-decent restaurant with a varied menu and convivial atmosphere. There are horse riding and fishing packages available, and hiking trails are nearby. May–Sept. Sites $25; RVs $35; cottages/cabins $65; doubles $109

Whitehorse

WHITEHORSE is the likeable capital of the **Yukon** and home to more than 25,000 of the region's 35,000 inhabitants. It's also the centre of the Yukon's mining and forestry industries and a busy, welcoming stop for thousands of summer visitors. Although greater Whitehorse spills along the Alaska Highway for several kilometres, the old **downtown** core is a forty-block grid centred on Main Street and mostly sandwiched between 2nd and 4th avenues. Though now graced only with a handful of pioneer buildings, the place still retains the dour integrity and appealing energy of a frontier town, and at night the baying of timber wolves and coyotes are a reminder of the wilderness immediately beyond the city limits. Nonetheless, the tourist influx provides a fair amount of action in the bars and cafés, and the streets are more appealing and lively than in many northern towns. You could easily spend a day or two here, stopping at some of the excellent cafés, restaurants and pubs or taking one of the many short trips into the surrounding hinterland – either way, Whitehorse is an ideal place to recoup after a lengthy road journey.

Brief history

The town owes its existence to the **Yukon River**, a 3000km artery that rises in BC's Coast Mountains and flows through the heart of the Yukon and Alaska to the Bering Sea. The river's flood plain and strange escarpment above town were long a resting point for Dene peoples, but the spot became a full-blown city when thousands of gold prospectors arrived in the spring of 1898, en route to Dawson City. Having braved the Chilkoot Pass (see page 822) to meet the river's upper reaches, men and supplies then had to pause on the shores of Lineman or Bennett lakes before navigating the **Miles Canyon** and White Horse rapids (for which the city is named) southeast of the current town centre. After the first boats attempting this were destroyed, the Mounties allowed only experienced boatmen to pilot craft through. The prospectors eventually constructed an 8km wooden tramway around the rapids and raised a shantytown at the canyon and tramway's northern head, allowing them to catch their breath before continuing to Dawson City.

The completion of the **White Pass & Yukon Route Railroad (WP&YR)** to Whitehorse put this tentative settlement on a firmer footing almost at the same time as the gold rush petered out. In the early 1900s the town's population dwindled to four hundred, down from ten thousand. A second boom came in 1942 when thousands of US Army personnel arrived to build the Alaska Highway, swelling the town's population almost overnight.

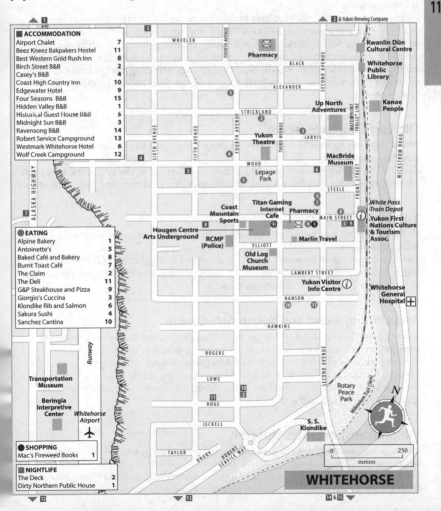

SS Klondike

2nd Ave at 300 Main St • Mid-May to Aug daily 9.30am–5pm; self-guided tours are free (check in with the office beforehand), and guided tours are offered by a rotating roster of partners (check with the visitors' centre)

One of the main things to see in town is the **SS Klondike**. Launched in 1937, it plied the river until 1950. One of only two surviving paddle steamers in the Yukon, it's rather sadly beached at the western end of 2nd Avenue, although it has been beautifully restored to the glory of its 1930s heyday. (It's actually the second SS *Klondike*; the original ran aground in 1936.) More than 250 sternwheelers once plied the river, taking 36 hours to make the 700km journey to Dawson City, and five days to make the return trip against the current. The other remaining paddle wheeler, the SS *Keno*, rests in Dawson City.

MacBride Museum

Front St & Wood St • May–Aug daily 9.30am–7.30pm; Sept–May Tues–Sat 10am–4pm or by appointment • $10 • ☎ 867 667 2709, ⓦ macbridemuseum.com

Housed in a log cabin, the **MacBride Museum** is packed with taxidermied animals (including an albino moose), an old WP&YR engine, pioneer and gold-rush memorabilia, as well as hundreds of marvellous archive photos and a display on the Asiatic peoples who crossed the Bering Straits to inhabit the Americas. Several outdoor exhibits showcase a replica RCMP office and the authentic log cabin (dating to 1899) of author Robert Service. For an extra $5 you can try your luck at panning for gold (summer only).

Old Log Church Museum

3rd Ave & Elliott St • Mid-May to early Sept Mon–Sat 10am–5pm (tours at 11.30am, 2.30pm & 4pm), Sun noon–4pm • $6 • ☎ 867 668 2555, ⓦ oldlogchurchmuseum.ca

The **Old Log Church Museum** is a modest museum devoted to the pre-contact life of the region's Indigenous peoples, whaling, missionaries, the gold rush and early exploration.

Yukon Brewing Co

102 Copper Rd • Tours: mid-May to Aug noon, 2pm & 4pm; Sept to mid-May Mon–Sat 2pm • $10 (proceeds go to local charities) • ☎ 867 668 4183, ⓦ yukonbeer.com

Local favourite **Yukon Brewing Co** puts on tours and tastings daily at their facility in the north of town a block north of Wal-Mart. Reserve the day ahead, or show up early as there is a maximum of ten visitors per tour.

Arts Underground and Yukon Arts Centre

Arts Underground 15-305 Main St • Tues–Fri 10am–5pm, Sat 11am–5pm • ☎ 867 667 4080, ⓦ artsunderground.ca **Yukon Arts Centre** 300 College Drive • Mon–Fri 10am–5pm, Sat noon–5pm • Donation • ☎ 867 667 8485, ⓦ yukonartscentre.com

Whitehorse has a thriving arts scene and **Arts Underground**, on the lower level of the Hougen Centre, is a good place to view, buy and get the inside scoop on local artists. Northwest of downtown, the gallery at the **Yukon Arts Centre** exhibits the work of regional and international artists.

Yukon Transportation Museum

Alaska Hwy, mile 917 (next to airport) • Mid-May to Aug daily 10am–6pm, Oct to mid-May Sun & Mon noon–5pm • $10 • ☎ 867 668 4792, ⓦ goytm.ca

On the bluff above town on the Alaska Highway is the excellent **Yukon Transportation Museum**; its displays, murals, historical videos, memorabilia and vehicles embrace

WALKS AROUND WHITEHORSE

A good self-guided walk is the route from downtown to **Schwatka Lake** and back, the trail for which begins from the bridge by the SS *Klondike*, and the 5km paved, river-hugging **Millennium Trail** is also pleasant. Both trails take you past the **Whitehorse Fishway** (daily: June 9am–5pm; July 9am–7pm; Aug 9am–9pm; donation; ☎867 633 5965), the world's longest wooden fish ladder, complete with interpretive displays and three underwater windows where you can watch chinook salmon bypass a hydroelectric dam as they swim upstream. Another popular 2km trail goes from the Robert Lowe Bridge (straddling the Miles Canyon, 9km south of Whitehorse) to **Canyon City**, a ghost town from the gold-rush era.

everything from dog-sledding, early aviation and the construction of the Alaska Highway to the Canol pipeline, the gold rush and the White Pass & Yukon Route Railroad.

Yukon Beringia Interpretive Centre

Alaska Hwy • May–Sept daily 9am–6pm; winter Sun & Mon noon–5pm • $6, $12 combo with Transportation Museum • ☎867 667 8855, ⓦ beringia.com

Next door to the Yukon Transportation Museum is the dynamic **Yukon Beringia Interpretive Centre**. Beringia was the vast subcontinent that existed 24,000 years ago when the Yukon and Alaska were joined by a land bridge across the Bering Sea to Arctic Russia. The centre's interactive exhibits, films and displays explore the First Nations history of the time. The flora, fauna and geology of that period are also covered and displays include the remains of a 12,000-year-old mammoth.

11

ARRIVAL AND DEPARTURE

WHITEHORSE

BY PLANE

Erik Nielsen Whitehorse International Airport (ⓦ hpw.gov.yk.ca/whitehorse_airport.html) is on the bluff above town, 5km west; the Whitehorse Shuttle Service ($10) meets all scheduled flights and services most downtown hotels (the service is complimentary for a few hotels, including the *Westmark, Coast High Country, Best Western Goldrush, Edgewater and Yukon Inn*). Taxis (☎867 667 4111, ☎667 4888, ☎393 6543) to the centre cost $35. The #3 McIntyre-Hillcrest City Bus services downtown from the airport ($2.50).

DESTINATIONS

The Yukon has several airlines operating scheduled services and several more offering tours and charter flights only. The idea of chartering a small plane may sound expensive, but often the prices are not prohibitive – at least by the standards of land transportation costs in the region – especially if you can get a group of people together.

Air Canada Jazz Calgary (May–Oct daily); Vancouver (3 daily).

Air North Calgary and Edmonton (May–Sept 5 weekly; Sept–May 4 weekly); Vancouver (Mon–Fri 2 daily, Sat 1 daily); Dawson City (Sun–Fri 1 daily); Inuvik and Fairbanks 3 weekly).

Charter airlines Alkan Air ☎867 668 2107, ⓦalkanair. com; Alpine Aviation ☎867 668 7725, ⓦalpineaviation yukon.com; Tintina Air (☎867 332 8468, ⓦtintinaair.com).

BY TRAIN

White Pass & Yukon Route Railroad Suite 4, 1109 1st Ave ☎867/633 5710, ⓦwpyr.com. Summer service (mid-May to mid-Sept) between Skagway, Alaska, to Whitehorse onboard WP&YR train and connect with bus in Carcross (passport required). Departs Skagway: Tues, Wed, Thurs, Fri & Sun at 7.30am. Return from Whitehorse: 7.30am Alaska time on Tues, Wed, Thurs, Sat & Sun. US$195 one way, US$235 return.

BY BUS

Since Greyhound pulled out of the region, there are no buses between southern Canada and the Yukon, however bus services operate within the Yukon. The bus station is at 2191 2nd Ave towards the northern end of downtown, but buses arrive and leave from a variety of locations.

DESTINATIONS

Dawson City Husky Bus (☎867 993 3821, ⓦklondike experience.com) operates a scheduled service from Whitehorse visitor centre (2nd Ave and Lambert St) to Dawson City (2 or 3 weekly; 7hr).

Haines Junction (Kluane National Park) Nature Tours Yukon (☎867 660 5050, ⓦnaturetoursyukon.com) and Who What Where Tours (☎867 333 0475, ⓦwhitehorsetours. com) both provide daily charter services from Whitehorse. Contact them for details.

GETTING AROUND

By bus Whitehorse Transit (✆ 867 668 7433) operates a bus service connecting the centre with the six suburban neighbourhoods, where you may need to go for some accommodation and restaurants; the fare is $2.50 (exact change only).

Bike rental Though you can cover the centre on foot, another good option is to rent a bike. Icycle Sports offer Fat Bike rentals in summer from the Whitehorse Cross Country Ski Club, 1 Sumanik Dr (Mon–Fri 9am–9pm, Sat & Sun 9am–6pm; ✆ 867 668 4477, ⊛ shop.icyclesport.com), half- and full-day rentals are $15–40. Kanoe People, 1147 Front St (✆ 867 668 4899, ⊛ kanoepeople.com), rents bikes starting at $25/4hr (no long term rentals).

INFORMATION

Yukon Visitor Information Centre 2nd Ave & Lambert St (mid-May to Sept daily 8am–8pm; rest of year Mon–Fri 8:30am–5pm closed noon–1pm, Sat 10am–2pm; ✆ 867 667 3084, ✆ 800 661 0494, ⊛ travelyukon.com). The main downtown office has information for the whole territory; pick up copies of the *Yukon Vacation Planner* and the *Visitor Guide* booklets, along with the *City Guides* to Whitehorse, Dawson Creek, Watson Lake, Inuvik and Haines Junction. Drivers can pick up a three-day free parking pass here.

Yukon First Nations Culture and Tourism Association For information on the Yukon's First Nations cultures, head here, in the White Pass & Yukon Route train depot at 1-1109 Front St (Mon–Fri 9am–5pm; ✆ 867 667 7698, ⊛ yfnct.ca), and pick up a copy of the *Yukon's First Nations Guide*.

TOURS AND ACTIVITIES

Downtown walking tour For some insight into Whitehorse's history, try the 45min downtown walking tour by the Yukon Historical & Museums Association (June–Aug Mon–Sat 9am, 11am, 1pm & 3pm; $4; ✆ 867 667 4704,

SKAGWAY TO WHITEHORSE: WALKING THE CHILKOOT TRAIL

No image better conjures the human drama of the 1898 gold rush than the lines of prospectors struggling over the **Chilkoot Trail**, a 53km path over the Coast Mountains between **Dyea**, Alaska, and **Bennett Lake** on the BC border south of Whitehorse. Before the rush, Dyea was a small village of Chilkat Tlingit, who made annual trips over the trail to trade with the interior Dene peoples. The Chilkat jealously guarded access to the **Chilkoot Pass** (1122m) – the key to the trail and one of only three glacier-free routes through the Coast Mountains west of Juneau. Sheer numbers and a show of force from a US gunboat opened the trail to stampeders, who used it as a link between the Pacific Coast ferry ports and the Yukon River, which then took them to Dawson City's goldfields.

For much of 1897, the US and Canada disputed the pass and border until the Mounties established a shack at the summit and enforced the fateful "tonne of goods" rule. Introduced because of chronic shortages in the goldfields, this obliged every man entering the Yukon to carry a tonne of provisions. Though it probably saved many lives in the long run, the rule caused enormous hardship: weather conditions and the trail's fifty-degree slopes proved too severe for pack animals, so men carried supplies for as many as fifty journeys. Many died in avalanches or lost everything during winters where temperatures could drop to -51°C and up to 25m of snow fall was possible. Still, the lure of gold was enough to drag 22,000 men over the pass.

PREPARATION

Today, most people make the fantastic journey across the mountains by train, car or bus from **Skagway to Whitehorse**. This route runs parallel to that taken by the restored **White Pass & Yukon Route Railroad** (mid-May to mid-Sept daily; train from Skagway to Carcross or Fraser, BC then bus to Whitehorse; US$129 Fraser, US$189 Carcross; ✆ 800 343 7373, ⊛ wpyr.com). Alaska is an hour behind the Yukon and venturing into the US requires a valid passport.

More and more people are **hiking** the old trail, which Parks Canada has laid out and preserved. Its great appeal lies in the scenery, natural habitats (coastal rainforest, tundra and subalpine woodland) and the numerous artefacts (old huts, rotting boots, mugs and broken bottles) still scattered about. The trail is well marked, regularly patrolled and generally fit to walk between June and September (expect snow throughout June); most hike it in **three or four days**, heading from south to north. Dangers include bears, avalanches, drastic changes in weather and exhaustion; there's a 12km stretch for which you should allow twelve hours. There are three warming huts en route but these aren't for sleeping in, so you have to **camp** at the nine sites

ⓦheritageyukon.ca), which departs from Donnenworth House at 3126 3rd Ave, next to LePage Park. Alternatively, join one of the free summer strolls organized by the Yukon Conservation Society, 302 Hawkins St (July & Aug Tues–Sat; ☎867 668 5678, ⓦyukonconservation.org), who offer 2hr walks that delve into the human and natural history of the city and territory.

Waterfront Trolley Tour Discover Whitehorse's fascinating waterfront history while aboard a beautifully restored, bright yellow 1925 Waterfront Trolley. Hop on, or off, at several stops along the river from the Chilkoot Centre and Shipyards Park to the SS *Klondike* (daily May–Sept; $1 one way; ☎867 667 6355, ⓦmacbridemuseum.com).

Tour operators/outfitters The building of the hydroelectric dam has tamed the rapids' violence but it's still possible to kayak through Miles Canyon to see its sheer walls up close. Kanoe People (see page 822) run multi-day guided canoe trips, as do Up North Adventures (☎867 667 7035, ⓦupnorthadventures.com), who also provide self-guided tours with drop off at Marsh Lake and pick up at Schwatka Lake. These operators offer riding and hiking excursions and winter tours involving dog-sledding, ice-fishing and snowshoeing; check online or call for pricing details. Guided six-hour mountain bike tours (from $130) of the surrounding hills can be arranged with Boréale Mountain Biking (☎867 336 1722, ⓦbe-yukon.com; full-day summer tour $175), across the river at Km6 of the Long Lake Road. A variety of day- or multi-day whitewater rafting trips (from $125) on the famed Tatshenshini River can be arranged at the Tatshenshini Expediting office (☎867 663 2742, ☎867 393 3661, ⓦtatshenshiniyukon.com).

11

ACCOMMODATION

Whitehorse has a surprising amount of **accommodation**, but in high summer much of it is booked up well in advance. If you arrive without a reservation, contact the visitor centre or try the string of **hotels** on Main Street between 1st and

along the trail: no backcountry camping is allowed. Pick up the *Chilkoot Trail* **map** ($9) from Skagway's Trail Center or Whitehorse's Parks Canada office.

RESERVATIONS AND PERMITS

The number of hikers crossing the Chilkoot Pass into Canada is limited to fifty per day, of which 42 places can be **booked in advance** ($12 reservation fee; 8.30am–4pm; ☎867 667 3910, ☎800 661 0486). The remaining eight places are offered on a first-come, first-served basis after 1pm on the day before you start out. Outside July to mid-August a reservation may not be needed. Order an advance **information pack** (same number, ⓦpc.gc.ca/chilkoot; or from the government offices, 300 Main St, Suite 205, Whitehorse; Mon–Fri 8am–noon & 1–4.30pm).

You don't need a **permit** for day-hikes on the US side, but you do for day-hikes on the Canadian side ($10), and if you're hiking the full length of the trail or spending a night ($61.30, but $34.30 if you're only hiking and overnighting on the Canadian side, $27 for US). Hikers need to go to the Chilkoot Trail Center in Skagway on Broadway at 2nd Ave (late May to early Sept daily 8am–5pm; ☎907 983 9234) to pick up or buy a permit and sign a register, and note that permits that are reserved and not picked up by noon on the day the trip is to start will be cancelled. Bring **identification** (a passport or enhanced driver's licence for North Americans; a passport for everyone else); you may be required to deal with Canadian customs at the Chilkoot Pass ranger station, but you're more likely to do so at the Alaska–Canada border post at Fraser or in Whitehorse.

TRANSPORT AND SUPPLIES

Dyea-Chilkoot Trail Transport (☎907 617 7551) offers shuttle bus service from Skagway to the trailhead at **Dyea**, 16km northwest of Skagway. Normal hours are 9am to 6pm, but transfers as early as 4.30am can be reserved with advance notice. Fare is US$30 for one, but US$15 each for two or more people.

The trail finishes at **Bennett**, from where there is no road access and no mobile phone service. Most people catch the daily service run by the WP&YPR railroad from Bennett to Whitehorse, Fraser or Skagway; or return to Skagway from Carcross. From June to August the railroad offers the Chilkoot Trail Hikers Service (check for departure days; US$50 one-way to Fraser, from US$95 to Skagway, US$63 to Carcross, US$99 train and bus to Whitehorse). Buy tickets before the hike or you'll incur a US$15 extra fee; for customs reasons the train doesn't stop at Log Cabin when travelling to/from Carcross and Skagway.

Besides the usual hiking equipment, also bring **9m of rope** to help sling your food and any scented items over the bear poles at each campground.

5th avenues; for **B&Bs**, visit ⊚ yukonbandb.org. The town has a good private **hostel** and while the Wal-Mart car park is free for RVs, Whitehorse is not bereft of far nicer **RV sites** and **campgrounds**.

HOTELS AND B&BS

Airport Chalet 91634 Alaska Hwy ☏ 867 668 2166, ☏ 866 668 2166, ⊚ airportchalet.com; map p.819. Directly opposite the airport and serviceable enough for its purposes. There is internet access in the lobby and a basic restaurant. $89
Best Western Gold Rush Inn 411 Main St ☏ 867 668 4500, ⊚ bestwesternbc.com; map p.819. A dependable choice with larger than average rooms, the historic hotel also features spa access, an exercise room and the frequently crowded *Gold Pan Saloon* where singers perform nightly. $180
Birch Street B&B 1501 Birch St, Porter Creek ☏ 867 633 5625, ⊚ birchstreet.ca; map p.819. A 10min drive from downtown, this quaint B&B offers cosy, yet spacious rooms with private/shared bathrooms and has easy access to nearby walking or cross-country ski trails. $100
Casey's B&B 608 Wood St ☏ 867 668 7481, ⊚ caseybandb.com; map p.819. One room and one two-bed suite in a downtown location with hearty breakfasts; kitchen and laundry facilities are available. $165
Coast High Country Inn 4051 4th Ave ☏ 867 667 4471, ☏ 800 554 4471, ⊚ coasthotels.com; map p.819. A pleasant and easy-going hotel at the far western end of 4th Ave, a 10min walk from downtown. It's been renovated recently and there's a popular bar-patio. Weekly rates are available and airport shuttle is included. $195
Edgewater Hotel 101 Main St ☏ 867 667 2572, ☏ 877 484 3334, ⊚ edgewaterhotelwhitehorse.com; map p.819. Nicely renovated hotel overlooking the Yukon River in the downtown area, with a bar and two popular restaurants. Rooms are well appointed and have comfortable beds and en-suite bathrooms. $199
Four Seasons B&B 18 Tagish Rd, Riverdale ☏ 867 667 2161, ⊚ 4seasonsyukon.com; map p.819. A relaxing and comfortable place to unwind after a lengthy road or river trip. Located less than a 5min drive from downtown, with three rooms (shared bathrooms) and a guest lounge. The host, Greg, is incredibly helpful. Dogs allowed. $99
Hidden Valley B&B 40 Couch Rd, Hidden Valley ☏ 867 633 6482, ⊚ yukonbedandbreakfast.com; map p.819. Located on the largest privately owned parcel of land in Whitehorse this is a superb place to relax and wind down in an attractive outdoor setting, with four comfortable private rooms. A 20min drive from downtown, shuttle service to

city centre and airport available. $145
Historical Guest House B&B 505 Wood St ☏ 867 668 3907, ⊚ yukongold.com; map p.819. This two-storey log home two blocks east of Main St was built in 1907 for Sam McGee and his family, the protagonist of a Robert Service poem (see page 835). A separate wing has the main lodging, with two double rooms and a suite, with modern facilities, all with private bathrooms. $115
Midnight Sun B&B 6188 6th Ave ☏ 867 667 2255, ☏ 866 284 4448, ⊚ midnightsunbb.com; map p.819. This large home on the northern edge of town has a quiet lounge and four comfortable en-suite rooms and serves up delicious breakfasts. Internet access also available. $155
Ravensong B&B 11 Donjek Rd, Riverdale ☏ 867 667 4059, ☏ 867 333 5619, ⊚ ravensongbb.com; map p.819. Lovely two-suite set-up in a quiet residential suburb 3min drive from downtown. Patio and barbecue available as are a hot-tub, laundry and wi-fi. Discounts offered for multi-night stays. $125
Westmark Whitehorse Hotel 201 Wood St ☏ 867 393 9700, ☏ 800 544 0970, ⊚ westmarkhotels.com; map p.819. This hotel with 181 rooms and a dining hall is very convenient to Main St and 2nd Avenue, but it's also the preferred temporary lodging of many tour groups and cruise passengers. $169

HOSTELS AND CAMPGROUNDS

Beez Kneez Bakpakers Hostel 408 Hoge St ☏ 867 456 2333, ⊚ bzkneez.com; map p.819. Cozy and friendly place at the western end of downtown (near the junction of 4th Ave and Robert Service Way), with a kitchen, laundry, internet access and use of barbecue on deck. Dorms $35 doubles $65; summer cabin $85
Robert Service campground ☏ 867 668 3721 ⊚ robertservicecampground.com; map p.819. A scenic 20min walk down South Access Rd, past the SS *Klondike* on the Millennium Trail. Set on the banks of the Yukon River, this site is specifically for tents and backpackers and gets very busy in summer. There are hot showers, clean bathrooms and freshly brewed coffee and baked treats are available daily. If the site is full, you could opt to pitch your tent in the woods above the lake, past the dam beyond the campground or along the bluff above town by the airport. Firewood $8. Mid-May to mid-Sept. Sites $26
Wolf Creek campground Off Alaska Hwy, 16km south; map p.819. This nearest government campground is operated by Yukon Parks. It has eleven sites, forty RV sites and there are no services, but wood and water are available. $12

EATING

Considering Whitehorse's size – and location – it has a remarkable number of very good cafés and restaurants; a similar sized city south of the 60th Parallel might struggle to match the quality of what's on offer here, both in terms of food and the overall geniality you'll encounter.
Alpine Bakery 411 Alexander St ☏ 867 668 6871

TRANSPORT IN THE YUKON AND NWT

Whitehorse provides the main **transport** links not only to most other points in the Yukon, but also to Alaska and the Northwest Territories. The best way to explore the Yukon is by renting a car or RV from Whitehorse, but a handful of tour operators offer various bus/train combination packages to several locations throughout the territory and into BC and Alaska. Public transport is limited; however, it will get you to surprisingly remote places, but times and schedules change: ask at the tourist office or call providers for the latest.

DISTANCES FROM WHITEHORSE

Anchorage 1165km	**Haines** 415km
Beaver Creek 457km	**Haines Junction** 158km
Burwash Landing 285km	**Inuvik** 1226km
Carcross 74km	**Prince George** 1880km
Dawson City 535km	**Seattle** 2831km
Edmonton 1982km	**Tok** 639km
Fairbanks 980km	**Vancouver** 2702km
Fort Nelson 946km	**Watson Lake** 436km

11

ⓦalpinebakery.ca; map p.819. The bread, pizza slices, soups, cakes and freshly squeezed juices are all made from organic ingredients at this popular bakery. Mon–Fri 8am–6pm, Sat 8am–4pm.

Antoinette's 4121 4th Ave ☏867 668 3505, ⓦantoinettesrestaurant.com; map p.819. Chef owner Antoinette moved from Trinidad and Tobago to Canada as a teenager and she's been serving comfort food with a Caribbean twist in Whitehorse for over a decade. Dishes include Yukon Fog (smoked soup with float, $11), Crispy Guacamole Salmon ($30) and Curry Chook Stew ($29). Tapas available 2–6.30pm. Daily 11am–late.

Baked Café and Bakery 100 Main St ☏867 663 6291, ⓦbakedcafe.ca; map p.819. This café, with a relaxed atmosphere and a decent selection of teas and coffees, is one of the best coffee bars in town. It brews up locally roasted beans, and delicious home-baked goods, sandwiches, soups and salads are also on hand. It also has a patio in summer. Mon–Fri 7am–7pm, Sat 8am–6pm & Sun 9am–5pm.

Burnt Toast Café 2112 Second Ave ☏867 393 2605, ⓦburnttoastcafe.ca; map p.819. An excellent alternative if you want to avoid the long queue at Klondike Rib and Salmon next door, this relaxed place serves up a varied modern-Canadian menu, with starters (think wild game potato skins) and mains (like elk and blueberry sausage) from $17–22. Perhaps the best place in town for weekend brunch (around $12). Mon–Fri 8am–9pm, Sat 8.30am–2pm & 5–9pm, Sun 8.30am–2pm.

The Claim 305 Strickland St ☏867 667 2202, ⓦtheclaim.ca; map p.819. For a rather boutique coffee experience, try the top-level pastries (some gluten-free) along with the seriously potent coffee menu selections here. Some savoury items on hand too for breakfast and lunch, in addition to some gourmet-ish jarred jams and other foodie items. Mon–Fri 7.30am–6pm, Sat 9.30am–5pm.

The Deli 203 Hanson St ☏867 667 7583; map p.819. Grab a sandwich and a home-made cake or stock up on beef jerky or European meats and cheeses at this restaurant in the retail Yukon Meat & Sausage. Mon–Fri 8.30am–5.30pm, Sat 9am–5.30pm.

★ **G&P Steakhouse and Pizza** 209 Main St ☏867 668 4708, ⓦgandpsteakhouse.com; map p.819. The family-run dining room, 40-years-old but replanted on Main St from the Alaska Hwy, is among the most friendly of Whitehorse's fine-dining establishments. Steak and (deep-dish) pizza, of course, but also bar snacks, pasta, salads and seafood (mains $24–36). Mon–Sat 4–10pm.

Giorgio's Cuccina 206 Jarvis St ☏867 668 4050, ⓦgiorgioscuccina.com; map p.819. Italian dishes (mains from $20) served in a setting with ancient Roman decorative flourishes. Mon–Thurs & Sun 4.30pm–10pm, Fri & Sat 4.30pm–10.30pm.

★ **Klondike Rib and Salmon** 2116 2nd Ave ☏867 667 7554, ⓦklondikerib.com; map p.819. An informal place for excellent northern specialities such as barbecue salmon, caribou, bison and elk (mains from $27, at lunch from $14). Extremely popular for dinner – expect to wait up to an hour in the queue, even on a Monday (no reservations). Mid-May to late Sept: Mon–Sat 11am–10pm, Sun 4–10pm.

Sakura Sushi 404 Wood St ☏867 668 3298, ⓦsakurawhitehorse.ca; map p.819. One of a couple of Japanese restaurants in town serving reasonably priced tempura, teriyaki, sushi and sashimi dishes. Mon–Fri 11am–3pm & 4.30–9.30pm, Sat noon–3pm & 4.30–9.30pm, Sun 4–9.30pm.

Sanchez Cantina 211 Hanson St ☏867 668 5858; map p.819. Established Mexican restaurant with a local following. You can eat in the authentic dining room, or if the weather's nice, on the breezy deck. Veggie and vegan friendly. Mon–Fri 11.30am–2.30pm & 5–9pm, Sat 5–9pm.

DRINKING

The Deck at the Coast High Country Inn (see page 824), 4051 4th Ave ☎867 667 4471; map p.819. Popular and lively, this pub has local brews by the Chilkoot Brewing Company and scrumptious barbecue food on the deck in summer (burgers, sandwiches and mains $12–25). Daily 11.30am–1am.

Dirty Northern Public House 103 Main St ☎867 663 3305, ⓦdirtynorthernyukon.com; map p.819. A somewhat younger, hipper crowd hangs at the *Dirty Northern*, lured in with the promise of ten beers on tap, a handful of in-house cocktails, live music (some nights) and tweaked pub food. And if you also hunger for a bacon vanilla ice cream sandwich, this is definitely the place to go. Daily 11.30am–2am.

ENTERTAINMENT

Frantic Follies at the Westmark Whitehorse Hotel ☎867 668 2042, ⓦfranticfollies.com. The widely touted Frantic Follies vaudeville act stage shows of banjo-plucking and frilly-knickered-dancing at the *Westmark Whitehorse Hotel* have been playing in town for around three decades, and often feels that way (late May–early Sept nightly except Mon 8.30pm; $24).

SHOP

Mac's Fireweed Books 203 Main St ☎867 668 2434, ☎800 661 0508, ⓦmacsbooks.ca; map p.819. Stocks an excellent range of books, guides, maps, nautical charts and pamphlets (summer daily 8am–10pm; winter 8am–9pm).

DIRECTORY

Car rental Budget, 4178 4th Ave (☎867 667 6200, ☎800 661 0411, ⓦbudget.ca); Rent-a-Wreck, 17 Chilkoot Way (☎867 456 7368, ☎whitehorse@rent-a-wreck.ca) and Driving Force, 213 Range Rd or at airport (☎867 668 2137, ☎800 936 9353, ⓦdrivingforce.ca). Most agencies may have restrictions for taking cars on gravel roads. If you're driving the Dempster Hwy your best option is to rent an RV from Fraserway RV, 9041 Quartz Rd (☎867 668 3438, ☎866 269 2783, ⓦfraserway.com).

Directory enquiries ☎411.

Emergency services Within Whitehorse and immediate surroundings ☎911; Yukon Road and Weather Conditions ☎511, ⓦ511.yukon.ca.

Hospital Whitehorse General Hospital, 5 Hospital Road ☎867 393 8700, ⓦwhitehorsehospital.ca.

Internet Free wi-fi at *Baked Café*. All the hotels have some sort of internet access. The public library, at 1171 1st Ave next to the Kwanlin Dün Cultural Centre, has free public access (Mon–Thurs 10am–9pm, Fri–Sun 10am–6pm). *Titan Gaming and Collectibles*, 10-305 Main St (☎867 668 5750), is the only internet café in town. They serve hot food, sandwiches, snacks and coffee (daily 10am–midnight; $3/15min, $5/30min or $7/hr).

Laundry Norgetown Laundry, 4213 4th Ave (daily: summer 8am–11pm; winter 8am–9pm; ☎867 667 6113).

Outdoor equipment and rental Canoes, kayaks, paddles and life jackets can be rented from Kanoe People (see page 822) or Up North Adventures (see page 823). At both places, standard canoe prices start from $40/day, $85/weekend (Fri night to Mon morning); kayak $5 more. For other outdoor gear, try Coast Mountain Sports, 309 Main St (☎867 667 4074; Mon–Sat 9am–6pm, Sun noon–5pm).

Police ☎911 (emergency) or ☎867 667 5555 (non-emergency only).

Postal outlet 211 Main St at Shoppers Plaza ☎867 667 2485; Mon–Fri 9am–6pm, Sat 11am–6pm.

Travel agent For ferry reservations and tickets for local events, contact Marlin Travel, 2101a 2nd Ave (Mon–Fri 8.30am–5.30pm; ☎867 668 2867, ⓦmarlintravel.ca).

Kluane Country

Kluane Country is the pocket of southwest Yukon on and around a scenically stunning 491km stretch of the Alaska Highway from Whitehorse to **Beaver Creek** at the border with Alaska. *Kluane* (pronounced 'Clue-ah-nee') comes from a Southern Tutchone word meaning a "place of many fish". Indeed, the area teems with fish, particularly at **Kluane Lake**, the Yukon's highest and largest stretch of water. Today the name is associated more with the all-but-impenetrable wilderness of **Kluane National Park**, a region containing the country's highest mountains, vast icefields and the greatest diversity of plant and animal species in the far North. The park's main centre is **Haines Junction**, at the intersection of the Alaska Highway and the Haines Road. Although

motels and campgrounds dot the Alaska Highway, the only other settlements of any size are **Destruction Bay** and **Burwash Landing** on Kluane Lake. Alaska/Yukon Trails as well as Interior Alaska **buses** (see page 821) ply the length of the Alaska Highway.

Haines Junction

A small, modern village nestled amid some dramatic mountain scenery, **HAINES JUNCTION** is the biggest service centre between Whitehorse (160km away) and Tok in Alaska. There are a handful of overnight possibilities and lots of tour and rental companies for river-rafting, canoeing, fishing, hiking, cycling, riding and glacier flights in Kluane National Park. Enquire at the visitor centre for information on outfitters.

INFORMATION

HAINES JUNCTION

Dä Kų Cultural Centre 208 Alaska Hwy (☎ 867 634 3300). This Champagne and Aishihik cultural centre is also home to Parks Canada's Kluane National Park office (mid-May to mid-Sept daily 9am–5pm; ☎ 867 634 7207, ⓦ parkscanada.gc.ca/kluane) and to the Haines Junction Yukon Visitor Information Centre (mid-May to mid-Sept daily 8am–8pm; ☎ 867 634 2345).

ACCOMMODATION AND EATING

Kathleen Territorial Campground The only campground within the park accessible from the highway, 27km south of Haines Junction. Gorgeous views of the lake, but it can get rather windy. Free firewood and no reservations. Parks Canada fee $15.70
Raven Hotel & Gourmet Dining 181 Alaska Hwy ☎ 867 634 2500, ⓦ ravenhotelyukon.com. Hotel on the Alaska Hwy just three blocks from the Cultural Centre. A delightful German breakfast is included in the room rate. $145
Wanderers Inn Backpackers 191 Backe St ☎ 867 634 5321, ⓦ wanderersinn.ca. Comfortable hostel with friendly and knowledgeable hosts. Shared areas are clean and well equipped; accommodation includes dorms (6-bed) and private rooms, as well as a family room with four single beds. Sites with access to facilities are also available. Dorms $42, doubles $100

Kluane National Park

KLUANE NATIONAL PARK contains some of the Yukon's greatest but most inaccessible scenery within its 21,980 square kilometres, and for the most part, you'll only see and walk the easterly margins of this UNESCO World Heritage Site from points along the Alaska Highway (no road runs into the park). Together with the neighbouring Wrangell-St Elias National Park in Alaska, the park protects the **St Elias Mountains**, though from the highway the peaks you see rearing up to the south are part of the subsidiary Kluane Range. Beyond them, largely invisible from the road, are St Elias's monumental **Icefield Ranges**, which contain Mount St Elias (5488m) and **Mount Logan** (5950m) – Canada's highest point – as well as Mount Denali (Mt McKinley; 6193m), part of the Alaska Range and the highest point in North America; these form the world's second highest coastal range, after the Andes. Below them, and covering more than half the park, is a huge base of mile-deep glaciers and icefields, the world's second largest non-polar icefield (after Greenland) and just one permanent resident, the legendary **ice worm**. Yet global warming is taking its toll on the icefields, with levels dropping by approximately 1.8m a year.

Unless you're prepared for full-scale expeditions, this interior is off limits, though from around $200 you can take plane and helicopter **tours** over the area; information on guided tours is available from the Whitehorse and Haines Junction visitor centres.

At the edge of the icefields a drier, warmer range encourages a green belt of meadow, marsh, forest and fen providing sanctuary for a huge variety of **wildlife**, including grizzlies, moose, mountain goats and a four thousand-strong population of white **Dall sheep**. These margins also support the widest spectrum of **birds** in the far North, some 150 species in all, including easily seen raptors such as peregrine falcons, bald and golden eagles, together with smaller birds like arctic terns, mountain bluebirds, tattlers and hawk owls.

Trails (see page.829) offer the chance to see some of these creatures, but the only **campground** within the park accessible from the highway is at *Kathleen Lake*; there is hotel and camping accommodation along the Alaska Highway.

Kluane Lake

The Kluane region might keep its greatest mountains out of sight, but it makes amends by laying on the stunning **Kluane Lake** along some 60km of the Alaska Highway. About 75km northwest of Haines Junction, and hot on the heels of magnificent views of the St Elias Mountains, the huge lake (some four hundred square kilometres) is framed on all sides by snow-covered peaks whose sinister glaciers feed its ice-blue waters. It's not part of the national park, but the **Tachäl Dhäl** (Sheep Mountain) park visitor kiosk sits at its southern tip (mid-May to early Sept daily 9am–4pm). There are two settlements along the lakeshore, both good places to go boating or fishing and find accommodation. The first is **DESTRUCTION BAY**; the second town, **BURWASH LANDING**, is 15km beyond and holds the Kluane Museum of Natural History (mid-May to mid-Sept daily 9am–6.30pm; $5; ☎867 841 5561, ⓦkluanemuseum.ca), with displays on Yukon wildlife and Southern Tutchone First Nations history. Burwash Landing is home to the Kluane First Nations government.

11

ACCOMMODATION   **KLUANE LAKE**

DESTRUCTION BAY
Congdon Creek The best overall local campground is the lovely Yukon government-run *Congdon Creek* site (with water) off the Alaska Hwy, 12km south of Destruction Bay;

there's heavy bear activity in the area and you must camp inside the electric fence. An interpretive trail goes from here around Kluane Lake (make noise and carry bear spray). **$12**
Cottonwood Park Campground ☎867 841 4066 &

WALKING IN KLUANE NATIONAL PARK

Kluane has only fifteen maintained **trails** but experienced walkers will enjoy wilderness routes totalling about 250km, most of which follow old mining roads or creek beds and require overnight rough camping. Several signposted single- and multi-day hike trailheads can be accessed from the highway, each mapped on pamphlets available from Haines Junction visitor centre, where staff also organize guided day-walks during the summer.

Six trails start from points along Haines Road, immediately south of Haines Junction. The path nearest town (7km south) and the most popular walk is the 15km round-trip **Auriol Trail**. The trailhead for the classic **King's Throne** walk (5km one way) lies 27km south of Haines Junction. It's fairly steep, but offers spectacular views of Kathleen Lake; continue past the maintained trail to the summit of the mountain to be rewarded with views of the icefields. The well-maintained **Rock Glacier Trail**, 50km south of Haines Junction, is a twenty-minute jaunt to a view of Dezadeash Lake. For a longer trek, the **Mush Lake Road** route (trailhead 52km south of Haines Junction) is 22km one-way and part of the 85km of the Cottonwood Trail. North of Haines Junction, paths strike out from the Tächäl Dhäl (Sheep Mountain) visitor centre on Kluane Lake. The **Sheep Mountain Ridge** (11.5km) is a steep, hard slog, but offers good chances of seeing the area's Dall sheep. The longer **Slim's River West Trail** (22.5km one way) is a difficult one but presents glimpses of the edges of the park's icefield interior. Backcountry permits ($10/night) are required for those planning **overnight** or multi-day hikes; register at the Haines Junction or Tächäl Dhäl visitor centres, where you can also pick up a mandatory bear-proof food canister.

About 17km north of Haines Junction and just outside the park boundaries on the Alaska Highway, the **Spruce Beetle Walk** is a 2km loop trail taking in a patch of forest devastated by the spruce beetle. Thriving in balmier winters, these persistent little borers operate like a slow-motion forest fire; they've infested and killed an estimated forty percent of the mature spruce trees in Kluane Country since the early 1990s. Look out for red pine needles – a sign of infestation; grey trees without needles have already succumbed.

☎ 613 968 6844, ⓦ cottonwoodpark.ca. Located 27km south of town, the *Cottonwood Park Campground* caters to hikers and cyclists with lakeside campgrounds, and they also have RV sites and a plush wilderness cabin to rent. Facilities include hot showers, drinking water, sanitary pump-out station ($10), a hot tub and store. Year-round,

cash only. Sites $35, RV $45

Talbot Arm Motel Destruction Bay ☎ 867 841 4461 ⓦ talbotarm.com. Conveniently sited on the highway, this motel is a little dated, but it has everything you need (a restaurant, café, store and petrol station). $110

Beaver Creek and the US border

BEAVER CREEK, Canada's westernmost settlement, is the last stop before Alaska. The customs post is a couple of kilometres up the road and the border is open 24 hours a day. Those not pushing deeper into Alaska but looping to Dawson City have a great journey ahead: just before Tok, the **Taylor Highway** (Hwy-5) bears northeast off the Alaska Highway back towards the Yukon border, passing through relatively unexceptional scenery until it hits the US–Canadian border at Little Gold Creek (May–Sept daily 8am–8pm). From here, the 105km road to Dawson City on the **Top of the World Highway** (see page 836) offers sensational views.

INFORMATION

Tourist office For full details on crossing the border, and what to expect on the other side, visit the Yukon tourist office, 1202 Alaska Hwy (mid-May to early Sept daily 8am–8pm; ☎ 867 862 7321).

ACCOMMODATION

1202 Motor Inn 121975 Alaska Hwy ☎ 867 862 7600, ⓦ 1202motorinn.ca. Close to the Alaska border, this comfortable motel has real backcountry character. Rooms are basic, but clean, with everything from a double with a shared bath, to a large family suite (complete with comfy sofa). RV and tent sites available, too. Sites $10, RVs $15, doubles $120

Buckshot Betty's Mile Across from the Fire Hall ☎ 867 862 7111, ⓦ buckshotbettys.ca. This well-respected

establishment, open year-round, contains eight rooms each with private entry and bath, kitchenettes and wi-fi. The on-site bakery and all-day dining room (7am–11pm, winter 7am–10pm) are big pluses. $120

Snag Junction ☎ 867 667 5648. This good but small (15 sites) government-run campground lies 10km south at the Snag Junction. Aimed primarily at campers (it's off grid), but there are three pull-thru sites. May–Oct. $12

Klondike Highway: Whitehorse to Dawson City

Most people approach Dawson City on the **Klondike Highway** from Whitehorse, a wonderful, lonely, 536km paved road running through almost utter wilderness. The highway loosely follows the original winter **overland route** to the goldfields first used in 1902; it took five days to complete the chilly journey in horse-drawn stages, with the trip costing an extortionate $125 per person (passengers were also expected to carry enough overproof rum to keep the drivers sufficiently lubricated). Today, the drive takes little more than six hours, but you could easily stretch that out by allowing for frequent stops and a detour along the **Silver Trail** to explore the historic silver-mining towns of Mayo and Keno.

Yukon Wildlife Preserve

Mid-May to mid-Oct daily 9.30am–6pm; mid-Oct to mid-May usually Fri–Sun only (call ahead to confirm hours) • $15 self-guided walk, or $22 for a guided bus tour • ☎ 867 456 7300, ⓦ yukonwildlife.ca

Eight kilometres from Whitehorse, take the turn-off for Hot Springs Road, which brings you 8km later to the **Yukon Wildlife Preserve**. The eleven types of mammal that graze the large expanses here are largely of the hoofed variety, but there's still something to be said for standing feet from a heavily-antlered caribou or watching a speck of a clumsy yet impressive moose slowly amble from the rear of its swampy enclosure to appear huge nearer your path. And the mountain goats are endlessly entertaining.

Takhini Hot Springs

Daily noon–10pm (extended hours in summer) • $12.50 • ☎ 867 456 8000, ⊛ takhinihotsprings.com

Two kilometres further down the road comes to the **Takhini Hot Springs**, where the water in the large pool is a toasty 36°C. You can camp or dock your RV here ($20–42) or park yourself in the hostel ($30, $100 for a private room) and if you don't want to pay for the privilege of a hot soak, use the public pool at the outflow point in the stream below, built by the locals.

Lake Laberge and Fox Lake

Back on the highway from Takhini Hot Springs, the road carves through a wide, tree-covered valley where you'll catch bursts of purple fireweed flowers. Some 40km north of Whitehorse, the road bypasses the 50km-long **Lake Laberge**, immortalized in Robert Service's poem *The Cremation of Sam McGee*. There is a government **campground** ($12) and beach here and the lake is popular for boating. Another 25km on the road toward the quite pretty **Fox Lake** you'll pass a fire burn, the first of many forest-fire-ravaged areas. The unfolding miles of bare grey skeleton trunks from a 1998 blaze reveal how slowly the trees in these parts recover.

Carmacks and around

CARMACKS is the first settlement of any note you'll hit. It has two petrol stations, a **visitor centre** (June–Aug) and a handful of accommodation options. Just after the bridge leaving Carmacks, the **Tagé Cho Hudän Interpretive Centre** (summer daily 9am–6pm or by appointment; ☎ 867 863 5831) has exhibits revealing something of the traditional lifestyle of the Northern Tutchone people. About 25km north of Carmacks, it's worth stopping briefly at the lookout for the formidable **Five Finger Rapids**, formed by five huge pillars that divide the Yukon River into narrow channels. The rapids look benign from above, but many a stampeder lost his belongings here, or worse, his life. A steep 1km trail leads down from the lookout to the water's edge.

Stewart Crossing and Mayo

The village of **STEWART CROSSING**, 60km north of Pelly Crossing, sits at the junction of the **Silver Trail**, a highway that strikes off northeast for three historic silver-mining towns that sprang up following the discovery of silver on Keno Hill in 1919. The first 62km of road is paved and there is a **visitor kiosk** (mid-May to mid-Sept) just after the turn-off for the Silver Trail. The winding 56km drive to **MAYO** passes through moose habitat and offers scenic views of the Stewart River, which once lured Klondike-area prospectors to the area in the early 1900s. Mayo has a **tourist office** in the same building as the **Binet House Interpretive Centre**, which gives a good overview of the area's history and geology.

Keno City

Push on from Mayo to tiny **KENO CITY**, a weathered collection of wooden buildings whose highlights include a mining museum (June–Sept daily 10am–6pm; ☎ 867 995 3103, ⊛ yukonmuseums.ca/museum/keno/keno.html) and the Alpine Interpretive Centre (same hours) next door which houses information and displays on area wildlife. Check out the house constructed with 32,000 beer bottles (the owner thought it would be good insulation).

Stewart Crossing to Dawson City

The scenery picks up considerably after Stewart Crossing for the last stretch of the Klondike Highway, with wide views of sweeping valleys, rounded mountains and drunken forests (the spruce trees here all lean to one side thanks to the underlying permafrost which stunts growth). At the 554km mark, a bright red hand-painted sign welcomes you to **Moose Creek**, Yukon's smallest town, home to "two great guys & gals and three friendly dogs", and a lovely little place to stop for a bite to eat or to spend the night, and the last place on the highway to fuel up before Dawson.

Some 40km before Dawson City is the turn-off for the **Dempster Highway** (see page 839). Just before Dawson City, the road wanders through tree-covered hills and then picks up a small, ice-clear river – the **Klondike**. The first small spoil heaps start to appear on the hills to the south, and then suddenly the entire valley bottom turns into a devastated landscape of vast boulders and abandoned dredge tailings. This continues for several kilometres until the Klondike flows into the much broader **Yukon River** and Dawson City comes suddenly into view.

INFORMATION

Carmacks visitor centre Carmacks has the main visitor centre at a pull-out on the east side of the Klondike Hwy 1km before entering town (daily June–Aug 9am–7pm; ☎ 867 863 6330, ⓦ carmacks.ca).

KLONDIKE HIGHWAY

Mayo tourist office 304 Second Ave, in the Binet House Interpretive Centre (mid-May to mid-Sept daily 10am–6pm; ☎ 867 996 2926).

ACCOMMODATION AND EATING

BRAEBURN AND TWIN LAKES

Braeburn Lodge 20km after Lake Laberge, ☎ 867 456 2867. *Braeburn Lodge*, opposite the airstrip, is a good place for a hearty cup of soup and a sandwich as well as their massive cinnamon buns ($10) that have become de rigueur along this stretch. Petrol and diesel also available, but no accommodation. Daily 7am–11pm.

Twin Lakes Campground Km308. A government campground, located off the Klondike Hwy on the beautiful shores of Twin Lakes. It has eighteen standard tent or RV sites with no services, but wood, water, a kitchen cook shelter (overlooking the lake) and boat launch are available. $12

CARMACKS

Coal Mine Campground & Canteen ☎ 867 863 6363, ⓦ coalminecampground.com. The riverside *Coal Mine Campground & Canteen* is at the junction of the Klondike Hwy and the Robert Campbell Hwy, the latter a scenic gravel road winding 590km east to Watson Lake. A relaxing place to take in the view of the Yukon River while munching on a burger or enjoying an ice cream cone. Bike rentals, showers, laundry and free wi-fi. Mid-May to mid-Sept 9am–9pm. Sites $20; RVs $35; cabins $80

Hotel Carmacks ☎ 867 863 5221, ⓦ hotelcarmacks. com. Located close to the banks of the Yukon River, this hotel offers standard rooms, each with a private bath, and two of them with kitchenettes. Eight cabins sleeping four, an RV park and general store with fresh groceries and a

petrol/diesel pump are close at hand. The neighbouring *Gold Pan Restaurant* is popular with locals and travellers. Open year-round (cabins summer only). RVs $40; cabins $95; doubles $169

KENO CITY

Keno City Campground ☎ 867 995 3103. The *Keno City Campground* has a number of good hiking trails and panoramic views of the Ogilvie and Wernecke mountains from the signpost on Keno Hill. Firewood and water available. $10

Silver Moon Bunkhouse ☎ 867 668 4206, ⓦ silvermoonbunkhouse.com. Rooms are cosy despite being sparsely decorated, and the property features shared baths and a communal kitchen. There's a standalone "honeymoon shack" if you're after some privacy ($165). $138

MOOSE CREEK

Moose Creek Lodge ☎ 867 996 2550, ⓦ moosecreek-lodge.com. Friendly staff on hand serving up coffee, home-cooked meals and baked treats, petrol and tourist information, plus there are three rustic cabins on hand to rent. Basic services, no internet, but a fabulous place to catch up on rest; the restaurant is open daily for breakfast, lunch and dinner. May–Sept. $125

Moose Creek Territorial Campground The *Moose Creek Territorial* has 34 sites, a sheltered kitchen shack, outhouses and hiking trails. Free firewood. $12

Dawson City and around

Few episodes in Canadian history have captured the imagination like the **Klondike gold rush**, and few places have remained as evocative of their past as **DAWSON CITY**, the stampede's tumultuous capital. For a few months in 1898 this former patch of moose pasture became one of the wealthiest and most famous places on earth – at one point Dawson was bestowed the exaggerated nickname "Paris of the North" – as multitudes struggled across huge tracts of wilderness to seek their fortunes in the largest gold deposit of its kind of all time.

An ever-increasing number of tourists and backpackers spend a day or two here, exploring the boardwalks, rutted dirt streets and dozens of false-fronted wooden houses, particularly those in the street grid behind **Front Street**, which runs parallel to the Yukon River. Parks Canada is restoring designated **National Historic Sites**, but in a spot where permafrost buckles buildings, snow falls in late September and temperatures touch -60°C during winters, there's little real chance of Dawson losing the gritty, weather-worn feel of a true frontier town.

11

THE KLONDIKE GOLD RUSH

There was nothing quite like the delirium of the 1898 **Klondike gold rush**. Over 100,000 people are estimated to have left home for the region, the largest single one-year mass movement of people that century. About 30,000 made it, but only four thousand found any gold. A couple dozen of these made – and lost – huge fortunes.

The first to prospect near the Klondike River was dour Nova Scotian **Robert Henderson**, the very embodiment of the lone pioneer. In early 1896 he panned 8¢ worth of gold from a creek in the hills above present-day Dawson City. He thought the creek would yield more and he panned out another $750 before returning downriver.

Henderson set about finding a route up the Klondike River to meet the creek he'd prospected. At the river's mouth he met **George Carmack** and two of his friends, **Skookum Jim** of the Dakla'weidi Clan and **Tagish Charlie** of the Tagish/Ilingit First Nation. Henderson told Carmack of his hopes, and then uttered the phrase that probably cost him a fortune: "There's a chance for you George, but I don't want any damn *Siwashes* staking on that creek." Henderson wandered off, leaving Carmack to prospect a different set of creeks – the right ones, as it turned out. On August 16, Skookum Jim found $4 of gold on **Bonanza Creek**. The next day Carmack staked the first claim and rushed off to register the find as Henderson prospected almost barren ground over the hills. Two weeks later, all of Bonanza had been staked and almost all the real fortunes had been secured by that winter.

In the spring of 1897, a thousand-odd miners from the West Coast arrived, drawn by vague rumours of a big find. The headlong rush followed the July 1897 docking of the *Excelsior* in San Francisco and the *Portland* in Seattle, with battered Yukon miners coming down the gangplanks dragging bags and boxes literally bursting with gold. The rush was on.

Thousands embarked on trips, but hundreds never returned. The most common route was to take a boat to **Skagway**, climb the dreaded **Chilkoot Pass**, pick up the Yukon River at Whitehorse and then sail 700km to **Dawson City**. The easiest and most expensive route lay by boat upstream from the mouth of the Yukon River in western Alaska. The largest single influx came when the ice melted in May 1898 and a vast makeshift armada drifted down the Yukon River. As for the gold, it's the smaller stories that resonate: the miner's wife who wandered the creek by her cabin picking nuggets from the water; the $1000 of gold found during the Orpheum Theatre's rebuilding in the 1940s, under the floorboards where it ended up fifty years before; or the $200 worth of dust panned nightly from a Dawson City saloon's beer mats in 1897.

By 1899 the rush was mostly over – not because the gold had run out, but because the most easily accessible nuggets had already been taken. The gold rush had made Alaska, while Edmonton sprang from almost nothing and Vancouver's population doubled in one year. It was the first of a string of mineral discoveries in the Yukon and the far North, a region whose vast, untapped natural resources are increasingly the subject of attention from multinational corporations as rapacious and determined as their grizzled predecessors.

Today, Dawson City has become something of a beacon for the arts set. The Klondike Institute of Art and Culture has a contemporary **art gallery** and a residence programme that brings over eighteen artists to town each year. In mid-July, the city hosts its annual **Dawson City Music Festival** (ⓦdcmf.com), which attracts scores of local and international musicians. The city also comes to life in mid-August during the annual **Discovery Days Festival**, which marks the discovery of gold in August 1896. Activities include a parade and arts festival; book accommodation well in advance if visiting at this time. Check ⓦdawsoncity.ca for more information.

The heritage buildings

Fuelled by limitless avarice, between 1898 and 1900 Dawson exploded into a metropolis of thirty thousand people – the largest city in the Canadian West and the equal of Seattle and San Francisco in its opportunities for vice, decadence and good living. There were opera houses, theatres, cinemas (at a time when motion-picture houses were just three years old), steam heating, three hospitals, restaurants, bars, brothels and dance halls which generated phenomenal business. Supply and demand made Dawson an expensive town: a single two-metre frontage fetched as much in rent in a month as a four-bedroom apartment in New York cost for two years.

Remnants of all this can be seen in the town's wealth of heritage buildings, two dozen of which are under the stewardship of Parks Canada (see box), though the exteriors of all the buildings are easily seen on your own.

The heritage buildings date from the earliest days of the rush but many of them have been destroyed by fire or permafrost. Most of these have been deliberately preserved in their tumbledown state. Elsewhere, restoration projects are in full flow, partly financed by profits from the town casino, which also funds the city's many visitor attractions. Permafrost precluded the construction of brick buildings with deep foundations, so restoration engineers have had to work doubly hard to save what are generally all-wood buildings, most notably the **Palace Grand Theatre** (1899) on the corner of 3rd Avenue and King Street. It's rumoured the theatre was originally built from the hulks of two beached paddle steamers.

Nearby, on the corner of King Street and 3rd Avenue, is the 1901 **post office**. On 3rd Avenue and Princess Street, **Harrington's Store** has a "Dawson as They Saw It" exhibition of photos (June–Sept daily 9am–4.30pm; free); near the same junction stands **Billy Bigg's Blacksmith Shop**; at 807 6th Ave is the cream-and-brown clapboard **Anglican Church**, built in 1902 with money collected from the miners. At 4th Avenue and Queen Street is **Diamond Tooth Gertie's Gambling Hall**, opened as the first legal casino in Canada, named after one of the town's more notorious characters. It's still operating, and is now also the world's northernmost casino. The **Firefighters Museum** in City Hall, across from the *George Black* ferry on Front Street, is also worthwhile, with a guided tour of old fire tenders, water pumps and other equipment. In a town built almost entirely of wood, these were once vital to Dawson's survival.

SS Keno

One of the town's more obvious old wooden constructions is the **SS Keno** riverboat, moored on the river just down from the tourist office. It was built in 1922 and ran up and down the Stewart River carrying ore from the mines around Mayo. Not all boats were as lucky as the *Keno*; the improvements to transport links made many riverboats redundant and some were beached downstream. Cross the river on the free ferry, walk through the campground and ten more minutes along the waterfront and you'll reach a **ships' graveyard**, strewn with the ruins of seven boats.

> ## VISITING DAWSON CITY'S HERITAGE BUILDINGS
>
> Parks Canada organizes programming for all its **National Historic Sites**, including tours taking in the **SS Keno** or **Dredge No. 4** (the massive mining machine used to drill into the earth for gold); others capitalize on some of the town's two dozen **heritage buildings** (June to mid-Sept several daily; $6.30 each; Ⓦ pc.gc.ca). In addition, one of these is open to the public for free one night a week on a rotating basis. Check the website for the latest details, as buildings may sometimes be closed for renovation work. **Tour tickets** are available at the tourist office, as are up-to-date schedules of events.

Dänojà Zho

1131 Front St, across from visitor centre • June–Sept Mon–Sat 10am–6pm; by appointment rest of year • $7 or with Parks Canada ticket • ☎ 867 993 6768, ☎ 867 993 7100, Ⓦ trondekheritage.com

The dramatic-looking **Dänojà Zho**, or "Long Time Ago House", also known as Tr'ondëk Hwëch'in Cultural Centre, uses exhibits, guides, videos and live demonstrations to explore both the traditional and present-day culture of the Tr'ondëk Hwëch'in, the region's original inhabitants.

Dawson City Museum

595 5th Ave • Mid-May to Aug daily 10am–6pm; Sept Tues–Sat 10am–2pm; rest of year by appointment • $9 • ☎ 867 993 5291, Ⓦ dawsonmuseum.ca

The **Dawson City Museum** is housed in the former Territorial Administration Building and has an excellent historical run-through of the gold rush from the first finds. Fascinating old diaries and newspaper cuttings vividly document the minutiae of pioneer life and events such as the big winter freeze of 1897–98, when temperatures reputedly dropped to -86°C. One of its highlights is the wistful, black-and-white film *City of Gold*, a wonderful award-winning documentary, which first drew the attention of the federal government to Dawson's decline in the 1950s. Tours of the museum building are available, and during winter the organization screens classic films – check with the visitor centre or website for times, and events.

Robert Service Cabin

8th Ave and Hanson Ave • Check at the visitor centre for tour times in July–Sept • $6.30 for cabin and poem recital, free from 2–3pm

Most Canadians hold **Robert Service** in high esteem and he has a place in the pantheon of Canadian literature. Verses like *The Shooting of Dan McGrew* and *The Cremation of Sam McGee* combine strong narrative and broad comedy to evoke the myth of the North. Born in Preston, England, in 1874, the poet wrote most of his gold-rush verse before he'd even set foot in the Yukon: he was posted by his bank employers to Whitehorse in 1904 and only made it to Dawson in 1908. He retired a rich man on the proceeds of his writing, spending his last years mainly in France, where he died in 1958. His **cabin**, which is a very accurate restoration, gives an idea of how most people must have lived once Dawson was reasonably established. During the summer people come here to pay homage and listen to a Parks Canada staffer read one or two Service poems.

Berton House Writers' Retreat

The unexceptional-looking **Berton House Writers' Retreat** almost opposite the Service cabin was built in 1901 and was the childhood home of another famous Canadian writer, Pierre Berton (see page 892), whose bestseller *Klondike – The Last Great Gold Rush 1896–1899* offers a superb insight into this most fascinating of times in Canadian history. The house now acts as a private retreat for Canadian writers.

11

> **MIDNIGHT DOME**
>
> The **Midnight Dome** is the distinctive hill rearing up behind Dawson City, half-covered in stunted pines and half-eaten away by landslips. From its summit at midnight on June 21 you can watch the sun dip to the horizon before immediately rising again – Dawson being only 300km south of the Arctic Circle. The Midnight Dome Road runs 8km to the summit (884m) from the Klondike Highway just outside of town. Without a car it's an extremely steep haul (ask at the tourist office for details of the trail), but more than worth the slog for the massive views over Dawson, the goldfields, the Yukon River's broad meanders and the ranks of mountains stretching away in all directions.

Jack London's Cabin

Corner of 8th Ave and Firth St • Hut and museum mid-May to mid-Sept daily; check with the visitor centre for tour times • $5

Jack London's Cabin is a somewhat unpersuasive piece of reconstruction (logs from the original were separated and half of them used to build a cabin in Jack London Square in Oakland, California). However, alongside the hut there's a great little museum of pictures and memorabilia, where docents tell stories of London's life and work during the summer (noon and 3pm). London knew far more than Robert Service of the real rigours of northern life, having spent time in 1897 as a ferryman in Whitehorse before moving north to spend a year holed up on Henderson's Creek above the Klondike River. He returned to California penniless but loaded with material that found expression in *The Call of the Wild*, *White Fang* and *A Daughter of the Snows*.

Bonanza and Eldorado creeks

Make a point of seeing the two creeks where it all started and where most of the gold was mined – **Bonanza and Eldorado**, both over 20km from Dawson City along rough roads to the southeast. Today, gold mining continues at a hectic pace as more claims are being staked and deposits discovered – most of these claims are still owned and definitely out of bounds to amateurs.

To reach **Bonanza Creek**, follow the Klondike Highway – the continuation of Front Street – for 4km to the junction with Bonanza Creek Road. The road threads through scenes of apocalyptic piles of boulders and river gravel for some 12km until it comes to a simple cairn marking **Discovery Claim**, the spot staked by George Carmack after pulling out a nugget the size of his thumb. Every 150m along the creek in front of you – the width of a claim – was to yield some 3000kg of gold, about $25 million in 1900 prices.

At Discovery Claim the road forks again, one spur running east up **Eldorado Creek**, the other following Upper Bonanza Road to the summit of **King Solomon's Dome**, where you can look down over smaller scarred rivulets, before returning in a loop to the Klondike Highway via Hunker Road. As time passed and the easily reached gold was exploited, miners increasingly consolidated claims or sold out to large companies which installed dredges capable of efficiently clawing out the bedrock and gravel. Numerous examples of these industrial dinosaurs litter the creeks, but the largest and most famous is the 1912 **No. 4 Dredge** at Claim 17 BD ("Below Discovery") off Bonanza Creek Road. It's an extraordinary piece of industrial archeology 66m long and eight stories tall, one that from the start of operations in 1913 until 1966 dug up as much as 25kg of gold a day. Modern mines are lucky to produce a quarter of that amount in a week. Tours from Dawson City are available (see page 837).

Top of the World Highway

When they're not shrouded by mid-morning fog (beautiful as well), the broad vistas you can snatch from the **Top of the World Highway** (Hwy-9), a summer-only gravel road, are spectacular. If you're hiking, venture across the Yukon River via the *George Black* **ferry** from Front Street (mid-May to mid-Sept daily 24hr; rest of year 7am–11pm, depending on whether the river is frozen; free; ☎867 993 5441) and pick up the trail. After 5km the road reaches a great panorama over the area and after 14km another **viewpoint** looks out over the Yukon Valley and the **Ogilvie Mountains** straddling the Arctic Circle; in late summer, many people pile out of their cars around here to pick **wild blueberries**. The road continues above the tree-line as a massive belvedere and can be seen switchbacking over barren ridges into the distance. It hits the **Alaska border** 108km from Dawson, where you can cross only when the customs post is open (mid-May to mid-Sept 9am–9pm). Be prepared to do only about 50km/hr, and ask at the Dawson tourist office about local difficulties and fuel availability. Set your clocks back one hour when entering Alaska.

ARRIVAL AND INFORMATION

DAWSON CITY AND AROUND

By plane Dawson City's airport is 19km southeast of the town on the Klondike Hwy. It's serviced by Air North, which provides links to Fairbanks, Whitehorse, Inuvik and Old Crow, and Alkan Air charter flights service Inuvik, Old Crow, Mayo and Whitehorse (see page 818). There are no scheduled airport shuttles, but a handful of companies offer that service for $30 – ask at the tourist office (or ask at your hotel). A local taxi service is Grab-a-Cab (☎ 867 993 3333).

By bus The bus to Alaska generally arrives and departs from behind the visitor centre.

Destinations Alaska/Yukon Trails (☎907 888 5659, ☎907 479 2277, ☎alaskashuttle.com) run to Fairbanks, Alaska (June to mid-Sept Mon, Wed, Sat 8am; arrives Fairbanks 6pm). Husky Bus (☎867 993 3821, ☎867 335 8833, ☎klondikeexperience.com/husky-bus) travels to Whitehorse (May & Sept Mon & Thurs at noon, June–Aug Sun, Tues, Fri; $119), with stops along the Klondike Hwy; they also run a trip to Tombstone Territorial Park on the Dempster Hwy (call for reservations). Inuvik MGM Services (☎867 777 4295) runs a bus up the Dempster Hwy ($310 one way) and back. Call for a reservation but note this is an on-demand service only and a minimum of eight passengers is required.

Tourist office Run by the Klondike Visitors Association and on the corner of Front and King streets (mid-May to mid-Sept daily 8am–8pm; summer ☎867 993 5566, off-season ☎867 993 5575; ☎dawsoncity.ca). It shares the building with Yukon Tourism and Parks Canada; all three offer tourist information, show films, run events and tours, and house historical exhibits. Download a free copy of the current *Dawson City Visitor's Guide* at ☎yukoninfo.com.

Northwest Territories Dempster Delta Visitor Centre Opposite the tourist office (mid-May to mid-Sept Mon–Fri 9am–7pm; ☎867 993 6167, ☎800 661 0750). An essential stop if you're heading north on the Dempster Hwy (see page 839).

TOURS AND ACTIVITIES

River cruises First Nations-owned Fishwheel Charter Services (☎867 993 6237, ☎fishwheelcharterservices. yolasite.com) runs intimate, 2hr boat tours ($65) up the Yukon River that take in a visit to a traditional fish camp; in the winter, dog-sledding and guided camping trips are offered. The *Klondike Spirit* is a side-paddler offering afternoon ($52.50) and dinner cruises ($110) June through Sept; tickets can be purchased at the *Triple J Hotel* at Fifth Ave and Queen St.

City and road tours Klondike Experience (☎867 993 3821, ☎klondikeexperience.com) offers trips to the Midnight Dome, a popular place to enjoy a view of Dawson City and its surroundings, tours that take in the city and goldfields, and day-trips to Tombstone Territorial Park along Dempster Hwy (from $95).

Flight tours Trans North Helicopters (☎867 993 5494, ☎tntaheli.com) and Great River Air (☎867 993 4359, ☎greatriverair.com) run flightseeing trips over the goldfields and the Yukon River.

Goldfields and gold panning You can pan for gold at Claim #6 (bring you own pan!) for free. Try Claim #33 on Bonanza Creek Rd ($15; 10am–5pm) if you want to rent a pan or shovel ($2); they claim "guaranteed gold". Gold Bottom Mine Tours (office on Front St near Princess St; ☎867 993 5023, ☎goldbottom.com) offers 3hr tours at 8.15am and 1.15pm ($60, $50 self-drive). In addition, Klondike Experience (☎867 993 3821, ☎klondikeexperience.com) visits the Discovery claim on its Tales of Dawson City tour (8.30am; $59). Visits to Dredge #4 are run seven times daily on the hour 10am–4pm from mid-May to mid-Sept by Gold Bottom Mine Tours (office on Front St near Princess St; $15, $25 with transport; ☎867 993 5023, ☎goldbottom.com).

Canoe rental The *Dawson City River Hostel* (see page 838) and the Dawson Trading Post store at 966 Front St (☎867 993 5316) rent canoes. Both can give you information on good trips from Dawson City, including the float down the Yukon River to the abandoned gold-mining town of Fortymile.

ACCOMMODATION

In July and August it's pretty much essential to book **accommodation** in advance. Rates are high in the half-dozen or so mid-range establishments, most of which have colourful, old-fashioned facades. Prices in all drop considerably outside the high summer period and many spots close between September and mid-May.

HOTELS AND B&BS

Aurora Inn 5th Ave & Harper ☎ 867 993 6860, ⓦ aurorainn.ca. A colourful exterior, cheerful staff and eighteen immaculate rooms make this one of the best picks in town. Airport transfer included. **$149**

Bombay Peggy's 2nd Ave & Princess St ☎ 867 993 6969, ⓦ bombaypeggys.com. Nine very comfortable and plush Victorian-style rooms with antique and custom fixtures in a heritage house of former ill-repute. March–Nov. Shared bath **$119**; en suite **199**

Bonanza Gold Motel and RV Park 2km south of Dawson City at the Km712 marker on the Klondike Hwy ☎ 867 993 6789, ☎ 888 993 6789, ⓦ bonanzagold.ca. A variety of comfortable rooms and suites all with mini-fridge and microwave, some with kitchenette. Also provided: a full-service RV site, laundry and wi-fi. RVs **$24**, doubles **$139**

Downtown Hotel 2nd Ave & Queen St ☎ 867 993 5346, ☎ 800 661 0514, ⓦ downtownhotel.ca. Centrally located hotel with 59 rooms which, though not flashy, are nonetheless a bit nicer and fresher then you might expect. In addition, it houses the *Jack London Grill*, one of the more reliable year-round places in town serving full menu breakfasts and a selection of hearty lunches and dinners. Free wi-fi and free transport from the airport, bus station and waterfront. **$140**

Eldorado 902 3rd Ave, at Princess ☎ 867 993 5451, ☎ 800 764 3536, ⓦ eldoradohotel.ca. A little old fashioned, with 52 central rooms, some with kitchenette. **$129**

Fifth Ave B&B 5th Ave near the museum ☎ 867 993 5941, ☎ 866 631 5237, ⓦ 5thavebandb.com. A spacious robin's egg-blue house with shared kitchen and single, double or triple rooms with shared and private bathrooms. Look out for the electric-blue exterior. Hearty breakfasts (in summer these are served next door at the *Aurora Inn*). **$125**

Klondike Kate's Cabins & Rooms 3rd Ave & King St ☎ 867 993 6527, ⓦ klondikekates.ca. Renovated, pretty and popular cabins, in this family owned business. There's a good restaurant on-site. April–Sept. **$140**

Whitehouse Cabins Front St ☎ 867 993 5576, ⓦ whitehousecabins.com. Seven guest rooms situated in three restored waterfront cabins with kitchenettes and open porches at the northern end of the street beyond the *George Black* ferry. Three wall-tent cabins as well. May–Sept. Cabins **$139**; wall-tent cabins **$119**

HOSTELS AND CAMPGROUNDS

Dawson City River Hostel ☎ 867 993 6823, ⓦ yukon hostels.com. Across the river from downtown, 200m to the left of the ferry dock. The "northernmost hostel in Canada" is a collection of bunks, tents, family rooms and private doubles in smart log cabins. Amenities include wood-fired showers and stoves, canoe ($250/16 days) and bike rental ($25/day), a small store, and transfers to Whitehorse (on demand). No electricity. Cash or PayPal only. Mid-May to Sept. Dorms **$22**; sites (per person) **$14**; doubles **$48**

Gold Rush Campground 5th Ave, at York ☎ 867 993 5247, ☎ 866 330 5006, ⓦ goldrushcampground.com. A bleak, fully serviced but busy place designed for RVs, and the most central campground with showers. May–Sept. Basic **$29**; full hook-up **$53**

Yukon River Campground ☎ 867 667 5648. Across the river from downtown, 500m to the right of the ferry dock. The main town campground for tents, but there are no showers (or running water). **$12**

EATING

There are numerous cafés around town, including several good snack places on Front St. Otherwise, most dining takes place in bigger hotels' restaurants.

Alchemy Café 878 3rd Ave at Princess St ☎ 867 993 6880, ⓦ alchemycafe.ca. Supplied with coffee from Whitehorse's Beans North and a variety of teas, this mostly organic café is a great place to laze away an hour or so. Limited but enjoyable menu of light fare and desserts – and the owner can also work on your iPhone (he's a certified Apple tech). March–Sept Mon–Fri 7.30am–5pm, Sat & Sun 9.30am–5pm.

Aurora Inn Restaurant 5th Ave and Harper St ☎ 867 993 6860, ⓦ aurorainn.ca. Hotel restaurant that serves grilled meats, burgers, seafood, schnitzel and a handful of tasty vegetarian mains ($20–45). For breakfast, there's a European-style breakfast buffet. May–Sept daily 7–10am, 5–10pm.

Cheechakos Bake Shop 902 Front St ☎ 867 993 5303. Offering home-baked breads, pastries, cakes and muffins along with breakfast and lunch sandwiches. May–Sept Mon–Fri 7am–5.30pm, Sat & Sun 9am–4pm.

★ **Drunken Goat Taverna** 950 2nd Ave ☎ 867 993 5868. One of the most popular restaurants in town, it specializes in Greek food, served in hearty portions and by a very friendly staff. Open year-round. Daily noon–10pm.

Klondike Kate's 3rd Ave & King St ☎ 867 993 6527, ⓦ klondikekates.ca. The excellent *Klondike Kate's* is the friendliest, most relaxed place in town for fabulous breakfasts and dinners. Their salmon specials are not to be missed (mains $18–30). April–Sept daily 4–10pm.

Riverwest Bistro Front St & Queen St ☎ 867 993 6339. The most popular café for breakfast is likely the *Riverwest Bistro*, which also plies guests with good coffee, soups, sandwiches and ice cream. May–Sept Mon–Fri 7am–5pm, Sat & Sun 8am–4pm.

Sourdough Joe's Front St & Princess St ☎ 867 993 6590. The popular venue has mouthwatering halibut fish and chips, seafood chowder and home-made burgers and fries. May–Sept daily 11am–10pm.

DRINKING AND NIGHTLIFE

Nightlife revolves around drinking in the main hotel bars, or spending an hour or so at *Diamond Tooth Gertie's Gambling Hall*.

Bombay Peggy's 2nd Ave & Princess St ☎ 867 993 6969, ⓦ bombaypeggys.com. Hotel bars provide more sedate alternatives to the gambling hall, among which the lounge at *Bombay Peggy's* hotel stands out for its fine atmosphere. Daily 3pm–1am.

Diamond Tooth Gertie's Gambling Hall 4th Ave & Queen St ☎ 867 993 5575. Canada's oldest legal gambling hall; you need to be over 19 to gamble and all proceeds from here and several other town sights go to the maintenance of the visitor attractions and to the community of Dawson. Three times a night, a singer and can-can girls grace the stage for some over-the-top knicker-flashing, tap-dancing and (mostly tame) titillating audience interaction. $15 entry. Mid-May to mid-Sept daily 7pm–2am, Fri–Sun opens at 2pm; off-season Fri & Sat only.

Sourdough Saloon At the Downtown Hotel, 2nd Ave and Queen St. The *Sourdough Saloon* is popular with locals and visitors alike. If you're game enough, volunteer for the Sourtoe Cocktail that involves a real pickled human toe. Daily 11.30am to midnight or 1am.

Westminster 975 3rd Ave ☎ 867 993 6029. If you want a taste of a real northern bar, opt for the *Westminster*, known locally as "The Pit": it's full of grizzled characters and most certainly not the place for a quiet drink or the faint-hearted. It hosts live music most nights. Daily 9am–1am.

SHOP

Maximilian's Gold Rush Emporium Front and Queen St ☎ 867 993 5486, ⓦ maximilians.ca. Stocks paperbacks on local history and the latest fiction, along with maple products, T-shirts and sundries. Summer daily 9am–8pm, winter Mon–Sat 10am–6pm, Sun noon–5pm.

DIRECTORY

Currency exchange and ATM CIBC Queen St, between Front & 2nd ☎ 867 993 5447.

Internet Free at the public library on 5th Ave and Queen St (Mon & Wed noon–6.30pm, Tues, Thurs & Fri 10am–6.30pm, Sat noon–4pm).

Laundry *Gold Rush Campground and RV Park* (see page 838) or Monte Carlo at 1043 2nd Ave.

Post office 3rd Ave between King and Queen sts (Mon–Fri 8.30am–5.30pm, Sat 11.30am–2.30pm).

Dempster Highway

Begun in 1959 to service northern oilfields, and completed over twenty years later – by which time all the accessible oil had been siphoned off – the 741km **Dempster Highway** between Dawson City and Inuvik in the Northwest Territories is the only road in Canada to cross the **Arctic Circle**. This route offers a tremendous journey through a superb and ever-changing spectrum of landscapes – mountains, open tundra, rivers, bogs, with thousands of wandering caribou and millions of migrating birds. In June the landscape bursts into colour as scores of tiny arctic plants suddenly bloom en masse, while in late August the tundra is ablaze in the most intense hues of red, yellow and orange imaginable. It's also hard to resist the temptation of crossing into the Arctic 445km north of Dawson City, a section that takes you over the most captivating stretch of highway. Yet the Dempster is a hard-packed **gravel road** and the journey to Inuvik (12–15hr) is not a breeze; the road is generally in good condition, but often very slippery when raining, so drive the speed limit and give plenty of room to oncoming traffic. Keep in mind this road is very much about the journey rather than the destination.

The highway is open year-round except for brief periods during the November freeze and April thaw. All distances given below (unless stated) are from **Kilometre 0** of the highway, which is at the junction of the North Klondike Highway, 40km east of Dawson City.

GETTING AROUND

DEMPSTER HIGHWAY

By bike If you're cycling or motorbiking – increasingly popular ways of doing the trip – be prepared for rough camping. Call at the Northwest Territories and Dempster Delta Visitor Centre (see page 837) in Dawson City for information and pick up a free copy of *The Dempster Highway Travelogue*, which outlines a detailed account of the journey ahead. If you're without your own transport you might pick up a lift here, or take the bus service run by MGM Services, Gray Line Yukon or by Husky Bus, which offers an on-demand service (see page 837).

By car The first fuel stop is right at the turn onto the Dempster, but It's a cardlock, meaning that only the company's credit card will unlock the pump. The next is 365km north at the *Eagle Plains Hotel and Service Station*. After that it's 193km to Fort McPherson, where there is mechanical service available, and thereafter there's nothing reliable until Inuvik. (There is fuel in Tsiigehtchic, but the pumps are not always on; you must request the station be opened at the main town building during weekday business hours, or enquire at the Northern Store grocery). Take a jerry can and make sure you have two spare tyres and your car is in good condition – the only other maintenance facilities are at Eagle Plains. It's worth checking on ☎ 800 661 0750 to see the status of the two ferry services on the route at Peel River (539km; free on demand, spring to late autumn daily 9am–1am, then ice bridge) and Tsiigehtchic (609km; same details) are running.

Road information Check road conditions along the Dempster at ☎ 511yukon.ca.

Dawson City to Eagle Plains

About 72km north of Dawson City is **Tombstone Mountain Territorial Park**, the first of the highway's three rudimentary government-run campgrounds. It's a magnificent, 2000-square-kilometre park packed with wildlife and archeological sites and an interpretive centre (mid-May to mid-Sept 9am–9pm) with a biologist/botanist on hand to offer guided nature walks.

At **Hart River** (Km80) you may see part of the 1200-strong Hart River Woodland **caribou herd**; unlike the barren-ground herds farther north these caribou have sufficient fodder to graze in one area instead of making seasonal migrations. Golden eagles and ptarmigan are also common along the Blackstone River (Km93), as are tundra birds like Lapland longspurs, lesser golden plovers, mew gulls and long-tailed jaegers. This river offers the best chance at **fishing** for arctic grayling – simply pull over on the highway or by the bridge and spend a few hours casting your line. At Moose Lake (Km105), **moose** can often be seen feeding, along with numerous species of waterfowl such as northern shoveller, American widgeon and the arctic tern, whose Arctic-to-Antarctic migration is the longest of any bird.

Chapman Lake (Km120) marks the start of the northern **Ogilvie Mountains**, a region that has never been glaciated and so preserves numerous plant and insect species and provides an important early wintering range for the Porcupine caribou herd; as many as forty thousand caribou cross the highway in mid-October – they take four days and have right of way. This rough stretch of road crosses the Ogilvie Mountains at **North Fork Pass** (1289m), the highest elevation on the highway, at Km139. Unique butterfly species breed at Butterfly Ridge (Km155), close to some obvious caribou trails which cross the region, and it should also be easy to spot Dall sheep, cliff swallows and bald eagles.

Beyond, the highway goes up to **Eagle Plains** and almost unparalleled access to the subarctic **tundra**, which in summer and autumn is a beautiful medley of colours, the vegetation having been coaxed to riotous life by hours of perpetual daylight.

ACCOMMODATION   DAWSON CITY TO EAGLE PLAINS

Eagle Plains Hotel and Service Station Km369 ☎ 867 993 2453, ⊛ eagleplainshotel.ca. The only proper accommodation on the highway within the Yukon is the 32 rooms at this hotel. It has fuel, a garage with mechanic, tyres, lounge, a restaurant and RV park. Doubles **$175**; sites **$18**

Engineer Creek Campsite Km194, at Engineer Creek.

Avoid fishing here, as the river has high iron concentrations. It's a government-run campground with fifteen RV/tent sites. No electricity, but there is water. April–Sept. **$12**

Tombstone Mountain Campground Km72. The first of the highway's three rudimentary government-run campgrounds with 30 RV/tent sites. April–Sept. **$12**

The Arctic Circle and beyond

Finally, after travelling 405km you cross the **Arctic Circle**, an imaginary line circumnavigating the globe at 66½°N, indicating the point on Earth where the sun will not set for at least one full day. From here on in, the further north you travel, the higher the midnight sun. A sign on the highway marks the crossover point.

Beyond is a government-run campground at **Rock River** – an important caribou hunting area for the Gwich'in for over 8000 years – and then the road climbs into the **Richardson Mountains** to meet the border of the NWT (Km465) before the less-than-arresting flats of the Peel Plateau and Mackenzie River and the run to Inuvik. The **time changes** at the Yukon–NWT border: NWT time is one hour ahead of Yukon time.

The tiny Gwich'in Dene village of **FORT MCPHERSON** is at Km574, soon after crossing the Peel River. It holds a service station, the *Peel River Inns North* and a small **visitor centre** (daily June–early Sept).

At Km609 is the minuscule settlement of **TSIIGEHTCHIC**, 80km south of Inuvik. It was founded as a mission in 1868 and acquired a Hudson's Bay post soon after; a red-roofed 1931 mission church still stands here.

ACCOMMODATION

THE ARCTIC CIRCLE AND BEYOND

Nitainlaii Territorial Campground 10km south of Fort McPherson (Km541, 76km after the NWT border). The unserviced government-run site has 23 non-powered spots; shelter, outhouse, potable water, and a pretty view. Stop by the Interpretive Centre for information on the natural and cultural history of the region. June–Sept; no reservations. **$15**

Peel River Inns North Fort McPherson, Km574 ☎ 867 952 2373, ☎ 888 866 6784, ⓦ peelriverinn.com. Small and comfortable inn with eight basic rooms and a grocery store next door. There's a shared kitchen, too. It's pricey, as it's the only Inn in town. **$199**

Rock River Government Campground Km445.8. This campground with twenty spots is set in a valley with dramatic views of the surrounding subarctic landscapes and makes a good base to start treks in the Richardson Range. Watch for northern wheatears and snowy owls. No electricity or services. **$12**

Vadzaih Van Tshik Campground Km692. On the run to Inuvik (see page 841), there's a scenic campground at Vadzaih Van Tshik which has eleven sites with water, shelter, firewood and toilets. June–Sept no reservations. **$15**

The Western Arctic

The **Western Arctic** region centres on **Inuvik** and encompasses the mighty delta of the **Mackenzie River** – North America's second longest river – and reaches across the Beaufort Sea to the border with Nunavut. The region also includes part of Victoria and Banks islands, the most westerly of Canada's Arctic islands. The delta ranks as one of the continent's great **bird** habitats, with swans, cranes and big raptors among the hundreds of species that either nest in or overfly the region during the spring and autumn. It also offers the chance of seeing pods of **beluga whales** and other big sea mammals, while local **Inuit** guides on Banks Island should be able to lead you to possible sightings of musk ox, grizzly bear, wolf and arctic fox.

After Inuvik, and the two villages on the short NWT section of the Dempster Highway, a year-round highway has opened to **Tuktoyaktuk**. The area's other settlements are **fly-in communities** reached from Inuvik. **Aklavik** is near – by NWT standards – and is the place to fly out to if you want a comparatively accessible taste of Inuit (Inuvialuit) culture. **Paulatuk** (on the coastal mainland) lies much farther afield, and serves as a base for more arduous tours into the delta and Arctic tundra. Inuvik, along with Yellowknife and Fort Smith, is one of the key centres of the accessible North, and one of the main places from which to take or plan tours farther afield (see page 844).

Inuvik

INUVIK ("the place of man") is the farthest north you can drive on a public highway in North America – unless you wait for the winter freeze and follow the ice road carved across the Mackenzie River and the Arctic Ocean to the north. Canada's first planned town north of the Arctic Circle, Inuvik is a battered spot begun in 1954 as an administrative centre to replace Aklavik, a settlement to the west wrongly thought to be doomed to envelopment by the Mackenzie River's swirling waters and shifting mudflats. Inuvik is an interesting melting pot of around 3500 people, with Dene, Métis and Inuvialuit living alongside the trappers, pilots, scientists and frontier entrepreneurs drawn here in the 1970s when a boom followed the oil exploration in the delta. Today, the local economy also relies on government jobs, services, tourism and the town's role as a supply and communication centre for much of the western Arctic. For 56 days from late June, Inuvik basks in round-the-clock sunshine – it's well worth timing your trip to coincide with the mid-July **Great Northern Arts Festival** (🌐gnaf.org), ten fabulous days of exhibitions and performances by local and international artists.

Wandering the town provides an eye-opening introduction to the vagaries of northern life, from the strange stilted buildings designed to prevent their heat melting the **permafrost** (which would have disastrous effects on the piles or gravel pads that serve as foundations), to the street-level "utilidors", which carry water and sewage lines – again, to prevent the permafrost melting.

The influence of Inuvialuit people in local political and economic life has increased, to the extent that the **Western Claims Settlement Act** of 1984 saw the government cede titles to various lands in the area, returning control to the Inuvialuit that which had been lost to the fur trade, the Church, oil companies and national government.

Igloo Church

174 Mackenzie Rd · ☎ 867 777 2236

A potent symbol of the Church's local role resides in the town's most-photographed building, the **Igloo Church**, or Our Lady of Victory, a rather incongruous cultural mix. The circular domed structure isn't always open; ask at the rectory for a glimpse inside and of the paintings by local Inuvialuit artist Mona Thrasher.

Inuvik Community Greenhouse

Corner of Loucheux Rd and Breynant St · ☎ 867 777 3267, 🌐 inuvikgreenhouse.com · Tours June–Sept Mon–Fri 5.30pm, Sat 5pm · $5

Behind the church is the **Inuvik Community Greenhouse**, the northernmost greenhouse in North America, blooming with flowers, fruit and vegetables that would otherwise not survive in the harsh climate. It's housed in a converted hockey arena and hosts a small community market on Saturday. Greenhouse tours are available in summer or you can get in touch to arrange a private tour ($10/person, min $40).

Inuvialuit Regional Corporation Craft Shop

3rd Floor, 107 Mackenzie Rd · ☎ 867 777 2737

The best place in town to pick up unique pieces by Northern artists – including one-off carvings and clothing made from polar bear, wolf or musk ox – is at the not-for-profit **Inuvialuit Regional Corporation Craft Shop**. It obtains its goods directly from local craftspeople, and every dollar goes back to them.

ARRIVAL AND DEPARTURE
INUVIK

By plane Flights with Air North from Whitehorse, Dawson City, Old Crow, Fairbanks and other points south service Inuvik's airport (☎ 867 777 2467), 12km south of town. First Air and Canadian North both have numerous northern connections and run weekly and daily flights from Edmonton; Canadian North also runs daily flights from Yellowknife (see page 795). A taxi (☎ 867 777 5888) from the airport should cost $35. The fly-in communities (see page 845) are served by Inuvik-based Aklak Air (☎ 867 777 3777, ☎ 866 707 4977, 🌐 aklakair.ca) or North-Wright Airways (☎ 867 678 2749, 🌐 north-wrightairways.com). **Destinations** Edmonton (3 weekly; 5hr); Whitehorse (flights vary according to season; 3hr 10min); Yellowknife (1 daily; 2hr 35min).

By bus The MGM bus service (☎ 867 777 4295, ☎ 867 678 0129) runs charter services along the Dempster Hwy to Inuvik.

11

TOURS FROM INUVIK

Most visitors to Inuvik take a **tour** of some description, and despite the remoteness of the NWT and the isolated nature of its communities, it is remarkably simple – if occasionally rather expensive – to find **tour operators** who offer a wide range of cultural, natural history and other trips. A full list of licensed operators can be found in the *Explorers' Guide to Canada's Northwest Territories* or by visiting ⓦ spectacularnwt.com; further information is on ☎ 800 661 0788 (in Canada) or ☎ 867 873 7200. Download a free copy of the *Inuvik Attraction and Service Guide* (ⓘ inuvik.ca), which provides a list of accommodations, tour operators, attractions and information on the surrounding communities – also available at most tourist centres in NWT and Yukon.

Day-trips from Inuvik include tours to the tundra, a traditional bush camp, boat tours on the Mackenzie River, beluga whale-watching, flights over the Mackenzie Delta and trips to the fly-in communities. Arctic Nature Tours and Up North Tours are the main operators and have a special bias towards wildlife. Trips include tours to the Babbage River (which, if the timing is right, offers a bird's-eye view of the Porcupine caribou herd) and bird and wildlife visits to Hershel Island, a Yukon territorial park in the Beaufort Sea that is still a prime hunting and fishing ground for the Inuvialuit (western Arctic Inuit). The companies also offer guided trips to Tuktoyaktuk and can arrange tours with guides based in Aklavik and Paulatuk.

TOUR OPERATORS

Arctic Adventure Tours ☎ 867 777 3535, ☎ 800 685 9417, ⓦ arcticadventuretours.com. Accommodation, tours of the Dempster and flight tours to Tuk, ice road excursions and dog-sledding. Also rents boats and vehicles.

Tundra North Tours ☎ 867 678 0510, ☎ 800 420 9652, ⓦ tundranorthtours.ca. Tours of Dempster Hwy, flight tours, cultural boat tours and winter excursions on snowmobile and ATV.

INFORMATION

Western Arctic Regional Visitor Centre Near the town's entrance at the eastern end of Mackenzie Road, at the junction with Loucheux Road, a 10min walk from the centre (June to early Sept daily 10am–6pm; ☎ 867 777 4727).

Tourist office 2 Firth St (☎ 867 777 8600, ⓦ inuvik.ca).

ACCOMMODATION

Arctic Chalet 25 Carn Rd ☎ 867 777 3535, ☎ 800 685 9417, ⓦ arcticchalet.com. The best accommodation option for budget travellers is the cabins (most with kitchenettes) at the excellent lakeside *Arctic Chalet*, 3km from town off the approach road. Doubles $140; full-service cabins $150; RVs $35

Capital Suites 198 Mackenzie Rd ☎ 867 678 6300, ☎ 877 669 9444, ⓦ capitalsuites.ca. In partnership with the local Gwich'in Zheh Gwizu', the *Capital Suites* offers a range of accommodation styles ranging from studios to one- or two-bedroom suites. Guests have access to free wi-fi, laundry facilities and a fitness room. $184

Eskimo Inn 133 Mackenzie Rd ☎ 867 777 2801, ⓦ mackenziehotel.com/eskimo.htm. One of the cheaper places in town, with 74 rooms ranging from standard to superior standard. On-site services include laundry facilities, dining room, lounge and free cable TV. Owned by the same people as the *Mackenzie*. $129

Happy Valley Territorial Campground ☎ 867 777 3652. At the northwest end of town on Franklin Rd off Mackenzie Rd, is the nearest local campground, with a view of the Richardson Mountains. June–Sept. Sites $15; RVs $22.50

Mackenzie Hotel 185 Mackenzie Rd ☎ 867 777 2861, ⓦ mackenziehotel.com. One of the finer places to stay in town offering fabulous northern hospitality. Rooms come with a microwave and fridge; some have a mini bar and jet bath. Facilities include an excellent dining room and lounge, and an exercise room. $214

EATING

Eating possibilities are largely confined to hotel dining rooms; at the time of writing *Café Gallery*, the only café in Inuvik, had closed.

Alestine's 48 Franklin Rd ☎ 867 777 3702. Summer-only operation with locally caught fish transformed into fish and chips, plus reindeer (try the reindeer tacos at $15), desserts and other items. Daily 5–9pm.

JamPaks 90 Mackenzie Rd ☎ 204 290 9416, ⓦ jampaks.ca. Billed as the world's first Jamaica-Pakistani restaurant, this pop up at Café Mackenzie is open just one day a week for eat-in or take-out. Jerk Chicken or sweet and sour meatballs are $25 and there are plenty of veggie choices too. Sat only 10am–9pm.

The Mad Trapper Pub 124 Mackenzie Rd ☎ 867 678

4102. A locals' place, which also puts on occasional live music. Mon–Sat 11am–2am.
The Roost 120 Mackenzie St ☎867 777 2727. This restaurant serves everything from pizzas, burgers and fried chicken to Chinese cuisine, and takeaway is also available. Daily till midnight.

DIRECTORY

Car rental You can rent a car from Arctic Chalet Car Rental, 25 Carn St (☎867 777 3535, ☎800 685 9417, ⓦarcticchalet. com), or at Driving Force Vehicle Rentals, 170 Airport Rd (☎867 777 2346, ☎800 936 9353, ⓦdrivingforce.ca).
Library and bookshop You can get more background on the area and access the internet at the Inuvik Centennial Library (Mon–Fri 10am–6pm, Sat & Sun 1–5pm; ☎867 777 8620), 100 Mackenzie Rd, and pick up maps, guides, books and charts at Boreal Books (Mon–Fri 10am–6pm, Sat 10am–5pm; ☎867 777 2198), 75 Mackenzie Rd.

Tuktoyaktuk

TUKTOYAKTUK, or simply Tuk, rests on a sandspit on the Beaufort coast about 138km north of Inuvik. It acts as a springboard for oil workers and tourists, both considered outsiders who have diluted the traditional ways of the whale-hunting Karngmalit peoples. The Karngmalit have lived and hunted in small family groups on this fascinating but inhospitable shore for centuries. The settlement's name means "Looks Like Caribou", reflecting its former reputation as a hunting ground for *tuktu*, or caribou. Many locals still hunt, fish and trap, but government, tourism and the oil business now pay most wages.

This is the most popular tour outing from Inuvik, either a drive of a few hours or a short low-altitude flight, which is worth paying for just to enjoy the scenery. Most casual visitors come during the summer to see pods of beluga and great bowhead whales, or to look at the world's largest concentration of **pingos**, 1400 volcano-like hills, formed by the combination of frost and abundant water, across the delta's otherwise treeless flats; two of the largest have been used as landmarks for centuries.

While in Tuk drop by the **community freezer**, located some thirty feet underground; the rooms are surrounded by permafrost and are used to store caribou meat and fish. The town is also well known for its traditional arts and crafts fashioned from soap stone, caribou antler, whale-bone and musk-ox horn. Carvings usually feature polar bears, *inuksuit* (piled stone way-markers that look vaguely like people), hunters and drum dancers.

ARRIVAL AND INFORMATION | TUKTOYAKTUK

By car In 2017, the 138km Inuvik-Tuktoyaktuk Highway (ITH) opened to traffic. This all-weather road – a packed gravel two lane highway – is a year-round link from Inuvik and begins from the end of the Dempster Highway.
By plane Flights from Inuvik have been scaled back since the road opened, but Aklak Air (☎867 777 3777, ☎866 707 4977, ⓦaklakair.ca) still operate a daily service.
Tourist information For more information on the settlement, or to enquire about outfitters and local accommodation options, contact the community office (☎867 977 2390) or try the Northwest Territories ⓦspectacularnwt.com.
Tours Inuvik's tour companies come out here, but for a local guide, Chuck Gruben's Guiding and Outfitting (☎867 977 2360, ⓔchuckgruben@hotmail.com) or Pokiak Guiding and Outfitting (☎867 977 2170, ⓔookpiktours@yahoo.ca) offer cultural, boat or dog-sledding tours.

ACCOMMODATION

Hunter's B&B ☎867 977 2558, ⓦhuntersbbtuk.ca. Your best option while in town, *Hunter's* accommodates six guests in two spacious bedrooms with shared baths ($200/ person). **$400**

The fly-in communities

Accessible only by air except in winter, when incredible snow roads are ploughed across the frozen delta, the region's several **fly-in communities** are close to some fascinating and relatively accessible Arctic landscapes, wildlife and cultures. All are served by Inuvik-based air routes (see page 842) and have simple grocery stores, though their prices make it wise to bring in some of your own supplies. Some have hotels, but you should be able to camp close to all; ask permission first at the hamlet offices. The best way to visit is with a tour company from Inuvik (see page 844), but even if you're going under your own steam it's still worth checking with the tour companies for discounted flight-only deals.

Aklavik

AKLAVIK, 50km west of Inuvik on the western bank of the Mackenzie delta, means "Place of the Barrenlands Grizzly Bear". A Hudson's Bay post (which you can still see) aimed at the trade in muskrat fur was established here in 1918, though for generations before the region had been the home of Inuvialuit families who traded and frequently clashed with the Gwich'in of Alaska and the Yukon. Today its inhabitants are proud not to have jumped ship when they were invited to leave their sinking town for Inuvik in the 1950s, and most are happy to regale you with stories of the mysterious "**Mad Trapper of Rat River**", one Albert Johnson, who is buried here. Johnson (supposedly a former Chicago gangster) arrived in Fort McPherson in July 1931, purchased guns and ammunition and later built a cabin-cum-fortress on the delta, not far from Aklavik. After local trappers accused him of tampering with their traps, a constable was sent to question him, but Johnson shot him through the door. A posse of Mounties and local men armed with guns and fistfuls of dynamite then laid siege to Johnson's cabin for fifteen hours but he managed to escape, shooting another Mountie in the process. Johnson grabbed world headlines briefly as he managed to elude capture for a further forty days in the dead of a brutal winter, but he was eventually shot on the Eagle River surrounded by seventeen men.

ARRIVAL AND INFORMATION AKLAVIK

By plane Flights from Inuvik on North-Wright Airways (ⓦ north-wrightairways.com) operate daily.
Tourist information For local information contact the hamlet office (ⓣ 867 978 2351) or visit ⓦ aklavik.ca for information on accommodation, tours and upcoming events.

ACCOMMODATION AND EATING

Aklavik Inn ⓣ 867 978 2461. In town, there are two stores, two restaurants and a two-room boarding house, the *Aklavik Inn*. You can prepare your own meals here or pay extra for half- or full board. **$225**

Paulatuk

PAULATUK, 400km east of Inuvik, is one of NWT's smallest permanent communities. Situated on a spur between the Beaufort and an inland lake, the settlement was started by the Roman Catholic Mission in 1935 as a communal focus for the seminomadic Karngmalit, who despite such paternalism have fought off the adverse effects of missionaries and trader-introduced alcoholism to hang on to some of their old ways. The village's name means "place of soot", a reference to the coal seams to the northeast, where the (literally) Smoking Hills take their name from the smouldering coal ignited years ago and still burning.

Hunting, fishing and trapping still provide their economic staples, along with handicrafts aimed at the tourists here mainly for the chance to watch or hunt big game. Key sites for the former activity are the cliffs of the Cape Parry Bird Sanctuary and the **Tuktut Nogait National Park** on the Parry Peninsula to the west, a calving ground for the migrating Bluenose caribou herd of 20,000. Local operators will take you out to both areas, and in spring run trips to look for polar bears on the Amundsen Gulf.

ARRIVAL AND INFORMATION PAULATUK

By plane Aklak Air flights (ⓣ 867 777 3777, ⓣ 866 707 4977, ⓦ aklakair.ca) operate three times weekly from Inuvik.
Tourist information For information on activities or accommodation contact the hotel or the hamlet office (ⓣ 867 580 3531) or drop by at the Parks Canada interpretive centre (Mon–Fri 9am–5pm; ⓣ 867 580 3233, ⓔ inuvik. info@pc.gc.ca), located in the *Paulatuk Visitor Centre Hotel*, for information on the park and on licensed guides.

11

ACCOMMODATION AND EATING

Paulatuk Visitor Centre Hotel ☎ 867 580 3051. The only reliable accommodation option is this place, which has ten rooms, kitchen facilities (basic meals available) and a small store; though it's best to bring your own supplies. They'll also help you arrange tours. **$285**

The Sahtu

The **Sahtu** embraces the Mackenzie River south of its delta as far as Tulita and the great swath of land across to and including **Great Bear Lake** to the east, the world's eighth largest lake. There's no year-round road access: you either drive on the famed winter access road, fly in, canoe the Mackenzie – no mean feat – or sign up with **fishing** and hunting charters that boat or fly you into the backcountry, home to some of North America's finest fishing lodges and lakes. In 1994 a road was built as far as Wrigley, 225km northwest of Fort Simpson (see page 849), but plans to push it through to Inuvik have been a long time in the making. In the meantime, most tours operate out of the area's nominal capital at **Norman Wells**, on the banks of the Mackenzie River in the lee of the Franklin Mountains, which separate the river and Great Bear Lake. The Sahtu has just four other communities: **Fort Good Hope**, north of Norman Wells; **Déline** on Great Bear Lake; **Colville Lake**, north of Great Bear Lake; and **Tulita**, south of Norman Wells.

Norman Wells

The region's largest transport hub and community, **NORMAN WELLS** overlooks the Mackenzie River. The town owes its economic well-being to **oil**: the local Dene long knew this region as Le Gohlini – "place where the oil is" – and explorer Alexander Mackenzie first noticed a yellow liquid seeping from the rocks in 1789. The stuff only began to be fully exploited in 1919 after Dene locals led geologists to the same spot. Drilling and refinement on an industrial scale began in 1932 and increased during World War II when the US government sponsored the building of the **Canol pipeline** to supply the Alaska Highway. The pipeline was abandoned in 1945 and its old route is now the **Canol Heritage Trail** (see box below).

You can follow the oil and Canol story in the **Norman Wells Historical Centre** (year-round, call for hours; free; ☎ 867 587 2415, ✆ normanwellsmuseum.com), 23 Mackenzie Drive, which is filled with photographs, modest displays and odd memorabilia. Alongside, the settlement's uniquely ecumenical **church** does double duty: Catholics sit on one side, Protestants on the other.

THE CANOL HERITAGE TRAIL

The **Canol Heritage Trail**, and the attached **Doi T'oh Territorial Park**, is becoming an increasingly popular **long-distance wilderness trail**. Stretching some 372km from Norman Wells to the Yukon border, the journey can take three to four weeks and ranks among the world's tougher treks, passing through some of the NWT's most spectacular ranges. The route meanders through the Mackenzie Mountains west of Norman Wells, across three challenging rivers (at least one must be crossed by raft) and through **grizzly bear** country. Unless you sign up for a tour to see this magnificent but utterly wild region, you should have **extensive backcountry experience**. If you do venture on the trail without a guide, inform the local detachment of the RCMP about your itinerary in either Dawson City (☎ 867 993 2677) or in Ross River, Yukon (☎ 867 969 2677).

Mountain River Outfitters and Canoe North Adventures (see page 848) provide both package tours and logistical support for individual hikers on the Canol trail.

ARRIVAL AND INFORMATION   NORMAN WELLS

By plane Canadian North flies daily to Norman Wells from Inuvik, Yellowknife and Edmonton, while First Airways flies four times weekly from the same locations (see page 795). North-Wright Air flies to Yellowknife and Inuvik (charters ☎ 867 587 2288, reservations ☎ 867 587 2333, ✆ north-wrightairways.com) and offers sightseeing flights. The airport is a 20min walk from the centre of the town.

Tourist office The town's tourist office is in the Historical Centre (see page 847) and has information on nearby hiking trails.

ACTIVITIES AND TOURS

Fishing trips For details of the many fishing-charter companies enquire locally or download a copy of the *Explorers' Guide* (☎ 800 661 0788, ✆ spectacularnwt.com).

Canoeing Mountain River Outfitters (☎ 867 587 2697, ✉ rickmuyres@gmail.com) runs day-trips up the Mackenzie River to Fort Good Hope and the Arctic Circle (mid-June to mid-Sept), provides logistical support for the Canol Trail and rents canoes and other outdoor equipment.

Canoe North Adventures (☎ 867 587 4440, ✆ canoenorth adventures.com) supplies logistical support and package tours of the surrounding rivers and lakes. They also rent out canoe and camping gear.

ACCOMMODATION AND EATING

Canoe North Lodge ☎ 867 587 4440, ✆ canoenorth adventures.com. Run by the outfitting company, the cosy facility here consists of a half-dozen doubles plus bunks and wall tents, shared baths, TV lounge, dining area and coffee bar. Prices are per person and breakfast is included. **$135**

Heritage Hotel 27 Mackenzie Drive ☎ 867 587 5000, ✆ heritagehotelnwt.com. With very few options in town, the *Heritage Hotel* is surprisingly good. They can organise fishing tours and other activities, and the on-site restaurant is a local favourite, too. **$250**

The Deh Cho Trail

Northern Alberta and the adjoining southern portion of the NWT were first opened up to trade courtesy of the mighty rivers that flow through these parts. Traders, particularly the Hudson's Bay Company, used routes along the Peace, Hay, Slave, Liard and Mackenzie rivers to maintain remote outposts and foster commercial relations with local First Nations people. Some of these far-flung communities have survived to the present day, and the circuit of roads connecting them has become known as the **Deh Cho Trail**, which local tourism organizations promote extensively in a bid to lure travellers away from the Alaska Highway.

The southern parts of this 3000km route weave its way through an all but uninhabited landscape of rippling hills, rivers, lakes, lonely farms and open prairie. Yet most of the route passes through a monotonous mantle of forest and after hours of motoring through it, the region's very modest communities appear as exceptional highlights. In truth, they offer very few attractions worthy of a stop. The sheer untrammelled wilderness is a boon for adventurers, especially **anglers** or **boaters**. Kayakers and canoers will find extraordinary rapids and waterfalls, and long-distance lake and river systems invite expeditions. But for most outdoor enthusiasts, the main reason to travel the Deh Cho Trail is to reach a trio of attractions off it: the impressive wilderness of **Nahanni National Park**, the bison and crane sanctuary of **Wood Buffalo National Park**, and **Yellowknife** (see page 853), the capital city of the NWT and one of Canada's most accessible and reliable places to enjoy the Northern Lights.

The Deh Cho loop incorporates the initial leg of the **Alaska Highway** (see page 813) before branching off near Fort Nelson onto the **Liard Highway**. This is a long, largely gravel road passing within sight of Nahanni National Park and close to **Fort Simpson**, from where the **Mackenzie Highway** (Hwy-1) pushes its way east and then south beyond the Alberta border (as Hwy-35) to **Peace River**. A number of highways there allow you to complete the loop back to BC.

INFORMATION   THE DEH CHO TRAIL

Deh Cho Connection See ✆ spectacularnwt.com for information (where to stay, route suggestions, driving advice) on all three of the provinces the trail touches (you can also find links to visitor centre websites of the communities alongside it).

GETTING AROUND

By plane Because the roads barely merit travelling for their own sake, flying is a tempting time-saving option, though it is expensive unless you organize flights well in advance. **By bus** The Hay River-based Frontier Coachlines, 16 102nd St (☏ 867 874 2566, ⓦ frontiercoachlinesnwtltd.ca), which

THE DEH CHO TRAIL

runs buses to Fort Providence, Yellowknife and Fort Smith. **By car** If you decide to drive, fuel up at virtually every community you pass and, if you are going to camp, prepare for the unwelcome nocturnal attention of bears.

The Liard Highway leg: North of Fort Nelson

Beginning 35km north of Fort Nelson, the **Liard Highway** – or BC Hwy-77, which becomes NWT Hwy-7 – pushes north through forested wilderness to the regional centre Fort Simpson. En route it passes the hamlet of **Fort Liard** and offers great views of Nahanni National Park from the road- and riverside **Blackstone Territorial Park** (19 campgrounds; $22.50; ⓦ nwtparks.ca/campgrounds) where there's also a couple of short hiking trails. The road conditions are generally very good even though the highway's surface is gravel for much of its length. Icy winter conditions pose a threat, as do bison that can wander onto the road at any time of year.

11

Fort Simpson

All means of access and facilities – including tour operators and outfitters – for the Nahanni National Park are in busy **FORT SIMPSON**, 150km to the park's east, at the confluence of the Liard and Mackenzie rivers. This spot has been inhabited for nine thousand years by the Slavey peoples and their ancestors, making it the longest continually inhabited region in the NWT. Most of the town's resources are along the main drag, **100th Street**, effectively a continuation of the primary road through town, while the bulk of the outfitters' offices are gathered north of the strip at the top of the nearly parallel Mackenzie Drive. At the southern end of Mackenzie Drive, you'll find the site of the old Hudson's Bay Company post and an area known as the "Flat" or the Papal Grounds, whose teepee and other developments date from the papal visit here in September 1987. If you're hoping to stay in town, be sure to book ahead.

ARRIVAL AND INFORMATION

By plane You can get to Fort Simpson by air twice daily (not Sat) from Yellowknife using either Air Tindi (☏ 867 669 8260, ☏ 888 545 6794, ⓦ airtindi.com) or First Air (see page 795). The main airport is 12km south of town, while a light plane and floatplane airstrip lies just to the northwest of downtown.

FORT SIMPSON

Tourist information Ask at the first building on the left as you come into town (mid-May to mid-Sept Mon–Fri 8.30am–8pm, Sat & Sun 9am–8pm; mid-Sept to mid-May Mon–Fri 1–5pm; summer ☏ 867 695 3182, winter ☏ 867 695 2253, ⓦ fortsimpson.com).

ACCOMMODATION

Deh Cho Suites 10509 Antoine Drive ☏ 867 695 2309, ☏ 877 695 2309, ⓦ dehchosuites.com. Beautifully decorated accommodation in a quiet area of town. Twelve suites and rooms with private bath, mini-fridges, wi-fi and satellite TV. Access to a barbecue, laundry facilities and shared kitchen supplied with breakfast options. $195

Fort Simpson Territorial Park campground The local campground, just southwest of the Papal Grounds in Fort Simpson Territorial Park, is operated on a first-come, first-served basis but has lots of space, showers and fire wood. RVs $22.50; RV hook-up $28

Janor Guest House 10003 99B Ave ☏ 867 695 2077, ⓦ janor.ca. Fort Simpon's best-kept secret. This quaint guesthouse, with six rooms (two with private bath), is

located downtown across from the high school. Continental breakfast included, and guests can pick veggies from the back garden to prep their meals in the shared kitchen. High-speed internet, laundry facilities and barbecue are also available, as is an airport shuttle. $150

Maroda Motel 9802 100th St ☏ 867 695 2201, ⓦ nahanni-inn.com. The small and low slung *Maroda Motel* is a couple of blocks south of, and smaller than, sister hotel *Nahanni Inn*. Half of the units have fully equipped kitchenettes and some rooms are pet friendly. $170

Nahanni Inn 10001 Marc Andre Ave ☏ 867 695 2201, ⓦ nahanni-inn.com. The 40-room *Nahanni Inn* is a fairly standard motel in Fort Simpson Territorial Park with coffee shop and dining room. $190

The Mackenzie Highway leg: Fort Simpson to Hay River

Though it takes its name from the lightly used leg that runs parallel to the Mackenzie River, the **Mackenzie Highway** is far more important for the section that hooks south through northern Alberta – providing the vital link for travellers driving between Edmonton, Yellowknife and Wood Buffalo National Park – to its "mile zero" at Grimshaw, Alberta. Though generally in excellent condition this road is about as dull as northern drives get: the highway ploughs through a tight corridor of seemingly endless evergreens in which views rarely open out, and little tempts you to get out and stretch your legs. The notable exceptions are the short and well-marked trails heading to occasional roadside cascades that have led local – and optimistic – tourism promoters to dub the highway the Waterfall Route.

The only stop of interest on the stretch of the Mackenzie Highway between Fort Simpson and the junction with Hwy-3 to Yellowknife (see page 855) is **Sambaa Deh Falls Territorial Park**, 150km east of Fort Simpson. From its campground, it's a ten-minute hike on an unmarked trail that heads upstream beside the river to a broad-shouldered, pounding waterfall. More impressive is the waterfall further downstream

11

NAHANNI NATIONAL PARK RESERVE

With gorges deeper than the Grand Canyon and waterfalls twice the height of Niagara, the vast **Nahanni National Park Reserve** (reserve office ☎ 867 695 7750, ⊛ pc.gc.ca/nahanni) ranks as one of North America's finest national parks and one of the most rugged wilderness areas anywhere in the world.

Designated a UNESCO World Heritage Site, the reserve is close to the Yukon border in the heart of the Mackenzie Mountains and surrounds the **South Nahanni River**, a renowned 322km stretch whose whitewater torrents, pristine mountains and 1200m-deep canyons have attracted explorers and thrill-seeking canoeists alike – this is home to one of the world's best whitewater runs. Unless you fit one of these categories or you fork out oodles of dollars for **guided trips** by boat or sightseeing by air, getting close to the best areas is difficult: the park is roadless and wild and there are no formal trails, although heavy use has made some routes well defined.

A **reservation** and **fee** system is in place for people wishing to use the park: the day-use fee is $24.50. There are strict quotas on visitors, so check the latest details whether you intend to visit independently or with a tour. For full information, contact the reserve office or the tourist office in Fort Simpson.

As for **tours**, operators in Fort Simpson cater to all levels of demand, from day-trippers wanting air tours of the big set-pieces to self-contained canoers and walkers on month-long expeditions who require no more than a drop-off or pick-up by air. **Day-trips** will likely depend on availability, so book well in advance. If you are in a party of fewer than three and just turn up, contact the airlines and ask to be put on a waiting list – they will contact you if they find others to fill a trip. The spectacular **Virginia Falls** is the park's most popular day-trip.

TOUR OPERATORS

Canadian River Expeditions ☎ 867 668 3180, ☎ 800 297 6927, ⊛ nahanni.com. Offers one- to two-week canoeing, kayaking and rafting trips (from $5775, plus park fee of $200).

Nahanni Wilderness Adventure ☎ 403 678 3374, ☎ 888 897 5223, ⊛ nahanniwild.com. Offers a variety of multi-day rafting, canoeing and hiking excursions on the Nahanni (from $6640).

North Nahanni Naturalist Lodge ☎ 867 695 2116, ☎ 888 880 6665, ⊛ nahannilodge.com. Offers other tours of the region and accommodation in a pleasant

backcountry lodge (from $2000 for five days).

Simpson Air ☎ 867 695 2505, ☎ 866 995 2505, ⊛ simpsonair.ca. Offers floatplane day-trips from $542.50/person, as well as a combined flight and cabin rental on Little Doctor Lake (contact for prices).

Wolverine Air ☎ 867 695 2263, ☎ 888 695 2263, ⊛ wolverineair.com. Take groups of three for a day-trip by floatplane to Nahanni for $2200, with stops at Virginia Falls (1.5hr stopover), Glacier Lake (1hr stopover) and for a few minutes at the idyllic Little Doctor Lake at the edge of the mountain range.

– in view of the highway and the campground turn-off – where waters plummet dramatically into a narrow gorge.

More waterfalls dot the road beyond the junction with Hwy-3 to Yellowknife, where the Mackenzie Highway is paved for its remaining 186km journey to the Alberta border. The most impressive of these falls are the 33m-high **Alexandra Falls**, located 72km shy of the Alberta border. South of Alberta's provincial border the Mackenzie Highway becomes **Hwy-35** and a string of campgrounds provides the only accommodation en route to the town of **High Level** (see page 852), 191km from the NWT border.

ACCOMMODATION AND EATING   THE MACKENZIE HIGHWAY LEG

Services along the NWT stretch of the Mackenzie Hwy are limited to *Lisa's Place*. A better selection of food and accommodation can be had 43km away at **Hay River** (see below).

Camping You can camp at: Lady Evelyn Falls Territorial Park near Kakiska and the junction to Hwy-3; at Louise Falls and Alexandra Falls in Twin Falls Territorial Park; and at the 60th Parallel Visitors' Centre (mid-May to mid-Sept

8.30am–8.30pm; ☏ 867 875 5570) on the Alberta border. Tent site $15, RV $28

Lisa's Place 230 Northern Lights St, Enterprise ☏ 867 984 3711, ⊛ lisasplacenwt.com. The only motel nearby is the basic *Lisa's Place* in the village of Enterprise; it also has a convenience store (with sandwiches on sale) and the only petrol station around (daily 7am–midnight). $95

Hay River

HAY RIVER – the gateway to the third largest lake in North America, and to **Fort Smith** and **Wood Buffalo National Park** (see page 853) – is a typical no-nonsense northern town. Situated on the **Great Slave Lake** at the mouth of the Hay River, it's been inhabited for thousands of years by the Dene people. White settlers had put it on the map by 1854, but it wasn't until the 1940s that the town became an important transport centre. It's now also one of the most important **ports** in the North, shipping freight up the Mackenzie River in huge barges to provide a precarious lifeline for High Arctic communities as far away as Inuvik and Tuktoyaktuk. If you're stuck in town, the best way to kill time is to wander down to the wharves for a look.

Across a bridge to the north, Vale Island centres on Mackenzie Drive and is home to the wharves, airport, the remnants of the old town, the campground and a series of passable and popular **beaches** (7km from the centre of New Town). The best sand is near the campground on the northeast side of the island at the end of 106th Avenue.

ARRIVAL AND INFORMATION   HAY RIVER

By plane Regular flights run to Yellowknife with Buffalo Airways and First Air; the latter also provides six flights per week to Edmonton.

By bus Frontier Coachlines (see page 849) run a bus service to Hay River.

Destinations Fort Smith (3 weekly; 7hr); Yellowknife (5

weekly; 12hr).

Tourist office Hwy-2 south of the New Town centre on the corner with McBryan Drive (mid-May to mid-Sept Mon–Thurs 8am–8pm, Fri–Sun 8.30am–9pm, mid-Sept to mid-May Mon–Fri 8.30am–5pm; ☏ 867 874 3180, ⊛ hayriver. com).

ACCOMMODATION AND EATING

Harbour Guest House 31 Capital Drive ☏ 867 874 2233. An economical but very pleasant choice along the beach on Vale Island; there's a deck with Great Slave Lake views. Shared kitchen, living room and dining room. $170

Hay River Campground You can camp (and swim) near the beach on Vale Island. 35 sites and a new shower block. Mid-May to mid-Sept. $18

North Country Inn 912 Mackenzie Hwy ☏ 867 874 5706, ☏ 877 362 4206, ⊛ ncinn.ca. If you'd rather be close

to downtown try this spot between New Town and the Vale Island bridge. Each room has a bathtub, a kitchenette and free wi-fi, and there's a launderette on site. $149

Ptarmigan Inn 10 J. Gagnier St ☏ 867 874 6781, ☏ 800 661 0842, ⊛ ptarmiganinn.com. For the most comfort after a long haul, try the downtown *Ptarmigan Inn*, which has a fitness centre, sauna and sports bar. It also has the nicest restaurant in town, *Keys Dining*. $161

11

High Level

You're only going to stop in **HIGH LEVEL** – 191km south of the NWT border and 250km north of Peace River – if you want a place to bed down. The huge stock of motel accommodation means room rates are very reasonable – yet many of the town's thousand guest rooms are block-booked in advance by seasonal workers. From here south to Manning – the next motel cluster – only a couple of basic campgrounds and the odd wind-blown store disturb the peace.

INFORMATION   HIGH LEVEL

Tourist office 10803 96th St, alongside Hwy-35 at the southern edge of town (summer daily 9am–8pm; rest of year Tues–Sat 9am–4pm; ☎780 926 4811).

ACCOMMODATION AND EATING

Aspen Ridge Campground 3km south of the centre on Hwy-35 ☎780 926 4540, ⍟aspenridgecampground.ca. The best option for campers with forty sites between tall trees. Each site has a fire pit, and firewood is available. May–Oct. Sites $20; RV $35

Flamingo Inn 9802 97th St ☎780 926 8844, ⍟flamingoinnhighlevel.com. A popular hotel with 24hr reception and an adjoining restaurant serving tasty pasta and stir-fry dinner specials. $99

Four Winds Centre 10310 97th St ☎780 926 3736, ⍟fourwindscentre.com. The 75 units here are usually the cheapest option among all the town's rooms, and the WINDS Lounge and VLT Game (until 3am) Room here are usually well-attended. $60

Quality Inn 9704 97th St ☎780 926 4222, ⍟qualityinnhighlevel.com. The hotel is a good bit smarter than other options in High Level, with rooms all boasting flat screen TVs. The steaks at the on-site steakhouse are the best in town. $120

Super 8 9502 114th Ave ☎780 841 3448, ☎800 454 3213. Standard rooms at this Wyndham hotel, although guests here do have access to a pool with a waterslide and a gym. Breakfast and parking (even RVs) are included. $129

Peace River

If you're travelling under your own steam you'll probably end up staying overnight in **PEACE RIVER**, 486km from Edmonton. The largest town in the region, it has a handful of standard **motels**. From Peace River, the Deh Cho Trail completes its loop by continuing to Grimshaw, where the Mackenzie Highway officially ends. You can take Hwy-2 from either back into BC.

INFORMATION   PEACE RIVER

Tourist office The tourist office operates out of the old station building at 9309 100th St (summer daily 10am–6pm; ☎780 624 2044, ⍟peaceriver.ca).

ACCOMMODATION AND EATING

Peace River Lions' Club ☎780 624 2120. For campers there's this 110-site place with showers (coin-operated) at Lions' Club Park on the west side of the river. April–Oct. $20; RVs $30

Peace Valley Inns 9609 101st St ☎780 624 2020, ☎800 661 5897, ⍟peacevalleyinns.com. The best choice in town, with a variety of rooms (some with fireplaces, double bathrooms or balconies) on the northern edge of downtown. Pub on-site, too. $119

Su Casa Café 9822 95th St ☎780 624 8262. This café tucked away near the river has authentic Mexican meals, delivered in huge portions. Tues–Fri 11am–2pm & 5–9pm, Sat 1–9pm.

Fort Smith and around

Beginning near Hay River, lonely Hwy-5 is the only overland route to **Fort Smith**, just over Alberta's northern border in the Northwest Territories, which in turn is the only conceivable base for exploring the adjacent **Wood Buffalo National Park** (see page 853). The drive's an easy 280km haul through forest and swampy muskeg, with the last 150km running within park boundaries on the park's only paved road. It's easy to spend an enjoyable couple of days touring here – and even Fort Smith, modest as it is, is a likeable base to soak up some Northern atmosphere.

Northern Life Museum & Cultural Centre

110 King St • June–Aug Mon–Fri 10am–5pm, Sat 1–5pm; Sept–May Mon–Fri 10am–noon and 1–5pm • Free • ☎ 867 872 2859, ⓦ nlmcc.ca

There are a handful of things to see around town before visiting the park, in particular its good local history institution, the **Northern Life Museum**, worth a look for its excellent collection of traditional artefacts, crafts and fur-trading memorabilia, including a replica birchbark canoe and archive photographs. In addition, there's a permanent exhibit on the traditions of Indigenous groups like the Chipewyan, the Cree and the Dene.

The rapids

If you fancy a short **hike** or two and a chance to see some of the region's famous white pelicans, try exploring the series of rapids beside town and upstream. All are linked by the Trans Canada Trail, but can be visited from trailheads starting beside the road to Fort Fitzgerald southeast of town. A map is available from the tourist office though the trails themselves are easy enough to follow. **Mountain Rapids**, about 8km southeast of Fort Smith, are of particular interest as the location of a white pelican colony, while **Pelican Rapids** – 12km from Fort Smith and a 45-minute walk through dense vegetation from the road – are most memorable for their thundering bulk. They're readily viewed at close quarters from tongues of granite Canadian Shield that jut into the centre of the watercourse.

ARRIVAL AND DEPARTURE

FORT SMITH

By plane The easiest access to Fort Smith and the park is by plane, but isn't cheap. Northwestern Air (☎ 877 872 2216, ⓦ nwal.ca) offers daily flights to/from Yellowknife (around $800 return) and Edmonton (roughly $1400 return). The airport is 5km west of town on McDougal Rd. For a taxi from here call Portage Cabs (☎ 867 872 3333) or Duck Soup Cabs (☎ 867 872 4747).

By bus Frontier Coachlines (see page 849) runs three buses per week from Hay River.

GETTING AROUND AND INFORMATION

Fort Smith's tourist office 108 King St in the recreation complex, beside the Northern Life Museum (daily June–Aug daily 9am–6pm, Sept–May Mon–Fri 9am–noon, 1–5pm; ☎ 867 872 8400, ⓦ fortsmith.ca).

National Park visitor centre Excellent centre a short distance west at 149 McDougal Rd (mid-May to early Sept daily 9am–6pm; late Sept to mid-May Mon–Fri 9am–noon & 1–5pm; ☎ 867 872 7960, ⓦ parkscanada.gc.ca/buffalo).

Maps and guides Can be found in the cluster of shops at the intersection of McDougal Rd and Portage Ave in the Rusty Raven (☎ 867 872 2606).

ACCOMMODATION AND EATING

Pelican Rapids Inn 152 McDougal Rd ☎ 867 872 2789, ⓦ pelicanrapidsinn.com. The town's hotels are similar in terms of quality, though the larger *Pelican Rapids Inn* is fractionally more convenient at the centre of downtown and home to the town's only restaurant. **$162**

Queen Elizabeth Territorial Park Campground There's a public campground in Queen Elizabeth Territorial Park alongside the Slave River on the northern edge of town. Sites **$15**; RVs **$28**

Whooping Crane Guest House 13 Cassette Crescent ☎ 867 872 3426, ⓦ whoopingcraneguesthouse.com. A very comfortable choice offering two large rooms in an octagonal log cabin or an apartment suite with lounge, full kitchen and bathroom. Each unit has a TV, small refrigerator, private bathroom and access to wi-fi. Guests also have access to bicycles. Delicious home-cooked breakfasts served daily. **$135**

Wood Buffalo National Park

Straddling the border between Alberta and the Northwest Territories, **WOOD BUFFALO NATIONAL PARK** is bigger than Switzerland, making it Canada's largest national park and the world's second-largest protected environment (the largest is in Greenland). Wild and vast, the park is limited to low hills, lakes, grasslands, boreal forest, salt plains and marsh. These drain into the Peace and Athabasca rivers and then into Lake Claire, forming one of the world's largest freshwater deltas in the process. To the casual visitor the landscape is subtle and unassuming – there are no real "sights" or scenic set pieces to compare with, say, the Rockies – but for dedicated naturalists, or those who are prepared to spend time (and money) letting the landscapes get under their skin, the park holds much of interest, embracing North America's finest limestone formations, classic swaths of coniferous forest and rare salt-plain habitats.

The park was created in 1922 to protect an estimated 1500 wood bison, but since then it has also become a vital refuge for around fifty other species of mammal, including black bear and lynx. The Peace–Athabasca Delta in the park's southeast corner boasts 227 species of wildfowl – no fewer than four major migration routes cross the area. The world's only river rookery of rare **white pelicans** is here and the park is the last refuge of the critically endangered **whooping crane** – discovered nesting in a remote part of the park in 1954 after it was assumed hunters supplying the decorative demands of European aristocrats had made them extinct. Though there were only 21 of the majestic birds in the park in 1954, there are over 230 today – about half the total world population (most of the others are in captivity). Each boasts a 2.4m wingspan and nests far from any human contamination on the park's northern fringes. The presence of the cranes, bison, and the various rare and unspoiled habitats saw the park declared a UNESCO World Heritage Site in 1983. Another claim to fame is that it's the most northerly breeding site for **red-sided garter snakes**. Able to hibernate in the warm cracks in the limestone bedrock during the winter, in spring these snakes join dozens of others for mating to create an unforgettable writhing mass.

Exploring the park

The best way to absorb the landscape of the park is probably from the air or on a tour (see page 855), or by paddling a canoe around the almost limitless Athabasca, Peace and Slave river systems that were once the main route for trade from the south. The easiest and cheapest way to see some of the park independently is to spend a long day driving a clockwise loop through its northeastern corner from Fort Smith. Completing this loop relies on the use of a sandy dirt road called **Parson's Lake Road**. Make sure you check on its current condition and suitability for your vehicle at the park tourist office in Fort Smith.

To follow this loop, drive southwest from Fort Smith on Hwy-5, turning off at 8km and following the road to Peace Point. Possible stops along here include the **Salt River Day Use Area** (after 27km), where you can hike the 750m Karstland Loop that acts as an introduction to the local geology, and is also the start of the straightforward 16.5km day-hike. Stop at a small roadside parking lot about 3km southwest along the road from the Salt River Day Use Area to reach the scenic highlight of this loop: **Grosbeak Lake**, a bleak salt lake flecked with salt-etched rocks which can be reached via an hour-long round-trip hike. The intersection of the main park road with the **Parson's Lake Road** comes after another 10km. This 42km-long, sandy and often impassable road is the best place to see bison, with good chances of spotting bears along the way also. The road finishes in a junction with a dirt road (close to Hwy-5) you can follow to the **Salt Plains Lookout** for fantastic views of the park and the chance to wander across these remarkable plains. From here the 30km back to Fort Smith on the sealed Hwy-5 quickly completes the loop.

As an alternative, you can canoe 12km downstream from Peace Point (10–12hr) to reach the most-visited backcountry area of the park, the meadowland and delta habitat of **Sweetgrass Station**, which is a prime viewing spot for buffalo, wolves and wetlands wildlife. For more information on the park's waterways, see the waterway guide at Ⓦpc. gc.ca/buffalo.

THE WOOD BISON OF WOOD BUFFALO

The largest land mammal in North America, the **wood bison** – commonly called the wood buffalo – is the longer-legged, darker and more robust relative of the plains bison. Like the plains bison, the wood bison were mercilessly hunted to the brink of extinction by the 1890s, which helped prompt the creation of **Wood Buffalo National Park** in 1922. Soon after its designation, local herds were bolstered in a dubious way by the introduction of some six thousand plains bison. As a result, some of the bison in Wood Buffalo National Park today show traits of plains bison, but an even more contentious consequence was the spread of tuberculosis and brucellosis – already rampant in the plains herd – to animals throughout the park. This has created a long-simmering row between conservationists and Alberta's beef lobby, with some asserting the only way to prevent the spread of the diseases (which they claim are highly infectious) to elk and to Alberta's valuable beef herds is to kill all the bison off. Those opposed to this plan point out the herd has been infected since the 1920s, yet the disease has survived by internal regulation and natural balance, with animals showing few outward signs of the diseases or of suffering. Furthermore, there has never been an instance of those diseases transferring to humans. Most locals, who are largely opposed to the cull, argue that killing or inoculating every animal would be a daunting task, given the immensity of the animals' range.

The two disease-free northern herds – that range around the Mackenzie Bison Sanctuary (which surrounds much of Hwy-3 to Yellowknife) and the Liard Highway near Fort Simpson – are kept that way by constant vigilance in a bison no-go area: any bison found here, disease free or not, are shot. Meanwhile, as a long-term management solution is debated, the park's buffalo – now around five thousand – continue to nibble contentedly.

TOURS AND ACTIVITIES

Tours One licensed operator is Taiga Tour Company (☎ 867 872 8096, ⓦ taigatour.com), which offers a full spectrum of paddling and birdwatching tours from around $1000/person, including three nights' accommodation; eleven-day expeditions can be arranged by snowmobile, dog-sled or canoe. Wood Buffalo Park also offers hiking tours and programmes for visitor groups. Phone ahead to the tourist

WOOD BUFFALO NATIONAL PARK

office (☎ 867 872 7960) to schedule your hike for less than $15/person.

Sightseeing flights Cheaper and far quicker are the sightseeing flights offered by Northwestern Air (☎ 877 872 2216, ⓦ nwal.ca) and Reliance Airways (☎ 780 464 7537, ⓦ andrewlakelodge.com/reliance-airways-ltd); prices start at around $125/person for 30min.

ACCOMMODATION

If you want to overnight in the park, the only serviced campground is at Pine Lake. **Backcountry camping** is allowed anywhere in the park if it's at least 1500m from Pine Lake or any road or trail. The park tourist office can advise on good spots and general precautions.

Pine Lake Campground 60km south of Fort Smith. Pine Lake is the easiest option and gives you access to its

day-use area, pleasant beach and lakeshore hiking trails. $15.70

Sweetgrass Station You can stay in the cabin (bunks) here free of charge, but must first register with the park tourist office in Fort Smith. Drinking water comes from the river and needs to be boiled and treated. To get here you'll need to canoe (see above) or charter a motorboat.

Yellowknife

Surrounded by endless expanses of northern lakes, forests and great wilderness, the NWT's capital city, **YELLOWKNIFE**, is named after the copper knives of the First Nations Slavey people. Today, this city of 22,000 attracts adventure seekers who come to experience the city's legendary hospitality, its Northern Lights, an array of cultural events and a mind-boggling selection of canoe routes and fishing spots. Despite its large-city size, Yellowknife has managed to keep its frontier-town atmosphere.

The city's high-rise core of offices and government buildings exists to administer the NWT and support its population in a region whose resources – despite the recent discovery of diamonds to the north in 1991 – should by all rights support only a small town. Even the Hudson's Bay Company closed its trading post here as early as 1823 on the grounds of economics and, except for traces of gold found by prospectors on the way to the Klondike in 1898, the spot was a forgotten backwater until the advent of commercial gold and uranium mining in the 1930s. This prompted the growth of the **Old Town** on an island and rocky peninsula on Great Slave Lake, and then in 1947 the **New Town** on the sandy plain behind it. In 1967, the year a road to the outside world was completed (Edmonton is 1524km away by car), Yellowknife replaced Ottawa as the seat of government for the NWT. Oiled by bureaucratic profligacy and the odd gold mine, the city has blossomed ever since.

Much of Yellowknife's accessible hinterland is an ideal playground for paddlers and naturalists, or for hunters on the trail of the region's 400,000-strong herd of caribou. Shops around town sell a variety of expensive northern First Nations crafts, but these are cheaper than you'll find in more southerly cities.

The Old Town

Visitors are steered carefully down the main street, Franklin Avenue (50th Avenue), and down the long hill from the new town to quaint Old Town cabins such as the **Wildcat Café** (see page 858). Elsewhere, the Old Town is a shakedown of pitted and buckled roads (the result of permafrost) and a few quaintly battered buildings on the aptly named Ragged Ass Road and Willow Road. These are more or less the only remnants of the old times.

Prince of Wales Northern Heritage Centre

Daily 10.30am–5.30pm, Thurs until 9pm • Free • ☎ 867 873 7551, ⓦ pwnhc.ca

The **Prince of Wales Northern Heritage Centre** is on the shore of Frame Lake, across from city hall in the downtown core. As Yellowknife's key attraction, the centre showcases the culture, heritage and history of the Northwest Territories. The permanent Tundra and Taiga galleries highlight the landscapes and cultures from above and below the treeline respectively, and other exhibits feature topics such as ice age mammals, the Yellowknives Dene First Nation, Indigenous Special Constables and the RCMP. The community exhibit and contemporary art spaces showcase different works every six months and the centre also includes a café, the NWT Archives and an interactive children's area.

Northwest Territories Legislative Assembly

Tours June–Aug Mon–Fri 10.30am, 1.30pm & 3.30pm, Sun 1.30pm; Sept–May Mon–Fri 10.30am • Free • ☎ 867 669 2230, ☎ 800 661 0784, ⓦ assembly.gov.nt.ca

---

YELLOWKNIFE'S FESTIVALS

Yellowknife itself springs to life during its many **festivals**; for more information on the city's events and other attractions, check ⓦ spectacularnwt.com and ⓦ visityellowknife.com.

Snowking Festival March ⓦ snowking.ca. One of the most intriguing of Yellowknife's festivals, with attractions during the month-long party that include a snow castle constructed on Yellowknife Bay, fireworks, art exhibits, a film festival and plenty of music and food.

Yellowknife Summer Solstice Festival June 21. A midsummer celebration is celebrated with street events, a golf tournament with tee-off times under the midnight sun, and a host of cultural and musical performances.

Folk on the Rocks Mid-July ⓦ folkontherocks.com. Annual event with 24 hours of song on five stages over one weekend, during which folk singers from across Canada and the US meet Inuit and Dene singers, folk dancers and the famous Inuit "throat singers" in an amazing medley of world music.

Just northwest of the centre, also on Frame Lake, stands the $25-million **Northwest Territories Legislative Assembly**, opened in 1993 (there are only nineteen members). It's an impressive piece of architecture, much of it open to public view. There is a café on-site (Mon–Fri 9am–5pm).

Ingraham Trail

Close to town you can walk the trails around **Frame Lake** and from the campground on Long Lake (see page 858). Alternatively, you can drive out on the **Ingraham Trail**, an 81km highway that was to be the start of a major NWT "Road to Resources" but was abandoned in the 1960s. There are plenty of boat launches, picnic sites and campgrounds en route, as well as short walking trails like the **Cameron River Falls** (48km from Yellowknife) and lakeside beaches where the hardier of the city's population brave the water.

ARRIVAL AND DEPARTURE   YELLOWKNIFE

11

By plane There are regular Canadian North and First Air flights to Edmonton, with Canadian North also flying to Calgary and both airlines to Iqaluit, Nunavut. Numerous smaller airlines serve most NWT and many Nunavut destinations. Yellowknife's airport is 5km west of the city on Hwy-3. A taxi from there costs around $20; call City Cab (☎867 873 4444) or Diamond (☎867 873 6666). Listed below are only the main direct scheduled flights operated by the big carriers.

Destinations Cambridge Bay (daily; 1hr 30min); Edmonton (2–3 daily; 1hr 35min); Fort Smith (1 daily; 1hr 30min); Inuvik (1 daily; 2hr 35min); Iqaluit (3 weekly; 3hr); Norman Wells (1 daily; 1hr 15min); Rankin Inlet (3 weekly; 53min).

By bus Frontier Coachlines (☎867 874 2566, ⊛frontier coachlinesnwtltd.ca) runs three buses weekly from Hay River via Fort Smith.

INFORMATION AND GETTING AROUND

Car rental Companies at or near the airport include Budget, 20 Old Airport Rd (☎867 920 9209, ☎800 383 9211); elsewhere try National, downtown at 5118 50th St and at the airport (☎867 873 3424, ☎920 2970, ☎800 387 4747) or Hertz Yellowknife (☎867 766 3838, ☎800 263 0600), also at the airport. The city offers free three-day visitor parking passes to visitors using cars to get around town. Passes can be picked up at the temporary visitor centre inside city hall or at the airport gift shop.

Useful websites See ⊛ykonline.ca and ⊛yellowknife.ca (where you can download a visitors guide).

ACTIVITIES AND TOURS

Outdoor equipment rental To rent camping gear, canoes, snowmobiles, fishing tackle and other outdoor equipment, or to take part in a guided river trip, contact Narwal Northern Adventures, 4702 Anderson-Thomson blvd (☎867 873 6443, ⊛narwal.ca).

Tours Along with Inuvik, Yellowknife is the headquarters of most of the far North's outfitters and tour operators. Many licensed outfits run fishing, wildlife, Arctic sightseeing, canoeing, kayaking, boating and other trips, most ranging from one- or two-day outings up to full-blown three-week mini-expeditions to unimaginably wild areas. You'll find comprehensive listings in the *Explorers' Guide* booklet, obtainable from national tourist offices before your trip. For more information, check with the temporary visitor centre inside city hall or see online.

ACCOMMODATION

Hotel prices in the city are high, so it's worth looking up one of the dozen or so **B&Bs** if you're on a budget. If you plan to camp near the city or anywhere else in the territory, it is worth visiting ⊛campingnwt.ca.

Bayside B&B 3505 MacDonald Drive ☎867 445 5003, ⊛baysidenorth.com. Located in the heart of Old Town on the shores of Great Slave Lake, this quiet place offers a cabin and four rooms with a downstairs all-day café (*Dancing Moose*; see page 858) overlooking the waterfront, with a wraparound deck that affords a spectacular view of the bay. Floatplane mooring facilities available if you're flying in. **$105**

Blue Raven B&B 37 Otto Drive ☎867 873 6328, ⊕tmacfoto@acrticdata.ca. Cosy three-room B&B high on the bluff at the edge of Old Town. There are three simple, modern rooms with shared baths and grand views from its wonderful sundeck of Great Slave Lake. Fireplace in winter. Excellent home-cooked breakfasts. **$105**

Embleton House 5203 52nd St ☎867 873 2892, ☎888 909 5203, ⊛embletonhouse.com. Friendly B&B in a

quiet district two blocks from downtown. The seven rooms range from modest doubles with shared bath to a suite with kitchen and skylight for watching the Northern Lights. $120
Explorer Hotel 4825 49th Ave ☎ 867 873 3531, ☎ 800 661 0892, ⊚ explorerhotel.ca. *The Explorer* is the largest hotel in town with 187 rooms, and indeed it's the largest in northern Canada, serving both tourists and business travellers. There's a good restaurant on-site (with room service), fitness centre, flat-screen TVs and iPod alarm clocks. $183
Fred Henne Territorial Park Campground ☎ 867 920 2472. The only campground is the fully serviced *Fred Henne Territorial Park* by Long Lake off Hwy-3 north of the airport (2 miles from Yellowknife). Trails run to town from here via Frame Lake – allow about an hour, or you can follow the Prospectors' Trail north from the site, a good way to get a taste of the wilderness that encircles Yellowknife. Sites $15; RVs $32

EATING AND DRINKING

Yellowknife is increasingly becoming known for its fantastic range of **restaurants** that serve up everything from traditional pub fare to unique northern cuisine such as caribou, musk ox and arctic char. Most of the hotels have good dining rooms and much of the **nightlife** revolves around their lounges.

Black Knight Pub 4910 49th St ☎ 867 920 4041. Scottish bar that nonetheless has a menu peppered with other countries' fare (nachos, French onion soup, stir-fry, butter chicken, bangers and mash, steaks, burgers, and, oh yes, Scottish stew), it's become a popular spot for its great range of malts and adjoining *Top Knight* nightclub. Mon–Sat 11am–2am.

Bullocks Bistro 3534 Weaver Drive ☎ 867 873 3474. Fish and chips meets fine dining in this informal, yet fairly high-end restaurant. You'll find simply prepared local whitefish, cod, pike and trout on the menu (mains $20–40), along with some delicious chowders and mouth-watering musk-ox stew. Reservations recommended. Tues–Sat noon–9pm, Sun & Mon 4–9pm.

Dancing Moose Café 3505 McDonald Drive ☎ 867 669 8844. Perhaps the best place in town for breakfast, this charming café, with a panoramic view, offers a choice of waffles, omelettes, eggs Benedict, as well as lunch items including soups, sandwiches and home-cooked comfort foods. Mon–Sat 8am–3pm.

Javaroma Gourmet Coffee 5201 50th Ave ☎ 867 669 0725. Successfully formulaic coffee house (they've roasted their own beans since 1996), with good fresh bagels, pastries and sandwiches and a medley of styles of coffee on offer (they've got two more cafés at the airport, too). Mon–Fri 7am–10pm, Sat 8am–10pm, Sun 9am–10pm.

Taste of Saigon 4913 50th Ave ☎ 867 873 9777. Authentic Vietnamese dishes including a hearty *pho*, which will warm you up on a cold winter's day. Mon–Sat 11am–9pm.

Trader's Grill 4825 49th Ave in the Explorer Hotel ☎ 867 873 3531. Another fine-dining establishment with a menu offering a wide choice of northern country food, including musk ox, caribou and lemon butter arctic char (dinner mains $31–42). Voted the best Sunday brunch in town (reservations recommended). Mon–Fri 7am–2pm & 5–9pm, Sat & Sun 8am–2pm & 5–9pm.

Vietnamese Noodle House 4609 50th Ave ☎ 867 873 3399. Short on atmosphere but long on noodles: everyone in town knows these can't be beat. Mon–Thurs 11am–5pm, Fri 11am–midnight, Sat & Sun 11am–8pm.

★ **Wildcat Café** 3904 Wiley Rd ☎ 867 873 4004, ⊚ facebook.com/wildcatyellowknife. An atmospheric and endlessly busy little café in a log cabin, this is Yellowknife's oldest restaurant, operating since 1937. This Canadian landmark has served everyone from royalty to prime ministers and international celebrities. Expect to share a table while you enjoy a taste of the region ranging from the grilled arctic char ($34) to bison stew ($21) or a veggie burger ($16). June–Sept Mon–Fri 11.30am–10pm, Sat & Sun 10.30am–9pm.

Zehabesha 5004 51st Ave ☎ 867 873 6400. It's most unlikely that many locals call this the best restaurant in town, as it offers previously unfamiliar Ethiopian dishes. But the flavours are striking, and the fantastic value for the large portions is an added bonus. Dishes top out at near $20. Daily 11am–9pm.

Nunavut

Home to only 38,000 people, **Nunavut** (meaning "Our Land" in Inuktitut, the **Inuit** language) covers almost two million square kilometres – a fifth of Canada's land surface and an area five times the size of California, stretching west from Hudson Bay then north through the great "Barrenlands" of the interior to the Arctic islands in the north. From its western edge to the tip of Baffin Island in the east is 2000km (the distance from Washington, DC, to Denver). From north to south it's even more of a span – 2500km, the distance from London to Moscow.

Long an amorphous political entity administered by the federal government, the Northwest Territories was formally divided on April 1, 1999, by a land treaty which split the old territories in two and created a new central and eastern Arctic territory termed Nunavut. The signing followed fifteen years of low-profile but effective negotiating and campaigning, and produced the largest land deal in Canadian history, in which the Inuit regained possession of their homeland (valued at $1.15 billion) in return for renouncing all their claims to the remainder of the NWT. One practical effect has been the **renaming** of most of its 28 settlements with Inuit names, though in many cases English-language names have continued to stick; both are provided in this book, with the more common appellation given preference.

Nunavut is the land of musk ox, polar bears, vast caribou migrations, millions upon millions of migrating songbirds and endless horizons of fish-filled lakes and rivers. The region is also home to ten-thousand-year-old glaciers, deep fjords, impressive mountain ranges and endless kilometres of open tundra. Besides the **wildlife** and breathtaking **landscapes**, there are a host of activities, including fishing and high-adventure outdoor pursuits. Add to these the wide spectrum of living **cultural treasures**, from Inuit printmakers and carvers to traditional drummers and "throat" singers.

Most of the region's communities are formed of indigenous Inuit and lie in the **Kivallliq region** on the arc of Hudson Bay's western coast, and encompassing **Baker Lake**, Nunavut's only inland community. In these settlements you will find that the Nunavummiut, or Inuit of Nunavut, continue to honour their traditional lifestyle, culture and ancestors. The remainder of Nunavut's population live even further north in the scattered communities dotting **Baffin Island** and its surrounding archipelago. The capital, at **Iqaluit** on Baffin Island, is home to nearly one-fifth of the territory's population.

Although you'll find an old way of life and stunning Arctic landscapes, don't be alarmed by the physical appearance of most villages; housing here is at a premium and many buildings and infrastructure suffer the effects of the Arctic's harsh and changing environment. Houses are built on stilts and sit high above the permafrost layer, while some are even cabled down to prevent them from blowing away during the fierce arctic winds. All building supplies, canned grocery goods and supplies must be shipped in by sealift, which arrives once or twice a year during the brief ice-free months between July and early October. Despite the rundown appearance of these places, it is the warmth and generosity of the Inuit who live there that make staying here an unforgettable experience.

GETTING AROUND AND INFORMATION   NUNAVUT

Getting around Exploring Nunavut is hugely rewarding, but far from easy – the separate communities aren't connected by highway. The landscapes are sublime but often inhospitable, so access is invariably by plane or helicopter and therefore expensive; we've listed the airlines that service some communities in the relevant account. The best way to see the area is with one of the many tour companies. For those wishing to trek or canoe the various parks and rivers on their own or in small groups, the best place to purchase topographical and regional maps is at the Ottawa-based World of Maps (☏ 800 214 8524, ⦿ worldofmaps.com).

Tourist information Nunavut publishes its own visitors' guide, the annual *Explore Nunavut Guide* (available free online ⦿ nunavuttourism.com), which is packed with information, a full listing of tour operators and outfitters. Information is also available at ☏ 866 686 2888, or internationally ☏ 800 491 7910, ⦿ explorenunavut.com.

It's also worth exploring Nunavut Parks at ⦿ nunavutparks. com.

Costs and money Hotel prices in the North are invariably per person, not per room, so double all rates if you are two people sharing a double room. Don't be surprised if you are required to share a room with a stranger – this is the North and hotel space is at a premium. Rates sometimes include meals, so are not as steep as they first appear, and note that alcohol is not available in some settlements. Most of the communities in Nunavut have no banks – the exception being Iqaluit and Rankin Inlet. If you are short of cash you could withdraw from the ATMs found in many of the smaller communities, usually at the Northern Grocery store or locally run Co-op stores.

11

Kivalliq (Mainland Nunavut)

Nestled along the western shores of Hudson Bay lie a handful of communities that are only accessible by air, boat or snowmobile from **Arviat** ("place of the bowhead whale") in the south through **Whale Cove** (Tikirarjuaq, "long point"), **Rankin Inlet** (Kangiqtiniq, "deep inlet") – the area's main transport and administrative centre – to **Chesterfield Inlet** (Igluligaarjuk, "place with a few houses") and **Coral Harbour** (Salliit, "large flat island") in the north. The region also includes **Baker Lake**, Nunavut's only inland community, which is renowned for its prints and beautiful soap-stone carvings.

Inland, the land is dominated by gently rolling hills and the vast openness of the tundra. Home to grazing caribou, musk ox, grizzly bears and millions upon millions of migrating songbirds, swans and geese, this region is a **naturalist's paradise**. Offshore, in the waters of Hudson Bay, lies one of the world's best spots to observe pods of beluga whale, seal and sea ducks – you may even encounter a polar bear patrolling the shores.

Rankin Inlet (Kangiqtiniq)

11

RANKIN INLET serves as the business and transportation hub for central Nunavut. The community was founded in 1955 when the North Rankin Nickel Mine opened, with many Inuit families moving from the land to Rankin Inlet to become miners or obtain other industry-related jobs. Although the mine closed in the mid-1960s the community remained, thanks in part to its craft industry, tourism and the entrepreneurial spirit of its residents.

The most prominent attraction is the huge *inuksuk* that sits on the rocks above town. Some of the more popular activities in summer include fishing trips and boat rides to the Marble Island, an important Inuit historical site, with old camps, sunken ships and artefacts from the whaling era. It's also worth hiring Pissuk Outfitting (☎867 645 4218, ☎867 645 3322) to take you to **Iqalugaarjuup Nunanga Territorial Park**, some 10km northwest from town on the Meliadine River. Once there, you can walk among the **Thule** sites and see storage caches, ancient fox traps, stone tent rings, kayak cradles and the remains of a sod house. In winter you can experience the traditional skill of igloo building or dog-sledding on the sea ice. If you're in town in late April or early May it's worth attending Pakallak Time, an annual **festival** where everyone joins in square dances, games and dog-team races.

ARRIVAL AND INFORMATION

RANKIN INLET

By plane First Air and Canadian North have direct flights to Rankin Inlet from Iqaluit and Yellowknife and connecting services from Ottawa and Montréal via Iqaluit. Calm Air (see page 795) has scheduled services from Churchill, Manitoba, to Rankin Inlet and most other Kivalliq villages. Chartering a flight to visit the interior can be arranged by contacting Kivalliq Air (☎867 645 2992, ☎888 831 8472, ⓦkivalliqair.com).

Tourist information There's a small regional Kivalliq Regional Visitor Centre at the airport (☎867 645 3838), and a post office at the *Siniktarvik Hotel & Conference Centre*. Contact the hamlet (☎867 645 2895) for information on outfitters, tours and other accommodation.

ACCOMMODATION

Katimavik Suites Hotel ☎867 857 2275, ⓦkatimaviksuites.com. An upper-end hotel with eighteen studio rooms and ten suites. Facilities include common kitchen areas, laundry facilities, TV and wireless internet. Per person $230

Nanuq Lodge ☎867 645 2650, ✉nanuq@qiniq.com. Well-equipped, friendly B&B which has internet and a small library of books of local interest. Complimentary afternoon tea and snacks are available, as well as assistance in setting up local tours. Per person $200

Siniktarvik Hotel & Conference Centre ☎867 645 2807, ⓦsiniktarvik.com. A basic, no-frills place to stay while in town. Conveniently located in the centre, this hotel has fifty rooms, each equipped with private bathroom, cable TV, telephone and wireless internet. A full-service restaurant is located on the main floor. Per person $209

Coral Harbour

CORAL HARBOUR or Salliit ("a large flat island in front of the mainland") is the only settlement on Southampton Island and one of the best places to see **arctic birds**, **walrus** and **polar bears** (on nearby Coats Island), as well as the beautiful Kirchoffer Falls, 24km out of town, and the Thule archeological sites at Native Point, 64km southeast of town. As the English name suggests, Coral Harbour refers to the fossilized coral originally formed some 450 million years ago when the local climate was much more tropical. Outfitters can take you to Fossil Creek Trail to see the best display of **fossils** in Nunavut, or to the East Bay and Harry Gibbons Migratory Bird sanctuaries to see thousands of snow geese, tundra swans, sandhill cranes and scores of other migratory species that gather here each year in spring.

ARRIVAL AND INFORMATION   CORAL HARBOUR

By plane Flights on Calm Air and on First Air arrive from Iqaluit via Rankin Inlet.
Tourist information Contact the hamlet (☎ 867 925

8867, ⓦ coralharbour.ca) for information on outfitters, tours and other accommodation options.

ACCOMMODATION

Leonie's Place ☎ 867 925 9751, ⓔ leoniesplace@ yahoo.ca. Shared double accommodation in eight rooms, each a nonsmoking with private bath. A large lounge with

common kitchen and TV is available for guests. Breakfast available for $15, lunch $25, dinner $40. Per person **$225**

Arviat

ARVIAT, 240km southwest of Rankin Inlet, is particularly known for its crafts and the McConnell River Migratory Bird Sanctuary, home to the snowy owl and thousands of nesting waterfowl. In autumn, beluga whales congregate in the bays around town and caribou are often spotted foraging nearby. The late autumn months are the best time to see polar bears feeding along the sea ice's edge. Residents here are proud of their traditions and welcome the chance to introduce you to throat singing, drum dancing or storytelling. Some 20km of gravel roads allow you to explore the area outside of town by four-wheel-drive (which can be rented from locals; enquire at the hamlet office), and there are hiking trails as well. The Sivulinut Elders Society hosts cultural events and drum dances in town.

ARRIVAL AND INFORMATION   ARVIAT

By plane There are daily flights to Arviat from Rankin Inlet and Winnipeg.
Tourist information For more information on the community, tours, outfitters and accommodation, visit ⓦ nunavuttourism.com or contact the Arviat tourism

office on ☎ 867 857 2921 or ⓔ info@visitarviat.ca. You can also call the summer-only Margaret Aniksak tourist office (☎ 867 857 2366) or the hamlet office (☎ 867 857 2841). Head to the well-stocked Northern Store for groceries.

ACCOMMODATION

Katimavik Suites ☎ 867 857 2752, ⓦ katimaviksuites. com. One of the better places to stay in town, this family-run business operates thirteen luxury suites and two apartments with en-suite bathrooms, kitchenettes and high-speed wi-fi. Per person **$230**
Padlei Inns North ☎ 867 857 2919, ⓦ arviathotel. innsnorth.com. The largest hotel in the community

accommodates forty guests in shared rooms. Each room is equipped with a private bathroom, TV, telephone and internet facilities. Traditional local and Canadian cuisine available at the restaurant. Hotel management can assist you with local outfitters. Per person **$250**

Baker Lake (Qamani'tuaq)

Some 260km west of Rankin Inlet at the mouth of the Thelon River is **BAKER LAKE**, or Qamani'tuaq ("far inland" or "huge widening of a river"), the Arctic's only inland Inuit community, which also marks Canada's geographic centre. It has long been a meeting place for members of different Inuit groups and provides a point of access into the **tundra** that characterizes the vastness of the region. This is a subtle landscape that's worth more than its "Barrenland" label suggests, particularly in summer, when the thaw brings to life thousands of tiny streams and lakes, and some three hundred species of wildflowers amid the lichens and grasses that provide fodder for huge herds of musk ox and caribou. Millions of wildfowl can also be seen, and the huge skies and flat horizons are also one of the best places in Canada to see the **aurora borealis** (see page 797) throughout autumn and winter. Also be sure to take in the **Inuit Camp**, which includes a demonstration by Inuit families of traditional activities (hunting, trapping and weaving).

A short walk east along the shore from the tourist office is the **Inuit Heritage Centre** (July & Aug hours vary; ☎867 793 2598), which features displays interpreting the culture of the Caribou Inuit. A visit to Baker Lake is not complete until you drop by the Jesse Oonark Centre or the Ookpiktuyuk Art Gallery, both of which showcase the beautiful soapstone carvings, wall hangings and fine jewellery the community is renowned for.

ARRIVAL AND INFORMATION
BAKER LAKE

By plane Calm Air has daily flights here from Rankin Inlet.

Tourist information The summer-only Vera Akumalik tourist office (hours vary; ☎867 793 2456) occupies a reconstructed 1936 Hudson's Bay Company post in the original lakeside building. Staff there can provide information on local tours as well as assist you in organizing a paddling trip on the Thelon or Kazan rivers, both taking you into the heart of the vast tundra. Visit ⓦbakerlake.ca or contact the tourist office or the hamlet (☎867 793 2874) for information on outfitters, tours and other accommodation.

ACCOMMODATION

Baker Lake Lodge ☎867 793 2905, ⓔbakerlakelodge@hotmail.com. Five basic cabins (with separate wash room) that can accommodate twenty people from late June to early Sept, and full dining facilities are available (extra charge for meals). Owners will assist you in planning trips to surrounding wilderness areas. Price includes pick-up from airport. Cabins per person **$85**

Community campground There's a small community campground located on the road to the airport. Free.

Iglu Hotel ☎867 793 2801, ⓦbakerlakehotel.innsnorth. com. This place offers two aircraft-hanger-like structures within which there's accommodation and also a restaurant with mediocre cafeteria food. Per person **$225**

Nunamiut Lodge ☎867 793 2127, ⓦnunamiut lodgehotel.ca. The Inuit-owned *Nunamiut Lodge* holds 32 rooms with private baths and cable TV. A solarium dining room affords gorgeous views of the lake; meals are a flat $20 for breakfast and $50 supper (a la carte lunch is served noon to 1pm only), and reservations are highly recommended. Owners will assist you with Inuit-focused guided tour packages. **$295**

Kitikmeot (the Arctic Coast)

Canada's last frontier, the **Arctic Coast** (or Kitikmeot region) encompasses the country's northern mainland coast from the Mackenzie River to Baffin Island, and – as "coast" is a relative term in a region where the sea is often frozen – numerous islands too, most notably a large part of Victoria Island. It is a barren, ice-carved and wind-scoured landscape of chilly lakes and low hills with not a tree to be seen. Braving this setting, which is also nearly completely dark and frozen for eight months of the year, is a permanent population of a few hundred. As recently as sixty years ago, the Inuit (see page 863) here had known little or no contact with the outside world. Few explorers encountered them, and even the most determined of Western agencies – the Church and the trading companies – failed to compromise a people who are still extraordinarily isolated by climate, distance and culture. Yet today, few of the Inuit live according to the ways of popular myth. Except on the odd trapping party, for example, government-built homes have replaced igloos, and rifles, snow bikes, outboard motors and light aircraft have superseded the bone tools, sledges and sealskin kayaks of a generation ago.

You have to be fairly determined to reach any of the region's seven communities, let alone explore the hauntingly beautiful icefields and tundra. Those that forge their way

THE INUIT

Distinct from all other Canadian Indigenous peoples by virtue of their culture, language and Asiatic physical features, the **Inuit** are the dominant people of a **territory** extending from northern Alaska to Greenland. They once led a **nomadic** existence in one of the most hostile environments on earth, dwelling in **igloos** during the winter and **skin tents** in the summer, moving around using **kayaks** (*qajaq*) or **dog-sleds** (*qamutik*). The latter were examples of typical Inuit adaptability – the runners were sometimes made from frozen fish wrapped in sealskin and caribou bones were used for crossbars.

Animals from the land and sea – caribou, musk ox, seal, walrus, narwhal, beluga whales, polar bears, birds and fish – provided everything: oil for heating and cooking, hides for clothing and tents, harpoon lines and dog harnesses and food. The Inuit **diet** was almost entirely meat based, and every part of the animal was consumed, usually raw, from the eyeballs to the heart. Delicacies included the plaited and dried intestines of seals, and whole sealskins stuffed with small birds and left to age until the contents had turned to the consistency of cheese. All food was shared among the community, and the successful hunter had to watch his catch being distributed among other families in the group, in accordance with specific relationships, before his own kin were allowed the smallest portion. **Starvation** was common – it was not unusual for whole villages to perish in the winter – and consequently **infanticide**, particularly of females, was employed to keep population sizes down. Elders who could not keep up with the travelling group were abandoned, a fate that also befell some offenders of the social code – though the usual way of resolving conflict was the **song-duel**, whereby the aggrieved would publicly ridicule the behaviour of the offender, who was expected to accept the insults with good grace.

It was a woman who often served as the **shaman**, or *angakok*, maintaining the group's communion with the supernatural. The deity who features most regularly in Inuit myth is a goddess called **Sedna**, who was mutilated by her father. Her severed fingers became seals and walruses and her hands became whales, but Sedna lived on as the mother and protector of all sea life, capable of withholding her bounty if strict taboos were not adhered to, including keeping land and sea products separate.

Sporadic **European contact** dates back to the Norse settlement of Greenland, and early missionaries did visit some Inuit. It wasn't until the early 1800s that the two cultures met in earnest. By 1860 commercial **whalers** had begun wintering around the north of Hudson Bay, employing Inuit as crew and food hunters in return for European goods. The impact on the Inuit was not really deleterious until the arrival of **American and European whalers** in 1890, when the liberal dispensing of alcohol and spread of diseases (smallpox and tuberculosis) led to a drastic decline in population.

By the early 1900s **fur traders** were encouraging the Inuit to stop hunting off the coast and turn inland, using firearms and traps. The accompanying **missionaries** brought welcome medical help and schools, but put an end to multiple marriages, shamanism and other traditional practices. More changes came when Inuit were employed to build roads, airfields and other military facilities during World War II, and to construct the line of radar installations known as Distant Early Warning system (DEW) in the Cold War era. As well as bringing new jobs, this also focused government attention on the plight of the Inuit.

The consequent largesse was not wholly beneficial: subsidized housing and welfare payments led many Inuit to abandon their hunting camps and settle in **permanent communities**. Without knowledge of English and French, these Inuit were left out of all decision-making and often lived in separate parts of towns administered by outsiders, and high levels of depression, alcoholism and violence became the norm. A 1982 ban on European imports of sealskins created mass **unemployment**, and although hunting still provides the basics of subsistence, the high cost of ammunition and fuel makes commercial-scale hunting uneconomical.

And yet it's not all gloom. Inuit co-operatives are increasingly successful and the production of **soapstone carvings** – admittedly a commercial adulteration of traditional Inuit ivory art – is very profitable. Having organized themselves into politically active groups and secured **land claims** such as Nunavut, the Inuit are now slowly rebuilding an ancient culture that was shattered in under half a century.

11

11

THE NORTHWEST PASSAGE

The fabled **Northwest Passage** across the top of Canada's Arctic continues to exert a romantic allure – and, in the wake of oil discoveries in the far North, an increasingly economic one. The world's most severe maritime challenge, it involves a 1500km journey from north of Baffin Island to the Beaufort Sea above Alaska. Some fifty thousand icebergs line the eastern approaches and thick pack ice covers the route for nine months of the year, with temperatures rising above freezing only in July and August. Perpetual darkness reigns for four months of the year and thick fog and blizzards can obscure visibility for the remaining eight. Even with modern technology navigation is extremely difficult: little is known of Arctic tides and currents; sonar is confused by submerged ice; and the featureless tundra of the Arctic islands provides only a few points of visual or radar reference.

John Cabot can hardly have been happy with Henry VII's 1497 order to blaze the northwest trail, the first recorded instance of such an attempt. The passage subsequently excited the imagination of the world's greatest adventurers, men such as Sir Francis Drake, Jacques Cartier, Sir Martin Frobisher, James Cook and **Henry Hudson** – cast adrift by his mutinous crew in 1611 when Hudson Bay turned out to be an ice-bound trap rather than the actual passage.

Details of a possible route were pieced together over the centuries, though many paid with their lives in the process, most famously **Sir John Franklin**, who vanished into the ice with 129 men in 1845. Many rescue parties set out to find Franklin's vessels, HMS *Erebus* and HMS *Terror*, and it was one of those searchers, **Robert McClure**, who – in the broadest sense – first transited the route in 1854. Entering from the west, he was trapped for two winters before sledging to meet a rescue boat coming from the east. Norwegian **Roald Amundsen** made the **first sea crossing** in 1906, but only after a three-year voyage. The first single-season traverse was made by a Canadian Mountie, **Henry Larsen**, in 1944 – his schooner, the *St Roch*, is now enshrined in Vancouver's Maritime Museum.

are usually looking to spot **wildlife**, **fish** or hunt for musk ox, caribou and polar bears. Increasingly, more tourists are visiting this region as part of a cruise through the famed Northwest Passage. Most visitors base themselves either at **Kugluktuk** (Coppermine) or at Victoria Island's **Iqaluktuuttiaq** (Cambridge Bay), the transport and service capital. Each main Arctic Coast community, remarkably, has **accommodation**, but reservations are vital and prices predictably steep. You need to come prepared: in some cases, even meals must be booked in advance. Basic groceries are usually available at stores, but there are no banks. Various **tour operators** run trips to and from the main centres; for extensive information, send for the *Explore Nunavut* booklet before you go (see page 859).

Cambridge Bay (Iqalukuuttiaq)

CAMBRIDGE BAY, or Iqaluktuuttiaq ("fair fishing place") lies to the north of the Arctic Circle on the southern shore of **Victoria Island**, Canada's second largest island. Today, it's the regional centre for the Kitikmeot communities and an important staging point for tours or for heading still deeper into the hinterland. It also operates as the administrative focus for the region's western lands, despite being a full 1300km from Iqaluit. Over the centuries the region was a summer gathering place for the Copper Inuit, attracted here by the abundance of good hunting. Kitikmeot Foods processes caribou and musk ox for export and the Ikaluktutiak Co-op runs a fishery that supplies arctic char nationwide (both concerns are open to the public for direct sales). The Hudson's Bay Company arrived in 1921, and purchased the *Maud*, explorer Roald Amundsen's schooner, for use as a supplies and trading ship. This little piece of Arctic history was used for years before being left to sink into disrepair and then, ultimately, into the harbour where its hulk can still be seen. Recently, the Canadian Government has given permission for a Norwegian team to salvage the *Maud* and return her to her native Norway.

By plane Scheduled flights arrive on Canadian North and First Air from Yellowknife; First Air flies between all the settlements except Bathurst Inlet and Umingmaktok, which can be reached by charter aircraft only.

Arctic Coast Visitors Centre (call ahead for hours, but generally Mon–Fri 8.30am–5pm; ☎ 867 983 2224). The region's main tourist office is an attractive modern building overlooking the bay. It has displays on the art, history and culture of the Copper and Netsilik Inuit, as well as on the age-old search for the Northwest Passage; staff there will provide you with details on outfitters, bike rentals, guided walking tours, fishing licenses and information regarding film and culture evenings. Contact the hamlet office (☎ 867 983 4650) for information on outfitters, tours and other accommodation options.

ACCOMMODATION AND EATING

You can camp 5km away at Freshwater Creek and – if you're self-catering – buy supplies at the Northern Store. You should also be able to camp on the shoreline of the bay, but ask at the hamlet office first, and make sure you're well away from, and out of sight of, any houses.

Arctic Islands Lodge 26 Omingmak St ☎ 867 983 2345. Located on the shores of the famed Northwest Passage the 25-room *Arctic Islands Lodge* offers comfortable rooms with private bathrooms, TV and wi-fi. Meals cost $30–60 at the coffee shop or restaurant located on the main floor. Singles $235; doubles $335

Green Row Executive Suites 10 Omingmak St ☎ 867 983 3456, ⓦ greenrow.ca. The small *Green Row Executive Suites* has eighteen central, self-contained suites with kitchenettes. Gym access, laundry facilities and a large common room are also available. $235

Kugluktuk (Coppermine)

KUGLUKTUK ("place of rapids") lies west of Cambridge Bay on the Canadian "mainland", sitting astride the **Coppermine River** close to the westernmost point of Nunavut. The river provides one of the continent's great **canoe trips**, with most canoeists (or rafters) joining tours or chartering a plane from Yellowknife (600km to the south) to the river's headwaters. The 325km trip downstream takes around ten days, offering sensational opportunities for **watching wildlife**. You can also strike lucky by walking or taking short tours from Kugluktuk itself. The most popular walk (20km one way) is to the **Bloody Falls**, so called because a party of Inuit were massacred here in 1771 following an argument with a group of Dene guides accompanying English explorer Samuel Hearne. If you don't fancy the walk, or only want to go one way – it is tough going in places – you can arrange a boat to drop you or pick you up; the tourist office has full details. In spring, the Nattiq Frolics celebrations feature dancing, a community feast, Inuit games and snowmobile racing.

By plane Access by air is provided through Canadian North and First Air from Yellowknife and other local communities.

Heritage Visitors Centre (July & Aug daily 8.30am–5pm, other times on request; ☎ 867 982 3570) In the summer they organize local walking tours and programmes. Contact the tourist office or hamlet office (☎ 867 982 6500) for information on outfitters, tours and other accommodation.

ACCOMMODATION AND EATING

Campground Camping is possible at Kugluk (Bloody Falls) Territorial Park. The campground below the falls is referred to as Onoagahiovik by the Inuit, the place where you "stay all night". Contact the Department of Environment's Kugluktuk office (☎ 867 982 7450).

Coppermine Inn ☎ 867 982 3333, ☎ 867 982 3340. Central motel rooms or self-contained units and breakfast, lunch and dinner (if you want them) should be reserved at least 2 days in advance. $225

Baffin Island

Baffin Island comprises half a million square kilometres of Arctic vastness, whose main attraction is **Auyuittuq National Park** on the Cumberland Peninsula, one of Canada's northernmost accessible national parks. With a treeless landscape, mountains towering over 1500m, icy glacial streams and 24-hour daylight from May to July, hiking in the

11

park offers one of the most majestic experiences in Canada. Yet with temperatures hitting a mere 10°C from June to August, it can be a harsh environment that will appeal only to the truly adventurous; expensive though they are, **package tours** are definitely recommended if this is your first venture into such a remote place. Bring all necessary gear with you, as supplies are limited here.

Iqaluit (Frobisher Bay)

The main gateway to Baffin Island – and capital of Nunavut – is rapidly growing **IQALUIT** (meaning "place of many fish"), whose population of seven thousand is predominantly Inuit. Since being selected as Nunavut's capital in December 1995, Iqaluit has seen tremendous change, with the construction of homes, commercial and government buildings continuing apace. Iqaluit has the most to see in terms of culture and in-town attractions of any settlement in Nunavut, but even these activities won't hold your interest for too long – the real draws are in the surrounding area.

Sights include a tour of the impressive **Legislative Assembly Building** (year-round by appointment; ☎ 867 975 5000), which houses a fine collection of Inuit art and a ceremonial mace fashioned from an ivory narwhal tusk and adorned with precious minerals mined throughout Nunavut. There's a superb collection of Inuit art and artefacts in the **Nunatta Sunakkutaangit Museum** (call for latest times; ☎ 867 979 5537), housed in a renovated Hudson's Bay trading post building. Enquire at the Unikkaarvik Visitor Centre (see "Information and Tours" below) for day-tours (by 30min boat ride in summer, by dog team or snowmobile in winter) to the **Qaummaarviit Territorial Historic Park**, located on an island a short distance from Iqaluit. Artefacts found there indicate the Thule had lived in the region some eight hundred years ago, and interpretive signs now explain the significance of tent rings, meat caches and gravesites, some of which can still be seen. Fabulous char-fishing awaits at nearby Sylvia Grinnell River.

ARRIVAL AND DEPARTURE

IQALUIT

By plane Getting to Baffin Island is only feasible by air. First Air and Canadian North (see page 795) make the round-trip daily from Montréal and Ottawa (3hr). Ticket prices can get as low as $900 return, but are usually nearer $1500. Both airlines also link Yellowknife to Iqaluit, via Rankin Inlet (5 weekly; 3hr 50min). Ask about cheap pass deals and other pre-booked flight deals if you're making international

flights into Canada: these are often much cheaper bought beforehand in conjunction with the carrier you're using to fly into the country.
Destinations Edmonton (6 weekly; 7hr–10hr 30min); Montréal (6 weekly; 2hr 15min–4hr 45min); Ottawa (4 daily; 3hr); Yellowknife (6 weekly; 4hr 50min).

INFORMATION AND TOURS

Tourist offices The main Nunavut Tourism office is here (☎ 800 491 7910, ☎ 866 686 2888, ⓦ nunavuttourism. com), as is the Unikkaarvik Visitor Centre (June–Sept Mon–Fri 9am–6pm, Sat 10am–4pm, Sun 1–4pm, rest of year closed Sun; ☎ 867 979 4636) at 220 Sinaa St, which features cultural exhibits and wildlife displays. Both centres provide

information, maps of the town and region, along with information about visiting the rest of Nunavut.
Tours Tour operators who run trips into the interior abound in Nunavut; consult ⓦ destinationnunavut.ca or contact the Iqaluit tourist office at ⓦ city.iqaluit.nu.ca for more information.

ACCOMMODATION

Iqaluit has many accommodation options including B&Bs, which tend to come and go. The main hotels charge more or less similar rates – around $250 per night – for similar facilities.

★ **Accommodations by the Sea** ☎ 867 222 3498, ⓦ staybythesea.ca. One of the better B&Bs in town is the very comfortable *Accommodations by the Sea*, with six bedrooms, full access to a kitchen, cosy living room and a

large balcony with a gorgeous view of the surroundings. Complimentary airport pick-up, and very helpful staff. $230
Capital Suites ☎ 867 975 4000, ☎ 877 669 9444, ⓦ capitalsuites.ca/iqaluit. Fully furnished suites complete with full kitchens, wi-fi and the comforts of home, and with friendly staff. $244
The Discovery ☎ 867 979 4433, ⓦ thediscovery.com. *The Discovery* offers a variety of accommodation styles

ranging from smart standard rooms to executive suites, all with private bathrooms, wi-fi and TV. There's a courtesy airport shuttle, too. One of the best places to eat in Iqaluit is the *Granite Room*, which serves delicious traditional Inuit food (arctic char, musk ox) and other Canadian dishes. **$275**
Frobisher Inn ☎ 867 979 2222, ☎ 877 422 9422, ⓦ frobisherinn.com. Very comfortable rooms with full amenities including internet; guests have use of a fitness centre. Gourmet coffees are served at the *Caribrew Café* while dining with full menu service is available at the *Gallery Hotel Restaurant*. Also offers complimentary airport shuttle. **$266**

Auyuittuq National Park

Straddling the Arctic Circle on the northeast coast of Baffin Island, **Auyuittuq National Park** is one of the most spectacular destinations in the Canadian North. The heart of the park is the massive **Penny Ice Cap**, a remnant of the ice sheet that extended over most of Canada east of the Rockies about eighteen thousand years ago, and the 110km **Pangnirtung/Akshayuk Pass**, a major **hiking route** which cuts through the mountains between Cumberland Sound and the Davis Strait. *Auyuittuq* is Inuktitut for "the land that never melts" but, despite the unrelenting cold, in summer the sparse tundra plants do bloom, and chance encounters with arctic hares and foxes, polar bears, Canada geese, snowy owls and gyrfalcons are a possibility. Just offshore you may spot narwhal, walrus, bowhead and beluga whale, as well as harp, ringed and bearded seals. Yet the main attraction is not necessarily the random, rare wildlife sightings but the sheer rugged beauty and raw power of the dramatic landscape.

Services within the park are extremely limited and the **weather** is highly unpredictable. Snowstorms, high wind and rain occur frequently, and deaths from hypothermia have been known even in summer. All-weather hiking gear is essential, as is a walking stick to assist you with the ice-cold stream crossings which occur every 200–300m and can be waist-high in July. There is no wood for fuel, so a camping stove is essential.

ARRIVAL AND INFORMATION

AUYUITTUQ NATIONAL PARK

By plane Daily 1hr First Air and/or Canadian North flights leave from Iqaluit to Pangnirtung, or Pang, the gateway to Auyuittuq National Park. The only transport for the 25km from Pang to Overlord, the south entrance of the park, is by freighter canoe, which the Inuit also charter for fishing, whale-watching and sightseeing trips. The rates on these "canoes" – which are like small fishing boats with outboard motors – are set by the Inuit cooperative, and work out at around $150/person one way (usually minimum of two passengers). The boats can only pass through the Pangnirtung Fjord after the ice break-up in July and only then during high tides (check at the park office for monthly tide charts). Arrangements for a canoe pick-up should be confirmed by radio from the few emergency shelters in the park. The best choices for transport to the park are Joavie, who runs Alivaktuk Outfitting (☎ 867 473 8721, ⓦ alivaktukoutfitting.ca), or Peter at Peter's Expediting & Outfitting Services (☎ 867 473 4060, ⓦ kilabukoutfitting. com, ⓔ peterkilabuk2005@qiniq.com). Both also arrange sightseeing tours around the region throughout the year.
Tourist office In the Angmarlik Visitor Centre (hours vary, summer only; ☎ 867 473 8737), which is located next to the Parks Canada office; enquire at the tourist office about homestay programmes with local families.
Safety orientation All visitors must participate in a mandatory safety orientation briefing held at the Parks Canada office (☎ 867 473 2500). Download the visitor information package at ⓦ pc.gc.ca/eng/pn-np/nu/auyuittuq/visit.aspx), where you can find information on this and other parks in the North.

ACCOMMODATION

Auyuittuq Lodge ☎ 867 473 8955, ⓦ pangnirtunghotel.com. The only commercial place to stay in Pang is the 22-room *Auyuittuq Lodge*, which also offers tasty meals at an additional cost (you can also order takeaway lunches for when you are out on the land). Per person **$239**

11

Contexts

History

Fully unified as late as 1949, Canada is a country of intertwining histories rather than a single national thread. Not only does each of its provinces maintain a considerable degree of autonomy, but each grouping of First Nations, Inuit and Métis peoples can claim a heritage that cannot be easily integrated into the story of white, European Canada. Such a complex mosaic militates against generalization, although Canadians themselves continue to grapple with the nature of their own identity. What follows is an attempt to define and clarify key events and themes.

The beginnings

The ancestors of the **Aboriginal peoples** of North America first entered the continent around 25,000 years ago, when vast glaciers covered most of the northern continents. It seems likely that North America's first human inhabitants crossed the land bridge linking Asia with present-day Alaska – they were probably Siberian hunter-nomads travelling in pursuit of mammoths, hairy rhinos, bison, wild horses and sloths. These people left very little to mark their passing, apart from some simple graves and the grooved, chipped-stone spearheads that earned them the name **Fluted Point People**. In successive waves the Fluted Point People moved down through North America until they reached the southernmost tip of South America. As they settled, so they slowly developed distinctive cultures and languages, whose degree of elaboration depended on the resources available in their various environments.

The migration of the Inuit

Around 3000 BC, another wave of migration passed over from Asia to North America. This wave was made up of the first group of **Inuit** migrants who – because the land bridge was now submerged under today's Bering Strait – made their crossings either in skin-covered boats or on foot over the ice. Within the next thousand years the Inuit occupied the entire northern zone of the continent, moving east as far as Greenland and displacing the earlier occupants. These first Inuit are now called the **Dorset Eskimos** after Cape Dorset, on Baffin Island, where archeologists first identified their remains in the 1920s, but they were assimilated or wiped out by the next wave of Inuit. These crossed into the continent three thousand years ago, creating the **Thule** culture – so called after the Greek word for the world's northernmost extremity. The Thule people were the direct ancestors of today's Inuit.

The Aboriginal peoples

The Aboriginal peoples of Canada, who numbered around 300,000 before the Europeans arrived, were divided into three main language groups: **Algonkian**, **Athapascan** (principally in the north and west) and **Inuktitut** (Inuit). Within these groups existed a multitude of cultures. None of these people had a written language,

c.23,000 BC	c.5000 BC	c.3000 BC
Human settlement of Canada begins via the land bridge over the Bering Strait.	First petroglyphs carved in Ontario.	First Inuit reach North America from Siberia.

the wheel was unknown to them and their largest draught animal, prior to the introduction of the horse (via the Spanish), was the dog. Yet over the centuries each of the tribes developed techniques that enabled them to cope and survive.

Inuit and northern forest peoples

Immediately prior to European arrival, Canada was divided into a number of cultural zones. In the extreme north lived the nomadic **Inuit** (see page 863), whose basic unit was the family group, small enough to survive in the precarious conditions. The necessarily small-scale nature of Inuit life meant they developed no political structures and gathered together in larger groups only if the supply of food required it – when, for example, the arctic char were running upriver from the sea to spawn, or the caribou were migrating. Immediately to the south of the Inuit, in a zone stretching from the Labrador coast across the Canadian Shield to northern BC, lived the tribes of the **northern forests**. This was also a harsh environment, and consequently these peoples formed small nomadic bands that followed the game on which they depended. Variations between the tribes largely resulted from the type of game they pursued: the **Naskapi** fished and hunted seals on the Labrador coast; the **Chipewyan**, occupying the border country between the tundra and forest to the west of Hudson Bay, mainly hunted caribou; and the **Tahltan** of BC combined hunting with seasonal fishing. Like the Inuit, the political structures of these tribes were rudimentary and, although older men enjoyed a certain respect, there were no "chiefs" in any European sense of the term. Decisions were generally made collectively with the opinions of successful hunters – the guarantors of survival – carrying great weight, as did those of their **shaman**, whose main function was to satisfy the spirits that they believed inhabited every animate and inanimate object.

The Iroquois-speakers

The southern zone of Canada, stretching from the St Lawrence River along the northern shores of the Great Lakes to southern BC, was climatically much kinder, and it's in this region that Canada's Aboriginal peoples developed their most sophisticated cultures. Here, along the banks of the St Lawrence River and the shores of the Great Lakes, lived the **Iroquois-speaking** peoples, who were divided into three tribal confederacies: the **Five Nations**, the **Huron** (see page 141) and the **Neutrals**. All three groups cultivated corn (maize), beans and squash in an agricultural system that enabled them to lead a settled life – often in communities of several hundred. Iroquois society was divided into matriarchal clans, whose affairs would be governed by a female elder. The clan shared a longhouse and when a man married (always outside his own clan), he would go to live in the longhouse of his wife. Tribal chiefs (*sachems*) were male, but the female elders of the tribe selected them and they also had to belong to a lineage through which the rank of *sachem* descended. Iroquoian society had its bellicose side, too. An assured winter supply of food enabled the Iroquois to indulge in protracted intertribal warfare: in particular, the Five Nations were almost always at war with the Huron.

The Ojibwa and the peoples of the Plains

To the west of the Iroquois, between lakes Superior and Winnipeg, lived the **Ojibwa**, forest hunters who learned to cultivate maize from the Iroquois and also harvested the wild rice that grew on the fringes of the region's lakes. Further west still, on the prairies,

c.1000 BC	c.500 BC	c.100 BC
Tobacco smoking big among the Iroquois; big tobacco pouches and pipes de rigueur.	Pacific Coast peoples carve prototype totem poles.	Good times in BC: the priapic Sechelt sculpture shows it isn't all about fishing on the West Coast.

lived the peoples of the **Blackfoot Confederation**: the **Piegan**, **Blackfoot** and **Blood** tribes. The economy of this latter grouping was based on the buffalo (or bison): its flesh was eaten; its hide provided clothes and shelter; its bones were made into tools; its sinews were ideal for bow strings; and its hooves were melted down to provide glue. In the late seventeenth century, the hunting techniques of these prairie peoples were transformed by the arrival of the **horse**, which had made its way – either wild or by trade – from Mexico, where the Spanish conquistadors had introduced them. The horse made the bison easy prey and, as with the Iroquois, a ready food supply spawned the development of a militaristic culture centred on the prowess of the tribes' young braves.

The peoples of the West Coast

On the **Pacific coast**, tribes such as the **Tlingit** and **Salish** were dependent on the ocean, which provided them with a plentiful supply of food. But there was little cohesion within tribes and people from different villages – even though of the same tribe – would at times be in conflict with each other. Yet these tribes had a rich ceremonial and cultural life, as exemplified by the excellence of their woodcarvings, whose most conspicuous manifestations were memorial or **totem poles**, which reached colossal sizes in the nineteenth century. **Weaving** was also highly developed.

European arrival

The first recorded contact between Europeans and the Aboriginal peoples of North America occurred around 1000 AD, when a **Norse** expedition sailing from Greenland landed somewhere on the Atlantic seaboard, probably in Newfoundland (see page 451). It was a fairly short-lived stay – according to the Icelandic sagas, the Norse were forced to withdraw from the colony they called Vinland because of the hostility of the natives. More certainty applies to the year 1492, when **Christopher Columbus** set off in search of the westward route to Asia. Columbus bumped into the West Indies instead, but his "discovery" of islands that were presumed to lie off India encouraged other European monarchs to sponsor expeditions of their own. In 1497, **John Cabot**, supported by the English king Henry VII, sailed west and sighted Newfoundland and Cape Breton. On his return, Cabot reported seeing multitudes of cod off Newfoundland, and his much-publicized comments effectively started the **Newfoundland cod fishery**. In less than sixty years, up to four hundred fishing vessels from Britain, France and Spain were making annual voyages to the Grand Banks fishing grounds around the island. Some of the fishermen soon established shore bases to cure their catch, and then they started to winter here – which was how settlement of the island began. By the end of the sixteenth century, the British and French pretty much controlled the cod fishery and Newfoundland became an early focus of Anglo-French rivalries, a colonial conflict that continued until England secured control of the island in the 1713 Treaty of Utrecht.

New France

Meanwhile, in 1535, **Jacques Cartier**, on a voyage paid for by the French Crown, made his way along the St Lawrence River, also hoping to find Asia. Instead he

200 AD	c.1000	1492
The seminomadic Beothuks colonize Newfoundland; also see 1829.	Vikings establish a colony in Newfoundland, but don't like it much and soon leave.	Christopher Columbus sails west for Asia, but finds the West Indies instead.

stumbled upon the Iroquois, first at Stadacona, on the site of Québec City, and later at Hochelaga, today's Montréal. At both places, the Frenchman had a friendly reception, but the Iroquois attitude changed after Cartier seized one of their tribal chiefs and took him back to France. For a time the Iroquois were a barrier to further exploration up the St Lawrence, but subsequently they abandoned their riverside villages, enabling French traders to move up the river buying **furs**, an enterprise pioneered by seasonal fishermen.

The development of the fur trade aroused the interest of the French king, who in 1603 commissioned **Samuel de Champlain** to chart the St Lawrence. Two years later Champlain founded **Port Royal** (see page 353) in today's Nova Scotia, which became the capital of **Acadie** (Acadia), a colony whose agricultural preoccupations were soon far removed from the main thrust of French colonialism along the St Lawrence. It was here, on a subsequent expedition in 1608, that Champlain established the settlement of Québec City at the heart of **New France**, and, to stimulate the fur trade, allied the French with those tribes he identified as likely to be his principal suppliers. In practice this meant siding with the Huron against the Five Nations, a decision that intensified their traditional hostility. Furthermore, the fur trade destroyed the balance of power between the tribes: first one and then another would receive, in return for their pelts, the latest type of musket as well as iron axes and knives, forcing enemies back to the fur trade to redress the military balance. One consequence of such European intervention was the **extermination of the Huron people** in 1648 by the Five Nations, armed by the Dutch merchants of the Hudson River.

New France consolidates

As pandemonium reigned among the Aboriginal peoples, the pattern of life in **New France** was becoming well established. On the farmlands of the St Lawrence River a New World feudalism was practised by land-owning *seigneurs* and their *habitant* tenants, while the fur territories – entered at Montréal – were extended deep into the interior. Many of the fur traders adopted native dress, learnt Aboriginal languages and took wives from the tribes through which they passed, spawning the mixed-race people known as the **Métis**. The furs they brought back to Montréal were shipped downriver to Québec City and then on to France. But the white population in the French colony remained relatively small – there were only eighteen thousand New French in 1713. In the context of a growing British presence, this represented a dangerous weakness.

The rise of the British

By 1670, Charles II of England had established the **Hudson's Bay Company** and given it control of a million and a half square miles adjacent to its namesake bay, a territory named Rupert's Land, after the king's uncle. Four years later the British captured the Dutch possessions of the Hudson River Valley, thereby trapping New France. Slowly the British closed the net: in 1713, they took control of Acadia, renaming it **Nova Scotia**, and in 1755 they deported its French-speaking farmers. When the Seven Years' War broke out in 1756, the French attempted to outflank the British by using the Great Lakes route to occupy the area to the west of the British colonies and then, with the help of their native allies, pin them to the coast. The British won the war by exploiting their naval superiority: a large force under the command of **General James Wolfe** sailed up the St Lawrence in 1759 and, against all expectations, successfully

1497	1534	1583
John Cabot bumps into Newfoundland – and a sea of cod.	Jacques Cartier claims Québec for the French; he plants a 10m cross on the shores of Gaspé Bay.	Humphrey Gilbert claims Newfoundland for England. Local expat fishermen give him a dog; he levies a fishing tax.

THE HUDSON'S BAY COMPANY

In 1661 two Frenchmen, **Medard Chouart des Groseilliers** and **Pierre-Esprit Radisson**, reached the southern tip of Hudson Bay overland and realized it was the same inland sea described by earlier seafarers. They returned to the St Lawrence River laden with furs, but the French governor promptly arrested them for trapping without a licence. Understandably peeved, they turned to England, where Charles II financed them and gave them two ships, the *Eaglet* and the *Nonsuch*. After a mammoth voyage, the *Nonsuch* returned with a fantastic cargo of furs and this led to the incorporation of the **Hudson's Bay Company** by Charles II on May 2, 1670. The Company was granted wide powers, including exclusive trading rights to the entire Hudson Bay watershed, now renamed **Rupert's Land**.

By 1760, there were HBC **trading posts** at the mouths of all the major rivers flowing into Hudson Bay. Each was commanded by a factor, who took his orders from London, though these instructions were often unrealistic, based on the idea of Aboriginal trappers bringing furs to the posts – the direct opposite to the Montréal-based North West Company, whose mainly francophone employees spent months in the wilderness working with the Aboriginals. There was intense competition between the HBC and NWC across the north of the continent, occasionally resulting in violence, but in 1821 the two companies merged. They kept the name Hudson's Bay Company and the British parliament granted the new company a commercial monopoly from Hudson Bay to the Pacific.

Local traders fiercely resented these extensive **monopoly** rights and, in a landmark 1849 case, a Manitoban jury found a Métis trader guilty of breaking the monopoly but refused to have him punished. Thereafter, in practice if not by law, the Company's stranglehold on the fur trade ended. Furthermore, the HBC's quasi-governmental powers seemed increasingly anachronistic and when a company official, **James Douglas**, became BC governor in 1858, the British government forced him to resign from the HBC. This marked the beginning of the end of the Company's colonial role.

In 1869, the HBC sold Rupert's Land to Canada. In return it received a cash payment, but, more importantly, retained the title to the lands on which trading posts had been built as well as one-twentieth of the fertile land open to settlement. Given that the trading posts often occupied those very sites that were to be the nucleus of the new cities that were sprouting in the West, this was a remarkably bad deal for Canada – and a great one for the HBC. Subsequently, the HBC became a major real-estate developer and retail chain, a position it maintains today.

---

scaled the Heights of Abraham to capture Québec City. Montréal fell a few months later – and at that point the French North American empire was effectively finished, though they held onto Louisiana until Napoleon sold it off in 1803.

Aboriginal consternation

For the Aboriginal peoples, the **ending of the Anglo-French conflict** was a mixed blessing. If the war had turned the tribes into sought-after allies, it had also subordinated Aboriginal to European interests. A recognition of the change wrought by the end of the war inspired the uprising of the Ottawas in 1763, when **Pontiac**, their chief, led an unsuccessful assault on Detroit, hoping to restore the French position and halt the progress of the English settlers. Moved largely by a desire for a stable economy, the response of the British was to issue a proclamation which confirmed the legal right of the Aboriginals to their lands

c.1600	1640s	1670
Beaver hats become fashionable in Europe; beavers dismayed.	The first Jesuit missionaries arrive in New France.	Hudson's Bay Company incorporated; they're after beaver pelts – beavers even more dismayed.

and set aside the territory to the west of the Appalachian Mountains and the Great Lakes as **Indian Territory**. Although colonial governors were given instructions to remove trespassers on "Indian Land", in reality the proclamation had little practical effect until the twentieth century, when it became a cornerstone of Aboriginal peoples' attempts to seek compensation for the illegal confiscation of their land.

The Canadiens

The other great problem the British faced in the 1760s was how to deal with the French-speaking **Canadiens** of the defunct New France – the term "Canadiens" was used to distinguish local settlers from those born in France, most of whom left the colony after the British conquest. Initially the British government hoped to anglicize the province, swamping the French-speaking population with English-speaking Protestants. Yet large-scale migration failed to materialize and the second English governor of Québec, **Guy Carleton**, realized – as discontent grew in the American colonies – the loyalty of the Canadiens was of vital importance.

Carleton's plan to secure this loyalty was embodied in the 1774 **Québec Act**, which made a number of concessions to the region's French-speakers: Catholics were permitted to hold civil appointments, the seigneurial system was maintained and the Roman Catholic Church allowed to collect tithes – all at a time when Catholics in Britain were not politically emancipated. The success of Carleton's policy was seen during the **American War of Independence** (1775–83), and later during the Anglo-American War of 1812. The Canadiens refused to volunteer for the armed forces of the Crown, but equally they failed to respond to the appeals of the Americans – no doubt calculating that their survival as a distinctive cultural group was more likely under the British than in an English-speaking United States.

The United Empire Loyalists

In the immediate aftermath of the American War of Independence, the population of what was left of British North America expanded rapidly, both in "Canada" – which then covered the present-day provinces of Québec and Ontario – and in the separate colonies of New Brunswick, Nova Scotia, Prince Edward Island and Newfoundland. The first large wave of migration came from the US as forty thousand **United Empire Loyalists** (see page 329) made their way north to stay within British jurisdiction. Of these, all but eight thousand moved to Nova Scotia and New Brunswick, the rest going to the western edge of Québec, where they laid the foundations of the future province of Ontario. This influx of English-speakers was partly countered among the Canadiens by the so-called *revanche du berceau* (revenge of the cradle) – an attempt, encouraged by the Catholic clergy, to outbreed the English-speaking population. The end result was that the population of "Canada", as defined at the time, trebled to 330,000 between 1783 and 1812.

The War of 1812

The Americans had secured their independence from the Crown, but tensions between Britain and the US still deterred potential colonists, a problem resolved by the **War**

1713	1755	1759
Treaty of Utrecht: France cedes its claims to Newfoundland and Acadia (in the Maritimes) to the English.	The English forcibly evict the French-speaking Acadians from the Bay of Fundy.	The British general James Wolfe dies during his successfu attack on Québec City; effectiv fall of New France.

of 1812. Neither side was strong enough to win, but by the Treaty of Ghent in 1814 the Americans recognized the legitimacy of British North America, whose border was established along the **49th Parallel** west from Lake of the Woods, in what is now northern Ontario, to the Rockies. **Immigration** now boomed, especially in the 1840s, when economic crises and shortages in Britain, as well as the Irish famine, pushed it up to levels that even the fertile Canadiens could not match. Between 1815 and 1850 over 800,000 immigrants poured into British North America. Most headed for **Upper Canada**, later called Ontario, which received 66,000 migrants in 1832 alone.

Faced with this human tide, the surveyors charted new townships as quickly as possible, but they simply couldn't keep pace with demand. One result was that many Aboriginal people were dispossessed in contravention of the 1763 proclamation. By 1806 the region's indigenous people had lost 4.5 million acres.

The division and union of Canada

Throughout the early and mid-nineteenth century, it was the English-speaking merchants who drove Canada's economic expansion. Seeking political changes that would enhance their economic power, they also wanted their own legislative assembly and the universal application of English law, which would not have been acceptable to the French-speakers. In the **Canada Act of 1791**, the British government imposed a compromise, dividing the region into **Upper** and **Lower Canada**, which broadly separated the two linguistic groups along the line of the Ottawa River. In **Lower Canada**, the French-based legal system was retained, while in **Upper Canada**, English common law was introduced. Both of the new provinces had an elected assembly, though these shared their limited powers with an appointed assembly and executive councils appointed by the provincial governor. This arrangement allowed the assemblies to become the focal points for vocal opposition, but ultimately condemned them to impotence. At the same time, the merchant elite built up chains of influence and power around the appointed provincial governments: in Upper Canada this grouping was called the **Family Compact**, in Lower Canada the **Château Clique**.

Responsible government

By the late 1830s considerable opposition had developed to these cliques. In Upper Canada the **Reform Movement**, led by **William Lyon Mackenzie**, demanded a government accountable to a broad electorate and the expansion of credit facilities for small farmers. In 1837 both Mackenzie and **Louis-Joseph Papineau**, the reform leader in Lower Canada, were sufficiently frustrated to attempt open rebellion. Neither was successful and both were forced into exile in the US, but the rebellions did bring home to the British Government the need for reform. This led to the **Act of Union** of 1840, which united Lower and Upper Canada with a single assembly. The rationale for this arrangement was the belief that the French-Canadians were incapable of handling elective government without Anglo-Saxon guidance. Yet the assembly provided equal representation for Canada East and West – in effect the old Lower and Upper Canadas. A few years later, this new assembly achieved **responsible government** almost accidentally. In 1849 the Reform Party, which had a majority of seats, passed an Act compensating those involved in the 1837 rebellions. The Governor General, Lord

1763	1780s	1813
New France is renamed "Québec" and formally delivered to England by the Treaty of Paris, 1763.	United Empire Loyalists flee the US and arrive in Canada by the thousands.	Americans occupy Toronto in the War of 1812.

Elgin, disapproved, but he didn't exercise his veto – so, for the first time, a Canadian administration acted on the vote of an elected assembly, rather than imperial sanction.

Foundation of the Liberal and Conservative parties

The **Reform Party**, which pushed through the compensation scheme, included both French- and English-speakers and mainly represented small farmers and businessmen opposed to the power of the cliques. In the 1850s this grouping became the Canadian **Liberal Party**, but attempts to establish a Canada-wide coalition fell apart in the 1860s with the emergence of "Clear Grit" Liberals in Canada West (Ontario). The Grits argued for "Representation by Population" – in other words, instead of equal representation for the two halves of Canada, they wanted constituencies based on the total population. As the English-speakers outnumbered the French, the "Rep by Poppers" slogan seemed a direct threat to French Canada. As a consequence, many French-Canadians transferred their support to the **Conservative Party**, while the radicals of Canada East (Québec), the **Rouges**, developed a more nationalist creed.

The **Conservative Party** comprised a number of elements, including the rump of the merchant elite who were so infuriated by their loss of control that they campaigned to break the imperial tie and join the US. Yet, when the party fully emerged in 1854, the old "Compact Tories" were much less influential than a younger generation of moderate conservatives, whose lynchpin was **John A. Macdonald**, who was to form the first federal government in 1868. Such moderates sought, by overcoming the democratic excesses of the "Grits" and the nationalism of the "Rouges", to weld together an economic and political state that would not be absorbed into the US.

Confederation

In the mid-1860s Canada had achieved responsible (parliamentary) government, but British North America was still a collection of **self-governing colonies**. In the east, Newfoundland was almost entirely dependent on its cod fishery, Prince Edward Island had a prosperous agricultural economy and both Nova Scotia and New Brunswick had boomed on the backs of their shipbuilding industries. Far to the west, on the Pacific Coast, lay fur-trading BC, which had just beaten off American attempts to annex the region during the **Oregon crisis**. This dispute was finally resolved in 1846, when the international frontier was fixed along a westward extension of the original 49th Parallel, but this was not the end of BC's problems. In 1858, **gold** was discovered beside the Fraser River and, in response to the influx of prospectors from the US, BC was hastily designated a Crown Colony – a process repeated in 1895 when gold was discovered in the Yukon's Klondike. Between Canada West and BC stretched thousands of miles of prairie and forest – the old Rupert's Land that was still under the loose authority of the Hudson's Bay Company (see page 873).

In the 1860s, during the **American Civil War**, the incoherent structure of British North America raised fears of a US invasion just as the "Rep by Poppers" agitation was making the status of the French-speaking minority problematic. These issues prompted a series of conferences to discuss the issue of **Confederation**, and after three years of intense debate the British Parliament passed the **British North America Act** of 1867. In effect this was a constitution for the new **Dominion of Canada**, providing for a federal

1818	**1829**	**1858**
49th Parallel agreed as the border between the US and Canada from Lake of the Woods in Ontario to the Rockies.	Shanawdithit, the last of the Beothuks, dies of tuberculosis in St John's, Newfoundland.	Gold discovered in British Columbia; the rush is on.

parliament to be established at Ottawa; for Canada East and West to become the provinces of **Québec** and **Ontario** respectively; and for each province to retain a regional government and assembly. All of the existing colonies joined the Confederation except BC, which waited until 1871; Prince Edward Island, till 1873; and Newfoundland, which remained under nominal British control until 1949.

The consolidation of the west

Having settled the constitution, the Dominion turned its attention to the west. In 1869, the territory of the Hudson's Bay Company (see page 873) was bought for £300,000 and the Crown assumed responsibility for the so-called **Northwest Territories** until Canada was considered ready to administer them. Predictably, the wishes of its population – primarily Plains Indians and five thousand **Métis** – were given no heed. The Métis, whose main settlement was near the site of modern-day Winnipeg, were already alarmed by the arrival of settlers from Ontario and were even more alarmed when government land surveyors arrived to divide the land into lots that cut right across their holdings. Fearful of their land rights, the Métis formed a provisional government under the leadership of **Louis Riel** and prepared to resist the federal authorities (see page 505).

In the course of the rebellion, Riel executed a troublesome Ontario Orangeman by the name of Thomas Scott, an action that created uproar in Ontario. Despite this, the federal government negotiated with a Métis delegation and appeared to meet all their demands, although Riel was obliged to go into exile in the US. As a result of the negotiations, Ottawa created the new province of **Manitoba** to the west of Ontario in 1870, and set aside 140 acres per person for the Métis – though land speculators and lawyers ensured that fewer than twenty percent of those eligible actually got their land. Dispossession was also the fate of the **Plains Indians**. From 1871 onwards a series of treaties were negotiated, offering Aboriginal families 160-acre plots and a whole range of goods and services if they signed. By 1877 seven treaties had been agreed (eventually there were eleven), handing over to the government all of the southern prairies. However, the promised aid did not materialize and the Aboriginal peoples found themselves confined to small, infertile reservations.

The Mounties arrive; the Plains Indians are colonized

In 1874, the federal government's increased interest in the Plains – spurred by the **Cypress Hills Massacre** of Assiniboine tribes the year before (see page 533) – was underlined by the arrival of the first 275 members of the newly formed **North West Mounted Police**, the **Mounties** (see page 524), forerunners of today's RCMP. Once the Mounties had brought a semblance of law and order, Ottawa passed the **Second Indian Act** of 1880, making a **Minister of Indian Affairs** responsible for the Aboriginal peoples. The minister and his superintendents exercised near-dictatorial control with almost any action that an Aboriginal person might wish to take, from building a house to making a visit off the reservation, subject to approval by a local official and, often, the ministry in Ottawa. The Act decreed that every Aboriginal applicant for "enfranchisement" as an ordinary Canadian citizen had to pass through a three-year probation period. They were also to be examined to see if they had attained a sufficient level of "civilization". If "enfranchised", the individual was counted as a so-called **non-status Indian**, as opposed

1862	1864	1870s
'And the rock poured me out rivers of oil" exclaims Hugh Shaw as he strikes Canada's first gusher in the oil fields of Ontario.	Confederation: representatives of Ontario, Québec, Nova Scotia, New Brunswick and PEI meet to discuss joining together.	The Mounties (the North West Mounted Police) pacify the Prairies and soon become the source of imperial legend.

GREY OWL: THE GREAT CON ARTIST?

In the 1930s, Wah-Sha-Quon-Asin, aka **Grey Owl** (1888–1938), established an international reputation as a frontiersman and proto-conservationist, travelling Canada, Britain and the US to spread the message and publishing bestselling books to wide acclaim. Yet, after his death, the truth slowly won out – and a very different truth it was.

Grey Owl was actually born **Archie Belaney** in Hastings, England. He emigrated to Canada at the tender age of 17 and, after spending time in Toronto, made his way north to Temagami, in Ontario, where he worked as a guide in the tourist camps and became fascinated by the customs of the local Ojibwa. Unusually for the time, Belaney married a young Ojibwa named **Angele** and they had a daughter, but Belaney was prone to drunken rowdiness and was run out of town after a brawl. He moved to **Biscotasing**, a railway stop and Hudson Bay trading post north of Sudbury, where he became a forest ranger, but his arrest warrant caught up with him and he had to leave town again – though not before making **Marie Girard**, another Aboriginal woman, pregnant.

During World War I, Belaney fought with the Canadian army in Flanders, where he was wounded in the foot. During his convalescence in England, he married his nurse, thereby adding bigamy to his many accomplishments. In the event, however, the call of the Canadian wilderness proved his marriage's undoing and Belaney returned to Biscotasing, stopping en route to see Angele for four days, during which another child was conceived. Back in Biscotasing, Belaney became the town drunk, living an anarchic life of fighting, drinking and trapping under his Grey Owl persona. For reasons that remain obscure, Belaney then had a change of heart, returning to Temagami to live with Angele and their two children in 1925, but he was off again after he met Anahereo, a 19-year-old Iroquois woman. Belaney and Anahereo moved to a hut in northern Québec, where their only companions were two beavers; it was these two animals (and a third that followed) that inspired much of Belaney's **writing** and prompted him to start a **beaver colony**. To raise money for the project he began writing and lecturing about his (fictional) life, a publicity campaign that secured him the post of **warden** of Riding Mountain National Park and later Prince Albert National Park in Manitoba.

Belaney's relationship with Anahereo collapsed, but it didn't take long for him to meet and marry a replacement, a French-Canadian who adopted the Indian name **Silver Moon**. Grey Owl made a lecture tour of Britain and the US in 1938, which included an audience with King George and the princesses Elizabeth and Margaret, but it left him so exhausted he died later the same year. Only then did his wives, friends and family find out the truth.

to the **status Indians** of the reservations. These distinctions persist today, with status Indians, of whom there are around 700,000, divided up into around six hundred Aboriginal bands. Some bands number fewer than one hundred and others more than five thousand, but all now have at least a degree of self-government as well as local fishing, hunting and land rights. Today, both status and non-status Indians can vote, but the former were only granted this right in 1960.

The Métis overrun

During the 1870s, most of the **Métis** had moved west into what was to become the province of **Saskatchewan** in 1905. They congregated along the Saskatchewan River in the vicinity of **Batoche**, but once again federal surveyors caught up with them and, in the 1880s, began to parcel up the land. In 1885, the Métis rose in **revolt** and, after the return of **Louis Riel**, formed a provisional government. In March they successfully beat

1882	1885	1885
"So this is Winnipeg; I can tell it's not Paris" Oscar Wilde exclaims on an extended lecture tour of North America.	Louis Riel, a Méti leader, is executed despite the jury recommending mercy.	The Last Spike goes in and Canada's first transcontinental railway is completed.

off a detachment of Mounties, encouraging the neighbouring Cree to raid a Hudson's Bay Company store. It seemed that a general insurrection might follow and indeed the Plains Indians were desperate: they were ravaged by smallpox, befuddled by the treaty system, and facing starvation following the **disappearance of the buffalo herds**. Yet Ottawa was having none of this: they dispatched a force of seven thousand men plus an armed steamer and after two preliminary skirmishes the Métis and the Cree were crushed. Riel, despite his obvious insanity, was found guilty of treason and hanged in November 1885.

The defeat of the Métis opened a new phase in the development of the West. In 1886 the **first train** ran from Montréal to Vancouver and settlers swarmed onto the prairies, pushing the population to 1,300,000 in 1911, up from 250,000 in 1890. Clifford Sifton, minister of the interior, encouraged the large-scale immigration from Eastern Europe of what he called "stalwart peasants in sheepskin coats". These Ukrainian, Polish, Czech and Hungarian **farmers** ploughed up the grasslands and turned central Canada into a vast granary, leading the Dominion into the "wheat boom" of the early twentieth century.

Two world wars

In the early twentieth century, Canada's burgeoning economy attracted immigrants by the thousand: in 1850, for example, Toronto had 30,000 inhabitants, 81,000 in 1882, and 230,000 in 1910. Most of these immigrants came from Britain, and when **World War I** broke out in 1914 the citizens of loyalist Canada poured into the streets to sing *Rule Britannia*. Thousands of volunteers thronged the recruiting stations – an enthusiasm that would cost many of them their lives: no fewer than six hundred and twenty thousand Canadians fought in the war, and casualties amounted to around ten percent.

Immediately after the war, Canada hit the economic buffers and, just when it appeared that matters were on the mend, the economy was hit by the stock market crash of 1929. During the **Great Depression** unemployment reached astronomical levels – between 30 and 35 percent – and economic problems were compounded by the lack of a decent welfare system. The hastily established Department of Welfare was only able to issue food and clothing vouchers, meaning that thousands slept in the streets. Fate was cruel too: Canada experienced some of the severest weather it had ever had, with perishing winters followed by boiling hot summers.

At the start of **World War II**, thousands of Canadians rushed to join the armed forces once again. The British were extremely grateful and Churchill visited Canada on several occasions, making a series of famous speeches here. The war also resuscitated the Canadian economy – as well as that of the United States – as Canada's factories switched to war production. Boatloads of British kids were also shipped to Canada to escape the attentions of Hitler's Luftwaffe. After the war, Canada set about the process of reconstruction in earnest, trusting its wartime leader – and longest-serving prime minister (22 years) – the Liberal **William Lyon Mackenzie King** to push things along. Almost without a break, the Liberals remained in power until 1984 and from their ranks came the two dominant political figures of the age, **Lester Pearson** and **Pierre Trudeau**.

1896	1917	1917
Gold discovered in the Yukon; the Klondike gold rush is on.	Tom Thomson, the greatest of all Canadian painters, drowns in the Ontario backcountry.	Battle of Vimy Ridge: for the first time Canada's army divisions act under a unified command; Canada's Gallipoli, without defeat.

Aboriginal peoples from 1900 to today

For Canada's **Aboriginal peoples** the early years of the twentieth century were grim. Herded onto small reservations under the authoritarian control of the Minister of Indian Affairs, they were subjected to a concerted campaign of **Europeanization** – ceremonies such as the sun dance and the potlatch were banned, and they were obliged to send their children to boarding schools for ten months of the year. Deprived of their traditions and independence, they lapsed into poverty, alcoholism and apathy. In the late 1940s, the academic Frederick Tisdall estimated that no fewer than 65,000 reservation Aboriginals were "chronically sick" from starvation. In addition, the Inuit were drawn into increasing dependence on the Hudson's Bay Company, who encouraged them to concentrate on hunting for furs rather than food, while the twin agencies of the Christian missions and the RCMP worked to incorporate the Inuit into white culture. Across Canada, a major consequence of the disruption of the traditional way of Aboriginal life was the spread of disease, especially tuberculosis, which was fifteen to twenty times more prevalent among the Aboriginal population than among whites.

In 1951, a new **Indian Act** increased both the autonomy of tribal bands and federal subsidies, but nonetheless Aboriginal people remained well behind the rest of Canadian society in all the key economic indicators. In 1969, the average income of a Canadian family was $8874, while 88 percent of Aboriginal families earned $3000 or less, with fifty percent earning less than $1000. In that same year, partly as a result of lobbying, all **Indian agents** were withdrawn from reservations, and Aboriginal political organizations started receiving government funding. Increasingly, these organizations focused on the need for full recognition of their Aboriginal rights and renegotiation of the treaties that had created the reservations.

Political stirrings: the Assembly of First Nations

The early 1980s saw the foundation of the **Assembly of First Nations** (**AFN**), which championed "Status Indians" in a number of legal actions over treaty rights and opposed federal plans to abolish the whole notion of "Status Indians". Many of these treaty cases were based on breaches of the 1763 proclamation, whose terms stated that Aboriginal land rights could only be taken away by direct negotiation with the Crown. One Grand Chief of the AFN, **Ovide Mercredi** – a lawyer and former human-rights commissioner – announced his objective was to secure equal status between the AFN and the provincial governments, a stance indicative of the growth in Aboriginal self-confidence, despite the continuing impoverishment of the reservations. The political weight of the AFN was made clear in the constitutional talks that took place over the establishment of an **Inuit homeland** in the Northwest Territories, a complex negotiation resulting in an agreement to create two self-governing territories in 1999 (see page 858).

Direct action and cultural resurgence

Despite the best efforts of the AFN, not all of Canada's Aboriginals, who comprise around three percent of the country's population, saw – or see – negotiation as their salvation: the action of armed Mohawks to prevent a golf course being built on tribal burial grounds at **Oka** in Québec in 1990 displayed an almost uncontainable anger against the dominant whites, and divided sympathies across the country.

1942	1949	1963
"There are no limits to the majestic future which lies before the mighty expanse of Canada with its virile, aspiring, cultured, and generous-hearted people." Winston Churchill butters up the Canadians during World War II.	Newfoundland joins Canada – but only just.	Trans-Canada Highway completed – all 7821km of it.

The Oka militants paved the way for more conciliatory voices to hold sway in the AFN, but the balance of power between those committed to negotiation as distinct from those favouring direct action is delicate. As a result, the AFN ploughs on with negotiations that rarely hit the headlines against a backdrop lit by occasional bursts of unrestrained rage.

More positively, there has been a resurgence in **fine and applied art**, and Aboriginal ceremonies, like the summer pow wows, now attract large crowds and more media attention. Aboriginal theatre groups have sprung up across Canada; there's a public television channel for Indigenous people, the **Aboriginal Peoples Television Network** (ⓦaptn.ca); and in 1996 a National Aboriginal Day, now called the **National Indigenous Peoples Day** was agreed and fixed for every June 21.

Québec and the future of Canada

Just as Canada's indigenous people drew inspiration from the worldwide national liberation movements of the 1960s, so did the **Québécois**. Ever since the fall of New France (see page 871), the francophones had been concerned about *la survivance*, the continuation of their language and culture. This anxiety had peaks and troughs but the Québécois establishment, comprising both the Catholic clergy and the province's politicians, kept a lid on the discontent, recommending accommodation with the British and later the federal authorities. Characteristically, this elite upheld the traditional values of a Catholic and rural New France, and Québec's industry and commerce developed under anglophone control. Thus, in early twentieth-century Montréal, a francophone proletariat worked in the factories of anglophone owners, a situation that stirred deep (historical) resentments. The elite was ill-equipped to deal with its own working class, which in turn helped spur the development of a new generation of Québec **separatists**.

Held in Montréal, **Expo '67** was meant to be a confirmation of Canada's arrival as an industrial power of the first rank. Yet when French president **Charles de Gaulle** used the event as a platform to announce his advocacy of a "free Québec", he ignited a row that has pretty much dominated the political agenda ever since. That same year, **René Lévesque** formed the **Parti Québécois (PQ)**, with the ultimate goal of full independence, hence the slogan *Maîtres chez nous* ("masters in our own house"). But in 1968 this was offset by the election of a determinedly federalist French-Canadian, **Pierre Trudeau**, as prime minister: the scene was set for a showdown.

An independent Québec? Referenda and turmoil

The **PQ** represented the political wing of a social movement that, at its most militant and extreme, embraced the activities of the short-lived **Front de la Libération du Québec (FLQ)**. In 1970, the FLQ kidnapped and murdered Pierre Laporte, the province's Minister of Labour, and an enraged Trudeau put the troops onto the streets of Montréal. This reaction benefitted the PQ, a modernizing party of the social-democratic Left, which came to power in 1976 and set about using state resources to develop Québécois economic interests such as the hydroelectric plant on James Bay. It also passed a contentious language law, **Bill 101**, which made French the province's official language and placed all sorts of restrictions on the use of English. This was too

1970	1995	1988	1999
The actions of the Front de libération du Québec (FLQ) create a national crisis; Pierre Trudeau takes control.	Second referendum on an independent Québec takes place; separatists fail again.	Abortion legalized – without any legal restrictions.	Nunavut becomes Canada's newest province, with the Inuit in the majority.

much for many anglophones, especially as the PQ also had plans for a referendum on secession, and thousands of them hot-tailed it out of Québec with the majority emigrating to Ontario. Yet, when the **referendum** came, in 1980, sixty percent of Québec's electorate voted "*non*" to separation, though if anyone thought this was the end of the matter, they were soon to be disappointed.

Shortly afterwards, Trudeau stirred the pot by **repatriating** the country's constitution under the terms of the **Constitution Act**, signed by Queen Elizabeth II in 1982. Trudeau made it unequivocally clear that, as far as he was concerned, Québec had no veto over constitutional amendments (as it maintained it did) and the Québec provincial government responded by refusing to sign the act – and still hasn't to this day. Three years later, the Liberals won control of Québec from the PQ, but in 1994 the PQ returned to office, promising to hold a **second independence referendum**. This they did in 1995, but the PQ lost again. Thereafter, Canada's politicians have made determined efforts to sort the issue out once and for all, but they have failed and, like the ball that keeps bouncing back, the PQ returned to office in 2012 and pledged to drive an independence agenda yet again. There were groans across all of English-speaking Canada. But those groans didn't last long: it turned out to be a very challenging two years for the PQ, which lost to the Liberal Party under Philippe Couillard in the 2014 general elections. This marked the PQ with this unfortunate distinction: the first single-term government since the Union Nationale government was defeated in 1970.

Into the twenty-first century

In the 1980s and 1990s, Canada seemed beset with problems: the Québec imbroglio was never ending; the NAFTA free trade agreement between the US and Canada destroyed the country's protective tariffs and caused thousands of redundancies; and the collapse of the North Atlantic cod fishery brought Nova Scotia and Newfoundland to the brink of economic ruin. There was also a crisis of political leadership with the prime minister, **Brian Mulroney**, becoming widely derided for incompetence, his party, the Progressive Conservatives (PCs), commonly accused of large-scale corruption. In 1993, the PCs reaped an electoral whirlwind when they were almost wiped out in the federal elections and the Liberals, under **Jean Chrétien**, were returned to office with a huge majority. A cautious politician, Chrétien had some success in rebuilding federal prestige, his pragmatic approach to politics proving sufficiently popular to see him re-elected for a second term in 1997 and a third in 2000, albeit with reduced majorities.

Paul Martin

In 2003, Chrétien reluctantly announced his retirement and the Liberals appointed a new leader, **Paul Martin**. Meanwhile, facing the prospect of further electoral defeats, Canada's two rightist parties – the Canadian Alliance (from the Midwest) and the Progressive Conservatives – belatedly managed to swallow their differences, uniting to form the **Conservative Party**, but were still unable to defeat the Liberals in the federal elections of 2004. The new Liberal administration, with Martin as premier, did not have an overall majority and its political weakness made the government shaky. Still, the Martin regime did manage to pass several progressive

2002	2003	2005	2010
Canadian troops join the Americans in Afghanistan for what turns into a ten-year stay.	Increasing prices make oil extraction from Canada's giant oil sands economic.	Same-sex marriage legalized.	The XXI Olympic Winter Games are held in the Vancouver area, marking the first time that the Olympics are hosted in British Columbia.

measures, including the Civil Marriage Act of 2005 and the Kelowna Accord dedicated to improving the lot of Canada's Aboriginal people. In the end, it wasn't the politics that did for Martin, but allegations of **corruption**, which swirled round the prime minister until the Liberals lost a vote of parliamentary confidence in late 2005. Shortly afterwards the **federal elections of 2006** produced a narrow victory for the Conservatives with **Stephen Harper** becoming the new prime minister of a minority administration.

From Stephen Harper to a new Trudeau

The Conservatives made a good showing in the federal election of 2008, strengthening Harper's position, but they still failed to secure an overall majority. Harper continued with his minority administration and even ventured into the Québec imbroglio, suggesting he would recognize that "the Québécois form a nation within a united Canada" – which had all the pundits rushing off to the dictionary to define "nation". Harper proved to be far from blunder free, but he was astute and he bided his time, undoubtedly benefiting from the relative soundness of the Canadian banking system, which had not been deregulated to the extent it had elsewhere: the financial crisis that broke across Europe and in the US in 2008 only ruffled the country's waters rather than creating a full-blown gale. Harper's reward came in the **federal elections of 2011** when the Conservatives won an overall majority – and the Liberals sank to third place. At last, unencumbered by the need to placate more centrist politicians, Harper could show his right-wing credentials. And, he did just that during his tenure: tightening immigration policy, diminishing federal funding increases for Medicare and adjusting environmental laws to boost oil extraction from the Athabasca oil sands and to aid mining companies. In 2011, Canada became the first country to withdraw from the Kyoto Protocol on global warming. Harper also trumpeted the country's royal traditions, welcoming the Duke and Duchess of Cambridge on their first official overseas trip as a married couple. In the same year, Canada pulled out its combat troops in Afghanistan, and by spring 2013, the government had fully ceased all operations in the country.

However, in the 2015 Canadian federal election, the Liberal Party, led by **Justin Trudeau**, son of former Prime Minister Pierre Trudeau, won by a surprise landslide, bringing Harper's tenure to an end. In November 2015, the charismatic 43-year-old was sworn in as Canada's Prime Minister, and after more than three decades Canada is once again helmed by a Trudeau. The young Trudeau acted on several of his campaign promises almost immediately: in a first for Canada, he unveiled a cabinet that is gender-equal – fifty percent women. When asked why, his answer was powerfully simple: "Because it's 2015." Trudeau moved fast on promised middle class tax cuts, welcomed 25,000 Syrian refugees and appointed an inquiry commission to investigate missing and murdered Indigenous women. His government also legalized recreational cannabis use and pardoned people with convictions for possessing up to 30 grams. Trudeau has pledged to tackle climate change and to usher in a new era of "positive politics" – although relations with the US are at a low point after Trump criticised him for being "meek and mild". Despite this, in 2018, after a year of wrangling, NAFTA (the North American Free Trade Agreement) was successfully renegotiated and sealed with a new trade deal name: the United States-Mexico-Canada Agreement.

2011	**2015**	**2018**
Canada ends its combat role in Afghanistan and coordinates efforts with the US and Britain to tighten sanctions on Iran.	In the October 2015 federal election, Justin Trudeau of the Liberal Party wins a landslide victory and is sworn in as Prime Minister in November.	Canada becomes the second country in the world to legalise recreational cannabis use.

The natural environment

Canada has just about every type of natural habitat going, from ice-bound polar islands in the far north to sun-drilled pockets of desert along the US border. Between these extremes the country's mountains, forests and grasslands support an incredible variety and profusion of wildlife – any brief account can only scratch the surface of what it's possible to see. National and provincial parks offer the best starting places, and we've listed some of the outstanding sites for spotting particular species. Don't expect to see the big attractions like bears and wolves easily; despite the enthusiasm of guides and tourist offices, these are encountered only rarely.

Eastern forests

Canada's **eastern forests** divide into two main groups – the Carolinian forest of southwest Ontario, and the Great Lakes–St Lawrence forest extending from the edge of the Carolinian forest to Lake Superior and the Gulf of St Lawrence.

The Carolinian forest

The **Carolinian forest** forms a narrow belt of largely deciduous hardwood trees similar to the broad-leaved woodlands found over much of the eastern United States. Trees are often typical of more southerly climes – Kentucky coffee tree, tulip tree, sassafras and sycamore among others, and more ordinary staples like beech, sugar maple and basswood. None of these are rare in the US, but in Canada they grow only here, thanks to the region's rich soils and relatively warm, sheltered climate.

Urban and agricultural sprawl threaten much of Ontario's Carolinian flora and fauna and today much of the original forest has shrunk to a mosaic of fragments protected by national and provincial parks. The forests are most often visited by tourists for the astounding October colours, but if you're looking for **wildlife** you might also catch Canada's only marsupial, the **opossum**, or other southern species like the **fox squirrel** (introduced on Lake Erie's Pelee Island); the **eastern mole**, which occurs only in Essex County on Lake Erie's north shore; and the **eastern vole**, found only in a narrow band around Lake Erie.

Carolinian birds and reptiles

Naturalists are equally drawn to the Carolinian forest for the **birds**, many of which are found nowhere else in Canada, especially during seasonal migrations. Most noteworthy of the more unusual species is the **golden swamp warbler**, a bird of almost unnaturally colourful plumage. More common visitors are hooded and Kentucky warblers, blue-winged and golden-winged warblers, gnatcatchers, and virtually every species of eastern North American hawk; sharp-shin hawks are common, and during autumn migrations thousands of broad-winged hawks might be seen in a single day near Port Stanley on Lake Erie's north shore. In the wetlands bordering the forests, particularly at Long Point on Lake Erie, you can search out **reptiles** found nowhere else in the country. Most impressive is the water-loving **fox snake**, a harmless animal that often reaches well over a metre in length, but is often killed because of its resemblance to the rattlesnake and venomous copperhead – neither of which is found in the region. Also present, but in marked decline, are several **turtle** species, especially Blanding's, wood, spotted and spiny softshell.

Great Lakes–St Lawrence forests

Occurring in one of the most densely populated parts of Canada, the mixed **conifer forests** of the **Great Lakes–St Lawrence** area have been heavily logged and severely affected by urbanization. Most of the trees are southern species – beech and sugar maple, red and white pines – but are mixed with the eastern hemlock, spruce, jack pine, paper birch and balsam fir typical of more northerly forests. This region is second only to southern BC in the number of bird species it supports. It also provides for large numbers of **white-tailed deer**, a rare beneficiary of logging as it prefers to browse along

FLORA AND FAUNA CHECKLIST

This is by no means an exhaustive list of all Canada's **flora and fauna** – simply an indication of the places and the seasons, you are most likely to see certain species and types of wildlife.

Bears Black bears: Glacier National Park, BC, and Banff, Jasper and Kananaskis Country, AB. Grizzlies: Glacier National Park, BC, and Khutzeymateen Estuary, north of Prince Rupert, BC (Aug)

Bison Wood Buffalo National Park, AB

Butterfly Migrations: Point Pelee, Lake Erie, ON (spring and autumn)

Caribou Dempster Hwy, YT (autumn)

Cranes and pelicans Last Mountain Lake, SK (late Aug)

Dall's sheep Sheep Mountain, Kluane National Park, YT (summer)

Desert species Cacti, sagebrush, rattlesnakes and kangaroo rats: around Osoyoos, BC (summer)

Eagles and owls Boundary Bay, south of Vancouver, BC (winter)

Elk Banff, Jasper and Kananaskis Country, AB (summer)

Polar bears Near Churchill, MB (autumn)

Prairie species Hawks, coyotes and rattlesnakes: in the Milk River region, AB (May and June)

Salmon Adams River sockeye salmon run near Salmon Arm, BC (Oct)

Sea birds Gannets, murres and black kittiwakes around Cape St Mary's, NFL. Waterfowl and sea birds in the Haida Gwaii, BC. Northern gannets on Bonaventure Island, Gaspé Peninsula, QC (June and July)

Sea otters and sea lions Off Pacific Rim National Park, Vancouver Island, BC (spring and summer)

Seals Haida Gwaii, BC (summer)

Snow geese Cap-Tourmente, QC (autumn)

Whales Beluga, fin, humpback, blue and minke whales: near Tadoussac, QC, and Bay of Fundy, NB. Killer whales (orcas): Robson Bight in Johnstone Strait, Vancouver Island, BC (all in summer). Grey whales: Pacific Rim National Park, Vancouver Island, BC (spring and summer)

clearing edges. In the evergreen stands on the north shore of the St Lawrence River there are also large numbers of Canada's smallest mammal, the **pygmy shrew**. These tiny animals must eat their own weight in food daily and can't rest for more than an hour or so – they'd starve to death if they tried to sleep through the night.

Grassland

Contrary to the popular image of Canada's interior as a huge prairie of waving wheat, true **grassland** covers only ten percent of the country. Most is concentrated in the southernmost reaches of Alberta and Saskatchewan, with tiny spillovers in Manitoba and BC. Two grassland belts once thrived in the region, **tall-grass prairie** in the north and **shortgrass** in the south. Farming has now not only put large areas of each under crops, but also decimated most of the large mammals that roamed the range – pronghorns, mule and white-tailed deer, elk, wolves, grizzlies, coyotes, foxes and cougars.

The most dramatic loss from the grasslands has been **bison** (or **buffalo**), the continent's largest land mammal. Once numbering an estimated 45 million, Canada's bison are now limited to just a few free-roaming herds. They're extraordinarily impressive animals – the average bull stands six feet at the shoulder and weighs over a tonne – and early prairie settlers were so struck with their size that they believed bison, not the climate, had been responsible for clearing the grasslands.

Once almost as prevalent as the bison, but now almost as rare, is the **pronghorn**, a beautiful tawny-gold antelope species. Capable of speeds of over 100kph, it's the continent's swiftest land mammal. Uniquely adapted for speed and stamina, the pronghorn has long legs, a heart twice the size of similar-sized animals, and an astonishingly wide windpipe. It complements its respiratory machinery by running with its mouth open to gulp maximum amounts of air. Though only the size of a large dog, it has larger eyes than those of a horse, a refinement that spots predators several kilometres away. Today, wolves and coyotes are more likely to be after the prairie's new masters – countless small rodents such as **gophers**, **ground squirrels** and **jackrabbits**. Birds typical of the grassland include ducks, grebes, herons, pelicans, rails, marbled godwit, the curlew, and raptors such as the **prairie falcon**.

Boreal forest

The **boreal forest** is Canada's largest single ecosystem, bigger than all the others combined. Stretching in a broad belt from Newfoundland to the Yukon, it fills the area between the eastern forests, grasslands and the northern tundra, occupying a good slice of every province except BC. Only certain **trees** thrive in this zone of long, cold winters, short summers and acidic soils: expect to see billions of white and black spruce (plus red spruce in the east), balsam fir, tamarack (larch) and jack pine, as well as such deciduous species as birch, poplar and aspen – all of which are ideal for wood pulp, making the boreal forest the staple resource of the country's **lumber industry**. If you spend any time in the backcountry you'll also come across **muskeg**: neither land nor water, this porridge-like bog is the breeding ground of choice for pestilent hordes of mosquitoes and blackflies – and Canada has 1.3 million square kilometres of it. It also harbours mosses, scrub willow and even the occasional orchid.

The boreal forest supports just about every **animal** recognized as distinctively Canadian: moose, beaver, black bear, wolf and lynx, plus small mammals and creatures such as deer, caribou and coyote from transitional forest-tundra and aspen-parkland habitats to the north and south. **Wolves** are still numerous in Canada, but hunting and harassment has pushed them to the northernmost parts of the boreal forest. Their supposed ferocity is more myth than truth; intelligent and elusive creatures, they rarely harm humans, and it's unlikely you'll see any – though you may well hear their howling if you're out in the sticks. **Lynx** are even more elusive. One of the northern forest's most elegant animals, this big cat requires a 150- to 200-square-kilometre range, making Canada's northern wilderness one of the world's few regions capable of sustaining a viable population.

Beavers and moose

Beavers are commonly seen all over the boreal regions of Canada. You may catch them at dawn or dusk, heads just above the water as they glide across lakes and rivers. Signs of their legendary activity include logjams across streams and ponds, stumps of felled saplings resembling sharpened pencils and dens which look like domed piles of mud and sticks. Lakes, streams and the margins of muskeg are all favoured by **moose**. A lumbering animal with magnificent spreading antlers, it is the largest member of the deer family and is found over most of Canada, but especially near swampy ground. It's also a favourite with hunters, and few northern bars are without their moose head.

Boreal birds

Forest wetlands also offer refuge for **ducks and geese**, with **loons**, grebes and songbirds attracted to the surrounding undergrowth. Canada's three species of ptarmigan – willow, rock and white-tailed – are also common, and you'll see plenty of big **raptors**, including the great grey owl. Many boreal birds migrate, and even those that don't – hawks, jays, ravens and grouse – tend to move a little way south, sometimes breaking out into southern Canada in mass movements known as "irruptions".

Mountain forests

Mountain forests cover much of western Canada and, depending on location and elevation, divide into four types: West Coast, Columbia, montane and subalpine.

West Coast forest

The **West Coast**'s torrential rainfall, mild maritime climate, deep soils and long growing season produce Canada's most impressive forests and its biggest trees. Swaths of luxuriant **temperate rainforest** cover much of Vancouver Island and the Pacific coast, dominated by Sitka spruce, western red cedar, Pacific silver fir, western hemlock, western yew and, biggest of all, **Douglas fir**, some of which tower ninety metres high and are 1200 years old. These conifers make valuable timber, and much of this forest is under severe threat from logging. Some of the best stands – a fraction of the original – have been preserved on the Haida Gwaii and in Vancouver Island's Pacific Rim National Park. Below the luxuriant, dripping canopy of the big trees lies an **undergrowth** teeming with life. Shrubs and bushes such as salal, huckleberry and bunchberry thrive alongside mosses, ferns, lichens and orchids. All sorts of animals can be found here, most notably the **cougar** and its main prey, the Columbian **blacktail deer**. **Birds** are legion, and include a wealth of woodland species such as the Townsend's warbler, Wilson's warbler and the orange-crowned warbler. Rarer birds include the Rufous hummingbird, which migrates from its Mexican wintering grounds to feed on the forest's numerous nectar-bearing flowers.

Columbia forest

The **Columbia forest** covers the lower slopes (400–1400m) of BC's interior mountains and much of the Rockies. **Trees** here are similar to those of the West Coast's warmer and wetter rainforest with Sitka spruce, which rarely thrives away from the coast, the notable exception. The undercover is also similar, with lots of devil's club (a particularly vicious thorn), azaleas and black and red twinberry. Mountain lily, columbine and bunchberry are among the common flowers. Few mammals live exclusively in the forests with the exception of the **red squirrel**, which in turn is preyed on by hawks, owls, coyotes and weasels. Bigger predators also roam the mountain forest, most notably the **brown bear**, a western variant of the ubiquitous **black bear**. Aside from the coyote, the tough, agile black bear is one of the continent's most successful carnivores and the one you're most likely to see around campsites and rubbish dumps. Black bears have adapted to a wide range of habitats and food sources, and their only natural enemies – save wolves, which may attack young cubs – are hunters. Scarcer is the famous **grizzly bear**, a far larger and potentially dangerous creature distinguished by its brownish fur and the ridged hump on its back. The grizzly is largely confined to the remoter slopes of the Rockies and West Coast ranges, where it feeds mainly on berries and salmon. Like other bears, grizzlies are unpredictable and readily provoked, so it's best to try and avoid unpleasant encounters.

Montane forest

Montane forest covers the more southerly and sheltered reaches of the Rockies and the dry plateaux of interior BC, where spindly Douglas fir, western larch, ponderosa pine and the **lodgepole pine** predominate. Like its eastern counterpart, the jack pine, the lodgepole requires intense heat before opening and releasing its seeds, and huge stands of these trees grew in the aftermath of the forest fires which accompanied the building and running of the railways. Plentiful voles and small rodents attract **coyotes**, whose yapping – an announcement of territorial claims – you'll often hear at night close to small towns. Coyotes are spreading northwards into the Yukon and Northwest Territories, and eastwards to Ontario, Québec, New Brunswick and Nova Scotia, a proliferation that continues despite massive extermination campaigns, prompted by the coyotes' taste for livestock. Few predators have the speed to keep up with coyotes – only the stealthy **cougar**, or wolves hunting in tandem, can successfully bring them down. Cougars are now severely depleted in Canada, and the BC interior and Vancouver Island are the only regions where they survive in significant numbers. Ponderosa and lodgepole pines provide fine cover for **birds** like goshawks, Swainson's hawks and lesser species such as ruby-crowned kinglets, warblers and pileated woodpeckers. In the forest's lowest reaches both the vegetation and the birdlife are those of the southern prairies – semiarid regions of sagebrush, prickly pear and bunch grasses, dotted with lakes full of common **ducks** such as the mallard. You might also see the cinnamon teal, a bird whose limited distribution draws birdwatchers to BC on its own account.

Subalpine forest

Subalpine forest covers mountain slopes from 1300m to 2200m throughout the Rockies and much of BC, supporting lodgepole, whitebark and limber pines, alpine fir and Engelmann spruce. It also contains a preponderance of **alpine larch**, a deciduous conifer whose vivid autumnal yellows dot the mountainsides to beautiful effect. One of the more common animals of this zone is the **elk**, a powerful member of the deer family, which can often be seen summering in large herds above the tree-line. Elk court and mate during the autumn, making a thin nasal sound called **bugling**; respect their privacy, as rutting elk have notoriously unpredictable temperaments. Small herds of **mule deer** migrate between forests and alpine meadows, using small glands between their hooves to leave a scent for other herd members to follow. Other smaller animals attracted to the subalpine forest include the golden-mantled ground squirrel and birds such as **Clark's nutcracker**, both tame and curious creatures, which often gather around campsites in search of scraps.

Alpine zones

Alpine zones occur in mountains above the tree-line, which in Canada means parts of the Rockies, much of BC and large areas of the Yukon. Plant and animal life varies hugely between summer and winter, and according to terrain and exposure to the elements – sometimes it resembles that of the tundra, at others it recalls the profile of lower forest habitats. In spring, alpine meadows are carpeted with breathtaking displays of **wildflowers**: clumps of Parnassus grass, lilies, Indian paintbrushes and a wealth of yellow flowers such as arnica, cinquefoil and glacier lily. These meadows make excellent pasture, attracting elk and mule deer in summer, as well as full-time residents such as **Dall sheep**, the related **bighorn** and the incredible **mountain goat**, perhaps the hardiest of Canada's bigger mammals.

Marmots, resembling overstuffed squirrels, take things easier and hibernate through the worst of the winter and beyond. In a good year they can sleep for eight months, prey only to grizzly bears, which are strong enough and have the claws to dig down into their dens. In their waking periods they can be tame and friendly, often nibbling contentedly in the sunnier corners of campsites. When threatened, however, they produce a piercing and unearthly whistle. The strange little **pika**, a relative of the rabbit, is more elusive but keeps itself busy year-round, living off a miniature haystack of fodder, which it accumulates during the summer.

Birds are numerous in summer, and include rosy finch, pipit and blue grouse, but few manage to live in the alpine zone year-round. One that does is the **white-tailed ptarmigan**, which, thanks to its heavily feathered feet and legs, is able to snowshoe around deep snow drifts; its white winter plumage provides camouflage.

Coastlines

Canada has three **coastlines**: the **Atlantic**, the **Pacific** and the **Arctic** (see page 862). Each boasts a profusion of maritime, dunal and intertidal life; the Pacific coast, warmed by the Japanese current, actually has the greatest number of species of any temperate shore. Yet few people are very interested in the small fry – most come for the big mammals, **whales** in particular.

TRAILING WHALES AROUND CANADA

Canada has the longest coastline in the world, which translates into excellent whale-watching. **Grey whales** are comparatively common in the Pacific, and are easily spotted from mainland headlands in the February-to-May and September-to-October periods as they migrate between the Arctic and their breeding grounds off Mexico. Once hunted close to the point of extinction, they've now returned in large numbers. **Humpback whales** are another favourite, largely because they're curious and follow sightseeing boats, but also because of their surface acrobatics and long, haunting "songs". They too were hunted to near-extinction, and though protected by international agreement since 1966 they still number less than ten percent of their original population. Vancouver Island's inner coast supports one of the world's most concentrated populations of **killer whales** or **orcas**. These are often seen in family groups or "pods" travelling close to shore, usually on the trail of large fish – which on the West Coast means **salmon**. The orca is the only whale whose diet also runs to warm-blooded animals – hence the "killer" tag – and it will gorge on walrus, seal and even minke, grey and beluga whales. For whale-watching tours, check the individual chapters, where recommended operators are listed.

Pacific sea otters, fur seals and sea lions

Another West Coast inhabitant, the **sea otter**, differs from most marine mammals in that it keeps itself warm with a thick soft coat of fur rather than with blubber. With binoculars, it's often easy to spot these charming creatures lolling on their backs, cracking open sea urchins or mussels with a rock and using their stomachs as anvils; they often lie bobbing asleep, entwined in kelp to stop them floating away. Northern **fur seals** breed on Alaska's Pribilof Islands but are often seen off the BC coast during their migrations. Like their cousin, the northern **sea lion**, a year-round resident, they are "eared seals", who can manage rudimentary shuffling on land thanks to short rear limbs which can be rotated for forward movement. They also swim with strokes from front flippers, as opposed to the slithering, fish-like action of true seals.

The Atlantic coast

The **Atlantic**'s colder waters nurture fewer overall species than the Pacific coast, but many birds and larger mammals – especially **whales** – are common to both. One of the Atlantic region's more distinctive creatures is the **harp seal**, a true seal species that migrates in late winter to breeding grounds off Newfoundland and in the Greenland and White seas. Most pups are born on the pack ice, and for about two weeks sport fluffy white coats that have been highly prized by the fur trade for centuries.

Tundra

Tundra extends over much of northern Yukon, the Northwest Territories and Nunavut, stretching between the boreal forest and the polar seas. Part grassland and part wasteland, it's a region distinguished by high winds, bitter cold and **permafrost**, a layer of perpetually frozen subsoil which covers over thirty percent of Canada. Yet the tundra is not only the domain of ice and emptiness: long hours of summer sunshine and the melting of topsoil nurture a carpet of wildflowers and many species of bird and mammals have adapted to the vagaries of climate and terrain.

Vegetation is uniformly stunted by poor drainage, acidic soils and permafrost, which prevents the formation of deep roots and locks nutrients in the ice. **Trees** like birch and willow can grow, but they spread their branches over a wide area, rarely rising over a metre in height. Over 99 percent of the remaining vegetation consists of perennials like **grasses and sedges**, small flowering annuals, mosses, lichens and shrubs. Most have evolved ingenious ways of protecting themselves against the elements: Arctic cotton grass, for example, grows in large insulated hummocks in which the interior temperature is higher than the air outside. **Wildflowers** during the short, intense spring can be superlative, covering seemingly inert ground in a carpet of purple mountain saxifrage, yellow Arctic poppy and indigo clusters of Arctic forget-me-not.

Tundra mammals

Tundra grasses provide some of the first links in the food chain, nourishing mammals such as the white **Arctic ground squirrel**, whose fur the Inuit use to make parka jackets. Vegetation also provides the staple diet of **lemmings**, among the most remarkable of Arctic fauna. Instead of hibernating these creatures live under the snow, busily nibbling away on shoots in order to double their weight daily – the intake they need merely to survive. They also breed almost continuously, which is just as well, for they are the mainstay of a long list of predators. Chief of these are **Arctic white foxes**, ermines and weasels, though birds, bears and Arctic wolves may also hunt them in preference to larger prey. Given their importance in the food chain, lemming populations have a marked effect on the life cycles of many other creatures.

A notable exception is the **caribou**, a member of the reindeer family and the most populous of the big tundra mammals. Caribou are known for their epic migrations, frequently involving thousands of animals, which start in March when the herds leave their wintering grounds on the fringes of the boreal forest for calving grounds to the north. The exact purpose of these migrations is still debated. They certainly prevent the overgrazing of the tundra's fragile mosses and lichens, and probably also enable the caribou to shake off some of the wolves that would otherwise shadow the herd (wolves have to find southerly dens at this time to bear their own pups). The timing of treks also means calving takes place before the arrival of biting insects, which can claim as many calves as predators – an adult caribou can lose as much as a litre of blood a week to insects.

The tundra's other large mammal is the **musk ox**, a vast, shaggy herbivore and close cousin of the bison. The musk ox's Achilles' heel is a tendency to form lines or circles when threatened – a perfect defence against wolves, but not against hunters, who, until the introduction of conservation measures, threatened to be their undoing. Canada now has some of the world's largest free-roaming herds, although – like the caribou – the Inuit still hunt them for food and fur.

Tundra birds

Tundra **birds** number about a hundred species and are mostly migratory. Three-quarters of these are **waterfowl**, which arrive early to take advantage of streams, marshes and small lakes created by surface meltwater: Arctic wetlands provide nesting grounds for numerous swans, geese and ducks, as well as the **loon**, which is immortalized on the back of the Canadian dollar coin. The red-necked **phalarope** is a particularly specialized visitor, able to feed on aquatic insects and plankton, though not as impressive in its abilities as the migratory **Arctic tern**, whose 32,000km round-trip from the Antarctic is the longest annual migration of any creature on the planet. The handful of non-migratory birds tend to be scavengers like the raven, or predators like the **gyrfalcon**, the world's largest falcon, which preys on Arctic hares and ptarmigan. Jaegers, gulls, hawks and owls largely depend on the lemming.

The Arctic coast

Fauna on the **Arctic coast** has a food chain that starts with plankton and algae, ranging up through tiny crustaceans, clams and mussels, sea cucumbers and sea urchins, cod, ringed and bearded seals, to beluga whales and **polar bears** – perhaps the most evocative of all tundra creatures. Migrating **birds** are especially common here, notably near Nunaluk Spit on the Yukon coast, which is used as a corridor and stopover by millions of loons, swans, geese and plovers, among others.

Books

Most of the books listed below are in print and in paperback and those that are out of print (o/p) should be easy to track down secondhand. Note also that while we recommend all the books we've listed below, we do have favourites – and these have been marked with ★.

TRAVELOGUES

★ **Will Ferguson** *Beauty Tips from Moose Jaw.* Humorist Ferguson spent three years crisscrossing Canada and this finely observed, semi-comic travelogue is the result. Beyond the amusing anecdotes, factual treasures and liberal doses of gentle skepticism, the book also serves to shed some light on Canada's psychogeography – no small feat in a country so vast. Required reading for both Canadians and anyone visiting the country. If you liked it, try the same author's *How to Be a Canadian: Even If You Already Are One.*

John Gimlette *Theatre of Fish: Travels through Newfoundland and Labrador.* Apparently following in the footsteps of his great-grandfather, Gimlette reaches parts of the province few have travelled in this lively, entertaining journal that is, at times, perhaps a little too colloquial for its own (stylistic) good.

Grey Owl *The Men of the Last Frontier; Tales of an Empty Cabin; Sajo and the Beaver People.* First published in the 1930s, these three books, which are often packaged together in one form or another, give a romantic description of life in the wilds of Canada at the time when exploitation was changing the land forever. Grey Owl's love of animals and the wilderness are inspiring and his forward-thinking,

ecological views are surprising.

★ **Paul Kane** *Wanderings of an Artist among the Indians of North America.* Kane, one of Canada's better-known landscape artists, spent two and a half years travelling from Toronto to the Pacific coast and back in the 1840s. His witty, racy account of his wanderings makes a delightful read.

Gary and Joanie McGuffin *Quetico: Into the Wild.* The McGuffins love canoeing and have produced several books on their assorted travels – and this is the latest. Remote Quetico Park is in northern Ontario.

Susanna Moodie *Roughing It in the Bush: or Life in Canada.* Intriguing narrative written in 1852, describing an English couple's slow ruin as they attempt to create a new life in southeastern Ontario.

★ **Jan Morris** *O Canada: Travels in an Unknown Country* (o/p). Musings from this respected travel writer after a coast-to-coast Canadian trip. Comprises a series of finely judged and beautifully written essays on each of Canada's principal cities. Published in 1992, some of Morris's observations are inevitably outmoded, but the book is still an excellent primer.

CULTURE, ART AND SOCIETY

Kevin Bazzana *Wondrous Strange: the Life and Art of Glenn Gould.* Scholarly, well-researched Gould reader giving the low-down of every facet of the man and his music – in 500-odd pages. Gould fans will love it.

Hugh Brody *Maps and Dreams* (o/p). Brilliantly written account of the lives and lands of the Beaver (Dane-zaa) First Nations (Indian) band of northwest Canada. For further acute insights into the ways of the far North see also the same author's *Among the Inuit.*

Stephen Brunt *Gretzky's Tears* and *Searching for Bobby Orr.* Two fascinating looks at ice hockey, the sport that helps define Canada. In *Gretzky's Tears*, Brunt, a sports columnist for the *Globe and Mail*, tells the story of the trade that sent Wayne Gretzky – considered by most to be the game's best ever player – to Los Angeles from Edmonton; the move helped transform hockey and had a huge impact on many Canadians. *Searching for Bobby Orr* is more of a character study of another famous Canadian player, whose sheer athletic talent changed the game during an era when hockey was just starting to become more of a "business";

greed, ego, naivetey and disillusionment were to follow.

Lovat Dickson *Wilderness Man: The Strange Story of Grey Owl* (o/p). The fascinating tale of Archie Belaney, the Englishman who became famous as his adopted persona, Grey Owl. Written by his English publisher, who was one of many not to discover the charade until after Grey Owl's death.

Christian F. Feest *Three Centuries of Woodlands Indian Art.* This attractively illustrated book covers every aspect of its subject in revealing detail. Published in 2007.

The Kino-Nda-Niimi Collective (editor) *The Winter We Danced: Voices from the Past, the Future, and the Idle No More Movement.* An invaluable and emotional collection of writing, poetry, lyrics, images and art contributed by First Native People and their allies, which gives an insight into the Idle No More protest movement. All proceeds go to the Native Youth Sexual Heath Network. Published in 2014.

Mark Kurlansky *Cod: A Biography of the Fish that Changed the World.* This fascinating book tracks the life and times of the cod and the generations of fishermen who have lived off it. There are sections on overfishing and the fish's breeding habits along with cod recipes. The Newfoundland cod fishery features prominently and you won't get a more balanced view as to what went wrong – and why the fishery became decimated.

Barry Lopez *Arctic Dreams*. Extraordinary, award-winning book combining natural history, physics, poetry, earth sciences and philosophy in a dazzling portrait of the far North.

★ **A.B. McKillop** *The Spinster and the Prophet: A Tale of H.G. Wells, Plagiarism and the History of the World*. In 1925 Toronto teacher and armchair historian Florence Deeks sued the great H.G. Wells for the then-fabulous sum of $500,000 for his supposed literary piracy of her manuscript about the history of the world. Did he do it? Was she simply an overwrought spinster? Read on.

Dennis Reid *A Concise History of Canadian Painting*. Not especially concise, but a thorough trawl through Canada's leading artists, with bags of biographical detail and lots of illustrations of major works. The third, updated edition of this book, which goes as far as 2000, was published in 2012. Reid has also compiled the book on Canada's greatest painter, *Tom Thomson*.

Jonathan Vance *A History of Canadian Culture*. Ambitious, 500-page attempt to master its subject with plenty of time to define what exactly culture is – as distinct from, or the same as, mass entertainment. Immaculate historical research, including – for example – plays written by sailors ice-bound in the Arctic.

HISTORY

Fred Anderson *Crucible of War: The Seven Years' War and the Fate of the British Empire in British North America, 1754–1766*. Lucid and extraordinarily well-researched account of this crucial period in the development of North America. At 800-odd pages, it's perhaps a little too detailed for many tastes, but it's a fascinating read. Included is the story of the fall of Fort William Henry, as celebrated in the film, *The Last of the Mohicans*.

Owen Beattie & John Geiger *Frozen in Time: The Fate of the Franklin Expedition 1845–48*. An account both of the doomed expedition to find the Northwest Passage and the discovery of artefacts and bodies still frozen in the northern ice; worth buying for the extraordinary photos alone. Published in 2004.

Carl Benn *The Iroquois in the War of 1812* (o/p). In 1812, the US was at war with Canada and one of its armies invaded and briefly occupied Toronto. The role played by the Iroquois people in the war was pivotal to Canada's survival and the ramifications of the conflict affected the Iroquois for generations to come.

★ **Pierre Berton** *Klondike Fever: the Last Great Goldrush 1896–1899*. Until his death in 2004, the prolific Berton was Canada's leading popular historian, writing a whole stream of eminently readable books on the key episodes of Canadian history. The *Klondike* is one of the most mesmerizing, but other equally appealing titles include *The Arctic Grail*, describing the quest for the North Pole and the Northwest Passage; *The Last Spike: the Great Railway 1881–1885*, an account of the history and building of the transcontinental railway; *Flames across the Border*, a detailed account of the US attack on Canada in 1813–1814; *Vimy*, an account of the World War I battle fought mainly by Canadians which Berton sees as a turning point in the nation's history; and *Niagara*, a simply wonderful account of everything that has ever gone on there, including details of

the assorted lunatics and publicity-seekers who have gone over the Falls.

★ **Robert Bothwell** *The Penguin History of Canada*. Quite simply the best general history book currently in print. Concise, fair-minded and well-written account and analysis of the country's economic, social and political history.

★ **John English** *Citizen of the World: The Life of Pierre Elliott Trudeau Volume One: 1919–1968* and *Just Watch Me: The Life of Pierre Elliott Trudeau: 1968–2000*. Two brilliantly written and researched volumes on Canada's best-known, most flamboyant (an uncommon characteristic in Canadian politicians) and definitely most divisive prime minister.

Gerald Friesen *The Canadian Prairies: a History* (o/p). Stunningly well-researched and detailed account of the development of Central Canada. A surprisingly entertaining book that's particularly good on the culture of the Métis and Plains Indians. Published in 1987.

Peter C. Newman *The Last to Die: Ronald Turpin, Arthur Lucas, and the End of Capital Punishment in Canada*. It's 1962 and Turpin and Lucas became the last people to be executed in Canada. Newman tells the tale – and tells it well. If this fits the bill, also try Newman's much-praised *Empire of the Bay: The Company of Adventurers That Seized a Continent* (o/p).

James Raffan *Emperor of the North: Sir George Simpson & the Remarkable Story of the Hudson's Bay Company*. Laudable and readable account of the rise and fall of the Hudson's Bay Company and its star employee, the redoubtable George Simpson.

★ **George Woodcock** *A Social History of Canada* (o/p) Erudite and incisive book about the peoples of Canada and the country's development. Woodcock, who died in 1995 was arguably the most perceptive of Canada's historians and his work has the added advantage of being very readable.

FICTION

★ **Margaret Atwood** *Surfacing*. Canada's most eminent novelist is not always easy reading, but her analysis, particularly of women and society, is invariably witty and

penetrating. In *Surfacing* the remote landscape of norther Québec plays an instrumental part in an extreme voyage c self-discovery. Other notable works include *Alias Grace*, dark and sensual tale centred around the true story of one of Canada's most notorious female criminals of the 1840s, and the Booker Prize-winning *The Blind Assassin*. Many of her later books – *The Year of the Flood* and *Lady Oracle* for example – are less specifically Canadian, and present a dystopian view of the world both present and future.

Douglas Coupland *Generation X: Tales for an Accelerated Culture*. This celebrated Canadian novelist, best known for his treatises on mass culture and media, has penned more than twenty books, from the seminal 1991 *Generation X: Tales for an Accelerated Culture*, which defined a generation via the stories of three drifting 20-somethings, to 2013's *Worst. Person. Ever.*

Robertson Davies *What's Bred in the Bone, The Rebel Angels and The Lyre of Orpheus*. For many years the leading figure of Canada's literary scene, Davies died in 1995 at the age of 82. Among his considerable output are big, dark and complicated webs of familial and social history which include wonderful evocations of the semirural Canada of his youth. A good place to start is these three titles, which together comprise *The Cornish Trilogy*. Similarly intriguing is *Fifth Business* and *The Cunning Man*.

Marina Endicott *The Little Shadows*. It's 1912 and a woman and her three daughters are trudging through the snows of western Canada to a vaudeville audition: they luck out and enter the greasepaint world. A subtle and soft novel of what happens thereafter follows.

Margaret Laurence *A Jest of God* and *The Diviners*. Manitoba-born Laurence epitomized the new vigour that swept through the country's literature during the 1960s – though the best of her fiction was written in England. Most of her books are set in the fictional prairie backwater of Manawaka, and explore the loneliness and frustration of women within an environment of stifling small-town conventionality.

Mary Lawson *The Other Side of the Bridge*. Intricate family/clannish stuff in small-town northern Ontario, on the edge of the lakes, rocks and forests of the Canadian Shield. Deftly written, as is Lawson's earlier *Crow Lake*.

Stephen Leacock *Sunshine Sketches of a Little Town*. Whimsical tales of Ontario small-town life; the best of a series based on Leacock's (1869–1944) summertime stays in Orillia.

Jack London *Call of the Wild* and *White Fang*. London spent over a year in the Yukon goldfields during the Klondike gold rush. Many of his experiences found their way into his vivid – if sometimes overwrought – tales of the northern wilderness. These are the pick.

Ann-Marie MacDonald *Fall on Your Knees*. Entertaining, epic-style family saga from this Toronto-based writer, who has an astute eye for characters and a fine storytelling touch. The novel follows the fortunes of four sisters from Halifax, against a backdrop that sweeps from World War II to the New York jazz scene.

★ **Alistair MacLeod** *No Great Mischief*. This evocative novel tells the tale of a family of Gaelic-speaking Nova Scotians from Cape Breton. Some of the episodes are brilliantly written and it was undoubtedly one of the best Canadian novels of the 1990s.

Anne Michaels *Fugitive Pieces*. This debut novel from an award-winning poet concerns survivors from the Nazis who emigrate to Canada. Their relationship deepens but memory and the past are never far away. A beautiful work.

W.O. Mitchell *Who Has Seen the Wind* (o/p). Canada's equivalent of *Huckleberry Finn* is a folksy story of a young boy coming of age in small-town Saskatchewan, with great offbeat characters and fine evocations of prairie life.

★ **L.M. Montgomery** *Anne of Green Gables*. Growing pains and bucolic bliss in a children's classic from 1908. Set on Prince Edward Islan.

Brian Moore *Black Robe*. Moore emigrated to Canada from Ireland in 1948 and stayed long enough to gain citizenship before moving on to California. *Black Robe* – the story of a missionary's journey into Aboriginal territory – is typical of the author's preoccupations with Catholicism, repression and redemption.

Lisa Moore *February*. An oil rig sinks and a husband dies off the wild shores of Newfoundland. Grief and redemption, sorrow and joy follow in the wake of calamity.

★ **Alice Munro** *Lives of Girls and Women; The Progress of Love; The Beggar Maid; Friend of My Youth; Dance of the Happy Shades; Who Do You Think You Are?; Something I've Been Meaning to Tell You; Runaway; The Moons of Jupiter; and Hateship, Friendship, Courtship, Loveship and Marriage*. One of the world's finest living short-story writers – she won the 2013 Nobel Prize for Literature, among many other awards – Munro deals primarily with the lives of women in the semirural and Protestant backcountry of southwest Ontario. Unsettling emotions are never far beneath the surface crust of everyday life. Among her more recent works, *Open Secrets* focuses on stories set in two small Ontario towns from the days of the early settlers to the present; her 2012 *Dear Life* ploughs a similar furrow; and *Too Much Happiness* has one of its best stories set at a college in London, Ontario. Otherwise, start with *Who Do You Think You Are?*

Howard Norman *The Haunting of L*. Curious novel of psychosis, deception and sexual shenanigans mostly set in Churchill, Manitoba. The writing is a tad patchy, but the best sections are disconcerting and effecting in equal measure.

Michael Ondaatje *In the Skin of a Lion*. This is the novel that introduces readers to the characters that appear in the more famous *The English Patient*. It's a highly charged work spanning the period between the end of World War I and the Great Depression in Toronto.

E. Annie Proulx *The Shipping News*. The 1994 Pulitzer Prize-winner is a rambling, inconclusive narrative of a social misfit who finds love and happiness of sorts in small-town

Newfoundland. Superb descriptions of sea, weather and all things waterbound make it an intriguing primer for a visit to the province.

Mordecai Richler *The Apprenticeship of Duddy Kravitz.* French-Canadian, working-class and Jewish – Yiddishkeit was Richler's (1931–2001) bag. He was the laureate of the minority within a minority within a minority. All his novels explore this theme with broad humour and pathos. In *The Apprenticeship*, his best-known work, Richler uses his early experiences of Montréal's working-class Jewish ghetto in an acerbic and slick cross-cultural romance built around the ambivalent but tightly drawn figure of Kravitz. Richler's pushy and ironic prose is not to all tastes, but you might also try *Solomon Gursky Was Here* or his later *Barney's Version*, a rip-roaring comic portrait of a reckless artist *manqué.*

Carol Shields *The Stone Diaries* (o/p); *Larry's Party* (o/p). Winner of the Pulitzer Prize, Shields was much lauded for the detail she found in the everyday. There are moments of great beauty and sensitivity in these books as they chronicle the experiences of bourgeois North American suburbia with unnerving frankness.

Susan Swan *The Wives of Bath* (o/p). At a Toronto girls' school in the 1960s, the protagonist, Mouse, struggles with notions of feminine beauty as her best friend struggles with gender identity. A wry novel written in a genre the author described as "sexual gothic".

Miriam Toews *A Complicated Kindness.* Novels set in the Amish/Mennonite communities ("bonnet rippers") were very much in vogue in the mid-2000s – and this version, set in Manitoba, is one of the best of its type. The protagonist is a 16-year-old girl rebelling against the strictures of her traditional community. Also by Toews: *Irma Voth*, about another young girl – Irma – struggling to make sense of the Mennonites, but this time in Mexico.

John Wyndham *The Chrysalids.* A science-fiction classic built around a group of telepathic children and their adventures in post-Holocaust Labrador. First published in 1955.

POETRY

Elizabeth Bishop *The Complete Poems, 1927–1979.* Though American by birth, Bishop spent much of her youth in Nova Scotia. Many of her early poems feed off her Canadian childhood and her fascination with the country's rough landscapes.

Leonard Cohen *Poems & Songs.* A fine collection from a 1960s survivor who enjoyed critical acclaim as a poet before emerging as a husky-throated crooner of bedsit ballads. See also his *Beautiful Losers*, one of the most aggressively experimental Canadian novels of the era and first published in 1966.

Robert Service *Special Service: The Best Poems of Robert W. Service.* Service's Victorian-style ballads of pioneer and gold-rush life have a certain charm and they capture the essence of the gold-rush period. Among them, *The Heart of the Sourdough* is one of the most memorable, or you could sample *The Shooting of Dan McGrew*.

SPECIALIST GUIDES

Kathy & Craig Copeland *Don't Waste Your Time in the Canadian Rockies.* An essential guide for anyone wishing to do more than just the more obvious hikes; structured around a ratings system that helps prevent you wasting your time – hence the title. A seventh edition was published in 2015.

Ben Gadd & Mike Grandmaison *The Canadian Rockies.* Widely available in western Canada's larger bookshops, this is a lovingly produced and painstakingly detailed handbook of walks, flora, fauna, geology and anything else remotely connected with the Rockies.

Language

Canada has two official languages – English and French – plus numerous First Nations, Inuit and Métis tongues. Tensions between the two main language groups play a prominent part in the politics of Canada, but Indigenous languages are more or less ignored except in the country's more remote areas, particularly in the Northwest Territories and Nunavut, where Inuktitut, the language of the Inuit, is spoken widely. In a brief glossary such as this there is no space to get to grips with the complexities of Indigenous languages, and very few travellers would have any need of them anyway: most First Nations peoples (including those in Québec) have a good knowledge of English, especially if they deal with tourists in any capacity.

Québécois French

Québécois French differs from its European source in much the same way as North American English differs from British English. Thus, although Québécois French vocabulary, grammar and syntax are very near European French, speech can pose a few problems.

Tracing its roots back to seventeenth-century vernacular French, Québécois French has preserved features that disappeared long ago in France itself, and it has also been affected by its close contact with English. The end result is a dialect that – frankly – is a source of amusement to many French people and bafflement for those educated in the French language back in Europe, not to mention other parts of Canada. Within Québec itself there are marked regional differences of pronunciation, so much so that Montréalers find it hard to understand northern Québécois.

The Québécois can be extremely sympathetic when visiting English-speakers make the effort to speak French – and most are much more forthcoming with their knowledge of English when talking to a Briton or American than to an English-speaking Canadian. Similarly easygoing is the attitude towards the formal *vous* (you), which is used less often in Québec; you may even be corrected when saying "*S'il vous plaît*" with the suggestion that "*S'il te plaît*" is more appropriate. Another popular phrase you are likely to encounter is "*pas du tout*" ("not at all"), which in Québec is pronounced "*pan toot*", completely different from the French "*pa du too*". The same goes for "*c'est tout?*" ("is that all?"), pronounced "*say toot*"; you're likely to hear this when buying something in a shop. With **pronunciation** there's little point trying to mimic the local dialect – generally, just stick to the classic French rules.

FRENCH PRONUNCIATION

French isn't an easy language for English-speakers to pronounce, despite the number of words shared with English, but learning the essentials is not difficult. Differentiating words is the initial problem in understanding spoken French; it's very hard to get people to slow down. If, as a last resort, you get them to write it down, you may find you can identify half the words anyway.

VOWELS

a as in hat
au as in over
e as in get
é between get and gate
è between get and gut
eu as in hurt
 as in machine
 as in hot
 as in over

ou as in food
u is a pursed-lip version of true
The following are extra-tricky nasal sounds:
an/am and en/em like Doncaster said through your
 nose
in/im like anxious
on/om like Doncaster said with a heavy cold
un/um like understand

CONSONANTS

Consonants are pronounced much as in English, except:
ç is an English s
ch is an English sh
h is silent
ll as in bayonet
r is growled rather than trilled
th is like an English t
w is an English v

FRENCH WORDS AND PHRASES

THE BASICS

good morning/afternoon/hello bonjour
good evening bonsoir
good night bonne nuit
goodbye au revoir
yes oui
no non
please s'il vous/te plaît
thank you (very much) merci (beaucoup)
you're welcome bienvenue/de rien/ je vous en prie
OK d'accord
How are you? Comment allez-vous?/Ça va?
Fine, thanks Très bien, merci
Do you speak English? Parlez-vous anglais?
I don't speak French Je ne parle pas français
I don't understand Je ne comprends pas
I don't know Je ne sais pas
Excuse me (in a crowd) Excusez-moi
Sorry Pardon/désolé(e)
I'm English Je suis anglais(e)
Scottish/Welsh écossais(e)/gallois(e)
Irish/American irlandais(e)/américain(e)
Australian australian(e)
I live in… Je demeure à……
Wait a minute! Un instant!
here/there ici/là
good/bad bon/mauvais
big/small grand/petit
cheap/expensive bon marché/cher
early/late tôt/tard
hot/cold chaud/froid
near/far près (pas loin)/loin
vacant/occupied libre/occupé
quickly/slowly vite/lentement
loudly/quietly bruyant/tranquille
with/without avec/sans
more/less plus/moins
enough/no more assez/ça suffit
Mr Monsieur
Mrs Madame
Miss Mademoiselle

NUMBERS

1 un/une
2 deux
3 trois
4 quatre
5 cinq
6 six
7 sept
8 huit
9 neuf
10 dix
11 onze
12 douze
13 treize
14 quatorze
15 quinze
16 seize
17 dix-sept
18 dix-huit
19 dix-neuf
20 vingt
21 vingt-et-un
22 vingt-deux
30 trente
40 quarante
50 cinquante
60 soixante
70 soixante-dix
80 quatre-vingts
90 quatre-vingt-dix
100 cent
101 cent-et-un
110 cent-dix
200 deux cents
1000 mille
2000 deux milles

DAYS

Monday lundi
Tuesday mardi
Wednesday mercredi
Thursday jeudi
Friday vendredi
Saturday samedi
Sunday dimanche
morning le matin
afternoon l'après-midi
evening le soir
night la nuit
yesterday hier
today aujourd'hui
tomorrow demain
tomorrow morning demain matin

MONTHS

January janvier
February février
March mars
April avril
May mai
June juin
July juillet

August août
September septembre
October octobre
November novembre
December décembre

TIME

minute minute
hour heure
day jour
week semaine
month mois
year année
now maintenant
later plus tard
What time is it? Quelle heure est-il?
It's 9.00 Il est neuf heures
...1.05 ...une heure cinq
...2.15 ...deux heures et quart
...5.45 ...six heures moins quart
...9.40 ...dix heures moins vingt
...10.30 ...dix heures et demie
noon midi
midnight minuit

QUESTIONS AND DIRECTIONS

Where? Où?
When? Quand?
What? Quoi?
What is it? Qu'est-ce que c'est?
How much/many? Combien?
Why? Pourquoi?
It is/there is C'est/Il y a
Is it/is there…? Est-ce que/Y a-t-il…?
How do I get to…? Où se trouve…?
How far is it to…? À quelle distance est-il à…?
Can you give me a lift to…? Pouvez-vous me conduire jusqu'à…?
Can you tell me when to get off? Pouvez-vous me dire quand descendre?
What time does it open? À quelle heure ça ouvre?
How much does it cost? Combien cela coûte-t-il?
How do you say it in French? Comment ça se dit en français?

ACCOMMODATION

Is there a campsite nearby? Y a-t-il un camping près d'ici?
tent tente
cabin chalet
hostel auberge de jeunesse
hotel hôtel
Do you have anything cheaper? Avez-vous quelque chose de meilleur marché?

full board tout compris
Can I see the room? Puis-je peux voir la chambre?
I'll take this one Je vais prendre celle-ci
I'd like to book a room J'aimerais réserver une chambre
I have a booking J'ai une réservation
Can we camp here? Pouvons-nous camper ici?
How much is it? C'est combien?
It's expensive C'est cher
Is breakfast included? Est-ce que le petit déjeuner est compris?
I'm looking for a nearby hotel Je cherche un hôtel près d'ici
Do you have a room? Avez-vous une chambre?
...for one/two/three people ...pour une/deux/trois personne(s)
...for one/two/three nights ...pour une/deux/trios nuit(s)
...for one week ...pour une semaine
...with a double bed ...avec un lit double
...with a shower/bathtub ...avec douche/salle de bain
...hot/cold water ...eau chaude/froide

TRAVELLING

bus autobus
train train
plane avion
car voiture
taxi taxi
bicycle vélo
ferry traversier
ship bâteau
hitch-hiking faire du pouce
on foot à pied
bus station terminus d'autobus
train station gare centrale
ferry terminal quai du traversier
port port
A ticket to… Un billet pour…
one-way/return aller-simple/aller-retour
Can I book a seat? Puis-je réserver un siège?
What time does it leave? Il part à quelle heure?
When is the next train to…? Quand est le prochain train pour…?
Do I have to change? Dois-je transférer?
Where does it leave from? D'où est-ce qu'il part?
How many kilometres? Combien de kilomètres?
How many hours? Combien d'heures?
Which bus do I take to get to…? Quel autobus dois-je prendre pour aller à…?
Next stop Le prochain arrêt
Where's the road to…? Où est la route pour…?

SOME SIGNS

Entrance/Exit Entrée/Sortie

Free admission Entrée Libre
Gentlemen/Ladies Messieurs/Dames
WC Toilette
Vacant/Engaged Libre/Occupé
Open/Closed Ouvert/Fermé
Arrivals/Departures Arrivées/Départs
Closed for holidays Fermé pour les vacances
Pull/Push Tirez/Poussez
Out of order Hors d'usage/Brisé
To let À louer
Platform Voie
Cash desk Caisse
Go/Walk Marchez
Stop Arrêtez
Customs Douanes
Do not touch! Défense de toucher!
Danger! Danger!
Beware! Attention!
First aid Premiers soins
Ring the bell Sonnez
No smoking Défense de fumer

DRIVING
turn to the left/right tournez à gauche/droite
straight ahead tout droit
car park terrain de stationnement

no parking défense de stationner/ stationnement interdit
tow-away zone zone de remorquage
cars towed at owner's expense remorquage à vos frais
one-way street sens unique
dead end cul-de-sac
no entry défense d'entrer
slow down ralentir
proceed on flashing green light attendez le feu vert clignotant
turn on headlights! allumez vos phares!
no overtaking défense de dépasser
passing lane only voie réservée au dépassement
speed vitesse
self-service libre-service
full service service complet
Fill the tank with… Faîtes le plein avec…
…regular …de l'essence ordinaire
…super …du super
…unleaded …du sans plomb
Check the oil Vérifiez l'huile
battery la batterie
radiator le radiateur
plugs bougies d'allumage
tyre pressure pression des pneus
Pump up the tyres Gonflez les pneus

A FRENCH MENU READER

BASIC TERMS AND INGREDIENTS
beurre butter
chaud hot
crème fraiche sour cream
dessert dessert
frappé iced
froid cold
fromage cheese
hors d'oeuvre starters
legumes vegetables
oeufs eggs
pain bread
poisson fish
poivre pepper
salade salad
sel salt
sucre sugar
tourte tart or pie
tranche a slice
viande meat

SNACKS
un sandwich/une baguette… a sandwich…
croque-monsieur grilled cheese and ham sandwich
oeufs au plat fried eggs

oeufs à la coque boiled eggs
oeufs brouillés scrambled eggs
oeufs durs hard-boiled eggs
omelette nature plain omelette

SOUPS AND STARTERS
assiette anglaise plate of cold meats
bisque shellfish soup
bouillabaisse fish soup
bouillon broth or stock
consommé clear soup
potage thick soup, usually vegetable

MEAT AND POULTRY
agneau lamb
bifteck steak
boeuf beef
canard duck
cheval horsemeat
côtelettes cutlets
cuisson leg of lamb
dindon turkey
escargots snails
foie liver
gibiers game

gigot leg of venison
jambon ham
lard bacon
porc pork
poulet chicken
saucisse sausage
veau veal

FISH AND SEAFOOD
anchois anchovies
anguilles eels
carrelet plaice
cervettes roses prawns
hareng herring
homard lobster
lotte de mer monkfish
maquereau mackerel
morue cod
moules mussels
saumon salmon
sole sole
truite trout

COOKING METHODS
à point medium done (steak)
au four baked
bien cuit well done (steak)
bouilli boiled
frit/friture fried/deep fried
fumé smoked
grillé grilled
mijoté stewed
pané breaded
rôti roasted
saignant rare (steak)
sauté lightly cooked in butter

VEGETABLES AND GRAINS
ail garlic
asperges asparagus
carottes carrots
champignons mushrooms

choufleur cauliflower
concombre cucumber
laitue lettuce
oignons onions
petits pois peas
poireau leek
pommes (de terre) potatoes
riz rice
tomate tomato

FRUIT AND NUTS
amandes almonds
ananas pineapple
cacahouète peanut
cérises cherries
citron lemon
fraises strawberries
framboises raspberries
marrons chestnuts
noisette hazelnut
pamplemousse grapefruit
poire pear
pomme apple
prune plum
pruneau prune
raisins grapes

DRINKS
bière beer
brut very dry
café coffee
citron pressé sweetened lemon juice
demi-sec sweet
doux very sweet
eaux de vie fruit spirit/liquor
jus d'orange orange juice
lait milk
sec dry
thé tea
vin rouge red wine
vin blanc white wine

Small print and index

A ROUGH GUIDE TO ROUGH GUIDES

Published in 1982, the first Rough Guide – to Greece – was a student scheme that became a publishing phenomenon. Mark Ellingham, a recent graduate in English from Bristol University, had been travelling in Greece the previous summer and couldn't find the right guidebook. With a small group of friends he wrote his own guide, combining a contemporary, journalistic style with a thoroughly practical approach to travellers' needs.

The immediate success of the book spawned a series that rapidly covered dozens of destinations. And, in addition to impecunious backpackers, Rough Guides soon acquired a much broader readership that relished the guides' wit and inquisitiveness as much as their enthusiastic, critical approach and value-for-money ethos. These days, Rough Guides include recommendations from budget to luxury and cover more than 120 destinations around the globe, from Amsterdam to Zanzibar, all regularly updated by our team of roaming writers.

Browse all our latest guides, read inspirational features and book your trip at **roughguides.com**.

Rough Guide credits

Editor: Georgia Stephens, Siobhan Warwicker
Cartography: Carte
Managing editor: Rachel Lawrence
Picture editors: Michelle Bhatia, Aude Vauconsant

Cover photo research: Michelle Bhatia
Senior DTP coordinator: Dan May
Head of DTP and Pre-Press: Rebeka Davies

Publishing information

Tenth edition 2019

Distribution

UK, Ireland and Europe
Apa Publications (UK) Ltd; sales@roughguides.com
United States and Canada
Ingram Publisher Services; ips@ingramcontent.com
Australia and New Zealand
Woodslane; info@woodslane.com.au
Southeast Asia
Apa Publications (SN) Pte; sales@roughguides.com
Worldwide
Apa Publications (UK) Ltd; sales@roughguides.com
Special Sales, Content Licensing and CoPublishing
Rough Guides can be purchased in bulk quantities
at discounted prices. We can create special editions,
personalised jackets and corporate imprints tailored to
your needs. sales@roughguides.com.

roughguides.com
Printed in China by CTPS
All rights reserved
© 2019 Apa Digital (CH) AG
License edition © Apa Publications Ltd UK
All rights reserved. No part of this publication may be
reproduced, stored in or introduced into a retrieval system,
or transmitted in any form, or by any means (electronic,
mechanical, photocopying, recording or otherwise) without
the prior written permission of the copyright owner.
A catalogue record for this book is available from the
British Library
The publishers and authors have done their best to ensure
the accuracy and currency of all the information in **The
Rough Guide to Canada**, however, they can accept
no responsibility for any loss, injury, or inconvenience
sustained by any traveller as a result of information or
advice contained in the guide.

Help us update

We've gone to a lot of effort to ensure that this edition of
The Rough Guide to Canada is accurate and up-to-date.
However, things change – places get "discovered", opening
hours are notoriously fickle, restaurants and rooms raise
prices or lower standards. If you feel we've got it wrong
or left something out, we'd like to know, and if you can
remember the address, the price, the hours, the phone
number, so much the better.

Please send your comments with the subject line
"Rough Guide Canada Update" to mail@uk.roughguides.
com. We'll credit all contributions and send a copy of the
next edition (or any other Rough Guide if you prefer) for
the very best emails.

Readers' updates

Thanks to all the readers, including Alan Blow, who have taken the time to write in with comments and suggestions.

Acknowledgements

Stephen Keeling would like to thank Laura Walbourne at Go Western Newfoundland; Gillian Marx and the team at
Newfoundland & Labrador Tourism; Heather MacDonald-Bossé at Tourism New Brunswick; Pamela Wamback at Tourism
Nova Scotia; Nancy Lockerbie at Fundy Trail Parkway; Daniela Resenterra and Anna Cooke at QuébecOriginal; Siobhan
Warwicker and Rachel Lawrence back in London; and lastly to Tiffany Wu, the world's greatest travel partner.
Rachel Mills For much-needed support arranging my research trip, I'd like to thank Destination BC, Tourism Tofino and
travel PR agency KBC. To Robin, thanks for being by my side and in my pod. And to the wonderful editorial team at Rough
Guides HQ, thanks for the dreamy commission.
AnneLise Sorensen says *merci beaucoup* and thank you to all who offered their wonderful hospitality, travel tips,
Québecois wine and cheese – and everything in between. A big thanks to the Insight Guides and Rough Guides editorial
team, including Rachel Lawrence, Siobhan Warwicker and Georgia Stephens, as well as all my talented co-authors.
Christian Williams would like to extend a particular thanks to Bill Macdonald for hospitality in Lake of the Woods; to
David at Canada DriveAway for record-beating service; and to Grace G Scott at Fiat for road support. At Rough Guides a
big thanks goes to all those involved in the book; particularly Rachel Lawrence for stepping in at short notice.

Photo credits
(Key: T-top; C-centre; B-bottom; L-left; R-right)

ABOUT THE AUTHORS
Stephen Keeling first travelled to Canada in 1993. He worked as a financial journalist for seven years before writing his first Rough Guide in 2005, and has since worked on books to Florida, Mexico, New England, Puerto Rico, Spain and USA among others. He lives in New York City.
Rachel Mills is a freelance writer and editor based by the sea in Kent. She is a co-author for the Rough Guides to New Zealand, India, Vietnam, Ireland and England, as well as Canada, and regularly writes for *The Telegraph*, DK Travel and loveEXPLORING.com. You can follow her travels on Instagram @rachmillstravel.
Writer, editor and photographer **AnneLise Sorensen** (annelisesorensen.com) journeys – and wine-tastes – around the world, contributing to numerous outlets including *New York Magazine*, Condé Nast, DK Top 10 Barcelona and Rough Guides to Spain, Scandinavia, Central America, New York and Canada. AnneLise splits her time between New York, California and Europe, and explores Canada regularly, from the bright lights of Toronto to the low lights of Montréal, fueled by its poutine, ice wine – and *joie de vivre*.
Christian Williams has longstanding links with Canada that include family ties and several mountain bike scars. He has written or co-authored some twenty books including the Rough Guides to Skiing and Snowboarding, Colorado, Tenerife, Germany, Austria and Berlin, his hometown.

Index

Map symbols

The symbols below are used on maps throughout the book

▬▬ ▪ ▪	International boundary	✗	Airstrip	⊙	Statue	✿	Viewpoint
▬▬ ▪ ▪	State/province boundary	★	Bus stop	⛪	Monastery	✗	Ski area
▬▬ ▬▬	Chapter division boundary	Ⓜ	Subway station	⊤	Gardens	开	Picnic area
▬▬	Motorway	Ⓗ	Helipad	⚡	Lighthouse	▮	Tower
▬▬	Pedestrianized road	⛴	Boat	⚠	Campsite	🏛	Monument
▬▬	Road	@	Internet access	❀	Waterfall	♦	Museum
▬ ▬ ▬	Unpaved road	ⓘ	Information office	◈	Spring/spa		Building
⊓⊓⊓⊓⊓	Steps	Ⓟ	Parking	≋	Rapids	⇌	Church
▪ ▪ ▪ ▪	Path	⊞	Hospital	🐘	Zoo	◯	Stadium
▬ ◆ ▬	Railway	⊠	Post office	⛟	Distillery	⊞	Cemetery
●▬ ▪ ▪◯	Cable car	⊠	Gate/entrance	▲	Mountain peak		Beach
▬ ▬	Ferry route	◆	Place of interest	峰	Mountain range		Park
▬▬	Wall	∴	Ruin	⫽	Mountain pass		Glacier
✈	Airport	⛳	Golf course				

Listings key

- ■ Accommodation
- ● Eating
- ■ Drinking/nightlife
- ● Shopping